HISTORY

EDITORIAL CONSULTANT **ADAM HART-DAVIS**

HISTORY

THE DEFINITIVE VISUAL GUIDE

FROM THE DAWN OF CIVILIZATION TO THE PRESENT DAY

**LONDON, NEW YORK, MELBOURNE,
MUNICH, AND DELHI**

DORLING KINDERSLEY

Senior Art Editors
Ina Stradins, Maxine Lea

Senior Editor
Angeles Gavira Guerrero

Art Editors
Alison Gardner, Mark Lloyd,
Francis Wong

Section Editors
Nicola Hodgson, Rob Houston, Constance Novis,
Ruth O'Rourke, Rebecca Warren, Ed Wilson

Designers
Brian Flynn, Kenny Grant,
Peter Laws, Matt Schofield,
Rebecca Wright

Editors
Sam Atkinson, Tom Broda, Kim Bryan, Mary
Lindsay, Ferdie McDonald, Sue Nicholson, Paula
Regan, Nigel Ritchie, Carey Scott, Giles Sparrow,
Steve Setford, Alison Sturgeon, Claire Tennant-Scull,
Miezan Van Zyl, Jo Weeks

DTP Designers
John Goldsmid, Laragh Kedwell,
Robert Strachan

Editorial Assistants
Tamlyn Calitz, Manisha Thakkar

Jacket Designers
Lee Ellwood, Duncan Turner

US Editor
Christine Heilman

Cartographers
Ed Merritt, John Plumer,
David Roberts,
Advanced Illustration Ltd:
Paul Antonio, Russel Ikin

Indexers
Indexing Specialists (UK) Ltd.

Production
Elizabeth Warman

Picture Researcher
Louise Thomas

Managing Editor
Sarah Larter

Senior Managing Art Editor
Phil Ormerod

Publishing Manager
Liz Wheeler

Art Director
Bryn Walls

Reference Publisher
Jonathan Metcalf

TALL TREE

Art Director
Ed Simkins

Managing Editor
David John

Designer
Ben Ruocco

Project Editor
Rob Colson

First American Edition, 2007
This edition published in 2012
Published in the United States by
DK Publishing
375 Hudson Street
New York, New York 10014

07 08 09 10 11   10 9 8 7 6 5 4 3 2 1

001–HD107–April/2012
Copyright © 2007, 2012 Dorling Kindersley Limited
All rights reserved

Published in Great Britain by Dorling Kindersley Limited.

A catalog record for this book is available from the Library of Congress.

ISBN 978-0-7566-7609-4

DK books are available at special discounts when purchased in bulk for
sales promotions, premiums, fund-raising, or educational use. For details,
contact: DK Publishing Special Markets, 375 Hudson Street, New York, New
York 10014 or SpecialSales@dk.com.

Color reproduction by Media Development Printing Ltd., UK
Printed and bound in Singapore by Star Standard PTE Ltd.

Discover more at
www.dk.com

Editorial Consultant Adam Hart-Davis

Writer, broadcaster, and photographer Adam Hart-Davis has presented history, science, and technology series on the BBC, ITV, and the History Channel, and is the author of more than 25 books. He is also the editor-in-chief of DK's *Science*.

Main Consultants

Professor Brian Fagan

Origins

Emeritus Professor of Anthropology, University of California, Santa Barbara, CA

Dr. Karen Radner

Rulers and Hierarchies

Lecturer in the Ancient Near East, University College London, UK

Professor Richard Lim

Thinkers and Believers

Professor in the Ancient Mediterranean World and Late Antiquity, Smith College, Massachusetts

Dr. Roger Collins

Warriors, Travelers, and Inventors

Honorary Fellow, School of History and Classics, University of Edinburgh, UK

Dr. David Parrott

Renaissance and Reformation

Fellow and lecturer in Modern History, New College, Oxford University, UK

James Freeman

Industry and Revolution

Postgraduate researcher, specializing in 18th and 19th century history, Cambridge University, UK

Professor Richard Overy

Population and Power

Professor of History, University of Exeter, UK

Contributors and Specialist Consultants

Contributors: Simon Adams, Lindsay Allen, Robin Archer, Debbie Brunton, Jack Challoner, Nick McCarty, Thomas Cussans, Erich DeWald, Brian Fagan, Emma Flatt, Abbie Gometz, Reg Grant, Alwyn Harrison, Ian Harrison, James Harrison, Michael Jordan, Ann Kay, Paul Kriwaczek, Keith Laidler, Siobhan Lambert-Hurley, Sarah Lynch, Margaret Mulvihill, Liz Mylod, Owen Miller, Sally Regan, Nigel Ritchie, J. A.G Roberts, Natalie Sirett, Giles Sparrow, Paul Sturtevant, Jenny Vaughan, Philip Wilkinson.

Consultants: Early Mesoamerica and South America Dr. Jim Aimers, UCL Institute of Archaeology, UK; **India** Professor David Arnold, University of Warwick, UK; **Food and diseases** Professor Kenneth Kiple, Department of History, Bowling Green State University, US; **Latin America** Professor Alan Knight, Department of History, University of Oxford, UK; **Japan and Korea** Dr. Angus Lockyer, Department of History SOAS, UK; **How We Know** Dr. Iain Morley and Dr. Laura Preston, McDonald Institute for Archaeological Research, University of Cambridge UK; **Consulting editor** Philip Parker; **China** J.A.G Roberts

CONTENTS

6
INDUSTRY & REVOLUTION

7
POPULATION & POWER

Foreword

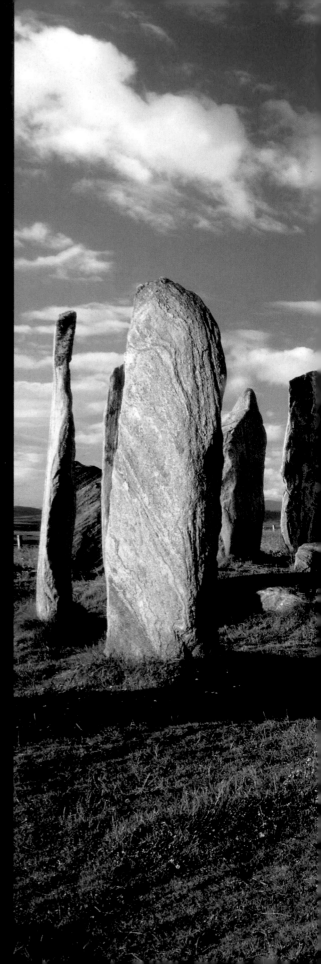

The history I learned at school was a mass of seemingly endless lists, formed of dates and the names of kings and queens. As a result, I hated it, and never saw the connections between the various strands of the subject. I now realize that history *is* important and that we can all learn from the triumphs—and mistakes—of our ancestors. Both utterly fascinating and hugely informative, *History* is a reference book that teases out the sparks of wars and revolutions, and uncovers the deep roots of great civilizations. It brings the subject to life, painting broad pictures of history's great sweep, aiming to excite and enthuse the reader by focusing on the most interesting, exciting, and dynamic people, events, and ideas of the past.

The photographs, maps, and graphics throughout *History* are spectacular, compelling you to dip in and discover what each page will reveal. This image shows some of the ancient standing stones at Callanish, Scotland, where 20 stone circles jut out from the bare, peaty landscape. The primary purpose of these stones, which have weathered through 4,000 years of human history, seems to have been to mark a curious lunar event that happens only once every 18.61 years—those early astronomers must have been persistent.

One of the joys of this book is that most subjects, however vast in scale, are presented within self-contained spreads. Some describe hundreds of years of ancient Egyptian civilization, or momentous periods of upheaval like the religious Reformation in 17th-century Europe or the Industrial Revolution of the 19th century. Others take as their theme much shorter periods of history, such as the English Civil War or the Russian Revolution. There are also spreads devoted to "Decisive Moments", key events that proved to be historical turning points, for example the assassination of Archduke Franz Ferdinand, which triggered World War I, or the 1755 Lisbon earthquake, which shook Europe to its very foundations.

But *History* isn't just about the events that have shaped us. A key strand in the book focuses on the ideas that have changed the world, exploring concepts such as democracy, evolution, and globalization. It also features biographies of some of history's most important and influential individuals from Alexander the Great to Adolf Hitler. And, as an enthusiast of science and technology, I am delighted to see coverage of the crucial innovations, inventions, scientific discoveries, and theories that have had an impact on the human story, from metalworking to the internet, and DNA to global warming.

ADAM HART-DAVIS

1

ORIGINS
4.5 MYA–3000 BCE

Evidence of the earliest hominins, the ancestors of modern humans, has been found in Central and East Africa, and dates back millions of years. Discoveries of early human remains reveal the remarkable ability to adapt to Earth's changing environment that has been so significant in the evolution of our species.

ORIGINS

4.5 MYA–3000 BCE

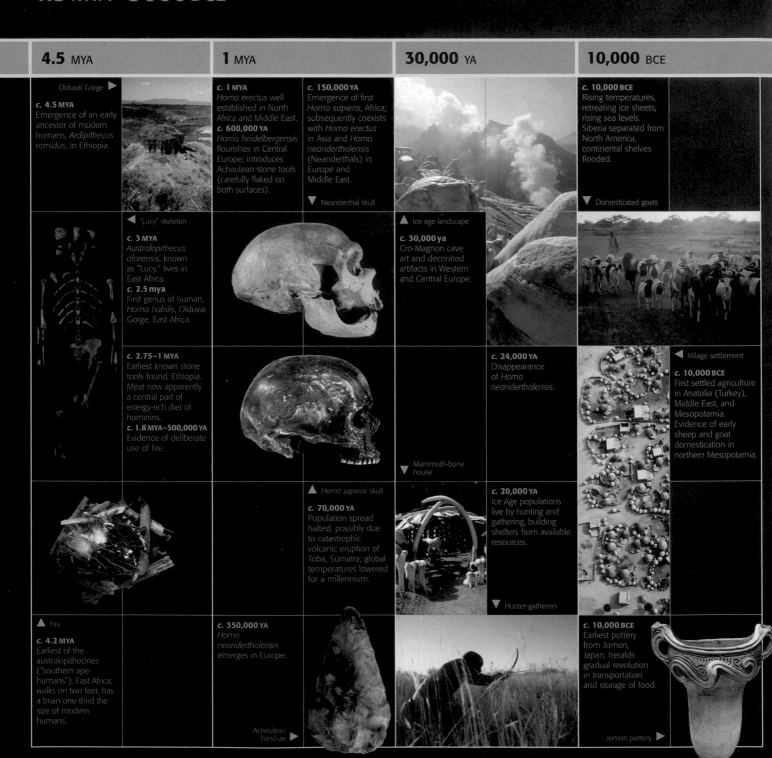

4.5 MYA	1 MYA	30,000 YA	10,000 BCE

Olduvai Gorge ▶

c. 4.5 MYA
Emergence of an early ancestor of modern humans, *Ardipithecus ramidus*, in Ethiopia.

c. 1 MYA
Homo erectus well established in North Africa and Middle East.
c. 600,000 YA
Homo heidelbergensis flourishes in Central Europe; introduces Acheulean stone tools (carefully flaked on both surfaces).

c. 150,000 YA
Emergence of first *Homo sapiens*, Africa; subsequently coexists with *Homo erectus* in Asia and *Homo neanderthalensis* (Neanderthals) in Europe and Middle East.

c. 10,000 BCE
Rising temperatures, retreating ice sheets, rising sea levels. Siberia separated from North America, continental shelves flooded.

▼ Domesticated goats

◀ "Lucy" skeleton

c. 3 MYA
Australopithecus afarensis, known as "Lucy," lives in East Africa.
c. 2.5 mya
First genus of human, *Homo habilis*, Olduvai Gorge, East Africa.

▲ Ice age landscape

c. 30,000 ya
Cro-Magnon cave art and decorated artifacts in Western and Central Europe.

c. 2.75–1 MYA
Earliest known stone tools found, Ethiopia. Meat now apparently a central part of energy-rich diet of hominins.
c. 1.8 MYA–500,000 YA
Evidence of deliberate use of fire.

c. 24,000 YA
Disappearance of *Homo neanderthalensis*.

◀ Village settlement

c. 10,000 BCE
First settled agriculture in Anatolia (Turkey), Middle East, and Mesopotamia. Evidence of early sheep and goat domestication in northern Mesopotamia.

▼ Mammoth-bone house

▲ *Homo sapiens* skull

c. 70,000 YA
Population spread halted, possibly due to catastrophic volcanic eruption of Toba, Sumatra; global temperatures lowered for a millennium.

c. 20,000 YA
Ice Age populations live by hunting and gathering, building shelters from available resources.

▼ Hunter-gatherers

▲ Fire

c. 4.2 MYA
Earliest of the australopithecines ("southern ape-humans"), East Africa; walks on two feet, has a brain one-third the size of modern humans'.

c. 350,000 YA
Homo neanderthalensis emerges in Europe.

Acheulean hand-ax ▶

c. 10,000 BCE
Earliest pottery from Jomon, Japan, heralds gradual revolution in transportation and storage of food.

Jomon pottery ▶

Measured against the estimated 4.5-billion-year age of Earth itself, humans–anatomically modern humans in particular–evolved remarkably recently. Modern man–*Homo sapiens*–appeared only about 150,000 years ago, rapidly migrating from African homelands to join other human species–*Homo erectus* in Asia and, across Europe and the Middle East, the Neanderthals. By about 24,000 years ago, *Homo sapiens*, socially more sophisticated, had become the sole human species. Then, in the Middle East, about 6,000 years ago, settled and increasingly complex societies emerged. With them came the first cities and the first states. It was the birth of civilization as we know it today.

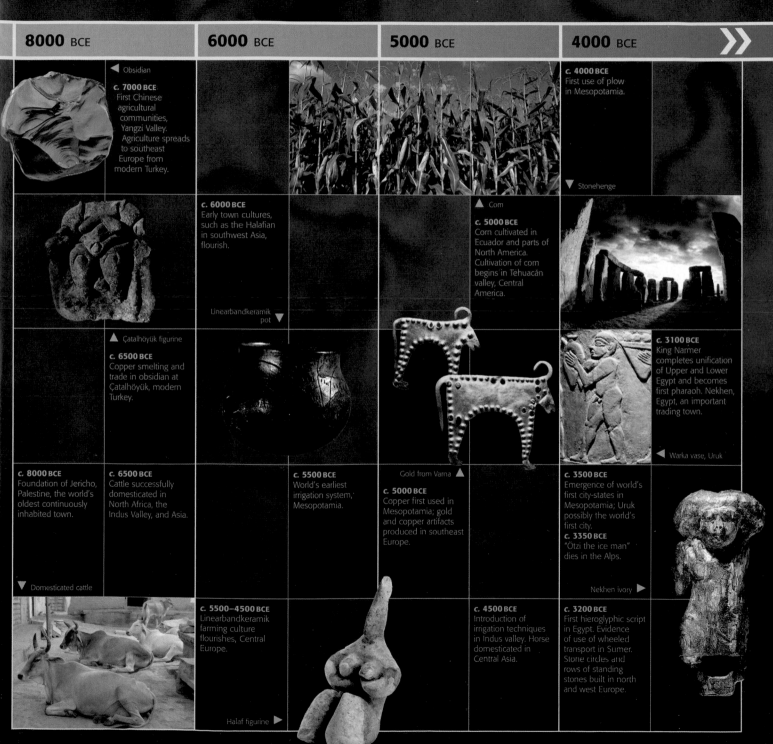

8000 BCE

◀ Obsidian

c. 7000 BCE
First Chinese agricultural communities, Yangzi Valley. Agriculture spreads to southeast Europe from modern Turkey.

▲ Çatalhöyük figurine

c. 6500 BCE
Copper smelting and trade in obsidian at Çatalhöyük, modern Turkey.

c. 8000 BCE
Foundation of Jericho, Palestine, the world's oldest continuously inhabited town.

c. 6500 BCE
Cattle successfully domesticated in North Africa, the Indus Valley, and Asia.

▼ Domesticated cattle

6000 BCE

c. 6000 BCE
Early town cultures, such as the Halafian in southwest Asia, flourish.

Linearbandkeramik pot ▼

c. 5500 BCE
World's earliest irrigation system, Mesopotamia.

c. 5500–4500 BCE
Linearbandkeramik farming culture flourishes, Central Europe.

Halaf figurine ▶

5000 BCE

▲ Corn

c. 5000 BCE
Corn cultivated in Ecuador and parts of North America. Cultivation of corn begins in Tehuacán valley, Central America.

Gold from Varna ▲

c. 5000 BCE
Copper first used in Mesopotamia; gold and copper artifacts produced in southeast Europe.

c. 4500 BCE
Introduction of irrigation techniques in Indus valley. Horse domesticated in Central Asia.

4000 BCE

c. 4000 BCE
First use of plow in Mesopotamia.

▼ Stonehenge

c. 3100 BCE
King Narmer completes unification of Upper and Lower Egypt and becomes first pharaoh. Nekhen, Egypt, an important trading town.

◀ Warka vase, Uruk

c. 3500 BCE
Emergence of world's first city-states in Mesopotamia; Uruk possibly the world's first city.
c. 3350 BCE
"Ötzi the ice man" dies in the Alps.

Nekhen ivory ▶

c. 3200 BCE
First hieroglyphic script in Egypt. Evidence of use of wheeled transport in Sumer. Stone circles and rows of standing stones built in north and west Europe.

« BEFORE

No one knows when human beings first appeared. Our only clues lie in fossils and stone tools. The journey started some time around six million years ago (mya) in Africa.

THE HUMAN FAMILY

Humans are classified as primates, a group that includes apes and monkeys. **Our closest living relatives are chimpanzees**, with whom we share almost 99 percent of our genes, but this tiny genetic difference is what makes us so far removed from apes.

CHIMPANZEE

OUR ROOTS

Sahelanthropus tchadensis **18 >>**, found at the southern edge of the Sahara in Chad, and dating to between 6 and 7 mya, may be the earliest human ancestor. Although very early, this skull seems more advanced in some ways than later species and it is **unclear how it fits into the evolutionary story**. Other very early ancestors about whom very little is known include *Orrorin tugenensis* and *Ardipithecus ramidus*. Some of these species came to a **dead end on the human family tree**. Others may have led directly to our own ancestors.

THE MOLECULAR CLOCK

Evolutionary biologists have developed a way of dating the evolution of more than 60 primate species. It is known as the molecular clock. The clock starts with the last common ancestor of all primates about 63 mya, and dates the **split between chimpanzees and humans to about 6.2 mya**. This is the moment when the human story truly begins.

The "cradle of humankind"

Olduvai Gorge in Tanzania is the most important prehistoric site in the world, where many finds that have furthered our knowledge of early human evolution have been made. The oldest artifacts found at the gorge—stone flakes and tools—are 2 million years old.

"**Human consciousness arose** but a **minute before midnight** on the geological clock."

STEPHEN JAY GOULD, EVOLUTIONARY BIOLOGIST, 1992

Our Remote Ancestors

The evolution of modern humans extends back millions of years. It is not easy to trace, as our evidence comes from scattered, unrelated finds, making it difficult to form a cohesive picture. The dominance of *Homo sapiens* is a comparatively recent development.

In the 19th century, Charles Darwin, the father of the theory of evolution by natural selection (see pp.340–41), identified tropical Africa as the cradle of humankind. Pioneering paleontologists Louis and Mary Leakey found evidence of this in the 1950s with discoveries in Olduvai Gorge, a deep gash in the eastern Serengeti Plains in Tanzania, East Africa (see left). It was in East Africa that our human ancestors evolved at least 4.5 mya (million years ago). A wide range of fossil finds provide evidence of a remarkable diversity of early hominins that flourished in this area.

> **HOMININ** The term used to refer to all early humans and their ancestors, including *Homo erectus*, *Homo ergaster*, *Homo neanderthalis* and *Homo sapiens*. Also includes all the Australopithecines, *Paranthropus boisei*, and *Ardipithecus*.

Earliest ancestors

One of the earliest known human ancestors is a small forest-living primate named *Ardipithecus anamensis*, which flourished in Afar, Ethiopia, some 4.5 mya. *Ardipithecus* was probably the ancestor of the Australopithecines—highly diverse hominins that appeared for the first time one million years later. The earliest found, *Australopithecus afarensis*, was famously nicknamed "Lucy" by the archaeologists who found her in 1974. Although it seems that this long-limbed hominin spent a great deal of time in the trees, some well-preserved footprints reveal that the species was bipedal (walked on two feet) (see p.18). As such, "Lucy" is an important link between us and our tree-dwelling ancestors.

The next generation

By 3 mya, the Australopithecines had diversified into many forms. They flourished throughout much of sub-Saharan Africa, especially in more open grasslands. These early humans were fully bipedal. Nimble and fleet of foot, species including *Australopithecus africanus* were skilled at scavenging meat from predator kills. Their brain size was also larger than their predecessors'.

The first humans

Ancestors of modern humans appeared about 2 mya in eastern Africa, quickly spreading to the west. Tools dating from 1.8 mya have been found in a dry stream bed at Koobi Fora on the shore of Lake Turkana, Kenya. The tools were made of stone from several miles away. It is not known who the tool users were, but they may have been some of the earliest humans, possibly a group who paused here and butchered antelope.

Handyman

Clearer evidence of the earliest toolmakers and their descendants has been found on the ancient lake beds at Olduvai Gorge in Tanzania. The tools

> **PALEOLITHIC A period covering the time from the first use of stone tools about 2.5 mya to the beginning of agriculture in about 10,000 BCE.**

INVENTION

STONE TOOLS

Homo habilis used the simplest stone technology, which was refined by *Homo erectus* into stone axes and cleaving tools for particular tasks such as butchering animals. The Neanderthals were the first to mount scrapers, spear-points, and knives in wooden handles. Modern humans developed more sophisticated technology, punching off parallel-sided blanks from carefully prepared flint nodules. They turned these blades into scrapers, chisels, and borers to work antlers, bone, and leather. After the Ice Age (see pp.22-23), hunters added tiny stone barbs to their arrows.

FLINT HAND-AX

are thought to date from about 1.8 mya, and were made by *Homo habilis* ("handy man"), who left what could be the remains of a camp by a lake, including a scatter of stone tools and broken animal bones. *Homo habilis* probably slept in trees, in relative safety from lions and other dangerous animals. In this predator-rich environment, humans were both the hunters and the hunted. The evidence from the Olduvai camp suggests that *Homo habilis* was breaking up parts of animal carcasses scavenged from predator kills.

At about the same time, what could be termed the first true human had appeared. Large-brained, with a receding forehead, and prominent brow ridges *Homo ergaster* had strong limbs similar to those of modern humans. These newcomers were hunters rather than scavengers.

DISCOVERY

FIRE

Fire is one of the most important discoveries ever made. Possibly around 1.8 million years ago and certainly by 500,000 years ago—the date is uncertain—early humans tamed fire, perhaps by taking branches from a blazing tree caused by a lightning strike. Creating fire at will was another step forward. The control of fire enabled humans to live in cold environments, and in deep caves, and provided protection against predators. The use of fire to cook also led to a greater variety of foods in the diet.

»

Homo ergaster was closely related to Homo erectus, the first humans to spread out of tropical Africa into Europe and Asia as part of a general radiation of mammals and their predators some 1.8 mya. Homo erectus was a skilled hunter and a brilliant opportunist, quick to take advantage of different environments—a key factor in the success of the human species.

These early humans soon settled in South and Southeast Asia, reaching Dmanisi in Georgia by 1.7 mya (see pp.24–25). They were well established in Western Europe by at least 800,000 years ago. Warmer conditions than today may have attracted Homo heidelbergensis to Northern Europe by 400,000 years ago. At about the same time, small bands of early humans were using long-shafted, aerodynamic wooden spears to hunt wild horses and larger game at Schöningen, Germany, and at Boxgrove in southern England.

The remarkable finds at Schöningen are the earliest preserved wooden tools yet discovered. Homo heidelbergensis lived in small, mobile groups. Each group probably returned to the same locations to hunt and forage at different times of the year. However, their communication and reasoning abilities were limited (see pp.20–21), which affected their ability to adapt and may be one reason why they do not appear to have settled in intensely cold environments or reached the Americas and Australia.

Adapting to different environments

By 500,000, early humans had adapted successfully to a wide variety of tropical and temperate environments, moving as far north as China, where numerous fragments of an evolving Homo erectus have come to light in Zhoukoudian Cave, near Beijing. The ability to use fire (see p.16) was crucial in making settlement possible in cold locations

HOW WE KNOW

THEY WALKED ON TWO FEET

About 3.75 mya, a volcanic eruption left a layer of ash at Laetoli, Tanzania that preserved the footprints of *Australopithecus afarensis* ("Lucy"). They were identified as those of a young adult who walked on two feet with a rolling gait, slower than that of modern humans. This bipedal posture—an important human anatomical feature that appeared before 4 mya—allowed our ancestors to live away from forests in open terrain.

3–2.4 mya
Site Africa

Brain size 375–500 cc

Australopithecus afarensis
Known as "Lucy," this early hominin was relatively short at 3 ft 3 in (1 m) in height, had shorter limbs than later species, and, significantly, walked on two feet.

2.5–1.8 mya
Sites Africa

Brain size 750 cc

Homo rudolfensis, a contemporary of *Homo habilis*, has been the subject of much debate concerning its age and relationship to the hominin species. It had a relatively large brain and was bipedal.

Human family tree
New discoveries of fossils that add to our knowledge of human evolution are being made all the time. The size and shape of the skulls help us to understand the abilities of our ancestors. Brain size is measured in cubic centimeters (cc), with an average modern human brain measuring 1,400 cc.

6.2–5.8 mya
Sites Africa

Brain size Unknown

Orrorin tugenensis is known to us through finds of large canine teeth. Little is known about the species, except that it may have been bipedal.

5.8–5.2 mya
Sites Africa

Brain size Unknown

Ardipithecus kadabba was one of the earliest species to be placed on the human tree. Like *Orrorin tugenensis*, this species had primitive canine teeth.

Homo rudolfensis

Ardipithecus kadabba

Orrorin tugenensis

Australopithecus afarensis

| 7 MYA | 6 MYA | 5 MYA | 4 MYA | 3 MYA | 2.5 MYA | 2 MY |

Sahelanthropus tchadenis

Ardipithecus ramidus

Australopithecus africanus

Australopithecus anamensis

Homo habilis

4.5–4.3 mya
Sites Africa

Brain size Unknown

Ardipithecus ramidus is a very early hominin. Fragmentary remains include large canine teeth found in Ethiopia, which are similar to those of the australopithecines.

6.7 mya
Sites Africa

Brain size 320–380 cc

Sahelanthropus tchadenis may be one of the first humans or may be more closely related to apes, as it shows a mixture of human and ape characteristics. Only the fragments of a skull have been found.

4.3–4 mya
Sites Africa

Brain size Unknown

Australopithecus anamensis is little known as few remains have been found. The jawbone from Kenya resembles that of a chimpanzee, while the teeth are closer to human teeth.

3.3–2.4 mya
Sites Africa

Brain size 400–500 cc

Australopithecus africanus was a slenderly built species. Its facial features appear to have been more human than earlier australopithecines. It had longer legs and shorter arms than modern humans.

2.5–1.8 mya
Sites Africa

Brain size 590–650 cc

Homo habilis had relatively long arms, marking it out from later humans. The species may descend from the australopithecines.

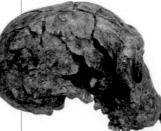

during the climatic swings of the Ice Age, but population levels remained very low and the survival of early humans must have been precarious at times.

The Neanderthals

By 200,000 years ago, *Homo neanderthalensis* had evolved in Europe and Eurasia. The Neanderthals had large brains and more rounded heads than their predecessors. Their body shape was also more recognizably "human," but it is believed that their reasoning power and speech were not as developed as those of *Homo sapiens*.

They were, however, expert hunters, who pursued animals such as bison with wooden and stone-tipped spears. They made sophisticated tools and dwelt in caves, rock shelters, and open camps. Theirs was a tough life in savage environments, and they probably lived for 30–40 years. Most experts agree that Neanderthals were not the ancestors of modern humans.

The appearance of modern humans

Intense controversy surrounds the origins of *Homo sapiens*—ourselves. Most geneticists use DNA evidence (see pp.26–27) to argue that modern humans first appeared in tropical Africa by about 180,000 years ago. The earliest fully modern human fossils come from Huerto, Ethiopia, and date to about 160,000 years ago. From Africa, *Homo sapiens* spread across the Sahara and into southwestern Asia by 100,000 years ago. No one knows when humans developed the abilities that set them apart from their earlier ancestors, but they were fully developed by 45,000 years ago, when the first modern humans settled in Europe alongside the Neanderthals.

The arrival of *Homo sapiens* may have spelled the end for the Neanderthals.

EXTINCTION AND SUCCESS

Although Neanderthals and *Homo sapiens* lived alongside one another, DNA evidence suggests **they did not interbreed**. Neanderthals died out, perhaps at the hands of *Homo sapiens*, who were successful in adapting to every corner of the globe. More than any other species, humans have used their skills to their own advantage.

2.75–1 mya

Sites Africa

Brain size 500–550 cc

Paranthropus boisei is the most extreme version of the early "robust" humans living in eastern Africa. *Boisei* flourished in the dry savanna areas that existed in Africa at that time and may have died out after climate change.

2–0.5 mya

Site Africa, Asia, Europe

Brain size 810–1250 cc

Homo erectus was a powerfully built human with massive brow ridges, a large face, and a long, low skull to accommodate a much larger brain.

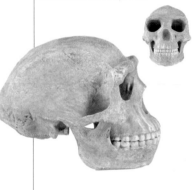

350,000–24,000 ya

Site Africa and Eurasia

Brain size 1125–1550 cc

Homo neanderthalensis may have lived alongside modern *Homo sapiens* in Europe. The species had a large brain and short robust build with powerful limbs.

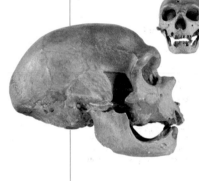

Paranthropus boisei

Homo erectus

Homo neanderthalensis

| 1.5 MYA | 1 MYA | 0.5 MYA | PRESENT DAY |

Homo ergaster

Homo heidelbergensis

Homo sapiens

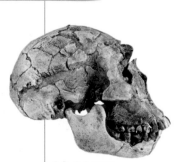

1.9–1.4 mya

Sites Africa

Brain size 600–910 cc

Homo ergaster was relatively tall, with a brain size well below that of modern humans. The skull was thick and the face long, with a "modern" projecting nose, a massive jawbone, and large teeth.

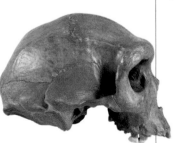

600,000–250,000 ya

Sites Africa and Europe

Brain size 1225–1300 cc

Homo heidelbergensis may have been an ancestor of *Homo neanderthalensis* in Europe. The skull had a large brow ridge like *Homo ergaster* and *Homo erectus* but its brain was larger.

From 150,000 ya

Sites Worldwide

Brain size 900–2000 cc

Homo sapiens roughly translates as "wise man." Our brain size is larger than earlier humans', and it is perhaps this which has enabled us to thrive in a variety of environments around the world.

The Art of Communication

Speech and language were key developments in human history, perhaps even more so than toolmaking. They turned the simple signs and grunts of our ancestors into increasingly sophisticated communication. Archaeology and studies of human anatomy help to indicate when these important traits evolved.

LOOKING AT THE EVIDENCE
Internal casts of human skulls (endocasts) reveal the relatively small brains of *Australopithecus* « 16–19 as apelike and incapable of speech.

A BRAIN FIT FOR THE JOB
The **brain size** of our early ancestors **grew gradually over millions of years**, allowing increasing levels of sophistication in communication and culture. *Homo sapiens'* brain measures 97½ cu in (1,600 cm³), almost three times the size of that of *Homo habilis*, whose brain capacity was 36½ cu in (600 cm³).

NO TALKING
Homo habilis « 16–19, who lived from about 2.5 million years ago, is thought to have had very limited communication skills, possibly using a range of **signs and grunts** to foster cooperation between members of a group.

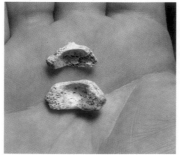

Discovering speech
The hyoid bone is found in the neck and is required for speech to occur. Finds such as these fossilized pieces of 400,000-year-old *Homo heidelbergensis* hyoid bone from Atapuerca, Spain, help date the first human speech.

O ur knowledge about when and how speech evolved remains a controversial area in the study of early human history. Articulate speech is an important threshold in human evolution because it opened up new vistas of cooperative behavior and the enrichment of human life. From archaeological evidence alone, it is difficult to know accurately when speech first developed. *Homo habilis* had a slightly more humanlike frontal lobe (where speech control is located) than earlier australopithecines. Other clues are found in the position of the larynx (voice box)—unlike all other mammals, the larynx of *Homo sapiens* is positioned low, permitting a wide variety of vocal

sounds. *Homo erectus*, from around 1.8 million years ago, was the first human with a lower larynx, and finds from Sima de los Huesos, in Atapuerca, Spain have shown that *Homo heidelbergensis* had developed a hyoid bone—a small, U-shaped bone that lies at the root of the tongue, between the larynx and pharynx—about 400,000 years ago. It was only about 300,000 years ago, however, that the base of the skull evolved, physically allowing fully articulate speech to develop.

The Neanderthal debate
Neanderthals may have had some capacity for speech and communication, and were apparently capable of

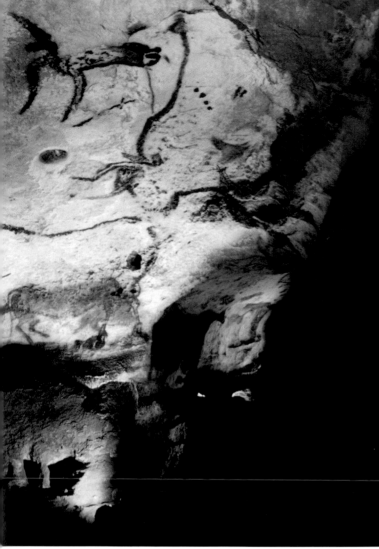

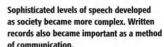

Artistic ability
17,000-year-old art from the Lascaux cave in France shows a high level of sophistication. Modern humans created these images that we can still relate to today.

Africa or southwest Asia. It appears that conscious thought evolved after modern human anatomy, for *Homo sapiens* flourished in tropical Africa at least 160,000 years ago, long before the appearance of the elaborate art traditions of the late Ice Age.

First artists

The creation of art requires reasoning and an ability to plan ahead and express intangible feelings. Some of the earliest known decorated artifacts, which were found in Blombos Cave in South Africa, are about 75,000 years old (see left) and are very basic. The full range of human artistic skills came into play during the late Ice Age, epitomized by the cave art, jewelry, sculpture, and carving of the Cro-Magnon people of Western Europe (see pp.26–27). The great bulls at Lascaux cave in France, and the polychrome bison at the cave at Altamira, in Spain, reflect human societies with complex religious beliefs and relationships with the spirit world. Although we do not know exactly what these paintings mean, it is clear that they had great symbolism for those who painted them. This knowledge would have been passed down through the generations by speech and song. For all later human societies, art has remained an important way of expressing our beliefs and knowledge of the world.

Sophisticated levels of speech developed as society became more complex. Written records also became important as a method of communication.

POWER THROUGH SPEECH

Speech and language enhanced cooperation between hunters, which led to the greater success of human societies around the world. **Groups could plan** game drives, negotiate exchanges of toolmaking stone, and **share intelligence** about food and water supplies.

KEEPING RECORDS

Cuneiform writing **62–63 »** developed in West Asia *c.* 3000 BCE as a means of recording commercial transactions

EGYPTIAN WRITING

and inventories. **Egyptian hieroglyphs** developed at around the same time.

WRITING HISTORY

By the end of the 3rd millennium BCE, writing was widely used for **recording history, philosophy, and science 102–103 »**.

PASSING ON KNOWLEDGE

Speech and writing allowed knowledge and cumulative experience to be passed on from generation to generation.

ABSTRACT THINKING

Today, symbols such as **road signs** are part of an **internationally understood language** we use every day.

ROAD SIGN SYMBOL

---

considerable intellectual reasoning. The discovery of a hyoid bone in Kebara Cave, Israel, dating to about 60,000 years ago, intensified the debate about Neanderthal linguistic abilities. The Kebara hyoid is almost identical to that of modern humans, which has led some anthropologists to claim that the Neanderthals were capable of fully articulate speech. Others disagree, pointing to the high position of the larynx, which would limit the sounds they could make. Some believe that Neanderthals had the communication skills of modern infants. The controversy is unresolved, but most scientists agree that Neanderthals did not have the advanced linguistic and communication skills of *Homo sapiens*.

Blombos beads
These 75,000-year-old perforated shell beads from Blombos Cave, South Africa, are perhaps the oldest known human ornaments in the world.

The great leap

Human language may have evolved because of the need to handle increasingly complex social information, perhaps about 250,000 years ago. As group sizes increased, so did an ability to learn language that could be used to articulate social relationships. It was only later—perhaps around 40,000 years ago during a time that has been referred to as the "Great Leap Forward"—that modern humans developed language of the kind we would recognize today.

Cultural explosion

Connected to the development of speech is the arrival of cognitive thought in early humans. This includes qualities such as perception of our place in the world, intelligence, and moral codes that come with more elaborate societies. None of these advances would have been possible without sophisticated speech. We don't know when *Homo sapiens* acquired the conscious thought and the abilities we have today, but it was at least 40,000 years ago, and most likely in tropical

---

HOW WE KNOW

BRAIN DEVELOPMENT

Research into the brain can reveal some evidence about the development of speech. Soft brain tissues do not fossilize, and are only preserved in casts of the inside of the skull case. The earliest signs of development of Broca's area, the part of the brain that controls speech, occur in *Homo habilis* about two million years ago. *Homo erectus* also shows signs of development in Broca's area, perhaps an indication of slowly evolving speech. However, any study of language abilities from casts is tentative. Unless a well-preserved hominin brain is discovered—which is unlikely—the amount that we are able to discover from Broca's area is limited, and tangible evidence from hyoid bones will still be needed to learn about fluent speech. Much remains speculative in our knowledge of the evolution of speech.

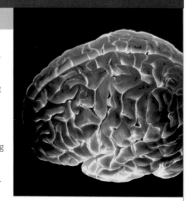

Understanding speech production
Broca's area—showing up red on this brain scan—is located in the left hemisphere of the frontal lobe. As our knowledge of the human brain grows, so does our understanding of how speech developed.

« BEFORE

Over millions of years, Earth has experienced a range of temperatures and climatic conditions that have played a part in the extinction or survival of whole groups of species, and changed the face of the planet.

THE ICE AGES

There is geological evidence (seen in rock surfaces and textures) for **four major ices ages** in Earth's history. The earliest of these is believed to have occurred around 2.7 to 2.3 billion years ago during the Proterozoic period.

HOT PLANET

Temperatures in the past were **generally far higher than today**. Following the extinction of dinosaurs about 65 million years ago, perhaps due to climatic change, average temperatures rose to about 82°F (28°C). Tropical rainforests proliferated on Earth.

THE BIG CHILL

The **abrupt cooling about 1.5 million years ago** that led to the last Ice Age, known as the **Pleistocene epoch**, probably resulted from small shifts in Earth's tilt toward the Sun.

The Ice Age

Much of human history unfolded during the dramatic climatic shifts of the most recent Ice Age, which began about 1.5 million years ago. Our ability to adapt to changes in climate has been crucial to the development of civilization but, adversely, may be the cause of future global warming.

Contrary to popular belief, an Ice Age is not a continual deep freeze, but a period of constantly fluctuating climate conditions punctuated by periods of intense cold. The earliest millennia of the last ice age—the critical period when our remote ancestors first colonized Africa— are little known. The information gleaned from deep-sea cores and ice borings gives us a much clearer picture of ice-age climate after Earth's magnetic field, generated deep inside our planet, abruptly reversed some 780,000 years ago. (It has not reversed since.) Deep-sea cores from the Pacific Ocean reveal at least nine major glacial (icy) periods that have come and gone over the past 780,000 years, the most recent of them ending in abrupt and irregular global warming between

HOW WE KNOW

DEEP SEA AND ICE CORES

Layers of sediment build up over time on ocean beds, and annual layers of ice are added to polar caps. By extracting cores of ice or deep sea sediment and looking at the composition, scientists can build a picture of climate change. Increases in atmospheric CO_2 (carbon dioxide) and CH_4 (methane)— both greenhouse gases—can be detected in the ice and indicate warming.

Similarly, the ratios of oxygen isotopes in the shells of microscopic marine animals reflect changes in sea temperature. The Vostok ice core from Antarctica provides evidence for the last 420,000 years, and shows that major shifts in temperature occur about every 100,000 years.

10,000 and 15,000 years ago. Sea cores give only a general impression of Ice Age climate change, but, as a rule, cooling proceeds relatively slowly and warming unfolds rapidly, as was the case at the end of the last cold (glacial) period. Glacial periods in the past have been longer than interglacials—brief, volatile intervals of warmer conditions during the Ice Age when the climate was as warm (or warmer than) today. These increases in temperature are caused by changes in Earth's path around the Sun and its rotation on its axis. Natural increases in greenhouse gases add to the warming. We are currently experiencing an interglacial period caused by these natural phenomena that began about 10,000 years ago.

Environmental change

The Ice Age witnessed dramatic shifts in global climate and major changes in natural environments. During glacial periods, huge ice sheets formed over Scandinavia, and covered most of Canada and parts of the United States as far south as modern Seattle and the Great Lakes. Great glaciers formed on the Alps and there were ice sheets on

[Graph: y-axis labeled "Degrees °F/°C" with values 39/4, 36/2, 32/0, 28/–2, 25/–4, 21/–6, 18/–8, 14/–10; right side labeled "Level of CO₂" with "High" at top and "Low" at bottom; x-axis labeled "Years before present" with values 400,000, 350,000, 300,000, 250,000, 200,000, 150,000, 100,000, 50,000, 0]

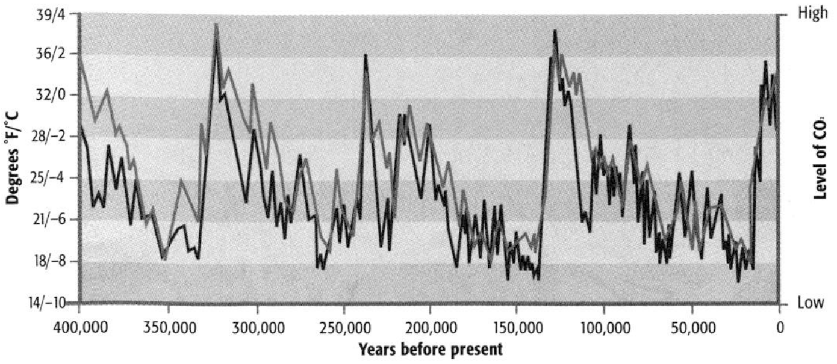

KEY

▬▬ Level of CO_2

▬▬ Temperature

Temperature variations of the Ice Age

Layers of sediment in ice cores taken from Vostok in Antarctica have enabled scientists to chart temperature variations over the past 420,000 years. The levels of CO_2 in the atmosphere have also been recorded and are linked to temperature rises, as can be seen here.

the Pyrenees, on the Andes, and on Central Asian mountains and high-altitude plateaus. South of the Scandinavian ice sheets, huge expanses of barren landscape extended from the Atlantic to Siberia. These environments suffered nine-month winters and were uninhabitable by ancestors of *Homo sapiens*, who lacked the technology and clothing to adapt to the extremes of temperature. It is no coincidence that *Homo erectus*, with their simple technology and limited cognitive skills, settled in more temperate and tropical

90

The number of meters (yards) sea levels around the world dropped at the beginning of the last Ice Age as water froze to form the ice caps of present-day Antarctica and the Arctic.

environments. The cold caused sea levels to fall dramatically as more water was converted into ice. Huge expanses of what are now continental shelves (land under shallow coastal waters) were exposed, linking land masses— Siberia was part of Alaska, and Britain was joined to Europe. Only short stretches of open water separated mainland Southeast Asia from Australia and New Guinea.

During interglacials, sea levels rose, ice sheets shrank, and forests moved northward as the steppe-tundra vanished. Humans moved north, following the animals they hunted and the plants they foraged, and adapting to a broad range of forested and grassland environments as well as arid and semiarid lands.

Humans and the elements

The Ice Age climate was volatile and the world's environments changed constantly, which meant that the opportunism and adaptive ability of humans was continuously challenged from one millennium to the next. These challenges may even have been

A harsh world

Temperature variations up to 10,000 years ago meant that humans could only survive by adapting to the changing conditions. Our ancestors became successful at surviving and thriving in the cold.

a factor in human evolution. Our earliest ancestors originated in tropical Africa and were basically tropical animals. During long periods of the ice ages, the Sahara was slightly wetter than today. The desert can almost be seen as a pump, drawing in animals and early humans during wetter periods, then pushing them out to the margins when the climate became drier. This was the ecological effect that allowed *Homo erectus* and the animals they preyed on to cross the desert and spread into more temperate environments some 1.8 million years ago.

A major interglacial raised temperatures, peaking around 400,000 years ago. By that time, *Homo erectus* was thriving in north Europe, but they could not adapt to the extreme cold of the glaciation that followed around 350,000 years ago. The few hunting bands living there probably moved southward to more temperate regions. By around 250,000 years ago, there are traces of early human settlement in Europe and parts of East Asia. The final interglacial peaked about 128,000 years ago, when Neanderthals (see p.19) were thriving in Europe. They adapted to the extreme cold of the last glaciation. After 50,000 years ago, modern humans had mastered all the global environments and were living in even the coldest and most extreme parts of the world.

10,000

The number of years ago that the current interglacial began. Based on past shifts, this warmer phase could last 100,000 years, although the influence of humans may affect this.

THE ABANDONED SITE OF CHACO CANYON

INCREASED VULNERABILITY

For most of human history, people have lived in small, highly mobile bands **30–31 »**. Farming **36–37 »** made humanity more **vulnerable to major climatic events** because people were unable to quickly move to avoid them. Such short-term events were a factor in the **rise and collapse of early civilizations**. One example of this is Chaco Canyon in New Mexico, a site that was settled between 900 and 1150 CE and was abandoned following drought and other unknown dramatic climatic changes.

THE EL NIÑO PHENOMENON

El Niño is a reversal in the flow of water in the Pacific Ocean that causes dramatic changes in the weather every two to seven years. El Niño is one of the most powerful influences on climate after the seasons. The phenomenon originates in the Southwest Pacific and results from interactions between the ocean and the atmosphere. El Niños have affected human history for at least 10,000 years. Major El Niños

EL NIÑO have **powerful global effects**, causing monsoon failures, and drought or flooding elsewhere. This thermal image highlights El Niño currents in white and red.

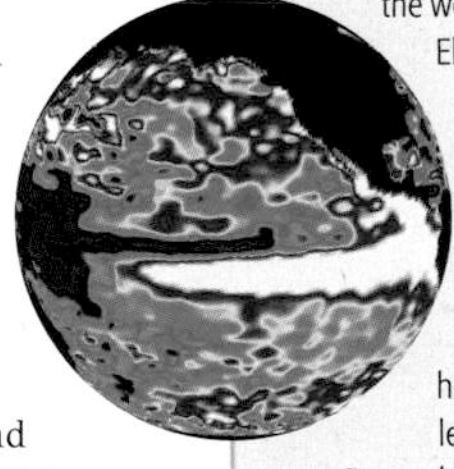

PERIOD OF STABILITY

As temperatures rose after the Ice Age, humans adapted to a rapidly changing world of **shrinking ice sheets and rising sea levels**.

MONSOON SEASON, INDIA

After 5,000 years of irregular warming and cooling, the world entered a warming period that has lasted into modern times. The Vostok ice core tells us this period is among the most warm and stable of the past 420,000 years.

THE FUTURE

The overuse of fossil fuels has increased **global warming**. The future effects of this human-made problem are still unknown.

> Earth is currently experiencing a warmer phase but is still affected by fluctuations in temperature and natural phenomena such as El Niño.

« BEFORE

The ancestors of modern humans (*Homo sapiens*) colonized Africa, Europe, and western Asia.

LIFE IN THE FREEZER
The last glaciation (colder period) of the Ice Age, when many areas were covered in ice, lasted from 100,000 to 50,000 years ago. During this period, sea levels were far below modern levels and **Siberia and Alaska were linked by land**. It was also **drier than today** and tropical climates were slightly cooler **« 22–23**. This was followed by a slightly warmer period before a return to extreme cold about 18,000 years ago.

ICY LANDSCAPE

ORIGINS OF MODERN HUMANS
The original ancestors of modern humans evolved south of the Sahara Desert in tropical Africa. The scattered **human population was very small**, and groups developed in isolation from each other.

EARLY MAN ON THE MOVE
Early *Homo erectus* fossils **« 19** indicate that they had settled in western Europe by 800,000 years ago. Neanderthals **« 19** spread into Europe and western Asia by 200,000 years ago.

FLINT HAND-AXES
This **technology,** developed in Africa 2.5 million years ago, was used for millions of years **« 17**.

FLINT HAND-AX

100,000 **The number of years since small groups of humans began to leave Africa. By 60,000 years ago genetically modern *Homo sapiens* were colonizing the Earth.**

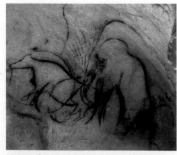
Mammoth cave painting
The walls of Lascaux Cave in France are alive with bison, mammoth, wild oxen, and stag. Cro-Magnon artists (see p.26–27) painted these powerful, ageless images in this Ice Age treasure trove of art some 17,000 years ago.

Out of Africa

Every human today is the descendant of a small group of modern humans who left Africa around 60,000 years ago to explore the planet. We can see the legacy of these journeys today in the diversity of races and cultures around the world.

Sixty thousand years ago, modern humans (*Homo sapiens*) were confined to tropical Africa and a small part of southwestern Asia. These were people with the same physical and mental abilities as ourselves, hunter-gatherers capable of adapting to any environment on Earth, be it one with nine-month winters and subzero temperatures, or steamy tropical rainforests. Then, during the last cold period of the last Ice Age, the most significant of all human migrations out of Africa began. Toward the end of the Ice Age 15,000 years ago, this vast population movement was complete. Late Ice Age hunting bands had settled all of mainland Africa and Eurasia and had crossed, or were about to cross, into the Americas. *Homo sapiens* had mastered tropical waters with canoes or rafts, had drifted or paddled to New Guinea and Australia, and penetrated as far south as Tasmania.

Survival of the fittest
Earlier forms of humans such as *Homo habilis* and *Homo erectus* had long vanished from Earth, forced into extinction on marginal lands where food was not plentiful, or killed by the newcomers, with whom they could not compete.

Colonizing the planet was not a deliberate project, undertaken by men and women set on occupying new lands or exploring the world that lay beyond their hunting territories. Rather, the complex population movements that took modern humans to the limits of the harsh late Ice Age world came about as a result of the necessities of hunting and plant collecting in a great diversity of natural environments. In more northern climates, meat was the staple food, while tropical and temperate groups made considerable use of wild plant foods. The secrets to survival were adaptability—the ability to adjust to sudden changes in climatic conditions by technological innovation—and sheer ingenuity, mobility, and opportunism. People responded to food shortages, drought, or extreme cold by moving elsewhere in a world where the total global population was perhaps no more than five million people, scattered in small groups over hunting territories large and small.

Many people may not have encountered more than a few dozen fellow humans during their lives, although we can only speculate about this, as the population figures can only be educated guesses.

Evidence of migration
Dozens of archaeological sites—caves, rock shelters, open camps, and huge garbage heaps, or "middens," of seashells and freshwater mollusks—document the great journeys made as humans spread around the globe. Klasies River Mouth in South Africa is one such site where caves were used as shelter by modern humans about 120,000 years ago, showing that by that date the first modern people had traveled from their origins in northeastern Africa (see pp.18–19).

The techniques of molecular biology are another way in which we can learn more about the movement of these early humans. By comparing certain strands of DNA (the substance found in every human cell that determines the characteristics we inherit), we can

1 **MILLION The estimated human population of Earth 500,000 years ago.**

work out how Earth was colonized by *Homo sapiens*, and when splits in the population occurred. This was a complex process involving constant movement by small numbers of people. We are only just beginning to comprehend the process of colonization, but one thing seems certain: all non-Africans are descended from what American biologist Stephen J. Gould once called "a single African twig" on the human family tree.

All people alive today have their ultimate roots in the so-called "African Eve" of some 150,000 years ago. This name stems from the fact that MtDNA (mitochondrial DNA) was passed from mother to offspring through every generation since the first *Homo sapiens*. We all share genetic information with "Eve," with each other, and with our ancestors (see p.27).

Human migration
This map shows key sites for our early ancestors, as well as the routes that *Homo sapiens* is thought to have taken from Africa around the world.

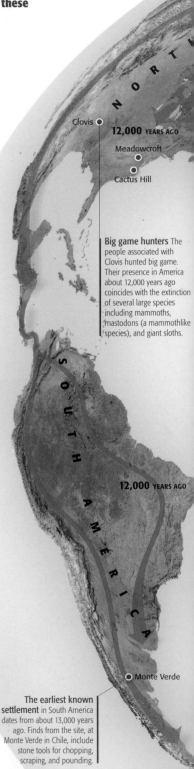

Clovis
12,000 YEARS AGO
Meadowcroft
Cactus Hill

Big game hunters The people associated with Clovis hunted big game. Their presence in America about 12,000 years ago coincides with the extinction of several large species including mammoths, mastodons (a mammothlike species), and giant sloths.

12,000 YEARS AGO

Monte Verde

The earliest known settlement in South America dates from about 13,000 years ago. Finds from the site, at Monte Verde in Chile, include stone tools for chopping, scraping, and pounding.

KEY

→ Migration of *Homo sapiens* around the world
● Site of early *Homo sapiens* find
○ Site of early Hominin find

Beringia Land Bridge

AMERICA

Kennewick

15,000 YEARS AGO

This mammoth bone carving found at Dolní Vestonice was made by hunters between 28,000 and 22,000 years ago.

ATLANTIC OCEAN

EUROPE

Schöningen
Boxgrove
Lascaux
Le Moustier
Altamira
Atapuerca
Dolní Vestonice

45,000 YEARS AGO

Dmanisi
Shanidar

60,000 YEARS AGO

AFRICA

160,000 YEARS AGO

Huerto
Hadar
West Turkana
Koobi Fora
Lake Turkana
Nariokotome
Olduvai
Laetoli

120,000 YEARS AGO

This archaeologist holds the remains of *Homo erectus*, which dates from about 1 million years ago, and was found on this site. The first modern humans in China occupied this site by about 40,000 years ago.

25,000 YEARS AGO
Zhoukoudian

ASIA

50,000 YEARS AGO

PACIFIC OCEAN

INDIAN OCEAN

Niah

Sangiran
Flores

Malakunanja

45,000 YEARS AGO

AUSTRALIA

Lake Mungo

The cave paintings of Altamira date from about 15,000 years ago and are famous for their dramatic representations of bison, boar, and red deer in charcoal and earth pigments by people of the Magdalenian (Paleolithic) culture of southern Europe.

"Lucy" (*Australopithecus afarensis*) was found in Ethiopia in 1974, dates from about three million years ago, and is an important example of an *Australopithecus* (see pp.16–17). This area of northeastern Africa is rich with early hominin remains and continues to yield finds that provoke new theories about our own evolution.

Blombos Cave
Klasies River Mouth

Klasies River Mouth Caves in South Africa were occupied by hunter-gatherers *c.* 120,000 years ago and have revealed some clues about how they lived. Some of the earliest known remains of *Homo sapiens* were found in the caves.

The earliest finds in Australia come from Lake Mungo. Tourists today visit a landscape of strange formations where over 20,000 years ago there was a lake and much human activity. Stone tools and animal bones found in the area have shown us much about the first Australians.

The bone house
This reconstruction of a shelter built from mammoth bones is based on the remains of a dwelling that was found by archaeologists in modern-day Ukraine. It demonstrates the ingenuity and adaptability of early humans to local conditions and resources.

Europe. These Cro-Magnon people—named after a rock shelter near Les Eyzies in southwestern France—were opportunists. They relied for their subsistence on a range of plant foods and fish, taking advantage of salmon runs, for example, when the rapidly changing climate of the late Ice Age allowed. Their success came not only from their superior mental abilities, but also from their ingenious multi-purpose flint tools, which worked almost like a modern Swiss Army knife. They used carefully shaped flint nodules to produce standardized, parallel-sided blanks, which they then turned into points, scrapers, and other tools. One of these artifacts—a chisel—allowed them to cut grooves in reindeer antlers, thereby "unlocking" a new technology for manufacturing harpoon heads, spear points, and other hunting weapons. Barbed, antler-tipped spears were especially effective on reindeer and other game. The Cro-Magnons produced other revolutionary items, including the spear thrower—a hooked stick that vastly increased the distance a spear could be thrown. They successfully used this new technology to hunt a

wide range of Ice Age animals, including bison, mammoth, and woolly rhinoceros. The eyed needle was another remarkable invention (see below). These people were also skilled artists and developed a distinctive visual tradition, which amplified their elaborate rituals and beliefs. One of the most famous examples of their art comes from the cave paintings of Lascaux in southwestern France, which are on a huge scale, and renowned for the skill of the artists who created them

Sometime after about 50,000 years ago, when glacial conditions in the north had improved and the climate was more temperate, modern humans moved into Europe and Asia. Tiny numbers of people were involved—in the hundreds—but by 45,000 years ago they were well established in the eastern European plains and in the Don Valley, now in Ukraine, and were moving rapidly across Central and Western Europe.

The Neanderthal controversy
Homo sapiens had settled alongside Neanderthal bands that had already been in Europe for about 200,000

years. DNA research on Neanderthal bones suggests that the newcomers did not interbreed with them, as had previously been believed. One theory is that Europe's indigenous inhabitants died out because they lacked the adaptability, mental abilities, and technology of modern humans. They survived in some parts of southeastern Europe until as late as 24,000 years ago before becoming extinct.

A thriving European culture
From about 40,000 to 10,000 years ago, a remarkable array of sophisticated, cold-adapted hunter-gatherer societies flourished in Central and Western

INVENTION
THE NEEDLE
The eyed needle was a groundbreaking invention. As early as 30,000 years ago, late Ice Age people in Europe and Asia made needles from polished bone and ivory slivers, perforated with sharp-pointed flints. They sewed tailored, layered garments that enabled them to work outside in freezing temperatures. It is believed that, like modern Inuits, they used cured and softened animal pelts, sewing the seams with fine thread made of animal and plant fiber. Without tailored clothing *Homo sapiens* would never have settled the Eurasian steppes or colonized the Americas.

The longest journey
The first *Homo sapiens* left Africa to colonize the planet about 60,000 years ago. By the end of the Ice Age 10,000 years ago, they had reached all the continents except Antarctica, adapting to different conditions wherever they went.

(see pp.20–21). For the first time, people had the skills to live in harsh environments like the Eurasian steppes, where there is little rainfall and dramatic changes in temperature with hot summers and very cold winters. Despite these skills, the Cro-Magnons appear to have moved south into sheltered locations, only moving north again as temperatures rose. Some of them constructed elaborate dwellings, like the intricate mammoth bone houses at Mezhirich in modern Ukraine (see left), built partially into the ground and roofed with hides and sod. Toward the end of the Ice Age, about 12,000 years ago, human society became more elaborate, as populations grew larger and new areas were colonized.

Siberia and the tundra

Homo sapiens migrated north from southwestern Asia and colonized the river valleys of Central Asia around 45,000 years ago. Small bands lived permanently in the bitter cold of the steppe-tundra—a windswept landscape featuring low-growing vegetation—that extended from central Europe all the way to Siberia far to the northeast. Enduring long winters, each band anchored itself on shallow river valleys like those of the Don and Dnieper in Russia, subsisting for the most part on animals such as the saiga antelope and large game, including the arctic elephant and the mammoth.

HOW WE KNOW

ADAPTING TO CHANGE

Study of the genes of modern populations can help to show how the early humans colonized the planet. Mitochondrial DNA, inherited through the maternal line back to a fictional "Eve" (see p.24), can be traced from an ancestral tropical African population to today. The male Y chromosome can also be used to trace through generations. From this evidence we know that 99.9 percent of the genetic code of modern humans is identical throughout the world. The differences in facial features and coloring are down to minor genetic mutations that have taken place over the last 150,000 years. Amazingly, the world's population outside Africa can trace their genetic history back to perhaps as few as 1,000 individuals who made the journey out of that continent. Chromosome mutations can be used to show when groups arrived in different parts of the world and to construct a genetic family tree that goes back to the Ice Age.

Between 35,000 and 18,000 years ago, some hunting bands moved northeastward across the steppe-tundra into the Lake Baikal region of Siberia and farther to the northeast. Some moved to, or formed, new groups, while others moved to find new hunting grounds or natural resources. A variety of circumstances linked to hunting and survival contributed to the movement of tiny numbers of these late Ice Age bands across an extremely inhospitable landscape. Such natural population movements led to vast areas of the globe being colonized.

Even earlier, from around *c.* 60,000 years ago, other groups moved east from northeast Africa and southwestern Asia into what is now India and Pakistan, and into the tropical forests of Southeast Asia. We know little of these movements—the groups probably skirted the Eurasian

A hunter's tool kit
As humans traveled around the globe and experienced different environments and climates, they adapted their weapons and tools to survive. These bone tools, found in France and dating to between 18,000 and 10,000 years ago, were used by hunters in Ice Age Europe.

FLORES FIND

Excavations in 2003 at Liang Bua Cave (right) on Flores Island, in Indonesia, yielded the remains of a tiny skeleton standing about 3 ft 6 in (1 m) tall. The bones display a unique mix of primitive and more advanced characteristics, and date to about 18,000 years ago. With a small skull (below), large brow ridge, and a delicate face, *Homo floresiensis* had slight legs like some early hominins, yet modern teeth. Questions have been raised over whether this is a separate species or a small *Homo sapiens*. Others suggest this is the remnant of a *Homo erectus* population, or the descendant of humans who drifted to the island, then developed unique anatomical traits in isolation. Unless more remains are found, *Homo floresiensis* may remain an intriguing, unsolved mystery.

》》 deserts and settled in northeastern China by 25,000 years ago, after the warmer south part of the continent had been explored.

Sunda, Sahul, and Asia

During the late Ice Age, a huge continental shelf—an area of land connecting the continents that is now covered by higher sea levels—known as Sunda extended from mainland Southeast Asia far into the Pacific. Only short stretches of open water separated New Guinea and Australia from this now-sunken land. Another landmass, Sahul, linked Australia and New Guinea themselves. *Homo sapiens* arrived in mainland Southeast Asia before 50,000 years ago. By 45,000 years ago—the date is controversial— a few hunting bands had crossed open water to Sahul and colonized what is now Australia. They may have crossed on primitive rafts or in dugout canoes. Modern humans had settled New Guinea by about 40,000 years ago, and crossed to the Solomon Islands by about 5,000 years later. Hunter-gatherers had settled throughout Australia, including Tasmania, by 30,000 years ago.

This was the outer limit of human settlement of the offshore Pacific until outrigger canoes (see pp.216–17) and open-water navigation techniques allowed people with domesticated animals and root crops to make the lengthy open-water passages

after 1000 BCE. The evidence of human life at Lake Mungo in Australia reveals details of hunter-gatherer life about 40,000 years ago. It is important as it captures a moment in time and a lifestyle that remained largely unchanged for thousands of years.

Reaching the Americas

Archaeologists have disputed the date of the first settlement of the Americas for over a century. Most now agree that native Americans originated in Siberia. Genetic and dental evidence links the two areas and backs up this theory. There are also linguistic ties that hint at population movements from Siberia to Alaska. But it is not known precisely when and how the first settlement took place.

Until about 10,000 years ago, a low-lying land bridge, Beringia, joined Siberia to Alaska

(see pp.24–25). Most scientists believe that the first Americans were Siberian hunters who crossed this bridge into Alaska at least 15,000 years ago, toward the end of the Ice Age.

Route south

More controversy surrounds the route by which the first Americans penetrated the heart of North America, something which is thought to have taken place at least 13,000 years ago. Huge ice sheets covered most of what is now Canada. One theory favors a movement south along the continental shelves of southeast Alaska and British Columbia, which was then a landscape of steppe-tundra. Another common hypothesis claims a rapid movement south along a narrow corridor between two ice sheets, one mantling the Rocky Mountains and the other extending east toward the Atlantic. The controversy is unresolved, but we know that small numbers of early American hunter-gatherers were south of the ice sheets, and some as far south as Chile, by at least 13,000 years ago.

The early Americans are best known from the remains of kills of bison, mammoth, and mastodon in North America. They are often labeled "big-game" hunters, which is misleading, as they relied on plant foods and adapted to temperate and tropical areas, as well as the bleak lands at the margins of retreating ice sheets. They did prey on indigenous species of large mammals, but, by 10,500 years ago, most of this "megafauna" was extinct, probably as a result of drier climatic conditions, perhaps speeded by some overhunting.

Early evidence

The archaeological record of the early Americas is sketchy. Key sites include a 12,000-year-old rock shelter in Meadowcroft, Pennsylvania, a scatter of stone tools from a site at Cactus Hill, Virginia, and a well-documented foraging camp at Monte Verde, Chile, dating to about 13,000 years ago. The first well-defined culture is that of the Clovis people, famous for their fine flint tools, who flourished between about 11,200 and 10,900 years ago. One controversial discovery is a 9,500 year-old skull from Kennewick, Washington State, which is believed to have caucasian features and may be an indication that some of the first settlers in America came from Europe. However, this has been the subject of much debate.

By 10,000 years ago humans had spread to every continent (except Antarctica) and had learned the skills needed to survive in different environments. Later explorers found their "new world" already inhabited by the descendants of those first settlers.

ADAPTING TO CHANGE

American Indian societies adjusted to warmer, often drier conditions, by intensifying the search for food, whether it be fish, game, or plant foods. By 4000 BCE, some foraging groups were experimenting with the **planting of native grasses 36–37 》》**, such as goosefoot.

LATER EXPLORATION

Europeans first came in **contact with American Indians** 500 years ago when they traveled the world in search of new land **230 》》**. Dutch settlers arrived in Manhattan in the 1800s and traded with the native population before establishing a permanent settlement there.

EUROPEAN SETTLERS IN AMERICA

AN ISOLATED CULTURE

The culture of the Australian Aboriginals developed in virtually complete isolation. Like other hunter-gatherer societies, they have **a complex relationship with their environment** and elaborate spiritual beliefs.

ABORIGINAL HUNTER

ATLATL

Atlatls (from an Aztec word) are throwing sticks or spear-throwers, first developed by Cro-Magnon hunters over 20,000 years ago. Spear throwers increase a spear's range and velocity—useful qualities for hunters who rely on stalking to kill their prey. The simplest atlatls are hooked sticks. A weight adds stability and velocity to the throw. Such weights, often called "bannerstones," are often found on native American sites, as they arrived with the first inhabitants of the region. The Aztecs later used them against Spanish *conquistadors* (see pp.230–31).

Oldest footprints

Hundreds of human footprints, preserved for over 20,000 years, have been found at Lake Mungo, Australia. At that time, the lake there would have been home to fish, mussels, and crayfish—all valuable food sources.

Clovis points

North American hunters made these flint spearpoints over 11,000 years ago. They are some of the few objects found from this early period. They would have been used to kill and cut up large prey such as mammoth.

Hunters and Gatherers

Hunting and foraging for food was the only way of life for all humans up until 12,000 years ago. It was a successful lifestyle that, in some ways, had significant advantages over a life of farming. Today, only a handful of hunter-gatherer societies survive, in the Amazon Basin and Africa.

We have been able to understand more about the hunter-gatherer diet from surviving artifacts such as carved stone and bone tools and decorative items (see pp.34–35), and also from hunting scenes in rock paintings, such as those at Lascaux, France, and Altamira, Spain. Rare finds of wooden digging sticks and flint sickle blades show that people dug for tubers and harvested wild grasses. Broken animal and fish bones, and fossil plant pollens, reveal details of the hunter-gatherer diet, as do deep shell middens (waste sites) crammed with the discarded shells of edible mollusks.

In addition, the few surviving hunter-gatherer societies can tell us first-hand about the dynamics of human existence before agriculture and animal domestication.

Mammoth hunters
Most hunter-gatherer bands were constantly on the move, camping near lakes and other strategic locations during the times of year when a particular plant food ripened or game was close by. At Dolní Vestonice, in what is now the Czech Republic, mammoth hunters lived in oval bone-and-timber huts (see p.26)

Gathered food
Wild plant foods, whether grasses, nuts, or tubers, were the dominant staple for most ancient hunter-gatherer societies. In most societies, women did the gathering.

The hunter's equipment
The earliest weapons took the form of simple flint arrowheads. As hunters became more sophisticated, weapons grew more specialized. The harpoon point, below, is carved from bone and suited to fishing. Arrows would have been used about 8,000 years ago for hunting.

overlooking a river valley and nearby swamps. Among the objects found at the site, which dates back to the last Ice Age, is the oldest known ceramic in the world—a "Venus" figurine (a carving shaped like a female figure) dating to between 29,000 and 25,000 BCE. Other carvings of bears, lions, and mammoths indicate a culture of some degree of sophistication. A similar date has been given to the Venus of Willendorf (see p.34) found in Austria. It has been suggested that these figurines represent fertility and the success of the hunter-gatherer group they are associated with.

Stone age transition
The line between nomadic hunting and gathering and settled farming is not always clear. Many communities may have stayed in one place while hunting, or moved around and cultivated crops. Ten thousand years ago, bands of Mesolithic (Middle Stone Age) fishers and hunters lived by the Baltic Sea, which at that stage was newly uncovered by retreating ice. Their diet mainly consisted of fish, supplemented by birds, plant foods, and game, caught

using stone-tipped arrows, antler harpoons, and wooden spears. Many groups in this area occupied the same settlements for generations, living along shorelines that shifted constantly.

Another site that has revealed details about a community that was hunting and gathering while on the move throughout the year is Star Carr in northeastern England. In 9000 BCE, a small group of Mesolithic people settled on waterlogged ground by a lake there. The wet conditions preserved flint tools, the remains of the elk and red deer they hunted, and the barbed spear points they used to kill them. Teeth and seeds tell us the site was occupied every year from March to June. These people adapted successfully to a rapidly changing post–Ice Age world by

BEFORE

Hunting and gathering, or foraging for food, is the fundamental way that humans and their ancestors lived. The success of the species depended on their ability to use Earth's resources to their own advantage.

HUMAN SCAVENGERS
Evidence from bones and flints has shown that early humans may have eaten the remains of animals killed by other predators rather than hunting for most of their food.

A VARIED DIET
As the first modern humans spread around the world **《 24–29** their diet changed in response to **locally available foods**. A process of trial and error would have been necessary while learning what foods were good to eat and what could potentially be harmful.

HAZELNUTS

CHANGING TO SURVIVE
Human societies throughout the world had to **adapt to radically different environments**. Predictability, seasonality, abundance, and **distribution of food resources** such as fish and nuts affected their choice to live a nomadic or more settled existence.

serrated edge

HARPOON POINT

FISHING SPEAR

twine binding

FLINT ARROW

flints stuck in groove of wooden shaft

flight of duck feathers

MESOLITHIC ARROW

reproduction shaft

BOW AND ARROW

Bows and arrows appeared during the late Ice Age and came into widespread use by about 10,000 BCE. At first, these would have been simple wooden bows used with stone- or bone-tipped arrows. The composite bow, made of sinews and bone or wood laminated together, is known from 1500 BCE, and reached North America in the first millennium CE.

INUIT BOW

AFTER »

Some hunter-gatherer groups had turned to farming by 10,000 BCE. Others continued to develop and innovate.

WHY NOT FARM?

From about 10,000 BCE there was a general transition from the hunter-gatherer lifestyle to farming. Some groups continued to forage for food, perhaps partly due to conditions in the part of the world they lived in, making growing crops or staying in one place impossible. Another reason may be that farming needs **more time spent devoted to food production and carries a greater risk of starvation** if crops fail. Some groups, such as the Haida people of North America and the Aboriginals in Australia, seem to have retained the hunter-gatherer lifestyle.

HAIDA HOUSE

CULTURAL COMPLEXITY

In areas of exceptionally rich food resources, much more **elaborate hunter-gather societies** developed after about 3000 years ago. In the Pacific Northwest of North America, for example, rich salmon and coastal fisheries and abundant lumber led to the development of complex societies under powerful chieftains.

INNOVATION

By 2000 years ago, the Norton people in North America had developed **sophisticated art** styles and an **elaborate harpoon weaponry** for hunting seals. By 1000 CE, the **ancestors of the modern-day Inuit** had settled in Canada.

MODERN INUIT SETTLEMENT

Hunting in the field
A modern San hunter takes aim with bow and arrow. His success depends on meticulous stalking to approach his quarry at close range. Many early hunters used vegetable poisons on their arrows, pursuing wounded animals for hours to kill them before predators struck.

maintaining a flexible way of life. Lepenski Vir in modern-day Serbia was also repeatedly used over many generations and has yielded a lot of information about a culture between two lifestyles. The site, used from as early as 6000 BCE, was situated on the banks of the Danube River, and the group's reliance on fishing was heavy. The fish sculptures found there (see pp.34–35) are significant early works of art and may be symbols of a religious cult, such was the importance of fish to this culture. The people lived in structures whose wide ends faced the river. Revisited for several hundred years, Lepenski Vir provides a portrait of a gradual changeover from nomadic life to more permanent settlement. The seminomadic lifestyle of Lepenski

Vir meant that people lived there for part of the year while also traveling to other areas. Finds at the site discovered some distance away provide the evidence for this.

A continuing way of life

Five thousand years ago, much of East and southern Africa was home to nomadic hunter-gatherer bands, which subsisted on a wide variety of animal and plant foods. Some sites, such as Gwisho in Central Africa, have revealed well-preserved wooden arrowheads and digging sticks, as well as traces of brush shelters. Many of these groups regularly visited rock shelters, including those at Nachikufu in present-day Zambia, Pomongwe in Zimbabwe, and Oakhurst rock shelter

in South Africa. These people, well known for their rock art (see pp.32–33), were the distant ancestors of the modern-day San hunter-gatherers, tiny numbers of whom still live in the Kalahari Desert of Botswana. Modern-day San have long been in contact with farmers, but the ancestry of their culture extends back to ancient times. As in other traditional hunter-gather cultures, the women are responsible for much of the food collection and hunting smaller animals, while the men hunt large prey.

BEFORE

There is little evidence that early humans before Neanderthals buried their dead or believed in a higher power.

NEANDERTHAL BELIEF

Neanderthals **《 19** first **buried their dead** at least 60,000 years ago.

CONSCIOUS THOUGHT

Homo sapiens is unique in **thinking and planning ahead**, and in conceptualizing ideas. Such cognitive abilities first appeared around 50,000 years ago, and perhaps even earlier **《 21**.

A wealth of grave goods

Two 25,000-year-old hunter-gatherers buried in Sungir near Vladimir in Russia lie surrounded by spears, bracelets, brooches, and thousands of ivory beads.

The Spirit World

Ever since humans became conscious of their own frailty and mortality, they have sought the answers to the eternal mysteries of life. Theories about the purpose of our existence and questions about what happens after we die will always be a part of the human experience.

It is difficult to know what the beliefs of humans were before the advent of writing. However, from the material remains left to us, we can piece together some of the ideas of the particular culture that created them. The main ways in which we know about prehistoric religion today are from images painted on cave walls, and from objects found in graves (grave goods). Death is often thought of as a link to another world, and the practices surrounding burial are always significant. The art of early humans found in caves and on bone carvings are indications of their beliefs outside of their everyday existence.

From about 40,000 years ago, the Cro-Magnons of western Europe developed a flamboyant artistic tradition that survives on cave walls and on beautifully carved and engraved antler tools (see pp.20–21). The cave engravings and paintings depict a wide range of animals, some of them long extinct, such as the mammoth and woolly rhinoceros; others, like wild horses, European bison, and reindeer are more familiar today. The animals on the cave walls reflect a harsh late Ice Age environment where people survived

for much of the year on meat. This reliance on hunting may have been inspired rituals that became the focus of cave art. By contrast, human figures in cave paintings are rare, and when they do occur are highly stylized or masked. Impressions of human hands and undecipherable signs do, however, appear on the walls of caves including Altamira in Spain, and Chauvet, Niaux, and Lascaux in France.

Magic and ceremony

Generations of archaeologists have argued over the meaning of Cro-Magnon cave art, which flourished until about 14,000 years ago. One theory is that the paintings were done by shamans (see box). In many hunter-gatherer societies, shamans were believed to act as intermediaries with

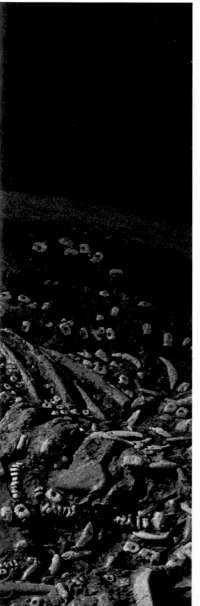

the spiritual world, using trances and hallucinogenic substances to pass into the realm of the supernatural. They were thought to communicate with ancestors, as well as retelling stories, and legends. They also passed ritual knowledge from one generation to the next. Late Ice Age shamans may have conducted ceremonies in caves, often painted with murals, where the acoustics lend themselves to chanting and singing, and in other less accessible caves far from daylight, where they may have felt closer to powers outside their immediate environment.

Surviving clues

In cultures that have survived up to more recent times we may find further clues to past beliefs. The American Indians and Australian Aboriginals live in worlds where the living and supernatural realms are treated as a continuation of one another. Both enjoyed elaborate ceremonial lives that included initiation ceremonies and seasonal rituals, as well as

commemorations of ancestral spirits. Hunter-gatherer societies that we know about today are almost universal in possessing complex beliefs and world views that are intimately connected to the natural world around them. Although we do not know that people in ancient cultures shared these rituals and beliefs, some of the artifacts and clues we have indicate this as a possibility.

Other forms of art provide further clues. The female figurines of hunter-gatherer societies (see p.30–31) may have been made as objects of worship, and related to a fertility cult. Carved antlers and bones similarly may have been connected with religious belief.

Grave goods

One of the earliest and most lavish burials found was in Sungir, Russia. The sheer richness and diversity of the artifacts accompanying the bodies

Aboriginal dreamtime
Australian Aboriginals enjoy a complex relationship with the supernatural realm that permeates their living world. Their art, such as this example from a cave wall, depicts mythic animals and humans and forms an important part of their spiritual beliefs—known as the Dreamtime.

shows that these people lived in a complex society with a strong hierarchical structure, and that they were concerned with what happened after death. One of the individuals, a girl of about eight years old, was found with the remains of over 5,000 ivory beads, which, it is estimated, each took over one hour to carve. The fact that such wealth accompanied the burials may indicate a religion in which these objects were needed to accompany the dead on a journey to another life. In other cultures food was left with the dead, suggesting a belief in an afterlife in which sustenance is required.

Some of the earliest buildings relating to religious belief may come from Çatalhüyök in Turkey from c. 7000 BCE, where murals are indications that the spaces were used for ritual purposes. However, until later periods when written records are preserved, our knowledge about belief and the afterlife can only be conjecture.

AFTER

Cultures throughout history have shared a belief in an afterlife and a higher power.

EGYPTIAN AFTERLIFE
The *Book of the Dead* is the common name for a collection of **funerary scripts** on papyrus, dating from c. 1600 BCE and thought to have been used by the ancient Egyptians as a set of **instructions for the afterlife 68–69 >>**. The grave goods placed in the pyramids of the Pharaohs to help them in the afterlife are further indication of a strong belief in another life.

BELIEF IN ANOTHER LIFE
A belief in the afterlife or reincarnation is still a part of human thought and is key to many religions, including **Hinduism, Buddhism, and Christianity 144–47 >>**.

CELTIC BELIEF
Deities connected with **death, fertility, and birth** are shown on the Gundestrup cauldron, dating from 2nd-century-BCE Denmark.

BOOK OF THE DEAD

GUNDESTRUP CAULDRON

HOW WE KNOW
THE SHAMAN TRADITION

Shamans—doctors, priests, or medicine men—still exist in some cultures, including this tribe from the Sepik Region of Papua New Guinea (see right), where the shaman is believed to possess supernatural powers. By observing their practices and rituals, it is possible to draw some useful parallels with early societies.

Archaeologist David Lewis-Williams argues that much of the cave art of the San hunter-gatherers of southern Africa was painted by shamans in hallucinogenic trances. These types of drug- or trance-induced experiences are still seen today in a few societies.

1 FLINT HAND-AX

6 CRO-MAGNON FLUTE

7 FLINT ARROWHEAD

2 DEER BONE CARVING

10 STONE CARVING

3 FLINT AXE

8 CARVED BONES

11 QUERNSTONE

4 "VENUS" FIGURINE

5 CARVED ROCK

9 CARVED PILLAR

12 SERRATED FLINT, BARBED FLINT, AND FLINT DAGGER

13 POTTERY CONE

Early Societies

These objects reflect the changes that were taking place in human society up to 3000 BCE. The shift from a hunter-gather lifestyle is revealed by the number of farming tools and pottery objects that were made at this time.

1 **Flint hand-ax** made by *Homo heidelbergensis* in Europe about 500,000–300,000 years ago. 2 **Deer's head carving** from bone, 8000–6000 BCE, from Riparo Gaban, Italy. 3 **Flint axe,** c. 4000–2300 BCE, used to harvest cereal crops. The original flint cutting edge has been fixed in a modern handle. 4 **"Venus" figurine** carved in limestone, c. 25,000–15,000 BCE, from Willendorf, Austria. Figures such as this have been found across Europe; they are always faceless and appear to be heavily pregnant. 5 **Carved rock** from approximately 75,000 years ago, discovered in Blombos cave near Stilbaai, South Africa. Considered to be one of the first examples of art, the piece is made from red ocher with a deliberately engraved design. 6 **Cro-Magnon flute,** c. 45,000 years old, discovered in a cave at Divje Babe, in the Idrijca valley in western Slovenia, and thought to be one of the earliest musical instruments. It is made from the femur of a young cave bear. 7 **Flint arrowhead** from around 10,000 years ago. Arrowheads such as this were created by skilled artisans by pressing a bone or antler tool against the edges to create a finely flaked thin artifact. 8 **Bone carvings,** c. 8700 BCE, from Dolní Vestonice, Czechoslovakia. They are believed to be an amulet (left) and a stylized female figure (right). 9 **Carved pillar,** c. 9000 BCE, from the Göbekli Tepe archaeological site in southeastern Turkey. These pillars may be part of an early temple. Other examples show various wild animals and birds. 10 **Stone sculpture,** c. 6000 BCE, showing both fish and human characteristics, from Lepenski Vir, Yugoslavia. Fish were important to the people who lived at this site. 11 **Quernstone,** a simple hand mill to grind cereal crops. This is a reconstruction of the type used by the first farmers c. 10,000 BCE. 12 **Serrated flint, antler harpoon, and flint point** mounted on a wooden shaft, made by modern humans during and after the late Ice Age, 18,000–10,000 years ago. 13 **Pottery cone** from Jordan, 3rd millennium BCE. 14 **Egyptian dagger,** c. 3500–3100 BCE, from Gebel el-Arak, Egypt, with scenes of battle and hunting carved on the handle, made from hippopotamus ivory, and a blade of the highest quality knapping. 15 **Naqada I bone figure,** 4000–3600 BCE. This is an example of one of the earliest three-dimensional representations of humans from ancient Egypt, found in graves of the predynastic period. 16 **Goddess figurine,** from El' Ma'mariya, Egypt, c. 3600–3500 BCE, made from painted terra-cotta. 17 **Pottery shard,** c. 4000 BCE, from Romania. As well as being useful, pottery was often strikingly painted and engraved as seen in this example. 18 **Carved spearthrower** in the shape of a mammoth, from the rock shelter of Montastruc, Tarn-et-Garonne, France. Approximately 12,500 years old, this tool is carved from reindeer antler. 19 **Foundation stone** engraved with cuneiform writing from the famous Sumerian city of Ur. This 4,000-year-old brick cone was placed in a mud-brick wall to record the foundation of a building. 20 **Egyptian comb** from the predynastic period, c. 3200 BCE. Carved from ivory, the animals include elephants and snakes; wading birds and a giraffe; hyenas and cattle. Parts of the comb's teeth can be seen along the bottom edge. 21 **Uruk pitcher** of limestone with animal carvings from Sumeria, 3500–3200 BCE.

14 EGYPTIAN DAGGER   15 NAQUADA I BONE FIGURE   16 "GODDESS" FIGURINE

17 POTTERY SHARD   18 CARVED SPEARTHROWER   19 FOUNDATION STONE   20 EGYPTIAN COMB   21 URUK PITCHER

BEFORE «

As the glacial period of the Ice Age «22–23 came to an end, conditions around the world improved for human life and the hunter-gatherer lifestyle began to die out.

OUT OF THE ICE AGE

Many of the advances in civilization were spurred on by **global warming**, which gave new opportunities to humankind.

EXPANSION

Human populations increased and spread as areas that had been glacial became temperate.

AGE OF TRANSITION

After the Ice Age, **large game animals died out** in many areas, and people turned to smaller animals and wild plant foods. Following a drought about 13,000 years ago, hunting bands in southwest Asia began planting wild wheat, barley, and other grasses to supplement strains of what grew in the wild.

BEGINNING OF FOOD PRODUCTION

Although people still lived as hunter-gatherers, moving around seasonally in search of food, by 12,000 years ago some groups had begun to exploit and control their own food supplies.

Corn, domesticated in central America by 5000 BCE, developed from a wild grass, teosinte, and is still found in Mexico. As it spread throughout much of the Americas, farmers developed strains that adapted to local conditions such as arid environments.

NORTH AMERICA

2500 BCE

5000 BCE

ATLANTIC OCEAN

Potatoes are a highland Andean crop, domesticated at an unknown date, but before 5000 BCE. Farmers in the Andes grew numerous potato varieties, adapted to different microenvironments high in the mountains. Potatoes were introduced to Europe in the 17th century.

5000 BCE

SOUTH AMERICA

KEY

■ Areas where farming originated
→ Spread of agriculture
○ Sites of early farming

Llamas were the only pack animal in the Americas, used by Andean traders for carrying textiles, fishmeal, and other commodities between the lowlands and highlands.

First Harvest

Everyone in the world lived by hunting and gathering 12,000 years ago. But only 6,000 years later, virtually every human society with the ability to farm and herd animals produced its own food.

Agriculture was not "invented" by one person in a sudden flash of genius. Hunting groups would have been aware that seeds germinated when they were planted in the soil. The switch from the hunter-gatherer lifestyle to one of agriculture and animal domestication was one that happened independently in various cultures around the world. It was partly prompted by climate change and was a momentous step forward for humankind—civilization as we know it today stems from the changes that took place from about 12,000 years ago.

In the area known as "the Fertile Crescent," which includes Turkey, Syria, and Iraq, people began to domesticate goats, sheep, and pigs by living in close proximity to wild herds and controlling their movements. Plants were gradually adapted from their wild varieties into crops that were tended and harvested. Einkorn, a variety of wheat, was the first domesticated cereal and was grown in the Fertile Crescent. The genetic changes to cereal grasses and animals that resulted from domestication occurred over a relatively short time. Key sites for early farming include Gobekli Tepe, Jericho, Çatalhüyök, and 'Ain Ghazal. In Abu Hureyra in the Euphrates Valley (modern Syria), a small foraging settlement became a compact farming community of mud-brick houses separated by courtyards and narrow alleyways. As the plants they had sought out became harder to find due to the drier climate, the people there began to cultivate the cereal rye. They also continued to hunt gazelles, and keep sheep. Analysis of bones (see left) has revealed that the number of domesticated sheep gradually outnumbered wild animals, and ground cereals became part of the diet. At Göbekli Tepe in Turkey, examples of what may be the earliest stone temples, dating from c. 9000 BCE, have been discovered. This was a community on the verge of becoming a permanent village with structured belief systems.

South and East Asia

Agriculture developed independently in South Asia. It is likely to have emerged in the Indus Valley of modern Pakistan, where farming villages such as Mehgarh were well established by 6000 BCE. Farmers in the Yangtze Valley in southern China had domesticated wild rice by at least 8000 BCE, probably at about the same time as along the Ganges River in India. In China, the Huang He (Yellow River) valley was an early center of millet and cereal cultivation, perhaps as early as 7000 BCE. Chinese agriculture became highly organized and intensive over later centuries, especially in the south. Northern Chinese farmers had to contend with frequent droughts and floods. In spite of these challenges, the sophisticated Yangshao village culture

> **NEOLITHIC** The last part of the Stone Age period, beginning *c.* 10,000 BCE in the Middle East, *c.* 5500 BCE in central Europe, and *c.* 4500 BCE in northern Europe. The introduction of farming is a key characteristic of the Neolithic.

HOW WE KNOW

TEETH AND BONES

The remains of domestic and wild animals can tell us a lot about the diet and lifestyle of our ancestors. By examining jaws and the growth patterns in teeth, one can establish the age and sex of an animal and whether it was wild or domesticated. From human remains we can learn a lot about diet and lifestyle. For example, the teeth of people from Abu Hureyra (see above) show heavy wear associated with eating ground cereals.

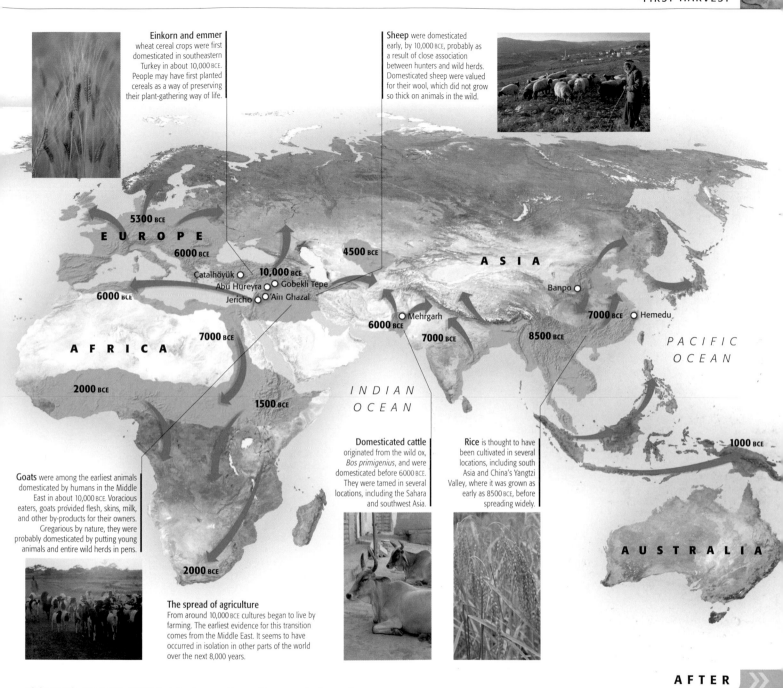

Einkorn and emmer
wheat cereal crops were first domesticated in southeastern Turkey in about 10,000 BCE. People may have first planted cereals as a way of preserving their plant-gathering way of life.

Sheep were domesticated early, by 10,000 BCE, probably as a result of close association between hunters and wild herds. Domesticated sheep were valued for their wool, which did not grow so thick on animals in the wild.

5300 BCE

E U R O P E

6000 BCE

4500 BCE

Çatalhöyük   10,000 BCE

A S I A

Abu Hureyra   Gobekli Tepe

Jericho   'Ain Ghazal

Banpo

6000 BCE

7000 BCE   Hemedu

6000 BCE   Mehrgarh

7000 BCE

A F R I C A

2000 BCE

7000 BCE

8500 BCE

PACIFIC OCEAN

1500 BCE

INDIAN OCEAN

Domesticated cattle
originated from the wild ox, *Bos primigenius*, and were domesticated before 6000 BCE. They were tamed in several locations, including the Sahara and southwest Asia.

Rice is thought to have been cultivated in several locations, including south Asia and China's Yangtzi Valley, where it was grown as early as 8500 BCE, before spreading widely.

1000 BCE

Goats were among the earliest animals domesticated by humans in the Middle East in about 10,000 BCE. Voracious eaters, goats provided flesh, skins, milk, and other by-products for their owners. Gregarious by nature, they were probably domesticated by putting young animals and entire wild herds in pens.

A U S T R A L I A

2000 BCE

The spread of agriculture
From around 10,000 BCE cultures began to live by farming. The earliest evidence for this transition comes from the Middle East. It seems to have occurred in isolation in other parts of the world over the next 8,000 years.

AFTER

of the north (see p.60), which practiced an early form of irrigation, was thriving by 5000 BCE.

First European farmers
Farming spread to Europe from southwest Asia by about 6000 BCE. It expanded across the Mediterranean, then northward, developing with slight variations in the associated crafts and architectural style as it spread.

Farming the Americas
The ancient native American population developed an expertise with wild plants. By 4000 BCE, many hunter-gatherer groups in the Americas were

growing sunflowers and other native plants as part of their vegetable diet. In the Andes Mountains in South America, hunters experimented with the cultivation of potatoes and other indigenous root vegetables.

The staple crops of native American agriculture—corn and beans—were both domesticated in Central America by 3500 BCE. Corn was domesticated from teosinte, a grass native to Central America. Many varieties developed. From the tropics, this vital staple spread to the Andes and into the North American southwest by 2500 BCE, before coming into use later in eastern North America.

Farming has had huge and far-reaching social effects beyond changing what humans eat.

GROWTH OF VILLAGES AND TOWNS
Food production tied people to cultivated land and grazing grounds, giving rise to **permanent settlements 38–39 »**.

TIME TO INNOVATE
Not everyone was needed in order to produce enough food to feed the community. **Individuals began to specialize** in a particular trade, such as pottery and metalwork **42–43 »**. Farming

produced surplus food. This was stored for times of need or traded, creating new trading possibilities. **Farming fed more people** within smaller areas, promoting **growth in population**.

GETTING MORE OUT
As populations increased, so did the **pressure on the land**. If favorable areas could not be sought out, **new techniques** had to be developed, such as the **irrigation systems** used in Egypt. The pressure on food production and the desire to produce more has continued to this day **290–91, 462–63 »**.

BEFORE

Early human populations were nomadic, moving around in search of food, as it became available.

DIGGING TOOL

LIFE ON THE MOVE Up to about 10,000 years ago, life revolved around the constant search for food. New areas were gradually colonized as groups of people sought to **exploit new sources of food**.

LIFESTYLE OF THE HUNTER
The way of life of the hunter-gatherers was highly successful and adaptable.

TEMPORARY SETTLEMENTS
Hunter-gatherer sites, such as hunting camps, were seasonal and impermanent. Examples we know about include Star Carr in Britain and Dolní Vestonice in Central Europe **« 30–31**. People on the move had fewer possessions, so they could remain mobile. This lack of material objects means that our evidence of this lifestyle is meager.

BIRTH OF AGRICULTURE
The switch to farming **« 36–37** began about 10,000 years ago. Tools, such as the **digging tool**, shown left, developed as part of this transition. The **first plow** was used at about the same time.

Village Life

The cultivation of domesticated crops and livestock brought with it permanent settlements and new ways of life, including the first settled communities and the beginning of religion and worship.

T he earliest farming villages were small huddles of mud-brick houses, nestled together and separated by narrow spaces. At Abu Hureyra, Syria (see pp.36–37), several hundred farmers lived in close proximity to their fields and each other. In another early settlement, 'Ain Ghazal, in modern Jordan, herds of goats were kept and wild animals were hunted. 'Ain Ghazal seems to have become a victim of its own success as its population grew and the land became overexploited, causing people to leave in search of more fertile lands.

Growing settlements
Jericho, in the Jordan Valley, was one of the first villages to grow successfully, over the period 9600–7000 BCE. By 8000 BCE it had become a small walled town, whose inhabitants lived in

beehive-shaped houses with stone foundations and plastered floors, many of which had private courtyards and ovens. Another highly successful, long-lived, and large settlement was Çatalhöyük in Turkey (see pp.36–37), which thrived from 7000 BCE and was inhabited for over 1,000 years. Its population lived in rectangular houses, built very close together, which were entered through the roof. The houses were whitewashed and painted with red geometric patterns. One reason for the site's success may have been its trade in the highly-prized black volcanic glass, obsidian, used to make cutting tools.

Surviving day to day
Cereal grains were the staple diet in all early farming communities across southwest Asia. Apart from bread or gruel (commonly oatmeal boiled in

water or milk), people in the first permanent village settlements lived on the meat and produce from their domesticated herds and supplemented their diet with wild game and wild plant foods.

One of the key features of these settlements, which marks them out from early hunter-gatherer sites, is the existence of storage facilities for food. This indicates that communities were planning for the season ahead and storing grain over the winter. These early farmers would have lived from harvest to harvest, and the danger of starvation was always present. In some ways, they had been better off as hunter-gatherers, as gathering food is less labor-intensive than producing it. They would have enjoyed more leisure time and less risk of disease brought about by overcrowding in villages (see pp.52–53). However, the benefits of farming—the ability to support more people from a smaller area—allowed populations to grow and society as we know it today to flourish.

Specialization
People now lived in crowded villages, with the same neighbors for generations. Men were probably responsible for herding animals, perhaps some of the work in the fields, and hunting, while women prepared food, and were responsible for foraging and food storage. Within such communities specific roles developed, as not everyone was required to find food. At the same time, some people became part-time specialists such as shamans (see pp.32–33) and spirit mediums, canoe builders, and potters. A network of family members would have helped each other in times of crop failure.

Burial rites
With more permanent settlements came new beliefs. Fertility of the soil was associated with new life. Ancestors were associated with the fertility of the land and were worshipped. Some of the dead at Jericho were decapitated and buried beneath the floors of their houses. Their relatives then modeled the revered ancestor's features in clay on the skulls and buried them in pits. At 'Ain Ghazal, collections of clay figurines were also buried in a deliberate fashion. Although the purpose of these ritualized objects is unknown, their existence indicates that people may have been practicing an early form of religion (see pp.40–41).

The rise of community life
In the first villages, people would have lived in close communities like this modern-day Tuareg village in Mali, Africa, on an island in the Niger River. Domesticated animals including goats and sheep would have been corralled and kept in areas between the houses.

INVENTION

POTTERY

Fired clay vessels are a feature of all early farming cultures around the world. Bowls were used for cooking and eating; large jars and round-bottomed pots held liquids or stored grain. Most early vessels were made by joining clay coils, or by shaping a pot from a clay lump.

Pots, such as this particularly sophisticated example, first appeared among the Jomon people of Japan before 10,000 BCE, and in Mali, West Africa, at about the same time. Most pottery was for strictly utilitarian purposes, but skilled potters also made fine-walled, elaborately decorated vessels for grave goods or ceremonial purposes.

Shrine figure
This ancestral figure from 'Ain Ghazal, dating from c. 7250 BCE, seems to stare into eternity. It stood on a house platform and was probably dressed in robes or costumes commemorating a revered ancestor.

AFTER »

The establishment of villages and farming communities led to population growth and new challenges for those who lived in them.

BIRTH OF THE CITY
Villages expanded into towns and cities **44–45 »**.

HEALTH RISKS
Growing population densities led to **unsanitary conditions**. Living in close proximity to animals allowed **new diseases 52–53 »** to spread from animal to human. Rising populations could also lead to famine and malnutrition.

INTENSIFICATION
Higher populations led to greater intensification of farming methods, such as irrigation.

EGYPTIAN DEPICTION OF IRRIGATION

BEFORE «

As human mental abilities developed, so did beliefs in powers greater than humankind and some kind of afterlife.

ART AND SHAMANS
Early art, such as **cave art and bone engravings « 20–21,** reflects an early human concern with interpreting and trying to influence the world around us through ritual.

FERTILITY
As farming took hold, societies made fertility goddesses, which indicates a desire to promote growth and life **« 30–31.**

GRAVE GOODS AND RITUAL
People buried grave goods with the dead from 40,000 years ago **« 32–33.** Farming communities such as Çatalhöyük, Turkey, had **rooms for ritual associated with the dead.**

ENGRAVED BISON BONE

West Kennet
The stone passageway in the West Kennet long barrow, in southern England, leads from a small forecourt to side chambers for the dead. West Kennet was built as a communal tomb *c.* 3650 BCE.

With the spread of farming across the world (see pp.36–37), an early form of religion developed out of a desire to worship ancestors, and to celebrate the seasons and the cyclical movements of the sun, moon, and stars. The most visible mark of Neolithic beliefs are the spectacular megalithic structures built after 4500 BCE in much of the Mediterranean world and in Western Europe, including Spain, France, Britain, and Scandinavia. Some of these sites are world-famous today.

Monumental sites
There are several types of monuments built using megaliths ("huge stones") that developed at this time and that continued to be used down to the middle of the 2nd millennium BCE. These include chambered tombs, "menhirs" (single upright stones), stone rows, and stone circles.

In Britain, causewayed enclosures—ceremonial spaces enclosed by banks with multiple entrance gaps—preceded henge monuments, which appeared around 3200 BCE. Henges consist of a circular or oval area enclosed by a bank, but usually have their associated ditch on the inside rather than the outside of the bank, and fewer entrances. Some contained wood or stone circles—Woodhenge in Wiltshire, England, is perhaps the most famous example of a wooden circle. Here, the only

Creating Stonehenge
In an earlier phase, Stonehenge consisted of a low circular bank with a ditch running along its inside and a row of timber posts along the inner side of that.

remaining evidence of the wooden structure is the post holes into which the timber posts were set.

Stone circles are most commonly found in southwestern England, western Scotland, and northwestern France, perhaps due to the supply of suitable stone blocks in those areas. The stone circle at Avebury, in Britain, is among the largest that survive. The stones may have indicated astronomical alignments and had religious significance. Similar purposes have been suggested for sites of standing stones and rows, such as the rows at Carnac, in France.

Long barrows were mounds used for communal burials. The barrows contained a number of bodies, which may have been exposed before final burial. Some, such as the one at West Kennet, in England, were built with internal stone chambers and used over several generations. Newgrange in Ireland (see below) and Gavrinis in Brittany are other examples of chambered tombs. Some of the stones at these sites are decorated with engraved abstract patterns of spirals, circles, and lozenges, referred to as "megalithic art." Cigar-shaped ritual enclosures with empty interiors (cursuses) are often associated with barrow sites.

Center of a sacred landscape
The most famous of all the megalithic sites is Stonehenge, England, which was developed, altered, and used over hundreds of years. Like other Neolithic

Rites and Rituals

The megalithic structures of the Neolithic period are awe-inspiring even today, and their mystery adds to their appeal. Frequently associated with burials and seeming to follow lunar, solar, or cosmic alignments, they are strongly tied to rituals linking humans to the wider landscape they inhabit.

monuments from *c.* 3000 BCE in northern Europe, it was part of a large sacred landscape that included sites of celebration and worship. Hills, lakes, mountains, rivers, and trees were all considered a part of the landscape that defined human existence. Many megalithic structures were constructed at the center of such a landscape and

Newgrange
The entrance to the burial mound in Ireland's Boyne Valley is blocked by this curb stone decorated with the concentric patterns that are common to megalithic art in northwest France and Ireland.

would have been visible from a distance; when newly dug, mounds in chalkland areas would have been quite conspicuous. Stonehenge is close to another circular structure, Durrington Walls, as well as Woodhenge, and a number of burial mounds, including those in the town of Amesbury.

The area around Stonehenge was farmed from around 4000 BCE. Then, in about 2950 BCE, a simple earthwork enclosure was dug containing a circle of wooden posts. Over the next 1,000 years, the site was developed in several stages. The outer circle of stones that we see today was put up by about 2550 BCE. Burials have been found around Stonehenge, along with finds that include amber and bone beads, showing that it was a site central to the rituals of life and death.

One possible reason these sites were built may have been to ensure the beneficial presence of ancestors at the heart of village life and to allow the living to maintain a connection with the spiritual world (see pp.32–33). Those who performed the rituals that took place here were thought to be able to communicate with the dead and would have been important members of the community.

These structures not only reflect developed beliefs, they also indicate an awareness of the natural world; some, such as Stonehenge, may have been built to mark the summer and winter solstices—critical events in farming societies. They are also striking feats of engineering and organizational ability. Many remain spiritual places today.

The megalithic structures in Europe are echoed around the world in later cultures. They can be seen at sites in many countries, including the US and Japan.

MOUNDBUILDER SITES

Elaborate funerary cults grew in North America after 1000 BCE. By 400 BCE the Hopewell people of the Ohio Valley traded objects like this as part of a cult, in which the dead were interred in mounds.

HOPEWELL CLAW

MISSISSIPPIAN CULTURE

This culture flourished in North America between 1000 and 1450 CE **212–13 »**. Public ceremonies marked the solstices, and the first harvest was celebrated in plazas surrounded by temples on top of earthen mounds.

FUNERARY CUSTOMS

Elsewhere around the world, funerary customs also played an important role in society. Japan's **Kofun** culture of the 3rd century CE and later is remarkable for its **keyhole-shaped burial mounds**. On the

KOFUN BURIAL SITE

AFTER »

other side of the world, an Anglo-Saxon King, who has been identified as **Raedwald,** was buried beneath a huge **mound at Sutton Hoo** in Suffolk, Britain, in his richly adorned ship, in 620 CE.

UPHOLDING TRADITION

The tradition of building elaborate sacred sites is still common today in cultures around the world in the form of Christian cathedrals, Islamic mosques, Buddhist temples, and even in the monuments erected to commemorate American presidents.

BEFORE

As settlements became more complex, trade and ties between communities grew and material culture became more developed.

BEFORE METAL
Flint was used to make the hardest and sharpest tools and weapons for thousands of years. From simple chopping devices, humans went on to produce tools for particular tasks, including scrapers, cutters, and hand-axes **《 17.**

PERMANENT SETTLEMENTS
As agriculture spread throughout southwestern Asia after 8000 BCE, settlements became more permanent. With permanent settlement came closer ties to the land and to a specific territory and its resources.

EARLY TRADE
Most communities exchanged commodities such as grain, building materials, and toolmaking stone. As a result, trade networks and relationships grew. The village of Çatalhöyük in Turkey, for example, specialized in trading obsidian, a highly prized volcanic glass used for making tools, particularly sharp knives.

OBSIDIAN

RITUAL AND WORSHIP
Both ritual and social life soon became more elaborate. At Çatalhöyük, what appear to be family shrines, where people commemorated their ancestors **《 32** and **worshipped a fertility goddess**, have been excavated, revealing distinctive goddess figurines made of clay.

GODDESS FIGURINE

Precious Metal

Humans had made tools out of stone, bone, and wood for thousands of years. The advent of copperworking around 8,000 years ago was the beginning of a long association with metals, and a significant watershed in human history, which led to even further innovation.

It seems that humans have always had a fascination with rare and beautiful materials, from exotic shells used as jewelry to shiny metals. Copper occurs both in its native form (uncombined with other elements and so needing little processing) or in the form of ore (a rock or mineral from which the metal can be extracted). Native copper is very malleable, with a distinctive reddish color. When it was first found, it was mainly used to make shiny ornaments. The earliest copper objects were hammered into shape to form crude axes and beads—examples of

ORE A rock containing naturally occurring mineral from which valuable metals or other constituents may be extracted.

these dating back to the 6th millennium BCE have been found in Turkey and the mountains of Iran. Copper ores are relatively common around the Mediterranean. Those found in surface outcrops are easy to identify by their distinctive green color. It was the discovery of copper smelting (heating the ore with charcoal to about 2,200°F [1,200°C] to extract the metal) that opened the door to a world of innovation, and the development of stronger and more practical items. This crucial discovery is believed to have been made at some point before 5000 BCE and may, theoretically, have

resulted from ore being dropped into a hearth by accident and reacting with hot embers. The earliest known use of gold and silver dates to a similar period. Gold was found in alluvial deposits in or along streams—which meant it did not have to be mined—and was valued for decorative and ritual purposes including grave ornaments (see right).

The first metalworkers smelted copper in open fires. They soon began to use holes lined with clay, then crucibles (containers designed to withstand the heat of the fire), to produce the metal more efficiently.

Trading up
The use of copper not only stimulated technological advances, but also led to significant cultural developments. As copper ore outcrops are patchily distributed, copper items and metal ingots of standard shapes and sizes became valued as tradable items. Culturally advanced in other ways, lowland Mesopotamia had no native metal or ore, which meant that both copper and gold, the two most prestigious ornamental metals, were imported from Anatolia (modern Turkey) and the Iranian Plateau. The traffic in these materials grew quickly, and growing lowland Mesopotamian towns began to exchange grain and other commodities for imported artifacts and ornaments. This trade came to involve both overland travel and transport along the Tigris and Euphrates rivers, where rafts made of wood and inflated goatskins probably came into use by 3000 BCE.

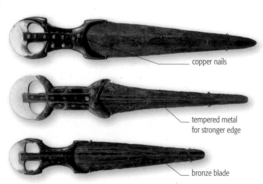

Egyptian daggers
These daggers from late predynastic Egypt date from c. 3000 BCE. They are made from bronze with copper nails and ivory detail on the handle. As technology developed, tools and weapons that had previously been cut from stone were made in metals, which were lighter and more pliable.

copper nails

tempered metal for stronger edge

bronze blade

Metalworking reaches Europe
The earliest copper mines in Europe have been found at Ai Bunar in southern Bulgaria, and date to around 5100 BCE. A large network of exchange

Metal moves west
Metalworking started in Anatolia and Mesopotamia (modern-day Turkey and Iraq) in around 5000 BCE, and spread westward and northward, reaching northern Europe by 2000 BCE. Its spread was facilitated by widespread trade, which was growing during this period.

KEY
- Metalworking 5000–4000 BCE
- Metalworking 4000–3000 BCE
- Metalworking 3000–2000 BCE
- ○ Site
- ••• Sporadic trade route
- → Spread of metalworking

ATLANTIC OCEAN

Scandinavia

BRITISH ISLES
North Sea
Stonehenge
Nebra
North European Plain
EUROPE
Volga
Don
Dnieper

Alps
"Ötzi the ice man"
Iberian Peninsula
Danube
Varna
Black Sea
Caucasus
Caspian Sea

Hissarlik
Ai Bunar
Anatolia
MESOPOTAMIA
Iranian Plateau
ASIA

Mediterranean Sea
Çatalhöyük
Uluburun

Atlas Mountains

AFRICA

Jericho
Uruk
Persian Gulf
Arabian Peninsula
Nile

1000 km
1000 miles

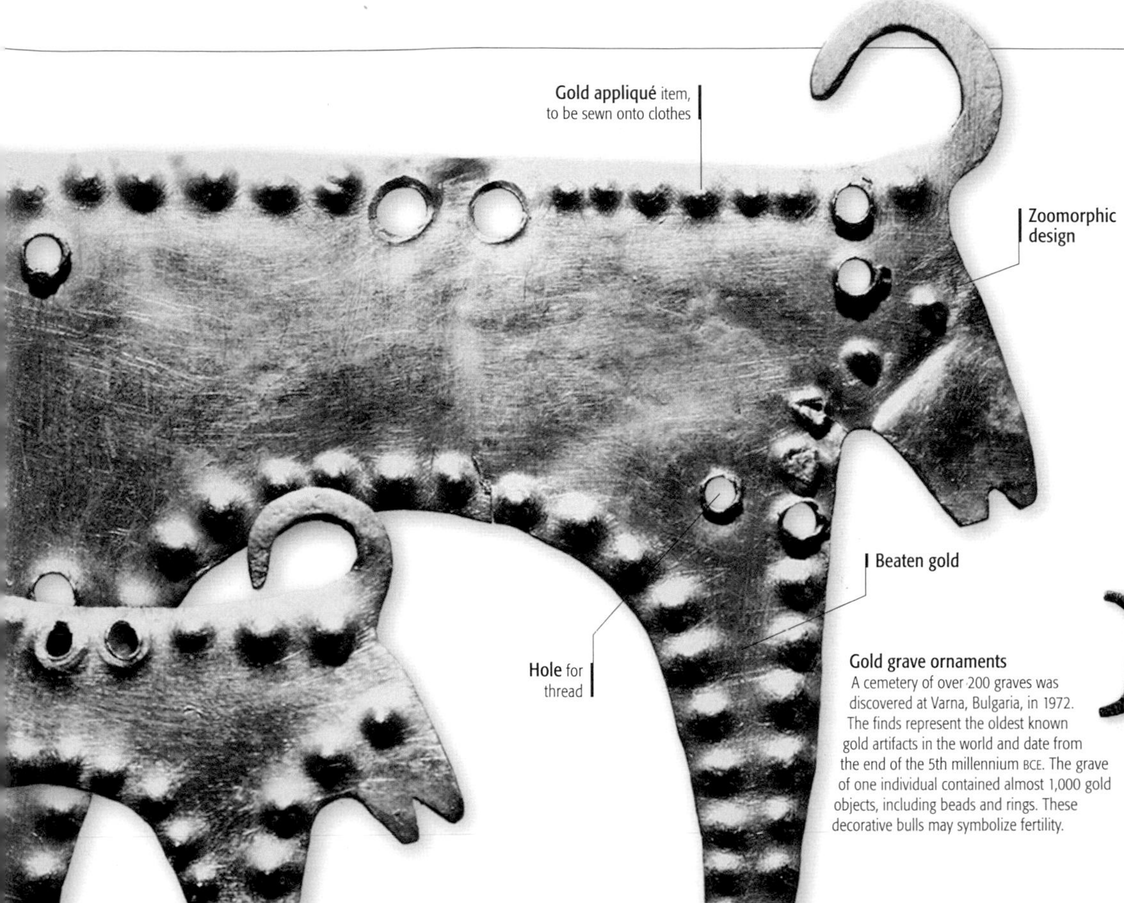

AFTER »

Gold appliqué item,
to be sewn onto clothes

Zoomorphic design

Beaten gold

Hole for thread

Gold grave ornaments
A cemetery of over 200 graves was discovered at Varna, Bulgaria, in 1972. The finds represent the oldest known gold artifacts in the world and date from the end of the 5th millennium BCE. The grave of one individual contained almost 1,000 gold objects, including beads and rings. These decorative bulls may symbolize fertility.

Hammered decorative detail

yielding fine gold and copper artifacts dating to about 4500 BCE. Copper metallurgy later developed in Italy and Spain from about 3500 BCE, and in Britain by *c.* 2000 BCE.

Copper tools and ornaments
Many of the innovations in copperworking came about as an indirect result of improved agricultural methods. Efficient arable farming in the Nile valley enabled villages to develop and thrive, maintained by a surplus of food. More efficient farming methods meant that not everyone was needed for food production, and so more

complex levels of social organization arose, with specialty roles developing within the community—from baker to potter, and weaver to metalworker. This specialization of trades allowed for innovation in the production of metal objects.

Beginning of bronze
The first copper-tin alloy—bronze— was produced in around 2500 BCE, although it did not come into widespread use until much later. Bronze is harder than copper and therefore more suitable for practical applications, such as weapons, armor, and tools.

had been established by this time, and objects made from copper were traded all over southeastern Europe. Rich graves have been discovered at Varna, on the Black Sea coast of Bulgaria,

The use of metal, from bronze to iron and steel, has transformed human civilization.

BEAKER CULTURE
Between 2800 and 1900 BCE, at the beginning of the Bronze Age, people of the Beaker Culture (so named for the distinctive shape of the pottery) lived across a large area of northern Europe. Both **flint and bronze tools**, such as these daggers, are associated with this culture.

BEAKER CULTURE TOOLS

COPPER INGOT

COPPER TRADE
As one of the raw materials for bronze, copper needed to be transported in increasingly large quantities. Handles on each end for carrying, and a uniform size, made ingots of the metal easier to transport, and trade and quantities easier to control. This copper ingot found in a hoard from Cyprus dates from about 1200 BCE.

BRONZE AGE A period defined by the use of bronze as the most important material for making tools and weapons. In the Middle East it is approximately 3000–1200 BCE.

IRON AGE
Iron was introduced in around 1200 BCE in the Middle East and eventually became used more than bronze, as it is tougher and **more suitable for use in tools and weapons**.

EARLY STEEL
Iron can be smelted only at about 2,900°F (1,600°C), though the metal can be worked at lower temperatures. Steel, an alloy (mixture) of iron and carbon, came into limited use as early as 500 BCE in China.

GOLD FEVER
In January of 1848 a work crew camped on the American River at Coloma near Sacramento, CA found a few tiny nuggets of gold. This discovery set off a mass of migration as half a million people from around the world descended on California in search of instant wealth.

GOLD NUGGET

INDUSTRIAL REVOLUTION
Steel only became a widely **mass-produced metal** with the advent of the Bessemer converter, which was developed in 1855 during the Industrial Revolution **295 »**.

HOW WE KNOW
OTZI THE ICE MAN

In 1991, the frozen body of a man dating to around 3350 BCE was found preserved in a glacier. He was nicknamed Ötzi, after the Ötztal Valley of the Alps where he was found. Scientific analysis has revealed many details about his life and violent death.

Arsenic, found in his hair, showed that he had worked with copper. A copper ax, an unfinished bow and arrows, and a flint knife were found alongside his body. His last meal, containing the primitive wheat einkorn, was preserved in his intestines. At the time of death,

Ötzi was fleeing attackers—a flint arrowhead lies in one shoulder and he parried a dagger attack with his hands before dying. Ötzi's bones show he suffered from arthritis, and the tattoos found on his body may have been put there for therapeutic purposes.

« BEFORE

The first settlements that developed from villages to towns were in modern-day Iraq. The change took place over a long period.

THE HALAFIANS

In what is now northern Iraq, the **Halafian culture** flourished after 6000 BCE. **Long-distance trade** of volcanic glass and brightly painted pots was one of the factors that led to larger villages and towns and to greater **contact between settlements**. Female figurines, like the one shown here, are characteristic of this society.

MESOPOTAMIA

Mesopotamia, which was also part of Iraq, was settled by village farmers as early as 6000 BCE. The communities living in the

south relied on long-distance trade for many commodities, and on **irrigation and wetland agriculture**. By 3500 BCE many southerners lived in growing towns—precursors of Mesopotamian cities 54–55 »

MORE COMPLEX SOCIETIES

By 4000 BCE, village life in southwestern and east Asia was firmly established. **Farming communities became larger and more organized.** Society became more stratified, with a growing social chasm between the rulers and the ruled.

HALAF FIGURINE

Treasure from Iraq
Naked men bearing offerings of fruit and vegetables approach the shrine of the goddess Innin (Inanna), an Earth goddess, on a carved stone vase of 3000 BCE found in her temple at Uruk. In 2003, looters stole the vase from the Iraq Museum in Baghdad; it was later recovered.

Egyptian market
Village markets with their visiting traders were a major part of community life at a time when all information was exchanged by word of mouth, and merchants brought news of the outside world. This modern-day Egyptian village is little different from the first villages thousands of years ago.

INVENTION

THE WHEEL

The wheel originated in Mesopotamia in the 5th century BCE and is believed to have developed from the potter's wheel. It is one of the most important inventions in human history as it revolutionized transport. By the 3rd millennium the use of wheels had spread east, where burials with wheeled carts took place. Chariots pulled by domesticated horses came into use in the Black Sea region of Europe and northern Mesopotamia after 3000 BCE and became valued by armies on the move. The scene below shows wagons with solid wheels and is taken from the Sumerian Royal Standard of Ur dating to c.2600 BCE.

Town Planning

Four thousand years after agriculture began, many farming villages in southwest Asia had grown into towns with over a thousand inhabitants. In southern Iraq, Egypt, and elsewhere, a few strategically placed communities became towns with neighborhoods, public buildings, and sacred precincts.

The world's earliest towns developed in Mesopotamia, perhaps as the result of a need to organize the construction of irrigation channels and canals fed by the Tigris and Euphrates rivers. At first, the towns were little more than agglomerations of villages and related families, but they soon became major centers of trade and vast irrigation works that transformed the countryside and produced several crops a year. Each clustered around temples and sacred precincts built on top of mud brick pyramids called ziggurats.

Uruk and Eridu

Uruk was the earliest Mesopotamian town and developed its initial phase between 4800–3800 BCE. By 2800 BCE

Uruk's town core covered an estimated 620 acres (250 hectares) and housed at least 5,000 people, with many more living in nearby villages. Its rulers governed satellite villages extending at least 6 miles (10 km) from the temple, but most people lived in the town, partly for protection, and also because everything was governed from the center. The growing town was the hub of major trade networks that brought metals, lumber, and other commodities from the highlands far upstream, in exchange for grain from the south's fertile soils. Uruk may even have maintained outlying colonies as far

Nekhen votive
An ivory statue from Nekhen in Upper Egypt depicts an early ruler wearing a ceremonial headdress.

away as the Zagros Mountains, several hundred miles to the north, to ensure control of major trade routes.

Eridu was another early town close to Uruk. Mesopotamian legends called Eridu the dwelling place of Enki, God of the Abyss, the fountain of human wisdom. The people believed that Enki had created order from the chaos of primordial waters. In its heyday, around 5,000 years ago, Eridu lay in a fertile landscape near the coast. Archaeologists have deciphered the complex history of

As the first towns became more complex, new ways of communicating within the community and with other sites became important.

WRITTEN COMMUNICATION

By 3100 BCE, written scripts like this one were in use in both Egypt and Mesopotamia. They developed from clay tokens used for recording commercial transactions. Only a few people were literate—scribes who **recorded and controlled all kinds of information** for the state **62–63 »**.

CUNEIFORM SCRIPT

CENTERS OF TRADE

In Egypt and Mesopotamia, **cities grew rapidly** to become major trading centers, with imposing public buildings. As urban populations rose, cities became the hubs of larger kingdoms and empires. At the same time, the volume of **long-distance trade** in commodities like iron ore and lumber grew quickly, as did the **demand for gold, silver, and other precious materials.**

GROWING AROUND THE YEAR

By 3000 BCE, **irrigation agriculture**, which used simple canals to divert floodwater to crops, began to give way to more elaborate agricultural landscapes with **networks of canals**. These larger areas produced food surpluses that saved labor, allowing rulers to engage in public works such as **pyramid building 56–57, 72–73 »**.

Enki's shrine, which began as a small mud-brick construction and went through at least six incarnations before becoming an imposing stepped pyramid adorned with brightly colored brick set in a 590-sq-ft (180-m²) enclosure.

The First Egyptian towns

In 4000 BCE, Egypt consisted of a valley of farmers living in small communities spaced along the Nile, which watered

FIRST EGYPTIAN RULER

HORUS AHA

King Horus Aha, often called Menes, is a shadowy figure in Egyptian history. He became the first ruler of a unified Egypt in about 3000 BCE. His predecessor, Narmer, an Upper Egyptian chieftain, may have unified Egypt with decisive military victories, but it was Horus Aha who assumed the role of divine king, the living god Horus on Earth. Like other early pharaohs, Horus Aha was buried at Abydos in Upper Egypt (see pp. 64–65). His power came from prowess in war and control of lucrative trade routes with Lower Egypt, even Mesopotamia.

their fields. It was a competitive world of small kingdoms, the largest of which were based on growing towns like Abydos and Nekhen in Upper Egypt. While Abydos was a sacred place—the ancient entrance to the underworld—Nekhen was a major pottery trading center. Nekhen's chieftains may have been the forerunners of the Egyptian rulers called pharaohs (see pp.56–57), for they are known to have supervised agriculture, and, like later kings, may have been considered living gods.

Town hierarchy

As towns grew, so society became increasingly hierarchical. One can liken these societies to a pyramid. At the top was the ruler, who may have governed as a living god as well as a secular leader. Beneath him were his immediate family and a small privileged class of high officials and priests. Lower down the scale came artisans, lesser functionaries, soldiers, and the commoners who were the manpower upon which all of society depended. Early Sumerian rulers and Egyptian pharaohs ruled by precedent (using the decisions of their predecessors rather than written laws), gave limited public

appearances, and lived in seclusion. Perhaps the very fact that they were not often seen in public led to the perception that they had supernatural powers.

A divine ruler's power came from his ability to control the labor of thousands of commoners. His authority came not only from a threat of force, but also from pervasive ideas and religious beliefs commemorated by art and writing on temple walls and reinforced by elaborate ceremonies. The latter were often displays of power that required imposing settings and conspicuous burial places such as pyramids.

For reasons that are still not fully understood, by the end of the 4th millennium BCE in Mesopotamia, almost everyone lived in cities. This was a rapidly changing world where wealth assumed increasing

Palette of Narmer
Dating to c. 3000 BCE, this slate palette, from a temple at Hierakonpolis, appears to show an early king and the unification of Upper and Lower Egypt.

importance. Life in early towns was unsanitary and chaotic with people living at close quarters.

Egyptian towns

In Egypt, town dwellers—even high officials—maintained close ties to relatives in areas surrounding the town. Little detail is known about the first Egyptian towns, which developed toward the end of the 4th millennium BCE, but they probably began as connected groups of growing villages. Different communities came together, perhaps for defensive reasons, under the rule of charismatic rulers. Some early Egyptian towns, such as Nekhen, became important trading centers and river ports, ruled by chiefs who competed with their neighbors. The roots of many of the most important cities in civilization began at this time.

2

RULERS AND HIERARCHIES

3000–700 BCE

As humans began to band together in organized communities,
more structured societies emerged. They began to develop greater
powers of communication, create complex belief systems, and form
cultured urban civilizations, particularly in the Middle East, India,
Europe, China, and Central and South America.

RULERS AND HIERARCHIES

3000–700 BCE

3000 BCE	2750 BCE	2500 BCE	2250 BCE
c. 3000 Beginning of Early Dynastic period of Mesopotamian city-states, including Sumerian-speaking Uruk and Ur. Start of Bronze Age in southeast Europe—in Minoan Crete and Cyclades islands of Greece. ▼ Administrative tablet, Uruk, Mesopotamia	**c. 2750** First Chinese bronze artifacts. **c. 2700** Mythical king Gilgamesh may have ruled Uruk in Mesopotamia. Silk weaving practiced in China.	**c. 2340** Sargon founds and rules the city of Akkad, uniting city-states of Mesopotamia into the first empire. Sargon of Akkad ▼	**c. 2100** 3rd Dynasty of Ur revives Sumerian civilization in southern Mesopotamia; King Ur-Nammu of Ur builds a ziggurat (stepped tower), now typical of Mesopotamian architecture, while renovating Ur's temple.

c. 2600
Rich array of grave goods buried at Royal Graves at Ur, Mesopotamia, indicate trade links extending as far as the Indus.
2613
Beginning of 4th Dynasty in Egypt—the age of the first true pyramids.

▲ Stamp seal from Mohenjo Daro, Indus Valley

c. 2500
Indus Valley civilization reaches its peak. Metalworking, in the form of copper, reaches across Europe to British Isles.

c. 2900
Early marble figurines made by the Cycladic culture of Greece.
c. 2800
End of Early Harappan phase of Indus Valley civilization, which began c. 3300 BCE.

Cycladic figure ▶

c. 2550
Outer stone circle erected at Stonehenge, Britain.
c. 2540
Great Pyramid of Khufu built in Giza, near Memphis, Egypt.

c. 2500–2350
Border conflict between Umma and Lagash in Mesopotamia is earliest international controversy recorded.
c. 2500–2350
Destruction of city of Ebla in Syria conserves the palace archives.

▲ Pepy II, 6th-Dynasty Egyptian pharaoh

c. 2200
First pottery in South America.
2181
Egyptian 6th Dynasty ends with collapse of Old Kingdom; First Intermediate Period of Egypt begins.

▲ Standard of Ur

2686
3rd Dynasty of Egypt heralds the beginning of the Egyptian Old Kingdom.

c. 2100
In Mesopotamia, decline of Akkadian empire founded by Sargon; rise of regional rulers of city states, notably Gudea of Lagash.

Gudea of Lagash ▲

2040
Mentuhotep II, ruler of Thebes, unites Upper and Lower Egypt and initiates Egypt's Middle Kingdom.

▼ Ziggurat of Ur

Caral ruins ▶

c. 3000–2750
First cities develop in South America; several settlements featuring temple complexes, such as Caral, emerge in coastal Peru.

c. 2650
Step Pyramid of Djoser built at Saqqara; start of great period of pyramid-building in Egypt.
c. 2600
Evidence for use of plow, Indus Valley.

Great Pyramid of Khufu, Giza ▶

▲ Shipbuilding, 5th-Dynasty Egyptian tomb

c. 2300
Beginning of Bronze Age in rest of Europe.

Complex civilizations developed along the river valleys of the Tigris and Euphrates in the Middle East, the Nile in Egypt, the Indus in India, and later, the Yellow River in China. Trade, increasing prosperity, and technological advances produced increasingly powerful centralized states, and in time, empires. These factors also brought many of these new societies in conflict with each other, particularly in the relatively highly populated Middle East, where Egyptians, Hittites, Assyrians, and Babylonians successively embarked on waves of military conquest. More enduring was Bronze Age China, which flourished from about 1800 BCE. In Europe, culture was most sophisticated in Crete, from around 2000 BCE.

2000 BCE

1800 BCE

1700 BCE

1600 BCE

c. 2000
Trading city of Ashur becomes predominant in north Mesopotamia. Middle Kingdom Egypt run by powerful officials, such as viziers.

▼ Middle Kingdom vizier, Egypt

1965
Sesostris I of Egypt conquers Nubia and extends southern frontier of Egypt to the second cataract of the Nile.
c. 1900
City of Erlitou develops on the Yellow River, China.

c. 1900–1700
Indus Valley civilization declines.
c. 1894
Old Kingdom of Babylon established in Mesopotamia.
c. 1890
Short-lived empire of Shamshi-Adad unites north Mesopotamia: a precursor to Assyria.

c. 2000–1800
Lapita people begin to settle Melanesia, in the Pacific, from Indonesia. Minoan civilization of Crete at its height; palace of Knossos built; Cretan Linear A script developed.

▼ Knossos palace, Minoan Crete ▶

◀ Shang bronze vessel

1965

c. 1800
Beginnings of Shang state, China. Possible sun worship in Scandinavia, indicated by bronze artifacts. Long-distance trade networks established in North America. In Peru, ceremonial center of La Florida built.

Phaistos disk, Crete ▲

c. 1763
Hammurabi, king of Babylon, defeats neighboring Elam and conquers and integrates kingdom of Larsa.
c. 1757
Babylon controls all of Mesopotamia.

c. 1755
Law code of Hammurabi of Babylon displayed on monumental stelae (memorial stones) in temples throughout Mesopotamia.

c. 1750
Massive ceremonial architecture at Sechin Alto, Peru. Possible date of the Phaistos disk, Crete.
c. 1730
Disintegration of Middle Kingdom Egypt; start of Second Intermediate Period.

▲ Hittite capital, Hattusha

c. 1650–1550
During Second Intermediate Period, Lower Egypt ruled by the Hyksos, a warrior elite of Asiatic origins; Upper Egypt ruled from Thebes by native kings.

c. 1700
Most cities of the Indus Valley civilization deserted.
c. 1680s
Development of leavened bread in Egypt.

c. 1627
Beginning of several years' global cooling, documented by tree rings, possibly indicates massive volcanic eruption, perhaps of Vesuvius (Italy) or Thera (Minoan–Mycenaean Greece).

c. 1650
Anatolian city-states unite as Hittite Old Kingdom, with capital Hattusha. Arrival of Aryan people in India.

c. 1600
Mycenae, Greece, emerges as center of civilization in Aegean; development of Linear B script by Mycenaeans.

Hittite statuette ▶

1595
Hittite king Mursili II sacks Babylon: end of Hammurabi's dynasty and the Old Kingdom of Babylon.
1500s
The Kassites, the warrior elite of the fallen Old Babylonian state, gain control over south Mesopotamia.

c. 1570
Egyptian rulers buried in rock-cut tombs in the Valley of the Kings.

▼ Akrotiri ruins

c. 1550
Aryans settle northern India. Rise of Egypt's New Kingdom, with new capital, Thebes, facing the Valley of the Kings. Volcanic eruption on island of Thera buries Minoan town of Akrotiri; Crete falls under Mycenaean control.

49

1500 BCE

Mid-1400s
Lapita people move beyond Melanesia to begin colonizing rest of Pacific. Mycenaean Greece at summit of power, with trading links from the Levant to Sicily.

◀ Mycenaean-style Minoan vase, Crete

▲ Mycenaean gold

c. 1500
Hittite Old Kingdom of Anatolia declines; kingdom of Mittani emerges nearby in north Mesopotamia.

c. 1500–900
Vedic-period Aryans expand over north India; hymns of Rig Veda composed.

▲ Hatshepsut's temple, New Kingdom Egypt

Early 1400s
Bronzeworking in Thailand and Vietnam. Copper worked in Sahara. Evidence of first metalworking in Peru. First pottery in Central America.

1400 BCE

Kassite Babylonian "boundary stone" ▶

c. 1400
Anyang becomes capital of Shang Dynasty China in place of Zhengzhou; first Chinese inscriptions on oracle bones. Nomadic cattle herding develops on the steppes.

◀ Pharaoh Akhenaten

c. 1350
Amarna Period of Egypt; Amenophis IV styles himself "Akhenaten," founds short-lived capital El-Amarna, advocates worship of Aten, the Sun, and instigates an artistic revolution.

Late 1400s
Warfare between New Kingdom Egypt, Hittite New Kingdom, and Mittani for control of the Levant.
1417
Egypt's New Kingdom reaches peak under Amenophis III.

1300s
First alphabets evident on Sinai peninsula (now in Egypt) and in city of Ugarit in the Levant. Kassite Babylonia, the Hittites, Mittani, and Egypt linked diplomatically and by intermarriage.

c. 1336
Priests of Amun restore religious and artistic orthodoxy in Egypt during young Tutankhamun's reign.

▼ Shang-Chinese oracle bone

Mid-1300s
City of Ashur breaks free from Mittani; its rulers proclaim themselves kings of Assyria.

1300 BCE

1200s
Middle Assyrian period: kings such as Tiglath-Pileser I build an Assyrian empire in northern Mesopotamia, Syria, and Anatolia. Cult of Osiris, involving the "Book of the Dead," popular in Egypt.

c. 1250
Stronger defenses around Mycenaean palaces indicate increasing threats.
1213
Death of Rameses II.

c. 1275
Egyptians under Rameses II fight the Hittites at the Battle of Kadesh.

▼ Egyptian "Book of the Dead"

c. 1258
Hittite king Hattusili III agrees Treaty of Kadesh with Rameses II of Egypt.

1200 BCE

c. 1200
Urnfield Culture emerges in Danube area of Europe. Olmec civilization develops in Mexico. Chavin civilization emerges in coastal Peru. Jewish exodus from Egypt to found kingdoms in the Levant.

Ugarit letter ▶

c. 1180
Hittite capital Hattusha destroyed by unknown invaders; Hittite state collapses.
1166
Death of Rameses III, Egypt's last great pharaoh.

◀ Rameses III battling the "Sea Peoples"

1154
Kassite dynasty of Babylon ended when city is sacked by neighboring Elam.
c. 1150
Mycenaean Greece collapses; start of Greek dark ages.

▼ Philistine mask

1100s
Mycenaean cities destroyed. Ugarit letters give account of maritime raids on the Levant coast. Egypt battles with the "Sea Peoples"—some linked with the Philistines. Chariots spread to China from Central Asia.

"I resettled them in their abandoned towns and houses. I imposed more tribute and tax on them than ever before: horses, mules, oxen, sheep, wine, and labor."

ASHURNASIRPAL II, KING OF ASSYRIA, 883–859 BCE

1100 BCE	**1000** BCE	**900** BCE	**800** BCE	»»

Olmec sculpture ▲

c. 1100
First fortified hilltop sites in Western Europe. Settlement established in Poverty Point, present-day Louisiana.

900s
Phoenicians major maritime power in Mediterranean; their alphabetic script widely used. Settled Ayran agricultural states in India. Adena culture develops in Ohio River valley. Polynesian culture evolves in Pacific.

c. 965
Solomon king of Israel.
c. 950s
Megiddo important royal fortress in Israel.
945
Civil war in fragmented Egypt.

◄ Phoenician script

c. 900
Kingdom of Urartu established in eastern Anatolia. Later Vedas composed in India. Nubian state of Kush established south of Egypt. Olmec site of San Lorenzo destroyed; Olmec site of La Venta assumes leading role.

c. 800
Rise of urban culture in Ganges valley. First ironworking south of Sahara. First phase of Celtic Iron Age. Italian city-states in central Italy. Greeks adopt Phoenician script. Evidence of writing in Central America.

Carthage ►

▲ King Jehu of Israel pays tribute to Shalmaneser III of Assyria

Late 900s
Assyria reintegrates lost territories by conquest; beginning of Neo-Assyrian period.
c. 926
Death of Solomon; Israel split into two kingdoms—Israel and Judah.

c. 850
Village established on Palatine Hill, Rome. Chavín politically and culturally dominant in Peru; Chavín cult of supernatural were-jaguar reaches height.

727–722
Shalmaneser V makes Israel an Assyrian province and deports "Lost Tribes" of Israel.
722
Accession of Sargon II of Assyria; moves capital to Khorsabad.
701
Assyria besieges Jerusalem in Judah.

1000s
Migrants, including the Philistines, settle in Syria and the Levant. Phoenicians expand across Mediterranean.
1069
Egyptian New Kingdom fragments into smaller kingdoms.

▲ Shang Dynasty Chariot burial, China

1027
Western Zhou Dynasty supplants Shang in China.
1006
According to Biblical tradition, Israelite kingdom united under David.

c. 900–700
Scythians adopt pastoral nomadism, expand across steppe, and build kurgans (burial mounds).
883
Ashurnasirpal II inherits Assyrian throne and moves capital from Ashur to Nimrud.

817
Traditional birth date of Jain teacher Parshvanatha.
814
Traditional date for founding of Carthage, a Phoenician colony in North Africa.

▼ Scythian kurgans

▲ Stele of Kawa, Kush

776
Pan-Hellenic athletics festival in Olympia.
771
Collapse of Western Zhou control in China; Eastern Zhou establish new capital at Luoyang; start of "Spring and Autumn" period.

c. 1050
Assyria loses territories to Aramaeans migrating into Middle East but survives as a state. Dark age throughout Middle East.
c. 1030
Aryans expand along Ganges valley in India.

▲ Zhou bronze vessel

c. 1000
Western Zhou record geography of China. Wet rice and bronze technology exported to Korea. Ironworking reaches central Europe. Greeks migrate to Asia Minor. Etruscans arrive in Italy.

753
Romulus founds Rome (traditional date).
c. 750
Amos, first great prophet of Israel. Works of Homer and Hesiod first written down. Kush conquers Egypt to its north.

Sargon II of Assyria ►

« BEFORE

Archaeological evidence suggests that prehistoric hunter-gatherers were robust and healthy. Their diets—mainly raw fruits, leaves, and vegetables, with some lean meat and fresh fish—were probably very well attuned to the needs of the human body.

MOVING AROUND

As they were constantly on the move, and not living in large groups, hunter-gatherers probably **suffered rarely from infectious diseases**. Life expectancy was low, but this probably had more to do with physical dangers than disease or want.

FLINT DRILL

MEDICAL INTERVENTION

During the Neolithic period, people began to make sophisticated stone tools and weapons. Some tools were used in **primitive attempts at surgery**. For example, flint-tipped dental drills, found in Pakistan, date back as far as 7000 BCE. Teeth in remains found nearby showed signs of skilful drilling to remove rotten dental tissue.

LIVING TOGETHER

As people began domesticating animals and crops, communities grew larger, and their inhabitants started living more closely together **« 38–39**. They lived close to their livestock, too, and this led to a **proliferation of diseases** that had not been a problem before. Waste was another hazard, and water supplies quickly became contaminated.

CHANGING DIETS

Settled, or sedentary, farming first appeared in the **Fertile Crescent « 36** in what is now the Middle East, around 10,000 BCE. An agricultural lifestyle brought with it diets very different from those of hunter-gatherers. There was less variety, and a single crop—often wheat—usually dominated. Repetitive tasks, such as grinding grain to make flour, caused excessive wear to people's joints, leading to arthritis. At the same time, **more food was cooked**, a process that can destroy vitamins and introduce toxins, while babies depended less on their mothers' milk. These changes led to populations of smaller stature and with weaker bones, as well as new conditions such as **anemia and scurvy**.

GRINDING GRAIN

EARLY HEALERS

Other medical interventions were practiced besides dentistry (see above). Often, serious bone fractures were successfully reset—remains show signs of regrowth. And in caves at Lascaux, France, archaeologists have found preparations of **medicinal herbs** dating back to 13,000 BCE.

At the beginning of the Bronze Age, around 3000 BCE, the civilizations of Mesopotamia (see pp.54–55), ancient Egypt (see pp.64–73), and the Indus Valley (see pp.58–59) were already well established. Busy, booming cities were surrounded by fertile land given over to agriculture, and farming became so efficient that only a relatively small proportion of the population needed to be involved in producing food. This led to the development of trade, mathematics and astronomy, writing, and a flourishing of cultural activities.

The price of progress

Along with the many benefits of their way of life, however, people in early civilizations suffered from some ill effects. Their diets were generally lower in fiber and higher in fat and salt than their hunter-gatherer predecessors. There is evidence that this led to an increase in conditions such as high blood pressure, heart disease, and cancer—a trend that began with the rise of agriculture several thousand years earlier, and continues today. This pattern was repeated elsewhere. In Central America, for example, early Maya people began relying on corn as a staple in civilizations originating around 1000 BCE. This led to a population explosion, but at the price of a dangerously restricted diet.

As the Bronze Age gave way to the Iron Age in Europe and Asia after about 1000 BCE, many killer diseases arose for the first time in human populations. Smallpox and anthrax are two good examples. In both cases, and in many others, the pathogens (disease-causing organisms) evolved to cross species barriers from livestock, and were able to take hold because people were living so close together in mostly unsanitary conditions. Rats, fleas, and lice thrived, and

carried diseases such as the plague and typhoid. In times of flood, drought, or war, these problems were heightened.

Explaining disease

No one in early civilizations could understand disease the way modern medical science does. Thus, it was normal to attribute the causes of disease to supernatural forces. People believed that they became unwell as the result of possession by evil spirits—demons—or because of angry gods or sorcery carried out by their enemies.

Just as explanations of disease appealed to the supernatural, so did most attempts to cure people. In most cultures, priests and sorcerers were at least as important as physicians—and exorcism of demons, sacrifice to the gods, shamanistic rituals, and counter-sorcery were commonplace. The Ebers papyrus, written in Egypt in the 2nd millennium BCE and discovered in the 19th century, contains a long list of "medical" incantations designed to turn away evil spirits.

Herbalism

Healing based on supernatural beliefs is an example of folk medicine. Herbal remedies also fall into this category. Many ancient treatments based on herbs or other plants evolved through trial and error, and are so successful that they are still used today for their analgesic (pain relief), antibiotic, or antifungal action. In Mesopotamia, for example (see pp.54–55), a willow bark extract was used to relieve headaches and reduce fevers. That extract is salicylic acid, the basis of aspirin.

Egyptian surgical instruments
In ancient Egypt, sharp bronze and copper instruments were used when embalming the dead, as well as for operating on the living.

Hole in the head
The earliest known surgery, dating back to 40,000 BCE, was trepanning—drilling a hole in the skull. This was probably done to release evil, disease-causing demons. The practice occurred in Central America, Europe, and Asia.

China has the strongest tradition of using herbs and roots in medicine. According to legend, one of its pioneers was the emperor Shen Nong, who is supposed to have lived in the 3rd millennium BCE. The story goes that he tested hundreds of different herbs, searching for ones with medicinal effects. He is also credited with the introduction of tea-drinking—for its remedial qualities.

The therapeutic use of plants is found in almost every corner of the world. The Olmec in Central America, for example (see pp.74–75), had areas of their gardens set aside for growing medicinal herbs. Papyri from ancient Egypt list remedies involving plants such as thyme, juniper, frankincense, and garlic—although there were others that used beer and animals' entrails. Herbalism is also central to Ayurvedic medicine, which originated in the Vedic period of India (see p.144) shortly before 1000 BCE. Ayurveda (literally "knowledge of life") is a holistic system that uses a combination of religion and science to create physical, mental, and spiritual well-being.

Organized approach

The Ayurvedic system is typical of the approach to science and technology that began to emerge—in China and India in particular—during the 1st millennium BCE. People began to think rationally, organize their thoughts, discuss them with others, and derive theories. This approach led not only to an encyclopedic knowledge of human anatomy and of a vast range of diseases, but also to well thought-out systems of diagnosis and treatment—the basis of modern medicine.

Sickness and Health

The desire to stay alive and healthy is a basic human instinct. It is no wonder, then, that people in early civilizations attempted to explain the origins of disease—and intervened to soothe pain, encourage healing, and effect cures. Some of these traditional approaches to medicine are still in use today.

The god Pazuzu, who as "king of the evil spirits" can ward off disease, looks down from the top of the amulet.

CHASTEBERRY (MENSTRUAL PROBLEMS)

ROSEHIP (SOOTHING TONIC)

GINSENG (STIMULANT)

Medicinal plants
The health-giving or healing properties of many roots, seeds, and leaves have been recognized since ancient times and confirmed by modern medical science.

The "heavenly domain" shows the symbols of the highest gods, such as the star of the goddess Ishtar.

Priests dressed in fish skins perform exorcism rituals at the bedside of the patient, probably a mother who has given birth. The lamp on the left indicates that this happens at night.

Pazuzu, who has a dog's head, a scorpion's tail, and bird talons, chases the malevolent Lamashtu back to the netherworld.

Lamashtu, the demonic goddess who preys on pregnant women and babies, has the naked torso of an old woman—with a pig and a dog drinking from her breasts. She carries a poisonous snake in each hand.

Purging demons
The Mesopotamians had a complex belief system of supernatural beings and forces. This Assyrian bronze amulet highlights the importance of these beliefs in explaining and treating disease.

HOW WE KNOW

SKELETAL HEALTH

Many of the ancient ideas about health and disease can be gleaned from the art, writing, and artifacts of the time. But equally important are human remains, such as bones, teeth, and other tissues. Skeletal remains are the most valuable, because they decay very slowly. They often show physical signs of deformity or malnutrition, and can also provide a physical record of certain medical interventions, including primitive surgery. Further details can be revealed under the microscope and by carrying out tests. Analysis of the chemical isotopes present and examination of the DNA can reveal subtle clues to what a person ate, how old they were, and how they lived and died.

HEALED BONE FRACTURE, ANCIENT EGYPT

AFTER

During the 1st millennium BCE, medicine became more systematic, but supernatural explanations and nonscientific folk remedies prevailed until after the scientific revolution of the 18th century.

ACUPUNCTURE
Acupuncture aims to **restore health** and well-being, and to **relieve pain**. Still one of the mainstays of Chinese medicine, it was probably developed in **Han China 128–29 >>** around 200 CE—although there is some evidence that it was used earlier. The locations

ACUPUNCTURE POINTS

of tattoos on a well-preserved body, nicknamed Ötzi after its discovery, tally very closely with important acupuncture points. Ötzi's body was discovered in 1991, in the Alps between Italy and Austria—he lived about 3350 BCE **<< 43**.

INDIAN PROGRESS
The Ayurveda system flourished across the Indian subcontinent. Its main exponent was **Sushruta**, whose 6th-century BCE work *Sushruta Samhita* describes more than 100 surgical instruments and 300 surgical procedures. Many historians of medicine refer to him as the **"Father of Surgery."**

ANCIENT GREEK MEDICINE
The **thinkers of ancient Greece 104–05, 130–131 >>** were among the first to apply careful observation and **rational thought** to philosophical questions, and this extended to medicine. Medical practice was dominated by the theory of "humors." According to this, the human body was composed of **four humors**: blood, phlegm, black bile, and yellow bile, and illness was the result of an **imbalance between them**. Although much of ancient Greek medicine was derived in isolation, Greek thinkers were influenced by Egyptian medicine, which had many excellent herbal remedies.

GALEN DISSECTING

ROMAN MEDICINE
Doctors in ancient Rome followed Greek medical practices, but while the Greeks had used philosophy to explain disease, the Romans reverted to explanations that depended on the whims of the gods. The greatest Roman physician and anatomist was **Claudius Galenus (Galen)**, who lived in the 2nd century CE. His ideas about **anatomy** were based on **careful observation**, but many were false. Nevertheless, they dominated Western medicine until the 16th century. Ancient Rome is celebrated for its initiatives on **public health**. Their water supplies, sewage and heating systems, and public baths were well ahead of their time.

BEFORE «

Settled life in Mesopotamia dates back 10,000 years. A rich archaeological record documents the growth of irrigation, agriculture, trade, writing, towns, and complex societies.

EARLY SETTLEMENT
Farming began c. 8000 BCE in the case of **Halaf culture «44–45** in the north and c. 6000 BCE in the southern, **Ubaid culture**.

HALAF POTTERY FIGURE

IRRIGATION AND ORGANIZATION
Settlements grew due to **irrigation programs**. The surplus crops grown were traded, **creating wealth**. The organization and control needed resulted in more complex, **layered societies**.

THE RISE OF URBAN CENTERS
By the 3000s BCE, the first **urban centers** were in place **«44–45**, with the southern **Sumer** region home to a thriving civilization by 3500 BCE.

FROM TRADING TO WRITING
The record-keeping needed to control trade used seals featuring symbols and pictures, followed by the development of early writing **62–63 »**.

SEAL SHOWING PLOWING WITH AN OX

The civilization of Mesopotamia thrived across an area that today includes Iraq, southwest Iran, east Syria, and southeast Turkey. Mesopotamia is Greek for "between rivers"—civilization here rested on a prime position between the Euphrates and Tigris rivers. This dependence on rivers echoes that of three other civilizations: those in contemporary Egypt (see pp.56–57) and the Indus Valley (see pp.58–59), and in China a little later (see pp.60–61).

As in Egypt, Mesopotamian crops relied on rich silts deposited by the river waters, while marshlands provided fish and waterfowl for eating, and reeds—used for roofing and baskets in Mesopotamia. Irrigation and land-reclamation programs required well-drilled marshalling of large numbers of people. This laid the foundations for what is thought to be the world's first stratified (layered) society—reaching its height of sophistication slightly ahead of Egypt.

City-states and empires
By around 3000 BCE, Mesopotamia was entering an era known as the Early Dynastic, which lasted 700 years. Civilization was focused initially on city-states in the south, an area often called Sumer after the Sumerian language widely spoken there. The pattern of Mesopotamia's history emerged at this stage: cities and city-states (see p.94), often linked by trading and diplomatic ties, would cooperate and compete, rise and fall. Certain city-states and city-based dynasties—Uruk, Kish, Akkad, and Ur—rose to control others for a while before being dominated by yet others. This contrasts with Egypt and its centralized rule, but bears some similarity to the later life of the Greek city-states (see pp.94–95). Great cities of the third millennium included Ur, Lagash, Kish, Eridu, and Uruk

Tomb treasure
The lavish jewels worn by Queen Pu-abi (Ur, c. 2500 BCE) feature precious metals and semiprecious stones from Ur's varied trading partners.

One figure is shown larger than everyone else. It is likely that this is the king, glass in hand, at his court, with this top row depicting a banquet scene.

The Cradle of Civilization

Mesopotamia, a fertile land embraced by rivers, was the site of the first complex societies. By 3000 BCE, competing city-states of great wealth and sophistication were flourishing here, with advanced irrigation and agricultural schemes, established trade, the first known writing, and grand palaces and temples.

EMPEROR, DIED c. 2284 BCE
SARGON OF AKKAD

Seen traditionally as a great warrior-king, Sargon established the Akkadian dynasty and ruled c. 2340–2284 BCE. He founded his capital city, Akkad, and created a centralized state that oversaw the first real empire in Mesopotamia. Few tales about Sargon can be verified. It has been suggested that he established himself as a successful independent ruler first and then began his expansionist policies. His military prowess could be explained by Akkadian techniques being more efficient than those of rival armies. We know about Sargon's rule from an ancient document called the Sumerian King List.

BRONZE CAST HEAD, 2334–2154 BCE, OF AN AKKADIAN RULER, PROBABLY SARGON

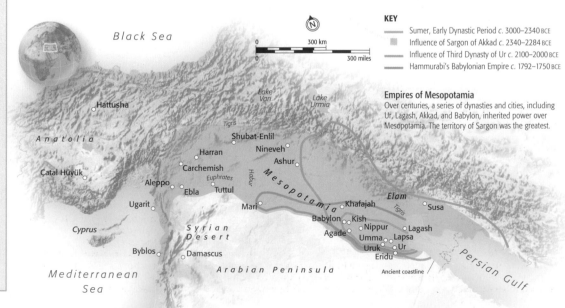

KEY
— Sumer, Early Dynastic Period c. 3000–2340 BCE
■ Influence of Sargon of Akkad c. 2340–2284 BCE
— Influence of Third Dynasty of Ur c. 2100–2000 BCE
— Hammurabi's Babylonian Empire c. 1792–1750 BCE

Empires of Mesopotamia
Over centuries, a series of dynasties and cities, including Ur, Lagash, Akkad, and Babylon, inherited power over Mesopotamia. The territory of Sargon was the greatest.

A courtier, one of several celebrating with their ruler, sits on a wooden stool and raises a cup in honor of the great occasion.

A court musician plucks at a lyre, decorated with the bull's head that appears repeatedly on examples of this apparently popular Mesopotamian instrument.

Standard of Ur
This object, whose purpose is a mystery, was found in the royal tombs at Ur. With 20-in- (50-cm-) wide wooden panels inlaid with shell, red limestone, and lapis lazuli, it reveals much about Mesopotamian life. This panel may show war booty being brought to court.

AFTER »

During the next millennium, a succession of cultures inherited the land between rivers.

AKKADIAN DECLINE
As the Akkadian empire faded, local leaders won regional power in Kish, Uruk, and Lagash. The rule of **Gudea of Lagash** saw his city's last thriving era. Irrigation systems were set up, temples rebuilt, and statues of Gudea were carved.

GUDEA OF LAGASH

THIRD DYNASTY OF UR
After the Akkadian era, the Third Dynasty of Ur (c. 2100–2000 BCE) fought off competing city-states to found a short-lived empire built on Akkadian achievements. The **kings of Ur** revived central rule to create a **Sumerian renaissance** harking back to the region's former glories.

OLD ASSYRIAN ERA
As the Ur dynasty faded, returning the south to rival city-states, the Assyrian city-state of Assur (c. 2000 –1800 BCE) **80–81 »** emerged as the center of a vast trade network in the north.

OLD BABYLONIAN ERA
Since c. 1900 BCE, the city of **Babylon**, north of Sumer, had been emerging as a dominant power. The Old Babylonian era (c. 1894–1595 BCE) saw the rule of **Hammurabi** (c. 1792–1750 BCE) and his famous **law code**, a rich source of information about life in the Babylonian state.

MITTANI AND BEYOND
The Hurrian people of **Mittani 78–79 »** dominated the north (c. 1600–1350 BCE), until control passed to the **Hittites 78–79 »** and the **Middle Assyrian kingdom 80–81 »**. In the south, the **Kassites 78–79 »** controlled middle-era **Babylonia** (c. 1400–1100 BCE). Around 1100 BCE, the Babylonian state collapsed along with other great Bronze Age powers **78–79 »**.

Oxen, sheep, and donkeys are apparently being brought in procession to the banqueting court. Perhaps they are being presented as spoils of war.

Heavily laden people in the procession are shown stooping visibly under the weight of sacks filled to the brim with foodstuffs and other valuable merchandise.

Fine detail in this scene gives insight into the clothing of the time. This figure is seen in a fringed skirt, while others sport woolen fleeces.

(see pp.44–45), Ebla, and Mari. By the 24th century BCE, many southern lands were under one king: Lugalzagezi of Umma. Farther west, Akkad became the center of a dynasty begun by Sargon (see left), whose influence expanded to the Mediterranean and Anatolia, resulting in the Akkadian language being used for official documents and diplomacy for many centuries to come (see pp.62–63, 66–67, 78–79).

A place for everyone
Mesopotamian society had a hierarchy and a centralized structure headed by rulers who were all-powerful but, unlike Egypt's pharaohs, were rarely thought to be divine. Grand royal palaces appeared throughout the region in the Early Dynastic era. We know of the sophistication and wealth of these palace cultures from discoveries such as the lavish, finely wrought

artifacts found in tombs at Ur where either royalty or priestesses (or figures combining both roles) were buried.

As in Egypt, specialists were needed to support such a society and its administration—a "professional" layer of experts such as bureaucrats, scribes, and merchants. In this urbanized civilization, many city-dwellers lived in impressive town-houses of locally sourced mud brick, mud plaster, and wooden doors.

A large labor force was needed to cultivate the land and run the great irrigation and building projects. However, there was some social mobility. Some laborers appear to have owned land or received rations linked to their work for central government.

Royal game
This game board of c. 2500 BCE, inlaid with shell and lapis lazuli, was found in a royal tomb in Ur. This game was popular right across the Middle East, Egypt, and India.

Rule and religion
In common with other civilizations of the time, politics and religion were intertwined. Rulers took a lead in directing religious matters, while priests and priestesses conversely took on "state" functions; some cities were ruled by priests. Each city had a massive central mud-brick temple (such as the famous Ziggurat at Ur, see p.73), which was the home-on-Earth of the city's god and where priests carried out rituals to win the god's favor. Keeping order was made easier by the people's belief that they must do the gods' bidding, to the extent that, when royalty died, palace staff entombed themselves with their king or queen. Around 74 bodies were found in one grave at Ur.

A world player
Poor in natural resources such as metal and stone, the Mesopotamians, like the Egyptians, were forced to forge wide-ranging trade (and so diplomatic) links

Precious lyre
Playing lyres seems to have been a part of court or temple life in Mesopotamia. A bull's or cow's head is a recurrent decoration.

over a region that included modern Iran, Afghanistan, the Persian Gulf, and the Indus Valley. This drove much of the progress and expansion of their culture and gave them a leading profile in world politics. Mesopotamia took the lead in many fields. Its art included exquisite jewelry, musical instruments, and beautiful stone carving dating back to 4th-millennium Uruk. In science, their numerical system based on the number 60 dates back to the Sumerians of the 3rd millennium BCE. It lives on today in our division of a circle into 360 degrees and in our splitting of the hour and the minute into 60 smaller parts.

BEFORE

The great Egyptian civilization of the Old Kingdom with its godlike pharaohs had its origins in earlier dynasties.

PRE-DYNASTIC EGYPT
The period between early Neolithic settlement and c. 3100 BCE is known as the Pre-Dynastic Era. Egypt existed in two parts—the north (Lower Egypt) and the south (Upper Egypt). Evidence discovered in tombs suggests a wealthy society, and that people believed in an afterlife.

NARMER

EARLY DYNASTIC ERA
The Early Dynastic Era (c. 3100–2686 BCE) covers the 1st and 2nd dynasties. **Menes, or Horus Aha** « 45, who united the kingdoms of Upper and Lower Egypt, is usually thought to be the first pharaoh. However, Narmer may have come first, or Narmer may be another name for Menes.

A SENSE OF IDENTITY
The Early Dynastic Era gave Egypt a strong sense of identity. It brought a sudden (as yet unexplained) rise to greatness, with more complex irrigation programs, grander royal tombs, a centralized state headed by a king with a semidivine identity, and a form of writing.

ARCHITECT AND PHYSICIAN

IMHOTEP

Imhotep is credited as the main architect of Djoser's "step pyramid." Djoser was the second pharaoh of the 3rd dynasty (c. 2686–2613 BCE) and Imhotep was his chief adviser and physician, as well as being the leading genius of his day. His step pyramid is seen as the building that helped establish the Old Kingdom as an era of remarkable achievement. The oldest surviving building made from cut blocks of stone, it was the first true Egyptian pyramid. Giza's great tombs adapted Imhotep's design, but filled in the stepped sides to produce what we now think of as the classic pyramid. Imhotep's skills as a physician were such that he was worshipped as a god in later ancient Egypt and Greece.

IMHOTEP

The Divine Pharaohs

Egypt's Old Kingdom (c. 2686–2181 BCE) flourished on the flood-enriched banks of the Nile River. It was an era of prosperity, relative stability, and strong centralized rule, during which the great pyramids were built and Egyptian society worshipped their mighty kings, or pharaohs, as "gods on Earth."

Old Kingdom society was tightly controlled by a centralized government headed by a highly powerful ruler, the pharaoh. Central to life, politics, and religion, which were all closely combined, was the idea that the pharaoh was a semi-divine figure who acted as mediator between the gods and his subjects.

As a religious and political leader, the pharaoh not only oversaw elaborate religious rituals that underlined his links with the gods, he also headed a vast, highly organized political and administrative bureaucracy, peopled by an army of advisors and officials, chief of which was an officer called a vizier. The bureaucracy also included local governors, who oversaw regions called *nomes* (former independent regions). Pharaohs are often seen as being despotic. However, although their word was law, the pharaohs did delegate a significant amount to the governors and, as the Old Kingdom progressed (see AFTER), gave them more and more power.

Kingdom of the Sun
The first pharaohs were believed to be earthly representations of the mythical figure Horus, son of the god Osiris, and Isis (see pp.68–69). Horus was strongly linked with Ra (or Re), creator of life and falcon-headed god of the Sun. The Sun cult became very important during the Old Kingdom and Ra emerged as a separate figure from Horus. "Ra" even became incorporated into pharaohs' names.

Through these connections, the pharaoh was the upholder of a justice system that aimed to reflect the cosmic order. He was also, vitally, the figure who worked with the gods to ensure that the Nile brought silt-rich annual floods each year, keeping the Nile Valley fertile enough to support the great Egyptian state.

The pharaoh was the ultimate all-seeing, all-knowing figure. He was often depicted dressed in a kind of kilt and false beard, bearing a crook, flail, and scepter, and with the double crown of Lower and Upper Egypt on his head.

A cobra, the "eye" of Ra, was shown rising up off his forehead. He was accompanied by the royal fan-bearer, and people fell prostrate before him. Egyptians did seem to realize he was a flesh-and-blood human, but they stood in awe of his sacred power.

"Gift of the Nile"
Ancient Greek historian Herodotus described the Nile's bounty as a "gift." The mighty river cut a huge valley in the northeastern corner of Africa (see pp.64–65). To the north, in Lower Egypt, the Nile's tributaries fanned out to create a wide, fertile delta, home to a high concentration of people. At the delta's south was the "capital city" of Old Kingdom Egypt—Memphis. Farther south, in Upper Egypt, the valley snaked away in a narrow strip, with towns clinging to its fertile banks.

The Nile's annual inundation left in its wake the rich black silt on which the Egyptians relied to grow their crops. Vast irrigation programs were

The pharaoh Khafre
Khafre, also known as Khafra, Chephren, or Khephren, was the fourth king of the 4th dynasty. This statue, showing him wearing a false beard and striped "nemes" headcloth, is from his pyramid-tomb complex at Giza.

Population of builders
This relief of an Egyptian shipyard is from a 5th-dynasty (c. 2494–2345 BCE) official's tomb at Saqqara. Ships were vital for travel along the Nile and for trade with some of Egypt's neighbors.

devised to direct the waters to wide areas of agricultural land. Marshlands along the banks provided waterfowl for eating (by wealthy people only) and the papyrus reed, used for making writing materials. The river waters themselves supplied fish and a means of getting from one place to another. The Egyptians, surrounded by vast stretches of arid, inhospitable desert, were only too aware of how dependent they were on this massive floodplain, As a result, lookouts were posted along the Nile in southern Egypt to spot early signs of high or low waters that would affect the annual harvest.

Society's pecking order
Society was fairly clearly divided into different levels. At the top was the royal family, presiding over court and administrative officials, such as scribes, and also priests. There was a strict pecking order, and showing duty and loyalty were top priorities.

The Great Pyramid of Khufu
The largest and oldest of the three Giza pyramids, this is what many people now think of as the greatest "true" pyramid ever. It probably took about 20 years to build, involving a workforce of thousands.

The Giza pyramid complex
The vast size of these royal tombs reflects the divine status of the 4th-dynasty kings. The most distant tomb is Khufu's "Great" pyramid; in the center is Khafre's; the smallest pyramid, in the foreground, is that of the pharaoh Menkaure.

Working the land
This fresco shows people harvesting wheat. The Egyptians created large areas for cultivation, using complex irrigation systems fed by the Nile.

It is said that most ordinary people in the Old Kingdom led miserable lives pressed into the pharaoh's service, building vast constructions or growing crops to feed the cities, in return for just enough sustenance to stay alive. However, evidence suggests that there was an independent local life, too, including markets where people sold produce and simple crafts. The fact that anyone could, theoretically, gain high office also contradicts the idea of a total dictatorship.

The age of the pyramids

The Old Kingdom is best known for its advances in stone building techniques, which saw fruition in the famous "step pyramid" at Saqqara, (see Imhotep, left) and then in the colossal royal pyramid tombs of the

Mallet
Simple, short-shafted wooden mallets like this were used with chisels to cut stone slabs with great precision and to produce fine relief carvings.

4th dynasty (c. 2613–2494 BCE). Built at Giza, close to Memphis at the edge of the desert, these are among the greatest building achievements in history. The Great Pyramid—the tomb of the pharaoh Khufu—was one of the Seven Wonders of the ancient world, and the only one that survives intact today. Just to the east of the pyramid lies the Great Sphinx, a massive part-lion, part-human statue, thought to have Khufu's features. The Giza pyramids are one of the earliest examples of using quarried stone. Huge blocks of limestone were transported from some distance away, cut with incredible precision, and lifted into place to make a perfectly fitted construction. No one knows exactly how this was achieved. Each pyramid may have been surrounded by a sloping bank, built

upward as the pyramid grew higher. The stone blocks may have been moved up the slope manually by using rollers and levers.

2 MILLION The number of limestone blocks, each weighing 16 tons (15,000 kg), used to construct Khufu's Great Pyramid at Giza.

A Middle Eastern power

Egypt became a major player in Middle Eastern politics during the Old Kingdom period. There is evidence of long-distance contact with many regions, including parts of modern Syria, Libya, Lebanon, and Sudan. Contact arose because Egypt wanted to keep its borders safe, and to trade for materials, such as wood. Borders cannot be maintained or crossed without negotiation, so Egypt must have started to develop the diplomatic skills for which it became famous.

AFTER »

There are countless theories about the Old Kingdom collapse; but no one knows for certain what happened.

NOBLES AND NOMES
By the 6th dynasty (c. 2345–2181 BCE), the pharaohs **granted certain powers to nobles and governors** of the regional districts, or **"nomes."** This may have gradually undermined the pharaoh's authority. It is also suggests that as the pharaoh lost control, others were able to take more power for themselves.

PHARAOH PEPY II

THE OLD KINGDOM COLLAPSES
At the end of the 6th dynasty, especially after the reign of **Pepy II**, the Old Kingdom started to fade and Egypt moved into a more uncertain time called the First Intermediate Period **64–65 ».** Royal authority weakened and Memphis lost some of its importance compared with other towns and cities.

WHY DID IT HAPPEN?
Links have been made with Egypt's dependence on the Nile, saying that **extreme flooding, drought, or both brought great destruction or famine.** This would have been especially disastrous if central authority was weak. Threats to Egypt's borders may also have been a factor in the Old Kingdom's decline.

Indus Valley culture grew largely out of developing farming cultures west of the valley.

EARLY FARMING CULTURES
Most notable was the Neolithic **Mehrgarh** culture, starting *c.* 7000 BCE in modern Pakistan.

HARAPPAN PHASES
The "Early Harappan" phase of the Indus Valley culture (*c.* 3300–2800 BCE) saw the first examples of the **Indus script**, more **sophisticated agriculture**, and **growing trade links**.

Indus Valley script
Indus valley seals are rich sources of imagery, featuring animal, human, and mythical figures alongside samples of the undeciphered script.

The Indus Valley civilization peaked between about 2600 and 1900 BCE, in what is often called its "Mature Harappan" period. It flourished across an extensive area of present-day northwest India, Pakistan, and Afghanistan, along the fertile Indus and Ghaggar-Hakra rivers.

At its height, the Indus Valley ranked among the first great early civilizations, in the company of Mesopotamia and Egypt (see pp.54–57). Like them, it depended heavily on farmland nourished by major rivers. Also in common with them, its people developed expert knowledge about how to harness and control the annual flooding patterns of the rivers.

Artistic skills
The refined artifacts produced in the Indus Valley region clearly show this to have been an advanced civilization. They include finely worked jewelry in gold and fired steatite (soapstone); figurines fashioned from bronze, terra-cotta, and faience; pottery; gold and silver ornaments; and seals. The latter often featured images of animals common to the area, such as elephants and zebu (oxen).

These artifacts seem to tell us that there was not only skill, but also prosperity and an elite class, which hints further at a society with different social and economic levels. There are quite a few different artistic styles, too, perhaps pointing to a diverse ethnic mix within the population.

Some Indus Valley artifacts, most famously the jewelry, have been found at sites elsewhere in the world, indicating widespread trading links. The Indus people relied heavily on trading arrangements and their partners included Mesopotamia (see right), Iran, and Afghanistan. Trading practice was boosted by advances in methods of transportation, especially in boats suited to long-distance travel along sea routes. Sets of weights have also been found among excavated artifacts, and the Indus people seem to have been among the first to develop a precise weights

Indus rulers
This famous figure from Mohenjo-Daro is known as "the priest-king", despite no evidence of rule by priests or kings.

Advanced sanitation
Highly developed plumbing included drains (above), some of which were covered, and latrines. To give each dwelling access to clean water, wells were built with high, sealed walls to avoid contamination problems.

Mohenjo-Daro
The city's grid pattern is visible here. Archaeologists have guessed at its structure by giving certain excavated areas names such as "Citadel Mound," "Lower Town," and "the Great Bath," but these remain contentious issues.

HOW WE KNOW

TRADE WITH MESOPOTAMIA

Maritime trading connections with Mesopotamia were especially important to the Indus Valley civilization. We know that they traded with Mesopotamia as Indus or Indus-influenced artifacts have been excavated there—notably a set of etched carnelian beads, like those below, found at the city of Ur in the tomb of Queen Puabi, *c.* 2550–2400 BCE.

CARNELIAN BEADS

Mysteries of the Indus

A fertile cradle of river-fed land, crossing parts of modern India, Pakistan, and Afghanistan, gave birth to the Indus Valley culture. People in its impressive, well-planned cities lived a refined life, but unlocking more about them is tantalizingly out of reach, as their script remains mostly undeciphered.

KEY
- ▪ Area of Harappan culture
- ○ Harappan site
- ● Site of Mehrgahr culture

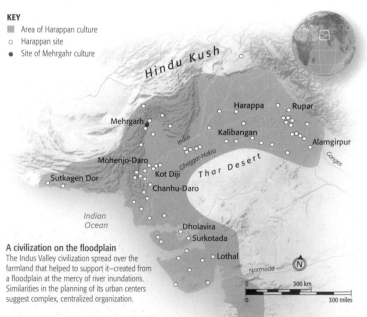

Hindu Kush

Harappa · Rupar

Mehrgarh · Kalibangan · Alamgirpur

Indus · Ghaggar-Hokra · Ganges

Mohenjo-Daro · Thar Desert

Sutkagen Dor · Kot Diji

Chanhu-Daro

Indian Ocean

Dholavira · Surkotada

Lothal

Narmada

N

0 — 300 km
0 — 300 miles

A civilization on the floodplain
The Indus Valley civilization spread over the farmland that helped to support it—created from a floodplain at the mercy of river inundations. Similarities in the planning of its urban centers suggest complex, centralized organization.

and measures system. Behind this system lay the kind of expert knowledge that explains why their city buildings were so impressive.

The world's first town planners?
A large number of settlements are associated with Indus Valley culture. The most spectacular, Mohenjo-Daro and Harappa (in modern Pakistan), were probably the world's first planned cities. Here were broad avenues and narrow side streets lined with spacious townhouses, all set out in a well-defined grid pattern. Remarkably, Indus cities thousands of miles apart were laid out in a similar way, suggesting a centralized state and local civic organization. Whether there was such a structure, and other details about government and society, remain largely a mystery, as although many distinct symbols appear on Indus artifacts, they remain undeciphered and their secrets locked away.

AFTER »

The Indus Valley civilization went into an unexplained decline, with most of its main cities deserted by *c.* 1700 BCE.

MOHENJO-DARO
The city suffered **severe flooding** in the 1700s BCE, and was laid waste by unknown attackers.

LIFE IN THE VALLEY
Part of the river system may have dried up, overstretching the cities' resources, although some southern settlements endured. Later Asian civilizations, such as the **Vedic 124 »** and **Hindu cultures** of the 1st millennium BCE, reveal cultural aspects of the Indus Valley civilization.

Bronze Age China

The Shang dynasty flourished from *c*. 1600 to 1100 BCE and was the first society to produce cast bronze on a large scale. Believed to be semidivine, the ruling Shang kings performed rituals to please their ancestors and gods. The artifacts that they used reveal a sophisticated society.

A "taotie"—the head of a ferocious animal with horns and bulging eyes—is hidden within the labyrinth-like decoration.

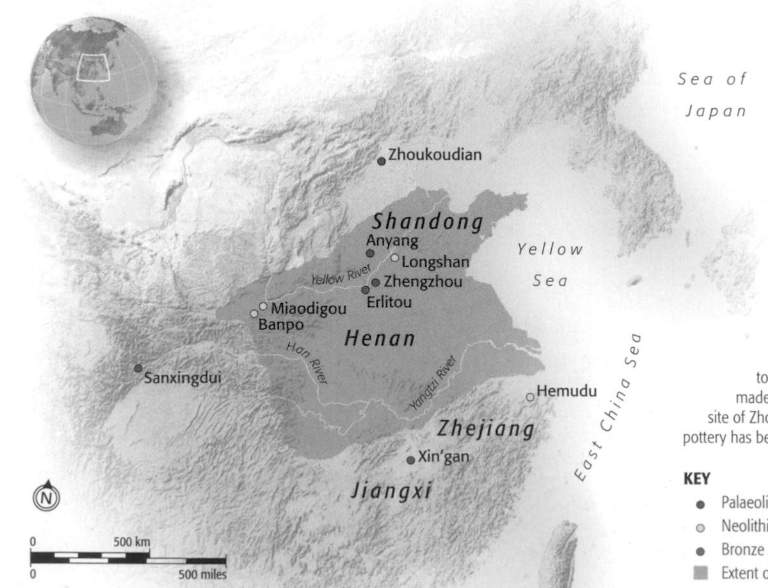

BEFORE

In the Neolithic period (8000–1500 BCE), the Chinese began farming millet and rice, and keeping animals. This required a static population, so people began to build houses, and to live together in villages.

NEOLITHIC HEMUDU

In 1973, a Neolithic (late Stone Age) settlement dating from *c*. 5000 BCE was discovered at Hemudu, in southeast China. The finds included terra-cotta pottery, wooden and bone articles, and the remains of pigs and buffalo. There were also some whistles made from the bones of birds, possibly used to attract birds to snares. The most exciting discovery was **evidence that the people of Hemudu cultivated wet rice**.

YANGSHAO CULTURE

The area of Yangshao, in the eastern province of Henan, was first excavated in the 1920s, and yielded some significant finds. In the **village of Banpo**, which was occupied *c*. 4500–3750 BCE, the inhabitants cultivated millet, used polished stone hoes and knives, and **wore hemp and possibly silk**. Their village had a residential area with about 100 houses and other buildings. They produced pots made of red clay, some decorated with spiral patterns, and others with human or animal designs painted on them.

YANGSHAO CLAY POT

LONGSHAN CULTURE

Soon after the discoveries at Yangshao, a completely different type of Neolithic pottery was found at Longshan, in Shandong province. It was much finer than Yangshao ware, and was black, decorated with rings and grooves, and often elevated on a circular foot. Some of **the pots may have been turned on a wheel**. Longshan culture, which also produced polished stone axes, spread along the middle and lower Yangzi (the longest river in China). In time, it overtook Yangshao culture, which was already dying out.

BRONZE AGE ERLITOU

The Xia dynasty was long thought to be a mythological one, but in 1959, **palacelike buildings, tombs, and bronze artifacts** from *c*. 1900–1350 BCE were found at Erlitou, in Henan. The bronze objects found there are the **oldest yet found in China**. Their shapes suggest that they may have derived from Longshan pottery.

The Bronze Age (see p.43) in China produced two major achievements: a developed system of writing, and the discovery of bronze. The highly prized metal, which was produced on a huge scale, was cast for weapons, tools, and vessels used exclusively by the noble classes for religious rituals. Early Bronze Age civilization in China was a rigidly hierarchical society, ruled by a supremely powerful king and his nobles. The people of the Shang— the second of China's ancient dynasties—believed that the king was invested with divine power from his ancestors, whose spirits were able to shape contemporary life if appeased with offerings. Bronze vessels were used for the sacrificial food and wine offered during these rituals, which can be seen as a precursor to the ceremonies of state used by later Chinese emperors (see pp.126–27). Much of what is known of Shang society has been gleaned from the study of the writings found on the "oracle bones" (see right).

The Shang state

In addition to support from aristocratic clans with whom they had family connections, Shang kings ruled their state with the assistance of officials. The Shang were frequently threatened by nomadic tribes from the inner Asian steppes (a vast belt of grassland that stretches from Europe to China), and the state was kept on a war footing. Nobles performed military duties in return for land. Shang kings waged wars against their neighbors, thereby obtaining slave labor and loot. They established new settlements, and cultivated captured land for farming. Despite being a warlike society, Shang civilization was based on agriculture and hunting. The production of bronze, too, resulted in a relatively settled society, as a static community was required to mine and smelt the ores that contain copper and tin, the metals needed for bronze casting.

Shang capitals

The Shang ruled over much of northern China and the center of the country. The most important capitals were Zhengzhou, the capital in the earlier period of the dynasty, and Anyang, which was occupied *c*. 1300–1050 BCE. At Zhengzhou, a defensive city wall 4 miles (6.4 km) long enclosed a large settlement; the wall and the buildings within were constructed of stamped earth. The houses and workshops that have been excavated, and the variety of artifacts found inside them, indicate that Shang society was highly organized and rigidly ordered. Outside the capital of Anyang, at

Shang dynasty China

Key Bronze Age sites include the early capital city of Zhengzhou, which later moved to Anyang. Pre–Bronze Age finds have been made at the Paleolithic (*c*. 100,000–10,000 BCE) site of Zhoukoudian, and Neolithic (8000–1500 BCE) pottery has been discovered at Banpo and Hemudu.

Zhoukoudian

Shandong
Anyang
Longshan
Zhengzhou
Yellow River
Erlitou
Miaodigou
Banpo
Henan
Han River
Sanxingdui
Yangtzi River
Hemudu
Zhejiang
Xin'gan
Jiangxi

Sea of Japan
Yellow Sea
East China Sea

0   500 km
0   500 miles

KEY
- Palaeolithic site
- Neolithic site
- Bronze Age site
- Extent of Shang influence

Strong handles were necessary for such a heavy pot to be removed from the fire.

Chariot burials
When an important person died, his chariot, charioteers, and horses were buried with him, as seen in this example found close to Anyang.

Xiaotun village, the remains have been uncovered of what was the ceremonial and administrative center of the late Shang state.

Burial customs

At Xibeigang, just north of Xiaotun, 11 huge graves have been found, which may belong to the 11 Shang monarchs who reigned at Anyang. When Shang kings died, they were buried in large cross-shaped graves. Their bodies were placed in wooden coffins surrounded by goods important to the deceased. The bodies of scores of slaughtered horses and human victims—possibly prisoners of war—were laid out on the ramps that led down to the burial chamber.

Bronze industry

The most prized archaeological finds from the Shang period are the bronze objects, made primarily for ceremonial purposes. The production of bronze was controlled by the king, and the quantity of bronze objects found indicates that it was a major industry, employing large numbers of skilled craftsmen. Early bronze technology in the West allowed an object to be cast from a single mold, but early Shang vessels were cast in several molds and the parts assembled later. Important finds of bronze vessels were made at the two capitals of Zhengzhou and Anyang. These vessels had ritual functions; some were intended for the preparation of sacrificial

meats, others for the heating of wine. Bronze was also used for musical instruments and for weapons, including swords and halberds, and hardware for chariots (see above).

Writing system

Along with a mastery of bronze, a complete writing system was created by the Shang, which had a huge effect on their organizational capabilities. Although some forms of early symbols appear on Neolithic pots and early Shang bronzes, the oldest inscriptions of complete sentences are found on oracle bones (see below). Over half of the known 2,500 symbols carved into the oracle bones can be read, and many closely resemble the Chinese characters of later times (see AFTER).

Bronze dagger
The highly ornamented handle of this dagger possibly depicts a stylized ram's head. Weapons such as this were probably used for ritual and sacrificial purposes.

Tripod shape is reminiscent of Longshan (Neolithic) pottery (see BEFORE)

Bronze ritual vessel
This highly patterned vessel was probably used by the Shang for the preparation of meat offerings.

AFTER »

Considered a tyrant, the last Shang ruler, Di Xin, was overthrown by the state of Zhou in the 11th century BCE. Many of the achievements of the Shang period, however, remain central to Chinese culture.

CHINESE CHARACTERS
The writing system created by the Shang developed over time into the Chinese characters in use today. The script was fixed in its present form during the Qin dynasty (221–206 BCE) **126–27** », and in 1716 the Kangxi Dictionary was published, containing over 47,000 characters. Studies in China have shown that full literacy requires a knowledge of 3,000–4,000 characters.

ANCIENT TEXTS

CALENDAR
The Shang created a lunar/solar calendar based on the zodiac, with ten "heavenly stems" and twelve "earthly branches." When combined together, the stems and branches formed cycles of sixty days or sixty years. The Shang model, although modified, **remains the basis for the traditional Chinese calendar**.

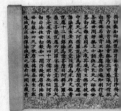

ANCESTOR WORSHIP
The Shang people worshipped many deities, most of whom were royal ancestors, and communicated with them through divination. This **veneration of ancestors** has remained an essential part of Chinese religious practice in modern times.

DIVINATION STICKS

HOW WE KNOW

ORACLE BONES

Sold in the 19th century as "dragon bones," an ingredient of Chinese medicine, "oracle bones" are actually the shoulder blades of cattle. Questions about the future would be scratched on the bones, to which a heated bronze tool was applied, and the resulting cracks were interpreted for an answer. Often, the predictions would be compared with the real event. They provide fascinating evidence not only of events in the Shang period, but also of early Chinese writing.

BEFORE

People used symbols to keep records long before the invention of true writing.

TALLY BONES
The **earliest** form of note-taking known in the Middle East, the **tally bone** dates back 30,000 years. The bones **recorded lunar months**, which governed the ritual cycles observed by **hunter-gatherers ‹‹ 30–31**.

CLAY TOKENS
From 9000 to 3000 BCE, people in the Middle East used **clay tokens** to record commercial transactions, sealing them into **clay envelopes** called **bullae**. A token's **shape** symbolized either **goods** (animals, grain) or specific **large numbers**. The example above is from **Uruk ‹‹ 44–45** and is dated to 3700–3200 BCE.

CLAY TOKENS AND BULLA

STAMP AND CYLINDER SEALS
A **seal ‹‹ 54–55** was a detailed engraved image **identifying the sender** of a message. The seal was pressed on wet clay by stamping, or rolling in the case of cylinder seals. Such seals appeared millennia before the development of writing.

HOW WE KNOW

THE ROSETTA STONE

Hieroglyphs were deciphered in 1822–24 by French Egyptologist and linguist Jean François Champollion. He used the Rosetta Stone—a stele of Ptolemy V bearing the same inscription in three scripts: hieroglyphic Egyptian (top), demotic Egyptian (middle), and Greek (bottom). He deciphered the Egyptian scripts by comparing identifiable words, such as names, in all three scripts, allowing him to work out the sound of each Egyptian sign from the Greek.

ROSETTA STONE

According to ancient tradition, writing was either invented by an individual or handed down to humanity by the gods. The Sumerian poem *Enmerkar and the Lord of Aratta* describes how King Enmerkar invented writing instantly to record a message too complicated for his messengers to memorize. We now know, however, that the development of writing was a gradual process, taking centuries. Our knowledge depends on surviving examples of ancient writing. Degradable materials, such as papyrus, bamboo, and parchment, have not endured, so the earliest surviving inscriptions tend to be found on monuments. These texts, such as the hieroglyphs on Egyptian tombs, are too sophisticated to be the first use of writing. In Mesopotamia (see p.54–55), however, people wrote on durable clay tablets that survive in

CUNEIFORM A writing technique widely used in the Middle East between 2500–330 BCE. Scribes used symbols made with wedge-shaped impressions pressed into clay or carved into stone. Many languages and civilizations used cuneiform, from Sumerian to Persian.

huge numbers, so the progression of their earliest writing can be traced. At early stages, writing was made up of

The Writing on the Wall

Writing—the symbolic representation of spoken language—and its development represents a massive step forward in the intellectual evolution of humans. The development of writing occurred independently in five different areas: Mesopotamia, Egypt, India, China, and Mesoamerica.

Message from a temple
This clay tablet was written in a temple of Mesopotamia in 3100–2900 BCE. The script is a kind of proto-cuneiform—an early, pictorial stage in Mesopotamian writing development. The tablet probably describes grain either distributed by or offered to a temple. Thousands of tablets such as this have been unearthed at Uruk in Mesopotamia (see pp.54–55). They recorded transactions and contracts made by the temples.

The barley symbol is very common in ancient Mesopotamian writing. Barley was one of the most important commodities and was used to make bread and beer—the two staples of the Mesopotamian diet.

Drawn symbols were used in proto-cuneiform. Drawing was a messy and time-consuming process compared to impressing standardized wedge signs, as was done later by cuneiform scribes.

A box of symbols represented one transaction or sentence. Writers of proto-cuneiform grouped signs in boxes, not lines or columns.

A seal impression acted as a signature. People involved in contracts authenticated them by pressing their seal into the clay, rather than writing their names. In this case, the seal image represents a hunting dog.

The walking (transport) symbol suggests the items specified elsewhere on the tablet were moved. The absence of verbs makes it impossible to say whether the transport was to or from the temple in which the tablet was found.

A transaction tablet was usually sized to fit into the palm of the scribe's hand, although much larger cuneiform tablets do exist.

Egyptian hieroglyphs
Formal writing in Egypt retained the use of pictorial symbols—hieroglyphs—for more than 3,000 years. This example from a 4th-century-BCE sarcophagus differs little in style from the earliest surviving inscriptions made in c. 3200 BCE. When reading hieroglyphs, the reader starts at the top on the side the signs face (in this case, right).

FROM PICTORIAL SYMBOLS TO CUNEIFORM

The earliest cuneiform, or proto-cuneiform, was pictorial and drawn into clay. At some point, all proto-cuneiform signs were rotated by 90 degrees. No one knows why. True cuneiform appeared when scribes began to form signs from impressed wedges.

Date	3200 BCE	3000 BCE	2400 BCE	1000 BCE
GIN "to walk"				
UD "day"				
MUSEN "bird"				
SE "barley"				

Cuneiform stylus
Cuneiform signs were formed by pressing a stylus into wet clay, each time producing a wedge shape. Cuneiform means "wedge-shaped" in Latin.

Numerals are expressed with these circular impressions. They mirror the shaped clay tokens once used to signify numbers (see BEFORE). They appear next to the sign for the commodity (barley). Before the invention of numerals, scribes had to draw a sign once for each item.

pictures of the things it records. Over time, these pictures were simplified and made abstract to make writing quicker and easier. In Mesopotamia, this process resulted in wedge-based cuneiform writing (see box, above). Many early scripts were logographic, meaning that each symbol represented an entire word or idea. A logographic system may use thousands of signs. Modern Chinese writing remains logographic, using around 12,000 symbols that allow written communication between the many different dialects of Chinese. Cuneiform and Egyptian hieroglyphic scripts, meanwhile, mixed logograms with symbols representing sounds. Such sound signs were combined to form words, which reduced the total number of signs to around a hundred in scripts such as Akkadian cuneiform. Egyptian and Maya hieroglyphs remained pictorial for decorative use in religious writing and inscriptions on monuments. For everyday use, however, the Egyptians developed a more efficient, abstract system called hieratic. It was written with fragile reed pens, which restricted the shapes the scribe could form. When written on papyrus, hieroglyphs were painted with brushes, allowing the scribe a freer hand.

Chinese writing also diverged, with different styles of calligraphy being developed for different uses. In most Chinese scripts, the meaning of signs was simplified as well.

The earliest writing records only objects (usually goods) and numbers (quantities of goods and measurements of time). Grammar was absent, so this writing cannot be read as language, but it aided the memories of people who knew its meaning already. It seems likely that others could have understood it with a little training. Writing was soon taken up by the rulers of ancient societies, however, and adapted to reproduce spoken language, allowing them to write literary, religious, and scholarly texts. From this point, special training was needed.

Spread of the written word

Cultures in the 3rd and 2nd millennia BCE were not really literate societies. Once writing became abstract, rather than pictorial, only a small number of merchants, administrators, and elites would have had enough schooling to read and write. It is thought that only one per cent of Egyptians were literate.

Ancient rulers used writing to manage the information on which their states ran, not to disseminate it. Royal political inscriptions might be combined with imagery, and it seems that the masses would have read only the images, while the writing was aimed at fellow elites and at posterity. Assyrian kings, for instance, buried inscriptions in the foundations of temples, recording their exploits so that future kings rebuilding those temples would read them.

Egyptian scribe
Education of scribes began in childhood, lasting at least 10 years, and included mathematics and accountancy. The scribal profession usually ran in families.

Writing systems became simpler and more sophisticated, but the spread of written communication was slow until printing was invented during the European Renaissance.

PHOENICIAN ALPHABETIC SCRIPT

ALPHABETIC SYSTEMS

At first, written symbols represented a variety of words, syllables, ideas, or sounds. The idea that every symbol should denote a sound was an innovation in the Middle East and led to the alphabet. The **first alphabetic writing**, with each sign representing a **consonant** but with **no vowels**, appeared in the 2nd millennium BCE, using adapted Egyptian hieroglyphs. The people of **Ugarit** in Syria developed a cuneiform alphabet, but the need for clay prevented it from spreading. Alphabets became important in 1000–700 BCE, being used for **Hebrew, Aramaic, and Phoenician** writing. The Phoenicians **82–83 »** used separate signs for vowels, **influencing Greek and Latin** writing.

AMERICAN SYSTEMS

The earliest surviving American writing is on 600 BCE **Zapotec** monuments in Mexico and **records the names of sacrificed captives**. Later inscriptions on **Maya monuments** record conflicts between city-states **140–41 »**. The **cultures of the Andes developed quipu 212 »**—a system that recorded numerical information with patterns of knots on webs of color-coded string.

ZAPOTEC CALENDAR

PRINTING

The spread of written material was hampered by the need to **copy by hand**. In Europe from 1454, with the **Gutenburg printing press 253 »** featuring **movable type**, books were produced quickly and cheaply on a large scale.

LETTERS OF MOVABLE TYPE READY FOR PRINTING

BEFORE

At the collapse of the Egyptian Old Kingdom **‹‹ 56–57** **centralized rule broke down and an unsettled time known as the First Intermediate Period (*c.* 2180–2040 BCE) began.**

FIRST INTERMEDIATE PERIOD
Egypt saw **civil war, drought** and **famine**, and oppression by local **tyrants**. However, the greater powers of nonroyals at the end of the Old Kingdom ushered in some broader-minded thinking, including a **better justice** system for all.

HERAKLEOPOLIS VERSUS THEBES
One of the **competing factions** was a dynasty of kings based at Herakleopolis, central Egypt. They were bitter rivals of the **Theban kings** farther south.

REUNIFICATION
In the 11th Dynasty, Thebes sealed its rise to prominence when Theban king, **Nebhepetre Mentuhotep II** (*c.* 2060–2010 BCE; right), defeated his rivals from Herakleopolis. He **reunified Egypt** and so took it into the **Middle Kingdom** era.

NEBHEPETRE MENTUHOTEP II

Egypt in Order and Chaos

Over 100 years of uncertainty and lack of centralized control followed the collapse of Old Kingdom Egypt. However, order and glory were restored once again with the great Middle Kingdom and New Kingdom eras, which were themselves separated by another period of some disorder.

Traditionally, ancient Egyptian history is seen as periods of order and prosperity separated by "intermediate" periods of chaos. Historians now think this is an overexaggerated contrast, but prosperous eras under strong centralized rule were certainly separated by times of division. Through all of this, however, ancient Egyptian culture and ways of life continued with surprising consistency for thousands of years—far longer than those of any other ancient civilization.

Middle Kingdom

Often said to last from Dynasty 11 to Dynasty 13, the Middle Kingdom (*c.* 2040–1730 BCE) saw Thebes becoming a major royal center, although the seat of government stayed near Memphis (see pp.56–57) at the new city of Itj-Towy. Middle Kingdom Egypt had a distinct character, but it was not as different from the Old Kingdom as once thought. In the 12th Dynasty, the royals regained a strong grip—perhaps as strong as in Old Kingdom times. The pharaoh took back some powers from nobles, but society did not return to a more feudal-type structure (in which powerless laborers worked for the pharaoh)—society was more democratic.

Rise of the bureaucrat

One of society's democratic features was that posts formerly held by royals passed to high-ranking "civil servants." Egypt was now run more like a corporation than an extension of the royal family.

Greater rights for ordinary people included access to mummification (see pp.68–69), and more interest was taken in the poor and needy. Money was spent not only on royal tombs but also on irrigation systems (for example, at Fayum near Memphis) that benefited all. The country's defenses were strengthened and new trade routes sprang up. Nubia, which came under Egyptian control, supplied not only gold and copper, but also the labor to mine these, as well as personnel for Egypt's army.

Keeping order
Powerful figures called viziers, as depicted by this 12th-dynasty statue, headed the administration of the Middle Kingdom. In the New Kingdom, one took control in Lower Egypt and another in Upper Egypt.

Disorder and restoration

The Middle Kingdom's stability dissolved when local governors pushed for more power. Civil war brought about another unsettled era—the Second Intermediate Period (*c.* 1730–1550 BCE; late Dynasty 13 to 17). During this time, a people called the Hyksos gained control and ruled Lower Egypt as pharaohs. Egyptian dynasties continued to rule Upper Egypt from Thebes. Theban rulers triumphed when the Hyksos were finally expelled under pharaoh Amose I, and the New Kingdom (*c.* 1550–1069 BCE; Dynasties 18 to 20) began. This era is often seen as a time of glorious "empire," with a militaristic, nationalistic outlook and new heights of wealth and power. The king's role as warrior–defender of his lands gained a new emphasis.

New kingdom power

During the New Kingdom, trade links extended and the art of diplomacy intensified, as seen in the famous Amarna letters and the treaty of Kadesh (see pp.66–67, 78–79). Egypt quashed threats to the throne, thanks greatly to warfare techniques borrowed from the Hyksos—especially the use of two-wheeled, horse-drawn chariots that were fast and lightweight.

The New Kingdom was an age of spectacular architecture and art. The lavish tomb contents of the pharaoh Tutankhamun (*c.* 1336–1327 BCE) were interred and the monumental buildings and statues of Rameses II (*c.* 1279–1213 BCE; see pp.66–67) were erected. Southern Theban culture prevailed, with Thebes being rebuilt and great temples erected to the sun god, Amun-Ra. Royalty was now buried in elaborate underground tombs, centered on Thebes' Valley of the Kings. Amenophis IV (1352–1336 BCE) took sun worship to extremes, bending his kingdom to the cult of Aten—worship of the sun's disk alone—and renaming himself Akhenaten in honor of his beliefs (see pp.68–69).

379 **The number of diplomatic letters in the archive of El-Amarna, Akhenaten's capital, recording Egypt's role as the world's leading power.**

Just as the Old and Middle Kingdoms had dissolved, so did the New Kingdom. It is unclear why outside threats (see AFTER) again became impossible to hold back. Rebellion and internal corruption may have played a part, but the truth remains a mystery.

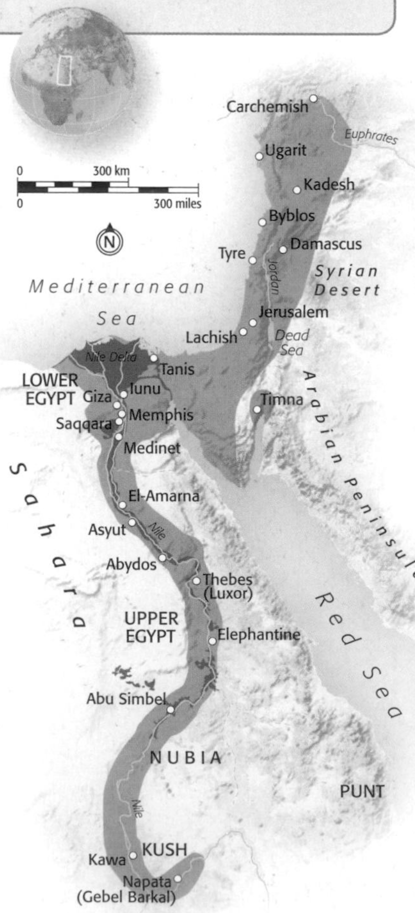

Carchemish
Euphrates
Ugarit
0
300 km
0
300 miles
Kadesh
Byblos
Tyre
Damascus
Syrian Desert
Jordan
Mediterranean Sea
Jerusalem
Lachish
Dead Sea
Nile Delta
Tanis
LOWER EGYPT
Giza
Iunu
Memphis
Saqqara
Timna
Arabian Peninsula
Medinet
Sahara
El-Amarna
Asyut
Nile
Abydos
Thebes (Luxor)
Red Sea
UPPER EGYPT
Elephantine
Abu Simbel
NUBIA
PUNT
Nile
KUSH
Kawa
Napata (Gebel Barkal)

KEY
Regions of control under Thutmosis III
Fertile land in the Nile valley

Height of Egyptian control
Egypt's lands reached their height under New Kingdom pharaoh Tuthmosis III (*c.* 1479–1425 BCE). Marked here are major centers of royal, religious, and administrative control during the Old, Middle, and New Kingdoms.

In-fighting
Private armies abounded during the Intermediate Periods, gathered by the leaders of regional factions fighting endlessly for control. This model army of Nubian archers is from the tomb of a governor of Asyut.

New Kingdom opulence
Queen Ankhesenamun anoints her young king, Tutankhamun, in a scene taken from a gold-inlaid throne entombed with the pharaoh in the Valley of the Kings. Tutankhamun's short reign continued the New Kingdom's grandeur and returned Egypt to its traditional religious practices after the Aten-cult worship of his predecessor, Akhenaten.

NEFERTITI

The most famous wife of Akhenaten (see p.64), Nefertiti seems to have taken a prominent role in her husband's rule. Art of the period frequently shows her alongside her king, sharing his worship of the sun's disk. She is even depicted in warrior-like poses suggestive of royal power. Nefertiti may have died in 1338 BCE, when all record of her disappears. Some believe that Smenkhkare, a mysterious figure who seems to have ruled jointly with Akhenaten for some of his reign, was in fact Nefertiti.

AFTER

Egypt's New Kingdom had become a vast empire, increasingly difficult to police. Late in the 20th dynasty, central authority again gave way to a destabilized spell—the Third Intermediate Period (c. 1069–664 BCE).

THIRD INTERMEDIATE PERIOD
Spanning Dynasties 21 to 25, this era lasted about **400 years** and saw a complex mixture of **foreign control** and **Egyptian independence**. **Native pharaohs** in Upper Egypt gave way to a period of **Libyan** control. Lower Egypt split into **many separate regions**.

KUSHITE RULE
By the 25th Dynasty, at the end of the Third Intermediate Period, Kushite rulers from **Nubia**, notably Piye (c. 747–716 BCE) controlled both Lower and Upper Egypt under their rule, so **reunifying Egypt**.

KUSHITE PHARAOH TAHARQA WORSHIPPING THE FALCON-HEADED GOD, HEMEN

ASSYRIAN OCCUPATION
Kushite sovereignty ended with the reigns of Taharqa and Tantamani (c. 690–656 BCE). Their rule gave way to nearly a **decade of occupation** by **Assyrians 80–81 >>** at the end of the Third Intermediate Period. Next came a brief Egyptian renaissance—the **Saite Dynasty 118 >>**.

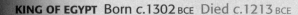

KING OF EGYPT Born c.1302 BCE Died c.1213 BCE

Rameses II

"All the lands… have fallen prostrate **beneath his sandals** for eternity."

PEACE AGREEMENT WITH THE HITTITES, *C.* 1258 BCE

The greatest pharaoh of the New Kingdom era (*c.* 1550–1069 BCE), Rameses II reigned supreme for almost 70 years and brought a stability and prosperity to Egypt. Like a present-day international statesman, he skillfully used diplomacy, military strategy, and propaganda to promote Egypt and, maintain his empire. In doing so he become a major figure in Middle Eastern politics.

The future Rameses II was born just before the 19th dynasty (*c.* 1295–1187 BCE), and became its third pharaoh. From his father,

Seti I, Rameses inherited an established empire that stretched from modern-day Syria in the north to Sudan (then Nubia) in the south. Like his father, he had territorial ambitions in Syria, but he had to contend with the threat from the Hittite Empire (see pp.78–79) further north in Anatolia.

His most famous confrontation with the Hittites was at the battle of Kadesh (or Qadesh) in Syria in *c.*1275 BCE. Rameses claimed this as a single-handed victory for himself, while others said the Hittites won decisively. The truth is probably somewhere in between, with neither side winning outright or making any major gains.

Portrait and cartouche
This impressive statue of Rameses II (left) stood in the temple of Luxor, in Egypt. The oval carving, or cartouche, (right) has symbols representing Rameses as king, and wearing the double crown of Upper and Lower Egypt.

Rameses the diplomat
Around 1258 BCE, after further skirmishes, the Hittites and Egyptians drew up a groundbreaking agreement, effectively ending hostilities between them (see right). Mindful of his role as a diplomat serving Egypt's wider interests, Rameses later underlined this new accord by making at least one Hittite princess one of his wives.

The new, friendly tone of relations between the two powers is also clear from the letters found in the archives of the Hittite capital, Hattusha. Like the famous "Amarna Letters" from the reigns of Amenophis III and Akhenaten (see pp.64–65), this correspondence is written on clay tablets in Akkadian cuneiform script (the language of

Rameses II as a boy
This limestone fragment from a stele (commemorative pillar) shows Rameses sitting next to hieroglyphs that indicate he is destined to become king of Egypt. He wears the side braid and a heavy ear decoration that were typical of a young Egyptian prince.

diplomacy, see pp.62–63), and features exchanges between a range of Middle Eastern powers and peoples. These lively letters are the earliest significant evidence of international diplomacy, painting a clear picture of long-distance trading, political agreements, and diplomatic and daily affairs. The letters between Egypt and the Hittites, and specifically between Rameses II and the Hittite king, Hattusili III, with whom the 1258 treaty had been made, discuss issues from international politics to medical problems and wedding plans.

Artistic license

An outstanding feature of Rameses' reign were his buildings. All over Egypt, monuments sprang up or old ones were added to. Giant statues and images of the pharaoh swiftly appeared, and craftsmen wrote inscriptions praising him on every available surface.

He created the new capital city of Per-Rameses in the Nile delta, close to modern-day Cairo. It was beautiful, and convenient for military forays into Asia. He also built the famous temples dedicated to himself and his favorite wife, Nefertari, at Abu Simbel, close to Egypt's modern border with Sudan. The four massive statues of Rameses at Abu Simbel are among the greatest achievements of Egyptian art. Their style was not subtle, but Rameses' creative lead helped the arts to thrive, as they had under his father.

Another major site was Rameses' vast mortuary temple, the Ramesseum. This was built on the west bank of the

Battle of Kadesh
This bas-relief from Abu Simbel portrays Rameses II fighting the Hittites single-handedly. He is seen astride a chariot, wielding a bow and arrow, and wearing the "crown of war."

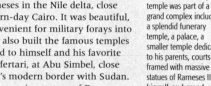

The Ramesseum
A symbol of the pharaoh's power and wealth, this funerary temple was part of a grand complex including a splendid funerary temple, a palace, a smaller temple dedicated to his parents, courts framed with massive statues of Rameses II himself, and grand avenues of sphinxes.

> " What will people say, when it is heard of **you** [his soldiers] **deserting me**."
>
> RAMESES' CLAIM THAT HE FOUGHT THE HITTITES SINGLE-HANDEDLY 1275 BCE

DECISIVE MOMENT

THE FIRST PEACE TREATY

The 1258 peace treaty between Rameses II and Hattusili III was first recorded on a silver tablet (contemporary clay copy shown below). An astonishingly modern document, it is seen as the first real international peace treaty, containing clauses on advanced concepts such as amnesty issues for refugees and extradition for fugitives. It is thought to be such a milestone in international relations that a copy of it hangs in the headquarters of the United Nations.

Nile at Thebes, the southern capital where Rameses created many new architectural projects. A palace, religious and political center, and also a seat of learning, the Ramesseum inspired the English Romantic poet Percy Bysshe Shelley's famous 1817 poem "Ozymandias."

Keeping control

Rameses II kept a tight grip on his lands and on his people. Government records that survive from his rule build a picture of a highly organized leader with a strong interest in law-making and order. With major centers at Per-Rameses and around Thebes, he ensured strong control over both Lower and Upper Egypt. He appointed

a tight web of able officials, including many old friends and many of his own very numerous (over 100) children.

There seems little doubt that Rameses II was a major figure in Middle Eastern history, despite his undoubted skill for self-promotion. His reign was the last great era of imperial glory for ancient Egypt, and he made his presence felt as far away as modern Turkey. He left a wonderful record of art and history, and a real taste of the grandeur and power of the pharaohs.

Rameses' mummy
Discovered in the 19th century, the mummy of Rameses II was later unwrapped to reveal his body. He was a tall man for the times, with a long narrow face, prominent nose, large jaw, and red hair. He is thought to be about 90 years old.

TIMELINE

■ **c. 1302 BCE** The future Rameses II is born to Seti I, whose family came from nonroyal stock, and his wife Tuyu. The crown prince Rameses is made regent while still young, to ensure that he will succeed his father.

■ **c. 1292 BCE** The young Rameses bears the rank of army captain at only about 10 years old (this title is probably honorary); accompanies his father on military campaigns to learn his craft.

■ **c. 1287 BCE** Rameses is married to Nefertari, who is around 13 years old and younger than her husband. Often said to be his favorite wife, she certainly seems to have been one of his chief wives for around 20 years. He may have had as many as eight wives, but also had a harem.

■ **c. 1279 BCE** Rameses is inaugurated as pharaoh, probably in his early to mid-twenties. He begins his reign by traveling south to officiate at his father's funeral in Thebes.

■ **c. 1277 BCE** Appears to have defeated some pirates, possibly Shardana people, who have been linked with the mysterious, controversial "Sea People." The defeated pirates appear to have been absorbed into the pharaoh's army.

■ **c. 1276 BCE** First campaign in Syria.

■ **c. 1275 BCE** Second foray into Syria culminates with the battle of Kadesh against the Hittites, who had long posed a threat to Egyptian power. His opponent is the Hittite king, Muwatalli. The building of Abu Simbel is probably under way.

■ **c. 1260s BCE** A large number of Hebrew peoples may be living in Egypt, perhaps forcibly "press-ganged" into the pharaoh's service. There may have been an historically important "Exodus" of these peoples from Egypt into Sinai at some point in the 1260s.

■ **c. 1258 BCE** After repeating his father's pattern of years of indecisive power struggles with the Hittites, Rameses and the current Hittite king, Hattusili III, draw up a famous peace agreement.

■ **c. 1259–1255 BCE** It is likely the temples at Abu Simbel are complete.

■ **c. 1256 or 1255 BCE** Probable date of death of Nefertari. Another wife, Isetnofret, now seems to become Rameses' principal queen.

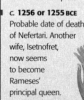

■ **c. 1245 BCE** Rameses marries the eldest daughter of the Hattusili III. She is called Maathorneferure.

NEFERTARI (MURAL FROM HER TOMB)

■ **c. 1230 BCE** Rameses probably marries another Hittite princess.

■ **c. 1224 BCE** One of Rameses' many sons, Merneptah, is named as his heir.

■ **c. 1213 BCE** Rameses' reign of about 66 years ends with his death, probably from an infection (possibly a dental abscess).

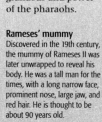

« BEFORE

The ancient Egyptians believed in many gods, and in an afterlife. Various gods rose to prominence and then faded again.

LIFE AFTER DEATH

Items found in graves from predynastic Egypt (before c. 3100 BCE) suggest that, even then, Egyptians performed **death-related rituals**.

PREDYNASTIC GRAVE GOODS

THE ORIGINS OF OSIRIS

Belief in Osiris is thought to have begun in the Nile Delta region and probably developed from the local god of a place called Busiris. Initially, Osiris may have been a **god of agriculture**, linked with fertility and the afterlife. He gained popularity throughout Egypt and by the middle of the Old Kingdom **‹‹56–57**, c. 2400 BCE, had become a dominant figure, associated with death and the **resurrection of the ruler**.

RIVALRY WITH RA

Before Osiris, the cult of Ra (or Re), god of the Sun and bringer of life, held center stage. Ra is depicted with a falcon's head, on which is carried the sun.

RA, THE SUN-GOD

HOW WE KNOW

INVESTIGATING MUMMIES

In the 5th–1st century BCE, historians such as the Greeks Herodotus and Diodorus Siculus provided the first reliable data on mummies. Since then, studying them has become an increasingly sophisticated science. DNA is analyzed (see p.465), and the mummy checked for the presence of diseases, to reveal more about its identity and the Egyptian way of life. Imaging techniques, such as X-rays and CAT-scans (below), can reveal a great deal without causing permanent damage.

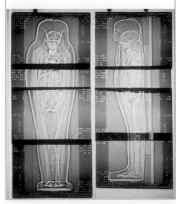

For the ancient Egyptians, the need and desire to please their gods were driving forces that influenced most aspects of their lives. They believed that the god Osiris judged them on the lives they had led and that those who had lived "good lives" would attain a happy eternity alongside the gods. He was thought to preside over their complex burial rituals, including embalming and mummification (see opposite), which they devised to ensure a passage through the underworld to an afterlife. Osiris's cult continued to develop during the Old Kingdom (c. 2686–2181 BCE). People came to believe that the pharaohs, Egypt's leaders, were reborn as Osiris after death. This powerful link to the Egyptians' belief in kings as gods was reflected in the "rebirth" elements of their burial rituals.

Cult of the people

After the collapse of the Old Kingdom (see pp.56–57), the popularity of the Osiris cult was assisted by the shift in government dynamics. With the pharaoh no longer an all-powerful figure, local officials gained in importance. In this slightly more democratic climate, the burial rites and the right to rebirth, once strictly confined to the pharaohs, were increasingly extended to ordinary Egyptians. At the height of Osiris's popularity, even mere mortals were believed to connect with the god at

His grandfather was Ra (see BEFORE) and his brother was Set, god of chaos. Osiris was husband (and brother) of Isis, a protective and magical goddess, and father of Horus, who was god of the sky and protector of the ruler of Egypt. Myth also told that the jealous and vengeful Set trapped Osiris in a coffinlike chest and threw it in the Nile River, then took his brother's position as king. Isis found and hid the body of her beloved husband, only for Set to discover it and tear it apart, scattering the pieces. It was said that Isis lovingly sought out all the remains and buried them where she found them (so aiding the spread of the cult). His body was then reassembled and bound with bandages, and he so became the first mummy. Isis revived Osiris by magic, and he traveled to the underworld to become king of the dead.

A matter of life and death

From these myths it is clear that the Egyptians' burial practices, particularly mummification and embalming, were a reflection of Osiris' own sufferings and the journey his soul made to the afterlife. Ideas about the soul and spirit were central to burial practices, and to beliefs in general. The Egyptians came to believe that each human being consisted not only of a physical body, but also of three spiritual parts. First, the *ka*, was part of a kind of "soul" and the essential life-force—a person's

Osiris figurine
The god was traditionally portrayed partly bandaged, as if being mummified.

A jury of 12 gods sits in judgment of the deceased. They pronounce their decision in a chamber often referred to as the "hall of Ma'at."

The deceased, Any, followed by his wife, walks into the "court," ready for the weighing of his heart and judgment by the jury of gods above.

The Realm of Osiris

The growth of the cult of Osiris, king of the dead, was immensely important to the ancient Egyptians. Osiris gradually became the dominant figure among a cast of potentially vengeful gods. These gods had strong moral codes, so living a good and honest life was vital if you were to gain eternity.

their death (this identification with Osiris was considered essential to reach eternal afterlife). Previously, such an honor was confined to their kings.

Family drama

Despite his growing importance, Osiris remained part of a broad and complex family of divine characters, each with a vital role to play in the Egyptian belief system. Tradition held that Osiris was the son of Geb, god of the earth, and Nut, goddess of the sky, and that he was once king of Upper Egypt.

"double." The *ba* formed another part of the "soul" and, in modern terms, an individual's personality. Finally, the *akh* was the form in which a deceased person existed in the afterlife, when the *ka* and *ba* were reunited.

It was typically believed that the *ka* and *ba* were released from the body at death and needed to find each other again in the afterlife in order to create a happy, eternal *akh*. The released *ka* returned to the dead body, feeding off it to stay alive. If the body was decayed or unrecognizable, the *ka* might not be

" **Homage to thee, Osiris**, lord of eternity, king of gods, **whose names are manifold.**"

THE EGYPTIAN BOOK OF THE DEAD, 1240 BCE

The bird-goddess Ma'at, keeper of truth and harmony, daughter of Ra and linked with Thoth, perches symbolically atop the scales of justice.

Osiris, the supreme judge of such ceremonies, sits among the jury of gods. He is wearing the crown of Upper Egypt.

Amun-Ra was an amalgamation of the sun god Ra and the god of the air, Amun. He has a falcon's mask and bears the solar disk on his head.

Any's heart, depicted with the Egyptian hieroglyph for "heart," lies in one pan of the scales of judgment.

The scales are supervised by the jackal-headed Anubis. Considered to be Osiris's son, Anubis was an underworld guide.

The Feather of Ma'at lies in the other pan. If the heart weighs the same as the feather, eternal afterlife is assured.

Thoth, chief scribe of the gods, notes the results of the weighing of Any's heart.

Ammit, a strange beast that is part lion, crocodile, and hippopotamus, waits to devour any heart that is found wanting.

AFTER

ROMAN-ERA MUMMY

The cult of Osiris survived beyond the ancient Egyptian period, and influenced newly developing belief systems.

CHANGING CULTS
By the Ptolemaic period in Egypt (323–30 BCE) **118–19 »** the cult of Osiris had begun to fade and **the cult of Serapis** was on the rise. This combined the cults of Osiris and the sacred bull Apis. Serapis was at first identified with Osiris, but then became entirely separate. Cults of Osiris and Isis lived on in various provinces of the Roman Empire **110–13 »**, with **temples to Isis** built in Roman London and Pompeii.

THE IMPACT OF OSIRIS
Many scholars believe that the ideas surrounding Osiris and his kingdom of the dead influenced the development of the world's major religions **144–147 »**. The belief in a god's rebirth and the idea that happiness in the next life could be achieved by being good can be reinterpreted as the concepts of **resurrection and salvation**. The performance of rites to connect humans with a divine presence is related to the idea of **sacrament**. These ideas are present in a variety of religions, including **Christianity**.

FREEMASONRY
Osiris lives on today within the "secret society" known as the **Freemasons**. Some of their beliefs and symbolism are connected to the figure of Osiris, partly as a way of evoking a sense of order and mystery **rooted in ancient wisdom**.

Osiris sitting in judgment
This papyrus scene, from the *Book of the Dead* of Any (New Kingdom, *c.* 1550–1069 BCE), shows Osiris deciding Any's destiny in a ceremony believed to take place after death. Any's heart is weighed against the feather of Ma'at, goddess of truth and justice. Bearing instructions on dealing with obstacles in the afterlife, a "book of the dead" was commissioned just before the subject's death, and always showed a favorable judgment.

---

able to feed and survive to reach the afterlife. This is why preservation was so important—to keep the "soul" alive after death.

Preserving the body
Embalmers washed the body, preferably in water from the Nile. They then removed the intestines, stomach, liver, and lungs and placed them in four vessels called canopic jars. The brain was removed through the nostrils, but the heart, considered to be the source of intelligence, was left in place. The body was then stuffed with

Organ storage
The removed organs were placed in canopic jars to prevent decay. The jar second from right represents Anubis, the main god of embalming.

linen (to keep its proper shape and appearance) and made whole again. It was soaked with preservative salts, resins, and oils, and decorated with protective charms, called amulets. Those shaped like a scarab beetle were especially potent as the insect's life cycle reflected the daily "rebirth" of the sun. The body was wrapped in linen bandages, placed in a coffin, and buried along with other amulets or items from everyday life to provide comfort in the hereafter.

IDEAS

THE CULT OF ATEN

During the period of Egypt's New Kingdom (*c.* 1550–1069 BCE), when Osiris worship was at its peak, the 18th-dynasty pharaoh Akhenaten created a breakaway cult of his own. He decided to worship the Sun's disc, in the form of a god called Aten. The cult, which some scholars cite as the first example of the worship of a single god (monotheism), came to an end at the close of Akhenaten's reign, after which the old order returned. This image shows Akhenaten with his chief wife, Nefertiti (see p.65), and one of their daughters (they are known to have had at least six) worshipping the Sun's rays.

1 DRINKING CUP 2 GILDED SUNSHADE 3 PENS

4 BALL

5 RINGS

6 BRONZE ANKH

7 EYE OF HORUS

8 AMUN STATUETTE 9 DAGGER AND SHEATH 10 FLY WHISK 11 ISIS AND HORUS 12 COSMETIC SPOON 13 FISH FLASK 14 CAT STATUE

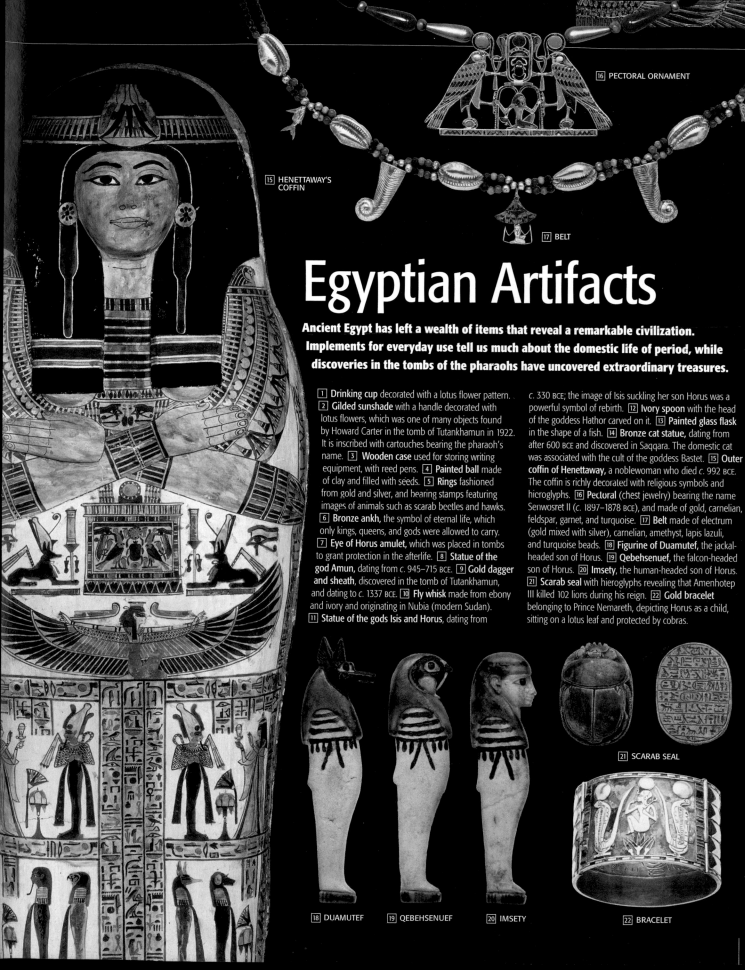

16 PECTORAL ORNAMENT

15 HENETTAWAY'S COFFIN

17 BELT

Egyptian Artifacts

Ancient Egypt has left a wealth of items that reveal a remarkable civilization. Implements for everyday use tell us much about the domestic life of period, while discoveries in the tombs of the pharaohs have uncovered extraordinary treasures.

1 **Drinking cup** decorated with a lotus flower pattern. . 2 **Gilded sunshade** with a handle decorated with lotus flowers, which was one of many objects found by Howard Carter in the tomb of Tutankhamun in 1922. It is inscribed with cartouches bearing the pharaoh's name. 3 **Wooden case** used for storing writing equipment, with reed pens. 4 **Painted ball** made of clay and filled with seeds. 5 **Rings** fashioned from gold and silver, and bearing stamps featuring images of animals such as scarab beetles and hawks. 6 **Bronze ankh,** the symbol of eternal life, which only kings, queens, and gods were allowed to carry. 7 **Eye of Horus amulet,** which was placed in tombs to grant protection in the afterlife. 8 **Statue of the god Amun,** dating from *c.* 945–715 BCE. 9 **Gold dagger and sheath,** discovered in the tomb of Tutankhamun, and dating to *c.* 1337 BCE. 10 **Fly whisk** made from ebony and ivory and originating in Nubia (modern Sudan). 11 **Statue of the gods Isis and Horus,** dating from

c. 330 BCE; the image of Isis suckling her son Horus was a powerful symbol of rebirth. 12 **Ivory spoon** with the head of the goddess Hathor carved on it. 13 **Painted glass flask** in the shape of a fish. 14 **Bronze cat statue,** dating from after 600 BCE and discovered in Saqqara. The domestic cat was associated with the cult of the goddess Bastet. 15 **Outer coffin of Henettaway,** a noblewoman who died *c.* 992 BCE. The coffin is richly decorated with religious symbols and hieroglyphs. 16 **Pectoral** (chest jewelry) bearing the name Senwosret II (*c.* 1897–1878 BCE), and made of gold, carnelian, feldspar, garnet, and turquoise. 17 **Belt** made of electrum (gold mixed with silver), carnelian, amethyst, lapis lazuli, and turquoise beads. 18 **Figurine of Duamutef,** the jackal-headed son of Horus. 19 **Qebehsenuef,** the falcon-headed son of Horus. 20 **Imsety,** the human-headed son of Horus. 21 **Scarab seal** with hieroglyphs revealing that Amenhotep III killed 102 lions during his reign. 22 **Gold bracelet** belonging to Prince Nemareth, depicting Horus as a child, sitting on a lotus leaf and protected by cobras.

21 SCARAB SEAL

18 DUAMUTEF   19 QEBEHSENUEF   20 IMSETY   22 BRACELET

BEFORE

Large-scale architecture was one of the earliest features of civilization.

NEOLITHIC BUILDING
Early Neolithic-period **<<36 stone structures** include walls in Jericho, now in Palestine (*c.* 8500 BCE), and a possible stone temple at Gobekli Tepe in Anatolia, now Turkey (*c.* 9000 BCE).

STONE BUILDINGS, GOBEKLI TEPE, TURKEY

TEMPLES IN MESOPOTAMIA
The oldest known structures in Mesopotamia are temples dating from the Ubaid Period (5900–4300 BCE). On sites long held **sacred**, the temples were rebuilt many times.

PITS AND MOUNDS IN EGYPT
Tombs in **predynastic Egypt** (before 3100 BCE) were simple, sand-covered pits. Early royal tombs were elaborations of this model, covering a rock-cut chamber with a **mound of sand**.

FIRST MONUMENTS IN THE AMERICAS
Mud-brick platforms called **huacas** appear along the coast of Peru **<< 74** from 4000 BCE. Used as **ritual sites**, they were often built in pairs.

Mortuary temple of Queen Hatshepsut
After the Old Kingdom came to an end, fewer pyramids were built and attention shifted to the mortuary temples. These were often built at the foot of cliffs, which were possibly viewed as natural pyramids.

Almost every form of ancient Egyptian monumental architecture can be interpreted as part of a temple. The pyramids were not isolated structures, but parts of mortuary (memorial) temple complexes. Egyptians believed that their kings became gods when they died, so the tombs were dedicated to their worship.

The first pyramid, the Step Pyramid, was built *c.* 2667–2648 BCE (see Imhotep, p.56) for pharaoh Djoser of the 3rd dynasty. The design probably evolved from the earlier sand mounds that covered tombs (see BEFORE). True pyramids appeared in the 4th dynasty, the first being built for pharaoh Snefru in *c.* 2580 BCE. It reveals a move toward the use of solar imagery in its imitation of the rays of the sun. The "Pyramid Texts," which were religious inscriptions on the walls of later pyramids, refer to the pharaoh ascending to join the god Ra (see p.68) on a solar barque—a mythical boat in which the sun rides.

Egyptian temples were carefully constructed models of the universe. The inner sanctum represented the ordered heart of creation, and the temple's outer walls, the cliffs at the edge of the Nile Valley, held back the chaos that lay beyond. Colonnades (rows of columns) and hypostyle halls (halls with pillars holding up the roof) represented the riverbanks, with the columns denoting reeds, while the ceilings symbolized the sky, and were decorated with images of stars and the sun. Palaces too were built along the same lines. Pharaohs gained such prestige from their building programs that some even appropriated the projects of their predecessors, erasing their names and claiming them as their own.

The step towers of Mesopotamia
In Mesopotamia (a region made up of what is now Iraq and parts of Syria, Turkey, and Iran, see pp.54–55), the

Structure of the Great Pyramid
The largest ever built, the Great Pyramid was made for Khufu, of the 4th dynasty. The pyramid was looted long ago. The limestone coating was plundered in 1356 CE to rebuild Cairo after an earthquake.

the outer surface was originally clad in limestone

the Upper Chamber, also known as the King's Chamber, contained the royal sarcophagus

the Great Gallery is a high but steep and narrow passage leading to the King's chamber

the subterranean Lower Chamber was neither finished nor used

the Middle Chamber, also misnamed Queen's chamber, was never finished

workers used this escape tunnel to leave after sealing the upper chambers

Building for Eternity

The construction of monuments, such as temples, palaces, and tombs, was one of the key features of developing civilizations. Most monuments had religious functions and were intended to legitimize the position of the rulers who built them by connecting them with the gods.

architecture, although its structure was different from that of the Egyptians, also had a religious purpose and shared similar functions. Mesopotamian gods were linked with particular cities, and temples in those cities were seen as their houses. Divination—the practice of foretelling the future—was a key part of the religion. The people believed that the gods controlled fate, so divination was used to determine the gods' intentions, and rituals were performed in an attempt to negotiate a better future. Astrology was a key part of this tradition, and ziggurats—the

Great Ziggurat of Ur
Ziggurats, such as this reconstructed example, were in constant use, with astrologers working all night, every night. They provided an unbroken view across the plain of Mesopotamia.

Choga Zanbil
Mud-brick architecture does not preserve well. No one knows exactly how this ziggurat in Elam (southwest Iran) looked when new.

tall, stepped towers attached to major temples—were also used as stellar observatories.

In Mesopotamia, the construction of temples was seen as both the king's privilege and his duty. Mud bricks did not endure long, so temples were often renovated or rebuilt. Royal palaces also became increasingly important there, especially under the powerful Assyrian Empire (see pp.80–81). They were centers not only for the royal court but also for the civil service. With a few exceptions, Mesopotamian kings were considered earthly governors appointed to rule on behalf of the gods, rather than being gods in their own right.

Symbolic riches
Ancient temples were not simply places of worship, but also important centers of administration. Most were part of large tracts of land that provided considerable income and trading power. Before it was destroyed at the

end of the 7th century BCE, the temple of Ashur—the city at Assyria's ancient heart—was the richest in the world.

The demonstration of power
To build monumental buildings required enormous resources, organization, and labor. These buildings acted as a potent demonstration of the ruler's power over his subjects, and periods of

> **CORVÉE** Most ancient societies used corvée labor to provide a regular supply of unskilled laborers. Corvée laborers worked on state building projects for a set amount of time each year instead of (or in addition to) paying taxes in the form of money or produce.

prosperity usually show evidence of new construction. When a kingdom lacked central authority, or access to resources, building stopped.

The Egyptian pyramids also provide evidence of ancient methods of construction. Rather than hundreds of thousands of slave laborers or conscripts working seasonally, as had been previously thought, the pyramids were built by 20–25,000 professional craftsmen and corvée laborers who worked year-round. Snefru's first pyramid was finished in only a few years, so he had first a new palace and then two more pyramids built. The decreasing size of pyramids after the 4th dynasty is probably due to an increase in the number of projects, rather than evidence that the 4th dynasty's grand projects had bankrupted the kingdom.

Monumental construction has continued to the present day all around the world.

MESOAMERICAN ARCHITECTURE
Olmecs **74–75 »** built the first monuments in Mesoamerica in 1000–500 BCE. Successive cultures in the region built **pyramid-shaped temples**. To them, everything possessed a spirit, and mountains were particularly powerful beings, so places of worship were constructed in their image. Pyramid building continued until the **Spanish conquest 230–31 »**.

GREAT PYRAMID, CHICHEN ITZA

THE SEVEN WONDERS OF THE WORLD
A list of the **Seven Wonders of the World**— the most breathtaking achievements of human construction—was publicized in the Greek world from the 2nd century BCE. Included were the **Pharos of Alexandria 97, 118 »** and the **Pyramids of Giza**—the only wonder surviving today. Also on the list were the **Hanging Gardens of Babylon** in Mesopotamia, described as constructed in tiers, like a ziggurat. No trace of the gardens has yet been uncovered.

LATER MONUMENTS
The Greeks **94–95 »** and Romans **110–13 »** continued the monumental tradition. In Europe, the building of stone monuments was revived by the medieval Christian church **196–97 »**.

IDEA

THE TOWER OF BABEL

The Biblical story of Babel may have begun as a reaction of Jewish exiles in 6th-century BCE Babylon to ziggurats. The Babylonians saw ziggurats, with their stepped levels leading progressively upward, as pathways to the heavens, providing access for astrology. Jewish writers were horrified by the thought of humans climbing to heaven, and wrote that a displeased God disrupted the project by diversifying and confusing the languages of the builders.

Early civilization in the Americas centered initially on the Andes in South America, and later on Mesoamerica to the north.

EARLY CITIES

One of the **first cities** in the Americas was **Caral**, 125 miles (200 km) north of modern Lima, Peru. The city, which was well established by c. 2500 BCE, included **pyramid structures** built around the same time as those at Giza, Egypt.

CARAL EXCAVATIONS, MAY 2001

MESOAMERICAN CULTURE

By c. 1500 BCE, **agricultural settlements** had formed in the area archaeologists call Mesoamerica (central Honduras and Costa Rica to northern Mexico). The main crops were corn, beans, squash, chilis, and cotton. There was **not yet an urban culture** to rival that at Caral.

VOTIVE OBJECT An artifact offered to a deity as a gift of some kind in order to thank or appease them, or enhance the success of prayers. Small "votive axes" carved out of jade were common in Olmec culture.

IDEA

WERE-JAGUAR MYTHOLOGY

The jaguar, found across Mesoamerica and South America, was viewed with reverential fear by the early cultures of these regions. It was often depicted as a "were-jaguar," which combined often infantlike human and jaguar features, typically with a downturned mouth, large lips, and oval eyes. The were-jaguar is especially associated with the Olmecs. It appeared as jade figurines and larger sculptures, and was carved into altars and other surfaces. Were-jaguar babies were common, usually shown held by a seated male figure (right). The were-jaguar's exact significance is unclear, but it may be a "transformation figure" used by shamans to connect with the gods or harness the animal's natural power.

FIGURINE OF SEATED MALE WITH WERE-JAGUAR BABY

The years between about 1500 and 900 BCE saw the first real stirrings of more advanced civilization in Mesoamerica. Agricultural skill and productivity improved, pottery became more complex (possibly through contact with Andean cultures in South America), and the temple-pyramid emerged. This was also the period when Mesoamerica's first great civilization sprang to life—the Olmecs.

Life in the lowlands

The Olmecs established themselves in the humid, fertile lowlands of south Mexico, and their culture was flourishing by about 1200 BCE. By around 800 BCE their influence had

Olmec civilization
The Olmecs' heartland was quite small, but its culture spread from the Valley of Mexico in the northwest into present-day Belize, Guatemala, Honduras, and El Salvador in the east.

KEY
● Olmec site
○ Related contemporary site
■ Olmec heartland
■ Area of related cultures

People of the Jaguar

The first great civilizations of Mesoamerica and South America rivalled those of Mesopotamia, Ancient Egypt, and China. In Mesoamerica, the Olmecs established a blueprint for later cultures in the region. At the heart of Olmec belief was jaguar-worship, which they shared with their South American counterparts.

spread out over a wider area of Mesoamerica. It seems that Olmec symbolism was adopted by various other groups in Mesoamerica, possibly as a result of trading links.

Olmec farming practices were not particularly advanced, perhaps because they did not need to be, since the staple crop, corn, grew in ready abundance. The Olmecs were hunters rather than pastoralists, because there were no large herd animals in the region that could be domesticated. Animals were not used for transportation and, unlike in Eurasia, there were no wheeled vehicles—which, in any case, would have been of little use in the wet and swampy Olmec heartland.

The rise of San Lorenzo

The first important Olmec center was San Lorenzo, on a plateau above the Coatzacoalcos River in the southern Mexican state of Veracruz. San Lorenzo was at its height between 1200 and 900 BCE. It was most likely a chiefdom rather than a city-state, with a hierarchy comprising an elite class, skilled workers, and laborers. The population was possibly only around 1,000.

The buildings at San Lorenzo were erected on earthen mounds and arranged around open plazas. They included temples and houses made of poles and thatch, and the city seems to have had an advanced drainage system. There were also many stone monuments, such as giant carved heads, altarlike

Giant head sculptures
The Olmecs are famed for their huge stone head sculptures, which were up to several yards (meters) tall and about 20 tons in weight. With distinctive flattened features, they are probably connected with Olmec gods.

structures, huge sculptures of seated people, and depictions of a variety of animals, most notably the jaguar (see left). Bloodletting and sacrifice may have been part of ritual practice, but this is purely speculation.

Near the San Lorenzo site, 1 mile (1.6 km) away at Cascajal, a stone dating from c. 900 BCE has been found bearing symbols that may be Olmec writing. This could suggest the Olmecs developed one of the first writing systems in Mesoamerica (see pp.62–63).

San Lorenzo seems to come to an end around 900 BCE. Evidence of widespread destruction of monuments has led some experts to suggest that there was a major uprising or invasion. Others think that environmental factors may have caused San Lorenzo's decline.

La Venta

The other major Olmec center was the city of La Venta, near the border of modern Tabasco and Veracruz states, which had a much larger population than San Lorenzo. Thriving between about 900 and 400 BCE, La Venta effectively took over from San Lorenzo as the principal Mesoamerican settlement. As at San Lorenzo, colossal stone heads and jaguar figures and imagery were found at La Venta, as well as temple-ceremonial complexes, including a giant pyramid. The major buildings at the site were all precisely aligned, perhaps linked with ideas about astronomy.

Olmec art was accomplished, especially its stone carving, including many small jade figures. Skilled relief carvings have been found at La Venta, along with other Olmec artifacts, including iron-ore mirrors that were worn around the neck. These may have been used by Olmec leaders as evidence of their "special" powers, as the mirrors could have been used to start fires or even project images.

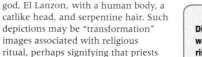

The Chavín of South America

To the South, the Peruvian Chavín culture began to develop in the Andes region around 1000 BCE, and then spread along a great strip of the Peruvian coast. The major excavated site associated with Chavín culture is that of Chavín de Huántar, high in the Andes, almost 185 miles (300 km) north of Lima.

Chavín de Huántar may or may not have been the center or birthplace of the culture, but it was certainly of great importance. At the heart of this sizable settlement, which could have been home to around 3,000 people, was a monumental ceremonial complex made of stone blocks and decorated with impressive relief carving.

As in Olmec culture, Chavín art often shows figures combining both human and animal features. At the center of the Old Temple at Chavín de Huántar is a sculpture showing the great Chavín god, El Lanzon, with a human body, a catlike head, and serpentine hair. Such depictions may be "transformation" images associated with religious ritual, perhaps signifying that priests could transform themselves into deities.

The buildings and site at Chavín de Huántar reveal the great engineering and architectural expertise of peoples in this part of the world, especially in the face of difficult terrain. Flat terracing had to be created to build the Old Temple, just as the Olmecs had to reshape the plateau at San Lorenzo, and the later Zapotecs would master the ultimate challenge of building Monte Albán (see p.140) on top of an artificially leveled mountain.

Chavín jaguar imagery
Several well-preserved panels depicting jaguars—important in Andean culture as well as Mesoamerican—have been found at Chavín de Huántar. They would have surrounded the impressive main plaza of this ancient site.

Different but often closely related cultures wove themselves into a complex web—rising, fading out, existing simultaneously, or persisting in some places more than others.

FROM OLMECS TO ZAPOTECS

Olmec culture had **peaked** by 600–400 BCE, but its **influence** was strongly felt in various **regional cultures** that persisted afterward throughout Mesoamerica, specifically the **Zapotecs** at **Monte Albán 142–43 ≫**, in the Oaxaca Valley of southeastern Mexico.

THE BIRTH OF MAYA CIVILIZATION

Maya culture **140–41 ≫** arose from **Native American** settlements in Mexico's Yucatán Peninsula and Central America. Significant **early developments** were taking place in the 600s or 500s BCE, and the culture had **really established** itself by around 200 BCE.

SOUTH AMERICAN CULTURES

While **Chavín culture** was declining by c. 200 BCE, other cultures (such as those of the **Paracas** and **Nazca** in Peru) were flourishing. Although regional in nature, they often had similar characteristics.

JAGUAR IMAGERY

The **jaguar** remained important to the **Maya culture**, and also to the much later **Aztecs**.

Olmec ritual
These small jade figures and upright artifacts are Olmec finds from La Venta. The figures have the part-human, part-feline features of the were-jaguar. The scene probably represents some kind of sacred ritual, with the artifacts being votive objects.

Chavín culture
Stretching from the Andes to the coastal plains of present-day Peru, Chavín culture developed the first coherent, recognizable style of Andean art. The Chavín also improved corn production and weaving techniques.

Andes

Amazon
Basin
Marañón

Chongoyapa
La Copa
Kuntur Wasi
Huallaga
Cupisnique
La Galgada
Chicama
Huaca de los Reyes
Punkuri
Chavín de Huántar
Cerro Sechín
Kotosh
Moxeke
Shillacoto
Huaura

PACIFIC OCEAN

Ancón
Chillón
Garagay

Andes

N

| 0 | | 300 km |
| 0 | | 300 miles |

KEY
▢ Chavín heartland
○ Early Chavín sites, 2000–850 BCE
◉ Chavín sites, 850–200 BCE

« BEFORE

Small Neolithic villages on Crete gave way to large Minoan settlements, as Crete led Europe into the early Bronze Age.

NEOLITHIC SOCIETY

Dating back to *c.* 6500 BCE, the Neolithic people of Crete probably **originated in Asia Minor**. Their simple life centered around rearing livestock, growing crops, and making basic pottery.

EARLY BRONZE AGE

The earliest evidence of the Minoan civilization is *c.* 3000 BCE. During the 3rd millennium BCE, **trading towns** on the Cretan coast **expanded.** Early trading partners included the people of the **Cyclades** (islands north of Crete in the south-western Aegean), whose culture emerged at the same time. On the mainland, too, **Europe was entering the Bronze Age,** with bronze reaching most regions in the 2000s BCE. Bronze ax heads were common and were invested with religious significance in addition to practical uses.

EARLY CYCLADIC FIGURINE

BULGARIAN BRONZE AGE AX HEAD

INVENTION

THE FIRST MOVABLE TYPE?

The Phaistos Disk is an archaeological mystery. Made of clay, both sides of the disk feature symbols arranged in a spiral, and each symbol has been pressed into the clay with a punch. The script is unique and has not yet been deciphered. Discovered in the early 1900s during excavations of the palace at Phaistos on Crete, it has been dated to the period 1850–1350 BCE. Its meaning and usage is not fully understood but, as it features reusable stamps, some archaeologists believe it to be the earliest form of movable printing type, predating anything comparable by 2,000 years.

PHAISTOS DISK

Europe's First Civilization

The first civilization to make its mark in western Europe was the Bronze Age culture of the Minoans, based on the Mediterranean island of Crete. Frescoes in the grand palaces depict a highly sophisticated way of life, and hint at a society where women played an unusually dominant role for the times.

Archaeologists named the ancient Cretan civilization "Minoan" after Minos, a mythical king of Crete (see pp.102–03). The Minoan civilization flourished between *c.* 3000–1400 BCE, peaking around 1600 BCE, during the late Bronze Age (see p.43). It is famous for its extensive trading links across the sea, well-planned cities, beautiful palaces and artifacts, goddess worship, and a tradition of "bull-leaping" (see right).

Intriguingly, however, what we know of Minoan culture is scant and based purely on their ruins as experts are unable to fully decode their writing, known simply as "Linear A." The Mycenaeans (see AFTER) modified Linear A to write the early form of Greek that they spoke. But while this Mycenaean script has been decoded using knowledge of Greek, the Minoans unknown, pre-Greek language still remains a mystery, and most of what they wrote down appears to be economic records.

Seafaring traders

An island location meant limited resources, so trade was crucial. As skilled seafarers, the Minoans employed a range of sophisticated vessels. They are often credited with having developed the first "navy," albeit used for trade rather than war. The Minoans' impressive trading network gave them influence across the Aegean Sea in the eastern Mediterranean, and far beyond. Minoan artifacts have been found in Egypt, modern Lebanon, Syria, Israel, and Cyprus. Not only were Minoan goods widely transported, but the Minoans themselves also settled in their trading destinations. Murals excavated at Tell el-Dab'a (ancient Avaris) in Egypt

Natural inspiration

This jar is from the late Minoan period (*c.* 1450–1400 BCE), when Mycenaean influence was evident. Natural imagery was popular, and octopuses would have been a common sight.

are Minoan in style and feature typical Cretan symbols such as bulls. Minoan-style paintings have also been unearthed at Tel Kabri in Israel.

Palace culture

Minoan life was characterized by highly developed urban settlements dominated by splendid palaces, which were home to Crete's rulers. The major cities on Crete were Knossos, Phaistos, Mallia, and Zakros, of which Knossos was the most opulent.

The cities, like those of Mesopotamia (see pp.54–55) and other civilizations of the time, were political, religious, administrative, cultural, and trading centers. Kings played both a political and a religious role and many government officials were likely to have been priests.

Minoan women
This detail taken from one of the stunning, brightly colored wall paintings at Knossos, shows a trio of refined Minoan ladies with attractively dressed hair, wearing fashionable clothes that left them exposed to the waist. There is evidence that Minoan women took a significant lead in many aspects of life.

sophisticated, multi-roomed houses. Those that did not follow a craft worked the land, providing for the cities that powered Cretan society; tasks would have included tending the vines and olive trees that produced large quantities of wine and oil.

Mythology and religion

Excavated artifacts give us an insight into Minoan religious practices and beliefs. People appear to have been buried with possessions or offerings, showing a belief in an afterlife. Cretan vases and frescoes are suffused with imagery featuring bulls, axes, snakes, and goddesses. All Minoan gods were female and one of the most popular was the "Snake Goddess," depictions of whom have been found in the ruins of houses and small palace shrines.

The bull image is widespread, being linked to King Minos. According to legend, his failure to sacrifice a bull sent by the sea-god Poseidon caused Minos' wife to give birth to the Minotaur—a creature that was half-man, half-bull. Minos trapped the Minotaur in a labyrinth, and young people were sacrificed to the creature every year.

Cretan frescoes also show young men and women leaping over bulls, which may have been performed for sport or for religious purposes.

Women in Minoan society

Women played an equal role to that of men in Minoan society, and participated in all occupations and trades, including the priesthood. Female "bull-leapers" are depicted alongside the men, and there is even evidence to suggest that Minoan society might have been "matrilineal" (with inheritance passed down the female line).

AFTER

The rich and highly successful Minoan civilization started to wane around 1500 BCE, but its complete decline took hundreds of years.

VOLCANIC ERUPTION
The **Thera eruption** in 1600 BCE (see above) may have resulted in the loss of the Cretan fleet, making Crete more vulnerable to outside powers and influence. Trade networks may also have been wiped out, causing "ripple-effect" damage throughout the whole region.

ARRIVAL OF THE MYCENAEANS
By 1500 BCE, the **Mycenaeans**, a late Bronze Age people from mainland Greece, had arrived on Crete. The Minoan and Mycenaean cultures had already influenced each other through trade. However, by 1400 BCE, the Mycenaeans **dominated Crete and the Aegean**. Their takeover may have been aided by an **earthquake** on Crete in the 1400s, which partially destroyed some Minoan cities.

JOINT DECLINE
The Mycenaeans adopted much Minoan culture, and a wonderful fusion of Minoan–Mycenaean styles flourished during this period. However, by 1200 BCE, the Cretan palace-cities were in decline **78–79 »**, and the **Greek Dorian** people moved in. The increasing use of iron for tools and weapons, and in trade, may also have put the Bronze Age culture at a disadvantage, and have been a factor in the civilization's decline.

Some scholars think that these main cities resembled small city-states (see pp.94–95), each ruling a specific part of the island and with a focus on trade. Minoan palaces themselves were vast sumptuous complexes with well-lit

1,000 The number of rooms thought to make up the famous frescoed palace at Knossos, "capital city" of the Minoan civilization.

rooms arranged around internal courtyards. The palaces had advanced drainage systems, similar to those in the Indus Valley (see p.58–59), and plumbing that featured interlocking clay pipes and flushing toilets.

A culture of craftspeople

Courtiers and wealthy families living in villas surrounding the palace would have owned exquisite artifacts and

gold jewelry for which the Minoans were famed. A distinctive feature of Minoan culture was its "Kamáres ware" pottery—including cups, jugs, jars, and enormous urns (*pithoi*), used to store food—with stylized designs often painted in black, white, and red.

Evidence suggests that many ordinary Minoans worked as craftspeople, making items for home use and export. The wealth that this industry created meant that they, too, lived in relatively

Bull-leaping
A Knossos palace fresco reveals the perilous art of bull-leaping in which young men and women took turns somersaulting over a bull's back.

Knossos palace
Around 1700 BCE, the Knossos palace complex was destroyed by an earthquake or an invasion. When rebuilt, the palace was even more splendid, with stone steps linking the different buildings on its hilly site.

Dolphin fresco
This beautiful fresco was discovered in a palace throne room. The Minoans moved from a decorative artistic style in their early days to the naturalistic style of art seen here.

« BEFORE

The Late Bronze Age « 43 began with the rise of several new powers.

THE HITTITES

The Hittite Old Kingdom formed in **Anatolia** (modern Turkey) in the 17th century BCE, but declined due to infighting. The New Kingdom emerged in the 15th century and expanded to challenge first **Mittani** (see below) and then **Egypt**. The state was divided into multiple kingdoms, each with a governor appointed by the great king, who ruled from the capital, **Hattusa**.

OLD-HITTITE GODDESS

KASSITE BABYLONIA

In 1595 BCE the **Hittite king Mursili II** sacked Babylon, ending the **Old Babylonian period** « 55. Babylonia then rose slowly as a power under the **Kassites**—an Indo-Iranian group that had immigrated centuries before. The Kassites were known for *kudurru* ("boundary stone") sculptures, which commemorated land grants.

KASSITE KUDURRU

MYCENAE

The civilization that **dominated Greece** in the Late Bronze Age (1600–1100 BCE), Mycenae « 77 controlled much of the **Aegean Sea** and absorbed the **Minoan civilization** « 76–77.

MITTANI

The kingdom of Mittani, populated by the **Hurrian people**, formed in **northwest Mesopotamia** in the 16th century BCE. Mittani **conquered Assyria 80–81** », holding it as a dependent state until the 14th century, as well as fighting Egypt for control of southern Syria. The **Mittanian capital, Washshukanni**, has not yet been excavated or even precisely located.

EGYPTIAN NEW KINGDOM

During its **New Kingdom** « 64–65 (1550–1069 BCE), Egypt became the **world's leading power** and the major force in the Middle East. Expansionist policies created an empire that, in the 15th century BCE, stretched from modern-day **Lebanon to Sudan** (ancient Nubia).

EGYPTIAN BRONZE AGE WAR CHARIOT

Rameses III battles the Sea Peoples

Pharaoh Rameses III smites his enemies in his battles against the "Sea Peoples" during the 12th century BCE. Long blamed for the Bronze Age collapse, the Sea Peoples may have been opportunists attacking weakened states.

The kingdoms of the Late Bronze Age—Babylonia, Mittani, Elam, Egypt, Mycenae, Alashiya, and the Hittite Empire—were potent powers, whose might was based on the war chariot. Where their frontiers met, they fought, but they made no attempt to conquer each other's core territories, so relative stability was maintained for four centuries from *c.* 1600 to 1200 BCE.

The flow of bronze
The key to this stability was the need for supplies of copper and tin to make bronze for weapons and tools. Copper was abundant, but the source of tin at the time was in distant Afghanistan. Long-distance trade in metals therefore needed to be maintained, and the states rapidly formed a diplomatic community,

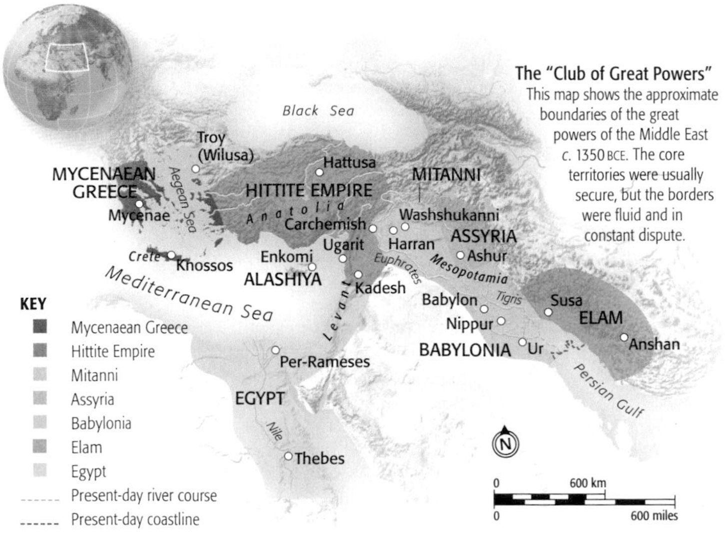

The "Club of Great Powers"
This map shows the approximate boundaries of the great powers of the Middle East *c.* 1350 BCE. The core territories were usually secure, but the borders were fluid and in constant dispute.

KEY
- Mycenaean Greece
- Hittite Empire
- Mittani
- Assyria
- Babylonia
- Elam
- Egypt
- ------ Present-day river course
- ------ Present-day coastline

Map labels: Black Sea, Troy (Wilusa), Hattusa, MITANNI, MYCENAEAN GREECE, HITTITE EMPIRE, Mycenae, Aegean Sea, Anatolia, Carchemish, Washshukanni, ASSYRIA, Crete, Khossos, Enkomi, Ugarit, Harran, Ashur, Euphrates, Mesopotamia, ALASHIYA, Kadesh, Babylon, Tigris, Susa, ELAM, Mediterranean Sea, Levant, Nippur, Anshan, Per-Rameses, BABYLONIA, Ur, Persian Gulf, EGYPT, Nile, Thebes

0 600 km / 0 600 miles

Bronze Age Collapse

In the Late Bronze Age of the Middle East, a diplomatic community of empires maintained a thriving international system based on bronze. Between 1200 and 1050 BCE, the records of these powers hint at tumult and upheaval—then most simply fall eerily silent, signifying a dark age of history.

based on intensive correspondence, dynastic intermarriage, and exchange of gifts. Whatever the current political balance and regardless of who was fighting whom, bronze was delivered.

Diplomacy also allowed the empires to make peace when strategically necessary. For instance, Egypt and Mittani initially fought over southern Syria, but Mittani made peace with Egypt to concentrate on the Hittite threat from the north. The Hittites later came into conflict with the Egyptians, but formed an alliance with them to repel the Assyrians. The Assyrians, formerly vassals of Mittani, were newcomers to the "Club of Great Powers," and it was some time before these upstarts were fully accepted.

Disintegration of kingdoms
The collapse began *c.* 1200 BCE. The first sign was that Mycenaean citadels in Greece were destroyed (see p.77), most likely by northern invaders. It seems that dispossessed Mycenaeans flooded outward looking for new lands. This is probably the origin of the story of Troy (see pp.102–03), which equates to a kingdom in Anatolia known to the Hittites as Wilusa.

What follows in the scant records available seems to be a cascade of mass migration, disruption, and destruction. Around 1180 BCE the Hittite Empire abruptly disappeared from history.

Most likely, marauding Mycenaeans drew Hittite forces away from Hattusa, the capital, which was then destroyed by tribes of northern Anatolia, leaving the rest of the empire to fragment.

The Egyptians fought off invasions by groups they called the "Sea Peoples," whom they blamed for the fall of the

Hittite capital
The ruins of Hattusa, destroyed around 1180 BCE, were unearthed at Bogazkoy in central Turkey. The palace was burned and the whole city abandoned.

Hittite Empire, although many of these groups seem to have had connections to former Hittite territories, meaning they were probably displaced by the empire's fall, rather than the cause of it. Egypt's New Kingdom declined and eventually fragmented in 1069 BCE.

Meanwhile, Babylonia's wars with Assyria and Elam resulted in Babylon's Kassite dynasty dissolving in 1154 BCE and Elam again disappearing from the

records a few decades later, when its capital, Susa, was sacked. Assyria also fell silent by 1050 BCE for over a century. The last few records speak of endless border skirmishes, as the kings attempted to hold back mass migrations of "Aramaeans" and "Mushki."

What happened?
This period is one of the most hotly debated subjects in ancient history. The events are known from only a handful of sources, such as the Ugarit letters (see right) and the Egyptian accounts of the Sea Peoples. After 1050, there are simply no records at all and the period 1050–934 BCE is termed a "dark age." The collapse represented only the removal of the top layer of culture, however—a dark age is simply a period in which the elite stop producing monuments and written records. The political map was redrawn, but the lives of most people would not have changed.

Although many kingdoms fell, only a few cities were utterly destroyed. Assyria and Elam were the only Bronze Age powers to return, but new kingdoms soon arose. The patterns of the Bronze Age were still deeply ingrained, but the new technology of iron would soon allow states such as Assyria (see pp.80–81) to break free of the old system of diplomacy and bid for world domination on their own.

AFTER »

New kingdoms, including the Hebrew states of Israel and Judah, were founded in the former territory of the Bronze Age powers.

ARAMAEAN KINGDOMS
Migrations were a key feature of the collapse, and the most significant migrants were the Aramaeans. By the 10th century BCE, a patchwork of **small Aramaean kingdoms** covered the Levant and northern Mesopotamia, and the **Aramaic language** was on its way to replacing Akkadian **« 54–55** as the Middle East's *lingua franca*. Aramaic was used in the Assyrian **80–81 »** and Persian **92–93 »** empires.

PHILISTINES
These people settled on the coast of the Levant at the end of the 2nd millennium BCE. They may equate to the **Peleset**—one of the "**Sea Peoples**" mentioned by the Egyptians—and are the **origin of the name Palestine**. Their architecture and culture appear Greek, suggesting that they began as displaced Mycenaeans **« 77**.

PHILISTINE FUNERARY MASK

IRON-AGE ECONOMY
Iron ore was more readily accessible than the ingredients for bronze, but the transition to an iron economy was highly disruptive, so the great powers stuck with bronze. After they fell, **iron came into common use**. By the 10th century BCE, Assyria was making the change, and the emerging new states were already using iron.

HOW WE KNOW

THE UGARIT LETTERS

Correspondence survives between the king of Ugarit, a regional ruler of the Hittite Empire, and the king of Alashiya, on Cyprus. The letters talk of hostile marauders plaguing the Ugarit area and are brought to a sudden stop soon after 1200 BCE by the city's destruction. They mention that the Hittites had called the bulk of Ugarit's forces away to fight elsewhere, leaving it defenseless. The marauders are never named but, as many cities around Ugarit were left unscathed, it is possible that they were displaced Mycenaean Greeks looking for a rich port to loot, as with the suspected fate of Troy.

LETTER AND ENVELOPE

BEFORE

Assyria rose to prominence in northern Mesopotamia ≪ 54–55 in the 14th century BCE, but its foundations were laid by rulers up to 600 years earlier.

OLD ASSYRIAN PERIOD

The Assyrian Empire's roots can be traced to the period c. 2000–1800 BCE when **Shamshi-Adad I** created a kingdom including the great trading city of **Ashur**, once an independent **city-state**.

MIDDLE ASSYRIAN PERIOD

By 1400 BCE, the Assyrians were vassals of their powerful neighbor, the **kingdom of Mittani** ≪ 78–79. As Mittani crumbled, Ashur broke free, its rulers proclaiming themselves "**kings of Assyria.**" Under Ashur-uballit I (1365–1330 BCE), Assyrian lands expanded over all of modern north Iraq, and Assyria came into conflict with Babylonia and the Hittites. Like other Bronze Age powers ≪ 78–79, Assyria declined in the 11th century BCE, but the state survived.

ASSYRIAN SOLDIERS

The Assyrians were Semitic people living in northern Mesopotamia (modern Iraq) and they reached the height of their empire—during the "Neo-Assyrian" era—in the 800s and 700s BCE. The Neo-Assyrian Empire built on the foundations of the Middle Assyrian period (1350–1000 BCE, see BEFORE), during which Assyria commanded much wealth and resources, improving agriculture and irrigation, erecting impressive buildings, and establishing key administrative centres.

Legendary warriors

The Neo-Assyrians were famed as fierce warriors and they showed innovative military prowess, which helped them to expand their territories. Chariot warfare had already become established during the Middle Assyrian period, when the Middle East was still in the Bronze Age (see pp.78–79). However, military success in the Neo-Assyrian period was aided by the Assyrians' effective adoption of new Iron Age warfare techniques. Their highly disciplined army featured a mix of chariots, infantry, and horseback

Life in an Assyrian military camp
This 9th-century relief from Ashurnasirpal II's palace at Nimrud shows a priest, bottom left, preparing to predict the future by studying a sheep's entrails. Foretelling the future was a prominent aspect of Assyrian life.

population movements were more like resettlements than deportations, because the people were given land and state assistance. This resettlement was the fate of the people known in Biblical tradition as the "Ten Lost Tribes" of the conquered Hebrew kingdom of Israel. They were moved to the Upper Habur area of northern Mesopotamia and the Zagros mountains of southwest Iran.

> **SEMITIC** A language group that includes Hebrew and Arabic, and a description of people from the Middle East who trace their ancestry to the biblical Noah and his son, Shem. The group includes both Jews and Arabs.

Food, probably a meat stew (perhaps from the butchered sheep), is being prepared on a stove.

Rulers of the Iron Age

By the 9th century BCE, a great Assyrian empire dominated the Middle East and stayed in control for two centuries. It is often seen as the first real "world empire," and much of its success can be traced to a stable political system and skillful exploitation of new Iron Age warfare techniques.

An Assyrian priest, recognizable by his hat, joins another man in butchering a sheep so that he can "read" its entrails.

Coded signs written by the gods were believed to be hidden in sheep's entrails.

ASSYRIAN KING, RULED 721–705 BCE

SARGON II

Coming to the throne in suspicious circumstances, Sargon II probably had a hand in the disposal of his brother and predecessor, Shalmaneser V. Sargon consolidated the gains of his father, Tiglath-pileser III, in Babylonia and the Mediterranean, and further enlarged the empire to Iran and far into Anatolia. With a vast workforce from all over the Middle East at his command and heavy tribute and taxes filling his coffers, Sargon built a new residence city called Sargon's Fortress (modern Khorsabad) in the Assyrian heartland— its palaces and temples bearing lavish stonework.

riders. This was the first army to use cavalry units, which, along with the Assyrians' use of iron weapons, gave them a great advantage over less advanced enemies. The fighting forces mixed a standing army of professional soldiers (including foreign mercenaries) under the control of the king with provincial contingents mustered as part of regional tax obligations.

Creating an empire

Famed too for the barbaric subjugation of their enemies, the Assyrians used impalement, mass execution, and the ruthless mass "deportation" of those who opposed them. But such methods were also used by other powers throughout the Middle East. The Assyrians certainly invented a new way of dealing with conquered people by moving them en masse to other parts of the empire and replacing them with other people from within the empire. However, the

Resettlement was designed to create a uniform population, although it created some hotbeds of dissent. The policy also made central Assyria a cultural melting pot. By the 7th century BCE, the royal entourage included scholars, craftsmen, and singers from Babylonia, Anatolia, Egypt, and Iran.

Stable foundations

Military effectiveness was crucially backed up by a relatively stable political system. Various factors contributed to this. The first was the royal bloodline, which was considered all-important, so that outsiders could not become king. A crown prince and heir apparent was selected as soon as a new king took the throne. There was always a successor, and he played an important role in running the empire. If the king died unexpectedly, the succession arrangement was already in place.

Second was the way in which power was delegated from the king to local officials. Assyria was organized into

Regional power
Assyrian governors often enjoyed great wealth. This mural detail is from a governor's residence at Til Barsip, during the reign of Tiglath-pileser III (744–727 BCE).

A servant sets out a bowl of soup, roasted animal ribs, and flat bread.

A fan is used by the servant to protect the meal from flies.

An Assyrian man is sliding food into or out of an oven.

The oven would have been used to bake bread or roast meat.

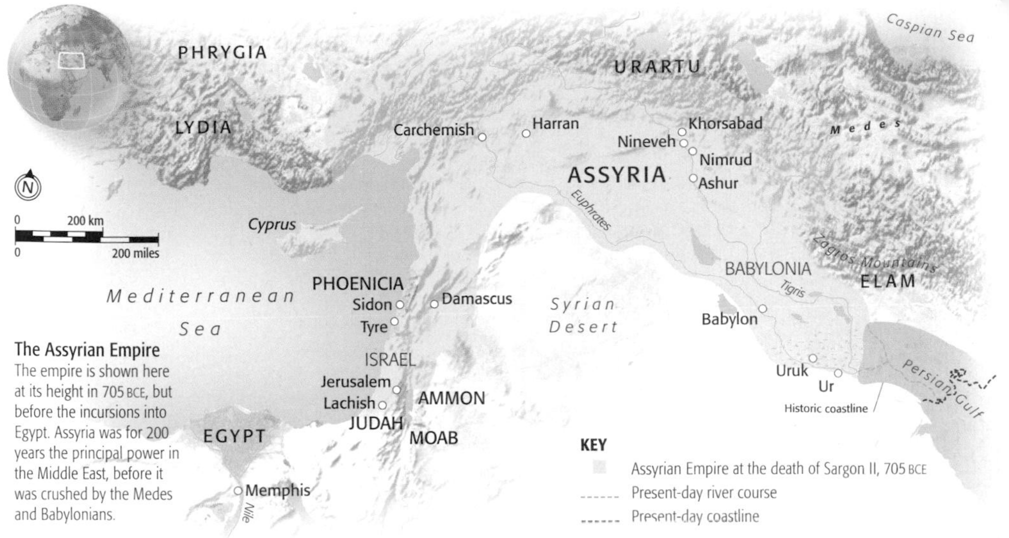

The Assyrian Empire

The empire is shown here at its height in 705 BCE, but before the incursions into Egypt. Assyria was for 200 years the principal power in the Middle East, before it was crushed by the Medes and Babylonians.

KEY

■ Assyrian Empire at the death of Sargon II, 705 BCE
------ Present-day river course
------ Present-day coastline

provinces, and newly conquered kingdoms were incorporated as provinces (with each one usually split up into two or more). The governors in charge of the provinces were directly appointed by the king. However, instead of governors being drawn from the local dynasty who had ruled before Assyria took over, or from the ruling family, the Assyrian king relied on eunuchs to represent his interests. As the eunuch governors could not have children, there was no danger that they would try to start their own dynasty.

The strong administration kept close control over the regions. It ensured that the provinces raised taxes and sent troops directly to wherever they were needed. At the top of the hierarchy, the king, the ultimate lawgiver, was aided by a powerful aristocracy from whom leading officials and army commanders were drawn. At the bottom, most of the population were peasants, paying their local lord with goods or services in return for protection. Village life changed little through successive kings.

Managing the empire

Assyrian rule had all the hallmarks of a strong empire: clever control tactics, good communication links, and varied trading connections. The Assyrians shrewdly sought to dominate areas that they had previously conquered in the Middle Assyrian period, which made it appear that they were reasserting their natural rights to those territories.

Parts of the empire were linked with a system of roads. "Royal roads" had stations for the express delivery of state correspondence using dispatch riders. This ambitious road network formed the basis of the later Persian system (see pp.90–91, 92–93). The roads were useful for overland trade, too. Strong trading links were developed with the Phoenician city-state of Tyre (see pp.82–83, 132), and Assyria built an impressive trading network across the Mediterranean as well as connections with the Arabs, and an ancient Iranian people called the Medes.

Tribute from Israel
Jehu, king of Israel, prostrates himself before the 9th-century-BCE Assyrian king Shalmaneser III. The scene is one of several such reliefs on a public monument erected at Nimrud in 825 BCE.

AFTER »

The Assyrian Empire, so aggressively built, could not withstand internal division.

KING SENNACHERIB

The Assyrian king **Sennacherib** (704–681 BCE), based at his spectacular capital, Nineveh, **aggressively defended** the empire's borders. His campaigns included sacking **the city of Lachish in Judah** (south of Israel), and **crushing**

SENNACHERIB'S CAPTURE OF LACHISH

Babylonia by **destroying its capital, Babylon**—although the city was later rebuilt by Sennacherib's son, **Esarhaddon**. Babylonia had once been a major Mesopotamian kingdom in the 2nd millennium BCE **« 55, 78–79** and emerged again from Assyria's shadow at the end of the 7th century BCE. **90, 92 »**.

CONQUEST OF EGYPT

Assyria conquered **Egypt « 65** in the 7th century BCE and ended the rule of the **Nubian dynasty**. They put the native Egyptian **Saite**

dynasty into power as puppet rulers, but Egypt then regained independence **118–19 »** under the Egyptian pharaoh Psammetichus I (664–610 BCE).

BROTHER WAR

The empire was weakened in 652–648 BCE by a war between **Esarhaddon's sons**: **Shamash-shumu-ukin**, whom he had installed as ruler of Babylon, and **Assurbanipal**, the eventual victor.

BABYLONIANS AND MEDES

On Assurbanipal's death, the empire endured a succession crisis, and when the **Babylonians and Medes** attacked and captured the city of **Ashur** in 614 BCE, the empire quickly disintegrated.

> "The Assyrian came down **like the wolf on the fold**, And his cohorts were gleaming in **purple and gold**."
>
> LORD BYRON, FROM HIS POEM "THE DESTRUCTION OF SENNACHERIB," 1815

BEFORE

By around 3000 BCE trading centers were developing in the eastern Mediterranean, the Arab peninsula, and Nubia.

MEDITERRANEAN MARITIME CITIES

By c. 3000 BCE, the maritime cities that would become the heartland of "Phoenician" (a later Greek label) civilization were developing or well established along the eastern Mediterranean coast. These included the cities of Tyre, Byblos, and Sidon (all in modern Lebanon).

THE ARABS

During the 3rd millennium BCE, states were flourishing in the better-watered parts of the Arabian peninsula. The "Magan" area (modern Oman) was an important trade partner for Mesopotamia **« 54–55**. Magan was valued for its **copper and diorite**, while it received goods such as textiles and wool.

NUBIA

Also during the 3rd millennium BCE, Nubia (modern Sudan) was forging links with Egypt by trading goods, providing a corridor to Africa through which Egypt obtained **ebony, ivory, gold, incense, and exotic animals**.

IVORY COMB, EGYPT'S OLD KINGDOM

THE INCENSE TRADE

Since ancient times, tales circulated about a "lost city" on the Arabian peninsula. Archaeological discoveries in the 1980s and 1990s, using images taken from space, appear to have found this city and identified it as Ubar (a region, not a city), in modern Oman. Items unearthed there include frankincense burners, and it is thought that this was a major Arabian trading post on the incense route, probably thriving by 900 BCE.

Incense was so precious, and its trade so important, because it masked unpleasant smells and was used in religious ceremonies. The trees from which aromatic resins are obtained grow only in Oman. This is why the incense, gold, and myrrh brought to Jesus by the three kings were such special gifts.

INCENSE BURNER

Tyre, Byblos, and Sidon formed the core of a great maritime trading network. These city-states on the east Mediterranean coast, a region known as Canaan in the 2nd millennium BCE and as Phoenicia to the Greeks, prospered between 1200–600 BCE.

The Phoenicians used maritime trade to expand a relatively small land base and keep at bay powers looking to control them. These included Egypt and the Hittites, from whose dominance Phoenicia emerged around 1200 BCE, and the ancient Greeks.

The Phoenicians' extraordinary seafaring prowess made them the control center for routes crossing the Mediterranean. Their trading links extended to Mesopotamia and, through the Red Sea, to Arabia and Africa. They were also successful merchants

Conquering Sea and Desert

During the 2nd millennium BCE, a variety of peoples in coastal and desert areas fringing more populated regions established vital trading networks that linked a cross-section of cultures.

and manufacturers, supplying a range of goods—from rich, exotic fabrics and glass to cedar wood—that found a lucrative market in Assyria.

A vast network of trading posts included Carthage in North Africa and Gades (Cadiz) in Iberia (Spain), close to the centers of tin production. Trade made Phoenicia an important force in international cultural exchange and spread the influential writing system that they developed (see pp.62–63).

The "Phoenicians," as the Greeks called them, are the same as the "Canaanites"; while the port of Ugarit (see p.79) was abandoned in the course of the collapse of the Late Bronze Age system, most other Canaanite cities survived intact and formed close trading links with the Philistines and other new arrivals.

Arab trade

Important trading networks were also established in the Arab world at this time. By the late 9th century BCE, there were major centers in southern Arabia (modern Yemen), including the Minaean and Sabaean kingdoms, and in the north. The lives of the seminomadic Arabs were transformed by the domestication of

the camel, around the 12th century BCE. This made it easier to create settlements in the desert, based around large oases, and to travel across arid regions in search of new resources.

Secrets of the desert

Camel trails marked out routes that became part of an "Incense Road," carrying incense and spices. Only the Arabs knew the secrets of traversing their dangerous desert routes. This knowledge made them powerful and wealthy, and they did their best to shroud their trails and sources in fabulous myth.

The Kingdom of Kush

A valuable nexus of trade routes was also thriving farther west, around the kingdom of Kush, in southern Nubia, bringing precious materials such as ivory and gold to the ancient world. By the 8th century BCE, Kush and its capital, Napata, were enjoying a glorious period as a major trade center freed from Egyptian domination. The value of Nubia's trade routes was one of the main reasons why Egypt had worked so hard, from about 2000 BCE, to exert control here, and the two cultures had a lasting impact on each other.

The earliest archaeological evidence for the Phoenician colony at Carthage dates to the second half of the 8th century BCE. Traditionally, the date of this trading post is given as 814 BCE.

ATLANTIC OCEAN

IBERIA

Gades
Mainaca
Lixus

Balearic Islands

Corsica
Sardinia
Nora

ITALY
Rome
Pithecusa

Hippo Regius
Utica
Carthage
Panormus

NUMIDIA
Hadrumetum
Thenae
Lilybaeum
Sicily

Sabrata
Oea
Leptis

Sahara Desert

Cyr

This stone slab (stela) from the Amun temple at Kawa shows a Nubian king called Ary, who may be the 8th-century BCE founder of the "kingdom of Kush" (in Egypt and Sudan), worshipping the gods Amun, Mut, and Khonsu.

Kawa

Trade across the desert and sea
All manner of goods, from many different sources, were transported across huge distances by networks that meshed Phoenician-controlled routes with the trade routes of Mediterranean, Middle Eastern, African, and Arabian peoples. For example, the 14th-century-BCE ship found wrecked off Uluburun (modern Turkey) was carrying goods from Mycenae, Canaan, Egypt, and Assyria. Its "nationality" is uncertain.

Senna

KEY

- ■ Phoenicia
- ○ Cities
- Phoenician trade centers and routes
- Incense trade centers and routes
- Gold and ivory trade centers and routes

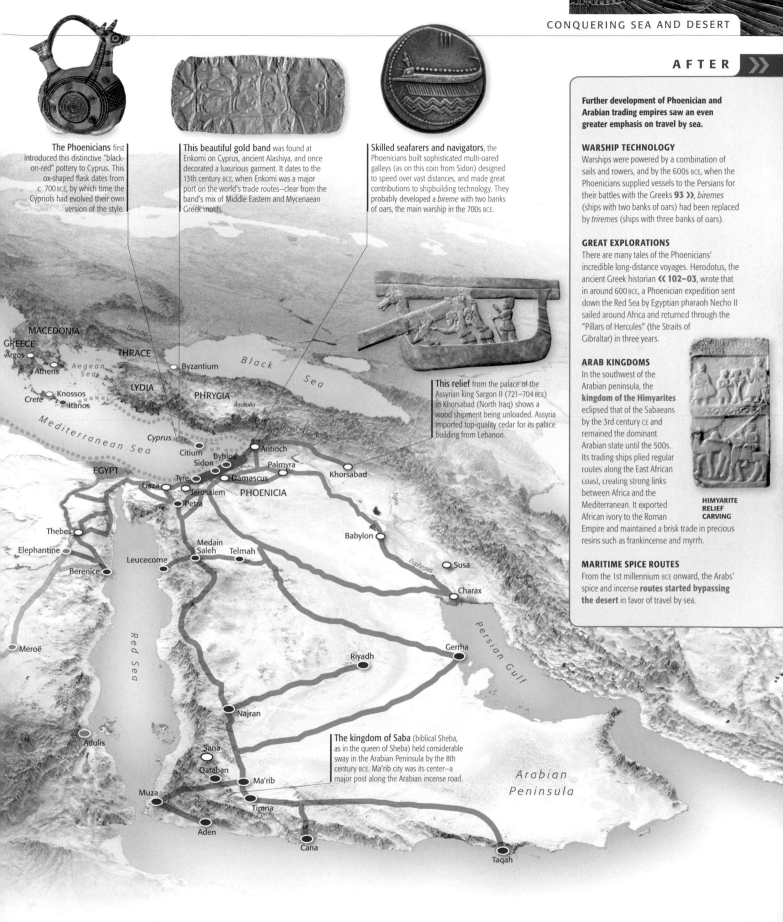

The Phoenicians first introduced this distinctive "black-on-red" pottery to Cyprus. This ox-shaped flask dates from c. 700 BCE, by which time the Cypriots had evolved their own version of the style.

This beautiful gold band was found at Enkomi on Cyprus, ancient Alashiya, and once decorated a luxurious garment. It dates to the 13th century BCE, when Enkomi was a major port on the world's trade routes—clear from the band's mix of Middle Eastern and Mycenaean Greek motifs.

Skilled seafarers and navigators, the Phoenicians built sophisticated multi-oared galleys (as on this coin from Sidon) designed to speed over vast distances, and made great contributions to shipbuilding technology. They probably developed a *bireme* with two banks of oars, the main warship in the 700s BCE.

This relief from the palace of the Assyrian king Sargon II (721–704 BCE) in Khorsabad (North Iraq) shows a wood shipment being unloaded. Assyria imported top-quality cedar for its palace building from Lebanon.

AFTER

Further development of Phoenician and Arabian trading empires saw an even greater emphasis on travel by sea.

WARSHIP TECHNOLOGY
Warships were powered by a combination of sails and rowers, and by the 600s BCE, when the Phoenicians supplied vessels to the Persians for their battles with the Greeks **93 »**, *biremes* (ships with two banks of oars) had been replaced by *triremes* (ships with three banks of oars).

GREAT EXPLORATIONS
There are many tales of the Phoenicians' incredible long-distance voyages. Herodotus, the ancient Greek historian **« 102–03**, wrote that in around 600 BCE, a Phoenician expedition sent down the Red Sea by Egyptian pharaoh Necho II sailed around Africa and returned through the "Pillars of Hercules" (the Straits of Gibraltar) in three years.

ARAB KINGDOMS
In the southwest of the Arabian peninsula, the **kingdom of the Himyarites** eclipsed that of the Sabaeans by the 3rd century CE and remained the dominant Arabian state until the 500s. Its trading ships plied regular routes along the East African coast, creating strong links between Africa and the Mediterranean. It exported African ivory to the Roman Empire and maintained a brisk trade in precious resins such as frankincense and myrrh.

HIMYARITE RELIEF CARVING

MARITIME SPICE ROUTES
From the 1st millennium BCE onward, the Arabs' spice and incense **routes started bypassing the desert** in favor of travel by sea.

The kingdom of Saba (biblical Sheba, as in the queen of Sheba) held considerable sway in the Arabian Peninsula by the 8th century BCE. Ma'rib city was its center—a major post along the Arabian incense road.

83

3

THINKERS AND BELIEVERS

700 BCE – 600 CE

The age of the great classical civilizations, including Greece, Rome, China, and Persia, was a period of remarkable innovation in science, philosophy, art, and politics. Vast empires rose and fell, systems of government that still influence society today were born, and great religions emerged. It is also the period when history was first written down.

THINKERS AND BELIEVERS

700 BCE–600 CE

700 BCE	600 BCE	550 BCE	500 BCE

c. 600
Ironworking in Nok, Nigeria. Greece continues colonization of Mediterranean with colony of Massalia, founded in southern France. First Greek coins. Paracas culture begins in Peru.

587
Neo-Babylonian Empire under Nebuchadnezzar II destroys Jerusalem's temple and exiles the Israelites.

▲ Cyrus Cylinder, proclaiming Persian sovereignty in Babylon

c. 500
Rice farming reaches Japan from China. Ironworking spreads to Southeast Asia and East Africa. Bronze coins used in China. Zapotecs develop hieroglyphic writing in Central America. Indian caste system in place.

▲ Hallstatt bird chariot, Celtic bronze, Europe

c. 700
Scythians from Central Asia settle in Eastern Europe. Rise of Greek city-states. Early Celtic Hallstatt culture in Europe. Agricultural villages in southeast North America.

c. 550
Cyrus the Great of Persia defeats Medes and founds Persian (Achaemenid) Empire. Rise of Sabaean and other states around Red Sea. Cast iron produced in China.
539
Babylonian Empire absorbed by Persia.

c. 650
First coins minted, Lydia, Asia Minor. Rise of "tyrants" in many Greek cities. Start of ironworking in China.
616
Traditional date for accession of Tarquin, Etruscan king of Rome.

◄ Hesiod

▲ Gate of Babylon

c. 563
Possible birth date of Siddhartha Gautama, the Buddha.
c. 551
Zoroastrianism official religion of Persia. Birth of Confucius.

510
Romans expel Etruscan royal family and establish republic.
505
Cleisthenes establishes democratic government in Athens.

▲ Persepolis relief

496
Rome defeats Latins at Lake Regillus.
490
Athenian Greeks defeat Persians at Battle of Marathon.

689
Babylon destroyed by Sennacherib of Assyria.
663
Assyrians sack Thebes in Egypt; their empire reaches its greatest extent.
660
Birth of Jimmu, legendary first emperor of Japan.

612
Assyrian Empire ended with sacking of Nineveh and Nimrud by Medes and Babylonians.
605
Birth of Lao-tzu, founder of Taoism.

▼ Homer's Odyssey

◄ Confucius

530
Etruscan influence at its height in Italy.
525
Persian Cambyses II annexes Egypt.
521
Persian empire reaches greatest extent under Darius I.

◄ Brick frieze of Darius's palace in Susa

Classical Greek vase ▶

Early 500s
Much of Middle East controlled by short-lived empire of the Medes; Mesopotamian region dominated by Neo-Babylonian Empire.

c. 520–460
Indian scholar Panini assembles Sanskrit grammar.
c. 515
Darius builds royal residence at Susa, former capital of Elam.

481
End of "Spring and Autumn" annals, first chronological history of China.
480–479
Xerxes' Persian invasion of Greece is defeated at Salamis, Plataea, and Mycale.

480
End of Archaic Period of Greek art; start of Classical Period.
478
Confederacy of Delos, later the Athenian Empire, founded.
c. 460
Persian administration adopts parchment.

Paracas textile, Peru ▶

Archaic Period Greek figure ▶

It has been estimated that in 1 CE, the great classical civilizations of Eurasia—Greece, Rome, Persia, India, and China—contained half the world's population of 250 million. These were more than formidably well-organized states and empires, with expansive, military, and materialistic ambitions. They were repositories of learning in the sciences and arts alike, and originators of great political systems—democracy in Greece, Confucianism in China—that have reverberated across the centuries. They also gave rise to a series of global religions—Buddhism, Judaism, and Christianity. Elsewhere, in Central and South America, Africa, and Japan, new civilizations were also emerging.

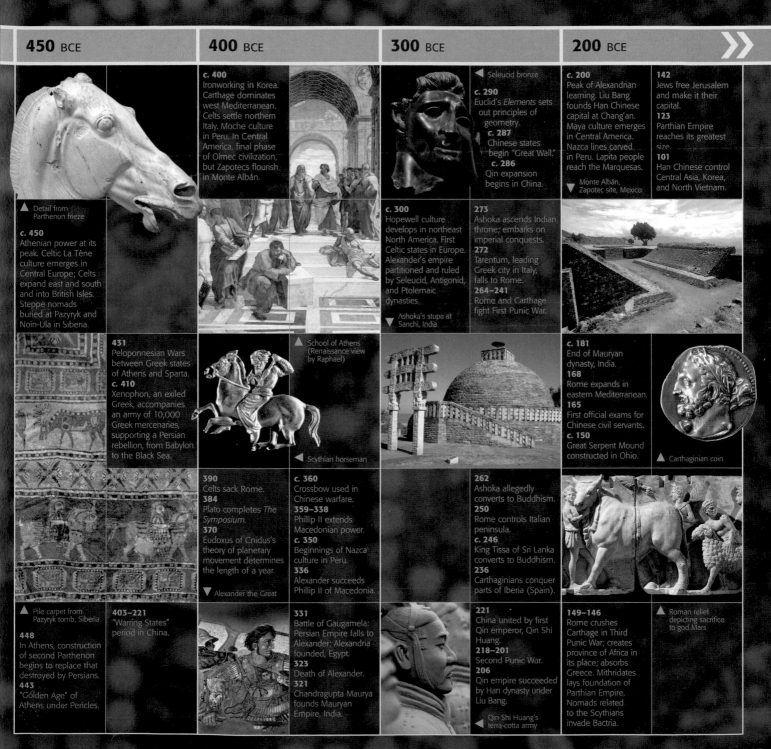

450 BCE

▲ Detail from Parthenon frieze

c. 450
Athenian power at its peak. Celtic La Tène culture emerges in Central Europe; Celts expand east and south and into British Isles. Steppe nomads buried at Pazyryk and Noin-Ula in Siberia.

431
Peloponnesian Wars between Greek states of Athens and Sparta.
c. 410
Xenophon, an exiled Greek, accompanies an army of 10,000 Greek mercenaries, supporting a Persian rebellion, from Babylon to the Black Sea.

▲ Pile carpet from Pazyryk tomb, Siberia

448
In Athens, construction of second Parthenon begins to replace that destroyed by Persians.
443
"Golden Age" of Athens under Pericles.

400 BCE

c. 400
Ironworking in Korea. Carthage dominates west Mediterranean. Celts settle northern Italy. Moche culture in Peru. In Central America, final phase of Olmec civilization, but Zapotecs flourish in Monte Albán.

▲ School of Athens (Renaissance view by Raphael)

◄ Scythian horseman

390
Celts sack Rome.
384
Plato completes *The Symposium.*
370
Eudoxus of Cnidus's theory of planetary movement determines the length of a year.

▼ Alexander the Great

403–221
"Warring States" period in China.

331
Battle of Gaugamela: Persian Empire falls to Alexander; Alexandria founded, Egypt.
323
Death of Alexander.
321
Chandragupta Maurya founds Mauryan Empire, India.

c. 360
Crossbow used in Chinese warfare.
359–338
Phillip II extends Macedonian power.
c. 350
Beginnings of Nazca culture in Peru.
336
Alexander succeeds Phillip II of Macedonia.

300 BCE

◄ Seleucid bronze

c. 290
Euclid's *Elements* sets out principles of geometry.
c. 287
Chinese states begin "Great Wall."
c. 286
Qin expansion begins in China.

c. 300
Hopewell culture develops in northeast North America. First Celtic states in Europe. Alexander's empire partitioned and ruled by Seleucid, Antigonid, and Ptolemaic dynasties.

▼ Ashoka's stupa at Sanchi, India

273
Ashoka ascends Indian throne; embarks on imperial conquests.
272
Tarentum, leading Greek city in Italy, falls to Rome.
264–241
Rome and Carthage fight First Punic War.

262
Ashoka allegedly converts to Buddhism.
250
Rome controls Italian peninsula.
c. 246
King Tissa of Sri Lanka converts to Buddhism.
236
Carthaginians conquer parts of Iberia (Spain).

221
China united by first Qin emperor, Qin Shi Huang.
218–201
Second Punic War.
206
Qin empire succeeded by Han dynasty under Liu Bang.

◄ Qin Shi Huang's terra-cotta army

200 BCE

c. 200
Peak of Alexandrian learning. Liu Bang founds Han Chinese capital at Chang'an. Maya culture emerges in Central America. Nazca lines carved in Peru. Lapita people reach the Marquesas.

▼ Monte Albán, Zapotec site, Mexico

142
Jews free Jerusalem and make it their capital.
123
Parthian Empire reaches its greatest size.
101
Han Chinese control Central Asia, Korea, and North Vietnam.

c. 181
End of Mauryan dynasty, India.
168
Rome expands in eastern Mediterranean.
165
First official exams for Chinese civil servants.
c. 150
Great Serpent Mound constructed in Ohio.

▲ Carthaginian coin

149–146
Rome crushes Carthage in Third Punic War; creates province of Africa in its place; absorbs Greece. Mithridates lays foundation of Parthian Empire. Nomads related to the Scythians invade Bactria.

▲ Roman relief depicting sacrifice to god Mars

100 BCE

1 CE

50 CE

100 CE

c. 100
Maritime trade spreads Indian influence to Southeast Asia. In India, *Bhagavad Gita* begun. Rise of Axum (Ethiopia). Romans introduce camel to Sahara. Celtic fortified settlements in Europe. Height of Adena culture in Ohio.

30
Suicide of Anthony and Cleopatra.
27
Octavian assumes title of Augustus as first Roman emperor.
4
Probable birth date of Jesus of Nazareth.

▼ Antiochus's sanctuary Commagene, Anatolia

▲ Jesus

c. 1
Kushans invade northwest India. Buddhism spreads in coastal Southeast Asia. Moche culture flourishes in Peru. Nabataeans, allied with Rome, control Red Sea trade.

43
Roman invasion of Britain.
47–57
Journeys of St. Paul.

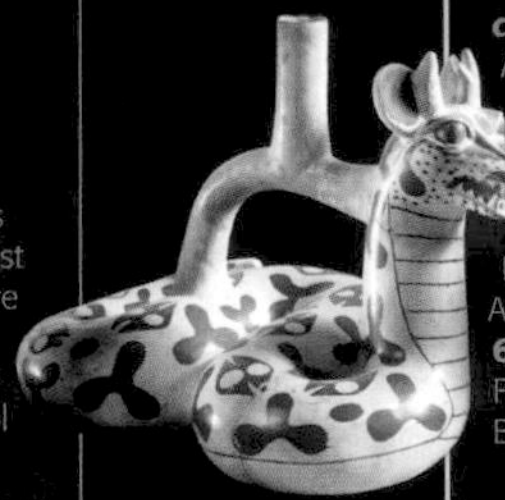

▼ Moche pottery, Peru

▲ Celtic cauldron, Gundestrup, Denmark

c. 50
Axum now major trading center.
60
Kushan Empire established in India and Central Asia.
65
First evidence of Buddhism in China.

c. 100
Teotihuacán, Mexico, expands; temples of sun and moon begun. Alexandria is center of Christian learning. Kushan emperor Kanishka propagates Buddhism.

Teotihuacán, Mexico ▶

117
Roman Empire at greatest extent.
122–28
Hadrian's wall built at Roman frontier in northern Britain.
132–35
Second Jewish revolt against Rome spreads the Jewish diaspora.

c. 150
Han China regains dominance of Central Asia. Christianity spreads west across Roman North Africa. Ptolemy of Alexandria's *Geographia*, first world atlas, completed. Peak of Nok Iron Age culture in Nigeria.

▼ Julius Caesar

2
First Chinese population census.
9
Romans retreat in Germany to the Rhine.
14
Augustus dies; stepson Tiberius succeeds him.

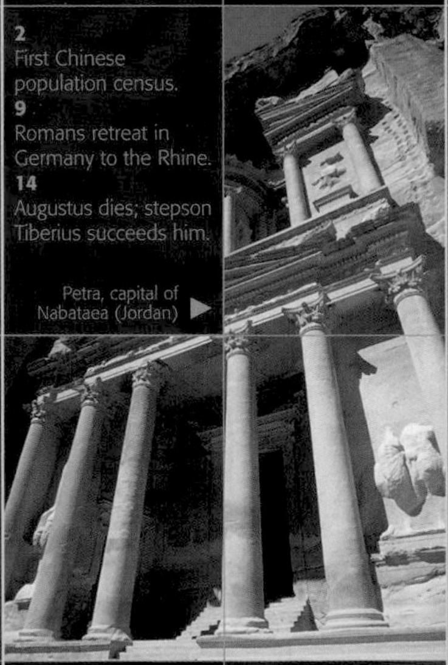

Petra, capital of Nabataea (Jordan) ▶

▲ Fresco, Pompeii

73
Peak of Han Dynasty military success.
79
Eruption of Vesuvius buries Pompeii and Herculaneum.

90
Gandhara (NW India) falls to steppe nomads.
89
Roman citizenship extended to all Italians.
63
Pompey captures Jerusalem and annexes Judaea; allies with Antiochus I of Commagene.

▼ Cleopatra

66–70
First Jewish revolt against Roman rule.
67
Roman emperor Nero orders construction of canal through isthmus of Corinth.

80
Flavian Amphitheater completed in Rome.
87
Embassy from Kushans of India to new Eastern Han capital of Luoyang.
99
Kushan embassy to Rome.

Roman colonnaded street, Apamaea, Syria

58–50
Julius Caesar's conquests in Gaul.
55
Xiongnu confederacy dissolves; southern group becomes tributary of Han China.
46
Julius Caesar declared dictator of Rome.

c. 25
Buddha represented for the first time, Gandhara, northwest India.
c. 30
Crucifixion of Jesus.
c. 40
Arawak people migrate down Orinoco and settle Caribbean.

▼ Flavian Amphitheater (Colosseum), Rome

166
Embassy of Syrian merchants to China; German tribes invade northern Italy.
180
Goths (Germanic Scandinavians) settle on Black Sea coast.

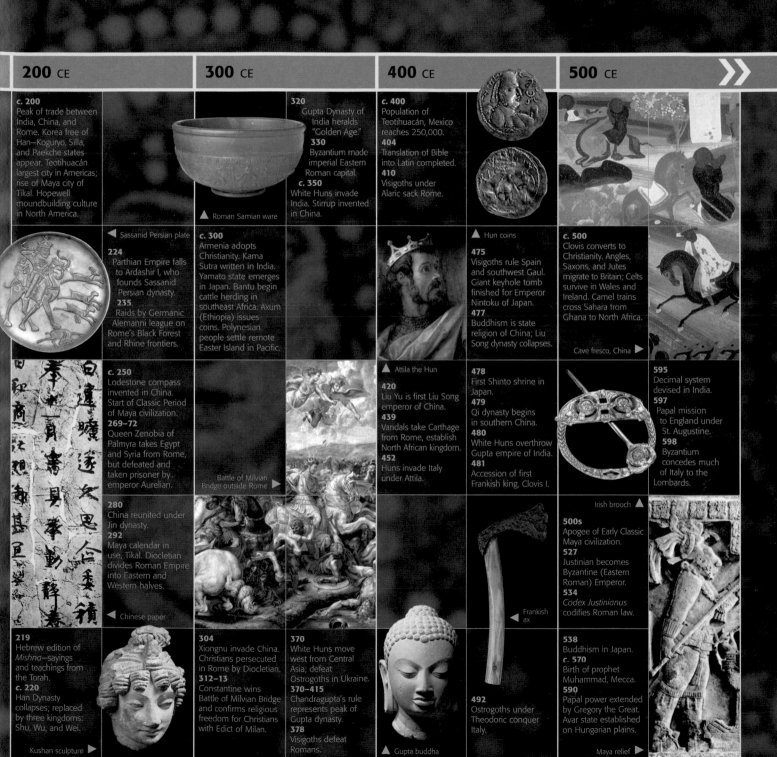

"I am **a citizen of the world.**" DIOGENES, GREEK PHILOSOPHER, c. 400–325 BCE

200 CE | 300 CE | 400 CE | 500 CE ≫

c. 200
Peak of trade between India, China, and Rome. Korea free of Han—Koguryo, Silla, and Paekche states appear. Teotihuacán largest city in Americas; rise of Maya city of Tikal. Hopewell moundbuilding culture in North America.

320
Gupta Dynasty of India heralds "Golden Age."
330
Byzantium made imperial Eastern Roman capital.
c. 350
White Huns invade India. Stirrup invented in China.

▲ Roman Samian ware

c. 400
Population of Teotihuacán, Mexico reaches 250,000.
404
Translation of Bible into Latin completed.
410
Visigoths under Alaric sack Rome.

◀ Sassanid Persian plate

224
Parthian Empire falls to Ardashir I, who founds Sassanid Persian dynasty.
235
Raids by Germanic Alemanni league on Rome's Black Forest and Rhine frontiers.

c. 300
Armenia adopts Christianity. Kama Sutra written in India. Yamato state emerges in Japan. Bantu begin cattle herding in southeast Africa. Axum (Ethiopia) issues coins. Polynesian people settle remote Easter Island in Pacific.

▲ Hun coins

475
Visigoths rule Spain and southwest Gaul. Giant keyhole tomb finished for Emperor Nintoku of Japan.
477
Buddhism is state religion of China; Liu Song dynasty collapses.

c. 500
Clovis converts to Christianity. Angles, Saxons, and Jutes migrate to Britain; Celts survive in Wales and Ireland. Camel trains cross Sahara from Ghana to North Africa.

Cave fresco, China ▶

c. 250
Lodestone compass invented in China. Start of Classic Period of Maya civilization.
269–72
Queen Zenobia of Palmyra takes Egypt and Syria from Rome, but defeated and taken prisoner by emperor Aurelian.

▲ Attila the Hun

420
Liu Yu is first Liu Song emperor of China.
439
Vandals take Carthage from Rome, establish North African kingdom.
452
Huns invade Italy under Attila.

◀ Battle of Milvian Bridge outside Rome

478
First Shinto shrine in Japan.
479
Qi dynasty begins in southern China.
480
White Huns overthrow Gupta empire of India.
481
Accession of first Frankish king, Clovis I.

595
Decimal system devised in India.
597
Papal mission to England under St. Augustine.
598
Byzantium concedes much of Italy to the Lombards.

Irish brooch ▲

280
China reunited under Jin dynasty.
292
Maya calendar in use, Tikal. Diocletian divides Roman Empire into Eastern and Western halves.

◀ Chinese paper

500s
Apogee of Early Classic Maya civilization.
527
Justinian becomes Byzantine (Eastern Roman) Emperor.
534
Codex Justinianus codifies Roman law.

◀ Frankish ax

219
Hebrew edition of *Mishna*—sayings and teachings from the Torah.
c. 220
Han Dynasty collapses; replaced by three kingdoms: Shu, Wu, and Wei.

Kushan sculpture ▶

304
Xiongnu invade China. Christians persecuted in Rome by Diocletian.
312–13
Constantine wins Battle of Milvian Bridge and confirms religious freedom for Christians with Edict of Milan.

370
White Huns move west from Central Asia; defeat Ostrogoths in Ukraine.
370–415
Chandragupta's rule represents peak of Gupta dynasty.
378
Visigoths defeat Romans.

▲ Gupta buddha

492
Ostrogoths under Theodoric conquer Italy.

538
Buddhism in Japan.
c. 570
Birth of prophet Muhammad, Mecca.
590
Papal power extended by Gregory the Great. Avar state established on Hungarian plains.

Maya relief ▶

Xerxes crossed the Hellespont as part of his Persian campaign to Greece in 480 BCE. The Hellespont was a narrow sea channel that had been both a frontier and pivotal point of empires. A boundary separating Europe and Asia, it was also a conduit of goods and communication between East and West.

Hatra was a rich trading city in territory disputed between Rome and Parthia (see pp.122–23) between 150 BCE and 224 CE. At times, it was one of several prominent semi-independent or client states (such as Commagene) between the great Roman and Parthian empires. Hatra's circular layout reflected Parthian city patterns, while the architecture revealed Roman influence.

This Greek depiction of northern nomads, known as the Scythians (see pp.138–39), demonstrates trading contact at the meeting point between settled and nomadic worlds. The Scythians were a group of related tribes sharing a common culture and related languages, who spanned the steppe lands from Siberia to southeast Europe.

BEFORE

The natural geographical zones of Eurasia have shaped the growth of powers, their conflicts, and their contacts. In many ways, Mesopotamia remained the heart of the ancient civilized world.

VALLEYS AND SETTLEMENT
Settled urban life began in the fertile valleys and floodplains of Egypt ≪ 56–57, Mesopotamia ≪ 44–45, and the Indus ≪ 58–59. These valleys became central to growing states during the period 3000–1000 BCE.

EXPANDING POWERS
Between 1550 and 700 BCE, the rich, ambitious monarchies of Egypt ≪ 64–65 and Assyria ≪ 80–81 expanded beyond their valleys into the disputed territory of the Levant—the area at the eastern end of the Mediterranean, roughly from modern Turkey south to the Sinai Peninsula. This was a fertile commercial crossroads and a gateway to the resources of the Mediterranean.

WORLD DOMINANCE
The Assyrians' heartland lay in the upper part of Mesopotamia, but in c. 800 BCE they dominated their neighbors more than any state had done before. They fought the mountain tribes to the north and east of their realm, but also developed diplomatic relations with them. The Assyrian Empire at last fell to the Babylonians in c. 612 BCE. Babylon was now at the center of the world again.

ISHTAR GATE, BABYLON

DESERTS AND FRONTIERS
In the second half of the 1st millennium BCE, the world's great powers became yet more mobile and ambitious. Peoples with roots as horsemen of the steppes, such as the Persians 92–93 ≫, combined rule of Mesopotamia with expansion from the Iranian Plateau to the desert of Central Asia. The same heritage of steppe horsemanship brought new military tactics to the Chinese warring states in 1000–500 BCE and, later, aided their unification 126–27 ≫.

Celts
Germanic peoples
Baltic peoples
Slavs
Dacians
ROMAN EMPIRE
Rome
Hellespont
MAURETANIA
Carthage
Athens
BOSPORAN KINGDOM
Sarmatians
CAPPADOCIA
COMMAGENE
Caucasus
ARMENIA
Mediterranean Sea
Berbers
Dura Europos
OSROENE
Caspian Sea
Sahara
Alexandria
Hatra
Seleucia
Nisa
KUSHAN EMPIRE
EGYPT
NABATAEA
DECAPOLIS
Ctesiphon
Babylon
Iranian Plateau
Bactra
Red Sea
KUSH
Persepolis
PARTHIAN EMPIRE
AKSUM
Arabs
Persian Gulf
Hindu Kush
HIMYAR
Arabian Sea
INDIAN STATES

Dura Europos was founded c. 303 BCE during Greek rule of Mesopotamia, on a trade route on the Euphrates River. The city then came under Parthian, Roman, and then Persian control. Its cultural diversity is reflected in its religious buildings, which include both the earliest preserved synagogue and this church.

Bisitun was a sacred mountain beside a site used successively as a staging post, garden, and palatial retreat. The mountain towered over the route from Babylon, on the low Mesopotamian plain, to the Iranian Plateau. In c. 515 BCE, Persian emperor Darius I (see pp.92–93) carved a monumental relief with an imperial inscription (below) proclaiming his sovereignty over both plateau and plain.

The Indus River was a central link in the route between the Persian Gulf and the interiors of India and Central Asia. The Indus Valley was also a contested frontier between powers including the Achaemenid Persian (see pp.92–93), Seleucid Greek (see pp.98–99), and Mauryan Indian (see pp.124–25) empires.

Kushan statues such as this are relics of a tribal power that in 1–250 CE consolidated a huge land empire between the Hindu Kush mountains and the Ganges River. Known to both Roman and Chinese imperial powers, the Kushans (see pp.138–39) formed a crucial zone of cultural exchange.

A series of empires spread across Eurasia in 700 BCE–600 CE, all shaped by their physical environment. The heart of the city-based empires remained in the south, from southern Europe through the Middle East to India and China. The steppe territory to the north continued to support an unsettled, nomadic life, largely uncontrolled by urban states (see pp.138–39). Nevertheless, great changes in the seats of power of both settled and nomadic people took place. Mesopotamia, once the center of a succession of empires (see BEFORE), became a border region from the 2nd century BCE. Enormous population movements of which we are only dimly aware today seem to have moved frontiers in the European steppe, Central Asia, and northwest China. At the same time, rulers resettled populations as a method of imperial control under the Assyrian, Babylonian, Persian, Roman, and Han Chinese empires.

Limitless ambition

The vast size of these empires was hard for their inhabitants to comprehend, but imperial powers used symbols to reflect the rich diversity of their lands. Assyrian and Persian rulers described the varied resources and people of their territory in inscriptions. Similarly, on unifying the fragmented states of China, the founding emperor of the Qin dynasty, Qin Shi Huang (see pp.126–27) shaped his vast tomb into a microcosm of the lands he ruled.

Views of the frontier

Each dynasty or empire developed its own ideas about the structure of the world. During Assyrian and Babylonian rule from the fertile, low-lying plains of Mesopotamia, mountains were seen as wild, chaotic places threatening danger. On the other hand, the mountainous homeland of the Macedonian Greeks and Persians helped to instill in them a hardy self-image. For these empires, great rivers, such as the Danube and Indus, marked the limits of their realm.

The rise and fall of dynasties and empires across Eurasia bequeathed a powerful idea of the inevitable fall of all worldly power. Later states with global ambitions looked back on a series of civilizations whose heirs they presumed themselves to be.

"BABYLON IS FALLEN"
Due to Babylon's dramatic role in the Bible, its fall became the archetypal example of the

"THE FALL OF BABYLON," JOHN MARTIN, 1831

decline of a once-great state. Its **apocalyptic destruction** was often depicted in art in the 19th century. Writers compared it with the **inevitable fate** of contemporary imperial and commercial powers, **Britain and the US**.

THE FORCES OF CHAOS
To the people of imperial city civilizations, invading nomadic tribes represented the forces of chaos. In Biblical and Islamic tradition, these forces were personified by the legendary **"Gog and Magog."** Waves of migrating people from the north and east, whether Scythians or Huns 138–39, 150–51 », were identified by the settled states with the peoples of Gog and Magog—threatening hordes on the borders of civilization.

ISLAMIC IMAGE OF GOG AND MAGOG

Frontiers of Power

From 700 BCE, ambitious powers began bidding for supremacy over all the known world. Each of these imperial movements, from Assyria to Rome, encountered barriers to its empire-building. Chief among them were the terrain and climate of the Eurasian continent, and the resistance of neighboring powers.

The shape of empires
A snapshot of the Eurasian landmass in c. 1 CE illustrates both the barriers to communication and unification, and the portions of land that were acquired and fought over by the main powers at that time.

The Great Wall of China began as a piecemeal chain of defenses, but during unification by the first emperor of the Qin dynasty, the sections were joined and reshaped to become a frontier wall against raids by northern nomads, such as the Xiongnu.

KEY
- Roman Empire
- Parthian Empire
- Han Empire of China
- Armenia
- Osroene
- Great Wall under the Han
- ▲ Mountain

‹‹ BEFORE

Earlier great powers of the Middle East set the scene for Persian conquest of the region.

ASSYRIAN EMPIRE

The Assyrian kings **‹‹ 80–81** had ruled lands between the Zagros Mountains of Iran and the Mediterranean. They led campaigns into **Egypt** and into the mountains of **Armenia**. When their **empire fell** in 612 BCE, they left rich cities and trade links open for exploitation by their successors.

DETAIL OF ISHTAR GATE, BABYLON, c. 580 BCE

NEW BABYLON

The bulk of Assyrian lands were taken over by a dynasty ruling from the ancient city of **Babylon ‹‹ 55, 79, 90**. These Neo-Babylonian kings rebuilt Babylon into an imperial capital. Although it fell to the Persian army less than a century later, Babylonian techniques of rulership were influential in the next 200 years, inspiring a text of Cyrus (see right) and the redevelopment of cities, such as Susa (see right).

O n the territorial margins of the great powers of Mesopotamia—Assyria and Babylonia (see pp.80–81 and BEFORE)—resided several small states and peoples. Among these were the Medes and Persians. Greek historians, influenced by Persian views, describe how the Medes first developed a luxurious empire to match their Mesopotamian neighbors. Of the Persians who attended their court, one individual, Cyrus, supposedly took over the Medes' empire from within. Archaeological remains do not back up this account, however. Contemporary chronicles unearthed in Babylon instead tell how Cyrus conquered lands surrounding Mesopotamia in the mid-6th century BCE before moving on the capitals of the heartland itself. First to fall was the Lydian kingdom in the west of modern Turkey. This conquest brought Cyrus within sight of Greece. Next to fall to Cyrus was the Babylonian king Nabonidus and his capital. Detailed Babylonian and Mediterranean records also recall the victories of Cyrus's son Cambyses, who invaded Egypt in 524 BCE. Cyrus's conquests of extensive areas in central Asia in the east are less well documented. With Cambyses' annexation of Egypt, the Persians—a small tribal elite from the Iranian plateau—had acquired a world empire within a generation, creating huge pressures on the leaders. When Cambyses died, his brother Bardiya seems to have been recognized as king. But the loudest voice in the following years is that of Darius I, who alleged in a

> " A Persian man has delivered battle **far indeed from Persia**"
>
> TOMB INSCRIPTION OF DARIUS I, 549–486 BCE

The **Persian Empire**

From provincial beginnings, a dynasty of kings—the Achaemenids—emerged to exert power across the continent of Asia from the Mediterranean to northwest India. The empire of the Persian kings was one of an unprecedented scale.

Persepolis
A griffin head designed to sit at the top of a column watches over Persepolis, the city developed by Darius I and his successors from 519 BCE. The structures included massive columned audience halls (right) and (in the distance) smaller royal palaces built of stone and mud-brick.

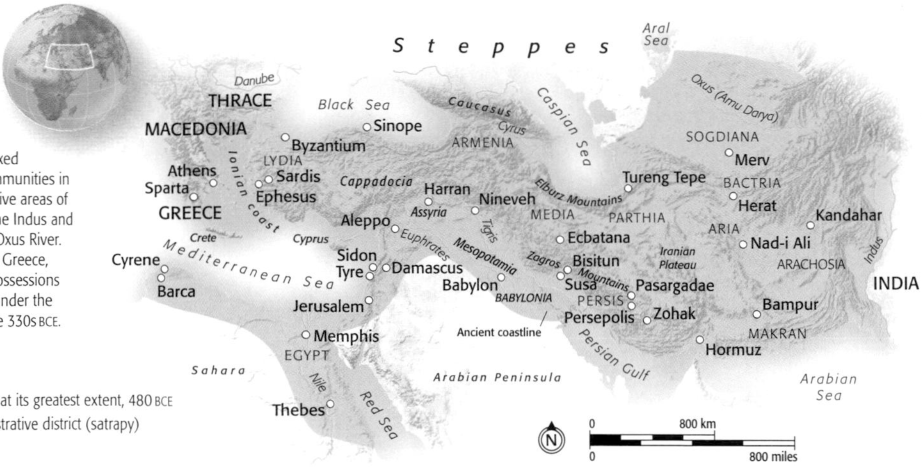

Persian Empire under Xerxes I (485–465 BCE)

By the time of Xerxes, Persian kings had annexed Egypt, many Greek communities in the Aegean, and extensive areas of central Asia, reaching the Indus and extending beyond the Oxus River. Despite retreating from Greece, Persia lost no further possessions permanently until Alexander the Great's conquests in the 330s BCE.

KEY

▨ Persian Empire at its greatest extent, 480 BCE

LYDIA Persian administrative district (satrapy)

(Map labels: Steppes, Aral Sea, Danube, THRACE, MACEDONIA, Black Sea, Sinope, Byzantium, Caucasus, Cyrus, Caspian Sea, Oxus (Amu Darya), SOGDIANA, Merv, Tureng Tepe, BACTRIA, LYDIA, Sardis, ARMENIA, Athens, Sparta, Ephesus, Cappadocia, Harran, Nineveh, Assyria, MEDIA, PARTHIA, Elburz Mountains, Herat, Kandahar, ARIA, Nad-i Ali, ARACHOSIA, GREECE, Crete, Cyprus, Aleppo, Euphrates, Mesopotamia, Tigris, Ecbatana, Iranian Plateau, Cyrene, Mediterranean Sea, Sidon, Tyre, Damascus, Babylon, BABYLONIA, Zagros Mountains, Susa, PERSIS, Pasargadae, Bampur, INDIA, Barca, Jerusalem, Persepolis, Zohak, Indus, Memphis, Ancient coastline, Hormuz, MAKRAN, EGYPT, Sahara, Arabian Peninsula, Persian Gulf, Nile, Red Sea, Thebes, Arabian Sea; scale 0–800 km / 0–800 miles, N)

AFTER

The Persian Wars between Greek city-states and the Persian Empire are seen by many as a period that defined ideas of "East" and "West." Afterward, the East would be regarded as foreign to the West, and vice versa. The Persian Empire also left more positive lasting legacies.

FALL OF AN EMPIRE
The last king of the Achaemenid dynasty, begun by Cyrus, was **Darius III**, who lost half of his empire to the invasion of **Alexander 96–97 ≫**. He was apparently imprisoned and killed by his own entourage in 330 BCE. Although Alexander cut a swath through the ruling elite and burned part of Persepolis, the structure and traditions of the Persian empire exerted a huge influence on the rulers and empires who followed **98–99 ≫**.

AN IMPERIAL LEGACY
Apart from the practical legacy of a functioning empire, over 200 years of Achaemenid Persian rule bequeathed other ideas. **Unifying notions** in **Greek** and **Jewish** communities are linked with their experiences in the Persian empire. The Achaemenid period was a catalyst for the development of states and identities across the Middle East. **Sassanid emperors 122–23 ≫** who ruled Persia centuries later identified themselves as **heirs to the Achaemenids**.

A royal heir

Under Darius, his son Xerxes, and subsequent kings, the image of the monarch carved into the walls of their palaces remained unchanged, emphasizing the continuity of their family line. Here, a royal heir in his court robe resembles the king exactly.

monumental inscription carved into the mountain of Behistun that Bardiya was an imposter whom Darius had removed. In the wake of this upheaval, Darius tried to create a harmonious image of the empire under his rule. The architecture at his capitals of Persepolis and Susa incorporated peaceful images of all the peoples of the empire. In a foundation document from Susa, Darius claimed that the building materials had come from far-flung corners of his realm, from India to the Ionian coast, and that many subject peoples had brought the splendid structure to completion.

Encounters with Greece

Darius and his successors emphasized harmony and productivity under their rule. Texts on the Persian kings, written by Greeks in small states scattered across the edge of Persian territory, instead concentrate on conflict. They had a complicated relationship with their neighboring superpower. When Persian-held Greek cities on the Ionian coast revolted in the 490s BCE, Athens and Eretria sent help from mainland Greece. The Persian leaders regarded this as rebellion by an otherwise cooperative people and sent a punitive expedition in 490 BCE, and another led by Darius's son Xerxes in 480 BCE. Although some cities came to terms with the Persians immediately, other Greek states staged valiant resistance. Their acts of defiance became defining moments in Greek consciousness of their independence of rule from the East (see pp.132–33).

A world empire

Despite withdrawal from Greece, Persia continued to wield influence in the Mediterranean, both politically and culturally. The Persian throne did not come under threat until the invasion of Alexander the Great (see pp.96–97) in 334 BCE.

The peoples who offered tribute to the Persian kings reached from

The Cyrus cylinder
This clay foundation document inscribed in Akkadian (see p.62–63), the traditional literary language of Babylon, gives Cyrus's carefully positive account of his conquest of the city in the 540s BCE, in which he was welcomed by the locals as a better ruler than his predecessor, the Babylonian king Nabonidus.

Scythians of the steppe to the north, to fortresses on the frontier of Upper Egypt in the south. The range of cultures encompassed by this scope stretched from the historic, settled cities of Babylonia, where an increasingly mixed elite resided, to newly emergent kingdoms on the Caucasus frontier, who sent detachments to the Persian army and copied elements of the Persian court in their architecture and luxury objects. The difficulties of administering such a vast and varied empire were significant; even a journey between two of several royal capitals could take up to three weeks. Official royal routes, supported by regular staging posts and carefully administered travel rations, provided a swift communication network. Across this network, orders, letters, luxury supplies and expert personnel were transported. Armies could be mustered more locally according to need. The ruling Persians spoke their own language (Old Persian), which was recorded only in the limited royal inscriptions appearing on monuments in the cites of the empire. Official communication was in Aramaic, a *lingua franca* (common language) inherited from Assyrian administration, but only a few fragments of such parchment and papyrus documents have survived. Letters from Egypt and records from Afghanistan illustrate how movements of officials and provisions were closely supervised by local administrators, under the authority of "satraps," who were usually Persian governors appointed by and answerable to the king. Such interconnections led to unprecedented transmission of ideas, goods, and people across vast distances.

HOW WE KNOW

THE PALACE OF SUSA

Despite their success, the Persians left no sustained historical account of themselves. The kings did, however, leave monumental statements on their palace walls about how they had wished to be seen. Images and texts found in Darius I's palace at Susa show Darius boasting of massive excavations for a platform for his columned halls. Glazed-brick reliefs on the exterior were inspired by the palaces of Babylon (see BEFORE). They show a Persian guard in colorful court robes.

PERSIAN EMPEROR 580–529 BCE

CYRUS

Folkloric tales of fate and heroism surrounded the early life of Cyrus, the founder of the Persian Empire, and were passed on by Greek writers. In his own words, Cyrus was "King of Anshan," an old city on the Iranian Plateau. He blended architectural styles from the lands he conquered in his garden-filled capital of Pasargadae. Cyrus also adapted local ideas about kingship to cast himself as a desirable ruler in the subject cities of Babylon and Jerusalem. Both Greek and Middle Eastern sources inspired a long tradition of viewing Cyrus as an ideal king.

« **BEFORE**

The period of Greek history leading up to the Archaic period was preceded the rich civilization of Mycenae and a period known as the "Dark Age" of Greece.

EARLY CIVILIZATION

Artifacts from Mycenae, Greece, are evidence of a rich Mediterranean civilization that existed before the rise of the city-states. The Mycenaean culture peaked in the 2nd millennium BCE.

THE "DARK AGE"

Between 1100 and 750 BCE, ancient Greece was in a "dark age" about which little is known. All of the future city-states were probably clusters of villages at this time.

EARLY ARCHAIC PERIOD

At the start of the Archaic Period (c. 750–480 BCE), increasing Mediterranean populations fueled the rise of cities such as Athens, Sparta, Thebes, and Corinth.

THE MAKING OF ATHENS

By the 7th century BCE, Athens was on the rise as a leading city-state. Central to its identity was its legal system. Around 621 BCE, Athenian magistrate Draco laid down a series of strict laws—probably the city's first significant legal code. Later, the Athenian statesman, Solon (c. 630–560 BCE), brought in laws that helped protect the rights of "ordinary" people.

SOLON

INVENTION

GEOMETRY

The period of the city-states saw philosophers and scholars such as Thales of Miletus bringing together mathematical principles from ancient Mesopotamia and Egypt to invent geometry, (*geo* meaning "Earth" and *metron* "measure" in Greek). The defining work on geometry was written by Euclid, a mathematician from Egypt, born c. 300 BCE, author of a treatise on geometry, the *Elements*.

11TH CENTURY RELIEF OF EUCLID

The leading centers of civilization in 6th- and 5th-century BCE Greece included Athens, Sparta, and Corinth. These communities are now referred to as city-states. Many of the architectural features of these city-states are shared by cities today. Typically, they were walled, with a central citadel or *acropolis* (characteristically a place of refuge housing a temple on raised ground), a main marketplace (*agora*), a sporting and socializing center (*gymnasium*), and one or more temples. Although termed "cities," population levels were low, and Sparta probably remained principally a cluster of villages. What was important, and central to the city-state concept, was that the inhabitants identified with their state first. So being a "citizen" of Sparta—a Spartan—was more important than being Greek. Beyond this, the city-states often varied greatly in character, each shifting through various types of government at different times. These included monarchy, tyranny (where there was one strong leader, not necessarily an unpopular one as implied by the modern use of the word), oligarchy (rule by a small group of people, typically nobles) and democracy. The eligible male citizens participated to varying degrees in many of these forms. This participation and idea of self-rule became one of the key characteristics of many of the city-states that came later.

City-states of the Greek model came to exist throughout the Aegean and its islands, in western Asia Minor (Ephesus), Sicily (Syracuse), southern Italy (Tarentum), Africa (notably Cyrene, in Libya), and in France (Marseilles).

Athens

A major figure in the story of the city-state was the Athenian magistrate Cleisthenes (c. 570–508 BCE) who instituted major reforms in the system of rule. He changed the Athenian tribal system and permanently altered Athens' political structure. He divided citizens into ten "tribes" (*phylae*), named after heroes. Attica (the area around Athens) was divided into three areas—coast, highlands, and city—and the tribes were made up of citizens from each of these areas and subdivided further into *demes*, the smallest voting districts of the polis.

The 5th-century statesman Pericles (c. 495–429 BCE) moved Athens farther toward a new kind of democracy (see

> **CITY-STATE** Often translated as *polis* in the context of ancient Greece. These states were independent, self-contained entities bound by the rule of law. They reached their height during the classical period, which lasted from c.480–323 BCE.

The Greek City-states

The rise of the *polis*—city-state—in ancient Greece was a major development in world politics. Great states such as Athens, Sparta, and Corinth provided a variety of models for ruling through a system of law, with Athens in particular paving the way to a groundbreaking idea: democratic government.

Parthenon treasure
This exquisite sculpture from the Parthenon in Athens is widely believed to have come from the workshop of Phidias, the most famous sculptor in ancient Greece.

The acroterion was a decorative feature above the pediment.

The eastern pediment was filled with sculptures depicting Greek mythology.

Sanctuary of Athena
This is one of several buildings clustered around the oracle at Delphi, a sacred site close to the Gulf of Corinth.

Theater at Epidauros
This vast 4th-century theater was built at Epidaurus, a city-state in the Peloponnese. The best-preserved theater to survive from ancient Greece, it seated around 12,000 people and has exceptional acoustics. The theater of the ancient Greeks influenced the development of both drama and theater design.

Temple of Apollo
From about 650 to 550 BCE, Corinth experienced a golden era. With colonies in the Adriatic and Macedonia, its command of several important harbors made it an important seafaring and trading center.

ARISTOTLE

Born in northern Greece, Aristotle was one of history's greatest philosophers and scientists (see pp.104-5). He wrote on a variety of subjects, including government. In his famous work, *Politics*, he analyzed many of the Greek city-states in an exploration of what might be the best form of government. In general, he had a great respect for the *polis* as a good way to govern and to make the most of people's talents.

pp.100–101). Juried courts were set up, therefore moving judicial power from the city council to its citizens. Its assembly became a democratic council where all male citizens, regardless of background or wealth, had an equal vote. Athens and the 5th-century city-states have come to be seen as the "birthplace of western democracy."

Athenian city-state life in the 5th and 4th centuries BCE also saw a remarkable flourishing of intellectual and artistic life. Playwrights including Aeschylus, Sophocles, and Euripides explored great philosophical themes that were later tackled by Plato and Aristotle (see left), and the thriving Athens that emerged from the Greek victory against Persia in the 4th century BCE saw its Acropolis rebuilt and the great Parthenon temple (below) completed.

Sparta and Corinth

Athens's great rival, Sparta, had a dual kingship from two royal lines—these kings ruled concurrently. Later, this rule was tempered by a council of aristocrats and an assembly of citizens (the *Homoioi*)—a society of equal male citizens willing to take arms for their state. Sparta also differed from the other Greek states in relying heavily on a serf population known as *helots*. In the 5th century BCE, a small, council-elected body called the *ephorate* came into being. Conceived to oversee government processes, they eventually seized power for themselves and sidelined the monarchy for a time. Sparta was famed for its army and military training.

Another powerful *polis*, Corinth, commanded a strong strategic position geographically on the narrow strip of land connecting mainland Greece.

The struggle for supremacy

The rise of hoplite warfare (see pp.116–17) in the 7th century BCE was central to the rise of the city-states. As the use of the phalanx formation became widespread (see pp.114–15), citizens who fought for their states expected some political say in return. Rivalry between city-states was constant, particularly between Athens and Sparta. Some events brought the states together, such as the Panhellenic games, which included the Olympic Games, and religious festivals. The city-states combined forces against the Persians in the 5th century (see pp.92–93), in an alliance effectively led by Sparta (although Athens was later dominant). Victory brought confidence and a sense of identity and unity.

A gold and ivory statue (now lost) of the goddess Athena by the famous sculptor Phidias stood in the center of the temple.

The many columns were fluted, without bases and with square capitals at the top.

The interior of the temple was divided into three aisles.

Distinctive three-stepped base leading into the temple.

The Parthenon
This breathtaking marble temple was built on Athens' acropolis between 447 and 432 BCE, on a wave of euphoria that engulfed the Athenians after their defeat of Persia. It was dedicated to the city's patron goddess, Athena.

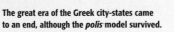

AFTER

The great era of the Greek city-states came to an end, although the *polis* model survived.

THEBAN DOMINANCE
From 371 to 362 BCE, the city-state of Thebes gained the upper hand. This **chaotic era** brought more city-state conflicts that weakened their power.

MACEDONIAN CONTROL
In 338 BCE, the Macedonian King Philip II **‹‹ 96–97** defeated the Greeks and formed the **League of Corinth** to support his own imperial plans.

THE CITY OF ROME
Rome grew in power **106–107 ››** and ruled over an empire using some of the ancient Greek models.

THE MIDDLE AGES AND THE RENAISSANCE
The 11th century CE saw the rise of **Italian city-states** such as Venice and Pisa. By the 13th–15th centuries, other examples flourished at Florence, Padua, Hamburg, and Flanders. The Renaissance rediscovery of **classical ideas and learning** in western Europe brought Plato and Aristotle's ideas on government to the fore **250–53 ››**.

RULER AND MILITARY LEADER Born 356 BCE Died 323 BCE

Alexander the Great

"There is **nothing impossible** to him who will try" ATTRIBUTED TO ALEXANDER THE GREAT

In less than a decade of warfare, Alexander of Macedon, known as "the Great," created one of the largest land empires the world has ever seen, stretching from Greece to northern India. His career of conquest was built upon that of his father, Philip II, king of Macedon in Greece. It was Philip who turned the kingdom of Macedon into a regional power in the Greek world. He created the army of heavy cavalry and pike-wielding infantry that became the instrument for Alexander's empire building.

From an early age Alexander was marked out among Philip's children as his most likely successor—he acted as regent of Macedon and keeper of the royal seal while Philip was making an expedition against Byzantium in 340 BCE. At the age of 18 he proved his courage and skill in war, leading a cavalry charge at the battle of Chaeronea in 338 BCE that crushed the Sacred Band—the famed elite Greek infantry from Thebes. Yet his right to the succession was by no means assured, for the throne did not necessarily pass to

Alexander in action
This Roman mosaic shows Alexander riding his horse Bucephalus into battle against the Persians at Issus in 333 BCE. Leading his army from the front, Alexander was never defeated in battle, despite fighting armies three times the size of his own.

Birthplace of an icon
The Macedonians originated as hill tribesmen in the mountains of northern Greece, although Alexander was born on the coastal plain, at Pella, where his royal predecessors had established their capital.

"A tomb now suffices him for whom the whole world was not sufficient"

SAID OF ALEXANDER AFTER DEATH

the eldest son and the king had several wives. There were rumors that Alexander's mother, Olympias, tried to have Philip assassinated before a son by another wife could grow old enough to succeed him. Alexander certainly acted ruthlessly to secure the succession once his father was dead, killing anybody at court who threatened his authority.

Heroic ambitions
When, in 334 BCE, Alexander led his army across the Hellespont—the body of water that separates Europe from Asia Minor to liberate the Greek cities under Persian rule in Asia Minor, he was fulfilling a plan previously announced by his father. But the astounding campaign of conquest that followed was entirely the expression of his own ambition. Alexander claimed descent in his father's line from the Greek hero-god Herakles (Hercules) and through his mother from the legendary hero of the Trojan War, Achilles. One of his first acts on crossing to Asia Minor was to visit the site of Troy as an act of homage to his ancestor. Later, in Egypt, his claims were raised a notch higher when a priest at the desert shrine of Ammon hailed him as the "son of Zeus," the king of the Greek gods, who was believed to be an ancestor of the Macedonian kings. Alexander's self-image as an heroic man of destiny chosen by the gods inspired his relentless drive to conquest.

Military leader
Alexander's army served him as the dedicated followers of a great fighting man. His elite cavalry, the Companions, were a tight-knit group with whom he fought, ate, and drank as the first among equals. On the battlefield Alexander led from the front. He liked to spearhead the cavalry charge and was often the first to storm city walls during a siege. He could be supremely reckless of his own safety, yet he was also thoroughly professional in organizing and motivating his cavalry and infantry in battle. His decisive victories over numerically superior Persian armies at Issus and Gaugamela showed a shrewd eye for the weaknesses of an apparently powerful enemy as well as an instinct for gambling on aggression. It was typical of Alexander's unresting ambition that the conquest of the mighty Persian Empire, achieved by 330 BCE, brought no end to his campaigning. He went on fighting, not just enforcing his claim to rule all the Persian domains, but also pushing farther into India.

Persian influence
Alexander saw himself as spreading Greek civilization by the sword. He founded Greek cities, the most famous of which was Alexandria in Egypt, and sought to Hellenize—to make Greek—the Persians whom he conquered. But his adoption of the mantle of the Persian Empire created great strains with his Macedonian followers. The traditions of Persian court ceremony were alien to Macedonians. The Macedonian veterans were also jealous when new Persian followers found favor with Alexander. Discontent came to a head in a series of mutinies that Alexander violently suppressed.

Alexandria's lighthouse
Alexander founded Alexandria as a Macedonian capital for Egypt. Its lighthouse was one of the seven wonders of the ancient world.

Noble savage
His fame in antiquity was unequaled, yet he left no creative legacy. Alexander was a ruthless man who killed both in anger and in cold blood. After Alexander died at the age of 32, his mummified body was taken to Egypt, where it remained on display for more than 500 years.

ALEXANDER IDEALIZED

HOW WE KNOW

LIVING GOD

This silver coin shows Alexander as the semidivine Herakles, distinguished by his lionskin cap. On other coins he is represented as the horned god Ammon, the supreme Egyptian deity. Alexander's close association with the gods and a suggested direct paternal link to Herakles, rather than Philip, enforced his own sense of destiny. According to one written source, Alexander attended banquets in Persia dressed as gods. The myth of his divinity was widely accepted and shrines were raised in his name.

ALEXANDER AS HERAKLES

TIMELINE

- **July 356 BCE** Born in Pella, Macedonia, the son of Macedon's ruler, Philip II, and his fourth wife Olympias.
- **343 BCE** The Greek philosopher Aristotle is brought to Macedon to educate him.
- **338 BCE** Plays a leading role in the defeat of Athens and Thebes at the battle of Chaeronea. His father makes himself leader of all the Greek city states except Sparta.
- **337 BCE** Philip marries a Macedonian woman, Eurydice. She bears him a son who could threaten Alexander's claim to inherit the throne.
- **336 BCE** Philip is assassinated by a bodyguard, Pausanias. Alexander succeeds to the throne and has Attalus, the chief supporter of Eurydice, killed.
- **334 BCE** Crosses the Hellespont at the head of an allied army. He visits the site of Troy and then conquers western Asia Minor, defeating a Persian army at Granicus.
- **November 333 BCE** Defeats Persian King Darius III at Issus in modern Syria, but the Persian ruler escapes.
- **332 BCE** Takes the cities of Tyre (Lebanon) and Gaza (Israel) after sieges. He proceeds to Egypt and is hailed as pharaoh. He visits the oracle of the god Zeus-Ammon at the Siwa Oasis and founds the city of Alexandria.
- **October 331 BCE** After a long march east from Egypt, he encounters the Persian army at Gaugamela. The Persians are utterly defeated and Darius flees for his life.
- **330 BCE** Darius is murdered by his Bactrian entourage. Alexander establishes himself as successor to the Persian throne. He suppresses a conspiracy in his army; his second-in-command Parmenion is among those put to death.
- **328 BCE** Falling into a rage during a drunken banquet, Alexander kills Clitus the Black, one of his leading Macedonian officers
- **327 BCE** Marries Roxana (Roxanne), a Sogdian princess. He bloodily suppresses a conspiracy by his royal pages, who oppose his adoption of Persian customs.
- **326 BCE** After invading the Punjab, he defeats King Porus at the battle of the Hydaspes. His beloved horse Bucephalus is killed. Reaching the Hyphasis River his soldiers mutiny and force Alexander to turn back, following the Jhelum, a tributary of the Indus River, to the sea.
- **326 BCE** He leads part of his army back to Persia in a march across the Gedrosian Desert that costs many soldiers their lives.
- **324 BCE** The Macedonians in Alexander's army mutiny as he recruits increasing numbers of Persians. Many Macedonian veterans are discharged. Alexander is plunged in deep grief when his closest friend, and rumored lover, Hephaestion dies.
- **June 11, 323 BCE** Alexander dies of a fever in Babylon, leaving no clear successor.

BEFORE

Alexander's conquests created an empire even larger than the Persian empire at its height. Anybody wishing to rule over it would have to take into account the legacy and traditions of Persia's Achaemenid rulers.

THE ACHAEMENID EMPIRE

The **Achaemenid Empire ‹‹ 92–93** reached its greatest extent under Darius I and his son Xerxes I in the 6th century BCE, and lost very little territory before Alexander **‹‹ 96–97** began his conquest in 334 BCE.

Divided into **satrapies** (provinces governed by men appointed by the king), it had several royal capitals. The ceremonial capital of **Persepolis** was largely destroyed by Alexander, but its great stairways, decorated with reliefs of **subject rulers** bringing tribute, survive.

BAS-RELIEF OF SUBJECT RULERS, PERSEPOLIS

The Conquests of Alexander the Great

In just ten years, Alexander conquered the Persian Empire, the largest empire the world had ever seen. His own empire now stretched from North Africa and the eastern Mediterranean to the Indus valley in northern India. On his death in 323 BCE, his generals fought to decide who would inherit the largest share of the spoils.

KEY

■ Empire and dependent regions of Alexander
— Route of Alexander the Great

The **Greeks** in **Asia**

The Achaemenid Persian Empire had ruled over an area extending from the Mediterranean to the Indus valley. It was all conquered by Alexander the Great in less than ten years, his army bringing with it ideas and tastes from Greek civilization that took root and flourished alongside local traditions.

B efore his death, Alexander had placed the key provinces in the conquered Persian empire under the control of trusted governors. However, he allowed local systems of government, to which the people were accustomed, to continue. Alexander appreciated the role of the Persians as an imperial people and, according to some accounts, tried to create a ruling race through intermarriage between his officers and Persian noblewomen.

The process of changing one mode of rule for another, he knew, was a delicate one and needed patience. He died in Babylon in 322 BCE (see p.97) before he realized his ambition of creating a completely unified empire

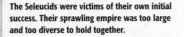

The Seleucids were victims of their own initial success. Their sprawling empire was too large and too diverse to hold together.

THE END OF THE SELEUCIDS

In the 2nd century BCE the Seleucids were driven from Persia and Mesopotamia by the **Parthians 122–23 »**. By 100 BCE the empire had been reduced to Antioch and a few other Syrian cities. They continued to exist only because powers such as Rome **106–15 »** and the **Ptolemaic dynasty 118–21 »** in Egypt did not see them as a serious threat. It was the Roman general **Pompey** who finally put an end to the Seleucid Empire, annexing Syria as a Roman province in 64 BCE.

THE PARTHIAN EMPIRE

The end of the Seleucid Empire left the Romans and the Parthians to contest the Middle East. When the Romans tried to invade Mesopotamia in 53 BCE, the Parthians defeated them at **Carrhae**, but the Romans had the better of later clashes, sacking the

Parthian capital of **Ctesiphon** three times in the 2nd century CE. The Parthians, originally a semi-nomadic steppe people, left much of the administrative structure of the Seleucid empire intact—coins with Greek inscriptions were minted as late as the 2nd century CE. All this changed after the Parthians were ousted by the Persian **Sassanids 122–23 »** in 236 CE.

GRAECO-BUDDHIST ART

Aspects of Hellenistic culture also survived farther east, in **Bactria** (in Afghanistan) and parts of northern India such as Gandhara. Between the 2nd century BCE and the 4th century CE many sculptures from Bactria and the so-called **Indo-Greek kingdoms 124–25 »** display a combination of the artistic styles of India, Persia, and Greece.

GREEK-INFLUENCED BUDDHA; BACTRIA, 3RD CENTURY CE

East meets West in Nemrud Dag, Turkey
In the 1st century BCE, the king of Commagene, Antiochus I, built a mountain-top shrine where the fine statuary depicts both Greek and Persian deities and uses a combination of eastern and western artistic styles.

---

embracing Macedonia, Greece, Egypt, and all the Persian territory he had conquered in Asia.

According to Plutarch's biography of Alexander, written nearly 400 years after the event, his body lay in its coffin for several days without showing any signs of decay, while his generals argued over who should succeed him.

The body, an important talisman for Alexander's potential successors, was embalmed to be taken home, but it was diverted to Alexandria in Egypt, where it was exhibited in a glass case.

Wars of succession

Alexander's wife Roxana had a son in August 332 BCE, but he never grew up to succeed his father—he was killed in 310 by one of the generals competing to take over the empire. Alexander had told his commanders that the succession lay with the "fittest." Bloody conflict to determine who this would be raged almost continuously from 323 to 279 BCE. By then, three main Hellenistic states had been established. The smallest was the Antigonid kingdom, which ruled in Macedonia and Greece. Constantly involved in wars with the Greek city-states (see pp.94–95), it eventually fell to Rome (see pp.106–15) in 168 BCE. The richest and most secure was the

Bactrian deities
This plate from Ai Khanoum (in modern Afghanistan) shows the Greek goddess Cybele in a chariot pulled by lions in front of a Persian priest at a fire altar.

Ptolemaic kingdom (see pp.118–19), which ruled Egypt and Palestine. It lasted until 30 BCE, when in the reign of Cleopatra VII (see pp.120–21), it was annexed by Rome. The largest of the successor states, however, was the Seleucid Empire, founded in 312 BCE by Seleucus I Nicator, when he secured Babylon and with it control of Persia, Mesopotamia, Syria, and much of Anatolia.

The three empires spread Greek ideas through their political institutions, town planning, and architecture. They were eager to show that they preserved the cultural freedoms of the Hellenic ideal, so the cities they built had all the attributes of a Greek city-state: an agora, or place for public debate, temples to all or one God, and spectacular theaters.

Greek culture in Asia

The Seleucid empire established many Greek-style cities to help control their huge territory. Seleucus I had a new capital, Seleucia, built in Mesopotamia, on the Tigris, near Babylon, but the capital was soon moved to Antioch in Syria. The Seleucids had a relaxed attitude to the religions practiced in their territories, and Greek ideas were accepted alongside old Persian, Jewish, and other local traditions.

In the course of the 3rd century BCE, the Seleucids had to abandon their eastern provinces of Bactria and Parthia, but that did not mean the end of Greek influence there. The distant Bactrian kingdom (in present-day Afghanistan) retained a magnificent Greek coinage, and archaeological sites such as Ai Khanoum (thought to be the city of Alexandria on the Oxus) reveal that Bactrian cities continued to follow Greek models with temples and other public buildings fronted by beautiful Corinthian columns.

To the west of the Seleucid sphere of influence, in present-day Turkey, Pergamum, an important new regional

HELLENISTIC The three centuries after Alexander's death in 323 BCE are called the Hellenistic Age, when post-Classical Greek culture spread far beyond its homeland. Greek ideas and artistic styles were adopted in Asia, Egypt, and, most importantly, Rome.

power, was emerging. Attalus I Soter, who ruled 241–197 BCE, took the title of king of Pergamum and made his city into a major center for literature, philosophy, and the arts. It had its own acropolis, magnificent temples, a theater seating 10,000 people, and a vast library. Another fascinating Hellenistic state was Commagene in the southeast of present-day Turkey, which broke away from the Seleucids around 162 BCE. It absorbed Persian influences from the east and Greek from the west. Antiochus I, who ruled from 70–38 BCE, built a monument to himself at Nemrud Dag, which is the most extraordinary fusion of Hellenism and Eastern culture.

IDEA

PHILHELLENISM

Admiration for Greek philosophy, poetry, and sculpture survives to this day, although it probably peaked in 18th- and 19th-century Europe. *The Apotheosis of Homer* (right) by Antonio Canova (1757–1822) embodies the spirit of admiration for Classical Greece. Philhellenism (love of Greek culture and the belief that theirs was the perfect way to order society) takes no account of the fact that Greek women had no vote or that Greek society depended on the labor of slaves.

BEFORE «

Ancient Greece was not a unified nation but a mosaic of around 150 city-states sharing a common language and religion; the two most important were Athens and Sparta.

A NATION OF CITY-STATES
After the destruction of the Mycenaean civilization (whose stories, including the *Odyssey*, were recorded by Homer), ancient Greece entered the Dark Ages, about which we know little **« 94**. Cities and their surrounding land became independent units known as city-states (*polis*).

SCENE FROM THE ODYSSEY

THE HOPLITE REVOLUTION
The city-states relied on their armies for their protection. Increased trade in the 7th century BCE began a military and political revolution. The new rich could now afford their arms and supplied regiments of hoplites (armored infantry) alongside the aristocratic cavalry. The need to act collectively in warfare led to a new form of government based on the shared interests of a broader section of society.

Athens' first lawgiver was Draco (*c.* 624 BCE). His severe penalties were designed to stop the aristocrats from taking the law into their own hands. In 594 BCE military defeat by the city of Megara and growing social tensions led to the appointment of Solon as supreme *archon* (magistrate). Since rural impoverishment had caused an agrarian (farming) and military crisis in Athens, Solon's solution was to abolish slavery brought about by debt, free the peasantry from feudal servitude, and make wealth rather than birth the prerequisite of political office, thus reducing the power of the aristocracy.

To encourage good governance (*eunomia*), he created a council (*boule*) to prepare the weekly business of the citizen's assembly (*ecclesia*), and a popular court of appeal (*heliaia*) for legal redress against abuses of power. Citizens were divided into four classes: aristocrat, "horseman," hoplite, and the poor (*thetes*), each of which elected 100 members to the council. Poor citizens could only vote at this stage.

In 560 BCE, the aristocrat Peisistratus took advantage of incessant internal feuding to seize power in a popular coup, initiating land reforms on behalf of the poor. It was against a backdrop of the increasingly harsh rule of his son that a progressive aristocrat called Cleisthenes overthrew this tyranny in 507 BCE, introducing the revolutionary reforms that would transform Athens into a formidable power and Greece's first true democracy.

Athens' democratic evolution
Cleisthenes created a future for Athens' citizens to match their potential. In place of *eunomia*, he promised *isonomia* (equality). To neutralize factional feuding, he tore up the old network of family and regional loyalties, redividing Athens into 139 voting districts (*demes*) arranged into 10 tribes (*phylae*) made up of citizens from each of the three regions—coast, interior, and city—in an elaborate system of checks and balances. Annual membership of an expanded council of 500 was chosen by

lot from each of the 10 tribes, which supplied the smaller 50-member group of council leaders (*Prytaneis*) to administer the daily affairs of government. Its composition was changed on a regular basis so that no one remained in power too long. Jury members for the courts were also chosen randomly to avoid corruption.

The 6,000-strong *ecclesia* convened weekly on the Pnyx, a site near the Acropolis, to vote on matters presented by the *Prytaneis* and elect the 10 generals (*strategoi*). Since Athens' defense could not be left to chance, these powerful officials, who controlled the army and the navy, could be reelected.

The effect of all these reforms was to reduce the powers of the aristocracy further while creating a united body of men loyal to Athens above all else. As a further safeguard, ostracism was introduced to banish any "dangerous" leaders from the city for 10 years.

Imperial power
With unity at home, Athens set about raising its profile abroad, investing in a powerful navy after its victory over the Persians at Marathon in 480 BCE, and acknowledging the growing importance of its oarsmen following an impressive naval victory over the Persians at Salamis in 490 BCE. Increasing colonization, dominance of the trade routes, the discovery of silver, and the creation in 477 BCE of the Delian League—an alliance with other city-states to protect themselves from future Persian invasions—made Athens the dominant power in Greece.

A brilliant orator called Pericles presided over a "Golden Age" of Athenian prosperity (451–429 BCE) and cultural preeminence. He consolidated the democratic "constitution" by compensating the poorer citizens for their time on jury service or attending the *ecclesia*, and limiting citizenship to those with two Athenian parents.

Democracy in Athens was suspended and quickly restored twice during the 5th century BCE. It was finally extinguished during the 2nd century BCE by an expanding Roman Empire.

> **DEMOCRACY** From the ancient Greek words "demos," meaning "people," and "kratos," meaning "power."

Birthplace of democracy
The Acropolis ("high city") of Athens was its spiritual center. The Parthenon (finished in 431 BCE), the temple at the top of the Acropolis dedicated to the goddess Athena, was built by the Athenian general Pericles following the defeat of the Persians, with money from the Delian League, as a symbol of Athens' glory.

> " … a man who takes no **interest in politics**… has no business here at all…"
>
> PERICLES, 495–429 BCE

The **Birth** of **Democracy**

The oldest and most stable democracy in ancient Greece developed in Athens, evolving constitutionally through monarchy, aristocracy, and tyranny before arriving at the principle of equality for all citizens. However, as in other Greek *polis*, women, slaves, and foreigners were excluded from participating.

KLEROTERION

KLEPSHYDRA (WATER CLOCK)

OSTRAKON (VOTING TABLET)

Objects of democracy
The *kleroterion* was used to select jurors. Slots in the device (fragment shown) held volunteers' names, and black and white balls were dropped down a tube to select them. Water clocks were used to time the speeches in the Assemblies. Citizens inscribed the names of overly ambitious politicians that they wished to ostracize from the city on an *ostrakon*.

AFTER »

It took a long time for the idea of democracy to become widely adopted; it was not until the mid-20th century that it became the most common form of government.

ROMAN VOTING

ROMAN DEMOCRACY
Republican government in ancient Rome was based on elected representatives (representative democracy) rather than Athenian-style direct democracy. **Power was shared** between the two Consuls, the Senate (aristocracy), and the Plebs (commoners). Over time, the Plebeian Assembly became the dominant legislature.

AMERICAN GOVERNMENT
The architects of the first modern democracies in the US **298–99 »** and France **302–03 »**, modeled them on the Roman Republic with representation limited to the wealthier classes only. The Athenians thought that representative democracy was tilted in favor of wealthier candidates. During the campaign for the 2008 **US presidential election**, the main candidates raised over $25 million each.

THE WORLD'S LARGEST DEMOCRACY
India's democracy governs a population of **over a billion people**.

From Myth to History

As Greece emerged from a "Dark Age" and writing was rediscovered, new ways of passing on knowledge and stories developed. For the first time in the Western world, history was recorded in prose, rather than verse—the poet became a historian and artistic license gave way to the goal of accuracy and explanation.

During excavations at the Palace of Knossos on the island of Crete in 1900, the British archaeologist Arthur Evans found a huge collection of written clay tablets. They had survived a fire that destroyed the palace some time after 1400 BCE. When the script, known as "Linear B," was deciphered, it turned out to be the first known example of early Greek writing. The art of writing then seems to have been lost to the Greeks during the so-called "Dark Age" (c. 1100–c. 750 BCE).

The subsequent development of the Greek alphabet and writing led to the recording of history. Before the 6th century BCE, history was recounted in the form of poetry and was mixed with folklore and myth, making it hard to separate fact from fiction.

Ancient Greece's most famous poet, Homer, (see below) is an important figure in the transmission of history in the Western world, although he probably never wrote down his own poems, and the subjects he used were a mixture of myth, folk memory, and fact. The story of the Trojan War, which may have been an actual event of the 13th century BCE, inspired both his epic poems, the *Iliad* and the *Odyssey*. In the first of these, two intense weeks in the story of the war are told. The *Odyssey* tells the tale of the Greek hero Odysseus's ten-year journey home from the Trojan War. Both stories show a desire to keep alive memory of past glories and hinge on Greek memories of an expedition to Troy in Asia Minor (Turkey). The actual events, if they happened at all, were not recorded in any surviving written accounts. This meant that over the intervening centuries, the facts were mingled with myth and travelers' tales to become the story we know today.

Fantasy and fact

One 19th-century archaeologist, Heinrich Schliemann, became obsessed with the story of the Trojan War and was determined to find evidence that it had actually taken place. Using the text of the *Iliad* as a guide, Schliemann found a vast city complex buried under various layers at Hissalik in northwest Turkey. One layer of the city had been destroyed by fire c. 1180 BCE. He was convinced that this was Troy, where the mythical Achilles had killed the Trojan hero Hector. Schliemann's archaeological practices destroyed a great deal of the value of the site. Later experts were appalled at what he had done and even questioned the authenticity of the many gold artifacts he claimed to have found. Schliemann went on to find more treasures at Mycenae on the Greek mainland, including the mask (see right) that he declared to be one of the leaders of the Greek siege of Troy, saying, "I have gazed into the face of Agamemnon." It is probable that it was in fact part of a royal burial treasure from a period before the Trojan War.

First written history

An early Greek writer to break away from this mix of myth and reality was Hecataeus of Miletus (c. 550–490 BCE), who is considered by some to be the first history writer. In one of his works, he set down in writing stories that had been passed down orally from generation to generation as well as recording family genealogies. Another writer, Simonides (c. 556–469 BCE), referred to events of the Persian invasion of 480 BCE in his poems.

It is a later writer, however, who is known today as the "father of history." Herodotus (484–425 BCE) wrote *The Histories*, which focused on the origins of the war between Greece and Persia that took place at the beginning of the 5th century BCE. He was interested in studying human nature and the world around him and recorded what he saw as he traveled the length and breadth of the ancient world. Although he came from Halicarnassus (modern Bodrum in Turkey), he also lived in Athens for a time. His travels allegedly took him to Egypt, Italy, Sicily, and Babylon, and his writing is full of entertaining detail about the customs and habits of the countries he visited.

Herodotus is remembered today because he was the first to write about events of his own time in prose rather than verse, and to organize his material systematically. He inspired later historians to break with the old epic tradition and write in this style, recounting real events rather than the mythical exploits of heroes and gods.

The work of Herodotus cannot, however, be relied upon as fact. His writing still depended, to some extent, on oral history and was colored by folklore and tradition. He claimed to have authenticated his information, but critics in antiquity argued that it was not wholly accurate. The later Greek historian and biographer Plutarch (c. 46–119 CE) had a very low opinion

Odysseus's voyage

This 3rd-century-CE Roman mosaic shows Homer's Odysseus on his epic journey. In this part of the story he is lured onto a rocky island by the singing of the Sirens.

> **HISTORY** The word was first used by the Greek writer, Herodotus. In ancient Greek the word meant "rational inquiry."

SCENE FROM THE EPIC OF GILGAMESH

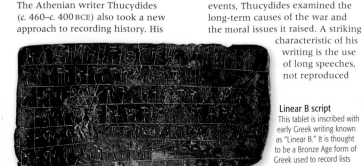

"The Mask of Agamemnon"
This astonishing burial mask was found at Mycenae in Greece by the archaeologist Heinrich Schliemann in 1876. He named the mask after the leader of the Greek troops during the Trojan War. It is part of a collection of royal treasure dating from *c.* 1600 BCE.

Over the centuries, written histories, like the folktales that preceded them, have been shaped by the values of the times in which they were recorded.

THE EPIC TRADITION
Old stories told in traditional ways **connect powerfully** with the listeners, as they are rooted in local landscape, history, and folklore. *Beowulf* is an English epic poem of the 10th century CE. The story concerns the struggle between forces of **good and evil**. In Cyprus, shepherds still tell stories about one-eyed giants, horned gods, and Bacchanalian feasts in nearby river beds.

BEOWULF MANUSCRIPT

MODERN MYTH AND HISTORY
Kathakali stories of Hindu myth, using dance and masks, costumes and music to accompany oral texts, are still **performed today**. The *Mahabharata* and the *Ramayana*, tales about the various Hindu divinities **145 »**, are told to people who may be **unable to read**, in the same way that the stories of Homer were told in ancient Greece.

KATHAKALI DANCER

word for word, but rewritten to express Thucydides's personal opinion. One famous example is the speech made by Pericles (see p.100), in which the city of Athens and all its achievements are praised in a funeral oration for those who had died in the war.

Despite their shortcomings—the inaccuracies of Herodotus and the poetic embellishments of Thucydides—the two Greeks are rightly acknowledged as the first true historians in the West. The era of recounting heroic deeds in epic poetry was over, and a new method of recording the past had begun.

of the accuracy of *The Histories* and called Herodotus "a father of lies."

Expressing a viewpoint
The Athenian writer Thucydides (*c.* 460–*c.* 400 BCE) also took a new approach to recording history. His famous *History of the Peloponnesian War*, written in 41 books, tells the story of the war between Athens and Sparta (see p.95). As well as recounting the events, Thucydides examined the long-term causes of the war and the moral issues it raised. A striking characteristic of his writing is the use of long speeches, not reproduced

Linear B script
This tablet is inscribed with early Greek writing known as "Linear B." It is thought to be a Bronze Age form of Greek used to record lists and inventories at Knossos.

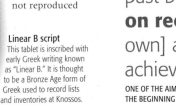

" To preserve the memory of the past by **putting on record** [our own] astonishing achievements… **"**
ONE OF THE AIMS OF HERODOTUS SET OUT AT THE BEGINNING OF "THE HISTORIES," C.440 BCE

HOW WE KNOW

VIEW OF THE WORLD

This map, from a woodcut made in 1867, shows Herodotus's view of the world, based on the descriptions found in his writings, with Asia Minor and the Middle East at its center. Although he did not venture far in modern terms—he was unaware of northern Europe, for example—he included an extraordinary amount of detail about the places he did visit, (Egypt, Africa, Italy, Sicily, and other parts of the Mediterranean), including the length of rivers and sizes of continents. Much of this was previously unknown.

For the first few hundred years of classical Greek civilization, scientific thought was not unlike that of earlier periods. Just as in Mesopotamia and Egypt, practical knowledge was used to help make life easier. Some individuals acquired skills in mathematics and astronomical observation, but they were used for practical purposes. Mathematics, therefore, was used in commerce and construction, and knowledge of astronomy in timekeeping.

When it came to accounting for natural phenomena, however, ancient civilizations tended to be far less practical. They relied unquestioningly on fanciful mythological explanations for everyday events. Myths involving supernatural gods were not tested— or even questioned.

After about 600 BCE, however, some began to question these ideas and wonder about the world around them.

Natural philosophers

These thinkers, or "natural philosophers," employed logic and reason to question the accepted myths. Thales of Miletus (c. 624–c. 526 BCE) is often referred to as the "father of science." Like many of the Greek scientific thinkers, Thales pondered the nature of matter. He suggested that all solids, liquids, and gases are ultimately made of water. This makes some sense—water is one of

Praising the gods
This clay tablet was left at a temple, and was dedicated to god of healing, Asclepius, from someone who believed their foot to have been healed through traditional rather than scientific medicine.

PYTHAGORAS

Pythagoras is best known for the mathematical law relating the sides of right-angled triangles: "the square of the hypotenuse of a right-angled triangle is equal to the sum of the squares of the other sides." In fact, the theorem was known long before Pythagoras, and there is no evidence that he even used it, or whether he even existed. His reputation for mathematical excellence comes from later Greek writers, particularly Aristotle. Modern academic study of Pythagoras' ideas shows that they were more religious than scientific. Pythagoras and his followers saw mystical relevance in mathematics.

(born c. 480 BCE) and his student Democritus (born c. 460 BCE) suggested that matter is made up of tiny, indivisible particles separated by empty space. Their ideas are similar to modern atomic theory.

All of these early thinkers grappled with philosophical concepts, such as change, infinity, and existence versus nonexistence (see pp.130–31). It is not important whether the theories were

mathematics in formulating their theories. Mathematics can be divided into geometry—the study of the relative position and size of objects, including Earth—and arithmetic— the study of numbers. Geometry had been used to help astronomers and architects, while arithmetic formed the basis of commerce. The natural philosophers used mathematics as a way of seeking truth.

Triumphs of Greek Science

Science is an attempt to understand and explain the world around us. The modern scientific method—a combination of observation, hypothesis, experiment, and theory—was established in the 17th century. But its roots lie with the ancient Greeks, who were among the first to think scientifically and search for plausible answers to life's mysteries through logic and observation.

« BEFORE

Some of the scientific ideas of the Greeks had been considered by earlier civilizations.

RATIONAL THOUGHT
In ancient India and China, philosophers thought about the world rationally, explaining causes of events by "laws," rather than myth.

EGYPTIAN ASTRONOMY
In Mesopotamia, the Babylonians and Egyptians had writing systems and calendars, and managed **impressive construction projects** **« 70–71** that required **exact measurements**.

EGYPTIAN CONSTELLATIONS

the few substances that we can observe directly changing between these three states. Another philosopher, Anaximenes (585–525 BCE), suggested that air was the "fundamental" substance, while Heraclitus (535–475 BCE) thought fire might fit the role. Inevitably, a more sophisticated and believable theory emerged, drawing on those that had gone before—the theory of the four elements, put forward by Empedocles (490–430 BCE). This theory explained many common phenomena in terms of the movement and interaction of air, earth, fire, and water.

Toward the end of the 5th century BCE, a new approach emerged. Leucippus

Euclid's theories
Euclid of Alexandria, a Greek mathematician (c. 325–c. 265 BCE) living in Egypt, wrote a geometry book called *The Elements* (a folio of which is shown here). His ideas on geometry and number theory remain key to mathematics today.

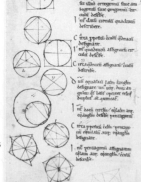

right or wrong, or even plausible, but that the people who constructed them were thinking rationally and philosophically, and were making observations to satisfy human curiosity. That can be seen as the true essence of science, and it had been missing from almost all earlier civilizations.

Philosophers in the ancient civilizations of India and China also employed reason and observation in their attempts to understand the world. They, too, formulated convincing theories similar to the theory of the four elements and atomic theory. In many cases, they made key discoveries before the Greeks. But the lineage of Western scientific thinking leads directly back to ancient Greece.

Science counts

Thales, and many of the other natural philosophers, importantly used

Some philosophers derived elegant mathematical proofs that provided insight into the nature of the world. One of them, Pythagoras (see above), went one step farther, suggesting not only that numbers describe reality, but that the world is literally made of numbers. Pythagoras was fascinated by the mathematical relationships between everything, including musical notes. The connection between mathematics and reality is still a central theme in science today.

Mathematics was also crucial to the scientific ideas of Plato (c. 427–c. 347 BCE), better known for his writings on ethics and politics. He suggested that each element is made of atoms with a particular idealized geometric shape. Plato supposed that the real world was an imperfect reflection of an ideal, "theoretical" and mathematically perfect world.

The Greek philosopher who had the greatest influence on the history of science was

The weight of the world
Legend has it that the Greek god Atlas was made by Zeus to hold up the universe as a punishment. This was the sort of idea that the Greek thinkers began to question, with their rational, scientific investigations and theories.

Many of the advances and ideas put forward by the ancient Greeks were lost in the centuries that followed. In many cases, it was not until relatively modern times that they were considered again.

ROMAN SCIENCE
Greek scientific knowledge was used by the Romans, although much was later lost and they tended not to be great theoretical thinkers.

ARAB SCIENTISTS
The ideas of the Greek natural philosophers passed to Arab scholars. In particular, the **Arabs translated the works of Aristotle into Arabic**. Great Arabic philosophers, such as Avicenna and Averroes, extended classical Greek thinking and added their own ideas and observations **174–77 》**.

MAPPA MUNDI

THE CATHOLIC CHURCH
Aristotle's flawed theories were **accepted as fact** by the Catholic Church in Europe, which dramatically set back scientific progress.

MEDIEVAL SCHOLARS
Geographical knowledge was revived with maps of the world (*Mappa Mundi*). This 11th-century example is from Winchester.

SCIENTIFIC REVOLUTION
In the 17th and 18th centuries, many **new thinkers** revived the spirit of scientific approach **266–67 》**.

NEW NATURAL PHILOSOPHY
Today, ancient Greek ways of thinking about matter and energy are still relevant; scientists of physics and chemistry ask much the same questions as Thales, Plato, and Aristotle.

Aristotle (384–322 BCE), a pupil of Plato. Aristotle reversed his teacher's idea about the role of mathematics. He maintained that truth was to be found only in reality—an idea known as empiricism. The theories of both remain important in scientific thinking today.

Using logic and observation, Plato and Aristotle deduced many previously unknown scientific facts. For example, they proved that Earth is round, not flat. Aristotle was perhaps the most prolific of the Greek natural philosophers. He wrote texts on a range of subjects, including botany, zoology, astronomy, anatomy, and physics. Aristotle's theories were plausible and well thought out, but were based on common sense, rather

MATHEMATIKA The ancient Greek word for "mathematics" is derived from a more general Greek word, *mathema*, which means "learning" or "study."

than rigorous logic and careful observation. Unfortunately, many were later discovered to be seriously flawed.

Later developments
During the final phase of the ancient Greek period in the 3rd and 2nd centuries BCE, great thinkers began to come full circle, applying the tools of Greek natural philosophy—mathematics and logic—to practical and technical challenges. For example, Archimedes (c. 287–c. 212 BCE) was a brilliant theoretical mathematician, but also a great engineer and inventor. Further developments were made at institutions such as the Museum and Library at Alexandria. Competition between centers of learning led to further innovations and the development of science.

INVENTION

HIPPOCRATIC OATH

The ancient Greeks' scientific way of thinking extended to the study of medicine. More than anyone, the physician Hippocrates (c. 460–c. 370 BCE), promoted a rational, scientific approach to medicine, giving it a firm footing as a professional endeavor. He placed importance on the careful observation of symptoms, and rejected traditional temple medicine theories about illnesses and their cures.

Even today, the ethical "contract" between doctors and patients is known as the Hippocratic Oath. We do not know whether Hippocrates was the author of the original, with promises to work "for the good of my patients according to my ability and my judgment and never do harm to anyone." It is preserved on papyri of later periods, such as this 3rd-century example discovered in Egypt.

« BEFORE

Before the rise of Rome, Italy was inhabited by several cultural groups. One of these was a Latin-speaking people who settled in villages, including Rome, in the hills above the Tiber River in about 1000 BCE.

EARLY DAYS
In the 8th century BCE, the highly developed **Etruscan civilization** flourished and spread across much of Italy; the Greeks established city-states in southern Italy and Sicily **« 94–95**; the Latin communities became more complex and Rome began to take shape as an important city.

ETRUSCAN RIDERS

THE BIRTH OF ROME
The date 753 BCE is traditionally given for the founding of the city of Rome. In legend, **Romulus and Remus**, twin brothers who were suckled by a she-wolf as babies, founded Rome. Romulus was also the name of the city's first king.

ROMULUS AND REMUS

The Rise of Rome

Ancient Roman civilization arose from multicultural beginnings, while Rome itself began life as a group of villages on the hills above the Tiber River. From these foundations arose the powerful Roman Republic, whose influence and territories spread around the world, with the great city of Rome at its heart.

B y 600 BCE, Rome had become a sophisticated city-state ruled by kings. It boasted specialized crafts, a rich aristocracy, monumental buildings, and organized social systems. The king ruled alongside a Senate and an Assembly. The Senate was a council of elders composed of the heads of various clans. It had the power to approve or veto the appointment of the king. The Assembly consisted of all male citizens of Rome; citizenship was granted only to those whose parents were native Romans. The Assembly's main function was to grant absolute power to the monarch once the clan leaders approved the candidate for king.

Rome stood at the crossroads of major trade routes connecting Europe with Asia and North Africa. Trade not only generated great commercial wealth for Rome, butt also brought the Romans in regular contact with several different cultures, such as the Greeks, from whom the Romans absorbed diverse influences. The Romans' Etruscan neighbors also had a profound effect on Rome, so much so that from the middle of the 6th century BCE the Roman monarchs were Etruscan. The Etruscans gave the Romans the toga, art, certain religious practices, forms of stone arch (see left), sewage systems, and chariot racing. The Greek influence, often passed on via the Etruscans, was strong in art and architecture (see pp.116–17), philosophy, and science and technology (see pp.104–05). The Etruscans also passed the Greek alphabet to the Romans, who developed it to create the basis for many modern western languages.

Roman engineering
The ancient Romans made considerable advances in building and civil engineering, mainly by clever development of principles obtained from other civilizations they came in contact with. While using fired bricks, tiles, and stone to great effect, they also perfected concrete, developing a form capable of hardening under water. From the 3rd century BCE , Roman builders became the first to use

INVENTION
THE ARCH

The Romans did not invent the arch, but they took its structural possibilities to entirely new levels. They became adept at working with the form and related structures such as the vault and dome, to help support monumental temples, amphitheaters, walls, aqueducts, viaducts, tunnels, lighthouses, and watermills. The Pons Aemilius (below) is the oldest stone bridge across the Tiber River in Rome, and dates from the 2nd century BCE.

CARTHAGINIAN GENERAL (247–182 BCE)
HANNIBAL BARCA

Hannibal fought with great valor against the Roman Republic in the Second Punic War (218–201 BCE). He captured the city of Saguntum in Spain, allied to Rome, then advanced on Italy. With Rome blocking the sea routes, Hannibal took 37 elephants and 35,000 men over the Pyrenees and Alps, as shown in this fresco. Despite heavy losses, he won many victories but was defeated at Zama in North Africa. Carthage was destroyed by the Romans, and Hannibal fled to Syria, where he later committed suicide.

Mixing business and ritual
This relief of the 1st century BCE shows animals being sacrificed to mark a census of citizens, which was done every few years. The figure in the toga (right of altar) is probably the censor (the magistrate taking the census).

The Romans' treatment of conquered peoples varied greatly. To those who seemed to them "civilized" enough and close in kinship, they granted rights similar to those of Roman citizens. Those who actively resisted them received much harsher treatment. Both these approaches were seen as effective ways of enforcing power and influence.

> **REPUBLIC** A society not ruled by a monarch in which power is shared between the aristocracy and the common people. The modern term is taken from the Latin *res publica*: "the public thing."

Mounting problems

Despite its extensive lands, by the 2nd century BCE, Rome was in a state of perpetual war, flux, and social discontent. Farms fell into disrepair while their owners were away fighting, and debts were mounting. While the city of Rome was at the heart of a growing empire, tensions arose as the republic's existing social and political institutions struggled to address new problems. The tensions reached a peak in 137 BCE when the Gracchi brothers, Tiberius and Gaius (tribunes of the Plebeians, or officials who represented Plebeian interests), pitted themselves against the Patrician Senate by proposing revolutionary social reform that included redistributing public land to the landless poorer classes. Armed struggle broke out and both brothers ended up dead. It was an episode that signaled the beginning of the Roman Republic's decline.

Senators
Members of the Senate were men of considerable personal wealth and standing and wore a toga with a broad stripe (*tunica laticlavia*).

Equestrians
These were upper/middle class men of wealth, often described as "knights." They wore a toga with a narrow stripe (*tunica angusticlavia*).

Plebeians
The common "class" included every freeborn male citizen not a senator or equestrian. It varied from the unskilled poor to wealthy merchants.

Latins
Latins were freeborn citizens from parts of Italy outside Rome. They had certain legal rights and were granted a form of Roman citizenship.

Foreigners
Freeborn inhabitants of Roman territory outside Italy were considered foreigners. They were granted a form of citizenship in the 3rd century CE.

Freedmen
Slaves who had been "manumitted" (liberated, via a specific ceremony, by their masters). They had rights, but their status changed over time.

Slaves
The non-free who had no rights and were bought and sold by their owners. Slaves were considered personal property under Roman law.

Roman social order
Roman society had strict class divisions. These were influenced by family background, wealth, citizenship, and freedom. The system frequently sparked controversy and dissent. Women had virtually no rights and belonged to the same class as their father or husband.

---

concrete extensively, constructing many large-scale engineering and building projects.

The coming of the Republic

Rome was ruled by seven kings before the last one, the Etruscan Tarquinius, was overthrown in 509 BCE in a coup staged by Roman aristocrats. Rather than install a new monarch, the Romans dismantled the institution and Rome became a republic.

The early republic had two consuls (to counter overreliance on one individual), who were elected annually. While the Senate was originally put in place to prevent despotism, it became the true decision-making authority. The law was upheld by magistrates, who also came from the Senate. These public figures were expected to show loyalty to the republic, self-sacrifice for the general good, and lead blameless lives as an example to others.

Citizens and slaves

Roman republican society was divided into the free and non-free (slaves). The most significant free people were citizens, who were able to elect the consuls. Citizens were further divided into Patricians (an elite landowning class), and Plebeians (all other citizens). The Senate drew its members from the Patrician class; therefore, the Republic in its early form

was largely a transfer of power from the king to the wealthiest classes in Rome. Rising Plebeian resentment at this often led to violence in a class conflict that became known as the "struggle of the orders."

The Patricians relied on the Plebeians, as they not only produced the food and supplied the labor that drove the Roman economy, but also formed the ranks in the Roman army (see pp.114–115). This reliance led the ruling classes to bring about social reforms. These included the "Twelve Tables" laws (most of the evidence of these laws is now lost to us), the election of the first Plebeian Council in 366 BCE, and the passing of a ruling in 287 BCE that the Plebeian Council's decisions would henceforth be binding for all citizens, including the Patricians. Rome's non-free people were slaves. From the 3rd century BCE the Romans used slave labor on a large scale for building projects.

Young boy and boar
Figurine of a young Roman boy in a tunic leading a sacrificial boar. This boy was probably a slave or attendant.

Military success

Roman armies won extensive lands for the Republic in wars that gradually took place farther afield and with increasing scale. By 264 BCE, Rome emerged from clashes with surrounding communities to dominate Italy, and by 146 BCE Rome had crushed the Carthaginians (see box left) in the Punic Wars, which broke out several times in the 3rd and 2nd centuries BCE, to dominate the entire western Mediterranean.

AFTER

The Roman Republic experienced great conflict in the 1st century BCE.

TIME OF TURMOIL
The 1st century BCE saw a mix of new gains and intensifying civil strife. Some of Rome's former allies, having fought for the republic, became

THE DEATH OF SPARTACUS

frustrated by Rome's domination over them and failure to grant them Roman citizenship.

SULLA'S DICTATORSHIP
The years 82–80 BCE brought the self-proclaimed **dictatorship of Sulla**. His struggles with rival Marius had already weakened the republic and

his rule increased patrician (upper class) power. During his dictatorship there were heightened levels of corruption within the Senate.

THE SLAVE REVOLT
In 72–71 BCE, Spartacus, a former auxiliary in the Roman army turned slave-gladiator, became **leader of a group of disaffected slaves** and rebels (see above) that swelled to around 120,000; they fought the Romans and dominated much of southern Italy. The Romans were ultimately victorious and **Spartacus was killed** in around 70 BCE. However, the uprising showed the dangers of employing slave labor on a massive scale.

ROMAN LEADER Born 100 BCE Died 44 BCE

Julius Caesar

"I love the name of **honor,** more than **I fear death**" JULIUS CAESAR

G aius Julius Caesar was born into a patrician (upper-class) Roman family of ancient lineage; he liked to trace his ancestry back to the kings of early Rome and the Roman goddess of love, Venus. The *gens Iulia* (the Julian family) were, however, neither especially powerful nor wealthy. Caesar grew up amid the intense political conflicts that wracked the declining Roman Republic (see pp.108–109). Aligned through his family and marriage with the reforming *populares* who wanted to break the power of the senate and empower a wider group of people from the lower classes, headed by his uncle Gaius Marius, Caesar was lucky to escape with his life when the group's rivals, the conservative *optimates*, triumphed under Sulla in 81 BCE. This setback slowed the career progress of the ambitious young patrician, for he was in his mid-30s before he achieved prominence.

Western hero
This imperious statue of Caesar was made in 17th-century France and is now in the Louvre, Paris. Caesar is a hero of Western civilization, partly through his own accounts of his military campaigns.

The first cesarean
A 14th-century illustration shows Caesar being born by cesarean section. This form of delivery is named after Caesar, although historians do not believe he was born by way of this procedure.

When Caesar's name did begin to attract attention, it was at first as much for scandal as for talent. He was a blatant womanizer notorious for his affairs with married women—he may have been the natural father of one of his eventual assassins, Marcus Brutus. In pursuit of public office, he spent far beyond his resources and fell heavily into debt. His political stance was that of a flamboyant populist, embracing policies such as the distribution of land to war veterans and the poor. He was widely distrusted among the Roman elite as unprincipled in the pursuit of money and power.

The conquest of Gaul
In 60 BCE, Caesar made a private agreement with the wealthy and powerful general and politician Marcus Licinius Crassus, and Pompey, Rome's most successful general, to work together to dominate Roman politics. Caesar was the junior member of the alliance (the Triumvirate), but it earned him election to the consulship, the most important office of state. This was followed by the appointment to

JULIAN CALENDAR

Based on a lunar calendar, the Roman year was only 355 days long, and was adjusted by occasional extra months. Caesar introduced a 12-month year of 365 days, with a 366-day leap year once every four years. To align Rome with the solar cycle, 46 BCE was made into a 445-day year. The Julian calendar then came into force in 45 BCE. It was in general use in Europe until the Gregorian calendar was introduced in 1582, and is still used by the Greek Orthodox Church.

The heart of the republic
The Forum, the heart of Rome, is where Caesar's supporter, Mark Antony, delivered a funeral oration over his body after the assassination. A temple to Caesar was later erected on the spot where he was cremated.

"I came, I saw, I conquered."

JULIUS CAESAR AFTER BATTLE OF ZELA

command in the Roman provinces of Gaul. There he showed outstanding energy and ruthlessness in years of campaigning against the Celtic and Germanic tribes of the region. Caesar went beyond the borders of his provincial command, making forays across the Rhine in Germany and north as far as the Thames River in Britain. Victories brought him both wealth and renown. They also gave him an instrument for attaining power: he shared the hardships and dangers of his legions on the march and in battle, praised and rewarded them, and in return they were loyal to him rather than to the Republic.

Rome's civil war

In late 50 BCE the Senate, under the control of Pompey, the distinguished military leader, called on Caesar to disband his army after his ten-year command in Gaul had come to a successful conclusion. Instead, Caesar

led his legions across the Rubicon, the stream separating Cisalpine Gaul (the region to the south of the Alps) from Italy proper. Easily occupying Rome, he took on Pompey in an armed struggle for control of the Roman world. After two years of fighting, the battle of Pharsalus in August 48 proved decisive for Caesar. Pompey escaped from the scene of his defeat, only to be murdered a month later in Egypt. Although Pompey's sons, Sextus and Gnaeus, continued the civil war until 45 BCE, Caesar's outstanding military skills had won him the supreme power he sought.

Reform and power

During his brief reign, Caesar revealed a zeal for innovation and reform. He halved the number of Roman citizens dependent on handouts of bread from the state by resettling the destitute in colonies in Italy and abroad, and reformed the calendar, see above. Yet he also exhibited great arrogance. For example, the Republic had in the past appointed a temporary "dictator," a leader with exceptional power

Caesar's death
Brutus steps forward to stab Caesar in this painting by 19th-century artist Vincenzo Camaccini. According to Latin author Suetonius, Caesar said: "You too, my child?", indicating that Brutus may have been his son.

Caesar's column
This column marks the place outside Rimini, Italy, where Caesar crossed the Rubicon in 49 BCE.

to cope with an emergency, but Caesar permanently assumed the role, and advertised the fact on coins.

Brutal assassination

In March 44 Caesar planned to lead an army on a campaign against the Parthians in the Middle East. A group of senators led by Gaius Cassius Longinus and Marcus Junius Brutus, inspired by an idealistic attachment to the Republic, and the desire to defend their own privileges, conspired to kill him before he left Rome. They stabbed him in the assembly hall, where he had come to address the Senate. Ironically, his death brought about the end of the Republic his assassins were trying to restore, and two years after his death, the Senate made him a deity. He is remembered today as a skilled orator, author, and military leader.

- **July 12 or 13, 100 BCE** Gaius Julius Caesar is born into a patrician family in Rome.
- **87** Caesar's uncle by marriage, the famous general Gaius Marius, seizes power in Rome.
- **83** Caesar marries Cornelia, the daughter of powerful patrician, Cinna; he becomes high priest of Jupiter.
- **81** Sulla, the enemy of Marius and Cinna, becomes dictator of Rome; dismissed from his priesthood, Caesar is forced into hiding.
- **80** Caesar takes refuge in Bithynia in Asia Minor, where it is alleged he becomes the lover of the Bithynian king, Nicomedes IV.
- **78** After Sulla's death, Caesar returns to Rome.
- **75** Kidnapped by pirates on a voyage to Rhodes, Caesar is ransomed. He then catches and crucifies his kidnappers.
- **69** After the death of his first wife, Caesar marries Pompeia, granddaughter of Sulla.
- **65** Appointed *curule aedile* (a public office of the Republic responsible for, among other things, the regulation of public festivals), Caesar courts popularity by organizing lavish festivities.
- **63** Caesar is elected *pontifex maximus*, chief priest of the Roman state religion; Cicero, the statesman, accuses him of involvement in the Catiline conspiracy, led by the Roman politician Catullus, and aiming to take over the republic.
- **62** Caesar divorces Pompeia.
- **60** Returning from a spell as governor of Further Spain, Caesar makes a deal to share power in Rome with Pompey and Crassus, forming the First Triumvirate.

COIN SHOWING CAESAR

- **59** Caesar's daughter Julia marries Pompey; he marries his third wife, Calpurnia. He is granted a five-year governorship of Cisalpine Gaul and Illyricum (in modern Albania); Transalpine Gaul is soon added to his command.
- **58** Caesar begins his conquest of Gaul by defeating the Helvetii tribesmen and Germanic king Ariovistus.
- **55–54** Caesar twice invades Britain and twice bridges the Rhine; his command in Gaul is extended for another five years.
- **January 10, 49** Defying a call from the Senate to disband his army at the end of his governorship, Caesar crosses the Rubicon (Fiumicino) into Italy, precipitating civil war.
- **June 23, 47** The Ptolemaic Queen Cleopatra, gives birth to Caesarion, probably Caesar's son.
- **August 47** Caesar defeats Pharnaces, king of Pontus and the Bosporus, at the battle of Zela.
- **March 45** Caesar defeats the last of Pompey's army at Munda in Spain, ending the civil war.
- **February 15, 44** Appointed dictator for life.
- **March 15, 44** Caesar assassinated by a group of conspirators set on restoring the Republic.

« BEFORE

POMPEY

The end of the Roman Republic was a long process, marked by the death of Julius Caesar in 44 BCE and Octavian's rise to power in 30 BCE.

POMPEY'S CONQUESTS

From 67 to 60 BCE, the great Roman general Pompey defeated pirates across the Mediterranean, gained lands for Rome in the Middle East, and formed the First Triumvirate alliance with Marcus Licinius Crassus and Julius Caesar.

THE RISE OF JULIUS CAESAR

By 51 BCE, Caesar was a major political figure **« 108–09**. The Roman Senate and Julius Caesar's former ally, Pompey, felt increasingly threatened by his growing power. In 49 BCE, Caesar took Rome, and war broke out between his and the Senate's forces, now led by Pompey. **Pompey was murdered** by allies of Caesar, who in 45 BCE became dictator for life–Rome's most powerful leader to date.

BLOODY TENSIONS

In 44 BCE, **Caesar was murdered** by a group of senators. His successors–the Roman general Mark Antony, and Octavian, Caesar's adopted son–became unable to work together, and divided Rome's empire into west (Octavian), and east (Antony). Friction between the two sparked **civil war**, further weakening the republic.

FADING OF THE REPUBLIC

Octavian defeated Mark Antony and Cleopatra **120–21 »** at the **Battle of Actium**, in 31 BCE. A year later, Octavian took over Egypt and became supreme in the Roman state.

PORTRAIT OF MARK ANTONY

The Roman World

The Roman Empire reached its greatest extent in 117 CE, at the start of the reign of emperor Hadrian (ruled 117–138 CE), as shown by this map. The great structures for which Rome has become famed–from walls and aqueducts to amphitheaters and temples–appeared all over the empire, and many still survive today.

The Colosseum, Rome, is a massive amphitheater that was originally called the Flavian amphitheater, as it was built by the Flavian emperors. The site of countless gladiatorial combats, its formal opening in 80 CE was marked by 100 days of gladiatorial games.

Emperor Hadrian supervised the building of this wall, which bears his name. Built on the northern border of the empire, Hadrian's Wall stretched for almost 75 miles (120 km), coast to coast across northern Britain.

Mosaics, buildings, and streets have survived at the site of the Roman city of Italica, close to modern Seville.

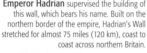

The Pont du Gard aqueduct (an artificial waterway) was built *c.* 19 BCE to carry water from Ucetia (Uzès) to Nemausus (Nîmes), France. With three tiers of arches and a height of nearly 165 ft (50 m), it was the highest aqueduct built by the Romans.

Mount Vesuvius erupted in 79 CE, burying Pompeii in ash (see p.112). It preserved a typical Roman town, complete with villas decorated with wall paintings, such as this example depicting a Roman girl.

The temple of Jupiter near Sbeitla, Tunisia, is one part of the impressive remains of the ancient Roman city of Sufetula, which probably originated as a fort during campaigns against Numidian rebels.

Map labels:

North Sea
78 CE
BRITANNIA 43 CE
Londinium
GERMANIA INFERIOR
GERMANIA SUPERIOR 83 CE
GERMANIA
Colonia Agrippina
Mogontiacum
Augusta Vindelicorum
Durocortorum
BELGICA
PANNONIA SUPERIOR 9 CE
Carnuntum
Aquineum
MOES INFER
ATLANTIC OCEAN
LUGDUNENSIS
RAETIA 58 CE
NORICUM 15 BCE
PANNONIA INFERIOR 9 CE
DACIA 106 CE
Virunum
Sarmizegetusa
Singidunum
GALLIA
Octodurum
ALPES GRAIAE ET POENINAE
ILLYRICUM
MOESIA SUPERIOR 29 BCE
Oescus
AQUITANIA 58–51 BCE
Burdigala
Lugdunum
Segusio
DALMATIA
Salonae 33 BCE
THRACIA 46 BCE
NARBONENSIS
121 BCE
Nemausus Ucetia
Cemenelum
ALPES COTTIAE
ALPES MARITIMAE
ITALIA
Rome
Ostia
MACEDONIA 146 BCE
Thessalon
27 BCE
Narbo
Pyrenees
197 BCE
TARRACONENSIS
Tarraco
SARDINIA ET CORSICA 238 BCE
Pompeii
EPIRUS 140 BCE
Nicopolis
Corinth
ACHAEA 146 BCE
HISPANIA
LUSITANIA 27 BCE
Emerita Augusta 181 BCE
BAETICA
Italica Corduba
197 BCE
Carales
Mediterranean Sea
SICILIA
Syracuse
Tingis
Caesarea
MAURETANIA CAESARIENSIS
Carthage
Sbeitla
AFRICA (PROCONSULARIS) 146 BCE
CR
MAURETANIA TINGITANA 44 CE
44 CE
NUMIDIA 48 BCE
Cyrene 74 BCE
CYRENAI
AFRICA
Leptis Magna 107 BCE
CRE

The remains of a colonnaded street (cardo maximus) at Apamea in Syria are 475 feet (145 m) long. The street would have been lined along both sides with buildings for public use.

By 27 BCE Octavian was, in effect, the empire's first "Emperor," taking the title Augustus (see pp.112). The Romans themselves did not consider that the republic ended with Caesar's death, and when Augustus came to power he did not paint himself as an all-powerful emperor figure. Instead, he claimed to have restored the republic and to have returned power to the Senate and the people. Augustus represented himself as "first among equals" with his fellow senators, although, in reality, he held supreme power.

The empire of Augustus started out with republican pretensions (rule by the Senate and Roman people), but while Augustus retained parts of the existing system, he grafted his own autocracy onto it. The republic's system of rule, based on competition among aristocratic families, was replaced by an imperial one in which a single aristocratic family dominated.

A worldwide empire

By the late 1st century CE, and the time of the emperor Trajan (ruled 98–117 CE), Rome headed an empire

praetors, who ruled in the emperor's name. By the 3rd century CE, separate leaders often attended to military matters. Within these provinces, cities looked much like Roman ones and were run according to a Roman-style system of law. One key feature of the 2nd-century empire was the rising status of these provinces and their great cities—for example, Ephesus in Asia Minor and Leptis Magna in North Africa (see map, left).

The urban centers of imperial Rome were linked by an impressive transport and communication network made

From **Republic** to **Empire**

As the structures of the republican system gave way to the empire, Rome found itself in command of vast, worldwide territories. The empire encompassed a diverse mix of peoples, and its politics, way of life, artistic achievements, and spectacular feats of engineering have had a lasting impact.

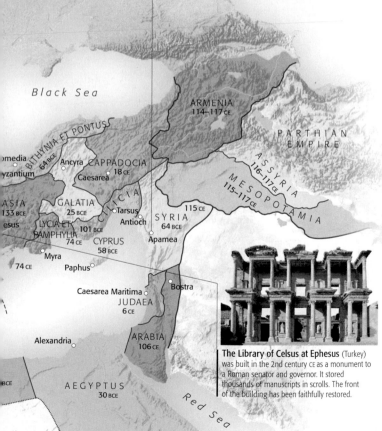

The Library of Celsus at Ephesus (Turkey) was built in the 2nd century CE as a monument to a Roman senator and governor. It stored thousands of manuscripts in scrolls. The front of the building has been faithfully restored.

KEY

DACIA — Province in reign of Hadrian
107 CE — Date of conquest or annexation by Rome
——— Boundary of Roman Empire
——— Province boundary
o — Provincial capital

of great wealth, which stretched across a vast area that took in all of the Mediterranean, the Middle East, and a large chunk of northern and central Europe. In the first two centuries of imperial rule, there were probably around 50 million people living in Roman lands.

The bulk of these lands were conquered during the days of the republic. The empire consolidated these areas and added a few new provinces, although these new acquisitions were also the first to be given up later on. Britain, Dacia (modern Romania), Assyria, and Mesopotamia (Iraq) were short-lived gains compared to other territories. Roman rulers were quick to crush any rebellion or threat (from outside or from within), often brutally. This is one reason why the empire was relatively stable during this time.

The expansion that was achieved was greatly helped by the work of emperors such as Trajan and Claudius. Another major factor in maintaining these lands was the Romans' legendary military might. Crucially, the empire had a standing army, unlike during much of the republic. Its soldiers were a professional, highly organized, and skilled machine, and loyal to the emperor (see pp.114–15).

An urban civilization

Ancient Roman civilization was highly urbanized, with a vast network of prosperous cities, filled with beautiful buildings that usually mirrored the city of Rome itself, such as temples and a public forum. The empire's extensive territories were divided into provinces ruled by governors called proconsuls or

possible by the Romans' unique talent for engineering—new roads, bridges, viaducts, harbors, and aqueducts were built throughout the empire.

"Warehouse of the world"

Good communication links also aided the empire's trade, although the road system often proved slow and Roman trade came into its own much more through the use of maritime transport. Rome's huge empire meant that it had at its command a »

INVENTION

THE ROAD SYSTEM

The empire was connected by thousands of miles of expertly made roads, typically consisting of stone slabs laid over rubble. Vital for allowing soldiers to move around as fast as possible—which is why Roman roads are often straight—they helped to control the vast territories. Much of the network in Italy centered on Rome, hence the proverb "All roads lead to Rome." Many Roman roads survive today, some in good condition—such as the Appian Way in Rome (below) which linked Rome with southeastern Italy.

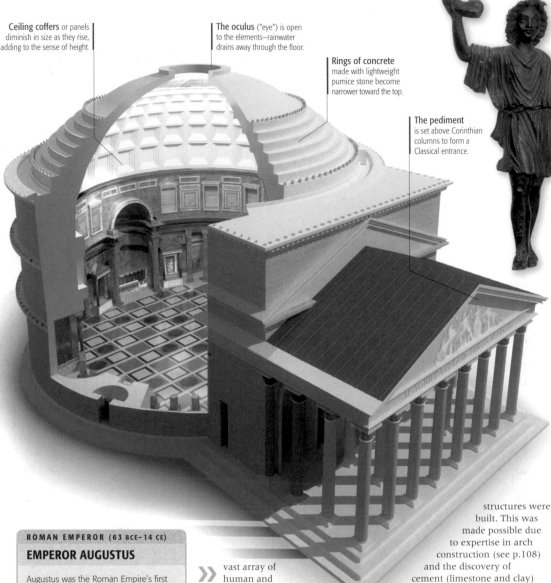

Ceiling coffers or panels diminish in size as they rise, adding to the sense of height.

The oculus ("eye") is open to the elements—rainwater drains away through the floor.

Rings of concrete made with lightweight pumice stone become narrower toward the top.

The pediment is set above Corinthian columns to form a Classical entrance.

Bronze household god
The Romans worshipped a variety of ancestral gods (*lares* and *penates*) as guardians of their homes. This bronze statuette holds a drinking horn, a typical attribute of a household god.

of Augustus (the city's principal public meeting place); Trajan's Column, completed in 113 CE, with reliefs celebrating two victories over the Dacians; and Constantine's Arch, finished in 315 CE, to mark the military might of Emperor Constantine I. The triumphal arch is a form that the Roman Empire made its own, and it has been copied up to the present day.

Life in the Roman Empire
Everyday life continued in many ways as it had done during the republic. Male citizens had varying freedoms, while women were mainly confined to the domestic arena. Slaves, with no

The Pantheon
Created as a temple in the 2nd century CE, the Pantheon in Rome is famed for its dome, the largest until modern times. Over 70 ft (21 m) high, with a diameter of over 140 ft (43 m), cement mixed with pumice near the top of the dome helps support the structure.

HOW WE KNOW

POMPEII

In August 79 CE, a massive eruption of Mount Vesuvius buried the nearby Roman city of Campania (now called Pompeii) in southern Italy under 20 ft (6 m) of ash and debris. Buildings were buried and people smothered. Neighboring cities, such as Herculaneum, were similarly affected. Excavation has revealed a perfectly preserved example of a sophisticated Greco-Roman city of around 20,000 people, with buildings such as a forum, amphitheater, and lavish villas. Even the remains of loaves in bakers' ovens were preserved. Many human bodies left their shapes in the ash, from which plaster casts have since been made (below), showing Pompeii's people as they fell.

EMPEROR AUGUSTUS

Augustus was the Roman Empire's first emperor. He was born Octavian, and was Julius Caesar's grand-nephew and adopted son. After Caesar's death he assumed the title Augustus, a name that had religious implications, and Princeps, meaning "first citizen." He brought an end to civil war, and appeared to be restoring the republic to its glory days, but in reality ruled as an autocrat. He held power for 41 years of relative peace, heralding the start of the empire that was to last for over four centuries.

》 vast array of human and natural resources, and a diverse web of trading connections. Its provinces traded all kinds of basic and luxury goods with each other, ranging from salt to mass-produced statues—which is why ancient Rome is often called the "warehouse of the world."

Throughout its many provincial cities and towns, the empire brought into being some of the really great works of ancient Roman architecture, engineering, and art. Imperial-era buildings and monuments took the Romans' love of impressive grandeur to a peak, proclaiming their wealth and power to the world.

Augustus oversaw the transformation of Rome, saying he "found [it] a city of bricks and left it a city of marble." Many magnificent

structures were built. This was made possible due to expertise in arch construction (see p.108) and the discovery of cement (limestone and clay) to make concrete.

The concrete revolution
The Romans had already made great inroads with the use of concrete (see pp.106), and by the time of the empire were using it very skillfully on a large scale. The immense load-bearing capacities of concrete, along with further advances in the application of architectural elements like the arch, meant that they could produce massive structures such as Rome's Colosseum, the enormous dome of the Pantheon (above), long aqueducts and viaducts (bridges), and harbors such as Caesarea Maritima in Judea in the Middle East. Other monumental imperial structures include three famous sights in Rome—the Forum

50,000 The number of spectators that could fit into the Colosseum in Rome. It was built between *c.*72 and 82 CE to stage a variety of "entertainments," including battle reconstructions, gladiatorial combat, dramas, and executions.

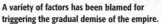

Port of Ostia
This great trading seaport lay at the mouth of the Tiber, close to Rome. Large merchant vessels unloaded goods onto barges to continue their journey into the city itself.

Hypocaust remains
These remains in a bathhouse reveal the Roman underfloor heating system (*hypocaust*). The floor, now gone, was raised by short pillars around which furnace-heated air circulated.

Mosaic
Wealthy Romans enjoyed fine interiors in their homes, such as this late-3rd-century mosaic from a villa in Sicily.

freedoms at all, were essential for keeping the wheels of Roman life running smoothly. In the country, up to a third of the population were slaves carrying out agricultural work to supply the towns and cities.

Housing took many different forms. The wealthy lived in magnificent villas with toilets, running water, and central heating. Often centered on a cool inner courtyard, these were filled with statues and artifacts (see pp.116–17) and decorated with beautiful mosaic floors and wall-paintings showing skill in the art of perspective—famous examples survive at Pompeii and in Rome itself, such as the House of Livia. These great houses were often designed and decorated by Greek artists living in these Roman cities. Such villas were the sites of lavish dinner parties. Food and drink was consumed on an excessive scale that has become legendary, and was accompanied by music and dancing.

Many poorer townspeople lived in crowded basic apartment blocks known as *insulae*. Remains of these buildings show similarities to modern apartment buildings, with uniform entrances and windows. The inhabitants of the *insulae* shared public toilet facilities.

Business, pleasure, and worship
Gathering for business or pleasure was a central part of Roman life. Meeting places such as markets, public "forum" areas, bath houses, and even communal toilets were popular spots, with private squalor offset by public grandeur. Meetings were often conducted outside, in open places, to discourage the secret plotting that characterized Roman rule.

Entertainment was also enjoyed in public arenas and theaters. This took the form of athletic games, gladiatorial combat, animal hunts, chariot races, plays and public execution of criminals. In the early centuries, the Romans of the empire believed in a range of gods and goddesses (see pp.142–43), both state and "household," to whom they built temples. For a long time these beliefs existed alongside the rising tide of Christianity (see pp.144–45).

Laws of the land
Augustus made some legal reforms, but the basic tenets of Roman law remained. Augustus had final say in determining if a law should be passed. Citizens charged with crimes often had patrons to defend them, and criminal law was administered by Roman magistrates. Punishments were harsh. By the first half of the 2nd century CE, Roman citizens pleading a miscarriage of justice were entitled to appeal to a higher court based in the city of Rome.

A variety of factors has been blamed for triggering the gradual demise of the empire.

ANTONINE PLAGUE
Around 165 CE, a plague (possibly smallpox), broke out in the empire and lasted for around 15 years. Huge numbers lost their lives—including two emperors. One consequence was a weakening of the social fabric of the empire.

5 MILLION The number of people estimated to have died of plague in the 2nd century CE.

476 Year the Roman Empire ended in the West.

THIRD-CENTURY CRISIS
The years from 235 to 284 CE were a chaotic time, with a **rapid succession of emperors** murdered one after the other. A variety of problems beset certain parts of the empire, including starvation, plague, inflation, high taxation, and "barbarian" attacks. Some regions, such as Gaul (France) and Britain, started to assert their own interests and threaten imperial authority. Such chaos made it easier for others to seize control, such as **Queen Zenobia** of Palmyra (modern Syria) in 272–73 CE.

DIOCLETIAN EDICT

FOUR EMPERORS
In 284 CE, the period of crisis in the 3rd century ended when Roman general **Diocletian** made himself emperor. He created the first imperial college of **four emperors** (the Tetrarchy) to oversee four sections of the empire. Diocletian issued an edict in 301 to attempt to stabilize the empire's economy. The second Tetrarchy broke down and partly prefigures the empire's later permanent split into east and west in 395 CE.

A SECOND ROME
In the early part of the 4th century CE, Roman emperor Constantine (280–337 CE) established a "second Rome" at Byzantium (modern Istanbul), renaming it Constantinople—a possible further cause of the empire's demise.

MOSAIC FROM CONSTANTINOPLE

Grooming kit
Wealthy Romans were well-groomed. This is a pocket set of tweezers, nail cleaner, and ear-scoop.

Gold coins
These coins, left in Kent, England, after the Roman invasion, represent over four years' pay for a Roman legionary. The owner may have intended to collect them in more settled times.

Silver ladle and spoon
Roman silverware came in various styles and showed great technical mastery.

Samian ware bowl
Bright red "Samian" pottery, known for its distinctive red coloring, was used widely during the early imperial period.

Gold bracelet
Snake-shaped bracelets were popular. This one dates from 1st-century CE Pompeii.

The Roman army was not a static organization but evolved over the centuries to meet diverse challenges and overcome new enemies. In its early days it resembled the ancient Greek hoplite army, which was primarily made up of men who volunteered to fight to protect their city. In Rome, changes began as soon as the empire expanded. By the time of Julius Caesar (see pp.108–09) in the 1st century, the army had become a well organized, mobile fighting force. The "classic" Roman army that we know most about today is that which Caesar (pp.108–109) began and Augustus (see p.112) honed. By the reign of Trajan (98–117 CE), this is the army that seemed unbeatable to its enemies.

A developing force

In the days of the early Republic (see pp.106–07) the army was staffed by volunteers from the aristocratic families. They provided their own weapons and uniform and trained for five or six years. Small units of men (centuries) worked as a team. They worked and lived together and fought with iron discipline, just as the Greek hoplites had done before them. As Roman power expanded, however, a professional army became vital. The general Marius (157–85 BCE) made many reforms, including opening the army to all. The practice of giving a piece of land to retired soldiers is also attributed to Marius. Caesar (100–44 BCE) oversaw a professional and well-led military force that Augustus (63 BCE–14 CE) maintained, with a stable number of legions to make up the army that would safeguard the empire. Length of service was standardized to 20 years. Every legion had an eagle standard (*aquila*).

Housesteads fort
This is the most complete Roman fort in Britain and was built c. 122 CE on Hadrian's Wall on the northern border of the empire.

a noble family, gained supremacy as a result of his outstanding military career.

All aspects of life were controlled by the army. Soldiers were not allowed to marry formally. If, however, they did take up with a local woman while stationed in a far-flung part of the empire, and they were together when

the nickname "Marius's Mules." Modern studies have estimated the weight based on rations for 16 days and a full set of equipment. At the end of a day spent on the march, they often had to set up a fortified military camp for the night, digging boundary ditches and setting up tents. Skilled engineers within the ranks also built bridges and roads, if necessary, in order to reach their destination. Training in physical fitness involved running, swimming,

The Roman Army

Perhaps nowhere can the formidable organization and ruthlessness of the Roman world be better seen than in its army. The professional standing army of several hundred thousand men at the height of the empire was a disciplined and well-trained fighting machine.

BEFORE

The Roman army was shaped by confronting enemies with successful armies of their own.

GREEK HOPLITE FORMATIONS
The ancient **Greek hoplites (infantry)** fought in organized formations. The hoplite "phalanx," in which they stood closely together with their shields locked together, allowed them to form **a united front** against the enemy—something the Roman army used during the republic.

ANCIENT GREEK HOPLITE SOLDIERS

SPARTAN POWER
From birth to death, life in Sparta **≪ 94–95** was tied to the army. Young boys were trained as soldiers, and the aim of the state was to produce a perfect and invincible hoplite army. Some of these values were echoed in the self-sacrifice demanded of Roman soldiers.

ALEXANDER'S ARMY
Alexander the Great's army of 30,000 infantry and 4,000 cavalry marched an average of over 20 miles (32 km) a day **≪ 96–97**.

The *aquilifer* (who carried the standard) was a coveted position. From this time, soldiers swore their allegiance to the emperor, which was key to ensuring their loyalty and in defending and protecting the empire's borders over the next two centuries.

TRIBUNE A junior officer.

CENTURION A soldier in control of each century of 80 men.

PRIMUS PILUS The chief centurion.

CUSTOS ARMORUM The soldier in charge of weapons and equipment.

LEGATUS LEGIONIS The commander of the legion.

PRAEFECTUS CASTRORUM The camp prefect, responsible for training and equipment.

IMMUNES Those who were excused from regular duties, including medical staff, surveyors, and armorers.

Life in the army

Although the life of a Roman soldier was dangerous and brutal, for many it was an escape from a life of poverty. It was also a way for those without money to gain political power and influence. Young men were expected to do military service as part of their education. Those from wealthier backgrounds saw the army as a step on the ladder to public office. One striking example of the positive effect a successful military career could have is Julius Caesar, who, although born into

he retired, she was given Roman citizenship in her own right.

Although the army was feared by many, it was scrupulously disciplined and generally dealt fairly with local people it came in contact with. Supplies were paid for, rather than taken, and a good general would not allow his troops to loot and pillage at random.

Fitness and training

New recruits had to be physically fit. They were expected to march up to 20 miles (30 km) a day, carrying all their equipment, which may have weighed 60 lb (30 kg) or more—earning them

wrestling, and throwing games. Exercises designed to build stamina might last for two days without rest. The men also practiced military drills and training, as in battle every soldier would be expected to follow commands and fight in formation. One of the most famous of these was the "tortoise" (*testudo*), in which rectangular blocs of soldiers stood together with their shields facing outward and upward toward the enemy.

The life of a Roman soldier was tough, but the discipline, effective leadership, and organization were key to its success for so long.

Army skills
Soldiers learned many skills. This roof tile, made by the 20th legion, features their charging boar emblem.

HOW WE KNOW

VINDOLANDA TABLET

These scraps of wood were found in a waterlogged trash pile near a Roman fort in northern England. They provide a detailed snapshot of life on the frontier of the empire from 97 to 103 CE. As well as personal letters from women and servants—including a birthday invitation—the tablets reveal details about the army. Work rotas, accounts, and reports give us an idea of everyday life as a Roman soldier.

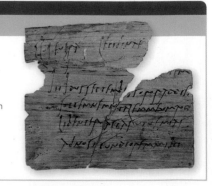

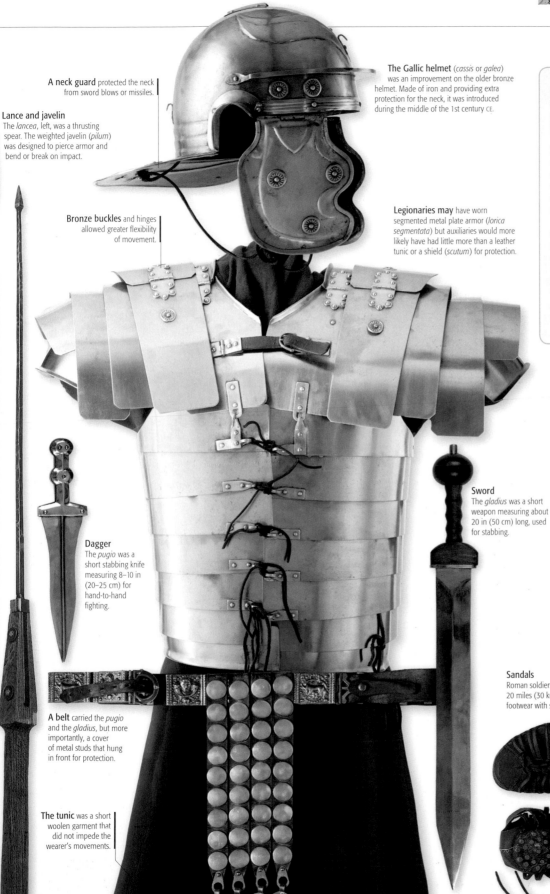

A neck guard protected the neck from sword blows or missiles.

Lance and javelin
The *lancea*, left, was a thrusting spear. The weighted javelin (*pilum*) was designed to pierce armor and bend or break on impact.

The Gallic helmet (*cassis* or *galea*) was an improvement on the older bronze helmet. Made of iron and providing extra protection for the neck, it was introduced during the middle of the 1st century CE.

Bronze buckles and hinges allowed greater flexibility of movement.

Legionaries may have worn segmented metal plate armor (*lorica segmentata*) but auxiliaries would more likely have had little more than a leather tunic or a shield (*scutum*) for protection.

Dagger
The *pugio* was a short stabbing knife measuring 8–10 in (20–25 cm) for hand-to-hand fighting.

Sword
The *gladius* was a short weapon measuring about 20 in (50 cm) long, used for stabbing.

A belt carried the *pugio* and the *gladius*, but more importantly, a cover of metal studs that hung in front for protection.

The tunic was a short woolen garment that did not impede the wearer's movements.

Sandals
Roman soldiers, who often marched 20 miles (30 km) a day wore leather footwear with steel studs.

AFTER »

The Roman army changed over time as enemies threatened the empire. The skills and legacy of the Roman army have influenced and inspired later fighting forces.

BARBARIANS AT THE GATE
After the middle of the 3rd century CE, the army was forced to evolve to deal with **new challenges at the frontiers**. The ability to adapt to changing conditions helped keep the empire together in difficult times **150–51 »**.

COMMUNICATION NETWORK
Much of the **road network**, built as the most direct route for the marching army, is still in use.

MODERN TANK WARFARE
The tank has taken the place of the tortoise as a **mobile fighting machine** and an armored unit to hold places of strategic importance.

ROMAN ARMY
146,720 MEN
28 LEGIONS

1 LEGION
5,240 MEN
10 COHORTS + 120 HORSEMEN

1 COHORT
480 MEN
6 CENTURIES

1 CENTURY
80 MEN
10 CONTUBERNIA

1 CONTUBERNIUM
8 MEN

Army organization
These figures are for the "classic" army of the 1st century CE. The total number, including auxiliaries such engineers, armorers, and doctors, may have been twice this size.

The Laocoön sculpture
This powerful group is one of the most famous of ancient classical sculptures. It may date from c. 200 BCE or later and the identity of its creator is uncertain. It shows the Trojan priest Laocoön and his two sons being attacked by snakes. One of the stories relating to Laocoön was that he was killed by serpents, along with his sons, as a punishment from the gods for having broken his vows of celibacy.

The sons look inward and upward toward their father, helping to create a balanced composition that focuses on the sculpture's main protagonist.

The twisting poses of the figures create a realistic sense of movement, and effectively express tortured writhing.

The agonized facial expression of Laocoön is one of the best examples of the increased realism in later ancient Greek art.

The human form is portrayed in marble in great realistic anatomical detail, although it remained within the idealized view of physical perfection.

The writhing serpents are shown wrapped around human limbs in a confusing mass that heightens the sense of torture.

BEFORE

Examples of early Greek art include striking symmetrical pottery and stone statues of idealized human forms.

EARLY POTTERY
Between the 10th and 8th centuries BCE, the "Geometric" style dominated Greek pottery. Its abstract, linear forms reveal the love of symmetry and proportion that was so important to Greek art.

GEOMETRIC STYLE VASE

ARCHAIC SCULPTURE
The "**Archaic**" period (c. 750–480 BCE) is famous for its *kouros* sculptures showing an idealized human form. These forward-facing nudes show the same symmetry as early Greek pottery. Bronze casting became popular in the 500s, which made side-on poses easier to create. This led to much greater realism in the sculpture of later periods.

KOUROS FIGURE

The art of the classical world took the form of statuary, painted pottery, wall paintings and mosaics, and architecture. In general, Roman art took the ideas of both the Greeks and the Etruscans (a people who dominated northern Italy by the 6th century BCE; see p.106) and developed it in new ways. While the Greeks loved idealized beauty, symmetry, and perfect proportion, the Romans showed a practical genius—clear in engineering feats such as the Colosseum (see pp.110–111). The Romans were influenced by Greek art through trading contacts and the changing fortunes of the Greek and Roman Empires: while the Greeks dominated parts of Italy in the Archaic era (see BEFORE), by 146 BCE, the

renders fabric with great realism. Polyclitus' *Doryphorus* (Spear Bearer) reveals a more realistic pose and musculature—informed by the Greeks' study of the human body, aided by observing naked athletes. It also displays a mathematically calculated ideal of beauty with perfectly proportioned limbs and body.

Realism

Classical styles continued into the Hellenistic period, but, while sculptures such as the famous Venus de Milo retain an ideal of female beauty, works

Classical black figure vase
Greek vases often had dark figures against a red clay background, as in this example, or red figures on black. The painters were highly skilled and the style evolved over time.

has been lost (except for vase painting), but many surviving Roman wall paintings give an idea of the lost art. Those from Pompeii (see p.112) and Herculaneum illustrate a particular talent for creating three-dimensional illusions of scenes such as mythological dramas on a flat surface, and for expertly rendering shading, highlights, and perspective.

AFTER

The art of ancient Greece and Rome has influenced many later cultures.

BYZANTINE ART
Domed buildings, perfected by the Romans, became a distinctive feature of the eastern Byzantine empire. The 6th-century CE church of Hagia Sophia, in the former Byzantine capital, Constantinople, is one example.

HAGIA SOPHIA, ISTANBUL

THE RENAISSANCE AND BEYOND
15th-century Europe rediscovered the art and architecture of Classical Greece and Rome **250–51 »**. Sculptors and painters, such as Raphael in Italy, gained a classical understanding of human anatomy, and architects created buildings informed by ancient Greek temples.

16TH-CENTURY PAINTING BY RAPHAEL

Classical Art

The art of ancient Greece and Rome—often known collectively as Classical Art—brought into being a wide range of different styles and approaches. These have had an enormous impact on Western art for many centuries, right up to the present day.

Romans controlled all of Greece. Generally speaking, art became more realistic over time, moving from the idealized form of the early period to the realism of the later Hellenistic period (c. 323–146 BCE).

Classical Greece
The Classical era of Greek history (c. 480–323 BCE) saw the flowering of "high Classical" art in an imperial Athens (see pp.100–01). The magnificent Parthenon temple (see pp.94–95) was built on the city's acropolis, adorned with sculptures created under the supervision of the sculptor Phidias. During the Classical period, sculpture began to show greater realism than the idealized style of earlier periods. Myron's *Discobolus* (Discus Thrower) is a masterly attempt to freeze realistic movement, and the unattributed Apollo Belvedere statue

were appearing filled with great emotion, dynamism, and expression—such as the Samothrace Nike (or Winged Victory), the Laocoön group (see left), and the Dying Gaul (see p.134).
Idealization and beauty now started to seem less important. Images appeared depicting characters from everyday life, such as a woman at a market or a boy strangling a goose.
Workshops in the ancient world at this time produced statues of all styles, in clay, marble, and bronze. These sold all over the world, to a rising number of private patrons. Before the Hellenistic era there had been little sense of "art" as a separate creative entity—statues were made to mark a grave, glorify a temple, or commemorate a war; vases often had practical uses. However, wealthy buyers who had seen statues of famous figures now wanted a portrait of themselves, or figures to decorate their villas. Seeing different styles gave rise to the first sense of a "history of art."

The art of Rome
Many of the Greek statues that survive today are actually Roman copies. In many ways the Romans simply copied the art of the Greeks, although they later went on to create their own artistic identity. Ancient Greek painting

The art of floor mosaics, using tiny pieces of colored stone (*tesserae*), was invented by the Greeks, but is the Romans who are famous for their mosaic work. Imperial Rome saw mosaic pavements and walls featuring ambitious schemes and imagery.
The Romans created monumental architecture and statues that celebrated the glories and wealth of their rule—Trajan's column and the Arch of Constantine, for example. Trajan's column was designed by a Greek architect, Apollodorus of Damascus, showing a continuing connection between Greek and Roman art. The Romans also used the Greek temple form, often placing it on a platform to make it more impressive and filling its panels with sculptures plundered from Greece. Their grand villas overflowed with statues, while Roman leaders used the power of art as propaganda. Without the Roman use of Greek art, much of its style and influence might have been lost to us.

> " **Beauty**consists in the proportions…"
>
> GALEN, GREEK PHYSICIAN, 129–C. 200 CE

ZEUXIS (5th century BCE) was one of ancient Greece's most famous painters. Ancient writers told a famous tale about Zeuxis painting an image of grapes that was so realistic that birds tried to peck it. Sadly, none of his work survives today.

Corinthian column
The Greeks created several different "orders" (styles) of columns for their buildings, which the Romans later adapted. This column is in the Greek Corinthian style, which was especially popular in Rome.

« BEFORE

After the New Kingdom « 64–65, Egypt suffered a series of invasions, until Alexander claimed it for himself.

BRIEF RENAISSANCE
The Assyrians « 65, 80–81 were ousted, and native Egyptian pharaohs presided over **a renaissance** of their culture—the Saite era, c. 664–525 BCE.

LATE PERIOD
Achaemenid Persians « 92–93 dominated in the years 525–400 BCE. Egyptians then ruled until 343 BCE, when the Persians returned to defeat **Nectanebo II**, the last native Egyptian pharaoh.

LATE-PERIOD EGYPTIAN GRAVE STATUE

ALEXANDER'S CONQUEST
In 332 BCE, **Alexander** « 96–97 seized Egypt from **Darius III** (the last Achaemenid king) when he conquered the Persian empire.

p.75) there had been a Greek presence in Egypt (see pp.116–17), and the Ptolemies—educated, like Alexander, as Greeks—created a distinctly Greek court and system of administration.

Cultural coexistence

The Ptolemies did not impose their culture on the Egyptians. While the ruling class enjoyed a Greek lifestyle, in all other layers of society, Egyptian culture continued much as before. Furthermore, the Greek rulers styled themselves as native monarchs, taking the title of pharaoh. They even built Egyptian-style temples, and worshipped native gods. The parallel Greek–Egyptian culture is illustrated by the Rosetta Stone, with its Greek, hieroglyphic, and demotic scripts (see p.62).

Ptolemaic rule

If the Ptolemies' cooperative policy was a shrewd political strategy, it paid off, because their rule brought stability to Egypt. Reforms were made to land

location opened Egypt up to the trade and cultures of the Mediterranean. With its library of legendary fame, it became the world's center of Greek learning.

The Romans

By the middle of the 1st century BCE, the Ptolemaic dynasty was weakened by leadership rivalries. Rome had been increasing its role in Egyptian affairs and was now effectively overseeing the country. Independence was completely lost in 30 BCE, when Cleopatra VII (see pp.120–21) the last Ptolemaic ruler, allied herself with the losing side in the power struggles in the Roman Republic (see pp.110–13). Octavian, the victorious Roman leader, incorporated Egypt as his own personal domain.

Alexandria continued to flourish and became a meeting point for Roman trade routes. It also remained a center for Greek culture, visited by scholars from across the Greek-speaking world. In the early days of Roman rule, the Egyptian government kept its strong

ALEXANDRIA HARBOR

In the 3rd century BCE, during Ptolemaic times, a great lighthouse was completed on Pharos Island, in the harbor of Egypt's cosmopolitan capital, Alexandria. This towering structure—destroyed by an earthquake during the medieval period—was one of the Seven Wonders of the ancient world. During the 1990s, archaeologists made some incredible finds underwater, including possible masonry from the lighthouse, and the remains of some impressive ancient statues. This image shows the recovery of a massive statue that may be one of the Ptolemaic kings.

▷ **Life on the Nile**
The Nile River remained a vital artery for the Egyptians in Ptolemaic and Roman times. This mosaic from c. 100 BCE shows life along the river's banks.

Greek and Roman Egypt

Ancient Egypt's later history is one of fascinating change and diversity. Absorbed into the empire of the Macedonian Alexander the Great, Egypt joined the Hellenistic (Greek) world under the Ptolemies, before becoming a province first of Rome, and then of the Byzantine Empire.

When Alexander, the Greek-educated king of Macedonia, died in 323 BCE, Egypt was part of his vast empire, and its control passed to one of Alexander's trusted generals, Ptolemy Lagus, who had been his governor there. By 304 BCE, Ptolemy was king of Egypt, and his descendants would rule for 300 years. The "Ptolemaic" period of Greek rule in Egypt came at a time when Greek culture had a wide influence across the Middle East and Mediterranean—a movement known as Hellenism (see p.99). Ever since Mycenaean times (see

ownership, and agricultural methods improved. Regional administration was organized using the existing Egyptian "nome" system of administrative districts. With an energetic flair for

350 ft (107 m)—the reputed height of the Pharos lighthouse at Alexandria, second only to the pyramids

business, the Ptolemies also began to replace the Egyptian barter system with an early form of monetary banking, created royal monopolies on certain goods, and zealously explored trade opportunities. Ptolemy I moved Egypt's capital from Memphis to Alexandria—the new port-city founded by Alexander—where it was to remain for 900 years. Alexandria became the prosperous symbol of Ptolemaic rule. Its north-coast

Greek culture, but the title of pharaoh became identified with the far-off emperor in Rome. Increasingly, however, Roman influences took hold. The Romans probably retained much of the Ptolemaic system of administration, but they slowly introduced many of their own practices in agriculture and everyday life. As Rome's power faded from the 4th century CE, Egypt came under the influence of the Christian Eastern Roman Empire based in Constantinople (once Byzantium, now Istanbul) and became a melting pot of different religious ideas.

Coptic Christianity

During the 1st century CE, Christianity spread to Egypt. By the later 4th century, it was the Roman Empire's official religion, and by the 6th, Egypt was strongly Christian. A devout Coptic church developed, which later became the principal Christian church in mainly Muslim Egypt. Copts held the "monophysite" belief that Christ was solely divine, and not both human and divine. In 451 CE the Eastern Roman Empire rejected the "monophysite" doctrine at the Council of Chalcedon (in modern Turkey), but the Egyptian Copts continued to adhere to it.

ΑΛΕΞΑΝΔΡΙΑ

Alexandria
This is a 6th-century Byzantine mosaic of the city, which was a leading center of Christianity by the 2nd century CE.

AFTER »

KHOSROW OF PERSIA ATTACKS THE BYZANTINES

Alexandria lost its status as the preeminent city of eastern Christianity to Constantinople (Byzantium 198–99 »). The Arabs' arrival in 642 CE dramatically changed Egypt again.

STRUGGLES OF PERSIA AND BYZANTIUM
Persian king **Khosrow II** wrested control of Egypt from the **Byzantine emperor, Heraclius**, and ruled briefly (616–28 CE) before Byzantium won control back, between 629 and 641 CE.

ARRIVAL OF THE ARABS
Egypt then passed to the **Arabs 174–77 »**. Caliph 'Amr ibn al-'As founded an encampment near Memphis that would later become Cairo, and introduced **Islam**, which dominates today.

THE LAST PHARAOH OF EGYPT   Born *c.* 68 BCE   Died 30 BCE

Cleopatra

"I will not be exhibited in his triumph."

CLEOPATRA REMARKING ON OCTAVIAN'S VICTORY PARADE, 30 BCE

A s a daughter of Ptolemy XII of Egypt, Cleopatra VII belonged to the Ptolemaic Dynasty (see pp.118–19) set up by the first Ptolemy, one of the generals of Alexander the Great (see pp.96–97). In theory, Egypt was independent, but in practice it was controlled by Rome. The Romans supported the Ptolemaic monarchs in return for financial favors. Cleopatra's father paid enormous sums to secure Roman backing, but this did not prevent Cleopatra's older sisters Tryphaena and Berenice from plotting against him.

When her father died in 51 BCE, Cleopatra, as eldest surviving daughter, ascended the throne with a younger brother. According to tradition, the king and queen were brother and sister as well as husband and wife, so she was expected to marry her brother, Ptolemy XIII. However, he and his chief minister Pothinus had other ideas—Ptolemy wished to be sole ruler, and by 49 BCE Cleopatra had been deprived of power and exiled. In 48 BCE, when the Roman political and military leader Julius Caesar (see pp.108–09) led a military campaign to Egypt, Cleopatra feared for her life. In becoming Caesar's lover, she was fighting for survival.

Caesar and Caesarion

With the help of reinforcements from Rome, Julius Caesar defeated an Egyptian army led by yet another of Cleopatra's sisters, Arsinoë IV. During the same campaign, Ptolemy XIII drowned—pulled into the Nile by the weight of his golden armor. Cleopatra was now free to rule Egypt with her youngest brother, Ptolemy XIV. Caesar had returned to Rome when she had their baby, whom she named Ptolemy Caesar, or Caesarion ("little Caesar"). Shortly

Cleopatra and Antony
This silver coin shows Cleopatra (left) on one side and her lover, Roman general Mark Antony (right), on the other.

Cleopatra as pharaoh
In this relief from a temple at Dendra, Cleopatra is depicted in the style of a pharaoh, wearing the crown of Hathor and a vulture headdress. She holds a staff and an ankh—the sign of life.

A legendary beauty
This 19th-century image depicts the glamorous Cleopatra of myth and legend. In reality, her success as a leader and a lover owed more to her intelligence and charm than her looks.

CLEOPATRA

afterward, on the official pretext of negotiating a treaty, Cleopatra visited Rome. At the time, it was common practice to display captives in triumphs (victory parades), so during Caesar's triumph, Cleopatra may have witnessed the exhibition of her sister Arsinoë.

After Caesar's assassination, Cleopatra returned to Egypt. It is likely that she organized the assassination of her co-ruler, Ptolemy XIV, replacing him with her son, Caesarion (Ptolemy XV). For the next three years, Cleopatra was careful to avoid the power struggle that broke out after Caesar's death. Instead, she restored order and prosperity to her own kingdom, where she was a popular and efficient ruler.

By 42 BCE the Roman general Mark Antony and Octavian (the future emperor Augustus, see p.112) were in control of the Roman world. They split power between them, Antony taking charge of the eastern Mediterranean. He summoned Cleopatra to Tarsus (in modern Turkey). and once again, she set out to conquer a conqueror, dazzling the Romans with her style and guile.

Antony and Cleopatra

At Tarsus, Cleopatra and Antony became lovers, but passion had yet to overrule politics. Before long, Antony had rejoined his Roman wife, Fulvia, in Greece, where she had fled after a failed rebellion against Octavian in Italy. By 40 BCE Fulvia was dead, which enabled Antony to seal another peace deal with Octavian by marrying his sister Octavia. In the meantime,

Cleopatra and Isis
This limestone stele shows Cleopatra (left) breastfeeding her son while making an offering to the goddess Isis. She later claimed to be the reincarnation of Isis.

Cleopatra had given birth to twins: a boy named Alexander Helios (sun) and a girl named Cleopatra Selene (moon). In 37 BCE, Antony came back to Egypt, and, while still wedded to Octavia, married Cleopatra. By the time he set off on an unsuccessful military campaign against the Parthians (see pp.122–23), she was expecting the baby she would name Ptolemy Philadelphus. Antony's next campaign, in Armenia, was victorious. His return to Egypt as a hero was followed by an event known as the "Donations of Alexandria." Seated on golden thrones,

Cleopatra and Antony proclaimed themselves as living gods—she Isis (see below) and he Dionysus/Osiris—and their children as the rulers of lands currently dominated by Rome.

After this, Octavian had no difficulty in persuading the Roman Senate to provide the means for an all-out war against Cleopatra, who was clearly determined to set herself up as a rival power. After her defeat by the Romans at the Battle of Actium, fought off the coast of Greece, she fled to Egypt with 60 treasure-laden ships, followed by Antony. Besieged at Alexandria, Antony killed himself, and Cleopatra, perhaps aware of her likely fate as the star of Octavian's triumph, also took her own life, supposedly with a poisonous snake hidden in a basket of figs.

Octavian honored Cleopatra's final request to be buried with Antony. She was 39. Her eldest son, Caesarion, was executed, but it is thought that the other children's lives were spared.

Cleopatra's decree
This papyrus document is a decree exempting a Roman citizen, Publius Candidus, from paying tax. Written in Egyptian demotic script at the royal chancellery in Alexandria, it has a note by Cleopatra stating: "Thus it shall happen." The Ptolemies, of whom Cleopatra was the last, were Greek-speaking. She was the first and only Ptolemy to learn Egyptian, the language of her subjects.

> ## "**Plato** admits **four** sorts of **flattery**, but she had a **thousand**."
>
> PLUTARCH, IN HIS BIOGRAPHY
> OF MARK ANTONY, *c.* 75 CE

IDEA

THE CULT OF ISIS

Daughter of the earth and sky, and sister-wife of the god Osiris, Isis was the principal goddess of ancient Egypt. When Osiris was murdered by the god Set, Isis found his body and performed rites that would return him to eternal life. Then she retired to raise her son Horus, magically conceived from her husband's corpse, until he was old enough to avenge his father. While the myth of Isis may have arisen as a representation of the flooding of the rich plains (Isis) by the Nile (Osiris), the cult of the sorrowing wife and loving mother spread far beyond its place of origin. Isis was adopted as a patron divinity of travelers, and had particular appeal to women.

THE GODDESS ISIS

TIMELINE

- **c. 68 BCE** Birth of Cleopatra, third daughter of Ptolemy XII of Egypt.

- **55 BCE** Cleopatra's sisters Berenice and Tryphaena are killed for deposing Ptolemy XII.

- **51 BCE** Ptolemy XII dies; Cleopatra VII becomes queen of Egypt with her brother, Ptolemy XIII.

- **49 BCE** Cleopatra is banished by Pothinus, chief adviser of Ptolemy XIII.

- **48 BCE** Julius Caesar arrives in Egypt and defeats the forces of Cleopatra's sister Arsinoë and Ptolemy XIII; Cleopatra is restored to power with another younger brother, Ptolemy XIV.

- **c. 47 BCE** Gives birth to a son, nicknamed Caesarion by the people of Alexandria in acknowledgment of his supposed father.

- **46 BCE** Back in Rome, Caesar celebrates with four triumphs (victory parades), the most splendid of which celebrates his victory in Egypt and features Cleopatra's captured sister Arsinoë in chains.

- **44 BCE** Cleopatra leaves Rome for Egypt after the assassination of Julius Caesar. Ptolemy XIV is assassinated, possibly by Cleopatra, and replaced by her son Caesarion (Ptolemy XV).

- **42 BCE** Octavian (right) and Mark Antony win the Battle of Philippi. Antony and Cleopatra meet in Tarsus and become lovers. **OCTAVIAN**

- **40 BCE** Cleopatra bears twins, Alexander Helios and Cleopatra Selene. The father is Mark Antony.

- **37 BCE** Antony returns to the Middle East and Cleopatra funds his military expeditions.

- **36 BCE** Cleopatra has another baby by Antony, Ptolemy Philadelphus.

- **35 BCE** Cleopatra delivers funds and much needed supplies for Antony's defeated army in Syria; Cleopatra and Antony return to Alexandria in Egypt together.

- **34 BCE** Antony returns from a successful military campaign in Armenia and celebrates his triumph in Alexandria. Vast territories and exalted titles are assigned to Cleopatra and her children in a ceremony known as the "Donations of Alexandria," which alarms Rome.

- **33 BCE** In Greece, Cleopatra and Antony organize land and naval forces in anticipation of war with Rome.

- **31 BCE** Cleopatra and Antony lose the Battle of Actium, but manage to return to Alexandria.

- **30 BCE** Rather than be taken to Rome by Octavian as a prisoner of war, Cleopatra kills herself, allegedly by poisonous snake bite.

RENAISSANCE VIEW OF THE DEATH OF CLEOPATRA

121

Trade links between Persia and China
This cave fresco in Dunhuang, China, from c. 600 CE, shows Sogdian merchants (from eastern Persia) on the Silk Road between the Sassanid Empire and China.

Parthian coins of King Gotarzes II
The Parthians retained the use of Greek on their coins—these were minted in 49–51 BCE—despite a fading knowledge of Greek during their empire.

The Greek–Macedonian empire of the Seleucids (see pp.98–99 and BEFORE) incorporated most of the Asian conquests of Alexander (see pp.96–97), including all of Persia and Mesopotamia. This empire was almost as vast as its predecessor—the first Persian empire of the Achaemenids (see pp.92–93)—but by the 3rd century BCE it had started to crumble as its many subjects asserted their autonomy.

Emergence of the Parthians
In the ruins of the empire, a people called the Parthians saw an opening. Once nomads who had settled in the northeast of the old Persian Empire, the Parthians had gained independence from Seleucid rule by 238 BCE. With

spread west from India along Parthian trade routes. These contacts denied Roman traders access to routes to China and India, leading to battles with the Roman armies. Parthia's most famous victory was the battle of Carrhae (or Harran, southeast Turkey) in 53 BCE, when the Roman army was utterly destroyed. Constant fighting with the Romans and nomads may have weakened the Parthians. They left little written record, so historians rely on their art and architecture, and foreign texts to paint a picture of the period.

> **THE PARTHIAN SHOT** A trick used by the Parthians that involved feigning a rapid retreat, only to turn around in the saddle to fire arrows at their pursuers.

Sassanid fortified settlement
Built high above the fertile Iranian plateau, Takht-e Solalman, or Solomon's Throne, was one of the holiest sites of the Sassanid Persians. It housed a Zoroastrian fire temple with an eternally burning flame.

fire altars were erected to Ormazd, or Ahura Mazda, god of light, truth, and life. Most Sassanid rulers, however, were tolerant of religions other than their own, and large populations of Jews and Christians inhabited the empire, especially in Mesopotamia.

In the early 7th century the Sassanids suffered a serious military defeat at the hands of the Byzantine Emperor Heraclius. From this point, the weakened empire lay at the mercy of Islamic forces invading from the south.

The Revival of Persia

Persia emerged from Greek rule under the control of the Parthian people. Parthian expansion coincided with that of the Roman Empire, and the two powers spent three centuries at loggerheads with each other. The Persians themselves regained control in 226 CE, founding the rich and opulent Sassanid dynasty.

« **BEFORE**

The first Persian Empire, based in southwest Iran, was ruled by the Achaemenid dynasty from c. 520 BCE << 92–93. When Alexander the Great << 96–97 swept the empire away in 334–323 BCE, the lands were not ruled by Persians for another 500 years.

THE SELEUCID DYNASTY
Alexander's conquests were partitioned after his death. Mesopotamia, Persia, and the east fell to a dynasty of **Greek–Macedonian rulers** founded by **Seleucus I << 98–99**, who had marched with Alexander's conquering army into Asia. Seleucus set up a new capital, **Seleucia**, on the Tigris River.

A GREEK–PERSIAN MIX
Greek and Persian cultures mixed << 98–99 in the territory ruled by Seleucus I and his **Persian wife,**
SELEUCID BRONZE **Apama.** Alexander had dreamed of a Greek–Macedonian–Persian empire with its component cultures taking strength from one another. He had encouraged **intermarriage** between his soldiers and locals.

AN EMPIRE LOST
The Seleucid empire weakened as the remote, **Central Asian Greek city states << 98–99** of **Bactria** (in modern Afghanistan) and other states farther west won independence. The empire retreated from India and Bactria c. 250 BCE.

expansion east, they took control of the silk routes from China and began strangling what was left of the Seleucid Empire itself. Under their king Mithridates I, Parthians overpowered Mesopotamia to control all lands from India to the Tigris River. Mithridates recognized the value of the Greek–Persian culture he was inheriting, so he allowed the defeated cities to retain their administrative systems, trading ties, and languages, while placing Parthian governors to oversee them.

Between Rome and China
The Romans defeated and annexed the Seleucid kingdom, thus becoming neighbors of the Parthians. So began an uneasy relationship that cast Parthia as the enemy of Rome for the next 300 years.

Parthians were well suited to frequent border skirmishes. In the north their frontiers were under constant threat from Steppe nomads (see pp.138–39), who they held at bay with a tactic of lightning cavalry strikes.

The Parthians had indirect contact with the Han Chinese, whose envoy Zhang Qian (see p.129) traveled to the west and returned with accounts of their empire. Buddhist ideas, meanwhile,

What is certain is that the Persians reemerged under Ardashir I of the Sassanid dynasty, who defeated the Parthians in 226 CE, restoring Persian rule until 640 CE.

The Persians back in power
From the Parthians, the Sassanids inherited control of land trade routes to the east. They also faced the Parthians' perennial problems of repelling nomads from the north and east and the Romans from the west. Ardashir's son, Shapur I, won a famous victory over the Romans at Edessa in 259 CE, capturing the Roman Emperor Valerian. Despite this initial success, war with the Romans and their successors, the Byzantines (see pp.198–99), continued through four centuries of Sassanid rule.

The Sassanids built a rich civilization based largely on agriculture and trade. Government was far more centralized than under Parthian rule, with local officials appointed by the king responsible for the building of roads and cities, which was paid for by central government.

Zoroastrianism, the traditional faith of the Persians, was elevated to the status of official state religion, and many new

Sassanid plate
This gold plate, typical of Persian artistic refinement, shows the king hunting on a camel—an image found on many Sassanid artifacts.

AFTER »

Persia was rapidly annexed by the Islamic conquerors, but Persian culture lived on in its art and literature.

DEFEAT BY THE ARABS
Arab Muslim armies 174–77 » routed the Sassanids at the **Battle of Qadisiyya** in 637 CE, and Muslims took over the institutions of power.

SEAT OF LEARNING
By 762 CE the **Abbasid caliphate 175 »**, having moved its capital to Baghdad, near Babylon, had become the world's greatest **center of scholarship**. Scholars of all religions made contributions to law, medicine, astronomy, mats, and philosophy.

PERSIAN HERITAGE
Persia's imperial past was not forgotten. Miniatures were painted and **epic stories** collected about the **PERSIAN QUR'AN** glories of the Achaemenid, Parthian, and Sassanid empires. Ferdowsi's **Shahnameh**, or **"Epic of Kings"** (c. 1000 CE), is a key work from this time.

MONGOL CONQUEST
In 1258, the **Mongols 166–67 »** destroyed the art and learning of centuries, although their Islamic successors sought to repair the damage.

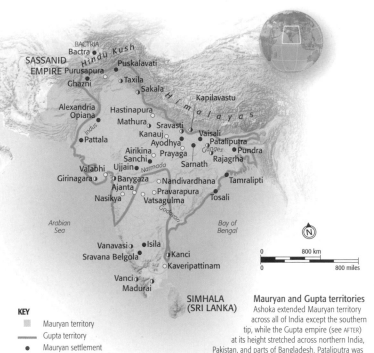

Mauryan and Gupta territories
Ashoka extended Mauryan territory across all of India except the southern tip, while the Gupta empire (see AFTER) at its height stretched across northern India, Pakistan, and parts of Bangladesh. Pataliputra was the capital of both regimes. Ayodhya was an important city and the eastern capital of the Kushan conquerors.

KEY
- ▪ Mauryan territory
- — Gupta territory
- ● Mauryan settlement
- ○ Gupta settlement

BEFORE

The Vedic period (c. 1500–500 BCE) is named after the Vedas—ancient Indo-Aryan texts that were produced during this time and that are central to the Hindu faith.

EARLY VEDIC PERIOD
Many local dynasties came into being, and by the 8th century BCE, India was divided into many small, competing kingdoms.

LATE VEDIC PERIOD
Around the 8th century BCE, large urban states known as *mahajanapadas* started to take shape in northern India. The northeastern **Magadha** area came to dominate the various warring regional powers. Its strategic position in the Ganges valley aided trade and linked it with flourishing ports in the Ganges river delta.

NANDA DYNASTY
In the 5th century BCE, just a few states, including Magadha, dominated India. By the 4th century, after countless wars, Magadha had emerged as the most powerful. Ruled by the prosperous **Nanda dynasty**, it set up complex irrigation projects and an efficient administration system, built a strong army, and established a royal center at the city of **Pataliputra** (modern Patna).

RISING RELIGIONS
Jainism and **Buddhism 144–47 ≫** were well established by the 4th century BCE, gaining ground against Vedic traditions—the origin of Hinduism.

India's First Empire

From their northeastern heartland, the Mauryans came to dominate India's massive subcontinent with what became its first real empire. This reached its greatest extent and enjoyed its greatest cultural flowering under the rule of Ashoka, who also played a major part in the rise of the Buddhist religion.

A round 321 BCE, the Nanda dynasty (see BEFORE) was toppled by Chandragupta Maurya, founder of the Mauryan dynasty and what would become the great Mauryan empire (c. 321–185 BCE). The emperor Chandragupta won a great deal of new territory, combining smaller kingdoms and uniting—often rather loosely—vast regions of India

Ashoka pillar
This is one of Ashoka's famous polished sandstone pillars bearing edicts inscribed in Brahmi script to help spread his ideas among his people. They are among the oldest deciphered original Indian texts.

under one ruler for the first time. The empire embraced much of the Indian subcontinent and part of Afghanistan.

The lands into which Chandragupta expanded included parts of the Macedonian empire won by Alexander (see pp.96–99) and by his successors the Seleucids. The Seleucids' attempts to repeat Alexander's success brought them headlong into the path of the advancing Mauryans, but Seleucus I Nicator ceded his claims to lands around the Indus in a pact with Chandragupta in 305 BCE.

Hellenistic (Greek) culture continued to have an influence in northern India, while Chandragupta based his administration partly on the Persian Achaemenid model (see pp.92–93). His highly efficient and impressive centralized system also owed much

to his minister, Chanakya, who produced one of the greatest treatises on politics, administration, and economics ever written—*Arthashastra*.

Chandragupta's legacy
At the core of Chandragupta's newly won empire was its glittering capital at Pataliputra. Under his sure hand, backed by strong military resources and an effective secret service, agriculture and trade flourished. He died around 297 BCE, having fasted to death. As a convert to Jainism, he spent his final days in ascetic repentance for a terrible famine that struck his people, which he was grief-stricken at being unable to hold back.

The second emperor was Chandragupta's son, Bindusara (c. 297–265 BCE). Little is known of his reign, but it seems

The Ashoka lions
Ashoka made this four-lion motif his symbol of imperial authority; it is now used as India's official emblem.

Sanchi gate
Four magnificent gateways lead to the Great Stupa at Sanchi. Dating from the first century BCE, these "torans" are decorated with intricate carvings that are one of the greatest artistic achievements of ancient Indian art. They show scenes from the life of Buddha and feature motifs such as Ashoka's famous four lions.

500 The number of war elephants presented by Chandragupta to Seleucus I Nicator in 305 BCE, in return for giving up his claims to Indian lands. He used the elephants in battles fought between Alexander's "successors," notably in the defeat of Antigonus at Ipsus in 301 BCE.

Great Stupa of Sanchi
Sanchi, central India, is home to one of the most impressive examples of Ashoka's stupa-building program in the 3rd century BCE. It was added to over subsequent centuries.

AFTER »

The 1st–3rd centuries CE saw the Kushans from the steppes of Central Asia ruling in the north while small dynasties came and went elsewhere. As these crumbled, the way was paved for the great empire of the Guptas.

DETAIL FROM AJANTA CAVE PAINTINGS

THE GUPTA EMPIRE
Around 320 CE, the region of Magadha gave birth to another great dynasty and empire, the **Guptas**, who dominated northern India until c. 540 CE. The Gupta dynasty's real empire-builders were its two first kings: **Chandra Gupta I** (c. 320–330) and his son, Samudra Gupta (c. 330–380). Great artistic achievements of this well-administrated, prosperous empire include the **Ajanta cave paintings** in western India. Some of these show episodes from the life of Buddha.

ART, RELIGION, AND SCIENCE
The Gupta era is often seen as the "classical" period of Indian culture, especially of **Hindu and Buddhist art**. The Guptas had a strong Hindu leaning, but Jainism and Buddhism also flourished. The classic image of **Buddha** developed, with a peaceful, reflective expression and curls flat against his head. Jain and Buddhist monks also created wonderful sculpted friezes at the **Udayagiri caves** (below). Wealthy patrons also encouraged architecture, dance, drama, and Sanskrit epics, while great advances were made in mathematics, astronomy, philosophy, logic, and medicine.

GUPTA-ERA BUDDHA

DEMISE OF THE GUPTAS
Under the fourth Guptan ruler, Kumara Gupta (c. 415–455), cracks began to appear in the empire as it faced incursions by **Hephthalite** nomads (or "White Huns") from the north. By the 6th century, the Guptas had pulled back to their original heartland, and India was again a patchwork of small kingdoms **180 »**.

UDAYAGIRI CAVES

---

that he successfully expanded Mauryan territories south into the Deccan, so that only the southern tip of India, plus the Kalinga area in the east (now in Orissa state), were not incorporated in the empire.

Bindusara's son, Ashoka, the third emperor (c. 265–232 BCE) was the last major ruler of the Mauryan dynasty and one of the great figures of ancient history. It was Ashoka who brought the empire to its greatest extent, gaining the Kalinga region after a particularly bloody battle. It was said that the waters of the Daya River, next to the battlefield, ran red with the blood of the many thousands fallen.

Ashoka is seen as presiding over a golden age. As his empire prospered, he promoted the arts and sciences and instigated a vast building program. This included a great many stupas (mound-shaped shrines), built to house supposed relics of Buddha.

At some point in his reign, Ashoka converted to the fast-growing religion of Buddhism. According to a story that mirrors the tale of his grandfather's repentance, he converted in remorse at the waste and bloodshed of the Kalinga War, turning his back on violence and embracing the peaceful Buddhist way of life. He sent missionaries to spread the word far and wide throughout Asia, including Sri Lanka, and in so doing played a major role in the development of Buddhism. He also spread the word through his edicts—sayings inscribed on stone pillars and rocks across India, Nepal, Pakistan, and Afghanistan. These set out his principles of peace, morality, respect, and humane rule, and of being the father who guides his people's spiritual welfare.

"All men are my children. What I desire for my own children... I desire for all men."
ASHOKA IN ONE OF HIS ROCK EDICTS, C.240 BCE

End of an era
The peace and prosperity of Ashoka's reign did not continue long after his death. Subsequent rulers lost territories and prestige, and there were squabbles over the succession. The last Mauryan emperor, Brihadratha, was assassinated c. 185 BCE by his chief aide, Pusyamitra, founder of the Sunga dynasty, which ruled central India until c. 73 BCE. India was now revisiting its chaotic, divided pre-Mauryan history. Small kingdoms arose in northern India, among them those of the so-called "Indo-Greek" rulers. The most famous of these was Menander (155–130 BCE), who may have battled with the Sungas.

INVENTION

DECIMAL NUMBER SYSTEMS

Indian mathematics advanced greatly under the Mauryans and Guptas (see AFTER). By the 4th century BCE, scholars were developing the idea of using combinations of units of different sizes. By the 1st century CE, they had devised a decimal-like system using the symbols shown here and refined the concept of zero as a "placeholder" to add and multiply numbers. The concept spread from India to the Islamic world and finally to the West, where it underlies the modern number system.

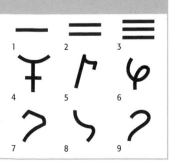

The **Unification** of **China**

The rise of the dynamic Qin state, which conquered the Warring States of China to create the Chinese empire, brought a period of stability and prosperity to China. Under the short-lived but ambitious rule of the First Emperor (221–206 BCE), the laws and infrastructure of imperial China first took shape.

Qin-dynasty coins
Round coins with a square hole, similar to those used in China until the late 19th century, first appeared during the Qin dynasty.

BEFORE

As China moved out of the Bronze Age, the Shang were defeated by the Zhou, the last of the pre-imperial dynasties.

THE ZHOU DYNASTY
The Zhou dynasty (1027–256 BCE) lasted **longer than any other in Chinese history**. During the Zhou period, bronze was widely used, and

ZHOU BRONZE

iron technology was introduced in China. The Zhou dynasty saw the **birth of the major indigenous Chinese philosophies**, including Confucianism **131 ≫**, and a system of government that had many **similarities to the European feudalism of the Middle Ages 188–91 ≫**.

THE WARRING STATES PERIOD
The Zhou rapidly **disintegrated into a number of independent states**, and from 481 BCE, the start of the era known as the Warring States Period, **regional warlords** were conquering smaller states around them to consolidate their rule.

The terra-cotta army
The First Emperor's mausoleum was constructed near Xi'an by 700,000 conscripts. In 1974 a chance find led to the uncovering of four pits containing over 7,500 life-size and lifelike terra-cotta soldiers, horses, and chariots (left). The scale of the mausoleum is a testament to the power of the First Emperor. Today, the terra-cotta army is visited by two million people every year.

One of the territories to survive the Warring States period was the state of Qin. The people of Qin were situated to the west of Zhou territory along the Yellow River valley—so far west that people said they shared the customs of the Rong and Di, non-Chinese groups regarded as uncivilized. In 316 BCE, Qin began a series of campaigns against the other warring states, and in 221 BCE the king of Qin defeated the last remaining state and declared himself Qin Shi Huang (see below), the First Emperor of Qin.

Qin Legalism
In 356 BCE, before the Qin had even begun to conquer the surrounding states, Lord Shang, an exponent of Legalist ideas, became chief minister of Qin. The Legalists opposed the Confucian ideals of filial piety and kingly benevolence (see p.131). Instead, they argued that the interests of the state came before those of individuals, that rulers should apply strict laws and punishments, and that the use of war as an instrument of state policy was acceptable. Lord Shang began a program of Legalist reform in the state of Qin, where all adult males were registered for military service. Perhaps unsurprisingly, considering its emphasis on the infallibility of the head of state, the First Emperor was an advocate of Legalism. During his reign, Li Si, the chief minister, put Legalist principles into practice and introduced measures that are still in effect throughout China today. Among these measures were the abolition of the feudal fiefs (see BEFORE), the standardization of the written script, the application of a strict legal code,

the establishment of official measures for weights and lengths, the issue of a unified currency, and even the regulation of the width of roads.

The Qin Empire
Though the Chinese empire had already been created by the conquest of the Warring States, Qin expansion continued southward. Expeditions were sent to modern Guangdong, on the south coast of China, and Chinese colonies were established there.

After campaigning against the steppe peoples in the north, the emperor ordered his general Meng Tian to construct a great wall to establish

QIN Pronounced "Chin"–a Chinese dynasty and a likely origin of the English word for China.

control over the Ordos region of Inner Mongolia, in order to help repel further incursions from the steppes. This was the first phase of the Great Wall of China, which was later rebuilt during the Ming dynasty (see pp.166–67). Meng Tian also constructed the Straight Road, which ran 500 miles (800 km) north from the capital Xianyang to the Ordos region to facilitate movement of military troops.

As well as constructing works that enhanced China's defenses, Qin Shi Huang also commissioned many grand public building projects—including palaces, bridges, and canals—to strengthen imperial rule in China.

An immortal tomb
As he grew old, the emperor became increasingly obsessed with finding the secret of immortality. This obsession led to the most ambitious building project commissioned by Qin Shi Huang—the construction of his own mausoleum—which began in 212 BCE. According to the description recorded a century later by the Grand Historian, Sima Qian, the tomb contained a model of the empire, which had rivers of quicksilver and a mechanism for operating the tides, and was guarded by traps that would shoot any intruders after the tomb was closed. Not far from this burial chamber (which has yet to be excavated) stood the terra-cotta army (see left), a legion of life-size pottery soldiers that were constructed to defend the First Emperor in death.

Qin Shi Huang died in 210 BCE on an expedition to the east of China in search of the island of Penglai, where immortals were believed to reside.

Fall of the Qin
After the death of the First Emperor, his son took power, but he was never as effective a ruler as his father, and he was forced to commit suicide by his chief minister two years later. China crumbled into civil unrest and much of Qin Shi Huang's work was lost. Palace archives were burned, destroying evidence of the period. Revolts and uprisings led to the demise of the dynasty less than twenty years after it had begun.

AFTER

The Legalist ideas of the Qin were rejected by the Han dynasty, but the influence of Qin Shi Huang was felt in China for centuries.

CHINA AS ONE
Following the short-lived Qin dynasty, the expectation that China should be **a unified state** remained strong up to modern times.

A NEW EMPIRE
The Han empire **128–29 ≫**, which followed the Qin dynasty, was to last for 400 years. The Han dynasty **rejected Legalist principles in favor of Confucianism**, and the influence of this philosophy in state affairs is still felt today.

LEGACY OF THE FIRST EMPEROR
Historically, **the rule of the First Emperor was seen in a negative light** by scholars, and his cruelty and obsession with immortality were highlighted. In more recent years, modern

MAO ZEDONG

China has come to reevaluate Qin Shi Huang's aims and achievements in political and social terms. Mao Zedong **424–25 ≫** praised the First Emperor for his achievements and endorsed his attack on Confucianism.

FIRST QIN EMPEROR (260–210 BCE)
QIN SHI HUANG

Later Confucian historians have painted a picture of Qin Shi Huang as a ruthless megalomaniac, a reputation that can be traced to two notorious acts committed during his reign. The first of these was the burning of many classical texts that were being used by officials to argue against his decisions, and the second was the alleged burying alive of 460 scholars for disagreeing with him. Yet whatever his failings as an ideal ruler, the achievements of the man who unified China for the first time cannot be underestimated.

« BEFORE

The autocratic actions of China's First Emperor, Qin Shi Huang, alienated the population, and his successors were unable to quell the widespread rebellion that broke out against them.

QIN DYNASTY

Qin Shi Huang's son, the Second Emperor, fell under the influence of the eunuch Zhao Gao, who persuaded him to execute Li Si, his father's first minister, by having him cut in two in the market place at Xianyang. The Second Emperor was forced to commit suicide in 207 BCE and was succeeded by his son. By then rebellion had spread and the **Qin dynasty « 126–27**, which was to have lasted "ten thousand generations," ended.

THE FIRST HAN EMPEROR

Liu Bang, who came from a poor peasant family, rose to prominence as the leader of a rebel band. At first he supported Xiang Yu, an aristocrat who hoped to revive the feudal states. In 206 BCE Liu Bang captured **Xianyang**, the Qin capital, negotiated the surrender of the last Qin ruler, and announced the repeal of the severe **Qin penal code**. His treatment of the inhabitants earned him a reputation for fairness. When Xiang Yu arrived, the city was looted and the royal family killed. The rebel leaders quarreled, and for the next four years they campaigned against each other. Although Liu Bang's forces suffered defeats, he continued to gather allies, and in 202 BCE he won a decisive victory at Gaixia in modern Anhui.

COUNTESS OF DAI'S TOMB

In 1972 the tomb of the Countess of Dai, dated *c.* 168 BCE, was found at Mawangdui in present-day Hunan province. The grave offerings included silk garments, lacquer bowls for wine and food, and wooden figurines of her servants. The beautiful painted banner draped over her inner coffin is one of the earliest surviving examples of Chinese painting on silk. It depicts the route her soul would take on its quest for immortality—to the magic island of Penglai and then to the gates of paradise. The tomb also contained silk manuscripts and a divination board, with markings similar to those found on bronze mirrors of the period.

PAINTED SILK BANNER

The Centralized State

The Han dynasty, founded by Liu Bang in 202 BCE, created a powerful centralized state with a highly efficient civil service that would serve as a model for future Chinese emperors over the next two millennia.

Liu Bang (see BEFORE) assumed the style of *huangdi* or sovereign emperor (see p.127), and used Han as the title of the new dynasty. He is usually known as Emperor Gaozu. During his reign, which lasted until 195 BCE, many of the features of the Chinese imperial system took shape.

Gaozu himself was the embodiment of the principle that a man of peasant origins but of outstanding virtue could become emperor. He began his reign by announcing an amnesty and measures to restore peace. In the west and in the area around the new capital that he established at Chang'an, he continued Qin practices, applying direct rule in the form of commanderies (districts ruled by a centrally appointed governor). But in the east and south he initially accepted the existence of ten kingdoms, whose rulers professed allegiance to him, although he later replaced them with members of his own family. In the commanderies he rewarded senior officials, military leaders, and leaders of non-Chinese groups who had submitted to the Han, by conferring on them the rank of marquis. This title allowed them to raise taxes for the state, retaining part of the money for themselves.

Promotion on merit

Gaozu formalized the system of bureaucratic government introduced under the Qin. The emperor was assisted by three senior officials, who were in turn supported by nine ministers, each with a defined area of responsibility.

Gaozu was contemptuous of scholars, but he recognized the importance of the Confucian ideals (see p.131) of education and public service. In 196 BCE he issued an edict on the recruitment of able persons to the imperial government. The sixth Han emperor, Wudi, took this process even further.

Writing brushes
The ink brush was invented before the Han period, but came into its own under the Han for keeping detailed records—first on silk and then on paper (see right).

Age of scholarship
Hsien Ti, the last of the Han emperors, who reigned c.189–220 CE, is shown in discussion with scholars who have been busy translating Confucian classical texts.

In 124 BCE he established an imperial academy where 50 students studied the classics in preparation for an examination. Those who passed became eligible for official appointments. The same year saw the most celebrated example of social mobility in Chinese history when Gongsun Hong, a former swineherd, was appointed chancellor.

Expansion of the empire
During Wudi's long reign (141–87 BCE) China made extensive territorial gains.

of the modern provinces of Guangdong and Guangxi and north Vietnam. All these military campaigns naturally cost money, so Wudi decided to augment tax revenues by imposing a state monopoly on salt and iron. This provoked a complicated debate over the degree to which the government should interfere in the economy.

Decline and usurpation
Wudi's successful reign came to a sad end, as the emperor in his later years became obsessed with his search for immortality, enlisting the help of the leading alchemists of the day. After his death the dynasty went into a period of decline, marked by weak emperors

> "To **learn without thinking** is fruitless; To think without learning is dangerous."
>
> CONFUCIUS, 551–479 BCE

The emperor's first concern, however, was to secure his northern frontier against invasion by the Xiongnu, a confederacy of nomadic steppe peoples originating in Mongolia (see p.139). In 166 BCE they had penetrated to within 100 miles (160 km) of Chang'an. In 138 BCE Wudi sent an envoy, Zhang Qian, to contact the Yuezhi, the traditional enemies of the Xiongnu, in the hope of forming an alliance. Zhang Qian failed to obtain their assistance, but his epic journey extended Chinese influence for the first time into the Western Regions (modern Xinjiang), helping establish trading links with Persia and opening up the Silk Road (see pp.184–85).

Wudi's greatest conquests were to the northeast and the south of the existing empire. In 128 BCE he sent an expedition to Korea, and 20 years later a longer campaign led to the establishment of four commanderies in the north of the peninsula. In 111 BCE he sent an expedition south to Guangzhou, and subsequently commanderies were established to administer the territory

and the excessive influence of the court eunuchs. One of the eunuchs' main duties was the care of the numerous imperial concubines, any one of whose sons could be named to succeed the emperor. This led to palace intrigues in which the eunuchs played an increasingly significant role. The economy, meanwhile, suffered from financial mismanagement, and there was widespread tax evasion. A further blow came in the early years of the 1st century CE with serious flooding of the Yellow River, which led to its changing to its southern course in 11 CE.

In 9 CE Wang Mang, who had been acting as regent for a succession of child emperors, usurped the throne. He ordered large private estates to be broken up, but was killed in 23 CE.

The Han ruled China for over 400 years (ignoring the brief interregnum of Wang Mang)—longer than any later dynasty. Their administrative structure was revived and retained by future Chinese rulers.

THE ROMAN AND HAN EMPIRES
The two great contemporary empires of Eurasia—the **Roman Empire ‹‹ 106–115** in Europe and the Han in China—both collapsed, but whereas the Roman Empire disappeared, the Chinese Empire was reunited at the end of the 6th century CE and survived for another 1,400 years. Important factors in the durability of the Chinese Empire compared to the Roman may have been the fact that China was a land empire and was held together by a common written

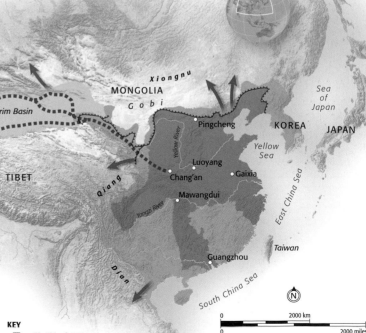

ROMAN COIN OF EMPEROR TRAJAN

language, the principles of Confucianism **130–31 ››**, and the ideal of ethical rule by an emperor. The Romans governed a sprawling empire populated by people speaking many languages.

AGE OF DIVISION
The fall of the Later Han was followed by a period of division between north and south. The north, at first fragmented into the **Sixteen Kingdoms**, was then dominated by the **Northern Wei dynasty**, while to the south a succession of **Six Dynasties** established their capital at Jiankang (modern Nanjing). In 589 CE China was reunited under the **Sui** dynasty and then in 618 CE by the **Tang dynasty 160–61 ››**, which ushered in a new period of stability. Under the Tang, long-distance trade between China and the Middle East revived along the **Silk Road 184–85 ››**, especially with the newly established **Islamic Caliphate 174–77 ››**.

The Later Han
In 25 CE Guang Wudi reestablished the Han dynasty, transferring the capital to Luoyang, which became the most populous city in the world. This was an age of scientific and technological progress; major inventions included paper (see below) and an instrument that indicated the direction in which an earthquake had occurred. In its

later years the Han court was weakened by factionalism, and China was menaced by the Xianbei, a new confederation of steppe nomads. Rebellions broke out, and Han generals, the most famous of whom was Cao Cao, contended for power. In 220 Cao Cao died and the dynasty collapsed.

INVENTION
PAPER
The invention of paper is traditionally credited to Cai Lun, a court eunuch who lived c. 50–121 CE. He soaked the bark of a mulberry tree and bamboo in water, pounded the mixture with a wooden tool, and then drained it through cloth, leaving only the fibers. This produced a type of paper that was light, cheap, and easy to make. His invention was adopted rapidly for documents and books and subsequently spread to the Islamic world and the West.

KEY
- Qin China in 206 BCE
- Territory added by Former Han Dynasty 206 BCE–9 CE
- Territory added by Later Han Dynasty 25–220 CE
- Great Wall under the Han
- Silk Road
- Main Han military expeditions

Han dynasty China
Under Wudi, the Han extended their control over south China. The Great Wall of China was originally constructed during the Han Dynasty and rebuilt in later periods.

‹‹ BEFORE

By Socrates' time (see right), Greek thinkers had begun to seek rational explanations, instead of adhering to traditional beliefs.

HESIOD

GREEK MYTHOLOGY

Homer's epics **‹‹ 102–03** of the 8th century BCE, retelling legends from Greek prehistory, underpinned all later classical education. **Hesiod's** poem *Theogony*, ("birth of the gods") *c.* 700 BCE, gives the first systematic account of Greek mythology, whose many gods were consulted through divination and oracles, such as the famous oracle at the Temple of Apollo in Delphi. Pre-Socratic philosophers questioned these traditional beliefs.

CONSULTING THE DELPHIC ORACLE

Xenophanes (*c.*570 BCE) wrote: "Homer and Hesiod have attributed to the gods everything that is shameful and blameworthy among men."

TRADING WISDOM

From about the middle of the 7th century BCE, the Greek world was transformed **‹‹ 94–95** as a commercial economy developed, with the market place, the **agora**, as the center of social life in every city. Exposure to new ideas through trade inspired thinkers to challenge traditional wisdom. Greeks exchanged social, political, and philosophical ideas and dared to imagine novel ways of governing society and of understanding the world. **Anaximenes** (*c.* 585 BCE) thought the origin of everything was air; **Heraclitus** (*c.* 534 BCE) thought it was fire **‹‹ 104–05**.

THE FOUNDERS

The Greeks recognized **seven sages** as founders of their intellectual tradition. The names varied but always included **Solon of Athens** (*c.* 630 BCE) **‹‹ 100–01**, whose maxim was "nothing in excess," and **Thales of Miletus** (*c.* 640 BCE) **‹‹ 104–05**, the first true philosopher. According to Plato, the other five were **Bias** of Priene, **Chilon** of Sparta, **Cleobulus** of Lindos, **Myson** of Chenae, and **Pittacus** of Mytilene.

" …the unexamined life is **not worth living**… "

SOCRATES, SPEAKING AT HIS TRIAL, 399 BCE

The School of Athens
This painting by Raphael—painted in 1509 for Pope Julius II—is proof of the enduring influence of Plato and Aristotle (walking in the center) and Socrates (leaving the picture on the left) on Western philosophy.

Classical Thought

During the 5th century BCE, under the brilliant leadership of Pericles, the city-state of Athens rose to become the political and cultural focus of the Greek world. The thinkers who lived and taught there prepared the ground for much of Western philosophy for the next 2000 years.

Philosophy is a method of rational inquiry used to attempt to understand the world and phenomena around us; it is also the study of the process of philosophical inquiry itself. Three philosophers who taught in Athens are credited with laying the foundations of all classical thought—Socrates, Plato, and Aristotle.

Socrates

Socrates was born around 470 BCE, and became famous for challenging conventional ideas that most people thought they understood. He did this by questioning what was meant by concepts such as "good," "evil," "courage," and "justice," to show people that their understanding of such terms lacked truth. He wrote nothing down, but his logical style of argument is portrayed in the works of his followers, particularly Plato and the soldier and historian Xenophon. His greatest concern was ethics, or how to live a good life. At the age of 70 his constant questioning was thought to threaten the Athenian state. He was condemned to death, and was forced to poison himself.

Plato

A follower of Socrates, Plato was born c. 428 BCE and developed his mentor's ideas. Many of his writings, such as *Symposium* and the *Republic*, were composed as dialogues on subjects such as ethics and justice, the nature of reality, and the immortality of the soul. He also tried to devise a perfect political system. He set up a school, called the Academy, on the outskirts of Athens, which continued to teach philosophy until the 6th century CE.

Aristotle

Plato's student Aristotle (see p.95) taught a different kind of philosophy from that of his master—more practical than theoretical—and insisted on the importance of observing facts (see pp.104–05). He spent three years as

ZENO THE STOIC
Zeno is said to have strangled himself at the age of 69, in accordance with the Stoic belief that a man has the right to determine his own death.

tutor to Alexander the Great (see pp.96–99), whose conquests spread Greek ideas widely in Asia and North Africa. Aristotle founded his own school outside Athens called the Lyceum. His books, compiled from lecture notes, covered subjects ranging from poetry, drama, ethics, and politics to mathematics, physics, logic, zoology, and anatomy. They remained the basis of Western and Islamic science and philosophy until the 17th century.

Many philosophical movements emerged from the work of Socrates, Plato, and Aristotle. Among the most important were Skepticism, Cynicism, Epicureanism, and Stoicism—the last two had the most enduring influence.

> **SKEPTICISM** A philosophical movement that denied the possibility of knowing the real truth with certainty.

> **CYNICISM** A philosophy that taught that virtue and asceticism, rather than pleasure and indulgence, led to happiness.

Epicureanism and Stoicism

Epicurus (born 341 BCE) taught that good and bad should be measured by the pleasure and pain they bring, and that the point of justice is to increase human happiness. He believed that the gods, if they exist at all, had no interest in human affairs and that there was no life after death. He thought that

Remembering mortality
Epicureans used the skull as a *memento mori* (which means "remember that you are mortal") to remind them of the importance of enjoying life while it is still possible.

events in the world were the result of the motion of atoms in empty space—an idea he possibly borrowed from Democritus (born 460 BCE). The Latin poet Lucretius brought Epicurus's ideas to the Roman world, where they strongly influenced writers like Virgil.

Stoicism was founded by Zeno of Citium (born 335 BCE). He divided philosophy into three elements: logic, physics, and ethics. He believed that underlying all matter was energy, which he called divine fire. Zeno claimed that universal human fellowship was more important than narrow loyalty and that man's duty was to accept what fate brings and to behave in accordance with nature.

Stoicism was an inspiration to the Romans who took over the Greek world from the 2nd century BCE (see pp.106–07). Roman thinkers such as Seneca the Younger, Cicero, and Cato the Younger adapted Stoic ideas to the new realities of the Roman Empire. The Roman values of bravery in battle, fortitude in the face of hardship, and the universal brotherhood of Roman citizenship owe their origins to the teachings of the Stoics.

IDEA

CONFUCIANISM

In China, Confucius (according to tradition, born 551 BCE) addressed ethical questions similar to those that concerned the Greeks. He emphasized truth, justice, correct social relations, and obedience to parents, believing that the family was the proper foundation for society and good government. He championed the golden rule: "Do not do unto others what you would not want for yourself." His collected sayings, *The Analects*, found a similar place in Eastern thought to Plato's *Republic* in the West.

AFTER »

Greek philosophical ideas became the common heritage of intellectuals in the Mediterranean world and beyond, well into the Roman period.

THE ROMAN ARISTOTLE
The Romans elaborated on Greek ideas. **Pliny the Elder** (born 24 CE) added to Aristotle's natural history and **Claudius Ptolemy** (born c. 90 CE) gave Aristotle's astronomy mathematical treatment. The poet **Horace** (born 65 BCE) was known as the Roman Aristotle for his analysis of literature and drama.

NEOPLATONISM
Plato's teachings on the nature of reality became a renewed doctrine—**Neoplatonism**—with **Plotinus** (born c. 205 CE). This had a **profound influence on Christian theology**, particularly through **St. Augustine** (born 354 CE), whose Neoplatonist ideas survived his conversion to Christianity.

MARCUS AURELIUS
Stoicism found a welcome in Rome, where it became the most popular philosophy among the

MARCUS AURELIUS

elite, idealizing self-control and detachment from emotion. The Emperor **Marcus Aurelius** (born 121 CE) gave expression to Roman Stoicism in his book *Meditations*.

LATER EPICUREANISM
In the US Declaration of Independence (1776) **298–99 »**, the right to **"life, liberty, and the pursuit of happiness"** is an Epicurean ideal.

ST. AUGUSTINE AT THE SCHOOL OF ROME

Even before the Greeks began pursuing geographical knowledge from 600 BCE, some people's experience of travel, trade, and communication was extensive.

MYTHICAL GEOGRAPHY
Early concepts of the shape of the world owe much to **myths « 102–03**. People had seemingly fantastical concepts of far-off lands. This schematic diagram of the world (left) dating to 1000–500 BCE describes mythical beings inhabiting the corners of the world. The perspective is **centered on the city of**

BABYLONIAN VIEW OF THE WORLD

Babylon in Mesopotamia (modern Iraq), and real locations, labeled with their names, surround it in rough correlation to reality. The tablet is a visual concept of the world rather than a guide to it.

DISTANT CONNECTIONS
Although some people traveled far in the ancient world, the knowledge of geography they acquired only gradually came to be expressed as maps or texts. Instead, the powerful showed off their connections with monuments in the landscape, or by displaying possessions from distant lands.

THE WEALTH OF TRADE CITIES
Since **Phoenician times «82–83**, cities that could control trade had become wealthy. Some city-states and kingdoms were built on their monopoly on goods such as **incense** or **silk**.

A Wider World

Links across the ancient world were forged by merchants, rulers, and migrants. Through increasing cultural exchange, societies gained knowledge of distant lands, and as awareness of the world grew, the far-flung connections of worldly and wealthy people were admired as marks of status.

Ivory from Africa
Unearthed in Nineveh, the capital of Assyria in 700 BCE, this carving is of elephant ivory, a material the Assyrians would have had access to through contacts with the Phoenicians. Such an exotic commodity from far-off lands would have conveyed status on its owner.

As empires united vast, multicultural regions (see pp.90–91), enterprising explorers and traders found new routes and access to valuable goods. The most luxurious or prestigious commodities were often those that had traveled the greatest distance. Silk that found its way from China to Rome changed hands many times en route, with each middleman taking his markup.

Ideas, stories, religions, languages, all traveled along the trade routes between the various lands. During the Hellenistic Period (see pp.98–99), Greek was a common language from Greece to India, and Greek gods, such as Zeus, made appearances as far afield as Bactria (modern Afghanistan). The Greek mythical hero Herakles (Hercules), also recorded in Bactria, appears as a statue over a major trade and military route through the Zagros Mountains of Persia (in present-day Iran, see pp.92–93). But here, his identity is blended with the hero Verethraghna of Persian tradition.

Later, as the spheres of influence of Rome, China, and Parthia expanded and overlapped, cultural interchange began to occur across the whole of Eurasia, and Buddhism spread from India to China via Parthian travelers on the Silk Road. It was a Parthian nobleman called An Shi Kao who, in 148 BCE, was the first to translate Buddhist texts into Chinese.

Traces of trade
The gradual spread of ideas and culture through trade and migration, although little documented, has left many archaeological traces. Artifacts unearthed far from home, such as African ivory in Assyria (see above), a hoard of Roman coins in India, or a Persian carpet in Siberia, provide clear evidence of long-distance trade. The occasional shipwreck can represent a detailed time capsule of information. Ancient writings also build the picture of trails taken by travelers. Documents

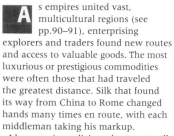

Roman road atlas
This view of the world, known as the Peutinger Table, is a medieval copy of a Roman original. It records journeys made across the Roman world and beyond before the 4th century CE. Distances are distorted unrecognizably to preserve the order of places and routes in a clear itinerary.

Greek in Central Asia
Common languages spread across vast, multicultural territories. Here, Greek is used on a 150-BCE coin of Afghanistan, unearthed in Turkey.

from the Persian capital Persepolis, for instance, note the rations given to official travelers, and the official stops they made across the empire from Sardis (today in western Turkey) in the west to India in the east. In the commercial world, itineraries were drawn up as guides for merchants. One surviving example, written by a Romanized author from Alexandria in Egypt in the 1st century CE, describes the Red Sea and Indian Ocean. It relates the ports and the goods, such as iron, gold, silver, myrrh, and slaves, available for import and export in each, and extends its account to the Ganges River and beyond, to China. Such knowledge was consolidated into an accurate geographical picture of the world by Greek and Roman map-makers. In the 2nd century CE, Ptolemy of Alexandria compiled *Geographia*—a world atlas that laid out instructions on charting the world with lines of latitude and longitude. It featured North Africa, India, Taprobane (Sri Lanka), and Sinae (China), including its capital, Chang'an.

Physical links

The transport networks of the ancient world were not so much constructed as evolved as common routes over millennia. In places, however, roads were cut deliberately by mobilizing forced labor. More often, a route was marked less by a physical road than by a maintained string of stages or settlements. States that expanded over wide areas needed to maintain regular communication by supporting these networks as a crucial aspect of their

Wealth of a caravan city
Petra was the capital of the Nabataean Arabs, who controlled the supply of luxury goods between Arabia and Mediterranean markets. The wealth of such a trade hub is evident in the surviving colonnades, temples, and tombs.

control. Roman skill in road-building grew as they gained control of Italy (see pp.106–07). Likewise, to send letters across their vast empire, the Persians developed a swift messenger system whose reputation for speed spread well beyond their empire. Xenophon, the Greek historian of the 4th century BCE, described relays of horses at stations spaced at one-day intervals and manned by officials. Whenever a letter arrived, the officials immediately sent it on with fresh riders and fresh horses.

Imagining new worlds

The imagination was important in forming ideas of the world. Old tales of exploration were remembered by the next wave of adventurers. When Alexander's army (see pp.96–99)

reached the edge of their known world, they imagined mythical heroes, such as Herakles, had explored the new horizon before them. The Greek historian Herodotus (see pp.102–03) wrote that the gold emerging from east of Persia was mined with the help of giant ants.

After 400 CE, expansion of the world's horizons slowed until geographical knowledge was revived first by medieval Arab and Chinese explorers, then by Renaissance Europeans **250–53 »**.

ARAB EXPLORATION

New impetus for exploration, trade, and the communication of ideas was provided by the contacts created between the Atlantic and the Far East by the Arab conquests **174–77 »**.

CLASSICAL WORLD VIEWS

Scholars relied on Classical views of the world for centuries after they were first produced. Both the **Peutinger Table** and **Ptolemy's world map 320 »** continued to be recopied by scribes into the **medieval period**. Columbus **224–25 »**

used Ptolemy's inaccurate calculation of Earth's circumference in attempting to sail west to India.

ARAB CARTOGRAPHY

The Muslim cartographer **Al-Idrisi** created a map for his patron, Roger II of Sicily, in the 12th century. Sicily was a contact zone between Muslims and Christians at the time. Al-Idrisi's map is oriented with south at the top, reflecting the outlook from Sicily toward the lands of Islamic rule. This map was one of the triggers for the pioneering Renaissance voyages that were to introduce the Old World to the New.

AL-IDRISI'S MAP

Nexus of trade
By c.1 CE, the world's trade routes had extended, through many intermediaries, from western Europe to China. China was largely self-sufficient, but imported desirable goods, such as spices from Southeast Asia and cavalry horses from Central Asia. Rome, in contrast, was a hub of commerce, dependent on trade. The empire imported food, slaves, animals, spices, silk, incense, and cotton.

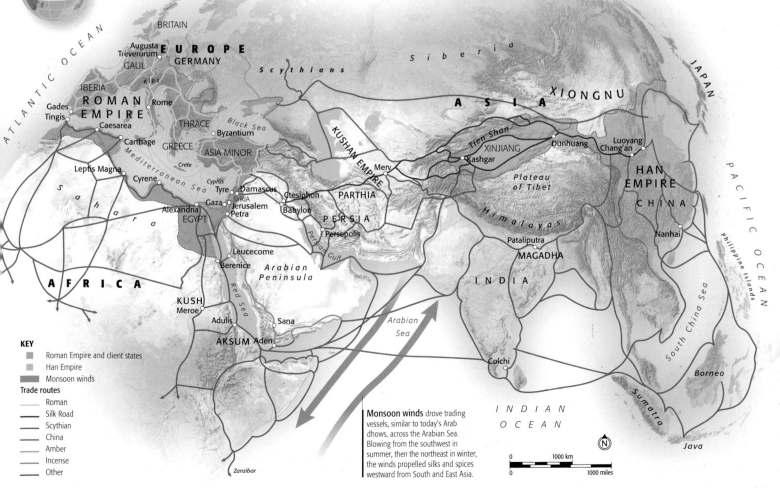

KEY

- ▨ Roman Empire and client states
- ▨ Han Empire
- ▨ Monsoon winds

Trade routes
- Roman
- Silk Road
- Scythian
- China
- Amber
- Incense
- Other

Monsoon winds drove trading vessels, similar to today's Arab dhows, across the Arabian Sea. Blowing from the southwest in summer, then the northeast in winter, the winds propelled silks and spices westward from South and East Asia.

0   1000 km
0   1000 miles

BEFORE

Some historians have linked Celtic origins with the Urnfield culture (so named because urns containing the ashes of the dead were placed in fields), which dates from around 1200 BCE and was based in France and Germany. It is also thought that Celtic ancestry may be rooted in the Eurasian steppes.

HALLSTATT CULTURE

Archaeological finds place the first Celts in **Hallstatt** (Austria) in around 700 BCE—the early Iron Age. The Hallstatt Celts seem to have been one of Europe's **first Iron Age cultures** and appear to have been wealthy and powerful. Their chieftains' graves contained valuable items such as bronze buckets and jewelry, suggesting trade with Greece and domination of several major European trading routes.

**HALLSTATT
BRONZE WAGON**

CELTIC ADVANCE

By around 500 BCE, the Celts had settled in pockets of France, Germany, and what is now the western part of the Czech Republic. About 100 years later, a significant spread of Celtic tribes into many parts of Europe began, notably into northern Italy. They settled in the Po valley before sacking Rome (c. 390 BCE). The extent of the Celtic "invasion" is a matter of debate.

CELTIC QUEEN (DIED 60 CE)

BOUDICCA

Queen of the Celtic Iceni people of eastern England, Boudicca (or Boadicea) led a bloody uprising against occupying Roman forces after the Romans ignored the will of her dead husband, King Prasutagus. The king had left his estate jointly to his daughters and to Rome, but Romans seized his entire kingdom and mistreated his family. Boudicca sacked Colchester and Londinium but was finally defeated, and is thought to have killed herself to avoid capture.

The word "Celt" refers to many groups of Europeans who spoke related Indo-European languages and migrated across Europe from the 5th century BCE. They are sometimes called "the first masters of Europe." Although the Celts were not one cohesive people, and were composed of numerous and fairly diverse groups, they displayed a common culture. This culture was typified by organization into tribes or clans, a nomadic or village life existence, and a strong warrior tradition.

The Dying Gaul
This copy of a Greek statue commemorates a Greek victory against invading "Gauls" (Celts) in the 220s BCE. The torc around the Gaul's neck is a sign of Celtic identity.

Celtic Warriors

Fierce warriors and skilled ironworkers with a love of feasting, the Celts swept across much of Europe during the 1st millennium BCE. Their advance brought them in contact with many of the cultures that shaped history, including the Greeks and Romans. Later, they played a part in the rise of Christianity.

By the 200s BCE, Celts and their culture were prevalent across a large swath of Western and Central Europe. In the 4th century BCE, they had already sacked (plundered) Rome. The next few centuries saw them reach the British Isles and move across Italy, France, Spain, Greece, Macedonia, and modern Turkey, sending delegations to Alexander the Great (see pp.96–97) in the 300s BCE and sacking Delphi, Greece, in 279 BCE. They met with varying fortunes, sometimes victorious and sometimes defeated. Where they did triumph, there was a significant exchange of cultures between the Celts and those they had conquered.

Tribal structure

Celtic society was an agricultural one of fortified villages, and was organized into many inter-fighting tribes or clans. The tribe was more important than the individual. Tribal structure was hierarchical, with a king or chief at the head; followed by noble-warriors and priests (druids); commoners, many of whom were farmers; and slaves. Druids had a very special status in Celtic society. They came from leading families and were exempted from paying taxes or taking part in fighting. The different tribes had cultural, rather than political, common ground. This lack of political cohesion was ultimately a weakness (see AFTER).

Beliefs and mythology

The Celts were illiterate, even at their height, but had a powerful oral tradition of storytelling and poetry. Epic poems of war exploits and glories are an especially important part of Celtic culture. Stories would also have been about Celtic beliefs and deities. Celtic mythology featured a strong belief in an afterlife—an "otherworld" realm less like a heaven and more of a parallel with the real world, much like the ancient Egyptian afterlife (see pp.68–69). The Celtic otherworld was peopled by gods and supernatural beings, such as Cernunnos, horned god of virility, nature, and plenty. The Celts believed that people journeyed to the otherworld after death, and great feasts were held as preparation for chiefs' burials. Woodland spirits were believed to inhabit the otherworld, and

A godlike figure appears to dip a man into, or remove him from, a cauldron, perhaps as an "Otherworld" rebirth or initiation ritual.

Noble horsemen may be riding away after rebirth in the cauldron. Their helmets have symbolic decoration such as crescent shapes, boars, or birds.

elements of the natural world were central to Celtic beliefs. Oak trees and mistletoe were thought to be sacred. The rituals performed by druids often took place outside, especially in woods.

Celtic art and crafts

Motifs from the natural world are important in Celtic art, too. The Celts were skilled metalworkers and they

CARTHAGINIAN COIN, IBERIA

The Celtic tribes lacked unity and were constantly fighting with each other. Greater, more unified powers subjugated them in most regions.

ROMAN RULE

By the 1st century CE, the spread of Roman power had ended Celtic domination in Italy, Gaul (after the Gallic uprising by **Vercingetorix** had been put down), and in England. In northern Italy, Celts had been incorporated as Roman citizens under Caesar **108–09 >>**, who had even raised two legions from this area for his conquest of Gaul. The Romans fought for control of Iberia (Spain),

with the **Carthaginians << 82–83** and native Celts, although the area remained "**Celtiberian,**" despite Carthaginian and Roman rule.

GERMANIC VICTORY

Germanic tribes fought against both the Romans and the Celts, and successfully pushed the Celts out of the Rhine Valley.

ON THE MARGINS

Subdued by Roman and Germanic forces, Celtic strongholds were increasingly pushed into the margins of their former lands. Ultimately, they

lingered on for longer in **Ireland** and other pockets where Celtic culture persists today, such as **Cornwall**, **Wales**, and the **Scottish Highlands**. It is likely that, during the 4th–6th centuries CE, the Anglo-Saxons further supplanted the Celts in England.

IRISH BROOCH

RISE OF CHRISTIANITY

Christianity reached the non-Roman-ruled Celtic people around the 4th century CE. **Celtic churches** played an important role in the early **spread of the Christian religion** in northern Europe.

Gundestrup cauldron
This Celtic silver vessel was found in a Danish peat bog in 1891. It dates from about the 1st century BCE, and it may have had a ritual purpose.

"The whole Celtic race is obsessed with war."

STRABO, ANCIENT GREEK HISTORIAN AND GEOGRAPHER, 1ST CENTURY BCE

spread their knowledge, especially of ironworking techniques, wherever they migrated. Gold and bronze were popular for luxury items—the Celts are famed for wearing gold torcs (neck bands with sculpted ends), as well as bracelets and impressive brooches. They were affected by foreign cultures, too. Some of the geometric and curvilinear shapes in Celtic art were influenced by the various peoples the Celts came into contact with, from the Greeks and Etruscans to steppe people such as the Scythians (see pp.138–39).

Weaponry, war, and dominance

Because a talent for warfare and horsemanship was central to Celtic culture, great artistic skill was poured into weaponry, armor, harnesses, and chariots. Some particularly fine weapons were borne principally as badges of honor and rank, or used for ceremonial purposes rather than in active service. These great warrior-people used shields, swords, and spears as weapons. Some Roman tools of war (such as the *scutum*, a type of shield) reveal Celtic influences. Chariots were used widely in earlier times and skilled horsemanship was greatly prized. Some Celtic tribes painted or tattooed themselves with plant dyes to look more alarming to their enemies.

The Celtic La Tène culture (named after an archaeological site in Switzerland) followed Hallstatt culture (see BEFORE) and grew in influence, becoming dominant between 450–15 BCE. Although it subsequently dwindled, Celtic culture persists today and Celtic languages are still spoken in Brittany (the Breton language), Wales, Scotland, Ireland, and the Isle of Man.

Warriors on foot with shields and spears, marching toward the left, may be dead soldiers approaching a ritual rebirth in the cauldron.

Musicians blow on long Celtic trumpets. This style of trumpet (*carnyx*) was held vertically and had a mouth shaped like a boar's head. It was played in battle.

Gundestrup detail
This is one of the panels on the Gundestrup cauldron, decorated with a scene of gods and men. Celtic mythology linked cauldrons with feasting and regeneration, and this particular panel, and the cauldron itself, may echo those beliefs.

2 DOG FIGURINE

6 HORNED HELMET

7 SPOON

8 HARNESS

11 HORSE MASK

3 HALLSTATT SCULPTURE

9 GUNDESTRUP CAULDRON

12 BRONZE BROOCH

4 HARNESS DECORATION

1 BATTERSEA SHIELD

5 CEREMONIAL AX

10 CHARIOT ORNAMENT

Celtic Metal

The Celtic clans were superb metalworkers, fashioning goods from bronze, iron, and gold. Ornate items have been discovered at sites in Central and Western Europe, and are distinctively decorated, often with images of animals and plants.

1 **The Battersea shield,** which was found in the Thames River, London. Dating from the 2nd century BCE, this was probably for display rather than battle, as it is made of thin bronze and intricately decorated. 2 **Bronze dog figurine,** which probably had some mythological or religious significance. 3 **Hallstatt bull sculpture** found on a site in Moravia, Czech Republic, and dating from c. 450 BCE. 4 **Harness decoration,** which was discovered in a grave in northern France. 5 **Bronze Hallstatt ornamental hatchet,** found in Austria. Dating from c. 650 BCE, it features the figure of a rider. 6 **Horned helmet,** possibly for ceremonial use, and dating to c. 250–50 BCE. It is the only helmet of its type to have been found in Europe. 7 **Carved metal spoon,** dating from the 6th century CE and discovered in Kilkenny, Ireland. 8 **Part of a harness** found in Cambridge, England and worked in bronze, with an engraved central design. 9 **Base of the Gundestrup Cauldron** (see pp.134–35), showing the ritual slaying of a bull. 10 **Enamel ornament,**

which would have decorated the chariot of a high-ranking horseman. It was found In Norfolk, England. 11 **The Stanwick Horse Mask,** a chariot fixture dating to the 1st century CE and discovered in Yorkshire, England. 12 **Bronze brooch** from c. 1000 BCE, and discovered in Austria. 13 **Ceremonial dagger** of iron and bronze, which was found in Britain. 14 **Enameled chariot hardware** found in Wales and dating from the 1st century CE. 15 **Chariot ornament** from 2nd century BCE. 16 **Bronze javelin heads.** 17 **The decorated bronze surface** of the back of a mirror, featuring a symmetrical clover leaf pattern, possibly belonging to a high-ranking woman. 18 **Bronze ornament** of the 1st century CE discovered in Ireland; its function remains unknown. 19 **Gold coins** dating from c. 1st century CE, and probably originating from northern France. 20 **Decorated bronze harness** discovered in an Irish peat bog. 21 **Silver pin brooch** decorated with animals. 22 **Bridle bit** worked in bronze and dating to the 2nd or 3rd century BCE.

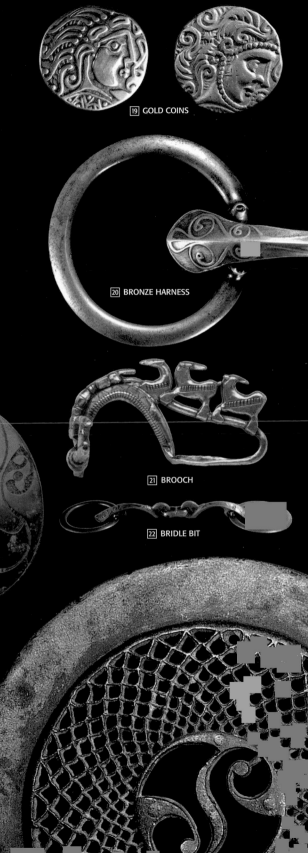

19 GOLD COINS

20 BRONZE HARNESS

21 BROOCH

22 BRIDLE BIT

14 CHARIOT HARDWARE

15 CHARIOT DECORATION

17 MIRROR

13 CEREMONIAL DAGGER

16 JAVELIN HEADS

18 BRONZE ORNAMENT

BEFORE

The steppes and prairies covering much of the Eurasian interior, especially in the west, were suited to varying degrees of farming and grazing.

KURGANS ON THE STEPPES

BRONZE AGE STEPPE CULTURE
By the Bronze Age **《 43** the Eurasian steppe peoples were living a mainly **agricultural life**. They kept horses and domesticated animals. Earthen burial mounds called **kurgans** were a major cultural feature from central Europe to Siberia.

MASS MIGRATION
By c. 2000 BCE a **major movement of steppe peoples** into adjacent lands seems to have begun, linked to **altered agricultural practices** and a search for **better farming conditions**.

In geographical terms, the Eurasian steppe can be divided into western and eastern regions. The western area begins in Hungary and stretches north of the Black Sea to the Altai Mountains in the east. The eastern portion, which is mostly at a higher altitude, runs east from the Altai range across Mongolia to Manchuria in China.

The western steppe, such as the fertile lands around the Danube, is wetter and greener. Moving eastward, summers become hotter, winters colder, and rain more scarce. Tribes of the eastern steppe often migrated west or south to areas of higher rainfall and fresh grazing pasture.

Scythian horseman
The Scythians are famed for creating beautiful artifacts, especially in gold, and for being formidable horsemen. This item, found at Kul Oba, in the Crimea, combines both aspects. It dates from the 4th century BCE.

skills were supplemented by a talent for fighting. Steppe society was organized into "kinship" groups (effectively extended families) and tribes. On occasion, tribes might assemble to create a larger body. Such gatherings were usually temporary, formed for a specific purpose, such as defense or attack. The rulers of steppe tribes were often thought to be divine.

Riding to victory
The early history of the horse's domestication is unclear, but by c. 700 BCE, horses were extremely important on the steppes, and were bred in large numbers. They were

Nomads of the Steppes

The steppes—grasslands stretching from Eastern Europe to China—have been home to nomadic and seminomadic groups for millennia. The history of the steppe people has been influenced by geography, while their territorial ambitions brought clashes with a range of powers that changed the world map.

HOW WE KNOW
THE PAZYRYK TOMBS

Pazyryk is a valley burial site in the Altai Mountains, in modern Kazakhstan, dating from the 5th to 3rd centuries BCE. Much of what we know about the Scythians comes from grave goods discovered in royal kurgans at Pazyryk. These goods included horses, burial chariots, and some of the earliest known textiles—felt and wool items such as appliquéd saddle-covers and colorful carpets (below).

Such migrations reinforced the nomadic lifestyle. It also brought various groups in contact with each other, which is why there are many cultural similarities between the different steppe peoples.

Life on the steppes
Relatively little is known about steppe life before the 11th century CE. We do know that the steppe tribes spoke Indo-European languages, and that

they kept domesticated animals, such as cattle and sheep. They often used animal caravans and rivers to transport goods, and their superb horsemanship

Mongolian herdsman
Nomadic pastoralism involves moving herds of domesticated animals over large distances. In some steppe regions it has changed little in thousands of years.

ideal animals for people who had to move over vast distances to find suitable pasture for their livestock, because they provided not only transportation but also meat and even milk.

By this time, the steppe people could fight very effectively on horseback, possibly having copied the techniques of the Assyrians (see pp.80–81). Crucial to the development of their fighting prowess were the composite

IDEAS

STEPPE BELIEFS

Steppe peoples were heavily influenced by the expansive skies of the open steppelands, which, as a major navigational guide, played a huge role in their lives. Some peoples certainly believed in a sky deity, a "heaven," and an afterlife, and shamanistic practices may also have been widespread. Shamans are people thought to have the power to cure sickness and communicate with the spirit world. Mirrors, a traditional shamanic tool, are believed to reflect secret truths and ward off evil spirits.

MONGOLIAN SHAMAN'S MIRROR

bow and stirrups. The composite bow is a short bow that is easy to fire from a horse, yet very powerful. The stirrup, which probably originated on the steppes around the 2nd century BCE, made it easier to ride well in full armor.

Steppe armies were skilled at launching sudden mounted attacks—usually raids rather than attempts at territorial conquest—and overran rival settlements with ease. Although some campaigns, such as the Cimmerian attack on Asia Minor c. 690 BCE, were large-scale onslaughts,

many raids were small affairs. The popular idea of invading hordes is misleading—a few fierce horsemen galloping in would seem overwhelming to an agricultural village.

Scythian and Kushans

The Scythians were a group of steppe peoples who had migrated from Central Asia to southern Russia by the 7th century BCE. Their warriors fought with bows and arrows, and axes. They wore felt caps and, except for some members of the aristocracy, no armor.

The Scythians possessed sizable territories at different periods, including a large area of the Middle East. One group, the "Royal Scythes," controlled an area around southern Russia, where stunning grave finds of gold artifacts point to a well-developed Scythian culture. By the 2nd century CE, the Scythians had been quashed by the Sarmatians, who were in turn defeated by the Huns (see pp.150–51).

THE AMAZONS, the famous female warriors of Greco-Roman legend, may have been based on Eurasian steppe women, who some believe took an active role in raiding and fighting.

Kushan head
This sculpture shows the mix of Greco-Roman and Indian influences that infused much of Kushan art.

Steppe nomads often integrated with people living in areas they invaded. In the 1st–3rd centuries CE, for example, the Kushans migrated from the fringes of Mongolia to the western steppe, into lands that once formed part of the Achaemenid Persian Empire (see pp.92–93) and the empire of Alexander the Great (see pp.96–98). Like the Parthians (see pp.122–23), the Kushans developed a settled, sophisticated culture that readily incorporated Greek, Persian, and Indian influences.

The Xiongnu

Xiongnu (or Hsiung-nu) is a term for a loose grouping of different steppe peoples (including some Scythians) whose warriors were raiding China by the 3rd century BCE. Some aspects of their culture seem to have been adopted from the Chinese regimes they attacked. The Xiongnu were a dominant force in Central Asia for five centuries.

Steppe peoples continued to make their mark on groups across Eurasia, from displaced Germanic tribes to rising Islamic powers.

THE HUNS

Between the 4th and 5th centuries CE, pastoral steppe nomads known as Huns **controlled huge swaths of Europe and Asia**, conquering other tribes they encountered, including the Germanic Ostrogoths. In the mid-5th century, some of those peoples **fought back** successfully against the Huns, and the **Eastern Roman Empire** also closed its borders. The Huns were soon a **spent force.**

HUN DINARS

TURKIC TRIBES

By c. 500 CE, the Turkic people (originally nomads in the Altai Mountains) **dominated much of the Asian steppe**. By c. 700 CE, their power had been weakened, and various Turkic tribes scattered westward following **wars with the Tang Chinese 160–61 ≫**. However, they remained a major presence, playing a key role in Middle Eastern history and the rise of Islam.

RISE OF THE MONGOLS

The Mongols managed to conquer and create a confederacy of all the nomads on the Mongolian steppes in the early 13th century **164–65 ≫**.

Paracas textile
The Paracas people of Peru made beautiful textiles. Many feature a godlike creature known as the "oculate being," depicted here wearing a gold diadem and holding a snake.

A dvanced American societies in this era had much in common: quarrying stone, creating beautiful artifacts, and worshipping multiple gods usually linked to nature (for example, the jaguar, the sun, and the moon). South American cultures were more advanced in their use of metals, but it was a Mesoamerican culture—the Maya—that left the most powerful and enigmatic monuments.

The Maya
The "Classic" period of Maya culture is normally dated from c. 300 to 900 CE. It flourished over a wide swath of Central America, especially the Yucatán and Guatemala's steamy lowlands. At its heart stood a large number of important cities. Originally ritual centers, many grew into populous city-states.

The Maya built huge, often pyramidal stone temples, such as those at Tikal in Guatemala, and showed a great talent

plotting the positions of the sun and moon and predicting solar eclipses. Their calendar had two main cycles: a 260-day sacred year (13 cycles of 20 days) and a 365-day solar year (18 months of 20 days each, plus an "unlucky" 5-day period, which the Maya spent appeasing the gods).

Monte Albán and Teotihuacán
While Maya civilization was thriving, the Zapotec people of southern Mexico were creating their major center at Monte Albán (see BEFORE). The ruins of the city's sacred and political center, dating mainly from c. 300 CE onward, show that this was another highly sophisticated society. A great central plaza is surrounded by monumental platforms, pyramids, staircases, and terraces. Other buildings include a ball court and an observatory. The architecture at Monte Albán shows influences from another significant

Early American Civilizations

Various advanced cultures flourished simultaneously in the Americas between the 1st century BCE and c. 400–600 CE—a period that includes part of the great Mesoamerican "Classic" eras. Perhaps the best known of these cultures was that of the Maya people, who with their stunning temples and scientific knowledge created one of the most extraordinary early American civilizations.

« BEFORE

The advanced societies of Meso- and South America in the 1st centuries CE built on the legacy of earlier cultures, the Olmecs in Mexico, and the Chavín in Peru.

OLMECS AND ZAPOTECS
Maya **writing**, their calendar, and understanding of astronomy all owe a debt to the **Olmec culture** « **74–75** that flourished c. 1200–400 BCE near the coast of the Gulf of Mexico. The **Zapotec** city of Monte Albán in the valley of Oaxaca, which first appeared at the time of the later Olmecs, remained an important center until c. 600 CE.

BALL COURT AT MONTE ALBÁN

CHAVÍN CULTURE
Chavín culture « **74–75**, widely diffused across Peru c. 1000–200 BCE, gave way to smaller coastal societies such as the Moche and the Nazca.

for carved stone reliefs, with some especially fine examples at Palenque in Mexico. Cities also featured palaces, open plazas, terraces, and courts where a sacred ball game was played. This seems to have been a strenuous affair in which the participants used their heads, hips, and shoulders to direct a rubber ball at its target.

Religious ritual played a major part in Maya life. They practiced forms of "auto-sacrifice" (self-mutilation involving the piercing of body parts), but more extreme scenarios involving torture and human sacrifice seem to be highly inaccurate and sensationalized.

Writing and the calendar
While the Olmecs developed a form of writing, some consider that the Maya should be credited with the first "real" Mesoamerican writing because theirs was more closely connected with actual speech. Their system comprised at least 800 glyphs (symbols).

The Maya also had a sophisticated calendar—probably using earlier Olmec concepts. This incorporated advanced astronomical knowledge that included

Moche stirrup-spouted jar
The Moche often combined different animals in their artifacts—this jar has the head of a deer, feline fangs, and a snake's body.

cultural center, that at Teotihuacán (see right), a huge city northeast of present-day Mexico City that flourished c. 300–600 CE and had cultural links across Mesoamerica.

Peruvian societies
In South America, various Peruvian cultures flourished up to about 400–600 CE. The people of southern Peru's Paracas peninsula were a mainly agricultural people, but were also extraordinarily talented weavers and embroiderers. Their art is preserved in the beautiful cloaks that the Paracas wrapped around mummified bodies.

The Nazca people lived on Peru's southern coast, with an important center at Cahuachi in the Nazca Valley. They created irrigation systems to support intensive grain production, as well as puzzling "lines" in the desert that remain a mystery today.

On Peru's northern coast, the Moche built a great administrative and religious complex at Sipán. Formidable warriors and inventive artists, they also created advanced valley irrigation techniques.

AFTER »

Meso- and South America continued to give rise to a variety of new cultures, while Maya civilization underwent a major shift.

SOUTH AMERICA
From around 600 CE, the **Tiahuanaco** and **Huari** cultures emerged in the highlands of Bolivia and Peru, respectively. The **Chimú** of coastal Peru created a large state that fell to the **Incas 212–13 »** in the 15th century.

TIAHUANACO GOD

THE LATE MAYA PERIOD
From the 9th century CE, a number of southern Maya centers were abandoned—due to a range of factors, including **depleted resources** resulting from **intense cultivation**—while northern ones such as **Chichén Itzá 210–13 »** were still thriving and expanding. The Maya culture lived on, and today there are around 6 million Maya in Mexico, Guatemala, and Belize.

Maya ritual
This carving shows a bloodletting "auto-sacrifice." Lady K'ab'al Xook pulls a thorny rope through her tongue as her husband, the king of Yaxchilán, holds a torch over her.

BEFORE

In earliest times, much religion seems to have been related to fertility or the seasons. As people's social organization changed, so did their conception of their gods.

EARLIEST SUPERNATURAL BELIEFS
Remains of Stone Age ritual burials **‹‹ 32–33** suggest that belief in the **afterlife** and the **spirit world** is at least 60,000 years old. Neolithic monuments and traces of ritual life **‹‹ 40–41** suggest a spiritual outlook reflecting the **cycle of seasons** and the **motion of the heavens**.

PREHISTORIC RELIGIOUS SYMBOLS
Religious artifacts from prehistoric societies **‹‹ 34–35** reveal more about beliefs, despite the lack of written evidence. Male and female figurines with exaggerated features may be related to a desire for **fertility and prosperity**. Ritual sites that contain animals—either their physical remains, or images—suggest the worshippers were preoccupied with the supply of **animals for food and materials**.

HIERARCHY OF GODS
Early religion often involved **polytheism—the worship of many deities**. With the emergence of more complex societies in the first towns **‹‹ 44–45**, the new social order was mirrored in religion: the gods were organized, like society, into a **hierarchy**, with the ruling god at the apex.

IDEAS

HUMANS BECOMING GODS

Individuals with power over others were sometimes given the status of a god. The deified ruler may have been seen as the earthly embodiment of a certain god, or may have been worshipped as a god in their own right, giving his or her subjects protection in return. Rulers deified in their lifetime or after their deaths became more common in the Mediterranean world after the 4th century BCE. Below, the Roman emperor Claudius is being deified right after his death in 54 CE.

Greek gods
Found in the Mannella region of southeast Italy, this Greek clay sculpture from the first half of the 5th century BCE features the Greek goddess and daughter of Zeus, Persephone, and the god of the underworld, Hades.

Gods and Goddesses

Gods and goddesses were believed to be responsible for many aspects of the human experience in the ancient world. The importance of a god was determined by their place in a hierarchical order. The worship of certain gods spread to far-removed places with the expansion of the ancient empires.

Before the spread of some notable "world religions" (see pp.144–47), most people practiced polytheism (see BEFORE). While some of their many gods held sway over a large area, others were gods of a single city or feature in the landscape, such as a river. The deities, who were often depicted with human features, influenced almost every aspect of life. Even the weather was believed to be the result of the current mood of an individual god or goddess.

Social or political changes could influence the way in which godliness was perceived. In times of war and territorial expansion, mortal leaders, such as Roman emperors (see left) were sometimes worshipped as if they were gods, which served to focus loyalty to that leader. As societies became more complex, the relationships between the gods became more elaborate and many cultures

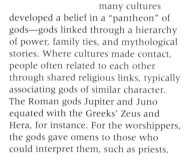

Gods and symbols
This Babylonian is paying his respects to the gods Marduk (symbolized by a triangular-headed spade) and Sin (a crescent moon).

developed a belief in a "pantheon" of gods—gods linked through a hierarchy of power, family ties, and mythological stories. Where cultures made contact, people often related to each other through shared religious links, typically associating gods of similar character. The Roman gods Jupiter and Juno equated with the Greeks' Zeus and Hera, for instance. For the worshippers, the gods gave omens to those who could interpret them, such as priests,

King of the Persian gods
The two sphinxes on this seal are supporting the winged Ahuramazda, patron god of the Persian monarchy (see pp.92–93). His appearance mirrors that of the king below. Seals transmitted religious images across great distances.

diviners, and oracles. In return the worshippers offered the gods gifts, sacrifice, or ritual tributes to secure their good will.

Supreme gods

In the same way that human societies have leaders, each pantheon also had a "supreme god." A god was recognized as supreme either by being given prominence by a ruler or city, or by being identified with key symbols in human life, such as a parent, or natural phenomena, such as the sun, sky, ocean, or storms. Gods became supreme gods when people came to think of them as "father" of a family of gods. One such god was Zeus, who was part-father, part-monarch of a quarreling cohort of Greek deities. A god could also be promoted to supreme deity if their city or people became dominant. Bel Marduk, for example, was the patron god of the city of Babylon from about 2000 BCE. When Babylon began

> "Men create gods **after their own image**…"
> ARISTOTLE, GREEK PHILOSOPHER, 384–322 BCE

to dominate southern Mesopotamia from 1780 BCE, Marduk's status was elevated and he acquired family ties with the gods of local regions and cities, eventually becoming supreme.

Gods in the landscape

A wide world of gods was imbued in the landscape itself, although physical evidence of their worship is hard to find, as it can be nothing more than a cluster of plaques by a spring. An ancient description of Persian religion revealed the practice of open-air rituals, and many Persian tablets record gods related to nature. Fertile places were revered across Asia and were the sites of gardens and Buddhist temples. Mountain sanctuaries could be the

> **MYSTERY RELIGION** One of many diverse religious cults involving a belief in death and regeneration or resurrection, which often required personal secret initiation. Early Christianity included many elements of a mystery cult.

focus of cults, such as that devoted to an ancient "Mother of the Gods" on mounts Sipylos and Dindymene in Anatolia. Mountains were sometimes used as billboards to promote a belief. The towering Buddhas in the cliff-face at Bamiyan in Afghanistan were sited strategically to overlook a major road to the East from Rome through Persia.

Migrant gods

Ever-wider cultural interconnections during the 1st millennium CE (see pp.132–33) enabled divine entities, such as the Buddha (see pp.144–47) to spread as never before. Gods could migrate with travelers, soldiers, and merchants across the entire Roman Empire. In London, temples to a rich variety of immigrant gods have been

Zeus' temple
The 5th century BCE temple of Zeus at Olympia in Greece contains a huge gold- and ivory-covered statue of the supreme god.

AFTER »

From 300 BCE–700 CE, the religious landscape was changed by the spread of the "world religions"—Hinduism, Buddhism, Judaism, Christianity, and Islam.

MONOTHEISM
Within pantheons of gods, lesser deities may diminish and disappear. If only one god remains, people's beliefs become **monotheistic 145 »**. Both **Judaism** and the **Zoroastrianism** of Persia have roots in earlier, polytheistic religions.

ENDURING EASTERN BELIEFS
The period 700 BCE–100 CE gave rise to most of today's established belief systems. In the East, **Taoism, Shintoism, and Confucianism « 133** all follow teachings more than 2,000 years old.

UNIVERSAL RELIGION
In antiquity, it was common for people to regard gods as the figureheads of their culture. Their religion was part of their ethnic identity, so it was **not encouraged in foreigners**. In multicultural kingdoms, tolerance of many beliefs was a fact of life. Some new religions, notably **Christianity 144–47 »** and **Islam 174–77 »** changed these ideas by proposing that, in theory, all humanity could and should share a single set of religious beliefs and practices.

uncovered. The gods included Serapis, who was first popular with the Greeks of Egypt (see pp.118–19), then hitched a ride with Roman settlement across Europe. Mithras, also worshipped in London, may have begun as the Persian Mithra. Such gods with "exotic" or Eastern origins, often the focus of "Mystery" cults requiring initiation, were popular with the shifting populations of the Roman world.

Exotic god
Dressed in a Phrygian cap and Persian clothing, and slaying a bull in Italy, the exotic origins of Mithras are highlighted in this Roman statue of the 2nd century CE.

BEFORE

Faith in a spiritual dimension to human existence probably evolved separately in many parts of the world among bands of Paleolithic hunter-gatherers.

GREEK GOD ZEUS

ANIMISM

The earliest belief of the hunter-gatherers is known as animism. In animism, all of **physical nature has a spiritual counterpart** and everything becomes part of a chain. Each object, living or inanimate, is a link, but the links are fluid so that a man can become a bird, an animal can be disguised as a rock, and a bird can transform into a cloud. The power for these changes stems from a world of vaguely defined guardian spirits.

MANY GODS

As tribes became settled into farming communities, pantheons of more **clearly identifiable gods** emerged. Each god was responsible for overseeing a part of the temporal world, and still acting as the guardian of his or her domain—such as Zeus, the Greek god of thunder and lightning and also the ruler of Mount Olympus. This is **polytheism** (meaning "many gods") **<< 142–43**, which early Christians dubbed "paganism," a derogatory term from the Latin *pagani*, meaning "peasants."

THE NEXT WORLD

The belief in an afterlife may extend back even farther in time than animism, because Neanderthal **<< 19** burial sites sometimes included medicinal herbs and other items, which could suggest that they thought the deceased was embarking on a **journey to another place**.

PANTHEISM A doctrine or belief presenting the natural world, including humankind, as being part of the divine. It is the predominant belief in Hinduism, but is rejected by beliefs that hold that God is transcendent—a being above the created world—such as Christianity and Islam.

Though many different religious sects and movements have flourished briefly throughout history, five great faiths have emerged and spread sufficiently to become major world religions.

Hinduism

The oldest of these five religious faiths is Hinduism, which has a range of very diverse traditions but no formal system of beliefs. The origin of the religion can be traced to about 1500 BCE, when it is believed that Aryan horsemen from Central Asia invaded the Indus Valley in northern India (see pp.58–59), accompanied by a creator god Indra and a pantheon of lesser deities (see p.143). These were the Vedic gods, who feature in the *Vedas*, the 3,000-year-old sacred texts that are central to the development of Hinduism. The religion evolved to focus on three main gods: a senior, somewhat remote deity called Brahma; Vishnu the creator; and Shiva the destroyer, along with their various consorts or *shaktis*.

From the 6th century BCE, Brahmanism became the dominant form of Hinduism and triggered the composition of the Brahmanic, Epic,

> "There is probably no subject in the world about which **opinions differ** so much as the nature of religion."
>
> JAMES FRAZER, FROM "THE GOLDEN BOUGH," 1922

no fixed abode," later known as Hebrews, came together under Moses and settled in Palestine. In 587 BCE Jerusalem, the city that the legendary King David had made the capital of Israel, was destroyed by the Neo-Babylonians (see p.92) and the Israelite elite deported to Babylon. Cyrus the Great (see p.93) allowed the exiles home in 539 BCE to form a religious state based on the Hebrew book of law (the Torah) and the Jewish

IDEA

MONOTHEISM

The religious faith of the Israelites rested in a universal god, a unique, unchanging, and physically unseen revelation that contrasted starkly with the polytheism of neighboring cultures in the ancient Middle East. Tradition has it that this omnipotent deity, also the God of Islam and Christianity, was first recognized by Abraham—one of the patriarchal ancestors of the Israelites.

Spreading the Faith

In the first millennium BCE the scope of religions, supported not just by local traditions, but by sacred writings, widened immensely. Hinduism and Buddhism spread across Southeast Asia, while the Middle East saw the expanding influence of Judaism, followed by its monotheistic offshoots, Christianity and Islam.

Holiest of holy sites
Christianity, Islam, and Judaism view this site in Jerusalem as holy. In the foreground people can be seen praying at the Western Wall, and behind it is the Dome of the Rock mosque.

and Puranic literature, including the great texts of the *Mahabharata* and *Ramayana*. Hinduism remains polytheistic (see BEFORE).

Buddhism

Buddhism emerged not as a belief in a god, but as an ascetic way of life. Its teachings involve the belief that death marks the transition to a new earthly life—reincarnation. The only way to escape this painful cycle of death and rebirth, known as *samsara*, is to achieve perfection, which is accompanied by an extinction of passions, or *nirvana*.

Buddhism evolved in part as a reaction against polytheistic Hinduism and attracted a body of disciples willing to practice asceticism (abstention from earthly comforts). The historical Buddha (distinguished from earlier wholly mythical characters) was born into the royal Shakya clan in northeast India (modern Nepal) in about 563 BCE. After his death in about 483 BCE his original companions established the *Theravada* ("doctrine of the elders") school that would become the basis of more conservative Buddhist teaching.

The first monotheistic faith

Judaism, the monotheistic (see above right) religion of the Jews, evolved from the older, ritualistic, temple-based cult attributed to Moses. The ancestors of the Jews, the wandering Israelite tribes or *habiru*, literally "people of

religion flourished, first under Persian control, then under Alexander the Great (see pp.96–97). When one of Alexander's successors, Antiochus Epiphanes, tried to introduce aspects of Greek cults, the resulting uprising led to a dynasty of priest-kings, the Hasmoneans. In 63 BCE Greater Judea was incorporated into the Roman order, and hard times followed, culminating in 70 CE when much of the population of Jerusalem was scattered (see p.146).

Followers of Jesus Christ

The second major monotheistic religion, Christianity, arose from Judaism. There is no evidence that Jesus envisaged founding a religious movement. It was only through his death on the cross, during which Christians believe he atoned for humanity's sins, that the early Church emerged. The first Christians met in private houses and had no formal dogma; only after several decades did formal places of worship appear. The new religion endured spates of often bloody persecution from orthodox Jews and also from Roman emperors, notably Nero in 64 CE and Domitian at the end of the 1st century CE. Rather than destroying the religion, however, persecution had the effect of reinforcing the convictions of its devotees. »

RELIGIOUS FIGUREHEAD (c. 4 BCE –c. 30 CE)

JESUS

Jesus of Nazareth was the inspiration for the religious movement of Christianity, which derives from Greek *christos*, synonymous with Hebrew *messiah*, meaning "a chosen one." Jesus probably saw himself as a social reformer, but to some Jews under Roman occupation he became the deliverer predicted in Jewish scripture. In the Christian gospels he is described as the son of God. For much of his life Jesus moved around the Sea of Galilee, accompanied by a local band of disciples and followers. Only after his journey to Jerusalem and his death by crucifixion did his following grow and his messianic fame spread.

HINDU AUM SYMBOL

BUDDHIST WHEEL OF THE LAW

JEWISH STAR OF DAVID

CHRISTIAN CROSS

Religious symbols
The Aum symbol represents the sacred Hindu syllable for God. The wheel of the law represents both the teachings of the Buddha and the cycle of death and rebirth. The six-pointed hexagram or Star of David is widely accepted as the symbol of Judaism, although it has only been adopted as such over the last 200 years. The cross in Christianity is symbolic of the death, and resurrection, of Jesus Christ.

The emergence of Islam
Islam emerged in the 7th century CE. It recognizes the transcendental god of Judaism and Christianity, but by the name of Allah. The Prophet Muhammad promoted a doctrine based on personal divine revelation, which was incorporated into the holy book of Islam, the Qur'an.

Traveling faiths
From their Asian beginnings, Hinduism, Buddhism, Judaism, Christianity, and Islam all spread out across the globe, carried in some cases by conquering armies, in others by migrants, traders, and missionaries.

Spread of Hinduism
Hinduism was firmly established on the Indian subcontinent by 700 BCE. From around 600 BCE, belief in reincarnation was established and Hinduism spread on a wave of popular fervor from India into Sri Lanka, Cambodia, and Malaysia. It reached Indonesia and the Philippines in about the 1st century CE. Hinduism also evolved into a wide range of branches and sects, each

devoting itself to a particular deity or aspects of a deity. The largest and most universal of these were the *Vaishnava* and *Shaivite* movements, worshipping the two main creator deities, Vishnu and Shiva. Much of the burgeoning popularity of Hinduism also stemmed from the set of religious texts known as the *Puranas*, committed to writing in 450–1000 CE, but known in oral tradition from much earlier. Despite a multitude of different facets, Hinduism became a powerful cohesive force among people who were disparate in language, culture, and social position.

Paths of Buddhism
In the centuries after the death of Gautama Buddha (c. 483 BCE), members of the Indian *sanghas* (communities of monks) elaborated his teachings and paved the way for the development of a host of schools. One of the principal branches, *Hinayana* Buddhism, following the ancient "way of the elders" or *Theravada*, arose in the 4th century BCE and spread mainly south and east from India into Sri Lanka, Myanmar, Cambodia, Laos, and Thailand. The other main branch, *Mahayana* (the "Great Vehicle") Buddhism developed later, in the 1st–3rd centuries CE, and became the dominant element in 300–500 CE, spreading mainly north and east. Among *Mahayana's* splinter sects is the influential *Vajrayana* school, also sometimes called tantric Buddhism. Other more austere *Mahayana* schools were carried by itinerant monks through China and thence to Japan, where further adaptation resulted in Zen Buddhism. The faith has been described as the "Vagrant Lotus" because its history has been one of migration from one culture to another. As a result, the Buddhism of India stands in sharp contrast with that found in Japan and Korea.

Jewish diaspora
The spread of faith often went hand in glove with politics, and Judaism was no exception. Dispersal began with the forcible deportation of the Jewish elite to Babylon in 587 BCE, thus triggering the *diaspora*—the scattering of Jewish communities outside the Land of Israel.

The process intensified when the Roman general Titus sacked Jerusalem in 70 CE, causing many inhabitants to flee. By the end of the 1st century the local population had largely recovered, rebuilding its faith through observance of the Torah. Although the Romans protected the right of Jews to practice their religion throughout most of the history of the empire, they targeted Judaism after several revolts in the 2nd century CE. The emperor Septimius Severus (193–235 CE) instituted a tax on self-identified Jews and forbade conversion to Judaism. From 527 CE the Byzantine emperor Justinian subordinated Jews to orthodox Christians. Jews continued to use the trade networks of the empire, however, establishing themselves wherever trade took place. By 600 CE they had founded settlements as far as Cordoba in Iberia, Cologne in Germany, Oxyrhynchus in Egypt, and Xarax at the mouth of the Persian Gulf. Jewish populations became particularly concentrated in Asia Minor and in Mesopotamia.

Footsteps of Christianity
The Roman Empire was also largely responsible for the spread of Christianity. Although successive emperors suppressed its fledgling communities, St. Paul was able to move freely across Europe and establish Christian cells in Corinth, Ephesus, Galatia, Thessalonica, and elsewhere. When Emperor Constantine the Great converted to Christianity early in the 4th century CE (see pp.148–49), expansion truly gained pace.
Even before the reign of Constantine, Christianity had extended rapidly into Syria and northwest into Asia Minor and Greece. In the 2nd century a thriving community of Greek-speaking Christians was established in the Rhone valley in France, and by 200 CE the Church was also well established

in North Africa, centered on Carthage. To the northeast, beyond the imperial frontier, a language barrier slowed progress, although by the 3rd century a church was founded at Edessa in modern Turkey. However, most missionary work was focused on Western Europe—in Italy, France, and Spain. Britain probably felt little influence until the mid-3rd century, but by 400 CE it was largely Christian.

PROPHET (c. 570–632 CE)

MUHAMMAD

Born in Mecca, Muhammad succeeded in ridding southern Arabia of polytheism and replacing it with the worship of a single God, Allah. In Islamic doctrine he is the "end of a line" of prophets, the ultimate deliverer of divine revelation. From about 610 CE he witnessed a series of angelic visitations that became the foundation of Islamic theology. In 622 CE, in a journey known as the Hegira, he fled Mecca to escape persecution and settled in Medina with a growing band of supporters. In 631 CE he returned to Mecca on a final pilgrimage, accompanied, it is said, by 120,000 devotees. He died in Medina at age 63.

MONK (c. 563–c. 483 BCE)

GAUTAMA BUDDHA

Also known as Shakyamuni and Siddhartha, he lived in northern India during the 6th and 5th centuries BCE. One of the many ascetic philosophers of his day, he achieved enlightenment—an awakening to the ultimate truth—at Bodhgaya and subsequently wandered for the rest of his life teaching Buddhist philosophy and gathering a community of disciples or *sangha*. He taught the Eightfold Path to enlightenment, which includes disciplined guidance on all aspects of morality, wisdom, and meditation.

Spreading the Christian faith
St. Paul (Paul of Tarsus) received a rabbinical education in Jerusalem. Originally an opponent of the early Christians, he was converted c.33 CE and became the leading Christian apostle, or missionary, especially among the non-Jewish communities. Upon arrest by the Roman authorities, he appealed to the emperor but was executed c.62 CE.

The basilica of St. Peter's in the Vatican City, Rome, is the focus of devotion for millions of Catholics worldwide. The original was destroyed in the early 16th century. Its replacement, which is topped by a magnificent dome designed by Michelangelo, took over a century to build.

Faiths spread throughout the world, and regional changes occurred where some religions were adopted by new cultures.

UNIVERSAL TEACHINGS
The guru—a revered teacher of spiritual matters – became central to Hinduism. New Hindu schools have arisen, aiming to make its thought more universal. A celebrated modernist, Sri Ramakrishna (1836–86) taught the **essential unity of all religions** and the Ramakrishna Mission spread far beyond India.

DISPERSION
The Jewish diaspora continued, and by the middle ages France and Spain had become two of its most important centers. During the 19th century an exodus of Jews took place from Russia and Poland, and in the Nazi holocaust **400–01 »** many of the old European communities were **virtually annihilated**. In 1947 the **modern state of Israel 414–15 »** was born, annexed from the indigenous population of Palestinians. Today, the main focus of diaspora Judaism is the United States.

REGIONAL DIFFERENCES
Buddhism evolved into **various regional forms** as its influence extended through Central and Southeast Asia, China, Japan, and most recently, the West.

GREAT CHANGES
By the 11th century, Christianity had split into two, the western Church under the papacy in Rome and the eastern Orthodox Church. In the 16th century it split again when **challenges to papal authority** resulted in the Reformation **256–59 »**.

The Hagia Sofia in Istanbul, Turkey, is a magnificent example of Byzantine architecture. It was dedicated as a church by the Roman emperor Justinian I in 537 CE, then in 1453 CE was converted into a mosque. In 1935 it was turned into the Ayasofya Museum.

Mount Kailas, on the border between Tibet and Nepal, is a holy place for Buddhists and Hindus alike. Pilgrims trek up the Humla valley to walk around the mountain, but no one has ever climbed its slopes.

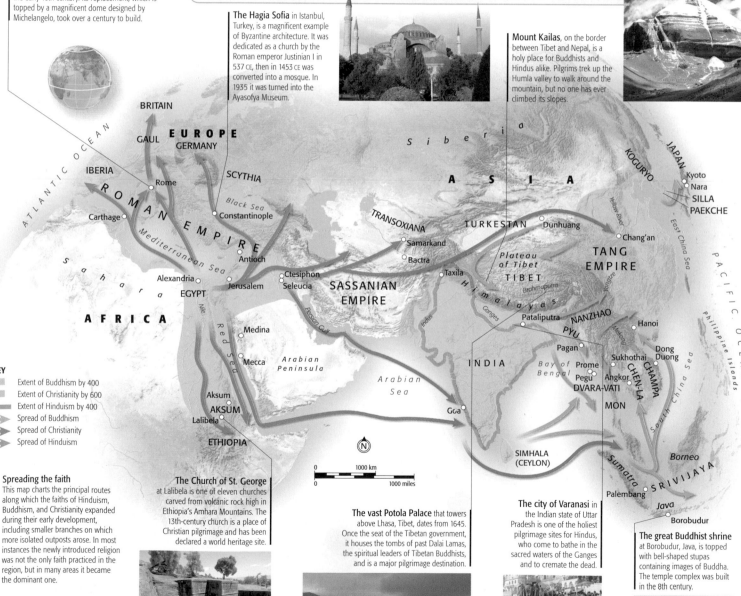

KEY
- Extent of Buddhism by 400
- Extent of Christianity by 600
- Extent of Hinduism by 400
- Spread of Buddhism
- Spread of Christianity
- Spread of Hinduism

Spreading the faith
This map charts the principal routes along which the faiths of Hinduism, Buddhism, and Christianity expanded during their early development, including smaller branches on which more isolated outposts arose. In most instances the newly introduced religion was not the only faith practiced in the region, but in many areas it became the dominant one.

The Church of St. George at Lalibela is one of eleven churches carved from volcanic rock high in Ethiopia's Amhara Mountains. The 13th-century church is a place of Christian pilgrimage and has been declared a world heritage site.

The vast Potola Palace that towers above Lhasa, Tibet, dates from 1645. Once the seat of the Tibetan government, it houses the tombs of past Dalai Lamas, the spiritual leaders of Tibetan Buddhists, and is a major pilgrimage destination.

The city of Varanasi in the Indian state of Uttar Pradesh is one of the holiest pilgrimage sites for Hindus, who come to bathe in the sacred waters of the Ganges and to cremate the dead.

The great Buddhist shrine at Borobudur, Java, is topped with bell-shaped stupas containing images of Buddha. The temple complex was built in the 8th century.

C·VAL·AVREL·CONSTANTINI
IMP·VICTORIA·QVA·SVBMERSO
MAXENTIO·CRISTIANORVM
OPES·FIRMATAE·SVNT

Battle of Milvian Bridge

In 312 CE, bitter rivals Constantine the Great and Maxentius met in battle outside Rome. Much was at stake, but foremost was the struggle for leadership of the western Roman Empire. Constantine went into the fray inspired by his Christian beliefs, while Maxentius put faith in pagan gods. The outcome was a turning point in the rise of Christianity.

In October 312 CE, Maxentius was making preparations behind Rome's walls to withstand a siege by Constantine. Previously, the two had separately been proclaimed emperor. Maxentius, being in Rome and having senate backing, perhaps had more legitimacy, but Constantine planned to take the city and claim the western empire as his alone.

Despite capturing some Maxentian strongholds as he crossed Italy that summer, Constantine must have felt some misgivings heading south from Gaul (France). He had a much smaller army than Maxentius, and its strength lay in a mobile cavalry that performed best in the open. However, before the battle, he apparently experienced a religious "conversion," which he may have felt put the Christian God on his side. Accounts include visions of a flaming cross in the sky and orders to place Christian symbols on his soldiers' shields.

As the battle began, Maxentius, fighting in the name of Mars, the Roman god of war, emerged into the open, giving Constantine the advantage. Maxentius had already dismantled Milvian Bridge to halt his opponent, so he and his troops had to cross the Tiber River using a bridge made from boats. In the ensuing battle, Constantine's cavalry disrupted enemy ranks with expert charges. Maxentius's troops had nowhere to go but into the Tiber, where many, including their leader, drowned. The next day, a triumphant procession, led by Constantine, marched through Rome with Maxentius's head on a spear.

Some view Constantine's "conversion" with cynicism, but he may have seen his victory at Milvian Bridge as a symbol of the power of Christianity. The influence of the faith had been gathering pace for three centuries, assisted by imperial edicts of religious tolerance. A few months after the battle, Constantine issued the Edict of Milan, which returned confiscated property to Christians and increased their status and political standing. His Christian leanings and massive church-building program helped the religion gain a hold in the west, shaping Byzantine culture (see pp.198–99), the Eastern Orthodox church, and medieval Christian society.

Fighting for Empire
This 16th-century fresco from the Vatican depicts the events at Milvian Bridge. In the center, the brightly lit Constantine can be seen pushing Maxentius and his troops into the Tiber River. Imperial standards bear crosses and, in the sky above, angels join in the battle.

> " …he saw… **a cross of light**… bearing the inscription, **'conquer by this'**."
>
> EUSEBIUS OF NICOMEDIA, BISHOP, 4TH CENTURY CE

A variety of factors have been blamed for starting the demise of the Roman Empire.

THE FADING OF ANTIQUITY

Under the *pax romana*, the Romans ruled a Mediterranean empire that was united by a Greco–Roman classical culture based on the value of the city. This classical civilization came to be threatened in places by **recurring civil wars**, economic pressures, and the wholesale influx of non-Roman people that took place toward the end of the 2nd century CE.

PERSIAN COIN

RISING PERSIAN POWER

The period of crisis in the Roman Empire during the 3rd century CE « **112–13** was, in part, caused by the newly **rejuvenated Persian Empire** under the rule of **Ardashir**, who became the first "king of kings" (*Shah-an-shah*) or emperor of the **Sassanid Empire** « **122–23** in 226 CE. Between 230–60 CE the Persians defeated the Romans on three occasions, capturing and killing Emperor **Valerian** in 260 CE.

FRONTIERS CRUMBLE

"Barbarian" pressure built up along the Rhine and Danube rivers in the 3rd century CE, leading to continual incursions. This had been a major migration route for thousands of years. The Romans had been fighting against a tide greater and older than themselves for a long time.

KING OF THE HUNS (406–453 CE)
ATTILA THE HUN

King of the "Huns" (steppe nomads from inner Asia) between 434 and 453, Attila was the scourge of the Roman world. By the 400s, the Huns controlled a sizable territory in Eastern Europe. Attila aimed to maintain a steppe empire placed strategically on the Hungarian plains, at the doorway to Western Europe. He subdued neighboring tribes and won victories over the eastern Romans, even extracting tribute money from them.

The date of 476 CE is often given as the end of the Roman Empire. This was the year Romulus Augustulus was deposed as emperor. He was, however, a "puppet" child king with a tenuous claim to leadership, and was emperor of only the western empire of Rome. He was removed by Germanic chief, Odoacer, who, though often portrayed as a barbarian warlord, was actually a former Roman commander in Italy.

Collapse would not occur for some time, and it is important to note that while the western empire declined, progress often pushed such groups into other lands—sometimes Roman territory—where they became allies of the empire and helped defend the Romans against Huns and other tribes.

Cooperation and conflict

In fact, it was not unusual for Germanic groups to become official Roman allies, or "federated" people gaining certain Roman-style rights. The situation was far more complex than a simple "barbarians versus Romans" scenario where one side rose and the other fell. Within the imperial system there were commanders and statesmen of Germanic blood. At different times, barbarians either sided with or fought against the Romans, as well as other barbarian groups. For example, the Goths defeated Emperor Valens in 378, at the Battle of Adrianople (Turkey), crushing the imperial army so severely that the Danube borders were left open

The last emperor
Romulus Augustulus is seen as the last emperor of Rome's western empire.

Decline and Fall?

The 5th century CE saw a massive shift in the world's map as the western Roman Empire faded, and a patchwork of new "barbarian" kingdoms dominated Europe. The eastern Roman Empire flourished as the Byzantine culture evolved there. It has been viewed alternately as a time of decline or one of transition.

the eastern Roman Empire, established in the early 4th century CE by Emperor Constantine (see pp.113, 149), thrived. Greco-Roman culture prospered there initially, although it evolved into a highly influential Christian Byzantine civilization that would last for another thousand years (see pp.198–99).

The time can be seen in a positive light and in some ways as one of continuity, rather than bleakly as the end of refined "civilization" when Europe was plunged into chaos. "Decline and fall" was the phrase famously coined by 18th-century English historian Edward Gibbon, to describe the end of the Roman Empire, but the period could also be viewed as one of transition.

The great migrations

By the 4th and 5th centuries CE, a variety of peoples—many from Eurasia's northern steppe lands—had gained a strong foothold in European and Middle Eastern territories once dominated by the Romans. Germanic kingdoms and tribes spread far and wide during these centuries—for example, the Visigoths in parts of France (a kingdom was founded at Toulouse in 418 CE), Spain, Greece, and Italy; Franks in France; the Vandals in North Africa (their kingdom was founded there in 429 CE); and the Sueves in Spain. In 410 CE the Romans officially withdrew from Britain, where the Celts prevailed before Angles and Saxons arrived on British shores.

In the later 4th century CE, westward-migrating Hunnic people defeated and forced semi-sedentary people living around the Black Sea area to flee. Their

Showing Roman soldiers striking heroic poses and in command of the situation, this is a powerful piece of imperial propaganda.

Distinctive beards, hairstyles, and clothing mark out the barbarians, who are all shown in agonized submission.

THE DECLINE OF ROME
The 5th and 6th centuries saw incursions from Goths, Visigoths, and Vandals, among other groups, contributing to the pressures on the Western Roman Empire.

383 Emperor Theodisius signs a peace treaty with the Goths, giving them land and autonomy in exchange for military service.

411 Iberian peninsula divided up between Germanic groups.

439 The Vandals **sack Carthage** and use it as a strategic base to control the Mediterranean.

455 Emperor **Valentinian III** is assassinated by rivals. Rome is sacked by the Vandals.

476 Warlord Odoacer takes throne from **Romulus Augustulus**, the last western emperor, and becomes first non-Roman "king" of Italy. The Western Roman Empire ends.

c.542 Justinianic **plague** starts to ravage the empire and continues for 200 years.

378 Goths, with **Alaric** as leader, enter Italy from the Balkans. **Emperor Valens** is captured and killed.

410 Visigoths, led by Alaric, **sack Rome**.

300 CE — **350** — **400** — **450** — **500**

297 Rome defeats the **Persian Empire**.

337 Death of Constantine the Great, the first Christian Emperor.

368 A long series of campaigns against the **Alemanni** (a Germanic tribe) on the Rhine frontier ends in Roman victory.

406 Germanic tribes cross Rhine to enter Roman Empire (Roman legions elsewhere, busy defending Italy against Alaric).

408 Goths, under Alaric, enter Italy again. Death of imperial general **Stilicho**, who had kept Germanic tribes at bay.

489 Theoderic the Ostrogoth takes Italy from Odoacer and becomes effective ruler until his death, though subordinate to the emperor.

535–53 The Eastern empire defeats Ostrogoths, retaking control of Italy and external territories.

This figure on horseback has been identified as Hostilian, who was a Roman general and a short-lived emperor before his death from the plague in 251 CE.

All the Romans in the relief are shown in armor, with clean-shaven faces wearing expressions of calm superiority.

This fine carving includes an incredibly detailed rendering of *lorica hamata*—a kind of metal-link armor worn by certain Roman soldiers.

Frankish ax
Lightweight throwing axes were popular weapons of the Franks in the 5th century CE.

for many years; Romans and Germanic people united to defeat Attila the Hun (see left) at the Battle of Châlons (France) in 451; the Visigoths had been Roman allies while also having a Gallic kingdom, but were then pushed south into Spain by Franks.

On some occasions the Romans tolerated, or were forced to accept, the settlement of barbarian groups on their lands. By 382 CE the Goths had assumed partial autonomy from the Romans and by 418 CE they were granted lands in Gaul (France). Where barbarians took over former Roman territories, they sometimes sought to supplant the old Roman aristocracy (as with the Vandals in North Africa), but in other places coexisted peacefully with them. There was much cultural cross-fertilization between the Romans and barbarians.

Weakening grip?
Another factor in the gradual fading of Roman power was the spread of plague and disease from the east. This led to severe shortages in the army and fewer people in general to support society. Various bouts of plague had spread through the empire in the 3rd century. Then the Justinianic plague broke out. Named after eastern Emperor Justinian, who retook the western empire in the mid-sixth century, it began in 542 CE and raged for 200 years. The effect on the population of the eastern Empire was devastating.

Other factors include a general decline in population, inflation, civil war, self-serving Roman corruption, and imperial overcultivation leading to loss of good agricultural land. These have variously been seen as reducing prosperity and resources, hastening the fading of the great urban centers of "classical" civilization and learning.

RELIGIOUS CHANGE
The rise of Christianity also played a major role in the new order. The "Arian" Christianity held by most

Germanic peoples was at odds with the more orthodox Christianity traditionally held by Roman peoples. Furthermore, the increasing power of the Christian church may have eroded some imperial authority (see AFTER).

Romans battling barbarians
The famous Ludovisi Battle Sarcophagus, an imperial Roman marble sarcophagus, depicts Romans battling against Ostrogoth barbarians during the 3rd century CE. It has been dated to around 250–60 CE.

Writhing figures struggling closely together convey the chaos and drama of hand-to-hand battle.

AFTER

The Roman Empire lived on in the east for 1,000 years as the Byzantine Empire, while new forces shaped the Western world.

BYZANTINE EMPIRE
After damaging wars with the Persians, the Byzantine or East Roman Empire **198–99 »** was too weak to face the challenges posed by Arab Muslim armies.

ARAB ADVANCE
Arab power, **united under the banner of Islam**, grew in the 7th and early 8th centuries with the capture of the Byzantine Levant, much of North Africa and Egypt, and attempts to take Constantinople **174–77 »**.

LATIN CHRISTENDOM
The pope shifted his loyalty from Constantinople's Roman emperor to Frankish king Charlemagne (747–814), **194–95 »**, crowning him Emperor of the Romans.

LATE ANTIQUITY
Distinctive communities that combined Germanic traditions, Latin Christianity, and aspects of Roman culture began to emerge in the post-Roman west, such as in Anglo-Saxon England.

ANGLO-SAXON BELT BUCKLE

4

WARRIORS, TRAVELERS, AND INVENTORS
600–1450

Contact between East and West increased in the medieval period, as trade routes expanded, leading to the spread of goods and ideas. Warrior tribes founded great empires in China and the Middle East, and in Europe the feudal system took hold, dominated by the might of the Christian church. In the Americas, Africa, and Asia, great civilizations flourished

WARRIORS, TRAVELERS, AND INVENTORS 600–1450

600	700	750	800

615
Persian conquests of Syria, Mesopotamia, and Palestine complete.
618
Tang dynasty established in China.

668
The Silla unify Korea.
692
Dome of the Rock Mosque completed in Jerusalem.
698
Islamic conquest of Carthage, North Africa.

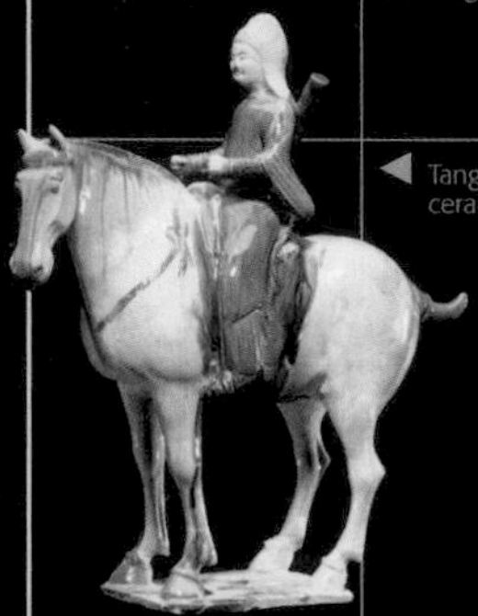

◄ Tang dynasty ceramic horse

◄ Lindisfarne Gospels

727
Byzantine emperor Leo III bans worship of religious icons.
c. 732
Muslims defeated by Franks at Poitiers, France, halting Muslim expansion into Western Europe.

◄ Camels carry goods across Sahara

800
Charlemagne crowned Emperor of the Romans by Pope Leo III.
802
Angkorian dynasty founded by King Jayavarman II in Southeast Asia.

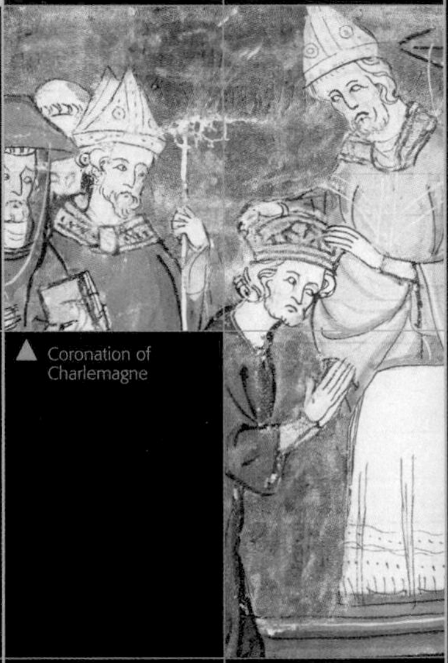

c. 700.
Lindisfarne Gospels written in England. Rise of Kingdom of Ghana, West Africa. Teotihuacán, Mexico, abandoned. North Peru dominated by Chimú state.

Chimú portrait beaker ►

c. 782
Scholars attracted to Charlemagne's court stimulate Carolingian Renaissance.
786
Harun al-Rashid, immortalized in *The One Thousand and One Nights,* becomes Abbasid caliph.

▲ Coronation of Charlemagne

622
Hegira (Muhammad's flight to Medina) marks start of Islamic era.
624
Muhammad's army defeats Meccans at Battle of Badr.
632
Death of Muhammad.

739
Byzantine army defeats Umayyads at Akroinon and expels Umayyads from Asia Minor.
c. 740
High point of Later Classic period of Maya, Central America.

◄ Harun al-Rashid

641
Islamic conquest of Egypt.
644
Islamic conquest of Persia.
661
Umayyad caliphate established.

▲ Battle of Badr

▼ Dome of the Rock mosque

750
Revolt against Umayyad caliphs leads to foundation of Abbasid caliphate.
753
Italy invaded by Franks under Pépin.
756
Breakaway Umayyad emirate established in Cordoba, Spain.

c. 790
Viking raids against Western Europe begin.
794
Emperor Kammu moves Japanese capital from Nara to Kyoto.

809
Death of Harun al-Rashid.
814
Death of Charlemagne.

843
Treaty of Verdun divides Charlemagne's empire into three: west and east portions roughly correspond to France and Germany.

711
Muslim invasion of Spain; Arab invasion of Sind in India.
725
Anglo-Saxon scholar Bede disseminates the AD dating system through Europe.

Maya stone lintel ►

760
Indian system of numerals adopted by Abbasid dynasty.
774
Lombards in northern Italy defeated by Franks under Charlemagne.

832
Caliph Al-Ma'mun establishes "House of Wisdom" in Baghdad: translates ancient Greek learning into Arabic.

Few would have predicted that the states chaotically established across Western Europe after 600 CE by the barbarian successors to Rome would prove anything other than destabilizing. At least until 1000, Europe was clearly marginalized, an obvious backwater. China, rejuvenated by the Tang and later dynasties, was superior in every sense, a technological powerhouse. Islam, legatee of ancient learning, explosively expansive, no less obviously imposed itself. Other societies—in the Americas, India, and Southeast Asia—promised much. Yet it was Christian Europe that would thrust itself upon the world. The process was never certain, but the results were decisive. Late-medieval Europe was poised to dominate the globe.

850

878
Alfred, king of Wessex, defeats Danes at Battle of Edington to halt Danish advance in England.

◀ Astrolabe

c. 850
Arab navigators perfect astrolabe. Cholas under King Vijayalaya gain power in south India.

▲ Chola bronze

c. 860
Cyrillic alphabet created in East Europe.
866
Vikings take city of York and establish a kingdom in northern England.

868
Diamond Sutra printed in China, the world's oldest surviving printed book.
874
Muslim Samanid dynasty established in Turkestan.

King Alfred ▶

900

c. 900
Beginning of golden age of Hindu temple-building in India.
906
Collapse of Tang dynasty, China. Magyars destroy Moravia (eastern Czech Republic) and begin to raid western Europe.

910
Foundation of reformed Benedictine abbey at Cluny, France.
911
Vikings found duchy of Normandy.

Viking longboat ▶

916
Foundation of Siberian Khitan empire, Mongolia
918
Foundation of state of Koryo in Korea.

932
Election of Otto I as German emperor.
936
Abbasid caliphs in Baghdad lose effective power to their Turkish troops, the Mamluks.

939
Kingdom of Dai Viet in Vietnam throws off Chinese rule.
947
Nomadic Qidan people invade northern China and establish Liao dynasty.

950

▼ Battle of Lechfeld

955
Otto I of Germany defeats Magyars at Lechfeld, halting their expansion west.
960
Song dynasty established in China.
966
Polish state founded by Mieszko I.

967
Fujiwara clan begins unification of Japan.
969
Fatimids of Tunisia assume control of North Africa from Tunisia to Egypt and relocate to new capital, Cairo.

▼ Fujiwara fan

972
King Edgar crowned at Bath, uniting English kingdoms. Formation of unified Hungarian state under Duke Geza.
986
Erik the Red begins Viking settlement of Greenland.

987
French Capetian dynasty founded.
c. 990
Toltecs take over Maya city of Chichén Itzá.

1000

▲ Chinese fireworks

1000
Stephen crowned as first king of Hungary.
1008
First Muslim raids into northern India, led by Muhammad of Ghazni.

1031
Fall of Umayyad caliphate of Cordoba during Christian reconquest of Spain.
1044
Formula for gunpowder published, China.
1045
First printing with movable type, China.

1013
Renewed Danish invasion of England.
1016
England, Denmark, and Norway united under King Canute.

▲ Chinese movable type

1047
Beginning of Norman conquest of southern Italy and Sicily.
1048
Fatimids lose control of Libya.

»

1050

1100

1150

1200

Battle of Hastings

1054
Final schism between Catholic and Orthodox Christian Churches.
1055
Seljuk Turks capture Baghdad.

1071
Battle of Manzikert: Seljuk Turks defeat Byzantines. Normans capture last Byzantine possessions in Italy.
1076
Empire of Ghana in West Africa falls to the Almoravids.

1076
Investiture controversy: Pope Gregory VII excommunicates German emperor.
1099
Capture of Jerusalem during First Crusade.

◀ **Seljuk Turks**

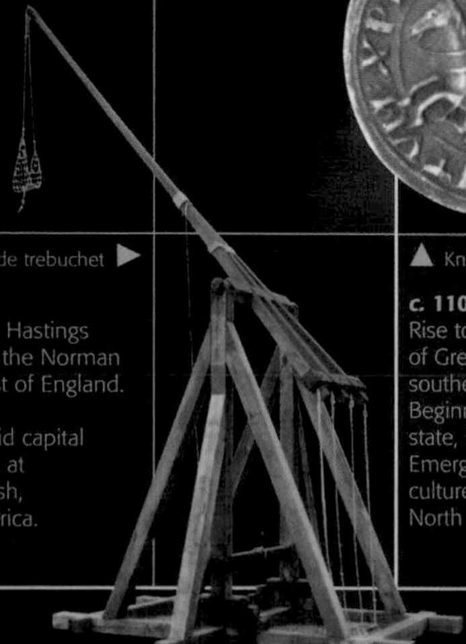

◀ **Crusade trebuchet** ▶

1066
Battle of Hastings leads to the Norman conquest of England.
1070
Almoravid capital founded at Marrakesh, North Africa.

▼ **Great Zimbabwe**

c. **1115**
Renaissance of Byzantine art under Alexius Comnenus.
c. **1118**
Crusading order of the Knights Templar founded.

1125
Chinese Liao dynasty defeated by Jin from Manchuria.
1130
Chinese Song dynasty moves capital to Hangzhou after Jin take control of northern China.

1122
Concordat of Worms ends the investiture controversy.
  1144
  Crusader state of Edessa falls to Muslims.
  1145
  Start of Second Crusade.

▲ **Knights Templar seal**

c. **1100**
Rise to prominence of Great Zimbabwe, southeast Africa. Beginning of Inca state, South America. Emergence of Pueblo culture, southwest North America.

1147
Almohads conquer city of Marrakesh from Almoravids and take control of North Africa.
1147
Almohads established in southern Spain.

◀ **Genghis Khan**

c. **1150**
Paris university founded.
c. **1162**
Birth of Genghis Khan, founder of Mongol empire.

1169
English conquest of Ireland launched.
1171
Ayyubid sultan Saladin overthrows Fatimid caliphate in Egypt.

▲ **Saladin**

1187
Crusader armies destroyed by Saladin at Battle of Hattin.
1189
Start of Third Crusade.
1192
Minamoto Yoritomo becomes shogun, Japan.

c. **1180**
Angkor empire of Cambodia reaches greatest extent under Jayavarman VII.
1185
Kamakura shogunate founded, Japan.

Angkor Wat ▶

1218
Mongols conquer Persia.
1227
Genghis Khan dies.
1235
Foundation of Mali kingdom, West Africa.

Byzantine relic survives Fourth Crusade. ◀

c. **1200**
Incas under Manco Capac settle in Andes near Cuzco; Aztecs enter Valley of Mexico.
1204
Constantinople taken during Fourth Crusade.
1206
First Muslim empire in India, the Delhi Sultanate, founded.

1206
Genghis Khan proclaimed leader of the Mongol tribes.
1209
Albigensian Crusade launched against heretics in southern France.

St. Francis of Assisi ▶

▲ **Architecture of Delhi Sultanate**

1215
Mongols capture Zhongdu (Beijing).
c. **1216**
Dominican and Franciscan monastic orders founded.
1217
Start of Fifth Crusade.

"The title Khan means in our language 'Great Lord of Lords.' And certainly he has a right to this title... He is indeed **the greatest lord** the world has ever known."

MARCO POLO, FROM "THE TRAVELS OF MARCO POLO," c 1298

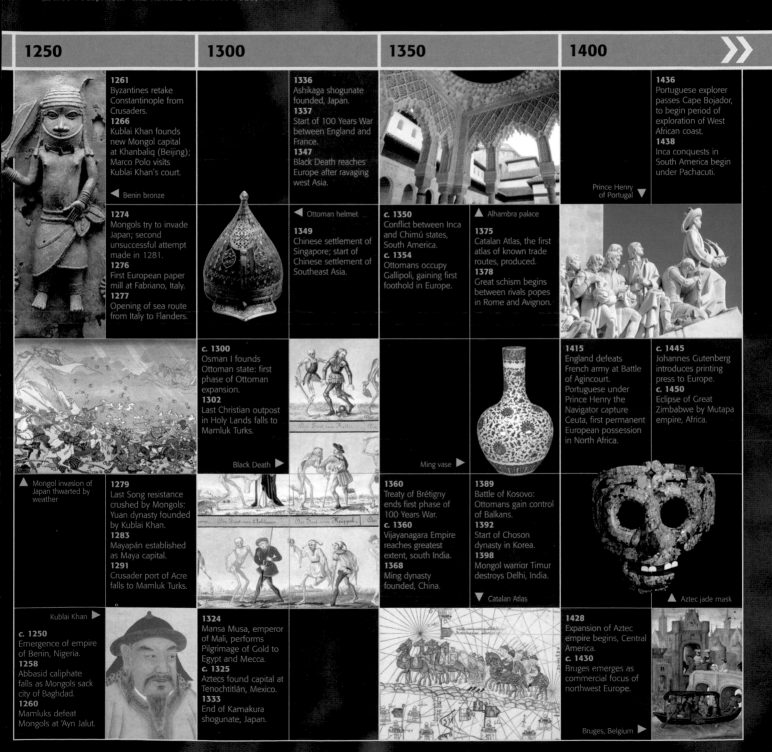

1250

1300

1350

1400

1261
Byzantines retake Constantinople from Crusaders.
1266
Kublai Khan founds new Mongol capital at Khanbaliq (Beijing); Marco Polo visits Kublai Khan's court.

◀ Benin bronze

1274
Mongols try to invade Japan; second unsuccessful attempt made in 1281.
1276
First European paper mill at Fabriano, Italy.
1277
Opening of sea route from Italy to Flanders.

1336
Ashikaga shogunate founded, Japan.
1337
Start of 100 Years War between England and France.
1347
Black Death reaches Europe after ravaging west Asia.

◀ Ottoman helmet

1349
Chinese settlement of Singapore; start of Chinese settlement of Southeast Asia.

c. 1350
Conflict between Inca and Chimú states, South America.
c. 1354
Ottomans occupy Gallipoli, gaining first foothold in Europe.

▲ Alhambra palace

1375
Catalan Atlas, the first atlas of known trade routes, produced.
1378
Great schism begins between rivals popes in Rome and Avignon.

1436
Portuguese explorer passes Cape Bojador, to begin period of exploration of West African coast.
1438
Inca conquests in South America begin under Pachacuti.

Prince Henry of Portugal ▼

c. 1300
Osman I founds Ottoman state: first phase of Ottoman expansion.
1302
Last Christian outpost in Holy Lands falls to Mamluk Turks.

Black Death ▶

▲ Mongol invasion of Japan thwarted by weather

1279
Last Song resistance crushed by Mongols: Yuan dynasty founded by Kublai Khan.
1283
Mayapán established as Maya capital.
1291
Crusader port of Acre falls to Mamluk Turks.

Ming vase ▶

1360
Treaty of Brétigny ends first phase of 100 Years War.
c. 1360
Vijayanagara Empire reaches greatest extent, south India.
1368
Ming dynasty founded, China.

1415
England defeats French army at Battle of Agincourt. Portuguese under Prince Henry the Navigator capture Ceuta, first permanent European possession in North Africa.

c. 1445
Johannes Gutenberg introduces printing press to Europe.
c. 1450
Eclipse of Great Zimbabwe by Mutapa empire, Africa.

1389
Battle of Kosovo: Ottomans gain control of Balkans.
1392
Start of Choson dynasty in Korea.
1398
Mongol warrior Timur destroys Delhi, India.

▼ Catalan Atlas

▲ Aztec jade mask

Kublai Khan ▶

c. 1250
Emergence of empire of Benin, Nigeria.
1258
Abbasid caliphate falls as Mongols sack city of Baghdad.
1260
Mamluks defeat Mongols at 'Ayn Jalut.

1324
Mansa Musa, emperor of Mali, performs Pilgrimage of Gold to Egypt and Mecca.
c. 1325
Aztecs found capital at Tenochtitlán, Mexico.
1333
End of Kamakura shogunate, Japan.

1428
Expansion of Aztec empire begins, Central America.
c. 1430
Bruges emerges as commercial focus of northwest Europe.

Bruges, Belgium ▶

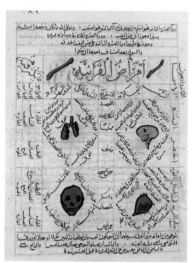

Avicenna's medical encyclopedia
Known as the "Prince of Physicians," the 11th-century Persian scholar Avicenna was a hugely influential figure both in the Middle East and in Europe, where his work *The Canon of Medicine* continued to be used as a standard medical text until the 16th century.

BEFORE

As the study of the Bible came to dominate intellectual activity in the West, knowledge of classical Greek learning declined.

CLASSICAL SCHOLARSHIP

Greek and Roman education included the teaching of **grammar**, **logic**, and **rhetoric** (the *trivium*) before moving on to **astronomy**, **arithmetic**, **music**, and **geometry** (the *quadrivium*). At Aristotle's Lyceum and Plato's Academy, students listened to their lecturers discuss philosophy and science.

ROMAN TEACHER AND PUPILS

DECAY OF CLASSICAL KNOWLEDGE

The classical approach continued into the early medieval period, but by now knowledge of the Greek language had largely died out in the West. **Christianity** was dominant, and education focused on **the Bible**. Some fragments of classical knowledge were preserved in texts such as the 6th century philosopher Boethius' *Consolation of Philosophy*. But by the 8th century, education in western Europe was structured almost entirely around the Bible, and scholarship had become largely cut off from Greek science and philosophy.

> **"Books** have led some to **learning** and others to **madness**."

FRANCESCO PETRARCH, "REMEDIES FOR FORTUNE FAIR AND FOUL," 1365

Diffusion of Knowledge

Knowledge of classical Greek and Roman culture declined in Western Europe in the early medieval period, but survived in the East. Muslim scholars preserved the works of classical Greek philosophers and, as this knowledge spread west, laid the foundations for the European intellectual revival.

During the late 8th and 9th centuries, something of a literary awakening occurred at the court of the Frankish emperor Charlemagne (see pp.188–89). Before Charlemagne, society lacked many of the basic educational skills; most priests were barely literate and the royal court had difficulty finding educated men to act as scribes and copy out manuscripts. To fix these problems, Charlemagne created schools and assembled the greatest scholars of the age at his court. A Northumbrian scholar, Alcuin of York, was recruited as head of the palace school. A standard curriculum was introduced, and the classical study of the *trivium* and *quadrivium* was reestablished (see BEFORE). Latin once again became the formal language of communication across Europe.

The Arab inheritance

Charlemagne's reforms were primarily concerned with creating an educated clergy capable of reforming the Frankish church. Works of classical Greek science and philosophy remained essentially unavailable in the Christian Europe. In Arab Spain, North Africa, and the Middle East, however, the situation

Astrolabe manual
Muslim scholars are shown using the astrolabe, an instrument for locating and predicting the position of the Sun, Moon, and stars. The astrolabe was introduced into Christian Europe via Muslim Spain in the 11th century.

was very different. The Arab societies inhabiting these regions had inherited many aspects of classical Greek culture. Until the 12th century, for example, virtually all that Christian Europe knew of Aristotle came via Boethius (see BEFORE). To Islamic scholars, Aristotle was "the Philosopher" and his works were standard texts. In the 9th–10th centuries, numerous classical Greek works were translated into Arabic, and a flurry of commentaries were composed.

Two individuals stand out during this period. The Persian scholar Avicenna produced a huge range of material covering almost every area of knowledge, from metaphysics to medicine. His *Book of Healing* is the largest encyclopedia of knowledge composed by one person in the period. Averroes (see below), a renowned philosopher, scientist, and lawyer, composed a series of commentaries on Aristotle that for centuries formed the key source for Aristotle's philosophy in the West.

The 12th-century renaissance

The diffusion of knowledge from East to West accelerated during the 12th century. In Spain, the Christian reconquest of lands previously held by Muslim rulers encouraged the spread of Islamic learning. In the 13th century, the Spanish king Alfonso X established a program of translation of Greek and Arab texts in Toledo, previously capital of the Muslim caliphate of Cordoba.

Other important hubs for the exchange of ideas included the Christian crusader kingdoms that were established in the Middle East in the 12th–13th centuries (see pp.200–201) and the Greek empire of Byzantium (see pp.198–99), which fell into the hands of the crusaders in 1204. By the 13th century, Latin translations of the most important classical texts were available to European scholars.

Scholasticism

The rediscovery of ancient philosophical works combined with the ongoing development of Christian theology led to the scholastic movement of the later Medieval period. Scholasticism was not a philosophy in itself, but rather a tool for learning that placed emphasis on logic and reasoning. The works of Plato

> **RHETORIC** Derived from the Greek word for "orator," rhetoric is the art of persuasion through spoken or written language. It was an important art in classical Greece, where public speaking was central to political life.

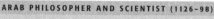

ARAB PHILOSOPHER AND SCIENTIST (1126–98)

AVERROES

Born into a learned and cultured family in the city of Cordoba (then part of Muslim Spain) Averroes was an expert in Islamic law and theology, as well as Arabic grammar and poetry. In 1153, he was invited to the court of the Almohad caliphs in Morocco, where he worked as a judge and physician, and wrote important works on medicine, philosophy, and law. He later fell out of favor and was exiled. Averroes' writings had a huge influence on European scholarship, but his greatest contribution was a series of commentaries on Aristotle that introduced medieval scholars to the works of the great Greek philosopher.

The growth of universities and the scholastic movement led to the humanist and intellectual movements of the Renaissance.

THE RENAISSANCE
The rediscovery of ancient Greek and Latin texts during the later medieval period stimulated interest in classical learning and led to the great **artistic and cultural flowering** of the 15th- and 16th-century **Renaissance 250–53 ≫**.

PICO DELLA MIRANDOLA

HUMANISM
The key intellectual movement of the Renaissance, humanism emphasized **human reason and dignity** rather than the Christian humility and obedience to authority that had been the focus of the medieval Church. The Italian writer **Pico della Mirandola** captured the new spirit in 1489 with his *Oration on the Dignity of Man*, a preface to 900 theses on religion and philosophy. Renaissance humanists, schooled in Greek and Latin from an early age and often learning Hebrew and Arabic as well, studied the poetry, grammar, rhetoric, and ethics of the classical authors in their original languages.

The Lindisfarne Gospel
Created by the monks of Lindisfarne in northern England in the 8th century, this illuminated Latin text is a striking example of early medieval religious art and scholarship. An Old English translation was added in the 10th century—the oldest surviving version of the Gospels in English.

themselves. In Paris, where the main subject was theology, the Church controlled the payment of staff. It took six years to earn a bachelor of arts degree, and a further 12 years for a master's degree and doctorate.

By the 14th century, universities had become central to intellectual life. Theology remained the most prestigious area of study, and all students were at least in minor orders (the lower ranks of the clergy). However, the first six years of study now focused on the seven liberal arts: arithmetic, geometry, astronomy, music, grammar, logic, and rhetoric—the classical *trivium* and *quadrivium*. In this way, the universities signaled a move away from an intellectual world entirely dominated by the Church.

Monastic scribe
Before paper became common, scribes used parchment or vellum for their work. Vellum was created by scraping down calf or sheep skins and smoothing the surface with a pumice stone or chalk.

Toledo translation school
Alfonso X "the Wise" of Castile in Spain was patron of a flourishing court of scholars who translated Arabic works on subjects ranging from astronomy to chess.

these authorities to the problems of Christian theology. Thomas Aquinas's *Summa Theologica*, for example, is a masterful synthesis of Aristotle's philosophy and Christian tradition (see p.195).

The universities
A better understanding of the classical art of debate, combined with a growing demand for education, led to the foundation of the first universities in the 12th–13th centuries. Medieval universities evolved from earlier cathedral schools and monasteries, and were created to study theology, law, medicine, and the arts.

Most universities did not have a central campus—classes were taught at masters' homes or in churches. In a university such as Bologna in northern Italy, where law was the most popular subject, students hired and paid the lecturers

and Aristotle were important for the followers of the movement, as they provided the basic tools for constructing arguments. But so were Christian authorities such as St. Augustine and, above all, the Bible. The scholastic method sought to apply the learning of

BEFORE ‹‹

After the fall of the Han dynasty, the Chinese empire divided into several kingdoms.

ARRIVAL OF BUDDHISM

Buddhism ‹‹144–47 had been brought to China from the Indian subcontinent by the 2nd century CE. During the **period of division** that followed the fall of the Han dynasty ‹‹128–29, Buddhism **spread quickly**, despite attempts to suppress the religion by Confucian officials. However, it was not until the Tang dynasty that **Buddhism was at the height of its influence** in China.

SUI DYNASTY

China was reunited in 589 CE under the **Sui dynasty**. The first Sui emperor, **Wendi**, built Chang'an (modern Xi'an), a **new capital city**, and enforced a **clear legal code**. His son, **Yangdi**, carried out a **costly program of canal building** and launched **ill-fated attacks on Korea**. The Sui dynasty fell to the Tang in 618 CE.

SUI DYNASTY FIGURINE

THE GRAND CANAL

The Sui emperor Yangdi commissioned a **Grand Canal** to run from Hangzhou to Beijing. The total length of the canal was 1,490 miles (2,400 km), and it remains **the longest canal in the world**.

CHINESE EMPRESS (625–705 CE)

WU ZETIAN

China's only empress to rule in her own right, Wu Zetian usurped the throne from her son the Ruizong emperor in 690 CE. Although judged to be a shrewd and ruthless ruler, she gave extravagant support to Buddhism and other foreign religions, and engaged in costly frontier campaigns. From 697 CE, she became enamored of the Zhang brothers. In 705 CE, her senior ministers had the brothers killed, and forced the empress to abdicate. She died later that year.

The reign of the Tang dynasty in China is widely regarded as a golden age of Chinese imperial power and culture. The dynasty itself was founded by Li Yuan, a frontier general, who in 617 rebelled against the Sui dynasty (see BEFORE). He took the capital Chang'an the following year, though it would be a further six years before the whole of China fell under his control. Under the title of Emperor Gaozu, Li Yuan inaugurated a new dynasty, which ruled over China for the next three centuries.

Taizong's reign

Gaozu's successor, the Emperor Taizong, was an intelligent and hard-working ruler, and his own reign (626–649 CE) became synonymous with a period of prosperity. Taizong improved the system of government that his father had established, and reformed the administrative system. State schools and colleges were set up, and government examinations were designed to ensure that the most talented individuals were placed in the highest official positions. For Taizong, this not only had the advantage of

> "Have I not heard that **pure wine** makes a **sage**, And even **muddy wine** Can make a man **wise**?"
>
> FROM "DRINKING ALONE IN THE MOONLIGHT" BY LI BAI, C. 701–62 CE

monk, perhaps curious to hear Xuan Zang's impressions of foreign countries. Buddhism continued to have a great influence on Chinese society until its suppression in the late Tang period.

Expansion of the empire

The Tang dynasty saw a remarkable period of Chinese expansion. In 657 Taizong's armies defeated the Turks at the battle of Issyk Kul in modern-day Kyrgyzstan, and advanced China's influence as far west as the borders of Persia. Taizong also launched expeditions against the kingdom of Koguryo in north Korea, though he died before he had established Chinese control over the area. At its greatest extent, in around the year 750 CE, Tang China claimed more land than the preceding Han dynasty, its borders reaching even farther west, south, and east than those of modern China.

Xuanzong's golden age

Following the reign of the ruthless Wu Zetian (see left) and several other short-lived rulers, the succession fell to the Emperor Xuanzong in 712 CE.

The Giant Buddha at Leshan
At 233 ft (71 m) tall, this stone Buddha in the Sichuan region of China is the world's tallest. Its construction began in 713 CE.

China's Golden Age

The peak of the Tang dynasty (618–907 CE) saw the flowering of Chinese art, architecture, and poetry. Silk Road caravans brought exotic goods from distant lands, and Chinese culture became the most cosmopolitan in the world.

delivering an efficient civil service, but also strengthened his own security. Unlike those drawn from China's rival aristocratic families, career officials had no power base of their own with which to threaten the Tang dynasty.

The rise of Buddhism

Though he promoted Confucianism and Daoism (see p.127) within the bureaucracy, Taizong personally embraced the Buddhist religion imported from India (see BEFORE). In 629 CE, the monk Xuan Zang journeyed to India to collect Buddhist texts. His travels were the inspiration for the famous Chinese novel *Record of a Journey to the West*, better known in the West as *Monkey*. When he returned to China in 645 CE, Taizong received the

Xuanzong was a clever and diligent ruler, and in the first part of his reign the fortunes of the Tang dynasty were revived. Sweeping reforms were made to the bureaucracy; large granaries were constructed to stockpile rice; military campaigns were fought against the Turkish, Tibetan, and Khitan peoples; a new network of frontier defenses was introduced, with permanent forces of professional soldiers; and contact was made with ambassadors from as far west as the Middle East. All of these measures led to a rich, powerful, and cosmopolitan state; China had reached a golden age.

As China's territory expanded, so did its cultural influence. Thousands of merchants, artisans, and diplomats from distant lands took up residence in the capital, Chang'an, which became

Little Goose Pagoda, Xi'an
Still standing today, this 15-story pagoda was built between 707 CE and 709 CE to house scriptures of the Buddhist faith.

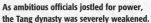

AFTER

As ambitious officials jostled for power, the Tang dynasty was severely weakened.

THE LATE TANG

After the fall of Xuanzong, successive emperors tried to **revive China's fortunes**, but to no avail. Powerful families evaded tax and the burden fell increasingly on those who were less able to pay. In 874 CE a significant **peasant rebellion** broke out. Huang Chao, the rebel leader, captured Chang'an and forced **Emperor Xixong** to flee. The emperor returned once the rebellion had been quashed, but his **authority had collapsed**. Military governors seized power, and in 907 CE the Tang dynasty was overthrown.

BUDDHIST STATUE

SUPPRESSION OF BUDDHISM

The increasing wealth and influence of Buddhism led to a **growing campaign of criticism** headed by Confucian scholars in the early 9th century. Anti-Buddhist feeling within the government reached its height in 845 CE, when **Emperor Wuzong** ordered the **destruction** of 4,600 **Buddhist monasteries** and the surrender of their lands to the state; 250,000 monks were secularized and thrown back into society, and Buddhism never regained its influence in China.

---

the world's largest city. Covering more than 30 square miles (77 km²), more than one million people lived inside its walls, and another million beyond them. Linked by a network of roads and canals to the rest of the empire, Chang'an was the terminus of the Silk Road (see pp.184–85), and traders from across Asia came to its great markets. Horses, essential for fighting against the nomadic tribes to the north and east, were imported from the Tarim Basin, and glass goblets came from Byzantium (see pp.198–99). Silk, ceramics, brick tea, and papers were traded in exchange. Foreign cultures were welcomed, and within the city walls were Daoist temples, Buddhist monasteries, Zoroastrian shrines, and Islamic mosques.

Three-glaze figurine
Developed in the 7th century, *sancai* (three-color) glaze, was widely used on vessels and figurines and is typical of the Tang dynasty. Its colors were green, amber, and cream.

Flowering of the arts
Xuanzong was a great patron of the arts, and during his reign Chinese painting and literature reached new

levels of sophistication. Two of China's greatest poets flourished in this period: Li Bai and Du Fu, known respectively as the Poet Immortal and the Sage Poet. Li Bai cultivated a reputation for eccentricity; many of his poems celebrate the joys of wine and women. The poems of Du Fu, by contrast, dealt with more serious moral and historical issues. Landscape painting evolved under the poet artist Wang Wei, who painted evocative winter scenes, and Wu Daozi developed a Chinese style of Buddhist sculpture. The court painter Han Gan was best known for his depictions of horses, a subject that continued to inspire artists in later periods.

The decline of the Tang
In the 730s CE Xuanzong's control over his government began to slip. A number of aristocrats began to displace the career officials. The most notorious of these was Li Linfu, who by 752 CE had made himself virtually a dictator. The emperor, who was 72 years old by this time, had ceased to play an active role in government.

He had become infatuated with Yang Guifei, who was his son's concubine and a famous beauty. After Xuanzong made her imperial consort, she persuaded him to promote her cousin Yang Guozhang to a senior position at court; when Li Linfu died, Yang took his place.

Among the professional soldiers who had been given commands along the frontier was an officer named An Lushan. He became a favorite (and possibly a lover) of Yang Guifei. The rivalry between An Lushan and Yang Guozhang at court led the former to raise a rebellion in 755 CE. The emperor was forced to flee from Chang'an. His military escort demanded the execution of Yang Guifei, blaming her for the emperor's misfortunes, and Xuanzong had no option but to accept. Though An Lushan was eventually defeated and the rebellion brought to an end, the Tang dynasty never recovered its former strength and glory.

INVENTION

PRINTING

The *Diamond Sutra*, the oldest surviving example of a printed book, was found in a walled-up chapel at Dunhuang on the Silk Road. With an inscription dated 868 CE, it predates the earliest European book, the Gutenberg Bible (see pp.256–57), by over 500 years. Seven strips of yellow-stained paper printed from carved wooden blocks are pasted together to form a scroll over 13 ft (4 m) long. It is one of the most important works of the Buddhist faith. It was called the *Diamond Sutra* because "its teaching will cut like a diamond blade through worldly illusion."

The Song Dynasty

The Song dynasty, established in 960 CE, reunited northern and southern China. Its extraordinary achievements in the arts and sciences outstripped developments in Europe at the time. However, aggression from the Jurchen people to the north gradually led to the surrender of northern China. The dynasty continued to rule in the south as the Southern Song, but was finally ousted by the Mongols in 1279.

« **BEFORE**

FIVE DYNASTIES SCULPTURE

After the fall of the Tang in 907 CE, the empire disintegrated.

CHINA DIVIDED
Between the rule of the Tang and the Song dynasties, the **Qidan Liao** (see below) controlled the northeast of China, while the south fragmented into the **Ten Kingdoms**. Northern China came under the rule of a short succession of **Five Dynasties** until the reunification of north and south was achieved by the first emperor of the Song dynasty in 960 CE.

ALIEN RULE AND SINICIZATION
In 907 CE, the **nomadic Qidan people** founded the **Liao** dynasty. From 947 CE the Qidan Liao ruled over part of northern China. In the south of their territory, they **recruited Chinese officials** and **modeled their institutions on the Tang**.

Zhao Kuangyin was a general under the Later Zhou, the last of the Five Dynasties (see BEFORE). In 960 CE he usurped the throne and founded the Song dynasty, taking the imperial name Taizu. With a mixture of guile and persuasion he reunified the disparate states of China, apart from the territory held by the Qidan Liao (see BEFORE). Establishing his capital at Kaifeng, Taizu revived the successful administrative system of the Tang government (see pp.166–67), albeit in a modified form.

Some of the magnificence of the Tang era returned to Chinese culture during the Song dynasty. There was a renewed interest in literature and the decorative arts. Artists experimented with brush effects, and landscape, animal, and bird paintings were particularly prized. Song dynasty architecture was also renowned, particularly for its tall structures and pagodas, palaces, and temple roofs.

An economic revolution?

The administrative and technological advances made by the early Song led to economic prosperity. Instead of carrying around large sums of copper coinage, Sichuan merchants began to trade in bills of exchange. These notes proved so successful that the government issued its first paper currency in 1024.

The country's infrastructure was also greatly improved during the Song period. The construction of an integrated system of internal waterways extended both the communications and trade networks. Large junks with four or six masts were developed, the magnetic compass was first used for navigation, and seafaring skills were improved. This led to an increase in maritime trade with the rest of East Asia, as well as with India and the east coast of Africa.

The innovations of the Song period affected China's population and urban growth. New methods of rice farming increased food output and allowed the population to double. Towns and cities grew along the main waterways and

Movable type
Between 1041 and 1048, Bi Sheng of Kaifeng invented the first printing system of its kind using clay characters held in wax within an iron frame.

along the southern coast, attracting at least ten percent of the population. Kaifeng became the greatest city in the world; in the 12th century its levels of trade were nearly 50 percent more than those of London at the turn of the 18th century.

Examinations and officials

Under the Song, the examination system established by the Han dynasty (see pp.128–29) was revived and expanded. Quotas were set for the number of candidates who could pass, and steps were taken to guard against cheating and to ensure the anonymity of candidates. Over 140 candidates a year were awarded the *jinshi*, the highest degree. In 1002, 14,500 men came to Kaifeng to take the imperial

The Zhang Zeduan silk scroll
The Spring Festival Along the River, by the Northern Song artist Zhang Zeduan, depicts bustling scenes of city life in Kaifeng, the Northern Song capital. Note the upward curve of the roofs, typical of the period.

examinations. The system attempted to ensure that talent, not birth or wealth, enabled a candidate to pass. More than 60 percent of successful candidates for the *jinshi* degree came from families that had not gained an appointment for an official in the bureaucracy for three generations. However, poor families were still unlikely to foster a successful candidate, as applicants needed to be wealthy or literate to enable them to prepare for the examinations.

From early in the Song period, scholars and officials were constantly proposing ideas for reforms to rectify the problems of the day. In 1068, Emperor Shenzong entrusted Wang Anshi, China's most famous reformer, with tackling the nation's problems. He identified the main cause of the state's weakness to be a shortage of funds, and raised money by imposing a government monopoly on tea, challenging wealthy families who were evading taxes, and offering interest-free loans to peasants

burdened with debt. To reduce the cost of the standing army, he required every household to supply men for a local militia. These reforms caused an outcry, Wang Anshi was dismissed, and the controversy that his acts had aroused permanently weakened the dynasty.

The Southern Song
The dynasty also had to deal with the challenge of non-Chinese regimes to the north. Part of northern China was already ruled by the Qidan Liao dynasty. In 1115 the Jurchen, a seminomadic people from Manchuria, established the Jin dynasty. In 1125 they overran the Qidan Liao, and two years later they captured Kaifeng. The Song court was forced to flee south, bringing an end to the retrospectively named Northern Song. The Southern Song emperors went on to fix their capital at Hangzhou. Although militarily weak, the Southern Song was also a period of continuing economic growth and social change.

Under the Southern Song, new philosophical ideas developed. Neo-Confucianists borrowed concepts from Daoism and Buddhism, and their ideas were synthesized by the scholar Zhu Xi. He emphasized the Dao, or "the Way," a philosophical path that individuals could follow through self-cultivation and the study of Confucian classics (see pp.131).

Neo-Confucian values were partly responsible for a deterioration in the rights of women during the Southern Song period. The remarriage of widows was discouraged, and women's property rights were curtailed. Footbinding—the practice of permanently disfiguring a young girl's feet to produce a supposedly attractive shape in later life—became well established during the Song period.

Song porcelain
The Song period is often regarded as the high point in ceramic production in China. Chinese porcelain was first manufactured in the 7th century, a thousand years before the secret of its production was discovered in Europe. True porcelain is made from kaolin, or China clay, the name deriving from Gaoling in Jingdezhen. Song porcelain was the most refined ever produced, and was characterized by the simple elegance of its shape, and its purity of color. The most famous Northern Song wares were created near Dingzhou in northeast China. After the fall of the Northern Song, manufacture was transferred to Hangzhou. In the south, Jingdezhen in Jiangxi was designated a center for the manufacture of imperial porcelain in 1004. It has continued as a major porcelain center to this day.

AFTER »

The Mongols took control of China from the Song, ruling as the Yuan dynasty (1279–1368).

THE MONGOLS TAKE CONTROL
The Mongols **destroyed the Jurchen Jin dynasty** in 1234, gaining control of north China. After more than 50 years of attacks by the Mongols, the Song fell in 1279 to **Kublai Khan**, the grandson of Genghis Khan **164–65** ».

MONGOL LAW
Kublai Khan **divided the population** into

KUBLAI KHAN

four classes: on top were the Mongols, then came peoples from Central Asia, then came the northern Chinese—who had been subjugated first by the Mongols—and lastly came the newly conquered Chinese of the Southern Song.

THE SILK ROAD
After the Mongol conquests, it was again safe for **merchants** and **missionaries** to use the Silk Road **184–85** ». The first European to record his journey was the Franciscan monk **John of Plano Carpini**, who reached Mongolia in 1246.

INVENTION
GUNPOWDER

A 9th-century Daoist text warned that mixing charcoal, saltpeter, and sulfur formed a dangerous combination; some who had done so had caused explosions and burned down buildings. By 919 CE gunpowder was being used in a flame-thrower, and by the end of the 10th century, simple bombs and grenades had begun to appear. In 1044, the formula for gunpowder was first published, 200 years before it appeared in Europe.

MONGOLIAN WARLORD Born c. 1162 Died 1227

Genghis Khan

"A man of great **ability, eloquence, and valor**."

MARCO POLO, *THE TRAVELS OF MARCO POLO*, 1298

Before he became known as Genghis Khan—a title he took in 1206 to proclaim his leadership of the Mongol tribes—the future warlord and conqueror was known simply as Temüjin. Born around 1162 to a minor chieftain in the mountains of eastern Mongolia, there was little in Temüjin's early life to indicate he would one day be ruler of the world's largest unbroken empire. When he was just five years old, his father was murdered and his family disinherited by their clan. For much of his childhood, Temüjin was forced to eke out a precarious nomadic existence with his siblings and their indomitable mother, Hoelun.

These early years must have done much to forge the great warrior and leader that Temüjin was to become. As the eldest male, Temüjin was the head of his family and quickly learned to make useful alliances. Having proved himself as a warrior by retrieving some stolen horses, Temüjin claimed a wife, Börte, from a neighboring tribe. He is said to have used her dowry of precious sable furs to win the favor of Toghrul

Engraving
According to a contemporary Persian chronicle, the Mongol emperor was a tall, long-bearded man with red hair and green eyes. This is how a 20th-century French artist depicted him.

Homage to a chief
Genghis Khan receives the homage of his vassals in this 14th-century Persian miniature. The white horse tails flying from his tent signify peace and diplomacy. Black horse tails meant war.

Battle scene
This Chinese painting depicts the Mongol cavalry in action on a mountain pass. Genghis Khan's highly disciplined army comprised battalions, or *tumens*, of 10,000 warriors, in turn divided into 1,000-man regiments.

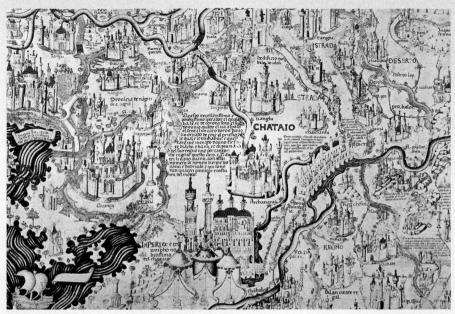

Mongolian Empire
This Italian map shows the empire of the Great Khan. *Chataio* (Cathay in English) was the name used by the Venetian traveler Marco Polo to describe northern China when he journeyed through the empire in the reign of Kublai Khan, Genghis Khan's grandson.

In 1227, while on campaign in Xi Xia, Genghis Khan fell from his horse, became feverish, and died. The vast empire he left to his sons stretched from Iran and Kazakhstan in the west, across central Asia and northern China to the Sea of Japan.

(also known as Ong Khan or "Prince King"), an old ally of his father's and leader of the Turkish-speaking Kerait people. When Börte was kidnapped, Temüjin called on Toghrul for help in rescuing her. Soon afterward, Börte had a baby, Jochi, who was acknowledged as Temüjin's son and heir—despite the possibility that he had been conceived while Börte was in captivity.

Campaigns and conquests
Having reclaimed his family's status and secured Toghrul's patronage, Temüjin began to earn his military reputation. Together with Toghrul, he harassed the Chinese empire north and west of the Great Wall. Sometimes he joined forces against other nomadic tribes, notably the neighboring Tatars, at the behest of the northern Chinese Jin dynasty. Another crucial ally at this time was his "sworn brother" Jamuka, of the Tangut tribe based in Xi Xia in northeast China.

Through a series of brilliant military campaigns and diplomatic maneuvers, which included the elimination of his

Mongol quiver
This ornate quiver was designed to hold the arrows that mounted Mongol horsemen were capable of aiming and firing at a full gallop. Mongol boys received intensive training in both horsemanship and archery.

former allies Toghrul and Jamuka, Temüjin made himself lord of all the Mongol tribes. In 1206, at a mass rally, or *kurultai*, Temüjin was proclaimed as Genghis Khan or "universal ruler."

For more than three decades Genghis Khan led the Mongol confederation in a string of victories and in campaigns that ravaged large areas of Asia and subjugated many millions of people.

Warrior and statesman
In conquering this huge empire, Genghis Khan frequently resorted to psychological warfare, using spies, propaganda, and terror as much as military force. Even today, the ruthless warlord who massacred the inhabitants of vanquished cities is hard to reconcile with the tolerant ruler, genuinely interested in the various belief-systems of his empire: Buddhism, Islam, Nestorian Christianity, Confucianism, and Taoism. Genghis Khan introduced a humane law code, the *Yassa*, across his empire, and outlawed the custom of kidnapping women. Moreover, in bringing order to the Eurasian landmass, he brought stability to the Silk Road (see pp.184–85), facilitating the renewal of East–West trade and cultural contact.

> "In military exercises **I am always in front** and in time of battle **I am never behind.**"
>
> WORDS ATTRIBUTED TO GENGHIS KHAN BY A CHINESE MONK, *c.* 1224

FOUNDER OF YUAN DYNASTY IN CHINA (1216–94)

KUBLAI KHAN

Genghis Khan was grandfather of another famous Mongolian emperor, Kublai Khan. While on his deathbed, the old warrior laid a hand on the young Kublai's head, a gesture interpreted as a sign of future greatness.

The Mongolian empire reached its greatest extent under Kublai Khan. Having inherited Mongolia and northern China, Kublai Khan added southern China to his dominion. He is celebrated as a unifier of China and the founder of the Yuan imperial dynasty. He is also the "Great Khan" of Marco Polo's travels, who entertained the Venetians and gave them passports for their journey.

GENGHIS KHAN'S COFFIN

The Mongol Yuan dynasty was destroyed by
economic turmoil and peasant rebellions.

YUAN DRAMA
The **earliest Chinese plays**, which were sung,
spoken, acted, and mimed, were written by
Chinese scholars in the Yuan period. Allegedly,
the plays contained **protests against the
Mongol presence**, and the popular response
to them was said to have contributed to the
collapse of the Yuan dynasty.

SUPPRESSION OF THE HAN
According to **Mongol law**, the indigenous people
of China, the Han Chinese, were the lowest class
within Chinese society. In the 1340s, a disastrous
flood of the Yellow River and **the conscripton
of thousands of Han peasants for forced
labour** led to widespread rebellion, and the
Yuan dynasty was finally overthrown in 1368.

ORIGINS OF THE GREAT WALL
Though the Great Wall that survives today
was constructed during the Ming dynasty,
its foundations were first laid by **Qin
Shihuang « 126–27** in 214 BCE,
when he connected the fortifications
of the small kingdoms of the **Warring
States** era to form a barrier that would
defend the empire against barbarians.

The **Ming Dynasty**

**The Ming, the last native Chinese dynasty, replaced the Mongol Yuan dynasty in 1368. During their rule
a new capital city was created at Beijing, and the Forbidden City was built within its walls. The Ming
period also saw China construct a defensive barrier against the outside world—the Great Wall.**

C hina under the Ming enjoyed
relative stability and saw the
development of a sophisticated
bureaucracy, but also witnessed a period
of imperial tyranny. In contrast to some
Western nations of the time, where royal
authority was challenged,
imperial power under the
Ming grew unchecked.
Hongwu, the first Ming
emperor, began life as a
poor peasant. During his
reign he reorganized the
army and attempted to
reform the land and
tax system. In
1380, Hongwu
abolished the

Typical Ming vase
The distinctive cobalt blue
glaze of Chinese porcelain,
developed by the Yuan, was
perfected under the Ming.

post of chief minister, revised the legal
code, and ensured that imperial power
could not be challenged in court. This
was supported by a surveillance system
operated by spies, secret agents, and
the "Brocade Guards," who carried out
major purges of corrupt officials.

Urban growth under Yongle
Hongwu's son usurped the throne in
1403 and reigned as Emperor Yongle.
He transferred the capital to Beijing,
and began building a magnificent walled
palace complex there, the Forbidden
City (see right), which nobody was
allowed to enter without permission.
Beijing became the main bureaucratic
and military center, but other cities
and towns also grew apace. Suzhou
and Nanjing became famous for their
sophisticated social life and lavish
festivals. Jingdezhen turned out blue-
and-white porcelain and Hangzhou
produced silk. Many of these cities

were connected by the Grand Canal
(see p.160); Linqing, one of the main
ports on the canal, handled 1.6 million
shiploads of freight annually.
A vigorous urban culture accompanied
the growth of Ming cities. The spread
of printing and the demands of a more
literate public led to a publishing boom.
Classic novels such as *The Romance of
the Three Kingdoms*, *Water Margin*, and
Journey to the West (otherwise known as
Monkey) came out for the first time in
print, and books with colored wood-
block illustrations were published.

Frontier strategy
After Yongle's death, the Ming dynasty
was threatened by a new group of ethnic
outsiders—the Mongol-speaking Oirat
peoples—who began a massive invasion
into Chinese territory in 1449. Emperor
Zhengtong rashly counterattacked, but
his forces were ambushed at Tumu and
he himself was taken hostage. The

The Great Wall
In 1474, construction began on the brickwork Great Wall that we know today. More than 1,500 miles (2,400 km) long, the wall stretched from the Jiayu Pass in the west to the Yalu River in the east. The wall was strengthened and maintained throughout the Ming period.

Oirat failed to take this opportunity to capture Beijing, and Zhengtong was eventually released. Nevertheless, the Tumu incident heralded the end of the expansionist policies of the Ming dynasty; from that point on, frontier strategy became much more defensive. Lacking the military resources to control the steppe regions that had been the source of the Oirat incursions, a barrier was built to contain the

The Forbidden City
In 1406, Yongle transferred his capital from Nanjing to Beijing. He ordered the construction of the Forbidden City, which, with 9,999 rooms, is still the world's largest palace complex.

CHINESE EXPLORER (1371–1433)

ZHENG HE

Ming rule saw the creation of a vast imperial navy. Between 1405 and 1433, the Muslim eunuch Zheng He commanded seven ambitious maritime expeditions. The first comprised 317 ships and 27,870 men, and put in at several Indian ports. On subsequent voyages, he reached Hormuz on the Gulf of Oman, and ships from his fleet put in at Jidda in Saudi Arabia. Zheng He's voyages took him to 37 countries, and resulted not only in increased trade for China, but also in the capture of pirates that had plagued Chinese waters. An account of Zheng He's voyages was written by the Muslim scholar Ma Yuan.

Mongol threat. Brick and stone were laid over the earthen walls first constructed by the Qin dynasty (see BEFORE) to create the Great Wall.

Trade with the West begins
Portuguese merchants first reached China in 1514, and in the 1550s they established a trading station at Macao on the southeast coast. In 1604, two Portuguese ships carrying 200,000 pieces of Chinese blue-and-white porcelain were captured by the Dutch. The contents were put up for sale in Europe and the auction set off a craze for Chinese porcelain. The beginnings of trade with the West marked a turning point in Chinese history; for the next 300 years, China's fortunes would be inextricably linked to its mercantile relationship with Western powers.

The decline of Ming power and authority was a protracted affair. The Manchu Qing dynasty finally took control in 1644.

MING BUREAUCRACY
The Ming had the most **effective central bureaucracy** in the world at the time, but by the end of the Ming period, the heavy hand of imperial control, court **intrigues**, and **factional fighting** between groups of officials had made a significant contribution to the fall of the dynasty.

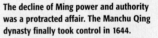

ADMINISTRATIVE SEAL

DECLINE AND FALL
By the late 16th century, the Ming dynasty was in decline. Weak emperors were **dominated by their advisors**, who increasingly influenced political decisions. In the north, **a new threat from the nomadic Jurchen** had arisen, as Nurhaci organized the tribes into the Manchu nation **240–41 ».** **Economic problems prompted peasant rebellions**, and in 1644 rebel forces under **Li Zicheng** took Beijing. Li was ousted in turn by the invading Manchus.

BEFORE ◄◄

The Asian mainland was the origin of Japan's first settlers and the source of later cultural and technological developments.

THE FIRST JAPANESE
The first inhabitants of Japan arrived from the Asian mainland around 30,000 BCE. By 8,000 BCE they were producing distinctive **jomon** (rope-patterned) pottery–possibly **the first pottery made anywhere in the world**. These early Japanese were hunter-gatherers.

JOMON POTTERY

ASIAN INFLUENCES
Around 300 BCE, the arrival of rice from East Asia revolutionized Japanese society. **Rice cultivation** required a peasant workforce living in settled communities. Large landowners became **regional rulers** who fought for access to water and fertile land. In the 6th–7th centuries CE, contact with Asia brought the Buddhist religion and with it **Chinese high culture** ◄◄ **160–61** including writing in the form of Chinese characters.

FUJIWARA JAPAN
Japan's line of **sacred emperors** is historically attested after the 3rd century CE. During the **Heian Period** (794–1185 CE), power devolved from the emperor to the **Fujiwara clan**, which controlled the imperial court and **dominated Japan** until the rise of the samurai.

BUSHIDO A code of conduct and a way of life practiced by the samurai. Bushido sought to unite learning and military prowess, and emphasized frugality, loyalty, mastery of martial arts and, above all, honor.

Twelfth-century Japan was a country with an elaborate, subtle, artistic culture that was developed at the imperial court in the capital, Kyoto. But in many areas outside the capital, life was lawless and unruly. In many provinces, clans (extended families) of samurai warriors ruled by force. Among the most powerful of them were two long-established families of high standing, the Minamoto and Taira. Their ancestors had been imperial princes who, in the 9th century, were dispatched from Kyoto to uphold the emperor's authority in distant provinces. There, fighting men flocked to serve them, and the two families became leaders of powerful warrior clans. From their provincial bases, in the 12th century the Minamoto and Taira returned to compete for supreme power in the capital, Kyoto.

Gempeii Wars
As the dominant family at the imperial court, the Taira at first had the upper hand. But, between 1180 and 1185 a series of fierce conflicts, known as the Gempei Wars, ended with the Minamoto family triumphant. At two decisive battles, in 1184 and 1185, the Taira were slaughtered in combat, driven to mass suicide, or captured and executed. Minamoto Yoritomo (see right), the head of the Minamoto clan, was established as the country's first military dictator, or "shogun," with his court at Kamakura, far to the east of Kyoto. The emperor was left in the old capital as a powerless figurehead.

Shogun rule
The rule of the shoguns, which was to continue until the mid-19th century, established the samurai as the dominant military and social elite. Originally rough fighting men at odds with the effete culture of the court, the samurai evolved into a striking mixture of the savage and the refined. The ideal warrior was as capable of dashing off a poem as he was of slicing off an enemy's head with his two-handed sword. In theory he subscribed to an austere code of honor and, rather than face defeat, would commit ritual suicide (*seppuku*) by cutting open the stomach (*hara kiri*). Warfare between samurai followed brutal but elaborate rules—for example, it was customary to cut off the head of a warrior you killed in battle and return it to his family stuck on a spiked board.

Fighting men
The dominant social position of men who were devoted to war as a way of life inevitably spawned violence in a country that had no external enemies. The sole foreign threat in the medieval period came from China. In 1274 and again in 1281, China's Mongol ruler, Kublai Khan (see p.165) attempted to invade Japan by sea from Korea. The samurai united to repel these invasions,

Fujiwara fan
Decorating fans was a typical activity of the refined court ladies.

"It is not the **way of the warrior** to be shamed and avoid death."

SAMURAI TORII MOTOTADA, 1600

The **Rise** of the **Samurai**

The samurai, an elite class of armored warriors, dominated Japan from the 12th century. Their fighting prowess and tradition of loyal service to the death—enshrined in the chivalric code of *bushido*—are the stuff of legend. But in reality, samurai ascendancy brought instability, violence, and civil war.

The Tale of Genji
Murasaki Shikibu's long novel *The Tale of Genji* was based on the author's experiences as lady-in-waiting at the imperial court in the early 11th century. It paints a vivid picture of Kyoto courtiers devoted to amorous intrigues and the delicate expression of emotions in verse.

Divine wind
The second attempt by the Mongols to invade Japan met with disaster. The Mongol fleet was scattered by a typhoon, remembered by the Japanese as the *kamikaze* ("divine wind").

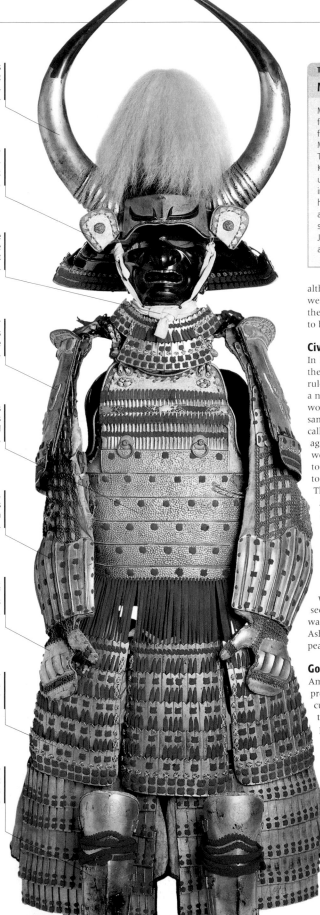

The buffalo horns decorating the helmet are made of carved, gilded wood.

The helmet, or *kabuto*, has a leather-covered sweepback to protect the neck.

The throat defense is attached to the mask, or *mempo*, that covers the lower face.

The shoulder guard, or *sode*, is suspended above the arm defense.

The breastplate is decorated with plates of gold lacquer tied with red silk knots.

The arm guard, or *kote*, combines metal plates with chainmail.

Gloves, or *tekko*, are made of small metal plates bound with string.

The skirts, or *kusazuri*, of the armor are split for ease of movement.

The greaves, or *suneate*, protect the samurai's lower legs

THE FIRST SHOGUN (1147–99)

MINAMOTO YORITOMO

Minamoto Yoritomo was involved in the feud between the Minamoto and Taira clans from an early age. In 1160 his father, Minamoto Yoshitomo, was executed by the Taira and he was exiled from the capital, Kyoto. Twenty years later he led a Minamoto uprising against the Taira. Although defeated in his first battle at Ishibashiyama in 1180, he went on to triumph both over the Taira and rivals within his own clan. He became shogun in 1192, marking the beginning of Japan's long feudal age. Yoritomo died in a riding accident.

although they were helped by bad weather. For the rest of the time, if the samurai were going to fight, it had to be against one another.

Civil war

In 1333, a major civil war began when the emperor Go Daigo challenged the rule of the shoguns. Aiming to found a new imperial age, in which emperors would exercise real power, with the samurai as their servants, Go Daigo called on warriors across Japan to rise against the shogunate. Many clans were willing to do this, but in order to seize power for themselves, not to restore control to the emperor. The most ruthless of the samurai, Ashikaga Takauji, expelled Go Daigo from Kyoto and enthroned an alternative emperor, who duly appointed Takauji as the first Ashikaga shogun. Go Daigo set up a rival court at Yoshino and samurai across Japan took up arms in favor of one or other emperor, depending on where their personal advantage seemed to lie. The resulting civil war lasted 60 years, before the third Ashikaga shogun, Yoshimitsu, restored peace to Japan in 1392.

Golden age

Ambitious and forceful, Yoshimitsu presided over a golden age of Japanese culture. He made his court at Kyoto the site of a cultural renaissance, patronizing the refined, stylized "Noh" drama (see p.243), collecting ink splash paintings, and promoting Zen, a distinctively Japanese variant on Buddhism that profoundly influenced the arts. Yoshimitsu spent lavishly,

building a pavilion coated in gold and surrounded by splendid gardens. In 1402 he negotiated formal trade links with the emperor of China, enabling him to import Chinese artifacts for his cultured capital.

Violence erupts again

But Yoshimitsu, and his equally cultured successor, Yoshimasa, presided over an unstable society. The *daimyo*, powerful and brutal warlords who had little allegiance to the shogunate, controlled vast areas in the provinces. While Kyoto practiced refinement, from 1467 Japan descended into permanent civil war between the private armies of rival *daimyo*.

AFTER »

In the 16th century, warfare in Japan entered a new era with the introduction of firearms. The fighting finally ended under the shogun Tokugawa Ieyasu, who reunited the country.

CHRISTIANITY
The arrival of Europeans in Japan from 1543 brought both guns and Christianity. A mission established by St. Francis Xavier flourished until the 17th century, when **Christianity was banned** and converts were persecuted.

ST. FRANCIS XAVIER

UNIFYING JAPAN
In the 16th century, ambitious *daimyo* sought to end Japan's endemic civil strife by unifying the country under a single strong ruler. **Odu Nobunaga** and his successor **Toyotomi Hideyoshi** took control of much of Japan in the 1560s–1590s. The unification of the country was completed by **Tokugawa Ieyasu 242–43 »**, who became shogun in 1603, founding a dynasty that was to rule for 250 years.

Warrior's armor
Samurai fought without shields, depending on armor for protection. The magnificent helmets and body armor were intended for display as well as defense. This fine example dates from the 19th century, when the samurai had mostly ceased actual fighting.

BEFORE

China was an important influence on the successive rulers of the Korean peninsula.

CHINESE INFLUENCE
In 668 CE, the Korean peninsula was unified by the Silla kingdom, which imported and adapted institutions, ideas, and technology from neighboring China. **Buddhism** became central to spiritual and political life during this period. During the **Koryo dynasty** (932–1392 CE), Buddhist art and scholarship flourished under state sponsorship. Among the ruling elite of scholar-officials, an intellectual import from Song-dynasty China ❮❮ **162–63** began to gain ground: **Neo-Confucianism**.

A NEW DYNASTY
In 1392, a Koryo general called Yi Songgye seized power, declaring himself the first king of the new **Choson dynasty**. This provided the opportunity for the Neo-Confucians to sweep aside the economic power and "corrupting" political and moral influences of Buddhism.

78 MILLION The number of Korean-speakers around the world who still use the letters of the phonetic han'gul script originally devised by King Sejong.

Korea in the Middle Ages

The Choson kingdom dominated Korea from 1392 to 1910, making it one of history's most enduring royal dynasties. King Sejong is credited with laying the foundations of this longevity during his 32-year reign (1418–50). His greatest legacy is the invention of han'gul—an alphabet for the Korean language.

At the heart of Sejong's project was the implementation of the Neo-Confucian view of the world, which had been established as the official ideology of the dynasty by Sejong's grandfather Yi Songgye (see BEFORE). For the Neo-Confucians, human society was an integral part of a universe that included the natural world and the heavens and was governed by a pattern called li or "principle." Although it appeared to be abstract, Neo-Confucianism was an intensely pragmatic philosophy that defined the way in which humans should relate to one another socially and the way that society, and the king in particular, should interact with the wider natural world. The role of the ideal Neo-Confucian sage-king was to bring order to heaven and earth according to the requirements of li, and most importantly, to harmonize all aspects of human behavior with the underlying universal order. This was an ideal that Sejong ambitiously sought to realize in a way that no other Korean king before or since has done.

At the start of the Choson period, the aristocracy, which had grown powerful under the previous Koryo dynasty (see BEFORE), was forced to seek power through a revitalized civil service examination system, based on similar Chinese systems (see pp.128–29). This new ruling class, which combined features of a hereditary aristocracy and a scholarly bureaucracy, came to be called the yangban and remained the most powerful class in Choson society until the beginning of the 20th century.

In addition to maintaining his own ruling dynasty and strengthening the bureaucratic state, Sejong placed much importance on ensuring the well-being of his people through innovations that improved their lives.

Sounds for the people
It is easy to identify King Sejong's most important innovation—the invention of the phonetic alphabet for the Korean language, called han'gul. As far as contemporary Koreans are concerned, it is a central aspect of everyday life and a source of national pride, but when the king first introduced the alphabet in the mid-15th century, the new writing system seemed to the intellectual elite of the time to be a vulgarization of written language. Writing in Korea had hitherto been limited to complex Chinese characters and was the exclusive property of the yangban. Many yangban resented these simple and relatively easy-to-learn new characters, which for a long time were used mainly by women.

The king explained his motivation for creating the script in his preface to a work illustrating the new writing system,

INVENTION
RAIN GAUGE

Rain gauges, such as this stone, iron, and bronze example, were designed in the 1440s, long before such equipment was used in Europe. Each gauge was standardized to 16.5 in (42.5 cm) in height and 6.5 in (17 cm) in diameter. Sejong had them installed in every county so that local magistrates could record rainfall and contribute to knowledge of the climate and improvement of agricultural techniques. Other scientific achievements of 15th-century Korea were the development of water clocks and the publication of books on medicine, pharmacology, agriculture, and astronomy.

The introduction of han'gul

The new Korean alphabet, today called han'gul, is thought to have been largely the work of King Sejong himself and is based on a careful analysis of the Korean language. It was first revealed in 1443 and then formally introduced by the king in 1446 in a ceremony depicted here in a modern Korean painting.

But han'gul was more than just a project to bring literacy to the lower levels of society. Like much that Sejong did, it was also an attempt to reflect the order of Neo-Confucianism. It divides the sounds of the Korean language into the two components of the universal principle—yin (dark, female, passive) and yang (light, male, active).

Alongside the new alphabet, King Sejong encouraged the advancement of sciences, particularly astronomy and meteorology, which sought to understand the function of the heavens (see left). His attention also extended into the reform of court music, the encouragement of refined painting that depicted the natural world, and the spread of new agricultural techniques to the country's farmers.

A society of unequals

The foundations of the Choson dynasty rested upon more than just the will of a determined, farsighted king. The Neo-Confucianism that dominated the thinking of Sejong and his officials reflected the reality of Choson's unequal society and actually helped to reinforce its rigid class structures.

The great majority of the population were peasants engaged in agriculture, paying taxes to the state and rent to landlords, and often finding themselves at the mercy of the floods and droughts that beset the Korean peninsula's fragile ecology, bringing with them famine and disease. Beneath the farmers on the social scale were various lowborn groups, including those involved in so-called "dirty occupations" such as butchery and leatherworking. There was also a large hereditary

Despite the many achievements of the 15th century, problems in the political system of the Choson dynasty began to appear.

INVASION FROM THE EAST

The 16th century saw the rise of a vicious rivalry among the scholar-officials who vied for position in the state bureaucracy and at court. The emphasis that Choson placed on literary scholarship and its favoritism toward a civil rather than military bureaucracy had serious consequences. When **Japan invaded** in the 1590s, the country was unprepared. After two invasions in six years brought devastation for the country and its people, the invaders were finally repelled with military aid from Ming China **‹‹ 164–65** and a series of naval victories courtesy of the famous admiral, Yi Sunsin.

RECOVERY AND RENOVATION

Choson recovered during the 17th century, but the **fall of China's Ming dynasty** to Manchu "barbarians" in 1644 was a profound shock. The rulers of Choson then saw themselves as the true defenders of civilization and Neo-Confucian orthodoxy. Two kings, Yongjo and Chongjo, ruled for much of the 18th century and the country prospered. A move away from Neo-Confucianism toward solving practical problems and an interest in new ideas from China and Europe followed.

slave class that is thought to have comprised in the region of 30 percent of the total population and remained a notable feature of Choson society until the 19th century.

In accordance with his ideology, Sejong sought to encourage appropriate relationships between the different classes and cultivate decorum in personal relations. In 1432, he ordered the publication of a didactic text on Neo-Confucian ethics called the *Illustrated Guide to the Three Bonds*, which was reprinted later that century with a han'gul text so that a general readership could benefit from its instructions. The three bonds of the title were those that occur between parents and children, between ruler and official, and between husband and wife. Each example of bond was illustrated with a series of short biographies and woodcuts depicting the stories of devoted sons and daughters, loyal officials, and faithful wives.

But the less lofty lives of the common people found an expression in the arts of this period, in particular through punch'ong ceramics. These developed from the refined celadon ceramics—crackle-glazed porcelain in a range of jadelike colors—favored by the Koryo court in previous centuries. The freedom of their incised and stamped designs has often been cited as a key feature of the Korean artistic style, and this apparently artless but graceful form of pottery had a deep influence on Japanese ceramics. Korea's impact on the art in Japan saw a dramatic increase after potters were taken from Korea back to Japan by invading armies in the late 16th century.

Hunmin Chong'um
The opening pages of *Correct Sounds for the Instruction of the People* contain Sejong's explanation of the new script in both Chinese characters and han'gul. The book was first printed in 1446 at the time of the introduction of the new phonetic script for the Korean language.

KOREAN KING (1397–1450)

KING SEJONG

The fourth king of a relatively young dynasty, Sejong came to the throne of Choson (Korea) in 1418 at the age of 22. He was the grandson of the dynastic founder Yi Songgye and became the first king to be extensively schooled from an early age in Neo-Confucian philosophy and ethics. Today, Sejong the Great is a national icon symbolizing Korea's first "golden age" and is seen by many millions of Koreans every day on the back of the 10,000-won note.

> **" I have ... designed 28 letters, which I wish to have everyone practice at their ease."**
>
> KING SEJONG, PREFACE TO "CORRECT SOUNDS," 1446

published in 1446: "The sounds of our country's language are different from those of China and are not easily conveyed in Chinese writing. Among the ignorant people there have been a great many who ... have been unable to express their feelings."

Chongmyo ritual
At Chongmyo Shrine in Seoul, the Choson kings frequently held elaborate Confucian rites as a way of honoring their royal ancestors.

Punch'ong ware
Freely decorated ceramics, such as this elegant vase, characterized the earthy aesthetics of the period.

« **BEFORE**

The Dong Son culture flourished in Southeast Asia during the 1st millennium BCE.

THE DONG SON

Remains of the Dong Son culture that created this drum (1st–2nd century BCE) were **discovered near Hanoi in Vietnam** in the 1930s. Dong Son culture was centered on **northern Vietnam**, but remnants have been found **across Southeast Asia** as far away as **Java** and **Sumatra**. Dongsonians had an organized society that later cultures in the region would draw upon.

DONG SON DRUM

HOW WE KNOW

BOROBUDUR TEMPLE

The Buddhist monument of Borobudur in Central Java remained largely hidden by jungle until its rediscovery in 1814. Careful study of carvings and inscriptions around the site suggests that it was constructed under the influence of the Srivjaya Empire in the 8th–9th centuries. Almost 21,500 sq ft (2,000 m²) of narrative sculptures provide information about Buddhist worship and daily life in Java in the period.

Lost Empires

Long seen as a way station for merchants and missionaries, Southeast Asia has also been home to peoples and empires whose commercial, spiritual, and artistic wealth were rivaled by none. This wealth depended on the movement of people, goods, and ideas across the vast waterways and fertile plains of the region.

Among the great numbers of people who migrated along the waterways of Southeast Asia, many moved from the islands of Java and Sumatra to the coasts of today's Vietnam and Cambodia. These people set up maritime trading centers that traded spices, woods, metals, and animal products from inland for merchandise from elsewhere in Southeast Asia, India, Persia, and Arabia. Many areas grew wealthy as a result of this trade, and the Champa kingdom in southern Vietnam became a great empire, its power and influence lasting from the 7th century CE until its defeat by the Vietnamese emperor 1471.

Rivers and floodplains

The fertile rivers of the Southeast Asian interior were another source of wealth. Communities around the river basins of the Mekong, Red, Chao Phraya, and Irrawaddy rivers grew prosperous from rice and livestock. But the rivers were also a source of conflict as the region's empires fought each other for control the most productive arable areas. As early as the 7th century CE, the rulers of the Khmer people, in modern Cambodia,

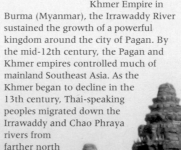
> "**Rice** is easily had … and **trade** is easily carried on."
>
> ZHOU DAGUAN, CHINESE DIPLOMAT, DESCRIBING KHMER CAMBODIA, c. 1290

had fought the declining Funan empire and the Champa city-states for control of the fertile Mekong River delta. While the power of Funan passed, the Champa and Khmer continued to quarrel over the floodplain. After 939, the Champa also had to contend with the northern Vietnamese state of Dai Viet, which was desperate to find territories south of the crowded Red River valley. The Champa preoccupation with the Dai Viet let the Khmer Empire strengthen its grip on the rice lands of the Mekong.

At the same time, to the west of the Khmer Empire in Burma (Myanmar), the Irrawaddy River sustained the growth of a powerful kingdom around the city of Pagan. By the mid-12th century, the Pagan and Khmer empires controlled much of mainland Southeast Asia. As the Khmer began to decline in the 13th century, Thai-speaking peoples migrated down the Irrawaddy and Chao Phraya rivers from farther north and took control of many former

Borobudur relief
The Buddhist monument at Borobudur features 2,672 carved reliefs showing both the Buddhist afterlife and the daily existence of the Javanese people.

Khmer lands. In 1238, they established the first Thai nation, the kingdom of Sukhothai, in central Thailand.

Island kingdoms

The peoples that remained on Sumatra and Java set up prosperous trading communities rivaling the coastal states of the mainland. By the 8th century, the Srivijaya Empire controlled most of Sumatra

C H I N A

PAGAN
c.850–1287
(c.1050–1287)

DAI VIET
939–1527
Thang Long

PACIFIC
OCEAN

HARIPUNJAYA

Pegu

Nakhon
Pathom

Angkor Vijaya

KHMER EMPIRE
c.802–1327
(c.1110–1280)

CHAMPA
921–1471

Andaman
Sea

Hainan

South
China
Sea

Philippines

Tambralinga

Kedah

Malay
Peninsula

Jambi

SRIVIJAYA
c.200–1320
(c.740–1025)

Palembang

Borobudur

Java

KADIRI
1045–1221

Bali

MATARAM
SINGHASARI

Sumbawa Flores Sea

Lombok

INDIAN OCEAN

Borneo

Java Sea

0   800 km
0   800 miles

N

Empires of Southeast Asia
Situated between India and China, Southeast Asia
has always been a region where products, ideas,
and faiths from abroad have been debated,
exchanged, accommodated, and fought over.

KEY

Core area of Pagan Empire
Outermost limit of Pagan Empire

Core area of Dai Viet Empire
Outermost limit of Dai Viet Empire

Core area of Champa Empire
Outermost limit of Champa Empire

Core area of Khmer Empire
Outermost area of Khmer Empire

Core area of Srivijaya Empire
Outermost limit of Srivijaya Empire

Core area of Kadiri Empire
Outermost limit of Kadiri Empire

c. 650–1320   Period of state's duration
(c. 740–1025) Period of state's apogee

AFTER

Both Christianity and Islam were exported to Southeast Asia by merchants and traders.

THE SPREAD OF ISLAM
Islam arrived in Southeast Asia with **Arab and Indian traders** from the east coast of India. By the **15th century**, Islam was the most popular religion in Java and Sumatra, transforming statecraft among the sultans and **religious custom** among the peoples of the islands.

EUROPEAN EMPIRE BUILDERS
After the Portuguese seized Malacca on the south of the Malay Peninsula in 1511, **European merchants and missionaries** began to emerge as major players in the commerce and statecraft of Southeast Asia **224–25 »**. They sought to channel trade through ports that they could control and **convert to Christianity**. Initially limited to the coastal cities, European influence spread across mainland Southeast Asia as **missionaries** traveled inland to convert people to Christianity and engage in commerce.

PORTUGUESE GALLEON

and the Malay Peninsula, dominating the shipping routes through the Straits of Malacca and imposing tolls on the highly profitable spice trade. Other maritime kingdoms, such as the Hindu Kadiri empire, grew in influence as the Srivijaya empire weakened in the 11th century.

The spread of religion
Merchants from India, China, and Sri Lanka brought religion as well as trade to Southeast Asia.

Hinduism first spread among the people of the islands and the mainland much as Mahayana Buddhism (see pp.144–47) later did in the 7th century—on the boats of traders. In Vietnam, Confucianism (see p.127) from China was also integrated into the daily workings of government and society.

The wealth from trade and agriculture financed the building of huge temples and monuments to the gods. Buddhist monuments such as

Borobudur in Java (see left) and the great Hindu temples of Angkor in the Khmer Empire testify to the impact these faiths had on the lives of the people. They also provide evidence of the Southeast Asian belief in the power of the gods to make or break the prosperity granted by the land, rivers, and sea.

Jayavarman II
The great Khmer ruler Jayavarman VII (c. 1125–1215) built vast temples and defeated the Champa, but his excessive spending also impoverished the empire.

Angkor Wat
Constructed in the 12th century during the reign of the Khmer ruler Suryavarman II and dedicated to the Hindu god of Vishnu, Angkor is the largest religious complex in the world. Measuring nearly 640 acres (260 hectares) in area, its outer wall encircles a temple 210 ft (65 m) tall and comprises over 2,600 ft (800 m) of carved stone.

« BEFORE

Prior to the rise of Islam, the Arabian Peninsula consisted of loosely organized federations of peoples and towns.

BEFORE ISLAM

The Arabian Peninsula has always been dominated by sparsely populated, arid desert. Its early inhabitants were mainly nomads such as the **Bedouin**, although there were some farmers around the oases. The few towns were trading centers for goods such as spices. Frankincense, a fragrant tree resin, was one of the most important products. The proximity of the **Silk Road 184–85 »** made it relatively easy for Arabian merchants to trade their goods.

FRANKINCENSE

PRE-ISLAMIC RELIGION

Pre-Islamic Arabs spoke a number of languages and followed a variety of religions, most of which were polytheistic, worshipping several different gods **« 144–45**. **Mecca**, later the most important religious site of Islam, was already a center of worship.

MUHAMMAD THE PROPHET

Muhammad was a merchant based at Mecca when he had his first revelation from God. Although some people accepted his teachings, the hostility of others forced him into **exile in Medina**. There, he gathered more followers, uniting the local tribes and raiding caravans until he managed to conquer Mecca itself. By Muhammad's death in 632 CE, the whole of the Arabian Peninsula was united under the new Islamic religion. The followers of Muhammad—Muslims—then **expanded** farther **toward Syria**, which brought them in contact with the two great empires of Persia and Byzantium.

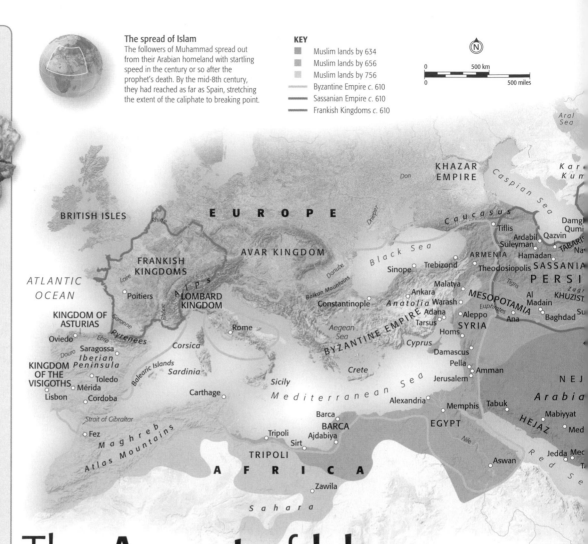

The spread of Islam
The followers of Muhammad spread out from their Arabian homeland with startling speed in the century or so after the prophet's death. By the mid-8th century, they had reached as far as Spain, stretching the extent of the caliphate to breaking point.

KEY
- ■ Muslim lands by 634
- ■ Muslim lands by 656
- ■ Muslim lands by 756
- — Byzantine Empire c. 610
- — Sassanian Empire c. 610
- — Frankish Kingdoms c. 610

0 500 km
0 500 miles

The Ascent of Islam

In 622 CE, Muhammad was forced into exile in Medina from Mecca for his beliefs. By 750, these beliefs had become the basis of a religion whose adherents governed an area stretching continuously from the borders of China to Spain. By 1450 Muslims were ruling in areas as far east as Indonesia.

Following the death of Muhammad in 632 CE, his successors, who were known as caliphs, carried Islam far beyond the confines of the Arabian Peninsula. Shortly after the death of the second caliph 'Umar ibn 'Abd al-Khattab in 644, the Muslims conquered the entire Persian Empire (see pp.122–23), as well as taking Syria and Egypt from the Byzantine Empire (see pp.198–99). The new rulers were tolerant toward the religions they found in their conquered territories, and did not force conversion. The constantly expanding area of the Islamic Empire was controlled by governors based in armed camps, each taking their instructions from Medina.

Despite their military successes, the Muslims were soon split by factional differences. The most remote

Kaaba
This 16th-century Turkish tile depicts the Kaaba at Mecca. Originally a site of pre-Islamic polytheistic worship, this square building is the holiest site in Islam, and all Muslims pray toward it.

governors were constantly trying to become independent, and there was tension between the "true" followers of Muhammad and those they believed were simply hungry for power. Things came to a head with the murder in 656 of the third caliph, 'Uthman ibn 'Affan, which led to outright civil war between 'Ali ibn abi Talib, a relative of Muhammad himself, and Mu'awiya ibn Abi Sufyan, a relative of the murdered 'Uthman. When 'Ali was

assassinated in 661, Mu'awiya took power, becoming the first caliph of the Umayyad dynasty.

Although this turbulent period saw a great deal of conflict, it also witnessed the collation and standardization of the Qur'an, the Muslim holy book. The second caliph even introduced a new Islamic "Hijri" calendar, which kept time by following the cycles of the moon, and dated its years from the time of Muhammad's flight to Medina.

The Umayyad dynasty

The Umayyads took their name from the clan to which the first Umayyad caliph, Mu'awiya ibn Abi Sufyan, belonged.

Dome of the Rock
The Dome of the Rock mosque in Jerusalem is the oldest surviving monument from the early period of Islam. First built in the 7th century, it has been restored and redecorated several times since. The site is sacred not only to Muslims, but also to Jews and Christians, and has been a lasting source of conflict.

While early caliphs had been chosen by community leaders, under the Umayyads the position became hereditary. To improve the government of their expanding empire, the Umayyads moved their capital to the more central Damascus, and borrowed institutions from the Byzantine and Persian rulers of the area, simply changing the administrative language to Arabic.

The Umayyads continued the conquests of previous caliphs, consolidating power over the former Persian Empire and extending the rule of Islam across North Africa. They built monumental shrines and places of worship to emphasize Islamic power, including the Dome of the Rock, on the site in Jerusalem where Muhammad is believed to have ascended to heaven, and great mosques at Damascus, Aleppo, and Medina. Although conversion was still by choice, special taxes on non-Muslims and religious restrictions on senior government positions encouraged the population to become increasingly Muslim and to adopt Arab customs, particularly in the east of the empire, in what are now Iraq and Iran.

Despite all this, factionalism remained rife, with several groups trying to seize power from the Umayyads. One major group still believed that only the descendants of 'Ali, who had lost in the civil war that brought the Umayyads to power, should rule. When one of 'Ali's sons was killed, they proclaimed him a martyr. The resulting dispute triggered one of the biggest splits in Islam and 'Ali's followers ultimately became the Shia branch of Islam.

In 750, several anti-Umayyad factions joined together to overthrow their rulers. The leader of the revolt was descended from another relative of Muhammad, named 'Abbas.

The Abbasid dynasty
The family of 'Abbas was largely based in the old Persian Empire—modern-day Iran, Iraq, and Afghanistan. They moved the capital east to the new city of Baghdad, which was closer to their center of power, located on major trade routes,

Arab astrolabe
The astrolabe was an astronomical device developed in the Islamic world that used the position of the sun and stars for navigation, and as a tool to locate Mecca.

and closer to fertile farming areas. The new rulers ruthlessly wiped out anyone they perceived as a threat, and replaced the old Umayyad officials with those loyal to them. The Abbasids used a system of intelligence to spy on officials in far-off countries, to make sure they did not get too powerful. They used the words of the Qur'an and Islamic law to justify their claims to power and to further secure their position. They also introduced a more formal system of taxation to pay for their armies and bureaucrats.

The Abbasid period is generally considered a golden age of Islamic art, science, and architecture. Arabic became increasingly important as both a religious and a political language. Large encyclopedias and collections of lore were commissioned, and translations made of Greek and Persian scientific treatises, philosophical works, and literary texts. (see pp.158–59). Without these Arabic copies, the modern world would probably know very little about Greek and Persian literature, and the technological advances of the scientific revolution (see pp.266–67) and after might have been much delayed.

Despite their best efforts, the Abbasids were unable to prevent further revolts and uprisings among their subjects. In the mid-10th century, the Buyids, a group of professional soldiers employed by the Abbasids, staged a coup and took over the caliphate. Content to operate out of sight, they allowed the Abbasids to retain their title, and the Abbasid caliphate survived in name until the arrival of the Mongols in the 13th century.

> **CALIPH** Muhammad's successors as leaders of Islam were known as caliphs (from the Arabic *Khalifat ar-Rasul Allah*, "the successor, representative of the Prophet of God"), and the area over which they ruled was known as the caliphate.

BATTLE OF BADR

The Battle of Badr was crucial to the foundation of Islam. Taking place on March 17, 624, it is one of the few battles mentioned in the Qur'an. The Quraishi rulers of Mecca, frustrated by early Muslim ambushes on caravans in the area, launched a concerted attempt to stop them, but despite overwhelming odds in their favor they were soundly defeated. This illustration of the pursuit of the defeated army comes from a later account of the battle. Victory consolidated the political position of Muhammad and forced the surrounding areas to take him seriously.

"[The] Arabs... will **stand in awe** of us **forever.**"
AMR IBN HISHAM, ISLAMIC COMMANDER AT BADR, 624 CE

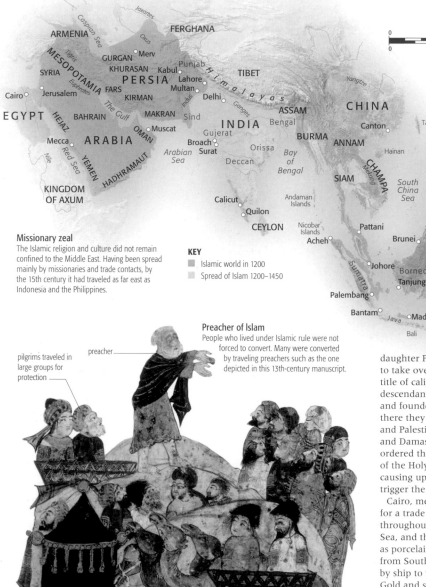

Missionary zeal
The Islamic religion and culture did not remain confined to the Middle East. Having been spread mainly by missionaries and trade contacts, by the 15th century it had traveled as far east as Indonesia and the Philippines.

KEY
■ Islamic world in 1200
■ Spread of Islam 1200–1450

pilgrims traveled in large groups for protection

preacher

Preacher of Islam
People who lived under Islamic rule were not forced to convert. Many were converted by traveling preachers such as the one depicted in this 13th-century manuscript.

daughter Fatima, emerged from Tunisia to take over North Africa and claim the title of caliph. 'Ubaydallah's "Fatimid" descendants conquered Egypt in 969, and founded the city of Cairo. From there they went on to conquer Syria and Palestine, reaching as far as Aleppo and Damascus. The Fatimid caliph ordered the destruction of the Church of the Holy Sepulcher in Jerusalem, causing uproar in Europe and helping trigger the Crusades (see pp.200–01).

Cairo, meanwhile, became the center for a trade network that extended throughout the Mediterranean, the Red Sea, and the Indian Ocean. Goods such as porcelain from China and spices from Southeast Asia were brought in by ship to the Egyptian Red Sea ports. Gold and slaves, meanwhile, were brought down the Nile from Ethiopia and the Sudan, to be traded in Cairo.

Alhambra palace
The Alhambra was built in the 14th century at Granada in southern Spain. The palace buildings are covered in tiles and plasterwork bearing Islamic geometric designs and inscriptions.

AL- The Arabic word for "the" forms the prefix of many scientific words that were adopted by medieval Europe along with the scientific knowledge of the Islamic world—for example, alkali, algebra, alchemy, algorithm, and almanac.

Most of the merchants were Muslim, although some Europeans from Venice and Genoa were also involved.

As well as being an important trading center, Cairo was also a site of religious learning. Al-Azhar University, founded by the Fatimids in the 10th century, is one of the oldest universities in existence. It attracted scholars from

Although the Islamic world was united by culture and trade throughout the whole medieval period, it did not always have one government. As the Abbasid dynasty concentrated its power in the east, the areas farthest from the new caliphate began to break away. First was Spain, which in 756 became an independent emirate, or principality, ruled by a branch of the exiled Umayyad dynasty. Shortly after this, independent governors also arose in Morocco, western and eastern Algeria, Tunisia, and Egypt.

By the 10th century, Islam had developed into three separate caliphates—the title "caliph" was by

now taken by the self-appointed head of any major Islamic community who felt the right to take it. In addition to the Abbasids in Baghdad, there was a Fatimid caliphate in Egypt, and an Umayyad caliphate in Spain.

The Isma'ili Fatimids
The Fatimid dynasty was founded in the early 10th century by an Isma'ili Shia Muslim named 'Ubaydallah. The Isma'ili Shia branch of Islam probably started as a secret movement in Iraq, though its missionary activity soon took its members all across the Islamic world. In 910 'Ubaydallah, who claimed descent from Muhammad's

ABBASID CALIPH
HARUN AL-RASHID

Harun al-Rashid was the fifth Abbasid caliph, ruling in Baghdad from 786–809. He is famous as a protagonist in many of the stories of *The Book of One Thousand and One Nights* (the "Arabian Nights"), but was also a significant historical figure.

Harun was the first caliph to appoint a vizier (from the Arabic *wazir*, meaning "helper") with many administrative powers—although his own vizier was removed from power in 803. He was also an important patron of the arts, presiding over part of the "Golden Age" that saw the emergence of classical Islamic culture.

Niujie mosque
One of the oldest mosques in China, Niujie was originally built in the 10th century CE. While Islamic empires never extended their influence to China, strong trade links between the two cultures ensured that Islam gained a foothold in East Asia.

Hassan tower
The huge 12th-century tower at Rabat in Morocco was designed as a minaret for an enormous mosque that was never completed.

Qutb Minar minaret
The Qutb Minar in Delhi, India, is the world's tallest brick minaret. The tower and mosque complex were built in the early 13th century by the founder of the Delhi sultanate.

Great Mosque of Djenné
Although the current mosque at Djenné in Mali is just over a century old, it stands on the site of a mosque first built in 1240. Following its construction, Djenné became West Africa's most important seat of Islamic learning.

Syria, Ethiopia, and the Maghreb, and is still considered the most prestigious site of Islamic learning in the world.

The Fatimid dynasty continued to rule Egypt until their conquest by the Kurdish warrior Saladin in 1171. Saladin used his Egyptian base to retake the Holy Land from the crusader settlers, but his Ayyubid dynasty fell within a century, overthrown by the Mamluks, originally Turkish slave soldiers, who had risen to become commanders of the Egyptian army.

The Umayyads in Spain
The emirate of Cordoba was founded in 756 by the exiled Umayyads, who ruled almost all of Spain. The title of caliph was taken by 'Abd al-Rahman III al-Nasir in 929, possibly as a reaction to the claims of the Fatimids.

The blending of Islamic ideas with Christian and Spanish influences produced a unique cultural fusion across the areas ruled by the Umayyad and the Almoravids, their Moroccan successors. The visual arts of Islamic Spain are expressed most fully at the Alhambra (see above), a palace built for the rulers of the kingdom of Granada. Spain became the wellspring from which Islamic and pre-Islamic knowledge flowed back into medieval Europe, and the influence of highly civilized "Moorish" Spain extended into neighboring Christian kingdoms. The availability of Islamic scholars and Arabic-speaking Christians made cities such as Toledo on the Moorish–Christian frontier a center for the translation of Arabic texts into Latin.

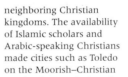

Hajj certificate
The *hajj*, or pilgrimage to Mecca, is one of the key duties of all Muslims. This certificate, dating from 1207 and depicting the Kaaba shrine, was proof that its owner had completed the pilgrimage.

Other Muslim lands
As traders carried their religion across the ocean with their goods, Islamic belief moved east. The 13th century saw the establishment of an Islamic sultanate in Delhi (see pp.180–81). From here Islam spread into Southeast Asia and the Indonesian archipelago. Muslim traders and missionaries also settled in western and eastern Africa, around Ghana, Senegal, and Sudan (see pp.182–83).

AFTER

Islam has continued to play an influential role in world history until the present.

FATE OF THE CALIPHATES
The Mongols ‹‹ 164–65 who invaded the Abbasid caliphate in the 13th century assimilated the local culture to become the Ilkhanid dynasty. The Mamluks halted the Mongol advance around 1260, and survived to be conquered in the 16th century by the **Ottomans 206–07** ››. After 1031, the Spanish caliphate dissolved into smaller states that were slowly conquered by Spanish Christians, the last falling in 1492.

FUNDAMENTALISM
The late 20th century saw the rise of a politicized Islam, advocating **strict adherence to the Qur'an** and revolt against secular governments, as seen in the Iranian Revolution led by Ayatollah Khomeini **442–43** ››.

AYATOLLAH KHOMEINI

1 STONE FIGURE

2 GLASS BEAKER

3 INCENSE BURNER

4 TIRAZ TEXTILE

5 PENDANT

6 CERAMIC BOWL

7 FRIEZE TILE

8 QUR'AN STAND

12 CERAMIC POT

13 HELMET

14 GOLD COIN

Islamic Treasures

The craftsmanship of the caliphate period was stunning, with even the most everyday objects featuring intricate and highly distinctive designs, often bearing religious inscriptions. Many different materials were used, including wood, metal, and ceramics.

1 **Stone figure,** dating from the late 12th–early 13th century. 2 **Glass beaker,** dating from 9th–10th century. 3 **Bronze incense burner,** dating from the 12th century and fashioned by the artist Ja` far ibn Muhammad ibn `Ali. 4 *Tiraz* (textile) **fragment,** dating from the 10th century, with a black ink and gold leaf inscription reading "In the name of God, the merciful, the compassionate." 5 **Pendant** from the Fatimid caliphate, which ruled over North Africa, Egypt, and Syria. It is a mixture of gold and enamel and dates from the 11th century. 6 **Enamel bowl** from Persia (Iran), dating from the late 12th–early 13th century, with the words "good wishes" inscribed upon it. 7 **Frieze tile** *c.* 1270–80, using abstract floral and leaflike patterns. 8 **Qur'an stand,** dating to 1360, and made from carved and inlaid wood. 9 **Brazier** in cast bronze, dating from the second half of the 13th century, and dedicated to the Sultan al-Muzaffar ibn Umar. 10 **Brass Seljuk ewer,** *c.* 1180–1210, with inlaid silver and bitumen, and inscribed with the words "Glory, prosperity, power, joy, happiness, permanent stability." 11 **Brass alam, or standard,** as carried in the annual Muharram ceremony, which commemorates the martyrdom of the grandson of the Prophet Muhammad, who died at the Battle of Karbala in 680 CE. 12 **Ceramic pot** dating from the second half of the 11th century and designed to hold medicine. 13 **Persian military helmet,** dating from the late 15th century and fashioned from iron and silver. 14 **Gold dinar coin** from Sicily. Struck during the reign of the Fatimid caliph al-Mustansir in the 11th century; the radiating lines on the piece are characteristic of the period. 15 **Mosaic miharab,** dating from 1354. These niches are placed in mosques to indicate the direction of Mecca, Islam's holiest city. 16 **Glass bottle,** dating from the late 13th century, and probably made in Syria. The enameled and gilded glass features images of warriors wielding maces, swords, lances, and bows and arrows. 17 **Gold armlet,** dating from 1030 CE and made in Persia.

9 BRAZIER

10 SELJUK EWER

11 ALAM

15 MOSAIC MIHRAB

16 GLASS BOTTLE

17 METAL ARMLET

The **Delhi Sultanate**

Kingdoms and empires rose and fell in India in the centuries before the Sultanate.

THE GUPTAS
The Gupta Empire (320–540 CE) **« 124–25** was a **period of stability and prosperity**. It ran from present-day Bangladesh to eastern Pakistan.

HARSHA
In 606 CE **Emperor Harsha** established a **powerful empire** across much of northern India. After his death the empire **fragmented into small kingdoms**.

THE CHOLAS
The **Chola Dynasty** (850–1200 CE) ruled all of south India. The empire was a crucial staging post for **Chinese and Arabic merchant ships**.

CHOLA BRONZE

ISLAM BEFORE THE DELHI SULTANATE
Arab traders had introduced Islam to the region by the 8th century, and there were incursions by Muslim armies from **Persia** and **Ghazni** (modern Iran and Afghanistan) in the 8th–11th centuries. Islam's impact at this stage was still very limited.

Although Islam was present in parts of South Asia from the 8th century, the establishment of the Delhi Sultanate (1206–1526) marked a new era. Immigrants from Central Asia and Persia brought concepts of kingship, built cities, and founded empires. India was incorporated into the cultural scope of Islam.

I n 1175, the nomadic Muslim chieftain Muhammad of Ghur (in present-day Afghanistan) advanced into India. Although the Indian armies were bigger and richer, the nomads had the advantages of horses and a centralized army. Sweeping eastward over modern-day Turkestan, Pakistan, and northern India, Muhammad's armies sacked Delhi in 1193.

After Muhammad of Ghur's death in 1206, one of his generals, the ex-slave Qutb-ud-din Aibek, gained control of his territories in India and established the Delhi Sultanate (kingdom). To celebrate this and to symbolize the assimilation of new territory into the wider Muslim world (see pp.174–77), he began to build what would become the tallest minaret in the world—the Qutb Minar. This 238-ft (72.5-m) tower came to symbolize the sultanate. As the empire expanded, successive sultans sought to demonstrate their power by building grand monuments around it.

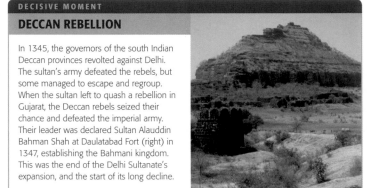

DECISIVE MOMENT

DECCAN REBELLION

In 1345, the governors of the south Indian Deccan provinces revolted against Delhi. The sultan's army defeated the rebels, but some managed to escape and regroup. When the sultan left to quash a rebellion in Gujarat, the Deccan rebels seized their chance and defeated the imperial army. Their leader was declared Sultan Alauddin Bahman Shah at Daulatabad Fort (right) in 1347, establishing the Bahmani kingdom. This was the end of the Delhi Sultanate's expansion, and the start of its long decline.

Sultans and slaves

The early sultans ruled over a fragile kingdom, and their authority was concentrated in a series of fortified towns. The nomadic tribes who made up the nobility did not have a strong tradition of hereditary kingship. Military slaves frequently became sultans, such

as Iltutmish in 1211 or Balban in 1266. Women, too, could become sultans if they could muster the support of the nobility, as Razia Sultana did in 1236.

Succession to the throne at Delhi was often secured through violence; during the Slave Dynasty (1206–90)—the first dynasty of the Sultanate—at least five

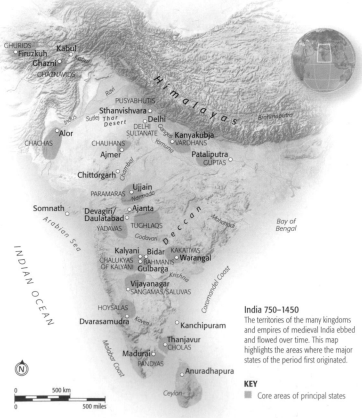

India 750–1450
The territories of the many kingdoms and empires of medieval India ebbed and flowed over time. This map highlights the areas where the major states of the period first originated.

KEY
■ Core areas of principal states

Sufi poetry
Amir Khusrau was court poet for several of the Delhi sultans and a follower of the Sufi (Islamic mystic) saint Nizammudin. His poetry, an example of which is shown here, is sung today in the devotional music called *Qawwali*.

of the 11 sultans were assassinated. In 1258, refugees fleeing the destruction of Baghdad by the nomadic Mongols (see pp.162–65) came to India, bringing with them new ideas of the divine right of kings and the rituals of the Persian courts of the Sassanids (see pp.122–23). Imperial authority grew stronger as a result, although tribal loyalties and intrigues remained divisive.

Throughout the period of the Delhi Sultanate, the sultans based their policies on pragmatism, rather than the *Sharia* (Islamic) law. Some Hindu temples in zones of military conflict were destroyed, but this had been a military tactic in India before the arrival of the Muslims and there does not seem to have been a policy of temple destruction. In settled areas, temple building and renovation was sanctioned by the state. Subjects were permitted to practice their own faiths, and the *Jizya* tax, which non-Muslims are supposed to pay in an Islamic state, was only enforced sporadically.

Expansion to the south
Between 1299–1305, sultan Alauddin Khilji launched a series of successful military expeditions against the various rich kingdoms south of Delhi, including the Yadava capital of Devagiri, the Somnath temple in Gujarat, Chittorgarh in Rajasthan, and Mandu in central India. In 1311, Alauddin sent his favorite slave, Malik Kafur, on a series of raids into the Deccan (the vast plateau region that covers much of southern India) in search of plunder. The Yadavas of Devagiri, the Kakatiyas of

Lodi Tomb
The Lodi Dynasty, the last dynasty of the Sultanate, ruled from 1451 to 1526. Several octagonal Lodi tombs still stand in Delhi.

> **1,600** The number of years that the inscribed iron pillar in the courtyard of the Qutb Minar complex has survived in the open air without any sign of rust. The great pillar dates back to the pre-Islamic empire of the Guptas.

Warangal, and the Pandyas of Madurai were all defeated. Their kings were reinstated, but had to acknowledge the sultan's overlordship and send him an annual tribute. After Alauddin's death in 1305, the southern kingdoms stopped paying tribute, and so in 1321 Sultan Ghiyasuddin Tughlaq sent his son Muhammad to annex them. The kings were replaced with governors.

The emperor's new capital
After he became sultan, Muhammad bin Tughlaq (reigned 1324–51) moved the capital 700 miles (1,100 km) south to Devagiri, now renamed Daulatabad. In 1327–28 he forced the elite to relocate to Daulatabad, but within two years the inadequate water supply compelled him to reinstate Delhi as the capital.

Meanwhile, the empire began to fragment. New kingdoms and political elites, both Hindu and Muslim, came to power in the Deccan region of south India. Telugu-speaking warriors established the Vijayanagar Empire to the south of the Delhi Sultanate in the 1330s, and in 1345 the governors of the Deccan rebelled against Delhi and founded the Bahmani kingdom (see left). By 1398, when the Mongol warrior Timur sacked and

AFTER

Competing empires to the south weakened the sultanate, but it was a fresh invasion from Central Asia that finally supplanted it.

THE DECCANI SULTANATES
By the end of the 15th century, the **Bahmani** kingdom had fragmented into **five rival sultanates**, constantly at war with each other. In 1565 the **Vijayanagar Empire** was defeated by a rare combination of these five provinces.

THE MUGHALS
In 1525, **Babur**—a descendent of both Timur and Genghis Khan **«164–65**—marched from Kabul to India. He defeated the last of the Delhi Sultans at the **Battle of Panipat** in 1526 and established the **Mughal Dynasty 244–45 »**. The Mughals ruled India until the British removed the last king in 1858 at the start of the **British Raj 352–53 »**.

destroyed Delhi, the sultanate was no longer a major power. It continued until 1526 when the last of the sultans, Ibrahim Lodi, was defeated at Panipat, but was by then just one of many states contending for power in northern India.

Qutb Minar Complex
The Quwwat-ul-Islam ("Might of Islam") mosque in Delhi was constructed by Qutb-ud-din Aibek, founder of the Delhi Sultanate, as a symbol of his power. The sandstone base of the Qutb Minar is visible in the background.

BEFORE

Growth in trade across the Sahara led to the formation of more centralized states south of the Sahara desert, such as the Ghana Empire.

MUSLIM TRADERS
Islam spread across North Africa from Arabia in the 7th century CE **<< 174–77**. The **introduction of camels** to Africa by Muslim Arabs made travel possible through the desert, enabling Arabs and North African Berbers to open the first regular trade routes between North Africa and regions south of the Sahara desert. Muslim traders created **trading networks** throughout the sub-Saharan regions of East and West Africa.

TRADERS WITH CAMELS CROSS THE DESERT

THE EMPIRE OF GHANA
In the 8th to 11th centuries, the Ghana Empire of West Africa grew powerful on the **trans-Saharan gold trade**. Its rulers became **Muslim** in the 11th century, but then it declined in influence and was supplanted in the 13th century by the Mali Empire.

" ... stones of marvelous size... with no mortar joining them..."
VICENTE PEGADO, CAPTAIN OF THE PORTUGUESE GARRISON AT SOFALA, 1531

Freestanding masonry
The wall of the Great Enclosure has a marble core, and is bounded on each side by horizontal, free-standing masonry. The wall contains 900,000 large granite blocks, and is decorated with a chevron pattern along the top.

South of the Sahara

Buoyed by trading links with Asia and Islamic North Africa, a number of prosperous empires and commercial centers formed in Africa to the south of the Sahara desert, including the Mali and Songhay empires in West Africa and Great Zimbabwe in south-central Africa.

The cosmopolitan trading towns along the Swahili east coast of Africa were the first to benefit from the commercial activity, their coastal position helping them to monopolize the maritime trade with India, Persia, and Arabia. By the 13th century, Muslim trading cities such as Kilwa, in present-day Tanzania, were at the center of a highly profitable mercantile network, importing textiles, spices, and ceramics from Asia and exchanging these for African gold, iron, ivory, and slaves.

Great Zimbabwe
The Swahili ports did not produce these goods themselves, but traded in turn with states from within the African interior. At one end of the supply chain lay the settlement of Great Zimbabwe, an important source of gold, and the hub of a prosperous trading empire that thrived in southern Africa during the 11th–15th centuries. In the language of the Shona people of the region, the word *Zimbabwe* meant "houses of stone," a term applied to the hundreds of stone-walled enclosures found throughout the Zimbabwe plateau. Great Zimbabwe is the largest of these, located on the southern edge of the plateau. The spectacular stone ruins today cover nearly 1,800 acres (7 km²) and are divided into hilltop and valley complexes.

Built at the head of the Sabi River valley, Great Zimbabwe was well placed to control the passage between the gold fields in the west and the trading cities along the Swahili coast. Local natural resources supported the

Soapstone bird
Likely representing the bateleur eagle, these bird carvings stood on walls and monoliths in Great Zimbabwe, and have become the national symbol of Zimbabwe.

region's economy: seasonal grazing was available for cattle and the soil was fertile enough to support the core cereal crops of sorghum and millet. Lumber and ivory were in plentiful supply. In the 12th–13th centuries, Great Zimbabwe also profited from taxes on the trading caravans that passed through the area.

City of stone
In the 13th–14th centuries, the people living in and around Great Zimbabwe probably numbered between 11,000 and 18,000, and most would have lived in huts, situated closely together. The ruling elite led a more privileged and comfortable existence, supported by the wealth provided by their control over the export of gold and ivory to the coast. Local granite was used to enclose the hilltop at Great Zimbabwe with stone walls, perhaps as a fortification.

The Great Enclosure
The outer wall of the Great Enclosure at Great Zimbabwe is 820 ft (250 m) in circumference, and as high as 80 ft (25 m). An inner wall runs along the outer wall, and forms a narrow passage that leads to the conical tower.

The Hill Complex
The buildings above the Great Enclosure may have been built as fortifications, although the walls offer no access to the top from which to repel attackers. Another theory is that it was created to show the power of the ruler.

Conical tower
The mysterious conical tower at Great Zimbabwe is 33 ft (10 m) high and 16 ft (5 m) in diameter. Its purpose is unknown, although it has been suggested that it was a symbolic grain bin.

Set in the valley below the hill, the drystone walls of the Great Enclosure probably served as a palace.

As well as local pottery and ornaments made from copper, bronze, and gold, archaeologists have found many objects of Asian origin, indicating the settlement's prosperity and extensive trade links. These include 13th-century glazed Persian earthenware, 14th-century Chinese dishes, and fragments of painted glass from the Middle East.

In the mid-15th century, however, Great Zimbabwe was abandoned. The end of Great Zimbabwe coincides with the vast conquest by the king of the Karanga, Mutota, who sought to extend his rule over the whole plateau between the Zambezi and Limpopo rivers, including the main gold-bearing areas. But Great Zimbabwe's decline was probably not a result of Mutota's expansion policy. More likely the land could no longer support the concentration of population, forcing many inhabitants to find new areas of woodland where plots could be cleared.

The Mali Empire
In West Africa, the first great empire to be established after the decline of Ghana in the 12th century (see BEFORE) was the Mali. The Mali Empire, like that of Ghana, was based in the Sahel, the savanna region running along the southern border of the Sahara. From the Sahel, it was possible for Mali, like Ghana before it, to exploit the trade across the Sahara to North Africa and control the exchange of gold for salt mined in the desert. The first capital of the Mali

West African terra-cotta head
The artists of Ile-Ife, near Benin in what is now Nigeria, were renowned for naturalistic sculptures of human heads, created to honor rulers they believed were divine.

empire, Niani, was sited by the Bure goldfields on the Niger River, where much of the wealth of the empire originated. Other trade goods included slaves and kola nuts, as well as glass beads and cowrie shells for currency.

Mansa Musa and Timbuktu
The Mali state was founded in 1235 by Sundiata Keita when he united the 12 Mandinke clans of Mali. But it was in the 14th century that the empire reached its peak under Sundiata Keita's grandnephew Mansa Musa (see below).

A devout Muslim, Musa is renowned for his spectacular "Pilgrimage of Gold" to the holy city of Mecca. Musa also extended the boundaries of the Mali Empire, uniting much of the Western Sudan (the huge West African savanna region to the south of the Sahel) under his rule. The Moroccan traveler Ibn Battuta, journeying through Mali in the 1350s, could write that he had enjoyed "complete and general safety" in the area.

During Mansa Musa's reign, the city of Timbuktu on the trans-Saharan trade route to North Africa became a wealthy commercial hub and a great center for scholarship (see right). Musa had the great Jingereber mosque built in Timbuktu; it still stands in the city today. North African and Egyptian scholars visited Musa's court, and he exchanged ambassadors with Egypt, Morocco, and Arabia.

The Songhay
By the early 15th century the Mali Empire was in decline. Subject states began to break away, including the Songhay kingdom, based around the city of Gao about 250 miles (400 km) downriver from Timbuktu. During the 1460s, the Songhay king Sunni Ali took control of much of the Mali Empire, including the city of Timbuktu and the crucial trade routes.

Like the Mali, the Songhay Empire depended for its great wealth on the goldfields on the Niger River and the trans-Saharan trade in salt and slaves. At its height in the 16th century, the Songhay Empire would exceed even that of the Mali in size and wealth.

500 slaves dressed in gold and carrying golden staffs as well as 80 camel-loads of gold accompanied Mansa Musa on his great pilgrimage to Mecca, according to the contemporary Arab historian al-Umari.

HOW WE KNOW

TIMBUKTU LIBRARY
The Sankore Mosque in Timbuktu was one of the most important centers of learning in Africa. Manuscripts preserved at Sankore (such as the one below) document the scholarship and the cultural sophistication of medieval Mali. As one West African proverb states: "Salt comes from the north, gold from the south ... but the treasures of wisdom come from Timbuktu."

AFTER »

From the 15th century, Portuguese and other European traders and colonists became ever more involved in African trade and politics.

BENIN
The empire of **Benin** rose to prominence in West Africa during the 15th century. Benin was well known for **hand-cast bronzes**, which could only be made with royal consent. The first **Portuguese** traders arrived in about 1485, and a strong political alliance and mercantile alliance was formed. They traded in ivory, palm oil, pepper, and, perhaps most significantly, in **slaves 280–81** ».

BENIN BRONZE PLATE

THE MUTAPA KINGDOM
Many of the people of Great Zimbabwe settled on the northeastern edge of the Zimbabwean plateau close to the Zambezi River, where they formed the **Mutapa kingdom**. In 1628, the Portuguese replaced the king with a puppet ruler, who later signed a treaty giving the Portuguese free rein to **mine minerals**. This was the first instance of the **Afro-European concession treaties** that would become widespread during the European colonization of Africa **360–61** ».

KING OF MALI (1312–37)

MANSA MUSA

Mansa Musa was the best known of the Islamic emperors of Mali, largely because of his hajj (pilgrimage) to Cairo and Mecca in 1324–25. He was said to have taken 60,000 porters and hundreds of servants decked in gold. During the trip, Mansa gave away or spent so much gold that it apparently took the economy of North Africa a decade to recover. Musa established sound economic and cultural relations with the countries he traveled through. He brought back with him an Arabic library, religious scholars, and the Muslim architect al-Sahili, who built the great mosques at Gao and Timbuktu.

Long-distance trade across Eurasia was stimulated by the demand for luxury goods—precious metals, spices, and silks—by the wealthy inhabitants of powerful empires.

EARLY TRADING LINKS

In Europe and Central Asia, the empires of Persia « 92–3, Greece « 94–9, and Rome « 110–15 opened up **communication and trade** as far east as the kingdoms of India. In the east, the **Qin and the Han dynasties** « 126–29 unified China. In 138 BCE the Han emperor Wudi sent Zhang Qian to seek allies to fight their enemies to the northwest of China. The knowledge he brought back of kingdoms to the west led to the opening of **new trade routes**. A network of trading links soon developed between East and West. Silk reached Rome from Han China through a series of intermediaries, principally the Parthians « 122–23.

TRADING IN IDEAS

Flourishing in India from the 3rd century BCE, **Buddhism traveled** north to Central Asia and then east along the Silk Road to China, where it was firmly established by the 4th century CE.

ALTERNATIVE TRADE ROUTES

Following the rise of Islam « 174–77 Arab traders used the seasonal **monsoon winds** to build up an extensive seaborne trading network around the Indian Ocean. In the 8th century CE they even found a **sea route to China** and traded directly with the **Tang** « 160–61. It must have been on the ships of Arab traders that Chinese goods from this era were transported to the east coast of Africa.

CHINESE VASE FOUND IN AFRICA

Constantinople was a major entry point to Europe for silk and spices, which were shipped to the west by Genoese or Venetian traders.

A subsidiary trade route ran north of the Caspian to Astrakhan in the Mongol Khanate of the Golden Horde, then on to ports on the Black Sea.

To the west of the desert and the Himalayas lies the important oasis town of Bukhara. Its citadel dates back to the 7th century CE.

The Mongols conquered Baghdad in 1258, putting an end to the Abbasid Caliphate (see pp.174–77). A new Mongol khanate, the Il-Khanate, was established in its place.

Ports on the Indian ocean exported goods to the Islamic countries to the west. The city of Ahmadabad later became a major producer of silk.

Delhi, capital of the Islamic Sultanate of Delhi (see pp.180–81) was a major center for the exchange of goods and ideas.

KEY

Major routes

Subsidiary routes

Sea routes

The Silk Road

A web of caravan trails, mountain passes, beacon towers, oases, and garrison forts fringing some of the most inhospitable parts of the planet, the Silk Road was the world's greatest thoroughfare in the 13th–14th centuries. Trade along the route flourished under the protection of the vast Mongol empire.

New world view
Narratives of 13th- and 14th-century travelers transformed European maps of Asia. This image of the Silk Road from the *Catalan Atlas* (1375) possibly shows Marco Polo traveling in a caravan.

B anditry and political instability were a constant threat to the routes that made up the Silk Road. It was in periods of relative peace, during the rule of the Tang dynasty (see pp.160–61) and later under the protection of the Mongols (see pp.164–65), that trade along the Silk Road truly thrived.

The empire of the Mongols

By 1250, Genghis Khan (see pp. 164–65) and his successors had conquered an area that stretched from the Yellow Sea to the Black Sea. Under Mongol protection the Silk Road flourished as a 4,000-mile (6,400-km) trade route, along which travelers and traders were able to move in unprecedented safety.

Kublai Khan (see p.165), who became Great Khan of the Mongols in 1260, later declared himself emperor of China. He founded the Yuan dynasty

that would rule China until 1368 and established his court at Dadu (modern-day Beijing). Before the 13th century, the idea of a journey from Europe to China was unheard-of, but taking advantage of the Silk Road, a few merchants and missionaries traveled all the way to Kublai Khan's capital. They included the Venetian merchants Niccolo and Maffeo Polo, who reached Dadu in 1266. There were apparently well received by the Great Khan, who wanted to learn about Christianity and Western science. Five years on, Niccolo and Maffeo's nephew, Marco Polo (see right), reached Kublai's court. Also in the 13th century, Rabban Sauma, a Chinese Christian, made a pilgrimage in the opposite direction, from Dadu to Jerusalem, and then on into Western Europe. The accounts of both journeys provide a fascinating glimpse into life along the Silk Road in medieval Asia.

Traffic of treasure

Silk was not the only valuable commodity traded along the Silk Road: there were spices, medicines, ivory, rare plants, exotic animals including leopards, and precious stones such as amber and lapis lazuli. Commodities from the west included textiles, gold, and silver. From China, caravans carried silk, paper, weapons, lacquer, and even rhubarb. Goods were sold or exchanged for other commodities en route in staging-post bazaars.

The products were carried on camels, horses, bullocks, and yaks, depending on the location. The two-humped Bactrian camel was Central Asia's hardiest beast of burden. It could withstand the searing heat and biting cold and survive without water between oasis towns. Great caravans plied the Silk Road, and camel trains of 400 animals were not uncommon.

The **Id Kah Mosque**, in Kashgar, was built in 1422, but includes older structures dating back to the 8th century, and began as a mosque in 996. Kashgar is situated at the meeting point of the northern and southern Silk Roads, and was the gateway to the West. Set up as a garrison town at the foot of the Pamirs by 76 CE, it gave access to the mountain passes into Central Asia, India, and Persia.

The Taklimakan desert was a major obstacle between China and lands to the west. The Silk Road split into two routes that skirted the desert—one to the north and one to the south.

Built in the 1st century BCE as a garrison town, Gaochang became an important religious center, where Buddhism was firmly established.

A vital oasis near the junction of the northern and southern branches of the Silk Road, Dunhuang flourished under both the Han and Tang. A hoard of fascinating documents, collected over the centuries by Dunhuang's Buddhist monks, was discovered in a cave in 1900.

VENETIAN MERCHANT AND ADVENTURER (1254–1324)

MARCO POLO

As a teenager, Venetian Marco Polo accompanied his father and uncle on their second expedition to China, where they reached the fabled court of Kublai Khan. Marco learned the Mongol language and the Great Khan employed him as roving envoy and governor for three years in eastern China. He returned to Venice in 1295, but the following year was captured in a naval battle against the Genoese. In captivity, he dictated an account of his travels to a fellow inmate. Marco Polo's *Travels* was the most detailed account of East Asia available to European readers. It was printed in 1483 and influenced the thinking of many later would-be explorers.

"I have not told half of what I saw"

MARCO POLO, 1324

The Silk Road under the Mongols
Although the Mongols under Kublai Khan did not complete their conquest of China until 1279, they had already won control of the north by the death of Genghis Khan in 1227. Northern China, together with conquests in Central Asia, Persia, and Russia formed a continuous swath of Mongol territories, all linked by the traditional routes of the ancient Silk Road.

The geometrical center of China, the city of Lanzhou on the Yellow River was a major trading hub for the Silk Road under the Han dynasty.

Kashgar

Gaochang

Dunhuang

CHINA

Lhasa

Lanzhou

Chang'an

The Tea and Horse Caravan Road traversed high, dangerous terrain on the way to Lhasa. Tea, introduced to Tibet during the Tang dynasty (618–907 CE), was carried along this route from southern China.

A former capital of China, Chang'an (modern-day Xi'an) marked the start of the Silk Road from the east. From here, trade also traveled east, to Korea and Japan.

AFTER »

A number of factors contributed to the decline of the Silk Road, which did not survive into the 15th century.

THE BLACK DEATH
Outbreaks of bubonic plague started in China in the 1330s, and the Silk Road was probably the principal means of transmission of the **Black Death 186–87 »** across Central Asia to Europe.

COLLAPSE OF MONGOL CHINA
Having secured the route since the mid-13th century, the Mongols lost control of China to the **Ming dynasty « 166–67** in 1368.

TRADE UNDER THE MING
In the early 15th century, the Chinese joined Arab, Persian, and Indian merchants trading in the Indian Ocean. The **treasure fleets** commanded by **Zheng He « 167** shipped goods such as blue-and-white porcelain to the Middle East and even to Africa.

NEW ROUTE
Trade between Europe and East Asia became possible via the **sea route to India 224–25 »** pioneered by Vasco de Gama in 1498.

ARCHAEOLOGY
The Silk Road was **rediscovered** by European explorers in the 19th century. It was given its name by a German geographer, Ferdinand Von Richthofen. A number of **ancient cities** in the Taklimakan region were excavated, including Dunhuang and Gaochang.

GAOCHANG

A NEW SILK ROAD
In 1998, representatives from more than 30 countries met to discuss the possibility of developing a modern **Europe–Caucasus–Asia** equivalent of the ancient routes.

BEFORE

Infectious diseases have a long history, and the first accounts date back to ancient times.

SMALLPOX IN EGYPT

The first known records of infectious diseases include the mummified remains of Egyptian pharaoh **Rameses V** dating back to *c.* 1140 BCE. His head appears to show skin lesions similar to those caused by **smallpox**.

EARLY VACCINATION

In ancient China it has been claimed that a lucky day was chosen on which to blow crusts from the skin of a **smallpox** sufferer into a patient's nose through a tube or quill. If the Chinese did inhale a powdered material from the sores of smallpox victims, this would be the **first recorded form of vaccination**.

PESTILENCE IN GREECE

The ancient Greek historian **Thucydides** (*c.* 460–401 BCE) recorded in painstaking detail the symptoms of the **great pestilence of 430–429** BCE, which devastated Athens, "so that it may be recognized by medical men if it recurs." Despite catching the disease himself, Thucydides survived to

THUCYDIDES

leave **a harrowing account of the death and despair** that the disease caused, accounting as it did for some 60,000 lost lives—a quarter of the population of Athens at that time.

FIRST EUROPEAN BUBONIC PLAGUE

From *c.* 542 CE a bubonic plague had reached Egypt and the Roman Empire, from Arabia: it became known as the **Plague of Justinian** (after the emperor Justinian I). Thus the Black Death was not the first such plague in Europe.

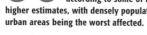

60 PERCENT of Europe's population died from the plague in the 14th century, according to some of the higher estimates, with densely populated urban areas being the worst affected.

YERSINIA PESTIS BACTERIUM

Medical researchers have extracted genetic evidence of the DNA code of the sausage-shaped *Yersinia pestis* bacterium (see right) from several plague burial sites in French and other cemeteries from the period 1348–1590. Historians studying medieval parish registers have also uncovered abnormally high mortality rates, which along with maritime records and contemporary accounts detailing symptoms, locations, and dates, have brought together random pieces of the plague's timetable and destinations.

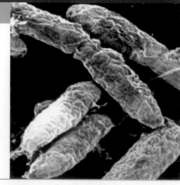

The bubonic plague that came to be known as the Black Death spread to Europe from central Asia, where it had already left a trail of devastation. It may have first reached Europe in the fall of 1346, when an army of Muslim Tartars laid siege to the flourishing Christian enclave of Caffa (the modern-day Ukrainian port of Feodosiya) on the Silk Road (see pp.184–85) and plague struck the besieging troops. Stories of infected corpses being catapulted over the walls into Caffa to spread the plague are probably unreliable. What is not disputed is that infected fleas on rats accompanied the besieged Christian merchants when they fled by boat back to the Mediterranean via Constantinople in 1347, and so they

Plague migration
Seaborne transportation carried the plague over vast distances. This map shows the spread of the plague through Europe, year on year from 1347. Only Iceland and Finland remained unscathed.

0 1000 km
0 1000 miles

The **Black Death**

Towns and villages of medieval Europe became littered with corpses, and death carts carried so many bodies that they could only be buried in deep pits. The medieval world had very little protection against a plague that was to wipe out one in three, and maybe more, of the population.

took the bubonic plague with them. Thus the most virulent epidemic then known, and still ever recorded, spread rapidly—and fatally—through much of the Western world.

Diverse strains

Plague is caused by a bacterium called *Yersinia pestis* (see below), which is carried by fleas on wild rodents. Transfer of bacterial infection occurs when the fleas feed on human blood.

There were three variants of the plague: bubonic, in which the patient develops buboes, or swellings, of the neck, groin, or armpit glands and from which this variant got its name; pneumonic, or blood-coughing, in which the lungs are infected because the infection is carried in the air and

inhaled; and septicemic, or blood-poisoning, in which the bacteria attack the blood system itself.

The bubonic variant was the most dramatic and obvious form of Black Death, as described by contemporaries such as the Italian writer Giovanni Boccaccio, who wrote of "certain swellings in the groin or the armpits ... some as large as a common apple." It took 3–5 days to incubate, and then within a further three days caused death in 80 percent of victims.

The pneumonic strain, with or without the boils, was 90–95 percent lethal within just a few days (today, with treatment, that percentage would probably survive) and could be transmitted directly from person to person—by sneezing, for example. The septicemic variant, though the least common, led to virtually instantaneous death. This most virulent form also caused a victim's skin to turn dark purple, almost black, and may account for the plague's epithet "black"—though this term was not used at the time.

Trail of death

How many perished under its macabre shadow is not known, but it is estimated that in Europe more than 25 million died from this plague pandemic. Other estimates rise to 50 million out of a population of 80 million in the 1300s. The plague returned repeatedly over subsequent generations, but never again with such devastating loss of life.

AFTER

The Black Death had a huge impact on medieval society. But it was not the last plague to strike Europe, and there may be others in the future.

AFTEREFFECTS

The traumatic decline in population led to a shortage of labor and a sudden rise in prices, as well as **irreversible social changes**. The European population did not recover until the 16th century. Over the next four centuries, another **nine major plague pandemics** hit Europe.

SARS: MODERN PLAGUE

MODERN PLAGUES

Precautionary measures now help to control the spread of disease. In Hong Kong in 2003, for example, tissue-paper masks were used to avoid contact with **SARS (Severe Acute Respiratory Syndrome)**—a variety of pneumonic plague. Scientists predict that drug-resistant infections may cause devastating pandemics in the future.

Dance of death
The Black Death touched every level of medieval society, lords and ladies, clergy, and the poor alike. This *Danse Macabre*—a reminder of the universality of death—was a recurrent moral and artistic theme in post-plague Europe.

Der Tod.   Der Tod zum Pabst.   Der Tod zum Kaiser.   Der Tod zur Kaiserin.   Der Tod zum König.

Der Tod zur Herzogin.   Der Tod zum Grafen.   Der Tod zum Abt.   Der Tod zum Ritter.   Der Tod zum Juristen.

Der Tod zur Edelfrau.   Der Tod zum Kaufmann.   Der Tod zur Aeblissin.   Der Tod zum Krüppel.   Der Tod zum Waldbruder.

Der Tod zum Herold.   Der Tod zum Schultheiss.   Der Tod zum Blutvogt.   Der Tod zum Narren.   Der Tod zum Krämer.

Medieval Europe

After the fall of the Roman Empire, Europe fragmented into many small states in which local leaders took power and, in some cases, carved out empires for themselves. The Frankish ruler Charlemagne and the Saxon Otto I both held territory that approached the size and power of the Western Roman Empire.

The most successful of the new states to emerge in the period after the end of the Western Roman Empire was the kingdom of the Franks. The Franks were a confederacy of Germanic tribes from the area around modern-day Belgium and Holland. Under their leader Clovis (*c.* 481–511 CE), the Franks conquered most of the old Roman province of Gaul and laid the foundations of an empire that would dominate Western Europe for centuries. Significantly for the future of Europe, Clovis also

Charlemagne reliquary
This silver container, made in the shape of a bust of the emperor, was reputed to have contained parts of his skull.

« **BEFORE**

As the power of the Roman Empire came to an end, other leaders took control of the areas that had been controlled by Rome.

WANING OF THE ROMAN EMPIRE
Over the course of the 5th century CE, **military and economic problems** led to the western Roman emperors being **unable to exercise direct rule** over their provinces **« 150–51**. Instead, power was delegated to a series of commanders from beyond the frontiers who established themselves with their followers. Rome lost control of **Britain** in around 410, **Southern and Western Spain** in 413, **Southwest France** in 418, **North France and the rest of Spain** after 451, and most of the **rest of France** in 473. Romulus Augustulus, the last Roman emperor, was deposed in 476 by **Odoacer**, leader of a federation of East Germanic tribes. Odoacer was crowned King of Italy.

POWER IN THE EAST AND WEST
Barbarians filled the power vacuum left by the end of the Western Empire in the 5th–6th centuries: **Visigoths** in Spain, **Ostrogoths** in Italy, **Vandals** in North Africa, **Anglo-Saxons** in England, and **Franks** in Gaul (France).
The Eastern Roman Empire survived and became known as the empire of Byzantium **198–99 »**, although further provinces were lost to Slavs in the Balkans and the Arabs in the Mideast and Africa in the 6th–7th centuries.

converted to Catholic Christianity while most of his rivals were Arians, regarded as heretics by the Roman population. In doing so, Clovis ensured that Catholicism, rather than the Arian form of Christianity, would eventually prevail through Western Europe. On his death, Clovis's kingdom was divided among his sons, and it continued to expand in the 6th century under his descendants, known as the Merovingians.

The Carolingians
The power of the Frankish kings declined in the late 7th century. Several died young, and rival aristocratic factions vied for power. One of these families, later known as the Carolingians, emerged as dominant as a result of the alliances with other noble houses made by its head, Pippin II. From 719 to 741 CE his illegitimate son Charles Martel ("the Hammer") controlled the kingdom, ruling in the name of a succession of Merovingian kings. Charles Martel defeated Arab raids from Spain and reimposed Frankish rule east of the Rhine. Anglo-Saxon missionaries such as St. Boniface were encouraged to set up monasteries and promote conversion in the conquered territories. In 751, Charles Martel's son Pippin III obtained the pope's approval to depose the last Merovingian king, and became the first ruler of the new Carolingian dynasty.

Charlemagne
Pippin's son, Charles the Great or Charlemagne, reigned for almost half a century from 768. He faced few internal challenges to his authority and was able to initiate a series of aggressive campaigns against the neighboring

> "A chief in whose shadow the Christian people **repose in peace** and who **strikes terror** into the pagan nations."
>
> ALCUIN OF YORK, LETTER DESCRIBING CHARLEMAGNE, *c.* 796 CE

4,500 pagan Saxon prisoners were beheaded on a single day in 782 CE, according to one contemporary chronicle, after the emperor Charlemagne ordered them to choose between Christian baptism and execution.

peoples. The king met with the leading lay and ecclesiastical nobles in an annual assembly each spring, in which new laws were agreed and plans made for campaigning later in the year. Frankish society was organized for almost continuous warfare, and the nobles depended on conquest for a continuing supply of treasure and new territories with which to support and expand their own followings.
Under Charlemagne, the Franks undertook 30 years of warfare against the pagan Saxon tribes to the east of the Frankish lands, forcefully converting them to Christianity. In 773, invited by Pope Hadrian I to save Rome from conquest by the Lombard (north Italian) king Desiderius, Charlemagne invaded northern Italy. Following the capture of the capital, Pavia, he proclaimed himself King of the Lombards. An expedition to the Ebro Valley in Spain in 778 was less successful, but Charlemagne's greatest triumph came in 796 with the collapse of the Avar Empire, centered in modern Hungary, as a result of Frankish attacks. He acquired the enormous treasure they had built up over the preceding three centuries, which he used to pay for new churches and monasteries, as well as building a new capital at Aachen in western Germany.

The Carolingian renaissance
Contacts with Italy and the Anglo-Saxon kingdoms enabled Charlemagne to attract scholars to his court, such as Alcuin of York, the Visigothic poet Theodulf, and the Lombard historian Paul the Deacon. Not only did the Frankish court become a center of learning to which the leading aristocratic

families sent their sons, these and other advisors also helped Charlemagne to carry out a program of reform of the Frankish church. This involved importing model texts from Italy, including works of liturgy, church law, monastic rule, and biblical scholarship. Higher levels of literacy were imposed on the clergy, and new laws were issued throughout the reign to counter errors and abuses in the Frankish church. A reformed and more legible script known as Caroline replaced that used in the Merovingian period, and continued in use throughout Western Europe until the 12th century.
In 802 CE, following the failure of two rebellions against him, Charlemagne imposed oaths of loyalty on all free men over the age of 12. His subjects swore loyalty to "my lord Charles, most

Charlemagne's coronation
Pope Leo III crowned Charlemagne emperor on Christmas Day 800 CE. Charlemagne said he did not want to be crowned by Leo, perhaps because by "giving" the emperor the crown, Leo appeared the more powerful of the two.

Battle of Lechfeld
In 955 CE Otto I decisively defeated the Magyars at Lechfeld, near Augsburg, in Germany. The battle ended the threat from the Magyars, who had taken advantage of divisions in Western Europe to mount their invasion.

adoption of the title was justified by the fact that the throne of the Eastern Roman Empire in Constantinople (see BEFORE) was held by a woman, the Empress Irene and so theoretically vacant. Charlemagne's seal included the Latin tag *renovatio Romani imperii* ("renovation of the Roman Empire") and he is portrayed on coins, in deliberate imitation of the Roman emperors, wearing a military cloak and laurel crown.

Charlemagne himself had doubts about a title that tied him so closely to Rome, and in 813 he held a purely Frankish ceremony for the coronation of his son, Louis the Pious.

After Charlemagne
Louis the Pious was an intelligent and well-educated man, but he lacked his father's leadership abilities. When he died in 840, the empire was divided between his three sons, who quarreled and in turn had multiple heirs, so the great Carolingian empire was further split. In addition, the security of Europe was threatened by invasions from several directions—Scandinavian Vikings from the north (see pp.202–03), Arabs from the south, and Magyars who had moved into what is now Hungary from farther east. Over the course of the late 9th and early 10th centuries, Western Europe fragmented into many small states, governed by local rulers and Carolingian heirs.

In 911, the last of the eastern Carolingian rulers, Louis the Child, died, and a group of German dukes banded together to choose a king for their lands. The resulting line of rulers, most of whom were from Saxony in eastern Germany, grew steadily more powerful. The most successful of them all was Otto I (reigned 936–73 CE). Otto benefited from a discovery of silver in the Harz Mountains in Saxony in 938, which gave him the wealth to pay for a huge army and build a string of fortified towns. He pushed the boundaries of his German empire eastward, inflicting a major defeat on the Magyars at the Battle of Lechfeld in 955 (see above).

Like Charlemagne before him, Otto cultivated the church, encouraging the conversion of non-Christians in his realm and founding new bishoprics. He appointed his own nominees as abbots and bishops and sought to strengthen the authority of the church at the expense of the secular nobility. »

pious emperor." This use of oaths to create a direct relationship between ruler and subjects reflects the lack of more complex administrative structures, such as had existed in the Roman Empire. Charlemagne made many administrative reforms and created a more efficient bureaucracy than had existed under his predecessors, but he continued to depend on a handful of officials drawn from the local aristocracy. Military action, in particular, required a large degree of consensus among the nobility.

Imperial authority
Charlemagne also sought to develop the imperial dimension of his rule, borrowing from the authority of the Roman emperors. In 800 he went to Rome to reinstate Pope Leo III and, on Christmas day, he was crowned "Emperor of the Romans." This

> " [Charlemagne] energetically **promoted the liberal arts** and praised and honored those who taught them."

EINHARD, HISTORIAN AND COURTIER, FROM "LIFE OF CHARLEMAGNE," c. 827 CE

ANGLO-SAXON KING (c. 849–899 CE)
KING ALFRED

Alfred the Great inherited the throne of Wessex (southern England) in 871 CE. At the Battle of Edington in 878, he defeated the Danes, who had already occupied north and eastern England and were attacking Wessex. Basing his style of rule on that of Charlemagne, he strengthened his kingdom against further attacks, building fortified towns and establishing a navy. Alfred, like Charlemagne, also promoted education and the arts. He left his kingdom much stronger than he found it, and he laid the foundations for his successors to unite England under a single ruler.

>> In 961 CE, Otto invaded northern Italy and was crowned emperor by the pope, John XII, cementing the relationship between the papacy and the emperor of what would later become known as the Holy Roman Empire.

Feudalism in Europe

The term "feudalism" is used to describe the system of relationships between kings and nobles in northern Europe during much of the medieval period. In many ways it was the same system used by the Carolingian emperors, who appointed noblemen to administer areas of their empire in return for a certain amount of power and land, sealing the relationship with an oath of loyalty.

The feudal system that evolved in England and France worked much the same way as the Carolingian example.

The king assigned a parcel of land (known as a fief) to a nobleman; in return for the land, the nobleman swore to be loyal to the king and promised to perform various duties. First and foremost, he had to devote a set number of days each year to military service for the king. He was obliged to attend the king's court, where he would give his advice on matters of policy and justice. He would also be asked to contribute payments for certain royal expenses—for example, when the king was building a new castle or a royal wedding was taking place.

A nobleman who entered into this kind of feudal relationship with the king was termed the king's vassal, and he referred to the king as his lord. Many noblemen

Knight's helmet
This 14th-century helmet was designed for full head protection. The wearer looks out through a narrow slit and there are tiny holes for ventilation.

apportioned part of their land to sub-tenants, who performed duties and swore allegiance in turn. This meant that the feudal system developed into a hierarchy of lords and vassals. The social networks that were involved could become very complicated, because it was possible for a vassal to accept lands from several lords. This kind of arrangement could lead to conflicting loyalties, especially if two lords were on different sides in a war. So vassals identified one of their superiors as their liege lord, the lord who took precedence over others.

France and England

The feudal system was most highly developed in France and England. Feudalism was already well established in France by the 10th century, when a

Dover castle
England's first Norman king, William I, built a castle at Dover following his conquest in 1066, but the massive stone tower and inner walls were the work of Henry II, who upgraded the building in the 1180s. The stronghold was designed to guard the country against invaders arriving by ship across the English Channel, and its thick walls made it one of the strongest castles of its time.

The king's gateway gives access to small walled area called the North Barbican, where attackers could be trapped.

Narrow slits allow archers to shoot out at attackers. Small windows prevent attackers from climbing in.

Battlements protect defending archers and provide a safe refuge.

The main floors of the great tower contain a ceremonial hall for the king and smaller private rooms.

The walls of the great tower are up to 21 ft (6.4 m) thick to protect the royal apartments from attack.

The forebuilding and entrance were guarded, acting as a barrier between the lord of the castle and intruders.

Spiral staircase in corner tower leads to storage areas below the castle.

In the field
In return for protection and the right to work their lands, peasants worked for the lord of the manor for an agreed number of days per year, as well as giving him a share of their produce.

Viking leader called Rollo agreed to give up raiding the coasts of France in return for the right to settle with his followers in the northern part of the country (see pp.202–03). Rollo became the vassal of the Carolingian ruler, Charles the Simple, and his people became known as the Normans. In 1066, Duke William of Normandy invaded England (see pp.192–93), became its king, and granted lands to many of his Norman followers in return for their fulfillment of feudal obligations. From this time onward, feudalism was firmly implanted in England.

Much of the rest of northern Europe was made up of a patchwork of smaller states, particularly those that formed part of the mainly Germanic Holy Roman Empire. Here the overlapping rights and responsibilities of emperor,

The inner bailey walls or courtyard housed the hall and other buildings to provide accommodation for the king's household, guests, and armed garrison.

dukes, and other secular and ecclesiastical princes made the political system more complex.

Knighthood and chivalry
The medieval knight fitted broadly into this system of feudal obligation. Having evolved initially from the heavy cavalry who had accompanied rulers such as Charlemagne, by the 11th century the knights had come to represent a distinct caste of professional fighting men. Their status was confirmed and enhanced through symbols and public ceremonies such as the "accolade"—a girding with a sword or hand on the shoulder. In return for this special status, the knight was expected to fight for his lord and to defend those groups, such as the clergy and the poor, who relied on his protection. The 12th-century writer John of Salisbury defined the knight's duties as being "to guard the church, to fight unbelievers, to venerate the priesthood, to protect the poor from injuries, to pour out their blood for their brothers."

Inevitably, the reality of knightly conduct did not always match up to this chivalric code. Toward the latter part of this period, in particular, feudal obligations were superseded by monetary arrangements. By the 14th century, knights would expect to be paid for their service and could themselves often pay a shield tax in lieu of service. Nonetheless, throughout this period knights remained a social and military elite.

The castle
Castles were the headquarters of the medieval feudal system. A castle was a multipurpose building. It was the home of a lord, his

family, and his servants. It was where business was done, the lord met his vassals, and courts of justice met. It was also a military base and a fortified building from which a whole region could be defended.

Some castles were royal residences. In a period when communications were poor, the best way for a monarch to exercise power in the kingdom was to travel continuously, so rulers usually had castles around the kingdom. Other strongholds were held by vassals on the king's behalf, who ruled as a part of their feudal duties. A castle usually had a courtyard (bailey), surrounded by a strong, fortified wall. Inside the bailey was the main accommodation, a grand hall and private rooms for the lord or king, heated by open fires and decorated with tapestries. In the towers or outer buildings were less luxurious rooms for the stables, garrison, and service buildings.

"The **faithful vassal** should ... counsel and aid his lord."
FULBERT OF CHARTRES, LETTER TO DUKE WILLIAM OF AQUITAINE, 1020 CE

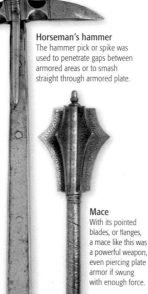

Halberd
The halberd was carried by foot-soldiers, who inflicted serious injuries with its sharp point. They also used the weapon to trip or maim a horse or to pull a knight off his mount.

Horseman's hammer
The hammer pick or spike was used to penetrate gaps between armored areas or to smash straight through armored plate.

Mace
With its pointed blades, or flanges, a mace like this was a powerful weapon, even piercing plate armor if swung with enough force.

ENGLISH KING (1027–87 CE)

WILLIAM THE CONQUEROR

William, Duke of Normandy, invaded England in 1066, defeated his English rival, Harold, in battle at Hastings, and became William I. He introduced feudal government to England and appointed many French noblemen as his vassals, meaning that the ruling class of England was mainly Norman for many years. William and his nobles built many castles, and he commissioned a famous survey, the *Domesday Book*, detailing the lands and wealth of his kingdom.

AFTER

The feudal system gradually died out as traders and merchants grew more powerful, and printing led to greater exchange of ideas.

CHANGES IN FEUDAL SERVICE
During the 14th and 15th centuries social changes made **feudal relations decline in importance**. Increasingly, vassals paid feudal dues in money rather than by military service. At the same time, the **middle classes**, who made their living by buying and selling goods, became more powerful.

RENAISSANCE
Writers and artists began to look back to ancient Greece and Rome for inspiration. This cultural rebirth, or **Renaissance 250–55 >>**, resulted in a new realism in painting, changes in architectural styles, and translations of classic texts.

SPREAD OF PRINTING
Around 1438, German metalworker Johannes Gutenberg invented a method of making metal printing type. This allowed printing of books and the **rapid circulation of ideas** in Europe.

Battle of Hastings

The Battle of Hastings was fought in southern England between an Anglo-Saxon army under Harold of Wessex and a force of invading Normans led by William of Normandy. The Normans were victorious and their leader became William I of England, known ever since as William the Conqueror.

In 11th-century England, several contenders vied to become king, largely because of the actions of Edward the Confessor (1003–66). In 1051, Edward told William of Normandy that he would be king after Edward's death, but when a Viking invasion looked likely in the early 1060s, Edward made a pledge to the Danish Svein Estrithsson too. Harald Hardraada of Norway had also been promised the throne by an earlier English king. However, English nobles wanted a native ruler, and Edward made yet another oath, this time to Harold of Wessex.

In January 1066, Edward died and Harold took the throne. But he soon faced a challenge— Harald Hardraada invaded northern England. Harold marched north to face his rival in battle and emerged the victor. At the same time, William of Normandy set sail across the English Channel with an invasion force, and landed on the south coast. As soon as he heard the news, Harold marched south, hoping to take the invaders by surprise.

William's scouts were watching for Harold's army, and soon after his arrival the Normans attacked. The two armies were well matched in numbers, with around 8,000 men each. At first, the English seemed invincible. Their footsoldiers fought in close, efficient formations and their axmen dealt fearsome blows. When a rumor spread that William had been killed, the Norman soldiers started to break up in disarray. But William held up his helmet to show that he was still alive. From then on, the Norman archers and mounted knights dominated the English, who were exhausted after their long march south. Finally Harold was wounded and then, after being set upon by Norman knights, he was killed. William claimed victory.

On December 25, 1066, William was crowned king of England. He quickly strengthened his position by granting lands to his nobles, thereby ensuring the spread of Norman power across the country. For many generations to come, England was ruled by kings from Normandy or other parts of France. The ruling class of England was Norman, the language of government and the court was French, and many senior churchmen were from Norman families.

The Bayeux Tapestry
This unique historical record is a 230-ft- (70-m-) long embroidered panel that tells the story of events leading up to the Battle of Hastings and the battle itself. Although it is thought to have been created in England, it tells the story from a Norman perspective.

"They are a **race inured to war**, and can hardly live without it."

WILLIAM OF MALMESBURY, FROM "DEEDS OF THE KINGS OF THE ENGLISH," DESCRIBING THE NORMANS, 12TH CENTURY

‹‹ BEFORE

Christianity survived the fall of Rome and prospered. Christian Europe expanded, and Church and State became intertwined.

SURVIVAL OF THE LATIN CHURCH
The decline of the Western Roman Empire and the **influx of barbarian peoples** in the 4th–6th centuries CE did not spell the end for Christianity in Western Europe. Many of the Germanic tribes were **Arian Christians**, a variant of Christianity at odds with Roman doctrine. Others, such as the Franks, entered as **pagans** but were **converted to Christianity**. Throughout the lands of the Roman Empire in Western Europe, Latin Christianity survived and, by the 6th–7th centuries, had **triumphed over Arianism**.

From the late 6th century under Pope Gregory the Great, and throughout the 7th–10th centuries, **Christian missionaries** began to spread Latin Christianity into the remaining pagan areas of Europe, such as Anglo-Saxon England, Denmark, and the Slavic territories of Central Europe.

THE EAST–WEST SCHISM
Long after the collapse of the Western Empire, the **Roman Empire in the East** continued to thrive **198–99 ››**. The Eastern Church under the **Patriarch of Constantinople** became gradually more estranged from the Latin Church, culminating in the **Great Schism of 1054**.

THE IMPERIAL CHURCH
Under the emperor **Charlemagne ‹‹ 194–95** church and state enjoyed a **close relationship**. Charlemagne made the church central to his government, using clerics as teachers and administrators, and used the spiritual authority of the church to **enhance his own authority** as emperor and defender of Christianity. In 800 he was **crowned by the pope** in Rome. This policy was adopted by other secular rulers such as the German emperor **Otto I ‹‹ 195–96** who used his influence over the appointment of clerics to strengthen his own authority at the expense of the nobility.

THE FIRST CRUSADE
By 1095, Christian Europe felt confident enough to mount a **military campaign** outside Europe in order to recapture the **Holy Lands** of the Middle East from the Muslims **200–01 ››**.

A CRUSADER

The **Power** and the **Glory**

Medieval Western Europe was dominated by a common religious culture. Under a series of strong-willed, reform-minded popes, the Church became more centralized, powerful, and assertive. But over time, the Church also grew increasingly intolerant and politically divided.

A t the start of the 11th century, Western Europe was emerging from a long period of raids by tribes outside its borders, including Vikings from the north (see pp.202–03), Muslims from the south (see pp.174–75), and pagan Magyars from the Eurasian steppes. By 1000 CE the worst of the raids were over and Latin Christendom ceased to feel on the defensive. Freed from the threat of pagan and Muslim aggressors, the Church grew more prosperous, self-confident, and assertive.

The church reform movement
With this increasing confidence came a desire for reform. This impulse was felt first in the monasteries, which had served as an important repository for Christian learning and observance during the previous centuries. Prior to the 11th century, individual monasteries spread across Europe tended to follow their own interpretations of the monastic rule, often under the control of secular lords and benefactors. The reform movement centered on the Burgundian

The monk in the white habit may represent Bernard of Clairvaux, abbot of the reformed Cistercian order.

An unidentified bishop wears a pallium, a yoke-shaped band of white wool, embroidered with crosses.

A senior cardinal (Niccolo Albertini di Prato) stands at the right hand of the pope in his broad-brimmed cardinal's hat.

Pope Benedict XI dominates the piece—as pope he is God's representative on earth and the supreme spiritual authority.

Several nuns wear the black and white habit of the Dominicans; others wear Franciscan and Carmelite habits.

Priests and monks from the Augustinian, Benedictine, Carmelite, Dominican, and Franciscan orders are shown engaged in prayers and debate.

The sheep symbolize the pope's human flock and are guarded by black and white dogs that represent the Dominican order—a play on the phrase *Domini canes*, Latin for "Lord's hounds."

monastery of Cluny and on Gorze in the Rhineland sought to impose a more consistent interpretation of the original monastic "Rule" of St. Benedict. Under the influence of Cluny, Europe's monasteries merged into more uniform "orders" with a renewed commitment to discipline, prayer, and study.

Other new monastic orders emerged in the period following the Clunaic reforms. In 1098 an abbey was founded at Cîteaux in France that gave its name to one of the most significant of these movements, the Cistercians. Under the influence of the charismatic preacher Bernard of Clairvaux, the Cistercians rejected Cluny's wealth to focus on manual labor, strict discipline, and austerity. Cistercian monks played a vital role in the settlement and cultivation of inhospitable and dangerous lands along the borders of medieval Europe.

Papal reform
This reforming impulse also drove the agendas of several influential popes of the late 11th century, who wished to see a Church in which the sacred was more clearly differentiated from the worldly. Popes such as Leo IX (1049–54) sought to limit practices such as clerical marriage and the purchase of church positions (simony). He also attempted to extend papal authority by making ceremonial journeys and summoning bishops to synods (church councils) held at major towns. In his campaign Leo was ably assisted by a group of

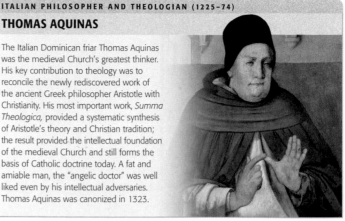

ITALIAN PHILOSOPHER AND THEOLOGIAN (1225–74)

THOMAS AQUINAS
The Italian Dominican friar Thomas Aquinas was the medieval Church's greatest thinker. His key contribution to theology was to reconcile the newly rediscovered work of the ancient Greek philosopher Aristotle with Christianity. His most important work, *Summa Theologica*, provided a systematic synthesis of Aristotle's theory and Christian tradition; the result provided the intellectual foundation of the medieval Church and still forms the basis of Catholic doctrine today. A fat and amiable man, the "angelic doctor" was well liked even by his intellectual adversaries. Thomas Aquinas was canonized in 1323.

reformers, one of whom, a Clunaic monk named Hildebrand, later became Pope Gregory VII—a key figure in the increasingly powerful papacy.

The investiture controversy
Gregory VII was determined to promote the authority of the papacy in both spiritual and temporal spheres—even if this meant clashing with the authority of the secular kings and princes. In 1075, shortly after he was elected, he composed a detailed statement outlining his status as the spiritual head of Christendom. In it Gregory claimed that, since the pope owed his position to God, he was superior in authority to all earthly rulers.

A major area of dispute between the resurgent papacy and secular rulers was over the appointment (investiture) of bishops and other senior church officials. Since the time of Charlemagne, (see pp.194–95) secular rulers had used their right to be involved in this process to ensure a compliant and sympathetic church. Gregory was determined that control over investiture should lie with the Church and, ultimately, with himself.

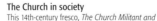

The Church in society
This 14th-century fresco, *The Church Militant and Triumphant* by Andrea da Firenze, presents an idealized view of the medieval social order. Enthroned in the center, the pope presides over the representatives of the Church to his right, and State to his left.

Demons and devils
A gargoyle looks out from Notre Dame cathedral, Paris. In the drama of medieval Christendom, demons and devils battled angels and saints.

Matters came to a head in 1076 when Gregory opposed the appointment of the archbishop of Milan by the German emperor Henry IV. A clash between the uncompromising pope and the formidable emperor seemed inevitable.

Henry persuaded the bishops of the German empire to declare the pope deposed; Gregory retaliated by excommunicating (excluding from the Church) Henry. When the German princes rebelled and elected an alternative emperor, Henry decided that he had no option but to do public penance and appeal to the pope to lift his excommunication. After four days of penance, Henry was granted absolution, but conflict between papacy and empire rumbled on. In 1122 a compromise was reached at the Concordat of Worms—but by then the controversy had divided Europe and caused almost half a century of civil war inside Germany.

Popes and antipopes
All over Christendom, the stage was set for a series of clashes between Church and State. In 12th-century England, Henry II clashed with Thomas Becket, Archbishop of Canterbury, about whether clergy should be subject to common law rather than that of the Church. »

The Holy Roman Emperor Charles IV holds the orb, symbolizing the emperor's special responsibility for the security of the Church.

King Charles V of France stands to the left of the emperor, representing the other secular rulers of Latin Christendom.

An unidentified noble occupies the final seat, his sword a reminder of his role as a defender of the Church.

The laity fills the right-hand side of the picture, with representative of various secular occupations. The man in white wears a golden garter showing he is a knight and a member of the English Order of the Garter.

Four pilgrims carry the symbols of the major medieval pilgrimage sites: a seashell for Santiago de Compostela, a veil for Rome, and a palm for the Holy Land.

Gothic stone angel
Serene figures such as this one from Reims Cathedral, France, were symbolic of the joys of heaven as well as a consolation for the sufferings of the faithful on earth.

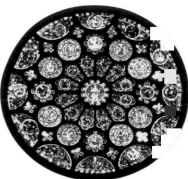

Burning of heretics
Watched by the French King Philip II Augustus, a group of Amauricien heretics are burned outside Paris in 1210. Philip II's reign also saw the launch of the Albigensian Crusade against Cathar heretics in southern France.

Large stained glass windows
let light and color flood in to the building, a feature typical of Gothic churches and cathedrals.

>> Becket's murder by a group of Henry's knights made him a martyr to the cause of church independence. The shrine containing his relics at Canterbury became a center of pilgrimage for people all over Europe.

By the late 14th century, the Church and the papacy itself were divided. Pope Urban VI, elected in 1378, alienated his supporters in the papal court, and the cardinals responded by electing a rival pope. This "antipope," Clement VII, established his papal court at Avignon in France. A European crisis developed as the German emperor recognized the Roman claimant, the French king supported his rival, and other states and kingdoms took one side or the other. The resulting split, or "Great Schism," between a succession of popes and antipopes undermined the prestige and authority of the papacy; for several years there were three rival claimants. The schism was eventually resolved in 1414 at the Council of Constance, with the pope in Rome recognized as legitimate.

New devotions
For all its power, the established Church was increasingly cut off from the spiritual life of the growing urban classes. Merchants, craftsmen, and their families could now read and write, ending the clergy's monopoly on the transmission of ideas. These people were often better educated than the clergy, and more open to new forms of religious devotion.

The growing impulse for a more personal, informal relationship with God is expressed in spiritual works such as Thomas à Kempis' *The Imitation of Christ*, published around 1418. These ideals also permeated poetry and art, which began to focus more on "Our Lady," the Virgin Mary. Mary was held to be more approachable and sympathetic than other saints, and the relic of her tunic

at Chartres cathedral was a major attraction for pilgrims from all over Europe. Such holy relics were considered miraculous, capable of inducing cures for all manner of physical and spiritual ills. For the well-to-do, a pilgrimage to a shrine was also a relatively pleasant way of doing penance and, hopefully, earning remission from time in purgatory.

Early in the 13th century, two new religious orders were founded. The Franciscan and Dominican friars were known as mendicants, from the Latin word for "beggars," for they renounced

personal property and were not attached to richly endowed abbeys. The friars were a part of the new urban culture, building churches and schools in the middle of towns and preaching in public squares. To support themselves, they depended on charity, putting them more closely in touch with ordinary people. The Franciscan friars, in particular, sought a return to the simplicity and poverty of the early Church, living among the people, caring for the poor or needy and preaching repentance.

Heretics and the Inquisition
The Dominican order had its roots in the campaign against the Albigensians, or Cathars, a heretical (holding beliefs contrary to the established teachings of the Church) movement in southern France who believed that the existence of evil contradicted the notion of one benign God. Wearing black and white habits, the Dominicans were dedicated to teaching and preaching, and emphasized religious orthodoxy and obedience to the papacy.

As the papacy came to define Christian doctrine with a new exactitude during the 13–14th centuries, there was a corresponding intolerance of unorthodoxy and of deviants such as the Albigensians. By the Synod of Toulouse in 1229, the ecclesiastical tribunals known as inquisitions had developed into a more formal institution charged with the suppression of heresy.

Medieval pilgrimage
A group of pilgrims leave Canterbury, site of the shrine of Thomas Becket and a major place of pilgrimage, in a version of the prologue to Geoffrey Chaucer's *The Canterbury Tales*.

Staffed by Dominicans, the medieval Inquisition operated mainly in France and Italy. The systematic persecution of heretics—and, increasingly, the persecution of any views that diverged from strict Roman Catholic orthodoxy—was the dark side of the highly organized and efficient medieval Church.

FOUNDER OF THE FRANCISCANS (c. 1180–1226)

ST. FRANCIS OF ASSISI

The son of a wealthy merchant in the Italian town of Assisi, Francis led a carefree youth. In 1209, he was inspired by a sermon to give away all his possessions. He began to live like a beggar, traveling barefoot, preaching repentance, and aiding the poor. In time he was joined by two companions, and they determined to live by the rule of poverty and simplicity that Christ had given to his apostles. In 1210, Francis gained the blessing of Pope Innocent III for his new order, the Franciscans. By his death in 1226, his followers, inspired by St. Francis' humble and compassionate example, numbered many thousands.

3,000 **SQUARE YARDS** of glass were used in the stained glass windows at Chartres cathedral. 152 out of 186 original stained glass windows at Chartres still survive today.

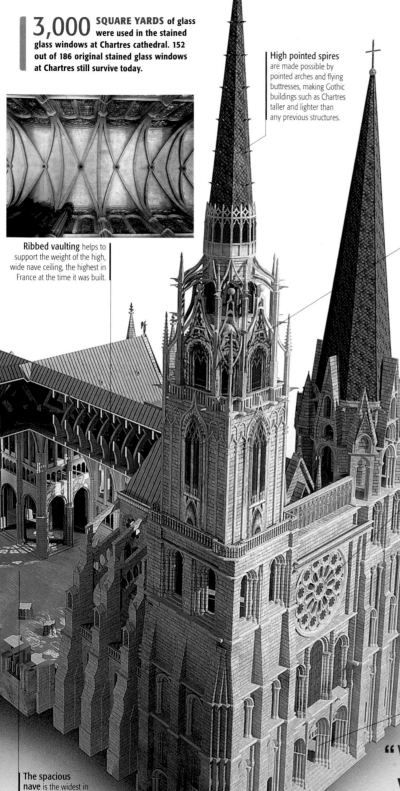

Ribbed vaulting helps to support the weight of the high, wide nave ceiling, the highest in France at the time it was built.

High pointed spires are made possible by pointed arches and flying buttresses, making Gothic buildings such as Chartres taller and lighter than any previous structures.

Chartres Cathedral
The great cathedral at Chartres is a striking example of the "Gothic" style of architecture that emerged in 12th-century France and flourished throughout the late medieval period. Gothic buildings, with their pointed arches, large windows, clustered columns, and soaring spires were intended to invoke the majesty and splendor of God. The main Gothic portion of Chartres was built in 1194–1220.

Flying buttresses surround and support the high walls and spires. Typically for a Gothic building, the buttresses at Chartres cathedral are turned into a decorative feature.

The west rose window depicts the Last Judgment. There are three rose windows in total, bathing the interior in a warm and golden light.

The spacious nave is the widest in France and permits an unbroken view along the entire length of the cathedral.

The royal portal features intricate carvings of religious scenes including Christ sitting in judgment. Statues of kings and queens symbolize the religious authority of the French monarchs.

Allegations of corruption and excess in the Church, as well as new ideas and forms of religious belief spread by new technology, undermined the unity of the Church.

THE REFORMATION
In the 16th century, the movement known as **the Reformation 256–59 ≫** ended the religious unity of Western Europe and resulted in the establishment of **Protestant churches** that owed no allegiance to the pope. The catalyst for the Reformation came in 1517, when a priest named **Martin Luther** nailed a list of propositions to the door of the Castle church in Wittenberg, Germany. He intended to start a debate and, thanks to the new technology of the **printing press**, his ideas for reform of the Christian church were being read and discussed throughout Germany within two weeks and throughout Europe within a month. By 1600, **Lutheran** churches were established in Germany and Scandinavia, **Calvinist** churches in Scotland, Switzerland, and the Netherlands, and **Anglican** churches in England and Wales.

THE GREAT BIBLE

VERNACULAR BIBLES
For **Luther**, as for other Protestant reformers such as **Calvin** and **Zwingli**, the authority to oppose the Church came from **Holy Scripture**, the **direct word of God**. To make holy writ readily available to ordinary men and women it had to be translated from **Latin**—the language of the clerical elite—into the **vernacular**, the spoken languages of everyday life. Luther lost no time in **translating the Bible** into German. This Bible facilitated the spread of Lutheranism from Germany to Scandinavia, Poland, and Hungary. Elsewhere, the momentum for the production of **printed Bibles in the vernacular** was equally unstoppable. The **first authorized edition of the scriptures in English**, the Great Bible, was produced by Miles Coverdale and published in 1538.

> "Where there is **charity and wisdom**, there is neither **fear nor ignorance**."
>
> ST. FRANCIS OF ASSISI, "ADMONITIONS," *c.* 1220

BEFORE

The Byzantine Empire grew out of the eastern Roman Empire, gradually acquiring a distinctive new Greek Christian culture that replaced the traditions of ancient Rome.

ANCIENT BYZANTIUM
According to legend, the Megaran king, **Byzas**, founded the Greek city of Byzantium in 667 BCE on the advice of the oracle at Delphi **‹‹ 94**.

FIRST DIVISION OF THE EMPIRE
In 293 CE the emperor **Diocletian** split the Roman Empire **‹‹ 110–13**, with two emperors (*Augusti*), one ruling in the east, the other in the west, assisted by two younger co-emperors (*Caesares*).

A NEW CAPITAL
When **Constantine ‹‹ 148–49** defeated his last rival to become sole emperor in 324 CE, he decided to build a new capital, Nova Roma (New Rome), at Byzantium. Completed in 330 CE, it became known as **Constantinople** after his death.

FINAL DIVISION
In 395 CE the Roman Empire was definitively split into eastern and western divisions by Emperor **Theodosius**, the eastern empire being ruled from Constantinople. The last western emperor was deposed in 476 CE, but by then the true rulers in the west were the Goths, Vandals, Franks, and other Germanic peoples **‹‹ 188–89**.

BYZANTINE EMPRESS (500–48 CE)

THEODORA

Daughter of a circus bear-keeper, Theodora was a comic actress and, some claim, a prostitute, before marrying Justinian in 523. When he became emperor of Byzantium in 527, Theodora proved herself a talented ruler in her own right. Her advice quelled the Nika riots of 532, probably saving the empire. She is regarded as an advocate for women's rights who used her position to help her society's oppressed, and she is venerated as a saint in the Orthodox church.

The term "Byzantine Empire" suggests a separate entity from the Roman Empire. The Byzantines, however, called themselves Romans and their realm Romania. Constantinople had been the capital of the Roman Empire since the reign of Constantine (306–37 CE), and the center of gravity of Mediterranean civilization had shifted to its eastern shores long before the final collapse

Hagia Sophia
Built by Justinian I in five years (532–37), the Hagia Sophia church (meaning "holy wisdom") was converted into a mosque in 1453 by the Ottomans. Despite later additions, it remains one of the finest examples of Byzantine church architecture.

The Byzantine Empire

A great metropolis when the capitals of Western Europe were little more than villages, Constantinople stood for more than a millennium at the heart of its empire, a center of religion and culture, and a military power forming a protective barrier that allowed Europe to emerge from the ruins of the Roman Empire.

of Rome. The city stood at a strategic position that controlled the trade routes between Asia and Europe, as well as the passage from the Black Sea to the Mediterranean.

When the German Odoacer deposed the last western emperor, Romulus Augustulus, in 476 CE, the Byzantine emperor Zeno became sole heir to the Roman Empire. One of his most significant acts was to persuade the Ostrogothic leader Theodoric, who was threatening to do in the east what other barbarian tribes had done in the west, to conquer Italy rather than take part of the eastern empire.

Rare Byzantine relic
A survivor of the sack of Constantinople in 1204, this gilt enamel reliquary is said to contain a fragment of the cross on which Jesus Christ was crucified.

Conquests and losses
The first emperor to attempt to regain lost territories in the west was Justinian, who reigned from 527–65. His armies won back North Africa from the Vandals and also reconquered much of Italy. In addition to these conquests, Justinian left a substantial cultural legacy in the form of magnificent churches and a thorough codification of Roman law.

In the east, however, things did not run so smoothly. The Persian Sassanids (see pp.122–23) broke a treaty made

BYZANTINE The word was not used regularly to indicate the eastern Roman Empire until after its fall in 1453. It is also applied to the empire's style of architecture, notable for its domes and mosaics, and is a derogatory term for complex, obscure political processes.

with Justinian and entered imperial territory in 540, seizing the city of Antioch. There followed an exhausting series of military clashes until the emperor Heraclius won a decisive victory over the Persians in 628. No sooner had he won control of the east, however, than the Muslim Arabs (see pp.174–77) invaded, and the empire lost its eastern provinces to Islam. Constantinople was besieged for four years in 674–78. It survived thanks to the secret weapon Greek fire, a flammable liquid used as a flamethrower, whose composition remains a mystery to this day.

The empire faced many enemies besides the Arabs, including the Lombards in Italy and the Bulgars in the Balkan peninsula, but somehow Byzantium survived. Heraclius introduced a system of government, in which the empire was divided into military provinces, called "themes," each governed by an independent *strategos* or general.

Orthodoxy
Despite the chronic instability of its empire and periodic outbreaks of plague, the city of Constantinople

The Mosaic of the Donors
Located above the imperial bodyguard's Vestibule of the Warriors, which today serves as the exit, the Mosaic of the Donors illustrates the consecration of the Hagia Sophia, its dedication to Christ, and Constantinople's status as capital of a Christian empire.

The emperor Justinian offers the Church of Holy Wisdom (the Hagia Sophia) to the Virgin Mary and the baby Jesus.

was the largest in the world. Part of its strength lay in its importance as a center of Christianity. The Byzantine church was the "Orthodox" church—in contrast to the various other forms of eastern Christianity that it considered heretical. The fact that the emperor was held to be God's representative on Earth gave him great authority, but could also cause serious problems. Leo III, who ruled from 717 to 741, banned religious icons because he said they were being worshiped as idols. This became known as the Iconoclast controversy. The empire erupted in protest, and the icons were restored, to be "venerated" but not worshiped. Controversies of this kind added to the growing distance between the churches of the east and west.

Revival and collapse

The empire's fortunes revived under the "Macedonian" emperors of the late 9th–early 11th centuries. It regained control of the Adriatic Sea, southern Italy, and all of Bulgaria. Cities grew and prospered, trade increased, and artistic and intellectual life flourished.

A shrinking empire
The gradual loss of Byzantine territory is evident through centuries of invasion from both the east and the west.

KEY
— Imperial frontier, c. 628
— Imperial frontier, c. 1030
— Imperial frontier, c. 1143
— Imperial frontier, 1328

0   500 km
0   500 miles

However, after 1025 Byzantium fell into difficulties again. A string of weak rulers after Basil II (928–1025) allowed the once-formidable armed forces to fall apart. At the same time, the empire was faced with new, ambitious enemies, such as the Normans, who had taken southern Italy by 1071. But the greatest danger came from the Seljuk Turks in Asia Minor (present-day Turkey). By 1080, most of Asia Minor had been lost and Byzantium's fatal decline had begun. Desperate, Emperor Alexius sent embassies to Western Europe asking for help. The result was the series of military expeditions known as the Crusades (see pp.200–01). However, instead of helping their eastern brothers, the crusaders mostly pursued their own interests. Intended to bring support to Constantinople, the so-called Fourth Crusade was the single most catastrophic event in Byzantine history. In 1204 a crusader army that was supposedly on its way to defend the Holy Land brutally sacked the city of Constantinople and dismantled the empire.

Bronze horses stolen from Constantinople
These horses once adorned the Hippodrome erected by Constantine in Constantinople. Looted by the Venetians in 1204, they were installed in St. Mark's Basilica, Venice.

The Virgin Mary and Jesus are depicted in the highly stylized form of Byzantine icons.

Constantine I, the first Christian emperor and founder of Constantinople, offers the city itself to Mary and Jesus.

AFTER ➤➤

In 1204 much of the Byzantine Empire was divided up between its crusader conquerors, but it survived and limped on until the fall of Constantinople to the Ottomans in 1453.

CONSEQUENCES OF THE SACKING
After the Fourth Crusade Constantinople was left underpopulated and in ruins. The city never really recovered. Chief beneficiary was the **Venetian Republic**, which took over much of the Byzantines' trade as well as shipping fabulous quantities of loot back to Venice.

CONSTANTINOPLE BECOMES ISTANBUL
On May 29, 1453, the **Ottoman Turks 206–07 ➤➤** took Constantinople, renaming it **Istanbul**, and making it the capital of the Ottoman Empire **246–47 ➤➤**.

STOPPING THE OTTOMANS
Once Byzantium had fallen, the Ottomans completed their conquest of the Balkans with ease. Their progress was finally stopped by the Habsburg victory at Vienna in 1683.

« BEFORE

ANGEL
GABRIEL

The spread of Islam on the borders of Europe coincided with the growth of a pious and aggressive warrior society in Western Europe.

THE SPREAD OF ISLAM
In 610 CE, following a visitation from the Angel Gabriel, the prophet Muhammad proclaimed the religion of Allah (God) among the tribes of the Arab Peninsula. Islam took root over much of Asia, North Africa, and parts of Europe **« 174–77**.

THE EUROPEAN SITUATION
By the 11th century, as opportunities for territorial expansion within Western Europe declined, an aggressive warrior society began to turn its attention to the lands outside Europe's borders. The Christian Byzantine empire **« 198–99** had long acted as a buffer between Western Europe and Asia, but in 1071 the Byzantine army was destroyed by the Muslim Seljuk Turks at Manzikert.

The Crusades

For more than two centuries, the Middle East became a battleground in which Christian armies from Europe, inspired by an ideology of legitimate religious warfare, fought Muslims for control of the Holy Land (Palestine).

n 1095 CE, in a small field outside the cathedral at Claremont in France, Pope Urban II made an impassioned appeal. He called for a military expedition to liberate the holy city of Jerusalem and free Christians from the yoke of Muslim rule. In exchange, Urban stated that any soldiers who died fighting the enemy would earn remission from all sins. The crowd erupted with cries of "God wills it!". Over the next two years alone, thousands of crusaders, as these soldiers became known, took the cross and joined this pilgrimage to the Holy Land.

Foundations of the crusade
Urban's sermon may have been the catalyst, but the roots of the crusades stretch farther

KEY
■ Muslim lands
■ Greek Christian (Orthodox)
■ Roman Church (Papal authority)

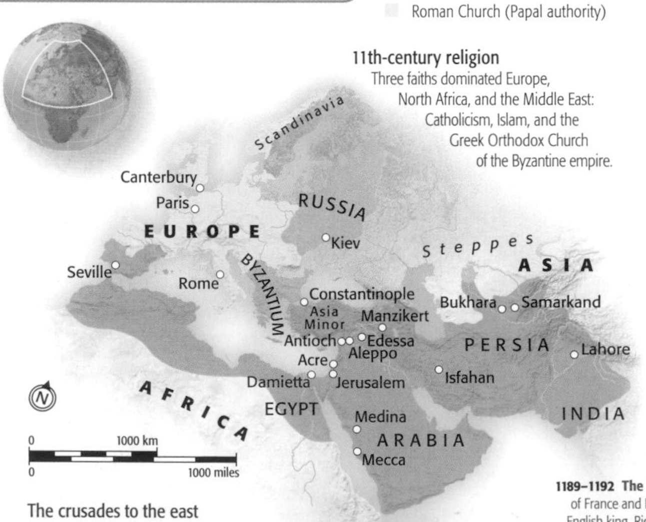

11th-century religion
Three faiths dominated Europe, North Africa, and the Middle East: Catholicism, Islam, and the Greek Orthodox Church of the Byzantine empire.

[map labels: Scandinavia, Canterbury, Paris, RUSSIA, EUROPE, Kiev, Seville, Rome, BYZANTIUM, Steppes, ASIA, Constantinople, Bukhara, Samarkand, Asia Minor, Manzikert, Antioch, Edessa, PERSIA, Lahore, Acre, Aleppo, Damietta, Jerusalem, Isfahan, INDIA, AFRICA, EGYPT, Medina, ARABIA, Mecca]

0   1000 km
0   1000 miles

The crusades to the east
There were several major expeditions from Europe to the Middle East and Egypt in the period 1095–1272 CE.

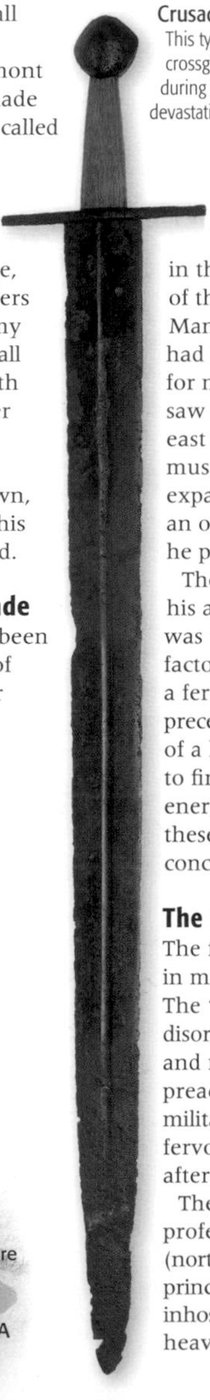

Crusader sword
This type of broad-bladed sword, with simple crossguard and pommel, became popular during the Crusades. It would have been devastating against lightly armored opponents.

back. Most obviously, Urban was responding to the political situation in the east: following the defeat of the Byzantine armies at Manzikert in 1071, the emperor had sent an appeal to the pope for military assistance. Urban saw the proposed expedition east as a chance to flex papal muscles and check the expansion of Islam, as well as an opportunity to conquer what he perceived as pagan areas.

The huge popular response to his appeal, although unexpected, was the product of a number of factors, including the growth of a fervent lay piety over the preceding centuries and the need of a land-hungry warrior class to find an outlet for their martial energies. The crusades united these impulses by legitimizing the concept of religious warfare.

The First Crusade
The first of the armies to enter Anatolia, in modern-day Turkey, met with disaster. The "people's crusade" was a ragged and disordered movement of peasants, knights, and religious zealots led by a charismatic preacher, Peter the Hermit. Lacking military discipline and blinded by religious fervor, the band was massacred soon after entering Seljuk Turk territory.

The army that followed was a far more professional body: a largely Frankish (northern French) force made up of several princely armies. Trekking overland through inhospitable country, they captured the heavily fortified town of Antioch in Syria

The Church of the Holy Sepulchre had been destroyed by the caliph in 1009. It was rebuilt after the crusaders conquered Jerusalem in 1099.

The Patriarch of Jerusalem was the spiritual leader of the kingdom and representative of the pope in Rome.

Mounted and heavily armored knights formed the heavy shock troops of the crusader armies.

The defense of Jerusalem
Crusader knights guard the Church of the Holy Sepulchre in Jerusalem. As the traditional site of Jesus's crucifixion and burial, this was the physical destination for pilgrims and crusaders alike.

1095 Pope Urban II preaches the crusade at the **Council of Clermont**. The response exceeds all expectations.

1145–49 The Second Crusade fails to recapture Edessa, lost 1144.

1189–1192 The Third Crusade is led by the kings of France and England and the German Emperor. English king, Richard I, makes a truce with Saladin.

1198 The Fourth Crusade never reaches the Holy Land. Crusader armies are diverted to fight the Christian Byzantine empire at Constantinople.

1217–21 The Fifth Crusade captures Damietta in Egypt but surrenders before reaching Cairo.

1248–54 The Seventh Crusade ends with the capture of Louis IX of France, who is ransomed for 50,000 gold bezants.

1291 Following the **fall of the port of Acre** the remaining Crusader states in the Holy Land are evacuated.

| 1050 CE | 1100 | 1150 | 1200 | 1250 |

1071 Seljuk Turks destroy the Byzantine army at the **Battle of Manzikert**. The Byzantine emperor appeals to the Pope for assistance.

1099 The First Crusade ends with the **capture of Jerusalem** and the formation of Christian crusader states in the Holy Land.

1187 After unifying the Muslims in the east, Saladin destroys the Christian armies at **the Battle of Hattin**. By the end of 1187, Saladin **recaptures Acre and Jerusalem.**

1228–29 The Sixth Crusade ends when Frederick II negotiates the return of Jerusalem and a 10-year truce with the Ayyubid Sultan of Egypt.

1244 Jerusalem is retaken from the Christians by the Ayyubids.

1270 Louis IX of France is diverted to Tunis in North Africa during the **Eighth Crusade**. He dies before he can set sail for the Holy Land.

The fleur-de-lis was the emblem of the king of France. Most of the leaders of the First Crusade were Frankish.

The imperial eagle was the emblem of the Holy Roman Empire. German emperors led armies to the east in 1145, 1189, and 1228.

SULTAN OF EGYPT AND SYRIA (1138–93)

SALADIN

Founder of the Ayyubid dynasty and unifier of Muslim states in the Middle East against the crusaders, Saladin was also renowned throughout Christendom as an honorable and chivalrous leader. Contemporary accounts abound with stories of his gallantry.

In 1187 Saladin annihilated the crusader armies at Hattin. When Jerusalem fell three months later, he allowed neither massacre nor looting. Although he failed to expel the crusaders from the Holy Land, and was defeated at Arsuf in 1191 by Richard I of England, Saladin paved the way for the later elimination of the Crusader states.

1,000 The number of beds in the pilgrim hospital run by the Order of St. John of Jerusalem, also known as the Knights Hospitallers. During the 12th century the knights adopted a military role.

Hospitallers, whose members took vows of poverty and chastity to dedicate their lives to the defense of the Holy Land. These warrior monks were the closest thing the crusaders had to a standing, professional army. They often pursued their own interests at the expense of their fellow Christians, but they built a fearsome reputation—after the battle of Hattin in 1187, the Sultan Saladin (see above) allowed the ransom of all prisoners except for the Templars and Hospitallers, whom he had executed.

The later crusades
Never again would the Muslim states of the Holy Land be so unprepared as they had been at the time of the First Crusade. A second crusade was organized in 1145, following the fall of Edessa, but failed to retake the city from Nureddin, a Muslim ruler who had united much of Syria against the crusaders. By the 1180s, most of the Muslim inhabitants of Syria and Palestine were united under Nureddin's successor, the sultan Saladin. In 1187 Saladin destroyed the armies of the crusader kingdoms at Hattin and seized Jerusalem, gallantly sparing the lives of the Christians in the city.

Subsequent crusades to Egypt and the Holy Land enjoyed some success but many setbacks. The Fourth Crusade, in 1198, never made it to the Holy Land, instead seizing the Christian city of Constantinople from Byzantium (see pp.198-99). Major expeditions from Europe were sporadic, and the fortunes of the crusader states altered with the balance of power in the east.

After the fall of the port of Acre in 1291 defense of the mainland territories became impossible. The remaining Christian cities were abandoned and the crusaders expelled from the Holy Land.

Siege machine
Long sieges, such as Antioch and Jerusalem in 1097–99, were common during the crusades. Siege machines such as this trebuchet were used by both sides to bombard opposing soldiers, fortifications, and siege towers.

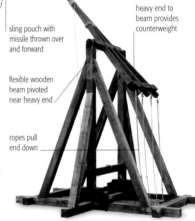

heavy end to beam provides counterweight

sling pouch with missile thrown over and forward

flexible wooden beam pivoted near heavy end

ropes pull end down

AFTER »

Greed and political expediency gradually came to undermine the ideals of the early crusades.

CRUSADES IN EUROPE
The crusading ideal of war against the enemies of Christianity in the Holy Land soon lost focus. As early as 1193 Pope **Celestine III** proclaimed a crusade against **pagans in northern Europe**. In 1209, **Innocent III** announced a crusade against **heretics** within France–the **Albigensian Crusade**. By the 1230s popes were using crusades as a political weapon against rivals.

END OF THE KNIGHTS TEMPLAR
Military orders such as the Templars grew immensely **rich and powerful**, attracting much criticism. In 1307, intending to seize their assets, **Philip IV** of France charged the Templars with **heresy**. Pope **Clement V** disbanded the order.

---

in 1098. A year later the crusaders arrived at Jerusalem. After a lengthy siege, the city fell. The crusaders slaughtered all Muslims and Jews in the city—a bloody climax that set the tone for much that was to follow.

Outremer
The crusaders now held a thin strip of coast in Palestine along which they established various crusader states, including the Kingdom of Jerusalem, the Counties of Edessa and Tripoli, and the

Templar seal
United in the service of Christ, two knights are shown sharing one horse.

Principality of Antioch. These territories were known collectively as *Outremer*, meaning "the land overseas."

In time, the crusaders built huge fortresses to defend these outposts, such as Crac de Chevalier. Despite this, their grip on the territories was never strong: they were often threatened by resurgent Muslim forces, and relied on further crusades from Europe to come to their aid.

The period also saw the formation of the military orders, the Templars and the

« BEFORE

Long before the Vikings spread across the continent, Europe had experienced raids by outsiders and established trade links with the east.

FLOCKING TO AN EMPIRE
In the 5th century many different peoples moved from farther east to trade, and often to settle in the relative **safety and prosperity** of the Roman Empire « 110–13.

PEOPLE PRESSURE
During the 4th and 5th centuries BCE immigrants arrived in such numbers that they destabilized a Roman world already in crisis « 150–51.

ROMULUS AUGUSTUS

BREAKING UP THE EMPIRE
The Roman empire in Western Europe ended when the boy-emperor, Romulus Augustus, was deposed by his own general, Odoacer, in 476 « 150–51. Without Rome's protection, many **small kingdoms, principalities, and lordships** were now more vulnerable to raiders.

There is a great deal of debate about why warriors from Denmark, Norway, and Sweden left their homelands and began to raid places in Western Europe in the 8th century CE. Most historians believe there was rapid population growth in Scandinavia during the 7th and 8th centuries, and, because of the harsh climate and rough terrain, there was limited land suitable for farming. This competition for land meant that not only was food in short supply, but local rulers began to fight among each other in order to expand their control over resources. One alternative, especially to a warrior society such as that of Scandinavia, was raiding. To the south

northeast coast of England, was pillaged by a Viking raid in 793 CE. Many of its monks were left dead. In 795 CE, monastic communities on the Scottish island of Iona, and Rathlin Island, off the northern coast of Ireland, suffered a similar fate. The situation was so bad that monks prayed for stormy weather so the "Northmen" would be unable to set sail.

The Vikings' focus on monasteries meant that contemporary writers, all of whom were monks themselves, often portrayed them as enemies of God. They recorded the calamities that befell their brothers with genuine anguish and horror. But while the Viking attacks were vicious and ruthless, they

and their sailors highly skilled. The ships were light, with shallow bottoms, and could be sailed far inland on rivers and lakes, taken out of the water, and dragged across land to another river.

Planning to stay
The nature of Viking involvement outside Scandinavia began to change during the 9th century. At first, they began to overwinter on islands in the Seine and at the mouth of the Loire River in France. Then, in 850 CE, Charles II of France gave a group of Vikings land to settle on in exchange for aid in a conflict against his brother, Emperor Lothar. Events like this gave the Vikings influence over local power

Raiders and Traders

From the 8th to 10th centuries, Scandinavians were both the terror of Europe and its most active traders and explorers. These people swept through the treasure houses of monasteries, founded towns and cities, and even became rulers in England and France. They were called the Vikings.

lay the Carolingian empire (see pp.188–89), Anglo-Saxon England, and Ireland; all were lands divided or weakened by internal power struggles.

Lightning attacks
The first Viking raids were carried out against soft targets, such as villages and monasteries, on the coast of Frisia (Netherlands) and eastern England. Monasteries were particularly attractive to the Vikings because they were rarely fortified, and were filled with spectacular treasures donated by local Christians. The monks were unable to defend themselves, and the Vikings, who were not Christian, had no qualms about sacking the monasteries and making off with gold and silver chalices, crosses, and book covers. The monastery at Lindisfarne, on the

were not deliberately anti-Christian, as some of the records suggest.

Vikings also threatened the relatively powerful Carolingian empire in the last years of Charlemagne's reign. His death marked a decline in central power and a rise in political instability. The Vikings exploited this power vacuum and expanded their attacks. By the 830s CE, they were able to raid the important town of Dorestad on the Rhine River three times.

Element of surprise
Early Viking raids were so effective because they struck unexpectedly. By the time locals could organize their defense, the Vikings were gone. They fought using the same basic weapons as their opponents, such as swords, spears, and axes. However, Viking longships were superior in design

Viking sword
Viking swords were often buried with their owners to accompany them on their journey to the hall of the dead warriors, Valhalla.

struggles, and encouraged them to settle outside Scandinavia. From this point on, even though they were often involved in raids, the Vikings became much more interested in acquiring land and establishing trade. Many kingdoms paid them off with huge amounts of silver and land in order to stop attacks. Between c. 991–c. 1014, for example, the English paid 150,000 lb (68,000 kg) of silver as tribute to Scandinavian kings, a payment known as Danegeld. A band of Vikings established the Duchy of Normandy in France when a chieftain named Rollo was given Rouen and the surrounding area

Viking war helmet
Viking helmets were similar to those used by other cultures at this time. The myth that their helmets had horns attached to them probably came about because Vikings were often compared to demons and devils.

HOW WE KNOW
ARABIC DIRHAMS

The Vikings raided and traded across an enormous geographical area. We know this through the types of coins found at Viking sites, in graves, and connected to towns. This 9th century hoard of Arabic dirhams was found at a Viking site in Scotland, and provides proof that Scandinavians sailed from the Baltic and along the rivers of Russia to reach the economic spheres of both Byzantium (see pp.198–99) and the Islamic caliphate (see pp.174–77). Arabic coins of a similar date have also been found at Viking trading centers at Birka in Sweden and Hedeby, Denmark.

Viking war spear
This spearhead was attached to a long pole, and thrown at the enemy, much the same way a modern javelin is thrown.

Viking war ax
The ax is the weapon that Vikings are most identified with. It could be wielded as a hand weapon or used for throwing.

Crystal necklace
This crystal necklace of Viking origin with Eastern elements demonstrates how Scandinavian craftsmen adopted the styles and techniques of the various cultures they came in contact with.

Iron trading weights
These brass-covered weights were found in Hemingby, Sweden. Each has been stamped with a different number of circles corresponding to its weight.

a square sail was attached to this mast

Viking brooch
Brooches are frequently found in Viking graves, and were used to fasten cloaks.

Gold bridle
Viking metalwork was complex and often consisted of intertwining animal shapes.

Viking longship
This ship was excavated from a royal burial site at Oseberg, Norway, and probably dates from 815–820 CE. While it is very similar to the type of ship used for everyday travel, it was almost certainly ceremonial in nature, as it is heavy and highly decorated.

longship was built of fine oak

Viking longship at sail
A viking longship was usually 70 ft (21 m) long and 16 ft (5 m) wide. The prow was carved with interlaced decorations, and a square sail was rigged to the mast.

15 oar ports were located on each side of the longship

by Charles the Simple *c.* 911 CE. Rollo's great-great-great grandson became William the Conqueror (see pp.192–93). Between 1016 and 1035, the Dane Cnut the Great ruled Denmark and England.

The Vikings also became great traders, sailing from Iceland to Russia and the Islamic empire. As early as 841 CE a permanent Viking settlement was founded at Dublin and the ancient English city of York. Vikings are even credited with being the founders of the Grand Duchy of Kiev, the forerunner of the kingdom of Muscovy and, later, Russia.

> "Behold the church of St. Cuthbert **spattered with the blood of the priests of God.**"
>
> ALCUIN OF YORK, 793

AFTER

The Viking Age came to an end during the 11th century. The kingdoms of Norway, Sweden, and Denmark evolved into more centralized states, as was happening elsewhere in Europe.

END OF THE VIKING AGE
Launching a lightning raid on a centralized state did not have the same effect as it did in the 9th and 10th centuries because, by 1500, these states had developed **organized armies and navies**. This meant that communities were able to defend themselves against attacks of the kind that the Vikings carried out.

ATLANTIC SLAVE TRADE
Raids later became central to the establishment of the Atlantic slave trade **280–81 »** in the 16th, 17th, and 18th centuries, where communities in western Africa bore the brunt of such attacks.

CARIBBEAN RAIDERS
Raid tactics similar to those of the Vikings were used during the same period in the Caribbean, where European navies, privateers, and pirates **sacked trading posts** and **preyed on shipping routes**.

THE HANSEATIC LEAGUE
Trading in the later medieval period (1100–1500) could be dangerous. In the 12th century, merchants from cities in northern Germany and the Baltic formed an alliance called the **Hanseatic League 276–77 »**. They traded between the Baltic, the Netherlands, and England, and carried goods from Arabia and beyond across the Russian steppes. Kiev and Novgorod, founded by Vikings, became gateways to the East. At its height, **merchants from over 60 cities** had joined, but by the end of the 15th century the league was in decline.

Battle of 'Ayn Jalut

United by Genghis Khan in 1206, the Mongols formed a group of tribes that embarked on a series of raids across Asia. By 1260, they had conquered an area stretching from the Pacific Ocean to the Mediterranean Sea, and were considered invincible. On September 3, 1260, the Mongols reached 'Ayn Jalut in Palestine, where they were met by the Mamluk Sultans.

The children and grandchildren of the Mongol leader Genghis Khan (see pp.164–65) took control of the Mongol tribes on his death in 1227. One of these grandchildren, Hülegü Khan, was given power over part of the Mongol army. He took this army into northwest Persia in 1255, raiding and looting as he went. In 1258 he defeated the Abbasid Caliphate (see pp.174–77), capturing and destroying the city of Baghdad and massacring the inhabitants. The Mongols now controlled Iraq and Persia. From here the Mongols pushed westward toward the Mediterranean. They overran Palestine and Syria, capturing the main city, Damascus, in 1259.

With Palestine and Syria conquered, Hülegü turned his attention to Egypt, the next major power to the west. He sent a message to its rulers, the Mamluks, asking them to surrender without a fight. Originally slaves taken from Turkish tribes and formed into an army by the previous rulers of Egypt, the Mamluks had overthrown the old government and taken power for themselves. Their new government was based on military principles, making it ideally suited for waging war and unlikely to give in to threats. The Mamluk response was to kill Hülegü's envoys and march toward the Mongol army in Palestine.

At the same time, Hülegü was informed that his brother, the Mongol Emperor (or "Great Khan"), was dying. With ambitions to gain control of the Mongol Empire for himself, Hülegü took most of the army with him and headed back to his brother.

Meanwhile, the Mamluks entered Palestine with an army equal in size to the Mongol force Hülegü had left behind. At 'Ayn Jalut—also known as Goliath's Spring—they defeated the Mongols, using their heavy cavalry to great effect. The Mamluks took control of Syria and Palestine, expelling the remaining Crusaders (see pp.200–01) in 1291.

The Mongols had never been so emphatically defeated before, and this halted their conquests to the west. The internal fighting that followed split the Mongol tribes into different sections. In Iraq and Persia, they became the Illkhanid dynasty and gradually took on the customs, religion, and language of the people they had conquered.

Mongol soldiers
This 13th-century Persian picture depicts Mongol soldiers in battle. The Mongol Empire was founded by Genghis Khan in 1206 and was one of the largest empires in history with an estimated population of 100 million people. At its height, it included territories from East Asia to central Europe.

> **"**It is for you to fly and **for us to pursue**… Fortresses will not detain us.**"**
> MESSAGE FROM HÜLEGÜ TO THE MAMLUKS DEMANDING THEIR SURRENDER, 1260

BEFORE

The Turkish tribes that founded the Ottoman Empire were originally semi-nomadic farmers who inhabited the steppes of Central Asia.

THE TURKS

Turkish tribes made early contact with the Islamic world through trade, warfare, and missionaries. They were also used as **slave warriors** by the Abbasid caliphate ‹‹ 174–75—the Islamic empire based in Baghdad—which led to the conversion of the Turks to Islam. The Ottoman lands in Anatolia bordered wealthy non-Muslim areas, which brought opportunities for expansion.

ANATOLIA

Before the influx of the Muslim Turkish tribes, Anatolia was ruled by the **Byzantine Empire** ‹‹ 198–99. It was inhabited mainly by small communities of settled Greek Christian farmers, interspersed with larger towns such as Nicaea (now the city of Iznik in Turkey).

The Rise of Ottoman Power

The Ottoman Empire was founded by a small group of nomadic Turkish warriors in Anatolia (modern-day Turkey). It lasted for 700 years, becoming a vast empire whose power and influence spanned the globe.

In the 10th century, the caliphate based in Baghdad (see pp.174–77) began to fragment into separate political entities, until it controlled only the provinces immediately around it. At the end of the 10th century, the remains of the caliphate were conquered by Turkish tribes from Central Asia. The Seljuk family who led the tribes took power as *sultans* (from the Turkish word for "authority"), restoring political authority to the caliphate, while exercising real power themselves through the figurehead caliphs. Although the Seljuks took over the existing system of government, their power was inherently unstable as it relied heavily on their nomadic warriors, who frequently clashed with settled peoples.

In 1071, the Seljuks defeated the Byzantine emperor in eastern Anatolia, and Byzantine rule was replaced by that of the Rum Seljuks, who were a branch of the Seljuk dynasty. This, and the fact Anatolia was well suited to the way of life practiced by the Turks, led to an influx of semi-nomadic tribes.

Disintegration

Another group of nomadic peoples from Central Asia were the Mongols (pp.204–05), who invaded most of Asia and parts of Europe. By 1258, the invading Mongol army had conquered most of Anatolia, Iran, and Iraq, replacing the Seljuks with the Ilkhanid dynasty (from the Mongol word for leader, *khan*). The Turks in Anatolia were forced to move westward into areas previously ruled by the Byzantines.

The Ilkhanid hold over Anatolia was never strong, and the peninsula soon began to disintegrate into multiple tribes and principalities. One of these small groups was led by Osman, son of Ertughrul, after whom the Ottoman Empire was named. This group was located in a strategically important area controlling the approach to Constantinople from the east. From here, the Ottomans managed to take over many Byzantine cities in Anatolia, which brought them more wealth and resources. The Ottomans then annexed land along the Dardanelles, which allowed them to control the crossing to Europe.

The creation of an empire

In the mid-14th century, the Ottomans aided the Byzantine emperor John VI Kantakouzenos in a civil war, and were rewarded with their first lands in Europe, on the Gallipoli peninsula. At the same time, the Ottomans expanded their lands in central and western Anatolia. After this, they spread into Europe, moving through eastern Thrace and across the Balkans. It was then that they probably encountered artillery for the first time.

Seljuk soldiers
This 13th-century stone relief depicts the armored warriors who maintained Seljuk power. The Seljuks were a Sunni Muslim dynasty that ruled parts of Central Asia and the Middle East in the 11th–14th centuries.

Ottoman war helmet
This battle helmet dates from c. 1500. Technological advances in warfare gave the Ottomans an edge in battle.

Finding a barrier blocking the route to the estuary on one side of Constantinople, the Ottomans dragged their ships overland to surround the city.

KEY

- ■ Nucleus of Ottoman Empire c. 1300
- ■ Conquests of Osman I, c. 1300–26
- ■ Conquests of Orkhan I, c. 1326–62
- ■ Conquests of Murad I, c. 1362–89
- ■ Conquests of Bayezid I, c. 1389–1402
- ■ Further Ottoman conquest by 1481
- ■ Vassal of Ottoman Empire by 1481
- ■ Under Venetian control c. 1450
- ● Siege

Ottoman Empire

The Ottoman Empire was very extensive until the end of the 15th century. At the center was Constantinople, whose fall to the Ottomans in 1453 is shown opposite. Its central location made its capture essential if the Ottomans were to rule in both Asia and Europe successfully.

HOLY ROMAN EMPIRE
LITHUANIA
Danube
Buda
HUNGARY
Dniester
Suceava
MOLDAVIA
Dnieper
Don
Venice
Zagreb
SLAVONIA
TRANSYLVANIA
Sea of Azov
KHANATE OF THE CRIMEA
Ravenna
DALMATIA
CROATIA
Belgrade
SERBIA
Argesh
WALLACHIA
Bucharest (Bükres)
Kefe (Kaffa)
PAPAL STATES
BOSNIA
HERZEGOVINA
Mostar
Danube
DOBRUJA
Rome
Adriatic Sea
REPUBLIC OF RAGUSA
Kosovo
Vidin
Nicopolis
Varna
Black Sea
Naples
NAPLES
Durazzo
ALBANIA
Balkan Mountains
Sofia
BULGARIA
Adrianople (Edirne)
Constantinople
1453: captured from Byzantines
Trebizond
Palermo
Corfu
THRACE
Gallipoli
Dardanelles
Bursa
Nicaea (Iznik)
Ankara
Erzurum
Sicily
Salonica (Selânik)
OTTOMAN EMPIRE
ANATOLIA
Malatya
Cephalonia
Aegean Sea
Athens
MOREA
Andros Tenos
Smyrna (Izmir)
Adana
Zante
Naxos
Aleppo
Monemvasia
Mediterranean Sea
Crete
Cyprus

0 300 km
0 300 miles

High towers aided the defenders. The Ottomans used siege towers to try to get the attackers to the same height, but these were also repelled.

Constantine XI Palaeologus, the last reigning Byzantine emperor, personally led the final defense of the city and died in the final attack.

The city walls withstood numerous assaults before being breached. The Ottomans tried to mine under the walls, but were thwarted each time.

The Siege of Constantinople
This 16th-century fresco shows the 1453 siege of Constantinople. The Ottomans had besieged Constantinople twice before but failed each time. Three days of looting followed its fall on May 29, 1453, and Sultan Mehmed II, who led the attack, spent much of the rest of his reign restoring and repopulating the city.

Ottoman artillery was far superior to Byzantine artillery. Huge cannons eventually breached the city walls, allowing them to enter.

Hagia Sophia Church in Constantinople was converted into a mosque immediately after the capture of the city.

The waters of the Bosporus protect Constantinople. Mehmet II fortified castles on either side of the Bosporus to prevent reinforcements.

AFTER

OTTOMAN SULTAN (1432–81)

MEHMED II

Mehmed II was sultan of the Ottoman Empire from 1451 to 1481. This 15th-century watercolor shows him in a peaceful pose. The reality was very different. One of Mehmed's first acts as sultan was to have his infant brother strangled to prevent further civil wars. His reign was one of ceaseless campaigning, which extended the empire to include most of the Balkans and Greece, Anatolia, the upper Euphrates valley, and sections of the Black Sea coast.

Later wars with Hungary, which was threatened by Ottoman expansion, led to the adoption of artillery-based military tactics. It was this development that made the Ottoman conquest of Constantinople possible.

Attacks by a neighboring principality in Anatolia in 1397 forced the Ottomans to take action, resulting in the conquest of most of eastern Anatolia. This bordered on the territory of the Mongol warlord Timur, whose empire stretched across Central Asia, southern Russia, Iran, and Azerbaijan. In 1402, Timur invaded Anatolia, capturing Bayezid, the Ottoman leader, and plundered Anatolia for a year. The remaining small portion of Anatolian territory, and Ottoman lands in Europe, were split between the sons of Bayezid. Civil war ensued for two

Fritware pottery
Produced in the Middle East in the 13th century, Fritware combined ground glass with clay to produce white ceramics.

generations. The eventual winner, Murad II, spent most of his life fighting to restore the lands the Ottomans had lost to Timur and securing his borders. He abdicated in 1444 in favor of his 12-year old son, but was recalled by his viziers (ministers) when the king of Hungary attacked the empire. At Murad's death in 1451, the Ottoman Empire dominated western and northern Anatolia and a large part of the Balkans. Murad was succeeded by one of the Ottoman Empire's most able leaders, Mehmed II (see left). After securing his borders, he laid siege to the city of Constantinople in 1453. Just 50 years after the near destruction of the Ottomans, despite civil war and in-fighting, they captured a wealthy imperial city, and brought down the remains of the Byzantine Empire.

The Ottoman Empire continued to be a preeminent cultural and military power into the 17th century and beyond.

IZNIK POTTERY
Iznik pottery became popular in the 16th century. Under sultans such as Suleyman the Magnificent (1520–66), the Ottomans enjoyed a golden age of cultural development **246–47** >>.

IZNIK POTTERY

THE JANISSARIES
Originally the sultan's household infantry, the Ottoman Empire used the janissaries in all its **major campaigns** of the 16th–17th centuries **246–47** >>. By the 18th century the janissaries even dominated government. After revolting in 1826, they were abolished. **JANISSARY**

« BEFORE

After the end of the Roman Empire, Europe's cities and trading networks fell into decline.

THE ROMAN EMPIRE

Under the Romans « 106–15, a wide network of cities and roads was established throughout Western Europe and **trade flourished**. Large towns were built even near the frontiers of the empire, such as at Trier in Germany. After 476 CE, when the last emperor was deposed in the West, **roads fell into disrepair** and some **towns were abandoned**. Political insecurity meant people hoarded their money rather than using it for trade, and the economy became reliant on **bartering**.

ROMAN GATE AT TRIER

Throughout the early part of this period, urban populations remained low. Some old Roman towns developed into religious centers, with bishops becoming the most powerful of the local lords. Other towns were used mainly as places for defense. Trading continued, but widespread unrest disrupted travel across Europe. With fewer coins being minted—a result of shortages of silver and political instability—people had to rely on exchanging one thing for another, or bartering.

From the 11th century onward, Western Europe began to stabilize. The supply of silver increased when deposits were found in the German province of Saxony. This meant that more coins could be produced and trade could be carried out more easily. However, it was the towns of the Italian peninsula that were first to benefit from these developments. Italy was ideally situated in the center of the

bankers, lending money to rulers across Europe. The Riccardi family of Lucca effectively financed the reign and costly wars of Edward I of England (1271–1307), for example, although they would later go bankrupt when subsequent English kings refused to pay back the loans. Pisa, Genoa, and Venice all became great ports. Venice

Wealthy Flemish couple
This oil painting by Matsys depicts a Flemish money-changer and his wife. The clothes, books, and glassware indicate the prosperity of the new merchant class.

Cities and Trade

Between 600 CE and 1450, the cities and towns of medieval Europe began to expand from simple defensive settlements into cosmopolitan centers of trade, power, and art. In Italy, cities became independent states, some building empires. In Northern Europe, the towns of Flanders became centers of manufacturing.

> "He who is not a **citizen** [city-dweller] is not fully a **man**."
>
> REMIGIO DE GIROLAMI, DOMINICAN FRIAR, 14TH-CENTURY FLORENCE

Bridging Britain and the Continent
This map from 1572 shows all the principal towns in Flanders, including Bruges and Antwerp. These towns were major manufacturing centers and, in the medieval period, specialized in processing English wool.

Mediterranean and was the natural crossroads for goods coming from east and west. Most importantly, many of its towns were effectively independent of overlords and emperors. The German Holy Roman Emperors Frederick Barbarossa and Frederick II were unsuccessful in their attempts to intervene in Italian affairs in the 12th–13th centuries (see right). This left the Italian cities free to run their own affairs and concentrate on trade.

Italian city-states

Textile production, banking, and shipping made enormous fortunes for the Italian cities and the families involved in these occupations. Tuscany, especially the cities of Florence and Siena, produced fine woolen cloth that was exported across Europe. Silk was produced around Milan and Pavia in the north. The Italians were also accomplished

Milanese gold ducat
This 15th-century gold coin could be transported more easily than the equivalent value in silver.

also managed to build an empire in the Balkans and Greece, making the city the principal maritime power in Europe.

The great success of Italy, however, was Florence, whose fortune was built on textile production and banking, and on its central position on the Italian peninsula. Florence was an oligarchy, a society ruled by the wealthiest merchants. During frequent struggles between the Germanic Holy Roman Empire and the Papacy in the 11th–12th centuries, it always backed the popes and gained privileged access to the lucrative Roman market as a result. The city aggressively guarded its position within Tuscany and eventually came to dominate the other banking cities of Siena and Lucca, and the port of Pisa. In time, one family, the Medicis, came to dominate the city.

The Italian city-states made many important economic advances. They issued gold coins, which made it easier to deal in goods of a high value than

BATTLE OF LEGNANO

The Battle of Legnano, on May 29, 1176, marked the point at which the city-states of northern Italy gained autonomy from the Holy Roman Emperor, Frederick Barbarossa. A group of these towns, called the Lombard League, objected to the emperor's interference in their internal affairs and, supported by Pope Alexander III, rebelled. The emperor looked sure to triumph when he laid waste the city of Milan. However, the Lombard League defeated his armies at Legnano, northwest of Milan, and he was forced to make peace.

when using silver coins. They also invented the modern financial practices of accounting and insurance to keep track of complicated transactions and prepare for losses due to shipwrecks.

Great trading networks

In northern Europe, the Flanders region grew rich and powerful during the 13th century. Like Italy, its geographical location was key to its development. It straddled an area of modern Belgium and the Netherlands that meant it was ideally positioned to benefit from trade with France, England, and the Holy Roman Empire.

Flanders was ruled by the counts of Flanders and Hainault, who encouraged trade by giving generous privileges to manufacturers. Huge annual fairs took place in the Flemish towns of Lille and Antwerp and farther south in the Champagne region of France. Here, Flemish merchants could sell the cloth that Flanders was famous for producing.

The three main cities of Flanders were Ghent, Bruges, and Ypres. Known simply as "the Three Cities," they housed the workshops where wool was processed into cloth and the homes of the great merchants and guilds. The woolworker and merchant guilds became very powerful and came to dominate politics in the trading cities.

30,000 The number of workers involved in Florence's cloth industry in the 1330s, according to the Florentine chronicler Villani, out of an estimated population of just 100,000.

Bruges: canals for pleasure and trade
Trade transformed small towns, making merchants and artisans wealthy; this image from about 1520 shows Bruges at the height of its wealth and power. Bruges' North Sea port and canals formed vital arteries for trade, linking the town to England, Genoa, and other trading centers.

Flanders imported most of its raw materials, including wool to make cloth, from England. Flanders itself grew corn and rye, which it exported, and plants to make dye for the cloth manufacturers. However, trade was often damaged by regulations brought in by English kings, who sought to encourage home-grown cloth production. From 1277, Flanders began to look elsewhere and started to trade more extensively with Genoa and other Italian cities.

Towers of San Gimignano
These towers in Tuscany were not built to protect the town from outsiders, but to defend rival family factions within the town from each other.

AFTER

The great centers of trade shifted away from Flanders and Italy during the 16th century.

ITALIAN CITY-STATES
A dispute between the French and Spanish over the **Duchy of Milan** turned Italy into a battlefield, damaging Italian trade. By 1527, the Holy Roman Emperor Charles V captured Rome and the city was sacked by his mercenaries, the Landsknechts.

After the **discovery of America**, the focus of trade shifted from the Mediterranean to the Atlantic. Countries such as England, Portugal, and Spain benefited, while Italian trade declined.

NORTHERN EUROPE
Flemish trade suffered as **English manufacturers** began to process their own wool, helped by Flemish immigrants. The **Hanseatic League**, a trading alliance of northern European towns, began to operate through the Baltic as far as England, providing a great stimulus for the northern economies.

LANDSKNECHT

BEFORE

The Maya, Aztecs, and Incas had the most advanced cultures of all the peoples living in America before the arrival of the Spanish.

THE MAYA
The **Maya** « **140–41** had lived in parts of Mexico, Guatemala, Belize, and Honduras for more than 1,000 years before the first great flowering of their culture *c.* 300 CE.

THE AZTECS
The **Aztecs** are thought to have arrived in **central Mexico** in the 13th century, either from northern Mexico or from the southwest United States, but their exact origins are unclear.

THE INCAS
Beginning as a tribe in Cuzco in the 12th century, the Incas **spread** throughout **the Andes** regions of modern-day Peru, Ecuador, and Chile.

MISSISSIPPIAN CULTURE
Mississippian culture of the **southeast United States** had much in common with Mesoamerican cultures: **agriculture** based on **corn**, towns with wide plazas, and giant ceremonial mounds.

Pre-Columbian Americas

Characterized by their advances in astronomy and the arts, the Maya, Aztecs, and Incas had the richest and most complex societies in pre-Columbian America. Although distinct cultures, they shared similar traditions, including ritualized religious worship and a belief in the value of education and spirituality.

Whereas the Aztecs and Incas subjugated neighboring peoples to create powerful empires, the Maya never formed an empire, nor did they have a single ruler or dominant capital city. They were a loose federation of city-states bound together by a common language, culture, and religion. The priest-rulers, who maintained power through their superior education and contacts with the gods, led the Maya to extraordinary achievements in mathematics, astronomy, architecture, fine arts, engineering, and writing.

Religious practices

Along with the Aztecs and Incas, the Maya had a pantheon of gods, and their religious practices were based on their interpretation of the cycles of nature. These gods were rarely discrete entities but instead combined a wide variety of forms and ideas. They could be both young and old, take both human and animal forms, and often had a counterpart of the opposite sex.

The supreme deity of the Maya was Itzam Ná, who was represented iconically as an old man; he was the inventor of writing and patron of learning and sciences. His wife, IxChel, was goddess of the old moon, as well as of weaving, medicine, and childbirth.

Religious rituals were performed to satisfy the gods and ensure order in the world. Ceremonies usually began with fasting and abstinence, followed by offerings of food,

Quetzalcoatl mask
This mask is thought to represent the Aztec god Quetzalcoatl, who is often depicted as a feathered serpent. It is made of cedar wood, covered in turquoise mosaic, and the teeth are made of shell.

ornaments, dancing, and an occasional human sacrifice, although not on the scale of the Aztecs (see right). During the ceremonies the priests might impersonate the gods, or use hallucinogens to enhance their powers of divination. Finally, there would be feasting and drunkenness.

Later Maya civilization

Around 800 CE, some lowland Maya city-states went into decline, and by 900 CE had all but collapsed. Many explanations have been proposed for this, ranging from natural causes, such as disease or climate change, to soil exhaustion, war, or loss of control by the priest-aristocracy, but no theory can be proven absolutely.

After *c.* 900 all the main Maya centers were in the northern part of the Yucatán. One, Chichén Itzá, was founded in the second half of the 8th century by a confederation of groups drawn from the Maya lowlands and the Itzá people, whose origins are unknown. The city, which appears to have experimented with new rituals and forms of shared government, was a thriving community in the 9th and 10th centuries, but collapsed after 1050.

The architecture of Chichén Itzá (see pp.212–13) is strikingly similar to that of Tula, the capital of the Toltecs 40 miles (65 km) to the north of Mexico City, which flourished at around the same time. It is not exactly clear which of these cities influenced the other, but there must have been

extensive cultural and trade links across central and southern parts of Mexico at this time.

The Aztec Empire

The Aztecs—or Mexica, as they called themselves—were the most powerful people in the Valley of Mexico during the 15th and 16th centuries. Their capital, Tenochtitlán (now Mexico City), was founded in the 14th century on an island in Lake Texcoco. The marshes that surrounded the city might seem an unpromising environment, but the Aztecs were expert managers of water. They not only built dams to trap the fresh water from the rivers that flowed into the lake, but also grew a wide variety of crops on *chinampas,* fertile artificial islands created in the shallow lake.

Aztec society was class-based, with nobility at the top and slaves at the bottom. Education seems to have

> "We beheld… **cities** and towns **on the water**… it was like the things of **enchantment**."
>
> BERNAL DIAZ DE CASTILLO, ON ENTERING THE AZTEC CAPITAL TENOCHTITLÁN, 1519

Carving on stone lintel at Yaxchilan
This carving shows the accession rituals of the ruler Bird Jaguar. His wife Balam-Ix, sitting opposite, performs a blood sacrifice by drawing a rope through her tongue.

HOW WE KNOW

MAYA ASTRONOMY

The pyramid of Kukulcán at Chichén Itzá is a solar calendar, built on top of an earlier lunar calendar. The pyramid is full of symbolism: the four stairways leading to the central platform at the top each have 91 steps, totaling 364— added to the central platform this makes 365, which is the number of days in the solar year. On either side of each stairway are nine terraces, which makes 18 on each face: a number that equals the number of months in the Maya solar calendar. The facing of each terrace contains 52 panels, representing the 52-year cycle during which the solar and religious calendars become realigned.

Stone sacrificial altar
The *cuauhxicalli,* which translates as "eagle gourd vessel," was used by Aztecs to make their most sacred offerings—human hearts.

been universal, with schooling provided for both boys and girls. A boy's education included training to fight in wars because the Aztecs were a culture with a proud warrior tradition. By 1520 they had an empire that stretched across Mexico from the Gulf of Mexico to the Pacific.

Like the Maya, the Aztecs had a large number of gods, related to the creation of the cosmos, to the sun, and to fertility, death, and war. The two main temples on the pyramid in Tenochtitlán were dedicated to Huitzilopochtli, the god of war and Tlaloc, the god of rain and water. Another important god was

Quetzalcoatl, the feathered serpent god of wind, creativity, and fertility. Although the Aztecs had a rich culture that showed particular respect for poetry and song, they are remembered more for their human sacrifices. They believed that if they did not satisfy the gods with sacrifices, the sun would not continue its journey across the sky.

Their rites took many different forms, some more brutal than others. One performed for the fire god, Huehueteotl, involved captives being anesthetized and thrown into a fire. Before they died, priests retrieved them using hooks and removed their hearts. »

Civilizations of America, c. 1520
The Incas occupied the Andes mountains of South America. The Aztecs were centered on Tenochtitlán, now Mexico City, while the Maya inhabited the Yucatán Peninsula.

KEY
- Aztec Empire
- Inca Empire
- Maya cultural region

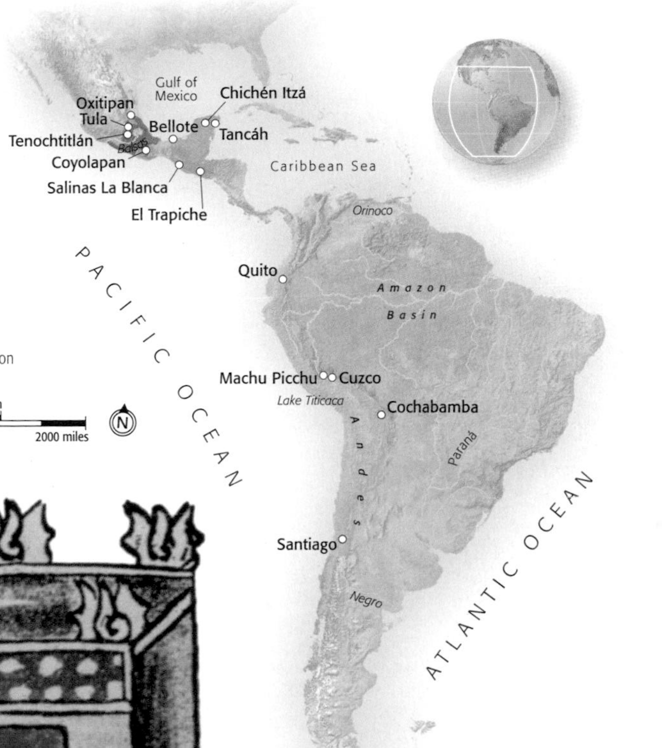

The beating heart was lifted into the air by the priest, who pronounced it "precious eagle cactus fruit" as an offering to the sun god.

The priest drove a flint or obsidian knife into the breast of the victim, killing him almost instantaneously, then slit the arteries around the heart in order to pull it from the body.

The fire in which the heart was burned was contained in a special vessel carved to represent an eagle.

The sacrificial victim was stretched out on his back over a stone by a number of assistants, usually four.

The victim's body was tossed down the staircase after the sacrifice.

Aztec sacrifice
In this depiction of an Aztec sacrifice, the pyramid temple represents the Sacred Snake Mountain, where, according to Aztec mythology, Huitzilopochtli, god of war and the sun, dismembered his sister, the moon goddess Coyolxauqui.

>> In contrast, the method of honoring Tezcatlipoca consisted of choosing the most handsome and brave prisoner of war to be an incarnation of this complex god, who is often considered to be the rival of Quetzalcoatl. After a year of being pampered, the prisoner's last month was spent in the company of four "goddesses" who met his every desire. He would then be sacrificed.

The Incas

In South America, the Incas used both conquest and peaceful assimilation to expand their empire, until it was the largest in pre-Columbian America. Expansion was remarkably rapid, only starting in earnest in the reign of Pachacuti, which began around 1438. He and his son, Tupac Inca, created a huge federal system consisting of four provinces, each overseen by an Inca governor. Following each new conquest, magnificent roads, many of them paved, were built to link it to the capital Cuzco

Lost city of the Incas
Machu Picchu is the best preserved of the known Inca settlements. Abandoned in the 16th century, it is a fine example of Inca architecture and planning. High-quality building work and numerous shrines suggest that the site had religious importance.

and the rest of the empire. The Incas had no horses, nor had they discovered the wheel; messages were carried by relays of runners, while llamas served as pack animals. Their superior organization enabled them to absorb many existing states, the largest being Chimor on the coast of northern Peru, home to the influential Chimú culture. By Tupac Inca's death in 1493, Inca rule reached north to Quito in Ecuador.

Like other American cultures, the Incas built temples devoted to their gods, of whom there were many—the sun god, Inti, being most important. Their worship included divination, and animal and human sacrifice. Although fairly rare, human sacrifice normally involved children taken from villages around the empire.

INVENTION

QUIPU

The Incas used collections of knotted colored threads, called *quipu*, to record information. Spun from llama and alpaca hair, there might be just a few threads in a *quipu*, or hundreds or even thousands. Like decimalization, the system is based on the number 10. *Quipucamayocs*—accountants in Inca society—would use the *quipu* to perform simple mathematics, calculate taxes, and keep records of labor or livestock, for example. They were also used for censuses and for tax accounting, and to track events and time. Inca historians used them to tell the Spanish conquistadors their history, although it is unknown whether the strings simply recorded important numbers or contained the history itself.

Culture and architecture

Elaborate architecture is one of the most important legacies of Inca civilization. The complex stone temples built by the Incas used a mortarless construction process that had been developed between 300 BCE and 300 CE by the Pucara peoples in lands to the south of Cuzco, around Lake Titicaca. Each stone was carved to slot exactly into the one below it. Final adjustments were made by lowering the rock onto the one below, raising it again, and chipping away any sections on the lower rock where marks in the dust indicated that the fit was not perfect. This attention to detail meant that buildings constructed by this method were extremely stable.

Machu Picchu

Apart from Cuzco itself, much of which was damaged by the Spanish conquistadors (see AFTER), the most complete remaining example of the Inca's careful planning and building techniques is Machu Picchu. Situated 40 miles (70 km) northwest of Cuzco, it is

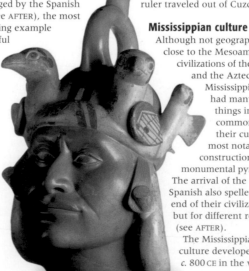

Chimú pottery
The Chimú, one of the many peoples whose lands fell to the Incas in the 15th century, produced strikingly sculpted pottery figures. Their civilization owed much to the earlier Moche (see p.140).

Temple of Kukulcán
Dominating the center of Chichén Itzá is the Temple of Kukulcán (Quetzalcoatl, the plumed serpent of the Aztecs and Toltecs). At the spring and fall equinoxes, the sun creates undulating patterns of triangles of light on the temple stairway. These link with the massive carvings of snakes' heads at the foot of the stairs, suggesting a giant serpent zigzagging down the face of the pyramid.

thought that Machu Picchu is a relatively recent construction, dating perhaps from the mid-15th century. The quality of the stonework, the high altitude of its position, and the many shrines that have been identified among its ruins seem to indicate that this settlement was much more important than a mere rural village. It has been suggested that Machu Picchu was one of a number of royal estates built by Pachacuti. According to Spanish chroniclers, these settlements were used as country estates when the Inca ruler traveled out of Cuzco.

Mississippian culture

Although not geographically close to the Mesoamerican civilizations of the Maya and the Aztecs, the Mississippians had many things in common with their cultures, most notably the construction of monumental pyramids. The arrival of the Spanish also spelled the end of their civilization, but for different reasons (see AFTER).

The Mississippian culture developed from c. 800 CE in the valley of the Mississippi River and spread to much of central, eastern, and southeastern North America. The Mississippian peoples lived in a highly structured society with close ties to the land: they relied on corn as their staple food. Key settlements were created at Spiro Mounds in eastern Oklahoma, Moundville in Alabama, and Etowah Mounds in northern Georgia; the most elaborate center was based at Cahokia Mounds in Collinsville, Illinois.

Cahokia was inhabited from the 7th to the 14th centuries and at its peak had around 30,000 inhabitants. The inhabitants made flat-topped mounds on which they built houses, burial buildings, and temples. More than 120 mounds were built, and many were enlarged several times.

It is thought that Cahokia went into a gradual decline beginning around 1200, and was completely abandoned by 1400. The inhabitants left no written records, and the city's original name is unknown—"Cahokia" refers to a nearby Illiniwek clan that was present in the area when French settlers arrived in the 17th century.

Monks Mound, Cahokia
Large Mississippian settlements were dominated by massive pyramidal mounds of earth that served as bases for temples—where the people could observe celestial events such as the summer and winter solstices—or the residences of the more powerful individuals.

The Mississippians were accomplished craftsmen, and archaeological excavations have revealed a range of ceramic vessels, some of them sculpted to look like trophy heads taken in warfare. Intricately carved pipes and ceremonial axes have also been found. Excavations carried out at the Spiro Mound have produced shell gorgets (decorative disks worn around the neck) with representations of warriors and snakes.

AFTER »

The arrival of the Spanish conquistadors (conquerors) had far-reaching effects on the peoples of Mesoamerica and much of South America, devastating traditions and ways of life that had existed for hundreds of years.

THE CONQUISTADORS
Arriving in Mexico in 1519, **Hernán Cortés 230–31** » heard about the wealthy Aztec city Tenochtitlán. With a group of Spanish soldiers and some local enemies of the Aztecs, he took control of the city in 1521. Most of the city was destroyed, but it was rebuilt by the Spanish as Mexico City, capital of the Viceroyalty of New Spain.

The **Spanish** reached the **Yucatán** in about 1524. Although individual independent centers did fall to the conquistadors, the Maya often put up a fierce fight. The last stronghold submitted in 1697.

In 1532, **Francisco Pizarro 231** » obtained permission from Spain to overcome the Inca, who had already been weakened by a civil war and smallpox. They finally fell to the Spanish in 1572.

THE FATE OF THE MISSISSIPPIANS
The decline of the Mississippian culture began before the arrival of the Spanish and French as a result of intertribal warfare and malnutrition, compounded by the spread of European diseases.

2 AZTEC LIP ORNAMENT

1 MAYA CODEX

8 GOLD NOSE PLUG

6 JADE VAMPIRE BAT MOSAIC MASK

7 CARVED STONE FROM TEMPLO MAYOR

12 FEATHER SHIELD

11 BALL MARKER

Aztec to Inca

A highly sophisticated level of craftsmanship is evident in the decorative and sacrificial objects crafted by the ancient civilizations of Meso- and South America, from the Aztecs, Toltec, and Mayan peoples of Mexico to the Inca and Chimu of Peru.

1 **Maya codex** (painted book) showing drawings of five gods and hieroglyphics. It was read from top to bottom and left to right. 2 **Aztec lip ornament** in the shape of an eagle head with bangles hanging from the underside of its open beak. 3 **Aztec labret** (lip ornament) made by the Mixtecs. These ornaments were inserted through a hole pierced through the skin below the bottom lip. 4 **Toltec mask** inlaid with mother of pearl from the Toltec city of Tula, 40 miles (65 km) northwest of modern-day Mexico City. It represents a coyote warrior. 5 **Toltec warrior** carved from stone and painted in battle dress. Its arms are raised to hold an altar or shrine. 6 **Zapotec vampire bat mosaic mask** carved of 25 pieces of jade, with yellow eyes made of shell. 7 **Carved round stone** found at Templo Mayor, Mexico City, showing the separated limbs, head, and torso of the Aztec goddess Coyolxauhqui. 8 **Mixtec nose plug** made of hammered gold. Such nose plugs were placed

above the top lip. 9 **Peruvian fan** made from macaw feathers, with a handle of braided brown wool. 10 **Aztec priest's sacrificial chert (stone) knife** with a carved jaguar handle. 11 **Maya ball marker**, consisting of a disk with a whorled emblem on top of a pillar. It was used for ball-court games, which were played by all Mesoamericans. 12 **Aztec feather shield**, stretched with spotted jaguar skin and decorated with strings of feathers. All Aztec warriors carried a feather shield. 13 **Chimu portrait** beaker from Peru made of beaten silver. This may have been a portrait of a real person and used for ceremonial purposes. 14 **Inca gold ornamental belt** made up of rectangular sections. 15 **Ornamental Maya incense burner** in the form of Chaac (Maya god of rain) wearing an elaborate headdress. 16 **Gold necklace** found in the Basin of Mexico. 17 **Aztec funerary urn** made of clay, found at Templo Mayor, Mexico City, depicting a bearded god.

14 BELT ORNAMENT

3 JADE LABRET

4 TOLTEC WARRIOR MASK

10 AZTEC SACRIFICIAL KNIFE

5 TOLTEC WARRIOR

9 FEATHER FAN

16 GOLD NECKLACE

13 PORTRAIT BEAKER

17 FUNERARY URN

15 MAYAN GOD OF RAIN

« BEFORE

Today's "Polynesians" are linked by language and DNA evidence to two prehistoric peoples.

POLYNESIAN ORIGINS

Polynesians today are descended from a southeast Asian group (probably from modern-day Taiwan), and a group indigenous to Melanesia (near Papua New Guinea). These two peoples gave rise to the **Melanesian "Lapita" culture**, whose pottery dates back as far as 1600 BCE. In the early centuries CE, these people split into many tribes and explored the South Pacific.

HOW WE KNOW

MOA BIRD

The enormous moa was one of many victims of the Polynesian expansion. These giant, wingless birds, up to 12 ft (3.6 m) tall, were hunted to extinction by Maori settlers of New Zealand. Later European expeditions collected remains for study by scientists such as Richard Owen (1804–92), below.

Polynesian Expansion

By approximately 700 CE, the Polynesians had reached all corners of the South Pacific, spreading across the uninhabited islands of Micronesia and reaching the extreme limits of their exploration and settlement at New Zealand and Easter Island, leading to a diverse range of cultures.

Archaeological evidence for the presence of Polynesian settlers from around 700 CE has been found in places as far flung as Samoa, Hawaii, and New Zealand. The islands, however, never formed a single empire of the type found elsewhere in the world—each group of settlers lived mostly in isolation, occupying territories that ranged in size from a small portion of an island, to a whole group of small islands. For this reason an incredible range of diverse cultures developed across Polynesia, each with its own way of life, customs, and tools. Some built huge stone cities, while others lived in villages on the beach. Contact with other groups among the isolated islanders was rare, while among groups sharing an island, war was frequent.

Across the ocean

The Polynesians were great shipbuilders, navigators, and sailors, and probably reached America more than a hundred years before the Vikings. They sailed on long voyages,

Polynesian pendant
Although the Polynesians did not use metal, they were able to create intricate tools and jewelry, such as this greenstone pendant.

into the unknown and often against the prevailing winds, to reach and populate far-flung islands. Often they brought their whole world with them—an entire family traveling together, their boats laden with all the possessions, tools, animals, and plants they would need in order to make a distant island their new home.

Some have argued that the colonization was largely accidental; without even a compass to aid their navigation, the Polynesians surely did not achieve this intentionally—they must have been blown off course. However, recent studies have shown

Double-hulled canoe
The Polynesians explored the ocean more extensively than anyone before in vessels like this. Supplies could be stored in the double hull.

that ancient Polynesian methods of navigation using the stars, birds, winds, currents, and tides would have been surprisingly reliable when crossing even the widest gulf of ocean. Some recent explorers have even repeated these epic journeys in replica boats. Although Polynesian islanders are often depicted as living at one with nature, in reality they altered

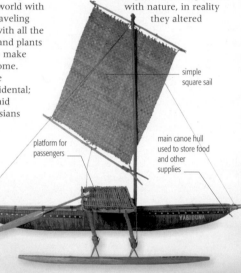

simple square sail

main canoe hull used to store food and other supplies

platform for passengers

887 The number of Moai statues found across Easter Island. Nearly 400 lie in the quarries where they were carved, but 288 were moved and erected successfully. The remainder were abandoned on roads.

INVENTION

STICK CHART

This stick chart from the Marshall Islands, in the Pacific Ocean, demonstrates one of the many unique methods the Polynesians used to navigate the seas. Made of sticks and shells, and bearing little resemblance to a normal map, it is a representation of local tides and currents. Rather than taking the chart on voyages, Polynesian navigators memorized them prior to departure, often with the aid of chants.

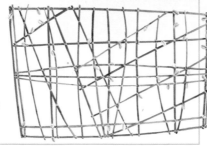

on when the Polynesians arrived; some claim it was as early as 300 CE, while recent studies claim a late date of about 1200 CE.

Archaeologists do know that around 1000–1200 CE, the trees of Rapa Nui began to disappear. Climate change

16 MILLION The number of palm trees thought to have stood on Rapa Nui before the arrival of humans.

and the arrival of seed-eating rats may have increased the speed of the decline, but it seems to have largely been triggered by the colonists' obsessive construction of giant stone heads called "Moai." These were carved in one piece from compressed volcanic ash and required wooden frameworks during the carving process, and wooden rollers for transport from the quarries to ceremonial sites along the coast.

No one knows for certain why the Moai were built, or what they represent; and as they were built over a long period of time, the tradition may have been influenced by a variety of changing

With the arrival of western ships, Polynesian isolation came to an end.

EUROPEAN CONTACTS

From 1567, European ships began to explore the islands of the South Pacific **224–25 »**. Colonists soon followed, crushing **indigenous cultures** with weapons, gods, and diseases. Some went down fighting—this spear is from the New Zealand Wars (1845–72), fought between the Maori and the British.

MAORI SPEAR

factors. However, as the heads replaced the trees, environmental disaster struck, and Rapa Nui's ecosystem collapsed. Birds had nowhere safe to nest, so they became extinct. The loose soil washed into the sea, leaving a lifeless landscape. The inhabitants could not even build boats for fishing—they resorted to cannibalism to stay alive, and began to tear down and deface the heads that had affected their environment so much.

Moai heads
Those Moai that made it to their final destination were erected along the coast of Rapa Nui, facing inland. According to one theory, they represent great chiefs from the island's history.

their environment just as much as any other group of settlers. Polynesians arriving on new islands brought with them domesticated animals, such as dogs, chickens, and pigs, and they (along with the rats which stowed away) were highly destructive. The Polynesians also brought new plants for farming, and chopped down trees to make boats, tools, and fire. In fact, one reliable method for dating the Polynesian expansion across the Pacific is to look for archaeological evidence of large flora and fauna extinctions.

Because of this, each of the Pacific islands today has its own unique ecosystem, consisting of the different plants and animals that

happened to survive the arrival of the Polynesians, mingled with whatever invading species were introduced to the island with the colonists.

Mysteries of Rapa Nui

Rapa Nui (also known as Easter Island) is one of the most isolated islands in Polynesia. It lies 1,290 miles (2,000 km) from the nearest island and is believed to have been named Easter Island because the first European visitor arrived on Easter Sunday in 1722. Historians still do not agree

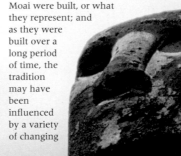

5

RENAISSANCE AND REFORMATION

1450–1750

Within 30 years of Columbus's first Atlantic crossing in 1492, a Spanish expedition had circumnavigated the globe. As European explorers set sail in search of new lands to conquer and colonize, commerce and trade expanded internationally. It was also an age in which established beliefs were questioned, leading to conflict and change.

RENAISSANCE AND REFORMATION

1450–1750

1450	1470	1490	1510

1455
Wars of the Roses, a dynastic struggle for the English throne.

▼ Gutenberg Bible

1477
Battle of Nancy: Charles the Bold killed; Habsburgs acquire most of the Burgundian territories.
1479
Union of Castile and Aragon (modern-day Spain) through marriage of Isabella I and Ferdinand.

1497
John Cabot reaches Newfoundland.
1498
First European voyage to India around Cape of Good Hope, Vasco da Gama. Columbus first European to reach South America.

▼ Columbus's landing

1520
First Portuguese trading mission to China. Magellan discovers navigable route south, around tip of South America.

◄ Self-portrait of Leonardo da Vinci

1471
Annamites expand south, invading Hindu state of Champa, South Vietnam. Final decline of Khmer civilization begins. Portuguese take Tangiers from Moors.

▼ Inca army supply depot

1480
Muscovy under Ivan III escapes Tatar Mongol domination.
1485
Battle of Bosworth: Henry VII of England defeats Richard III and establishes Tudor dynasty.

c. 1510
Height of Italian renaissance.
1513
Ponce de León claims Florida for Spain.
1514
Battle of Çaldiran: Ottomans defeat Safavid Persians.

1453
Constantinople captured by the Ottomans; Byzantine Empire falls.
c. 1454
Gutenberg Bible printed in Germany.

1492
Christian reconquest of Spain completed as Muslim Granada falls to Spain. Christopher Columbus makes first Atlantic crossing and lands in Caribbean Islands off the coast of the Americas.

1502
First shipment of African slaves sent to Cuba to work in Spanish settlements, beginning triangular slave trade between Europe, West Africa, and Americas.

1516
Ottomans under Selim II conquer Syria, Egypt, Hejaz, and Yemen.
1517
Martin Luther writes the *95 Theses*, triggering the Reformation.

Ferdinand Magellan ►

1467
Onin War in Japan begins marking start of century-long "Era of Warring States."

◄ Printing press

1468
Songhoy recapture Timbuktu from the Tuaregs and become leading power in West Africa.

1472
Marriage of Ivan III of Russia to Zoe, niece of Byzantine emperor; Ivan takes title of czar.
1475
Chimú conquered by Incas; greatest imperial expansion begins.

Isabella I ►

1494
Treaty of Tordesillas: the New World divided between Spain and Portugal. Italian wars begin with Charles VIII's invasion of Italy to lay claim to Naples.

Seville port ►

1529
Vienna besieged by Ottomans. Peace of Cambrai relinquishes France's rights in Italy, Flanders, and Artois. Charles V renounces claims to Burgundy.

◄ Martin Luther

Europe after 1450 benefited from a scientific as much as a philosophical revolution. The Renaissance was more than a matter of the rediscovery of the continent's ancient learning—it sparked a spirit of scientific inquiry that provided key technological advantages over the rest of the world. It was as much a desire for knowledge for its own sake, as for commerce and colonization, that underpinned the voyages of exploration that established mid-18th century Europe as the world's first global power. This expansion was made in the face of formidable opposition. At least until 1700, Ming, later Qing, China; Mughal India; and Safavid Persia were Europe's equals, while Ottoman Turkey presented a persistent threat.

1530

1532
Francisco Pizarro lands in Peru and encounters, captures, and kills Inca emperor Atahuallpa.
1533
Pizarro conquers Inca capital, Cuzco.

▼ Silver censer

1534
Henry VIII of England breaks with Rome. Ottoman–Safavid war; Ottoman capture of Baghdad. Jacques Cartier explores Strait of Belle Isle and St. Lawrence.

◄ Henry VIII

▲ Gold Inca armlets

1536
Wales and England formally united under Act of Union. Henry VIII begins dissolution of monasteries in England; crushes Catholic rebellion.

1550

1545
Council of Trent called to counter threat of Protestantism. Silver discovered at Potosí, Bolivia.
1547
Battle of Mühlberg: Protestant League of Schmalkalden defeated by Emperor Charles V.

1550
Suleyman mosque begun in Istanbul.
1552
Henri II of France assists the German protestants in overturning authority of Charles V in Germany.

Sultan Suleyman ►

1555
Charles V concedes "Accord of Augsburg," giving German princes freedom to select protestant or Catholic religion.
1556
Mughal Emperor Akbar begins personal rule.

▲ Elizabeth I

1558
Elizabeth I becomes Queen of England. Akbar conquers region of Gwalior in central India. England loses Calais, last French possession.

1565
Beginning of Ivan IV's "reign of terror" in Russia. Spain claims Philippines. South American Indian population decimated by European diseases.

Smallpox in Americas ►

1570

1571
Battle of Lepanto: Ottoman expansion in Mediterranean halted. Portuguese invasion of Zambezi.
1576
Mughal forces capture Bengal in north India.

▼ Battle of Lepanto

c. 1570
Flemish cartographer Mercator presents new world-map projection.
1570
Portugal founds colony in Angola; starts slave trading.

▼ Mercator map

1585
Spain establishes first permanent European colony in Philippines, Cebu. Treaty of Nonsuch provides English military assistance for Dutch rebels in their struggle against Spain.

1586
Japan begins reunification.
1588
Accession of Shah Abbas to throne of Safavid Persia rolls back Ottoman territorial gains. Spanish Armada fails to conquer England.

1590

c. 1590
Maori population rise causes strain on resources; warfare increases.
1592
Japan invades Korea; Repulsed by Chinese troops and Korean navy.

Mariner's Mirrour ◄ c. 1590

1593
Beginning of "Long Turkish War" between Habsburgs and Ottomans.
1595
Henri IV seeks to unite religious divisions in France by declaring war on Spain.

◄ Maori eel trap

1600
Battle of Sekigahara gives Tokugawa Ieyasu control of Japan. British East India Company established.
1602
Founding of Dutch East India Company.

1590
Peace treaty negotiated between Safavid Persia and Ottomans. Toyotomi Hideyoshi achieves unification of Japan; capital moved to Edo (modern Tokyo).

▼ Japanese tea ceremony

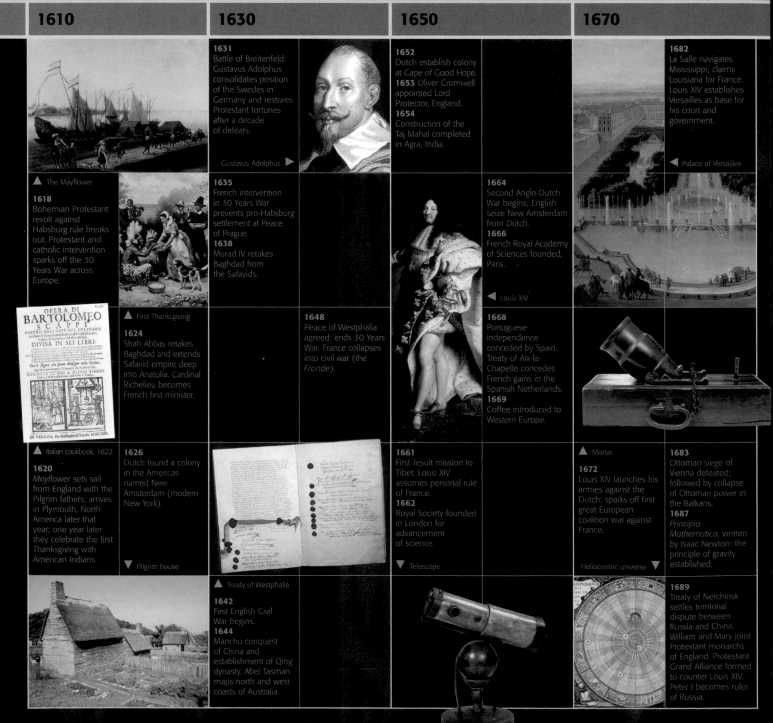

▲ The Mayflower

1618
Bohemian Protestant revolt against Habsburg rule breaks out. Protestant and catholic intervention sparks off the 30 Years War across Europe.

▲ First Thanksgiving

1624
Shah Abbas retakes Baghdad and extends Safavid empire deep into Anatolia. Cardinal Richelieu becomes French first minister.

OPERA DI
BARTOLOMEO
SCAPPI
MASTRO DELL'ARTE DEL CVCINARE,
...
DIVISA IN SEI LIBRI.
...
IN VENETIA, Per Alessandro de Vecchi. M.DC.XXII.

▲ Italian cookbook, 1622

1620
Mayflower sets sail from England with the Pilgrim fathers; arrives in Plymouth, North America later that year; one year later they celebrate the first Thanksgiving with American Indians.

1631
Battle of Breitenfeld: Gustavus Adolphus consolidates position of the Swedes in Germany and restores Protestant fortunes after a decade of defeats.

Gustavus Adolphus ▶

1635
French intervention in 30 Years War prevents pro-Habsburg settlement at Peace of Prague.
1638
Murad IV retakes Baghdad from the Safavids.

1626
Dutch found a colony in the Americas named New Amsterdam (modern New York).

▼ Pilgrim house

▲ Treaty of Westphalia

1642
First English Civil War begins.
1644
Manchu conquest of China and establishment of Qing dynasty. Abel Tasman maps north and west coasts of Australia.

1652
Dutch establish colony at Cape of Good Hope.
1653 Oliver Cromwell appointed Lord Protector, England.
1654
Construction of the Taj Mahal completed in Agra, India.

1648
Peace of Westphalia agreed: ends 30 Years War. France collapses into civil war (the *Fronde*).

◀ Louis XIV

1661
First Jesuit mission to Tibet. Louis XIV assumes personal rule of France.
1662
Royal Society founded in London for advancement of science.

▼ Telescope

1682
La Salle navigates Mississippi; claims Louisiana for France. Louis XIV establishes Versailles as base for his court and government.

◀ Palace of Versailles

1664
Second Anglo-Dutch War begins; English seize New Amsterdam from Dutch.
1666
French Royal Academy of Sciences founded, Paris.

1668
Portuguese independence conceded by Spain. Treaty of Aix-la-Chapelle concedes French gains in the Spanish Netherlands.
1669
Coffee introduced to Western Europe.

▲ Mortar

1672
Louis XIV launches his armies against the Dutch: sparks off first great European coalition war against France.

Heliocentric universe ▼

1683
Ottoman siege of Vienna defeated; followed by collapse of Ottoman power in the Balkans.
1687
Principia Mathematica, written by Isaac Newton: the principle of gravity established.

1689
Treaty of Nerchinsk settles territorial dispute between Russia and China. William and Mary joint Protestant monarchs of England. Protestant Grand Alliance formed to counter Louis XIV. Peter I becomes ruler of Russia.

> "The church says that the Earth is flat, **but I know that it is round,** for I have seen the shadow on the Moon, and I have more faith in a shadow than in the Church."

FERDINAND MAGELLAN, LEADER OF THE FIRST EXPEDITION TO CIRCUMNAVIGATE THE GLOBE, c. 1519

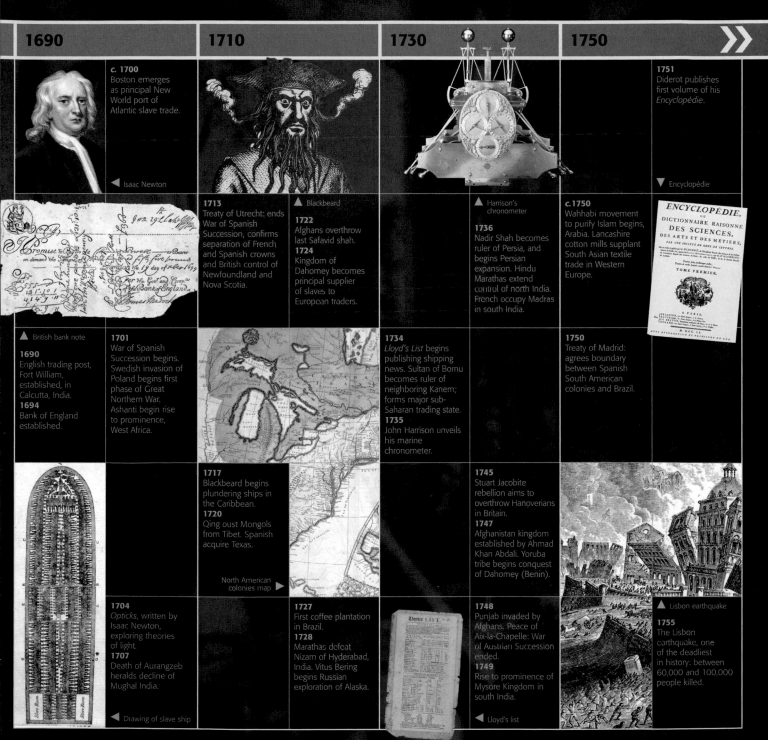

1690 · 1710 · 1730 · 1750

c. 1700
Boston emerges as principal New World port of Atlantic slave trade.

◀ Isaac Newton

1713
Treaty of Utrecht: ends War of Spanish Succession, confirms separation of French and Spanish crowns and British control of Newfoundland and Nova Scotia.

▲ Blackbeard

1722
Afghans overthrow last Safavid shah.
1724
Kingdom of Dahomey becomes principal supplier of slaves to European traders.

▲ Harrison's chronometer

1736
Nadir Shah becomes ruler of Persia, and begins Persian expansion. Hindu Marathas extend control of north India. French occupy Madras in south India.

c.1750
Wahhabi movement to purify Islam begins, Arabia. Lancashire cotton mills supplant South Asian textile trade in Western Europe.

1751
Diderot publishes first volume of his *Encyclopédie.*

▼ Encyclopédie

ENCYCLOPÉDIE, ou DICTIONNAIRE RAISONNÉ DES SCIENCES, DES ARTS ET DES METIERS,

TOME PREMIER.

▲ British bank note

1690
English trading post, Fort William, established, in Calcutta, India.
1694
Bank of England established.

1701
War of Spanish Succession begins. Swedish invasion of Poland begins first phase of Great Northern War. Ashanti begin rise to prominence, West Africa.

1734
Lloyd's List begins publishing shipping news. Sultan of Bornu becomes ruler of neighboring Kanem; forms major sub-Saharan trading state.
1735
John Harrison unveils his marine chronometer.

1750
Treaty of Madrid: agrees boundary between Spanish South American colonies and Brazil.

1717
Blackbeard begins plundering ships in the Caribbean.
1720
Qing oust Mongols from Tibet. Spanish acquire Texas.

North American colonies map ▶

1745
Stuart Jacobite rebellion aims to overthrow Hanoverians in Britain.
1747
Afghanistan kingdom established by Ahmad Khan Abdali. Yoruba tribe begins conquest of Dahomey (Benin).

1704
Opticks, written by Isaac Newton, exploring theories of light.
1707
Death of Aurangzeb heralds decline of Mughal India.

◀ Drawing of slave ship

1727
First coffee plantation in Brazil.
1728
Marathas defeat Nizam of Hyderabad, India. Vitus Bering begins Russian exploration of Alaska.

Lloyd's LIST

1748
Punjab invaded by Afghans. Peace of Aix-la-Chapelle: War of Austrian Succession ended.
1749
Rise to prominence of Mysore Kingdom in south India.

◀ Lloyd's list

▲ Lisbon earthquake

1755
The Lisbon earthquake, one of the deadliest in history: between 60,000 and 100,000 people killed.

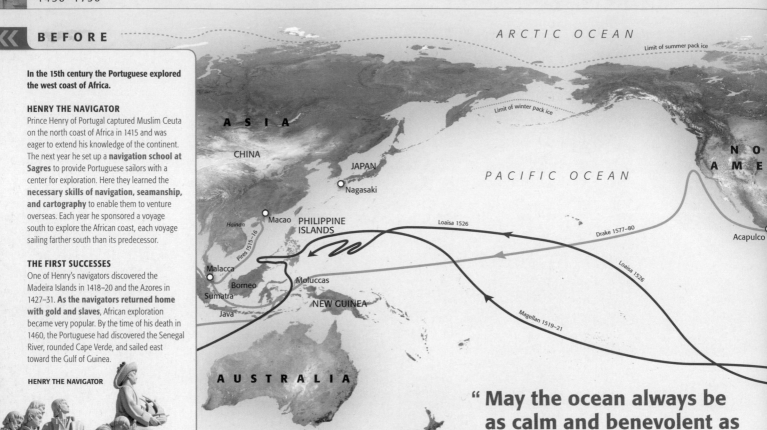

« BEFORE

In the 15th century the Portuguese explored the west coast of Africa.

HENRY THE NAVIGATOR

Prince Henry of Portugal captured Muslim Ceuta on the north coast of Africa in 1415 and was eager to extend his knowledge of the continent. The next year he set up a **navigation school at Sagres** to provide Portuguese sailors with a center for exploration. Here they learned the **necessary skills of navigation, seamanship, and cartography** to enable them to venture overseas. Each year he sponsored a voyage south to explore the African coast, each voyage sailing farther south than its predecessor.

THE FIRST SUCCESSES

One of Henry's navigators discovered the Madeira Islands in 1418–20 and the Azores in 1427–31. **As the navigators returned home with gold and slaves**, African exploration became very popular. By the time of his death in 1460, the Portuguese had discovered the Senegal River, rounded Cape Verde, and sailed east toward the Gulf of Guinea.

HENRY THE NAVIGATOR

ARCTIC OCEAN

Limit of summer pack ice

Limit of winter pack ice

ASIA

CHINA

JAPAN

Nagasaki

PACIFIC OCEAN

NO
AME

Macao

Hainan

PHILIPPINE ISLANDS

Pires 1515–16

Loaisa 1526

Drake 1577–80

Acapulco

Malacca

Borneo

Sumatra

Java

Moluccas

NEW GUINEA

Loaisa 1526

Magellan 1519–21

AUSTRALIA

Expedition routes
This map shows the major European ocean voyages of the 15th and 16th centuries. Each line color corresponds to the country of the explorer, whose name and expedition date appear above the line. Arrows indicate the direction of travel, and major ports or stopovers are indicated with white dots.

"**May the ocean always be as calm and benevolent as it is today**. In this hope I name it the **Pacific Ocean**."

FERDINAND MAGELLAN ON FIRST ENTERING THE PACIFIC OCEAN, NOVEMBER 27, 1520

Voyages of Discovery

In little over a century, European navigators left their continent and sailed the world, opening up new sea routes to India and the east. They discovered a continent previously unknown to them, and began a process that eventually resulted in the total European colonial and economic domination of the world.

PORTUGUESE EXPLORER (1480–1521)

FERDINAND MAGELLAN

Magellan was a Portuguese soldier and adventurer who had taken part in four expeditions to India and Malaya. He quarreled with the Portuguese king, Manuel I and left the country in 1514 to enter the service of Spain. In 1519 he proposed a voyage west to the Spice Islands, which promised great wealth to Spain if successful. Magellan set out in 1519 with five ships and about 260 men. He sailed south across the Atlantic, and in November 1520 through the straits that now bear his name and into the Pacific. He then crossed the ocean, the first European to do so, reaching the Philippines in April 1521, where he was killed in a local war. His deputy, Juan Sebastian del Cano, took charge, eventually returning to Spain in September 1522 with only one ship and 17 members of the crew.

At the start of the 15th century, European knowledge of the world was surprisingly limited. Sailors used world maps based on the cartography of Ptolemy, a Greek geographer who had died 13 centuries earlier, in 168 CE. Europe, the Mediterranean, and western Asia were reasonably well mapped, but Africa was vague in shape, as no one knew how far south it stretched, and the Americas were missing altogether. Poor ship design that restricted oceangoing voyages and primitive navigation instruments kept ships close to the coast. At best, navigators used dead reckoning—intelligent guesswork based on speed through the water, winds, and currents—to assess their location.

The development of the oceangoing caravel (see right) by the Portuguese and new navigation instruments transformed this situation. The magnetic compass, the astrolabe, which measured the height of the Sun at noon, and the cross-staff and quadrant, which measured the height of a star, all helped navigators determine their latitude, or how far north or south they were. Lack of accurate marine chronometers (see p.282) meant that longitude—distance east or west—was not accurately calculated until the mid-18th century.

New technology, new worlds

Armed with this new maritime technology, the Portuguese tentatively explored the coast of Africa. Diogo Cão sailed around the Gulf of Guinea and then headed south, exploring the Congo River before making his final landfall at Cape Cross in what is now Namibia in 1486. Two years later, Bartolomeu Dias rounded the Cape of Good Hope and sailed into the Indian Ocean, while in 1498 Vasco da Gama crossed the Indian Ocean to Calicut in southern India. These expeditions

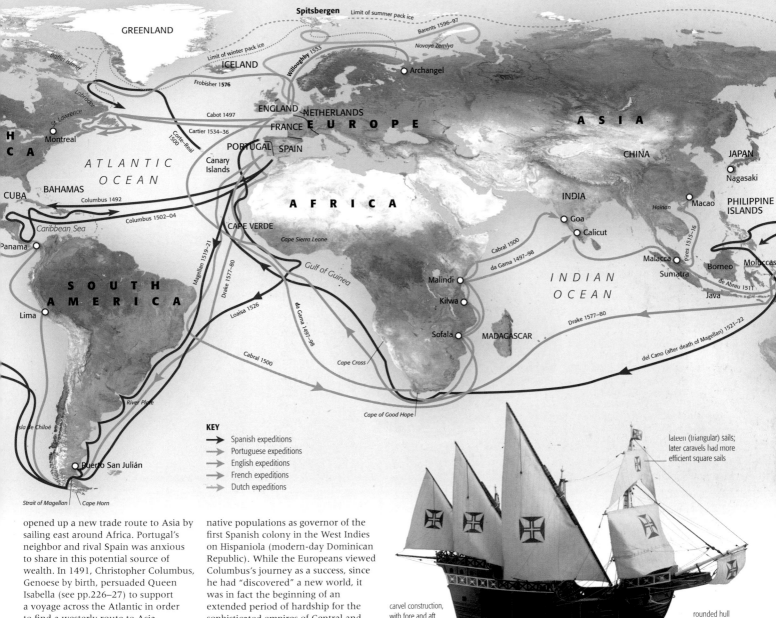

Spitsbergen — Limit of summer pack ice
GREENLAND
Barents 1596–97
Novaya Zemlya
Limit of winter pack ice
ICELAND
Archangel
Baffin Island
Frobisher 1576
Willoughby 1553
Labrador
Cabot 1497
ENGLAND NETHERLANDS
FRANCE EUROPE
Cartier 1534–36
ASIA
St Lawrence
Corte-Real 1500
Montreal
PORTUGAL SPAIN
ATLANTIC OCEAN
Canary Islands
CHINA
JAPAN
Nagasaki
CUBA BAHAMAS
Columbus 1492
AFRICA
INDIA
Hainan
Macao
PHILIPPINE ISLANDS
Columbus 1502–04
CAPE VERDE
Cape Sierra Leone
Goa
Calicut
Cabral 1500
Malacca
Pires 1515–16
Caribbean Sea
Panama
Magellan 1519–21
da Gama 1497–98
Malacca
Sumatra
Borneo
Moluccas
Gulf of Guinea
da Gama 1497–98
INDIAN OCEAN
de Abreu 1511
Java
SOUTH AMERICA
Drake 1577–80
Malindi
Lima
Loaisa 1526
Kilwa
Drake 1577–80
da Gama 1497–98
Cabral 1500
Sofala
MADAGASCAR
del Cano (after death of Magellan) 1521–22
River Plate
Cape Cross
Isla de Chiloé
Cape of Good Hope
Puerto San Julián
Strait of Magellan | Cape Horn

KEY
➤ Spanish expeditions
➤ Portuguese expeditions
➤ English expeditions
➤ French expeditions
➤ Dutch expeditions

opened up a new trade route to Asia by sailing east around Africa. Portugal's neighbor and rival Spain was anxious to share in this potential source of wealth. In 1491, Christopher Columbus, Genoese by birth, persuaded Queen Isabella (see pp.226–27) to support a voyage across the Atlantic in order to find a westerly route to Asia.

He set sail in 1492 with three ships, using dead reckoning to calculate his position. Like other navigators of his day, he knew that the world was round—it is a myth that the common belief of the time was that the world was flat—but accepted Ptolemy's incorrect calculation of its size. Thus when he stumbled upon the islands of the Caribbean (see pp.228–29) he assumed these were outlying islands of Asia. Three further voyages, in 1493–96, 1498–1500, and 1502–04, failed to convince him that he had found not Asia but a previously unknown continent—the Americas.

Columbus in context
Columbus has been much criticized in recent years both for his geographical ignorance and for his treatment of the

native populations as governor of the first Spanish colony in the West Indies on Hispaniola (modern-day Dominican Republic). While the Europeans viewed Columbus's journey as a success, since he had "discovered" a new world, it was in fact the beginning of an extended period of hardship for the sophisticated empires of Central and South America and the other peoples of the continent. However, had Columbus not made this first landing, another navigator would have done so within a few years. But he was first, and as a pioneer, he opened up the prospect of European expansion overseas.

Around the world
The desire to seek new trade routes to Asia continued to preoccupy European sailors and merchants. The Spanish explored a route to the west. In 1519 Ferdinand Magellan (see left) set out to sail to the rich Spice Islands (the Moluccas in modern-day Indonesia). In so doing he started a voyage that, after his death in 1521, was completed by his deputy, who, with the 17 surviving members of the crew, became the first Europeans to sail around the world.

lateen (triangular) sails; later caravels had more efficient square sails

carvel construction, with fore and aft planks flush to each other

rounded hull with high bow and stern

The caravel
The Portuguese voyages of the 15th century were made possible by the development of the caravel, so named because of its flush-planked carvel construction. The caravel was lighter than its predecessors and more seaworthy, enabling it to venture far from land. A small ship, only 60 ft (20 m) long, it carried a crew of about 25.

Both routes to Asia were arduous, so French and English navigators explored the coast of Canada hoping to find a northwest passage to Asia, a feat not achieved until the Norwegian Roald Amundsen completed the voyage in 1906 (see pp.320–21). English and Dutch navigators also sought a northeast passage around the top of Siberia—again, a feat not achieved until 1879 by Finn Nils Nordenskjöld.

AFTER ▶▶

Competing Spanish and Portuguese discoveries in the Americas and Asia created a clash between these two maritime nations.

TREATY OF TORDESILLAS
In 1494 Pope Alexander VI negotiated a treaty that **divided the world along a line** drawn south across the Atlantic Ocean: west of the line was Spanish, east was Portuguese. The treaty was useful when the Portuguese began to colonize Brazil, but problems arose in the Spice Islands of Southeast Asia. The treaty was vague about what happened on the other side of the world.

QUEEN OF SPAIN Born 1451 Died 1504

Isabella of Castile

"I... am ready to **pawn my jewels** to defray the expenses of it..."

ISABELLA TO COLUMBUS, SPEAKING ABOUT HIS PROPOSED VOYAGE TO ASIA, 1492

According to a contemporary chronicler, Isabella I of Spain was a neglected child: "The Queen, Our Lady, from childhood was without a father and we can even say a mother… She had work and cares, and an extreme lack of necessary things." Isabella's father, John II of Castile (a Spanish kingdom), died when she was three, at which point her depressed mother shut herself away. Her young brother died of a plaguelike illness in 1468, and her older half-brother, the mentally unstable Henry IV, perceived her as a threat. However, Isabella emerged from this Cinderella-like childhood an extremely strong-willed and intelligent young woman.

As a leading contender for the throne of Castile, Isabella attracted many suitors—including the king of Portugal and brothers of the kings of England and France—but she herself decided to marry Ferdinand of Aragon: "It has to be he and absolutely no other." In marrying the young prince of Aragon—whom she had yet to meet—17-year-old Isabella risked the wrath of Henry, who had not given his consent. But Isabella knew that this was the marriage most likely to bring her power. In 1469 they were married in the Spanish city of Valladolid, and for much of the next 10 years they fought for recognition of their right to become joint rulers of the unruly kingdom of Castile.

Love and war

In 1474 Henry died and civil war broke out. However, within a few years it was clear that Isabella and Ferdinand were winning on every front. By 1476 they had set up the *hermandad* ("brotherhood"), a network of local

Catholic New World
This 17th-century altarpiece from Guatemala reveals the impact of Spanish culture in the Americas. Isabella regarded it as her sacred duty to bring Christianity to her subjects in the New World.

Isabella the Catholic
Isabella's strong will helped bring about fundamental changes in Spain. Her reign led to the permanent unification of Spain (which had previously been a collection of kingdoms) and her decision to sponsor Christopher Columbus's journey to find a new route to Asia laid the groundwork for an era of global commerce and trade.

Fall of Granada
Isabella's greatest achievement was the conquest of Granada, the last Moorish kingdom in Spain. She and her husband are pictured (left) accepting the submission of their new Muslim subjects, but in practice, promises of religious toleration were not kept.

Having achieved so much for "God's cause," Isabella had time for other activities. She and Ferdinand agreed to sponsor the "enterprise of the Indies," the first transatlantic voyage of Christopher Columbus (see pp.228–29), which led to the development of a global Spanish empire (see pp.234–35).

Isabella's final years
In her final years, Isabella was distressed by a succession of family tragedies. She had five children: Isabella, John, Joanna, Maria, and Catherine. Both Isabella and Maria married into the Portuguese royal family, while John and Joanna married the daughter and son of the Habsburg Emperor Maximilian I. The first husband of Catherine was Arthur, Prince of Wales; the second, Henry VIII of England.

But Isabella's son and heir, John, died soon after his wedding, and this loss was followed by the death in childbirth of Isabella's eldest daughter, Isabella. Then, before he was two, her grandson Michael died in her arms. Since it was clear that the unhappy Joanna la loca ("the mad") had lost her reason, all hope for the future of the dynasty rested with Isabella and Ferdinand's Habsburg grandson, the future Holy Roman Emperor Charles V. It is thought that these events contributed to a decline in Isabella's health, and her death in 1504.

Family portrait
This painting in a Dominican monastery in Avila shows Isabella, Ferdinand, and their children John and Joanna at prayer before the image of the Madonna and Child.

militias that formed a basic police force, and eventually became the basis of a national Spanish army.

In 1477 Isabella and Ferdinand entered the city of Toledo in triumph—they were the unchallenged monarchs of Castile. Their partnership was carefully worked out. In keeping with their motto *"Tanto monta, monta tanto, Isabel como Fernando"* ("It's the same thing, Isabella is the same as Ferdinand"), they issued joint decrees and approved coins and stamps. Although Ferdinand's name preceded Isabella's on state documents, her coat of arms came first. They were a united front, fully supporting each other's decisions.

The Catholic Monarchs
Isabella may have viewed the turmoil of her childhood as a sign of God's displeasure with the weak rule of her half-brother Henry. Her sense of duty and passion for order and unity led to the establishment of the Spanish Inquisition in 1478. This was a court run by the Catholic Church with the aim of ensuring royal subjects remained faithful Christians. Within Isabella's own lifetime, this institution—whose first victims were Jews and conversos (Christians of Jewish ethnicity)—became a byword for cruelty and terror. By 1492, the year of the fall of Granada, those who died because of its denunciations may have exceeded ten thousand in number.

In 1480 Isabella and Ferdinand announced their intention to go to war against Granada, the last Moorish (Muslim) kingdom in Spain (see pp.174–75). In 1492, after being besieged for a year and a half, Granada surrendered. For this victory, Isabella and Ferdinand were congratulated by

the monarchs of Europe, and awarded the title of the "Catholic Monarchs" by the pope. In addition to forming the final episode in the centuries-long battle by the Christian church to reclaim the Iberian peninsula, Granada's conquest was widely seen as compensation for the loss of Constantinople to Muslim Ottoman Turks in 1453 (see pp.206–07).

New-found wealth
This 15th-century gold coin was minted in Seville with the images of both monarchs. Spain had access to vast amounts of silver and gold in the Americas.

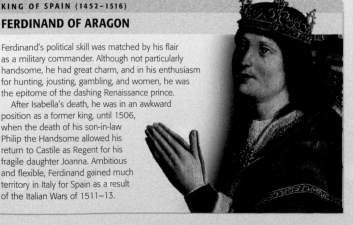

KING OF SPAIN (1452–1516)

FERDINAND OF ARAGON

Ferdinand's political skill was matched by his flair as a military commander. Although not particularly handsome, he had great charm, and in his enthusiasm for hunting, jousting, gambling, and women, he was the epitome of the dashing Renaissance prince.

After Isabella's death, he was in an awkward position as a former king, until 1506, when the death of his son-in-law Philip the Handsome allowed his return to Castile as Regent for his fragile daughter Joanna. Ambitious and flexible, Ferdinand gained much territory in Italy for Spain as a result of the Italian Wars of 1511–13.

TIMELINE

- **1451** Birth of Isabella, daughter of John II of Castile and Isabella of Portugal.
- **1452** Birth of Ferdinand II of Aragon.
- **1454** John II of Castile dies; Isabella's half-brother Henry IV accedes to the throne.
- **1468** Isabella's younger brother Alfonso dies.
- **1469** Isabella of Castile marries Ferdinand of Aragon.
- **1470** Birth of Isabella's eldest daughter, Isabella.
- **1474** Henry IV of Castile dies; Isabella and Ferdinand claim the throne.
- **1476** Isabella and Ferdinand set up the *hermandad*, a collection of local militias that act as a peacekeeping organization.
- **1478** Birth of Isabella and Ferdinand's son and heir, John; the Spanish Inquisition is established.
- **1479** A treaty with Portugal brings order to Castile; birth of Isabella and Ferdinand's daughter Joanna; Ferdinand inherits the throne of Aragon, thereby bringing two Spanish dynasties together under the same monarchs.
- **1480** Parliament confirms Isabella's succession as Queen of Castile; the monarchs announce their intention to go to war against Granada.
- **1481** Dominican priest Tomas de Torquemada is appointed by Isabella as Grand Inquisitor. As a result, treachery and heresy become indistinguishable in Spain, and nonconformists, Jews, and dissidents are rigorously persecuted. Torquemada is likely to have been the author of the infamous decree of 1492, which expelled the Jews from Spain.
- **1482** Birth of Isabella and Ferdinand's twin daughters, only one of whom (Maria) survives.
- **1485** Birth of Isabella and Ferdinand's youngest daughter Catherine.
- **1492** Fall of Granada, last Moorish kingdom in Spain; Ferdinand and Isabella agree to support the expedition of Christopher Columbus. Isabella gives him numerous entitlements to the new lands he discovers, which he compiles in his *Book of Privileges*.
- **1493** In the Papal Bull (a decree) *Inter Caetera*, Pope Alexander VI refers to the couple as *Reyes Catolicos* (The Catholic Monarchs).
- **1497** John marries Margaret of Austria; Joanna marries Philip of Flanders.
- **1498** John dies suddenly; young Isabella, Queen of Portugal, dies in childbirth.
- **1499** Isabella and Ferdinand's daughter Maria marries Manoel of Portugal.
- **1500** Death of Isabella and Ferdinand's grandson Michael; their youngest daughter Catherine (Catherine of Aragon) marries Prince Arthur of England.
- **1504** Isabella dies.

THE BOOK OF PRIVILEGES

Columbus lands in the Caribbean

The arrival of a small, Spanish-sponsored fleet on the Caribbean island of San Salvador was to have dramatic effects on both sides of the Atlantic Ocean. European explorers would be galvanized by the discovery of what eventually proved to be two whole new continents, while the native populations were about to enter a period of prolonged suffering and repression.

Christopher Columbus was born in Genoa around 1451, going to sea at an early age. For eight years he sought sponsors for a plan to sail west from Europe to eastern Asia and the island kingdom of Cipangu (Japan). By finding a direct sea route to Asia, he hoped to open the wealth of the region for European trade. He finally won backing from Isabella of Castille (see pp. 226–27) in 1491.

Columbus set off from the Spanish port of Palos on August 3, 1492. His fleet consisted of a three-masted cargo ship, the *Santa Maria*, carrying 40 men, the smaller *Pinta*, with 26 men, and the four-masted *Niña*, with 24 aboard. The fleet dropped anchor in the Canary Islands, southwest of Spain, for repairs, but on September 6 it finally resumed its journey across the Atlantic.

On the evening of October 11, 1492, Columbus, aboard the *Santa Maria*, thought he saw "a light to the west. It looked like a little wax candle bobbing up and down." Two hours after midnight, Rodrigo de Triana,

lookout on the *Pinta*, sighted land. Columbus had crossed the Atlantic.

He claimed the island he had found for Spain, naming it San Salvador, and traded with the Arawak natives (calling them "Indians," in the belief that he was off the coast of Asia). The island's true location is unclear—for years, it was assumed to be present-day San Salvador in the Bahamas, but in 1986 a team from the US National Geographical Society judged it must have been Samana Cay, 78 miles (125 km) southeast, and a later study concluded it was probably Grand Turk, 200 miles (320 km) farther southeast.

On October 14, Columbus set off in search of gold. He explored three small islands before sailing to Cuba, and then to Hispaniola (Dominican Republic and Haiti), where he established the first European transatlantic settlement since the Vikings (see pp. 202–203), 500 years earlier. On January 16, 1493, he set off back to Spain, convinced that he had sailed to Asia and back.

Columbus makes landfall
Columbus was captivated by the island he named San Salvador (meaning "Saint Savior"). "Everything is green and the vegetation is like that in Andalusia in April." He did not, however, discover the gold he sought, nor did he realize that this was not an outlying island of Asia, but part of a new continent—the Americas.

" …in honor of **God** who guided us and **saved us from many perils.**"

COLUMBUS'S WORDS AFTER CLAIMING SAN SALVADOR FOR SPAIN, OCTOBER 12, 1492

On the eve of European conquest, three highly advanced civilizations occupied much of Central and South America.

MAYANS

The Mayan states ◀◀ 140–41 clustered around the Yucatán Peninsula in what is now southeast Mexico. All **16 states were independent**, and in 1480 there was a major war for regional supremacy. The lack of a single ruler made these states more difficult to conquer.

AZTECS

The Aztec Empire ◀◀ 210–13 was based around the city of Tenochtitlán (on the site of present-day Mexico City). Under Itzcóatl (reigned 1428–40) and his successors, the empire expanded rapidly, so that by the reign of Moctezuma II (1502–20), **over 10 million people** were subject to Aztec rule, which stretched from the Caribbean across the valley of Mexico. Central to their belief system was the need to provide human sacrifices for their sun god Huitzilopochtli.

15th CENTURY MAP OF TENOCHTITLÁN

INCAS

During the reigns of Pachacuti (1438–71) and his son Tupac Yupanqui (1471–93), the Inca empire, established around 1230 in the South American Andes, grew rapidly ◀◀ 210–15. By 1525, the empire was at its greatest extent, stretching from modern-day Ecuador in the north to Chile in the south. The empire was **rich in gold** and had a 12,500-mile (20,000-km) network of roads.

GOLD INCA KNIFE

> "Shipmates and friends. There lies **the hard way**, leading to Peru and wealth."
>
> FRANCISCO PIZARRO, ON GORGONA ISLAND OFF THE PACIFIC COAST OF COLOMBIA, 1526

Contact Americas

Forty years after Columbus first set foot in the Americas, the Spanish had built a vast empire in North, Central, and South America. With remarkable ingenuity and treachery, and considerable bravery, two small bands of soldiers felled two mighty empires and initiated three centuries of Spanish rule.

CONQVISTA DE MEXICO POR CORTES. AC.7

The Spanish came to the Americas for a variety of reasons. They sought wealth in the form of gold, spices, and other goods. They came to claim land for their king, and saw the locals as inferiors to be subdued and exploited. They came to convert, for in their eyes this was a godless continent. And they came for adventure—Vasco de Balboa was an unsuccessful pig breeder, Hernán Cortés a failed law student—but the Americas gave men such as these a chance of gold and glory. Initial conquest and settlement was confined to the Caribbean islands. The first permanent mainland settlements were founded from 1510 and included Vasco de Balboa, soon to become the first European to see the Pacific, and Francisco Pizarro. Balboa found gold, and learned of a rich land across the Pacific called Birú (Peru). By now, the Spanish were realizing that this new world was rich, but its wealth was not to be taken easily. In 1518 the Spanish governor of Cuba sent 11 ships under the command of Cortés to explore the coast of the Yucatán peninsula for gold. Cortés learned of a great empire inland, and on August 16, 1519 set out from the Mexican coast with 15 horsemen, 400 soldiers, and a few hundred porters. Using local guides and interpreters, he arrived at Tlaxacala, an independent city and enemy of the Aztec empire. With the Tlaxacalan army as willing allies, he approached the Aztec capital, Tenochtitlán, in November 1519.

▷ **Spanish stronghold**
The Spanish fort of San Lorenzo del Chagres was built on the Caribbean coast of Panama and guarded the route across the isthmus to the Pacific Ocean.

The Aztec emperor Moctezuma was fearful of the Spanish, aware of their military reputation and ruthlessness. He placated them with gifts and housed them in a palace in his island capital. The Spanish were also wary, as they were now effectively prisoners. Cortés launched the desperate scheme of taking Moctezuma prisoner, though

this simply encouraged the Aztecs who were hostile to the Spanish presence to chose another leader.

Tenochtitlán began its descent into chaos when Cortés's soldiers massacred a large number of young Aztec nobles taking part in a festival of feasting and dancing. As the city rebelled, Moctezuma proved powerless to calm the Aztecs; he was stoned by his own people and later died of his wounds. Cortés fought his way out of the city, losing three-quarters of his men in the disastrous "Night of Sorrows." However, the Aztecs failed to deliver the death blow to Cortés's bedraggled survivors. Boosted by large numbers of new soldiers attracted by rumors of huge wealth, and by a vast auxiliary army of native peoples anxious to throw off the yoke of Aztec dominance, Cortés undertook a second, and this time definitive, siege of Tenochtitlán, forcing the Aztecs into a final surrender after a desperate struggle in August 1521. While Cortés set about organizing his new territory, others

Inca Gold Armlets
Gold jewelry in the Inca empire was a sign of wealth and power. Gold was also used for ceremonial items.

◁ **The capture of Tenochtitlán**
The destruction of the Aztec capital by Cortés in 1521 is shown in this somewhat fanciful late 18th-century painting by an unknown Spanish artist. The splendor of the city on its island in Lake Texcoco is clear, though not, perhaps, the brutality of the conquest.

▽ **Inca storehouses**
The Incas were great stonemasons, building depots to store their harvested crops, and roadside hostels for royal messengers and other travelers.

were exploring to the south. Birú excited the Spanish, who sent an expedition along the Pacific coast in 1522 that found no gold but confirmed reports of a rich empire inland. Further expeditions continued to map the coast, and two of these were led by Francisco Pizarro, an illiterate but brave 51-year-old soldier.

In 1527 Pizarro landed at Tumbes, an Inca outpost (see pp.210–13), trading goods for gold, silver, jewels, and cloth. With this treasure, he returned via Panama to Spain and sought permission to mount an armed expedition.

By 1531 he was back with three ships and 180 men. Reaching Tumbes, he found it ruined by a civil war between Atahuallpa (see right) and his brother Huáscar for control of the Inca empire. Learning that Atahuallpa and his army were across the mountains at Cajamarca, Pizarro, with his 106 footsoldiers and 62 horsemen, set out on a trek to meet Atahuallpa. They were received by an imperial envoy bearing gifts from the emperor, who was camped with his army outside the city. Pizarro lured Atahuallpa into Cajamarca, took him hostage, and was offered an enormous ransom. With the treasure amassed by July 1533, and panicked at rumors of an Inca counterattack to liberate Atahuallpa, Pizarro and his officers executed the emperor. The Spanish then marched on the capital, Cuzco, and seized control of the entire Inca empire.

An uneven struggle

Both Aztec and Inca empires fell to remarkably small Spanish armies. But the Spanish had guns, horses, and armor, and ruthlessly exploited their opponents' weakest points: the repressive rule of the Aztecs over their subject peoples, and the Inca civil war. From a strategic point of view, they

recognized that both empires were highly centralized states ruled over by all-powerful emperors. Capture the emperor and the state was paralyzed. Following the conquest, the Spanish exploited the religion of the Aztecs, using their desire for captured enemies to sacrifice to turn them into allies on the battlefield. Pizarro was also helped by the superb Inca road network that enabled his troops to cross otherwise inaccessible terrain. Perhaps most importantly, though, the Spanish brought with them diseases to which the Americans had no resistance. Diseases decimated local populations as the Spanish took control of their lands. In everything but numbers, the Spanish had the advantage and the luck.

AFTER »

TOBACCO

« BEFORE

LLAMAS IN PERU

Until the end of the 15th century, the New World and Old World had entirely separate agricultures, and most of the serious diseases of Europe and Asia had not crossed the Atlantic.

DOMESTICATED CROPS

New World domesticated crops—those whose growth was controlled by farmers—included **corn, tobacco, cocoa, and cotton**. The Old World was equally productive, but apart from cotton it shared few crop types with the Americas. Among its most important crops were **wheat, rice, and tea**.

DOMESTIC ANIMALS

Europe and Asia had an abundance of domesticated animals—such as **horses, cattle, goats, sheep, chickens, and pigs**—but in the pre-Columbian Americas the only equivalents were **turkeys, guinea pigs, dogs, alpacas, and llamas**. The Americas, however, had an incredible range of wild animals, hence much meat in the diet was obtained through hunting and fishing.

DISEASE

Before Columbus, the Americas had enjoyed a long period of population growth. Nevertheless, **mortality rates remained high** from diseases such as tuberculosis, and waterborne parasites caused illness. The Europeans suffered similarly, but **they went on to export some of their deadly diseases**.

Columbus's very first voyage in 1492 (see pp.228–29) introduced new species to the Americas—he brought 28 horses, three mules, and an assortment of sheep, goats, cattle, chickens, dogs, and cats. Apart from the dogs, these were all unfamiliar creatures to the indigenous Americans, but Spanish colonization in the 16th century quickly expanded stock holdings. The numbers of domesticated animals imported by Europeans grew at different rates depending on the species, and brought different social effects. Sheep, goats, pigs, and chickens bred rapidly (the Europeans found excellent grazing land), and became useful not only as sustenance for the colonists, but also as foods to trade with native Americans for fruits and vegetables. Geographically, grazing animals also spread quickly—by 1519 sheep flocks could be found from northern South America up to the southwestern corner of what is today the United States.

Horses and cattle

Horse and cattle numbers grew more slowly because of the animals' longer breeding cycles and smaller numbers of offspring. Nevertheless, during the 16th century they spread through Peru and Chile and reached northward through New Spain, which covered Central America and much of southern North America. Horses were central to the early Spanish military conquests— many native Americans were at first terrified of horses, believing them to be divine creatures—but they also introduced effective transportation, providing the future means for a wider

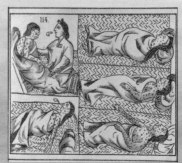

Deadly trade
An early colonial artwork shows the lethal effect of smallpox on the native Americans. The first major smallpox outbreak in the Americas occurred between 1520–24, but epidemics returned regularly until the late 1800s.

The Great Exchange

Columbus's arrival in the Americas in 1492 began one of the greatest revolutions in global food habits ever seen. Plants and animals previously separated by some 3,000–4,000 miles (5,000–6,000 km) of ocean would now be exchanged.

European colonization of North America. American Indians later fueled the growth of cattle herds with a newly acquired love of beef and leather.

Transatlantic foods

The "exchange" of animal foods between the Old and New Worlds was mainly one-sided, with Europe importing its domesticated animals into the Americas. The exchange of plant life, by contrast, ran both ways. The European colonists attempted to grow all the traditional Old World Crops in the Americas, with sugar cane, bananas, and lemons, for example, all doing well in the tropical climate. Grain crops such as wheat grew better in mountainous regions and later found perfect growing conditions in the temperate plains of North America. By the end of the 16th century, sugar cane was growing in huge amounts in the Caribbean, Peru, Brazil, and Mexico, with entire forests being cleared for its growth. Exported in the opposite direction were crops that changed the diets of much of Europe

and Asia, including corn, beans, potatoes, and tobacco. Potatoes were introduced across Europe between 1570 and 1600, and two centuries later they would be one of the most important crops of the Old World, alongside corn. Cacao (a base ingredient of chocolate) transformed European confectionery, while tobacco introduced a whole new pastime. Tomatoes became staples of Mediterranean cooking, while chili peppers introduced new spices to Old World palates.

Destruction and disease

This great exchange steadily transformed the world's diets, but also had dramatic human consequences. Along with food, the Europeans also brought diseases that devastated indigenous populations, principally smallpox, measles, bubonic plague,

New cuisine
This Italian cookbook from 1622 was an effort to teach Italians how to cook the exotic foods arriving from the Americas, such as tomatoes.

Potatoes and wheat
Wheat, an Old World crop, grows alongside potatoes in a hilly region of South America. Wheat needs cooler temperatures to grow, and the first attempts to grow the plants in the American tropics largely failed.

typhoid fever, scarlet fever, cholera, whooping cough, diphtheria, mumps, and (from Africa) malaria and yellow fever. The only major disease that possibly traveled in the opposite direction was syphilis, although many experts dispute its origins.

Compounding the horrors of disease were the social effects of Old World agriculture in a New World setting. Local communities were displaced to make room for grazing cattle, or were forced to labor on farms and plantations. New types of weeds choked native plants. Serious overgrazing problems occurred in places such as New Spain, with large areas turned practically to desert, having been stripped of vegetation and suffering from soil erosion. For better or worse, the New World had imported much more than just plants and animals.

The Great Exchange had far-reaching implications across the world, irrevocably changing the global ecosystem.

EXPORT OF TEA
Tea was first imported to the Dutch settlement of New Amsterdam in North America in 1650, and during the second half of the 17th century its popularity spread along the eastern seaboard. By the 19th century, **tea clippers were making regular tea runs from Europe** to Boston, New York, and Philadelphia.

TEA CLIPPER

CHANGED LIVES
In the late 1400s the native population of North and South America numbered around 40 million, but by the late 1700s that **figure had fallen by 70–90 percent**, mainly because of European-introduced diseases. The consequent collapse of the local workforce in the Americas contributed to the creation of the **transatlantic slave trade**, in which millions of Africans were forcibly shipped to the Americas to live and work on plantations **280–81 ≫**

Plains horses
The introduction of horses had a profound effect on the history of the Americas. Horses had existed on these continents previously, but were hunted to extinction by 7000 BCE. Once American Indian nations of the plains (stretching from the Rocky Mountains to the Mississippi River) mastered the use of the horse, it transformed their way of life. They were now able to travel faster and farther than ever before, and their hunting efficiency increased exponentially.

EARLY SILVER

Silver is documented as being used as far back as the 3rd millennium BCE in the Middle East. It became the **most common coinage metal in Europe** from the 5th century BCE onward. Ironically, although the pre-Columbian civilizations of the Americas **‹‹ 210–13** had silver, it was cacao beans and spiny oyster shells that were used as payment. Silver was mainly used to make jewelry.

PLUNDERING THE NEW WORLD

Imports from America included pearls, sugar, dyestuffs, and cowhide, but gold and silver were most highly prized. It was the **quest for gold and silver** that drove the Conquistadors and the early colonial ventures **‹‹ 230–31**. Gold and silver were plundered during the conquest. At first soldiers seized or bartered objects belonging to the native Americans. When these supplies were exhausted, gold was prospected by natives washing out surface gold from stream beds. Silver, however, required mining.

Spanish Silver

From the 1540s onward, the Spanish New World was shaped by the discovery, exploitation, and trading of silver around the world. The steady stream of silver into the Empire's coffers allowed Spain to become the superpower of its day, producing such imperial adventures as the Great Armada of 1588.

The discovery of silver at Potosí (present-day Bolivia) in April 1545 was not the first time the Spanish colonialists had encountered this precious metal. It was already being mined in the arid hills of New Spain (present-day Mexico), and in Peruvian mountain sites previously exploited by the Incas. In 1540, Spaniards began mining silver at Porco, located like Potosí to the southeast of Lake Titicaca. But five years later, the discovery of an entire mountain of silver ore (the biggest single concentration of this precious metal ever found) changed everything. Potosí quickly sprawled into a shanty village, growing in the next century to become the largest city in the New World with a population between 100,000 and 160,000. A royal

mint, established there in 1585, still stands today and, at some 13,600 ft (4,150 m) above sea level, Potosí remains the highest human habitation in the Americas.

Real exploitation of the Potosí mines took off around 1560 when a new and more productive method of refining silver came into use. The new process required mercury, for which the main source was the Almadén mines in Spain, but it yielded more silver than traditional smelting, and made it worthwhile to extract lower-grade, less concentrated seams of ore. The mercury was imported in leather

Mestizo madonna
Catholic veneration of the Virgin Mary, adopted by Spanish American mestizo society (of mixed native American and European descent), produced this icon.

bags from Spain and became an important trade in itself. Silver mining also boosted the demand for supplies of beef, leather, and tallow candles. Mules were used to carry supplies to the mines and bring back silver, so ranching and mining grew together.

Hard labor was soon in great demand, driving the import of African slaves (see pp.280–81). As both Mexico and Peru became wealthy from their mineral resources, the numbers of preyed on by privateers, or swept under in storms, but the impact on the Spanish Crown was relatively light and the *flota* continued to ensure the regular supply of silver and the royal share, the *quinto real* (the royal fifth). From the 1580s Philip II could expect two to three million ducats a year from the treasure fleets, and this flow of coins gave him the freedom to make his audacious attacks on other European powers (see pp.272–73).

The accountants take over
It was not just the sailors who ensured the silver took a secure route, but also the civil servants. They ran an extensive and accountable system of bureaucratic government that was set up to replace the violent, quarrelsome, and independent-minded Conquistadors. The Council of the

Silver mining
The conical mountain of Cerro Potosí became the chief source of the Spanish Empire's dazzling wealth after the discovery of silver there in 1545. The huge outcrop of silver ore was soon honeycombed with mine workings, as shown in this engraving from the 18th century.

slaves increased—imported for the mining industry, and to work as servants. Many native Americans were used as forced labor, but others were paid as skilled craftsmen to produce fabulous silverwork.

The first transatlantic convoys
From 1503 to 1660 some 16,000 tons of silver were shipped to Seville (compared with 185 tons of gold), tripling the existing silver resources of Europe. Seville was the "mistress" port, enjoying a monopoly on all these precious cargoes until 1680. Each *flota* (a convoy escorted by armed galleons) sailed from Vera Cruz, Cartagena, and Nombre de Díos to Seville over two months. The system worked—there were only two occasions when whole convoys were intercepted and defeated (once in 1628 by Dutchman Piet Heyn and once by the English Admiral Robert Blake in 1657). Individual galleons, so large and laden with bullion and guns, were often wrecked by poor navigation,

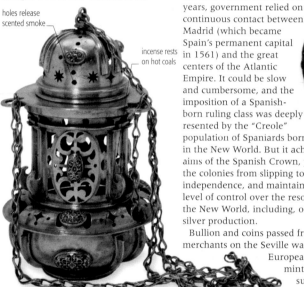

holes release scented smoke

incense rests on hot coals

Censer
An elaborate silver church censer from about 1630, suspended by chains and used for burning incense in Catholic ceremonies, shows the direct link between the prosperity of Spanish–American society and silver production.

chain to swing censer back and forth

> "The last load of silver… arrived **just in time** to pay the German infantry and cavalry we are recruiting."
> LETTER FROM FRANCISCO DE ERASO, FINANCIAL ADVISOR OF EMPEROR CHARLES V, 1558

The mistress port
Seville was already a thriving trading port when, in 1503, it was given a monopoly on silver brought back by the fleets from Mexico and Peru. Between 1516 and 1525, 499 ships left Seville port for the Indies.

Indies, established in Spain from 1522, was charged with the business of the new Imperial territories, presenting reports and policy documents to the King, and acting as the link between Spain and the administrators in the Americas. In order to maintain crown control of the new colonies, all the major posts in the colonial administration, from the Viceroys of New Spain (Mexico) and Peru, from judges to senior churchmen, were either fixed-term appointments or always chosen from the Spanish elites—never from those already in the New World. For the next 200 years, government relied on continuous contact between Madrid (which became Spain's permanent capital in 1561) and the great centers of the Atlantic Empire. It could be slow and cumbersome, and the imposition of a Spanish-born ruling class was deeply resented by the "Creole" population of Spaniards born and bred in the New World. But it achieved the aims of the Spanish Crown, preventing the colonies from slipping toward independence, and maintaining a high level of control over the resources of the New World, including, of course, silver production.

Bullion and coins passed from silver merchants on the Seville waterfront to European royal mints, bankers such as the Fuggers and

Philip II
Spain's King Philip II was a bureaucratic ruler, issuing decrees, laws, and rules from his fortress-monastery El Escorial. He relied greatly on advisers and officials to run both his government and his armies.

the Genoese, and the newly created bourses in Antwerp and Bruges (see pp.276–77). In exchange came weapons, powder, and troops. Even Elizabeth I (see pp.260–61) and the merchants of England sought to ensure their share of the treasure through loans. The silver trail stretched east via Italy to the Eastern Mediterranean, and across Persia and India into East Asia, where it was the one commodity in steady and undiminishing demand from Europe in exchange for spices, silks, and Chinese porcelain. Silver, in effect, became the foundation of a global economy.

AFTER

The influx of Europeans had a lasting effect on the American continents. It was over 300 years before the emigrants shook off their colonial shackles.

REVOLUTIONARY TIMES
Spanish and Portuguese rule in South America began to crumble during the Napoleonic Wars of the early 1800s **306–07 》**. Napoleon's invasion of the Iberian peninsula **304–05 》** undermined Spain's power and inspired

independence movements and revolutionaries. This led to the Spanish–American Wars of Independence **318–19 》** and the Mexican Revolution.

HYBRID CULTURE
Modern festivals such as the *Día de los Muertos* or "Day of the Dead" are a living reminder of how Spanish Catholicism was bolted onto earlier native traditions to create a vibrant and unique celebration.

DAY OF THE DEAD ARTWORK

The **Pilgrim Fathers**

The arrival of 102 settlers in Plymouth, Massachusetts on December 11, 1620 is one of the legendary stories of US history. These men, women, and children are lauded as the Pilgrim Fathers, the founders of what became the United States. Yet they were by no means the first Europeans to settle in the country.

« BEFORE

The first Europeans to visit America were adventurers rather than settlers.

ALGONQUIN INDIANS

FRENCH CANADA
Frenchman **Jacques Cartier** explored the St. Lawrence River from 1535 to 1542, and renamed Hochelaga, Mont Réal (Montreal). Fishermen and fur traders followed.

HOCHELAGA

Permanent French settlers arrived later–after the foundation of Québec in 1608.

SURVIVAL TECHNIQUES
To survive in this **new and hostile environment**, the French formed alliances with local tribes, notably the Algonquin Indians. The Iroquois tribe later became allies of the British.

In the century after Columbus arrived in the Americas (see pp.228–29), European contact with North America was remarkably limited. The Spanish, obsessed with gold and conquest, concentrated on exploiting the wealthy empires of Central and South America. To the north, the French explored the rich fishing and fur-trapping regions of the St. Lawrence River. Those European navigators who did visit America were more concerned with finding a route around it to Asia than exploring the continent itself.

While the Spanish established bases to protect their bullion fleets, such as St. Augustine in Florida, and the French traded in Canada to the north, it was the English who first attempted colonization of the eastern seaboard. In 1584 the English adventurer Sir Walter Raleigh established a settlement on Roanoke Island, but lacked the resources to sustain it. The settlement is believed to have been destroyed by the local Croatoan Indians in 1590. By then the defeat of the Spanish Armada in 1588 (see pp. 260–61) gave the English the incentive to attempt to intervene in the relatively undefended and undercolonized continent of North America. In 1607 the Virginia Company of London took advantage of this, and set up a colony in Jamestown, Virginia.

The Pilgrims
The men and women who settled Jamestown came to acquire land and hopefully wealth. Those that landed at New Plymouth in 1620 came to escape religious persecution in Europe. Often described as Puritans, they were more accurately religious dissenters who had left England for the Netherlands in 1608, but then decided to build their own society in a new land. Armed with a Virginia Company land grant, they set sail in the *Mayflower*. After a two-month voyage, they arrived in the New

1630, Catholics in Maryland in 1634, religious freethinkers in Rhode Island in 1636, and Quakers in Pennsylvania in 1682. Other colonies, notably the Carolinas, were given by the English king to supportive noblemen.

Dutch and Swedish trading companies also joined the colonial scramble. The Dutch West India Company, started in 1621, established Fort Orange (present-day Albany) on the Hudson River in 1623. It then purchased Manhattan from the native Canarsees for 40 guilders in 1626. Farther south, the Swedish West Indian Company set up New Sweden on the Delaware in 1638. The Dutch ended Swedish rule in 1655, but were then conquered by the British in 1664. English rule thus stretched the length of the east coast, from New England in the north to the Carolinas and, in 1724, Georgia in the south.

Labor and work

The English saw their colonies as "transplantations" of English society to a "New World"—the word "plantation" was used to describe both Jamestown and Plymouth—and made no attempt to meet their neighbors. The English colonists preferred to create closed, self-sufficient communities. When their efforts failed, as they often did, the settlers seldom conciliated the natives, but instead tried to defeat, destroy, or drive them away. To the English, the native American was an obstacle to be overcome, not a valuable resource to be exploited.

This proved a problem as the colonies grew in strength. Those in the north became successful merchant communities, where farming was for food, not export, and so had little need for local labor. Those in the south, however, required workers. The growing of tobacco and other export crops led to the development of large farming estates. These were worked first by white indentured servants from England, but then increasingly by African slaves (see pp.280–81), the first 20 of whom arrived on a Dutch ship in Jamestown in 1619.

The Mayflower
This painting shows the 12-year-old *Mayflower* in Delft Harbor at the start of its voyage to the Americas. It was a merchant ship with a crew of 25–30, and was previously used to transport wine.

Plymouth area. A year later, the settlers celebrated their first successful harvest with a dinner, an event still celebrated every November as Thanksgiving.

The settlers, who called themselves "Saints" or "Strangers" depending on their religious beliefs—the name "Pilgrims" was applied later—received help initially from two American Indians, Samoset and Tisquantum (Squanto), who spoke English as well as their native language, Algonquin. Indeed, Squanto had been taken to England in 1605 by an English seafarer and stayed for nine years. The Pilgrims were not the first Europeans to settle live in the area, as the seaboard was well known to English fishermen from the early 1500s, many of them wintering on its sheltered coast and gathering stocks of food for the journey home.

Religion and trade

Many English colonies on the eastern seaboard were religious in origin: Puritans settled in Massachusetts in

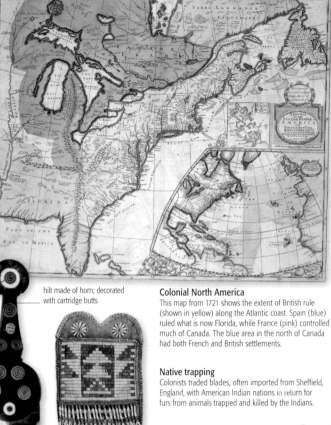

Colonial North America
This map from 1721 shows the extent of British rule (shown in yellow) along the Atlantic coast. Spain (blue) ruled what is now Florida, while France (pink) controlled much of Canada. The blue area in the north of Canada had both French and British settlements.

Native trapping
Colonists traded blades, often imported from Sheffield, England, with American Indian nations in return for furs from animals trapped and killed by the Indians.

hilt made of horn; decorated with cartridge butts

steel blade

animal skin sheath decorated with porcupine quillwork

Pilgrim housing
This reconstruction of the Plymouth settlement shows how the settlers built their homes: a simple wooden frame covered with wood slats and roofed with thatch kept out the worst of the elements.

Inside a Pilgrim house
The furniture was made from local wood, the curtains and bedding spun from homegrown flax or wool. There were no luxuries—anything that the settlers could not make, they did without.

AFTER »

Settlers started to object to being ruled from overseas without having any rights.

COLONIAL RULE
By 1750 most of the **13 colonies** were governed in much the same way. Each had a local assembly—Rhode Island's

COLONY ASSEMBLY MEETING HOUSE

met in the Meeting House in Newport (above right)—and a governor appointed or approved by the monarch. Each colony made its own laws and was **internally self-governing**. They were therefore relatively independent, with political and social institutions that differed quite markedly from those in Britain.

IMPERIAL RULE
Colonies were **subject to the British parliament and government**, which regulated their trade and currency to prevent them from competing with British industries. When in 1765 the British government began to levy direct taxes on the colonies to pay for its recent colonial wars, the colonists strongly objected to paying without having proper representation in the British Parliament. This was one of the **major causes of the American Revolution 298–99 »**.

Spain, Portugal, and France were nations under the rule of autocratic monarchs and their courtiers. Any overseas trade was firmly tied to royal finances.

The Portuguese established the pattern for empire-building: within 15 years of their arrival in the Indian Ocean in the 1480s, they had destroyed Arab naval power. Portugal had limited population and natural resources, but a wealth of nautical and navigational expertise. By forging an empire, it could tap into the lucrative Asian spice trade, giving it greater financial security. Bases at Malacca, Ormuz, and Goa in the Indian Ocean, established by Portuguese navy general Afonso da Albuquerque, ensured control of the Persian Gulf and major spice trade routes to the east. Macau, in Southern China, followed in 1517, and by the 1560s, Portugal imported 50 percent of Europe's spice supply and 75 percent of its pepper. At the same time, the Portuguese were importing the first African slaves to Brazil (see pp.280–81), ensuring that the colony became the world's largest sugar producer.

Between 1580 and 1640, Portugal and Spain operated their empires in parallel under the king of Spain. Spain's trade bureaucracy ensured that the monarch received 20 percent of all precious metals mined in the New World, in exchange for protective convoys. New colonies in the Philippines ensured a transit point between America and China, while Portugal helped Spain dominate East Asian trade, carrying gold and silver to China and bringing back silk via the Pacific and Atlantic oceans.

It was the mercantile commercial philosophy of the French Richelieu and later Colbert that drove France's

> " Let it be known that if you are **strong in ships** the commerce of **the Indies is yours**."
>
> FRANCISCO DE ALMEIDA, FIRST PORTUGUESE VICEROY OF INDIA, c. 1507

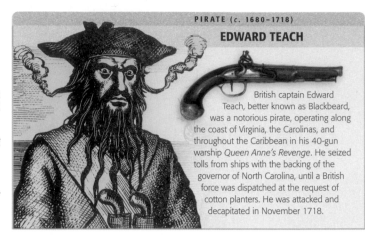

PIRATE (c. 1680–1718)

EDWARD TEACH

British captain Edward Teach, better known as Blackbeard, was a notorious pirate, operating along the coast of Virginia, the Carolinas, and throughout the Caribbean in his 40-gun warship *Queen Anne's Revenge*. He seized tolls from ships with the backing of the governor of North Carolina, until a British force was dispatched at the request of cotton planters. He was attacked and decapitated in November 1718.

colonial ambitions under Louis XIV (see pp.278–79). France's empire was a state creation, and at first excited little enthusiasm among the French merchant classes. One notable exception was the fur trade created in New France (Canada), along the trading network around the Great Lakes.

Trade for France's rulers, as for Spain's, meant reaping the benefits of colonial resources in order to safeguard a position in Europe. In both countries, the interests of merchants themselves came a poor second.

Empires of merchants

Traders and adventurers were at the forefront of England and Holland's "private-enterprise" empires. Both

Wampum fur trade belt
Belts of small seashells, called wampums, were made by Iroquois natives along the New England coast. Dutch traders used wampum beads as currency in the fur trade with the Iroquois from the early 1600s.

Trade and Empire

Between the late 15th and 18th centuries, many European nations developed large trading empires stretching to Africa, Asia, and the Americas. Imperial growth tended to follow one of two patterns—centralized, bureaucratic, and monarchical, or mercantile and occasionally chaotic.

BEFORE

Advances in navigation opened new doors.

EXIT THE DRAGON

In 1405–33, seven major Chinese naval expeditions explored and traded across the oceans as far west as Africa. Chinese trade and empire could have been carried farther, but the project was abandoned—largely due to imperial mistrust of foreigners.

MARINER'S MIRROUR 1588

NAVIGATION AIDS

From the 15th century onward, improvements to maps and navigation manuals allowed European sailors to venture across the world's oceans. *Mariner's Mirrour* was the first book to show standardized symbols for buoys, channels, safe anchorages, and submerged rocks.

were helped by the establishment of banks, bourses, and joint-stock companies (see pp.276–77), and particularly the East India Companies. Shareholders accepted the need for private defense forces, navies, and fortifications to safeguard their commercial interests, but they were not interested in ruling subject peoples.

With the focus on commerce rather than empire, the Dutch built up the most extensive trade network of any European power, including a toehold in Japan. Ships of the Dutch West India Company spurred the Caribbean sugar plantations, and carried the first slaves to the tobacco plantations of Virginia (see pp.280–81).

England was another latecomer to empire-building, content to harass and plunder Spanish convoys, but somewhat overshadowed by the Dutch. England's East India Company was founded two years before the Dutch, but its less sophisticated financial system and preoccupation with internal affairs gave the Dutch a better start. This changed around the end of the 17th century. New Navigation Acts set out a framework for colonial trade and monopolies, the Hudson's Bay Company traded out of Canada, and the 1715 Treaty of Utrecht gave England a monopoly on supplying slaves to the Spanish American empire. As a result, English foreign trade doubled by 1780.

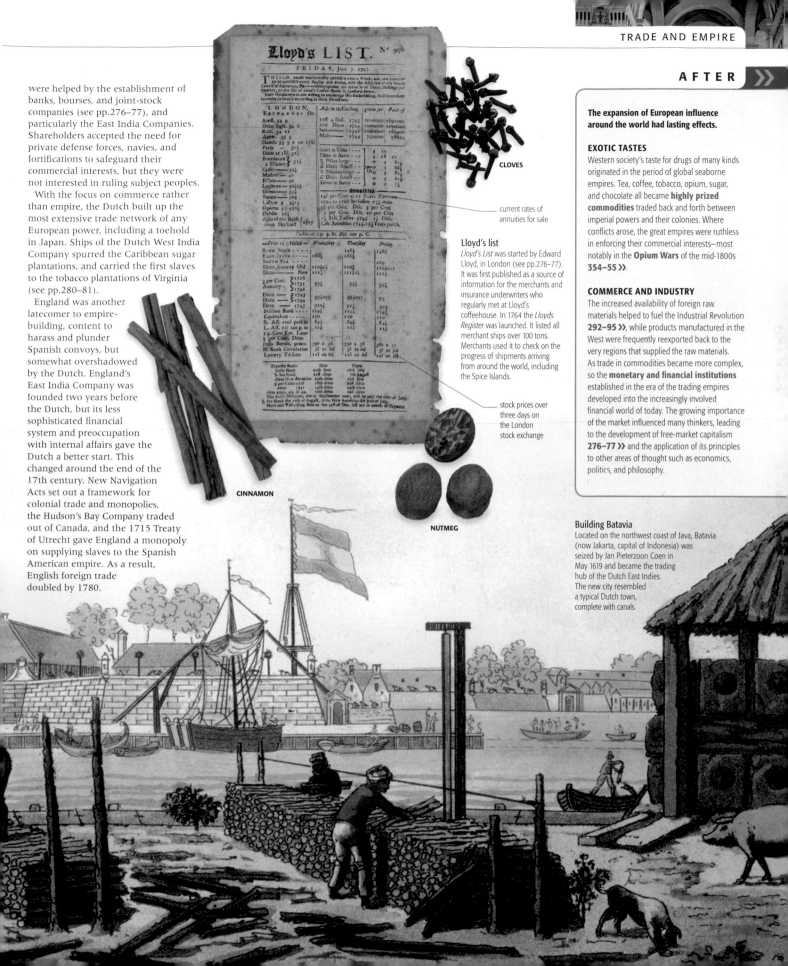

CLOVES

current rates of annuities for sale

Lloyd's list
Lloyd's List was started by Edward Lloyd, in London (see pp.276–77). It was first published as a source of information for the merchants and insurance underwriters who regularly met at Lloyd's coffeehouse. In 1764 the *Lloyd's Register* was launched. It listed all merchant ships over 100 tons. Merchants used it to check on the progress of shipments arriving from around the world, including the Spice Islands.

stock prices over three days on the London stock exchange

CINNAMON

NUTMEG

The expansion of European influence around the world had lasting effects.

EXOTIC TASTES
Western society's taste for drugs of many kinds originated in the period of global seaborne empires. Tea, coffee, tobacco, opium, sugar, and chocolate all became **highly prized commodities** traded back and forth between imperial powers and their colonies. Where conflicts arose, the great empires were ruthless in enforcing their commercial interests—most notably in the **Opium Wars** of the mid-1800s **354–55 »**.

COMMERCE AND INDUSTRY
The increased availability of foreign raw materials helped to fuel the Industrial Revolution **292–95 »**, while products manufactured in the West were frequently reexported back to the very regions that supplied the raw materials. As trade in commodities became more complex, so the **monetary and financial institutions** established in the era of the trading empires developed into the increasingly involved financial world of today. The growing importance of the market influenced many thinkers, leading to the development of free-market capitalism **276–77 »** and the application of its principles to other areas of thought such as economics, politics, and philosophy.

Building Batavia
Located on the northwest coast of Java, Batavia (now Jakarta, capital of Indonesia) was seized by Jan Pieterzoon Coen in May 1619 and became the trading hub of the Dutch East Indies. The new city resembled a typical Dutch town, complete with canals.

BEFORE

While the last few emperors of the Ming dynasty were distracted by internal rebellion, a new power was gathering in the north.

THE JURCHEN BANNERS

The Jurchen people were descended from the founders of the **Jin dynasty ‹‹ 163**. By the 16th century the Jurchen were living near Jilin in modern-day northeast China, where they hunted, farmed, and traded extensively with the Chinese. In 1616, the Jurchen leader **Nurhaci** founded the Later Jin dynasty and began to organize his people, as well as the Mongols and Chinese who had submitted to Jurchen rule. The entire population were enrolled into **four military units** called banners, each being identified by the color of their standards.

300 Jurchen families were formed into one *niru*, or company.

25 *niru*, or 7,500 families, were organized under one banner.

FROM JURCHEN TO MANCHU

Nurhaci's successor, Huang Taiji, introduced Chinese-style institutions among the Jurchen. In 1636 he changed the name of his people to Manchu (a word of unknown origin) and in 1637 renamed the Later Jin dynasty, adopting the dynastic name **Qing**, meaning "clear." The banner system was expanded by the conquests of Huang Taiji to include eight Manchu, eight Mongol, and eight Chinese banners by 1644.

By the early 17th century, the Ming dynasty (see pp.166–67) was beset by internal popular rebellions and the threat of a Manchu invasion. In April 1644, the rebel leader Li Zicheng took Beijing, and the Ming emperor committed suicide. Li tried to persuade Wu Sangui, the most powerful commander on the frontier, to join him. Instead Wu negotiated with the Manchus, allowing them to pass freely through the Great Wall. The Manchus took control of Beijing in June and Li Zicheng fled. Fulin, the six-year-old son of Huang Taiji (see BEFORE), became the Shunzhi emperor, thus inaugurating the Qing dynasty (1644–1911).

Imperial Poetry
Emperor Kangxi was an accomplished poet as well as a sponsor of the arts. The poetry in this album is attributed to him.

The Manchus continued their advance south, crushing any resistance from Ming loyalists. They also ordered all male Chinese to show that they submitted to Qing rule by shaving their foreheads and adopting the queue, a long braided ponytail, which was compulsory in China throughout the Qing period.

Having gained control over China, the Qing instituted a bureaucracy that relied on features retained from the Ming administration, which included the system of government examinations. Few Manchu could speak Chinese, and even fewer had any experience of office, so all senior posts within the bureaucracy were assigned to both a Manchu and a Chinese official, a policy that helped somewhat in easing the resentment felt by the Chinese at being ruled by alien invaders.

The Prosperous Age

Shunzhi showed great promise as a ruler, but he died of smallpox at an early age. It was his three successors who were responsible for consolidating Qing power in China.

Shunzhi's son, the Kangxi emperor, was the longest-reigning emperor in Chinese history. Though born a Manchu, Kangxi became the epitome of a Chinese emperor. He read and commented on

The Three Emperors

The reigns of the Three Emperors, Kangxi (1661–1722), Yongzheng (1722–35), and Qianlong (1736–95), are known collectively as the "Prosperous Age," a period when the Chinese empire expanded to its greatest extent and its population doubled.

RUSSIAN EMPIRE
Nerchinsk
Amur River
Ussuri
Zunghar
1757
Outer Mongolia
1696
Manchuria
Sea of Japan
Xinjiang
Rehe
1757
Inner Mongolia
Beijing
KOREA
JAPAN
Yellow River
1717, 1750
Yellow Sea
TIBET
Xi'an
Shanghai
East China Sea
Lhasa
Chengdu
Nanjing
Yangtze River
NEPAL
KEY
BHUTAN
Changsha
INDIA
ASSAM
Taiwan
BURMA
Guangzhou
Macao
Bay of Bengal
ANNAM
LAOS
South China Sea
HAINAN

N
0   2000 km
0   2000 miles

KEY
▮ Under Manchu control by 1644
▮ Under Manchu control by 1660
▮ Qing acquisitions by 1770
➜ Main Qing campaigns

Qing territory
The Treaty of Nerchinsk, 1689, defined the border between China and Russia. In 1750, Qianlong declared Tibet a Chinese protectorate. In 1757 a Zunghar rebellion was mercilessly crushed, and their territory was incorporated into the empire.

more than 50 memorials every day, and traveled extensively. He was a patron of the arts and encouraged scholarship. During his reign he crushed a major internal rebellion and led successful campaigns against the Zunghar people of Mongolia.

Emperor Yongzheng, who may have usurped the throne, succeeded Kangxi. Yongzheng insisted on the use of the Manchu language at court and raised the salaries of officials to discourage corruption. To ensure ideological conformity he ordered that the Sacred Edict, which exhorted subjects to revere the emperor, be read out twice a month at Confucian temples.

The reign of the fourth Qing emperor, Qianlong (see right), saw the boundaries of China reach their farthest extent (see left). The addition of territory led to an expansion of the economy, as well as a significant population increase.

Missionaries

The first Christian Jesuit mission in Beijing had been established in 1598. When the Manchus came to power, they continued the Ming practice of

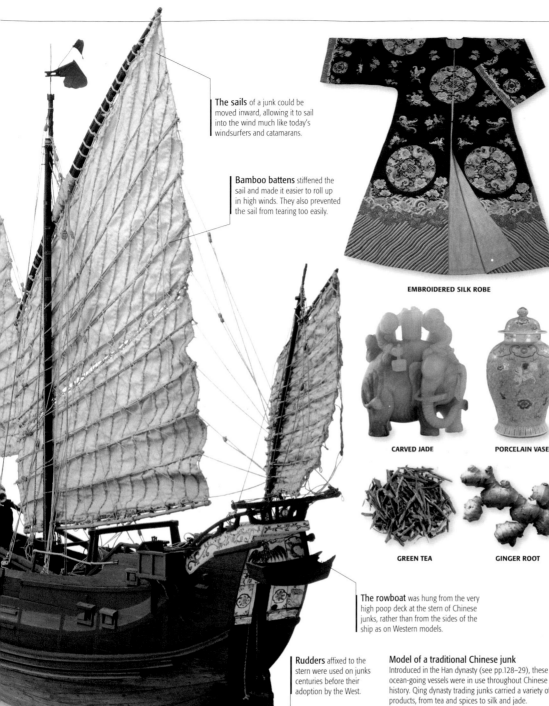

The **sails** of a junk could be moved inward, allowing it to sail into the wind much like today's windsurfers and catamarans.

Bamboo battens stiffened the sail and made it easier to roll up in high winds. They also prevented the sail from tearing too easily.

EMBROIDERED SILK ROBE

CARVED JADE

PORCELAIN VASE

GREEN TEA

GINGER ROOT

The **rowboat** was hung from the very high poop deck at the stern of Chinese junks, rather than from the sides of the ship as on Western models.

Rudders affixed to the stern were used on junks centuries before their adoption by the West.

Model of a traditional Chinese junk
Introduced in the Han dynasty (see pp.128–29), these ocean-going vessels were in use throughout Chinese history. Qing dynasty trading junks carried a variety of products, from tea and spices to silk and jade.

QIANLONG

Qianlong projected an image of himself as a model Chinese ruler, attending to affairs of state in the morning and painting and writing poems in the afternoon. Though not particularly gifted, he was a prolific poet; more than 40,000 poems have been ascribed to him. The later years of his reign were marred by the growing power of his favorite, Heshen (see AFTER).

AFTER

The last few decades of Qianlong's rule saw the "Prosperous Age" come to an end.

QING CORRUPTION
In 1775, the imperial bodyguard **Heshen** became a favorite of Qianlong, and he began to build a network of corrupt patronage. Qianlong gave him control of the imperial revenues, and allowed him to appoint his henchmen to senior official posts. Heshen is considered to have begun a trend of corruption that continued through the 19th century, gradually undermining the status of the Qing dynasty.

THE OPIUM TRADE
Opium, grown in India, was smuggled into China by British firms. Until 1821 imports of opium averaged 4,500 chests a year. Then the price was lowered, and by 1830 the trade had soared to 18,956 chests. Opium smuggling surged again to more than 40,000 chests a year in 1834, costing 34 million silver dollars and causing a significant drain on imperial revenues. Chinese attempts to curb the trade led to the Opium Wars 354–55 ».

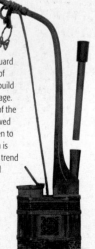
OPIUM PIPE

300 MILLION The population of China in 1762, according to government estimates.

employing Jesuits for various official tasks. Kangxi gave Father Adam Schall responsibility for preparing the imperial calendar, for example. When a mistake was detected, Schall was accused of treason and narrowly escaped death. Other Jesuit priests were engaged as diplomats, architects, artists, and mathematicians. In 1692, after Jesuit missionaries had cured the emperor of malaria, Kangxi issued an "edict of toleration," which permitted the teaching of Christianity. However, when the pope forbade all Chinese Christians from performing the rites of ancestor worship, the preaching of Christianity in China was forbidden.

The tea trade
China had long-standing commercial links by land with Central Asia and by sea with Southeast Asia. From the late Ming period, China also had dealings with the European powers. By the 18th century, Britain had become China's major Western trading partner. Interest in Chinese ceramics and silk was still strong, but tea quickly became China's leading export. However, the Chinese would only accept silver in exchange for tea, and it was British attempts to create a demand for a substitute that led to the trade in opium (see AFTER). Under the Qing, foreign trade was regulated closely and from 1760 it was confined to the city of Guangzhou. Complaints over trade restrictions led the British government to send the Macartney embassy to China in 1792 (see p.354).

241

Japan's Great Peace

In the 17th century, Japan shut the door to the outside world. Anybody venturing abroad and daring to return would be executed. For the next 250 years a newly unified Japan was steered along a path of *sakoku*, or national seclusion, and developed its economy and a unique cultural identity.

Imagine a 17th-century city of towering stone walls, long wooden parapets, huge gatehouses, and massive moats, all sprawling out from the largest castle in the world. This bustling town-port with artisans, traders, and laborers is Edo (present-day Tokyo), a city twice the size of the largest cities in Europe at the time, such as London and Paris. Its busy thoroughfares were filled with people from different classes, all of whom were beneficiaries of a new period known as

« BEFORE

Before the Edo period, Japan was a politically divided and unstable country.

CIVIL WAR
From the 12th to the late 16th centuries, Japan experienced intermittent civil war **« 168–69.**

THE COMING OF PEACE
The battle of **Sekigahara** was the last great field battle between two Japanese armies. The victor, Tokugawa Ieyasu, the son of a *daimyo* (warlord) took the title of **shogun** (military dictator).

the "Great Peace" or Edo Period. Early-modern Japan was experiencing a period of previously unknown calm that was to last over 250 years.

Shogun authority
Under the newly installed shogun (see pp.168–69) ruler Tokugawa Ieyasu, Edo became the military capital of Japan. The emperor and his court—though revered—were consigned to ceremonial stature at Kyoto, which was Japan's capital at that time. The Imperial court, powerless but prestigious, conferred the title shogun and Ieyasu manipulated this "support" to his advantage. But the key players in the pacification of Japan were the

> " [Edo] is on most days **more crowded than** a public street in any of the most populous towns of **Europe**."
>
> DUTCH TRADER ENGELBERT KASMPFERER, 1621

daimyo (see pp.168–69), regional leaders who controlled the provinces. The shogun, while exercising control from Edo, had to work with these local magnates, in order to maintain power in distant provinces that were difficult to reach. It was an uneasy alliance veering between accommodation and manipulation: the *daimyo* had to obey the shogun on important policies, and their wives and children had to live in Edo periodically to act as collateral, but they exercised a good deal of freedom and control in their local areas. They were allowed to demand physical labor and duties from local villagers, including taxes and rent.

The great change
Under the shogunate, Japanese society was put through a largely successful experiment of "social engineering." The population was labeled as to whether they were samurai, farmers, craftsmen, or merchants. At the apex of the system were the warrior class, the samurai, who were the only individuals allowed to carry weapons. As a class, samurai were controlled by the military leaders and worked as government officials, guards, policemen, or for local authorities, serving either the shogun or one of the local *daimyo*.

The great change in Japanese society was the elevation of farmers—who made up 80 percent of the population, and whose labor was critical to the economy—to the second rank of society. Although at the mercy of the *daimyo* and samurai, the peasant farmers enjoyed a high degree of village autonomy. They elected leaders and formed collective assemblies that decided on local issues. They paid taxes (in rice) as a village unit and were granted individual rights to cultivate the land registered to them. In

Edo, largest town
This print by the Japanese artist Ando Hiroshige reveals an 18th-century view of Edo, which was the one of the largest cities in the world throughout the 18th century. Today the Japanese view Edo, upon which Tokyo grew, as the home of their traditional culture, and people born in Tokyo are still known as *Edo-ko*, or children of Edo.

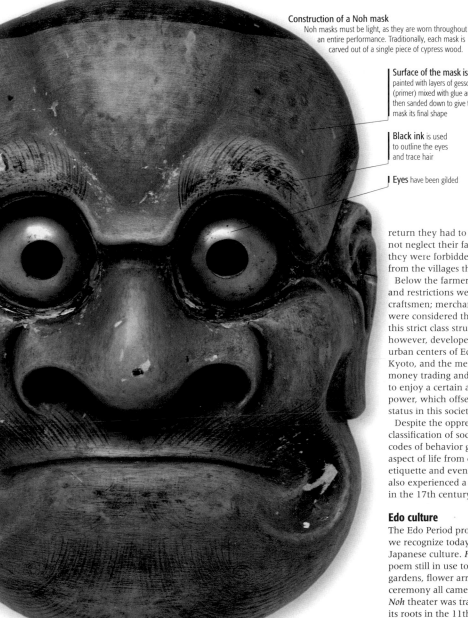

Construction of a Noh mask
Noh masks must be light, as they are worn throughout an entire performance. Traditionally, each mask is carved out of a single piece of cypress wood.

Surface of the mask is painted with layers of gesso (primer) mixed with glue and then sanded down to give the mask its final shape

Black ink is used to outline the eyes and trace hair

Eyes have been gilded

Tea ceremony
A colored woodcut of a classic Edo era scene: geishas at a formal tea ceremony. *Cha-no-yu*, as it is called, was—and still is—considered a traditional art in Japan.

return they had to ensure that they did not neglect their farms, which meant they were forbidden to move away from the villages they occupied.

Below the farmers in terms of rights and restrictions were the artisans and craftsmen; merchants and shopkeepers were considered the lowest rank in this strict class structure. Commerce, however, developed in the expanding urban centers of Edo, Osaka, and Kyoto, and the merchant class made money trading and brokering, coming to enjoy a certain amount of financial power, which offset their "low class" status in this society.

Despite the oppressively rigid classification of society and the strict codes of behavior governing every aspect of life from clothing to social etiquette and even tea drinking, Japan also experienced a cultural renaissance in the 17th century.

Edo culture

The Edo Period produced much of what we recognize today as traditional Japanese culture. *Haiku*, the 17-syllable poem still in use today, was born; zen gardens, flower arranging, and the tea ceremony all came into their own; and *Noh* theater was transformed. *Noh* had its roots in the 11th century in the

provinces. It originally consisted of acrobatic and juggling displays, but the addition of operatic dance and recital transformed it into a highly stylized and symbolic drama. As with all other forms of cultural life in the Edo period, *Noh* theater was strictly governed and the lower classes were forbidden to learn the techniques of the art form. Kabuki, *ukiyo-e*, porcelain, and lacquerware all developed and thrived during this period. *Ukiyo-e*, or "pictures of the floating world," was an art form that proved highly popular for its depictions of sensual courtesans, erotic prostitutes, and flashy kabuki actors. The *Ukiyo-e* style broadened from screen prints into wood-block prints to show scenes of Edo and landscapes, as typified by Hiroshige (see left). The genre also later proved influential to Western artists such as Vincent van Gogh, Claude Monet, Edgar Degas, and Gustav Klimt.

AFTER

The 18th and early 19th century in Japan were marked by severe famines, increasing social tensions, and repeated but unsuccessful attempts at political reform.

DECLINE OF THE SHOGUNATE
By the beginning of the 19th century, a growing number of Japanese saw the **shogunate system as inflexible and unresponsive** to new challenges **356–57 »**.

JAPAN'S MODERNIZATION
Japan was **forced to open** its borders by the US in 1854 and its **Westernization** began **356–57 »**. The Bank of Japan (including a modern mint) was established in 1882.

JAPANESE COINS

Noh and Kabuki

There are four main categories of Noh masks, each representing a different Noh genre: god, demon, warrior, woman. Noh plays deal with a universal truth, displayed on stage in a kind of visual metaphor. The masks used in Noh theater use neutral expressions, which means that the actors have to use great skill to bring the characters "to life." Pictured to the right are a 14th-century warrior mask and two Edo-period masks.

While Noh theater's restraint and elegance appealed to upper-class Japanese society, Kabuki theater, which was garish and bawdy, was embraced by the merchant class.

NOH WARRIOR

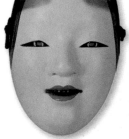

NOH DEMON

NOH WOMAN

THE MUGHAL DYNASTY
After an initial period of expansion and consolidation, the Mughal Empire remained a stable and vibrant entity for over 170 years (1556–1719). A long, slow decline ended with the empire's dissolution in 1857.

The Great Mughals

One of the most powerful states of the 17th century, the Mughal Empire had a complex administrative system that enabled it to rule over more than 100 million people across most of the Indian subcontinent. The splendor and sophistication of its court was world-famous.

The decisive battles in Babur's (see left) conquest of north India were his defeat of the Afghan Sultan of Delhi, Ibrahim Lodi, at Panipat in 1526 and his success over a confederacy of Rajput kings at Kanua the following year. Using firearms and an experienced and efficient cavalry, he had consolidated Mughal (Persian for Mongol) rule over the rich cities and productive lands of northern India from his capital at Agra by his death in 1530.

His son, Humayun, met with less success. By 1540, he had lost his father's kingdom to the Afghan ruler, Sher Shah Sur, and had been forced into exile at the Safavid court in Persia. In mid-1555, with Persian support, he restored Mughal rule by defeating Sher Shah's weaker descendants, thus duplicating his father's conquests. However, he died just seven months later, leaving the empire to his 12-year-old son, Akbar, with an influential noble, Bairam Khan, as his regent.

Together, they extended Mughal control over northern India, in the region bounded by the Indus and Ganges rivers, to form an imperial heartland that, in time, was framed by palace fortresses at Agra, Allahabad, Ajmer, and Lahore. After he came of age in 1560, Akbar achieved a further series of military successes; by his death in 1605, his empire reached from Kashmir in the north and Afghanistan in the northwest, to Bengal in the east and the Deccan plateau in the south.

Structure and tolerance
To consolidate his position, Akbar established a centralized system of government. This was administered by warrior-aristocrats (*mansabdars*) of various ranks who could be appointed to bureaucratic or military positions and were accompanied by their own households or troops. The most senior *mansabdars* were paid with land grants (*jagirs*). They had the right to collect taxes from this land, but could not own, govern, or occupy it.

Akbar had a policy of religious tolerance, which was evident in his own marriages to women of different faiths, whom he did not force to convert to Islam. This was a shrewd

The first Mughal emperor
Babur, founder of the Mughal Empire, is shown here capturing sheep from the Hazara tribe. Babur is remembered as much for his literary prowess as for his military achievements. This picture is from his memoir, the *Baburnama*, which provides a frank insight into his life.

BEFORE

On the eve of its conquest by the Muslim Mughals, India was very fragmented.

MUSLIM AND HINDU INDIA
Muslim rule over India's predominantly Hindu population began in the north with the **Delhi Sultanate** (1206–1526) **‹‹ 180–81**. The south was dominated by the Hindu **Vijayanagar Empire**. The center consisted mainly of Muslim sultanates, while the **Hindu Rajputs** and **Lodi Afghans** quarreled over the north.

BABUR IN AFGHANISTAN
To the northwest, in Central Asia, **Babur**, a descendant of Genghis Khan **‹‹ 164–65**, had been exiled from his home in Ferghana by the Uzbek Shaibani Khan. He seized Kabul, capital of Afghanistan in 1504, then moved on to India.

Mughal territory
The Mughal Empire experienced three main phases of expansion, which corresponded to the reigns of Babur, Akbar, and Aurangzeb. This map shows the extent of empire at the end of each of their reigns.

KEY
— Babur's domains, 1525
— Babur's acquisitions prior to Mughal expulsions, 1539
■ Akbar's domains, 1556
■ Areas held by Mughals at Akbar's death 1605
□ Additional areas acquired up to the death of Aurangzeb, 1707

Map labels: UZBEKS, Balkh, AFGHANISTAN, Herat, Hindu Kush, Kabul, Qandhar, Qalat, SAFAVID EMPIRE, Srinagar, Lahore, Plateau of Tibet, Multan, Thatta, Thar Desert, Delhi, Fatehpur Sikri, Agra, Ajmer, Aravali Range, Chitor, Ahmadabad, Vindhya Range, Satpura Range, Illichpur, Ajodhya, Allahabad, Patna, Murshidabad, Garhgaon, AHOMS, Chatgaon, Calcutta, ARAKAN, AVA, Katak, Bay of Bengal, Arabian Sea, Bombay, Junnar, Ahmadnagar, Bidar, Golkonda, Gulbarga, Hyderabad, Goa, Masulipatam, Deccan, Western Ghats, Eastern Ghats, Sira, Mangalur, Arkat, Madras, Shrirangapattanam, Calicut, Tanjore, Cochin, Madurai, Jaffna, INDIAN OCEAN, SAVULUS Ceylon, Himalayas, Brahmaputra, Ganges, Narmada, Mahanadi, Krishna, Godavari, Indus, Sutlej, Ravi, Chenab

0 500 km
0 500 miles

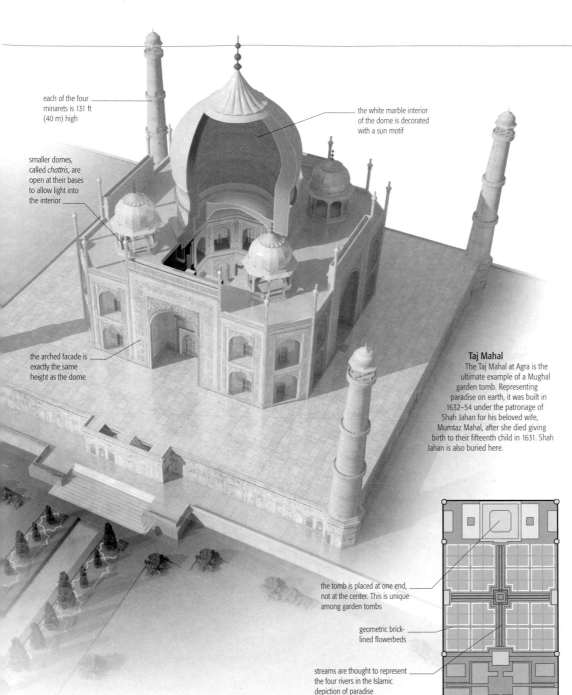

each of the four minarets is 131 ft (40 m) high

the white marble interior of the dome is decorated with a sun motif

smaller domes, called *chattris*, are open at their bases to allow light into the interior

the arched facade is exactly the same height as the dome

Taj Mahal
The Taj Mahal at Agra is the ultimate example of a Mughal garden tomb. Representing paradise on earth, it was built in 1632–54 under the patronage of Shah Jahan for his beloved wife, Mumtaz Mahal, after she died giving birth to their fifteenth child in 1631. Shah Jahan is also buried here.

the tomb is placed at one end, not at the center. This is unique among garden tombs

geometric brick-lined flowerbeds

streams are thought to represent the four rivers in the Islamic depiction of paradise

Red Fort
Repeating scalloped arches of red sandstone in the Red Fort at Delhi. The Red Fort, or Lal Quil, was at the heart of Shah Jahan's new city. From 1648 it functioned as his imperial palace and the Mughal administrative center.

AFTER »

In the 18th century, Mughal sovereignty became limited to Delhi and its hinterland.

BAHADUR SHAR II

END OF MUGHAL RULE
The emperor retained some authority within India as a whole as the *shahanshah*, or "king of kings." His court patronized religious and cultural developments.

EAST INDIA COMPANY
During the early 19th century, any remaining authority was eroded systematically by the expanding **East India Company 352 »**. A final attempt to restore Mughal rule was connected to the Indian Mutiny of 1857. This led to the dissolution of the Mughal Empire and the establishment of British crown rule in India **352–53 »**. The last Mughal emperor, Bahadur Shah II, died in exile in Burma in 1862.

The paradise garden
The Taj Mahal garden is thought to represent paradise; the word "paradise" is from the ancient Persian for "walled garden." Mughal formal gardens, *charbaghs* (four gardens), were based on those of the Persians, who saw great significance in the number four. The design was brought to India by Babur. The plan of the Taj Mahal garden (left) shows the use of units of four.

political move that would help to unite the many faiths of his empire. He also allowed the Hindu Rajputs to negotiate entry into his nobility if they offered their daughters in marriage. Eventually, he relied more on Rajputs and Persians than on his own Central Asian nobles.

Reform and the arts
During his reign, Akbar also reduced the influence of Muslim scholars (*'ulama*), abolished taxes on Hindu pilgrims and non-Muslim residents (*jizya*), and introduced the Bengali calendar, a solar calendar to replace the Muslim lunar cycle. At his new palace at Fatehpur Sikri near Agra, he held

religious debates in a custom-built *ibadat-khana*, or "house of worship," that gave representation to different faith groups. These policies were highly pragmatic in a country that was predominantly non-Muslim, but they were also a reflection of his eclectic spirituality, further revealed in his establishment of a cult based on the worship of light and sun (*din-i-ilahi*).

Music and art also interested Akbar. He induced the famed singer and musician, Tansen, to join his court, and began patronizing what became known as north Indian classical music. At Fatehpur Sikri, he established a school of Mughal painting, combining Persian

and Indian influences in a style that was to reach its peak during the reign of his son, Jahangir (1605–27).

Peak and decline
Jahangir's son, Shah Jahan (1628–58), contributed more artistic treasures, such as the Taj Mahal at Agra and a majestic new capital at Delhi, which included the Red Fort and the Jama Masjid. These huge projects were also symbols of Mughal wealth, dependent on flourishing agriculture and trade. From his accession in 1658, the last "great" Mughal, Aurangzeb oversaw the expansion of the empire to its largest extent. Yet his reign also

signified the beginning of the end. He was often away from his capital on military campaigns, and he depleted the treasury attempting to defeat the Marathas in the south who were trying to establish their own empire. Some scholars also believe his strict interpretation of Islam offended his Rajput collaborators and Hindu subjects.

The empire was further weakened by a rapid succession of rulers following Aurangzeb's death in 1707. In 1739, Nadir Shah, the Safavids' successor, sacked Delhi and seized the Mughal treasury. The empire was all but dead. In 1857, the British deposed Babadur Shah II, the last Mughal emperor.

The Ottoman Empire

For over 600 years the Ottoman Empire dominated the political and religious life of the Middle East, viewed with awe by the Christian West, and a byword for wealth, power, unimaginable opulence, and—in its latter years—widespread corruption.

The harem of the Topkapi Palace
This 18th-century miniature by Fazil Enderuni shows concubines bathing in the Topkapi Palace harem. All concubines were non-Muslim captives taken in war or bought from slavers.

T he emergence of the Ottomans as a world power began with the rule of Mehmed II in 1451. Mehmed led his army west to attack Christian Constantinople, capital of the once-great Byzantine Empire (see pp.198–99). Using the world's largest cannon to pound the allegedly "impregnable" walls, and with more than 160,000 men against the defenders' 7,000, he swiftly crushed all resistance. On May 29, 1453 Constantinople fell. Mehmed pushed on into Europe, seizing territory, until his failure to take Belgrade in 1456 brought the conquest to a halt and left the Ottoman Empire's border with Western Europe static for the next 60 years.

Meanwhile, the Ottoman eastern borders were threatened by the rise of the Persian Safavids. It was not until the Battle of Chaldiran in 1514 that Selim I humbled the rival dynasty. A great expansion followed. Selim led his troops east and south, taking Jerusalem's holy sites and conquering Cairo in 1517. Selim's son, Suleyman, known as "The Magnificent" in Europe for his wealth and power, proved no less a conqueror than his father. Despite his success, Suleyman's personal life ended in tragedy.

Suleyman's two favorite sons, Mustafa and Bayazid, were accused of conspiring against him. To save his throne, Suleyman was forced to have them both executed. He never

Dagger and scabbard
Ottoman weaponry was renowned for its beauty and functionality. This dagger and scabbard, richly encrusted with semiprecious stones, was probably the possession of an Ottoman noble.

recovered from this loss and, a sad and broken figure, became a virtual recluse in the Topkapi Palace, leaving his Grand Vizier (chief minister) to run the empire. While both Mustafa and Bayazid had been trained to rule, the grieving Suleyman had left Selim, his untutored surviving son, in the febrile atmosphere of the harem (the women's area of the palace). This neglect had disastrous consequences for Ottoman rule.

Ottoman decline

Many historians date the beginnings of decline from the accession of Selim, known as "the Drunkard." With no political or military training, Selim's formative experiences were food, drink, and women. On his accession Selim handed over control of the empire to his vizier. This set the pattern for the next century of Ottoman rule, with catastrophic results.

Without a strong ruler, government corruption flourished, and the indifference of the bureaucracy to predatory local officials eroded public support for the regime. Lacking the controlling hand of the sultan, the

BEFORE ≪

The Ottoman Empire was forged in a bloody furnace of continual intrigue and conflict.

THE CREATION OF THE EMPIRE
In the 13th century a band of **Turkish warriors** led by **Ertughrul** and his son **Osman ≪ 206–07** came to Anatolia from the Central Asian Plains. Ertughrul came to the aid of the Seljuk Sultan Kaihusrev II and was rewarded with land, which grew to become the *Osman-li*, the Ottoman Empire.

SIPAHI WARRIOR

JANISSARIES
Osman's son, **Orhan**, formed the "akinci" (standing cavalry formations) and the celebrated "janissaries" (highly trained infantry). With this formidable army, Orhan and his son **Murad I** seized most of the Balkans, and achieved the Ottoman goal of conquering Anatolia. The **Sipahis** were mounted warriors in the army recruited from land-owning Turks. They considered themselves an elite force.

EMPIRE ACHIEVED
After defeat by the Mongols at Ankara in 1402, the reigns of **Murad II** and **Mehmed II ≪ 207** finally saw the Ottoman empire restored.

RULER OF OTTOMAN EMPIRE (1520–66)

SULEYMAN

This king is known as "Suleyman the Magnificent" in the Western world and in the Islamic world as *Kanuni*, "the Lawgiver"—a tribute to the prosperity his reign brought to the Ottoman Empire. Suleyman believed himself to be the spiritual heir to both Alexander (see pp.96–97) and Caesar (see pp.108–09), and claimed title to all the lands they had ruled over. Within a year of his accession, his armies had taken Belgrade, and by the time of his death the Ottomans controlled large parts of southeast Europe, the North African coast, and the Middle East. His rule saw a cultural renaissance of Islamic civilization. His support of the arts and the rule of law that he implemented remain his legacy.

KEY
- Ottoman Empire and vassals 1512
- Ottoman conquest, 1512–1639
- Vassal border
- Frontiers before 1600
- Frontiers after 1600
- Borders of empire 1800

Map
The Ottoman Empire was a considerable force in world politics from the 14th century until the early 20th century. This map shows the borders of the Ottoman Empire at the height of its power.

0   1000 km
0   1000 miles

various elements of government—the Diwan (supreme Court), grand vizier, and janissaries (elite army units)—all vied for power. The Sublime Porte (Ottoman Government) presented a united face to its enemies, but a century of nepotism and greed slowly ate it from within.

Although there had been a few attempts to stem the tide of misgovernment, it was only in the 1650s with Mehmet Kopprulu, grand vizier to Mehmet IV, that a systematic and enduring effort to root out corruption began. He also planned a resumption of Ottoman conquest, but died before his plans came to fruition. His brother-in-law, Kara Mustafa, continued Mehmet's expansionist policies, marching on Vienna, the capital of the mighty Habsburg Empire, in 1683. However, a combination of innovative cavalry tactics and superior artillery resulted in Mustafa's defeat.

With this defeat a steady European encroachment on Ottoman lands began, and for most of the 18th century they were at war with one or more European powers. Mahmud I brought respite to the weary empire, capturing Belgrade, and holding it under the Treaty of Belgrade of 1739. But given the ongoing corruption within government, further losses seemed inevitable.

The Blue Mosque
Built for Sultan Ahmed I between 1609–16 by master architect Sedefhar Mehmet Aga, the Sultan Ahmed mosque in Istanbul is lined with more than 20,000 handmade ceramic tiles.

Calligraphy
This is the exquisite *tugra*—a form of calligraphic monogram or seal—of Sultan Murat III and dates from 1575. Initially *tugras* were used only on official documents such as *fermans* (orders of the Sultan), but later they began to appear as a symbol of sovereignty on stamps, coins, and flags. *Tugras* even appeared on ships, mosques, and palaces.

AFTER ≫

After 1750, the Ottoman Empire's story is one of slow, continuous decline.

LOSING GROUND
In the early 1800s, reforms were introduced to stabilize the Ottoman Empire, but its **slow dismemberment** continued. The Greeks seized independence in 1829, and the Russo-Turkish War of 1828–29 led to further losses **330–33 ≫**. Bosnia-Herzogovina rebelled in 1875, and in another war with Russia in 1877–78, the Empire ceded Romania, Serbia, and Montenegro. Turkey—what was left of the Ottoman Empire—became known as "the Sick Man of Europe."

END OF EMPIRE
Two more **Balkan Wars** (1912–13) saw the empire lose most of its remaining European territory. By the end of **World War I 372–75 ≫** in 1918, the empire effectively ceased to exist, the Treaty of Sèvres of 1920 formally confirming its dissolution.

OTTOMAN COAT OF ARMS

Battle of Lepanto

The largest battle fought by galley fleets in the Mediterranean, the Battle of Lepanto was a clash between the Ottoman Turks and the Holy League of Spain, the Papacy, Venice, and Genoa. The aim of the Europeans was to save the island of Cyprus from the westward advance of the Ottomans, who already occupied most of Hungary and threatened Vienna and the Austrian lands. The result was a huge defeat for the Ottoman forces.

The Ottomans, from northwestern Turkey (see pp.246–47), had taken territory from the Byzantine Empire (see pp.198–99). In 1453 they conquered the empire's capital Constantinople (modern Istanbul), and in the next few years they took over most of its lands, from Serbia and Bosnia in the west to Anatolia in the east. By the early 16th century they were expanding again, destroying the power of Hungary at the Battle of Mohacs in 1526, and laying siege to Vienna in 1529—although they had to pull back from the city when they ran out of supplies and winter came.

In 1570, the Ottomans invaded the island of Cyprus. By moving into the Mediterranean, they threatened the freedom of wealthy cities such as Genoa and Venice to continue to travel and trade freely in the region (see pp.208–09). The Habsburg rulers of the Holy Roman Empire (see pp.188–89) were concerned they would be attacked again, and the Catholic Church also felt threatened by the Muslim Ottomans. As a result, Venice, Genoa, Spain (ruled by Philip II), and the Papacy formed an alliance, called the Holy League, in order to defend the Mediterranean against the Ottomans. The League assembled a huge fleet of some 210 ships commanded by Don John of Austria, illegitimate son of the Habsburg emperor, Charles V. In 1571, Don John spotted the Turkish fleet, rather bigger than his own, off Lepanto (now Navpatkos), on the western coast of Greece. Both fleets were made up mainly of galleys, large warships powered by oarsmen. Don John also had six galleasses, powerful hybrid vessels with sails as well as oars, and with heavy cannons mounted along their flanks.

The ships of the League attacked quickly. The Turks preferred to fight by ramming their enemy's ships, but Don John deployed the formidable firepower he carried. The tactics were a resounding success. The Ottoman commander, Ali Pasha, was killed, as were thousands of his men.

The Holy League destroyed the Turkish navy, but they did not destroy the Turks. The Ottomans built a new fleet, which was afloat within a year. The Turks kept control of Cyprus and the rest of their empire. But they did not expand farther westward, as they might have done if they had won.

Don John of Austria goes to war
This painting by 16th-century Italian artist Andrea Micheli depicts the Battle of Lepanto, which was the last battle fought by galleys. The Holy League sank or captured around 200 of the Ottoman ships, losing only 15 of their own.

"Strong **gongs groaning** as the **guns boom** far... "
G. K. CHESTERTON, BRITISH AUTHOR, FROM THE POEM *LEPANTO*, 1915

The Renaissance

During the 15th and 16th centuries, art and learning flourished in cities and at royal courts in many parts of Europe, but especially in Italy. The works of the exceptional individuals who made this "renaissance" are among the marvels of the world.

The Renaissance was part of an ongoing process that changed the shape of European culture over many centuries. The term "Renaissance" refers to a "rebirth" of interest in the legacy of ancient Greece and Rome, but the texts of pre-Christian writers had in fact been copied and read in Christian Europe at least from the time of Charlemagne (747–814 CE; see pp.188–89). The paintings of artists such as Giotto, and the writings of Dante, Petrarch, and Boccaccio in the 14th century are among many works that prefigured the Renaissance. The period of the Renaissance is, however,

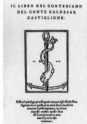

Early book
Baldassare Castiglione's *Book of the Courtier* (1528) was a guide to behavior at a Renaissance court.

conventionally dated to around 1450–1550, as a time of exceptional curiosity and inventiveness in European art, architecture, ideas, and technology.

Wealth and culture
Economic prosperity was the basis for the Renaissance. Art and learning were luxuries that could be afforded through the increasing wealth of a social elite. The major centers of Renaissance cultural activity were the thriving city-states of Italy, such as Florence, Milan, and Venice, prosperous cities in Germany, and the Flemish Netherlands (see pp.208–09, 276–77). Grown rich on the proceeds of banking, trade, and manufacture, cities spent freely on cultural luxuries out of civic pride or to enhance the prestige of local rulers such as the Medici family in Florence or the Sforzas in Milan. Wealthy kings such as Matthias Corvinus in Hungary and Francis I in France also patronized artists and intellectuals as a way of advertising their own power and status. Renaissance popes such as Alexander VI (pope from 1492 to 1503) and Julius II (1503–13) made Rome another focus of excellence, lavishing money raised from their Christian flock on extravagant artistic and architectural projects such as St. Peter's Basilica.

The Classical world
The Renaissance was still far from the modern world of science and reason—astrology and alchemy (see p.266) were major fields of study, and one

see pp.188–89

Dante standing before Florence
Domenico di Michelino painted this image of the poet Dante alongside his native city, Florence. Florence was home to many artists, including architect Brunelleschi, who designed the famous cathedral dome, visible on Dante's left.

Humanist group
Painted by Domenico Ghirlandaio around 1490, this detail from a fresco in the church of Santa Maria Novella in Florence shows a group of humanist scholars including Marsilio Ficino, head of the Platonic Academy.

Michelangelo's David
This massive marble statue was made by Michelangelo for the city of Florence in 1504. Its celebration of the nude male form reflects the influence of classical antiquity, but its subject is the biblical hero David.

of the period's most famous books was *Malleus Maleficarum* (1486), a treatise on hunting witches. Renaissance intellectuals and artists were in a sense backward-looking; self-consciously seeking to learn from and emulate the achievements of the ancient world and to reconcile the best of the wisdom of ancient Greece and Rome with their Christian faith. But they were also inspired by a confident belief in progress through free enquiry and fresh inventions.

Humanism
The loose international network of scholars who spearheaded the Renaissance are known as "humanists," reflecting the degree to which they placed humankind, rather than God, at the center of their world-view. A typical treatise published by humanist Pico della Mirandola in 1486 was entitled "On the Dignity of Man." These scholars studied ancient texts more critically than had been done before, reading in Greek as well as in Latin, which had long been the

«

BEFORE

In medieval times, some artists and thinkers were already breaking with tradition.

THE FIRST RENAISSANCE
Historians have identified an early "renaissance" in 12th century Europe. **Contact with the Muslim world and the Byzantine Empire** gave access to the works of Islamic and ancient Greek philosophers and scientists **« 158–59**.

GIOTTO
Florentine artist Giotto di Bondone (c. 1267–1337) initiated a **revolution in European painting** a century before the Renaissance proper. His religious frescoes broke with the conventions of Christian art, showing realistic figures engaged in dramatic scenes.

DIVINE COMEDY
In his epic **Divine Comedy**, describing a journey through Hell and Purgatory to Paradise, Florentine poet Dante Alighieri (1265–1321) combined the classical past with a medieval Christian view of the universe.

DANTE'S INFERNO

language of the educated in Europe. They also strove to establish an accurate text for the Bible—the famous humanist Erasmus regarded his Greek version of the New Testament as his major achievement. Humanists were often employed as tutors for the children of the rich and powerful, and they devised influential systems of education, focusing on subjects such as Latin, history, grammar, and rhetoric.

Feats in architecture

Architecture was an area in which the emulation of antiquity was most fruitful. One of the first great achievements of the Renaissance was the dome built for the cathedral in Florence by Filippo Brunelleschi. Brunelleschi had studied the ancient ruins in Rome, including the domed Pantheon (see pp.110–13), before embarking on the work. Completed in 1436, it was the largest dome ever built, a nearly miraculous feat of engineering as well as an aesthetic masterpiece. Domes were established as a crowning feature of the most ambitious Renaissance buildings, including St. Peter's Basilica in Rome,

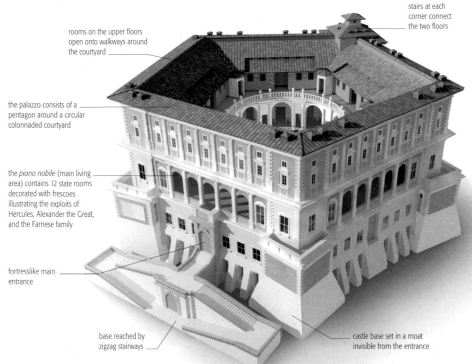

stairs at each corner connect the two floors

rooms on the upper floors open onto walkways around the courtyard

the palazzo consists of a pentagon around a circular colonnaded courtyard

the *piano nobile* (main living area) contains 12 state rooms decorated with frescoes illustrating the exploits of Hercules, Alexander the Great, and the Farnese family

fortresslike main entrance

base reached by zigzag stairways

castle base set in a moat invisible from the entrance

while antique-style columns, arches, and statues (see pp.116–17) abounded in palaces, villas, and churches.

Artists and art

In painting and sculpture, the influence of ancient Greece and Rome was evident, for example, in the interest in an ideal version of the naked human body, seen especially in the painting and sculpture of Michelangelo Buonarroti. Artists also added classical pagan mythology to their subject matter (see pp.142–43), although usually for the private enjoyment of wealthy connoisseurs. Christian and biblical themes predominated in art for public display. As well as a desire to match the art of antiquity, however, there was a novel drive to represent the visual world with illusionistic precision. Flemish artists such as Jan van Eyck led the way with oil paintings that represented human features and the surfaces of objects with astounding accuracy of detail. In the second half of the 15th-century, Italian artists such as Piero della Francesca and Andrea Mantegna pioneered the use of linear perspective, intended to create a perfect illusion of three-dimensional space on a flat »

Villa Farnese

Commissioned by the wealthy Farnese family, the Villa Farnese in Caprarola is considered a masterpiece of late Renaissance architecture. Architect Giacomo Barozzi de Vignola worked on the building from 1559–73.

The Birth of Venus

Painted around 1483, Sandro Botticelli's famous painting is unusual in having an overtly pagan (non-Christian) theme drawn from classical mythology. This was possible because it was produced for Lorenzo de Medici's private villa, not for public display.

Sistine ceiling

Commissioned by Pope Julius II in 1508, the ceiling of the Sistine Chapel in the Vatican is one of the masterworks of Florentine genius Michelangelo Buonarroti. Depicting scenes from the Old Testament, the frescoes took four years to complete.

CLASSICAL SCHOLAR (1466–1536)

ERASMUS

Dutch humanist Gerhard Gerhards, better known by his pen-name Erasmus, was ordained as a priest but lived as an independent scholar. In works such as *In Praise of Folly* (1509), he criticized the corruption of the Church, advocating a life governed by firm moral and religious principles. Erasmus's writings were among the first printed books to achieve a wide readership and they helped prepare the way for the Protestant Reformation (see pp.256–57).

"Our century, like a **golden age** has restored... the liberal arts."

MARSILIO FICINO, FLORENTINE PHILOSOPHER, 1492

surface. Associated with geometry and optics, painting was part of the mainstream of intellectual development in the Renaissance.

Overtaking the ancients

The striving for an exact depiction of the world in art was related to a wider trend toward the close observation of nature, rather than reliance on received wisdom. This produced clear advances on the knowledge inherited from the ancients. For instance, the dissection of corpses by the Brussels-born anatomist Andreas Vesalius at the University of Padua allowed the long-accepted views of Galen, the revered medical authority of antiquity, to be superseded. The geographical notions of the ancient Greek Ptolemy were corrected thanks to the efforts of European explorers and mapmakers. Nicolaus Copernicus challenged the current Christian view of the universe by asserting that the Sun, not Earth, was at the center of the solar system (see p.266).

Craftsmanship

Underpinning the achievements of the celebrated geniuses of the Renaissance was a widespread culture of practical ingenuity and skilled craftsmanship. Fine craft objects, such as the elaborate suits of armor made by the metal-workers of Nuremberg and Augsburg, or the products of Venetian or Florentine goldsmiths, were collected as avidly as any painting or sculpture. More practically, it was during this time that gunpowder weapons came into general use in European warfare

Timepiece
The first clocks marked with minutes appeared in the 1570s (see below), but truly accurate timekeeping was not possible until pendulum clocks were introduced in the 17th century.

A dagger carries an abbreviated Latin inscription, AET. SVAE 29. This gives the age of the subject, France's ambassador to England Jean de Dinteville, as 29.

Jean de Dinteville is depicted with his friend, French envoy Georges de Selve. The objects between them suggest their wealth and learning.

The celestial globe, showing the constellations, was the latest model, made by German astronomer Johannes Schöner. Its presence echoes the terrestrial globe below.

The scientific instruments are devices for navigation and time measurement. They are resting on a valuable Turkish rug, imported from the Ottoman Empire.

The Ambassadors
Painted by German artist Hans Holbein at the court of English king Henry VIII in 1533, this painting shows the Renaissance's fascination with scientific instruments as well as its taste for hidden meanings and visual tricks.

In the foreground is a distorted representation of a skull, an obvious symbol of mortality. The skull appears correctly if viewed from a precise low point to the side of the painting.

The open book is a Lutheran hymnal, open at the hymns "Come Holy Ghost" and "Man Wilt Thou Live Blessedly." It probably hints at the religious conflicts of the Reformation.

(see pp.272–73). Mechanical clocks, which had first started to appear in the towers of Italian cities in the 14th century, became more widespread. Navigational instruments such as magnetic compasses were essential tools of expanding seaborne trade.

The printed word

By far the most influential product of European enterprise, however, was the printing press. Fresh thinking became readily available through the relative speed with which new printed books could be produced and distributed. Literature in the vernacular—everyday languages such as English, Italian, and French, rather than scholarly Latin—received an enormous boost. Humanist scholars were able to circulate accurate, standardized versions of major texts. The most important of these was the Bible. Providing people with direct access to what was regarded as the word of God was a prime cause of the great religious upheaval of the Reformation (see pp.256–57).

Political turmoil

The cultural developments of the Renaissance took place within a context of acute political and religious conflicts. The Italian city-states that were such dynamos of creativity were also the site of vicious power struggles. In Florence the dominant Medici family was twice driven into exile by popular uprisings, in 1494 and 1527, and twice restored to power. Civil conflicts were complicated by the intervention of the armies of the kings of France and the Habsburg emperors, who fought one another in Italy in a series of wars from the 1490s to the 1550s. Rome was laid waste by an imperial army in 1527. Observing these conflicts at close hand inspired Florentine Niccolo Machiavelli to write his cynical political handbook *The Prince* in 1513 (published in 1532), advising the wise ruler to use any methods, however immoral, to stay in power. Whether or not this was good advice, it certainly described the normal practice of Renaissance political leaders. Machiavelli's model for *The Prince* was the ruthless Cesare Borgia (1476–1507), the illegitimate son of Pope Alexander VI, who was suspected of many murders, including that of his elder brother.

Niccolo Machiavelli
Author of *The Prince*, Machiavelli based his pragmatic political philosophy upon his experiences as a diplomat in the service of Florence.

Challenge to the Church

Religious disputes grew out of a discontent with the state of the Church that was simmering throughout the 15th century. Much of the thrust of Renaissance humanism, especially in the works of Erasmus, consisted of an attack on the ignorance and corruption of the clergy, including successive popes, and calls for a return to a purer form of faith. On the other hand, Renaissance artists, as purveyors of luxury goods sometimes with pagan connotations, found their works under attack from religious reformers.

Religious revival

Between 1494 and 1498, a radical monk, Girolamo Savonarola, won control of Florence and led an orgy of book-burning and destruction of works of art in his campaign against wealth and corruption. One of the main provocations for the Reformation that challenged papal authority from 1517 was outrage at the money being spent on commissioning men such as Raphael and Michelangelo to beautify Rome. The atmosphere

of religious revival in the Reformation and the Counter-Reformation (see pp.258–59) was broadly hostile to the spirit of free inquiry and invention that animated the Renaissance. In the second half of the 16th century, both zealous Protestants and Catholics cracked down on the "free-thinking" that undermined their religious orthodoxies. But in the longer term, there was to be no turning back from the development of scientific and philosophical inquiry, the dissemination of knowledge and culture in printed books, and innovation in the arts.

Mercator map
Representing the latest knowledge of geography, this map was created by Flemish cartographer Gerardus Mercator in 1587. Mercator's projection, his famous method for representing the globe on a flat surface, was still in widespread use four centuries later.

> " It is much safer for a prince to be **feared than loved** if he is to fail in one of the two."

NICCOLO MACHIAVELLI, FROM "THE PRINCE," 1532

Renaissance clock
The introduction of spring-powered timepieces at the start of the 16th century allowed smaller portable clocks such as this to be made for domestic use.

AFTER

Renaissance thinkers came in conflict with the Church, but their achievements lived on.

RELIGIOUS REACTION
In 1542 the Catholic Church established the Congregation for the Doctrine of the Faith in Rome as a body to **suppress ideas contrary to the Church's teaching.** In 1564 Pope Pius IV established an **Index of Proscribed [banned] Books,** which included the works of Erasmus and Copernicus. Giordano Bruno, a wide-ranging thinker in the Renaissance tradition, was **burned at the stake** in Rome after the Congregation found him guilty of heresy in 1600.

ART AND ARCHITECTURE
Through the 16th century, European painting, sculpture, and architecture developed in a less naturalistic direction, **valuing expression above harmony and true proportion**. This more artificial style has been labeled "Mannerism" by art historians. Mannerism evolved into the exuberant Baroque style dominant in the 17th century.

GALILEO
Working in Italian cities including Pisa, Padua, and Florence, Galileo Galilei (1564–1642) built on the **Renaissance spirit of inquiry and observation** to lay the foundations of the Scientific Revolution 266–67 ≫.

LATE RENAISSANCE
In some countries the Renaissance is generally agreed to have flowered at a later date. In both England and Spain, the height of the Renaissance did not occur until the second half of the 16th century and early 17th century, when writers, musicians and artists such as Thomas Tallis, Edmund Spenser, William Shakespeare, El Greco, and Miguel Cervantes all flourished.

INVENTION

THE PRINTING PRESS

The first effective press for printing books using movable metal type and oil-based ink emerged in 15th century Europe. Its invention is attributed to Johannes Gutenberg, a German artisan and entrepreneur. The Bible that he published in 1455 was the first book printed in this way. The new technique spread, with presses established in Paris in 1470 and London in 1476. The most prestigious early printer, Aldus Manutius, set up the Aldine Press in Venice in 1494. By 1500 some 35,000 different books were in print. Much cheaper than hand-written works, printed books revolutionized the diffusion of knowledge.

> "**A spring of truth** shall flow from it…"

GUTENBERG, 15TH CENTURY

heavy platen or printing plate

tympan

bar to lower platen

leather ink ball, stuffed with horsehair

sliding coffin

sturdy wooden frame

Leonardo da Vinci

ARTIST AND INVENTOR Born 1452 Died 1519

"All our **knowledge** has its origins in our perceptions."

LEONARDO DA VINCI

One of the great geniuses of the Italian Renaissance (see pp.250–53), Leonardo was the illegitimate son of a peasant woman; his father married a Florentine heiress eight months after his birth. Raised in the countryside outside Florence, he received little formal education, and only learned Latin, the basic accomplishment of an educated man of his day, in adulthood. Instead, he studied the animals and landscapes around him. It was characteristic of Leonardo that, at a time when artists and philosophers were fixated on learning from the classical past, he concentrated on direct observation of the human and natural world.

It is possible to present Leonardo's career as that of an ambitious artisan and entrepreneur, a poor boy making good use of opportunities for profit and advancement. He had the good fortune to be born near Florence, home to the finest concentration of painters, sculptors, and architects in 15th-century Europe. At about age 14, he was apprenticed to Andrea del Verrocchio, a leading sculptor whose studio had recently branched out into painting. Leonardo's outstanding talent, especially in the relatively new medium of oil painting, was unmistakable, and in his mid-20s he was able to set up a studio of his own.

Leonardo's paintings are now his most famous achievement, but in the 15th century, even with his own studio, an artist was only a craftsman touting for commissions. The next step up was to be taken on by a prince as a member of his household. Thus, in about 1482, Leonardo proposed his services to Ludovico Sforza, the ruler of

Ducal commission
This document from Cesare Borgia, lord of the Romagna, dates to 1502, commissioned "architect and engineer" Leonardo to survey palaces and fortresses.

Florence Cathedral
During his apprenticeship in Florence, Leonardo helped place the orb and cross on top of the city's famous cathedral dome.

Self-portrait
Leonardo drew this haunting self-portrait when he was in his mid-60s, three or four years before his death. The long hair and beard give him the air of a traditional sage or seer.

INVENTION

FLYING MACHINE

From an early age Leonardo was obsessed by the idea of flight. He studied birds on the wing, commenting that "a bird is a machine operating according to mathematical laws." This model is a full-size realization of his design for an ornithopter—a machine powered by flapping artificial wings. It could never work because human muscles are not strong enough in proportion to the weight of a human body. Indeed, none of Leonardo's flying machines were practical; they were simply flights of imagination.

AN ORNITHOPTER

experiments. They include studies of the movement of water and speculations on the nature of the cosmos, as well as reflections on fossils, and on the principles of flight. They also include the record of one of his greatest achievements, the systematic exploration of human anatomy. Leonardo obtained about 30 corpses for dissection, from which he produced the most refined, accurate, and annotated sketches.

A modern thinker

Leonardo's idiosyncratic personality and free-ranging mind could easily have brought him into conflict with the authorities. His homosexuality was both a sin and a crime in the society he inhabited, even if it was not generally disapproved of in sophisticated circles. Dissecting corpses was of dubious legality and almost got him into trouble in Rome in about 1515. He seems to have had no fixed religious beliefs and certainly did not allow Christian doctrine to set limits to his thinking. In his declining years, Leonardo was respected, even revered. Around 1515 he appears to have suffered a stroke. Unable to undertake major works, he found a sympathetic patron in the French King Francis I, who appreciated the prestige of having such a renowned figure in his employ. It is reported that Francis said he could never believe there was another man born in this world who knew as much as Leonardo. Few of Leonardo's paintings have survived, but their scarcity has if anything enhanced his legendary status.

Milan. Judging that the warlike Milanese ruler might have more need of a military engineer than of an artist, Leonardo listed at length the "infinite variety of machines for attack and defense" that he could create, including armored cars, portable bridges, and cannons, before mentioning as an afterthought his skills at painting and sculpture.

A man of talent

Leonardo's all-around skills, including his ingenuity at designing machines, were exactly what Renaissance princes were looking for, and he rarely lacked employment for the rest of his life. Even at the end of his career, he was engaged by the French monarchy as firstly "engineer" and then "painter and architect." Leonardo's boundless imagination and experimentation led to many failures and disappointments. For Ludovico Sforza he designed one of the largest equestrian statues ever conceived, but it is unlikely that it could have been cast and only a clay model was built. His *Last Supper*, considered one of the ultimate masterpieces of Western art, was painted using an innovative technique that meant it started decaying almost as soon as it was finished. In the service of the ruler of Florence from 1503, he produced a

Anatomical drawing
Leonardo's sketch of a cross section of a human skull showed impressive anatomical details, which are due to the autopsies he preformed.

grandiose project for a canal linking the city to the sea, which was never built, and he also undertook to paint the Anghiari fresco for the Palazzo Vecchio, which was never completed. The machines he dreamed of were ingenious and forward-thinking but mostly impractical.

In fact, much of Leonardo's most remarkable work consisted of writings and sketches in his private notebooks, material that remained unpublished until long after his death. It was in these notebooks that Leonardo's fertile, inquiring, adventurous mind and eye found full expression. The pages are packed with an astonishing number of ideas, observations, projects, and

"Art is **never finished**, only abandoned."

LEONARDO DA VINCI

The Last Supper
Leonardo painted *The Last Supper* in the refectory of the church of Saint Maria delle Grazie in Milan, using a mix of tempera and oil, rather than a traditional fresco technique. As a result, the paint soon began to flake off.

« BEFORE

The Catholic Church dominated Europe throughout the medieval period and into the 16th century.

EARLY REFORMERS
The Lollards from England in the 14th century and the

HUSSITES

Hussites from Bohemia in the early 15th century both proposed reforms of the Catholic Church **to end corruption** and purify church doctrine.

THE GREAT SCHISM
Pope Clement V moved the papacy to Avignon in France in 1309 to avoid **internal feuding in Rome**. An attempt to return the papacy to Rome in 1379 led to the election of two rival popes, causing a **schism << 194–95**. A Church meeting in Germany in 1417 elected a third pope to replace the two rivals.

RENAISSANCE EXCESS
The building of a vast new basilica in Rome was funded by the **sale of indulgences**, or pardons for sins, which typified the **extravagance** of the Catholic Church in the 15th century.

ST. PETER'S BASILICA, ROME

120 The number of years it took to build St. Peter's Basilica in Rome. Pope Leo X financed construction partly through the sale of indulgences and used the leading artists of the Renaissance (see pp.250–53) to design and decorate it.

The **Reformation**

A simple but effective protest against corruption in the Catholic Church in 1517 soon turned into a major force for religious change known as the Reformation. It transformed the political, social, and economic face of Europe over the next few centuries, and its legacy can still be seen around the world today.

Martin Luther's (see below) challenge against the Catholic Church in Wittenberg, Saxony, came after the arrival in the area of German preacher Johann Tetzel, who was selling indulgences (see BEFORE) to raise money for Pope Leo X. Indulgences had long been criticized by Catholic theologians (scholars of religion) but their financial success ensured the practice was too lucrative to end. Luther's response, on October 23, 1517, was to post a document bearing 95 theses (statements) on the door of the town church. Luther's theses were not radical, but they attracted a wide audience, and due to recent advances in printing methods (see p.253) they were widely distributed and read. Luther's initial criticism of the church focused on the sale of indulgences, but he went on to attack the core Catholic teachings of transubstantiation (the belief that bread and wine change into the body and blood of Christ when received during communion), clerical celibacy, and papal supremacy. He also called for a reform of religious orders such as monasteries, and a return to the simplicity of the earlier church.

The Lutheran church

Luther's challenge to the established church won him many followers, but he initially wished only to reform the existing church rather than set up an entirely new system. Several attempts were made to reconcile Luther with the religious authorities, until, in 1521, he

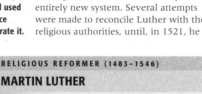

PROLO

Leather bindings enclose parchment pages. About 170 copies of the Bible were printed, its 1,200 pages appearing in two separate volumes.

The Gutenberg Bible
The world's first printed Bible was produced, in Latin, by the German printer Johannes Gutenberg in 1455. Bibles in the vernacular, or common language, first appeared during the Reformation.

RELIGIOUS REFORMER (1483–1546)

MARTIN LUTHER

A university-educated priest and friar, Martin Luther became a professor of theology (the study of religion) at Wittenberg University in 1512. His disagreements with the Catholic Church hierarchy over its conduct led to a revolt against the institution in 1517 that soon spread across Europe. Luther was a reluctant revolutionary, preferring at first to reform the Church from within, but once excluded from the Church in 1521, he proved to be an energetic and skilled leader, making good use of the new printing technology to write and distribute pamphlets publicizing his views. His belief in order, and his conservative political views, put him at odds with many who wished to develop more radical religious doctrines.

> " Here I stand. I can do no other. **God help me**. Amen. "
>
> MARTIN LUTHER, ADDRESSING THE DIET OF WORMS, APRIL 18, 1521

Decorative margins and headings were inscribed by hand before the printed sheets were bound together.

Gothic printed type modeled on German hand-written script.

"… the **only supreme head** on Earth of the Church in England."

DESCRIPTION OF HENRY VIII OF ENGLAND IN THE ACT OF SUPREMACY, 1534

was summoned to present his views at an imperial Diet (parliament) at Worms in front of Holy Roman Emperor Charles V, who ruled over much of Europe. Luther refused to retract his views and, having already been excommunicated (expelled from the church) by the pope, was now outlawed by the emperor. His response was to set up his own independent church. He also set to work translating the Bible into German; previous editions of the Bible had been transcribed in Latin—Luther's edition would allow people to read the Bible in their native language for the first time.

Part of the power of Luther's teachings lay in their appeal to German identity. Germany at this point was made up of many independent states, nominally controlled by Emperor Charles V. German princes wishing to exert their power against the dominance of Charles V saw Luther's teachings as a way of breaking both imperial and church control over Germany. What began as a religious debate soon became a political revolt. In 1524 the Peasants' War broke out in southwest Germany as a result of economic hardship in the region. A league of German princes, supported by Luther, crushed the revolt in 1526 with great loss of life. The revolt horrified Luther as much as it did the secular leaders it was aimed at. One by one, the north German states of Saxony, Hesse,

Brandenburg, Brunswick, and others adopted Lutheranism. Each state took control of the church, strengthening the hold of the ruler over his people.

Worldwide appeal

The appeal of Lutheranism was not restricted to Germany. In 1527 Gustavus Vasa, the ruler of Sweden (which had only gained independence from Denmark–Norway in 1523), seized church lands to provide funds for his new state. He then reformed the new state church along Lutheran lines. A similar process saw the adoption of Lutheranism in Denmark–Norway in 1536. In England, a break with the church in Rome came about after the pope refused Henry VIII a divorce from his wife, Catherine of Aragon. Henry replaced the Pope as head of the English church.

Political fallout

The political response to the Lutheran reformation was led by Emperor Charles V. However, his vast territorial domains in Europe brought him in conflict with, among others, France. War between these two sides, as well as between Charles and the growing might of the Muslim Ottoman empire in the Mediterranean and Balkans (see pp. 246–47), meant he could not devote all of his resources to crushing the Lutherans in Germany. Charles defeated the Lutherans in battle at Mühlberg in 1547, but he could not crush them politically. A religious and political compromise was finally reached by the Peace of Augsburg in 1555, by which the emperor allowed each prince within the empire to choose between Catholicism and Lutheranism and impose that belief upon his subjects.

The Renaissance papacy
Pope Leo X became a cardinal while still a child. He promoted the sale of indulgences to pay for the rebuilding of St. Peter's Basilica, prompting Luther's protest against this practice in 1517.

THE REFORMATION
The Protestant Reformation began in Germany in 1517 and had a profound and disruptive effect across Europe well into the next century.

1517 Martin Luther posts his **95 Theses** on a church door in Wittenberg, Saxony, in eastern Germany.

1518 The Swiss Reformation begins under the leadership of **Ulrich Zwingli**.

1519 Charles I of Spain becomes Holy Roman Emperor Charles V.

1521 Luther is excommunicated by the pope and **outlawed** by the Holy Roman Emperor Charles V.

1524–26 The **Peasants' War** rages in southern Germany; north German states adopt Lutheranism.

1540 Pope Paul III acknowledges **Jesuit** religious order and makes them the chief agents of the **Counter-Reformation**.

1545 The **Council of Trent** meets for first time to define Catholic policy.

1560 The **Calvinist reformation** begins in Scotland.

1555 The **Peace of Augsburg** ends the religious wars in Germany.

1563 The **Anglican Church** is established in England.

1562–98 French wars of religion begin between Catholics and French Protestants (Huguenots).

1568–1648 Protestant **Dutch rebellion** against Catholic Spanish rule.

1580 The Protestant queen of England, Elizabeth I, has the Catholic **Mary Queen of Scots** executed.

1593 Protestant king of Navarre **Henri IV converts to Catholicism** to secure the throne of France.

1598 The **Edict of Nantes** brings an end to the French wars of religion by allowing Protestant worship in France.

1618–48 30 Years War starts as a religious conflict, but ends as a national power struggle; the peace that ends the war grants religious freedom to Calvinists.

| 1500 | 1520 | 1540 | 1560 | 1580 | 1600 |

>> Luther himself was conservative in theology and in his respect for order, but many of those who followed him were far more radical.

Zwingli and Calvin

In Zurich, Switzerland, Ulrich Zwingli (1484–1531) converted the city along Lutheran lines: his 67 theses of 1523 were adopted by the city council as official doctrine. However, he disagreed with Luther about the nature of the Eucharist (the bread and wine received during communion) and began to lead the Swiss Church in a more radical, anti-hierarchical direction. His death in 1531 while defending Zurich against the Catholic cantons (provinces) of Switzerland slowed the momentum of the reformation in Switzerland. Calvin (see below), who was starting to create a new religious center in the city of Geneva, subsequently emerged as the key figure associated with protestant reform in Switzerland.

Calvin had converted to the new reformed faith in 1533 and settled in Geneva in 1536. There he developed a more austere form of Protestantism, based on his own reading of scriptures and his rigorous academic training, stressing predestination—God's control of all human actions. Though Calvin himself did not develop any practical theory of resistance to "ungodly authority," such as the Catholic Church or Catholic rulers, many of his successors were prepared to justify violent resistance through his teachings. Like Luther, he stressed both an individual's direct relationship with God without a papal or priestly intermediary and the primacy of the Bible—now widely distributed in modern languages

RELIGIOUS REFORMER (1509–64)
JOHN CALVIN

Born in France, John Calvin prepared for a church career in Paris, but in 1533 experienced a "sudden conversion" to the reformed faith. He wrote the *Institutes of the Christian Religion* (1534), rejecting papal authority in favor of justification by faith alone. He settled in Geneva in 1536, where he sought to create a society in which the demands of "godly behavior" were strictly enforced by a combination of church and civil authorities. The duty of the citizen was to interpret the Bible and create a godly society.

Warhaffte Abbildung des Heil: Concily oder Kirchen-Versamlung zu Trient, so Anng
A° 1545 vnd geendet 1563 Wie solche Herr oberster Melchior Lussy Ritter vnd Lan
Alls gewester Abgesandter von den 7. Lobl: Chat Cantonen in seinem Wahnha
Abmahlen Lassen: Diese Taffel hat Herr Haubtman Felix Leonti Keÿser
-aman zu Ehren vnd gedächtnus Hochermelten Herren Lussis als seines gewes
Herren Copieren, und in das Capuciner-Convent vbersetzen Lassen A
A Ist das orth wa Herr Lussy in dem Concilio   Den sitz gehabt, der Keÿserliche
portugösische, vnd venetianische Abgesandte   hatte den vor Rang, Wie B. di
aber nach ihme, der spanische Aber sasse beÿ   dem Herzen Secretario ga

Council of Trent
The Counter-Reformation was conceived in the Italian Alpine town of Trent, then under Austrian Habsburg rule. Here, in the cathedral, the Church Council met in 1545–47, 1551–52, and finally in 1562–63, to reform the doctrines and practices of the church to meet the threat posed by the Protestant Reformation.

Pope Paul III convened the first session of the Council of Trent in 1545; the second and third sessions were convened by Julius III and Pius IV.

Catholic cardinals and bishops and leading Catholic theologians attended the council; no Protestants attended.

COUNTER-REFORMATION

The Counter- (or Catholic) Reformation set out to challenge the appeal of the new Protestant churches by reforming and remodeling the Catholic Church, drawing on a great mass of reformist sentiment and enthusiasm within the church that had been building up since the late 15th century. It strengthened the spiritual institution of the papacy, reformed old and formed new religious orders, most notably the Jesuits, who set up schools and missions to preach Catholic virtues, and clarified church doctrines. Congregations were lured back into church through increased use of ornament and spectacle, best personified by the glorious new churches in the Baroque style in Austria and Italy—the spectacular ceiling of St. Ignatius Church in Rome (right), dating from around 1707, shows the missionary work of the Jesuits.

and not the Latin of the church—as the foundation of all preaching and teaching. Unlike Luther, however, who believed in the political subordination of the church to the state, Calvin preached that church and state should act together to create a "godly society"

St. Bartholomew's Day Massacre
The French wars of religion reached a bloody climax on St. Bartholomew's Day (August 24) 1572, when the French regent, Catherine de Medici, authorized the massacre of about 200 Huguenot leaders meeting in Paris for her daughter's wedding. Catholic mobs then went on a rampage, killing thousands more Huguenots.

Reformation in Europe
By 1600 the religious map of Europe was largely settled. Lutheran churches were well established in Germany and Scandinavia, and Calvinist churches in Switzerland, the Netherlands, and Scotland. The Anglican religion was established in England and Wales. France, Spain, Portugal, Italy, southern Germany, and Poland were largely Catholic, although Calvinist beliefs were strong in south and west France, while Austria was evenly split.

KEY

Catholic

Protestant

—— Frontiers 1590

in which religious beliefs and strict codes of conduct should shape every aspect of daily life. Calvinism took hold in Scotland, the Netherlands, and in large parts of France, where followers were known as Huguenots, and in areas across the German states, Bohemia, and Transylvania. Calvinism also inspired the Puritan movement in England and, later, North America, whose members wished to purify the Anglican church of its remaining Catholic elements, notably the authority of bishops and the "popish" adornment of church vestments, ornaments, and music.

The Catholic response
The initial Catholic response to the Reformation was to excommunicate (exclude from the sacraments of the church) those who rebelled against it. As it became clear that it could not crush the Reformation, the Catholic Church began to reform itself, drawing on a groundswell of internal calls for church reform that long predated the emergence of Luther.

Meeting in three sessions at Trent in the Italian Alps from 1545–63, the Catholic Church initiated a Counter-Reformation (see box). The Catholic Counter-Reformation succeeded in its aims, strengthening Catholicism both theologically and politically, although a more authoritarian orthodoxy was instituted. Poland, Austria, and Bavaria now became solidly Catholic. But while Germany remained largely at peace, the strong Calvinist (Huguenot) presence in France prompted a lengthy religious war that was only ended with the granting of religious toleration in the Edict of Nantes in 1598. By the end of the century, perhaps 40 percent of Europe's population followed one or other of the reformed beliefs.

AFTER

The impact of the Reformation continued to be felt well into the 17th century.

WARS OF RELIGION
Religious fervor continued to inflame European politics. The **30 Years War 262–63 ≫** of 1618–49 began as a religious conflict between Catholic Austria and Protestant Bohemia (in the present-day Czech Republic), although in its later stages it became a political struggle for supremacy between France and the equally Catholic nations of Spain and Austria. The **Wars of the Three Kingdoms** in the British Isles (including the English Civil War **264–65 ≫**), which developed after 1639, were largely caused by Charles I's emphasis on an Anglican church, which stressed ritual and the importance of the sacraments, actions that were regarded as "popish" by the Calvinist Scots and Charles' enemies among the puritan English. Not until the signing of the **Treaty of Westphalia** ending the 30 Years War in 1648 did **religion become secondary to the state** in European politics.

QUEEN OF ENGLAND Born 1533 Died 1603

Elizabeth I

"I have the body but of a **weak and feeble woman**, but... the **heart... of a king**" ELIZABETH I AT TILBURY, 1588

From her earliest years, England's future Queen Elizabeth I was surrounded by danger and intrigue. Her birth was a disappointment to her father, Henry VIII, who was desperate for a male heir. He had declared himself head of the English Church so he could divorce and marry again, in an effort to produce a son with his new wife. Elizabeth was two-and-a-half when her mother, Henry's second wife Anne Boleyn, was executed on his orders, accused of adultery. Declared illegitimate, Elizabeth was relegated to court life, finding safety in discretion. After Henry's death in 1547 she was taken under the protection of his widow and sixth wife, Catherine Parr, and educated together with her half-brother, the future Edward VI.

Her elder half-sister Mary's accession to the throne in 1553 placed Elizabeth in a perilous situation. The Catholic Mary

Gloriana
Elizabeth I's style of dress expressed both her love of finery and her desire to present an image of power and magnificence.

The Tudor Rose
The symbol of the Tudor dynasty, of which Elizabeth was the fourth monarch, was created by Henry VII.

Henry VIII
Elizabeth I's father was a true Renaissance man. He was highly educated, fluent in several languages, and adept at sports such as tennis. He was also an avid huntsman. One of Henry's lasting legacies is the establishment of the Church of England.

The Spanish Armada
The sea was described as "groaning under the weight" of the Spanish fleet sent to attack England in 1588. The decisive defeat of the armada was Elizabeth's finest hour.

had every reason to distrust a sister who could be put forward as a Protestant candidate for the throne. Elizabeth survived by steering clear of plots against Mary and maintaining a facade of loyalty. The worst she suffered was a brief imprisonment in the Tower of London, in 1554.

The Golden Age
The early deaths of her siblings brought Elizabeth to the throne at the age of 25. From the start of her reign, she chose her advisers well, especially her chief secretary of state, William Cecil. The goal she set them was the survival of her person and her state—a goal dictating

caution, suspicion, and ruthlessness when required. Elizabeth refused to endorse Protestant extremism, insisting on royal control over the Church but trying to avoid complex issues of doctrine. Plots and rebellions by English and Irish Catholics plagued her reign, and she had her cousin, Mary Queen of Scots, imprisoned and eventually executed as a dangerous Catholic claimant to the throne. Elizabeth similarly attempted to avoid involvement in the religious wars racking Europe, but was reluctantly drawn into backing the Protestant Dutch against Catholic Spain.

The Virgin Queen
Elizabeth's role in the cultural flowering that occurred in England during her reign and the feats of English mariners is hard to assess. She supported the arts financially, although her taste in theater was more for clowning than for refined wit. Adventurers such as Sir Francis Drake enjoyed her fitful support, backed when their schemes served her purposes. For the last two decades of her reign, England was at war with

Drake knighted
Elizabeth I knighted Francis Drake on board his ship, the *Golden Hinde*, after his round-the-world voyage. The knighthood was a calculated political gesture, effectively giving royal backing to his plunder of the lands of the Spanish empire.

Royal offering
These gold-embroidered textile gloves were presented to Elizabeth I on a visit to Oxford University in 1566.

WRITER AND POET (1564–1616)

WILLIAM SHAKESPEARE

William Shakespeare, son of a Stratford-upon-Avon wool dealer, was one of the actors and dramatists financially supported by Elizabeth I. He is considered to be the greatest writer of the English language, and is believed to have written at least 37 plays and 154 sonnets. He excelled at both comedy and tragedy, and his works explored the universal human experience. *Twelfth Night* was written specifically to be performed at court for Elizabeth I.

Spain. Elizabeth's advisers tried to seek national security through an advantageous marriage between the queen and a foreign prince. Although Elizabeth toyed with proposals, she accepted none. Her aversion to marriage was simple. Unmarried she ruled; once married, she inevitably would have had to cede part or all of her power to her consort, as were the conventions of the day.

In Elizabeth's later years, the deaths of favorites and counselors left her an isolated figure. Yet she never lost her popularity with her people. In her final speech to parliament before her death, she deftly balanced her arrogant sense of an untrammeled "divine right" to rule with her aspiration to lead by popular consent: "Though God hath raised me high," she stated, "yet this I count the glory of my crown, that I have reigned with your loves."

TIMELINE

- **September 7, 1533** Anne Boleyn gives birth to the future Elizabeth I in Greenwich Palace; she is recognized as heir presumptive to the throne ahead of her half-sister Mary, daughter of Henry's first wife Catherine of Aragon.
- **May 19, 1536** Anne Boleyn is executed; Elizabeth is declared illegitimate and loses her right of succession to the throne.
- **June 1543** An act of parliament restores Elizabeth to the line of succession, after her brother Edward VI and sister Mary.
- **January 28, 1547** Henry VIII dies; Elizabeth becomes a ward of his widow, Catherine Parr. He is succeeded by his son, Edward VI.
- **March 20, 1549** Catherine Parr's fourth husband, Thomas Seymour, with whom Elizabeth has been closely associated, is executed for treason.
- **July 19, 1553** Elizabeth's Catholic sister Mary accedes to the throne.
- **March 18, 1554** Elizabeth is imprisoned in the Tower of London for alleged complicity in a rebellion against Mary led by Sir Thomas Wyatt; she is released on May 19.
- **July 25, 1554** Mary marries Philip II of Spain in Winchester Cathedral; Roman Catholicism is restored as the primary religion in England.
- **November 17, 1558** Elizabeth accedes to the throne on the death of Mary; she is crowned in Westminster Abbey on January 15, 1559.
- **May 8, 1559** The Act of Supremacy asserts the Queen as head of the Church of England, restoring the Anglican Church in place of Mary's Catholicism.
- **1564** Elizabeth makes her favorite, Robert Dudley, the Earl of Leicester.
- **November 9, 1569** The Catholic Earls of Northumberland and Westmoreland lead the Northern Rebellion against Elizabeth.
- **February 20, 1570** The Northern Rebellion is defeated.
- **April 4, 1581** Elizabeth knights Francis Drake after he completes a voyage around the world.
- **1585** Anglo-Spanish War begins: Elizabeth supports the Netherlands, in revolt against Spanish rule.
- **July 1588** The Spanish Armada, an attempt by Philip II of Spain to invade England, fails.
- **1590–96** Edmund Spenser's epic poem *The Faerie Queene*, in praise of Elizabeth (or Gloriana in the poem), is published.
- **August 4, 1598** William Cecil (later known as Baron Burghley), Elizabeth's chief adviser since the start of her reign, dies.
- **November 30, 1601** Elizabeth makes her last address to Parliament.
- **March 24, 1603** Elizabeth dies in Richmond Palace, Surrey.

LETTER FROM ELIZABETH I TO DRAKE

> " Germany… is a place of dead men's skulls… and **a field of blood.** "
>
> EDWARD CALAMY, ENGLISH PREACHER, 1641

Defenestration of Prague
Protestants assembled in Prague's Hradschin Castle, where they threw two Catholic regents out of a window in protest for violating guarantees of religious freedom.

Battle of White Mountain, 1620
This was the first major military encounter of the 30 Years War. The Catholic League and imperial forces had a numerical advantage over the Protestant troops, routing them in just two hours.

The 30 Years War

The Habsburg-controlled Holy Roman Empire sought to reestablish its imperial authority against an array of disparate enemies from 1618 to 1648. Initially a civil war between rival religious factions in Germany, the 30 Years War became a battle for European supremacy.

BEFORE

Religious divisions, dynastic ambition, and the impact of the Reformation **<< 256–59** all had a role in sowing the seeds of the 30 Years War.

HELMET OF CHARLES V, HOLY ROMAN EMPEROR

HOLY ROMAN EMPIRE
The Frankish king, Charlemagne (742–814), was the empire's first ruler **<< 188–89**. By the end of the 16th century **the empire included much of Germany**, part of the Netherlands, Bohemia (Czech Republic), and many states in Italy.

THE STRUCTURE OF GERMANY
During the Reformation, Holy Roman Emperor Charles V allowed the princes of each state within his realm to choose their state's religion **<< 256–59**. **Many German states adopted Protestantism**, causing tension within the Holy Roman Empire.

Throughout the 16th century, the Catholic Church was the only continent-wide institution in Western Europe, remaining part of the daily routine of millions of its inhabitants. But the words of Martin Luther, John Calvin, and the Reformation (see pp.256–59) had challenged the previously unquestioned authority of the pope. The result was the agreement in 1555 of the Peace of Augsburg. The Holy Roman Emperor, Charles V, along with the Imperial Diet (legislative assembly) headed by the empire's great princes, agreed that each ruler in the empire should be able to choose between Catholicism or Lutheranism (but not Calvinism) for their realm's religion. This gave Lutherans equal rights under the imperial constitution.

Tension still existed between Catholics and Protestants, however. In 1607 a riot between the two sides broke out in the south German city of Donauwörth. The emperor authorized Catholic Duke of Bavaria, Maximilian I, to restore order. When the duke imposed a rigorous Catholic settlement on the city, German protestants formed a defensive Protestant Union led by Calvinist Frederick V, ruler of the Rhineland Palatinate. This was swiftly followed by the formation of the Catholic League led by Maximilian I. The Imperial Diet tried to resolve the ill will, but the more radical Protestants walked out and the Diet did not meet again until 1640.

The real flashpoint came in 1617. A Habsburg duke, the devoutly Catholic Ferdinand of Styria, was

Plug bayonet
Musketeers during the 30 Years War used their muskets as clubs when too close to fire, relying on pikemen to defend them. Later, the plug bayonet, fitted into the gun's muzzle, was a better close-quarters weapon.

named Crown Prince and Emperor Matthias's successor as King of Bohemia, a primarily Protestant realm. As a result of his push for a Catholic Reformation in Bohemia, Protestant nobles rebelled in 1618 with the "Defenestration of Prague" (see left). Regents representing Ferdinand

ENDEMIC WAR
The 30 Years War was a series of conflicts spurred by religious bigotry and imperial paranoia that divided Europe from 1618–48. For the people living in central Europe, this period was one of continuous warring.

1620 Ferdinand crushes Bohemian revolt in the **Battle of White Mountain**.

1619 Death of Habsburg Emperor Matthias; Ferdinand becomes Holy Roman Emperor.

1629 Treaty of Lübeck marks the Danish defeat and end to involvement in the 30 Years War.

1632 Swedish king **Gustavus Adolphus** is killed at the battle of Lützen, Saxony, Germany.

1634 Battle of Nördlingen; Swedes are crushed by HRE.

1635 France intervenes, preventing pro-Habsburg peace.

1643 Battle of Rocroi, NE of Rheims, France. Spanish army crosses into France, stopping to besiege Rocroi.

1648 Treaty of Westphalia ends 30 Years War.

1645 France defeats Bavarian army at **Alerheim**.

1618	1628	1638	1648

1618 Members of **Bohemian aristocracy revolt** after Ferdinand becomes King of Bohemia in 1617 and pushes Catholic reform.

1626 Danish King **Christian IV** intervenes to help German Protestants against Holy Roman Empire.

1631 First **Battle of Breitenfeld**, outside Leipzig, Germany. Swedish–Saxon Alliance is formed against Ferdinand. An imperial army invades Saxony in an attempt to break the alliance.

1637 Death of Emperor Ferdinand II.

1642 Second **Battle of Breitenfeld**. Swedish general Torstensson ravages Habsburg lands in Austria.

1647 Truce of Ulm is signed by Bavaria, Cologne, France, and Sweden.

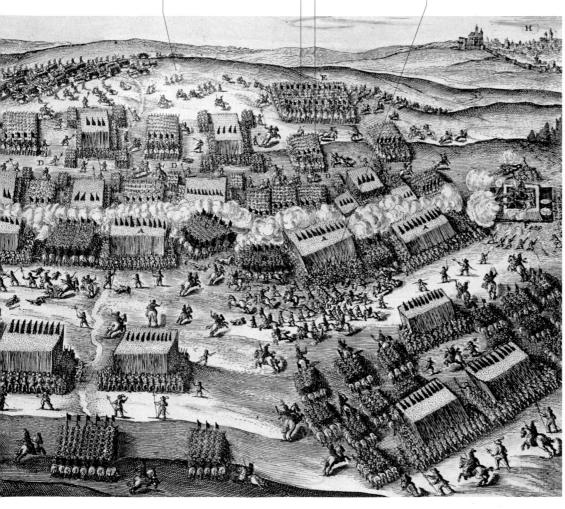

The site of the battle was a small, low hillside just outside Prague where 23,000 Austrian imperial and Catholic forces faced about 21,000 Protestants of the Bohemian Estates' army and the Czech nobility under Frederich V, king of Bohemia.

Imperial forces outnumber the Estates forces, though the latter had well-trained mercenaries and the advantage of being on higher ground.

The Estates army formed two echelons of footsoldiers, about 5,000 cavalry, and reserves. The right wing flanked an arboretum, the left backed against a hillock.

Blocks of troops were typical of this period: being less spread out, they were easier to command. However, any accurate artillery shell or side-on cavalry charge on such a formation spelled disaster, as the target was larger.

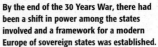

AFTER

By the end of the 30 Years War, there had been a shift in power among the states involved and a framework for a modern Europe of sovereign states was established.

EMERGENCE OF SOVEREIGN STATES
The Peace of Westphalia paved the way for the concept of the sovereign state. **Fixed geographical boundaries** for the many countries involved were established and states of the Holy Roman Empire were **granted full sovereignty**. It was recognized that citizens were bound to the laws of their own government rather than those of neighboring powers, whether religious or secular.

THE RISE OF FRANCE
The end of the war left Germany decentralized and divided into many territories. A politically weakened Spain recognized the Dutch Republic —and later Portugal—as independent. France continued to war with Spain until 1659, when it emerged as the **dominant Western power**.

RELIGIOUS TOLERANCE
Calvinism, Lutheranism, and Catholicism were all recognized as **legitimate faiths**. While religious conflicts still occurred, there were no further great religious wars in mainland Europe.

DECLINE OF THE MERCENARY
The hiring of mercenaries had been commonplace in realms that lacked standing armies. However, the size of these armies had grown massively, making them **very costly to maintain**. They also caused great destruction as the soldiers attempted to live off the land, often taking from civilians. These limitations gave rise to the idea of the national "professional" army.

7 MILLION The estimated number of dead in the 30 Years War. It was the most costly war in terms of human life to be fought on European soil until the two world wars of the 20th century.

were publicly slung out of Hradschin Castle windows onto the moat some 50 ft (15 m) below, although they were unharmed.

With the election, on Matthias's death in 1619, of Ferdinand as King of Bohemia and Holy Roman Emperor, the Habsburg's religious issues became an imperial one. The Bohemian rebels appointed Calvinist Frederick V as king of Bohemia; he took the throne and called for support from the Protestant Union in his revolt. Spain lent Ferdinand financial aid, as well as troops, which, together with the newly mustered Catholic League army led by Count Tilly, marched into Bohemia to crush the German Protestant rebellion.

After the battle of White Mountain on November 8, 1620 (see above), Bohemia lost its independence, and Protestantism in the region was exterminated.

Murky motives
Various countries supported the cause of the Protestants for their own ends, political or territorial, entering into war with the Habsburgs at different times. Cardinal Richelieu of Catholic France supported the rights of the German princes against the Catholic Habsburgs, led by state politics and trading interests rather than any shared cause.

Self-interest of the sovereign state was also behind the intervention of the Dutch Republic and Sweden in the war, rather than any anti-Catholic solidarity with the German protestants. The Dutch had trading rights to protect across Europe and the rest of the world.

Sweden was a small country of peasant farmers and a preeminent gun foundries industry. Under the decisive leadership of Gustavus Adolphus II (see p.272), Sweden became a power on the Baltic coast. Having crushed Count Tilly at the Battle of Breitenfeld in 1631,

Gustavus was killed at the ensuing battle of Lützen in 1632. The desire for peace, and resentment against marauding armies looting their land, was now overwhelming in Germany, and the Peace of Prague was forged in 1635 between the Holy Roman Empire and most Protestant states.

Reconciliation between Catholics and Protestants in Germany was imminent, but Richelieu, displeased to see the Habsburgs retain power, entered into the war against them that year, with Swedish support.

The theater of war now spread to most of Europe, with fighting between the Dutch Republic and France against Spain. With the Treaty of Westphalia in 1648 Habsburg power in Europe was fatally checked.

Peace of Westphalia
Signed on October 24, 1648, this document ended the 30 Years War, establishing that more than one religion could coexist in Habsburg Europe.

The English Civil War

The conflict between monarchy and Parliament had its origins in Charles I's belief in the Divine Right of Kings. The English Civil War was really three wars fought between Parliamentarians and royalists in 1642–46, 1648–49, and 1649–51.

> "**God** has brought us to where we are…"
>
> OLIVER CROMWELL, ADDRESSING THE ARMY COUNCIL, 1654

O n August 22, 1642, Charles I raised his battle standard at Nottingham, signaling the start of a civil war that split England down the middle, pitting brother against brother and father against son. By the time it was over, around 10 percent of Britain's population was dead.

This war was not just the product of a quarrel between Parliament and the king. Religion also played a key role, as for many Parliamentarians, Catholicism and tyranny were inseparable. In 1640 Charles had recalled Parliament in order to raise money to quell a revolt in Calvinist (see pp.258–59) Scotland against his clumsy attempts to impose "popish" reforms, such as the Anglican prayer-book, upon them. However, instead of granting him cash, they countered with their own catalog of recriminations, fueled by 11 years of grievances. He was forced to dismantle the institutions of absolute rule

Statue of Charles I
The reign of Charles I was characterized by religious conflict. Combining charm with stubbornness, his absolutist tendencies, (see p.279) put him on a collision course with Parliament.

and lost his right to dissolve Parliament. Rumors of his complicity in an Irish rebellion against Protestant English rule increased the tension. When news reached Charles that Parliament intended to impeach (charge with improper conduct) his Catholic queen, Henrietta Maria, he took drastic action. In January 1642, he entered the House of Commons with an armed force, intending to arrest five leading radical MPs for high treason. Forewarned, they took refuge in the City of London, which considered Charles's actions an outrage. Fearing for his safety, Charles went north to raise an army, while his queen went abroad to raise funds to pay for it.

The years of conflict

While the king commanded the loyalty of Wales, the west, and the north, Parliament controlled London, the east, and the south. The initial battles were inconclusive—a draw at Edgehill was followed by victories for the royalists, or Cavaliers, at Landsdown and Adwalton Moor in 1643, and for the Parliamentarians, or Roundheads, at Turnham Green and Newbury. Numerical supremacy and Scottish involvement led to Roundhead victories at Marston Moor in 1644, and at Naseby and Langport in 1645.

BEFORE

Since the 13th century, the English monarch had needed Parliament's approval to raise taxes; its increasing interference infuriated the Stuart kings.

THE TUDOR REFORMATION
When the pope refused **Henry VIII** a divorce from his first wife, Henry rejected the pope's authority and declared himself head of the Church of England in 1534. **The Reformation ‹‹ 256–59** that followed was consolidated during **Elizabeth I's ‹‹ 260–61** reign by legislation making **Protestantism** England's national religion. Since she was childless, she was succeeded in 1603 by her Stuart cousin, **James VI of Scotland**.

KING JAMES I
James's belief in the **Divine Right of Kings** (that the king was god's representative on Earth with unlimited authority) antagonized Parliament. He quarreled with them over taxes and religious laws.

KING CHARLES I
Relations between James's son **Charles I** and Parliament disintegrated further, exacerbated by his anti-Puritan **‹‹ 259** policies. By 1629, he had dissolved Parliament three times, governing alone during the "Eleven Years Tyranny" (1629–40). He enforced royal authority through the Courts instead and raised money by selling titles.

The conspirators meet and Lady d'Aubigny (left) shows them Charles's Commission of Array (a royal commission summoning his officers to war)—to be proclaimed once Charles sends word of his advance.

The conspirators intend to seize the Tower of London and secure the forts, while Royalist forces from Oxford meet up with the advancing Cornish forces under Sir Ralph Hopton.

The Guildhall is the planned storehouse for the conspirators' magazine (arms and gunpowder).

With suspicions aroused, the Commons orders the detention of the King's emissary Alexander Hampden on May 22. On May 31, they order the arrest of the suspected conspirators on the evidence of a spy.

Parliamentarian uniform

The New Model Army, formed in 1645 by Parliament, was England's first professional army. The foot regiments, comprised of pikemen and musketeers, were provided with the distinctive red tunic shown here.

Foiled royalist plot

This propaganda print was probably intended for popular consumption. It is a graphic account of the "Malignants' plot" against Parliament that was unearthed on May 31, 1643.

red coat was the only uniform item officially issued to the New Model Army

soldiers were often issued swords, also called tucks

woolen breeches

colored bow, which was used to fasten breeches

The plan is to arrest the leading parliamentarians, including their (Puritan) leader John Pym, along with two members of the House of Lords.

The conspirators are hanged at the Tyburn gallows. Responding to the Covenant, the King issues a proclamation making all who support it guilty of treason. The die is cast.

In response to John Pym's report on the royal plot, the Commons accepts the imposition of a vow of support for Parliament known as "the Covenant," which is sent around the country as a test of loyalty. On June 15 the City of London observes a day of Thanksgiving to celebrate the prevention of this "wicked plot."

After the fall of Oxford in 1646, Charles's surrender to the Scots at Newark marked the end of the first civil war.

Parliament's supporters now split into those who wanted to share power with the king, and a more radical group, supported by the army generals, that wanted a republic. Despite his confinement, Charles continued to bargain with various parties, finally making a deal with the Scots to adopt Presbyterianism (their system of church government) in England in return for their support. The royalists rose again in July 1648 and the Scots invaded England. The New Model Army (see caption, left) easily suppressed these uprisings before crushing the Scots at Preston. They then marched on Parliament and dismissed most of its members. The 58 who remained—known as the Rump Parliament—were ordered to set up a High Court to try the king for treason. Charles I was found guilty and beheaded on January 30, 1649. This was truly revolutionary; monarchs had been deposed or killed before, but never legally executed. Parliament now abolished the monarchy and the House of Lords, declaring England a republic or "Commonwealth."

The Lord Protector

Before the civil war, Oliver Cromwell was a landowner and Puritan Member of Parliament. By the war's end, he was Parliament's most powerful military leader. He spent the next two years campaigning in Scotland and Ireland, crushing local uprisings and bringing them

Charles I's death warrant
On January 29, 1649, Charles I was found guilty of being a traitor. His death warrant, shown here, is endorsed by many signatures, including that of Oliver Cromwell.

firmly under English control. His defeat of a Scottish army loyal to Charles I's son (later Charles II) at Worcester in 1651 finally brought an end to the civil war. In 1653, Cromwell dismissed the Rump Parliament, unhappy at its failure to pass any reforms. After being appointed Lord Protector for life—a role that effectively made him a military dictator—he divided England and Wales into 10 districts ruled by army generals. His rule, based on strict Puritan principles, included the banning of most public entertainments. In September 1658, Cromwell died and was succeeded by his son Richard. With no power base, he was helpless against the army generals and resigned after less than a year.

Statue of Cromwell
A devout military leader and shrewd politician, Oliver Cromwell became king in all but name.

AFTER

In 1660 the monarchy was reinstated to restore national unity. A second revolution to restore Protestantism was followed by a Bill of Rights (1689) that marked the start of a more limited, constitutional monarchy.

THE RESTORATION

After Cromwell's death, **the throne was offered to Charles II** on the condition that he supported religious toleration and pardoned those who had fought his father. Puritan rules were swiftly dropped—theaters and music halls reopened, and public festivals, such as Christmas, were restored. Nell Gwyn, a former orange-seller turned actress, became one of the king's most popular mistresses.

NELL GWYN

THOMAS HOBBES

Hobbes, one of England's most influential political thinkers, lived through the bloodshed of the civil war. His book *Leviathan*, published in 1651, **advocates strong government** at the expense of personal freedom, arguing that humankind's natural state is one of unending conflict.

THE "GLORIOUS REVOLUTION"

The openly Catholic **James II**, who succeeded Charles II in 1685, alienated his subjects by placing religion above politics. His advisers secretly invited the Dutch Protestant prince, **William of Orange,** to take over the throne in 1688.

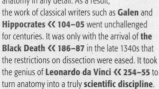

Throughout the late medieval period, physicians and "natural philosophers" began to develop what was later known as the "scientific method."

CUTAWAY OF A MAN

ANATOMISTS

Taboos surrounding the desecration of corpses prevented physicians of the 2nd–14th centuries from studying human anatomy in any detail. As a result, the work of classical writers such as **Galen** and **Hippocrates « 104–05** went unchallenged for centuries. It was only with the arrival of **the Black Death « 186–87** in the late 1340s that the restrictions on dissection were eased. It took the genius of **Leonardo da Vinci « 254–55** to turn anatomy into a truly **scientific discipline**.

ALCHEMISTS

A mix of **proto-science and superstition**, alchemy was the forerunner of chemistry that developed from the 11th century into the Renaissance (1300–1650 CE) **« 250–53**. Practitioners used methods we would recognize today in pursuit of a mythical "philosopher's stone" attributed with a variety of powers, such as the ability to give everlasting life or to make gold.

ALCHEMISTS AT WORK

For almost 1,500 years, (from about 200 CE) European thought was overshadowed by the legacy of the classical world. Just as the Catholic Church reigned supreme in religious affairs, so too in matters of "natural philosophy" (the general term for science before the 19th century) nearly all thinkers deferred to ancient authorities such as Plato, Hippocrates, and Aristotle (see pp.130–31).

Despite this, the new way of thinking had a long gestation. Arab scholars took many Greek ideas and developed them further (see pp.174–77). As their works began to filter back into European libraries, they helped to inspire a growing recognition that not everything the Greeks said was accurate. During the 18th century, failings were exposed in a number of areas, and a new method of philosophy, in which observation and experiment took precedence over authority, began to establish itself.

The knowledge explosion

The scientific revolution could not have taken place without the printing press (see p.253), and the rapid spread of information that printed books brought with them. Suddenly, ideas could be transmitted accurately and rapidly across the entire European continent. At the same time, the onset of trade with remote parts of the world and the discovery of a whole new continent—the Americas—meant that there was far more to investigate (see pp.230–31). Collectors, such as the Dane Ole Worm, created "cabinets of curiosities"—early

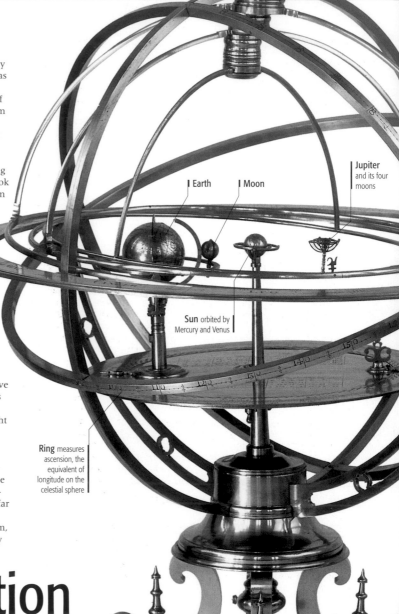

| Earth | Moon

Jupiter and its four moons

Sun orbited by Mercury and Venus

Ring measures ascension, the equivalent of longitude on the celestial sphere

Scientific Revolution

The 16th and 17th centuries saw a metamorphosis in European thinking about the natural world. The Renaissance had transformed art, and the Reformation loosened the ties of religious dogma. A third revolution produced a new view of the universe.

THE HELIOCENTRIC UNIVERSE

The idea that the universe orbited Earth is an ancient one. Celestial objects were thought to be mounted on spheres. However, there were problems—Mercury and Venus never strayed far from the Sun, and Mars occasionally reversed its motion. In 1543, Polish priest and astronomer Nicolaus Copernicus published the first widely read proposal for a new system with the Sun at its center (pictured right), and the Earth the third of six planets orbiting around it.

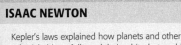

Celestial sphere c. 1700

This armillary sphere is an astronomical teaching device, developed by Greek and Arab astronomers. It is a skeletal representation of the "celestial sphere" used for measuring astronomical coordinates. From the early 17th century onward, the Sun was placed at the center of the sphere, as shown here.

Ring measures declination, the equivalent of latitude

Plane of the solar system

Timekeepers

Improvements in time measurement aided both astronomy and navigation. The weight-driven brass lantern clock was one step forward, although this Japanese version from the mid-17th century still does not have a minute hand. The pendulum clock invented by Christiaan Huygens in 1656 marked a further advance in precision.

ENGLISH PHYSICIST (1643–1727)
ISAAC NEWTON

Kepler's laws explained how planets and other celestial objects followed their orbits, but could not explain why. The realization that the force of gravity found on Earth might extend out into space, and be generated by other objects of sufficient mass, came from Isaac Newton. Newton was a brilliant but tempestuous individual, fascinated by mathematics, astronomy, optics, and alchemy. During the last two decades of his life, he was the most revered "natural philosopher" in Europe. The universal laws of motion and gravitation, and the model of the behavior of light that he discovered, remained the foundations of physics for two centuries.

NEWTON'S TELESCOPE

equivalents of today's natural history museums. Exotic plant species brought back from around the world were cultivated in botanical gardens, and the collection of new specimens became an increasingly important part of exploratory and trading missions overseas.

The growing interest in novelty undermined the reliance on the ancients, as it became clear that they had not, after all, known everything. The classical geographers had nothing to say about the new lands now being discovered, and since the authorities were also silent about the many new species of plant and animal, the scholars of the time had no choice but to investigate for themselves, and start to draw their own conclusions.

Written in the stars

Improved technology was also undermining other long-held theories. The most celebrated casualty of the entire revolution was the ancient, Earth-centered model of the universe. Italian physicist and astronomer Galileo Galilei is often credited with discovering that Earth and the other planets orbit the Sun, using one of the first telescopes. However, the idea had been in the air for several decades (see left). Galileo's discovery in 1610 of the four moons orbiting Jupiter showed that Earth was not the center of all motion in the universe, and his observation of the Moon-like phases of Venus showed that it must be orbiting the Sun. The most persuasive evidence for this theory came from the observations of Danish

astronomer Tycho Brahe. He used another refined form of technology—a precise measuring device known as a mural quadrant, developed from Arabic astrolabes (see p.175).

However, these observations alone could not have created a new theory—they merely disproved the old one. The crucial leap was made by Brahe's one-time student, German astronomer Johannes Kepler. Careful study of Brahe's measurements allowed him to develop a set of laws, published in 1609, that showed how the planets follow elliptical, rather than circular, orbits around the Sun. The acceptance of Kepler's laws involved a brutal divorce from classical ideas of circular perfection, and was not helped by the lack of a model to explain what force kept the planets on their elliptical courses—that had to wait until the century's end, and the breakthroughs of Isaac Newton (see above).

Advances in biology

While astronomy and physics were undergoing their revolution, medicine and anatomy were also in a period of rapid change. The discovery of a lost text by Galen in the early

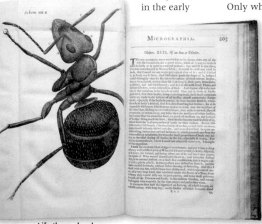

Life through a lens
The first book of microscope observations was Robert Hooke's *Micrographia* of 1664, which described and illustrated Hooke's observations of insects, plants, and living cells. This illustration of an ant shows more detailed anatomy than was previously possible.

16th century intrigued the Flemish anatomist Andreas Vesalius, who discovered that Galen had clearly never dissected a human body. Vesalius' great atlas of anatomy, *De Humani Corporis Fabrica* (1543), inspired a new generation to continue the study of anatomy without undue deference to authorities from the past.

One great battleground between traditionalism and the new approach was the nature of the circulatory system. Galen taught that the blood did not circulate through the body, but rose and fell in "tides," along with the body's other "humors" (phlegm, and black and yellow bile). Imbalances in the humors supposedly caused a variety of ailments, and much of medieval medicine focused on how best to regulate them.

Only when Galen's description of the heart was proved wrong did physicians begin to question this theory. In 1603, Italian anatomist Hieronymus Fabricius discovered valves within certain blood vessels, but it was not until 1628 that William Harvey, personal physician to Charles I of England, announced his discovery that the valves only worked in one direction. Blood vessels must therefore form two distinct groups—arteries taking blood away from the heart, and veins carrying blood back toward it.

Harvey's discovery met with fierce resistance, not only because it undermined Galen, but also because, with no visible connection between

Mountains on the Moon
Using a telescope Galileo discovered the varying terrain of the Moon (shown here), and spots on the Sun.

arteries and veins, it relied on tiny "capillaries," too small to be seen, to complete the system. By stating the evidence rather than attacking rival ideas, Harvey formed a template for later scientific publications. In 1661, improvements to the recently invented microscope finally allowed direct observation of the capillaries, vindicating Harvey and confirming the supremacy of the new method of observation, experiment, and deduction.

AFTER

After the scientific revolution, science became established as the best method to explain and predict natural phenomena.

SCIENCE AND SOCIETY
The 17th century saw the foundation of many scientific societies across Europe. Establishment of true **scientific method** inspired thinkers in many other fields, giving rise to economic, social, and political sciences among others.

THE RATIONAL UNIVERSE
Newton's "clockwork" model of the universe following immutable physical laws inspired Enlightenment philosophers **270–71 »**, yet left many in fear of an essentially meaningless Universe. **Darwin's theory of evolution 340–41 »** had a similar traumatic effect.

TECHNOLOGY AND EMPIRE
The rise of science led to rapid technological advance in Western Europe, culminating in the **industrial revolution 292–93 »**. The growing supremacy of Western technology ensured longevity of the nascent European empires.

Lisbon Earthquake

The Lisbon earthquake was the one of the worst natural disasters in European history. Up to 100,000 people perished in the earthquake itself and in the tsunami and fire that followed. The physical shockwaves were felt around the world; but the event also caused people to question established beliefs.

In the 18th century, Lisbon, situated on the southwest coast of Portugal, at the mouth of the Tagus River, was a grand, affluent city that formed the hub of a vast global empire. But by 10:00 am on November 1, 1755, an earthquake measuring an estimated 9 on the Richter scale (the highest number on the scale being 10) had reduced Lisbon to a scene of utter devastation. Cracks as wide as 16 ft (5 m) appeared in the ground, swallowing buildings and people.

In panic, many inhabitants had fled toward the port at the mouth of the river, clambering aboard the ships moored there in the belief that they would be in a safer place. But the earthquake was followed by a massive tsunami, a huge wall of water some 20 ft (6 m) high, that crashed into the city and roared up the river, causing further death and destruction. All along the coast of Portugal, towns were inundated by catastrophic floods. Agadir in North Africa was flooded, leaving thousands dead, and the wave traveled as far as northern Europe and across the Atlantic as far as Barbados. Once the ground had stopped shaking and the waters had receded, the third disaster, fire, struck Lisbon. The flames continued to burn for six days. These three catastrophes resulted in the destruction of three-quarters of Lisbon's buildings, including the city's vast royal library, which held priceless works of art and historical records detailing Portuguese expeditions to Southeast Asia.

The earthquake had struck on All Saints' Day, one of the holiest days in the Christian calendar. Priests saw the timing as an indication that God was punishing people. The earthquake caused others to question the very existence of a higher being. The event became a key topic of discussion for thinkers of the Enlightenment (see pp.270–71), who began to look for the causes of such disasters in the natural world, rather than blaming the wrath of God. The French writer and philosopher Voltaire used the earthquake to attack blind faith in God; while the German philosopher Immanuel Kant argued that the causes of the disaster should be examined scientifically, and that it is the responsibility of humanity to prepare itself for such events.

Disaster strikes
As the earthquake struck, Lisbon's buildings rocked backward and forward. Ships were torn from their anchorages and buildings collapsed, killing most of the people inside.

"I assure you this once opulent city is nothing but ruins..."
REVEREND CHARLES DAVY, AN EYEWITNESS, 1755

The **Enlightenment**

The German philosopher Immanuel Kant described the Enlightenment as "… man's release from his self-inflicted immaturity," meaning that people should use their reason without taking direction. His motto, *Sapere aude*! ("Dare to know!") encouraged readers to challenge outdated traditions.

This detailed scene from a pastry cook's kitchen shows the various tasks involved in pastry making. The *Encyclopédie* paid particular attention to everyday professions, eager to preserve artisan skills and techniques for posterity.

The Enlightenment was an intellectual "current" that flowed across Europe and beyond during the 18th century thanks to an explosion in printing and the widespread use of the French language. The thinkers, known as *philosophes*, applied ideas from advances in science (see pp.266–67) to change the way that people thought about government and society, seeking to replace superstition, tyranny, and injustice with reason, tolerance, and legal equality.

Madame de Pompadour
A woman renowned for her beauty and wit, Jeanne Poisson (1721–64) was installed in Versailles Palace as Louis XV's mistress. She was an avid patron of artistic and intellectual projects.

From 1750, a "republic of letters" emerged in Paris, aided by the existence of literary salons and the *Encyclopédie* (see right). "What does it mean to be free?" asked Francois-Marie Arouet—better known as Voltaire—probably the most famous *philosophe* of them all. "To reason correctly and know the rights of man. When they are well known, they are well defended."

Questioning received wisdom led the *philosophes* to attack many things: general ignorance and intolerance;

outdated privilege among nobles and clergy; absolutism or tyranny in all its forms, such as the royal *lettres de cachet* that allowed anyone to be locked up without evidence; and the Church (for encouraging superstition and persecution).

The Swiss thinker Jean-Jacques Rousseau railed against moral decadence and inequality in his essays on *The Arts and Sciences* (1749) and on *Equality* (1755), which challenged basic Enlightenment beliefs by arguing that social progress had helped to corrupt human nature. His bestselling novels *La Nouvelle Heloise* (1761) and *Emile* (1762) tapped into a rich vein of "sentimentalism" and made him the darling of the chattering classes. But he soon found himself an isolated figure, in conflict with other *philosophes*.

Spreading ideas

The most influential tool for spreading Enlightenment values was the 28-volume *Encyclopédie*, which boasted an impressive array of contributors, including Jacques Turgot, Voltaire,

The *Encyclopédie* (1751–72)
Diderot and d'Alembert edited this 28-volume magnum opus over 20 years. Its 17 volumes of text and 11 volumes of engravings contained 72,000 articles and over 2,500 plates.

Frontispiece for the first volume of the *Encyclopédie* or "Reasoned Dictionary of the Sciences, Arts and Trades."

ENCYCLOPÉDIE,

OU

DICTIONNAIRE RAISONNÉ

DES SCIENCES,

DES ARTS ET DES MÉTIERS,

PAR UNE SOCIÉTÉ DE GENS DE LETTRES.

Mis en ordre & publié par M. *DIDEROT*, de l'Académie Royale des Sciences & des Belles-Lettres de Prusse ; &, quant à la PARTIE MATHÉMATIQUE, par M. *D'ALEMBERT*, de l'Académie Royale des Sciences de Paris, de celle de Prusse, & de la Société Royale de Londres.

Tantùm series juncturaque pollet,
Tantùm de medio sumptis accedit honoris! HORAT.

TOME PREMIER.

A PARIS,

Chez { BRIASSON, *rue Saint Jacques, à la Science.*
DAVID l'aîné, *rue Saint Jacques, à la Plume d'or.*
LE BRETON, Imprimeur ordinaire du Roy, *rue de la Harpe.*
DURAND, *rue Saint Jacques, à Saint Landry, & au Griffon.*

M. DCC. LI.
AVEC APPROBATION ET PRIVILÉGE DU ROY.

‹‹ BEFORE

The roots of the Enlightenment lay in the Renaissance and English political and intellectual culture.

MONTAIGNE'S "ESSAYS"

HUMANISM
A cultural movement of the Renaissance
‹‹ 250–53, humanism **laid the foundations** for the Enlightenment by emphasizing the dignity and reason of man. Humanists such as the French moralist **Michel de Montaigne** wrote essays questioning anything and everything.

POLITICAL REFORMS
In 1688, the English king James II was overthrown and replaced by William III. **Subsequent political reforms** inspired French writers, such

as **Voltaire**. He promoted the English legal system, religious toleration, and its constitutional monarchy as alternatives to French absolutism in his *Lettres Philosophiques* (1734); it was immediately banned.

ENGLISH ROOTS
Enlightenment thinkers adopted **three English philosophers** as their "patron saints": Francis Bacon (1561–1626) for his development of scientific method based on experiment and observation; John Locke (1632–1704) for his political theory and empiricism (acceptance of knowledge based only on direct experience); and Isaac Newton (1643–1727) for his unifying scientific laws and discoveries.

FRANCISCI BACONI, BARONIS DE VERULAMIO... OPERA OMNIA...

FRANCIS BACON'S "THE ADVANCEMENT OF LEARNING"

and Rousseau under the editorial guidance of Denis Diderot and Jean d'Alembert. Its aim was to assemble and disseminate all existing knowledge in clear, accessible prose and to educate public opinion by "changing accepted habits of thought." Banned twice for its anti-Catholic tone, its survival relied on the support of the state censor.

A more effective way of spreading similar ideas was through satire. The

political theorist Montesquieu started this trend with *Lettres Persanes* (1721), which depicted French and European customs through the eyes of Persian visitors, poking fun at the Church, Court, and French society. Voltaire perfected it in *Candide* (1759), an account of a naïve young man's adventures, by exposing the hypocrisies of the institutions and attitudes that he encountered.

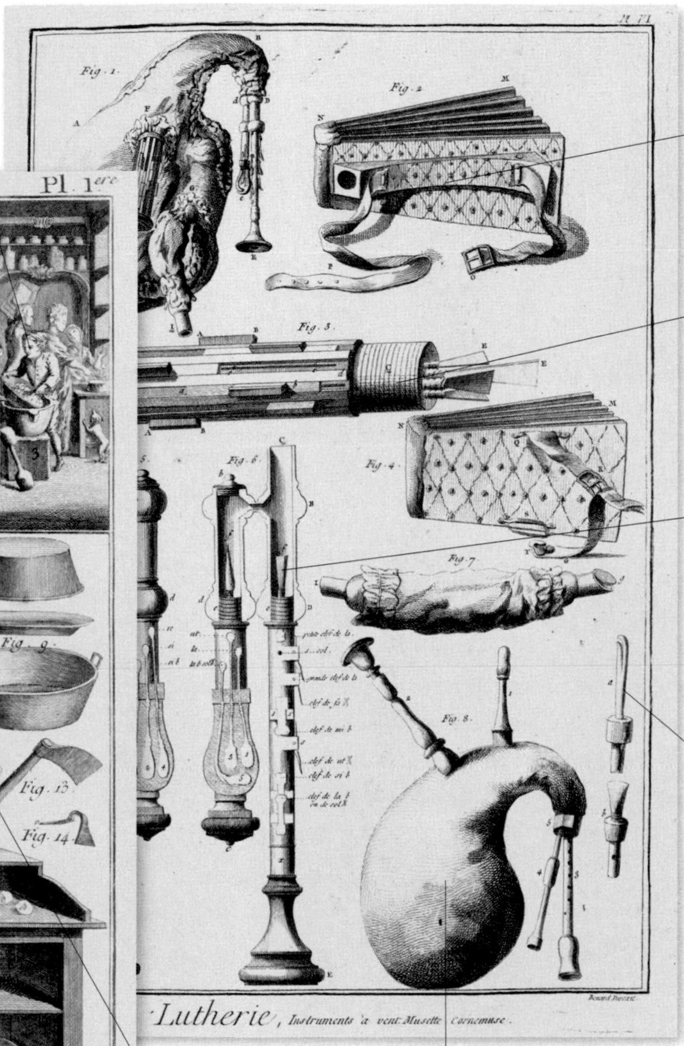

Detailed legends precede each set of labeled plates, which are grouped by themes, such as artisans and musical instruments.

The soufflet was a type of bellows to which a sound-producing object such as a chanter (see below) could be attached.

The four-reed drone fitted onto the *musette de cour* shown above it; a type of bellows-blown bagpipe. Finger-holes were uncovered by moving sliders.

The chanter fitted onto the end of the *musette*. With three keys and seven finger-holes, it gave a range of one octave; annotation relates each finger-hole to its note.

Other mouthpieces for the bagpipes are illustrated—the editors intended the engravings to be as comprehensive as possible.

Lutherie, *Instruments à vent Musette Cornemuse*

The tools of the trade of a pastry cook (*patissier*) are shown here, including bowls of varying sizes, a baking tray, a mortar and pestle, and a rolling pin.

A fully inflated cornemuse (a type of bagpipes) shows the positioning of the mouthpiece, fingering tubes, and venting tube.

AFTER

The Enlightenment provoked both radical change and growing criticism of its ideas.

REVOLUTIONS
Increasing demands for political representation helped pave the way for the **American and French revolutions**. The Founding Fathers incorporated many of Montesquieu's political ideas, including the **separation of powers**, into the US constitution **298–99 »**. However, in France, a combination of revolutionary wars and the "Terror" **302–03 »** served to **dissolve Enlightenment optimism** in a sea of blood.

ROMANTIC BACKLASH
Enlightenment ideas were so widespread by the second half of the 18th century that few failed to share confidence in the "Cult of Reason." But the 19th-century Romantic movement **338–39 »** emphasized emotion, imagination, and a love of nature over reason and industrial progress.

ENLIGHTENED MODERNITY
After the horrors of World War II **392–403 »**, the United Nations (UN) was founded in 1949 to resolve international relations based on the Enlightenment idea of **universal citizenship**. In practice, the self-interest of modern nation states often comes first.

UNITED NATIONS

"The consent of **the people** is the **sole basis** of a government's authority."

JEAN-JACQUES ROUSSEAU, "THE SOCIAL CONTRACT," 1762

One of the most popular targets of the *philosophes* was the Church, which some saw as one of the main obstacles to reform. They argued that for states to be progressive, politics and religion should be kept apart. Yet many also believed that religion was necessary for upholding the social order, creating an insoluble conflict. Anticlerical sentiments, spread by satirical prints and novels, were fueled by anger at the Church's corruption and abuse of power. Freemasons lodges sprang up across Europe as secular spaces for disciples of the "Cult of Reason" to gather and exchange ideas.

The other main target was royal absolutism. The French king and his ministers were often in dispute with the *parlements*—French law courts dominated by the aristocracy. Montesquieu transformed the political debate by proposing, in his bestselling treatise *Spirit of the Laws* (1748), a limited monarchy based on a three-way division of powers between the executive (king), the legislature (parliament), and the judiciary.

This was a time when thinkers believed that a rational, scientific approach could be applied to almost any subject. Scotsman Adam Smith's analysis of capitalism, in his book *Wealth of Nations* (1776), invented the new science of economics, while Kant's *Critique of Pure Reason* (1781) presented a more scientific approach to philosophy and knowledge.

IDEA

ENLIGHTENED DESPOTISM

Enlightenment ideas on the state, attacking outdated traditions, filtered down to some of Europe's rulers, including Empress Maria Theresa of Austria, Catherine II "the Great" of Russia, and Frederick II "the Great" (left) of Prussia, who briefly employed Voltaire as his advisor. Frederick tried to govern his subjects as the "first servant of the state." His "revolution from above" created an enlightened welfare state with a modern bureaucracy and law system, transforming Prussia into a semiconstitutional state. Prince Karl Frederick of Baden went one step farther, abolishing serfdom outright.

« BEFORE

Decades of war in Europe resulted in advances in military tactics and techniques, although the development of improved weaponry was slow to follow.

BATTLE-READY

The 30 Years War (1618-48) **‹‹ 262–63** put **Europe on an all-out war footing**. Innovative tactics were employed by field commanders, and training manuals, maps, and field glasses began to be more widely used. But the idea of a permanent or **"standing" professional army** as a fixed piece of machinery of state (just like the nonmilitary civil service) was still in its infancy.

TECHNOLOGY OF WAR

Despite the fact that gunpowder had been developed 400 years before **‹‹ 162–63**, it remained highly volatile and liable to explode at any time. The **copper and bronze weaponry** made to fire it was slow in development and far from uniform in design or ammunition. Cannons varied in size and were classified by ball weight, the largest being referred to as the "90-pounder." **Giant cannons** known as bombards could weigh 5 tons (4,500 kg) and throw an iron ball nearly half a mile (1 km). These cannons were useful for demolishing fortifications.

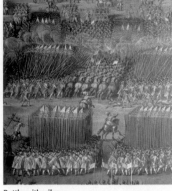

Battle with pikes
As military tactics became more sophisticated, full-on cavalry charges and standardized artillery became integral to more sustained and offensive tactics than the older pike-style warfare, shown above.

D uring the 17th century, Europe became an almost permanent theater of war, witnessing more battles than in any other place or time. If there was a dispute to settle, then war was the way to do it—diplomacy came when treaties were made.

From the late 17th century, trade—not religion or dynasty—became the dominant cause of conflict between Europeans. The nascent nation-states were increasingly concerned about their freedoms to trade, and thereby to profit and to protect monopolies both on the high seas and in overseas possessions. This became the dominant factor in state formation.

Quarrels about trade around the world were now a concern of European states-in-the-making. For example, from 1652 to 1674, two former republican allies—England and the Dutch Republic—embarked on three Anglo-Dutch Wars centered around trade, colonial possessions, and shipping rights. France and Denmark also entered the conflicts periodically.

The initial cause was an act passed by the English parliament that forbade any foreign ship to carry, and therefore trade, English goods. The Dutch carried massive quantities of English goods in their ships, which made them huge profits that they were prepared to fight to protect. The Treaty of Breda (1667), which ended the second Anglo-Dutch War, was the first multinational peace settlement, concerned as much about Europe's overseas interests as its European boundaries. Significantly, the wide-ranging Peace of Westphalia that had ended the 30 Years War

Masters of War

By the 18th century, Europe had emerged from a series of violent wars fought over religion. Such conflicts were quickly replaced with battles over trade rights both in Europe and in the ever-increasing number of European colonies abroad. The increasing sophistication of military tactics across the continent outpaced advances in artillery design and production.

Stalemate
The Four Days' Battle was fought on June 11–14, 1666 as part of the Second Anglo-Dutch War, (1665–67). It was fought at close quarters between an English fleet of 56 ships under the Duke of Albemarle and a larger Dutch fleet commanded by their great admiral Michiel De Ruyter.

KING OF SWEDEN (1594–1632)

GUSTAVUS ADOLPHUS II

Gustavus Adolphus II came to the throne of Sweden in 1611 and is considered the father of modern military tactics. He promoted a more standardized and much lighter artillery, more compact supply trains, offensive tactics (a quick offensive campaign gave the enemy little time to prepare its defense), and provisioning troops by negotiation, not looting. To achieve this he needed well-trained and disciplined troops, and Gustavus ensured that his men were regularly paid. His military innovations in troop formations and combinations led to a permanent increase in the size of European armies. Sweden was a major power in Europe by the time of his death.

Mobile musket
This flintlock musket from 1741 is the precursor of the rifle. More portable and accurate than earlier guns, it also had a fixed ring bayonet.

> "The masterpiece of a successful general is to **starve his enemy**."

FREDERICK II OF PRUSSIA, ATTRIBUTED

only 19 years earlier (see pp.262–63) contained almost nothing about non-European matters in its collection of treaties, which demonstrates how rapidly Europe's overseas possessions had grown in importance.

On a war footing
One effect of frequent wars was that large and properly equipped armies and navies had to be maintained, and this required centralized and bureaucratic states to run them. Countries now developed national armed forces as they became an integral element of nation-building. The Dutch were a typical example of how a government's administration and finances were now geared to the ability to mobilize for war and buttress the state's power.

With Europe's political geography much more stable at home, the "standing army" of well-drilled, better provisioned, and uniformed troops that

did not "stand down" (disband) every winter slowly became the norm. The days of the mercenary captains raising private armies for a fee were numbered. Militarism, the central aim of which was the financing and organizing of professional armies, was increasing so that by the 1690s, France, fighting a European coalition, could mobilize upward of 340,000 troops. Even at peace the French standing army numbered 150,000 troops, compared

with 55,000 in the 1660s. Prussian mobilization in the 18th century could raise an army of 185,000 from a population of only five million. Warfare came of age with key developments in the study of strategy, siege tactics, topography, and ballistics. Weapons and ammunition were also refined, and logistics became more of a science as soldiers were now part of the state's permanent expenses. The emphasis switched to defense from aggression.

bronze siege mortar

wooden mounting

Early mortar gun
Developed in the 17th century by a Dutch military engineer, the Coehorn siege mortar gun was a cannon used to fire shells at right angles.

Europe's military power grew in sophistication and scope, soon to be "exported" to the rest of the world.

NAPOLEONIC WARFARE
Warfare went through another modernization during the Napoleonic period **306–07 »** with the **formation of military training schools**. During the Napoleonic Wars (1799–1815), Napoleon Bonaparte introduced the method of deploying massed artillery at a specific point in a battle, thereby giving him sensational victories.

EUROPE'S FIRST PROFESSIONAL ARMY
Russia had the first European army in which **all the men wore uniforms** and private soldiers were decorated for bravery—almost unknown in the rest of Europe. Troops were directly recruited and financed by the state—**peasant conscripts served for life** until 1793.

THE SEVEN YEARS WAR
The Seven Years War **296–97 »** involved both Europe and colonies in the Americas for the first time. It is considered to be the first truly global conflict in history.

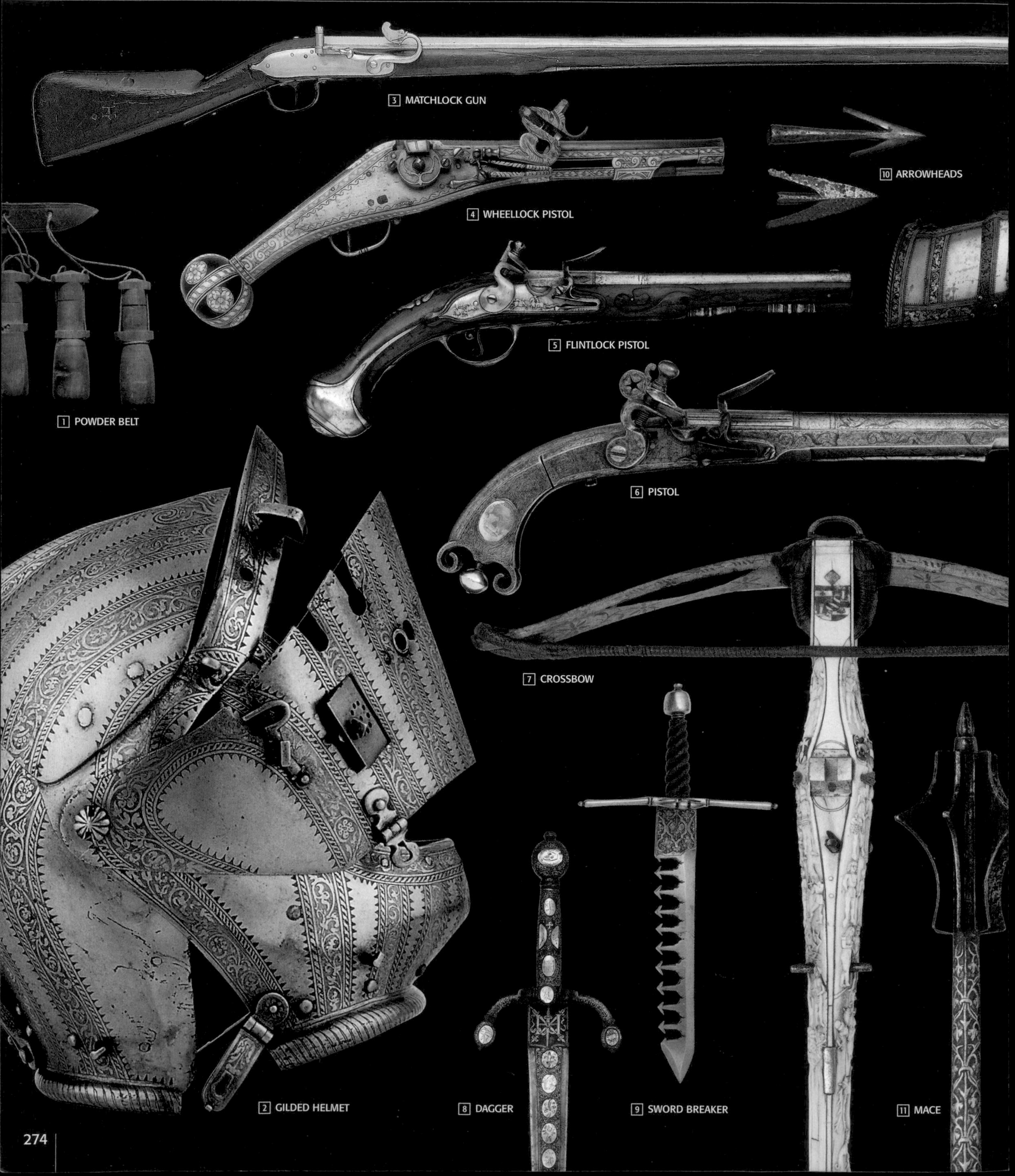

3 MATCHLOCK GUN

4 WHEELLOCK PISTOL

10 ARROWHEADS

5 FLINTLOCK PISTOL

1 POWDER BELT

6 PISTOL

7 CROSSBOW

2 GILDED HELMET

8 DAGGER

9 SWORD BREAKER

11 MACE

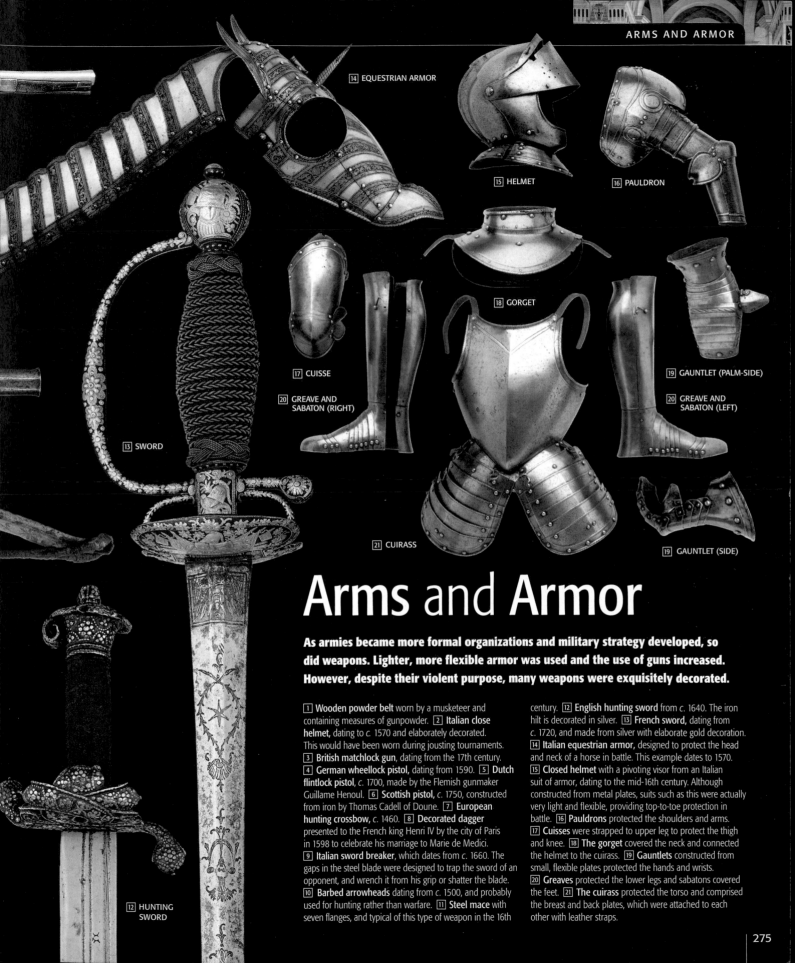

14 EQUESTRIAN ARMOR

15 HELMET

16 PAULDRON

18 GORGET

17 CUISSE

19 GAUNTLET (PALM-SIDE)

20 GREAVE AND SABATON (RIGHT)

20 GREAVE AND SABATON (LEFT)

13 SWORD

21 CUIRASS

19 GAUNTLET (SIDE)

12 HUNTING SWORD

Arms and Armor

As armies became more formal organizations and military strategy developed, so did weapons. Lighter, more flexible armor was used and the use of guns increased. However, despite their violent purpose, many weapons were exquisitely decorated.

1 **Wooden powder belt** worn by a musketeer and containing measures of gunpowder. 2 **Italian close helmet,** dating to c. 1570 and elaborately decorated. This would have been worn during jousting tournaments. 3 **British matchlock gun,** dating from the 17th century. 4 **German wheellock pistol,** dating from 1590. 5 **Dutch flintlock pistol,** c. 1700, made by the Flemish gunmaker Guillame Henoul. 6 **Scottish pistol,** c. 1750, constructed from iron by Thomas Cadell of Doune. 7 **European hunting crossbow,** c. 1460. 8 **Decorated dagger** presented to the French king Henri IV by the city of Paris in 1598 to celebrate his marriage to Marie de Medici. 9 **Italian sword breaker,** which dates from c. 1660. The gaps in the steel blade were designed to trap the sword of an opponent, and wrench it from his grip or shatter the blade. 10 **Barbed arrowheads** dating from c. 1500, and probably used for hunting rather than warfare. 11 **Steel mace** with seven flanges, and typical of this type of weapon in the 16th

century. 12 **English hunting sword** from c. 1640. The iron hilt is decorated in silver. 13 **French sword,** dating from c. 1720, and made from silver with elaborate gold decoration. 14 **Italian equestrian armor,** designed to protect the head and neck of a horse in battle. This example dates to 1570. 15 **Closed helmet** with a pivoting visor from an Italian suit of armor, dating to the mid-16th century. Although constructed from metal plates, suits such as this were actually very light and flexible, providing top-to-toe protection in battle. 16 **Pauldrons** protected the shoulders and arms. 17 **Cuisses** were strapped to upper leg to protect the thigh and knee. 18 **The gorget** covered the neck and connected the helmet to the cuirass. 19 **Gauntlets** constructed from small, flexible plates protected the hands and wrists. 20 **Greaves** protected the lower legs and sabatons covered the feet. 21 **The cuirass** protected the torso and comprised the breast and back plates, which were attached to each other with leather straps.

The **Rise** of **Capitalism**

From the 15th century, capitalism—investing and trading goods for profit—became a key force in European economies, politics, culture, and even warfare. The establishment of overseas empires, and the creation of trading centers to finance them, spurred this new wave of global commerce.

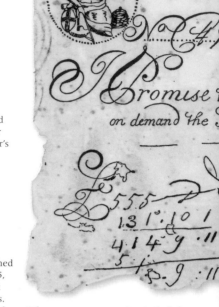

The discovery of the Americas (see pp.228–29) and the development in the 15th century of ocean-going ships capable of sailing vast distances (see pp.224–25) kick-started the modern era of capitalism. The enterprise of investing money to make money now had a global reach with potentially massive profits, simply because of the scarcity of the precious commodities—from silver to silk, porcelain to pepper—and the large distances involved. The value of goods from the East was so huge in Europe that it paid for the costs of such voyages many times over.

The return on investment might be high, but so were the risks. Ships often succumbed to storms, reefs, and pirates, with the result that all of the goods accrued over many months would be lost in an instant. Investment in ships, rigging, guns, and crew, as well as refurbishing and filling the ships with outgoing stock, was also huge. Such undertakings tied up large sums of money for long periods, sometimes years, before any profit could be realized. In Europe, a glut of a certain commodity could depress prices. So a large number of speculators needed to be persuaded to share the risk.

Edward Lloyd's coffee shop
Ship owners meet at Lloyd's coffeehouse to discuss future voyages with underwriters—men who insure things against loss for a premium. This gathering developed into insurance giant Lloyd's of London.

Merchant capitalism

The need to secure the required investment saw the creation of joint stock companies. Investors bought into the companies—even if they had no personal links to its trading activities—by buying stocks in them on the open market. They could sell their stocks but, crucially, could not withdraw their capital. An investor's share in the company's stock could also be sold at whatever price the buyer and seller agreed on. The Muscovy Company was the first joint-stock enterprise established in England in 1555, but the Dutch East India Company was the most famous. It was chartered by the States General in 1602 and consisted of a grouping of six provincial chambers each with its own capital and share distribution of total profits. They appointed 17 general directors, the Heeren XVII, who became the central management. The Heeren XVII controlled the administration of factories and territory in the East Indies, the marketing of imported goods to Amsterdam, and how ships were to be freighted and employed.

Even the Bank of England, when it was founded by royal charter in 1694, was organized at first on joint-stock lines to raise money for what were effectively trade-based wars against France. No other joint-stock banks were permitted in Britain until 1826.

Dutch trader's manual
A Dutch trader's manual from the 1500s with pictures of coins, which was used to conduct business.

Other company enterprises included the United Company of Merchants of England (1600), Companhia Geral do Comércio do Brasil (1649), Compagnie de Chine (1698), the French East India Company (1723), Compagnie de Sénégal (1673), the Royal African Company (1672), the Dutch West India Company, the Hudson's Bay Company (1670), and the South Sea Company (1711)—the name of each often giving away the nature of the enterprise.

The lynchpin of capitalism

A vital innovation, the joint-stock company enjoyed a much more long-term and independent existence than other companies, as it built up its capital and a buoyant market for its shares over time. In return for being given a commercial monopoly abroad and the authority to negotiate with Asian and Indian rulers, these companies provided protection on the ocean and employed their own armed ships and troops

◀◀

BEFORE

In the medieval period, the attitude of the Catholic Church to usury (money with lending interest charged) prevented capitalism from developing. The papal ban on levying interest was not repealed until the 15th century.

EUROPE'S FIRST BANKERS
In the 12th century, the Italian cities of Genoa and Venice saw the rise of **Europe's first bankers ◀◀ 208–09**, with the earliest forms of bills of exchange and double-entry bookkeeping, which is the basis of modern banking and accounting systems. The Genoese had helped finance the Crusades **◀◀ 200–01** and profited from lucrative trading rights and shipping contracts in the Middle East. They had also unwittingly brought **the Black Death** back to Europe **◀◀ 186–87**.

> " ... freedom of trade is based on **a primitive right** of Nations..."
>
> HUGO GROTIUS, FROM "CONCERNING THE LAW OF PRIZE," 1604

Royal exchange
As a London cloth merchant who supplied the tapestries for Henry VIII's Hampton Court, Richard Gresham had visited Antwerp's trading center. He recognized its vital trade link, and urged the establishment of a similar center in London. In 1565 his son Thomas established the Royal Exchange of London, shown here.

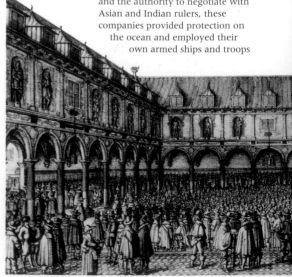

Paper money in the UK
The first British bank notes, issued by the Bank of England from the mid-1690s, showed the image of Britannia. From 1727, Scottish bank notes featured the monarch's head.

New banking services
A handwritten check for £70 dates to 1725. Its function is much like a modern check. A large range of financial services offered by banks were provided by legal clerks, merchants, and goldsmiths in the 18th century.

> " Apart from myself there dwells no one in Amsterdam who is not **engaged in trade**." RENE DESCARTES, 1600s

Papal paper money
The Bank of the Holy Spirit at Rome was Europe's first national bank, established in 1605 by Pope Paul V. This note (above) was issued for circulation in the Papal States under Pope Pius VI in 1786.

to protect their coastal factories and trade. In effect, they made local war and peace.

Specialist traders now emerged to arrange deals between buyers and sellers of stocks and shares (in an enterprise or commodity with which they had no direct connection) in return for a cut on each transaction. They were called brokers. In London the brokers gathered at first in coffeehouses, and a system of stockbroking

gradually became established. The first coffeehouse in London opened in 1652 (coffee itself being a valuable commodity and newly fashionable refreshment). At Edward Lloyd's coffeehouse, merchants, brokers, ship owners, and sea captains met to discuss investment and insurance for new voyages. At Jonathan's coffeehouse in Change Alley, brokers negotiated with investors to buy and sell shares in joint-stock companies and trading ventures.

In 1698, stock dealers were expelled from the Royal Exchange (see left) for rowdiness and began their dealings in the streets and coffeehouses nearby, in particular in Jonathan's Coffeehouse. It was in these coffeehouses that brokers also came up with the idea of producing lists of share prices and shipping departure data.

In the same year, John Castaing began publishing a twice-weekly newsletter of share and commodity prices, called *The Course of the Exchange and other things*, which he sold at Jonathan's. It is the earliest written evidence of organized trading in stocks in London and the precursor of the famous insurance

exchange Lloyd's of London and the Lloyd's Register of Shipping (see pp.238–39).

A "bourse" is born

From the early 16th century in Antwerp, merchants had a base within which to trade—a Bourse. It was custom-built and regulated as a market for the sale and purchase of trading companies' shares and stocks. The Bourse—the continental term for a stock exchange—became the symbol of capitalism and an expanding economy, in which ships were chartered, cargo insured, and stocks and shares bought and sold. After the siege of Antwerp in 1585, trading moved to Amsterdam.

The Dutch formalized the idea of a stock exchange building to market shares: in 1609 the *Amsterdamsche Wisselbank* (Amsterdam Exchange Bank) was founded, which made Amsterdam the financial center of the world until the Industrial Revolution (see pp.292–95). As with marine insurance, double-entry bookkeeping, and other business techniques, the bank was copied from Italian models.

AFTER

As a global economy began to emerge, financial institutions became privatized and monarchs and state governments began to lose their dominion over the economy.

CAPTAINS OF INDUSTRY
Adam Smith's *Inquiry into the Nature and Causes of the Wealth of Nations* (1776) supported the massive growth in the banking industry. The **Industrial Revolution 292–95** >> helped spur a new system of ownership and investment, and moneyholders were able to reduce the State's intervention in economic affairs. The captains of industry had arrived.

LLOYD'S OF LONDON
Within the vast atrium of the Lloyd's of London building stands the Lutine Bell. It was rescued from HMS *Lutine*, which sank in 1799 with its crew and cargo of gold and bullion. Now mainly reserved for ceremonial purposes, it was traditionally rung once for the loss or delay of a ship and twice for its safe arrival.

THE LUTINE BELL INSIDE LLOYD'S OF LONDON

KING OF FRANCE Born 1638 Died 1715

Louis XIV

" L'Etat, c'est moi." (I am, myself, **the state**) LOUIS XIV, KING OF FRANCE

Louis XIV was only four years old in 1643, when he succeeded his father, Louis XIII, as king of France. During the regency of his mother, Anne of Austria, the effective ruler of France was her chief minister, Cardinal Mazarin. When Mazarin died in 1661, the 23-year-old King Louis XIV was expected to appoint a chief minister of similar caliber. Instead, he announced his intention of being his own first minister, and ruling as an absolute monarch (see right).

Expensive wars
For the first 20 years of his personal reign (1661–81), Louis was constantly waging war. He began with an attack on the Spanish Netherlands in 1667 to gain land, but his territorial ambitions there were thwarted by an alliance between Holland, England, and Sweden. In 1672, having detached England from that alliance, he invaded Holland, but under William of Orange the Dutch managed to stand firm against him. Although this campaign led to the formation of another European alliance against France, Louis did make some territorial gains along France's frontiers.

In 1688 he was at war again, against a "Grand Alliance" that included Holland and England, both now ruled by William of Orange. A factor in this alliance for the Protestant member states was Louis' revocation of the Edict of Nantes in 1685 (see pp.258–59), which meant that Huguenots (French Protestants) no longer had the right to practice their faith in France. The War of the Grand Alliance lasted until 1697. There were a few years of peace until 1700, when the death

of the king of Spain led to the War of the Spanish Succession (see right).

To fund his constant military campaigns, Louis XIV relied on his director of finances, Jean-Baptiste Colbert. Colbert improved the tax collection system, brought

The Sun King portrait
This magnificent portrait by Hyacinthe Rigaud of the "Sun King" fits contemporary descriptions of Louis XIV. By all accounts, Louis was attractive, with a strong nose, piercing eyes, and a healthy complexion.

Royal family tree
Louis XIV was a member of one of the most powerful and widely distributed royal dynasties in Europe, the Bourbons. His mother, Anne of Austria, was a member of another great dynasty of the period: the Habsburgs.

Theater
Madeleine Béjart was the leading lady of the theatrical company managed by Molière, the genius of French comedy whose plays entertained Louis and his court.

Palace of Versailles
Once established at Versailles, Louis' court become a magnet for all the talent in France, and a monument to French cultural and political prestige.

industry under state control, and did what he could to boost French naval power. He was also in charge of the royal household's finances, a responsibility that included the cost of Versailles.

The court of the Sun King

Versailles began as a modest hunting lodge near Paris, where the young Louis XIV entertained his intimate friends. In the late 1660s Louis started to devote more attention to the project of reconstructing and extending the old hunting lodge into a royal palace. There was method behind Louis' extravagant plan to build a great royal palace. By making Versailles the permanent base of the royal court and the seat of government from 1682, Louis created a hugely attractive nexus of power and influence, which the nobility found irresistible, and which persuaded them to trade provincial power for influence and rewards at Court, under the direct auspices of the king. Above all, the Court was a center of conspicuous consumption and magnificence, principally intended to glorify the "Sun King," as Louis was styled by artists paid to glorify him. And, like the sun god Apollo, Louis wished to appear a great patron of the arts, provided that the artists obeyed the various controls imposed by the royal academies. At the heart of the royal palace, which at its height was the size of a small town containing upwards of 10,000 people, were the apartments of Louis, his Spanish Queen, Marie Thérèse, and the royal mistress. It was usual for the current royal mistress to enjoy court honors, and the children resulting from the relationships were acknowledged by the king.

The Sun King died at the age of 77, in the 56th year of his personal rule. His final years were clouded by bereavement, military defeat, and a catastrophic country-wide collapse in the French economy. The sudden deaths of his son, the dauphin (heir apparent), his grandson, and his elder great-grandson—all within a matter of months—meant that his kingdom passed to his five-year-old great grandson, Louis XV.

Sun motif
This gilded sun emblem made of carved wood is found on the walls of the palace of Versailles. Sun motifs served as logos for Louis XIV's golden reign.

IDEA

ABSOLUTE MONARCHY

From the moment of his coronation (pictured, right) Louis XIV demonstrated his belief that he had a "divine right"— God-given duty—to rule France as an absolute monarch, without consulting parliaments, ministers, or senior nobles. Blessed with stamina, confidence, and a passion for order, he was an extraordinarily capable ruler. Even when he was at war, he insisted on daily progress reports about the construction of Versailles. Other monarchs envied his power and his palace; the scale of the palace of Versailles was mimicked all over Europe.

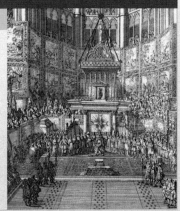

TIMELINE

1638 Birth of Louis, long awaited first-born child of Anne of Austria and Louis XIII of France.

1643 Death of Louis XIII; Anne of Austria and chief minister Cardinal Mazarin effectively rule France.

1648–53 The period of internal troubles and civil war in France known as the Fronde.

1648 Treaty of Westphalia brings to an end the Thirty Years War (see pp.262–63).

1659 Treaty of Pyrenees brings peace with Spain, cemented by a proposed marriage alliance between Louis XIV and the Spanish princess, Marie Thérèse.

June 9, 1660 Marriage to Marie Thérèse of Spain.

LOUIS XIV'S MARRIAGE

1661 Death of Cardinal Mazarin; Louise de la Vallière becomes the official royal mistress; Louis begins his personal rule; birth of Louis' eldest son, the dauphin Louis.

1666 Death of Anne of Austria.

1667 Louis XIV establishes the French Academy of Science.

1668 Treaty of Aix-La-Chapelle marks France's successful annexation of part of the Spanish Netherlands.

1672–78 France goes to war against the Dutch .

1682 The full court moves to the new palace of Versailles, 12 miles (19 km) west of Paris; birth of Louis' first grandson, the Duc de Bourgogne.

1683 After the death of his wife, Louis XIV marries his long-term companion Madame de Maintenon in a secret ceremony.

1685 Louis XIV revokes the Edict of Nantes, ending the freedom to worship of French Protestants (Huguenots), hundreds of thousands of whom leave France; the indignation of Europe's Protestant powers, Holland, England, and Sweden contributes to the formation of the Grand Alliance against France.

1689 William of Orange, now also king of England, leads the Grand Alliance against France.

1700 Charles II of Spain (half-brother of Louis' queen, Marie Thérèse) dies without heirs. His bequeaths the throne in the first instance to Louis XIV's grandson, the Duc d'Anjou, who becomes Philip V of Spain.

1701–13 War of the Spanish Succession is triggered by counter-claims to the Spanish throne by Holy Roman Emperor Leopold I and Louis' expansionist policies. The war ends in 1713 at the Treaty of Utrecht, with Philip V left on the Spanish throne, but the Spanish Empire partitioned.

1711–12 Deaths of Louis XIV's eldest son (the dauphin), grandson (the Duc de Bourgogne), and elder great-grandson.

1715 Louis XIV dies at Versailles; he is succeeded by his only surviving legitimate descendant, his great-grandson, who becomes Louis XV.

« BEFORE

The Afro-European slave trade began in around 1440, when Portuguese traders began to ship captured Africans to work on plantations, to feed Europe's growing demand for sugar.

SUGAR PLANTATIONS
The first sugar plantation was established by the **Portuguese in Madeira**, an island off the northwest coast of Africa, in 1452. At first, **Africans were kidnapped** and forced into slavery to work on plantations, but in 1458 a deal was brokered with African rulers to **purchase slaves**. Up to the mid-17th century, 90 percent of the 140,000 slaves imported from Africa were bought by the sugar planters of the West African islands (the Canaries, Madeira, São Tomé, and Cape Verde). The rest were shipped to the Americas.

SUGAR CANE

The Slave Trade

The brutal trade in African slaves began in the mid-15th century and reached its height in the 18th century. All together, around 10 million Africans were captured, shackled, and shipped to the Americas to work on sugar, cotton, and tobacco plantations.

Although African slave labor was used in the production of other commodities, such as minerals, coffee, cocoa, indigo, cotton, and tobacco, it was Europe's craving for sugar that brought European traders to Africa to buy and barter slaves. The Swedes, Danes, French, British, Dutch, and Portuguese established over 30 slave forts along the West African "Gold Coast," and a series of ports for exporting slaves stretched over 2,000 miles (3,200 km) from the Senegal River south to Angola in Senegambia, Dahomey (Benin), and Ouidah.

Slaves in Africa
Slavery was already part of Africa's tribal economy and society—more so than land ownership—before the arrival of the European traders. For example, women and children whose menfolk had been killed in battle were usually enslaved, becoming part of a tribal ruler's extended family. The East Africa slave trade was also well-established, with captured slaves transported north across the Saharan desert and east into Arabia, the Middle East, and India by Arab and Ottoman slave traders.

African chiefs were complicit in providing the European seafarers with slaves. However, they did not want the Europeans to settle inland. (In any case, the Europeans themselves were deterred by the difficulties of travel in Africa's interior, and the threat of disease.) As a result, African chiefs leased out land along the coast so the Europeans could establish trading forts. African slaves captured in raids or after battle were transported to the forts by their African captors, then sold to the European traders. Some African rulers were especially accommodating. For

example, in 1726 the King of Dahomey suggested that the Europeans should establish plantations in his kingdom—he would supply the slaves.

Money without morals
With only a toehold on the African coast, Europeans were unable to monopolize the slave trade. Slaves

Slave ship
This horrific image shows how many slaves could be packed into the hold of the slave ship, *Brookes*, to maximize profit. In 1789, anti-slavery campaigners published 700 posters of the drawing, sparking the beginning of the end of the slave trade in Britain.

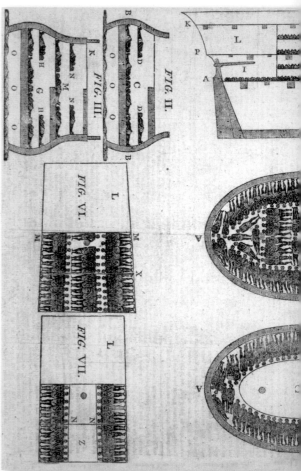

The triangular trade
The global triangular trading system had profit on every leg. Slave ships left European ports for West Africa laden with iron, wine, guns, and textiles. These were exchanged for slaves, who were transported across the Atlantic to sell to plantation owners. The ships then returned to European ports with a cargo of sugar, coffee, and tobacco.

Liverpool
Bristol
Lisbon
Seville
Ottoman Empire
Richmond
Charleston
New Orleans
Cuba
Haïti
Cartagena
AFRICA
St. Louis · Cape Coast
Elmina · Ouidah
Brass
Zanzibar
Luanda
Benguela
Salvador
Potosí
Rio de Janeiro
Buenos Aires
Cape Town

0 3500 km
0 3500 miles

KEY
Slave routes
→ European slave traders
→ Arab slave traders
→ Ottoman slave traders
● African slaving centers
Goods routes
→ Tobacco, sugar, cotton
→ Metals, tobacco, sugar, coffee
→ Iron, cloth, shells, guns

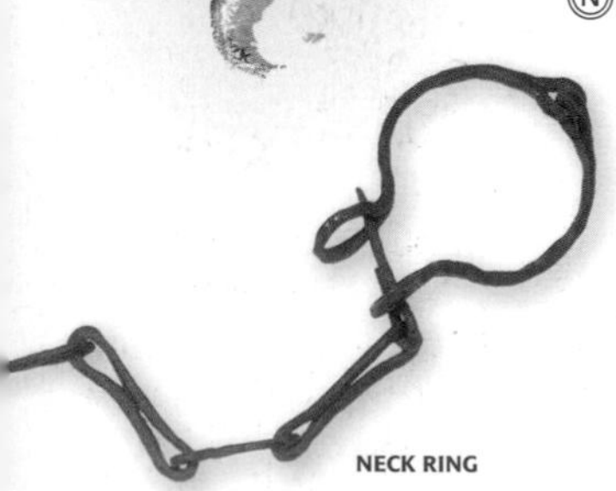

NECK RING

Instruments of torture
Slaves were seen as chattel, or goods, not as human beings, demonstrated by the assortment of heavy iron shackles that they had to endure. Male slaves were chained up in gruesome ankle and neck chains.

FOOT SHACKLES

" There was nothing to be heard but the **rattling of chains**, smacking of whips and groans and **cries** of our... men.**"**
OTTOBAH CUGOANO, FREED SLAVE, 1787

were collected directly from leased forts in exchange for goods, such as guns or alcohol, or ships plied the Gold Coast hoping to pick up a cargo of slaves from private dealers.

For the mercantile companies, shareholders, captains, and other traders involved, there appeared to be no moral qualms at all: slaves simply oiled the wheels of a well-organized and highly lucrative business. For example, by the 1780s the plantations of the French colony Saint-Domingue (Haiti) accounted for 60 percent of France's overseas wealth, supplying

Branding iron

When they were bought, all male slaves were forcibly branded with a hot iron as proof of ownership.

40 per cent of all the sugar and 60 percent of all the coffee consumed in Europe.

The middle passage

Slaves from the African coastal forts were packed on ships bound for South, Central, and North America— a journey called the "middle passage." In the 16th–19th centuries, some

54,000 trade voyages were recorded. This peaked in the 1780s at 78,000 slaves a year, with half of them carried on British ships.

A typical middle passage journey took around 10 weeks. Each ship carried 140—600 slaves in appalling, cramped conditions. Men were chained together in a suffocatingly small space between the deck and the hold. Women were usually left unchained and were allowed on deck to help with the cooking. However, they risked constant sexual harassment and rape by the European crew.

Hygiene on board ship was crude. Few ships were equipped to deal with bodily functions and, as they were shackled together, it was particularly hard for the men to avoid catching dysentery and smallpox—the two biggest onboard killers. After a month at sea, a slave ship stank of sweat, urine, feces, and vomit. It was said that a slave ship could be smelled two days before it actually arrived in a port.

Each morning, the slaves were dragged up onto deck and their shackles were inspected. Any slave who had died during the night was unchained and thrown overboard. Rations included boiled mash of horse beans and yams, biscuits, rice, plantain, and occasionally meat. One food bucket was usually shared among many, resulting in quarrels— and infection.

Captains and crew succumbed to disease and death as much as their cargo. In 1787, of the slave-ship crews that embarked from Liverpool in England, less than half returned alive.

Auctioned

Arriving in Brazil or the Caribbean islands, the slaves were sold at auction, then delivered to their new owners. This was often followed by a period of "seasoning"—about a year in which the slave either succumbed to disease or survived to live a life of human bondage and misery.

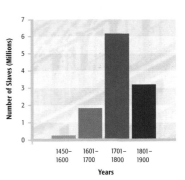

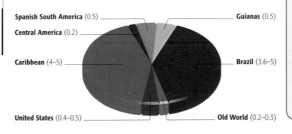

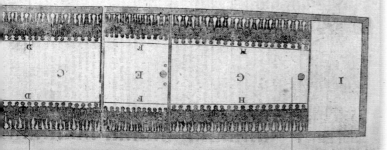

Slaves were shackled in rows between the hold and the deck, lying on their back or sides. Each slave had only around 12 in (30 cm) space around them.

This diagram shows how 482 slaves could be packed on board. This ship had previously carried as many as 609 slaves (351 men, 127 women, and 113 children).

Men were chained together at the front of the boat; women were held in a separate area. Most transported slaves were between 16 and 45 years old.

Food and water were stored in the hold below the slaves. Both food and water were rationed so there was enough to last the voyage. Any slave refusing to eat out of misery or rebellion was whipped.

Number of slaves exported from Africa
Records suggest that between 1450 and 1700, 2 million Africans were enslaved, rising to 6 million in 1701–1800. Accounting for those dying in transit to forts and on slave ships, the figure is probably closer to 12 million.

AFTER »

The slave trade was finally abolished in England in 1807, after years of campaigning by antislavery groups.

ANTISLAVERY CAMPAIGN

Thomas Clarkson, a leading antislavery protester in England, gathered evidence such as shackles and the oral accounts of former slave captains to publicize the horrors of the trade. The fight gained momentum when it was taken up in parliament by William Wilberforce **308–09 »**. The Abolition of the Slave Trade Act was passed in England in 1807, followed by the **Emancipation Act of 1833**, which made owning slaves illegal. A string of legislation followed, with slavery abolished in the US in 1865, Cuba in 1886, Brazil in 1888, ending with Sierra Leone in 1927 and the Gold Coast in 1928.

ANTISLAVERY POSTER, BOSTON, 1851

SLAVERY TODAY

Modern-day human rights campaigners point out that the fight against slavery is far from over. It is estimated that there are **over 27 million slaves** in the world today, including people in forced labor, women and girls trafficked for work in the sex industry, and children kidnapped and forced to fight as soldiers.

CHAINED SLAVES IN ZANZIBAR

Destination and number of slaves exported from Africa (in millions)
Most slaves bought by European traders were shipped to the Caribbean or Brazil, altering the population dynamics: by 1800, half of Brazil's population was of African origin.

Spanish South America (0.5)
Central America (0.2)
Caribbean (4–5)
United States (0.4–0.5)
Guianas (0.5)
Brazil (3.6–5)
Old World (0.2–0.3)

« BEFORE

Some Pacific lands were settled many millennia before they were charted by Europeans in the late 18th century.

AUSTRALIA AND NEW ZEALAND
The **Maori**, from Polynesia, settled New Zealand by about 1400 **« 216–17**. But arid Australia remained uninviting except to the **Aborigines** who landed there 40,000 years earlier.

UNCHARTED TERRITORY
To Europeans, *Terra Australis Incognita* (Unknown Southern Continent) was a hypothetical landmass somewhere in the Pacific Ocean **320–21 »**.

INVENTION
HARRISON'S CHRONOMETER

The problem of determining longitude on an endless horizon was one of the greatest challenges for sailors navigating the Pacific Ocean in the 18th century. John Harrison (1693–1776) had no formal training in clock-making but built five marine timekeepers, the best of which could keep time at sea to within about one second per day—a staggering positioning accuracy of about 1,600 ft (500 m)—solving the navigational problem. This huge clock was his first prototype, called H1. It measures about 3 ft x 3 ft (1 m x 1 m) and weighs 72 lb (33 kg). It performed admirably at sea.

NAUTICAL CHRONOMETER

uses 24-hour dial; runs without pendulum or any lubrication

two 5-lb (2-kg) weights counteract the movement of a rolling ship

£20,000 The prize offered by the British government in 1714 to the person who could solve the longitude problem. John Harrison eventually won the prize in 1764, though the full amount was not given to him until 1773.

Exploring the Pacific

Less than 250 years ago the Pacific Ocean remained the last great unknown area on Earth, at least to European explorers and traders. European superpowers were rapidly exploring the rest of the world from the 15th century onward, yet the Pacific Ocean remained a mystery for another 400 years.

B y the middle of the 18th century, Europeans had mapped the coastlines of North and South America, Asia, and Africa, and vast empires were well underway in these areas. So it may seem odd that the Europeans did not attempt to colonize the islands of the Pacific Ocean until the late 18th century.

The problem of the Pacific
Simply put, there was nothing to lure the Europeans to the Pacific—no tales of El Dorado, no indigenous empires to conquer and convert, and no lucrative trade to exploit. There were also geographical, technological, and logistical barriers: the Pacific covers an area larger than all the continents'

landmass combined, and the prevailing winds also narrowed the sea routes available. Earlier Polynesian voyagers—the Maori who had sailed to New Zealand and the discoverers of the Hawaiian Islands (see pp.216–17)—had steered their canoes by means of the sun and the stars, and patterns in the ocean's currents and waves. European sailors had effective sextants, compasses, and other navigational aids, but they still could not determine longitude. This is the measurement of the position of a point east or west of the prime meridian (where longitude is 0°). It can be calculated by comparing the time at any point to the time at the prime meridian, but to know the time at Greenwich (the British meridian) after

a voyage to the other side of the world required an extremely accurate clock. The ability to determine longitude was vital—it would allow sailors to chart their precise location and that of the islands they visited. The Solomon Islands, for example, were sighted and reported in 1568 but were not

Maori war canoe
The Maoris had giant war canoes (*waka taua*), which carried 70–140 armed warriors. Led by a Maori chief (*rangatira*), a war canoe had a hull carved out of a single tree trunk and an intricately carved prow.

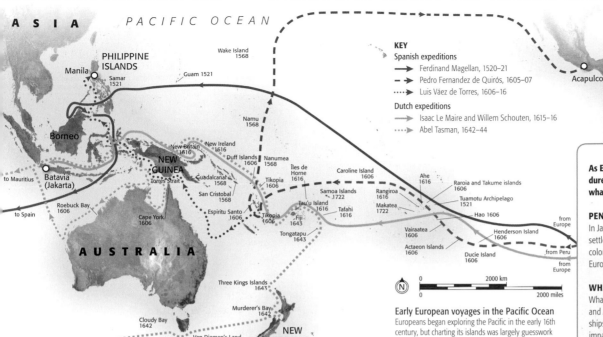

PACIFIC OCEAN

ASIA

PHILIPPINE
ISLANDS
Manila

Samar
1521

Wake Island
1568

Guam 1521

Acapulco

KEY

Spanish expeditions
→ Ferdinand Magellan, 1520–21
⇢ Pedro Fernandez de Quirós, 1605–07
⋯⋯ Luis Váez de Torres, 1606–16

Dutch expeditions
→ Isaac Le Maire and Willem Schouten, 1615–16
⋯⋯ Abel Tasman, 1642–44

Borneo

Namu
1568

New Britain
1616
New Ireland
1616
NEW
GUINEA
Torres Strait
Duff Islands
1606
Nanumea
1568
Îles de
Horne
1616
Caroline Island
1606
Ahe
1616
Raroia and Takume islands
1606
Tuamotu Archipelago
1521

to Mauritius

Batavia
(Jakarta)

Guadalcanal
1568
San Cristobal
1568
Tikopia
1606
Samoa Islands
1722
Rangiroa
1616
Makatea
1722

to Spain

Roebuck Bay
1606

Espiritu Santo
1606
Tikopia
1606
Tau'u Island
1616
Tafahi
1616
Hao 1606

from
Europe

Cape York
1606

Fiji
1643

Vairaatea
1606
Henderson Island
1606

from Peru

AUSTRALIA

Tongatapu
1643

Actaeon Islands
1606
Ducie Island
1606

from
Europe

Three Kings Islands
1643

0   2000 km
0   2000 miles

Cloudy Bay
1642

Murderer's Bay
1642

Early European voyages in the Pacific Ocean
Europeans began exploring the Pacific in the early 16th century, but charting its islands was largely guesswork until Cook's voyages of 1768–79 (see pp.320–21).

from Mauritius

Van Diemen's Land
(Tasmania)

NEW
ZEALAND

AFTER

As European settlers arrived, some under duress, the Pacific region began to develop whaling and agricultural industries.

PENAL COLONIES
In January 1788 **the First Fleet of convicts** and settlers arrived from England to set up the penal colony of New South Wales, which began the European settlement of Australia **320–21 »**.

WHALING
Whaling was a lure in the Pacific for Europeans and Americans from 1789 onwards. Whaling ships called in to refuel all over the Pacific. They impacted on the islands' native communities as well stimulating further **maritime expansion**.

SHEEP FARMING
British settlers in Australia and New Zealand introduced sheep to temperate regions of the continent. Today, Australia is the **biggest fine-wool producer in the world**.

MERINO SHEEP GRAZING IN AUSTRALIA

properly charted until 1793. Accurate chronometers (see left) were invaluable as they allowed sailors to measure exact longitude for the first time. Other obstacles to colonization included malaria, settlers' reliance on imported livestock, the poor quality of land for farming, and tropical storms.

Spanish monopoly
The biggest disincentive to exploring the Pacific region was reflected in a Dutch East India Company report on Abel Tasman's voyages to Tasmania and New Zealand: "No riches or things of profit, but only the said lands."

Maori eel trap
A Maori eel trap (*hinaki*) was finely woven from vines and allowed eels to swim in, but not out. It was placed in lakes or waterholes.

The Spanish Empire claimed the exclusive right of navigation in Pacific waters. They used the Pacific primarily to ship South American silver to the Philippines to trade with China and the East Indies. Spain's greatest rival, the Dutch East India Company, concentrated on its possessions in the Indonesian archipelago, discouraging its captains from long, fruitless, and costly ocean voyages in the region. Breakthrough voyages, such as Luis Vaez de Torres' 1606 sailing between New Guinea and Australia that proved the former to be an island, received no publicity. The

Spanish did not want Dutch and English ships passing through the Java Sea to the Pacific and on to South America.

The race for land begins
When British Captain James Cook (see pp.320–21) set out for Tahiti on the *Endeavour* in 1768, his orders were to observe the transit of Venus, a rare astronomical event when the planet passes across the disk of the Sun. But the British also wanted to forestall any French ambitions of gaining land in the area. The second, secret purpose of Cook's voyage was to survey the vast Pacific Ocean to see if Tahiti was the possible gateway to the landmass of a southern continent, Australia.

6

INDUSTRY AND REVOLUTION

1750–1914

From the middle of the 18th century, the world experienced radical change. Political revolutions challenged established governments, aiming to throw off the shackles of oppression and privilege. New methods of mechanization and transportation resulted in an age of industry and manufacturing that gave birth to new cities and consolidated empires.

INDUSTRY AND REVOLUTION

1750–1914

1750	1760	1770	1780

1758
Britain defeats France at Fort Duquesne, Pennsylvania; Britain takes Senegal from the French. Battle of Zorndorf between Prussia and Russia; result favors Prussia.

◀ Frederick the Great

▲ Adam Smith

1772
Partition of Poland by Austria, Prussia, and Russia.
1773
Boston Tea Party, a protest against British taxes on American colonies, occurs.

▼ Captain Cook's first landing in Australia

1776
US Declaration of Independence; British abandon Boston.

Articles of ▶
Confederation

1762
Catherine the Great comes to the Russian throne. France cedes upper Louisiana to Spain.
1763
Treaty of Paris; British supremacy in North America confirmed.

1781
Battle of Yorktown: George Washington and French allies defeat British; Articles of Confederation ratified. Massacre of Xhosa by Boers, South Africa.

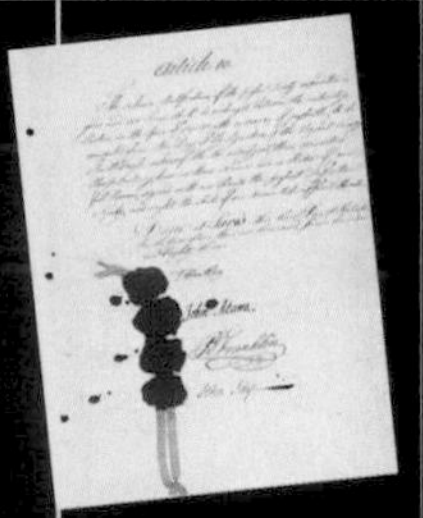

▲ British East India Company

1756
The Seven Years War begins; of the major European powers Hanover, Britain, and Prussia (led by Frederick the Great) clash with France, Austria, and Russia.

1768
Russian–Ottoman war. James Cook begins his first Pacific voyage (to 1771).

1784
India Act: British take direct control of Indian territories.

◀ Treaty of Paris

▲ Bridgewater canal

1760
Boer settlement of South African interior. Work on Britain's first "modern" canal, the Bridgewater Canal.
c. 1760
Enlightenment, led by thinkers such as Adam Smith and Voltaire.

1775–83
American Revolution.

▼ US Declaration of Independence

1777
Treaty of San Ildefonso: Spanish possession of Uruguay and Portuguese possession of Amazon basin confirmed.
1778
France joins America in Revolutionary War. Cook's third Pacific voyage.

1757
Victory at Battle of Plassey secures Bengal for the British East India Company; Prussia defeats Austria at Battle of Leuthen; gives them control of Silesia.

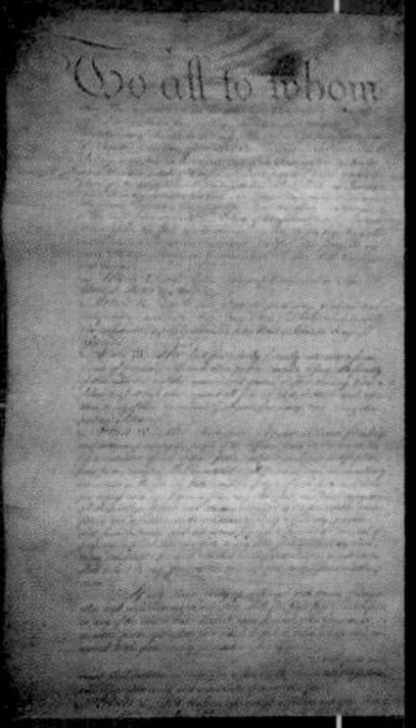

▲ Battle of Zorndorf

1759
Anglo-Prussian force defeats French at Minden, north Germany; Britain takes Quebec from France.

1769
Egypt declares independence from Ottomans.

▼ Captain Cook's chronometer

▲ Tennis Court Oath

1782
Britain sues for peace with American rebels. Native revolt in Peru quashed by Spanish.
1783
Treaty of Paris: American independence recognized by British.

1789
Tennis Court Oath; French Revolution begins. George Washington elected first president of the United States (to 1797).

The American and French revolutions transformed Western political expectations. If the results were contradictory—the United States emerging as a fully functioning democracy, France destabilized for almost a century—demands for political liberation echoed through the 19th century. These demands took place against a background of Western domination, supported by rapid industrialization, expanding trade, and population growth. It was an era of unprecedented European global supremacy and imperial expansion on every continent. Yet by 1914, these apparently impregnable powers were poised to tear themselves apart in the world's bloodiest war.

1790   1800   1810   1820

1805
Battle of Trafalgar; Britain defeats Franco-Spanish fleet. Battle of Austerlitz: France defeats Austrians and Russians. Lewis and Clark explore territories of Louisiana Purchase and reach the Pacific.

◀ Napoleon Bonaparte

1828
Russia acquires Armenia, declares war on Ottomans, takes Varna, Bulgaria. Egypt agrees to withdraw from Greece. Agricultural innovation, such as Morton seed drill, continues.

◀ Simón Bolívar

▲ Execution of Marie Antoinette

1793
Louis XVI and Marie Antoinette executed; beginning of "Terror" led by Maximilien Robespierre.

Maximilien Robespierre

1806
France defeats Prussia; serfdom abolished in Prussia.
1809
Anti-Spanish uprising in Mexico starts revolts across Latin America. Sweden cedes Finland to Russia.

▲ Treaty of Vienna

1812
Napoleon invades Russia; occupies Moscow, but forced to retreat. Egypt reclaims Mecca and Medina from Ottomans.

1821
Greek War of Independence (to 1829) against Ottomans. Venezuela and Mexico achieve independence.
1823–26
First Anglo-Burmese War.

Anglo-Burmese War ▶

1792
Louis ... erthrown; French republic declared; France declares war on Austria, Prussia, and Piedmont.

1798
Napoleon Bonaparte invades Egypt; French fleet destroyed by British at Battle of the Nile. Ceylon becomes British colony.

1803
Britain declares war on France (to 1815). Cape Colony, South Africa, restored to Dutch. Louisiana Purchase: France sells territory between Mississippi and Rockies to US.

Battle of Trafalgar ▶

1815
Napoleon escapes Elba; defeated at Waterloo; exiled to St. Helena; French monarchy restored. Serbia throws off Ottoman rule. Britain takes control of India.

1799
Brumaire Coup brings Napoleon to power as first consul. Britain assumes control of south India.

Napoleon's sword from Brumaire Coup ◀

1824
Ottomans joined by Egyptians against Greek nationalists. Peru becomes independent from Spain, aided by Simón Bolívar.
1826–28
Russo-Persian War.

1829
Ottomans negotiate Greek and Serbian independence. First passenger railroad in US.

▼ Morton seed drill

1804
Napoleon assumes title of Emperor of France. Napoleonic Code introduced.

▲ Battle of Maipu

1813
Battle of the Nations; allies defeat France; British cross into France.
1814
Anti-French allies occupy Paris, Napoleon exiled to Elba. Congress of Vienna to set out future of Europe.

1818
Chilean independence from Spain confirmed by victory in Battle of Maipu. Shaka unites Zulus, South Africa.
1819
US buys Florida from Spain. Colombia gains independence.

Abolition of slavery in Britain ▶

1830

1840

1850

1860

1840
Opium War, China, fought by the British and the Chinese; British troops force the Chinese to negotiate. Maoris obliged to accept British rule in New Zealand.

▼ Treaty of Nanjing

1854
Crimean War (to 1856): Britain and France ally with Ottomans, declare war on Russia. Britain recognizes independence of Orange Free State, South Africa.

Opening of Great Exhibition, London

1865
Union victory in American Civil War; South devastated; Lincoln assassinated. French colony established in Senegal, West Africa.

◄ Otto von Bismarck

▲ *Liberty Leading the People*, Eugene Delacroix

1830
Revolution in Paris topples Charles X; Louis-Philippe crowned king of France. Belgian War of Independence (to 1831). First wagon train to California.

1851
Pseudo-Christian Taiping rebels march north through China: immense devastation. Great Exhibition opens, London.
1852
Britain acknowledges independence of Transvaal Boers.

1857
Indian Mutiny; revolt attempts to end British rule. Last Mughal emperor exiled by Britain. France and Britain declare war on China: take Guangzhou.

▼ Indian Mutiny

1838
Battle of Blood River: Boers massacre Zulus.
1839
Mahmud II introduces reforms to Ottoman Empire. Charles Darwin publishes diary of voyage on HMS *Beagle*.

◄ Johann Wolfgang von Goethe

1846
Japan refuses US demands to open trading links. Mexican-American War begins (to 1848): Mexico defeated. US claims California.

1861
Abraham Lincoln elected president of the US; the slave states cede from the Union; American Civil War begins (to 1865). Serfdom abolished in Russia. Italy unifies.

1831
Belgium achieves independence from Netherlands. Mass immigration to US from Ireland begins.
1832
Russia annexes Duchy of Warsaw. Death of Johann Wolfgang von Goethe, Germany.

1842
Treaty of Nanjing: China cedes Hong Kong to Britain, opens ports to foreign trade. Webster–Ashburton Treaty: US–Canadian border agreed.

1859
Second Italian War of Independence; Giuseppe Garibaldi serves as major general. Suez Canal begun. Charles Darwin's *Origin of Species* published.

◄ Giuseppe Garibaldi

1834
Slavery abolished in British empire; Boers move north.

Beagle specimen ▶

1848
Gold discovered in California, prompting California Gold Rush. Karl Marx and Friedrich Engels publish *The Communist Manifesto*.

◄ *The Communist Manifesto*

1862
Taiping rebels attack Shanghai. Otto von Bismarck prime minister of Prussia. Foreigners expelled from Japan.
1863
Slavery outlawed in Confederacy, but not abolished until end of Civil War.

▲ Pistol used to assassinate Lincoln

1867
Austro-Hungarian dual monarchy. Bismarck chancellor of North German Confederation. Meiji restored, Japan. US purchases Alaska from Russia.

"A people destined to achieve great things for **the welfare of humanity** must one day or other be constituted a nation." GIUSEPPE MAZZINI, ITALIAN REVOLUTIONARY AND PATRIOT, 1861

1870 | 1880 | 1890 | 1900 »

1870
Franco–Prussian War: France capitulates.
1871
German unification: France cedes Alsace–Lorraine to Germany. Paris Commune revolt suppressed. Modernizing reforms, Japan.

Anglo-Egyptian war ▶

1880
Boers drive Britain from Transvaal.
1881
Britain recognizes self-government in Transvaal. Anti-Jewish pogrom in Russia; mass Jewish immigration to US.

1894
Ottomans massacre nationalist Armenians. Britain occupies Buganda and Uganda. French conquer Dahomey. First Sino-Japanese war begins (to 1895).

1900
Anti-Western Boxer Rebellion, China; European forces occupy Beijing.
1901
Commonwealth of Australia proclaimed. Queen Victoria dies.

Albert Einstein ▶

◀ Early X-ray

1897
Greek–Ottoman war: Ottomans force concessions from Greeks. Cuba granted autonomy. Anti-British uprisings, northwest frontier of India.

1905
Russian revolution: Czar Nicholas II grants limited concessions. Norway gains independence. Special Theory of Relativity proposed by Albert Einstein.

1909
Reformist "Young Turks" oust Ottoman sultan, Abdul Hamid II. Ottomans recognize independent Bulgaria.

Young Turk Revolution ▼

▲ Bell box telephone

1875
Anti-Ottoman revolts in Balkans.

1876
Serbia and Montenegro declare war on Ottomans: Serbia defeated. Alexander Graham Bell patents telephone, US.

1895
Battle of Weihaiwei: crushing Japanese victory over China; Japan annexes Taiwan. Anti-Spanish uprising, Cuba. First X-ray, Germany.

Le Petit Parisien

1877
Britain annexes Transvaal, South Africa. Phonograph, Thomas Edison, US.
1878
Serbia, Montenegro, and Romania gain independence from Ottoman Empire.

1882
Germany, Austria, and Italy form anti-French alliance. Nationalist revolt in Egypt prompts British occupation.
1884
Berlin Conference negotiates European partition of Africa.

▲ Early Benz Velo

1889
First Italian colony, Eritrea, Africa. Rhodesia colonized. Brazil declared a republic. Eiffel Tower constructed, Paris.

1910
Monarchy overthrown, Portugal: republic proclaimed. China invades Tibet. Japan annexes Korea. Mexican Revolution begins.

◀ Phonograph

▼ Mexican Revolution

▲ Boer soldiers

1885
King Leopold of Belgium acquires Congo. Madagascar becomes a French protectorate, Tanganyika a German protectorate. First automobile, Daimler and Benz, Germany.

1899
South African (Boer) War (to 1902). Britain and Egypt agree to share power in Sudan. Germany occupies Rwanda.

Eiffel Tower ▶

« **BEFORE**

Despite advances in farming practices and knowledge, pre-18th-century food production was inefficient and reliant on manual labor.

ENCLOSURE

The enclosure system was first developed in England in the 12th century, and saw the division of large, commonly-owned fields into small, privately-owned plots. Laborers were forced from the fields by land owners thanks to a series of Enclosure Acts. This practice spread through Europe during the 19th century.

ENCLOSURE SYSTEM

NEW METHODS

By the mid-17th century many farmers began to treat **farming as a science**. They adopted new winter feeding methods, which made fresh meat available year-round. Improved seeds in Holland and later in England yielded new varieties of fruit and vegetables, and numerous new horse-drawn threshers, cultivators, grain, and grass cutters were used.

POPULATION GROWTH

In 1750 the world population began to boom. Although this had happened before, each time the population had ceased to grow because agriculture could not feed the extra people. However, by 1750 the onset of agricultural technology allowed this population growth to be sustained.

The mid-18th century witnessed a dramatic increase in world population. The British economist Thomas Malthus (see right) believed that this rise would eventually be halted by a shortage of food. He had not accounted, however, for vast improvements in agricultural practice.

In 1701, Jethro Tull had developed the horse-drawn seed-drill, a machine for efficiently planting seeds, while a four-year system of crop rotation dispensed with the need to replenish fields by leaving them unfarmed for a season. These changes would have been impossible under the old common-field system, but a spate of Enclosure Acts (see BEFORE) during the 19th century allowed landowners to evict peasants from the land, and experiment with new farming techniques without the consent

Mechanical reaping

Cyrus McCormick's mechanical reaper of 1831 was a boon to wheat farmers in the American Midwest. It could do the work of three men, and was soon exported around the world.

Changing practices

Rural scene like this one in Norfolk, England in 1887 had remained relatively unchanged for centuries. Eventually, with the introduction of steam power, horse-drawn plows became obsolete.

The Food Revolution

The Agricultural Revolution that began in the mid-18th century saw a massive increase in food production. The dramatic increase in efficiency fed a rising population, allowing it to expand further. Workers moved away from the fields and into the factories, providing labor to help drive the Industrial Revolution.

THOMAS MALTHUS

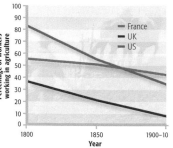

Thomas Malthus was born into a wealthy family and enrolled at Jesus College, Cambridge, in 1784. In 1798 he published his *Essay on Population*, arguing that the growth in population was far outstripping that of food production. Although derided by many, he was the first to write about the economic situation of the lower classes. Malthus believed that if left unchecked, population would always exceed the level of food available. He saw starvation and disease as "positive checks" on population growth and voluntary abstinence as a form of birth control as "preventative checks."

Agricultural labor
The technological innovations of the 19th century changed the way the labor force was deployed. As food production increased, workers moved away from agriculture, into industry.

The involvement of technology in food production continues in the 21st century, though not without controversy.

FAST-FREEZING
Clarence Birdseye developed advanced techniques for freezing food in the 1920s. The popularity of frozen food increased during World War II **392–405 ≫**, as it used less packaging than canning.

ADDITIVES

As more people moved to cities, food had to be transported and stay fresh for longer. This was made possible by the introduction of additives to prevent food decay.

FOOD MOUNTAIN

FAMINE VERSUS PLENTY
The 20th century witnessed increasing concern about commercial and intensive agriculture **462–463 ≫** which led to **large food surpluses** in developed countries, while the other parts of the world suffered from **famine**.

GM FOODS
Since James Watson and Francis Crick broke the genetic code in 1953, the **engineering of genes** has been possible. Genetically modified food products appeared in stores in the 1990s. However, the industry stalled due to misgivings about the safety of GM foods **462–63 ≫**.

---

of other farmers. In the US, the mechanical reaper, invented by Cyrus Hall McCormick in 1831, further reduced the need for farm labor. Steam power invaded the countryside with the introduction of the Fowler steam plow in the 1850s.

In the second half of the 18th century better livestock was introduced with selective breeding, by British agriculturalists Robert Bakewell and Thomas Coke. This increased profit and food supplies. In the mid-19th century, the British scientists Joseph Gilbert and John Lawes demonstrated that plants required nitrogen and other nutrients, improving techniques for farming crops.

Food preservation
These food cans date from the Boer War (1899–1902). During wars, demand for canned food increased. At home, it was a status symbol among the middle classes.

Around the world
As Europeans explored the globe, they carried with them their farming methods and crops (see pp.232–33).

In 1788, the first European settlers arrived in Australia, and influenced early practices in wool production. In the US thousands had moved west in the 1850s to escape poverty and overcrowding in east coast cities such as Boston and New York. But lack of wooden fences meant farmers could not keep cattle off their crops. The invention of barbed wire (made commercially successful by Joseph Glidden in 1874) solved this problem and transformed farming in the Midwest in the process. Prairie grassland was hard to cultivate, but the development of farm machinery, such as John Deere's sodbuster plow, changed this situation. High-yield crops from the Americas, such as peanuts, started making their way to China and East Asia, where, after their

introduction, significant increases in population took place. These crops from the Americas triggered an agricultural revolution in Africa. Corn and sweet potatoes reached the western shores of Africa with slave traders, who introduced them into that continent to provide food for their human cargoes.

Preservation and transport
Equally important to this improvement was that crops could be preserved and distributed efficiently and safely. Although drying and salting had been used for millennia, new preservation techniques were invented during the 18th and 19th centuries. In 1795, French chef Nicolas Appert developed a process for preserving food in airtight bottles after sterilization. This process was patented in England by Peter Durand in 1810, including the provision of using "tin canisters." The rights to this were bought by engineers Donkin, Hall & Gamble, who set up the world's first canning factory in 1813 in London. Modern refrigeration began in the 1850s when the French inventor Ferdinand Carré pioneered the vapor compression system.

Preserved food made its way around the world on steam railroads and steamships (see pp.292–95). This also enabled agriculture to pursue price and profit globally, rather than focus on a small, local economy, allowing farmers to import specialty seeds, foods, and livestock that suited their terrain.

At last, the population could expand without risk of starvation. A period of high productivity and low food prices meant people did not spend all their money on food. Amid this wealth, however, was the Irish potato famine (see right), which ravaged the Irish population.

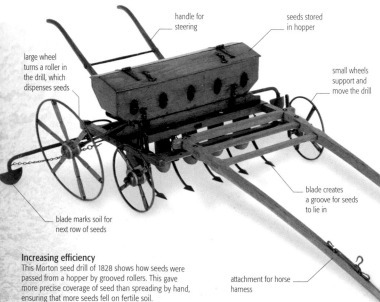

Increasing efficiency
This Morton seed drill of 1828 shows how seeds were passed from a hopper by grooved rollers. This gave more precise coverage of seed than spreading by hand, ensuring that more seeds fell on fertile soil.

handle for steering

seeds stored in hopper

large wheel turns a roller in the drill, which dispenses seeds

small wheels support and move the drill

blade creates a groove for seeds to lie in

blade marks soil for next row of seeds

attachment for horse harness

THE IRISH POTATO FAMINE

In 1846, blight—a fungus that damages plants—ruined the potato crop in Europe, leading to starvation for many people in Ireland, where potatoes were a staple food. There was another blight in 1847, accompanied by an outbreak of typhoid. All attempts to deal with the problem failed and Ireland's population was decimated in this, the last peacetime famine in Western Europe. By 1851, the population of Ireland had fallen from 8.5 million to 6.5 million. Many people had died, while others had emigrated, principally to the US.

Abundant raw materials and significant technological advances created the conditions for industrialization in Britain, which then spread to Europe and the US.

BRITAIN FIRST
Access to cheap imports, such as cotton, silk, and wool, from its colonies gave Britain an advantage in being able to industrialize faster than the rest of Europe.

RAW
MATERIALS

IRON MASTERS
Two key innovations made by British ironworks owners contributed to industrialization. First, in 1709, Abraham Darby's use of **coke** (processed coal that burns at **much higher temperatures**) instead of charcoal reduced the cost of ironmaking, due to coke's relative abundance. Secondly, Henry Cort's "puddling" and "rolling" processes of the 1780s produced a **purer form of iron** that was **malleable** and more useful to industrial processes than the brittle "pig iron," or "cast iron."

TRANSPORTATION NETWORK
Transportation was another vital element during industrialization. Raw materials had to be moved to the point of manufacture, and finished goods went to cities and ports for distribution. Britain had a network of navigable rivers, which it enhanced by building canals. The Bridgewater Canal, Manchester, cut in 1761, was followed by other canals that were connected to major rivers.

BRIDGEWATER
CANAL

4,250 MILES **(6,800 km) of inland waterways were built in England between 1760 and 1800.**

FOLLOWING THE SEAM
The **rich belt of coal** that runs through the industrial north of England also runs through Silesia, the Ruhr Valley, and across the Atlantic to Pennsylvania, which would also become **heavily industrialized** when that coal was exploited.

FREEDOM TO TRADE
An empire unhindered by continental Europe's **internal frontiers** and **trade barriers** gave Britain a trading advantage. Slave plantations in America and the West Indies **« 280–81** had given Britain a supply of cheap cotton, and when slavery was abolished in 1807, trade with the colonies continued. Even after the American Revolution **298–99 »** the United States was still an important market.

The **Industrial Revolution**

The world we live in today owes much to the industrialization that took place first in Britain, in the late 18th century, and swept across Europe and North America during the 19th. It transformed the western world from a rural society to an urban one, and set the foundations for modern capitalist society.

The term "Industrial Revolution" implies a sudden and universal change, but it was not a single event, rather a series of technological innovations, social developments, and economic growth spurts that fed into each other. Britain was fortunate in having the conditions it needed to be the industrial pioneer. Firstly, there was a natural abundance of the raw materials: water, iron, and coal. Secondly, there was available capital: interest rates were low, and members of an increasingly wealthy middle class, looking for ways to invest their money, were eager to support new inventions and technology. Finally, Britain had an unusually large market for its manufactured goods, with an expanding empire, and a dominance of the seas, along with a strong merchant navy to trade and transport goods around the world.

The steam engine powered the revolution. Invented by Thomas Newcomen in 1712, the improvements

"I sell here, Sir, what the world desires to have—**power**."

MATTHEW BOULTON, BRITISH ENGINEER, 1776

Child labor
Child labor was cheap, and in demand, as small hands could reach into machines. These children spinning cotton in South Carolina, in 1903, have bare feet, because nails on their shoes might produce a spark, causing a fire.

made by James Watt (see below) have remained an essential element of steam engines ever since. When, in the 1770s, Watt went into business with Matthew Boulton, an entrepreneur and factory owner, they manufactured steam engines to Watt's patented design. These went on to power all stages of industrial production—pumping the mines; powering machinery in the factories and mills; and driving the steamships and railroad locomotives.

The "iron horse"
The huge demand for steam resulted in an increased need for coal. Improvements in both the mining of coal and its distribution via canals, and later, railroads, dramatically cut its cost. The use of refined coal (coke) to smelt iron (see BEFORE) further fueled industrialization by enabling engineers to build better tools and machines. Iron was also used as a building material for

(see BEFORE)

Forging a revolution
These men working in a Minnesota metalworks formed part of a large but unprotected workforce. By the late 19th century, Minnesota was one of the largest producers of iron ore in the US.

Steam powered
Trains, like this British one from 1908, were both the product and driving force of the Industrial Revolution. They were enabled by the growth of coal mining, and transported raw materials and goods at high speed.

and became increasingly concentrated in towns. Textile production rapidly mechanized; by 1835 there were more than 120,000 power looms in textile mills. "Domestic" or "cottage" work (where home-workers were paid per item produced), ran alongside factory work, where workers operated machines that carried out just one task in a production line.

Reaction to progress
The Industrial Revolution undoubtedly improved productivity, and drove technological and economic progress, but it also became synonymous with appalling living and working conditions. Men, women, and children flocked to the cities, but with so many seeking

> **TRADE UNION** An organization devoted to protecting the interests of its members, who are drawn from a specific profession or trade.

employment, the value of their labor was reduced, and they worked long hours for low pay. Many formed trade unions, but workers' conditions improved only slowly: legislation passed was limited in scope, and frequently ignored by factory owners.

Opposition to industrialization also came from skilled workers, who had been made obsolete by mechanization, and unemployed factory workers. Rioting, and the wrecking of

bridges, ships, and railroads. By 1850, about 2 million tons of iron had been used for railroad tracks and there were 6,214 miles (10,000 km) of train tracks around Britain. Known as "iron horses," locomotives could pull huge loads and reach speeds of up to 40 mph (65 km/h). The speed and efficiency of the railroads made the growth of the great manufacturing cities possible, and by the 1840s, it had cut the cost of moving goods by up to 50 percent. Railroad timetables changed timekeeping, with the standardized use of Greenwich Mean Time (GMT) replacing local time across Britain.

Dark satanic mills
With the harnessing of steam power, factories and mills no longer needed to be sited near natural resources such as rivers,

INVENTION

THE STEAM ENGINE

In 1712 Thomas Newcomen built an "atmospheric engine" in which a vacuum produced by condensing steam caused atmospheric pressure to pull down a beam. This device was useful for pumping water out of coal mines. Sixty years later James Watt improved its efficiency, and added modifications for driving machinery. In 1804 Richard Trevithick put a high-pressure steam engine on wheels to make the first steam locomotive, and in 1830 the *Rocket* pulled the first passenger train on George Stephenson's Liverpool–Manchester railroad.

≫

machinery, was carried out by gangs known as "Luddites." The British government sent troops to control them, and at a mass trial in 1813, more than 50 people were sentenced to death or penal transportation to Australia (see pp.350–51), where they would be forced into unpaid labor.

Continental challenge

The first phase of the Industrial Revolution took place largely in Britain, but not exclusively so: Britain's

American colonies had shipbuilding and iron-production industries; and some German states began to industrialize their metalworking. At the start of the period, France's total industrial output was close to Britain's, but progress was stalled by the French Revolution (see pp.300–03). The first Continental nation to industrialize was Belgium, from 1820 onward.

A second wave, sometimes called the Second Industrial Revolution, took place in Germany, Switzerland, and the US after the development of their

railroads from 1840 to 1870. German industrialization accelerated massively after unification in 1871 (see pp.333), and by the turn of the century, both Germany and the US had overtaken Britain's industrial output.

European industrialization was made possible not just by technology, but also by the availability of a workforce recently freed from serfdom—those

◁ **Eiffel Tower**
Finished in 1889, Gustave Eiffel's tower, made from 18,038 separate pieces of iron, was a sign of France's industrialization. The tower was the world's tallest structure for 41 years.

"Avarice, the spur of industry."
DAVID HUME, SCOTTISH PHILOSOPHER, "OF CIVIL LIBERTY," 1742

△ **French railroad construction**
As with industrialization itself, railroad building in France suffered a false start. France's first railroad opened as early as 1832, but subsequent development was hindered by political and financial problems.

▷ **Trading fuel**
London's Coal Exchange (1849) was symbolic of the Industrial Revolution in two ways: the existence of the exchange was evidence of the increased value of coal, while the building itself, with its 72-ft- (22-m-) iron and glass dome, would not previously have been possible.

SPREAD OF THE INDUSTRIAL REVOLUTION
From Britain, industrialization with its mechanization, market economy, and profound social change swept in waves across Europe, the United States, and Japan.

1802 First **Factory Act** passed in Britain. Modest regulations imposed on working conditions.

1849 The first continental use of coke in iron-making occurs on the Ruhr.

1837 Term "Industrial Revolution" coined by Louis-Auguste Blanqui to describe the changes in Britain during the preceding 50 years.

1850 Britain owns half the world's ocean-going ships, contains half the world's railroads, and produces more than half of Europe's steam horsepower (but produces less horsepower than the US).

1900–14 Industrialization in **Japan**, **Austrian** part of **Habsburg Empire** and, to a lesser degree, **Spain** and **Hungary**.

1828 First modern **blast furnace** goes into operation, in Silesia.

1855 **Bessemer** process developed in England.

1895 Huge acceleration of industrialization in **France**.

1750	1775	1800	1825	1850	1875	1900

1771 Richard Arkwright develops the first water-powered mill in Derbyshire, England.

1781 The **condenser** steam engine is first used in Europe.

1830–70 Railroad networks completed in **Britain**, **Belgium**, and **Germany**, accelerating industrialization in those countries. French coal and iron output had doubled by the early 1850s.

1870s onwards "2nd industrial revolution": Massive acceleration in industrialization, particularly in **Germany** and the **US**, which began to challenge Britain's supremacy.

1890s Russia and Sweden begin massive program of railroad building and industrialization.

1905 Italy's industrialization, based on chemicals and textiles.

▽ Forth Rail Bridge, Edinburgh
Completed in 1890, this was the world's first steel cantilever bridge. It cost the lives of 57 of its 4,000 construction workers.

△ British coal miners lead pit ponies
Coal fueled the industrial revolution, and in Britain output increased almost sixfold in fifty years, from 11 million tons in 1800 to 65 million tons in 1854.

△ Trade and transportation
National and international transport networks were vital to the continued momentum of the Industrial Revolution. London's Albert Dock was opened in 1880 as the second of the Royal Group of Docks.

tied for life to work their landowner's land—which was abolished in France during the 1790s, in Germany from 1811 to 1848, and in Russia and Poland in the 1860s. In the US, immigrants moving to North America from Europe brought new skills and labor.

17 The number of men employed by German steel manufacturer Krupp in 1826–this number rose to 122 in 1846 and 70,000 in 1910.

The age of steam and steel
The second wave of industrialization was founded on new industrial enterprises: chemicals, engineering, and steel production, aided by the Bessemer process (see right).

Railroads provided the momentum for continued industrialization. In addition to transporting raw materials and finished products, they also affected the economies of industrializing nations. Not only did they connect previously disparate economic regions, but financing railroads required new approaches to investment, such as a shift from private to joint-stock banking (see pp.276–77), which provided greater access to capital for industry in general.

Similarly, the progression from sail to steamships had an impact on global trade. Foodstuffs and raw materials could be bought from the cheapest supplier, and the market for finished products increased. Improved communications, such as the invention of the telegraph and telephone (see pp.344–45), enabled businesses to respond relatively quickly to changes in the marketplace. They were also able to establish links with the farthest parts of the world which, thanks to the developments of the Industrial Revolution, had become intimately linked with their own.

Until the advent of the steam locomotive, the fastest form of transportation on Earth was a galloping horse. Industrialization changed everything: the dominance of agriculture was over, cities now ruled, and the consumer society was born.

THE THIRD WAVE
After the first phase of the industrial revolution in Britain, and the second in Belgium, Germany, and the US, economic growth was slowed by a **worldwide depression**. Recovery was triggered by a **third wave of industrialization** from the 1890s onward in countries including Russia, Sweden, France, Italy, and Japan. Where the first wave had centered on textiles and iron production, and the second on heavy engineering and steel, the third wave saw the application of industrial processes to **chemical and electrical engineering**,

car manufacture, and increasingly, **armaments**.

LUGER PISTOL

ARMING FOR WAR
Bessemer invented his steel-making process (see below) after the French complained that a **new artillery shell** he had invented for use in the Crimean War was **too powerful** for their cast-iron cannons. The advent of steel sparked an **arms race** that changed the face of warfare forever with the introduction of mass-produced guns, heavy artillery, and tanks.

OMINOUS SIGNS
German dominance in industrial production and weaponry toward the end of the 19th century led its increasingly nervous neighbors to accelerate industrialization. Russia, France, and Italy all **invested in arms manufacturing**, and Russia improved its railroad network specifically for transporting troops to defend its borders.

INVENTION
BESSEMER PROCESS

Steel-making was one of the key characteristics of the second phase of the Industrial Revolution. Previously, engineers had used cast iron (strong when compressed) or wrought iron (strong under tension). On October 17, 1855, building on previous investigations in this field, English metallurgist Henry Bessemer filed a patent for a means of producing mild steel by blasting cold air into molten iron in a "Bessemer Converter." This reduced the amount of carbon in the iron, making a stronger, more versatile product used for railroad lines, shipbuilding, and armaments.

« **BEFORE**

The war of 1756–63 followed an eight-year conflict that had involved many of the same powers, although they did not consistently fight on the same sides.

SCHÖNBRUNN PALACE

WAR OF THE AUSTRIAN SUCCESSION

The death of the Austrian Habsburg emperor **Charles VI** in 1740 prompted war in Europe. France and Prussia attempted to prevent his heir, **Maria Theresa**, from acceding to the Austrian throne—the summer seat of which was the Schönbrunn Palace, in Vienna—and her husband, **Francis of Lorraine,** from becoming Holy Roman Emperor. The Aix-la-Chapelle peace treaty of 1748 confirmed both Maria Theresa and her husband on their respective thrones, but left **Austria weakened** against the growing power of **Frederick II's** Prussia, which had snatched the rich province of Silesia from Austria during the war. Although the treaty formally brought peace to Europe, it also left many **issues dangerously unresolved**.

PRUSSIA EMERGES

Prussia's annexing of Silesia saw it emerge as a significant figure on the European stage, leading to diplomatic overtures from Britain and France.

COLONIAL CONFLICT

Alongside the war in Europe, Britain and France continued their **colonial rivalry** overseas. Britain captured Louisbourg on Cape Breton Island in Canada from the French in 1745, only to lose Madras in India to France the next year, although the British Royal Navy won a **number of notable victories**. The **Treaty of Aix-la-Chapelle** returned both gains to their original owners, but the conflict remained intense.

The War of the Austrian Succession ended in 1748 without proper resolution (see BEFORE). Tensions over colonial possessions continued between Britain and France, while Austria plotted to regain the province of Silesia, which Frederick II of Prussia (see right) had seized in 1740.

A state of uneasy peace lasted until 1756, when Frederick signed a treaty with Britain to protect Hanover, in northwestern Germany. This powerful new alliance gave Maria Theresa of Austria an excuse for a "diplomatic revolution," when she allied with her former enemy, France, and strengthened ties with Empress Elizabeth of Russia, to safeguard against a British and Prussian alliance. In a preemptive strike, Frederick II marched 70,000 of his troops into Saxony, which was sandwiched between Prussia and Austria. Fighting broke out almost immediately.

Far-flung hostilities

This new conflict soon spread beyond Europe, as Austria and Prussia's allies, France and Britain, had already been battling in the Americas and East Asia. Fighting between the colonial rivals had erupted the previous year, over control of the Ohio River Valley.

In India, war broke out in 1756, when an ally of the French, the Nawab of Bengal, captured the British trading base at Calcutta, and held 145 prisoners overnight in a small cell in Fort William: subsequent British exaggeration of the numbers held, the number of deaths, and the size of the cell turned the incident known as "the Black Hole of Calcutta" into an imperial myth.

A turning point

In Europe, Frederick had failed to achieve a decisive victory in Saxony, and found himself surrounded by hostile nations. But in June 1757 the statesman William Pitt the Elder took charge of the British war effort. Frederick won a great victory at Rossbach, in Saxony, over the French, another over the Austrians in Silesia in December, and defeated the

The **First Global Conflict**

For seven years, the major nations of Europe waged war not just on the European continent itself, but also, for Britain and France, in their colonial possessions overseas in the Americas and Asia. The Seven Years War was the first approximation to a world war, and gave birth to a new, truly global empire.

KING OF PRUSSIA (1712–86)

FREDERICK II

Frederick II, king of Prussia from 1740, is perhaps the archetypal 18th-century enlightened despot (see p.271). He believed in absolute power, but generally used it for the good of his subjects, establishing religious toleration, abolishing torture as an instrument of state power, and freeing the slaves on his own estates. An able and cultured man—he corresponded with the French philosopher Voltaire, and wrote music for the flute, which he played well—he was also a ruthless figure on the European stage and a brilliant military commander, raising Prussia to the first rank of European powers.

> "In the end God will have pity on us and **crush this monster**."

AUSTRIAN EMPRESS MARIA THERESA, SPEAKING OF FREDERICK II, 1757

Russians at Zorndorf, Prussia, in August 1758. In India, British general Robert Clive (see pp.352–53) defeated the Nawab of Bengal at Plassey in June 1757, while the British navy routed the French off the Indian coast in 1758–59.

The turning point of the war came in 1759, the British "year of victories." The first years of the war in America had seen French success, but James Wolfe turned the tide for the British, by capturing Louisbourg in 1758, and then by defeating general Montcalm in Quebec, the capital of French North America, in 1759. In Europe, an Anglo-German army defeated the French in Hanover, while the French navy was crushed off the coast of Brittany.

The seizure of French Montreal in 1760, and Pondicherry, in India, in 1761 effectively marked the end of the war, despite the entry of Spain on the French side in 1761. With the succession in 1762 of the pro-Prussian Peter III in Russia, all nations were ready for peace. The 1763 Treaty of Paris saw Britain take French North America, and all French lands east of the Mississippi, as well as parts of the Caribbean, and every French fort in India. Spain gave Florida to Britain, but received French lands west of the Mississippi in return. With the French excluded from North America and India, Britain now controlled a massive colonial and trading empire.

The Battle of Zorndorf

Frederick II of Prussia followed up his decisive defeats of the French and Austrians in 1757 with an equally impressive victory over the Russians at Zorndorf in western Poland on August 25, 1758.

The end of the war saw Britain victorious, but also vulnerable.

AMERICAN REVOLUTION
French **revenge** on Britain was swift. France helped America in its war of independence against Britain after 1777 **298–99 》**.

THE BIRTH OF THE BRITISH RAJ
The end of French power in India left Britain without a rival in its **conquest of the entire subcontinent**. By the 1830s, Britain had gained Bengal and Bihar in the east, and ruled over much of the south and center **352–53 》**.

BRITISH RULE IN INDIA

POLAND
A byproduct of the war was the **end of Poland** as an independent nation. Squashed between Prussia, Austria, and Russia, Poland was divided by the three powers after 1772. In 1795, it was absorbed piecemeal by Russia, Prussia, and Austria, and did not reappear until 1918.

« BEFORE

In the 18th century, settlers in Britain's American colonies became increasingly intolerant of European rule and paying taxes from which they did not benefit.

COST OF WAR
Britain was ceded French territory in North America during the Anglo-French wars (1754–63) but the cost was high, and the British felt the colonials had failed to pay their share.

PROTEST
Until the 18th century, British **North America was subject to English law**. Settlers thought the new laws passed after 1763 to raise money

BOSTON TEA PARTY

for the British extremely irksome. The Stamp Act, a direct tax on paper, caused riots. In 1773 a group of Bostonians disguised as American Indians threw a cargo of highly taxed EIC tea into Boston Harbor. The American slogan was **"no taxation without representation."**

INTOLERABLE ACTS
The British response to this episode was rapid. In 1774, laws were passed in reprisal that the Americans dubbed "Intolerable Acts." Intended to restore order, instead they **united the colonies in further protest**. Fiery leaders began to emerge—they cried out that the actions of the British government were illegal and stirred the colonists to take further action.

The war between the North American colonies and Britain in 1775 was the predictable climax of years of bitter quarrels between the two sides (see BEFORE).

The first shots were fired in a minor skirmish. On April 19, 1775, General Thomas Gage, commander of the British forces in North America, dispatched troops to seize an arms cache in Concord, a town just outside Boston. In Lexington, Kentucky, the British encountered a small force of American militia (armed civilians). It is unclear which side fired the first shot, but later it was referred to as "the shot heard around the world." When the British made it back to Boston, they were besieged by militias, and had to wait there for reinforcements. With

On June 15, 1775, George Washington became commander of the new Continental army. He immediately began turning the militias into a more professional fighting force. Washington failed in his attempt to invade Canada in 1775. His men also suffered a major blow in the summer of 1776 when the British captured New York. However, news of the revolts had spread, and the colonists' cause was rapidly gaining momentum.

Independence
The American colonists made their decisive break with Britain on July 4, 1776, when their leaders agreed to the Declaration of Independence. The declaration stated that "life, liberty and the pursuit of happiness" were the

The Articles of Confederation
Adopted by Congress—the formal assembly of government representatives—in 1777, this was the first governing document, or constitution, of the United States, and was ratified by all thirteen states in 1781.

American Declaration of Independence

Until the end of the 18th century, Europe and its colonies were dominated by monarchies. The American Declaration of Independence undermined the old order and proclaimed a new republic in which people would be free to govern themselves.

their arrival on May 26, Gage decided to capture hill positions that overlooked Boston. The resulting Battle of Bunker Hill in June 1775 was a disaster. Although they captured the hill positions, half the British troops were wounded or killed, and they failed to break the American siege of Boston.

"unalienable rights of all men," and when a government tried to destroy these rights, it was "the Right of the People to alter or abolish it, and to institute new government." The signing of the Declaration of Independence was a momentous event, and made a peaceful settlement with the British much less likely. It was largely the work of Thomas Jefferson (see left).

Washington had won important battles in what is now New Jersey—in Trenton on December 26, 1776 and Princeton on January 3, 1777—which reinforced his reputation. On March 2, 1776, with a force of over 17,000 men and a buildup of artillery stocks, the Americans began bombarding the blockaded British troops in Boston. They were forced to depart for Halifax, Nova Scotia. Although the British went on to capture New York, an American victory at nearby Saratoga in October 1777 stirred French interest in an alliance with the colonies. On February 6, 1778 France and America signed treaties of alliance. It was a major turning point—the Americans were no longer fighting alone.

All hope of a British victory ended on October 19, 1781. Lord Cornwallis was forced to surrender at Yorktown, Virginia, after an 18-day siege.

AMERICAN PRESIDENT (1743–1826)

THOMAS JEFFERSON

Thomas Jefferson was the third president of the United States. An intellectually outstanding figure of the period, Jefferson was chosen as the principal drafter of the Declaration of Independence at the age of 33. He served as governor of Virginia during the American Revolution and afterward became the first US secretary of state.

Jefferson's vision of the newly created US—as a loose union of self-governing states with central government having limited powers—gave birth to the Democratic Republican Party. Jefferson founded the University of Virginia and died on the 50th anniversary of the Declaration of Independence.

Declaration of Independence
This painting by John Trumbull depicts the committee of five who drafted the Declaration of Independence, presenting it to the Continental Congress on July 4, 1776.

"Oh, God! It's all over."
PRIME MINISTER LORD NORTH, ON HEARING OF THE SURRENDER OF THE BRITISH TROOPS TO THE AMERICANS, 1781

The British prime minister at the time, Lord North, broke down and sobbed when he heard the news.

Birth of a nation

After the British withdrew, Loyalists were allowed to remain, but about 2 percent opted to emigrate to Canada and the Caribbean.

The British government gave the Americans their independence in return for a trade agreement that would benefit both sides. The Treaty of Paris, signed in 1783, gave the Americans a western border on the Mississippi, and control of the Old North West—an area extending from the Ohio and Mississippi rivers to the Great Lakes.

Conflicts over the issue of slavery threatened to divide the nation, but the new republic had great political hopes, which they set out in the 1781 Articles of Confederation, and later the Constitution of June 21, 1788. George Washington was elected as the first president in 1789, giving the federal

Stars and Stripes
Dating from about 1830, this hand-sewn flag has 13 stars and 13 stripes, to commemorate the 13 original colonies that rebelled against the British.

(central) government exclusive power in the conduct of diplomacy, commerce, and war. Congress was to consist of two chambers, the Senate and the House of Representatives. In addition, a Supreme Court was set up to interpret laws and safeguard the Constitution, which stated that all men were born equal, and had an equal voice in government.

French territories were incorporated into the United States, but the growing north–south divide eventually led to civil war.

FURTHER EXPANSION
The **new nation quickly expanded** to the south and west. Ohio became a state in 1803, Indiana in 1816, Illinois in 1818, and Alabama in 1819. In 1803 President Jefferson purchased the Louisiana territory from France **310 ››**.

WAR OF 1812
Fought under the motto **"free trade and sailor's rights,"** the War of 1812 against Britain was a result of British maritime policies during the Anglo-French wars when American sailors were seized and forced into the British navy. President James Madison saw the war as a way to **strengthen republicanism**, and believed it could secure possession of Canada as a bargaining chip against Great Britain. Although three attempts were made to invade Canada, all of them ended in failure. The war

was, however, the first step in establishing the US as a serious, and permanent, presence in **international politics**.

CIVIL WAR
The US was divided on **the issue of slavery**. For years, slaves were used on southern plantations, but in the north slave labor was forbidden. Eventually, seven southern states split from the Union when Abraham Lincoln **316–17 ››**

CONFEDERATE OFFICER'S CAP

was elected president and, in 1861, formed the **Confederate States of America 314–15 ››**. They were later joined by four other states. Civil war broke out, as the North tried to save the Union. The war ended in 1865 with victory for the Union, but it led to economic disruption. **Slavery was abolished,** but Abraham Lincoln was assassinated in the month the war ended.

Storming of the Bastille

In the summer of 1789 a revolution broke out in France against the despotic government of Louis XVI. Many different factors caused this revolution, but the one event that symbolized the collapse of royal power in the face of widespread popular dissent was the storming of the Bastille prison on July 14, 1789.

Built between 1370 and 1383 as part of the walled defenses of Paris, the Bastille first became a prison for high-ranking state prisoners during the early 17th century. It also served as an arsenal, storing large quantities of gunpowder and arms. In 1789 the prison was defended by 18 cannons and 12 smaller artillery pieces manned by a regular garrison of 82 *invalides*—veteran soldiers no longer fit for active service—and reinforced by 32 grenadiers from a Swiss mercenary regiment summoned to Paris by the king some days before.

On July 14, rumors spread through Paris that troops were marching on the city to crush dissent against the king. Responding to this threat, a crowd of between 600 and 1,000 strong, armed with weapons seized from the Hôtel des Invalides, a military hospital, assembled in front of the Bastille to acquire its arsenal and defend their city from attack.

At around 10:30 a.m. the first of two delegations met the governor of the Bastille, Bernard-René de Launay, asking him to distribute its weapons to the crowd. Both delegations were unsuccessful. By 1:30 p.m., the crowd had lost patience, and surged into the undefended outer courtyard. Gunfire rang out, although it is unclear which side first opened fire. At around 3 p.m., a detachment of 62 mutinous Gardes Françaises arrived at the prison armed with two cannons, which they placed in front of the gates leading to the inner courtyard. As fighting intensified, de Launay threatened to blow up the fortress; but the soldiers within the garrison surrendered, forcing him to open the gates.

At 5:30 p.m., the crowd stormed the prison. The governor was led away to the *Hôtel de Ville*, the town hall, where he was stabbed to death, along with at least two defenders. One defender and 98 attackers died in the actual fighting, with another 73 attackers wounded.

The news of the fall of the Bastille spread quickly across France, prompting uprisings in many cities. In reality, the prison was an almost empty symbol of royal tyranny—it held a mere seven prisoners—but the storming did signify that power had now passed from those who discussed political change to those who took direct action to achieve it.

First blood
One of the first victims of the storming of the Bastille was its governor, Bernard–René de Launay, shown here, surrounded by soldiers. He was seized by the mob, stabbed to death, and then decapitated. His head was stuck on a spike and paraded through the streets of Paris.

"It was the **best** of times, it was the **worst** of times."

CHARLES DICKENS, *A TALE OF TWO CITIES*, 1859

BEFORE

Revolution in France

A violent upheaval shook France at the end of the 18th century as several causes of disaffection came together at one explosive moment: national bankruptcy, the burgeoning ambitions of the bourgeoisie, the king's lack of authority, and growing social discontent caused by high taxes and rising bread prices.

In the 1780s, France faced a mounting crisis. A century of foreign wars had left the country with huge debts and threatened bankruptcy.

IMMEDIATE CAUSES

France's humiliation by England in the **Seven Years War** (1756–63) **❮❮ 296–97**, losing its North American colonies, motivated heavy French expenditure on the **American Revolution** (1775–83) **❮❮ 298–99**. Its effect was to put financial reform at the top of the political agenda. Under the *ancien régime* (pre-revolutionary "old order"), French society was divided into three estates: clergy, nobility, and commoners. Nearly 40 percent of the land was owned by the nobles and clergy who made up less than 3 percent of the population and were exempt from taxes, placing the tax burden on the bourgeoisie (middle class) and peasantry. Enlightenment ideas **❮❮ 270–71** against tyranny led the growing professional classes to demand a greater role in the running of the country. Bad

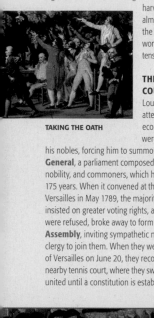
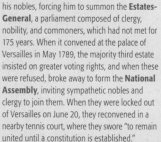

harvests (1788–89) almost doubled the price of bread, worsening social tensions.

THE TENNIS COURT OATH
Louis XVI's attempts at economic reform

TAKING THE OATH

were blocked by his nobles, forcing him to summon the **Estates-General**, a parliament composed of clergy, nobility, and commoners, which had not met for 175 years. When it convened at the palace of Versailles in May 1789, the majority third estate insisted on greater voting rights, and when these were refused, broke away to form the **National Assembly**, inviting sympathetic nobles and clergy to join them. When they were locked out of Versailles on June 20, they reconvened in a nearby tennis court, where they swore "to remain united until a constitution is established."

The formation of the National Assembly on June 17, 1789 (see BEFORE) was the first step toward revolutionary change. Louis XVI's dismissal of Jacques Necker, the popular finance minister, on July 11, along with the concentration of troops outside Paris, provoked agitation in Paris for arms amid rumors of a royal clampdown. Several days of rioting ended with the July 14 capture of the Bastille prison (see pp.300–01), symbolizing an important blow against the oppressive forces of the *ancien régime*, while placing Paris and mob violence at the center of events.

The revolt spread to the countryside, where wild rumors resulted in the "Great Fear," in which peasants attacked their landlords, burning their châteaux. On August 4, National Assembly deputies voted to abolish feudal privileges (see pp.190–91), sweeping away an entire system of property ownership in one stroke. On October 5, Parisian women, frustrated by bread shortages and the king's indecision, marched to Versailles to force his move to Paris, where he could be more closely monitored.

Between 1789–91, the National Assembly passed a series of reforms that further undermined the *ancien régime*. These included publishing the "Declaration of the Rights of Man,"

reforming the army, dividing France into 83 *départements*, selling off the Church's land, and forcing the clergy to take a civic oath to the state. This last measure split the Church, alienating the conservative peasantry and sowing the seeds of future counterrevolution.

A new constitution showed the National Assembly's distrust of the masses by dividing the population into active (higher-income voting) and passive (non-voting) citizens.

This period also saw the growth of political clubs—such as the Cordeliers and Jacobins—that tried to exert pressure on the Assembly. The Jacobins were the first real political "party," with clubs dotted throughout France.

In June 1791, the king attempted to flee abroad, but was captured at Varennes, east of Paris, by a postmaster. This marked a key turning point, for it lost the king his people's trust.

Threatened on all sides
In April 1792, a new Assembly declared war on Austria and Prussia, hoping to distract attention from

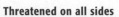

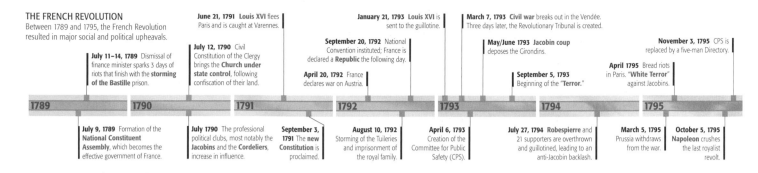

THE FRENCH REVOLUTION

Between 1789 and 1795, the French Revolution resulted in major social and political upheavals.

June 21, 1791 Louis XVI flees Paris and is caught at Varennes.

January 21, 1793 Louis XVI is sent to the guillotine.

March 7, 1793 Civil war breaks out in the Vendée. Three days later, the Revolutionary Tribunal is created.

July 11–14, 1789 Dismissal of finance minister sparks 3 days of riots that finish with the **storming of the Bastille** prison.

July 12, 1790 Civil Constitution of the Clergy brings the **Church under state control**, following confiscation of their land.

September 20, 1792 National Convention instituted; France is declared a **Republic** the following day.

May/June 1793 Jacobin coup deposes the Girondins.

November 3, 1795 CPS is replaced by a five-man Directory.

April 20, 1792 France declares war on Austria.

September 5, 1793 Beginning of the "**Terror**."

April 1795 Bread riots in Paris. "**White Terror**" against Jacobins.

1789	1790	1791	1792	1793	1794	1795

July 9, 1789 Formation of the **National Constituent Assembly**, which becomes the effective government of France.

July 1790 The professional political clubs, most notably the **Jacobins** and the **Cordeliers**, increase in influence.

September 3, 1791 The **new Constitution** is proclaimed.

August 10, 1792 Storming of the Tuileries and imprisonment of the royal family.

April 6, 1793 Creation of the Committee for Public Safety (CPS).

July 27, 1794 Robespierre and 21 supporters are overthrown and guillotined, leading to an anti-Jacobin backlash.

March 5, 1795 Prussia withdraws from the war.

October 5, 1795 Napoleon crushes the last royalist revolt.

domestic problems. While saluting the revolution with one hand, the king plotted with the other, hoping that French defeat would restore his fortunes.

A series of military defeats brought panic to Paris. A Prussian manifesto that threatened the French people if any harm came to Louis inflamed the Parisian radicals, who stormed the Tuileries on August 20, deposing the king. At the same time, a revolutionary Commune took control of the city and encouraged the massacre of 1,200 "counter-revolutionary" prisoners, provoking international horror. A third, more radical Assembly (the Convention) was elected and a crucial victory at the battle of Valmy on September 20 helped to restore national confidence.

"The Incorruptible"
Maximilien Robespierre, a radical politician, was the effective leader of France during the Reign of Terror.

The next day, the Convention declared France a Republic. In January 1793, the king was found guilty of "the crime of being a king" and guillotined, sending shockwaves through Europe.

Foreign invasion once more threatened the nation, and France became more militarized. It relied on conscription and revolutionary zeal for its citizen armies, fighting a series of revolutionary wars that were bankrolled by loot from newly "liberated" countries. At the same time, a major counterrevolution, provoked by mass conscription, broke out in Brittany and the Vendée (western France). Atrocities became commonplace on both sides.

Execution of Marie Antoinette
When Queen Marie Antoinette was guillotined on October 16, 1793, few mourned. Deeply unpopular, she was found guilty of treason by the Revolutionary Tribunal.

IDEA
HUMAN RIGHTS

The French Revolution's most lasting legacy was its *Declaration of the Rights of Man and Citizen*, published on August 26, 1789. Inspired by the political writings of John Locke and Jean-Jacques Rousseau, this bold document stated that all "men are born and remain free and with equal rights," and that the duty of government was to preserve these "natural and inviolate rights… liberty, property, security and resistance to oppression" through a constitution, rooted in the rule of law. Although originally neglecting women's rights, its universal appeal made it the basis for the constitutions of many countries as well as the UN's *Universal Declaration of Human Rights*, published in 1948.

LA DÉCLARATION

> "**Virtue** without which **terror is deadly**; **terror** without which **virtue is impotent**."

MAXIMILIEN ROBESPIERRE, FEBRUARY 5, 1794

Faced with mounting military and economic problems, the government founded the Revolutionary Tribunal, to provide instant justice, and the Committee for Public Safety (CPS), to centralize power. Meanwhile, increasing conflict within the Convention culminated with the expulsion of a faction known as the Girondins on June 2, and the rise to power of the Jacobins.

The Jacobins and the "Terror"
Under Robespierre's leadership, the Jacobins aimed to create a new "Republic of Virtue." "Citizen" became the common form of address, a new revolutionary calendar was introduced, towns were renamed, and the education system reformed.

On September 5, 1793, "terror" was made "the order of the day" and "war" declared on those suspected of counter-revolutionary sympathies, creating an oppressive climate of informers and instant justice. In 10 months, 20,000 "enemies of the revolution" were executed across France. A decisive military victory over Austria in June 1794 eased the pressure, but there was no letup in the daily flow of victims to the guillotine. Robespierre and his supporters were finally toppled by fearful fellow deputies, and this was followed by an anti-Jacobin backlash (the "White Terror") and a return to more moderate policies. In 1795, the CPS was replaced by a five-man Directory. Royalist–radical tensions pulled France in both directions and two elections were annulled. In 1799, a coup d'état installed Napoleon Bonaparte (see pp.304–05) as leader—five years later, he became emperor of France.

AFTER

The success of the French Revolution, and its spirit of "liberty, equality, fraternity," helped to inspire wars of independence far beyond Europe.

IMPACT OVERSEAS
In 1791, **Toussaint l'Ouverture** led a successful **slave revolt** in the French colony of Saint-Domingue (Haiti). From 1808, **revolutionary nationalism** inspired the wars of independence against Spain in Latin America **318–19 »**.

LEGACY IN FRANCE
While the revolution failed in some ways, the legacy of popular insurrection established a radical tradition in Paris that continues today. **Charles X**'s attempts to return to the past provoked one revolt in 1830, while his successor Louis-Phillipe's misjudgment of the mood for reform in 1848 provoked another **330 »**, which spread across Europe. In 1871, there was a short-lived and bloody **Paris Commune** based on the one from 1792. In 1968, Paris students almost toppled de Gaulle's government. Today, the French still protest to show their discontent.

PARIS RIOTS 1968

A REVOLUTIONARY TEMPLATE
Vladimir Lenin **377 »** studied the French Revolution as a **model for change**. During the **Russian Revolution 376–77 »**, he adopted the need for revolutionary terror along with a citizens' army to defend against invasion and civil war. **Rebuilding society from scratch** found echoes in the Chinese Cultural Revolution **424–25 »** and in Cambodia's attempt to relocate the towns to the countryside (1975–79).

EMPEROR OF FRANCE Born 1769 Died 1821

Napoleon Bonaparte

"**Death is nothing**, but to live defeated and inglorious is to die daily." NAPOLEON BONAPARTE

The future French emperor Napoleon Bonaparte was born Napoleone Buonaparte, a member of a poor Corsican noble family of Italian origin. A wild island of bandits and vendettas, Corsica became a part of France in 1768, the year before Napoleon's birth. When he was nine years old Napoleon learned French at school so he could attend the military school at Brienne-le-Château in France, but he always spoke with a strong Italian accent. His family was poor enough to have his school fees paid by the state.

That he was an able man was evident at an early stage and, after graduating in 1784, he went on to complete a two-year course at the Royal Military School in Paris in 12 months, proving

notably strong in math, geography, and science. He was commissioned as a sublieutenant of artillery at the age of just 16.

Revolutionary opportunities

On the death of his father in 1785, Napoleon was elected as head of his family, despite not being the eldest son. Corsica remained the focus of his life for some years, to the neglect of his army career. It was only after his family left the island in 1793 because of their pro-French views that Napoleon shifted his ambitions to France. A superb opportunist, he seized the chances for rapid advancement opened up by the French Revolution (see pp.302–03). Appointed a brigadier-general by the Jacobins, a prominent political club of

Portrait of Napoleon
Napoleon carefully controlled his public image, employing only the finest portrait artists of the day to present his desired view of himself to the people. This picture of Napoleon was painted c. 1807 by Hippolyte (Paul) Delaroche.

Peacemaker
On September 30, 1800, Napoleon signed the Treaty of Mortefontaine, ending a smoldering naval conflict between France and the US, brought about by US reaction to the French Revolution.

Carve up
Drawn in 1805, this caricature by the cartoonist James Gillray demonstrates the greed of great powers. The British prime minister, William Pitt the younger (1759–1806), and Napoleon are carving up the world—the Frenchman seizing a slice of Europe while Britain takes most of the rest.

NAPOLEONIC CODE

The Civil Code, drawn up on Napoleon's orders between 1800 and 1804, is often regarded as his most enduring legacy. His personal influence upon the code favored patriarchal authority and "family values." At Napoleon's insistence, the code states: "The wife owes obedience to her husband." Men under 25 could not marry without their parents' consent. Although divorce was permitted, it was difficult to obtain. Napoleon's code broadly upheld the rights and freedom of conscience established by the French Revolution.

COPY OF NAPOLEONIC CODE

Imperial insignia
In his imperial crest, Napoleon alludes to Emperor Charlemagne, his 9th-century predecessor (ivory hand of justice) and the Roman Empire (eagle).

Retreat from Moscow
As the French withdrew from Russia in 1812, Marshall Ney (center) inspired the rearguard of the Grande Armée to resist the Russian cossacks.

"Bonaparte's whole life, civil, political and military, was a fraud."

DUKE OF WELLINGTON, 1835

the Revolution, at the age of 24, he survived their fall and relaunched his career by providing artillery to defend their successors, the Directorate, against an uprising in October 1795 (see right). France fought all the major European powers, either individually or in coalitions, between 1793 and 1815 (see pp.306–07). Once Napoleon was made head of the Army of Italy in March 1796, there was no looking back. Reviving a moribund force, he had a spectacular series of victories, including defeat of the Papal army, that made him a French hero.

Supreme power
Napoleon was not content with being recognized as a superb general. Only supreme political power could satisfy the scope of his grandiose ambition to create an empire. Brought in as the military muscle to back a political conspiracy against the Directorate in 1799, he effortlessly shifted into the leading role in government as First Consul, and from there to absolute imperial power in 1804. Napoleon was a hard-working, intelligent head of government who supervised the creation of a new legal, administrative, and educational system in France. He was, however, also a man inspired by a sense of destiny, who believed in his

carefully nurtured public image as savior of France and successor to the Holy Roman Empire of Charlemagne (see pp.188–91).

Military genius
Napoleon genuinely desired peace—on his own terms—but spent almost the entirety of his years in power at war. He demonstrated his military genius time and again, maneuvering large-scale armies quickly to engage the enemy in decisive battle with maximum application of force. It was a style of warfare that often required his men to sustain heavy casualties in the pursuit of victory. Nevertheless, he was popular with the soldiers and

his presence on the battlefield always heartened them. He knew how to use titles and decorations—including the *Légion d'honneur*, which he instituted—to reward and inspire effort.

Downfall
Napoleon's character undoubtedly had defects. He was often dishonest, lying in battlefield dispatches to aggrandize his own role. By the time he invaded Russia in 1812, his grasp of the realities of power had begun to waver. Overreaching was always likely to be his downfall. He was finally defeated at Waterloo in 1815 and imprisoned on St. Helena, an island in the Atlantic. To the last, he devoted himself to the service of his self-image, writing his memoirs in captivity. He left a legend, but not the imperial dynasty that he had hoped to found.

Deathbed scene
Horace Vernet depicted the dead Napoleon crowned with laurel leaves, as a Roman emperor would have been, and with Christ-like features. Napoleon's admirers believed he was poisoned by the British, but he probably died of stomach cancer.

- **August 15, 1769** Born in Ajaccio, Corsica.
- **1779–84** Attends military school.
- **September 1785** Commissioned as a sublieutenant in the artillery after a year at the Royal Military School in Paris.
- **1791–93** Elected a lieutenant-colonel in the Corsican National guard.
- **June 1793** Flees from Corsica with his family.
- **August 10, 1794** Briefly arrested because of his links with the Jacobins, a radical political group.
- **October 5, 1795** Suppresses an attempted royalist coup in Paris. The Directorate gives him command of the Army of the Interior.
- **March 9, 1796** Marries Josephine de Beauharnais.
- **March 1796–April 1797** As commander of the Army of Italy, claims a series of victories over Austria, and Piedmont in Italy.
- **May 1798–August 1799** Leads Army of the Orient to invade Egypt and Palestine.
- **November 9, 1799** Back in France, he takes part in a coup that establishes a new government, the Consulate; the following month he becomes its leader (First Consul).
- **June 14, 1800** Defeats the Austrians at Marengo in Italy.
- **December 24, 1800** Survives an assassination attempt by royalists.
- **August 2, 1802** Declared Consul for life.
- **December 2, 1804** Crowns himself Emperor of France in Notre Dame Cathedral, Paris.
- **December 2, 1805** Defeats the Austrian and Russian armies at Austerlitz.

FRENCH CURRENCY BEARING NAPOLEON'S IMAGE

- **October 14, 1806** Defeats Prussia at the twin battles of Jena and Auerstadt.
- **July 15, 1809** Marriage to Josephine annulled; marries the Austrian Archduchess Marie Louise in March the following year.
- **March 20, 1811** His son is born, styled by Napoleon as the King of Rome.
- **June 1812** Invades Russia, but retreats in October.
- **October 16–19, 1813** Defeated at Leipzig by the forces of Prussia, Sweden, and Austria.
- **April 6, 1814** Abdicates after Paris is occupied by the Allies (Prussia, Russia, and Austria); he is exiled to the Mediterranean island of Elba.
- **March 20, 1815** Escapes from Elba and enters Paris.
- **June 18, 1815** Defeated at Waterloo in Belgium by the British and Prussian armies.
- **July 15, 1815** Surrenders to the British.
- **May 5, 1821** Dies a prisoner on the island of St. Helena.

« BEFORE

In 1792 France was declared a Republic **<< 302–03**. The change in government occurred during a series of wars in Europe and beyond.

REVOLUTIONARY WARS

The French Revolutionary Wars (1792–1802) were initially fought to protect French borders from other European powers.

NAPOLEON'S SABER

However, they brought in their wake **a citizen's army** inspired by revolutionary principles, an aggressive foreign policy, and a war economy dependent on forced enlistment, conquest, and loot, all of which facilitated Napoleon Bonaparte's rise to power **<< 304–05**.

RISE OF NAPOLEON

Having been tainted by association with the Jacobins after Robespierre's fall, Napoleon redeemed himself in October 1795 by crushing the last popular revolt in Paris, and then by conducting a **brilliant military campaign** in Italy—he was welcomed as a hero on his return to Paris in 1797. Following a highly popular but less successful campaign into Egypt, he returned to Paris in 1799 to seize power through a **military coup**.

Once in power, Napoleon behaved like an enlightened despot (see pp.270–71). He banned democracy, and set up a network of police spies responsible for censorship and for arresting his political opponents.

Following an assassination attempt in 1800, Napoleon was able to harness widespread support for his own dynastic ambitions, to fend off any attempt to restore the Bourbons—the royal family that had ruled France between 1589 and 1792—and to establish himself as the French leader. In 1804 Napoleon crowned himself "first Emperor of the French," in a ceremony overseen by the Pope, thereby sanctifying his position.

The building of an empire

Between 1805 and 1815, Napoleon's armies took on seven different coalition armies made up of various European powers. He won his most notable victories in 1805 at Austerlitz in the modern Czech Republic against the Austrians and Russians; in 1806 at Jena in Germany against the Prussians; and in 1807 at Friedland against the Russians, in their own country, forcing them to sue for peace. In 1812, at the height of his power, France's rule comprised 130 administrative regions.

Napoleon's ambitions outside Europe were more low-key. In 1803, he abandoned France's claims to the Americas by selling Louisiana to the US for $15 million (see pp.310–11). In the French West Indies, sugar plantations were disrupted by slave revolts and foreign invasion, although Saint-Domingue (now Haiti) was the only one to gain its independence in 1804.

Napoleon's empire grew in two stages: 1800–07 and 1807–12. During the first stage, he incorporated the Low Countries (the Netherlands and Belgium), northern Italy (Piedmont), and western Germany under his rule, emulating Charlemagne's achievements of 1,000 years earlier (see pp.188–89). In 1806, the Confederation of the Rhine unified the small German states, such as Bavaria and Saxony, into kingdoms allied to France. French legislation, such as the Napoleonic Code, took root in this "Inner Empire."

After 1807, his conquests included southern Italy, Spain, northern Germany, Illyria (the southern Balkans), and the Duchy of Warsaw (Poland). Charles Talleyrand, Napoleon's scheming foreign advisor, warned against extra expansion during this period, and these regions often

The Battle of Trafalgar
On October 21, 1805, the English Admiral Horatio Nelson sank 22 French and Spanish ships in the pivotal sea battle of the Napoleonic wars, sealing Britain's naval supremacy for the next 100 years.

The Napoleonic Wars

Between 1805 and 1815, Napoleon's armies conquered most of western Europe in a series of notable victories, creating an empire with 44 million French subjects. However, his plans to invade England were thwarted by naval defeat at Trafalgar, and his obsession with conquest led to a disastrous campaign in Russia. Napoleon was finally brought down at Waterloo in 1815.

rejected France's influence. Napoleon, however, was obsessed with restoring the Roman Empire by mastering Italy and conquering Britain. However, his dynastic aspirations reflected an increasingly dictatorial character prone to errors of judgment, such as overthrowing the Bourbon dynasty in Spain and replacing it with his own dynastic successor, his brother Joseph, thus provoking the Peninsular War—a long and disastrous campaign that raged between 1808 and 1813 and became known as "the Spanish ulcer."

Defeat and downfall

The destruction of two French fleets by English admiral Horatio Nelson at Aboukir Bay, Egypt, in 1798, and Trafalgar off the coast of Spain in 1805 scuppered Napoleon's plans for invading Britain. However, he insisted on

Napoleonic Empire
In 1812, at the height of France's conquests, more than 44 million subjects lived within the empire, some ruled directly from Paris, some by proxy rulers.

KEY

▪ French territory ruled directly from Paris
▪ Dependent state

0 — 500 km
0 — 500 miles

crippling England economically, by maintaining a maritime blockade, and it was this that eventually led to his downfall. It caused unnecessary wars against Portugal (1808–13) and Russia (1812), creating two simultaneous fronts and provoking his most disastrous defeats. These were epitomized by the humiliating retreat from Moscow in 1812, when he lost more than half a million men.

These campaigns left him vulnerable to a legacy of European resentments and military exhaustion following his defeat at Leipzig in 1813. He was finally defeated at Waterloo in 1815, by Prussia, and the Duke of Wellington's Allied army of British, Dutch, Belgians, and Germans.

IDEA
MASS CONSCRIPTION

Between 1792 and 1815, mass conscription supplied the 4 million men who fought in Napoleon's campaigns, including his first major success in Italy against the Austrians (1796–97, pictured below). In 1805 and 1812 he raised two vast armies, known as "*grandes armées*," from across his empire to fight in his Austrian and Russian campaigns. The first had 200,000 men and the second more than 600,000. Napoleon owed much of his success to these armies. It is estimated that around a million soldiers died in creating Napoleon's empire.

"History is a set of lies…
people have agreed upon."

NAPOLEON, FROM HIS MEMOIRS, 1823

AFTER ≫

Following Napoleon's resignation in 1814, Europe's rulers met at the Congress of Vienna to carve out a new balance of power.

POST-NAPOLEONIC EUROPE
Most of the hereditary monarchies overthrown by Napoleon were restored, allowing 30 more years of reactionary rule. Indeed, both Napoleon's son and nephew (right) went on to rule France.

NAPOLEON III

REPUBLICAN MOVEMENTS
Nationalist republican movements were quick to break out—first in Serbia, Greece, and Belgium; then, in 1848, in a wave of urban revolts that ultimately lead to Italian (1861) and German (1871) unification **330–33 ≫**. Napoleon's fall also paved the way for Britain to become the world's leading imperial power.

NAPOLEON'S DREAM
The **unification of Europe**, started by his legacy of a new legal code and metric system of weights and measures, was realized in 1957 in the shape of the EEC (now the EU) **452–53 ≫**.

POLITICIAN AND ABOLITIONIST Born 1759 Died 1833

William Wilberforce

"**We are all guilty**… in this **wretched** business."

WILLIAM WILBERFORCE, SPEECH TO THE HOUSE OF COMMONS, 1789

The third of four children born into a well-to-do Yorkshire family, Wilberforce grew up in an age when the institution of slavery was considered socially acceptable. He attended Hull Grammar School, in northern England, and from 1768 was brought up by an uncle who introduced him to Methodism, an offshoot of the Church of England. In 1776 he entered St. John's College, Cambridge. Before graduating he decided on a career in politics and fell in with William Pitt the Younger, later British prime minister. Wilberforce returned to Hull in the fall of 1779, running as an independent candidate, and won the parliamentary seat at a personal cost of over £8,000 ($34,000).

An evangelical parliamentarian

Between 1784–85, Wilberforce began a period of intense religious reflection. He consulted John Newton, rector of St. Mary Woolnoth, London, a former sailor who became an antislavery campaigner thanks to his early experiences as a slave ship master. Wilberforce became a fervent supporter of evangelical Christianity, joining the "Clapham Saints" under John Venn. In the spring of 1786 he returned to the House of Commons (the elected house of the British Parliament) committed to God, and eager to target immorality and vice. In 1787 he moved to Bath, in western England, where his interest first arose in championing the cause of black African slaves, but, contrary to popular accounts, he was not a founder member of the London Committee for the Abolition of the Slave Trade, and he attended no meetings until June 1791. In 1787 he declined the committee's request to represent the cause in Parliament, and only later agreed to the job "if no one else could be found."

He once made a pithy observation that "the first years that I was in Parliament I did nothing to any good purpose;

Member of Parliament

William Wilberforce portrayed at a time when he was regularly suffering defeats in the House of Commons at the hands of the powerful lobby of West Indies plantation owners.

St. John's College, Cambridge

The Second Court of St. John's College, Cambridge, where Wilberforce enrolled as an undergraduate in 1776. Here William Pitt the Younger (1759–1806), who himself later became British prime minister, inspired Wilberforce to enter politics.

my own distinction was my darling object." It was not unknown for him to be on his feet for up to three hours, making speeches to Parliament, for which he was dubbed the "nightingale of the Commons." His ideal of Christian charity did not always extend to his rivals, and he snubbed the real workhorse of the abolition movement, Thomas Clarkson, almost until the end of his life.

Spurning advice

In the spring of 1791, ignoring prudent advice, Wilberforce urged the parliament to completely abolish the slave trade; the confrontation immediately failed. Undeterred, he took a prominent abolitionist role in the Commons debate of April 1792 when he made his famous "Africa! Africa!" speech. This also suffered defeat. Wilberforce doggedly pursued the dream of a total abolition bill each year from 1795–1799, but it was regularly thrown out by the powerful West Indies lobby, representing those with financial interests in the region.

Pitt's government fell early in 1801, replaced by that of Henry Addington. By January 1802, however, Wilberforce had become seriously disillusioned,

House of Commons
William Pitt the Younger, the British prime minister, addressing the House of Commons in 1793, about a year after the failure of a pivotal antislavery debate.

Abolition
This engraving, by the British artist Joseph Collyer, shows the figure of Britannia examining the bill abolishing the British slave trade, on March 23, 1807.

> "Africa! Africa! Your **sufferings** have... arrested my heart."
>
> WILBERFORCE, HOUSE OF COMMONS, 1792

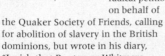

Symbol of suffering
A sculpture of a kneeling and chained enslaved African man, whose image was identified with the antislavery movement.

writing to Addington that he proposed to give up as the "active and chief agent in terminating the trade." Pitt was returned to power in 1804 and Wilberforce's biographers claim that the "abolition business" had again become his chief care, yet he only attended three meetings of the Abolition Society that year, and a further three in 1805.

William Pitt died prematurely in 1806. A Whig government under Addington was returned, and in 1807 the antislavery trade bill was trundled out again. Wilberforce spoke only briefly, late in the debate. Lord Howick, a leading advocate of abolition, delivered the main motion, dispensing with rhetorical flourishes and presenting hard economic facts. The House of Lords was won over and passed the Trade Abolition Bill on March 23, 1807.

At this time, he consistently denied interest in abolition. When debate was launched in earnest in 1823, he became a virtual bystander in the House of Commons and also in the recently formed Anti-Slavery Society. He was persuaded to table a radical petition on behalf of the Quaker Society of Friends, calling for abolition of slavery in the British dominions, but wrote in his diary, "I wish that Buxton or Whitmore should take chief management of the slave's concerns and let me give occasional assistance as my indifferent health and infirmities will allow."

In July 1828 he wrote scathingly to the new emancipation champion, Fowell Buxton, about the Duke of Wellington's pro-slavery position, yet he still took no more active involvement other than the symbolic chairing of an Anti-Slavery Society meeting in 1830. He passed away on July 29, 1833, without witnessing the final enactment of the emancipation bill on August 20, which was prompted less by the work of any individual than by a major slave uprising in Jamaica at the close of 1831.

Withdrawing from public life

Wilberforce increasingly claimed bouts of malaise that prevented him from attending debates that he guessed were likely to prove unpopular. Rhetoric also worked against him. On July 29, 1811 he wrote to a friend complaining of adverse press treatment, claiming, "I am often left out and more frequently dismissed with a much shorter account of what I have said...". He began to question if he should resign his seat in Parliament, and on September 8, 1812 declared his intention to step down. A month later he took on the seat of Bramber in Sussex.

ABOLITIONIST (1745–97)

OLAUDAH EQUIANO

Born in what is now Nigeria, Equiano wrote an influential autobiography, which was published in 1789 and detailed his life as a slave. Captured in West Africa at age 11, he was shipped to Barbados, and then to Virginia, where a Royal Navy officer bought him, taught him to read and write, and named him Gustavus Vassa after the Swedish king. Sold again, he was taken to Montserrat, in the Caribbean, where he bought his freedom. He moved to London in 1786 and became involved with the abolition movement. He married an English woman in 1792, but died five years later.

TIMELINE

- **August 24, 1759** Born in Hull, the third of the four children of Robert and Elizabeth Wilberforce.
- **1776** Enters St. John's College, Cambridge, with two scholarships, after attending St. Paul's School in London.
- **September 1779** Runs for and wins the parliamentary seat of Hull at a personal cost of over £8,000 ($34,000).
- **1784–85** Begins a period of intense religious reflection, consulting John Newton, antislavery campaigner. He joins the "Clapham Saints" and becomes a fervent evangelical Christian.
- **May 22, 1787** The London Committee for the Abolition of the Slave Trade is founded by Thomas Clarkson and others.
- **October 30, 1787** Wilberforce makes his first contact with the London Committee.
- **1788** Awarded Master of Arts Degree.
- **February 11, 1788** Gains William Pitt's support for the unpopular move to place responsibility for examining the slave trade and abolition with the Privy Council.
- **May 12, 1789** Makes his first major speech in the House of Commons.
- **April 19, 1791** Opts for confrontation and brings a full abolition motion before the House of Commons against advice. The motion is defeated by a large majority.
- **June 7, 1791** First attends a meeting of the London Committee.
- **April 2, 1792** Robustly denies interest in slave emancipation. Full anti-slave-trade debate in parliament overwhelmingly defeated.
- **May 30, 1797** Marries Barbara Ann Spooner, a landowner's daughter, after a two-week courtship.
- **1802** Organizes Society for the Suppression of Vice.
- **March 23, 1807** Bill against the slave trade carries in the House of Lords after a successful motion, presented by Lord Howick and Sir Samuel Romilly.
- **1812** Wilberforce resigns from his Hull seat. He represents Bramber, in Sussex, until retirement.
- **March 18, 1823** Presents radical petition in the Commons on behalf of the dissident Society of Friends for abolition in all British Dominions.
- **June 11, 1823** Wilberforce gives his last speech in the House of Commons.
- **1825** Retires from Parliament.
- **1830** Makes his last public appearance, chairing a meeting of the Anti-Slavery Society.
- **July 29, 1833** William Wilberforce dies in London.
- **August 3, 1833** State funeral held for Wilberforce in Westminster Abbey.

JOHN NEWTON

« BEFORE

During the 18th and early 19th centuries, Britain, Spain, France, and Russia all laid claim to parts of North America, often without consideration for the American Indian nations who already lived there.

REVOLUTION

In 1783, under the **Treaty of Paris**, 13 North American colonies under British rule gained independence **« 228–29** and formed the United States of America.

ESTABLISHING BOUNDARIES

With the Treaty of Paris, the northern border with British Canada through the Great Lakes was agreed. In 1783 **Britain returned Florida to Spain**, which also controlled the Louisiana Territory. Spain ceded the Louisiana Territory back to France in 1800.

TREATY OF PARIS

NEW STATES

The **1787 Northwest Ordinance** allowed the formation of up to five new states to the northwest of the US on land ceded by various states to the US government. This increased the conflict between settlers and natives. In 1795, 12 American Indian nations were persuaded to sign the **Treaty of Greenville,** giving land to the United States. They were then moved to vacant land in the west.

Ceremonial skull
This buffalo skull was painted by the Blackfoot nation for their ceremonial Sun Dance. The rights of such American Indian nations were usually swept aside by settlers and the US government.

Pioneer spirit
Settlers, such as this family, traveled west across the Great Plains, often in large convoys for safety. The wagons carried all their worldly goods, plus tools for farming and building.

From its beginnings, squashed between the Atlantic Ocean in the east and the Appalachian Mountains in the west, the United States quickly expanded westward to the Mississippi River and beyond. The land between the Appalachians and the Mississippi was ceded by the British at independence. Expansion across the Mississippi began after the Louisiana Purchase in 1803, whereby the French sold the entire Louisiana Territory (see BEFORE) to the US. In May 1804, US president Jefferson sent Meriwether Lewis, his secretary, and William Clark to explore this practically unknown area. The pair set off from St. Louis and sailed up the Missouri River.

DECISIVE MOMENT

FIRST TRANSCONTINENTAL RAILROAD

On May 10, 1869 at Promontory Point, Utah, a grand ceremony marked the opening of the first railroad to cross America. The 1,086 miles (1,738 km) of eastern Union Pacific track and the 690 miles (1,100 km) of the western Central Pacific track were linked. Leland Stanford, president of the Central Pacific Railroad, swung a silver hammer at a golden spike—a bolt made of gold—to symbolically join the tracks. Envoys from the Union Pacific Railroad also took a turn at hammering it home. The US now had its first transcontinental railroad.

Expanding the Frontier

The independent United States of America that emerged in 1783 was, in reality, the United East Coast. The land to its west appeared to be limitless. In the century that followed independence, the frontier was pushed west across the continent until American dominion stretched from ocean to ocean.

With the help of Shoshone guides, they crossed over the Rocky Mountains, and in December 1805 they reached the Pacific coast. The route was hard, but they met friendly Indians and returned with details of the new frontier.

Division of the land

An agreement with Britain in 1818 straightened out the northern border with Canada along the 49th parallel line of latitude. Another agreement in 1842 confirmed the northeast border in Maine. To the south, Florida was acquired from Spain between 1813 and 1819. This led to conflict with the Seminole nation. To deal with hostilities, the government passed the Indian Removal Act in 1830, giving the US president power to move tribes west across the Mississippi to the "Indian Territory" (now Oklahoma). The Cherokees were the first to arrive, having been displaced by the discovery of gold in their home in Georgia. In 1838, the "Trail of Tears" involved the enforced removal of about 17,000 Cherokees; 4,000 died, often from disease contracted in transportation camps.

Californian gold rush
The discovery of gold in the Lower Sacramento Valley in December 1848 lured prospectors west to California. They arrived by land and sea to seek their fortune, often carrying few possessions apart from a tin bowl to pan for gold.

American immigrants
From 1892 to 1954, 12 million people passed through the main immigration center of Ellis Island, New York. Like these children, all were given a health check before being allowed to enter.

The United States continued to expand into the 20th century. There were many opportunities to purchase or otherwise take control of land beyond its shores.

FIRST CATCHES
Alaska was bought from Russia in 1867 and **Hawaii, Midway Island, and Wake Island** were annexed in 1898.

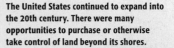

FARTHER AFIELD
A war with Spain, precipitated, among other disagreements, by the **sinking of the battleship USS Maine** off the coast of

BATTLESHIP MAINE

Cuba in 1898, brought **Puerto Rico, Guam,** and the **Philippines** under American control. The following year, the US acquired **Samoa** as a naval base and refueling station for ships trading with Asia. In 1917, the **Virgin Islands** were purchased from Denmark to protect Caribbean sea routes.

RELINQUISHING CONTROL
The US has given up some of its empire. The **Philippines gained independence in 1946,** while three former Japanese island groups in the western Pacific held since 1945 became independent in 1994–96. The **Panama Canal Zone,** American since 1903, was returned to Panama in 1999.

45 The number of states in the Union in 1900

" It is our **manifest destiny to overspread the continent** allotted by Providence for the free development of our yearly multiplying millions. "

JOHN L. O'SULLIVAN, NEW YORK *MORNING NEWS*, DECEMBER 27, 1845

In 1846, Oregon Country was split with the British, again along the 49th parallel, providing a Pacific frontier.

Further expansion came quickly. In 1836, Texas had become independent from Mexico. Its annexation by the US in 1845 led to war with Mexico, bringing California, Nevada, Utah, Arizona, and New Mexico into the nation in 1848. The Gadsden Purchase from Mexico in 1853 provided the land for the South Pacific Railroad to California and so confirmed the southern border. With the purchase of Alaska from Russia in 1867, the US completed its continental growth.

Land of opportunity
As politics and war settled the frontiers, countless intrepid migrants settled the land. Families traveled west from the Mississippi along designated trails.

The numbers were impressive. Three years after the opening of the Oregon Trail through the Rockies in 1841, 5,000 settlers a year were making the challenging journey.

Through the 1862 Homestead Act, the government offered farmers ownership of 160 acres of public land after they had farmed it for five years. Nebraska had been described by an army expedition in 1820, as "wholly unfit for farming," yet 72,000 people flocked there in four years to build houses of earth, and live off the soil. Land was not the only draw; the discovery of gold in California in 1848

Alaskan check
In 1867, the year before this check was issued, the US negotiated the purchase of Alaska with the Russian imperial government.

attracted 80,000 prospectors within a year. Others went west to start up new businesses or seek adventure.

The completion of a transcontinental railroad in 1869 (see left), and three more by 1883, further opened up the west. The railroads brought new settlers west and also helped farmers already there, as cattle and grain could be transported easily to cities back in the east.

The massacre of the Sioux ghost dancers at Wounded Knee on December 29, 1890 ended the wars with the American Indians. America had overcome the obstacles to its occupation of the continent.

311

5 KWAKIUTL TRANSFORMATION
MASK

8 INUIT FINGER MASK

6 DAKOTA
WAR
CLUB

7 THOMPSON NATION
WAR CLUB

9 PAIUTE CRADLEBOARD

1 HAIDA TOTEM POLE
OR GRAVE POST

3 ARAPAHO GHOST
CLUB

2 TSIMSHIAN SOULCATCHER

4 TLINGIT FIGHTING
KNIFE

13 FOX NATION BEAR
CLAW NECKLACE

10 DELAWARE
HEALTH DOLL

11 MOHAVE WARRIOR DOLL

12 HOPI KACHINA DOLL

14 SENECA PESTLE AND
MOHAWK MORTAR

15 INUIT ULU

American Indian Cultures

From farmers on the fertile Atlantic seaboard to the dwellers of the frozen Arctic, the native American Indian tribes were as diverse as the vast continent they inhabited. This is reflected in the rich and varied artifacts that represent these cultures.

1 **Haida totem pole or grave post**, which was probably erected in the honor of a deceased chief. 2 **Tsimshian soulcatcher** carved from ivory or bone and used by a shaman (traditional healer) to capture the soul of a sick person and return it to their body. 3 **Arapaho ghost club** used in the ceremonial "Ghost Dance" performed by the plains people in the late 19th century. 4 **Tlingit fighting knife** with an iron blade and abalone-inlaid ivory handle. 5 **Kwakiutl transformation mask**, which was fixed to a dancer's head with wickerwork and animal sinews. By manipulating draw cords attached to the beak, this mask changed from a fierce eagle into a human face. 6 **Dakota war club** made from tinned iron, topped with a carved stone, and trimmed with a feather and hair. 7 **Thompson nation war club** carved from birchwood and used for hunting beavers. 8 **Inuit finger mask** worn by women at ritual ceremonies to emphasize their flowing hand movements. 9 **Paiute cradleboard**, which was used to carry a baby; the

hoop was made from hide and slipped over the mother's head. 10 **Delaware doll** carved from wood; this female effigy was a spirit guardian of health. In the fall, the Delaware people honored her with a feast and offerings. 11 **Mohave warrior doll** sold by Mohave people as a souvenir at train stations in the 19th century. 12 **Hopi** *kachina* **doll** used to teach children about *kachina* (spirit beings). 13 **Fox nation bear claw necklace**, which was probably the property of a chief or renowned warrior. Three beads separate each claw; the collar is made from otter skin. 14 **Seneca pestle and Mohawk mortar** used by Iroquois woman to pound corn kernels into meal. 15 **Inuit ulu (knife)** with an ivory handle and steel blade; it was used by Inuit women to skin and butcher seals. 16 **Pomo shell currency**, which was taken south by traders and used as money by many of the California Indians. 17 **Malecite canoe** made from white cedar, covered with bark of white birch, and waterproofed with resin from the black spruce.

16 POMO SHELL CURRENCY

17 MALECITE CANOE

BEFORE

The Civil War was the result of years of conflict between the north and south.

NEW MEMBERS OF THE UNION
In the years following independence **‹‹ 298–99**, more territories joined the original 13 colonies of the United States (known as the Union).

SLAVERY
The Constitutional Convention of 1787 allowed **individual states to permit slavery**; northern states abolished it, while southern states kept it.

THE NORTH–SOUTH DIVIDE
The issue of slavery itself revolved around **state versus federal** rights, and whether a slave was a person's property, the right to which was guaranteed by the US Constitution. Admitting new free states (a state where slavery was outlawed) to the Union would be problematic, as it would upset the balance between slave and free states and possibly provoke a **federal move to abolish slavery**.

THE MISSOURI COMPROMISE
This 1820 amendment to the Missouri statehood bill balanced admission of slave and free states, but in 1857 the Supreme Court ruled it unconstitutional, in favor of slave-owning states. With increasing numbers of free territories wishing to gain Union status, and an armed raid in 1859 by antislavery militant John Brown to free slaves at Harpers Ferry, Virginia, the **southern states began to feel threatened**.

JOHN BROWN

> "The war is over—the **rebels** are our countrymen again."
> ULYSSES S. GRANT, 1865

The American Civil War

In 1861 the United States split apart over the issue of slavery. It fought a lengthy, bloody civil war that lasted until 1865. Thousands were killed, and while the issue that caused the war was resolved, its divisive legacy lasted for years.

The catalyst for war was the election in November 1860 of the first Republican Party president, Abraham Lincoln (see pp.314–15), against a divided Democrat opposition. Lincoln opposed slavery in territories wishing to achieve Union membership, and won the votes of every free state (see BEFORE) but one. The southern states voted for a pro-slavery Democrat, John Breckenridge. The impact of the result was immediate.

On December 20, 1860, South Carolina voted to leave the Union. By June 1861, 10 more states had joined these rebels, known as the Confederacy, but not every slave state joined: Kentucky remained neutral, while Delaware, Maryland, and Missouri were loyal to the Union. Virginia joined the Confederacy, causing West Virginia to separate and become a Union state.

The first shots were fired by Confederate cannons on April 12, 1861; their target was the Union-held Fort Sumter in Charleston Harbor, South Carolina. Three days later, Lincoln issued a call for loyal state governors to send 75,000 militia troops to protect Washington, DC. The war had begun.

A country divided

The two sides were not well matched; the Union had the larger population (22 million compared to 9 million in the South, of whom 3.5 million were slaves it would not arm) and greater resources. The Confederacy, however, had the better generals. Its simple strategy was to defend itself from attack and win recognition as an independent state. The Union government had no option but to attack the Confederacy by blockading its coastline and seizing its capital of Richmond, Virginia.

Both sides required troops and issued regular calls for volunteers. When numbers were insufficient, conscription was introduced, by the Confederacy in 1862, and the Union the next year. By the war's end, 50 percent of the eligible population in the Union had been mobilized, as were 75 percent of the Confederacy. Both armies were mainly white; Congress initially would not allow free African-Americans or escaped slaves—totaling about 500,000—to join the Union army, but changed the law after emancipation (the freedom of the slaves) in 1863. Almost 200,000 joined up, although they were paid less than white troops and could not become officers. In the Union, many women joined the Sanitary Commission, which ran kitchens and hospitals, and raised funds.

AMERICAN GENERAL (1822–85)

ULYSSES S. GRANT

Ulysses S. Grant trained at West Point military academy but failed to make a success of army life, and then saw his Missouri farm fail during the 1857 depression. His military training won him the rank of colonel when war broke out, and early successes and aggressive tactics—notably at Shiloh in 1862—earned him promotion. In March 1864 Grant was appointed by Lincoln as overall commander of the Union troops. In July 1866 he took control of the US army, until becoming Republican president in 1869. His tenure was marred by scandal, but he held office until 1877.

Battle of Gettysburg
Total casualties for both sides at Gettysburg are estimated to have exceeded 46,000, with the dead left on the battlefield. This was the first conflict to be extensively documented by war photographers.

Standard issue
Both armies used versions of this .58-caliber rifle-musket. In the north it was known as the Springfield, after the Massachusetts armory in which it was made.

Victories and defeats
Superior Confederate leadership led to early success, notably with Stonewall Jackson's victory at Bull Run, Virginia in July 1861, reprised in August 1862, when Union forces failed to push the Confederates away from Washington. The turning point was Confederate general Robert E. Lee's attempt to invade the Union, and his defeat at Gettysburg, Pennsylvania in a three-day battle in July 1863.

In the west, Union general Ulysses S. Grant (see left) held Shiloh, Tennessee in April 1862, and then took Vicksburg on the Mississippi in July 1863, cutting Arkansas, Louisiana, and Texas off from the rest of the Confederacy. In the fall of 1864, Union general William Sherman began to advance through Georgia to the sea, before moving north through the Carolinas. In Virginia, Grant's victories against Lee reduced the Confederate army to barely 60,000 troops. The fall of the Confederate capital on April 3, 1865 led to Lee's surrender to Grant at Appomattox Court House on April 9. The Union had won.

The reckoning
This was the first modern technological war. Railroads transported men and supplies to the front, messages were telegraphed, iron-clad warships fought for the first time, and photographers and journalists brought the war to people every day via newspapers. The human toll was immense: 360,000 Union dead and 275,000 wounded, 258,000 Confederate dead and 100,000 wounded. Economically, the south was ruined.

The main outcome of the war was emancipation. Lincoln had initially fought to preserve the Union, not free the slaves, but abolitionists in the north, and the effect of escaped slaves fighting in the Union army, changed his mind. On January 1, 1863 Lincoln's Emancipation Proclamation had freed the slaves in the Confederacy, though he did not have the constitutional authority to abolish slavery, nor the power in the south to do so. Lincoln himself did not live to see the effects of this action: he was shot at a theater in Washington on April 14, 1865, and died the next day.

84th Regiment
This flag belonged to the 84th Regiment, United States Colored Troops, and is inscribed with some of the battles in which they participated, alongside a larger force of Union army volunteers.

Confederate flag, Snodgrass Hill
The 2nd Battalion Hilliard's Alabama Legion attacked Snodgrass Hill during the Battle of Chickamauga, Georgia, September 1863. Their flag was pierced 83 times by Union troops.

Although the end of the war led to the reunification of the country, it took years for the new laws to be accepted.

EMANCIPATION
The Emancipation Proclamation of 1863 became the 13th amendment to the Constitution in 1865. The 14th amendment, passed in 1868, gave the **former slaves US citizenship** (American Indians had to wait until 1924), and the 15th amendment of 1870 guaranteed their **right to vote**. In many cases, however, these were paper rights, as racial discrimination lasted for the next century.

EMANCIPATION PROCLAMATION

RECONSTRUCTION
After the war, the south was occupied by federal troops. From 1866–77 Congress attempted **"Reconstruction" in the South**. Former Confederate officials were prohibited from holding public office, veterans were required to pledge allegiance to the Union, and newly freed slaves ran in state elections. Confederate states were readmitted to the Union only after they had accepted the 14th amendment. However, the founding of the white supremacist Ku Klux Klan in Tennessee in 1865 showed the reluctance of some Southerners to accept emancipation.

84TH REG'T
U.S. Colored Infantry
Port Hudson La July 1863
Pleasant Hill La April 1864
Mansura La May 1864
Bayou De Glaise La May 1864
White Ranche Texas May 1865

16TH PRESIDENT OF THE UNITED STATES Born 1809 Died 1865

Abraham Lincoln

"Government **of the people, by the people, for the people,** shall not perish from the Earth." ABRAHAM LINCOLN, GETTYSBURG ADDRESS, NOVEMBER 19, 1863

A braham Lincoln grew up in Kentucky, in what was then America's wild western frontier. His father, Thomas Lincoln, was a farmer and carpenter who set his son to hard manual labor from an early age. Abraham disliked his father and his limited world of subsistence farming. He became a lifelong believer in technological progress and financial economy as escape routes from the backwardness into which he had been born.

Lincoln had little schooling, but was encouraged in self-education by his stepmother Sarah. Eloquent and ambitious, by the time he was 30 he was a lawyer and, as a member of the liberal progressive Whig Party, held a seat in the Illinois House of Representatives. In higher social circles his backwoods manners were seen as rough and gauche, yet he was successful enough to persuade a plantation-owner's daughter, Mary Todd,

Wartime president
This photo-portrait of Lincoln was taken by Alexander Gardner in November 1863. It shows the president's stubborn resolve, but also reveals the sadness and strain that afflicted him as a wartime leader.

On the campaign trail
In 1858, Lincoln's public debates during the Illinois contest for the Senate attracted nationwide attention. Lincoln was at this time clean-shaven, adopting a beard in 1860 to improve his electoral chances.

CAMPAIGN BUTTON, 1864

A united front
In the presidential election of 1864, Lincoln ran with Democrat Andrew Johnson as his vice-presidential running mate. With war-weariness widespread, Lincoln's reelection was far from a foregone conclusion.

to marry him in 1842. Mary actively promoted her husband's political career, but was violently jealous and given to bouts of wild extravagance. As a couple, they did not find happiness; the death of two sons in childhood preyed on Mary's mind, while Lincoln himself was prone to fits of depression.

Elected to the US Congress in 1846, Lincoln's first foray into Washington, D.C., was not a success, so he returned to Illinois to dedicate himself to the law and making money. It was the eruption of the slavery issue through the Kansas–Nebraska Act of 1854 that propelled him back into politics. Lincoln participated in the formation of the Republican Party to resist the spread of slavery in the expanding United States. His attitude to slavery had been formed as a child, since his family attended antislavery Baptist churches. But it was above all his personal experience of self-advancement that determined his views. Lincoln felt that his rise from humble origins showed that any free

Man of letters
Lincoln wrote this letter to his Secretary of War, Simon Cameron, in May 1861, recommending that his friend, Alexander Sympson, be given a contract to supply the army with horses. In other letters, Lincoln constantly urged his generals to prosecute the war with greater energy and resolution.

A Presidential visit
Lincoln visits the Union army camp at Antietam in October 1862. He is flanked by intelligence chief Allan Pinkerton (left) and General John A. McClernand, one of the Union army's many lamentably unsuccessful military commanders.

> "Let us strive on to finish the work we are in; to **bind up the nation's wounds.**" ABRAHAM LINCOLN, INAUGURAL ADDRESS, MARCH 4, 1865

man could make something of himself. Slavery denied an individual the chance of self-betterment.

The reluctant abolitionist
Although he denounced slavery as morally wrong, Lincoln did not adopt an abolitionist stance, accepting that slavery would persist in the southern states. Even so, his antislavery position during public debates with Illinois Democrat Stephen A. Douglas in 1858 made him a figure of hate for Southerners. His statement that the United States government "could not endure permanently half-slave and half-free" was seen as an invitation to civil war.

As an inelegant, awkward westerner with limited political experience, Lincoln was not the obvious choice for Republican presidential candidate in 1860, but he slipped through as a compromise between conflicting factions. With the Democrats divided, he won the presidency with less than 40 percent of the popular vote. Diehard Southerners had made it clear his election would provoke secession (withdrawal) from the Union. So bitter was the atmosphere that Lincoln had to sneak into Washington in disguise to take up his office because of the threat of assassination.

Lincoln at first fatally underestimated the strength of secessionist sentiment and the force that would be required to overcome it. However, with the outbreak of civil war in 1861 between the northern states (the Union) and southern states (the Confederacy), Lincoln showed an unflinching will for victory. His position as president was precarious. He was despised by the political elite, opposed by factions on both wings of his own party, and threatened by discontented generals. He had to maneuver and compromise to maintain the support for the war. Yet with almost no

military experience, he showed a better grasp of the principles of warfare than most of his generals. It was not until 1864 that he found in Ulysses S. Grant a commander-in-chief whose implacable will matched his own.

Lincoln's legacy
Even in the thick of the war, Lincoln found a chance to advance the material progress in which he so firmly believed. He oversaw the creation of a National Bank, laid the foundations for the building of the Pacific Railroad, and prepared the way for the carving up of the prairies into small farms with the Homestead Act. On slavery, it was only after his reelection in 1864 that he was able to press for a constitutional amendment to abolish the practice and to advocate full citizenship and voting rights for black Americans.

Lincoln's unequaled rhetoric, both in his Gettysburg Address of 1863 and his second inaugural speech of 1865, gave the war a dignity it would otherwise have lacked. His assassination by fanatic John Wilkes Booth at the moment of victory for the Union army was a national tragedy.

THE GUN THAT SHOT LINCOLN

Assassination at Ford's Theatre
Watching the play *Our American Cousin*, alongside his wife Mary, Lincoln was shot in the head by John Wilkes Booth. He was carried to a boarding house opposite the theater, where he died early the following morning.

MARY LINCOLN

Mexican revolutionaries
A Mexican rebel group, *c.* 1911, shoots from a boulder overlooking a desert valley filled with factories. Thousands of laborers and landless peasants fought to reclaim lost lands.

« **BEFORE**

When the Spanish and Portuguese arrived, native Latin American cultures were to be subdued under colonial rule for 300 years.

CONQUISTADORS

The Spanish *conquistadors* (conquerors), bold and brutal adventurers, established **Spain's claim to the New World**. In 1513, Vasco Núñez de Balboa was the first European to see the Pacific. Eight years later, Hernán Cortés's Spanish expedition **conquered the Aztec Empire** of Moctezuma II in Mexico, and in 1532 the Spanish brought down the **Inca Kingdom** of Peru « 230–31. Mexico and Peru had rich silver and gold mines, and Mexico City became the capital of New Spain.

MOCTEZUMA HEADDRESS

SPANISH AND PORTUGUESE SETTLEMENT

In the 16th century, Spanish colonists advanced north into what is now Florida and California, and south to today's Venezuela and Argentina. In the 18th century, **precious metals** and stones were discovered, and coffee cultivation began in Brazil. The Portuguese **explored Amazonia**, and formalized their claim to it in 1750.

Latin America Liberated

The people of Latin America span the entire continent of South America, Central America, Mexico, and the islands of the Caribbean. They share a history of conquest and colonization by the Spaniards and Portuguese, a struggle for liberty, and centuries of political instability.

W hen Napoleon turned on his Spanish allies in 1808 during the Peninsular War (see pp.304–07), events took a disastrous turn for Spain. With the Spanish king and his son Ferdinand taken hostage by Napoleon, leaders jostled for power across Spanish America and juntas filled the void. Not many lasted long, but by 1810, progress toward independence was underway.

The independence movements in South America rose from opposite ends of the continent. From the south came José de San Martín. In 1817, San Martín, a former Spanish military officer, directed 5,000 troops across the Andes from Argentina and struck at a point in Chile where loyalist forces had not been expecting an invasion. San Martín then freed the Spanish stronghold of Peru.

From the north came Simón Bolívar (see RIGHT). Bolívar's forces invaded Venezuela in 1813, waging a ferocious campaign, but the rebels achieved only short-lived victories. In 1817 a larger and revitalized movement for independence emerged, and won the struggle in the north. Bolívar was named president of Gran Colombia in 1819, a union of Venezuela, Colombia, Panama, and Ecuador. The tide had

turned in favor of independence, and by 1821 further military campaigns had liberated New Granada and Venezuela. In the central Andes, the southern and northern armies attacked in a pincer movement to crush the remaining loyalist strength, and in 1824 Peru gained its independence.

In Mexico, a unique movement emerged in 1810, led by a radical priest, Miguel Hidalgo y Costilla.

Battle of Maipú
José de San Martín led his rebel troops over the heights of the Andes to fight Spanish royalists. The Battle of Maipú, in 1818, gained Chile liberty from Spanish domination. The Spanish army was so demoralized—2,000 died and 3,000 were captured—that San Martin was also able to liberate Peru.

Revolutionary poster
Urging peasants to unite under the name of Zapata, the commander of the Liberation Army of the South, this poster says, "The land should belong to those who work it." Large landed estates were forcing peasants from the land.

Plundered resources
Coffee was a nonnative crop introduced by the Europeans. Before 1800 it was mainly produced by slaves on plantations controlled by colonists.

Hidalgo appealed to the indigenous Mexicans to eject from the village of Dolores the wealthy classes of Spanish descent. This became known as the *Grito de Dolores* ("Cry of Dolores"). Hidalgo's untrained army grew to number 80,000 as it conquered towns and larger cities, and threatened Mexico City itself. After a dramatic defeat, Hidalgo was captured in 1811 and executed. But by then Mexican independence was on its way to being realized, and was achieved in 1822.

Brazilian independence

In Brazil, the discovery of a conspiracy against Portuguese rule in 1789–98 showed that some groups there had already been contemplating the idea of independence in the late 18th century. The reliance of the Brazilian upper classes on African slavery, (see pp.280–81) however, favored their continued ties to Portugal. The key step in the relatively bloodless end of colonial rule was the flight of the Portuguese court from Lisbon to Rio de Janeiro in 1808, to escape Napoleon's invading troops. After 13 years, King John returned to Portugal, leaving his son Pedro as regent. Dom Pedro I proclaimed Brazil independent in 1822, with himself as emperor. In 1831, however, he abdicated, leaving his five-year-old son, Dom Pedro II, as regent, until 1840, when he was made emperor. He reigned until 1889, when he was deposed, and a republic was proclaimed.

Building new nations

The former Spanish America split into more than a dozen separate countries. Adapting models from northern Europe and the US, republics were set up across the region. The earliest were in Venezuela, Chile, and New Granada in 1811–12. Factional fighting caused the first constitutional governments to fail, however, and the unrest led to more centralized regimes by the mid-19th century. Governments changed rapidly in most regions, and the use of force became common. Military men, "caudillos," rose to positions of dominance and consolidated their power through strategic alliances.

In many countries, difficult financial circumstances contributed to political instability. But by the 1860s and 1870s, manufacturers from England, the US, and other nations were welcomed, and there was a surge in demand for sugar, coffee, wheat, and beef. Traditional exports such as silver recovered, and exceeded previous production levels.

When domestic funding was scarce, European investment helped to provide money for improved infrastructure. Foreign firms, from countries such as

> **JUNTA** A Spanish word for a governing group, often used to refer to military officers who seize power and establish an authoritarian government.

Britain, constructed railways, streetcar systems, and electricity networks. Latin America underwent a thorough integration into the world economy. While urban populations flourished, however, rural life remained poor.

The Mexican Revolution

In 1876 General Porfirio Díaz forcibly seized power in Mexico and set up a dictatorship. He opened up the country to foreign investment and allowed the owners of foreign estates to take more of the Indian peasants' lands. Resentment of these policies exploded in the revolution of 1910. Díaz was overthrown in 1911, but fighting broke out between rival factions. Díaz's successor, Francisco Madero, failed to carry out promised agrarian reforms and was overthrown in 1913. President Álvaro Obregón (1920–24) finally implemented them and fighting ceased.

SOUTH AMERICAN REVOLUTIONARY LEADER (1783–1830)

SIMON BOLIVAR

Simón Bolívar was a South American patriot, and hero of the struggle for independence from Spain. Born an aristocrat, Bolívar began his revolutionary career in Venezuela in 1813, after visits to Europe and the US, where he had absorbed anticolonial ideas. He was called "El Libertador" ("The Liberator"). Bolívar spent his remaining years unsuccessfully trying to forge a union of the newly independent states.

" … **experience** comes from bad judgment."
SIMON BOLIVAR, ATTRIBUTED

AFTER

After centuries of colonial rule, industrialization and democracy came to Latin America only slowly.

NEW CONSTITUTION FOR MEXICO
In 1917, President Venustiano Carranza began to create the **modern Mexican state** with **land reforms** and more limits on the Church's power.

CARRANZA

NEW INDUSTRY
Shortages of goods caused by the two World Wars were an **incentive to industrialization**. The Great Depression of the 1930s **384–85 »**, however, hit Latin America hard. Heavy industry was not established until the 1950s. Brazil, Mexico, and Argentina became Latin America's leading producers of iron, steel, and machinery.

THE DAWN OF MASS POLITICS
Latin America has often been politically unstable. Many countries have swung between **extremes of left and right**, but most countries are now democracies **422–23, 438–39 »**.

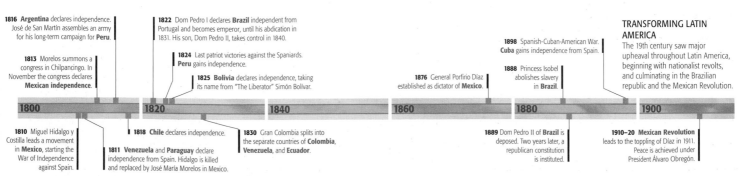

1816 Argentina declares independence. José de San Martín assembles an army for his long-term campaign for **Peru**.

1813 Morelos summons a congress in Chilpancingo. In November the congress declares **Mexican independence**.

1822 Dom Pedro I declares **Brazil** independent from Portugal and becomes emperor, until his abdication in 1831. His son, Dom Pedro II, takes control in 1840.

1824 Last patriot victories against the Spaniards. **Peru** gains independence.

1825 **Bolivia** declares independence, taking its name from "The Liberator" Simón Bolívar.

1898 Spanish-Cuban-American War. **Cuba** gains independence from Spain.

1888 Princess Isobel abolishes slavery in **Brazil**.

1876 General Porfirio Díaz established as dictator of **Mexico**.

1810 Miguel Hidalgo y Costilla leads a movement in **Mexico**, starting the War of Independence against Spain.

1818 Chile declares independence.

1811 Venezuela and Paraguay declare independence from Spain. Hidalgo is killed and replaced by José María Morelos in Mexico.

1830 Gran Colombia splits into the separate countries of **Colombia**, **Venezuela**, and **Ecuador**.

1889 Dom Pedro II of **Brazil** is deposed. Two years later, a republican constitution is instituted.

1910–20 Mexican Revolution leads to the toppling of Díaz in 1911. Peace is achieved under President Álvaro Obregón.

1800   1820   1840   1860   1880   1900

TRANSFORMING LATIN AMERICA
The 19th century saw major upheaval throughout Latin America, beginning with nationalist revolts, and culminating in the Brazilian republic and the Mexican Revolution.

« BEFORE

A great age of world exploration began in the 1400s, and lasted for over 400 years.

EARLY MAPPING
At the beginning of the 15th century, European sailors used maps based on the writings of ancient Greek geographer **Ptolemy**, showing Europe, the Mediterranean, and western Asia. The voyages of explorers such as **Christopher Columbus « 228–29** and **Ferdinand Magellan « 224–25** were instrumental in helping cartographers more accurately map the globe. However, European knowledge of the Southern Hemisphere was still sketchy. A Dutch

1486 ENGRAVING OF PTOLEMY MAP

map from the late 1500s shows an area labeled **Terra Australis Nondum Cognita** ("not yet known southern land"): it was thought Earth's land was equal in size north and south of the equator.

BRITISH EXPLORER (1728–79)
CAPTAIN JAMES COOK
One of five children, James Cook was born in Yorkshire, northern England, the son of a farm-hand. Apprenticed into the Merchant Navy, Cook studied astronomy and navigation and, after joining the British Royal Navy in 1755, made a name charting parts of Canada during the Seven Years War (see pp.296–97). He led three voyages to the Pacific, and was greatly respected by his crew, believing in good diet and hygiene. Despite mainly successful efforts to forge friendly relations with the Polynesians he visited, Cook was killed in Hawaii in 1779.

Completing the Map

Led by the desire to discover new land and lay claim to its riches, to open trade routes, or simply in a spirit of adventure, explorers of the 18th and 19th centuries mapped the continents of Australia, Africa, and North America, and set out to conquer the poles.

The continuing belief in the mid-18th century was that some vast southern continent must exist south of the equator to balance the Asian landmass in the north (SEE BEFORE). In 1768, Captain James Cook's reputation as a cartographer earned him the leadership of a British expedition to the Pacific. With instructions to chart coastlines and annex trading posts in the name of the British Crown, Cook's first Pacific voyage (1768–71) took him around New Zealand and along the coast of eastern Australia.

Matthew Flinders later

Cook's chronometer, K1, 1769
Invented by John Harrison, the chronometer (see p.282) allowed the measurement of longitude. Cook was one of the first to know his exact position while sailing uncharted waters.

circumnavigated Australia (1801–03), proving it was one large island. The west coast Swan River colony, founded in 1829, confirmed British claims to the whole continent, but few ventured deep into the interior until 1860, when Robert Burke and John Wills left Melbourne and headed north. By the following year they had crossed Australia.

Into Africa
Africa posed a great challenge to explorers, as there were still many blank spaces in European maps of the continent. The British, Portuguese, French, and Germans were all eager to lay claim to its lands, with various religious, commercial, political, and colonial agendas. Major exploration of Africa's interior began when a Scot, Mungo Park, traveled in the Niger Valley (1796–1805). Later in the 19th century several explorers, including Richard Burton,

Mapping continents
In 1866, Dr. David Livingstone set off on a journey to find the source of the Nile. His maps, such as the one above of central Africa, changed mapping of Africa.

John Hanning Speke, and Verney Cameron, endured great hardships to continue their explorations. The Scottish missionary David Livingstone attempted to open up trade routes favorable to Britain. He navigated lakes and rivers, including the Zambezi River and Victoria Falls, crossing Africa from east to west. Livingstone and Henry Morton Stanley (the man who was sent to find Livingstone when he went missing in 1866–71) were important in mapping this enormous continent. The last gaps in Africa's map were not filled in until the 1920s.

The Americas

The first European to make the long trek across North America

Stanley's pith helmet
Henry Morton Stanley was sent to Africa to find Livingstone. On finding him, in 1871, he doffed his hat, and uttered the now famous words, "Dr. Livingstone, I presume."

was the Scottish-Canadian explorer Alexander Mackenzie in 1793, as he searched for the Northwest Passage—a water route to the Pacific Ocean. In 1804, with settlements becoming overcrowded and people migrating west, US president Thomas Jefferson sent Meriwether Lewis and William Clark to explore Louisiana and the mountains and plains beyond it. They crossed the US from east to west by canoe, horse, and foot, reaching the Pacific Ocean in 1805.

A test of endurance

The North (Arctic) and South (Antarctic) poles were so inhospitable they offered little chance for exploitation, but there was prestige in being the first nation to conquer them. In 1893, Norwegian Fridtjof Nansen had failed to reach the North Pole. Competition to be the first to reach the pole intensified. A pair of Americans, Frederick Cook in 1908 and Robert Peary in 1909, both made claims to have reached the North Pole—claims that remain in dispute to this day.

While navigators of many nations had charted the coastline of Antarctica in the extreme south, it took an American expedition led by Lieutenant Charles

Wilkes (1840) to confirm that it was a continent. In 1911, two expeditions landed separately on the Ross Ice Shelf, about 900 miles (1,450 km) from the South Pole. Both the Norwegian Roald Amundsen and the Englishman Robert Falcon Scott sought to demonstrate their technological prowess and endurance. With husky-drawn sleds, Amundsen reached the pole on December 14, 1911. Halfway there, Scott sent his ponies back and dragged the sleds by hand. He reached the South Pole a month after Roald Amundsen, but died of starvation on the return journey.

Through such feats of human endeavor, geographers were able to draw the first accurate outline of the world. By the turn of the 20th century, all seven continents—Europe, Asia, Africa, North and South America, Australia, and Antarctica—were on the map.

> "**So we arrived**, and planted our flag at the geographical South Pole. **Thanks be to God!**"
>
> ROALD AMUNDSEN, NORWEGIAN EXPLORER, 1912

AFTER

In the 21st century, little uncharted territory remains on Earth. However, human endurance and scientific curiosity have kept polar and space exploration alive.

POLAR EXPLORATION
The **first crossing of Antarctica** was accomplished by the British **Vivian Fuchs** and the New Zealander **Edmund Hillary** in 1957–58. American **Ralph Plaisted** became the first to reach the **North Pole using surface transport** in 1968.

SPACE HIGHLIGHTS
In April 1961, the Russian cosmonaut **Yuri Gagarin** became the first person in space. In July 1969, the US made history when Apollo 11 successfully landed on the Moon **458–61 »**

1969 MOON LANDING

Polar dispute
This 1909 French cartoon depicts Peary and Cook, who both claimed to be the first to reach the North Pole. The fray that followed discredited both men

Cook in New South Wales
On August 22, 1770, Captain James Cook (center, raising hat) declared the southeastern coast of Australia British and named it New South Wales. Eighteen years later, to ease prison overcrowding, the British government sent the first fleet of around 750 convicts to settle at Sydney Cove.

« BEFORE

Since the advent of agriculture, people have lived in communities. The city has evolved as a center of commerce and power.

HERCULANEUM, ITALY

ANCIENT CITIES

Towns and cities emerged in Asia and Egypt in the 4th millennium BCE **« 44–45**. Larger towns grew into **densely populated walled cities**, with streets running at right angles to each other, to form a grid pattern. Ancient Greek **« 94–95** and Roman cities **« 110–13,** like Herculaneum, became centers of intellectual, religious, and commercial life.

THE MEDIEVAL PERIOD

After the fall of the Roman Empire **« 150–51** western European cities declined. In the medieval period towns began to expand again, often around a castle or monastery **« 188–91**.

REVIVAL OF CITY LIFE

Town planning was revived during the Renaissance **« 250–53,** and the grid pattern was popularized in 17th-century America.

The cause of the phenomenal growth of cities from the 19th century onward is fairly straightforward—the ascendancy of industry over agriculture—but the effects of this change in lifestyle were far more complex. The mechanization of agriculture (see pp.290–91) and the abolition of serfdom in Europe left an excess of labor in rural areas, and that labor force flooded into the cities when the Industrial Revolution (see pp.292–95) provided a new form of employment in the shape of factories and workshops.

Many centers of industry developed in cities that had existed for centuries. Others expanded from small villages, or developed as new cities where raw materials were available, or main roads or rail routes converged. Industrial buildings and railroad yards tended to be close to the city's center, with the

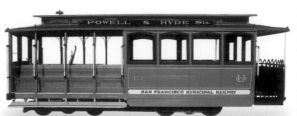

Urban transportation
The need for mass transit capable of dealing with steep hills led to the development of San Francisco's cable car system in 1873. The cable car's popularity resulted from its replacing horse-drawn transport.

workers—who had no transportation— living in cheap housing within walking distance of the factories. In many heavily industrialized cities, a "factory culture" arose, in which the populations of whole streets and even neighborhoods were connected by their employment at one particular local mill or factory.

Flocking to the cities

This urban expansion was apparent throughout the industrialized world. In 1850, London, Paris, Constantinople (now Istanbul), and St. Petersburg were the only European cities with more

City Living

Humans have lived together in cities since ancient times, but in 1800, urban areas were home to just 3 percent of the world's population. The massive explosion of urbanization that accompanied the Industrial Revolution saw that figure rise to 15 percent in the space of 100 years.

than 500,000 residents—just 50 years later, 23 European cities had passed that landmark, and nine had more than a million inhabitants: London, Paris, Berlin, Vienna, St. Petersburg, Manchester, Birmingham, Moscow, and Glasgow. However, despite this massive increase in city living, at the turn of the 20th century, the majority of people—even in industrialized nations—still lived in the country.

Squalor, space, and sanitation

For those who were forced to move to the cities, life was often squalid and miserable. In the first half of the 19th century, the influx of people to the cities outstripped the facilities available, which meant that in some poor urban areas, food supply and sanitation were so bad that the high mortality rate (both from malnutrition and from diseases caused by overcrowding, such as cholera and typhoid) kept urban growth relatively slow. Indeed, not all cities experienced continuous growth—

1.7 MILLION
The number of people living in Chicago in 1900. The population more than tripled in the 50-year period from 1850 to 1900.

some even declined. Water was polluted with human filth, the air with industrial pollution, and rats and insects quickly spread disease. Not surprisingly, the situation was worst in the world's most populous cities, such as London, Paris, Constantinople, and particularly Peking (now Beijing), which in 1800 was the only city with more than a million inhabitants.

The appalling conditions in the working-class slums close to his father's cotton mill in Manchester, in northern England, inspired German philosopher Friederich Engels to write *The Condition of the English Working Class in 1844*. It impressed the political philosopher Karl Marx (see pp.334–35), and provided valuable information for the socialist movement (see pp.336–37). It also added to the demands for improved health and sanitation in city slums. Such developments meant that urban populations began to expand naturally, rather than as a result of rural immigration, prompting the expansion that took place between 1850 and World War I.

Urban planners also came to realize that space was as important to health as sanitation. One result of this was the provision of "green lungs"—city parks

UNDERGROUND RAILROADS

In many of the world's cities, underground railroads are referred to as the "Metro," after the world's first example: the Metropolitan Railway in London (now part of the Metropolitan Line), which opened with steam traction on January 10, 1863. Putting the railroad underground by cutting or boring a tunnel was a means of providing rapid, frequent, and cheap transportation around a crowded city. Continental Europe's first underground railroad was the Tünel, opened in Istanbul in 1875, though it only covered 1,880 ft (573 m). The first subway in the US opened in Boston in 1897.

aimed at improving people's health and comfort—and another was the emergence of model towns. While industrialists are often characterized as exploiting the masses, many were philanthropists. In 1786, Scottish cotton magnate David Dale built the model town of New Lanark (see pp.336–37) for his workers, and his example was followed by several other industrialists during the 19th century, including his son-in-law, Robert Owen. In 1898,

Sir Ebenezer Howard published *Tomorrow: the Peaceful Path to Real Reform*, in which he outlined his vision of the "Garden City," an idealized town incorporating extensive green spaces. This was a great influence on 20th-century urban planning. »

Manhattan, New York
Elevated railroads, such as this one in Manhattan, photographed in 1895, allowed expanding cities to accommodate multiple modes of transportation.

WILLIAM LE BARON JENNEY

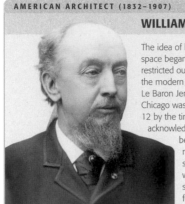

The idea of building up instead of out to maximize living space began in the medieval period, when city walls restricted outward expansion. But the man who inspired the modern skyscraper was American architect William Le Baron Jenney, whose Home Insurance Building in Chicago was 10 stories when completed in 1885 and 12 by the time it was demolished in 1931. It is generally acknowledged to be the first skyscraper, not simply because of its height but also because of its method of construction. Jenney's use of steel girders, a skeleton frame, and a "curtain wall" (hung from the frame rather than supporting the building) paved the way for modern skyscrapers.

The first such town was Letchworth, in Hertfordshire, England, in 1903. Harvey's idea was adopted by the American architect Walter Burley Griffin in his work on Canberra, the capital of Australia.

The spread of urbanization

As cities expanded, so did their infrastructures. Urban transit networks improved, with innovations such as urban trams in 1832 in New York City, underground railroads in London in 1863 (see p.323), and the elevated railroad, in 1867, again in New York City. The improvements in transport led more middle-class workers to move away from downtown areas, giving rise to the concept of suburban living and the commuter belt—residential areas on the periphery of a city. This in turn led to expansion of the suburbs, which in some cases meant cities absorbing entire towns and villages into their urban sprawl and filling the spaces that once

separated them with new housing and facilities. In some countries this resulted in legislation limiting the extent of expansion and the creation of "green belts" around cities.

City living was not simply about the buildings in which people lived and worked; it also affected their habits and ways of thinking. City-dwellers had greater anonymity than rural villagers, which gave them greater license in many aspects of their lives. This included sexual practices—infidelity and prostitution were higher in the cities—and religion: atheism was markedly higher in urban areas, which led to an increase in church-building and to the establishment of institutions like the Salvation Army, to bring people back to religion.

Leisure and pleasure

By the end of the 19th century, two new social phenomena had emerged: the leisure industry and consumerism. These arose from a combination of

"Hell is a city much like London…"

PERCY BYSSHE SHELLEY, ENGLISH POET, 1819

▽ **Glasgow, Scotland**
Glasgow's population increased twentyfold from 1780 to 1900, by which time it was known as "the Second City of the Empire." This picture, from 1860, shows the cramped conditions resulting from a population boom.

▽ **Moscow, Russia**
This wide, shop-lined street, photographed in 1890, is typical of the ambitious building program that was undertaken in Moscow in the late 19th century.

◁ **Piccadilly Circus, London**
Despite being built in the early 19th century, by the time of this photograph, taken in 1910, the roads of London's Piccadilly Circus were having to accommodate early motor cars (see pp.344–45), as well as more traditional horse and carts.

◁◁ **Manchester, England**
By the end of the 19th century, Manchester was a thriving industrial city. Market Street (shown here) is one of the city's main thoroughfares.

△ Chicago
By 1900, thanks to industry and railways, Chicago was the second-largest American city. Good transport links encouraged trade, such as markets, like this one on South Water Street.

△ Paris, France
Paris expanded rapidly from the 1840s due to the arrival of the railroads. During the 1850s, Napoleon III ordered a massive remodeling by Georges Haussmann, who replaced entire medieval districts of narrow, cramped streets with the wide boulevards, such as this one, for which the city is now famous.

World's biggest cities
These graphs show the extraordinary population growth in the world's top five cities. The list of top cities changes between 1800 and 1900 from mainly Asian cities to European and American ones.

factors: the spread of mass production, which reduced costs and thus lowered retail prices; the availability of the technology for mass entertainment such as cinema (see pp.344–45); the concentration of people in the cities to consume products and entertainment; and the fact that by 1900, for the first time, standards of living in the industrial West had risen so significantly that most people had some disposable income.

Not only were people earning more money, but the focus of their lives was undergoing a gradual shift away from the workplace—average working hours were shorter, leading to a division between work and leisure time. Rising income enabled people to decide what they did with that spare time. By the early 20th century, a wide range of diversions were available, including popular theater, music hall, motion pictures, and professional sports. Much of this entertainment directly or indirectly used the technologies whose development had led to urban growth: directly, in developments such as cinema, and indirectly in that railroads and transportation systems improved people's access to these leisure facilities.

3 PERCENT The proportion of the global population living in towns of over 200,000 people in 1800.

15 PERCENT by 1900.

30 PERCENT by 1950.

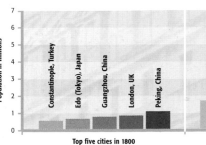

Population in millions

Top five cities in 1800: Constantinople, Turkey; Edo (Tokyo), Japan; Guangzhou, China; London, UK; Peking, China

Top five cities in 1900: Chicago, US; Berlin, Germany; Paris, France; New York, US; London, UK

Cities continue to expand, draining rural areas of their population, concentrating wealth, and creating new benefits and problems.

CONTINUED GROWTH
The number of people worldwide living in cities has **continued to rise** since the medieval period.

6.2 MILLION The average size of the world's 100 largest cities in 2000.

SLUMS AND SHANTIES
As urbanization continued to accelerate during the 20th century, the new phenomenon of the shanty town appeared on the **fringes of cities** in Africa, Asia, and South America, where there is a **wide gap between rich and poor**. Shanty towns are haphazard collections of unlicensed **makeshift houses** that are built from any available waste materials. The rural poor are drawn to shanty towns in the hopes that living **close to the city** might bring them employment, housing, health services, education, and utilities, but for the vast majority it is a false hope. Conditions are far worse than those they have left behind in the country, with hunger and poverty made worse by crime and disease. According to the United Nations, more than half the world's population now lives in cities, almost one-third of that number in slum areas or shanty towns.

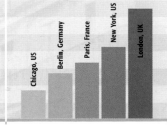
SHANTY TOWN LIFE

LIGHT POLLUTION
In urban areas, problems are caused by an **excess of artificial light**. These include adverse effects on human health and disruption of ecosystems governed by sunlight.

INNER CITY CONGESTION
During the 20th century, the problems of overcrowding in cities changed from those encountered during the 19th century. Problems of food supply and sanitation were replaced by those of **pollution and traffic congestion**, together with the perennial problem of overcrowding. Long a feature of third-world cities, bicycles are now commonly seen on the roads of developed first-world cities as people attempt to reduce pollution and find a quick route through the congestion 474–75 ».

A CITY CYCLIST

12 MPH The average speed of traffic in London in the year 1900 and in the year 2000.

BEFORE «

The theories of ancient Greece « 104–05 dominated medical thinking for 2,000 years.

GREEK MEDICAL THEORY
In ancient Greece (c. 500 BCE), it was believed that health depended on the body **maintaining a balance** of four fluids, or **"humors"**—blood, yellow bile, black bile, and phlegm. Each humor had its own characteristic qualities, combinations of hot, cold, wet, and dry. Blood, for example, was hot and wet. Disease was thought to arise when there was an imbalance of humors.

TEMPERAMENT

An **excess** of a particular humor was thought to give people their character, or **"temperament."** A sanguine temperament was believed to produce an excess of blood, which made the person cheerful, even-tempered, and optimistic, though feverish.

SKETCH FROM VESALIUS'S WORK

THE TRAVELS OF GREEK MEDICINE
These ideas spread from ancient Greece across the globe and dominated medicine for 2,000 years. They traveled across Europe during the Roman Empire, then spread to the Middle East, and to European colonies. While the core theories remained constant, doctors added to the Greek understanding of anatomy. In the 16th century, the Belgian physician **Andreas Vesalius's** groundbreaking *On the Workings of the Human Body* contained detailed anatomical sketches.

In the 18th century, doctors researching human anatomy realized that some diseases, such as cancer, produced swellings in the solid parts of the body or changes to the appearance of organs such as the lungs and liver. The idea that disease was located in the solid parts of the body, not the fluids (see BEFORE), was firmly established by Parisian research into pathology in the early 19th century. In the city's huge hospitals, doctors carefully recorded the progress of many of the diseases suffered by hundreds of patients they treated. Those who died were dissected, to discover how their illness had affected the organs in their body. Using this approach, doctors were able to monitor the progress of many diseases, and to make precise distinctions between diseases of the heart and of the lungs, for example.

During the rest of the century, doctors explored the structure of the human body in finer detail. They described the various tissues that made up the organs and, using improved microscopes, began to explore the cells that formed the tissues. While some researchers studied the minute structures of the human body, others began to research the functions of the organs. By experimenting on animals, their patients, and sometimes themselves, doctors began to understand

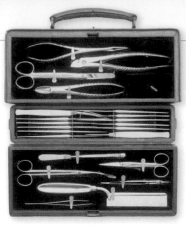

19th-century surgeon's kit
Although antisepsis is often associated with the British surgeon Joseph Lister and the use of carbolic acid, safe surgery owed much to simple ideas—like making surgical instruments from steel, and sterilizing them after every operation.

Germ Warfare

In the 19th century, a number of significant developments in medical science greatly increased doctors' knowledge of anatomy and disease. Coupled with the transformation of hospitals into specialized treatment centers came a crucial understanding of the spread of infection and how to halt it.

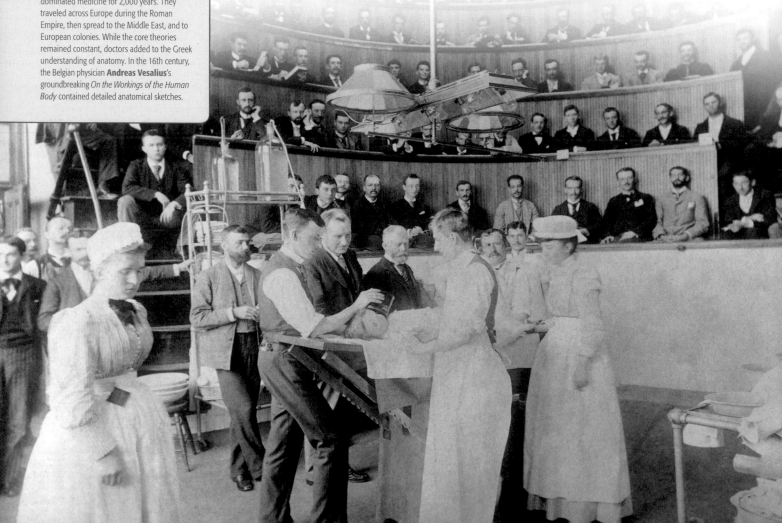

"A **hospital**... should do the **sick no harm**."

FLORENCE NIGHTINGALE, BRITISH NURSE AND PHILANTHROPIST, 1859

SCOPES AND X-RAYS

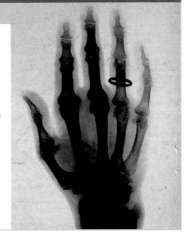

The idea that disease was located in the body's organs led to a string of inventions helping doctors to "see" inside of living patients. In 1816 René Laennec created the first crude stethoscope when he rolled up some papers into a tube, and discovered he could hear sounds made by the lungs and heart. The 19th century saw the invention of a number of "scopes" for seeing into the ear, eye, and the throat. The ability to see inside the living body became a reality in 1895 when Wilhelm Röntgen discovered that X-rays passed through flesh but not bone. X-ray images, such as this one from 1895, became an invaluable tool in helping doctors to repair damaged limbs.

the role of the liver and pancreas in the digestive system and the function of the kidneys. This in turn gave them new ways of diagnosing illnesses, such as identifying kidney disease by analyzing the chemicals found in a patient's urine.

Surgery

Once doctors began to think of disease affecting the solid organs of the body, they realized they might be able to cure patients by cutting out the diseased part. However, in the 18th century, surgical operations were used only as a last resort, because of the pain involved in cutting into the patient's body, and the high probability of wound infection.

From the beginning of the 19th century, surgery began to change with the introduction of anesthetics—the British surgeon Robert Liston's use of ether during an amputation had an impact throughout Europe. Now surgeons could work more slowly, reducing blood loss by tying up blood vessels, and carefully cutting out damaged or diseased tissue. Around the same time, they tackled the problem of wound infection: first by keeping their instruments and the wound clean, and later by using antiseptics to kill the germs that caused infection. At the end of the 19th century, modern aseptic techniques were introduced to eliminate contamination from the operating room: staff wore gowns, masks, and rubber gloves, and every instrument was sterilized. This allowed surgeons to operate safely, and to devise a range of operations to cure diseases.

Therapy

Although the practice of bloodletting—draining a patient of blood in the hope it would cure their illness—was still used in the 19th century, by 1900

doctors had abandoned most of the old "humoral" therapies (see BEFORE). However, there were still few effective remedies. Opium was used to relieve pain, but as an addictive substance it was not without risk. Doctors could treat serious injuries and broken limbs with the aid of anesthetics and improved surgical methods. Quinine (made from the bark of the cinchona tree) was used to treat malaria, and digitalis (made from foxgloves) was an effective treatment for heart conditions. In 1897, aspirin (based on a chemical found in willow bark) was launched. Salvarsan, the first synthetic drug, was introduced in 1910, and was prescribed in cases of syphilis. However, many remedies did not cure disease, but only soothed the symptoms—for example, cough syrup eased coughing, and poultices reduced

30 SECONDS was said to be all it took for the 19th-century surgeon Robert Liston to amputate a human leg—without administering an anesthetic.

swellings. Bed rest, nutritious food, and careful nursing were still the basis of medical care for most forms of illness.

Caring for the sick

Hospitals were crucial to the development of new medical ideas and practices, and in turn these medical innovations completely transformed the nature of the hospital. In the medieval period, hospitals across Europe were originally linked to monasteries and abbeys and were created to offer food and shelter—literally, hospitality (see pp.200–01).

They cared for the poor, the sick, and religious pilgrims. In the 18th century, hospitals were still charities caring for the sick and poor. In the 19th century, they became centers for treatment, open to all who could afford to pay. Operating rooms were built to allow students to view surgery, with specialized lights and equipment, and lined with glass and tiles that could be easily cleaned. Some teaching hospitals invested in new equipment, such as the first X-ray machines (see above). They also began to offer specialty treatments for complaints of the ear and eye, or conditions affecting children. As a result, hospitals treated a greater number of seriously ill patients, and the amount of staff, especially nurses, grew enormously to provide round-

Early operating theatre
This 1898 photograph of an operating room reveals that the idea of asepsis (the reduction of contamination) spread very slowly. The surgeon wears an apron, but no mask, and the room is filled with observers wearing ordinary clothes.

objective lens

stage for specimen slide

primary lens to focus light source

Microscope
From 1830, the microscope played a crucial role in understanding the structure of the body. Doctors diagnosed cancer by examining tissues under the microscope, and confirmed infection by identifying disease-causing bacteria.

In the late 19th and 20th centuries, the greatest medical developments came in the form of new treatments.

VACCINES
Smallpox vaccination had been developed in the 1790s, based on the **chance observation** that milkmaids who caught cowpox (a mild disease) did not catch smallpox. Other forms of immunization were developed as doctors began to understand how the body resisted disease. In the 1880s, French scientist Louis Pasteur developed a vaccine against rabies based on a **weakened form of the virus**. This was followed by vaccines against tetanus and diphtheria in the 1890s. **Mass immunization** against common childhood diseases came in the 20th century—with a vaccine against polio in 1957 and against measles and mumps in the 1960s.

LOUIS PASTEUR

NEW DRUGS
The first drugs that treated infections were produced in the 1930s, but they were replaced by the **discovery of penicillin**, which became available in the 1940s **464–65 >>**. Before then, most drugs were derived from plants, but since the 1950s, **synthetic drugs** have predominated.

the-clock care. Nurses, who were almost always women, played a crucial role in the new hospitals. They kept the wards scrupulously clean and neat to limit the possibility of infection, monitored patients' symptoms, and administered medicines. However, even experienced and skilled nurses were expected to follow the doctors' directions at all times.

While the relatively well-equipped hospitals were able to treat a wider range of conditions, many people, particularly the poor, continued to die of infectious diseases transmitted by bacteria and viruses. Cholera, typhoid fever, tuberculosis, and influenza killed thousands. Children were particularly vulnerable, and many died from measles, mumps, diphtheria, and scarlet fever. Doctors could do little to cure these diseases, but they could control their spread. Increased supplies of clean water and improved sanitation helped to clean up cities (see pp.322–25) and stop the spread of waterborne infections. Patients suffering from infectious diseases were isolated in special hospitals, or in their homes. Quarantine was used, so those traveling from areas where disease was present were forced to stay away from towns until it was certain that they were not carrying an infection.

Our Country

In the late 18th century, nationalism emerged in Europe and the American colonies as a force for liberty, equality, and fraternity. But during the 19th century, nationalism revealed its uglier side, proving to be an equally strong force for militarism, oppression, and racism.

« BEFORE

Until the 18th century the idea of the nation-state was linked to the monarchy and, in smaller states, people were unified by shared language and culture.

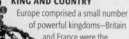

KING AND COUNTRY
Europe comprised a small number of powerful kingdoms—Britain and France were the oldest, with the Netherlands, Portugal, Spain, and Sweden emerging between the 15th and 17th centuries. Only in politically **FRENCH MONARCH'S CROWN** independent kingdoms was there any sense of nationhood. This was reinforced by **loyalty to the crown**, the flag, and, later, by patron saints.

CULTURAL NATIONALISM
In smaller states and principalities—territories ruled by a prince—political loyalties were localized, but a sense of unity was provided by **common language and culture**. Around 1765 German historian Friedrich Meinecke observed a single national spirit even "where 20 principalities could be seen during a day's journey."

The term nationalism describes a loyalty to one's nation, pride in its history and culture, a belief that the nation's interests are of primary importance, and a patriotic desire to achieve or maintain its independence.

Nationalism emerged as a political force in the late 18th century, and since then, the idea that nations have the right to form their own political states has shaped the map of the world as we know it today. This ideal, known as national self-determination, inspired major upheavals, such as the American Revolution (see pp.298–99), provided the impetus for smaller nations to seek independence from large empires, and encouraged nations divided into a collection of small states, or principalities, such as Germany and Italy, to seek unification.

Nations or nationalism?
Although the word "nation" is commonly used to describe a state or country, it is technically a group of people united by ethnicity, culture, language, and/or religion. A state is

defined as a geographical territory with its own independent government. These are not always the same thing— for example, the Kurdish people are a nation with no defined state, while South Africa under apartheid (see pp.454–55) was a state whose nations were forcibly divided (hence its new self-image as a multicultural "Rainbow Nation"). A country whose

Liberty Leading the People
This painting of the July Revolution of 1830 that made Louis-Philippe the French king is both a depiction of and an act of nationalism. The artist Eugene Delacroix wrote: "If I haven't fought for my country at least I'll paint for her."

> "**Our country**… may she always be in the right; but our country, **right or wrong.**"
>
> STEPHEN DECATUR, US NAVAL OFFICER, 1816

FRENCH SOLDIER (1790–UNKNOWN)
NICOLAS CHAUVIN

Chauvin was an idealistic young soldier whose fierce patriotism remained undiminished even though he was wounded numerous times while serving in Napoleon's Grand Army (see pp.304–07). Napoleon decorated Chauvin with the Saber of Honor, but when his brand of unquestioning nationalism fell out of fashion, he found himself satirized in several French plays. As a result of his unfortunate fame, the name "chauvinist" is now applied disparagingly to those who display excessive belief in the superiority of their country or of any other cause they embrace.

state boundaries correspond to those of a particular nation is described as a nation-state.

The precise origins of nationalism are unclear. One idea, called primordialism, is that nations are simply the outward territorial expression of the divisions between people of different ethnicity or culture. This idea of "cultural nationalism" was first expressed by the 18th-century German philosopher Johann Gottfried von Herder. He believed that nature had separated nations by "languages, inclinations, and characters." Opposition to this idea states that the concept of nationalism came first, followed by the artificial creation of nations, for political or economic reasons. In the 20th century, Czech-born British social philosopher Ernest Gellner said: "Nationalism is not the awakening of nations… it invents nations where they do not exist." More recently, it has been proposed that national identities evolve by merging with new ethnic and cultural influences.

Today the idea of the nation-state is well established, but that was not always the case. Until the medieval period, most people's loyalties were specific: to their tribe, religious leader, or feudal landlord. As people developed a sense of nationhood (see BEFORE) they began to demand the right to self-government. In America and France the liberal ideals of freedom, equality, and brotherhood (fraternity) led to nation-states that granted their citizens unchallengeable rights and were governed in the name of the people.

Consequences of nationalism

Once nation-statehood had been achieved, some less savory aspects of nationalism emerged. Napoleon tried to impose the French identity on much of Europe (see pp.304–07), and the belief that the United States had a "manifest destiny" (see pp.310–11) to take over North America came at the expense of the native population. The idea that the nation-state should cherish itself above all others could lead to racism, religious intolerance, and imperialism. The British politician Cecil Rhodes said, "If there is a God, then He would like to see me… color as much of the map of Africa British red as possible." Britain's imperialism went on to encourage nationalist movements within the territories of its empire.

AFTER 〉〉

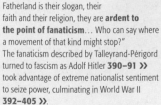

Throughout the 20th century, nationalism showed its two faces, freeing some while subjugating others.

FANATICISM AND FASCISM

In 1815 French foreign minister Charles-Maurice de Talleyrand-Périgord wrote of German nationalists:

NAZI PROPAGANDA

"The unity of the German Fatherland is their slogan, their faith and their religion, they are **ardent to the point of fanaticism**… Who can say where a movement of that kind might stop?" The fanaticism described by Talleyrand-Périgord turned to fascism as Adolf Hitler **390–91** 〉〉 took advantage of extreme nationalist sentiment to seize power, culminating in World War II **392–405** 〉〉.

FREEDOM

Nationalist movements brought independence to former European colonies throughout Africa and Asia, such as Egypt, Indonesia, and Algeria **412–13** 〉〉.

REACHING EXTREMES

Nationalism was also the root of civil war and genocide in, for example, the former Yugoslavia **450–51** 〉〉, and the terrorist activities of **nationalist groups** such as the IRA in Northern Ireland **436–37** 〉〉 and ETA in Spain.

Europe Redefined

Nationalism was one of the 19th century's most potent political ideologies. Over the course of the century, popular and state-led movements inspired by emerging concepts of national identity radically redefined the borders of Europe, replacing traditional monarchies with modern nation-states.

During 1814–15, statesmen from the powers that had brought down Napoleonic France (see pp.304–07) gathered at Vienna to decide how to redraw the borders of Europe (see BEFORE). The resulting settlement was essentially conservative—an attempt to contain the seeds of nationalism that had shattered the old order of Europe. Most of the monarchies that had been overthrown by Napoleon's armies were restored. In Spain, King Ferdinand VII was given back his father's throne; Italy was divided once again into scores of principalities; the 39-state German

Confederation was formed; Austria was given back most of the territories it had lost in Italy; Norway and Sweden were joined under a single ruler; and Russia was handed Finland and given effective control over the new kingdom of Poland.

But the forces to which the age of revolution gave birth were not so easily contained. Traditional loyalties to the old dynasties of Europe had declined; in their place came new loyalties to national groups and demands for nation-states. Over the following century, the old order of Europe would be fundamentally transformed.

National independence
Nationalist movements took two main forms in the 19th century: the political form of advocating independence from an alien rule; and the introduction of nationalist ideology to unite divided

Giuseppe Garibaldi
The Italian soldier and statesman Giuseppe Garibaldi became the hero of the Italian nationalist movement known as the *Risorgimento* ("resurgence").

against a foreign oppressor. In 1830, revolution also broke out in Belgium (part of the Kingdom of the Netherlands), and an independent Belgian state was formed in 1831.

A wave of radical agitation swept across Europe in 1848. In Paris the Bourbon monarchy, restored to the French throne in 1814, was overthrown and replaced by a republic. On hearing of events in France, the people of Vienna, Budapest, and Prague rose up against the Habsburg rulers of the Austrian Empire. For a time, this empire (which covered much of central and southeastern Europe) showed signs of collapse, but the revolutions of 1848 failed within the Habsburg territories.

National unification
The national impulse that led to the division of the Ottoman Empire into independent nation-states could also act as a force for unification. In 1814,

1859. With the help of France, Piedmont repelled Austria, leaving the way open for Cavour to take control of most of northern and central Italy.

The following year the charismatic Italian patriot Giuseppe Garibaldi invaded southern Italy with an army of a thousand volunteer "Red Shirts" and conquered Sicily and Naples. By 1871, the unification of Italy was essentially complete. »

IRELAND

ATLANTIC OCEAN

Bay of Biscay

Oporto

PORTUGAL
Lisbon

Madrid

SPAIN

GIBRALTAR
to Britain

« BEFORE

In the 18th century a number of national revivals made the concept of national identity a significant force in European politics.

MAGYAR RENAISSANCE
When **Joseph II**, the energetic ruler of the Habsburg Empire from 1780–90, decreed that German replace Latin as the empire's official language, the Hungarians (Magyars) in his empire reacted by insisting on the right to use their own tongue. This sparked a **renaissance** of Magyar Hungarian **language** and **culture**.

TREATY OF VIENNA

NATIONAL REVIVALS
The Magyar national reawakening subsequently triggered national revivals among the **Slovak, Romanian, Serbian,** and **Croatian** minorities within Hungary. In 1789, a **revolt** broke out in the **Austrian Netherlands** in reaction to the emperor's centralized policies, and in **Ireland** a swell of nationalism and a mass rebellion for **democratic rights** erupted against British rule in 1798. These revivals later blossomed into the nationalist movements of the 19th–20th centuries.

TREATY OF VIENNA
The **French Revolution « 300–03** and the conquests of **Napoleon Bonaparte « 304–07** shattered the old order of Europe and undermined many of the old certainties. The 1815 **Treaty of Vienna** was an attempt to redraw the borders of Europe and secure peace and stability.

"Let him who **loves his country** ... follow me." GIUSEPPE GARIBALDI, 1882

groups within a state. Large, ethnically diverse states such as the Ottoman Empire (see pp.246–47) were particularly vulnerable to the first type of nationalist movement. During the first part of the 19th century, there was a series of uprisings by Greeks, Serbs, Romanians, and other ethnic groups within the Ottoman Empire. Serbia was semi-independent by 1817, and Greece declared its independence from the Ottomans in 1829. The Greek War of Independence, in particular, caught the imagination of writers and artists such as the poet Byron (see pp.338–39) and the painter Delacroix, helping stimulate a romantic ideal of national struggle

the Congress of Vienna had divided the Italian peninsula into a patchwork of independent states. In spite of this, the idea of a single Italian nation had potent popular appeal. A revolutionary society known as the *Carbonari* (coal-burners) agitated for national unification and organized insurrections, and in 1831 the Italian patriot and author Giuseppe Mazzini formed the political movement known as "Young Italy," which called for one Italian nation—"independent, free, and Republican." Italian statesmen were quick to grasp the opportunities. Cavour, the Prime Minister of Piedmont in northern Italy, provoked a war against Austria in

The sick man of Europe
This cartoon depicts Abdul Hamid II, the last Ottoman emperor (ruled 1876–1909), having his empire whipped out from underneath him by Bulgaria and Austria. Bulgaria became independent from the Ottomans in 1908.

NORWAY

FINLAND

SCOTLAND

Christiania

SWEDEN

Helsingfors

St. Petersburg

Edinburgh

Stockholm

GREAT
BRITAIN

North Sea

Dublin

DENMARK

Baltic Sea

Riga

Moscow

ENGLAND

Copenhagen

WALES

MECKLENBURG

Hamburg

Danzig

RUSSIAN
EMPIRE

Amsterdam

POMERANIA

WEST
PRUSSIA

EAST
PRUSSIA

London

NETHERLANDS

HANOVER

Hanover

PRUSSIA

Berlin

BRANDENBURG

POSEN

Vistula

Warsaw

Brussels

Cologne

Rhine

Posen

PRUSSIA

Elbe

THURINGIAN
STATES

SAXONY

SILESIA

POLAND

Brest-Litovsk

Seine

Paris

BAVARIA

BAVARIA

Stuttgart

Prague
BOHEMIA

Cracow

Kiev

Dnieper

Loire

WÜRTTEMBERG

HOHENZOLLERN

Munich

Vienna

GALICIA

Dniester

FRANCE

BADEN

PR. OF
NEUCHÂTEL

Geneva

SWITZERLAND

AUSTRIAN EMPIRE

Bordeaux

NAVARRA

Lyon

AUSTRIA

Buda
Pest

HUNGARY

MOLDAVIA

Odessa

SARDINIA

Milan

LOMBARDY-
VENETIA

Venice

TRANSYLVANIA

ANDORRA

PARMA

MONACO

MASSA AND
CARRARA

MODENA

MILITARY FRONTIER

Bucharest
WALLACHIA

Sebastopol

Marseille

Belgrade

Danube

Black Sea

LUCCA

TUSCANY

SAN
MARINO

PAPAL
STATES

Barcelona

Corsica

MONTENEGRO

Balearic
Islands

Rome

THRACE

Constantinople

SARDINIA

Naples

KINGDOM OF THE
TWO SICILIES

Corfu
to Britain

OTTOMAN EMPIRE

ANATOLIA

Salonica

Palermo

Mediterranean

Ionian
Islands
to Britain

Smyrna

Athens

Cyprus

Malta
to Britain

Sea

Crete

Changing European boundaries, 1815–1914
Independence and unification during the 19th century
altered Europe's borders dramatically. The lines on this
map show the borders as they were in 1815, while
the areas of color document the territorial changes that
had happened by 1914.

KEY

Great Britain	Spain	Switzerland
Norway	France	Italy
Denmark	Belgium	Austro-Hungarian Empire
Sweden	Netherlands	Montenegro
Russian Empire	Luxembourg	Albania
Portugal	German Empire	Serbia

Romania
Bulgaria
Greece
Ottoman Empire
— German Confederation, 1815
--- Frontiers, 1815

N

0   250 km
0   250 miles

A show of strength
Prussian troops parade in the Champs Elysées in Paris in January 1871 after their takeover of the city during the Franco-Prussian War. Such displays showed off military strength, and helped build nationalistic pride.

>> Another politician who understood the power of the desire for national unity was the Prussian statesman Otto von Bismarck (see below). At the time of the 1848 revolutions, Germany was a loose confederation of states, of which the most powerful was Prussia. Bismarck's primary objective was to secure the supremacy of Prussia in Central Europe, but by encouraging the other German states to unify under Prussia, he was also the architect of the German nation.

The process began in 1864, when Prussia joined forces with Austria to annex the duchies of Schleswig and Holstein from Denmark. Two years later Bismarck was ready to deal with Austria, Prussia's chief rival for dominance in Germany. Allied with Italy and several smaller German states, Prussia defeated Austria—who counted the German states of Saxony and Bavaria among their allies—at the Battle of Königgrätz. Final unity came when the southern principalities of Germany joined Prussia in its war against France in 1870. A German victory led to the proclamation of a unified German Empire in 1871. Bismarck was appointed chancellor.

National identities

The principle that nations share a unique, common identity based on a common culture and history was well established by the late 19th century.

National identity
National symbols and rituals such as the flag and Pledge of Allegiance, shown in this US school (c. 1900), could help to forge the identity of a young nation such as the US, which was largely made up of immigrants.

National languages became paramount, often at the expense of regional dialects. During the struggle to unify Italy, for example, the Italian dialect spoken in Tuscany was chosen, and energetically promoted by writers such as Alessandro Manzoni, who revised and republished his great patriotic novel, *The Betrothed*, in this new national language. Symbols of national identity, such as music and literature, flourished. Sports was a focus of national pride. Military campaigns cemented a growing patriotic fervor with symbolic state emblems and flags. National Days were created, education systems enforced a standard curriculum, and fanfares, marches, and national anthems became prolific across Europe.

In some areas, a particular national identity was enforced by the state in an attempt to suppress or maintain control over other ethnic groups. In Hungary, where the ethnic Hungarians (Magyars) were outnumbered by non-Magyar minorities, the government enforced Magyar as the only legitimate language of administration—a policy known as "Magyarization." Anyone who opposed this policy was liable to be charged with "incitement to national hatred." In 1900, the Russian czar proclaimed Russian the state language of Finland in an attempt to suppress Finnish national identity—the "Russification of Finland."

Militarism

As liberal nationalism, which had focused on civil rights and a constitution, gave way to imperialist nationalism, based on national pride and expansion, a strong army became essential. Until Napoleon, armies were essentially professional forces whose manpower was drawn from the less socially and economically useful elements of the population. The old idea of loyalty to the king was replaced in the Napoleonic armies (see p.307) with loyalty based upon national patriotism fired by the idea of social revolution. This made it possible for Napoleon to raise the type of mass armies that came to characterize the national armies of the 19th and 20th centuries. The entire population was expected to contribute to the war, and conscription was gradually introduced across Europe. Consequently, armies began to expand to record size.

Mass armies required large supplies of arms. The Industrial Revolution (see pp.292–95) enabled mass production, and advances in technology changed warfare. The Russo-Turkish War of 1877–78 was the first war in which modern repeating rifles were uniformly used, increasing the accuracy of fire, and breech-loading cannon, which loaded from the rear for safety and efficiency, replaced front-loading cannon. By the outbreak of the Russo-Japanese War (1904–05), the use of indirect heavy artillery fire was standard practice. The result was that the armies of the early 20th century had an unprecedented killing capacity.

CHANCELLOR OF GERMANY (1815–98)

OTTO VON BISMARCK

Otto von Bismarck became prime minister of Prussia in 1862. His ambition was to unite Germany under Prussian leadership—a result he believed could only be achieved by force. Victory in the Franco-Prussian War (1870–71) persuaded the other German states to join together to form an empire. He became the first chancellor of the unified Germany. Although conservative, Bismarck introduced some social reforms in an attempt to reduce the appeal of socialism.

" It is **not by means of speeches** and majority resolutions that the great issues of the day will be decided—that was the great mistake of 1848 and 1849—**but by blood and iron**."

OTTO VON BISMARCK, SEPTEMBER 30, 1862

AFTER >>

Nationalism and a desire for independence dominated events in Europe in the years leading up to World War I.

EUROPEAN NATION-STATES
In the years preceding World War I, nationalism in many countries had turned **intolerant, imperialist, and expansionist**. Colonial acquisitions were greeted with enthusiasm and there was a growing sense that nations were in competition with each other. Italians, Serbs, Romanians, Greeks, and Bulgarians dreamed of extending their national borders to include their people who were living outside of their nation-state. This **expansionist nationalism** pitted the nation-states against each other. In 1912, a coalition of Bulgaria, Serbia, Montenegro, and Greece invaded, occupied, and partitioned the Ottoman Empire's European provinces. Disagreement over the spoils led to the **Second Balkan War** (1913) in which Greece and Serbia gained large territories.

INDEPENDENCE
The Russification of Finland in the late 19th century caused such resentment among the Finns that on the outbreak of the Russian Revolution **376–77 >>** **Finland declared itself independent.** A war of independence and civil war was fought in 1918, and Finland officially became a republic in 1919.

FINLAND DECLARATION OF INDEPENDENCE

Poland had disappeared from the map in 1785, partitioned between Russia, Prussia, and Austria. In 1915, the Germans expelled the Russians from Poland and promised Poland independence. However, the Poles joined the Allies in World War I and their pleas for **freedom** were finally answered in **Versailles** in 1919 when an independent republic was recognized **375 >>**.

Similarly, Ireland had also been fighting to shake off alien rule. In 1916, the Easter Rising was crushed by the British **436 >>**. In 1921, however, the British signed a treaty with the Irish majority party Sinn Féin to bring about Irish Independence, except for the six northern counties, and in 1922 the Irish Free State came into being.

WORLD WAR I
By the early 20th century, **nation-states** replaced small principalities in Europe. In Africa and the East, Europeans were continuing to annex territories for reasons of national pride and **economic advantage 350–53 >>**. These were also joined by a new generation of powers, whose interests were largely economic. Foremost among them were the US and Japan. But nationalism had within it the seeds of destruction. Rivalries between the powers intensified and their ambitions came into conflict. The result was to be **World War I 372–75 >>**.

THE REPUBLIC OF IRELAND'S FLAG

POLITICAL PHILOSOPHER Born 1818 Died 1883

Karl Marx

"The history of all… society is the history of **class struggle**."

KARL MARX, FROM "THE COMMUNIST MANIFESTO," 1848

Revolutionary socialist and philosopher Karl Marx was born into a well-to-do German Jewish family in Trier. His father had converted to Christianity to avoid persecution by the Prussian authorities. Karl was sent to university to become a lawyer like his father, but instead immersed himself in the study of philosophy and radical politics. Rebelling against his social origins, he became an atheist and a savage critic of the prosperous middle classes.

When Marx was a young man in the 1840s, Europe seemed to many people to be ripe for revolution. Marx became a political journalist, plunging energetically into arguments against the authorities and fellow radicals with whom he disagreed. At the same time, in unpublished manuscripts, he developed a complex philosophy of history, purporting to explain the alienated state of humans in the modern world and to justify a future transformation of society.

Marx and Engels

In 1844 Marx formed a close friendship with Friedrich Engels, the son of a wealthy cotton-mill owner. Marx and Engels shared the belief that

Victorian patriarch

Despite his enthusiasm for violent revolution, Karl Marx, pictured here in 1875, was a gentle father and husband. He reserved an intellectual hatred for people with whose political views he disagreed.

Student days

In 1836, Marx enrolled as a law and philosophy student at the Friedrich Wilhelm University in Berlin (above), now called Humboldt University.

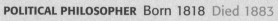

Forging friendships

Marx formed his lifelong friendship with Friedrich Engels (right in picture) in Paris in August 1844. The son of a German industrialist, with a business in Lancashire, England, Engels provided Marx with financial support as well as intellectual collaboration.

Cartoon of Paris Commune, 1871
In 1871 a revolutionary government, the Commune, briefly seized power in Paris. Marx had no influence on the uprising, but hailed it as "the glorious harbinger of a new society."

Radical journalism
Marx (left) and Engels (center) collaborate on the *Neue Rheinische Zeitung*, a radical newspaper that they edited in 1848–49, a time of revolutionary upheaval in Europe. Marx was an excellent journalist, writing with humor and style as well as insightful political analysis.

TIMELINE

- **May 5, 1818** Karl Marx is born in Trier, on the lower Rhine.
- **1835** Studies law at the University of Bonn.
- **1836** Moves to the Friedrich-Wilhelms-Universität in Berlin, where he studies for five years, leaving with a doctorate.
- **1842** Marx becomes editor of the *Rheinische Zeitung* newspaper in Cologne; it is shut down the following year because of his radical articles.
- **June 19, 1843** Marries Prussian aristocrat's daughter Jenny von Westphalen.
- **October 1843** Moves to Paris.
- **August 28, 1844** Friedrich Engels meets Marx in Paris and shows him his work on *The Condition of the Working Class in England*; their lifelong collaboration begins.

JENNY MARX, C. 1840

- **January 1845** Expelled from Paris, Marx and Engels move to Brussels, Belgium.
- **1847** Marx and Engels join the Communist League; Marx publishes *The Poverty of Philosophy*, a critique of French anarchist Pierre-Joseph Prudhon's *The Philosophy of Poverty*.
- **February 21, 1848** *The Communist Manifesto* is published.
- **March 1848** Arrested and expelled from Brussels, Marx moves to Paris, where a revolution has overthrown the monarchy.
- **June 1848–May 1849** Marx returns to Cologne and edits a radical newspaper, the *Neue Rheinische Zeitung*; when the paper is suppressed he returns to Paris.
- **August 1849** Again expelled from Paris, Marx moves to London, where he settles for the rest of his life.
- **1852** Becomes London correspondent of the *New York Daily Tribune*, a source of income for the next decade.
- **April 6, 1855** Marx's best-loved son, eight-year-old Edgar, dies; in all, four of Marx's seven children die between 1850 and 1857.
- **October 1864** Elected to the General Council of the International Working Men's Association (the First International).
- **1867** Volume one of his masterpiece, *Das Kapital*, is published.
- **1868** Marx and the anarchist Bakunin begin a struggle for control of the First International.
- **1871** Marx writes *The Civil War in France* after the crushing of the Paris Commune uprising.
- **September 1872** At the Hague Congress of the First International, the followers of Bakunin quit the organization; the seat of the International is moved to New York, where it goes into decline.
- **December 2, 1881** Marx's wife Jenny dies.
- **March 14, 1883** Marx dies; he is buried in Highgate Cemetery, London.

industrial workers, inspired to rise up against the capitalists who exploited their labor, could be the vehicle for revolutionary change. In 1847, Marx and Engels both joined a small subversive organization known as the League of the Just, soon renamed the Communist League. For this they wrote *The Communist Manifesto*, a powerful appeal for the overthrow of society by a worldwide workers' revolution. It was a timely document, for in 1848 there were revolts in many cities across Europe, including Paris, Berlin, and Vienna. Marx contributed to the agitation with his writings, though neither he nor the Communist League had any significant impact on events. After the suppression of the uprisings in 1849, life for radicals such as Marx became impossible in continental Europe. He moved to Britain, a relatively liberal country that was tolerant of the activities of political refugees.

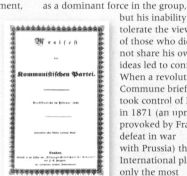

The Communist Manifesto
The *Manifesto* of 1848 is the most succinct statement of Marx's and Engels' ideas.

Theorizing revolution

In the 1850s the prospect of a triumph for the workers' revolution seemed remote, and the Communist League withered away. Marx instead devoted himself to an immense theoretical effort, intended to place the revolutionary critique of capitalist society on a secure scientific and philosophical basis. Although he earned some money from journalism, Marx did not work to support himself and his growing family, depending mostly on handouts from Engels. Thus he was free to write full-time, becoming a familiar presence in the British Museum Reading Room in London. The major result of his labors was the first volume of his analysis of capitalism, *Das Kapital*, in 1867.

By then Marx had resumed practical political activity. In 1864 he joined the International Working Men's

Association, an attempt to coordinate the efforts of assorted left-wing groups. Marx immediately established himself as a dominant force in the group, but his inability to tolerate the views of those who did not share his own ideas led to conflicts. When a revolutionary Commune briefly took control of Paris in 1871 (an uprising provoked by France's defeat in war with Prussia) the International played only the most marginal role in events. Yet after Marx wrote a pamphlet in praise of the uprising, the International received much of the blame (or credit) for it, giving Marx unprecedented notoriety.

Still, there was no reason in the last decade of Marx's life to suppose that he would become one of the most

> "The **workers** have nothing to **lose**... but their **chains**."
>
> KARL MARX, FROM *THE COMMUNIST MANIFESTO*, 1848

influential figures in history. His writings, combining German philosophy and economic analysis, were often dauntingly intellectual. Yet a conviction spread that Marx had proved the inevitability of the fall of capitalism and of a workers' revolution. After his death, Marxism was adopted as a belief system by revolutionary groups, and became the official ideology of states such as the Soviet Union and Communist China. What Marx himself would have thought of the actions carried out in his name we cannot know, although Engels claimed that Marx once declared: "I am not a Marxist."

IDEA

COMMUNISM

Marx saw history as a struggle between social classes. In 19th-century Europe, the bourgeoisie, or middle class, owned the means of production—factories and machinery. By paying the working class (proletariat) less than their labor was worth, the bourgeoisie accumulated capital. Laws and government were arranged to defend their power. According to communist ideals, it was the historic role of the working class to carry out a revolution, establishing a "dictatorship of the proletariat" and creating a classless society free of exploitation or want.

Throughout history, different economic systems governed the production and distribution of goods and services in society.

FEUDALISM
Feudalism was the system of land ownership that predominated in Western Europe during the Medieval period **<< 188–91**. Land was held by a **vassal** on behalf of a lord or a king, in return for loyalty and military service. **Serfs**, mostly unfree peasants, labored for the vassals in a state of virtual slavery in return for the right to farm some of the land for themselves.

MERCANTILISM
During the 17th and 18th centuries a trading system called mercantilism, operated in Europe, particularly England, France, and the Netherlands. It aimed to amass national wealth, especially in the form of gold bullion.

GOLD BULLION

CAPITALISM
Modern capitalism has existed in a recognizable form since the 16th century **<< 276–77**. Under this system the **means of production are privately owned** and goods are produced for a profit. Capitalism promotes a free market that is regulated by supply and demand.

HUMANISM
Humanism, a belief in the dignity and value of people, emerged during the Renaissance **<< 250–53** in Europe. Humanist values run counter to the harsh treatment of working people during the Industrial Revolution **<< 292–93**, and they made an important contribution to the development of socialist thinking.

Consequences of industrialization
The drive by 19th-century industrialists to maximize profits resulted in dirty and dangerous conditions for most working people–both in factories like these Pittsburgh steel mills and in overcrowded, inadequate housing. Disease was rife, and made worse by air and water pollution. These appalling conditions were the subject of numerous campaigns by social reformers.

> "From each according to his ability, **to each according to his need**."

KARL MARX, FROM "CRITIQUE OF THE GOTHA PROGRAM," 1875

Workers Unite!

While factory owners enjoyed huge profits during the Industrial Revolution, the new working class was impoverished. This inequality gave rise to political ideas that aimed to organize and inspire the workers, so that they could share the wealth they had created.

The hope of making the world a fairer place had existed for centuries. However, it was largely in response to the Industrial Revolution (see pp.292–95) that this idea developed into a political philosophy called socialism. Socialism seeks to share wealth by putting it in the hands of its creators—the working class. However, a central issue of socialist debate was whether this could be achieved gradually or through a revolution in which the working class seized power.

Socialism in practice
Early 19th-century socialists included Robert Owen, a Welsh industrialist, who came to believe, along with other "Utopian Socialists," in the construction of societies in which property was owned collectively. After establishing an experimental model community around his cotton mill at New Lanark in Scotland (see below), he continued to attempt to found cooperative communities, most significantly in New Harmony, Idaho, though this was not a success. One of the more radical beliefs for the age held by Utopian socialists was that men and women should have equal rights.

In France, Henri Saint-Simon, often called the "father of French socialism," looked for a society in which there would be equal opportunities for all, while his followers proposed an end to private property. Among the many other radical ideas to emerge in the early 19th century, particularly in continental Europe, was anarchism, which held that the state itself could be replaced by a system of voluntary cooperation between workers.

From the 1840s, the German-born philosopher and economist Karl Marx (see pp.334–35) brought together several strands of revolutionary thought to produce a coherent political theory, which he named "scientific socialism." Marx viewed history as a series of class struggles that would

ultimately lead to the end of capitalism and the arrival of an ideal, classless society without private property, and free from exploitation and want—a theory he called communism. He published his beliefs in the *Communist Manifesto* (1848), which he wrote with Friedrich Engels. Marx believed that such change could only be reached through a process of violent revolution.

The rise of Marxism
It is highly unlikely that many working class people read the work of Marx or other socialist figures, but their discontent was evident. In 1848 Europe was shaken by a series of revolutions, which erupted as a result of various factors, including high unemployment. Although all the revolutions were quashed, labor movements emerged strong. Many of these were greatly influenced by the theories of Marx.

Marx played a more direct role in one of these movements in 1864, when a group of workers and intellectuals formed the International Working Men's Association, or First International. Marx dominated the movement with his revolutionary theories. However, an alternative version of socialism, known as "social democracy," was beginning to gain momentum in Germany and spreading to other European nations. Inspired by the work of the German philosopher Ferdinand Lasalle, social democrats asserted that it was possible

French newspaper report
Karl Marx featured on the front page of the newspaper *L'Illustration* in November 1871. Nine months earlier Parisian workers had set up the Commune, a short-lived government that was hailed as the first example of "the dictatorship of the proletariat"–or communism.

for a fair government to free workers from want and exploitation. This form of socialism is still prevalent in European politics today.

For Marx, such a compromise was unacceptable. In his eyes, capitalism and the growth of socialism were steps toward revolution and communism. The revolution Marx sought eventually took place in Russia, though he had envisaged it happening in more industrialized societies, like Britain. In 1917, under the leadership of Vladimir Ilyich Lenin, Russian socialists overthrew the prevailing government and created the Union of Soviet Socialist Republics (see pp.376–77).

New Lanark
In 1800 Robert Owen set up a model community at this mill in Scotland. New Lanark provided decent conditions for the workers and education for their children and still succeeded in making a profit.

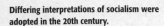

Differing interpretations of socialism were adopted in the 20th century.

SOCIALISM IN ONE COUNTRY

While Karl Marx saw socialism as an international movement, Lenin's successor, **Joseph Stalin 378–79** ≫, concluded that socialism must be built in one country—the Soviet Union. He **isolated** the nation from the rest of the world, and its economy, and those of other European countries modeled on the same system, was almost **entirely state-run** until the collapse of the Soviet Union in 1991 **446–47** ≫. Similarly, in China **424–25** ≫, after the Communist Party came to power in 1949, the economy was largely state-run.

TRADE UNIONS IN BRITAIN

From the early 19th century, British workers organized themselves into associations called **trade unions** to protect their common interests. The **Labour Party** grew out of the trade union movement and was formed in 1906 by socialist politician **James Keir Hardie**.

JAMES KEIR HARDIE

SOCIAL DEMOCRACY

Political parties espousing social democracy have held power for long periods during the 20th century—particularly in the Scandinavian countries, Germany, and France. They created societies in which wealth was—at least partially—redistributed among all their citizens.

May Day poster
This Italian Workers' Party poster is advertising a rally on *Primo Maggio*, which means "first of May." Many countries celebrate May Day in honor of the achievements of workers' movements.

Membership card
The holder of this card was a member of *Parti Ouvrier Français*, or the French Workers' Party. It was founded in 1882, as a result of a split within France's first socialist party, the *Fédération des Travailleurs Socialistes de France* (Federation of French Socialist Workers).

The Romantic Movement

The art movement known as Romanticism revolutionized art and philosophy in the late 18th century and the period that followed. Elevating the importance of self-expression, intuition, emotion, and the imagination over reason, Romanticism saw the beginning of the distinction between art and science.

« BEFORE

Before Romanticism, Enlightenment thinkers sought answers to profound questions in science and reason. Romanticism challenged this.

CLASSICISM
The Classical art movement of the Renaissance **« 250–53** imitated that of the ancient Greeks and Romans **« 116–17**, which was characterized by **precision, elegance, and simplicity**. Classicists followed the formal rules of art set down by ancient cultures.

THE ENLIGHTENMENT
The Enlightenment **« 270–71** spread a spirit of inquiry across Europe and its colonies during the 18th century. **Valuing reason, science, and progress**, its ethos was summarized by the English poet Alexander Pope: "Nature, and Nature's laws lay hid in night: God said, Let Newton be! and all was light." Inspired by Isaac Newton's **« 267** scientific inquiry into the world, Enlightenment thinkers had a thirst for knowledge that coincided with **a period of great scientific discovery and exploration**.

CHALLENGING IDEAS
French philosopher René Descartes advocated **doubting everything** until rational grounds had been established for believing it, which led enlightened thinkers to **challenge previously accepted truths**. Among them were Scottish economist **Adam Smith** (left), whose *Inquiry into the Nature and Causes of the Wealth of Nations* revolutionized economics and social thinking, and the French philosopher Jean-Jacques Rousseau, whose works were an inspiration for the French Revolution **« 302–303**.

ADAM SMITH

THE ROLE OF ART
Until Romanticism the word "art" was synonymous with "craftsmanship," and the word "artist" was used interchangeably with "artisan." Craftsworker-painters were connected to the courtly, religious, and corporate institutions in society, and the nature of their art was guided by the patron, who funded and commissioned the work, rather than the artists themselves.

"The Little Girl Lost"
This illustrated poem is part of *Songs of Experience*, a poetic collection written and illustrated by the English Romantic poet and engraver William Blake. Its celebration of emotion and imagination is typical of Romantic poetry.

R omanticism emerged as a reaction to the 18th-century Enlightenment ideals of rational thought and order (see BEFORE). It was the French philosopher Jean-Jacques Rousseau (see p.270) who first voiced the need for a counterpoint to the "Age of Reason." He was concerned that emotion and imagination were being overwhelmed by the importance placed on rational thought. Romanticism found its first expression not in France but among German writers, as a form of "cultural nationalism" (see p.326); the ideals of

Romanticism gave Germans a sense of national unity at a time when "Germany" was little more than a fragmented group of states. Led by Johann Wolfgang von Goethe (see below) with his novel *The Sorrows of Young Werther*, German writers and poets advocated *sturm und drang* ("storm and stress"), flouting convention by rebelling against their rational educations and emphasizing emotion in their work.

The German pioneers also established other motifs that would become characteristic of the movement. These included a respect for traditional folk art and customs, a sense of wonder at the marvels of nature, and an enthusiasm for ancient mystical and pagan beliefs. Above all, emotion was considered

> **" Romanticism** is… neither in choice of subject nor exact truth, but in a way of **feeling."**
>
> CHARLES BAUDELAIRE, FRENCH POET, "THE SALON OF 1846," 1846

superior to reason. This led to the cult of the artist as hero, capable of expressing thoughts and feelings beyond the realms of ordinary people.

Art for art's sake
The Romantic ideal was that art should be a form of self-expression rather than a commodity, and that artists should not be treated as hired hands. Painters began to distance themselves from their craft-based heritage and increasingly art became an imaginative product rather than merely a possession of the artist's patron. This reinforced the Romantic idea of the artist as a gifted individual, intrinsically different from "ordinary" people—a status indulged to its fullest by the English poet Lord Byron, and the German composers Ludwig van Beethoven and Richard Wagner.

Many painters abandoned the strict rules of classicism and instead brought personal significance to their work. Epitomized by the work of William

GERMAN WRITER AND THINKER (1749–1832)

JOHANN WOLFGANG VON GOETHE

Goethe was a major inspiration for the Romantic movement, of which he eventually came to disapprove. In 1773 he wrote the archetypal Romantic drama *Götz von Berlichingen*, about a young genius rebelling against the conventions of society. He went on to create more misunderstood heroes, but Goethe's masterpiece was the classically-influenced *Faust*, a reworking of the tale of a disillusioned scholar who sells his soul to Satan.

Gothic revival
Romanticism celebrated the medieval Gothic style in art, literature, and architecture. Above is Keble College, Oxford, England, controversial for its use of Gothic-style red brick rather than traditional stone.

"universal nightmare" for all other composers, because no one would ever be capable of bettering it.

The cult of the individual

Romanticism fundamentally changed the way society views art and the artist, reintroducing the classical idea that the creative act sets the artist apart. This contributed to a separation of arts and sciences and to the notion of the *avant garde*—of artists ahead of their time, pioneering new ways of thinking. Part of this was the cult of the individual, encapsulated in William Blake's comment: "I must create a system or be enslaved by another man's; I will not reason or compare: my business is to create."

The Death of Byron
Lord Byron is depicted lying on his deathbed by the Flemish Romantic painter Joseph-Denis Odevaere. Byron, who tried to help liberate Greece from Ottoman rule, is presented as a classical Greek hero.

AFTER

Blake and J.M.W. Turner in England, Théodore Géricault and Eugene Delacroix in France, and Caspar David Friedrich in Germany, Romantic painters explored the subjects of nature, individual consciousness, and the cultural history of their nations. Similarly, poets explored themes of childhood, subjective experience, and the mysteries of the natural world,

often using traditional poetic forms. Lord Byron became the embodiment of the Romantic ideal. He presented himself as a restless hero, in perpetual search of a deeper understanding through his work.

Perhaps the best expression of Romanticism is found in classical music. From the powerful symphonies of Ludwig van Beethoven, the Romantic songs of the Austrian Franz Schubert, and the epic operas of Richard Wagner, 19th-century composers produced many masterpieces that are still popular today. On hearing Beethoven's Ninth symphony, the French composer Claude Debussy declared that it was a

Art song
This is Franz Schubert's 1814 handwritten score of *Gretchen am Spinnrade*, a selection of text from Goethe's *Faust*. It is a typical example of a *lied*, or "art song"—a musical rendering of a literary text.

Artistic movements continued to spring from reactions to what was going on in society, as well as influencing social change themselves.

PRE-RAPHAELITES
In 1848 a growing reaction against materialism and industrialization in Britain contributed to the foundation of the Pre-Raphaelite Brotherhood by British artists John Everett Millais, Dante Gabriel Rossetti, and William Holman Hunt. They sought refuge in **legendary worlds** and yearned for a return to the spirituality of the medieval period and the Renaissance **‹‹ 250–53**. They had strong links to the literary world, and Rossetti and his sister Christina were both notable poets.

REALISM
As art became more of a commodity for the middle classes to acquire, its subject matter became tied to their values. Realism was a reaction against idealization in art and a rejection of literary or exotic subjects. French painter Gustave Courbet embodied its ideals, believing that an artist should only paint **scenes of everyday life**.

NATIONALISM
The German Romanticism that valued the folk tales and legends of German literature and music became corrupted into an extreme form of nationalism **328–29 ››**.

"PROSERPINE" BY ROSSETTI

In Judeo-Christian cultures, the Biblical story of the Creation was so fundamental to the way people viewed the world that challenges to it were almost unthinkable.

ADAM AND EVE

CREATIONISM

Creationism is the belief that the universe and everything in it was created by a god. Jewish and Christian creationists believe that the world was created exactly as stated in the Bible. Based on a **literal reading** of this, the Church believed that the **world was created between 6000 and 4000 BCE**, and that Earth and its species of plants and animals, including humans, are unchanging. The young Charles Darwin was influenced by theologians such as William Paley, who argued that the natural world was too complex not to have had a creator.

CHALLENGES TO CREATIONISM

In 1785 Scottish geologist James Hutton proposed that the Earth is being **continuously reshaped by steady change**, not by Biblical events such as the Creation and the Flood. This "steady state" view was later added to by British geologist Sir Charles Lyell, in his *Principles of Geology* (1830). Other challenges came from Darwin's grandfather, Erasmus Darwin, who in 1794 noted a **progressional change** in animals. French naturalist Jean-Baptiste de Lamarck also proposed a **theory of progressive development** in his *Philosophie Zoologique*, published in 1809.

Scientific specimens
Darwin collected these specimens (two fish and an eel) during his five years on HMS *Beagle*, between 1831 and 1836.

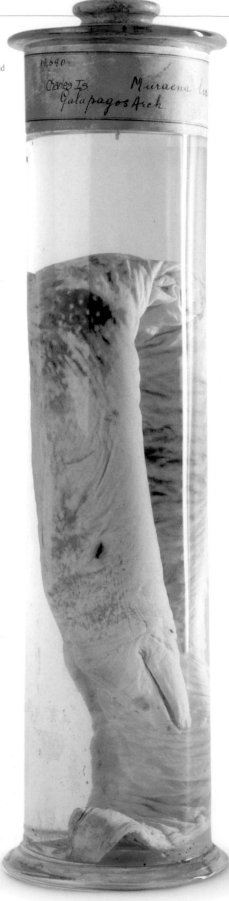

"Man with all his noble qualities… still bears in his bodily frame the indelible stamp of his lowly origin."

CHARLES DARWIN, FROM *THE DESCENT OF MAN*, 1871

Origin of Species

The theory of evolution is often called "Darwinism," after the British naturalist Charles Darwin. In 1859 Darwin published the results of his research in the first evolutionary theory based on scientific evidence. His controversial work known as *On the Origin of Species* changed our view of the world.

BRITISH NATURALIST (1809–82)
CHARLES DARWIN

Charles Darwin showed little motivation in school, causing his father to comment: "you will be a disgrace to yourself and your family." Darwin studied medicine and law, but dropped out of both, before finally completing a degree in divinity and later embarking upon a career as a naturalist on HMS *Beagle*'s scientific expedition around the coast of South America. After the voyage, he gained wide respect for the papers he published describing his findings, and then, plagued by illness, he painstakingly prepared the publication that was to change the course of scientific history. Darwin was respected by his scientific peers, including the biologist T. H. Huxley. Upon his death, Darwin was buried in London's Westminster Abbey alongside the physicist Isaac Newton.

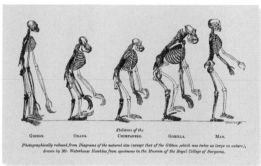

Evolving forms
T. H. Huxley (see pp.342–43) was the foremost exponent of Darwin's theories. This frontispiece to his *Evidence as to Man's Place in Nature*, 1863, reveals the similarities in the skeletons of (from left to right) gibbon, orangutan, chimpanzee, gorilla, and human.

Although the uproar caused by *On the Origin of Species by Means of Natural Selection* might suggest otherwise, the idea that humankind and animals had evolved from more primitive creatures was nothing new, even in Darwin's day. The first theory that all living creatures are descended from shellfish was proposed as early as the 6th century BCE. Some 2,500 years later, in 1844, Scottish encyclopedist Robert Chambers scandalized Victorian society by anonymously publishing *Vestiges of the Natural History of Creation*. Chambers argued that fossil evidence suggested that animal species had changed over time, contradicting the Biblical notion that they had been unchanged since their creation by God. Chambers' ideas were unscientific and unsubstantiated, but the very idea of evolution was enough to ensure that the book sold in huge numbers.

Natural selection

From 1831 to 1836, Darwin traveled as a naturalist aboard HMS *Beagle*, on a scientific survey of South American waters. During the voyage he found evidence to support the geologist Charles Lyell's idea that the world had evolved through gradual processes (see BEFORE), but it was not until several years later that Darwin began to forge his own theory. In the meantime he read Thomas Malthus's 1798 "Essay on the Principle of Population" (see p.291), which argued that the size of an animal population is limited by its food supply. When Darwin's friend, the ornithologist John Gould, realized that the species of finches that Darwin had brought back from his voyage shared common ancestors, Darwin wondered why. He concluded that those animals most suited to acquiring food would survive and pass on their characteristics to their offspring, while the unsuited would die out—a concept that Darwin called "natural selection," but British philosopher Herbert Spencer later called "the survival of the fittest."

Darwin began to work on what he called his theory of "transmutation" in 1842. By 1844 he had written 230 pages, but set it aside, partly because of ill health, but also because he was troubled by his conclusions. Darwin finally published when it emerged that zoogeographer Alfred Wallace was working on a similar theory. Charles Lyell persuaded Darwin to submit a paper to London's Linnean Society (a biological society), which was read on July 1, 1858, the same night as Wallace's essay. Darwin's *On the Origin of Species* was published in 1859.

5,500 The number of biological and anatomical specimens Charles Darwin collected during the voyage of the *Beagle*, the details of which were put in 12 catalogs.

The Descent of Man

The novel element in Darwin's theory was natural selection. His version, that individuals compete with each other for resources, differed from Wallace's idea that they competed against the environment. Humanity's descent from the apes was a minor part of *On the Origin of Species*, but his 1871 book, *The Descent of Man*, argued that it was

walking on two legs that led humankind to evolve differently. This was controversial, gaining both support and criticism from scientific and religious figures. Zoologist Ernst Mayr (1904–2005) said that it "demanded the rejection of some of the most widely held and most cherished beliefs of western man" (see pp.342–43).

Darwin's finches
Darwin's illustrations of some of the species of finches he discovered in the Galápagos Islands. The realization that the separate species were all derived from common ancestors influenced Darwin's theory of natural selection.

AFTER

Although Darwin's theory has been highly influential, and is widely taught, debate over the origin of life on Earth continues.

EVOLUTIONARY SYNTHESIS
As Darwin completed his book, Austrian botanist Gregor Mendel was researching **heredity in plants**. In the 20th century, after years of neglect, Mendel's work led to the new science of **genetics**, which explains how the mutations necessary for natural selection occur and are passed on. Scientists have since formed Darwin and Mendel's work into the modern theory of "**neodarwinism**."

INTELLIGENT DESIGN
Many people still doubt that complex living things such as human beings could have been created by entirely natural processes. They prefer an alternative theory of "intelligent design." In this theory, God created a universe that would run itself: one analogy is of God as **cosmic watchmaker**. Popular in the 19th century, the idea was revived in the late 20th century.

Before the 17th century, religion was practically unchallenged as a framework for understanding the world, but the scientific revolution offered alternative explanations for our existence.

GALILEO AND THE INQUISITION

In 1632, Italian scientist Galileo Galilei asserted his belief that Earth revolved around the Sun—a theory first put forward a century earlier—in his book *Dialogues on the Two Chief World Systems*. The Catholic Church banned it, and the Inquisition (a religious tribunal) « 196 forced

GALILEO FACES THE INQUISITION

Galileo (above) to denounce his own work as heretical. He was placed under house arrest, but during his confinement he wrote *Discourses Upon Two New Sciences*, which later inspired Isaac Newton « 269 to scientific discoveries that further challenged Biblical doctrine.

SOCIETIES AND ACADEMIES

During the 17th century the emergence of **scientific societies** such as the Royal Society in Britain and the Académie des Sciences in France provided forums for debate and encouraged the **formalization of the scientific method**. The societies also gave science respectability, though it continued to face opposition from the Church.

NEWTON'S GOD

Isaac Newton's scientific discoveries were criticized because it was thought that they had **demystified the world,** but Newton was

MECHANICAL MODEL OF THE SOLAR SYSTEM

devoutly religious: he did not present **science as an alternative to God**, and nothing in his work intentionally excluded God from the universe he described. Newton believed that God was the force behind the natural systems his science had sought to explain, with the universe as a clockwork machine (above) created by God.

THE ENLIGHTENMENT

Newton's discoveries caused a **revolution in physics** and inspired a new intellectual and philosophical movement known as the Enlightenment « 270–71, whose thinkers based their work on **reason and evidence**, rather than superstition and accepted beliefs.

"Was it through his grandfather or his grandmother that he claimed his **descent from a monkey**?"

BISHOP WILBERFORCE, ADDRESSING THOMAS HUXLEY AT A MEETING OF THE BRITISH ASSOCIATION FOR THE ADVANCEMENT OF SCIENCE, 1860

O n June 30, 1860 science clashed with religion on a stage at Oxford University's Museum Library. Weighing in on one side of the debate were Bishop Samuel Wilberforce and the Anglican Church; on the other was English biologist T. H. Huxley, armed with a copy of *On the Origin of Species*, published by Charles Darwin, the British naturalist, the year before (see p.341). Darwin's book, which advanced the theory that all creatures had evolved through natural selection, critically undermined the literal interpretation of the Bible, which held that God created the world, including humans, during a period of six days around 6,000 years ago. But religion was more than ready to defend

VANITY FAIR. July 24, 1869.

50

STATESMEN, No. 25.
"Not a brawler."

No. 38.

Price 6d.

No. 117.

Heated debate
Cartoons from the magazine *Vanity Fair* show Bishop Samuel Wilberforce (left) and T. H. Huxley. Their debate became known as "the moment that science clashed with religion."

Science vs. God

In 1859 Charles Darwin published *On The Origin of Species by Means of Natural Selection*, in which the naturalist put forward his theory of evolution. This sparked a public debate over the roles of religion and science in providing the means by which humans understood the world around them.

its position. Bishop Wilberforce attacked Huxley over a perceived lack of evidence, while Huxley quipped that he would rather be descended from a monkey than a bishop.

Hard evidence

This challenge to previously accepted ideas was not a deliberate attack on religion by science, but came simply from the fact that discoveries were being made that were at odds with Christian doctrine. As a Christian himself, Darwin found the situation very difficult and was reluctant to publish his theory for fear of the public's reaction, ruefully referring to himself as "the Devil's Chaplain." Philosophers had been challenging the literal interpretation of the Bible since the Enlightenment (see p.270–71), but in the late 18th and early 19th

centuries, scientific evidence added a new dimension to the debate. From 1785 to 1835, four scientists—James Hutton, Georges Cuvier, William Smith, and Sir Charles Lyell—provided

The Creation of Adam
Michelangelo's depiction of God creating Man adorns the ceiling of the Sistine Chapel in Rome. It is part of a series of panels depicting stories from the book of Genesis, the first book of the Bible.

VANITY FAIR.   Jan. 28, 1871.

OF THE DAY NO. 19.

Price 6d.

e-Man among the Inqut-ring Redskins."

metaphorical, with the six days of creation being interpreted as epochs, or geological time periods. The idea that humans themselves were descended from apes—derided as the "monkey theory"—was much harder to accept. Some found a way to reconcile the information with their religious beliefs. The novelist and theologian Charles Kingsley wrote: "I have gradually learnt to see that it is just as noble a conception of the Deity to believe that He created primal forms capable of self-development as to believe that He required a fresh intervention to fill the [voids] which He himself had made."

IDEA

THE PERIODIC TABLE

In 1869 Dmitri Mendeleev, a Russian chemist, wrote the name of each chemical element on a card with its chemical properties and atomic weight. Having noticed repeating (or "periodic") patterns in them, he arranged the cards in a grid according to property (by row) and weight (by column); the modern periodic table has reversed this system. His grid also allowed him to predict the existence and properties of unknown elements, which were not discovered until later.

"Irrationally held truths may be more harmful than reasoned errors."

T. H. HUXLEY, "THE COMING OF AGE OF 'THE ORIGIN OF SPECIES'," 1880

The march of science

During the 19th century, the elevation of science from a hobby of the eccentric to a respected and even admired discipline was marked by the use of a new word: its practitioners became known as "scientists," where previously they had been called "natural philosophers."

Science gained credibility alongside religion, rather than instead of it, and Christianity proved resilient to change. The reduction of the Church's influence by the state following the French Revolution in 1789 (see pp.302–03) resulted in greater religious freedom throughout Europe, with a move away from state religions toward more numerous denominations. Competition between them resulted in the strengthening of religious loyalties, while a rise in atheism in urban areas

led to increased church building in many European cities.

Scientific progress continued, with people experiencing its effects through technology and medical advances. Governments began to address the need for scientific education: research-based university departments were established, as were scientific and technical institutions. As scientific knowledge filtered through society, it became more accessible. Despite the fears of the Church, society was not faced with a stark choice between science or God. Instead, these advances led in many cases to the acceptance of both science and belief.

rock and fossil evidence that suggested that Earth was much older than had been thought, casting doubt on Biblical chronology and the story of creation, though 19th-century geology was not sufficiently developed to make accurate estimates of Earth's age.

The Church was able to cope with these new theories relatively easily. Many Christians were willing to consider Biblical chronology as

Geological evidence

The discovery of fossilized ancient creatures such as these ammonites (prehistoric mollusks) seriously undermined the teachings of the Bible regarding the age of Earth and the way it was created.

AFTER

Science has continued its attempts to explain the universe, while the issue of Creationism still causes debate today.

"Science without religion is lame, religion without science is blind."

ALBERT EINSTEIN, PAPER FOR CONFERENCE ON SCIENCE, 1940

BIG BANG

In 1927 Georges Lemaître, a Belgian scientist and Catholic priest, proposed that the universe was created by the explosion of a "quantum singularity," or "big bang"—a state of nothingness, existing outside space and time, containing the potential for everything there is, has been, or will be.

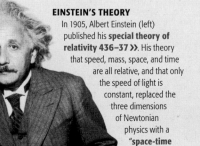

ALBERT EINSTEIN

EINSTEIN'S THEORY

In 1905, Albert Einstein (left) published his **special theory of relativity 436–37 >>**. His theory that speed, mass, space, and time are all relative, and that only the speed of light is constant, replaced the three dimensions of Newtonian physics with a **"space-time continuum."**

CREATIONISM The belief that the universe was created by a god, rather than being formed by a process of evolution.

CREATIONISM

In mainstream Western thinking, scientific theories have largely replaced Creationism. However, there is still a vociferous creationist minority, and in modern usage Creationism usually refers to Christian fundamentalists who oppose the teaching of scientific theories such as evolution and the Big Bang.

« BEFORE

From the advances of the 17th century, scientific progress gathered momentum, leading to many 19th-century innovations.

SCIENTIFIC REVOLUTION
During the 17th century, drastic changes took place as European science was revolutionized by the ideas of people like Galileo Galilei and Isaac Newton « **268–69**. By the late 17th century, **dramatic advances** had been made in mathematics, astronomy, and biology.

INDUSTRIAL REVOLUTION
In the late 18th century, Western Europe began to industrialize rapidly « **292–95**. Coal was used to power steam engines that drained mines and eventually drove machinery.

MECHANICAL CALCULATION
In the 1840s **Charles Babbage**, an English mathematician, worked on the development of an **Analytical Engine** which, had it been completed, would have been capable of performing calculations

ADA LOVELACE

similar to the early computers of the 1940s. **Ada Lovelace**, a woman fascinated by mathematics, saw the possibilities of the machine. In 1843 she published the **first known computer program**.

Ingenious Inventions

The four essentials of technological advances are the right idea, the method to execute it, the perfect moment in time, and the availability of the right materials. The 19th century saw these elements merge in an explosion of technology, which introduced mass production and fed mass consumption.

The Industrial Revolution (see pp.292–95) had brought with it an increase in population and urbanization as well as an emerging "middle class," which profited from industrial growth. Factories were filled with a labor force as agricultural manual work gave way to mechanization. Manufacturing produced cheaper goods for a mass market, encouraged by the rise in wages and standards of living. The traditional workplace, and the home, were being rapidly transformed.

Few men had a greater impact on life in the 19th century than Michael Faraday. Faraday discovered that an electric current was produced in a coil of wire when a magnet was moved through the coil.

His experiments with electricity in the 1830s led to dramatic developments in the sphere of communications. In 1837, British scientists William Cook and Charles Wheatstone patented the electric telegraph, a method of sending messages through wires to a remote receiver. Telegraphy expanded across the world. By 1876 the inventor Alexander Graham Bell, a Briton living

in the US who had spent much of his professional career working with the deaf, developed the telephone. This innovation went on to eclipse the telegraph.

Another electrical discovery in 1887 further revolutionized communications, when a German scientist named Heinrich Hertz proved the existence of radio waves. An Italian entrepreneur, Guglielmo Marconi, was convinced that Hertz's work could lead to messages being sent over long distances without the use of cables and was soon transmitting "wireless" signals. In 1906 Marconi achieved his final goal by transmitting speech over the airwaves using radio transmissions.

Other inventions were rapidly changing the world. By the turn of the 20th century wars were being

fought with more advanced weapons, food was preserved in new tin cans (see pp.290–91), and domestic refrigeration was evolving. Cars emerged on the roads, shipbuilding was prolific, railroads stretched across continents, and the first plane was about to take off. In the US, Wilbur and Orville Wright progressed by way of gliders to a fabric-covered wooden biplane. On December 17, 1903 they made a flight in the world's first powered plane; by the early 1930s the modern airplane was beginning to take shape (see pp.458–61). Domestic life was being slowly transformed by sewing machines, washing machines, electric stoves, electric heaters, and vacuum cleaners. Families had clearly defined "leisure time." They listened to gramophones, which played flat discs, and, in March 1895, people thrilled to the sight of flickering pictures when a film of workers leaving the Lumière factory during their lunch hour was shown. Cinema was born.

Gatling gun
Richard Gatling's mechanical gun of the 1860s consisted of six barrels mounted in a revolving frame. It was easy to use, reliable, and effective.

Can opener
While early tin cans were opened with a hammer and chisel, lighter steel cans made the can opener possible. "Bull's head" pierce-and-pry openers, like this one, appeared in the 1860s.

Tin can
A discovery in 1810 that food could be preserved by heating it and sealing it in jars led two British men, Bryan Donkin and John Hall, to develop tin cans.

Berliner gramophone
Emile Berliner created the forerunner of modern records and record players. This 1890s model plays grooved flat discs, which were cheaply produced.

Bell "Box" telephone
Alexander Graham Bell had transmitted speech along a wire by 1876. This early Bell telephone has a combined trumpetlike mouthpiece and earpiece.

Debrie Parvo camera
In 1908, 60 years after the earliest models, Frenchman Joseph Debrie developed the "Le Parvo" camera. At one time it was the most used camera in the world.

Benz Velo
The Benz Velo of 1895 was the world's first standardized car. Powered by a single-cylinder engine, there were two forward speeds and no reverse gear.

Carbon filament bulb
The carbon filament lamp of the 1870s used heated strips of carbon, housed in glass bulbs like this one, to generate light.

Remington No. 1 typewriter
The first popular typewriter was invented by the American Christopher Sholes in 1868. It was made by Remington, like this 1876 model.

Eastman Kodak Brownie
In the early 1900s the American George Eastman developed cheap cameras such as this example, and amateur photography was born.

Wright *Flyer*
On December 17, 1903 the Wright brothers' *Flyer* took off near Kitty Hawk, North Carolina. With Orville Wright as pilot, the plane rose to 10 ft (3 m) and landed heavily after 12 seconds. Of the three flights that day, the longest lasted 59 seconds.

AMERICAN INVENTOR (1847–1931)

THOMAS EDISON

Edison was a self-taught inventor. At the age of seven he set up his first chemistry laboratory at home. Attending school for only three months, from the age of 12 he began devoting all of his spare time to scientific experimentation. Edison's large-scale research laboratories were the first of their kind in the world, issuing 1,093 devices patented in his name, including an improved telephone, a successful electric lamp, and the first movie projector.

AFTER »

Science continued to progress in the 20th century, making technology accessible, and breaking down barriers to communication.

THE DAWN OF TELEVISION
In 1926 the Scottish engineer John Logie Baird **transmitted pictures and words** using radio waves **458–61 »**.

PLASTICS
Domestic products were increasingly made of plastic **458–61 »**. The **first versatile domestic plastic** was Bakelite, invented in 1909.

COMPUTER REVOLUTION
The first electronic computers were developed in secret in Britain and the United States during World War II. The **miniaturization** of computers by the use of silicon chips in the 1960s changed communication and industry **478–79 »**.

Cash register
The American James Ritty invented the cash register in 1879 to stop theft by cashiers. The keys operated gears that added together the money paid in.

Leclanché cell
This late 19th-century Leclanché cell is an early example of a battery. Most batteries today are Leclanché cells encased in metal.

Diving helmet
This helmet is part of a watertight diving suit from 1839, which allowed the diver to operate at depths down to 300 ft (100 m).

<<

BEFORE

Growing populations in Europe in the 16th–17th centuries led to the search for new lands.

CONQUISTADORS

The Americas were the greatest attraction for European settlers. Within 50 years of its discovery in 1492 << **228–29**, Spanish conquistadors (conquerors) had occupied more than 1 million square miles (2.6 million km²) of the new continent and named it "New Spain" << **230–31**.

EXPLORERS OF AFRICA

In 1652 the Dutch founded a **settlement** at Cape Town, southern Africa, to provision their ships. Mungo Park, a Scot, then **explored** the Niger Valley in 1796–1805. Others, such as David Livingstone, soon followed << **320–21**.

PIONEERS IN NORTH AMERICA

Spain founded a colony in Florida in 1565, but after their defeat by Britain in 1586 << **260–61**, Britain became the **dominant power**. By the end of the 18th century the British had driven the Dutch and the Swedes from North America, and the French from Canada << **296–97**. Migration to America gathered pace after the American Revolution << **298–99**.

The world in 1900

European influence stretched across the world. Britain, Russia, and France were the preeminent powers, but Portugal, Germany, and Denmark all controlled parts of Africa, Southeast Asia, and South America.

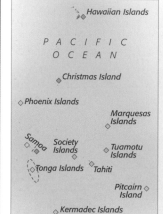

KEY

- ■ Ottoman Empire
- ■◇● Britain and possessions
- ■◇● France and possessions
- ■◇ Denmark and possessions
- ■◇● Spain and possessions
- ■◆● Portugal and possessions
- ■◇ Netherlands and possessions
- ■◇● German Empire and possessions
- ■◇ Russian Empire and possessions
- ■◇ Japan and possessions
- ■◇ Italy and possessions
- ■◆● US and possessions

The Imperial World

In the space of 400 years, Europeans transported the civilization of their continent into every corner of the world. Imperialism—empire-building—expanded so rapidly that by 1900, extensive areas of the inhabited world were governed by Europeans.

Many factors drove imperial expansion. The newly discovered continents of the world offered huge wealth, for example, but once this was realized, traders preferred to do business under their own administration. When Britain seized South Africa, it was because they wanted to deal with the British, rather than native Africans or the Dutch Afrikaner settlers, called Boers.

These new worlds provided exotic luxuries, such as spice from the Indies, tobacco and silks, and, with the onset of the Industrial Revolution (see pp.292–95), a steady supply of raw materials such as cotton. It also became apparent that they were an abundant source of cheap labor.

Another factor in imperial growth was the political rivalries of the major European powers. French imperial ambitions were designed to restore France's reputation after the crushing defeat in the Franco-Prussian War (see pp.306–07). For Germany, the colonies

were a symbol of prestige. In some cases, colonization was simply a matter of claiming a nation before another power could get there. This was particularly so in the "Scramble for Africa" (see pp.360–61).

There were also strong ideological motives. Many felt it their duty to spread Christianity, believing it was, in the poet Rudyard Kipling's words, the "white man's burden" to "civilize" the native population.

European success

Europeans had the men, money, ships, and guns to succeed in their ambitions, and military superiority helped invading nations to subdue local resistance.

The colonial nations found Australasia and North America sparsely inhabited. But elsewhere, such as India, they

discovered populous nations with sophisticated systems of government already in place. This necessitated a different approach to colonization. Communities of merchants were established, with garrisons to protect them, and only rarely did the colonists take formal control. In India, British control of the country (see pp.352–53) by the British East India Company only occurred after a long period of trading.

19th-century spice box

Throughout history, the country that has controlled the spice trade has been the richest. In the 19th century, Britain's maritime prowess established it as the leading colonial power.

Empire and migration

New lands beckoned European settlers. Population pressure at home, combined with improved overseas transport,

led to large-scale migration. In the 19th century, as the frontier of the US moved west (see pp.310–11), millions arrived from across the Atlantic Ocean. The miseries of the Industrial Revolution led many to emigrate. In Victoria, Australia, the discovery of gold in the 1850s triggered a rise in the population from 76,000 to 540,000 in just ten years. Colonists exported their dress, language, and religions around the globe. Western hairstyles, fashion, and

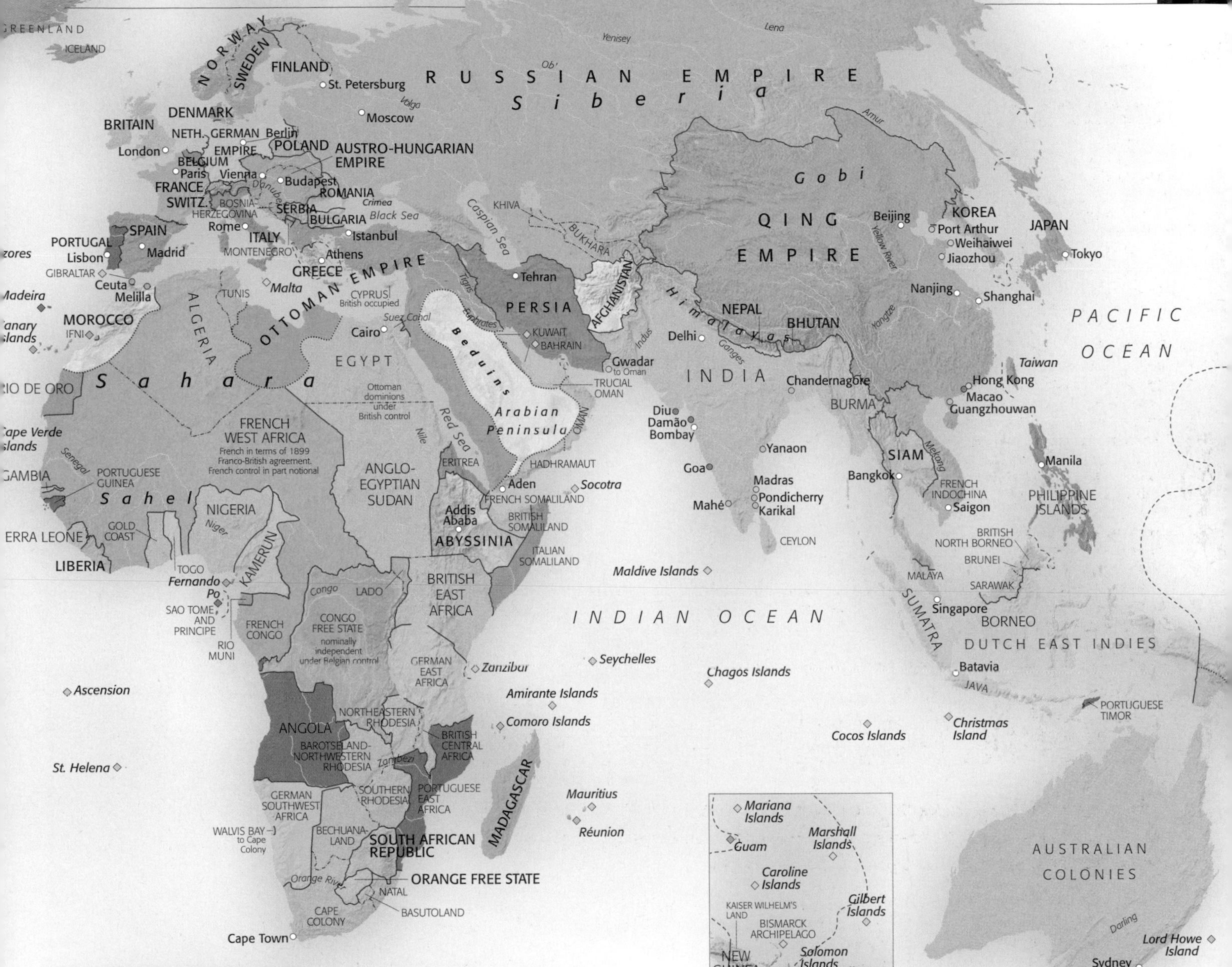

GREENLAND
ICELAND

NORWAY
SWEDEN
FINLAND
St. Petersburg

R U S S I A N   E M P I R E
Siberia

Lena
Yenisey
Ob'
Moscow
Volga

DENMARK
BRITAIN
NETH. GERMAN Berlin
London
BELGIUM EMPIRE POLAND AUSTRO-HUNGARIAN
Paris Vienna EMPIRE
FRANCE Danube Budapest
SWITZ. ROMANIA
BOSNIA- SERBIA
HERZEGOVINA Crimea
Rome ITALY BULGARIA Black Sea
MONTENEGRO
SPAIN Athens Istanbul
PORTUGAL Madrid GREECE
Lisbon
GIBRALTAR Malta O T T O M A N   E M P I R E
Ceuta CYPRUS
Melilla British occupied
MOROCCO TUNIS
IFNI Cairo
ALGERIA EGYPT
Sahara

RIO DE ORO
Cape Verde Islands
GAMBIA
ERRA LEONE
LIBERIA

Ottoman dominions under British control

Suez Canal
Tigris
Euphrates
Red Sea
Nile

P E R S I A
Tehran
KUWAIT
BAHRAIN
Gwadar
to Oman
TRUCIAL
OMAN

Arabian Peninsula
Beduins
HADRAMAUT

A N G L O -
E G Y P T I A N
S U D A N

ERITREA
Addis Ababa
FRENCH SOMALILAND
Aden
Socotra
BRITISH SOMALILAND
ABYSSINIA
ITALIAN
SOMALILAND

FRENCH
WEST AFRICA
French in terms of 1899
Franco-British agreement.
French control in part notional

Sahel
NIGERIA
GOLD COAST
Niger
Senegal

PORTUGUESE
GUINEA

TOGO
KAMERUN
Fernando Po
SAO TOME AND PRINCIPE
RIO MUNI
FRENCH CONGO
Congo
LADO
CONGO
FREE STATE
nominally
independent
under Belgian control

BRITISH
EAST
AFRICA

GERMAN
EAST
AFRICA

Zanzibar

AFGHANISTAN
KHIVA
BUKHARA
Caspian Sea
Indus

Gobi
Q I N G
E M P I R E
Amur
Yellow River
Beijing
Port Arthur
Weihaiwei
Jiaozhou
Nanjing
Yangtze
Shanghai

KOREA
JAPAN
Tokyo

NEPAL
BHUTAN
Himalayas
Delhi
Ganges
I N D I A
Chandernagore
BURMA
Diu
Damão
Bombay
Yanaon
Goa
Madras
Mahé Pondicherry
Karikal
CEYLON

Hong Kong
Macao
Guangzhouwan

Taiwan

SIAM
Bangkok
FRENCH
INDOCHINA
Saigon

P A C I F I C
O C E A N

PHILIPPINE
ISLANDS
Manila

BRITISH
NORTH BORNEO
BRUNEI
MALAYA SARAWAK
Singapore BORNEO
SUMATRA
DUTCH EAST INDIES
Batavia
JAVA

Maldive Islands

I N D I A N   O C E A N

Seychelles
Amirante Islands
Comoro Islands
Chagos Islands
Cocos Islands
Christmas Island
PORTUGUESE
TIMOR

Ascension
NORTHEASTERN
RHODESIA
BAROTSELAND-
NORTHWESTERN
RHODESIA
Zambezi
BRITISH
CENTRAL
AFRICA

ANGOLA
St. Helena

GERMAN
SOUTHWEST
AFRICA
WALVIS BAY
to Cape Colony
BECHUANA-
LAND
SOUTHERN
RHODESIA
PORTUGUESE
EAST
AFRICA
MADAGASCAR
Mauritius
Réunion

SOUTH AFRICAN
REPUBLIC
Orange River
ORANGE FREE STATE
NATAL
CAPE
COLONY BASUTOLAND
Cape Town

AUSTRALIAN
COLONIES

Darling
Lord Howe
Island
Sydney

NEW
ZEALAND

Mariana
Islands
Guam
Marshall
Islands
Caroline
Islands
Gilbert
Islands
KAISER WILHELM'S
LAND
BISMARCK
ARCHIPELAGO
NEW
GUINEA
PAPUA
Solomon
Islands
Ellice
Islands
Santa Cruz
Islands
PACIFIC
OCEAN
New
Caledonia
Fiji

AFTER

Deportation

By the mid-19th century, the French government reduced prison costs by sending "undesirables" to their far-off colonies. This woodcut depicts the deportation of prisoners from Toulon to Cayenne on the steamboat *Ceres*.

administration were all emulated, and Japan was able to modernize rapidly by adopting European ideas (see pp.356–57). However, despite being of European descent, the Boers of South Africa moved into the Natal, Orange Free State, and Transvaal regions of the country, so eager were they to escape British rule (see p.361). By 1900, much of the inhabited world was governed, directly or indirectly, by Europeans, or those of European descent.

After World War II, most colonies were granted, or won their independence. Today, only a few remnants of the great colonial powers survive.

THE END OF COLONIALISM

Portuguese possessions were some of the last colonies to become independent 412–13 ≫. In North and South America and Australia, **European rule left a permanent stamp.** In China, it left scarcely a trace.

AFRICA

Africans increasingly gained independence after World War II 392–405 ≫, but economic difficulties often caused **political instability** in the new nations. This often led to dictatorships—by 1976, 21 African countries had military governments.

AFRICAN IMMIGRATION TO EUROPE

Economic and political development failures in Africa, and new immigration and refugee policies in Europe, saw **mass migration** by African

peoples. Between 1960–89 an estimated 70,000–100,000 highly skilled African workers went to Europe, but they often faced discrimination.

INDIGENOUS PEOPLES

Indigenous peoples such as the forest people of the Amazon, the tribal people of India, and the Inuit of the Arctic **lost their land** during colonization. There is still a threat of territorial invasion, and the plundering of resources, in these places.

BRITISH QUEEN Born 1819 Died 1901

Queen Victoria

"We are not **interested** in the possibilities of **defeat**."

QUEEN VICTORIA, TO ARTHUR BALFOUR, MEMBER OF PARLIAMENT, 1899

Q ueen Victoria, the longest-reigning monarch in British history, was the only child of the Duke of Kent, fourth son of George III, and his German wife, Princess Victoria of Saxe-Coburg-Saalfield. Fair-haired and blue-eyed, she spent most of her childhood in the seclusion of London's Kensington Palace, and had little contact with her uncle, William IV. She was 11 when she found out her royal destiny, at which point she famously declared: "I will be good."

On the death of William IV in 1837, the 18-year-old Princess Victoria acceded to the throne. Until then, she had slept in her mother's room, and one of her first decisions, on moving into Buckingham Palace, was to insist on a bedroom of her own. In political matters,

Victoria's first prime minister, the fatherly Lord Melbourne, was her early mentor, but within a couple of years he was replaced by the love of her life, Albert of Saxe-Coburg-Gotha.

A royal courtship

As one of Victoria's German cousins, Albert was considered an appropriate husband. He was just three months younger than Victoria—in fact, the same midwife had assisted at both of their births—but he was mature for his age. He was an

A picture of royalty
A photographic portrait of the "great white queen." Photography, an invention of her reign, made Victoria an international icon, spreading her image around the world.

Prince Albert
Albert was married to Victoria for 21 years. After his death, Victoria reputedly made decisions based on what she thought he would have done.

The Victorian family
As a loving couple with a happy home life, the queen and her consort, seen here with some of their nine children, exemplified respectable "Victorian" family values.

intelligent, deeply serious young man, fluent in several languages and acutely conscious of his duties as the unofficial king of England. But it was his looks as much as his character, and his recommendation by Victoria's uncle, Leopold I of Belgium, that persuaded her to propose to this "perfect being." She was drawn to his appearance, adoring his "exquisite nose" and "beautiful figure," which she described as "broad in the shoulders."

Love and marriage

Victoria and Albert presented the public with the novel spectacle of a young and serenely happy royal family. In the space of 17 years, they had nine children: four sons and five daughters. The birth of the Princess Royal ("Vicky") in 1840 was followed, a year later, by the birth of a son and heir, the future Edward VII. For the birth of her eighth baby, Prince Leopold, Victoria had pain relief in the shape of newly available chloroform. She found it "soothing, quieting and delightful beyond measure," and this royal endorsement made it easier for other women to opt for pain relief in childbirth.

To reach their new homes at Balmoral in Scotland and Osborne on the Isle of Wight, the royal family took advantage of the railroads, another recent invention. For Victoria, Balmoral Castle, with its specially designed turrets and tartans, was a

Exhibiting the world
Victoria arrives for the opening of the Great Exhibition "of the works of industry of all nations" at the Crystal Palace in London's Hyde Park.

First Boer War
This jug, bearing Victoria's image, commemorates the First Boer War, 1880–81, in which Transvaal Boers resisted British efforts to annex South Africa, winning self-governance under nominal British oversight.

"dear paradise" and "… Albert's own creation, own work, own building, own laying-out." Her beloved husband's interest in art and design culminated in the Great Exhibition of 1851, for which 112,000 items from across the world were displayed in the Crystal Palace, a glass and iron exhibition hall in Hyde Park, London, of roughly 21 acres (85,000 m²).

The widow of Windsor

Albert's sudden death from typhoid in 1861 was a shock from which Victoria never fully recovered. As the "widow of Windsor," she withdrew from public life and lost some of her early popularity. But time was on her side. Partly as a result of Albert's steadying influence, she had removed herself from direct involvement in political conflicts, so that the Crown eventually came to be seen as above party politics, a neutral guarantee of constitutional stability. Even so, Victoria had strong personal opinions on the major issues and

Victoria Cross
This military decoration for conspicuous bravery was created by Queen Victoria in 1856.

personalities of the day. She disliked the great Liberal leader, William Ewart Gladstone, because he spoke to her as if she were "a public meeting." She had a much better relationship with his rival, Benjamin Disraeli, who coaxed and flattered the widowed queen into renewing her interest and participation in public life. It was Disraeli who had Victoria proclaimed Empress of India, a title and a role in which she took great interest and pride.

By 1887, the year in which she celebrated her Golden Jubilee, the 50th anniversary of her reign, Victoria had regained her early popularity. Ten years later, on the occasion of the Diamond Jubilee of 1897, the queen-empress commanded global esteem and affection. The spectacular celebrations in London were attended by representatives of her 387 million subjects around the world. Soon afterward, her health began to fail, and she was 81 when she died in January 1901. By that time, she was related to so many royal families that she was popularly known as the "grandmother of Europe".

End of an era
The funeral procession of Queen Victoria, February 1901. She was laid to rest in the Frogmore mausoleum at Windsor Castle, alongside Albert.

"We are **not** amused."

QUEEN VICTORIA, ATTRIBUTED, 1900

TIMELINE

■ **May 24, 1819** Alexandrina Victoria is born at Kensington Palace, London.

■ **June 26, 1830** William IV becomes King of the United Kingdom of Great Britain and Ireland, and with no legitimate children to succeed him, his niece Victoria becomes heiress presumptive.

■ **1830** The Regency Act of 1830 assures that Victoria cannot become queen until she is 18.

■ **May 24, 1837** Turns 18 and becomes eligible to assume the throne should her uncle die.

■ **June 20, 1837** Becomes Queen of the United Kingdom of Great Britain and Ireland when William IV dies of heart failure.

■ **June 28, 1838** Coronation ceremony at Westminster Abbey, London.

■ **February 10, 1840** Marries her cousin Prince Albert of Saxe-Coburg-Gotha in the Chapel Royal at St. James's Palace, London.

■ **May 6, 1840** England issues its first postage stamp, costing one penny, which bears the image of Queen Victoria.

■ **June 10, 1840** The first of a total of seven attempts on her life is made when Edward Oxford fires two bullets into her coach—she is pregnant at the time.

■ **November 21, 1840** Her first child, the Princess Royal Victoria Adelaide Mary, is born. Victoria and Albert will have a further eight children.

■ **May 1851** Victoria opens the Great Exhibition in Hyde Park, London, which showcases international culture and industry.

■ **1853** Chloroform administered to Queen Victoria in childbirth.

■ **1855** Livingstone names the Victoria Falls on Africa's Zambezi River after the Queen.

■ **1856** Balmoral Castle is completed.

■ **June 26, 1857** Victoria Cross awarded for the first time; 62 soldiers and sailors receive it.

■ **December 14, 1861** Devastated by the death of Albert, Victoria sinks into depression and starts a period of isolation, withdrawing from public life.

■ **May 1, 1876** Proclaimed the "Empress of India" by the British Prime Minister Benjamin Disraeli.

SHILLING SHOWING QUEEN VICTORIA

■ **1887** Golden Jubilee marks her 50th year as monarch. The celebrations help to draw Victoria back into public life.

■ **September 22, 1896** Victoria's reign surpasses that of George III as the longest in English, Scottish, and British history.

■ **1897** Diamond Jubilee is celebrated with a procession to St. Paul's Cathedral in London, and a thanksgiving mass.

■ **January 22, 1901** Dies of a cerebral hemorrhage at Osborne House on the Isle of Wight, bringing to an end a reign of nearly 64 years.

From 1511, the Portuguese, Dutch, Spanish, English, and French bargained and fought for control of Southeast Asia and Australasia.

EUROPEAN PROFITS
The Portuguese captured the Malaysian peninsula in 1511, moved on to the Spice Islands (the Moluccas) in 1513, and then China, Japan, and Indonesia. The Spanish arrived next, setting up **plantations** in the Philippines in 1565. Two **private trading companies** followed—the English East India Company (1600), based in India, and the Dutch East India Company (1602), which set up colonies in Asia.

COOK IN BOTANY BAY

CLAIMS ON AUSTRALIA
In 1770, James Cook **<< 320–321** explored Australia's fertile east coast, and claimed New South Wales for Britain. In 1829, Britain claimed the whole of Australia, and in 1840, annexed New Zealand too. In both cases, this action preempted French colonization.

The European colonization of Australia began in 1788 with the establishment of a British penal colony in Botany Bay (modern Sydney), New South Wales. Until then, Britain had transported convicts to North America, but the American Revolution (see pp.298–99) made this impossible. The use of Britain's new Australian colony for this purpose had been proposed in 1779, by English botanist Sir Joseph Banks. The natives seemed more peaceful than the Maoris of New Zealand—and this was to prove

and armed resistance proved ineffectual. Foreign diseases, to which the Aboriginal population had little resistance, also caused widespread mortality. A smallpox epidemic broke out in 1789, followed by influenza, typhus, chicken pox, whooping cough, tuberculosis, and syphilis.

A stolen generation
The prevalent view of Aboriginals is of a desert people, but this is only because they were driven into arid areas that were of no interest to British settlers: in

Waitangi with the Maoris in 1840. The chiefs ceded sovereignty in return for protection and guarantees against further encroachment on their lands.

However, the treaty was not upheld, and the settlers' continuing demands for land led to the New Zealand (or Maori) Wars, fought between 1843–47 and 1860–72. The Maoris were equipped with firearms acquired through decades of trading, and fought back staunchly. The first outbreak of war was contained relatively quickly, but the second became a protracted

Colonial Resistance

Resistance to the European colonization of Australia, New Zealand, and Southeast Asia brought very different outcomes for the indigenous populations. In Australia and New Zealand, it led to the subjugation of the Aboriginals and Maoris; in Southeast Asia, to eventual independence.

Dene-Harding revolver
The explosive power of European firearms such as this Dene-Harding revolver ensured that the colonizing powers swiftly overcame indigenous populations.

their downfall. When James Cook landed in 1770 (see BEFORE), there were 300,000–350,000 Aboriginals in Australia. Over the next 150 years, this figure declined by 80 percent. Initially, relations between native inhabitants and settlers were amicable, but as the colony expanded, the Aboriginals resisted. Their arrows and spears were no match for British guns, however,

1788 the Aboriginal population was concentrated in the same fertile areas as the most populous parts of modern Australia. British governors were instructed to protect the Aboriginals, but they often imposed British values and, in the late 19th century, even removed native children (the "Stolen Generation") from their families, and moved them into state institutions.

Maori wars
Maori resistance to European settlers in New Zealand was more fierce. Both Dutch explorer Abel Tasman and Cook received violent receptions, but Cook noted that tribal differences made united resistance unlikely. By the early 19th century, European and US seal and whale hunters were trading with the Maoris. As disputes among tribes and between Maoris and settlers were common (and to preempt French and American interests), Britain negotiated the Treaty of

guerrilla campaign that cost the lives of around 1,000 Europeans and some 2,000 Maoris.

3 MILLION acres of Maori land was confiscated in the 19th century, and most Maoris were confined to New Zealand's less fertile North Island

75 PERCENT of the Maori population still lived there at the end of the 20th century

The Dutch East Indies
During the 17th and 18th centuries, the Dutch monopolized trade with the Spice Islands (so named because prized spices, such as nutmeg, originated there), and took control of most of what is now Indonesia. In the 1790s, the Dutch East India Company (see BEFORE) collapsed and the Dutch government took over. From 1830 it forced Indonesian peasants to grow export crops, such as indigo and coffee, at set prices and, from 1870, allowed Dutch investors to lease land and establish plantations. This led to an outbreak of nationalist resistance, and the Dutch fought a series of wars between 1821 and 1901. Ultimately,

Ticket of leave
After being transported to Australia in chains, some convicts who had served a proportion of their sentence with good behavior were granted a Ticket of Leave (TOL) passport and allowed restricted travel.

Conflict in Burma
From 1823–87, the British fought three wars to gain control of Burma (now Myanmar), and in 1886 the country was proclaimed a province of British India.

political organization brought success, with Sukarno's Indonesian National Party finally forcing independence in 1949.

French Indochina
The first Europeans in Indochina (Vietnam, Laos, and Cambodia) had been French missionaries, who took Roman Catholicism to Vietnam during the 17th century. The murder of French Christians there provided the pretext for Emperor Napoleon III to invade in 1858, but resistance was strong, both from the Chinese, who claimed sovereignty over Vietnam, and from the indigenous population. In 1863, France took control of southern Vietnam and established a protectorate in Cambodia. Between 1874 and 1884,

"The loss of America what can repay?
New colonies seek for at Botany Bay."

JOHN FREETH, ENGLISH POET, *c*. 1731–1808

Maori *wahaika*
Weapons such as this *wahaika*—a short club made from wood, whale-bone, or stone—were used for close fighting. By the time of the Maori Wars, the Maoris had also acquired firearms.

the French set up more protectorates in northern and central Vietnam. In 1887, these were incorporated, along with Cambodia, in the Union of French Indochina. Territories ruled by Siam (which are now known as Laos) became a protectorate in 1893. The French tried to impose French culture on the Union. However, along with communism, it was Gallic education that inspired the Indochinese to seek the French ideals of *liberté, egalité,* and *fraternité* (see pp.302–03).

British Malaya
Britain first established a presence in Malaya in 1786, and in 1826 formed a colony called the Straits Settlements, which included Malacca and Singapore. During the 19th and early 20th century Britain set up protectorates over a number of Malay states including part of Brunei and North Borneo. By 1914, Britain had colonial control of British Malaya (now known as Malaysia).

The British established highly profitable tin mines and rubber plantations in Malaya. However, rather than exploiting the indigenous population, they imported Chinese labor for the mines, and Indian workers for the plantations, while encouraging the Malays to farm for a living. The result was a more peaceful coexistence than in many other European colonies in Southeast Asia.

AFTER »

World War II irreversibly altered the balance of world power, and led to the dismantling of the European empires.

ASIA AFTER IMPERIALISM
Britain granted commonwealth status to Australia in 1901, and New Zealand in 1907, recognizing their self-government within the empire. British Southeast Asian colonies were made independent between 1957 and 1984. Indonesia became independent from the Dutch in 1949, and in 1954 the French lost Indochina, leading to the division of Vietnam **412–13** ».

MIXED FORTUNES
After European withdrawal, the Philippines, Indonesia, and Vietnam all experienced civil unrest or war,

while Japan and, later, Malaysia, Singapore, and Indonesia went on to achieve such rapid economic growth that they were dubbed the **"Tiger economies" 456–57** ».

AUSTRALIA'S ABORIGINALS
While Southeast Asian independence meant self-representation for indigenous people, the same was not true in Australia. The **Aboriginal population declined** to 60,000 in 1921 and the interwar period saw **renewed confiscation** of land.

In 1938, on the 150th anniversary of European colonization, Aboriginals declared Australia Day, the national holiday, to be a day of mourning.

SUKARNO, FIRST INDONESIAN PRESIDENT

BEFORE «

A rich supply of lucrative resources led to competition between European powers for a stake in India. As the Mughal Empire's controlling grip on the area weakened, British influence increased.

RICHES OF THE EAST

Europe's craze for spices made India very alluring. The **lucrative** spice trade had tempted **the Portuguese** to India since the mid-15th century. By the 16th century, India was visited by **Italians, English, French, and Dutch,** all eager to trade, seek adventure, or spread Christianity in the area.

EAST INDIA COMPANIES (EICs)

To rival Portugal, **the EICs were formed by England (1600) and the Netherlands (1602)** « 276–77. These companies acted as trade organizations, and later provided a military presence in the region.

ENGLISH EAST INDIA COMPANY COAT OF ARMS

MUGHAL EMPIRE

The English EIC prospered, and worked with the ruling Mughal emperors « 244–45 well into the 19th century. However, as the **British fortunes rose, the fragile Mughal Empire went into decline**.

BRITISH INVOLVEMENT

Short reigns, protracted war, and peasant revolts undermined the Mughals. Indian provinces became more independent of central rule, paving the way for **British interference**.

The **British Raj**

The desire for power and wealth has led nations to expand their influence far beyond their frontiers. India became the jewel in the British Empire's crown, and the British Raj (Hindi for "rule")—which ran from 1858 to 1947—was the culmination of decades of British involvement and domination in the Indian subcontinent.

A t the turn of the 18th century, the long-established English East India Company (see BEFORE) enabled Britain to enjoy unprecedented privileges in India, with footholds in economic, political, and military life. To protect this situation, the EIC had increased the number of troops deemed necessary to defend its establishments. Rivalry with other trading companies, especially the French, was fierce and led to the Seven Years War (see pp.296–97), a slow, stuttering campaign for British expansion and control. In 1756, under Robert Clive, a soldier and statesman described as "the conqueror of India," the British claimed the richest Mughal province, Bengal, in the northeast of the country. This became the foundation of British rule in India. The recapture of Calcutta by Clive in late 1756, the storming of nearby French Chandernagore in early 1757, and Clive's success at Plassey in June of that year were milestones in the British domination of India. Finally, in 1763, the Mughal Emperor Shah Alam II formally inducted the EIC, and Clive, into the Mughal hierarchy. As *Diwan* (chancellor) for Bengal, the EIC received a title that amounted to

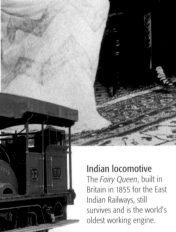

Viceroy Curzon at the Maharajah's Palace
Nathaniel George Curzon (fourth right) was Viceroy of India from 1898 to 1905, and ruled in place of the monarch. Devastating famines, and a dispute with Lord Kitchener, chief of the Indian army, led to his resignation.

sovereignty over the province. The British gained administrative powers throughout India and became more of a government than a trading concern.

British influence knew no bounds, from the building of roads, an extensive railroad network, and schools, to an administrative system of officials that emerged as a model for the British civil service. There was an agreement to allow Christian missions to operate in India, aided by influential figures in London such as the antislavery campaigner William Wilberforce (see pp.308–09). Hinduism was seen as something from which the people were to be emancipated. This evangelical zeal led to the eventual erosion of British tolerance and support of Indian faiths.

Indian locomotive
The *Fairy Queen*, built in Britain in 1855 for the East Indian Railways, still survives and is the world's oldest working engine.

subject to increased supervision from the British government. When its royal charter—sovereign permission to operate as a corporation—was renewed in 1813, the EIC had to surrender its monopoly of trade in India, allowing other corporations to operate in the region.

The Indian mutiny

Under the EIC, there was some rebellious behavior among Indian soldiers (sepoys) serving in the British army, who were aggrieved at their treatment. These sepoys bore the brunt of the First British–Afghan war (1838–42) and were shipped to China to fight in the Opium Wars (see pp.354–55).

By the late 1770s the East India Company was burdened with massive military expenditure and was in dire financial straits. India was of huge national importance to Britain, and so the British government decided to overhaul the EIC. The Regulating Act of 1773 resulted in the EIC's becoming

The Siege of Lucknow
The British Garrison in Lucknow, in northern India, was besieged by Indian rebels on July 1, 1857. Despite the large numbers of mutineers, the siege was finally ended by Sir Colin Campbell's relief force in November 1857.

"The key of India is London."

BENJAMIN DISRAELI, ADDRESSING THE HOUSE OF LORDS, MARCH 1881

impose tariffs or subsidies on imports and exports. Instead, they invested in the country's infrastructure, especially trains, which assisted economic development, and irrigation works. On the tea estates that proliferated from the 1850s, indentured labor was widely employed. Most Indians lived in abject poverty, a state not helped by severe famines in the second half of the 19th century. Conditions for migrants were miserable and mortality rates high. Their plight, and the continued deployment of Indian troops on imperial service in other countries, stirred nationalist feelings, resulting in an awakening Indian political consciousness.

INDENTURED LABOR A type of labor that binds apprentice to master. The employer offers little pay, but provides food and lodgings.

In December 1885, the Indian National Congress, or Congress Party, met for the first time in Bombay (now Mumbai). As the main nationalist political party, it was initially moderate and widely representative. By the beginning of the 20th century, however, a younger, more politically militant generation of Indians emerged, calling for independence from British rule (see pp.408–11).

AFTER »

The flash point was reached in 1857, in Meerut, northern India, when rumor spread that the British had introduced a new rifle and cartridge into the Indian Army. The cartridges, which soldiers had to bite open, were lubricated with a grease containing pig and cow fat, offending both Hindu and Muslim soldiers. The revolt spread across the country, and was finally quelled in 1859 after much bloodshed. In 1858 a royal decree stated that all EIC rights were to be handed over to the British Crown. Victoria assumed the role of Queen of India and Britain. The reign of the EIC was over, and the British Raj had begun.

Christian miniature
Indian artists often painted Christian subjects in order to appeal to the increasing Christian population of the country and patrons of the British Raj.

Rule Britannia

Initially, after the Indian Mutiny and the decline of the EIC, many policies remained unchanged, yet British attitudes toward Indians shifted from openness to insularity. As more British families arrived with their servants, private clubs were set up that became symbols of wealth and snobbery. Facilitated by new railroads, exports such as cotton, wheat, and tea enriched the British, yet profits rarely reached native pockets. Despite the fledgling nature of industries such as textiles, and their potential for collapse, the British insisted on an economic policy of *laissez-faire*, or free trade, refusing to

In the 20th century, demands for Indian independence grew. Indian sovereignty was accompanied by the division of the country.

THE FREEDOM STRUGGLE
At the end of the 19th century, calls for Indian independence were growing. In 1905, Lord Curzon **partitioned Bengal**, dividing it into two states. This led to a nationwide protest.

RELIGIOUS DIVIDE
Bengal's population was mainly **Hindu in the west** and **Muslim in the east**. Partition was reversed in 1911 after great political unrest.

PARTITION OF INDIA
The move for **Indian independence** was galvanized by the arrival of **Mahatma Gandhi 408–09** ». Committed to ridding his native land

FLAG OF PAKISTAN

of foreign rule, his charismatic personality helped to unite the country in the struggle. After arduous constitutional negotiations, the British agreed to transfer power on **August 15, 1947**. As they left India, the **largest mass migration in history** took place. Freedom led to partitioning, with the creation of the independent nations of **the Dominion of Pakistan and the Union of India 410–11** ».

SRI LANKA
Sri Lanka (**Ceylon** before 1972) lies 19 miles (31 km) off the coast of India. Parts of Sri Lanka were colonized by the Portuguese and Dutch in the 16th and 17th centuries. The whole country was **ceded to the British Empire in 1815**. A nationalist movement arose in the early 20th century and independence was granted in 1948.

« BEFORE

The **Opium Wars**

By 1838, use of opium, a highly addictive drug, was spiraling out of control in China. Increasingly concerned by the British trafficking of the narcotic, the Chinese government took prohibitive action, leading to a series of conflicts between the two countries.

The Opium Wars of the mid-19th century were the culmination of more than 50 years of strained Anglo-Chinese relations.

THE LADY HUGHES

In 1784 a British merchant ship, the *Lady Hughes*, fired a cannon salute and **accidentally killed two Chinese officials**. Chinese law required that whoever was responsible should be surrendered to the authorities. The gunner was reluctantly handed over, and he was immediately strangled. Thereafter, Westerners **refused to submit to Chinese law**.

THE MACARTNEY EMBASSY

In 1792, **Lord Macartney** led a large British delegation to the summer palace of **Emperor Qianlong** at Rehe to request the accreditation of a British minister at court, the opening of more ports, and the provision of an island base. He was granted an audience but **refused to perform the kotow**, the respectful ceremonial three prostrations and nine head knockings. Qianlong accepted Macartney's gifts but **rejected all the envoy's requests**.

Opium smoking
Opium imports were sanctioned under the 1858 Treaty of Tianjin and, in consequence, opium growing and addiction to the drug spread throughout China. In 1906, opium cultivation was finally banned and opium dens were forced to close. The apparatus for opium smoking was confiscated and burned in public bonfires.

In an attempt to curb the opium problem, the Chinese government appointed a leading official, Lin Zexu, to suppress trade in Guangzhou, a port city in the south of the country. On his arrival, Lin confiscated all opium stocks, and forced foreign residents to sign a bond agreeing to stop trading in the drug. The British government, having learned that its citizens had been imprisoned, sent an expeditionary force to China.

This force blockaded Guangzhou and, moving north, threatened the capital Beijing. Negotiations followed that left neither side satisfied. In 1842, a larger expeditionary force brought about a Chinese surrender, ending the First Opium War. China was compelled to negotiate the Treaty of Nanjing (see right), which ceded Hong Kong to Britain, admitted missionaries, controlled external tariffs, opened five treaty ports, and removed Westerners from Chinese jurisdiction. However, the relationship between Britain and

Sword used in Opium Wars
The outcome of the conflict between Britain and China was largely determined by weaponry. Chinese swords—like this example, captured by a British naval officer in 1842—were no match for British firearms.

China remained uneasy, and war flared up again in 1856. In this Second Opium War (also known as the Arrow War), the British were joined by the French. By 1860 China had been defeated, and was forced to grant further privileges to Britain, which were later extended to other Western powers.

The Taiping Rebellion

China in the mid-19th century was not only under attack from foreign powers, it was also under threat from a series of internal rebellions, the largest of which was the Taiping Rebellion.

In 1836, a Christian teacher, Hong Xiuquan, had a series of dreams that led him to believe he had a mission to restore China to Christianity. He made converts among peasants and miners in Guangxi, south China, and in January 1851 declared the establishment of the *Taiping Tianguo*, the Heavenly Kingdom of Great Peace. In 1853, Taiping rebels

agreement that envoys of both sovereigns will sign the treaty, in English

signatures of the three Chinese ambassadors, Qiying, Yilibu, and Niu Jian

agreement that envoys of both sovereigns will sign the treaty, in Chinese

signature of Henry Pottinger, the British ambassador to China

The Nanjing Treaty
The Treaty of Nanjing, 1842, was the first of the "unequal treaties," which gave benefits to Western powers without offering reciprocal advantages to the Chinese state.

The Chinese Army 1880
China's first modern army, the Anhui Army, which was raised by statesman Li Hongzhang to campaign against a series of mid-19th-century rebellions, adopted Western-style drills and Western-style weapons.

captured Nanjing, and established a state in which gambling and opium smoking were both banned, Taiping Christianity was the only religion, land was to be shared out equally, and women were given equal rights.

In 1860, a Taiping assault on Shanghai was defeated by the Western-trained "Ever-Victorious Army." In 1864, the Hunan army—organized on a network of personal loyalty and financed by a new tax on internal trade—recaptured Nanjing. Hong Xiuquan committed suicide and the rebellion came to an end, though pockets of Taiping resistance continued until 1868.

Missionaries

Christian missionaries gained the right to preach, travel, and own property in China under the unequal treaties (see above). After 1860, the number of Protestant and Catholic missionaries operating in China rose sharply. Missionaries initially concentrated on converting the population, but later ran schools and hospitals. Their presence

threatened the position of the Chinese scholar-officials, and anti-missionary incidents occurred, the most notorious being the massacre of French Sisters of Charity at Tianjin in 1870.

Self-strengthening

After the Opium Wars, the scholar Wei Yuan suggested "building ships, making weapons, and learning the superior techniques of the barbarians." The first "self-strengthening" projects began in the 1860s. In 1866 Wojen, a Mongol Grand Secretary, complained that self-strengthening ideas were not compatible with traditional Confucian government. Nevertheless, in 1872 the statesman Li Hongzhang started a steamship company to compete with foreign shipping on the Yangzi, and later established coal mines that led to the building of China's first railroad.

However, Japan's dramatic defeat of China's army and navy in the Sino-Japanese War (see below) seemed to indicate that attempts at self-strengthening were a failure.

AFTER ≫

In the wake of the Opium Wars, China experienced a period of unrest, both domestically and internationally.

SCRAMBLE FOR CHINA
China's defeat in the Sino–Japanese War precipitated a **scramble for territory**: Russia obtained an agreement to extend the Trans–Siberian railroad across Manchuria in northeast China; Germany seized Qingdao in the north; France obtained commercial concessions in the southwest; and Britain gained a 99-year lease on the "New Territories," opposite Hong Kong Island.

THE EMPRESS DOWAGER
In 1856, a concubine named **Yehonola** gave birth to the future Tongzhi emperor. As Empress Dowager Cixi **she dominated the court until 1908.** She has been accused of having murdered her daughter-in-law, of misappropriating naval funds, and of supporting the Boxer Uprising (see below).

EMPRESS DOWAGER CIXI

THE BOXER UPRISING
The Boxers United in Righteousness—so called because of the ritual "invincibility" boxing they practiced—attacked Beijing in May 1900 in a backlash **against Christian missionaries**. Britain sent 2,000 troops to stop them, but the Empress Dowager ordered the Imperial army to turn them away. Westerners were executed and thousands of **Chinese Christians were killed**. In the aftermath of the siege, Chinese officials were executed and compensation was paid to the West.

DECISIVE MOMENT

SINO-JAPANESE WAR

The origins of this conflict lay in a struggle between China and Japan over influence in Korea. Despite expectations of a Chinese victory, the contest was one-sided. First the Huai army was defeated at Pyongyang in present-day North Korea. Then, in September 1894, the Chinese Beiyang fleet engaged the Japanese fleet off the mouth of the Yalu River, at the border of North Korea and China. Four Chinese ships were destroyed; the rest took refuge at Weihaiwei. China was forced to sign the Treaty of Shimonoseki, recognizing Korean independence, and ceding Taiwan to Japan.

« BEFORE

Japan's history reveals that it has rarely been at peace. For centuries, the Imperial court and the warrior classes wrestled for control.

REUNIFICATION OF JAPAN
From the mid-15th to late 16th centuries, Japan was riven by **civil wars,** and by 1560 a handful of **warring families** vied for supremacy **« 168–69**. The emperor remained as a **figurehead**, without power, and three outstanding leaders:

TOKUGAWA IEYASU

Oda Nobunaga, Toyotomi Hideyoshi, and Tokugawa Ieyasu displayed **superior military tactics** and **shocking acts of brutality** to unify Japan. Ieyasu was made a shogun in 1603, and was recognized as the greatest power in the land.

TOKUGAWA RULE
With Japan reunified, Ieyasu's aim was to maintain control. **All foreign influences were discouraged**, and from 1635 Japanese subjects were unable to leave Japan–those Japanese who were overseas at the time were refused reentry on pain of death. Christianity was banned, and foreign merchants and missionaries expelled. With its **borders closed,** contact with outsiders could be strictly regulated by the shogun **« 242–43**.

A CLOSED COUNTRY
For two centuries, descendants of the Tokugawa shoguns kept the peace, and the population prospered. But from the early 19th century, environmental and political troubles caused the **shoguns' grip on power to slip**. Famine and earthquakes caused thousands of deaths, trade within Japan widened the gap between rich and poor, and foreigners sailed into Japanese waters.

Rising Sun

The "Land of the Rising Sun," as it is known to most Japanese, has had a turbulent history. For centuries it was a society ruled by fierce warlords, and for over 200 years it was closed to the rest of the world. Ambitious and industrious Japan quickly caught up with the West, but success came at a heavy price.

Japan's development from a land of feudal lords into a world power began in the 19th century. During the reunification of Japan (see BEFORE), the country was closed to foreign visitors and trade, but in 1853 the American government sent Commodore Matthew Perry to Edo (Tokyo) in command of four warships. Perry demanded the opening of Japanese ports for trade, making it clear he would return. Resistance seemed futile in the face of superior naval power. In 1854, Perry returned with an even larger fleet, and the shogunate (military rulers) signed the Treaty of Kanagawa. Japan was forced to open its borders.

Westernizing society
Similar treaties with Britain, France, Russia, and the Netherlands followed. They too were successful in demanding rights to trade, and Japan gradually lost control over its own customs duties. The Japanese people viewed these unequal treaties as humiliating, and a series of rebellions brought nearly 700 years of shogunate rule to an end. Following the Meiji Restoration (see right), the

Tokyo–Yokohama railroad
This poster, dating from 1875, celebrates the Tokyo terminus of the railroad, built in 1872 with the aid of foreign engineers. The image was issued only seven years after the Meiji Restoration opened Japan to foreign ideas.

new regime thought that Western ideas might make Japan stronger and more able to compete. A popular slogan of the day was "*oitsuke, oikose*" ("catch up, overtake"). The old feudal class system was restructured from "samurai warrior–farmer–artisan–merchant" to "nobles–samurai descendants–commoners." In 1873, conscription was introduced so that all men, not just those from the noble class, as previously, could join the military. In 1877, in a further move toward Westernization, Tokyo University was established, and employed several foreign teachers. A modern mint was set up, and in 1882 the Bank of Japan opened with a standardized decimal currency based on the yen.

Population shift
Perhaps the greatest symbol of Japan's modernization was the railway. The first was opened in October 1872, and within 15 years 1,000 miles (1,600 km) of track had been laid. It had a profound effect on the country and its economy. Suburbs grew as people now lived away from their place of work, and the age of commuting had begun.

> **SHOGUN** Prior to 1868, shoguns ruled Japan. They were hereditary leaders who commanded armies that included a warrior class known as the samurai.

Japan at war
After years of turmoil, there was a revived sense of national identity and pride in Japan. The cry was not only "*oitsuke, oikose*" but also "*fukoku kyohei*" ("rich nation, strong army"). Japan was not to be toyed with. In the spring of 1894, Korea called for military aid from China to put down a rebellion. China obliged, and so did Japan. The rebellion was swiftly dealt with, but both sides had interests in Korea and stayed on. The Japanese were determined to fight, and officially declared war on August 1.

The Sino-Japanese War had begun. In the battles that followed, Japan proved superior, especially at sea. The naval base of Port Arthur in Manchuria, on the northeast coast of China, was seized in November, and the Chinese fleet destroyed at Weihai in the eastern province of Shandong in February 1895. The Treaty of Shimonoseki in April 1895 saw China abandon its interests in Korea and cede territory to Japan, including Taiwan. Japan also gained rights in Manchuria, which had rich natural resources of lumber, iron, oil, gold, and uranium.

This was the first major step in Japan's empire-building in Asia. Russia reacted by persuading the French and German governments that Japan should give up its stronghold in Manchuria because it caused instability. Japan bowed to pressure and reluctantly agreed. When Russia refused to withdraw its troops from China, following an uprising against foreign influences known as the Boxer Rebellion (see pp.354–55), the increasing tension with Russia eventually erupted into war in 1904.

Japan was by now an impressive military force, while Russia was severely disadvantaged by the 1905 Revolution (see pp.376–77). Japan was triumphant. The ensuing Portsmouth Treaty, signed in September 1905, recognized Japan's interests in Korea and granted them occupation of the Liaodong Peninsula in Manchuria. Japan quickly established control over Korea. It disbanded the army and annexed the nation in 1910 with no international opposition.

Japan had succeeded in its aims—it was now taken seriously by Western powers. The unequal treaties, which had caused so much bitterness, were revised and full tariff (customs) control restored in 1911. In a mere half-century, Japan had gone from being virtually dismissed as a backward country to a major world power.

Modern power
A Japanese naval squadron is shown here steaming in to bombard Port Arthur, Manchuria, and attack Russian ships. During the Russo–Japanese war, Japan proved militarily superior, especially at sea.

"Enrich the country, strengthen the military."
JAPAN'S NATIONAL SLOGAN DURING THE MEIJI ERA, 1868–1912

As Japan entered the 20th century, it seemed stable. This soon changed. Economic depression and dissatisfaction with Japan's role in world affairs eventually led to war.

DISCONTENT
During World War I 372–73 >> industrial production grew fivefold and exports more than trebled in Japan. After the war, **prices collapsed and economic recession** set in. Rural incomes fell sharply and the gap between rich and poor, city and countryside widened. Both the military and public became increasingly angry, and many **blamed the influence of Western ideas**.

AN UNEASY ALLIANCE
Japan maintained an **uneasy relationship** with foreign powers. Japan attended the Versailles Peace Conference in 1919 374–75 >> where the victors of World War I met to negotiate peace treaties with the defeated Germany. But **Japan did not always feel a true equal**. In 1920, Japan was one of the founding members of **the League of Nations 374–75 >>**, which was set up to work toward disarmament and diplomacy, but it was upset that its proposal for a racial equality clause in the league's charter was rejected. To compound matters, the Washington Arms Limitation Treaty of 1922 limited Japan to three warships, compared with five American and five British.

NATIONALISM
After years of trying to gain respect abroad without success, **Japanese frustration** with Westerners **turned to contempt**. Fiercely ambitious, Japan was set on a path of confrontation with Western powers 402–03 >>.

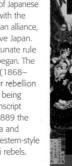

EMPEROR HIROHITO OF JAPAN (1901–89)

DECISIVE MOMENT

THE MEIJI RESTORATION
After US naval officer Matthew Perry demanded the opening of Japanese ports in 1854, the shoguns seemed incapable of dealing with the foreign threat. A group of leading samurai (warriors) formed an alliance, believing that only the restoration of the emperor could save Japan. In 1868 a short civil war brought the nearly 700-year shogunate rule to an end. Emperor Mutsuhito was restored and a new era began. The period of modernization that followed was called the Meiji (1868–1912), but not all were content. In 1877 there was a major rebellion in Kyushu. Traditional forces, including samurai infuriated at being barred from carrying swords, were defeated by the new conscript army. The emperor promised a national assembly, and in 1889 the first-ever formal constitution adopted outside North America and Europe was proclaimed. In this woodcut, Meiji officers in Western-style uniforms are shown accepting the surrender of the samurai rebels.

« BEFORE

Since the 8th century, interaction between the Islamic world and the West has been marked with conflict and unease.

MUSLIM EXPANSION

The Prophet Muhammad was both a political and a spiritual leader. By the time of his death in 632 CE, all of Arabia was **united under Islam**. His first successor, Abu-Bekr, proclaimed a Holy War against Byzantium and Persia. Palestine was captured and Egypt seized. In 711 CE a force of 7,000 Arabs invaded southern Spain **«« 174–77**.

SELJUK TURKS

At the beginning of the 11th century a great wave of Seljuk Turks **«« 177, 206**, led by Tughril Beg, conquered Iran. His successor, Alp Arslan, led the Seljuks to conquer Georgia, Armenia, and much of Asia Minor. They overran Syria and in 1071 defeated the Byzantine emperor Romanus IV in eastern Turkey **«« 199**. This gave the Seljuk Turks a reputation as defenders of Islam and was a major factor in starting the Crusades **«« 200–01**.

SELJUK BOWL

OTTOMAN EMPIRE

A number of Islamic states emerged during the 16th century. The largest was the Ottoman Empire **«« 246–47**, which grew from its original base as a Turkish warrior state in western Anatolia. Ottoman forces took Constantinople in 1453 **«« 207** and Syria and Egypt in 1516–17. In South Asia, Babur founded the Mughal Empire **«« 244–45**. Islamic teachings were carried around the world by missionaries and merchants.

MILITARY LEADER (1881–1922)

ENVER PASHA

Enver Pasha was born in the Black Sea town of Apana in 1881. Enrolling with the military, he was posted to Greece, where he joined a secret group hoping for modernization of the Ottoman Empire. In 1908 Pasha was one of the leaders of the Young Turks that rebelled against the rule of the Sultan Abdul Hamid. During World War I, as minister of war, he aligned Turkey with Germany and Austria–Hungary. On defeat in 1918, Pasha fled to Turkistan, where he was killed in 1922.

Modernizing the empire
Constantinople, at the heart of the Ottoman Empire, was modernized from the 1870s onward with constructions such as the Galata Bridge (pictured), electric lights, a water system, streetcars, and telephones.

The Young Turks Revolt

Five times a day millions of Muslims face Mecca to pray. Peace is the avowed aim, but the spread of Islam has not been without its conflicts. During its history, Muslim societies, such as the Young Turks and the Ottoman Empire, have struggled to define themselves in the modern world.

From the 11th century onward, Islam, under the leadership of the Turks (see BEFORE), had consolidated its hold on the Middle East and made further gains in India, East Asia, and Europe. However, by the 18th century, Europeans came to dominate much of the Muslim world from north Africa to southeast Asia, and this Western imperialism prompted a religious and political crisis.

Some believed that Islam could be restricted to private life and that public life might embrace modern, European ideas about technology, education, and law. One prominent modernist was Jamal Al-Din Al-Afghani (1838–97). Al-Afghani was a major catalyst for Islamic reform. He traveled all over the Muslim world strengthening communities in the hope of driving out the Western powers, but he was convinced that science and technology could be successfully adopted by Islamic countries without compromise to their religion or culture. In the late 19th century, other modernists, such as the Indian Syed Ahmad Khan (1817–98), recommended the reformation of Islamic society along similar lines. He was responsible for founding the Muhammedan Anglo–Oriental College at Aligarh, northern India, in 1875, where Muslims could study Western ideas without alienating themselves from their religion.

Rejecting the West

Conservative Muslim leaders were convinced that Muslim impotence in the face of Christian imperialism was a result of divergence from Islam and deviation from their traditions. Many called for a total rejection of Western ideas. Some concluded that where Muslims no longer lived under Islamic rule in an Islamic territory, they were now in a state of warfare requiring armed struggle, known as *jihad*. A series of *jihad* revivalist movements led to the emergence of Islamist states in Nigeria, Libya, and the Sudan.

During the 19th century, European expansion became an increasingly important force in Muslim societies, and the major states that remained independent responded by undertaking a wide range of reforms. In the Ottoman Empire (see BEFORE) reforms began with attempts by Selim III, who reigned between 1789–1807, to institute a *Nizam-i cedid*, or "New System" of military and bureaucratic organization. His successor, Mahmud II, went on to restore the power and authority to the central government that had been usurped by powerful local lords. Mahmud II's successor, Abdülmecid I, who reigned from 1839–61, embarked on a program of reform that would become known as the *Tanzimat* ("reorganization"). As the empire sought to modernize, it gained the support of the British, and the Crimean War (1853–56) found Britain and the Ottomans allied against Russia. In 1876 Abd al-Hamid II came to the throne, and Russia declared war

> **ISLAMISM An ideology that considers Islam to be both a religion and a system of government. Islamist states are guided by *sharia*–Islamic religious law.**

on the Ottoman Empire in 1877, in an attempt to liberate the Balkan Peninsula from Ottoman rule. In a swift campaign, the Russians drove the Ottomans back and forced them to sign the disastrous Treaty of San Stefano in 1878. This treaty deprived them of most of their European territories, including Bulgaria. Further territorial losses included the loss of Tunisia to the French in 1881 and Egypt to the British in 1882. In order to maintain greater control over the remaining empire, Abd al-Hamid continued the reform process. Great changes were made in education, military affairs,

> **"Turkey is a Muslim country, and Muslim ideas and influence must preponderate."**
> YOUNG TURKS (COMMITTEE OF UNION AND PROGRESS), 1910

LA RÉVOLUTION EN TURQUIE

Sanglant combat autour d'Yildiz-Kiosk. -:- Victoire des Jeunes-Turcs

The victorious Young Turks
This illustration from *Le Petit Journal* shows the Young Turks' successful revolution of 1908. After they marched on Constantinople, the sultan surrendered himself as a prisoner in his palace, the Yildiz Kiosk.

joined by Macedonian rebels as well as large numbers of Young Turks. This group called itself the Committee of Union and Progress (CUP). Abd al-Hamid was forced to give in to the revolutionaries' demands. A constitution was adopted and a parliament created and the Young Turks of the CUP, led by a triumvirate—a group of three people who share power—of whom Enver Pasha (see left) would become the best known, were in command of the empire.

The Young Turks continued the Ottoman reform process, opening schools to women and overseeing legislative progress in women's rights. However, they made a disastrous foreign policy decision. An appraisal of Germany's military capability led them to break neutrality and enter World War I in 1914 on the side of Germany and Austria-Hungary (see pp.372–75).

Revolutionizing the army
Enver Pasha (center) holds a *chibouk*, a traditional smoking pipe. Pasha had trained in Germany and wanted to improve the efficiency of the Ottoman Armed Forces along German lines.

AFTER

and bureaucracy, but he was intolerant of opposition to his rule from groups who thought his reforms were too mild.

In 1902 a meeting in Paris brought together the leadership of the "Young Turks"—a coalition group composed of fervent nationalists wishing to save Turkey from decay and ruin. In the early 1900s, Bulgarian and Macedonian terrorists started bombing Ottoman government buildings, demanding total independence. The two rebellions eventually joined in 1908 when an army regiment stationed in Macedonia rebelled and fled into the hills. It was

The 20th century witnessed continued polarization between the Islamic world and the West.

END OF THE OTTOMAN EMPIRE
At the end of World War I **372–75 ≫** the Allied Powers began the dismemberment of the Ottoman Empire. This led to parts of Turkey

being distributed to Greece. Mustafa Kemal—a Turkish soldier and statesman, widely known as Atatürk—led a successful resistance against this during the Turkish War of Independence (1918–23).

ISLAMIST RESURGENCE
The late 1960s signaled a turning point in Islam. The Arab–Israeli War in

MUSTAFA KEMAL DURING THE TURKISH WAR OF INDEPENDENCE

1967 and the loss of Jerusalem to Israel **414–15 ≫** was a blow to Muslim pride, provoking a call for a return to Islam. The Arab oil embargo of 1973 was a catalyst for resurgence, as was the Iranian revolution of 1978–79 **442–43 ≫**.

FUNDAMENTALISM
The attack on the World Trade Center on September 11, 2001 marked a new era in Islam's continuing internal and external struggle to deal with the challenge of the West **466–67 ≫**.

BEFORE

Europeans began colonizing the African continent as early as the 15th century.

PORTUGUESE EXPLORATION

Portuguese explorers began charting the coast of Africa in 1419. In 1575, the Portuguese built their first colony in what is now **Angola**.

CAPE COLONY

In 1652, the Dutch East India Company **‹‹ 276** founded **Cape Town** as a colony where Dutch ships could stock up on provisions for their onward voyages east.

SLAVE SHACKLES

OTTOMAN INFLUENCE

Between the 16th and late 19th centuries, northern Africa was loosely under the control of the Ottoman Empire **‹‹ 246–47**. Consequently, many aspects of Turkish culture took root in the region. The most profound example of these was **Sufism**, a mystical tradition within Islam.

SLAVERY

From 1500 to 1880, Europeans shipped an estimated **15 million African slaves** to the Americas, where they worked on plantations or in domestic service **‹‹ 280–81**.

ZULU WARRIOR KING (c. 1787–1828)

SHAKA ZULU

In 1816, Shaka became king of the Zulus of southeastern Africa. He revolutionized the Zulu army by introducing strict and arduous training regimens, new battle formations, and new weapons, such as the long-bladed *assegais* (a spear). Shaka led the Zulus in raids on neighboring Nguni villages, which they razed. In this way he systematically expanded his territory and created a powerful kingdom that covered vast areas of the southern coastal and interior regions of Africa, which are known today as KwaZulu-Natal. Shaka was assassinated by his half-brother Dingane.

The Scramble for Africa

Motivated by accounts by explorers and missionaries of vast untapped resources in the heart of the African continent, rival European countries raced to gain possession of African territory during the late 19th century. The race became known as the "Scramble for Africa."

Although several European trading nations had secured coastal settlements around Africa by 1600, by the early 19th century the interior of the continent remained largely uncharted by Europeans, partly because many explorers feared contracting malaria in the vast tropical expanses. In 1820, the development of quinine, an effective treatment for the disease, allowed the exploration of the tropics. By 1835, Europeans had mapped most of northwestern Africa. From the 1840s the Scottish missionary David Livingstone journeyed extensively in central and southern Africa. Expeditions in the 1850s and 1860s by Richard Burton, John Speke, and James Grant located the great central lakes and the source of the Nile. By the end of the

Privileged few

Like this British official, government staff based in Africa in the early 20th century enjoyed many privileges, including servants who tended to their every need.

century, Europeans had charted the courses of the Nile, Niger, Congo, and Zambezi rivers, and the world now knew about the vast resources of Africa. In 1869, the opening of the Suez Canal, a direct trade route from Europe to Asia, focused European attention on the continent's economic and strategic importance. This interest was intensified by the Industrial Revolution (see pp.292–95) and the urgent need for raw materials and new markets, and so it was not long before European countries began to scramble for African territory.

In 1875, on the eve of this territorial carve-up, the European colonial presence was still fragmented. There was the former Ottoman territory of Algeria, whose conquest by France had begun in the 1830s; a few Spanish settlements; Angola, which was held by Portugal, along with trading posts on the west coast; and British and French trading stations in west Africa. The Cape Colony was administered by the United Kingdom, and just north of Cape Colony there was the Orange Free State and the Transvaal. These two states were established by Boers (Afrikaners of Dutch origin), after the Great Trek of 1835–36. This was a mass migration of 12,000 Boers, known as the "pioneers," who left Cape Colony in a search for new pastureland and to escape unwelcome British rule.

The African continent at this time was in turmoil. Much of the southern interior had been depopulated in the first quarter of the century by the territory-hungry Zulus under Shaka's leadership (see above). States such as Egypt were expanding. There were Islamic holy wars, called *Jihads*, taking place in the west. Cultural groups were being torn apart by the continuing slave trade, and new states were

emerging in East, Central, and West Africa. The Europeans capitalized on these disruptions, conquering territory with reasonable ease. In some cases, such as the Anglo-Zulu wars in 1879, they used military force; in others, African and European leaders agreed joint control over territory.

Divided continent

The competition between the Europeans often resulted in violent conflict. In southern Africa the first of two wars between the Boers and the British took place from late 1880 to early 1881 (see right), while North Africa became a theater for Anglo-French rivalry. Between November 15, 1884 and February 26, 1885, the Berlin Conference was convened by German Chancellor Otto von Bismarck (see p.333) in an attempt to settle rival claims. At the conference it was agreed that imperial powers could only claim colonies if they had agreed treaties with chiefs, and had administrative powers in the region.

By the close of the century, virtually all the continent was under European control. Portugal expanded its empire to include Mozambique; Belgium took over the enormous Congo region;

> **"If I could, I would annex other planets."** CECIL RHODES, BRITISH-BORN SOUTH AFRICAN MINING MAGNATE, POLITICIAN, AND COLONIZER OF RHODESIA

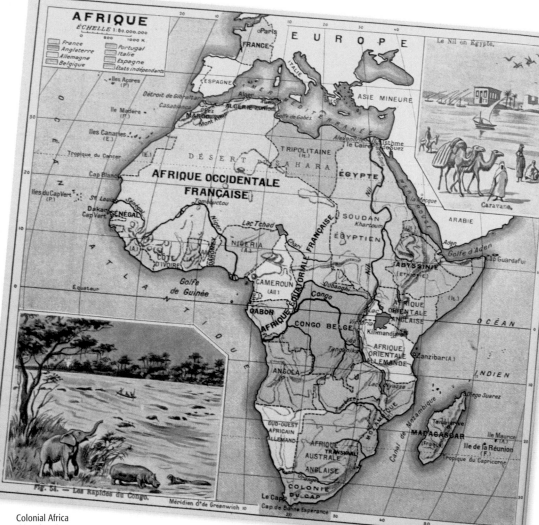

Colonial Africa
This early-20th-century map shows how Africa was divided between European powers. They exploited the continent's resources to benefit industry and commerce in their own countries.

BOER WARS

In retaliation for the British annexation of the Transvaal in 1877, Transvaal Boers (below) launched the first Anglo-Boer war in December 1880. In March 1881 the British admitted defeat and granted the Transvaal self-rule. A second Anglo-Boer war was fought between October 1889 and May 1902. After a long, hard-fought struggle, the British, aided by Canadian troops, won and absorbed the Boer republics of the Orange Free State and Transvaal into the British Empire.

AFTER

After World War II, Africa's colonial rulers faced demands for self-rule. By 1978, most countries were independent. White minority rule in southern Africa lasted longer.

AFRICAN NATIONALISM
Almost two million Africans served in the armies of their colonizers during World War II. When the soldiers returned home, they yet again faced the exploitation and indignities of colonial rule. Discontent grew, and many men joined the **independence movements**, which had been increasing in strength since before the war. Most African countries gained independence between 1956 and 1968 **412–13 》**, and by 1978 European rule had almost disappeared.

MAJORITY RULE
There were long and protracted struggles for **black majority rule** in Zimbabwe and South Africa. Majority rule was achieved in Zimbabwe in 1980 when **Robert Mugabe**, leader of Zanu PF, was voted into power. The **ANC** and the Inkatha Freedom Party (IFP) fought for majority rule in South Africa until 1994 when, led by Nelson Mandela, the ANC won the country's first multiracial elections **454–55 》**.

INKATHA FREEDOM PARTY ELECTION POSTER

and Germany gained new colonies in southern Africa. France and Britain acquired new territory in West Africa, and Britain also built a network of colonies in East Africa running from South Africa to Egypt. By 1914, the French had occupied Morocco and the Italians had conquered Tripoli. Only Ethiopia remained fully free, having beaten an Italian force at the Battle of Adowa in 1896.

Africa under foreign rule
Although the styles of rule adopted by the colonial powers varied, in general the Europeans made no attempt to develop their colonies, exploiting them as sources of raw materials and markets for their manufactured goods. Africans were excluded from decisions that affected their lives, and European settlers established themselves in relatively temperate areas of Africa

British in Egypt
These Scottish soldiers are pictured in front of the Sphinx at Giza in the summer of 1882, just after their victory at the Battle of Tel-el-Kebir, a dispute between the British and the Egyptians over the control of the Suez Canal.

where the land was fertile, often banishing Africans from the best land. The Europeans also brought changes to the African way of life. They imposed property taxes, and to pay these taxes Africans were forced to undertake waged labor, working on railroads, plantations, and mining operations. By forcing Africans into these jobs, Europeans caused resentment. This grew into violent anticolonial resistance, which spread across the continent in the early 20th century.

In 1904–05, the Herero of central Namibia rose up against their German rulers. In 1905, the Maji-Maji rebellion erupted in German East Africa.

In 1912, Zulus united to form the South African National Congress, which became the African National Congress, or ANC (see pp.454–55), to further the rights of native peoples. This marked the beginning of an organized movement for self-rule in Africa.

7

POPULATION AND POWER

1914–present

The modern age has seen the two bloodiest and costliest wars in human history, conflicts that spanned the globe. It has been a period of opposing political beliefs and ruthless dictators, of rapidly expanding populations and diminishing resources. But it has also been one of startling technological innovation and unprecedented prosperity.

POPULATION AND POWER

1914–present

1910	1915	1920	1925

1915
Italy enters World War I on Allied side; US invades Haiti and Dominican Republic. Nationalist risings in Dutch East Indies. Ottomans massacre or deport around one million Armenians.

Bolshevik banner ▶

1920
Ottoman Middle East territories mandated to Britain and France; German African territories to Britain, France, and South Africa. US senate rejects Versailles Settlement.

Red Army badge ◀

1925
Civil war in China. Nationalist uprisings in Syria. John Logie Baird creates first television picture. Edwin Hubble discovers galaxies beyond our own and the expansion of the universe. Locarno Treaty signed.

1914
Great Powers vie for influence in the Balkans; assassination of Austrian Archduke Franz Ferdinand in Sarajevo sets the "powder keg of Europe" alight.

▶ Assassination at Sarajevo

▼ Over the top

1918
Treaty of Brest-Litovsk: Russia surrenders Ukraine to Germany. World War I ends: Ottomans surrender; armistice agreed with Germany and Austria. Spanish influenza, six million die in Europe.

1921
Irish Free State created. Bolshevik victory in Russian civil war; six million die in famine. Nationalist uprising in Turkey. Washington disarmament conference.

◀ Michael Collins

1926
Chinese heartland united under Chiang Kai-Shek. Anti-Dutch communist revolt in Indonesia. Italy becomes a one-party state under Mussolini.

Stalin ▶

1917
Russian Revolution: czar abdicates, liberal government under Kerensky; Bolshevik revolution under Lenin; armistice agreed with Germany. US enters World War I on Allied side.

▼ Poppy

Lenin ▶

1927
Oil discovered in Iraq. Chinese nationalists purge communists. First nonstop solo transatlantic flight by Charles Lindbergh. Talking pictures first introduced to cinema.

1914
Austria declares war on Russia and sets World War I in motion; Germany invades France and the Ottomans ally with the Central Powers.

1919
Paris peace treaties: breakup of German and Austrian empires. League of Nations founded. Rutherford splits the atom. First powered transatlantic flight, Alcock and Brown.

▼ Spanish flu

1923
Turkish republic under Atatürk; secular reforms launched. Nationalist Kuomintang government in China. Hyperinflation in Germany. Military coup in Spain.

◀ Hyperinflation

1924
Death of Lenin leads to power struggle in USSR. Military coups in Chile and Brazil. Hitler imprisoned following attempted coup. Exchange of Turkish and Greek populations ends Turkish–Greek conflict.

1929
Wall Street Crash leads to global economic depression. First Five Year Plan in USSR: massive industrialization and collectivization of farms. Communists establish Jiangxi Soviet, South China.

▲ Collectivization

World War I, far from being the "war to end all wars," not only led to the political and economic turmoil that engulfed Europe in the 1920s and 1930s, but also sparked the Russian Revolution, ushering in the world's first communist state, the USSR. This was the beginning of an ideological confrontation that lasted until 1991. World War II, though in part a consequence of the Great Depression, was also directly spawned. It proved even more bloody, with a final death toll of more than 50 million. It left Europe prostrate, and directly contributed to decolonization across Africa, the Middle East, and Southeast Asia. In some regions an era of sustained economic growth followed the conflict.

1930 · 1935 · 1940 · 1945 »

1932
Famines in USSR leave around five million dead. Iraq gains independence. Kingdom of Saudi Arabia proclaimed. Chaco War: Bolivian claims to northern Paraguay. Disarmament conference in Geneva.

1948
State of Israel proclaimed: first Arab–Israeli war. Berlin blockade. Communist regimes Poland, Czechoslovakia, and Hungary. Burma and Ceylon independent. Korea partitioned. Gandhi assassinated.

▼ Hiroshima

▲ Depression in the US

1933
Hitler appointed chancellor in Germany. Dollfuss establishes authoritarian rule in Austria. Communist Party purged in USSR. Roosevelt president of US: launches "New Deal." World Economic Conference in London.

▲ Nuremberg rally

1938
Germany annexes Austria and, with British and French agreement, Sudetenland. Royal dictatorship in Romania. Japanese "New Order" proclaimed in Asia.

▼ Spanish Civil War

▲ Spitfire Mk V

1942
Battle of Midway: US repulses Japanese carrier fleet; German invasion of USSR stalls at Stalingrad; Axis forces defeated at El Alamein; US invades North Africa; killings begin at Auschwitz.

1930
Communists establish Pu'an Soviet in China. Allied troops leave Rhineland. Military revolution in Brazil: Getúlio Vargas in power. Over 3,000 banks fail in US. Frank Whittle invents jet engine.

▲ Gold "Jew" star

1940
German forces conquer Denmark, Norway, Holland, Luxembourg, Belgium, and France; Italy declares war on Britain and France; Battle of Britain; Japan allied with Germany and Italy.

1945
Russians storm Berlin; Hitler commits suicide; German surrender; US drops atomic bombs on Hiroshima and Nagasaki; Japanese surrender. United Nations formed.

Mahatma Gandhi ▶

1934
Death of Hindenburg: Hitler becomes Führer of Germany; one-party rule established; "Night of the Long Knives"; rearmament begins. USSR joins League of Nations. Communist "Long March" in China.

1936
"Great Terror" in USSR: start of show trials and purges. Spanish Civil War begins. Germany remilitarizes Rhineland. Anti-Comintern Pact between Germany and Japan. Military dictatorship in Mexico.

1941
German invasion of USSR; "Final Solution" ordered; Japan attacks Pearl Harbor: US enters war on Allied side; Japan invades Malaya, Burma, Philippines, and Dutch East Indies.

1944
900-day siege of Leningrad lifted. D-Day landings: second front in France; Paris and Brussels liberated; Battle of the Bulge: German offensive checked; Germans fire V2 rockets at London.

◀ Hitler

Soviet secret police poster ▶

▼ Pearl Harbor

毛主席革命路线胜利万岁

1937
Italy resigns from League of Nations; joins anti-Comintern Pact. US Neutrality Act passes into law. Sino-Japanese war: Japan sacks Nanking. Anti-French uprising in Tunisia. Authoritarian "New State," Brazil.

1939
Germany advances into Czechoslovakia. Franco imposes right-wing dictatorship in Spain. German–Soviet Non-Aggression Pact. Germany invades Poland; Britain and France declare war.

1947
India and Pakistan independent: widespread violence. US sponsors Marshall Plan. UN agrees partition of Palestine. GATT agreed, US. Sound barrier broken in US.

▲ Chairman Mao

1949
Mao's Communists victorious in Chinese civil war. East and West Germany established, the former as part of the Communist Bloc. NATO formed. USSR acquires atomic bomb.

1950

1955

1960

1965

1950
Korean War: first major Cold War armed confrontation. US military support for French in Indochina. China invades Tibet.

◄ The Peróns

1956
Hungarian uprising suppressed by USSR. Suez Crisis: failed Anglo-French invasion of the canal. Morocco and Tunisia gain independence from France and Sudan from Britain.

1962
Cuban missile crisis. France concedes Algerian independence. Uganda, Jamaica, Trinidad and Tobago gain independence from Britain. First transatlantic television pictures.

▼ Algerian independence

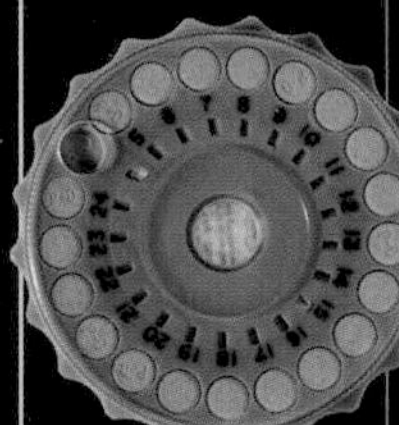

1968
"Prague Spring" crushed by USSR. Martin Luther King Jr. assassinated: race riots in US. Saddam Hussein seizes power in Iraq. Apollo 8: first manned lunar flight.

◄ Contraceptive pill

1955
Creation of Warsaw Pact. Soviet military support for Egypt. Widespread nationalist riots in Algeria and Morocco. Perón ousted in Argentina. US military intervention in Iran.

Korean War poster ►

Suez Crisis ►

1960
Decolonization of Africa: 12 French colonies gain independence, plus Congo (from Belgium), Nigeria and Somalia (from Britain). Hawaii is the 50th state of the US.

▼ Berlin Wall

▲ Vietnam

1952
Military coup in Egypt. Mau Mau uprising in Kenya. Founding of the European Coal and Steel Community. Comet: world's first jet airliner, Britain. First hydrogen bomb built.

1954
France defeated in Southeast Asia: Laos, Cambodia and (partitioned) Vietnam independent. USS *Nautilus*, first nuclear-powered submarine. Unitary state of Indonesia declared.

1961
John F. Kennedy president of US. Berlin Wall built. Military coup in South Korea. South Africa leaves Commonwealth. Bay of Pigs: US-backed attempt to topple Castro. Yuri Gagarin is first human in space.

1965
US troops in Vietnam. Voting Rights Acts, US: increases numbers of black voters. Indo-Pakistan War over Kashmir. Marcos takes power in the Philippines. Over five million women in the US are using the contraceptive pill.

1957
Treaty of Rome: founding of EEC.
1958
China's "Great Leap Forward": forced industrialization, around 20 million die. Fifth Republic in France: de Gaulle president.

1963
US and USSR end atmospheric testing of nuclear weapons. Assassination of Kennedy. Civil war in Sudan. Federation of Malaysia: Singapore, Sarawak, Sabah, and Malaysia.

▼ Funeral of JFK

▲ Pontiac Chieftain

1953
Anti-Soviet uprisings suppressed in Poland and East Berlin. Death of Stalin. Double helix structure of DNA discovered by Crick and Watson. Polio vaccine developed. Mount Everest climbed.

1959
Communist revolution in Cuba: Fidel Castro imposes Soviet-style regime. Tibetan uprising crushed by China. Boeing 707: the first long-haul commercial jet airliner.

◄ Che Guevara

1967
Six-Day War: Israel takes Sinai, Gaza Strip, West Bank, Golan Heights, and Jerusalem. Biafran War with Nigeria. Martial law imposed in Greece.

▲ Seeing into space

1969
SALT talks between US and USSR. Gaddafi seizes power in Libya. Sectarian violence in Northern Ireland. Apollo 11: the first Moon landing.

"I think that people want peace so much that one of these days **governments had better get out of the way** and let them have it." DWIGHT D. EISENHOWER, US PRESIDENT, 1953

1970 1975 1980 1985 »

Bloody Sunday

1975
Death of Franco: democracy and monarchy restored in Spain. Communist regimes in Laos and Cambodia. Civil war in Lebanon. Angola and Mozambique gain independence from Portugal.

Iranian revolution ▶

1980
Saddam Hussein launches Iran–Iraq War. Anticommunist union, Solidarity, formed in Poland. Majority black rule in Zimbabwe. First fax machines and domestic camcorders in Japan.

1982
Falklands War: Britain retakes islands after Argentinian invasion. US initiates START talks with USSR. Martial law imposed in Bangladesh. Martial law in Poland: Solidarity outlawed.

▲ Mikhail Gorbachev and Ronald Reagan

1971
Third Indo-Pakistan War: independent Bangladesh. Mogadishu Declaration denounces white rule in South Africa. Idi Amin seizes power in Uganda.
1972
Protesters clash with British army in Northern Ireland: Bloody Sunday.

1981
Ronald Reagan president of US. Militant campaign for independent Sikh state in Punjab. Israel withdraws from Sinai. First flight of US space shuttle, Columbia. IBM PC launched.

Iran–Iraq war ▶

1985
Mikhail Gorbachev launches reform of USSR: *glasnost* and *perestroika*. State of emergency declared in South Africa. Israeli withdrawal from Lebanon.

▲ Pinochet protest

1973
Yom Kippur War: OAPEC raises oil prices by 200 percent; sparks global recession. US troops withdrawn, Vietnam. Pinochet's military coup ousts Allende in Chile. Britain, Ireland, and Denmark join the EEC.

1976
Death of Mao in China; coup by "Gang of Four." Syria intervenes in Lebanon: imposes Arab peace force. First black homelands (bantustans) in South Africa; race riots in Soweto.

Margaret Thatcher ▶

1986
Superpower summit in Iceland: US and USSR agree to disarm. Democracy restored in Brazil. Collapse of Marcos regime in the Philippines. US bombs Libya. Nuclear reactor explodes at Chernobyl.

Fall of the Berlin War ▶

1970
Military rule in Somalia. US, USSR, and Britain negotiate Nuclear Non-proliferation Treaty. Allende elected president of Chile. First jumbo jet enters service in the US.

1977
Egypt–Israeli peace talks. Military coup in Pakistan. Gaddafi imposes "Islamic socialism" in Libya.
1978
Camp David Peace Treaty: Egyptian–Israeli rapprochement.

War in Afghanistan ▼

1979
USSR invades Afghanistan. Shah of Iran ousted: Ayatollah Khomeini imposes Islamic republic. Khmer Rouge overthrown in Cambodia. Margaret Thatcher prime minister of Britain.

Commodore PET ▼

1983
Democracy restored in Argentina. Martial law lifted in Poland. Islamic law introduced in Sudan: civil war. Foundation of militant Islamic terror group, Hezbollah, in Lebanon.

1974
Coup in Ethiopia: Haile Selassie ousted. Turkey invades Cyprus. Indonesia invades East Timor. President Nixon resigns in US. Death of Salazar: democracy in Portugal.

◀ Steve Biko

DRUM
STEVE BIKO
A SPECIAL REPORT IN WORDS AND PICTURES

1987
Intifada uprising in Gaza Strip and West Bank: Arab–Israeli tensions heightened. INF Treaty: US and USSR agree to cut nuclear stockpiles.

▲ Romanian revolution

1989
Collapse of Iron Curtain: Eastern Bloc governments toppled; Solidarity elected in Poland; Berlin Wall breached. Partial elections in USSR.

1990

1995

2000

2005 onward

1991
UN coalition expels Iraqi forces from Kuwait. Baltic republics assert independence from USSR. USSR dissolved, replaced by CIS. Slovenia and Croatia independent: at war with Serbia.

◀ Nelson Mandela

▲ Boris Yeltsin

1996
Taliban captures Kabul: declares it to be a fundamentalist Islamic state. Russian pullout leaves Chechnya de facto independent. Yeltsin wins Russian elections: communists narrowly defeated. DVDs launched in Japan.

2002
Euro introduced in 11 of 15 EU countries. Renewed Palestinian attacks on Israel. Mugabe wins rigged election in Zimbabwe: attacks on opponents. UN weapons inspections in Iraq.

◀ Twin Towers attack

2005
Muslim fundamentalist bombings in London: 52 die. Israel withdraws from Gaza; Syria withdraws from Lebanon. General election in Iraq: 98.8 percent turnout. Kyoto Protocol on climate change comes into force.

2008
Global financial crisis sends stock markets plummeting. Terrorist attacks in Mumbai, India; 175 die. Barack Obama is elected president of the United States.

2006
Sudan rejects UN peacekeeping force, launches genocide in Darfur; around 400,000 die. Renewed Israeli–Hezbollah conflict in Lebanon. North Korea tests nuclear weapon. Montenegro votes to split from Serbia.

2009
Bushfires in Australia kill 173. Hamid Karzai re-elected president of Afghanistan but Taliban attacks worsen. Outbreak of H1N1 "Swine flu" pandemic. Earthquake in Sumatra kills 1,000 people.

▼ Ads promote global companies

1990
Iraqi invasion of Kuwait: UN coalition forces sent to Persian Gulf. Moves to end apartheid in South Africa. Free elections held in East Germany; Germany reunited.

▼ Oslo Accords: Clinton, Arafat, and Rabin

1993
"Velvet Divorce": Czech Republic and Slovakia formed from Czechoslovakia. Oslo Accords: PLO and Israel agree limited Palestinian autonomy. Democracy restored in Cambodia. HIV/AIDS epidemic in southern Africa.

◀ Petronas Towers

1998
India and Pakistan test nuclear weapons. Serbs and ethnic Albanians clash in Kosovo. Economic crisis in Indonesia: overthrow of Suharto government. "Good Friday" peace deal, Northern Ireland.

2003
Widespread ethnic conflict in Darfur, Sudan. US-led coalition invades Iraq: takes Baghdad; Saddam Hussein ousted; widespread violence and terror attacks; UN lifts sanctions. First manned Chinese space flight.

▼ Fall of Saddam Hussein

LG

1997
Britain returns Hong Kong to China. Asian financial crisis. Adult sheep, "Dolly," cloned. Coup in Zaire. Israeli pullout from Hebron, West Bank. Microsoft is world's most valuable company.

▼ NATO troops in Kosovo

1999
Russia restarts Chechen war. Serbian "ethnic cleansing" of Kosovan Albanians: NATO intervention. Renewed Indian–Pakistani clashes over Kashmir. Democracy restored in Indonesia. US and UK begin air attacks on Iraq.

2007
Iran develops nuclear program despite international pressure and UN sanctions. Devolved government returns to Northern Ireland. Sectarian conflict between Sunni and Shia militias escalates in occupied Iraq.

2010
Earthquake in Haiti leaves 230,000 dead. Deepwater Horizon oil platform explodes in Gulf of Mexico, starting oil leak that takes six months to plug. Aung San Suu Kyi is released from house arrest by Burmese military.

▼ AIDS ribbon

1994
Civil war in Rwanda: 500,000 Tutsis massacred; two million Hutus flee. ANC wins multiracial elections in South Africa. Chechnya asserts independence: Russian invasion. US invades Haiti: democracy restored.

2001
Al-Qaeda terror attacks on New York and Washington, DC: President Bush commits US to "war on terror." US–UK coalition forces bomb Afghanistan: Taliban overthrown.

2004
Muslim fundamentalist bombings in Madrid: 191 die. Chechen separatists storm school in Baslan, Russia: 350 die. Indonesian earthquake sparks tsunami, in SE Asia and Indian Ocean: 210,000 die. Ten new countries join EU.

Wind power ▶

"…those who do not remember the past are **condemned to repeat it.**"

GEORGE SANTAYANA, "THE LIFE OF REASON," 1905–06

Boomtown
In 2006, China's economy grew by 10.7 percent. It was once one of the world's weakest economies but is now among the strongest. The growth in China's cities reflects this newfound wealth.

◄ Shanghai

The Assassination at Sarajevo

The spark that caused the European tinderbox to ignite into World War I was lit in the Bosnian capital of Sarajevo. The assassination of Archduke Franz Ferdinand, heir to the Austro–Hungarian throne, triggered a series of reactions that would lead to a full-scale European war within five weeks, a war that soon spread around the world.

The archduke and his wife Sofia were making an official visit to Sarajevo to inspect military maneuvers. Austria–Hungary had occupied the Turkish province of Bosnia–Herzegovina since 1878 and fully annexed it in 1908. Neighboring Serbia resented this, as the province was mainly populated by Serbs, so relations between the two states were tense.

As the royal couple drove to an official reception at the town hall, a bomb was thrown into their car. It bounced off the rear canopy and exploded under the car behind, injuring two royal aides and 18 others. After the reception, the archduke changed his route out of the town but on the way, his driver took a wrong turning and halted. By chance, a group of conspirators involved in the earlier incident but not detained by the police were loitering there. One of them, Gavrilo Princip, a 19-year-old student, leaped onto the car's running board and shot the royal couple at point-blank range, hitting the archduke in the neck and his wife in the abdomen. They both died within a few minutes.

It was clear that Princip had not acted alone. He and his five fellow assassins were members of the Black Hand, a secret nationalist society led by Colonel Dragutin Dimitrijevic, head of Serbia's military intelligence. Austria–Hungary then accused the Serbian government of complicity in the assassination. It also asked its ally, Germany, for support against Serbia. When this was confirmed, Austria–Hungary issued an ultimatum on July 23 that would have effectively ended Serbian independence. Serbia's reply was received in the Austrian capital just two minutes short of the 48-hour deadline. It had agreed to almost all of Austria's demands, but also appealed to Russia for help and offered to refer the dispute to the International Court. The reply was rejected. The next day, July 26, Austria–Hungary mobilized its forces, declaring war on Serbia on July 28. The countdown to war had begun.

Arrest
Soldiers arrest 19-year-old Gavrilo Princip after the assassination of Archduke Franz Ferdinand and his wife, Sofia, in Sarajevo.

"The lamps are going out all over Europe. We shall not see them lit again **in our lifetime**."

SIR EDWARD GREY, BRITISH FOREIGN SECRETARY, AUGUST 3, 1914

BEFORE

The origins of the world war lie in European rivalries stretching back more than 40 years.

TRIPLE ENTENTE

German unification in 1871, **≪ 330–33** and its rise to military and industrial power, combined with its commercial and imperial ambitions in Europe, the Middle East, and Africa, alarmed its neighbors. The German defeat of France in 1871 had made the two countries bitter enemies. Germany constructed **defensive alliances** with

first Austria-Hungary and then Italy, while France looked to Russia and Britain. A naval **arms race** between Britain and Germany added to the growing military tension.

SCHLIEFFEN PLAN

RUSSIAN THREAT Fearing war on two fronts, against France and Russia, in 1905, the German chief of the general staff, General von Schlieffen, drew up a plan for Germany to deliver a **knockout blow against France**, before turning to face the huge, but slow-to-mobilize, Russian army.

The beginning of the twentieth century saw Europe divided into two armed camps. Germany had formed an alliance with Austria-Hungary in 1879 (see BEFORE) as it felt threatened by the hostile nations at its borders and needed to protect its interests in Central Europe and the Balkans. France, Russia, and later Britain formed their own alliance, in part to protect themselves against possible German aggression.

The road to war

The spark that caused the war was the assassination of Archduke Ferdinand, heir to the Austro-Hungarian throne, by a Serb fanatic in Sarajevo, capital of Austrian Bosnia (see pp.370–71).

Austria accused Serbia of complicity in the murder, and gained German support. Austria refused a compromise with Serbia and, on July 28, declared war. Continental war was unavoidable as both sides honored commitments to their allies. Russia mobilized its troops in support of Serbia, and when German demands for it to stop were refused, Germany declared war on Russia on August 1. Knowing that France would support Russia, Germany then declared war on France on August 3 and implemented the Schlieffen Plan (see BEFORE) sending its army through Belgium in an attempt to knock France out of the war, before turning its attention on Russia. Britain initially held back, but honored its

guarantee of Belgian independence, agreed by treaty in 1839, and declared war against Germany on August 4.

Deadlock

The initial German advance was halted in early September, 50 miles (80 km) east of Paris, by a combined French and British army. Both sides then raced north toward the English Channel to try to break through around the side of their enemy's lines. When this failed, the two sides dug in along the length of the Western Front. Stalemate lasted there until almost the end of the war, as the defensive capabilities of the machine gun prevented any significant advance by either side. Allied attempts to break the deadlock at Neuve

The **Great War**

In July 1914 a war broke out in the Balkans that within days spread to the rest of Europe. That war was expected to be over by Christmas but it dragged on for more than four years. At the time it was known as the Great War. We know it now as World War I.

Going over the top
The order to climb out of the relative safety of the trench and advance—assaulted by gunfire and weighed down by weapons and heavy equipment—across the mud of no-man's-land toward the enemy was often met with terror.

The Western Front

The main front between the opposing German and Allied armies stretched in a huge "S" shape from the English Channel to the Swiss frontier, about 470 miles (760 km).

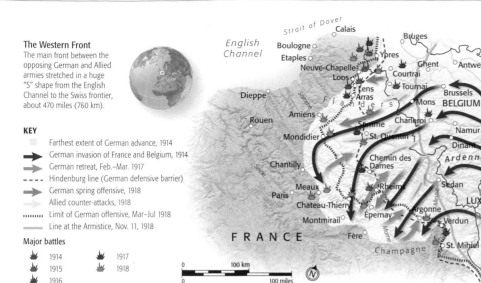

KEY

■ Farthest extent of German advance, 1914
→ German invasion of France and Belgium, 1914
⇒ German retreat, Feb.–Mar. 1917
--- Hindenburg line (German defensive barrier)
⇒ German spring offensive, 1918
⇒ Allied counter-attacks, 1918
······· Limit of German offensive, Mar–Jul 1918
— Line at the Armistice, Nov. 11, 1918

Major battles

⚜	1914	⚜	1917
⚜	1915	⚜	1918
⚜	1916		

Strait of Dover
English Channel
Calais · Bruges · Ghent · Antwerp
Boulogne · Ypres · Courtrai
Etaples · Neuve-Chapelle · Tournai · Brussels · Maastricht
Loos · Lens · Mons · BELGIUM
Dieppe · Arras · Charleroi · Namur · Liège
Rouen · Amiens · Somme · St. Quentin · Dinant · Ardennes
Mondidier · Chemin des Dames · Sedan
Chantilly · Rheims · LUXEMBOURG · Mosel
Paris · Meaux · Chateau-Thierry · Épernay · Argonne · Verdun
Montmirail · Fère · St. Mihiel · GERMANY
FRANCE · Champagne

0   100 km
0   100 miles

N

Trench life

Infantrymen wait in a trench near the front line for the order to go over the top. Conditions in the trenches were appalling—muddy, waterlogged, and infested with rats.

Chapelle, Ypres, and Loos in 1915, and the Somme in 1916, were hugely costly (57,470 British troops were killed or injured on the first day of battle on the Somme) and failed to break German lines. German attacks on the French city of Verdun throughout 1916 were intended to make France "bleed to death." By the time the battle ended in stalemate, there were more than 750,000 French and German casualties.

The other fronts

The Eastern Front was far more fluid. A Russian advance into German East Prussia was halted at Tannenberg in August and the Masurian Lakes in September. German and Austrian advances into Russia in 1915 were countered by a major Russian offensive into Austria in 1916.

In the Balkans, Serbia repelled an Austrian invasion, but the entry into the war on Germany's side by the Ottoman Empire in November 1914 and Bulgaria in September 1915 tipped the scales. By January, Serbia and its ally Montenegro were overrun, while Romania was defeated the following year. An Allied attempt to force the Ottomans out of the war by invading the Gallipoli peninsula in Turkey failed miserably in 1915. Italy, once a German ally, joined the war in April 1915 on the Allied side, lured by potential territorial gains, but soon became bogged down in battles with Austrian troops on the Isonzo River in the far northeast of the country.

All the main protagonists except Austria had extensive overseas empires (see pp.346–47). British and French imperial troops occupied German colonies in Africa and the Pacific, the Japanese seizing German colonies in the western Pacific and China. British and Indian troops also invaded Ottoman Mesopotamia (now Iraq), while in 1916 the British incited the Arabs to revolt against Ottoman rule.

At sea, the expected clash between the naval fleets of Britain and Germany never really happened. There were battles in the South Atlantic and at Jutland in the North Sea, but although German U-boats did substantial damage to Allied shipping, the British navy was the stronger force. »

> "What a bloodbath… Hell cannot be this **dreadful**."
>
> ALBERT JOUBAIRE, A FRENCH SOLDIER AT VERDUN, 1916

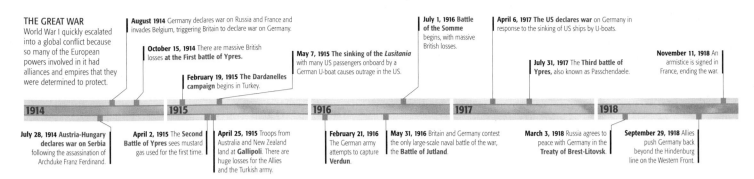

THE GREAT WAR
World War I quickly escalated into a global conflict because so many of the European powers involved in it had alliances and empires that they were determined to protect.

August 1914 Germany declares war on Russia and France and invades Belgium, triggering Britain to declare war on Germany.

October 15, 1914 There are massive British losses **at the First battle of Ypres.**

February 19, 1915 The Dardanelles campaign begins in Turkey.

May 7, 1915 The sinking of the _Lusitania_ with many US passengers onboard by a German U-boat causes outrage in the US.

July 1, 1916 Battle of the Somme begins, with massive British losses.

April 6, 1917 The US declares war on Germany in response to the sinking of US ships by U-boats.

July 31, 1917 The Third battle of Ypres, also known as Passchendaele.

November 11, 1918 An armistice is signed in France, ending the war.

1914 **1915** **1916** **1917** **1918**

July 28, 1914 Austria-Hungary **declares war on Serbia** following the assassination of Archduke Franz Ferdinand.

April 2, 1915 The Second Battle of Ypres sees mustard gas used for the first time.

April 25, 1915 Troops from Australia and New Zealand land at **Gallipoli.** There are huge losses for the Allies and the Turkish army.

February 21, 1916 The German army attempts to capture **Verdun.**

May 31, 1916 Britain and Germany contest the only large-scale naval battle of the war, the **Battle of Jutland.**

March 3, 1918 Russia agrees to peace with Germany in the **Treaty of Brest-Litovsk.**

September 29, 1918 Allies push Germany back beyond the Hindenburg line on the Western Front.

1917 was a difficult year for all sides. The Allied naval blockade of Germany and the German U-boat campaign against Allied merchant shipping led to severe food shortages: Germany ran out of wheat flour during the winter, while Britain had run out of sugar by April, and had only enough wheat to last six weeks.

Mutiny and revolution
The French army mutinied in April as a result of the losses it had endured. Riots in Russia in March led to the abdication of the czar, and when the Bolsheviks (see pp.376–77) seized power in November, they signed a ceasefire with Germany. The Italians had weakened the Austro-Hungarians, but when the Germans attacked in November, only the swift deployment of British and French troops saved Italy.

The Allies launched a new attack on the Western Front at Arras in April, and in July at Ypres. Both failed, with 250,000 casualties at Ypres.

US joins the war
Two events were to break the stalemate. In February 1917, Germany announced it would attack all foreign ships, in order to starve Britain out of the war. The threat to US shipping was clear, but Germany tried to divert American attention by encouraging Mexico to

Women at work
With men away fighting at the front, women were required to work in industry, services, and on the land. By the end of the war, one million British women worked in munitions (as pictured left) and engineering works.

attack the US. Publication of a telegram sent by the German foreign minister to Mexico outraged Americans, and in April the US declared war.

The second event was the mass use of tanks by the British at the Battle of Cambrai in November 1917. Tanks were one of the few developments in military technology during the war, along with airships and planes for reconnaissance, or bombardment.

The final nine months
In March 1918, Germany and Russia signed a peace treaty at Brest-Litovsk. Germany now shifted all its troops to the Western Front, and attacked on March 21 before US troops arrived. But the Germans outran their supplies and the attack was halted on July 18. A mass tank advance by the British at Amiens on August 8 and French–US attacks to the south then forced the Germans back into Belgium.

Germany's Bulgarian allies sued for peace at the end of September, while the Italians won a massive victory against the Austro-Hungarians in October. The Austro-Hungarian and Ottoman empires then both signed an armistice with the Allies. In Germany, food and fuel shortages led to the country collapsing from within. After the naval fleet mutinied at Kiel, Kaiser Wilhelm II abdicated and the new government agreed armistice terms. At 11 am on the morning of November 11, 1918, the war came to an end.

Land Army
Women worked the land. It was vital both in the US and in Europe, where U-boat attacks and an economic blockade reduced food supplies.

KEY
- Mobilized military
- Military dead

War casualties
The human cost of the war was immense: a total of around 65 million men fought during the war, of whom 8.5 million died and 21.2 million were seriously injured. An estimated 6.6 million civilians also died from the fighting, or blockade, and disease.

Troops in millions

Russia · France · British Empire · Italy · US — Allied Powers

Germany · Austria-Hungary · Turkey · Bulgaria — Central Powers

AFTER

The war had short-term political effects in redrawing the map of Europe, but had longer-lasting social and economic consequences.

POSTWAR PEACE TREATIES
Under the **Versailles Treaty** signed in June 1919, Germany reluctantly accepted guilt for causing the war and agreed to pay **reparations** (war damages). It lost its colonies to the Allies as "mandates"—territories under the supervision of the League of Nations, an international organization founded to promote peace through diplomacy—and gave up territory to France, Belgium, Denmark, and Poland. Germany's armed forces were limited in size; the Rhineland was **demilitarized** and the industrial Saar region became a League of Nations mandate.

THE MAP OF EUROPE REDRAWN
The treaties of **St Germain** with Austria (September 1919), **Neuilly** with Bulgaria (November 1919), and **Trianon** with Hungary (June 1920) **redrew the map** of Central and Eastern Europe, with defeated nations paying war reparations. _Anschluss_ **392 》,** union between Austria and Germany, was forbidden. The **Treaty of Sèvres** with the Ottoman Empire was agreed in August 1920 but later rewritten at Lausanne in July 1923.

WOMEN AND WORK
The **mobilization of women** into war industries and agriculture temporarily raised their economic status, although most returned to work in the home at the end of the war. As a result of their war work, **women gained the vote** in Britain in 1918 and in America in 1920 **434–35 》.**

REMEMBRANCE
The profusion of red **Flanders poppies** growing along the Western Front after the war inspired the British Legion to sell paper poppies to raise money for injured soldiers. On or near **November 11** each year, commemorations are held across Europe to remember those who were killed or injured.

POPPY APPEAL

TOTAL WARFARE
World War I has been identified as the first "total war" in history, as the entire national economy, industry, and population were directed toward winning the war. British success in this **total mobilization** was one of the main reasons it, and the Allies, overcame Germany.

"No more slaughter, no more mud and blood…"

LIEUTENANT R. G. DIXON, BRITISH SOLDIER, NOVEMBER 11, 1918

When Nicholas II succeeded to the throne as Czar (Emperor) in 1894, Russia was dangerously divided between the wealthy aristocracy and the discontented poor.

NICHOLAS II

Nicholas was an **autocrat,** believing that only he had the authority to rule Russia; however, he lacked the strength of will to fulfill this role. To remain a dominant European force, Russia desperately needed to industrialize, but with modernization came inevitable **demands for civil rights** from impoverished Russian workers. There were few freedoms for the predominantly peasant population. Nicholas, a natural conservative, repeatedly failed to work with moderate forces and reform society, losing the opportunity to transform Russia into a modern nation.

BOLSHEVIKS AND MENSHEVIKS

The **Russian Social Democratic Labor Part**y (RSDLP) was formed in 1898, and was heavily influenced by the theories of Karl Marx **« 334–35**. In 1902, the party divided into two strands; the **Bolsheviks**, led by Lenin (see right) who advocated change

JAPANESE WAR FLAG

through violent revolution, and the more moderate **Mensheviks**, who believed in a more gradual process of change.

RUSSO–JAPANESE WAR

In 1904 Russia became involved in a **war with the Japanese** over competing ambitions in Korea and Manchuria (northeast China) **« 356–57**. Weakened by successive defeats, Russia signed the **Treaty of Portsmouth** in 1905, bringing an end to the conflict.

1905 REVOLUTION

As Russia suffered defeats abroad, violence erupted at home. Petrograd (St. Petersburg) experienced **a brutal massacre** when 200,000 disaffected workers and their families **marched on the Winter Palace** (the residence of the czar) to demand better pay and working conditions. The protesters were met by Cossack cavalry who, sabers drawn, charged the crowd, killing many. Across Russia, the **population rose up** against the czar. Discipline broke down among troops and at Odessa, **sailors mutinied** against the appalling conditions on the battleship *Potemkin* (the subject of a 1925 film by Sergei Eisenstein).

POSTER FOR "BATTLESHIP POTEMKIN"

The Russian Revolution

Described by US journalist John Reed, a first-hand observer of the event, as "Ten Days That Shook the World," the October Revolution of 1917 saw the Bolshevik Party seize power in Russia, after decades of discontent. The Bolsheviks went on to create the world's first Communist state.

In the wake of the 1905 revolution (see BEFORE), Nicholas II agreed to instigate a new constitution for Russia, which included the formation of an elected parliament, or Duma. However, the czar retained the ability to disband the Duma at will, which he duly did when the assembly met in 1906 and 1907. Two subsequent Dumas met in 1907–1912 and 1912–17, although they were in almost constant conflict with Nicholas, who struggled to remain in control of the worsening political situation. The outbreak of World War I in August 1914 briefly united Russians against a common German enemy.

The war did not go well for Russia. By 1917, having sustained enormous losses on the battlefield and with the war effort creating high prices and food shortages, resentment toward the czar increased. Industrial workers across Russia began a crippling general strike. With violence erupting on the streets of

Petrograd and Moscow, Nicholas was finally forced to abdicate. The Duma handed over power to the Provisional Government, which aimed to establish a liberal democracy. But discontent was still in the air, as the government refused to withdraw from the war. The power was increasingly contested by the Petrograd Soviet of Workers and Soldiers, one of many workers' councils (soviets) springing up all over the country. The Petrograd Soviet had the crucial support of troops garrisoned in the capital. It denounced the new government as "bourgeois" (middle class), and claimed to be the only true representative of the Russian people.

Peace, land, and bread

In April 1917, Lenin (see right), a key member of the revolutionary Russian Bolshevik Party, returned to Petrograd from exile in Western Europe. Lenin was convinced that collapse of world capitalism, as predicted by Karl Marx, was imminent. His aim was to

supervise a proletarian (workers') revolution, with the rallying cry of "peace, land and bread, [and] all power to the Soviets." In April the Bolshevik newspaper *Pravda* ("Truth") published Lenin's demands for the overthrow of the government and withdrawal from the "imperialist" war.

Lenin's antiwar stance gained mass support in July, when a Russian offensive ended with huge casualties. For three days, soldiers and workers rioted in Petrograd in an uprising so damaging that the prime minister, Prince Lvov, resigned. He was replaced by Alexander Kerensky, who branded Lenin a German spy. Lenin fled to Finland and the prospect of revolution seemed to recede.

However, Lenin's followers soon received assistance from an unlikely source. General Lavr Kornilov, the Russian army's commander-in-chief, believed that the country would descend into anarchy if the Bolsheviks were to gain ground, and in August

> " History will not forgive us if we do not **assume power** now."
>
> LENIN, 1917

May Day protest
On May 1, 1917, a massive labor demonstration took place in Petrograd. Every Soviet (workers' council) in Russia was represented at the march. Many carried banners bearing political slogans.

Street fighting
Supporters of Lenin flee the gunfire of Provisional Government forces in Petrograd, July 1917.

In the aftermath of the Russian Revolution, the Bolsheviks faced both internal and international opposition. They acted ruthlessly to tighten their grip on power.

THE ROMANOV FAMILY

EXECUTION OF THE ROMANOVS
After his abdication Nicholas II and his family were kept under **house arrest**, moving in the spring of 1918 to Ekaterinburg in the Urals. On July 17, as anti-Bolshevik forces were advancing, Nicholas, his wife, their five children and servants were taken into the cellar of the house and shot. There is no evidence of a direct command from Lenin: the **death sentence** was passed by the local regional Soviet. The family's execution removed one of many threats to the Bolsheviks' rule.

CIVIL WAR
In 1918 the anti-Bolshevik **White Army** launched attacks against the new regime. They received military support from many countries including Britain, France, and the US. During the next three years the **Bolshevik Red Army** fought invasions in the Baltic, the Caucasus, Siberia, and Ukraine.

RED ARMY BADGE

BIRTH OF THE SOVIET UNION
By the end of 1920 the counter-revolutionaries were defeated and absolute Bolshevik military and political power was established. Russia was renamed the **Union of Soviet Socialist Republics (USSR)** or **Soviet Union** in 1922.

NEW ECONOMIC POLICY
During the civil war, the Soviet economy teetered on the **brink of collapse**, and money became virtually worthless. With the urban population and the army close to starvation, the state seized surplus food from peasant farmers without payment. In 1921 Lenin's "**New Economic Policy**" replaced these seizures with a regulated tax and as trade increased, the economy revived.

COMINTERN
Also known as the "Third International," Comintern was founded to promote **worldwide revolution**. Stalin 378–79 ≫ dissolved the association as a gesture of goodwill to the Allies in **World War II** 380–81, 392–405 ≫.

COMINTERN MEMBERSHIP CARD

BOLSHEVIK Founded by Lenin in 1912, the Bolshevik Party was committed to a workers' (proletarian) revolution and the overthrow of the imperial regime.

1917 he ordered troops into Petrograd to protect the government. Fearing that Kornilov intended to seize power for himself, Kerensky asked the Bolsheviks for assistance, which they duly provided, in the form of a mass of workers, who persuaded the troops to turn around.

The Kornilov affair seriously weakened the Provisional Government, and in October Lenin secretly returned to Petrograd. He announced to the Bolshevik Party's Central Committee that the time for revolution had arrived, entrusting the military organization of the revolution to Leon Trotsky (see pp.380–81).

October Revolution

On October 25—according to the old Russian (Julian) calendar, November 7 in the modern (Gregorian) one— Trotsky's men executed an almost bloodless coup in Petrograd. Armed squads of pro-Bolshevik revolutionaries occupied key positions such as train stations, banks, post offices, and telephone exchanges. The battleship *Aurora*, flying the Bolshevik Red Flag from its mast, dropped anchor in then Neva River with its guns trained on the Winter Palace, where Kerensky's government was in session. After the firing of a single blank shell from the ship and two shells from another gun position, the government surrendered.

That night, Lenin issued a powerful address to the Russian people, entitled "To All Soldiers, Workers, and Peasants," in which he promised to transfer the lands of the aristocracy, the church, and crown to peasant committees and to establish the workers' control over Russia's industries. The people of Russia would at last become their own masters. The Bolsheviks moved quickly to secure supremacy over other political groups, ensuring that soviets took over control across Russia, and ensuring that they alone would form the new government.

Lenin's immediate concern was to make peace with Germany and end an exhausting and costly war. Firmly believing that revolution would soon spread across the capitalist world, he accepted Germany's peace terms, failing to anticipate the furious international reaction against his new Russia that was about to be unleashed.

RUSSIAN LEADER (1870–1924)

VLADIMIR ILYICH LENIN

Lenin became politicized after his elder brother was hanged for his part in a plot to kill Czar Alexander III. In 1895 he was exiled to Siberia for revolutionary activities. On his release, Lenin spent several years in Europe, where he studied Marxist theory. His 1902 essay *What is to be done?* argued for a workers' revolution, under the leadership of a strong government. Lenin came to power in the October Revolution, but died less than seven years later. However, his politics provided the inspiration for further Marxist revolutions in many countries.

LEADER OF THE SOVIET UNION Born 1878 Died 1953

Joseph Stalin

"I believe in one thing only, the power of human will."

JOSEPH STALIN

The future dictator of the Soviet Union was born in 1878 in Georgia, in the southeastern Russian Empire. Joseph Dzugashvili (not yet "Stalin," or "Man of Steel") attended a theological college in the Georgian capital, Tblisi, where he became involved in radical politics. He joined the Marxist Social Democratic Labor Party (SDLP), and with Lenin sided with the Bolshevik faction (see p.377) when the SDLP split in 1904.

Many Russian Marxists, including Lenin (see pp.376–77) were forced to live in exile, devoting themselves to complex theoretical debates. In Russia, Stalin engaged in practical subversive activities, ranging from armed robbery to distributing illegal pamphlets. His efforts attracted the attention of both the Bolshevik leadership and the police. After several arrests, Stalin was facing exile in Siberia when he was unexpectedly freed after the overthrow of the Czar in March 1917 (see pp.376–77).

Father of the people
Stalin's official portrait of 1940 is intended to suggest his farsighted wisdom. The photograph shows no sign of the smallpox scars that disfigured him from childhood.

Information card
Stalin was arrested several times before 1917. This is a police record of one of his crimes. The future dictator was photographed and his fingerprints were recorded.

Rise to power
Stalin proved himself a tough enforcer of Lenin's policies during the upheavals that brought the Bolsheviks to power in 1917 and the Civil War that followed. Hard-working and devious, once the Soviet Union was established he became one of the most powerful men in the country. In 1922 Stalin was appointed General Secretary to the Central Committee of the Communist Party. He exploited this post to fill Party positions with his appointees and expel his enemies. Lenin belatedly turned against Stalin, calling for someone "more tolerant… more polite." But by then, Stalin's hold was too strong. Stalin's maneuvering after Lenin's death in January 1924 was a masterly exercise in political manipulation. He

pitted his rivals for power against one another, then used his control of the Party to ensure that it expelled or demoted them. By the time Leon Trotsky—once fellow Bolshevik and now bitter rival—was exiled from the Soviet Union in 1929, Stalin had established himself as the country's undisputed leader.

In an early example of his taste for rewriting the past, Stalin celebrated his 50th birthday that year, discreetly adjusting his birth date to 1879. The celebrations initiated the personality cult that was to continue for the rest of

his life. Hailed by his propagandists as "the Universal Genius" and the "Man of Steel," factories, towns, and even mountains were named after him across the Soviet Union, and every reference to him was couched in terms of groveling flattery (see pp.380–81).

Socialism in one country
In 1924, Stalin proposed the slogan "Socialism in One Country." In practice, this meant building up the power of the Soviet Union, the one country where Marxist revolution had succeeded. Stalin was acutely

conscious of Russia's economic and cultural backwardness, and he despised the peasant majority. His successor, Nikita Khrushchev, wrote: "for Stalin, the peasants were scum." From 1928–29, Stalin aimed to transform the Soviet Union into a major international power, and the process of the collectivization of agriculture and industrialization (see p.380–81) reflected his belief in the use of terror to achieve radical change. During the 1930s, millions of Soviet citizens were killed by the state, used as slave labor in prison camps, or died in famines to

IDEAS

STATE CENSORSHIP

Stalin's censors distorted the past to preserve the myth of his infallibility. Individuals who had fallen out of favor were eliminated from the historical record. Retouching photographs was a striking aspect of this enforced amnesia. In charge of the secret police in 1936–38, Nikolai Yezhov, known as the "Poisoned Dwarf," was responsible for the worst of the Stalinist purges. When he was also executed on Stalin's orders in 1940, all traces of his association with the Great Leader were eradicated. Thus Yezhov's image was removed from this photo taken at the Moscow–Volga canal.

ORIGINAL PHOTOGRAPH

RETOUCHED VERSION

> # "The death of one man is a tragedy. The death of millions is a statistic."
>
> JOSEPH STALIN, ATTRIBUTED

TIMELINE

- **December 18, 1878** Born Joseph Vissarionovich Dzugashivili in Gori, Georgia, son of a cobbler.
- **1901** Joins the Marxist Russian Social Democratic Labor Party.
- **1912** Joins the Bolshevik Party Central Committee and becomes editor of *Pravda*.
- **1913** After several arrests, Stalin is sentenced to exile for life in Siberia.
- **March 13, 1917** Freed from exile.
- **October 9, 1917** Joins the Bolshevik Committee to make an armed seizure of power.
- **March 1919** Joins the Politburo, the most powerful body of the Bolshevik regime.
- **April 3, 1922** Appointed General Secretary to the Communist Party's Central Committee.
- **December 1922** In his "last testament," Lenin calls for Stalin to be removed from his post.
- **January 21, 1924** Lenin dies. Stalin, Zinoviev, and Kamenev exclude Trotsky from power.
- **October 19, 1926** Trotsky, Zinoviev, and Kamenev expelled from the Politburo.
- **1928** The collectivization of agriculture and rapid industrialization is begun.
- **February 1929** Trotsky is exiled from the USSR.
- **1932–34** Around four million die in the Ukrainian famine caused by Stalin's policy of collectivization and requisition of grain.
- **December 1934** Arrests and executions within the Communist Party follow Sergei Kirov's assassination.
- **1936–38** Around 690,000 executed in "The Great Terror."
- **August 1939** Stalin makes a neutrality pact with the Nazis, secretly agreeing the partition of Poland between Germany and the Soviet Union.
- **August 21, 1940** Trotsky murdered in Mexico by an agent of Stalin.
- **July 3, 1941** Calls for Soviet resistance to the German invasion.

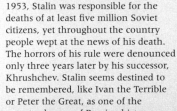

ALLIED PROPAGANDA

- **July 28, 1942** Decrees the death penalty for unauthorized retreat by the army.
- **November–December 1943** Stalin meets US president Roosevelt and British prime minister Churchill in Tehran; and again in Yalta in 1945.
- **March 1948** Coup in Czechoslovakia completes the Stalinist takeover of Eastern Europe.
- **July 1948–May 1949** USSR blockades Berlin, trying to evict the US, British, and French forces.
- **June 25, 1950** With Stalin's backing, North Korea invades South Korea, starting the Korean War.
- **1952** Allegations of a plot by Jewish doctors to assassinate Stalin and other Soviet leaders.
- **March 5, 1953** Stalin dies at his dacha under mysterious circumstances. (see pp.380–81.)

---

which Stalin's policies contributed. His aims were achieved, but at an astounding human cost.

Behind closed doors

The situation in the country was mirrored at Stalin's "court" in the Kremlin, Moscow, where his entourage lived in constant fear of arrest, torture, or execution. The assassination of Sergei Kirov, a member of Stalin's inner circle, in 1934 precipitated a wave of arrests and executions—although it is possible that Stalin himself had Kirov killed. Between 1936 and 1938, Stalin unleashed the secret police on the Communist Party leadership and army officers. Thousands were executed after grotesque "show trials" in which they confessed to absurd crimes.

Wartime leader

World War II showed Stalin at his best and worst. Shrewd and cunning, he entered an alliance with Nazi Germany in 1939 that arguably gave him time to strengthen his military position before the German invasion of the Soviet Union in June 1941. Yet he showed poor judgment in refusing to believe evidence of the imminent German attack. His military policy of "no retreat, no surrender" vastly inflated Soviet losses in the early battles of the war, yet he later bowed to his generals' judgment. His reign of terror over the Soviet people was unrelenting, but he sensibly encouraged patriotism and even allowed a revival of religion to

Opposing views
This German cartoon satirizes the Stalinist state by showing it as fighting against itself. In sharp contrast, this statue depicts Stalin as a regal leader.

boost morale. He handled the wartime alliance with the United States and Britain in masterly fashion, winning the trust of US president Franklin Delano Roosevelt, and the grudging respect of the British prime minister, Winston Churchill.

Postwar and death

Victory over Nazi Germany in May 1945 took Stalin to the pinnacle of power, but he became increasingly paranoid as ever more bizarre plots against him were allegedly uncovered by his secret police. Stalin's suspicion of the Western powers made the ideological struggle between the communist nations and the capitalist West—the Cold War—seem inevitable (see pp.406–07). By the time he died in

1953, Stalin was responsible for the deaths of at least five million Soviet citizens, yet throughout the country people wept at the news of his death. The horrors of his rule were denounced only three years later by his successor, Khrushchev. Stalin seems destined to be remembered, like Ivan the Terrible or Peter the Great, as one of the monster-heroes of Russian history.

World leader

The Soviet Union played a vital role on the side of the Allies in World War II. Stalin used his military advantage to bargain for greater Soviet influence in eastern Europe. He is pictured here with Churchill (left) and Roosevelt (center) at the Yalta Conference, where the leaders planned the future of postwar Europe.

BEFORE ≪

In the 19th and early 20th centuries, Russia's rocky path led it from despotic Czarist rule through revolution, civil war, and the creation of a new state. In 1920 the Union of Soviet Socialist Republics was formed.

SIBERIAN WORK CAMPS

During the 19th century, political activists and criminals were sent to work in forced labor camps in Siberia (northeast Russia). Stalin vastly extended the use of these work camps.

PRISONERS IN SIBERIA, 1897

SOVIET DEMOCRACY

Lenin held Marxist ≪ 334–35 beliefs and strove to achieve a "dictatorship of the proletariat." After seizing power for the workers, the Communist Party's role was to guide them. In theory, workers held political power through locally elected councils, or "soviets," but there was heavy state control and power was centralized in the Party.

W hen Lenin came to power after the Russian Revolution (see pp.378–79), he quickly established a highly centralized system of government. He banned all rival political parties, and empowered the Communist Party's dominant Central Committee to expel anyone who failed to follow the party line. Disagreements with Trotsky (see right) and other members soon led Lenin to favor Joseph Stalin, a rising star in the party. Stalin was already a member of the Politburo, the most powerful body of the regime, which made decisions on foreign relations, war, economics, and domestic policy, and the Orgburo, which was responsible for the Party's internal affairs. In 1922 he was appointed General Secretary of the Central Committee. After Lenin's death in January 1924, Stalin plotted to discredit and expel Central Committee members who opposed his leadership, most notably Leon Trotsky (see opposite). All his rivals would eventually meet with violent deaths.

Stalinism

Over the course of Stalin's rule, Lenin's version of communism mutated into what became known as Stalinism. Between 1928–37, Stalin instituted the first and second Five Year Plans, huge and ambitious schemes that aimed to transform the Soviet Union into an industrialized society. While the rest of the developed world was suffering economic depression, Stalin achieved extraordinary growth (see pp.384–85).

Agriculture in the Soviet Union was also transformed. Frustrated by his dependence on a rebellious peasantry to provide grain for the exports needed to finance his industrial plans, Stalin enforced a policy of "collectivization." Land belonging to peasants and kulaks (prosperous rural farmers) was confiscated and turned into vast farms that were collectively run and worked by cooperatives. It was initially

"Death solves all problems— no man, no problem." JOSEPH STALIN

30 MILLION The number of Russians who moved into cities and industrialized regions between 1928 and 1937, the time of Stalin's Five Year Plans.

The Hammer and Sickle

In 1921, with revolution achieved, and civil war at an end, the Soviet Union entered a 20-year period of relative peace. Lenin and the Bolshevik Party could turn their attention to the task of transforming the former Russian Empire, putting Karl Marx's vision of communism into practice.

Soviet farm tractor
In the 1930s, the first Soviet tractors were produced. They were kept at district stations and could only be used with party permission, thus keeping the farms under tight political control.

MARXIST REVOLUTIONARY 1879–1940

LEON TROTSKY

Leon Trotsky was a key figure in the Russian Revolution, a brilliant Marxist theorist, and a believer in international "permanent revolution." In the early days of the Soviet Union he served as the People's Commissar for Foreign Affairs and created the Red Army. After a power struggle with Stalin, he was expelled from the Soviet Union in 1929. Sentenced to death in his absence by a Moscow court—allegedly for plotting Stalin's death—Trotsky found asylum in Mexico. In 1940 a Stalinist agent, who had befriended Trotsky, assassinated him by driving an ice pick into his skull.

disastrous, producing reduced grain yields, violence, and famine. But over time, agriculture adjusted and living standards slowly began to rise.

The "Great Terror"

Such rapid growth and change came at a price. Throughout his rule, while Stalin cultivated a propaganda image of himself as father of his people—benign, even godlike—the Soviet people suffered appalling hardships. Living standards were often subhuman, work was compulsory, and absenteeism a crime. Criticism of the communist system could lead to a sentence in those same forced labor camps created by the Czars to crush dissent (see left). A network of new prison camps was erected west of Moscow to house the thousands who fell foul of Stalin's demands. The period 1936 to 1938, known as the "Great Terror," saw the secret police launching witch-hunts against the party elite and the army. Political opponents were forced to confess to plotting against Stalin and summarily executed. In two years, some 690,000 people were executed and many thousands more imprisoned or exiled.

The Soviet Bloc

The German invasion of the Soviet Union in 1941 caught Stalin by surprise, but after a bitterly fought war, his nation was ultimately victorious. At the 1945 conferences of Yalta and Potsdam, intended to secure lasting peace in the postwar world, Stalin secured the territories of eastern Poland and the Baltic States for Russia. New communist regimes emerged in Bulgaria, Romania, Hungary, Czechoslovakia, and East Germany. These became known as the Soviet Eastern Bloc, and were organized under Moscow's control, replicating Soviet policies and institutions. The Soviet Union had become the only world power to rival the United States. Relationships with its western allies quickly soured after the war. Russia and the Eastern Bloc became engaged in what would be termed the Cold War with the capitalist West (see pp.406–07).

Symbol of socialism
These figures raise the hammer, symbol of the industrial worker, and the sickle, symbol of the peasantry. "Socialist Realism" was the only art style permitted under Stalin.

The official truth
Pravda, meaning "truth," was the official newspaper of the Soviet Union between 1918 and 1991. Often used to parrot the views of the Communist Party, many regarded the paper as telling everything but the truth.

Ideal peasants
Without mechanized equipment, a Soviet women's brigade uses crude rakes to gather up the hay harvest on a collective farm, in this 1941 photograph. Images such as this one tried to show that the peasants were happily carrying out Stalin's severe agricultural policies; the reality was often very different.

Heroic images
This poster links Stalin with the revered Lenin, and typifies the heroic images Stalin used to promote himself.

AFTER ››

Despite the hardships that the Soviet people had suffered during Stalin's rule, there was genuine grief on his death in 1953. However, his legacy was a difficult one for the leadership of the Soviet Union.

DEATH OF STALIN

Stalin died in **mysterious circumstances** after eating dinner with close political colleagues, including **Lavrenty Beria**, former head of his secret police, and Stalin's successor Nikita Khrushchev. It has been suggested that he had swallowed warfarin, a type of rat poison. His body was embalmed, and displayed in the Lenin Mausoleum in Red Square. After Stalin's crimes were exposed, his **remains were removed** in 1961, and reburied in the Kremlin wall.

DE-STALINIZATION

Khrushchev swiftly began a process known as **De-Stalinization**, introducing basic legal rights, **allowing writers and artists greater freedoms**, and releasing huge numbers of political prisoners. Khrushchev also **encouraged foreign visitors** to the Soviet Union, but travel abroad for citizens remained strictly controlled. In 1956, Khrushchev denounced Stalin's regime of "suspicion, fear, and terror" in a secret speech to the inner circle of the Communist Party and a report was issued to the public pointing to some of Stalin's mistakes. The dominance of Stalinism finally began to diminish and a lesser cult of Lenin returned. That year, riots broke out in Poland, and the Hungarian people rebelled against Soviet rule. The **Hungarian uprising 448–49 ››** was brutally repressed by the Soviet Red Army.

KHRUSHCHEV

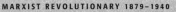

1 RED ARMY POSTER

2 RED CAVALRY POSTER

3 "RED WEDGE" BY EL LISSITSKY

4 "LENIN SWEEPS THE WORLD CLEAN"

5 ANTI-IMPERIALISM POSTER

6 POSTER BY ALEXANDER RODCHENKO

7 FILM POSTER

8 FIVE YEAR PLAN POSTER

9 INDUSTRIALIZATION POSTER

10 SOCIALIST POSTER

11 COLLECTIVIZATION POSTER

13 WORLD WAR II POSTER

15 ANTIFASCIST POSTER

16 ANTI-CAPITALISM POSTER

12 YOUTH MOVEMENT POSTER

14 ANTI-NAZI POSTER

17 COLLECTIVE FARM POSTER

Soviet Propaganda

During the rule of the Communist Party in Russia, every aspect of artistic production was controlled by the state. Propaganda produced during the period celebrated the glory of the socialist government and its policies and achievements, while damning its enemies.

1 **Red Army recruitment poster** (c. 1918–19), which reads "Have You Enlisted?" **2** **Ukrainian recruitment poster** for the Bolshevik cavalry from the Civil War period (c. 1918–20). **3** **"Red Wedge,"** an iconic Civil War poster by El Lissitsky (1919). The red wedge represents the Red Army driving into the heart of the White Army. **4** **"Lenin Sweeps the World Clean"** (c. 1920), a poster showing the Soviet leader ridding the world of the enemies of communism– the monarchy, the church, and capitalist businessmen. **5** **Anti-imperialism poster** by Dmitri Moor, depicting imperialism as a monster encircling industry and keeping the workers from the means of production. **6** **"Books in all branches of knowledge"** (1925), a famous and much-imitated poster by Alexander Rodchenko advertising the Leningrad branch of the state publishing house. Rodchenko's friend, Lilja Brik, shouts the word "books." **7** **Soviet film poster,** advertising *Moulin Rouge* (1928). **8** **Poster promoting Stalin's Five Year Plans** (1931) and showing women working in industry. **9** **"Industrialization is the Path to Socialism"** (1928), a poster promoting the rapid industrialization of the Soviet Union. **10** **Poster declaring "We are Building Socialism"** (1930) and showing images of vast factories, strong workers, and busy production lines. **11** **"Join Us"**–two idealized agricultural workers call out to persuade workers to join them on a *kolkhoz*, a type of collectivized farm (1930). **12** **Poster** calling for young workers to join collective farms (1930–31). **13** **Stalin** portrayed as a great leader with the military might of the Soviet Union behind him at the outset of World War II (1939). **14** **"Death to the Child Murderers"** (1942), a World War II poster showing a Nazi boot trampling a Russian peasant girl. **15** **Secret police poster** (1937) warns against "spies and deviants [and] Trotskyite-Bukharinite agents of fascism." **16** **Anti-US poster** from the Cold War period (c. 1955) showing a caricature of an inflated Statue of Liberty supporting a fat capitalist. **17** **Postwar poster** using an image of a typically romanticized worker to promote collective farming (late 1940s). **18** **"Glory!"**–a poster showing Yuri Gagarin, the first man to enter space, with fellow cosmonauts (1960).

18 SPACE RACE POSTER

« BEFORE

The Great Depression

The US stock market collapsed in October 1929, triggering worldwide economic recession. Authoritarian regimes rose to power as people lost faith in democratic governments.

BEFORE

After World War I the world economy slid into a recession that resulted in mass unemployment. Much of Europe experienced high rates of inflation.

NORTH AMERICA AFTER THE WAR

The postwar recession was reasonably short-lived in North America. Factories that produced goods for the war effort soon adapted to producing consumer goods, such as radios and cars, and from 1922 until 1927 the North American economies showed consistent growth.

EUROPE AFTER THE WAR

European agriculture and industries failed to adjust to the reduced demand of peacetime trade, so when millions of soldiers returned home, many could not find jobs. Germany, which had machinery confiscated by the victors, struggled to make **war reparation payments** « 374–75 to the Allies, who in turn had trouble paying off war debts, and **recovery loans** provided by the US.

HYPERINFLATION IN GERMANY

As the Germans thought they would win the war and intended to force the losers to pay for their costs, they chose not to finance it through taxation. Instead, the government ordered the *Reichsbank*, or central bank, to print more and more money to cover its ever-increasing war expenses. The *Reichsbank* continued to print money until 1923, when the purchasing power of the money in

circulation plummeted as the price of everything in Germany inflated rapidly (hyperinflation). At the peak of hyperinflation the exchange rate was **one trillion marks to the US dollar.** Paper money was worth so little that people burned it to heat their houses.

WORTHLESS MARKS

BREAD **In 1918 in Germany a loaf of bread cost 0.63 marks. During the hyperinflation crisis the price rose to 201,000,000,000 marks in November 1923.**

During the early 1920s the American economy flourished, but by 1927 the country was overproducing goods for which it did not have a market. Agricultural and factory production soon slowed down, leading to the loss of millions of jobs. Despite the downturn in demand for goods and rising unemployment, financiers and bankers continued to speculate recklessly on New York's Wall Street stock exchange, relying on borrowed money and false optimism.

The Wall Street Crash

In October 1929, stock prices began to decline and investors lost confidence in their shares, opting to sell them all. The first day of real panic, October 24, is known as "Black Thursday." The panic began again on "Black Monday," and on "Black Tuesday," October 29, 16 million shares were sold, and prices on the stock market collapsed completely in what became known as

In the news
The Crash affected all Americans, even making the headlines in this entertainment newspaper.

173 MILLION shares sold on US stock exchange in 1921.

451 MILLION shares sold in 1926.

1,125 MILLION shares sold in frantic trading in 1929.

the Wall Street Crash. Fortunes were lost and companies failed overnight. Wages for those still fortunate enough to have work fell dramatically. Many banks had made loans to businesses and people who could no longer repay

them. Some banks also lost money in the Crash—when people hit by the economic depression needed to withdraw their savings, the banks often did not have the money to give them. This caused other bank customers to panic and demand their cash, so many banks were ruined. As people lost their jobs and savings, mortgages on many homes and farms were foreclosed and the properties were repossessed. Many people were forced to take shelter in shantytowns, which were nicknamed "Hoovervilles" out of resentment for President Herbert Hoover, who refused to provide aid to the unemployed.

Government intervention

As a result of the Crash, US investors withdrew many foreign loans, causing the collapse of the system of international loans set up to handle war reparations (see BEFORE). European countries, including Germany, needed these loans to pay for their imports, and were unable to do so once the funds were taken away. This affected trade between Europe and North America directly. Other parts of the world were also badly hit as much of their trade relied on selling food and raw materials to Europe and North America. The price of commodities, or traded goods, dropped drastically,

---

EFFECTS OF DEPRESSION
The economic slump that gripped the US spread across the globe. Ill-conceived government measures exacerbated the hardships suffered in many countries.

1929 US loans to and investments in Europe end, causing a worldwide **slump in productivity** and prices.

1929–33 Stalin collectivizes Soviet agriculture.

May 1931 Austria's largest bank collapses, which in turn sets off a series of **banking collapses** all over central Europe.

Winter 1931 to 1933 Britain introduces protective import tariffs, but in the **Ottawa Agreements** gives preferential rates for its overseas territories.

March 9–June 15, 1933 The American Congress passes Roosevelt's **New Deal** program.

| 1929 | 1930 | 1931 | 1932 | 1933 |

October 24–29, 1929 The Wall Street Crash follows panic selling of stocks and shares.

October 28, 1929 The London stock exchange collapses.

June 17, 1930 The Smoot-Hawley Tariff, the highest tax on imports to the US in history, is signed into law by the American Congress.

June 20, 1931 President Hoover halts war reparations by Germany as part of an effort to limit the financial fallout of the banking collapse.

January 30, 1933 Hitler becomes **German chancellor,** winning the post by exploiting popular resentment of the depressed economic and social conditions.

On the road
Evicted from their farm in Missouri, this family traveled to California in search of work on the farms there.

In an effort to avoid the economic problems that arose after World War I, delegates from 44 Allied nations met in 1944 to plan for the end of World War II.

INTERNATIONAL MONETARY FUND
New **rules for financial and commercial transactions** between states in the developed world were drawn up and the **International Monetary Fund** (IMF) was established to implement international monetary rules.

WORLD BANK
The World Bank was established to provide **financing and advice** for the economies of developing countries. World Bank activities focus on the development of heath, education, rural development, and legal institutions.

became dictatorships (countries ruled by one person with no recognized opposition). Some states set about building empires to secure supplies of raw materials. In October 1935, Italy's fascist leader, Benito Mussolini (see pp.386–87), ordered the invasion of Abyssinia in East Africa. Hitler (see pp.390–91) began a program of active expansion, annexing Austria in March 1938. In response, Britain and France began to rearm, and World War II (see pp.392–405) erupted in 1939. The renewed war in Europe created new jobs in armament factories, revitalizing the world economy and ending the economic depression.

"I pledge you, I pledge myself, to a **new deal** for the **American people**."

FRANKLIN D. ROOSEVELT, DEMOCRATIC PRESIDENTIAL NOMINATION ACCEPTANCE SPEECH, 1932

falling to 45 percent of 1929 values in 1932. Nations sought to protect their own industries. President Hoover introduced the Smoot-Hawley Tariff in 1930, imposing a 42–50 percent tax on imports, and European governments responded with similar protectionist measures. This made matters worse, as it crippled international trade.

Hoover was criticized heavily for the way he handled the Depression and he was voted out of office in 1932 when Franklin D. Roosevelt won a landslide victory on the promise of a "New Deal," a series of relief programs devised to restart the economy and provide new jobs (see right). Roosevelt extended US government responsibilities into new economic areas and created social welfare assistance on a national level. Ultimately this large-scale government intervention worked and was adopted by other liberal democracies.

Rise of the far-right

Mass unemployment and poverty caused great anger, leading to civil unrest in some countries. Many people turned to right-wing leaders who promised to restore national prosperity by force if necessary (see pp.386–87). Between 1929 and 1939, 25 countries

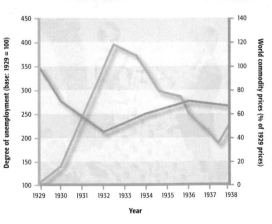

Commodities
There was a direct relationship between world commodity prices and employment between 1929 and 1932. When commodity prices fell to their lowest value in 1932, unemployment peaked. In the same year, commodity prices began to recover and unemployment began to decline in response.

KEY
Unemployment
World commodity prices

Soviet growth
Soviet economics followed a different path from those countries affected by the Great Depression. GNP rose as **Five Year Plans** for industrial growth and the state collectivization (see pp.380–81) of agriculture transformed the way the economy was run. The Soviet Union moved from being a rural and traditional economy to an urbanized, industrial base and emerged from this period of growth as a world power.

IDEA

NEW DEAL

Roosevelt's New Deal was a series of programs that aimed to tackle economic depression and rescue millions of Americans living in need. The program vastly increased the scope of the federal government's activities. Business practices were reformed and welfare policies were introduced. Huge public projects were set up, creating millions of new jobs. One successful project was run by the Tennessee Valley Authority. It built more than 20 dams and hydroelectric stations, turning the Colorado river basin into a vast wealth-producing area.

BEFORE

After the atrocities and humiliations of World War I, nationalist right-wing ideals took hold in many European countries.

ACTION FRANÇAISE

CHARLES MAURRAS

Founded in France in 1898, *Action Française* was an extreme **right-wing movement** led by Charles Maurras; his political vision included the reestablishment of the French monarchy. The group distributed a daily bulletin of the same name.

THE GERMAN IDEAL

In the 19th century, the concept of an eternal, ideal German *Volk* (people) and *Volksgeist* (spirit of the nation) began to emerge. The philosopher **George Hegel** spoke of the German spirit as the **"spirit of the new world"** and Friedrich Nietzsche envisioned a "master morality" in which strength triumphs over weakness, unrestricted by the "tyranny" of virtue. These concepts appealed to Hitler, who twisted them to suit his own purposes.

THE PAN-GERMAN PARTY

Georg Schönerer founded the Pan-German Party in the 1880s in Austria. Its aim was to **unite all German-speaking peoples** under German rule. The Party had a presence in the Austrian Parliament, but Schönerer's violent racism, which had led to his imprisonment for assaults on Jews, was too extreme for the politics of the day.

ITALIAN NATIONALISTS SEIZE FIUME

In 1919, Italian patriots, led by the poet **Gabriele D'Annunzio**, occupied the Italian-speaking port of Fiume on the Croatian coast. This action, which had popular support in Italy, was born of fury at gaining a mere 9,000 square miles in post–World War I peace settlements.

Fascism

World War I left Europe exhausted. Unemployment was rife as economies struggled to adapt to peacetime conditions. Disillusioned with their existing forms of government, many people were drawn to a new brand of nationalism known as fascism.

National Socialist Party poster
The Nazi Party promised to bring stability and order to Germany after the economic and social upheaval of the 1920s. It appealed to the people's basic demands, as this election poster from 1932 shows, with its promise of "Work, Freedom, and Bread."

The emergence of fascism and Nazism in Europe was made possible by a range of conditions. Economic hardship after World War I was a primary factor. In addition, the period 1918–20 was marked by political instability. Violence and lawlessness erupted across much of Eastern Europe, Germany, Italy, and Spain, between communists (see p.335) and their political opponents. Political thinking on the left was fractured, with communist, socialist, and trade union groups often in conflict with each other. On the right of the political spectrum, the nationalist philosophies of fascism began to gain ground. Fascists loathed communism's internationalist thinking and had no faith in democratic government. Many, including Hitler and Mussolini, were veterans of World War I (see pp.372–75) and resented the old ruling elites who had led them into

a disastrous war. With no attachment to church or monarchy, fascists put all their faith in love of their nation, favoring a strong, ordered state.

The massive human and economic costs of the World War I left Italy's government undermined. In 1920, bands of "Blackshirts"—adopting the Roman symbol of the *fasces* (see right), which represented their belief in collective strength and authority over individual freedom—began to take the law into their own hands, attacking

> **FASCISM** A radical nationalist ideology. Fascists believe in strong, authoritarian leadership and a collective, classless society bound by racial allegiance.

socialists and striking trade unions. In the absence of government authority, the Fascists were widely seen as the protectors of law and order. In October

Italian coin
"Fascist" comes from the Roman *fasces*—a bundle of sticks (weak on their own but collectively strong) surrounding an ax—a symbol of authority.

1922, Fascist leader Benito Mussolini, ordered his Blackshirts to march on Rome and seize power. King Victor Emmanuel III refused to back his Prime Minister's request for military support and invited Mussolini to form a new government. In 1926 Mussolini assumed absolute power, dissolving all other political parties and brutally silencing political opponents. Known to his people as *"Il Duce,"* or "the Leader," Mussolini cultivated an image of himself as Italy's one true leader, the choice of the masses. In reality, Italy was a police state.

The right-wing governments of Germany and Italy backed the nationalists in the Spanish Civil War. Fascist parties continue to draw support to the present day.

SPANISH CIVIL WAR
In 1936, fighting began in Spain between the socialist and republican left and nationalists led by **General Franco 388–89 »**. A bitter civil war ensued which lasted until the nationalist victory in 1939. **Hitler 390–91 »** and Mussolini both sent military aid to support Franco while **Stalin 378–79 »** supported his opponents.

GENERAL FRANCO

NEOFASCISM
Political groups of the far right have continued to emerge since World War II. Some, termed Neo-Nazis, believe in reviving Hitler's national socialism. Neofascist groups share elements of Nazi beliefs and tend to concentrate on a nationalistic, anti-immigration stance. These groups have included *Alternativa Sociale* in Italy, led by Mussolini's granddaughter Alessandra; the French *Front National*, founded by Jean-Marie Le Pen; and Jörg Haider's Austrian Freedom Party.

Nuremberg Rally
In the 1930s the Nazis held annual rallies for the party faithful at Nuremberg, as in the picture above. Thousands of soldiers stand listening to Hitler speak.

March on Rome
Mussolini's Blackshirts, shown above, were ordered to march on the Italian capital, Rome, in 1922. The Blackshirts, also called *"squadristi"* or squadrons, acted as paramilitary forces for the Fascist Party.

In 1918 the government of Germany's new Weimar Republic also faced huge problems. Germans were scarred by defeat in World War I and resentful of the peace settlements under which territory had been lost (see p.375). Economic troubles were made worse by war reparation payments imposed on Germany by its victorious enemies. In 1919, an Austrian-born soldier, Adolf Hitler, joined a small Munich-based political group: The German Worker's Party. Hitler had ambitions for power. His tirades against capitalists, communists, and Jews (at whose door he laid blame for all Germany's ills), would soon catch the public ear. His party was renamed the National Socialist German Workers Party (the NSDAP or Nazi Party, see pp.390–91).

Although the Nazi Party had much in common with Mussolini's Fascists, it also had a quasireligious element, with its all-powerful Führer who demanded submission and a zealous belief in the superiority of the German race. Taking up Hegel's idealist concept of nation (SEE BEFORE), Nazism's goal was to unite all German-speaking people in a great German *Reich*, or empire (see p.393), that would last for a millennium. The Nazis believed races such as the Slavs and Jews were racially inferior to Aryans (white Caucasian people, the purest having blue eyes and blonde hair) and as such they would be banished from the *Reich* to preserve Aryan racial purity. Later, the Jews were to be wiped out in the "Final Solution" (see pp.400–01).

Mass movements with fascist ideologies arose in many countries during the 1920s and 1930s. The Austrian government had fascist leanings well before the country was annexed by Germany (see pp.392–93). In Britain, the politician Oswald Mosley formed the British Union of Fascists. Mosley's "Blackshirts" acted as guards at political rallies and fought with left-wing and Jewish groups.

ITALIAN LEADER (1883–1945)
BENITO MUSSOLINI

Mussolini rose to political prominence before World War I in the Italian Socialist Party. In 1915 he broke with the socialists over intervention in World War I and became a radical nationalist. In 1919 he founded the Blackshirts and the Italian Fascist Party in 1921. He became Prime Minister of Italy in 1922. Italy fought alongside Nazi Germany in World War II, and when the Allies invaded Italy in 1943, Mussolini was stripped of his powers, though he led a Social Republic in the north of the country until he was shot in April 1945.

"The truth is that men are tired of liberty."

BENITO MUSSOLINI, APRIL 7, 1923

BEFORE

When Spain lost control of its American colonies, it began to lose its political stability.

REIGN OF ALFONSO XIII
Defeat in the 1898 Spanish-American War **<< 318–19** damaged Spain's monarchy. **Republican movements** pressed for greater democracy, and support for anarchism took root. In response to violent strikes, King Alfonso XIII became increasingly dictatorial. In 1921 Spain was defeated in a **rebellion by tribes in its Moroccan colony**, which aggravated the economic crisis, and domestic violence escalated. In September 1923 **General Miguel Primo de Rivera** led a *coup d'état* and became military dictator until he lost the army's support and resigned in 1930. In 1931 King Alfonso agreed to municipal elections. The

ALFONSO XIII

result was overwhelming majorities for those who were in favor of a republic, and Alfonso was forced into exile. He died in 1941.

SECOND REPUBLIC
The left-wing Second Republic alienated many groups with its reforms. In 1933, a **right-wing election victory** led to a general strike on October 4, 1934 and an armed rising in Asturias, northern Spain. When the left-wing **Popular Front** won the 1936 general election, their radical rhetoric alarmed conservatives. Tension mounted as street battles between rival groups and widespread strikes paralyzed the nation.

ANARCHISM is a political belief that society should have no police, government laws, or other authority.

Spanish Civil War

The Spanish Civil War is regarded as the first ideological conflict between international fascism and international communism. Some of the military tactics that were employed during the fighting foreshadowed those later used in World War II.

On February 21, 1936 Spain's new left-wing Popular Front government promised liberty, prosperity, and justice, but some people considered their policies to be too progressive. On July 17 and 18, Spanish military forces based in Morocco revolted against the elected government. They expected little opposition, but supporters of the Second Republic and its government resisted, and Spain found itself in the grip of civil war. The Republicans received weapons and volunteers from the Soviet Union and Mexico, and aid from supporters of liberal democracy, communism, and the anarchist movement. Left-wing parties, such as the Socialists and the Anti-Stalinist Marxist Party, which was formed in 1935, also supported the government. The insurgents, who became known as the Nationalists, had the backing of monarchists, Catholics, and the Falange

Fallen soldier
This photograph shows a Republican militiaman being shot at Cerro Muriano on the Cordoba front on September 5, 1936. It was taken by Hungarian photographer Robert Capa.

"Better to **die on one's feet** than to **live on one's knees**."
DOLORES IBARRURI, SPANISH WRITER AND POLITICIAN, JULY 18, 1936

War of words
US writer and journalist Ernest Hemingway observes a member of General Lister's Loyalist Vth Army Corps on the east bank of the Ebro River on November 5, 1937. A new kind of war journalism emerged during the Spanish Civil War, with eyewitness accounts of the brutality of war reported in the first person.

Call to arms
During the Spanish Civil War, recruiting posters were an important means of communication as many people were illiterate. The Nationalist poster (c. 1936) on the left and Anti-Fascist forces poster on the right are designed to carry a clear message without needing to be read.

to Spain to protect the Popular Front government. Their ranks included anyone who was opposed to fascism, and Spain became the *cause célèbre* for left-leaning intellectuals across the Western world. The British government, which proclaimed itself neutral, warned that Britons who enlisted on either side would be liable to two years in prison, and urged other states to prevent the dispatch of volunteers. Despite this deterrent, thousands of foreign idealists made their way to Spain, many of them to defend the capital city, Madrid.

Guernica
Spanish artist Pablo Picasso painted this mural for the Spanish pavilion at the Paris World's Fair (an exhibition). It expresses his feelings about the destruction of the Basque town of Guernica by German air raids in 1937.

(a Spanish fascist party). The fascist Italian and German governments also became involved, supplying troops and weapons, which gave the civil war a dramatic international character.

On July 19, 1936, General Franco (see below), a leader of the insurgent forces, assumed command of the Army of Africa based in Morocco and took it to Spain. This army played a key part in gaining Nationalist control of southwestern Spain. At the outbreak of the war, the Republican Army was about one-third larger than the Nationalist Army. However, by the time the Army of Africa arrived in Spain, the figures were close to equal.

International Brigades
Socialists and communists from all over Europe formed groups of volunteers called International Brigades and went

Battle for Madrid
At the outbreak of war, Madrid was controlled by the Popular Front government. Franco was anxious to capture the capital, and bombing raids began on August 28, 1936. On September 30, he captured Toledo, which is only 40 miles (65 km) from Madrid. Toledo had been in Republican hands since the beginning, despite the onslaught from thousands of Nationalist soldiers. Its capture was a huge morale boost for the Nationalists and did much to enhance Franco's reputation. By November 1, 25,000 Nationalist troops under General José Varela had reached the western and southern suburbs of Madrid. Five days later, Varela's men were joined by the German Legion Kondor (a unit from the *Luftwaffe*, see p.392) and the siege of Madrid began. It was to last for nearly three years.

Nazi medal
The Spanish Cross, or Legion Kondor Cross, was a campaign medal instituted on April 14, 1939 to recognize those Germans who served in the Spanish Civil War on the side of General Franco.

the Basque town of Guernica, an event foreshadowing episodes that occurred in World War II.

Franco was under pressure from both Hitler (see pp.390–91) and Mussolini to obtain a quick victory by taking Madrid, so he blockaded the road that linked the city to the rest of Republican Spain, and his troops attacked Guadalajara, 40 miles (65 km) east of the capital, on March 8, 1937. The Republican Army counterattacked, making use of Soviet tanks, and many lives were lost.

Infighting
Meanwhile, there was serious infighting among Republicans in Barcelona. On May 6, 1937, death squads assassinated a number of prominent anarchists, and rioting followed. These events severely damaged the Popular Front and led to the formation of a new government under the leadership of Juan Negrín. Negrín was a Communist sympathizer, and this enabled Joseph Stalin (see pp.378–79) to influence the Spanish government.

In April 1938, the Nationalist Army broke through the Republican defenses in the north, and Franco moved his troops toward Valencia with the aim of encircling Madrid. Negrín, eager to show that the Republican government was still viable, insisted on a policy of attack, rather than defense. However, at the Battle of Ebro (July 25– November 16, 1938), the Republicans were all but destroyed as an effective fighting force. On January 26, 1939, Barcelona fell to the Nationalist Army. It was a stunning victory. With further victories in Catalonia, Vinaroz, and other towns along the eastern coast,

Franco believed the war was over and urged the Republicans to surrender. On January 27, 1939, British prime minister Neville Chamberlain recognized the Nationalist government headed by Franco. The Nationalist Army entered Madrid virtually unopposed on March 27, 1939. Four days later, Franco declared the end of the war.

> **ARMY OF AFRICA** A highly professional army formed of Spanish troops, members of the Spanish Foreign Legion (modeled on the French Foreign Legion), and Moroccans from Spanish Morocco, known as *Regulares*.

AFTER »

After the Spanish Civil War, Franco took control as the country's dictator.

FOREIGN WITHDRAWAL
A committee in London drew up a plan to enable those who had fought in the **International Brigades** to return home. After months of negotiation, the other European powers finally gave their approval to the plan.

INTERNATIONAL BRIGADE STAMP

FRANCO IN POWER
The methods Franco used to restore order included censorship, banning strikes, and ensuring that the Nationalists formed the only legal political party. His **enemies were sent to prison camps**, where many thousands died.

SPAIN AND WORLD WAR II
Despite Hitler's efforts, Spain remained neutral in **World War II 392–405 »**, though Franco sent Germany supplies of scarce raw materials. He was penalized for this by the Allies, and Spain was barred from the **United Nations 397 »**.

FRANCISCO FRANCO

Franco was born into a military family. He joined the army and served in Morocco from 1910 to 1927. In 1926 he became the youngest general in Spain, and by 1936 he was chief of staff for the military. After leading the Nationalist movement to victory in the Spanish Civil War, Franco dominated Spanish politics and was the formal head of state. He wore the uniform of a captain general, a rank traditionally reserved for the king. Within three years of his death in 1975, Spain became a fully constitutional monarchy.

Fascist victory
In December 1936, Benito Mussolini (see p.387), Italy's fascist ruler, began to supply the Nationalists with men and equipment. After failing to take Madrid in a full frontal assault in 1937, Franco's forces launched a campaign to conquer the Basque Provinces, Asturias, and the industrial areas of northern Spain. During this offensive, the first large-scale aerial bombing of civilians took place, including the infamous German raid that destroyed

59 THOUSAND foreign volunteers joined in the fight

500 THOUSAND people lost their lives during the conflict

25 THOUSAND people died from malnutrition

20TH CENTURY DICTATOR Born 1889 Died 1945

Adolf Hitler

"When starting and waging a war, it is **not right** that matters, **but victory**."

HITLER, 22 AUGUST 1939

The Führer
Nazi propaganda photos depicted Hitler as the towering leader–führer–of his people. He was totally convinced by his personal myth, seeing himself as a "man of destiny" leading the German people to greatness.

W orld War I was the pivotal event in the life of German dictator Adolf Hitler. Before the war, this son of a minor official in the Austro-Hungarian Empire was a failed artist, nursing fantasies of greatness but in reality living an aimless, embittered existence on the margins of society. Four years serving on the Western Front put Hitler in touch with the shared experience of millions of Germans: the participation in modern warfare at its most destructive and of a defeat so painful that it had to be met with denial.

Like many other ex-servicemen, Hitler found it impossible to demobilize mentally, regarding himself as a frontline soldier ("*Frontkämpfer*") for the rest of his life.

Speaker and politician
Hitler had no particular interest in politics before or during World War I, nor had he expressed any particular dislike of Jews. But amid the political and social chaos of postwar Germany, he adopted views by which many Germans explained away the collapse of their country: that the war had been lost through a "stab in the back" by socialists and Jews, and that Germany

Hitler the soldier
This image shows Hitler as a corporal in the German Army in April 1915. As a "runner" carrying messages to the frontline trenches, he was wounded three times. In 1918, he was awarded the Iron Cross (right) for bravery under fire.

Mein Kampf
Hitler wrote his autobiographical political statement *Mein Kampf* (My Struggle) while in prison for nine months for his part in the Munich Putsch of 1923 (see right). Published in 1925, the book expressed his hatred of Judaism and Communism and his ambition to establish a German empire in the east.

IDEAS

NATIONAL SOCIALISM

Much of the "national" element of the ideology behind Hitler's National Socialist German Workers' Party (the Nazi Party) appealed to the masses because it was in line with a long tradition of German nationalism. For example, belief in the creation of a self-sufficient "Greater Germany" incorporating all ethnic Germans within its borders. The term "socialism" was associated with ethnic exclusivity rather than equality. Hitler strongly opposed Marxist socialism and purged from the party all those who wanted socialism in the sense of workers' power or the overthrow of capitalism. The core of National Socialism was not class war, but race war. Hitler intended to create a military state along racial lines. While the supposed evil power of the Jews would be crushed and "inferior" races such as the Slavs would be used as slave labor, the privileged German "Volk" would unite in solidarity behind the heroic leadership of their Führer.

"Who says I am not under the special protection of God?" ADOLF HITLER, MARCH 23, 1933

Hitler off duty
Hitler relaxes with Eva Braun, the woman who was his companion from 1932. Hitler married her in his Berlin bunker on April 29, 1945; they both committed suicide the following day.

was the victim of an international Jewish conspiracy. It was while mixing in political extremist circles in Munich that Hitler chanced upon an exceptional talent. When he addressed political meetings in beerhalls, his speeches stirred the crowd in a way no other agitator could achieve. His hypnotic ability to dominate and sway his listeners' emotions gave him the first intoxicating experience of power. By the mid-1920s, through the failed Munich Putsch, a coup in which Hitler tried to overthrow the government; his subsequent nationally publicized trial; and the publication of *Mein Kampf*; Hitler had reinvented himself as the messianic leader of a German national revival. His image was manufactured and dramatized by the Nazi Party propagandists, but it depended on a steely self-belief.

Rise to power
Hitler was an opportunist who exploited a democratic system he despised to obtain absolute power, never wavering from his long-term goals—establishing a dictatorship; overturning the Versailles peace treaty that had marked the end of World War I; defeating "world Jewry"; and creating a German empire to the east in the Slav lands

taken from Germany in 1919. In the political maneuvers and campaigns from 1929 to 1935 that brought him to absolute power in Germany, he showed a ruthless instinct for his opponents' weaknesses, alternating savage rhetoric and physical intimidation with gestures of moderation. Inherently given to fits of rage, he learned to manipulate this side of his personality for effect, raging one moment, soothing the next. Those who thought they could control him—the military, politicians, businessmen— underestimated his power, to which they all eventually submitted.

Once in control, Hitler took little interest in the day-to-day business of government. While his subordinates worked to fulfill what they guessed to be "the Führer's will," the Führer himself dabbled in grandiose architectural projects, such as the huge Königsplatz in Munich, or enjoyed the Alpine views at his Berchtesgaden retreat. Hitler was a teetotal vegetarian obsessed with cleanliness—he had no taste for luxurious

Final days
On April 20, 1945, looking tired and haggard and facing imminent defeat, Hitler appeared in the Reichs Chancellery garden in Berlin with some of his officers. Ten days later, he committed suicide.

self-indulgence. His only intimate relationship was with Eva Braun, and little is known about it.

Having assured his dictatorial control of Germany, Hitler turned his obsession to the pursuit of power in foreign and military affairs. He used the same tactics to get his way on the world stage as he had in domestic politics— alternating threats of violence with offers of peace, and taking outrageous risks to achieve his aims.

War and downfall
In September 1939, Hitler invaded Poland and finally tipped Europe into war. The startling success of German arms fatally confirmed Hitler's view of himself as an infallible leader. By the end of 1941 he had gone to war with both the Soviet Union and USA, and taken direct control of the German armed forces. When the tide of war turned against Germany, Hitler's mental and physical state deteriorated and his grasp on reality weakened. Yet he never lost his savage desire for power. Obsessed with his own historical greatness, Hitler was quite prepared to see Germany destroyed to create a grandiose funeral pyre for his ego. Eventually, holed up in his Berlin bunker, Hitler realized he had been defeated. As the Soviet army advanced into the city, he committed suicide.

TIMELINE

- **April 20, 1889** Born in Braunau, Austria, the son of a customs official.
- **1907** Fails the entrance exam for the Viennese Academy of Fine Arts.
- **May 1913** Moves from Vienna to Munich to evade military service in Austria.
- **August 1914** Joins the German Army as a volunteer at the outbreak of World War I.
- **August 1918** Awarded the Iron Cross, First Class, after four years' service as a dispatch runner on the Western Front.
- **1919** Comes in contact with the German Workers' Party (DAP) in Munich.
- **July 1921** Becomes leader of renamed National Socialist German Workers' Party (Nazi Party).
- **November 9, 1923** Attempts to overthrow the German government in Munich Putsch.
- **December 1924** Released from prison after serving nine months for treason.
- **March 1932** Belatedly takes German nationality and contests presidential elections, narrowly losing to Paul von Hindenburg.
- **January 30, 1933** Appointed chancellor through a backstairs deal with conservative German politicians and forms government.
- **March 23, 1933** Exploits crisis caused by a fire at the Reichstag (House of Representatives) on February 27; pushes through the Enabling Act to gain exceptional powers for four years.
- **June 30, 1934** Purges the SA (Stormtroopers), the Nazi Party's paramilitary wing, in the "Night of the Long Knives"—more than 80 people are murdered.
- **August 19, 1934** Becomes dictator of Germany after the death of Paul von Hindenburg.
- **March 7, 1936** Sends German forces into the demilitarized Rhineland in defiance of the Versailles peace treaty.

AUSTRIAN STAMP 1945

- **March 12–13, 1938** Germany annexes Austria in the Anschluss.
- **September 29–30, 1938** Wins British and French backing for the German takeover of the Sudetenland area of Czechoslovakia at the Munich Conference.
- **September 1, 1939** Orders invasion of Poland, triggering World War II.
- **March 30, 1941** Addresses his generals about the planned invasion of the Soviet Union and calls for "a war of annihilation"; the invasion is launched on June 22.
- **December 11, 1941** Declares war on the United States after the Japanese attack on Pearl Harbor.
- **December 19, 1941** Takes personal command of the German armed forces.
- **July 20, 1944** Survives an assassination attempt at his headquarters at Rastenburg.
- **April 30, 1945** Shoots himself in his bunker in Berlin as the city falls to the Soviet Red Army.

BEFORE

Scarred by World War I, Britain and France sought to avoid war with Nazi Germany but were thwarted by Hitler's ambitions.

MUNICH PACT

The Munich Pact was agreed between Britain, Germany, Italy, and France in 1938. It ordered the surrender of German-speaking areas of Czechoslovakia to Germany. Anglo-French **appeasement** of Hitler's wishes is criticized, but in 1938 neither nation could challenge Germany.

HITLER'S QUEST FOR *LEBENSRAUM*

The need for *Lebensraum*, or "living space," informed Hitler's plans for war. He believed that

for the "superior" **Aryan race ≪386–87** to dominate, Germany needed more land. He targeted neighboring territories with ethnic German populations. In 1938 Hitler entered Austria. *Anschluss* (the union with Austria) was followed by occupation of the Czech provinces, Bohemia and Moravia, in violation of the Munich Pact.

ANSCHLUSS

The Blitz
After defeat in the Battle of Britain (see right), Hitler launched 57 consecutive nightly bombing attacks on London, known as the Blitz. In this image, a German Heinkel 111 bomber flies over the Thames River in London during a bombing raid.

Beat
'FIREBOMB FRITZ'

BRITAIN SHALL NOT BURN

BRITAIN'S FIRE GUARD IS BRITAIN'S DEFENCE

Pushing the war effort
This poster was issued by the British Ministry of Home Security to encourage citizens to join the Fire Guard. Fire Guards, known as "the Midnight Watch," were volunteer patrols who extinguished fires after German air raids. The poster's tone is typical of the propaganda produced by the wartime government to promote the war effort.

Blitzkrieg

On September 1, 1939, Nazi Germany invaded neighboring Poland. France and Britain declared war two days later. Well-equipped German forces then pushed into Scandinavia and the Netherlands, crushing all opposition. Within a year, a seemingly invincible German army had conquered vast tracts of Europe.

Germany's assault on Poland began with the airforce (*Luftwaffe*) blanket-bombing roads, railroads, towns, and villages, sending terrified local populations fleeing ahead of the German advance. The chaos of refugees on the roads disrupted Polish counterattacks, and the German land invasion swept across the country at astonishing speed. This was *blitzkrieg*. The response of the British and French (the Allies) to German progress was hesitant. In the next two weeks, they did little more than survey the situation, while the German armed forces, or *Wehrmacht*, soon had the Polish capital, Warsaw,

surrounded. Poland capitulated when the Soviet Union, which had made a pact of nonaggression with Hitler, invaded from the east. There then followed several months of little military action, known as the "Phony War," in which the Allies built up weapon stocks and dropped leaflets to persuade the German people of the evils of their Nazi leaders.

On April 9, 1940, Hitler invaded Denmark and Norway in a preemptive strike against the British, who had threatened to occupy Scandinavia. The Phony War was over. On May 10, Hitler pushed westward toward France, conquering the Netherlands,

Belgium, and Luxembourg in just two days, to arrive at the French border. Both British and French commanders believed that the *Wehrmacht* would be held at the Maginot Line, fortifications

> **BLITZKRIEG** The tactic used by the German army to invade Poland. Meaning "lightning war," it involved swift, intense attacks that aimed to destroy the enemy quickly. It often included bombing raids.

constructed along the German border, and by the Belgian forests of the Ardennes, which they considered impassable for tanks. However, the Nazis swiftly broke through and advanced to Abbeville, on the north French coast, trapping British and French forces. The French begged the British for more military support, but the British Prime Minister, Winston Churchill, persuaded that France was lost, kept forces in reserve to protect Britain from German attack. From May 27 to June 4, Allied troops were evacuated from Dunkirk.

On June 22, 1940, it seemed that Germany had all but won. In an act of revenge, Hitler forced France to sign an armistice (peace agreement) in the same railroad car where the terms of Germany's defeat were agreed at the end of World War I (see pp.372–75). Hitler's popularity in Germany reached new heights. Each German offensive had achieved victory, and for many

Evacuating Dunkirk
A total of 693 ships rescued 340,000 British and French troops, such as those stranded on the beach above, from the northern French port of Dunkirk. The British people sailed their own fishing boats across the English Channel to support the Royal Navy's fleet. Churchill described the event as a "miracle of deliverance."

Air power
RAF Fighter Command had a numerical advantage over the German fighter force for most of the Battle of Britain. The British built 1,900 fighter planes, such as this Spitfire, the Germans built only 775.

SPITFIRE MK V

German citizens, untouched by war in their homeland, the process was easy.

Turning points
The Battle of Britain was waged from August to October 1940, and proved to be a turning point in Hitler's fortunes. The battle, fought by air, was intended as a prelude to German invasion. The *Luftwaffe* targeted airfields and ports along the English Channel, but the Royal Air Force's (RAF) early warning systems gave Britain the advantage. Hitler abandoned "Operation Sealion," his invasion plan, and began to target British cities instead (see left).

Perhaps if Hitler had consolidated his gains in Western Europe, Germany might have been victorious. But Hitler chose to invade Russia. Stalin's demand that Romania return Bessarabia to Russia, and his annexing of the Baltic States in 1940, infuriated Hitler. By

1941, Germany and its allies had overrun Yugoslavia and Greece, and with Romania, Hungary, and Slovakia in support, Hitler was confident of a broad front for the attack. In June 1941, Germany invaded Russia. Initially, the campaign, "Operation Barbarossa," made rapid advances, but the Soviet Red Army and a bitter Russian winter put paid to *blitzkrieg* tactics. Long battles ensued, some lasting many months, with enormous suffering and loss of life on both sides. In August 1942 a fierce battle began at Stalingrad (see p.394), which resulted in a German defeat. The tide of war had begun to turn.

(see pp.372–75)

BRITISH PRIME MINISTER (1874–1965)
WINSTON CHURCHILL

Born into the British aristocracy, Winston Churchill joined the army in his youth and served with the 4th Queen's Own Hussars, which gave him valuable firsthand knowledge of war. He entered parliament in 1899, holding many posts, including Secretary of State for War during World War I. As British Prime Minister (1940–45 and again in 1951–55) he resisted calls to settle a peace with Hitler, insisting that Britain should go down fighting. He is famous for his pugnacious war leadership and brilliant oratory. He was a prolific writer and was awarded the Nobel Prize for Literature for his book *The Second World War*.

The Axis in Europe
The alliance between Nazi Germany, Fascist Italy, and later Japan was known as the Axis. It was formalized in the Tripartite Treaty signed in 1940. Other minor powers became Axis satellites, supporting Germany's war aims.

AFTER

In France, the government collaborated with the Nazis, but here, as throughout occupied Europe, resistance movements formed.

VICHY FRANCE
After France's defeat **Marshal Pétain** took control of the French Government and agreed to the division of France into an **occupied zone** and a **nonoccupied Vichy zone**. Vichy France was administered by the French Government under Petain, on condition of full collaboration with the Germans. Petain sympathized with Nazi ideology. He replaced France's motto of "Liberty, Equality, Fraternity" with "Work, Family, Fatherland," and formed a militia that sent French Jews to die in Nazi concentration camps.

FIGHTING BACK
Resistance movements rose up against the Nazis all over occupied Europe. The *Maquis*, a French organization, attacked German installations and helped stranded British airmen. In Poland, partisans blew up bridges to stop German supplies from reaching battle zones. In Yugoslavia, **communist partisans** were led by **Josef Tito 450 》**, who narrowly escaped capture to go on and lead the country after the war.

TITO'S PARTISANS

Map

KEY
— Frontiers, 1937
···· Frontiers, Nov 1942
Greater German Reich
German occupation
Italian territory
Axis satellite
Finnish territory
Neutral
Allied territory
Allied occupation, 1941

NORWAY — Oslo
SWEDEN — Stockholm
FINLAND — Helsinki — Leningrad
North Sea
Baltic Sea
DENMARK — Copenhagen
UNITED KINGDOM
IRELAND
London
Channel Is.
NETHERLANDS
Hamburg — Danzig
EAST PRUSSIA
Riga
Moscow
REICHSKOMMISSARIAT OSTLAND
Kaunas — Minsk — Smolensk
U S S R
BELGIUM
GERMANY — Berlin
NORD
Paris — LUX.
Warsaw
BIALYSTOK
OCCUPIED FRANCE
SUDETENLAND
Prague
GENERAL GOVERNMENT
Cracow — Kiev — Kharkov
Nuremberg
REICHSKOMMISSARIAT UKRAINE
Stalingrad
FRANCE
Munich
Vienna SLOVAKIA
GALICIA
TRANSNISTRIA
ATLANTIC OCEAN
Bordeaux
VICHY FRANCE
SWITZ.
AUSTRIA
Budapest
HUNGARY
Odessa
Toulouse
Milan
N. SLOVENIA
CRIMEA
Turin
Trieste
Nice
BANAT
ROMANIA
Black Sea
Marseilles
Corsica
CROATIA — Belgrade — Bucharest
S. DOBRUJA
PORTUGAL
Lisbon
Madrid
SPAIN
Balearic Is.
SERBIA
Sofia
BULGARIA
Istanbul
Rome
MONT.
MACEDONIA
ITALY
Gibraltar
Sardinia
ALBANIA (annexed by Italy 1939)
Corfu
GREECE
TURKEY
MOROCCO (Fr.)
ALGERIA (Fr.)
Sicily
Mediterranean Sea
TUNISIA (Fr.)
Malta
Kythera
Athens
Crete
Dodecanese Islands

0 — 500 km
0 — 500 miles
N

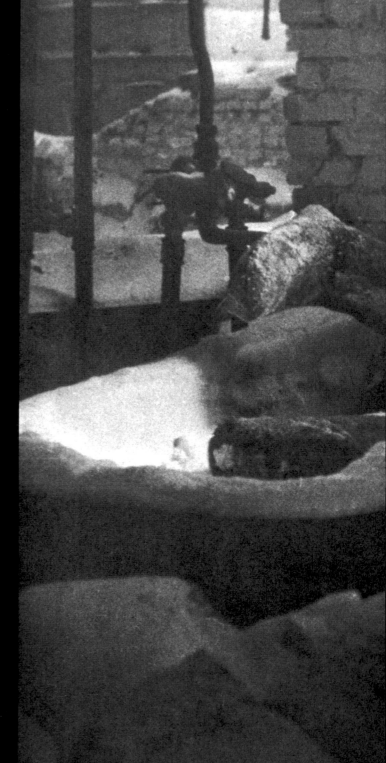

Stalingrad

In the early hours of February 2, 1943, the last German general still fighting in the Russian city of Stalingrad surrendered to the Soviet Red Army. At noon a German Luftwaffe reconnaissance aircraft circled over the city. The pilot radioed back to base: "No more sign of fighting in Stalingrad." The most decisive battle on the eastern front during World War II was over.

The industrial city of Stalingrad stood on the west bank of the Volga River in southern Russia. It controlled the vital river and rail connections that carried oil supplies to the armament factories of central Russia and to the Soviet Red Army itself. The city was not the original target for the Germans. Operation Blue, the German offensive that began on June 28, 1942, aimed to capture the Caucasus oilfields to the southwest and establish a secure position on the Volga. The Soviets responded to the German advance by concentrating their forces in Stalingrad, threatening the northern flank of the German army. On July 23, Hitler ordered General Paulus and his Sixth Army to capture Stalingrad at all costs.

The assault began on August 23 with sustained air attacks. The same afternoon, German troops reached the Volga, north of the city. By September 3, Stalingrad was surrounded, with the only means of escape east across the river. The battle became intense. Stalin, the Soviet leader, had ordered "Not One Step Backward," for this city bore his name and could never be

surrendered. Hitler was equally determined. German air and artillery shelling reduced buildings to rubble, but the Soviet troops held fast. As the Germans advanced into the city, the Russians fought them house by house. The two sides were often so close they fought each other from different stories of the same building.

On November 19, with the Russians now occupying a narrow strip along the riverbank, the Red Army launched Operation Uranus, an audacious attack on German positions from the rear. Four days later, the Germans were surrounded. A German attempt to rescue their trapped army failed in December. The battle raged into the New Year and, worn out by constant Soviet attacks, cold, and hunger, the remnants of the German army finally surrendered on February 2. The cost to both sides was immense: since November, the Red Army had lost 479,000 men, but, crucially, German losses were also high, with 147,000 deaths and 91,000 troops captured. The myth of German invincibility was shattered. The Red Army could now go on the offensive against Nazi Germany.

Fighting for each floor
A Soviet sniper perches in a bathtub as he takes aim from a ruined building. Every inch of the city was fiercely defended. Snipers were well suited to close combat, picking off German troops one by one. They won the title of "noble sniper" if they killed more than 40.

"The **God of War** has gone over to the other side."

ALFRED JODL, GERMAN MILITARY OFFICER, FEBRUARY 1943

BEFORE

From the start of World War II, governments sought ways to unite people in the war effort. When the US entered the war in 1941 the Allied cause was bolstered.

PROPAGANDA
Governments at war mobilized their citizens with **propaganda**; posters were a favored means of communicating **war aims**. All sides used propaganda to encourage people in the **war effort** and **boost morale**.

US POSTER

THE ANGLO–AMERICAN ALLIANCE
The Alliance was signed in December 1941 as the US entered the war. It set up joint British and American military command for all Anglo-American operations. The pact was born of the close political understanding between the British leader, **Winston Churchill ‹‹ 392–93**, and US president **Franklin D. Roosevelt ‹‹ 384–85**. The two nations entered a period of cooperation, which helped Britain in the war.

Innovations in military technology played a key role in determining the outcome of World War II. One of the greatest battles of the war was fought at sea. The German navy began to target US merchant ships carrying weapons, raw materials, food, and eventually troops across the Atlantic Ocean to Britain. German submarines, or U-boats, sank three million tons of Allied shipping over the course of the war. Churchill later admitted that the threat to the lifeline of US supplies was the one thing that really terrified him; without it, Britain might have been starved into submission. The Battle of the Atlantic, as this theater of war became known,

was won partly by the development of longer-range aircraft that could reach U-boats. Support from the Canadian and US navies played a major role, as did better intelligence, and the development of centimetric radar to find submerged U-boats.

Desert warfare
Tanks and aircraft played a decisive role in the campaigns in North Africa, where mobility was crucial for crossing the deserts. Mussolini (see p.387) had wanted to extend the Italian empire by invading Egypt in 1940. Desperate to protect British interests in Africa, troops from Britain and Commonwealth countries (former British colonies, see

pp.346–47) were sent in to stop him. Initially the British drove the Italians back to Libya, despite Italy's superior numbers of troops and equipment. To aid its weaker ally,

1240
The number of days Australian troops held out under siege at Tobruk against Rommel's forces before being relieved by Allied troops.

Germany sent in the Afrika Korps under Field Marshal Rommel. By May 1941 he had won back all the territory lost by Italy. It was not until October 1942 and the British victory under

Total War

As the war in Europe raged on, the Atlantic Ocean and the deserts of North Africa became backdrops for fierce battles. Securing vital supply lines from the US enabled Britain and its allies to drive back the German and Italian troops. With the Red Army advancing from the east, Nazi Germany was surrounded.

Depth charge
Coastguards stand on the deck of the US Cutter *Spencer* watching the explosion of a depth charge blast a Nazi U-boat out of the water. The U-boat's target was the large convoy of merchant and troop ships seen on the horizon. Allied support and the advances in radar technology ensured Britain's Atlantic lifeline to the US and Canada stayed open.

Storming of Bardia 1942
The Allies captured territory held by the Italians with relative ease early on in the North African Campaign. Here, Australian troops storm the town of Bardia in Libya. German Field Marshal Rommel's Afrika Korps came to Italy's assistance and fighting continued in Egypt, Algeria, Morocco, and Tunisia.

General Montgomery, at El Alamein, that Rommel's advance was checked. The next month, the "Torch Landings" in Morocco and Algeria brought Allied reinforcements with US tanks and fresh troops. Within six months, after fierce fighting in Tunisia, the Axis powers (see p.393) were defeated in Africa.

The Axis surrender in North Africa was followed by the successful Allied invasion of Sicily, after which Hitler's key ally, Italy, secretly surrendered. In 1944, while the Red Army drove Axis forces out of the Soviet Union, Allied troops invaded Normandy, France (see pp.398–99). After the liberation of France, Germany made one last stand at the Battle of the Bulge in the Ardennes, Belgium, where more than 80,000 US troops and a similar number of

Germans were lost. Once Belgium and the Netherlands were liberated, the Allies entered Germany from the west and Russia invaded from the east. The Red Army's arrival in Berlin in April 1945 was followed by Hitler's suicide and unconditional German surrender. Victory in Europe was declared on May 8, 1945.

The Road to Berlin

By 1943, after Germany's defeat at Stalingrad (see p.394) and victories for British and US forces in Africa, the Allies held the advantage. British and US forces landed in Italy, while Soviet troops swept across Eastern Europe. With the D-Day landings (see p.399) in 1944, and Allied bombings, the Nazis faced attack on all fronts.

Relief at the end of war in Europe was tempered by grief at the immense loss of life and a resolve to achieve world peace.

ENDING THE WAR
After the Red Army took Berlin, the end of the war in Europe (VE Day) was officially declared on May 8, 1945. Huge celebrations took place, particularly in London. **War with Japan** continued until VJ Day on August 15 **402–03** »

SOVIET TROOPS RAISE THE FLAG IN BERLIN

COSTS OF WAR
The costs of World War II were immense. In terms of loss of human life, the statistics are appalling. The financial costs have been estimated at over $2 billion.

DEAD 25 million Russians, 6 million Poles, 5 million Germans, 400 thousand French, 300 thousand Britons— almost 60 million died worldwide.

YALTA AND POTSDAM CONFERENCES
In 1945 leaders from Britain, the Soviet Union, and the US met at conferences at Yalta (in Ukraine) and Potsdam (Germany) to deal with the **political and economic issues** raised by the war. Among the measures decided on were the creation of a new world peacekeeping organization, **the United Nations**, and the division of Germany into four zones of control, each administered by an Allied power.

KEY
— Greater German Reich, 1942
→ Allied offensives
● city severely bombed
✕ major battle
● partisan resistance
— frontiers 1942

Murmansk

Norwegian Sea

ATLANTIC OCEAN

Shetland Is.
Orkney Is.

NORWAY SWEDEN FINLAND

Glasgow
North Sea
IRELAND GREAT BRITAIN
Oslo Stockholm Helsinki
USSR
Liverpool Birmingham
Baltic Sea ESTONIA LATVIA
Moscow
London HOLLAND Bremen Copenhagen
Hamburg Hanover Königsberg E. LITH
Essen PRUSSIA Minsk
D-day landings 1944
St. Lô GERMANY Berlin 1945
BELG. Düsseldorf Warsaw Kursk
Caen Cologne Dresden 1945
Paris Frankfurt Prague POLAND Red army advance 1944
FRANCE Mannheim Kiev UKRAINE
Stuttgart Munich Stalingrad
Bay of Biscay SWITZ. AUSTRIA SLOV. HUNGARY ROMANIA
VICHY FRANCE Milan
Turin Genoa CROATIA Crimea
Marseille ITALY SERBIA Ploesti
PORTUGAL Corsica Bucharest Black Sea
SPAIN Balearic Is. Anzio BULGARIA
Sardinia Cassino MONT. ALBANIA
Mediterranean Sea Sicily Aegean Sea TURKEY
1943 GREECE Leros
MOROCCO North African landings 1942 Malta Kos Rhodes
ALGERIA Crete Cyprus
TUNISIA LIBYA El Alamein
EGYPT

0 — 500 km
0 — 500 miles
N

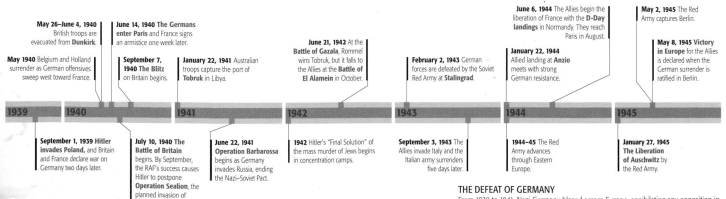

pp.398–99
p.393
p.394
p.399
402–03

May 26–June 4, 1940 British troops are evacuated from **Dunkirk**.

June 14, 1940 The Germans enter Paris and France signs an armistice one week later.

June 6, 1944 The Allies begin the liberation of France with the **D-Day landings** in Normandy. They reach Paris in August.

May 2, 1945 The Red Army captures Berlin.

May 1940 Belgium and Holland surrender as German offensives sweep west toward France.

September 7, 1940 The Blitz on Britain begins.

January 22, 1941 Australian troops capture the port of **Tobruk** in Libya.

June 21, 1942 At the **Battle of Gazala**, Rommel wins Tobruk, but it falls to the Allies at the **Battle of El Alamein** in October.

February 2, 1943 German forces are defeated by the Soviet Red Army at **Stalingrad**.

January 22, 1944 Allied landing at **Anzio** meets with strong German resistance.

May 8, 1945 Victory in Europe for the Allies is declared when the German surrender is ratified in Berlin.

1939	1940	1941	1942	1943	1944	1945

September 1, 1939 Hitler invades Poland, and Britain and France declare war on Germany two days later.

July 10, 1940 The Battle of Britain begins. By September, the RAF's success causes Hitler to postpone **Operation Sealion**, the planned invasion of Britain, indefinitely.

June 22, 1941 Operation Barbarossa begins as Germany invades Russia, ending the Nazi–Soviet Pact.

1942 Hitler's "Final Solution" of the mass murder of Jews begins in concentration camps.

September 3, 1943 The Allies invade Italy and the Italian army surrenders five days later.

1944–45 The Red Army advances through Eastern Europe.

January 27, 1945 The Liberation of Auschwitz by the Red Army.

THE DEFEAT OF GERMANY
From 1939 to 1941, Nazi Germany blazed across Europe, annihilating any opposition in neighboring territories. With troops fighting in North Africa and facing the Soviet Red Army outside Moscow, German forces had conquered vast territories by the winter of 1941. Yet in April 1945 the Allies were swiftly advancing on the German capital, Berlin.

D-Day

After almost four years of planning, a combined American, British, Canadian, and Free French force launched Operation Overlord, aiming to wrest control of Europe from Nazi Germany. Beginning on D-Day with a five-pronged attack on the coast of northern France, the operation was to prove a crucial turning point in World War II.

The largest of the five assault areas was at Colleville-sur-Mer, codenamed Omaha Beach. Heavy Allied air and naval bombardment, effective at the other landing points, had made little impact on the well-prepared German defenses at Omaha, where the US 29th Infantry Division—untested in combat—attacked alongside the US 1st Infantry Division. Horrendous weather had forced General Dwight D. Eisenhower, Supreme Commander of the Allied forces, to delay the attack for 24 hours. The mission launched with little improvement in conditions, but further delay would have set the operation back by several weeks.

The adverse weather wrought havoc with the Allied landing craft: some sank in the rough seas, while German mines ripped through others. Of 29 amphibious tanks launched at Omaha Beach, 27 sank with their crews still trapped inside them. Many of the soldiers emerging from the landing craft were swept off their feet by heavy surf and drowned as they attempted to wade ashore, while others proved easy targets for German fire, picked off from the clifftops as they struggled up the beach, weighed down by wet gear and heavy sand. The average age of the dead was 22. By early afternoon, American troops had managed to secure a small strip of beach, 6 miles (9.7 km) wide, and around 2 miles (3.2 km) deep. This patch of land came at a cost of 3,000 casualties.

Encountering less resistance at beaches codenamed Utah, Gold, Juno, and Sword, the Allies landed 150,000 troops by nightfall. Six days later they had linked the five beachheads into a continuous front and begun using artificial "Mulberry harbors" to land armored vehicles, heavy artillery, and more troops with which to further the advance. On June 27, after two weeks of intense fighting, American forces captured Cherbourg; on July 9 the British and Canadians overcame two Panzer divisions to take Caen; and on July 25 the tanks of the US 7th Army advanced south through Saint-Lô, breaching the German defenses. This was the vital breakthrough that led to the liberation of Paris on August 25 and, in early September, the crossing of the Siegfried Line into Germany.

Omaha beach
The first wave of troops to land at Omaha Beach arrived just before dawn. Photographer Robert Capa landed with them. Waist-deep in the icy sea with bullets tearing into the water around him, he captured the intense struggle as they fought their way onto the beach.

"We will accept nothing less than **full victory**."
GENERAL DWIGHT D. EISENHOWER, D-DAY ORDER SPEECH, 1944

BEFORE

Genocide–the murder of a group of people, for their religion or race, for example–has long been part of human life. The Holocaust is the result of such a policy, but it was not the first genocide of the 20th century.

ANTI-SEMITISM IN EUROPE AND RUSSIA

Anti-Semitism has its roots in the Roman Empire when **early Christians attacked Jews**, blaming them for the death of Jesus Christ. During the Crusades of the 11th century **« 200–01**, Jews were expelled from many western European nations **« 227**. Numerous Jews died in **pogroms** (organized massacres) in Russia in the late 19th century.

> **ANTI-SEMITISM** Discrimination, hostility, or prejudice directed at Jews as a religious, racial, or ethnic group, expressed in actions that can range from individual hatred to state-prosecuted persecution and violence.

ARMENIAN MASSACRE

In April 1915, the government of the Turkish Ottoman Empire accused the 1.75 million Armenians under its control of collaborating with the enemy, Russia. Over seven months, **600,000 Armenians were killed.** In addition **500,000 were deported** to what is now Iraq. Of these, only 90,000 survived. A further **400,000 Armenians lost their lives** when the Turks invaded the Russian Caucasus in 1918. The **massacres continued until 1922**, when the remaining Armenians were driven from Turkey.

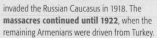

POSTER FOR ARMENIAN RELIEF

A central feature of the world view of the German dictator Adolf Hitler (see pp.390–91) was an alleged struggle between Germany, as the only state capable of rescuing European civilization, and an international Jewish conspiracy to subvert and dominate the world. He picked up these views from the popular anti-Semitism of the time, which saw Jews both as parasitical capitalists and as revolutionary Bolsheviks (see p.376). Either way, Hitler saw the Jews as an evil, implacable enemy of Germany who should be driven from the *Reich*.

The Nazis in power

Hitler took power in January 1933 and began a slow process of reducing the civil rights and economic position of the country's half-million Jews. They were removed from civil service and from many of the professions in 1933–4 and their shops and businesses boycotted. Thousands took refuge in exile abroad, and by 1939 fewer than half of Germany's Jews remained. In September 1935 the notorious Nuremberg Laws stripped Jews of their German citizenship and prohibited marriage or sexual relations between German Jews and ethnic Germans, or "Aryans" (see pp.387). In 1936 a program was set in motion to strip Jews of their assets, and by the outbreak of war, most Jewish property had been taken by the state or bought at reduced prices, to be sold on to "Aryan" owners. It was not until November 1938 that the Jews were threatened with widespread violence. A pogrom, known as the "Night of Broken Glass" (*Kristallnacht*), led to the destruction of 7,500 businesses and the

Poster advertising "the Eternal Jew"
In the film made by Joseph Goebbels, Hitler's Minister of Propaganda, scenes of Polish Jews living in Warsaw were intercut with images of rats. The Star of David had to be worn by all Jews under Nazi control from 1941.

"Kristallnacht"
The shattered glass of the many Jewish properties that were attacked on November 9–10, 1938 gave the night its name.

death of 91 Jews. After this 8,000 Jews were expelled from Berlin and around 25,000 Jewish men sent for a short spell in German concentration camps, where they were subjected to a brutal regime of punishment and labor.

Jewish isolation

Initially, Hitler's goal was to exclude the Jews from Germany. The Nazis reached an agreement with the Zionist movement to speed up emigration to Palestine (see pp.414–15). But by 1939, as thousands more Jews came under German control in Austria and areas of Czechoslovakia, it proved difficult to get other countries to accept Jewish immigrants. At the Evian Conference

5–6 MILLION Jews were killed, including 3 million Polish Jews.

212 THOUSAND Roma and Sinti gypsies were also exterminated.

70 THOUSAND disabled people in Germany were killed.

The Holocaust

The word "Holocaust" comes from two Greek words: *holo*, "whole," and *kaustos*, "to burn." The term is most closely associated with the deliberate attempt to annihilate the Jewish race in Europe from 1941 to 1945, probably the most shocking and far-reaching act of the age.

Death factory
At Auschwitz–Birkenau, train tracks lead to the main guardhouse, which prisoners called the "gate of death." From 1940, three labor and death camps were built here; more than 1 million Jews died here from 1941 to 1945, when the Soviet Red Army liberated the camps.

in France in July 1938 on the refugee question, only 2 out of 32 countries present agreed to accept higher quotas of Jews. Britain restricted Jewish access to Palestine due to the growing civil war there between the Arab population and Jewish settlers. The last emigrants left Germany in 1941.

Ghettoization and murder

The German invasion first of western Poland in September 1939, and then of the USSR in June 1941, radically and tragically transformed Germany's anti-Semitic policies. With 3.1 million Jews in Poland and 2.7 million in the western

" ... Europe will be **combed through** from west to east [of all Jews]."

MINUTES OF THE WANNSEE CONFERENCE, JANUARY 20, 1942

USSR, as well as more than a million in occupied France, the Low Countries, the Balkans, and Scandinavia, the Nazi authorities' reliance on emigration and small-scale attacks to "clear" Jews was no longer feasible. In Poland, the *"Einsatzgruppen"* (action groups made up from the SS—the elite core of the Nazi Party, whose leaders controlled the police and security) herded Jews into restricted areas of towns known as ghettos. Thousands more were sent to labor camps, where they worked for

the German war effort. As German troops swept into the USSR, the SS shot, or gassed in mobile vans, as many Jews as they could find. In Kiev, 33,771 Jews were marched out to the Babi Yar ravine and shot on September 29–30, 1941, one of many such incidents.

The "Final Solution"

Although a written order from Hitler has never been found, historians now date a decision on the "Final Solution of the Jewish Question" to late 1941. On January 20, 1942, Reinhard Heydrich, head of the Gestapo, summoned senior bureaucrats to a villa at Lake Wannsee in Berlin to ensure their support for his plans. Jews were now to be transported to camps in Eastern Europe, where they would be worked to death, or killed on the spot. Death was caused by mass gassing in sealed chambers, and the disposal of the bodies took place in huge crematoria staffed by Jews themselves. The death camps—Auschwitz, Belzec, Chelmno, Majdanek, Sobibór, and Treblinka—were supplied with trainloads of Jews from occupied and Axis Europe, except for Bulgaria, whose king refused to cooperate.

The killing was on a vast scale. Reports filtered out to the Allies, and the Auschwitz camp was photographed by a US reconnaissance plane in August 1944, but photo-interpreters were more concerned with a nearby chemical factory. Only when the Soviet Red Army advanced westward in 1944–45 did the camps cease work and the Holocaust end, with the total defeat of Nazi Germany in May 1945.

Ghetto roundup
Across Poland and occupied Russia, Jews were herded into walled or fenced ghettos in poor urban areas, where they had little or no food.

Mass murder
After death, Jews were stripped of everything, even their hair and the gold in their teeth. These shoes come from one day of gassing at Auschwitz.

Death train
Jews across Europe were rounded up and sent to the five main death camps in Poland. Many thought they were being sent to work in factories.

The Holocaust ended in 1945, but its legacy is still with us. Jews now have a homeland, but it is not without problems, and large-scale massacres of people solely due to their race or beliefs have continued to occur.

STATE OF ISRAEL

International revulsion at the Holocaust led the United Nations to create a **Jewish state of Israel** inside a partitioned Palestine in May 1948 **414–15 ≫**. The **Law of Return** (1950) made Israel **home** not only for its inhabitants, but **for all Jews**, wherever they might live.

"ETHNIC CLEANSING"

Genocide did not begin or end with the Holocaust. Anti-Jewish pogroms broke out in Poland in 1947, resulting in the deaths of some Jews who had survived Auschwitz, while 2 million Cambodians were killed by their revolutionary government in the **"killing fields"** of Year Zero in 1975–79. More recently, **750,000 Tutsis** were massacred by the majority Hutu tribe in Rwanda in 1994, while Serbs systematically killed thousands of Muslims in Bosnia in 1992–95 **450–51 ≫**.

RWANDAN REFUGEES

YAD VASHEM

The Jewish national **Holocaust memorial** at Yad Vashem, Israel, remembers those who died, and focuses on the resistance of Jews to Nazi terror. Memorials now exist in many European cities, notably Berlin, and a **National Holocaust Day** is commemorated in many countries on January 27, the anniversary of the liberation of Auschwitz. Yet **"Holocaust denial"** has gained ground in recent years, as some historians and politicians have tried to rewrite, or even obliterate, historical events for their own ends.

« BEFORE

Japan's desire to build an empire in Asia and the Pacific drew it into conflict with China and met with condemnation from the US.

JAPANESE EXPANSION IN ASIA
In 1931 the **Japanese took control of Manchuria 424–25 »** a vast region now in northeast China, and established the state of **Manchukuo** there. China was the first target in Japan's plan to create an empire in Asia and the Pacific, and it soon began to stage incursions into Chinese territory. In July 1937 a minor incident, involving a missing Japanese soldier, caused Japanese and Chinese forces to open fire on each other at the Marco Polo Bridge near Beijing. The conflict quickly escalated, leading to the **second Sino-Japanese war** and ultimately to both countries' involvement in World War II. Although European colonial interests were affected, they were absorbed by growing problems in Europe and resisted involvement.

US FREEZES DEPOSITS
German victories at the beginning of World War II encouraged Japan to start **empire building** in earnest. It signed the **Three-Power Pact** with Germany and Italy in 1940 and occupied French Indochina (Vietnam). The US responded by freezing Japanese deposits in the US and embargoed exports of crucial materials, such as aviation fuel, to Japan.

War in the Pacific

In 1941 Japan attacked the US navy base at Pearl Harbor, throwing down the gauntlet to all Western powers seeking to restrict the expansion of the Japanese Empire. The US and Britain immediately declared war on Japan. World War II had arrived in Asia and the Pacific and was now truly global.

US president Franklin D. Roosevelt had transferred his navy's battleship force to Pearl Harbor, Hawaii in April 1940, to deter Japanese aggression. The combined effects of war with China and foreign trade embargoes left Japan desperate for oil and other raw materials available in European colonies in the Southeast Asia and the East Indies. The Japanese raid on Pearl Harbor destroyed many US battleships and killed around 3,000 US personnel, reducing the threat to Japan's southward expansion.

Having gained an advantage, Japanese leaders put their plans into action. Their aim was to construct an imperial perimeter around Southeast Asia and the central Pacific. Pearl Harbor was followed by the Japanese invasion of most of their target territories, including Burma, British and Dutch Borneo, Hong Kong, and the Dutch East Indies. Between March and June of 1942, the Japanese survived fierce confrontations with Allied forces to conquer Singapore, Guam, and the Philippines, and established control in Indonesia, Malaya, and Burma. Having ousted the old colonial regimes, Japan made attempts to win over the mass of Asian peoples so that they would support them in the war. A degree of independence was granted to a few

Burma river patrol
Forces were sent into Burma to protect British colonial interests in the country. In the picture above, British troops patrol villages along a river as they search for Japanese soldiers.

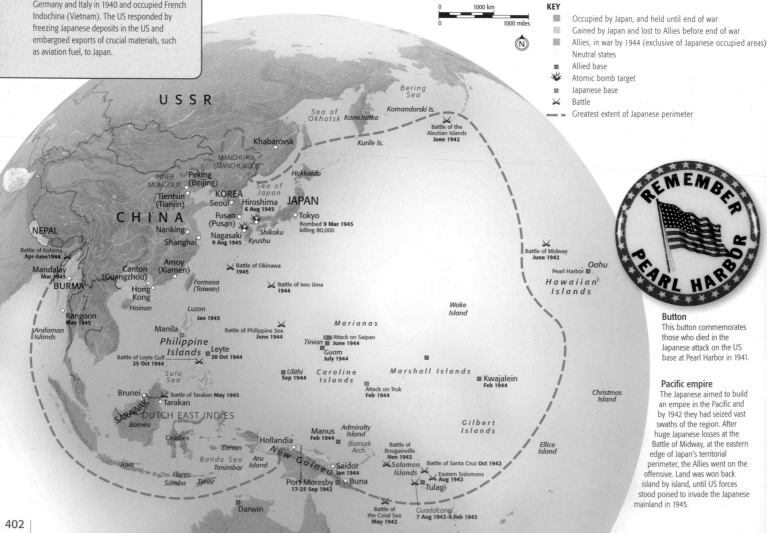

KEY
■	Occupied by Japan, and held until end of war
■	Gained by Japan and lost to Allies before end of war
■	Allies, in war by 1944 (exclusive of Japanese occupied areas)
	Neutral states
■	Allied base
⚹	Atomic bomb target
■	Japanese base
⚔	Battle
– – –	Greatest extent of Japanese perimeter

0   1000 km
0   1000 miles

Button
This button commemorates those who died in the Japanese attack on the US base at Pearl Harbor in 1941.

Pacific empire
The Japanese aimed to build an empire in the Pacific and by 1942 they had seized vast swaths of the region. After huge Japanese losses at the Battle of Midway, at the eastern edge of Japan's territorial perimeter, the Allies went on the offensive. Land was won back island by island, until US forces stood poised to invade the Japanese mainland in 1945.

Pearl Harbor
Japan carried out a surprise bombing raid on the American fleet at Pearl Harbor, Hawaii, on December 7, 1941. Thousands of American lives were lost, as well as many battleships, as seen engulfed in flames above.

territories, including Indonesia and Burma, in return for guaranteed loyalty to Japan. The Japanese were often guilty of barbarism. Atrocities were committed against Chinese citizens and in Japan's notorious prison camps, where medical experiments were conducted on prisoners of war.

Turning points

The Japanese advance was checked in May 1942 when a naval force heading for southern New Guinea was defeated in the Coral Sea. A far more significant defeat came at the Battle of Midway in early June. The Japanese Admiral Yamomoto assembled a powerful force of aircraft carriers, battleships, submarines, and destroyers with the intention of surprising the US fleet at the American-held Midway Islands. However, US intelligence had cracked the Japanese code and the US Navy was well-prepared for their arrival. In the ensuing battle, Japan lost its main fleet of aircraft carriers and hundreds of pilots.

The Allied counteroffensive

As was the case in Europe, the tide of war in the Pacific turned in favor of the Allied Powers during 1943. This change was in many ways due to the

extraordinary military and industrial resources of the US. Once the US war effort was mobilized, Japan began to struggle to match its enemies, and Allied troops began to recapture occupied territories. In early 1945, British troops invaded Burma, under Admiral Lord Louis Mountbatten and Field Marshal Sir William Slim, liberating the country in May.

During 1944 and 1945, US power at sea and in the air began to have a decisive effect. A sea blockade of Japan cut off all imports, strangling the Japanese war economy. Another decisive US naval victory at the Battle of Leyte Gulf in October 1944 opened the way for America to regain the Philippines. In February 1945 the US invaded the island of Iwo Jima, gaining a base for fighter escorts to support

US bombing raids on mainland Japan. Around 80,000 people died in the US fire-bombing of Tokyo. Victory in the Pacific was in sight for the Allies, but still Japan refused to surrender.

On August 6, 1945, the Allies dropped an atomic bomb on the Japanese city of Hiroshima (see p.405), and three days later on the city of Nagasaki. As news of the devastation sank in, the Soviet Union broke a neutrality pact with Japan by declaring war and invading Japanese-occupied Manchuria. These events persuaded the Japanese to sign an unconditional surrender on September 2, 1945.

Kamikaze
A Japanese volunteer *kamikaze* pilot flies his explosive-laden plane into a US battleship. Japan introduced this desperate tactic in 1944. By the end of the war, over 2,000 such suicide attacks had been launched.

After the war, communists won power in China, causing nationalists to flee. The US presence in Japan lead to political change.

COMMUNISTS SEIZE POWER IN CHINA
During World War II, Chinese political factions had united against the Japanese, but open civil war reignited in 1946. In 1949, the **communist People's Liberation Army** won emphatic victories against forces of the Guomindang Nationalist Party at Huai-Hai and Nanjing, forcing the nationalists to retreat. **Mao Zedong**, leader of the Chinese Communist Party, declared the **People's Republic of China 424–25 ››**.

CHINESE REGIME IN TAIWAN
After his defeat, the nationalist leader **Chiang Kai-shek** fled China with 600,000 troops and two million refugees. Chiang refused to acknowledge Mao's government and established his alternative government in Taipei on the former Japanese colony of Taiwan.

US OCCUPATION OF JAPAN
Japan was occupied by the Allies until 1952. Its war machine was destroyed and war-crimes trials held. In 1947, a new constitution introduced universal suffrage (the right to vote) and banned Japan from having an army. In the 1950s, a memorial park was built in the center of Hiroshima in remembrance of the nuclear attack.

HIROSHIMA PEACE PARK

US GENERAL (1880–1964)
GENERAL MACARTHUR

US General Douglas MacArthur was the Supreme Allied Commander in the Pacific. He was born into a military family and began his distinguished military career in World War I. He rose to the rank of Army Chief of Staff in the interwar years. At the end of World War II he became Supreme Allied Commander in Japan and oversaw the drafting of a new Japanese constitution. In 1950–51 he led UN forces in Korea (see pp.406–07).

Hiroshima

Around 7:15 am, Japanese radar detected three American aircraft flying south at high altitude. Because the planes were thought to be on reconnaissance, the air raid alert was lifted. At 8:16 am, the unchallenged leading B-29 bomber, named *Enola Gay*, dropped "Little Boy" over the city of Hiroshima. A nuclear weapon had been exploded in warfare for the first time.

The decision to bomb Hiroshima, and Nagasaki three days later, was made by US president Harry Truman. The war against Nazi Germany had ended in May, but Germany's ally, Japan, refused to surrender. Any invasion of Japan would result in a huge loss of both military and civilian life, as well as massive physical destruction. Truman therefore decided to use atomic bombs to force Japan to surrender. Hiroshima was chosen because of its industrial and military significance. The Hiroshima bomb exploded 1,950 ft (600 meters) above the city with a blast equivalent to 13 kilotons of TNT. An estimated 90,000 people were killed instantly; another 50,000 died by the end of the year. About 90 percent of Hiroshima's buildings were damaged or destroyed.

The physics that made this bomb possible grew out of the realization that the atom was not stable and indivisible but had the potential to release immense amounts of energy. In 1938, German scientists Otto Hahn and Fritz Strassmann split uranium atoms by bombarding them with neutrons. The process used, known as nuclear fission, had obvious

military uses, and scientists in the UK and US grew concerned that Germany might use it to make bombs. On August 2, 1939, Albert Einstein and the Hungarian physicist Leó Szilárd wrote to President Roosevelt urging him to take action. He set up the Uranium Committee to pursue research. After the US entered the war in December 1941, the "Manhattan Project," under the direction of J. Robert Oppenheimer, developed a nuclear bomb.

Three devices resulted from this work: the "Trinity" test of a plutonium bomb detonated in Alamogordo, New Mexico; the enriched-uranium bomb detonated over Hiroshima; and the plutonium bomb dropped on Nagasaki. In 1949, the USSR exploded its first atomic bomb. Britain, France, and China soon followed. Today, Israel, India, Pakistan, and North Korea have joined the nuclear club. The threat of nuclear war might have acted as a deterrent and kept the peace between the main nuclear powers. The ability to destroy the world, however, has made our planet an infinitely more dangerous place.

Atomic cloud
The devastating force of the explosion threw a huge mushroom cloud thousands of feet into the sky. The searing heat of the bomb was so intense it vaporized people, and caused a firestorm that destroyed the city.

"My God, what have we done?"

ROBERT LEWIS, COPILOT OF THE *ENOLA GAY*, 1945

« **BEFORE**

Historic distrust and ideological differences between the Soviet Union and the United States led to tension in the wartime alliance.

US IN SIBERIA

Antagonism between the Soviet Union and the US began in the **Russian Civil War ‹‹ 377** when the US intervened in Siberia (northeast Russia). Between 1918 and 1920, US troops fought on the side of the White Army against the Bolsheviks. Although the US later sent aid to the fledgling Soviet state, diplomatic relations were not in place until 1933.

US TROOPS IN SIBERIA

CLASH OF IDEALS

Even as their wartime alliance defeated **Nazi Germany ‹‹ 392–97**, relations cooled between the Soviet Union and the Western powers. In the US there was unease about the rise of European communism **‹‹ 335**, an ideology that advocated worldwide revolution and the end of capitalism. The West, led by the US, was equally mistrusted by the Soviet Union.

COMMUNIST POSTER

The Cold War

After World War II global politics became polarized as countries around the world allied themselves with either the United States or the Soviet Union. The East–West divide between communism and capitalism dominated world events for the next 40 years.

W hen the Allied powers met at Yalta and Potsdam to shape postwar Europe (see p.397), Stalin's insistence that Soviet borders be extended to cover eastern Poland and the Baltic states raised anxieties about his expansionist ambitions. Between 1945–47, the Soviets gained in influence as communist governments were founded in other Eastern European states (jointly known as the Eastern Bloc). With Britain's status as a world power damaged by six years of war, it became clear that the only Western power with comparable strength to the Soviet Union was the United States. In 1947 the British prime minister, Winston Churchill, had to request US support in Greece, where a civil war was raging between the royalist government and communist

partisans. The request prompted US President Truman to pledge assistance to all states trying to defend democracy against external threat. This became known as "The Truman Doctrine." Truman argued that the spread of communist regimes must be combated or America's national security would be at risk. This marked a new phase in US foreign policy called "containment." Over the next few years, through measures such as the Marshall Plan (see p.452), the US poured millions of dollars in financial and military aid into non-communist European states, bolstering their economic recoveries. The Soviet Union saw US containment measures

as imperialist and aggressive. It reacted by strengthening its own power base. In 1947 Andrei Zhdanov, a senior Soviet official, stated that the world was split into two camps: Western imperialists and socialist anti-imperialists. He set up the Cominform, an organization that supervised the strict ideological conformity of Eastern Bloc regimes with Moscow's party line. The first confrontation of the Cold War occurred in Berlin.

YOU DIE FOR HIM
KOREA
WAR PROFITS

Korean War propaganda
The Korean communists produced anti-capitalist propaganda, such as this poster. It aims to demoralize US troops, stating they will die for capitalist greed.

Berlin Airlift
Berlin's children greet one of the British and American transport planes that flew a total of 2.3 million tons of food, medicines, and fuel into their beleaguered city in 1948 and 1949.

TWO CAMPS ON THE BRINK

At several points throughout the Cold War, tensions almost reached boiling point, but direct conflict or "hot" war between the US and the Soviet Union was avoided.

1961 The building of the **Berlin Wall** is ordered by Walter Ulbricht, leader of East Germany, to stop the flow of refugees across the border from East to West Berlin.

1961 The US funds and organizes Cuban exiles in a bungled attempt to invade Cuba at the **Bay of Pigs** and depose the communist leader Fidel Castro.

1964–73 The US enters the **Vietnam War** to back the South Vietnamese army against North Vietnamese communists, the Vietcong. By the time a ceasefire is signed, 58,000 US lives and many more Vietnamese are lost.

1970 The **Nuclear Non-proliferation Treaty**, signed by the US and the Soviet Union to build an effective system of controls to prevent the spread of nuclear weapons, comes into effect.

1983 US President Reagan announces the **Star Wars** program, which gives the US space-based protection against attack from the Soviet Union, which he calls the **Evil Empire**.

1987 The **Intermediate-Range Nuclear Forces Treaty** is signed by presidents Reagan and Gorbachev, ending the arms race.

1950	1955	1960	1965	1970	1975	1980	1985

1950–53 US and South Korean forces fight against North Korean and Chinese troops in the **Korean War**.

1955 The Soviet Union and the Eastern Bloc formalize their military and political alliance in the **Warsaw Pact**.

1962 The discovery of Soviet missiles in Cuba leads the US to threaten the Soviet Union with attack unless installations are dismantled. For 14 days war seems imminent until Khrushchev agrees to US President Kennedy's demands.

1970–75 The **Cambodian War** breaks out between the communist Khmer Rouge and Cambodia's republican government. The republicans are backed by the US but the Khmer Rouge triumphs.

1979 Soviet troops enter Afghanistan to prop up the failing communist regime.

1985 Gorbachev comes to power in the Soviet Union. He reforms the country's failing institutions and opens up talks on nuclear disarmament.

1989 On November 9, the East German government opens gates along the Berlin Wall. Citizens set about dismantling it.

After World War II, Germany was divided into four zones, each separately administered by the US, France, Britain, and the Soviet Union. The German capital, Berlin, was situated deep in the Soviet zone and was split into four allied sectors. In 1948 the Western allies planned a separate West German state, uniting the US, French, and British zones. The Soviets tried to stop this by cutting off land routes into the Western sectors of Berlin, leaving only air access. For the next year, as diplomatic battles raged, the Berlin Airlift (see below) brought supplies to besieged Berliners. By 1949 division of Germany appeared to be inevitable. The German Democratic Republic was created in East Germany and the Federal Republic of Germany in the west. Berlin remained a divided city. In 1961 the barbed wire partitions were replaced by the Berlin Wall (see p.426).

The Cold War hots up

The superpowers' possession of weapons of mass destruction generated much of the fear and paranoia that characterizes the Cold War era. Initially the US was the only nation in possession of nuclear weapons, but once the Soviets tested their own nuclear bomb in August 1949, any future conflict carried the threat of global destruction. In 1953 the Soviet leader, Nikita Khrushchev, promoted a policy of "peaceful coexistence" with the West, and periodic attempts were made on both sides to create a thaw in relations. However, there were many flash points that reignited tensions and suspicions, bringing the world to the brink of catastrophe. In 1962, crisis was narrowly averted after a tense standoff when Soviet missile installations were discovered in communist Cuba. The superpowers continued to stockpile nuclear arms, reasoning that nuclear war could only be prevented if each side had an equal capacity to destroy the other. A range of arms agreements were negotiated during the Cold War, but disarmament was not considered to be a possibility.

Cuban missile crisis
Nuclear weapons were mobilized in Havana (above) as the US and the Soviet Union threatened each other with nuclear attack in an escalating argument over the building of Soviet nuclear installations in Cuba.

SIGNING THE NATO TREATY

On April 4, 1949 the North Atlantic Treaty Organization (NATO) was founded by the leaders of the United States, Canada, Britain, France, and several other European countries. NATO was, first and foremost, a military alliance that guaranteed assistance between member states and, crucially, allowed the US to maintain military bases in Europe. In 1953, Greece and Turkey entered NATO but a Soviet request for membership was rejected.

AFTER

The reforming political leader Mikhail Gorbachev unintentionally set off a chain of events that would break up the Soviet Union.

COLLAPSE OF COMMUNISM

In 1985 **Gorbachev** started to campaign for economic and political reforms known as *glasnost* and *perestroika* **446–47 »**. Two years later he became president and modernized the Soviet system, encouraging the creation of a private sector and openness with the West. He aimed to keep a one-party political system, but his social reforms sparked a chain reaction that led to the collapse of the Communist Party as Russians demanded choice in their leaders.

DISSOLUTION OF THE SOVIET UNION

In the Baltic States, Kazakhstan, and other parts of the Soviet Union, nationalists rose up to demand independence from Moscow. Gorbachev tried to hold the Soviet Union together, imposing sanctions and sending troops into Georgia and Azerbaijan. In 1990 **Boris Yeltsin** resigned from the Communist Party and began to campaign for its dissolution. In 1991 he emerged as the new Russian leader. He banned the Communist Party and dissolved the Soviet Union.

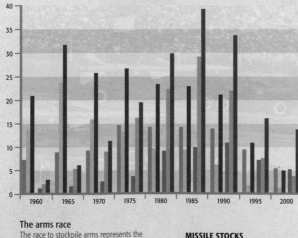

The arms race
The race to stockpile arms represents the superpowers' Cold War conflict in graphic terms. Each side rapidly developed the capacity to destroy the world many times over, but both continued to manufacture weapons at huge expense, competing to develop missiles that were ever more efficient.

MISSILE STOCKS

US	RUSSIA
Strategic	Strategic
Tactical	Tactical
Stockpile	Stockpile

POLITICAL AND SPIRITUAL LEADER Born 1869 Died 1948

Mahatma Gandhi

"Silent suffering… speaks with an unrivaled eloquence." GANDHI, 1923

Mohandas Karamchand Gandhi, known as Mahatma ("Grand Soul"), was born into the *vaisya* caste of Hindu society, traditionally devoted to trade. His father was prime minister of the tiny princedom of Porbandar, part of British-ruled northwestern India. Typical of privileged sectors of Indian society at that time, his life was shaped both by old Indian customs, such as an arranged marriage at an early age, and by the influence of European attitudes and ideas.

The young Gandhi was skeptical about his family's Hindu practices, however, including the avoidance of meat, and leapt at the chance to study law in Britain. Ironically, it was as a student in London that he first encountered the *Bhagavad Gita*, a sacred Hindu text that was to influence him profoundly, and he became a committed vegetarian.

When Gandhi went to South Africa as a 23-year-old lawyer in 1893, he had no clear purpose in life except to make money, at which he proved thoroughly successful. But the experience of the discrimination, prejudice, and mistreatment suffered by Indians in South Africa's racially divided society drew him into political activism. He led a series of mass campaigns during which he devised the method of political struggle he called *satyagraha* ("love-force" or "truth-force," see right). This was nonviolent civil disobedience, conceived by Gandhi as a moral and spiritual effort, seeking to bring about a change in the hearts and minds of the oppressors by

Handwritten letter
This letter was written in 1914, the year in which Gandhi definitively quit South Africa after two decades of campaigning for the Indians' rights.

Gandhi the lawyer
As a young London-educated lawyer, Gandhi looked the epitome of a Westernized Asian. He did not adopt traditional Indian dress until 1913.

Father of the nation
In his white "dhoti," Gandhi cut a strikingly odd figure at international political conferences. To the Indian masses, though, he seemed a reassuringly familiar type of holy man.

Young companions
The aging Gandhi is seen here with his "walking sticks"—his great-nieces Manu and Ava—at Birla House in New Delhi.

adherence to the truth and by the readiness to suffer. Gandhi certainly suffered himself, undergoing imprisonment and coming close to being lynched by a racist mob.

Adopting the simple life

When Gandhi returned to live in India in 1915, he was not only a seasoned leader of political protest but also a man with a distinctive set of attitudes based on the rejection of modern industrial civilization. As he was influenced by Russian author Leo Tolstoy and English social critic John Ruskin, he embraced the simple life, believing in the virtue of small artisan communities. He had made a vow of chastity (announced to his wife in 1906), seeking spiritual fulfillment through the renunciation of the passions. He also rejected modern medicine in favor of alternative remedies and a focus on diet.

Gandhi established a community, or *ashram*, at Ahmedabad, northwestern India, where he could live according to his principles, but he soon resumed campaigning. India was entering a period of great upheaval, shaped by both the British government's

commitment in 1917 to progress toward a degree of Indian self-rule, and simultaneous oppression by the British authorities in the Raj, notably the massacre of 379 demonstrators at Amritsar in April 1919. In a very short time, Gandhi swept to the forefront of Indian political life, launching a campaign of total noncooperation with the British, and a boycott of British goods, which attracted mass support. After taking over leadership of the Indian National Congress, he made it into a vital nationwide organization.

Spiritual values

Gandhi never had a politician's attitude, however. His goal was not the attainment of power but the spiritual and moral transformation of Indian society. His advocacy of nonviolence ran into difficulty as early as 1922, when a nationalist mob killed 22 policemen at Chauri Chaura, northern India. Gandhi responded by calling off his first noncooperation campaign, but critics pointed out in following years

Meeting the viceroy
Lord Mountbatten, the last British viceroy (governor) of India, and his wife were on close terms with Gandhi during the period preceding Indian independence in 1947.

that when he stirred up political dissent, in practice, it always led to violence. For much of the 1920s and 1930s Gandhi focused on breaking down communal barriers between Hindus and Muslims, and overthrowing the Hindu caste system—a system of inherited social classes. He also campaigned against industrialization, himself learning to use a hand spinning wheel as a symbol of his great belief in village crafts.

An undisputed leader

Despite these challenges, Gandhi remained both nationally and internationally the most renowned leader of the Indian independence movement. No other Indian leader could have led such an effective protest as the famous "Salt March" of 1930, a symbolic defiance of the British tax on salt. No other leader talked so effectively to the British ruling class, who were fascinated by his exotic dress and manner. And his moral authority in India was immense.

In 1942, reluctantly, he launched the "Quit India" movement, provoking brutal repression from the British authorities. The drift of events saddened his final years. The British decided to grant India independence after World War II, but the rise of Muslim separatism led to partition between India and Pakistan (see pp.410–411), which Gandhi loathed. Even worse was the violence that the subcontinent was plunged into. Fasting and pleading with Hindus and Muslims, Gandhi occasionally managed to halt the slaughter in one place, only for it to break out in another. His conciliatory attitude toward Muslims enraged Hindu extremists. On January 20, 1948 he was shot dead in Delhi by Hindu fanatic Nathuram Godse.

"Truth never damages a cause that is just."

GANDHI, FROM "NONVIOLENCE IN PEACE AND WAR", 1948

IDEA

SATYAGRAHA

Gandhi's principle of *satyagraha*, a nonviolent political struggle, was influential after his death. It became, for example, a point of reference for Martin Luther King Jr. as leader of the American civil rights movement (see pp.432–33), for the founders of the Campaign for Nuclear Disarmament (CND), and for some within the anti–Vietnam War protest movement (see pp.430–31). For Gandhi, *satyagraha* was more than simply a way of achieving political objectives through civil disobedience. He saw it as a path to spiritual improvement through truth, love, and suffering.

TIMELINE

- **October 2, 1869** Gandhi is born in Porbandar, Gujarat.
- **May 1883** Is married, at age 13, to 10-year-old Kasturba Makhanji.
- **1888–91** Studies law at University College, London, and returns to India as a lawyer.
- **April 1893** Travels to Durban, South Africa, to join an Indian law firm.
- **1894** Begins 20 years of campaigning against discrimination and exploitation of Indians in South Africa.

GANDHI AT HIS LAW OFFICES

- **1899–1902** During the Boer War, Gandhi forms an Indian Ambulance Corps.
- **September 11, 1906** Calls for resistance to the registration of Indians in Transvaal, initiating his first campaign of *satyagraha*.
- **May 1915** Returning to India, he founds the Satyagraha Ashram at Ahmedabad.
- **December 1921** Elected leader of the Indian National Congress.
- **February 1922** Halts the noncooperation campaign in shock at mob violence.
- **March 1922** Arrested and tried for sedition. Gandhi is sentenced to six years and serves two.
- **December 1928** Congress launches a campaign for dominion status for India.
- **January 26, 1930** Millions of Indians take Gandhi's pledge to pursue "purna swaraj"—complete independence.
- **March 12– April 6, 1930** Leads the "Salt March" from Ahmedabad to Dandi; he is arrested on May 4.
- **February 14–March 5, 1931** Released from prison. Gandhi negotiates a pact with British viceroy Lord Irwin to end civil disobedience.
- **September–December 1931** Gandhi represents Congress at a Round Table Conference on Indian constitutional reform in London; on his return to India he is arrested.
- **October 24, 1934** Disillusioned with politics, he resigns from Congress.
- **August 9, 1942** Gandhi and Congress leaders are arrested after the launch of the "Quit India" movement for independence from Britain; Gandhi is held in the Aga Khan Palace near Poona.
- **November 1946** Begins a solitary campaign to halt massacres and seek conciliation between Hindus and Muslims.
- **January 30, 1948** Gandhi is assassinated at Birla House, New Delhi.

NEWSPAPER REPORT OF GANDHI'S DEATH

The **Partition** of India

British rule in India ended in 1947 and the subcontinent was partitioned along religious lines to form the Hindu-majority state of India and the Muslim-majority state of Pakistan. Many millions of Muslims and Hindus caught on the wrong side of the border were forced to flee their homes.

BEFORE

Denied civil and political rights, Indians became increasingly disenchanted with British rule in the late 19th century. By the 1920s there was a mass anticolonial movement demanding home rule for India.

GOVERNMENT OF INDIA ACT
The **British Raj ≪ 352–53** made some limited concessions to Indian civil rights. In 1909 the **Government of India Act** allowed a very small number of Indians to sit on legislative councils, but their responsibilities were minimal.

INDIAN RIGHTS
The **Indian National Congress (INC)** was founded in 1885 by Western-educated Indians campaigning for Indian rights. Although the Congress represented all Indians, its members were mainly Hindu. In 1906 some Muslims broke away from the INC to form the **Muslim League**.

CIVIL DISOBEDIENCE
During the 1920s, under the leadership of **Mahatma Gandhi ≪ 408–09**, the INC demanded Indian independence. In a long campaign of civil disobedience, known as *satyagraha*, Gandhi encouraged the boycotting of British goods, the nonpayment of taxes, and passive or **nonviolent resistance**.

VIOLENT RESISTANCE
Not all Indians used peaceful means to resist British rule. When World War II ≪ **392–405** broke out, many Indians supported Britain's enemies. The Bengali leader, Subhash Chandra Bose, formed the 20,000-strong Indian National Army, which fought alongside Japanese forces.

INDIAN NATIONAL ARMY

After World War I (see pp.372–75), Britain promised India a major role in governing itself, in return for Indian support during the war. In 1919 a further Government of India Act (see BEFORE) was passed. It created an Indian parliament to which Indian ministers could be elected to hold positions of responsibility in departments such as health, education, and agriculture. However, only the wealthiest Indians, who formed a tiny percentage of the population, were allowed to vote for the parliament, and the British still held the real power, controlling all the other departments. Another act in 1935 allowed more Indians to vote, and the British kept only the most crucial departments—revenue, defense, and foreign affairs. These concessions did not go far enough for independence campaigners (see BEFORE). At the end of World War II, in 1945, the British agreed to hand over full power.

Direct action
As independence drew closer, the leader of the Muslim League, Muhammad Ali Jinnah, started to demand a separate Muslim state. The idea was resisted by Hindus, including Gandhi, who believed that India should remain united. In response, Jinnah declared August 16, 1946 "Direct Action Day." On that day Muslims protested all over India to voice their demand for a separate homeland. Tragically, the protest in Calcutta escalated into violent fighting between religious groups, and thousands of people died.

Drawing the line
Lord Mountbatten, the last viceroy of India, saw that the only way for the British to withdraw was to partition India and to transfer power to two governments. Among the major Indian leaders, only Gandhi refused to agree to partition. He even urged Mountbatten to offer Jinnah the premiership of a united India rather than a separate

Constitutional Assembly crowd
A crowd of people gathered outside the Constitutional Assembly in Karachi as the ceremony to symbolize the transfer of power from Britain to Pakistan took place. During the ceremony, Lord Mountbatten read a message from George VI pledging the support of the British Commonwealth (nations that were formerly part of the British Empire) to Pakistan.

ETHNIC TENSIONS

Ethnic and religious rivalries caused the partition of India. **Territorial disputes** arising from the partition have led to a series of conflicts between neighboring states.

1940 | **1950** | **1960** | **1970** | **1980**

1947–49 India and Pakistan go to war when Pakistan supports a Muslim insurgency in the independent province of **Kashmir**.

1958–60 Disputes arise between Pakistan and India over the rights to water in the Pakistani **Punjab** region.

1966 The Tashkent agreement commits the countries to resolve differences through peaceful means and noninterference in each other's foreign affairs.

1971 Civil war breaks out between West and East Pakistan. After the war ends, East Pakistan becomes **Bangladesh**.

1989 Pakistan begins its "moral and diplomatic support" of Muslim militant groups operating in the Kashmir valley. India accuses Pakistan of supporting terrorism.

1946 Jinnah calls for "direct action." Riots erupt and thousands of people are killed.

1947 Partition of the Indian subcontinent leads to a **mass migration** of people and the deaths of one million.

1965 Pakistan launches an offensive in the Indian-held parts of **Jammu and Kashmir**. India invades **Lahore** in retaliation.

1972 The Simla Treaty between the two countries paves the way for the diplomatic recognition of an independent Bangladesh by Pakistan.

1999 War briefly breaks out between India and Pakistan near the Indian Kashmiri town of Kargil.

Muslim nation. Congress president Jawaharlal Nehru, however, would not agree to this plan, nor would his most powerful Congress deputy, Vallabhbhai Patel. Neither felt they could work with Jinnah and were eager to get on with running an independent India.

In July 1947 Britain's Parliament passed the Indian Independence Act, ordering the demarcation of the dominions of India and Pakistan and dividing the assets of the world's largest empire. Under the partition plan, Pakistan had two wings—East and West Pakistan. These were located thousands of miles apart, in the mainly Muslim east and northwest of the region, respectively. India was formed from the remaining area, with the exception of the northern province of Kashmir, which was free to accede to India or Pakistan. On August 14, 1947 Pakistan gained

Partition riots
Violent gangs roamed the streets of Calcutta during riots that erupted as soon as partition was declared. The sectarian attacks claimed the lives of 4,000 people.

Nehru releases a dove
The Indian prime minister, Nehru, launched a dove of peace at his 65th birthday celebrations in 1954. Nehru held office from 1947 to 1964.

independence and Jinnah became its first governor-general. At midnight the next day, the independent state of India emerged with Nehru as its first prime minister. As soon as the new borders were announced, more than 12 million Hindus, Muslims, and Sikhs fled from their homes on one side of the borders to what they believed was refuge on the other side. They traveled on foot, in bullock carts, and on trains. The massive exchange of population left behind a trail of death and destruction. Within two months, about a million people were slaughtered in fierce religious riots. The Sikh population, who were caught on the Pakistani side of the new border, suffered the highest percentage of casualties. Most Sikhs eventually settled in India's much-reduced border province of Punjab.

Territorial and ethnic issues continue to cause conflict in the Indian subcontinent.

CONFLICT OVER KASHMIR

India and Pakistan have contested possession of the Muslim-majority state of **Kashmir** since 1947, when the Hindu ruler, Maharajah Hari Singh, gave the province to India. Wars were fought over the territory in 1947–48 and 1965. Since 1989 there has been an independence movement in the Indian-administered part of Kashmir. India blamed pro-Kashmiri militants for the attacks on their parliament in 2001 and on Mumbai hotels in 2008.

SIKH SEPARATISTS

No provision was made for Sikhs when India was partitioned between Muslims and Hindus. From the early 1980s Sikhs began to demand their own state, which they hope to call **Sikh Khalistan**, meaning "Land of the Pure."

NUCLEAR STANDOFF

India and Pakistan conducted nuclear tests in 1998, causing concern in the international community. The UN Security Council criticized the two countries and urged them to stop all nuclear weapons programs. Tensions were reduced in February 1999 after Pakistan and India signed the **Lahore Declaration**, pledging to intensify efforts to resolve all the issues between them. However, the threat of nuclear conflict still remains between the two countries.

COLONIAL RULE
Calls for independence by nationalist movements in many overseas territories forced European powers to withdraw.

1930 The Indian National Congress makes a symbolic declaration of **Indian independence**.

1945 Ho Chi Minh declares an Independent Republic in **Vietnam** and Sukarno declares **Indonesian** independence.

1956 The revolution of the king and the people sees **Morocco** win independence from France and agree the restoration of control over some Spanish-ruled areas.

1957–75 Independence from British, French, Spanish, Dutch, Portuguese, and Belgian rule is achieved by the majority of **African** and **Caribbean nations**.

1997 Hong Kong, a British territory since its victory in the Opium Wars of 1842, is finally handed back to **China** on July 1, 1997. This is judged to be the last action of the British Empire.

| 1900 | 1925 | 1950 | 1975 |

1915–24 Growing nationalist sentiments in **Sri Lanka** lead to the formation of the Youth Leagues who lobby for **self-rule** and withdrawal from the British Empire.

1922 Demonstrations against Britain's long-term occupation of Egypt lead to **Egyptian independence** but Britain continues to dominate Egyptian affairs.

1946 The formation of the international Pan-African Federation promotes **African independence**.

1948 The creation of the modern state of **Israel**. Indian independence from British rule is followed by the **partition** of the subcontinent into **India** and **Pakistan**.

1999 Macao returns to Chinese control after 442 years of Portuguese rule.

End of the Colonial Era

The decline of Europe's empires gathered momentum after World War II as domination of poorer nations by colonial powers came to be considered unacceptable. The transition from empire led to the creation of self-governing nation states in much of the world, but this created many new conflicts.

In 1945, the old justification for empire—that "inferior" races needed the guidance of "superior" Western civilization—came into question. In the aftermath of war there was a real desire to build a new and better world (see p.397). Many colonies had remained deeply impoverished and underdeveloped to suit the economic needs of empire. However, European powers were now forced to admit that this could no longer be accepted and some countries reluctantly began to prepare for a withdrawal from imperial territories.

End of empire
Unfortunately, this new recognition of the rights of "Third World" countries to self-govern coincided with the advent of the Cold War (pp.406–07). The transition to independent status of some former colonies was complicated by the superpowers—the US and the Soviet Union—who competed for influence over the people's choice of government. In the colonies themselves there was conflict between different social, political, and ethnic factions over who should govern. In many cases, European powers caused resentment by trying to hold on to their interests in resources, such as oil and gemstones, even after independence was granted.

As a result, transitions to independence were often marked by civil wars and intervention from foreign powers.

Withdrawal from colonies
In Indonesia, resentment of their Dutch imperial masters was so intense that Japanese invaders were initially welcomed during World War II. The Dutch were unwilling to surrender their interests in Indonesian oil and rubber. They invaded in 1945 to re-establish control, but conceded Indonesian independence in 1949, although they continued to occupy Western New Guinea. A full Indonesian Republic was not created until 1960. During World War II the German-backed Vichy regime in French Indochina, which incorporated Vietnam, Laos, and Cambodia, also collaborated with Japan. In 1945 the

Vietnamese nationalist Ho Chi Minh took advantage of the Japanese surrender to declare an Independent Democratic Vietnamese Republic. French troops invaded the new republic and by 1946 had taken control of the south of the country, while Minh's army (Viet Minh) held the north. The French Indochina War lasted from 1946–54, when massive French losses at the Battle of Dien Bien Phu finally precipitated a settlement. The country was divided into North and South Vietnam. Tensions between the two nations later escalated into the Vietnam War (see pp.430–31).

In the British colony of Malaya, an initially peaceful transition to self-government developed into conflict in 1948. Hostility toward Britain's intention to maintain business interests in Malay rubber and tin combined with political and ethnic divisions in the population to create civil unrest. An armed insurrection by the communist minority resulted in the death of three European plantation managers in June

‹‹ BEFORE

By the early 20th century the spread of nationalist ideas led to the growth of independence movements in the colonies.

COLONIES AND EMPIRES
Before World War II, European powers still **dominated much of the world**–Africa was largely divided between the British, French, Belgian, and Portuguese ‹‹ 360–61; much of Asia and the Caribbean also remained under imperial rule. In the Middle East, mandates granted by the League of Nations gave Britain and France administrative powers over the region.

COLONIAL ECONOMIES
Colonial territories tended to be under-industrialized, and in many the standard of living was very low. They supplied raw materials to power European industry, but the **development of their own national economies** was not seen as a priority.

RISE OF NATIONALISM
Increasingly, **citizens demanded the right to self-govern**. The imperial powers began to make some concessions toward power-sharing but remained determined to hold on to economic control of the natural resources of their colonies.

PRESIDENT OF EGYPT (1918–1970)

GAMAL ABDEL NASSER

From an early age, Nasser was interested in the fight for Egyptian independence. During World War II, he was involved in plans for a military coup to oust British forces from Egypt. These plans never reached fruition, but in 1952 Nasser spearheaded the Egyptian Revolution, becoming president (1956–70). Nasser's victory in the Suez Crisis of 1956 (see right) established him as a figurehead for Arab nationalism.

Ships scuttled in the Suez Canal
Ships sunk by Egyptian forces block the entrance to the Suez Canal. On the extreme right of the picture, a British naval salvage vessel attempts to clear the channel.

Dutch leave Indonesia
As Indonesia gains independence in 1949, servants carry 300 portraits of former Dutch governors out of the colonial residence, marking the end of over 340 years of imperial rule.

the fact that European governments had divided the continent along arbitrary borders that paid no attention to tribal boundaries (see pp.360–61).

150,000 The estimated death toll in the French–Algerian conflict.

As imperial powers withdrew, many nations also descended into civil war.

When the Belgian government abruptly granted independence to the Congo in 1960, violence erupted as different Congolese factions struggled to gain control of the nation's remarkable natural wealth. The Congo's nominally democratic government, installed at independence, failed in 1965 when Lieutenant General Mobutu seized power in a military coup.

After independence

Through the 1960s and 70s, transitions to independence became generally peaceful and independence was established across most of the world. However, independent government in the Third World has not equalized the distribution of global wealth and power. While former colonies such as Hong Kong and Singapore (see pp.456–57) have flourished post-empire, many others are among the world's poorest nations.

Paris riots
Growing opposition in France to French suppression of the Nationalist Movement in Algeria exploded into riots on the streets of Paris as French protesters clashed with the French Army and the notorious CRS riot squad in 1961. A ceasefire was called in Algeria in 1962. Later that year the Algerian people voted for independence.

AFTER »

In many cases, democracies established post-empire failed to survive, and military or one-party rule was established.

MILITARY REGIMES
In some countries power was seized in military coups, such as that led by Idi Amin in Uganda in 1971. **Ethnic violence and political repression** were rife under the military regimes.

DEMOCRACY
With a few exceptions, such as the independent Republic of Ghana, democracies established post-empire have failed in much of Africa. Elected national parliaments have often been **unable to establish unity** in countries, such as Sudan, that are divided along tribal lines.

INDEPENDENCE ANNIVERSARY, GHANA

1948, which led to armed confrontation. British troops defeated the Chinese guerrillas in 1952 and withdrew from Malaya in 1957 once the Federation of Malaya had been established.

The Suez crisis
The most significant crisis of British and French withdrawal from empire came in 1956 when President Nasser (see left) nationalized the Suez Canal. The canal, which links the Mediterranean and Red Sea through Egyptian territory, had been under British and French control since its construction in 1869. It represented a key route for the transport of raw materials to Europe. Anglo-French forces attacked Egypt to wrest the canal back from Egyptian control, but the United Nations, US,

and Soviet Union all refused to support the imperialist invasion. Humiliated, Britain and France withdrew. The crisis ended in a victory for Arab nationalism and signaled the decline of the old powers of Europe.

African conflicts
France's determination to maintain control of Algeria in northern Africa led to guerrilla fighting between the Algerian *Front de Libération Nationale* (FLN) and French security forces from 1954. By 1960, the violence had escalated and the independence issue was bitterly dividing the French nation. French army generals in Algeria then attempted a coup d'état. Independence was agreed in 1962. The struggle left deep scars on both French and Algerian national consciousness.

The dismantling of colonies in Africa spawned many territorial wars between African Nations. This was due in part to

BEFORE

In the 1880s, Jews known as Zionists began to emigrate to Palestine to avoid religious persecution in Europe. By 1897 they were demanding their own state, and in 1917 the British agreed to the foundation of a Jewish state in Palestine.

EARLY ZIONISTS

ZIONISM

Zionism became an organized political movement in 1897 when its founder, Theodor Herzl, convened the First Zionist Congress. The congress called for a Jewish state in Palestine.

SYKES–PICOT AGREEMENT

When the Ottoman Empire **«246–47** collapsed during World War I **«372–75**, France and Britain signed the 1916 Sykes–Picot agreement, dividing the Empire's Middle Eastern territories between them. France gained the mandate for Syria and Lebanon, and Britain was granted the mandate for Iraq and Palestine.

MANDATE An Ottoman or German territory that was handed to another country to run after World War I.

THE BALFOUR DECLARATION

The 1917 Balfour Declaration was a policy drawn up by the British government that accepted the need for a Jewish homeland in Palestine.

The Promised Land

According to the Bible, the land of Palestine was promised by God to the Jewish people. In 1948 the modern Jewish state of Israel was established in the region, causing fury among Palestinian Arabs and in the wider Arab world. It has proved one of the most contentious political acts of modern times.

The period of British rule in Palestine, which formally began in 1919 when the British Mandate (see BEFORE) was granted, was marked by controversy and violence. The majority Arab population strongly contested the Jewish settlers' claim on their country, and some Arabs resorted to aggressive attacks against Jews, their homes, and their businesses. The Jews, feeling that the British authorities were giving them insufficient protection, began to form local defense groups, known collectively as the Hagannah, to protect their communities. During the 1930s the Hagannah turned into a paramilitary organization, developing military training programs and sourcing arms from Europe.

The British withdraw

Guerrilla violence between Arab groups and the Hagannah became increasingly difficult for the British to police, so in 1939 they called together Arab and Jewish delegations to the St. James Conference, also known as the Round Table Conference, to find a solution to the ongoing tensions.

Jewish refugee
Like many of the Jews who emigrated to Israel in the 1950s, this Yemeni girl stayed at the Shaar reception center in Haifa when she first arrived in the Jewish state.

No agreement was reached at the conference, so the British formed their own policy, which was stated in the McDonald White Paper of 1939. In it the British made concessions to the Arabs on a wide range of issues, the most important of which was a restriction on the free settlement in Palestine of Jewish refugees. This seemed like a death sentence for those Jews trying to flee Nazi Europe (see pp.400–01) to Palestine. Supporters of the Arab and Jewish sides held international conferences during 1946, but the year ended without any workable solutions to the problem. Caught between Arab and Jewish demands, a cash-strapped British government declared its mandate in Palestine "unworkable" in February 1947 and referred the matter to the United Nations. The UN proposed a partition plan, which allocated about 44 percent of the area for an

Arab state and 56 percent for a Jewish state, with Jerusalem under international administration. On November 29, 1947 the UN General Assembly voted 33 to 13, with 10 abstentions, in favor of the Partition Plan. The Jews agreed with their decision but the Arabs did not, arguing that the plan ignored the rights of the majority of people living in Palestine.

> "In Israel, in order to be a **realist** you must believe in **miracles**."
>
> DAVID BEN-GURION, OLORA MANIFESTO, 1948

UN Partition plan
Under the plan the Jews would receive the northern coastal plain, eastern Galilee, and the Negev. The Arabs would get a section of desert bordering Egypt (the Gaza Strip), the Samarian and Judean highlands, and the southern coast.

Wreck of Altalena
In June 1948 crowds gathered on the Tel Aviv beachfront to see the wreckage of the burnt-out Altalena. It had sailed from France to Israel carrying arms for the Irgun (a splinter group of the Hagannah) and about 900 immigrants. Ben-Gurion refused to let it land in respect of a truce with the Arabs, and ordered warning shots to be fired. One hit the vessel and it burned.

Beirut
LEBANON
Tyre
Damascus
SYRIA
Golan Heights
Haifa
Sea of Galilee
Qunaytirah
Mediterranean Sea
Nablus
Jordan
Tel-Aviv
SAMARIA
Amman
Jaffa
Jerusalem
Gaza
Jericho
Gaza Strip
West Bank
Dead Sea
JUDEA
Hebron
Rafah
El Arish
Beersheba
TRANSJORDAN
ISRAEL
Negev
Sinai Peninsula
Eilat
Aqaba
Gulf of Aqaba

KEY
- Proposed Arab state
- Proposed Jewish state
- Proposed international zone
- Border of British mandate 1923

0   100 km
0   100 miles

DAVID BEN-GURION

David Ben-Gurion was born in Poland. He moved to Palestine in 1906 and became a prominent member of the Zionist movement, leading the struggle to establish a state of Israel. Ben-Gurion became Israel's first prime minister in 1949. Until his retirement in 1970, he played a major role in Israeli life, developing the state's policies and institutions, and guiding Israel through years of conflict.

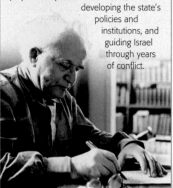

Despite this, Britain withdrew and on May 14, 1948 the Jewish state of Israel was established. It was recognized by the US, the Soviet Union, and other UN members, but not neighboring Arab countries, which refused to accept Israel as a state.

Troubles in the homeland

One of the first tasks for Israel's new leader, David Ben-Gurion, was to create the Israeli Defense Force from the Hagannah and other Jewish paramilitary organizations. Israel had real and immediate needs to defend itself as, once it was established, the country was invaded by Egypt, Syria, Transjordan (later Jordan), Lebanon, and Iraq, beginning the Arab–Israeli War of 1947–49, the first in a series of conflicts between Israel and the Arab world (see AFTER). A further threat to security was the Palestine Liberation

Evacuation of Jerusalem
This man was among thousands of Jews who were evacuated from Jerusalem by British troops in 1948. The city had come under siege from Arab militias who, in reaction to the Partition Plan, tried to dispossess the 100,000 Jewish people living in the city.

Organization (PLO). Formed in 1964 when various Arab guerrilla groups and political factions joined together, the PLO's stated aim was the destruction of Israel through armed struggle. The PLO sponsored innumerable guerrilla raids on Israeli civilian and military targets, giving the organization a worldwide reputation as a terrorist group. In the 1980s, Yasser Arafat, chairman of the PLO since 1969, took on the role of statesman and used diplomacy to achieve the group's ends. However, some Palestinian extremists believed Arafat gave too many concessions to the Israelis during diplomatic talks.

Entry visa
Dated January 1939, this visa allowed the German Jewish holder to emigrate to the British Protectorate of Palestine. By November of the same year restrictions had been placed on the numbers of Jews allowed to settle in the region.

Despite intervention by the international community, tensions between Middle Eastern Arabs and Jews erupted into conflict periodically after Israel was established.

SECOND ARAB–ISRAELI WAR

In 1956 **Egypt nationalized the Suez Canal Company << 412–13**, taking the waterway out of French and British control. Since tensions were also growing between Israel and Egypt over the Egyptian-held Gaza Strip, which Israel believed was a base for guerrilla activity, **Israel, Britain, and France joined forces** to invade Egypt.

SIX-DAY WAR

In response to the massing of Arab forces on its borders, **Israel launched a preemptive strike against Egypt, Jordan, and Syria** in June 1967. After six days, all the parties agreed to a ceasefire, under which Israel gained control of the Gaza Strip, a large part of the Sinai Peninsula, the West Bank, and the Golan Heights, collectively known as **"occupied territories."**

YOM KIPPUR WAR

In 1973 **Egypt and Syria launched a surprise attack** on Israel on Yom Kippur, the Jewish Day of Atonement, a day on which they knew the Israeli military would be participating in religious celebrations. The Arab forces made significant advances before Israel rallied and pushed the invaders back beyond the 1967 ceasefire lines.

MOVES TOWARD PEACE

In 1978 President Anwar Sadat of Egypt, Prime Minister Menachem Begin of Israel, and President Jimmy Carter of the US signed the Camp David Accords. The accords established a **"Framework for Peace"** in the Middle East, leading to the Israel/Egypt Peace Treaty in 1979.

ISRAELI OCCUPATION OF LEBANON

In an attempt to curtail cross-border attacks by the PLO based in Lebanon, Israel invaded in 1978 and in 1982; they became an occupying force there until 2000. In response to the killing of three Israeli soldiers and the capture of two others by **Hezbollah**, a Lebanese Islamic paramilitary group, Israel reinvaded in 2006.

OSLO ACCORDS

The Intifada (a Palestinian uprising against Israeli rule) persuaded Israel to join talks. The Oslo Accords agreed that Israel would withdraw from parts of **the West Bank and Gaza Strip**, allowing an interim Palestinian government in those areas. Subsequent peace efforts failed and opinions on both sides hardened. Islamist groups such as Hamas and Islamic Jihad gained ground in areas ruled by Palestine, while Israeli hardliners pushed through a policy of isolating these areas by building a "peace wall."

RABIN, CLINTON, AND ARAFAT

SCIENTIST Born 1879 Died 1955

Albert Einstein

"The most **beautiful** experience we can have is the **mysterious.** It is the source of all true **art and science."** ALBERT EINSTEIN, 1930

German-born physicist Albert Einstein had a largely uninspiring school career, although he displayed a natural talent for mathematics and a love of learning. After graduating from a technical university with a teaching certificate, Einstein found a job at a patent office in Bern, Switzerland, in 1903. Two years later, while still working there, Einstein submitted his doctoral thesis and published four scientific papers. Three of these were to be profoundly important in the history of science.

The first of Einstein's 1905 papers concerned the puzzling phenomenon known as the photoelectric effect, in which electrons are ejected from atoms of metal when light shines onto them.

Instead of the ejection rate gradually building with the intensity of light shining onto the metal surface, the effect suddenly "switches on" when the frequency of light rises past a certain threshold. In order to explain this effect, Einstein showed that light energy must be delivered in discrete packets, or "quanta."

German physicist Max Planck (1858–1947) had used quantization as a mathematical trick in 1900, but had

Einstein the icon
Albert Einstein contributed hugely to our understanding of the universe–from atoms to stars and galaxies–and became an iconic figure.

Young Einstein
Around the time of this photograph, Einstein–here with sister Maja–received a magnetic compass from his father. He later said that he had found inspiration wondering why compass needles turn.

School certificate
There is a myth that Einstein struggled at school. This certificate tells a different story–in physics and math he scored a maximum 6.

never supposed it to be literally true. Einstein's paper was the beginning of quantum theory—a field of physics that provides insight into the behavior of light, atoms, and subatomic particles. Einstein remained at the heart of its development for the rest of his life.

Einstein's second landmark paper of 1905, entitled *On the Electrodynamics of Moving Bodies*, outlined his Special

Theory of Relativity. The starting point in this paper was the fact that the speed of light is always the same, however fast an observer is moving relative to a light source. He used this to prove that time does not run at a single, "universal" rate—clocks moving relative to each other tick away seconds at different rates (though the effect is only noticeable at very high relative speeds).

Einstein's last publication of 1905 was a bold extension of Special Relativity. Working from the fact that the speed of light could not be exceeded, Einstein

IDEA

THEORIES OF RELATIVITY

The principle of relativity dates back to the scientific revolution of the 17th century (see pp.266–67). First identified by Italian physicist Galileo Galilei, it states that physical laws should behave in the same way in all isolated frames of reference unless they are being affected by external forces—in other words, natural laws are the same whether one is in motion or not. This is because all motion is relative—there is no universal, fixed reference point.

Einstein's Special Theory of Relativity (1905) reconciles this principle with the fact that light always travels at the same speed relative to an observer no matter how fast they travel relative to its source. In order to do this, Einstein explained how time and distance measurements become distorted at high relative speeds. The bizarre results of special relativity are used routinely by experimental physicists.

In 1915, Einstein extended Special Relativity to create his General Theory of Relativity. This theory explains gravity as a distortion of space-time, the four-dimensional "fabric" of the universe.

The two theories of relativity have been tested countless times and have never yet failed. One effect of general relativity (illustrated by this Hubble Space Telescope image) is a phenomenon called gravitational lensing, in which light from distant stars and galaxies is deflected and warped as it passes close to stars and galaxies.

TIMELINE

- **March 14, 1879** Albert Einstein is born in the small town of Ulm, Germany. The Einsteins move to Munich the following year.

- **1892** At age 13, Einstein begins his studies at the Lutipold Gymnasium (Munich).

- **1896** In order to avoid military service, he renounces his German citizenship, and begins studying mathematics in Zurich, Switzerland.

- **1901** Einstein graduates from the ETH, a technical institute in Zurich, with a teaching certificate. He is awarded Swiss citizenship.

- **1903** Marries his first wife, Mileva Maric, whom he met at college. He begins work at the patent office in Bern.

- **1905** In Einstein's "Wonderful Year," he writes four groundbreaking scientific papers, which are published in the German physics journal *Annalen der Physik*. He also gains his doctorate from the University of Zurich.

- **1911** Accepts a professorship at Charles University, Prague. From here, he publishes the first element of his General Theory of Relativity: the idea of gravitational redshift.

- **1912** Returns to Switzerland, becoming a professor at the ETH in Zurich.

- **1914** Einstein becomes director of the Kaiser Wilhelm Institute in Berlin and professor of theoretical physics at the University of Berlin.

- **1915** Publishes his General Theory of Relativity.

- **1917** Einstein publishes an important paper in which he proposes a "cosmological constant," which would help to explain the expansion of the universe. He also publishes a paper in which he suggests "stimulated emission" could be possible—this is the principle behind the laser, which was not invented until the 1950s.

- **1919** A total eclipse of the Sun on May 29 provides crucial proof for Einstein's General Theory of Relativity. Einstein's divorce is finalized, and he is married for the second time, to his cousin Elsa Löwenthal.

- **1922** Einstein is awarded the 1921 Nobel Prize for Physics "for his services to Theoretical Physics, and especially for his discovery of the law of the photoelectric effect."

- **1933** Einstein and his wife move to Princeton, New Jersey. Einstein takes up a position at the Princeton Institute for Advanced Study.

- **1939** Writes to US president Franklin D. Roosevelt, warning him that Nazi Germany may be building a nuclear weapon.

- **1940** Becomes a US citizen.

- **April 18, 1955** Dies of heart failure. He is cremated, but beforehand, his brain is removed and preserved.

LECTURING IN THE US

> "Do not worry about your difficulties with **mathematics**. I can assure you mine are **still greater**." ALBERT EINSTEIN

proved that mass and energy, too, are relative quantities, just as time and space are. Furthermore, he showed that mass and energy are two aspects of the same thing, mass-energy. It was in this paper that he derived his most famous equation, relating mass (m) and energy (E), via the square of the speed of light (c^2): $E = mc^2$. This relationship is the basis of nuclear power: inside a reactor, atomic nuclei are broken apart and lose mass, producing large amounts of energy in agreement with Einstein's theory. This famous equation is also the source of the devastating energy of nuclear weapons.

Recognition

In 1907 Hermann Minkowski, one of Einstein's teachers, showed that time is equivalent to the three dimensions of space, and is intertwined with them. He visualized "space-time" as a four-dimensional "fabric" of the universe.

However, few other physicists paid attention to this work at the time. Einstein, meanwhile, set about generalizing his Special Theory of Relativity to include gravity. He realized that time slows down in intense gravitational fields—and one result of this is that light bends as it passes close to very massive objects, such as the Sun. Einstein was able to explain gravity as a

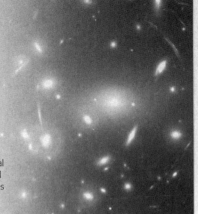

Einstein and politics
Einstein's Zionism brought him in contact with Israel's first prime minister, David Ben-Gurion (above). By 1946, Einstein was already proclaiming the need for nuclear disarmament (right).

distortion of space-time, and published his ideas in 1915, as the General Theory of Relativity.

A total solar eclipse in 1919 provided a chance to test Einstein's new theory. A team of physicists photographed the area of the sky surrounding the Sun during the eclipse. Stars in the dark sky around the obscured Sun appeared slightly out of place—a result of their light bending as it passed close to the Sun. The shift was inexplicable using the traditional "Newtonian" (see p.269) idea of gravity, but it matched Einstein's theory exactly.

Einstein became a worldwide celebrity. He won the 1921 Nobel Prize for Physics (the first of many honors), and stayed at the forefront of discovery during a period when physicists were beginning to unravel the universe's fundamental mysteries. He was celebrated beyond the academic life of science, becoming a cultural icon, and one of the few scientists known by nearly everyone.

Political life

One consequence of Einstein's fame was that people sought his opinions on a wide range of topics. He was acquainted with many world leaders, wrote widely in newspapers, books, and magazines, and became involved with many political causes. In his later years, he lobbied against racism in the US and against nuclear weapons. He was a pacifist and vegetarian.

A German-born Jew, Einstein had Zionist (see p.414) aspirations, and was in favor of establishing a Jewish homeland in the Middle East. Having seen the rise of Nazism in Germany at first hand, it was inevitable that he would become involved in the formation of the state of Israel (see pp.414–15). He was even asked if he would become its president.

Although Einstein's theories are only truly understood by physicists, most people recognize that his work radically changed our understanding of the world, and appreciate that this brilliant man was one of the most enduring characters of the 20th century.

The American Dream

From the end of World War II in 1945 to the early 1960s, America's dream of "life, liberty, and the pursuit of happiness," as stated in the 1776 Declaration of Independence, was lived out by the majority. It was a time of wealth, peace, and unity, though not without its downsides.

ONLY ONE!
this No-Frost Gas Refrigerator-Freezer
gives you so many modern automatic features...yet saves you money!

IT'S THE NEW
RCA WHIRLPOOL
...and naturally it's Gas!

◀◀ BEFORE

During World War II many marginalized sectors were thrust into central roles, only to be sidelined again when the war ended.

ROSIE THE RIVETER

WOMEN AND THE WAR

Women played a crucial role in the US victory in World War II ◀◀ 392–405. They served in the auxiliary army and navy services, and also the air force, flying new aircraft from factories to military bases or repairing those damaged in conflict. Many women moved from low-paid administrative or catering jobs into better-paid munitions or engineering work, but were rarely paid as much as men earned. Most women in industry lost their jobs when men returned from the war in 1945.

SEGREGATION

Segregation remained legal in the United States until well after World War II, despite the US having fought against the Nazis, who held an explicitly racist ideology. President Truman desegregated the armed services in 1948, prohibited segregation on interstate travel, and outlawed discrimination by employers and unions. However, the reality for African-Americans was still a life as a second-class citizen 432–35 ▶▶.

A merica emerged from World War II as the richest and most powerful nation on Earth. The only one of the wartime Allies not to be occupied or bombed, its industry—supplying its own military needs as well as some of those of Britain and the USSR—had provided full employment to its workforce and ended the Great Depression (see pp.384–85) of the 1930s. This economic boom continued in peacetime. National output doubled between 1946 and 1956, doubling again by 1970. Most personal incomes nearly tripled between 1940 and 1955.

The new middle class

This buoyant economy created a new middle class that made up 60 percent of families, who spent their money on consumer goods. Some 83 percent of American homes had a television by 1958, and two-car families doubled from 1951 to 1958. The US had 6 percent of the world's population (150 million in 1950), consumed one-third of the world's goods and services, and made two-thirds of manufactured goods.

Compared to the starch-rich and relatively expensive diet of their forebears in 1900, food was affordable and varied. The average American in the 1950s had a choice of green vegetables, frozen goods, fresh meat, and fast food. Consumption of hot dogs increased from 750 million in 1950 to 2 billion a decade later. As a result of an improved diet, children were on

Consumer Society

After World War II, Americans viewed consumption as a patriotic activity that helped aid economic recovery. The most sought-after items included refrigerators, cars, televisions, washing machines, toasters, and vacuum cleaners—all items that would modernize their lives.

G.E. DESIGNS NEW 32 lb. 'PERSONAL' TV
Goes where you go...

average two or three inches taller in 1950 than they were in 1900, women could expect to live to 71 instead of 51, and men to 65 rather than 48.

The flight to the suburbs

One urgent need for this new class was decent housing. Inaugurated for the second time as president in 1937, Franklin Roosevelt saw "one-third of a nation ill-housed, ill-clad, ill-nourished." The postwar economy provided food and clothes, but good housing was still in short supply. A rising birthrate was met with a falling number of new home starts. Millions of Americans lived in cramped or inadequate housing.

One answer came from pioneer Bill Levitt, who won a contract in 1941 to build 1,600 row houses for shipyard workers in Norfolk, Virginia. Frustrated by union rules and having to organize numerous skilled workers to build and equip a single house, he divided the building process into 27 separate steps, training 27 teams of workers to carry out each one. The fastest workers earned the most pay. It was the principle of the production line. After the war, Levitt applied the same

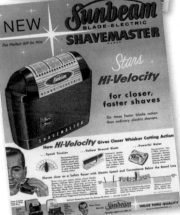

NEW Sunbeam
BLADE-ELECTRIC
SHAVEMASTER
The Perfect Gift for Him
Stars
Hi-Velocity
for closer, faster shaves

Six times faster blade action than ordinary electric shavers.

How Hi-Velocity Gives Closer Whisker Cutting Action

VALUE THRU QUALITY

Pontiac Chieftain

The American dream and the open road came together in stylish automobiles like the soft-top Pontiac Chieftain. Gas was cheap, and young people had diners, shopping malls, and drive-in movies at their disposal. Cars such as the Pontiac and the Cadillac became status symbols of the new wealth and freedom that Americans enjoyed during the 1950s.

"Private **affluence** amid public **squalor**."

J. K. GALBRAITH, US ECONOMIST, ON THE DISCREPANCIES IN AMERICAN SOCIETY IN "THE AFFLUENT SOCIETY," 1958

Jazz music
After the artistic excesses of Charlie Parker and bop music in the 1940s, 1950s jazz cooled down to find a new audience, with musicians like trumpeter Miles Davis (above) and college circuit favorite, pianist Dave Brubeck.

Suburbia
The mass production of housing resulted in streets with row after row of identical houses. Singer Malvina Reynolds critiqued the 1950s blandness with her song "Little Boxes," in which she sang "Little boxes on the hillside, ... Little boxes all the same ... And they're all made out of ticky tacky and they all look just the same."

The flip side
The American dream was not enjoyed by everyone. The 1950s was a conservative decade, based on white, middle-class family values where men went to work and wives stayed at home—only 36 percent of women worked in 1955. Women shared the dream, but relied on men to create it. African-Americans had no such dream. Segregation in jobs, housing, education, and democratic rights was rife, most notably in Southern states. The country was also in the grip of the Cold War (see pp. 406–07), giving rise to internal troubles such as the McCarthy witch-hunts (see below).

Eating out
With increased disposable income, young couples could spend money on recreation, drinking after work, or eating out regularly at the local diner. Such facilities were, however, still segregated in many southern states.

principles to his first development of 2,000 two-bedroom houses for war veterans on Long Island. Each house cost $6,900, with no down payment for veterans and a mortgage guaranteed by a federal housing bill. Levittown, as it became known, grew in four years to 17,447 houses and a population of 82,000 people. There were some rules: no fences, no clotheslines, no shrubs more than 4 ft (1.2 m) high along the lot line, and, controversially, no African-Americans, although that exclusion ended in 1949. The houses were all identical, but their inhabitants soon personalized them, adding porches and patios and building extra rooms. Some 13 million new homes were built from

1948 to 1958, almost all of them in new suburbs. This turned many American cities into social doughnuts, with a rich commercial and business center surrounded by a poor, largely African-American-inhabited inner ring of social housing, surrounded in turn by largely white suburbs.

Teen culture
As America grew richer, it also got younger: 40 million Americans were born from 1950 to 1960. By 1964, 40 percent of the population was under 20. The idea of the "teenager" emerged as young people developed their own culture.

Popular music had been divided according to race and, partly, class. Crooners dominated white popular music with movie and musical hits. Country and western was popular among the white working class, while African-Americans had blues, gospel, and, in the late 1940s, rhythm and blues. A new hybrid music—merging African-American rhythm and blues and white country and western—by white singers Bill Haley in 1954 and Elvis Presley in 1956, gave young people their own music. Rock 'n' roll was the music of rebellion and teenage angst, echoed in the movies of James Dean and Marlon Brando. It fed the emerging counterculture. Jazz, the Beat poets, novelists like Jack Kerouac, abstract expressionists Jackson Pollock and Mark Rothko, and folk and protest songs of Woody Guthrie and, later, Bob Dylan, defined American culture as much as rock 'n' roll or movies.

> **MCCARTHYISM** The practice, named after Senator Joe McCarthy, of accusing individuals of belonging to the Communist Party or communist organizations despite little supporting evidence. It raised fears of a "red menace" against American society in the Cold War.

Senator McCarthy
In 1950, the senator from Wisconsin alleged he had the names of 547 card-carrying communists in the State Department, and another 205 communist sympathizers. His anticommunist witch-hunt struck a chord as the Cold War with Russia intensified, but when he attacked the army in 1954 he was censured by the Senate.

AFTER »

In the 1960s and 1970s the reality of the "dream" was laid bare.

VIETNAM
The 1950s American dream became a nightmare in the 1960s, as arguments about civil rights **434–35 »** and increasing opposition to the Vietnam War **430–31 »** led to race riots and mass demonstrations in many cities. What appeared to be a cohesive, affluent society was revealed as divisive and fractured along lines of race and class.

IMMIGRANTS
The idea of the American dream is still powerful for many Hispanic immigrants. However, the reality is often harsh. Many immigrants work in seasonal jobs with low pay and few prospects.

LATINO (HISPANIC) WORKERS

The Death of Kennedy

On Friday November 22, President John F. Kennedy and his wife Jacqueline visited Dallas, Texas, to drum up support for the 1964 US presidential election. As the motorcade drove through Dealey Plaza, at least three gunshots rang out, killing the president instantly. The American people had lost a president they loved, and they had been robbed of their future.

Three days after John F. Kennedy's assassination, the world stopped again, united in grief. The funeral of the 35th president of the United States was watched by a million people lining the procession route, and millions more on television. During his brief time in office, the charismatic young president had come to epitomize the hopes of his nation—belief in a better future and the energetic pursuit of progress. With his murder the mood of bright optimism was shattered.

The assassination became the subject of huge controversy. A lone gunman, Lee Harvey Oswald, was arrested shortly after the shooting and charged with murder. He never came to trial; two days later he was shot dead while in police custody by Jack Ruby, a gangster who later gave contradictory reasons for the killing.

Kennedy's successor, Vice President Lyndon Johnson, quickly established an official investigation into the assassination headed by Earl Warren, Chief Justice of the United States. After a 10-month investigation, the commission concluded that Oswald had acted alone, as had Ruby, and that there was no conspiracy to kill the president. Many people have refused to accept these conclusions, but no firm evidence has ever come to light to suggest otherwise.

After the assassination, the body of the president was flown back to Washington. It first lay in repose in the East Room of the White House, and on Sunday afternoon was taken to lie in state in the Capital Rotunda. A brief memorial service was held. Over the following 18 hours, 250,000 people lined up in near-freezing temperatures to pay their respects.

On Monday the funeral procession returned to the White House and then moved on to St. Matthew's Roman Catholic Cathedral. Heads of state and representatives from 92 countries attended the service. It was at the height of the Cold War (see pp. 406–07), yet even the USSR sent a representative. The Archbishop of Boston led the mass, at which Kennedy's writings and speeches were read. The coffin was taken to Arlington National Cemetery, where Mrs. Kennedy lit an eternal flame over the grave. America now faced an uncertain future without JFK.

A son salutes
Moments after his father's casket was carried down the steps of St. Matthew's Cathedral, John F. Kennedy Jr., whose third birthday it was that day, saluted his father. His uncle Bobby Kennedy, who stands behind him, was himself assassinated just five years later.

"The **greatest leader of our time** has been struck down by the foulest deed of our time."

LYNDON B. JOHNSON, US PRESIDENT, NOVEMBER 27, 1963

Viva la Revolución

After World War I, Latin America entered a period of social unrest and political change that was created in part by the impact of economic crisis. Populist movements, some authoritarian, others revolutionary, swept new regimes to power. In some countries, governments were imposed on the population by the military.

The Peróns
Juan Perón and his wife Eva address an economic planning meeting in Buenos Aires. Although Eva Perón was not elected, she was influential in her husband's government. They enjoyed cult status in Argentina, and Eva's death in 1952 resulted in scenes of mass mourning.

BEFORE

300 years of colonial rule by the Spanish and Portuguese came to an end in Latin America at the beginning of the 19th century.

INDEPENDENCE FROM COLONIAL RULE
The transition from colonial rule to self-government in Latin America **‹‹318–19** was generally smooth in terms of economic stability. In the early years of the 20th century, many Latin American countries had **flourishing economies**, based on the **export of crops and minerals** to North America and Europe.

85 PERCENT of land in Brazil was owned by one percent of the population in 1910.

THE MEXICAN REVOLUTION
Mexico's popular uprising of 1910 preceded and influenced the revolutions in Russia **‹‹376–77** and Eastern Europe. **Porfirio Diaz's** military regime was overthrown in 1911, but widespread conflict continued as Mexican soldiers, workers, and peasants joined in a **struggle for civil rights and agricultural reform**. Although briefly calmed by the Constitutional Congress of Mexico in 1917, violence flared again in the 1920s.

DEPRESSION AND INDUSTRIALIZATION
The **world economic crisis** triggered by the market crash of 1929, and the ensuing Great Depression **‹‹384–85**, devastated Latin America's export market and **created shortages** in imported manufactured goods. The political response was to create economies that could provide for their own populations without reliance on foreign markets. The 1930s saw **rapid industrialization** and urban growth.

SOCIAL UNREST
In trends similar to those of 19th-century Europe **‹‹336–37**, the growth in Latin America's **urban workforce** led to a rise in **political activism** and **calls for social and political change**.

"The Arsenal"
This 1928 mural by Mexican artist Diego Rivera shows his wife, the painter Frida Kahlo, handing arms to workers. Rivera and Kahlo belonged to the Mexican communist party. The fall of Diaz's regime (see above) in Mexico set a precedent that popular uprising could succeed.

In 1930, economic problems led the Brazilian military to install Getulio Vargas as provisional president. Although it operated as a dictatorship—a government ruled by one person with absolute power and no recognized opposition, or restriction from the country's law—his government permitted liberal measures such as social and welfare reforms. For several years, Vargas followed a modernization program, but, alarmed at the growth of communist support in the 1930s, he began to model the state along fascist lines (see pp.386–87), proclaiming an *Estado Novo* ("New Order"). Hitler's Germany became a major customer for Brazilian goods, and Vargas supported the Axis powers (Germany, Italy, and Japan) at the start of World War II.

In 1941, Vargas changed his allegiance to the Allies (Britain, the US, the USSR, and France). This caused the military to force Vargas from office in 1945. He was democratically reelected in 1951, but committed suicide in 1954, after the army demanded his resignation.

Perón's "Third Way"
In Argentina, a populist government came to power in 1946 led by Juan Perón. "Peronism" was a contradictory mixture of progressive social values and authoritarian rule that Perón called the "Third Way." He transformed manufacturing in Argentina, launching an iron and steel industry, and ship and car production. Radical change came as women were given the vote, and corporations were nationalized. At the height of his popularity, Perón and his second wife Eva, known as "Evita,"

Castro's camp
This photograph, taken around 1957, shows the bearded revolutionary leader Fidel Castro with commanders of his rebel army at a secret camp in Cuba. The rebels were poorly armed, but Castro's guerrilla tactics won the conflict.

commanded huge mass support. Comparisons have been made with fascist regimes, and although he never pursued mass violence, he did crush any opposition to his rule. Argentina also provided a safe haven for Nazi war criminals after World War II.

Cuba breaks with the US
In Cuba, the military regime of Fulgencio Batista was overthrown after a long struggle with revolutionaries. Having trained in Mexico, Fidel Castro landed in Cuba in 1956 with an army of political exiles, including Che Guevara (see RIGHT). A guerrilla war ensued, in which small groups of armed rebels carried out repeated attacks to wear down the enemy, before the rebels seized power in 1959. Castro swiftly ended US dominance of Cuba's economy. Taking aid from the USSR, he implemented radical reforms including a Soviet-style agricultural policy (see pp.380–81). The 1962 Cuban Missile Crisis (see pp.406–07) further damaged US–Cuban relations. The US continues to impose an economic embargo on Cuba, but Fidel Castro's regime still survives.

Chile's brief democracy
In 1970 an increased desire for extreme political change, or radicalism, brought socialist Salvador Allende to the Chilean presidency. Concerns were raised in the US when Allende established diplomatic relations with communist regimes in Cuba, China, North Korea, and North Vietnam. He attempted to restructure Chile's unstable economy, but was soon threatened by a variety of political opponents. Eager to influence the next regime, the US backed General Augusto Pinochet's military coup against Allende in 1973. When attackers entered the presidential palace, Allende was found dead from a gunshot wound.

REVOLUTIONARY (1928–1967)

ERNESTO "CHE" GUEVARA

Che Guevara was born in Argentina in 1928. As a young man, he traveled extensively in Latin America, and became convinced that only revolution would solve the problems of poverty and social inequality that marked the continent. A visit to President Guzman's populist regime in Guatemala in 1953 confirmed Che's enthusiasm for radical political solutions and, in 1956, he joined Fidel Castro's rebel army. In 1965, Che left Cuba with the intention of sparking revolutions in other countries. He was captured by the CIA—the US secret service—in Bolivia in 1967, and executed by the Bolivian army.

AFTER

After authoritarian, often military-backed regimes in the 1960s and 1970s, many Latin American nations became more democratic.

COUNTERREVOLUTION
In the 1970s, the revolutionary and socialist ideals of previous decades were swept aside. **Military regimes 438–39 ››** were established in many countries, including Uruguay and Argentina.

ANTI-AMERICANISM
Left-wing presidents such as Venezuela's **Hugo Chávez** (from 1999) **438 ››** and Bolivia's **Evo Morales** (from 2006) have increasingly spoken out against US policy in Latin America.

« BEFORE

The Manchu Qing dynasty declined throughout the 19th century, as China increasingly fell under European influence. A period of chaos and rule by regional warlords followed its collapse.

OVERTHROW OF THE MANCHU EMPIRE
In 1905, the political revolutionary, Sun Zhongshan (Sun Yat-sen), founded the Revolutionary Alliance with the aim of **driving out the Manchus** and establishing a republican government in place of monarchical rule. **Nationalist soldiers seized Wuchang** on October 10, 1911, and within weeks south China's provinces had broken away from the empire. When the Manchus asked the commander of the Northern Army, **Yuan Shikai**, for support, he **encouraged the emperor to abdicate**, and in March 1912 he became president of the republic. In January 1916 he accepted an invitation to **become emperor**, but shortly afterward he gave up the position and died.

THE NATIONALIST PARTY
In 1912 the Revolutionary Alliance, led by Sun Zhongshan, became the **Nationalist Party**. Yuan Shikai expelled Nationalist Party members from parliament and they moved south to Guangzhou. There Sun Zhongshan, with help from the Soviet Union, **reorganized the party**. After the death of Sun Zhongshan in 1925, the party's leadership passed gradually to **Jiang Jieshi** (Chiang Kaishek).

WARLORDS FILL THE VOID
From 1916, China had no effective central government and was controlled by **regional warlords**. They included: **Zhang Xun**, the "pigtailed general," who briefly restored Puyi, the Manchu emperor; **Feng Yuxiang**, the "Christian General," who barred his troops from gambling; and **Yan Xishan**, the "Model Governor" of Shanxi, who supported educational reform.

THE MAY FOURTH MOVEMENT
On May 4, 1919, it was announced at the Paris Peace Conference « 375 that former German colonies in China were to be given to Japan, and major **demonstrations erupted**. The incident gave its name to the radical May Fourth Movement, which **attacked Confucianism** « 131, called for a "literary revolution," and welcomed a **wave of new ideas**.

CHINESE COMMUNIST PARTY (CCP)
Founded by revolutionaries who had been involved in the May Fourth Movement, the first congress of the CCP was held in July 1921, and was attended by a young Mao Zedong (see right).

> "**Communism** is a hammer which we use to **crush the enemy**."
> MAO ZEDONG, 1950

China's Long March

After the fall of the Manchu dynasty in 1911, China experienced a long period of political turmoil. The Nationalists reunified the country, but were frustrated by the 1937 Japanese invasion. The Communists came to power in 1949, and over the next 25 years attempted a revolutionary transformation of society.

In 1923, the Chinese Communist Party formed an uneasy alliance with the Nationalist Party (see BEFORE), and in 1926 supported them in the Northern Expedition to reunify the country. But the alliance collapsed in April 1927, when the Nationalist leader, Jiang Jieshi, ordered hundreds of Communists in Shanghai to be killed.

The Communist leaders fled to the countryside to plan insurrections. Mao Zedong (see right) led a revolt called the Autumn Harvest Uprising, and after defeat by the Nationalists, retreated to the southern province of Jiangxi. There, Mao formulated a new revolutionary strategy combining the formation of the Red Army—the military arm of the Communists—with land reform, and a promise to emancipate China's women.

The Nanjing decade
Jiang Jieshi's defeat of the Communists strengthened the position of the Nationalist Party, and in 1928 it effectively took control of the country, establishing its capital at Nanjing and reunifying China. Over the next decade, it reformed the currency, and established modern banks. New schools and colleges were opened, and railroads and roads were improved.

Great endurance
Crossing 18 mountain ranges and 24 major rivers, the Long March lasted 368 days and cost thousands of lives.

The Long March
In October 1934, the Communists abandoned their Jiangxi base, broke through a Nationalist blockade, and began the "Long March" to shake off their enemies. A trek of around 6,200 miles (10,000 km), it took

"Long live the victory of Chairman Mao's Revolution"
In a typical piece of propaganda, this celebration of the leadership of Mao Zedong, produced for the 50th anniversary of the creation of the Chinese Communist Party, shows him surrounded by adoring supporters.

perpetrated a massacre of around 300,000 men, women, and children that became known as the Rape of Nanjing. The Nationalist government relocated 1,000 miles (1,600 km) up the Yangzi River, while the Communists operated behind Japanese lines.

Civil war and communist victory

With the Japanese attack on Pearl Harbor in 1941 (see pp.402–03), the Sino-Japanese hostilities became absorbed in the wider conflict of World War II, and Japan was ultimately defeated by the Allies. By July 1946, another civil war in China had broken out. While the Nationalist government was being seriously damaged by galloping inflation, the Communists were gaining rural support with revolutionary land reform in favor of the peasants. Manchuria fell to the Communists, and when, in January 1949, around 300,000 Nationalists surrendered, Mao's troops marched triumphantly into Beijing. On October 1, 1949 the communist People's Republic of China (PRC) was established. Jiang Jieshi and two million of his supporters fled to the island of Taiwan, where they established the rival Republic of China.

Consolidation

The People's Republic then occupied all territory claimed by China, including Tibet. Mao negotiated the Sino-Soviet Treaty of Alliance and Mutual Assistance and, in 1950, when the Korean War broke out (see pp.406–07) China intervened on the side of North Korea. In China, the First Five Year

Mao's "little red book"
"Father is close, mother is close, but neither is as close as Chairman Mao." 900 million copies of *Quotations from Chairman Mao* were printed.

Plan, launched in 1953 with Soviet assistance, achieved spectacular increases in industrial output. Reforms banned arranged marriages, and the subjugation of women. Farming was collectivized, so peasants handed over their land to agricultural producers' cooperatives.

The radical years

In 1958, Mao Zedong introduced the radical policy known as the Great Leap Forward. Industrial and agricultural cooperatives were amalgamated into communes—with collective kitchens and daycares—and industrial targets were raised.

At first it seemed as if spectacular increases of output had been achieved, but later evidence showed that these policies had caused disastrous famines and the death of millions of people. In 1966, the Cultural Revolution was launched, with the aim of cleansing the country of "bourgeois" influences. Children were recruited as Red Guards and, to rekindle the spirit of revolution, were encouraged to report their schoolteachers and relatives if they failed to display sufficient communist fervor. Brandishing their "little red books" (see above) the Red Guards attacked the Four Olds: old ideas, old culture, old customs, and old habits.

CHINESE COMMUNIST LEADER (1893–1976)
MAO ZEDONG

The son of a rich peasant, Mao moved to Beijing from Hunan province at the time of the May Fourth Movement (see BEFORE), where he first encountered communist ideas. He joined the Chinese Communist Party at its inception in 1921, taking control in 1935 after proving his leadership during the Long March. As head of the country from 1949 until his death in 1976, Mao's attempts to implement his radical ideas led to disastrous famines. However, "Mao Zedong Thought" had far-reaching effects, and after his death the Party declared that it would remain "a guide to action for a long time to come."

AFTER ⟫

China's Cultural Revolution saw millions "reeducated" through forced labor and thousands executed. The terror did not end until the arrest of the Gang of Four in 1976.

GANG OF FOUR
Mao's wife **Jiang Qing**, party chief **Zhang Chunqiao**, critic **Yao Wenyuan**, and **Wang Hongwen**, a factory worker, expected to succeed Mao after his death. Instead, they were **arrested**, and found guilty of **plotting to seize power**.

THE FOUR MODERNIZATIONS
In 1978, Premier Deng Xiaoping announced the modernization of agriculture, industry, science, and defense, to make China a **great economic power** by the early 21st century **472–73 ⟫**.

TIANANMEN SQUARE
When **pro-democracy** students demonstrated in Tiananmen Square, Beijing, Premier Li Peng instructed the army to act. On June 4, 1989, troops opened fire on the protesters, killing 400–800.

TIANANMEN SQUARE PROTESTER DEFIES TANKS

more than 80,000 soldiers and workers northwest through harsh terrain, fighting the Nationalists all the way. By the time they established headquarters at Yan'an in October 1935, only about 8,000 of the original marchers had survived, and Mao had taken command of the Communist Party.

War with Japan

Japanese encroachment on Chinese territory had begun in 1931 with the seizure of Manchuria. In 1937, Japanese forces invaded China and

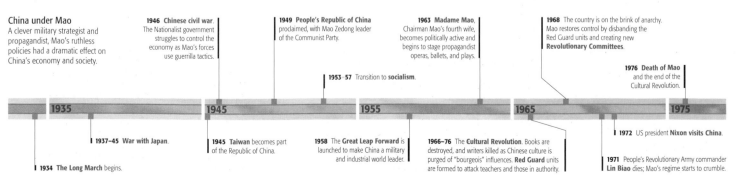

China under Mao
A clever military strategist and propagandist, Mao's ruthless policies had a dramatic effect on China's economy and society.

1946 Chinese civil war. The Nationalist government struggles to control the economy as Mao's forces use guerrilla tactics.

1949 People's Republic of China proclaimed, with Mao Zedong leader of the Communist Party.

1963 Madame Mao, Chairman Mao's fourth wife, becomes politically active and begins to stage propagandist operas, ballets, and plays.

1968 The country is on the brink of anarchy. Mao restores control by disbanding the Red Guard units and creating new **Revolutionary Committees**.

1953–57 Transition to **socialism**.

1976 Death of Mao and the end of the Cultural Revolution.

1935   1945   1955   1965   1975

1937–45 War with Japan.

1945 Taiwan becomes part of the Republic of China.

1958 The **Great Leap Forward** is launched to make China a military and industrial world leader.

1966–76 The **Cultural Revolution**. Books are destroyed, and writers killed as Chinese culture is purged of "bourgeois" influences. **Red Guard** units are formed to attack teachers and those in authority.

1972 US president **Nixon visits China.**

1971 People's Revolutionary Army commander **Lin Biao** dies; Mao's regime starts to crumble.

1934 The Long March begins.

Berlin Wall

The peace of a Sunday morning in 1961 was shattered as Berliners woke up to the sounds of military vehicles unloading coils of barbed wire and concrete posts in the streets. In central Potsdamer Platz, men used pneumatic drills to break up the cobblestones and set up concrete pillars. These disturbing scenes were the first signs of a physical division of Berlin.

In February 1945, the leaders of the US, USSR, and Britain met in Yalta (now in Ukraine but once part of the Soviet Union) to plan Europe's future after the defeat of Nazi Germany. They agreed to partition Germany and its capital, Berlin, into four zones of occupation divided between their three countries and France. Berlin lay deep inside the Soviet zone, but access between the western zones of the city and the three western zones of Germany was guaranteed along specified land and air links.

The agreement fell apart as the Cold War (see pp. 406–07) gained pace in 1946–47. The election of an anti-communist mayor for Berlin in early 1948 and the planned creation of a federal state with a common currency in the western zones of Germany annoyed the Soviets. On June 24, 1948, they blocked traffic from entering the city from the west. The British and Americans responded with a massive airlift of supplies to sustain West Berlin until an agreement with the Soviets was reached in May 1949.

For the next 12 years, Berlin remained the uneasy epicenter of the Cold War. The western half became linked with West Germany, while the eastern half became the capital of communist East Germany, both created in 1949. Economic disparities between west and east led thousands of East Germans and Berliners— almost 200,000 in 1960 alone—to cross the open frontier between east and west in search of a better life.

In 1961 the East German government decided to act. Crossing points between East and West Berlin were sealed off with barbed wire and concrete posts. In places, this barrier ran down the middle of streets to keep from touching West Berlin's soil. It even bisected a cemetery. The border between East and West Germany was sealed. Russian tanks waited outside the city, while the Americans sent 1,500 troops to reassure West Berlin.

Over the next 19 years, the wall was strengthened with reinforced concrete blocks 12 ft (3.6 m) high and set back from the original fence to create a heavily armed "no-man's land" in between. The wall became the symbol of a divided world, but ultimately symbolized the futility of such confrontation. Its fall on November 9, 1989, ended the Cold War.

A city divided
Many families were split up when the wall was built. This photo, taken in 1962, shows a young woman standing precariously at the top of the western side of the wall to speak to her mother in East Berlin. About 5,000 people escaped from the east through gaps in the wall.

"You cannot be **held in slavery** forever."

WILLY BRANDT, MAYOR OF WEST BERLIN, BROADCAST, AUGUST 1961

« BEFORE

Advances in science and mass production techniques transformed the way people lived after World War II.

POST WAR
In the late 1940s and early 1950s the world was reeling from the effects of World War II « 392–405, but by the mid-1950s the mood was changing. The US experienced **economic growth**, as did Germany, France, and Italy. In Britain, food rationing, which had been in place since 1940, ended in 1954. Employment rose throughout Europe, and with it came the beginnings of a **consumer boom**.

90 PERCENT of all Americans owned a TV set by 1960

1 IN 3 families in the UK owned a car in 1959

NEVER HAD IT SO GOOD
In 1957 the British prime minister Harold Macmillan said, "Most of our people have never had it so good," a sentiment that echoed around the developed world. People bought **luxuries and labor-saving devices**, developments in communication began to change the way people lived, and television took off as a mass medium.

ELVIS PRESLEY

ROCK 'N' ROLL
In 1955 Bill Haley and the Comets released the song "Rock Around the Clock," unleashing a new musical style: rock 'n' roll. It was **music for a new generation**—teenagers—and it shocked older, more conservative people. The greatest and most controversial star of the new genre was Elvis Presley.

BIRTH OF "POP"
Pop is **short for "popular,"** and in the 1950s it spawned Pop Art, which British artist Richard Hamilton called "**glamorous** and big business!"

Black Panthers March
An African-American civil rights group founded in 1966, the Black Panther Party marched for "land, bread, housing, education, clothing, justice and peace." It became an icon of the counterculture revolutions of the 1960s.

The Sixties

The 1960s witnessed the rise of new forms of entertainment and a new political and social agenda. The changing attitudes to youth, gender, class, place, and race challenged the established order.

At the end of World War II in 1945, soldiers returned home and started the families they had put on hold for four years. This led to an unusually steep rise in the population curve known as the "Baby Boom." In the United States alone, some 70 million "baby-boomers" became teenagers and young adults during the 1960s.

As the decade opened, it was a time of youthful optimism when anything seemed possible. And for the first time, the phrase "generation gap" was used. Where previously young people had aped their elders, new music such as rock 'n' roll empowered the younger generation, and adults were often left dumbfounded by what they considered the strange behavior of the youth.

Swinging sixties
In an age of increased middle-class affluence, the population had greater employment opportunities and a new buying power. In response to this, music and fashion became mass-market industries and were quick to cater to the demands of the youth market. The growing popularity of television helped spread popular culture around the globe, so trends could take off rapidly. Programs such as *Top of the Pops* in the UK and the *Ed Sullivan Show* in the US made the 1960s swing to the beat of pop music. In 1962, the Beatles emerged from Liverpool's Cavern Club. Their first album, *Please Please Me*, became famous around the globe within a year. They grew immensely popular, sparking such intense devotion in their fans that it became known as "Beatlemania." At one time during the 1960s, they had the top five records on the US Billboard Hot 100 list, and the Beatles remain the best-selling pop band of all time.

Music groups provided the inspiration for fashion, from neat mod styles and blue jeans, to Elvis jumpsuits and the ethnic clothing of singers such as Joan Baez. This fashion revolution burst onto the retail scene, led by designers like Mary Quant. Hems went up, then down. Adults found it hard to tell boys from girls. Both dressed in T-shirts and jeans; boys grew long hair; girls copied the model Twiggy by cutting theirs in a short "gamine" style. The unisex look had arrived. Boutiques sprang up to sell the new fashions, which were colorful, cheap, and informal. French New Wave cinema blossomed and also influenced style.

Permissive society?
Politics became more radical in the 1960s. There were many who felt that some laws were outdated and belonged to a bygone era. In 1966 the UK abolished the death penalty, and in the US support for the death penalty was at an all-time low. Gay rights came to the fore, and in the UK in 1967 new laws were passed that allowed adult homosexuals to behave as they wished in private. Abortion became legal in the UK, and legal in some US states. But not everyone welcomed these changes. Some insisted it would make society more permissive, or willing to accept what had once been considered "deviant" behavior. Others believed that these changes were the sign of a more tolerant society, willing to accept all people equally.

In 1963 Betty Friedan published *The Feminine Mystique*, reigniting the movement for women's rights. Friedan and journalist Gloria Steinem challenged remaining areas of sexual inequality, giving birth to a wave of radical feminism known as the Women's Liberation movement. More

The Beatles
The Beatles' 8th album, *Sgt. Pepper's Lonely Hearts Club Band* was released in 1967, and is often voted the most influential album of all time.

Isle of Wight festival
Three music festivals were held on the Isle of Wight, situated off the south coast of England, at the end of the 1960s. The 1969 festival, shown here, was attended by 150,000 people. In 1970 it became the largest-ever music festival, with over 600,000 people in attendance.

THE CONTRACEPTIVE PILL

Before the development of "the Pill," women all over the world used a variety of different birth control methods, which were often ineffective and sometimes dangerous. American nurse Margaret Sanger was a lifelong advocate of birth control and underwrote the research necessary to create the first human birth control pill, described as the most significant medical advance of the 20th century. Between 1962 and 1969, the number of users worldwide rose from approximately 50,000 to one million.

women went out to work, challenging conventional ideas of women as housewives and homemakers. Above all, the emergence of the contraceptive pill (see left) liberated women, offering them a reliable method of birth control for the first time.

Turn on, tune in, drop out

Known as the "Summer of Love," 1976 was the height of the hippie movement. Hippies embraced rock music, mystic religions, and sexual freedom, and many experimented with drugs such as marijuana and LSD (lysergic acid diethylamide), a drug that was claimed to open the mind to previously uncharted areas. In June 1967, Monterey, California, held the first open-air mass pop festival, which was attended by over 200,000 people. Its potent combination of youth culture and pop music is seen as the apex of all that the 1960s stood for. However,

The New Wave

A Bout de Souffle (*Breathless*), 1960, directed by Jean-Luc Godard, is one of the best-known films of French New Wave cinema.

the optimism of the decade soon started to unravel, influenced by the assassinations in the US of Senator Robert Kennedy and Martin Luther King Jr. (see pp.432–33) in 1968. Around the world, students protested at the increased involvement of US troops in the Vietnam War (see pp.430–31). The US saw race riots in the inner cities, and the civil rights movement shifted from a nonviolent position when elements of it were taken over by radical extremists.

In France, the student revolt of May 1968 in Paris linked up with a general strike of 10 million workers, who called for the overthrow of Charles de Gaulle's government.

The end of the decade was marked by two important rock festivals held in

1969—Woodstock in New York and the Altamont Free Concert in California. At Woodstock, 450,000 people attended the three-day festival, gathering in the spirit of love and sharing, but at Altamont, a black fan was stabbed to death by a gang of white Hells Angels.

"The thing **the sixties** did was to show us the possibilities and the responsibility that we all had. It wasn't the answer. It just **gave us a glimpse of the possibility**."

JOHN LENNON, LAST RADIO INTERVIEW, DECEMBER 8, 1980

see pp.432–33
see pp.430–31

The 1970s saw an abrupt end to the idealism that characterized the 1960s.

1970s
In 1973 the world experienced an oil crisis **440–41 »**, which affected the economies of developed nations. In Britain there was a **downturn in economic fortunes** and unemployment was on the increase.

PUNK
The commercialism of pop music was soon challenged in the 1970s by Punk music. An **antiestablishment** and **rebellious** movement, it was epitomized by bands such as the Ramones in the US and the Sex Pistols in the UK.

SEX PISTOLS

GLOBAL POP
In the 1980s MTV was launched, and pop artists became global stars. In 1985 the Live Aid concert was watched by **1.5 billion viewers** across 100 countries.

440–41 »

« BEFORE

The anticommunist foreign policy of the United States clashed with Vietnamese nationalists who wished to unite their country under communist rule.

LIBERTY LOANS

The American public's support for its armed services dates back to World War I, when **people bought billions of dollars of Liberty Loans** to finance the war effort. There was similar mass support for American troops during World War II and the Cold War « 406–07, of which Vietnam was part.

US POSTER FOR LIBERTY LOANS

TRUMAN'S POLICY

The US had fought alongside the communist USSR in World War II « 392–405, but relations between the two broke down as the Cold War began. In 1947, faced with a possible communist threat to Greece and Turkey, President Truman pledged "**American support for free peoples** who are resisting attempted subjugation by armed minorities or by outside pressures." Known as **the Truman Doctrine**, this guided US foreign policy throughout the Vietnam War.

COLONIAL VIETNAM

In 1941 **Ho Chi Minh**, a Vietnamese nationalist and communist, **created the Viet Minh** to fight Japanese occupation. He declared the country independent after Japan's defeat in World War II in 1945 « 402–03. When the French resumed their colonial control « 412–13, a bitter war began that ended in French defeat in 1954. The **Geneva Accords** of 1954 **divided Vietnam** temporarily into a communist north and a pro-American south.

The Vietnam War

The Vietnam War was the longest and bloodiest of the many conflicts of the Cold War. The American army was technologically superior, but was defeated by the far more effective tactics of the Vietnamese nationalist and communist army wishing to unite their country and free it from foreign control.

The division of Vietnam in 1954 (see BEFORE) did not bring peace to the country. The US wished to prevent the spread of communism throughout Southeast Asia, believing that one country after another would fall to communist regimes (the so-called "domino effect") and was prepared to use military action to prevent this. The Geneva Accords had stipulated that joint elections should take place in 1956 to decide the future of a reunified Vietnam—these elections never took place. In 1955, US president Dwight D. Eisenhower helped the anticommunist Ngo Dinh Diem to take power in a corrupt election in the south, and sent hundreds of military advisors to support the new government.

North Vietnam did not accept the partition of their country and launched attacks on South Vietnam. Anti-Diem South Vietnamese—labeled Viet Cong ("Vietnamese Communist") by Diem, although many were nationalists—took up arms to fight Diem's government, led by the National Liberation Front, an alliance of political groups based in North Vietnam.

Eisenhower's support for South Vietnam increased under his successor, John F. Kennedy. By the end of 1963, South Vietnam had received $500 million in US aid. In August 1964 the USS *Maddox* was conducting electronic surveillance of the North Vietnamese coast in the Gulf of Tonkin. The ship was fired on by two torpedo boats challenging its presence in North Vietnamese waters. It fired back, sinking one boat. On August 7, the US Congress passed a resolution approving retaliatory raids against North Vietnamese naval bases and

Viet Cong
Viet Cong fighters lacked the sophisticated weaponry and equipment of the US military, but they had the advantage of local knowledge and support.

Protests at home
US protests against the war were supported not just by traditional pacifists but also by a much larger constituency of peace campaigners, including civil rights campaigner Dr. Martin Luther King Jr. The war divided US society as no event had done that century.

> "We are **determined to fight** for **independence**, national unity, democracy and **peace**."
>
> HO CHI MINH, NORTH VIETNAMESE LEADER, MAY 8, 1954

The effect of the Vietnam War was felt for many years afterward, but Vietnam is now a peaceful and prosperous nation.

CASUALTIES OF WAR
One million Vietnamese troops on both sides **lost their lives** in the war, along with **4 million** Vietnamese civilians and **58,000** US troops. More than 153,000 US troops were seriously wounded; **the total number of Vietnamese casualties is unknown**.

UNIFICATION
The Paris Peace Accord held until renewed fighting broke out in January 1975. A final **communist offensive captured Saigon** on April 30 and reunified the country in 1976 as the Socialist Republic of Vietnam. Thousands who feared for their lives under the new government fled Vietnam in boats, many drowning before they could reach safety in neighboring countries. More than **1 million refugees** from the conflict eventually **settled in the US**.

VETERANS
More than 660 US servicemen were taken prisoner during the war; 591 of these were repatriated under the peace accord. However, **2,400 men are still missing in action**. Veterans' associations in the US are a vocal force in modern US politics.

MODERN VIETNAM
In 1986 the Vietnamese government relaxed its previous hard-line communist economic policies in favor of a more liberal policy of *doi moi* ("renovation") and **began to welcome foreign investment**. In 1995 Vietnam joined the Southeast Asian economic group ASEAN. War damage was immense due to heavy US bombing and the country continues to rely on overseas aid for reconstruction.

Wounded in action
The sight of young American troops wounded in action appeared on US television news night after night and did as much to turn American opinion against the war as any political debate.

Civilian casualties
Many Vietnamese civilians were caught up in the war: US bombing raids targeting Viet Cong only served to alienate those it claimed to support.

US troop deployment

The first US marines arrived in South Vietnam in March 1965. By July that year, more than 50,000 were in the country, as well as increasing numbers of US airmen and sailors. Numbers escalated to a peak of 543,500 troops in April 1969. In addition, 320,000 South Koreans, 47,000 Australians, and contingents from the Philippines, Thailand, and New Zealand fought alongside American troops. The Viet Cong and North Vietnamese troops received military aid and financial support from communist China and USSR, although no ground troops were committed. However, they did have the advantage of fighting on home soil, often with the active support of the local people.

The American plan in Vietnam was to attack North Vietnam from the air to stop it from aiding the Viet Cong. Operation "Rolling Thunder" targeted bridges, roads, railroads, airfields,

factories, fuel depots, and military installations, but failed to achieve its objectives. North Vietnam had a formidable air defense system, and kept supplies flowing to the south along the Ho Chi Minh Trail, a 12,500-mile (20,000-km) network of tracks and paved roads through the jungles of North Vietnam and neighboring Laos and Cambodia. The trail was well defended by antiaircraft batteries and hidden from observation by the jungle through which it passed. By 1970, 18,000 tons of supplies flowed down the trail each month.

The US tried to deny the Viet Cong jungle cover by spraying Agent Orange, a chemical deployed to defoliate the jungle. It also used napalm, an incendiary liquid that burned everything it touched. Such tactics deprived local farmers of their crops and therefore their livelihood and

further alienated the US-backed South Vietnamese government from the people.

US withdrawal

The Vietnam War was opposed by increasing numbers of Americans who did not see why their troops were fighting a war with no just cause. The first major antiwar demonstrations took place in 1965, and grew in strength as more and more young men were drafted, or forced into military service. Television brought the reality of the war into American homes on a daily basis. The last five years of the war were bloody and painful for both sides. The US started peace talks in Paris in August 1969 in order to find an orderly way out of the conflict. The talks continued until a peace accord was signed on January 27, 1973. US troops left South Vietnam to the Vietnamese 60 days later.

oil refineries and authorized Kennedy's successor, Lyndon B. Johnson, "to take all necessary steps, including the use of armed forces" to defend South Vietnam. Without a formal declaration of war, the US had committed itself to military conflict in Vietnam.

Hand-made Viet Cong machine gun
The USSR and China supplied North Vietnam with most of its weapons, but its fighters also made their own arms—such as this machine gun—as well as using weaponry captured from the US.

CIVIL RIGHTS LEADER Born 1929 Died 1968

Martin Luther King

"Our lives begin to end **the day we become silent** about things that matter."

MARTIN LUTHER KING JR.

Martin Luther King Jr. was born into a family committed to the struggle for civil rights (see pp.434–35). Both his father and his grandfather were preachers who had spoken out against the denial of rights black people were subjected to in the US. As a student, he became familiar with the ideas of nonviolent protest of Mohandas Gandhi (see pp.408–09). What King knew of Gandhi chimed with his Christian faith; he once said, "I went to Gandhi through Jesus." King came to believe that by suffering violence without responding in kind, campaigners might build up an irresistible moral force for change. King was recently married and newly established as a Baptist pastor in Montgomery, Alabama, when the Montgomery Bus Boycott, protesting against segregation on the city transit system, propelled him onto the national stage. King did not start the

A gift for eloquence
Martin Luther King's personal courage, eloquence as a public speaker, and unswerving dedication to nonviolence made a vital contribution to the progress achieved by the civil rights movement in the US in the 1950s and 1960s.

The King family
Martin Luther King Jr. and Coretta Scott King had two sons and two daughters between 1955 and 1963. All four of the King children grew up to follow in their parents' footsteps, becoming civil rights activists.

Dexter Avenue Baptist Church
It was during his time as pastor of Dexter Avenue Baptist Church in Montgomery, Alabama, from 1954 to 1960, that King became an acknowledged leader of the civil rights movement. His predecessor as pastor, Vernon Johns, had also been a tireless campaigner against racial discrimination.

boycott in December 1955 and only reluctantly agreed to lead the campaign. He nearly pulled out when his home was bombed, but said he "heard the voice of Jesus saying still to fight on." When the boycott was shown on national TV, King's speeches and great dignity had an immediate impact.

In 1957 the Southern Christian Leadership Conference (SCLC) was formed to build on the success of the Montgomery Bus Boycott. King became the leader of the SCLC, which was a more radical alternative to the long-established National Association for the Advancement of Colored People (NAACP). While unswerving in his commitment to nonviolence, King was prepared to pursue civil disobedience energetically, breaking laws he considered unjust and provoking confrontation with racist authorities and the police. He did not then, or later, control the civil rights movement, which was a popular mass protest to which many individuals and groups made their diverse contributions. But King's charismatic example both inspired activists to engage in civil disobedience and attracted the support of white liberals for the movement.

Relentless campaigning

In the first half of the 1960s, King's influence was at its peak. He linked local direct action against segregation and for black voter registration in the southern states of the US to pressure at a national level for civil rights legislation. Many traditional black community and religious leaders felt King was too radical, for example, in backing the campaign of sit-ins at segregated lunch counters and other public facilities by the Student Nonviolent Coordinating Committee (SNCC) in 1960. President John F. Kennedy and his brother, Robert F. Kennedy, repeatedly urged him to moderate his position. But in 1963 King raised the campaign to a high pitch of intensity, encouraging confrontation between protesters and police in Birmingham, Alabama—confrontations that resulted in police violence that shocked world opinion—and mounting a "March on Washington" by around 250,000 demonstrators.

Running for US president
King had planned to run in the 1968 elections with anti-Vietnam War campaigner Dr. Benjamin Spock.

Outlawing discrimination

The passage of the Civil Rights Act in 1964, making many forms of discrimination illegal, and the Voting Rights Act the following year were the culmination of King's campaigning efforts. Awarded the Nobel Peace Prize, he stood at the height of his world fame. But at the same time his support among African-Americans was wavering. King's integrationist views—he wanted all races to have equal rights in a desegregated society—had always been rejected by black separatists. Many young African-Americans also began to turn away from nonviolence, asserting the right to use force in self-defense. Young activists launched the aggressive slogan "Black Power," while King appeared hesitant and indecisive.

From 1965 onward King grappled with causes and with his conscience. His attempt to establish contact with African-Americans in the ghettos of Chicago in 1966 was only partially successful. His outspoken opposition to US involvement in the Vietnam War

offended many African-Americans, who were proud of their sons' service in an integrated army. His shift away from rights and race to poverty was seen as controversially "socialist" in an American context.

Assassination in Memphis

The hatred provoked by King's views had always made him a target. He was under covert surveillance by the

"I have a dream…"
King salutes the crowd in front of the Lincoln Memorial during the "March on Washington" on August 28, 1963. This was the occasion for King's "I have a dream…" speech, arguably his most inspired and inspiring flight of oratory.

Federal Bureau of Investigation (FBI), whose head, J. Edgar Hoover, alleged that King was a communist and was trying to use evidence of his alleged sexual promiscuity to blackmail him. On April 4, 1968 King was shot dead on a balcony of a motel in Memphis, Tennessee. A petty criminal, James Earl Ray, was convicted of the killing, though his guilt has been contested. King's death sparked rioting and arson in cities across the US: an ironic memorial to a man of nonviolence. His place in the pantheon of American heroes is now secure.

Homage to King
A poster advertising an event in honor of King by a French antiracism group, held in Paris on April 9, 1968, three days after his death.

"We, as a people, will get to the Promised Land."

MARTIN LUTHER KING JR., SPEECH IN MEMPHIS, TENNESSEE, APRIL 3, 1968

US CIVIL RIGHTS CAMPAIGNER (1913–2005)

ROSA PARKS

Born Rosa McCauley, Rosa Parks was an active campaigner against sexism and racism from the 1930s. Her refusal to give up her seat to a white man on a segregated bus and her subsequent arrest in Montgomery, Alabama, on December 1, 1955 ignited the civil rights movement and the Montgomery Bus Boycott. Rosa Parks grew famous, but she was forced out of her job in a department store and left Alabama for Detroit, Michigan. She later became especially active in aiding black youths. In 1996, Parks was named the "Mother of the Modern Day Civil Rights Movement" by the US Congress.

TIMELINE

- **January 15, 1929** Martin Luther King Jr. is born in Atlanta, Georgia, son of a Baptist pastor; the name entered on his birth certificate is Michael.
- **1948** Graduates from Morehouse College in Atlanta with a degree in sociology.
- **1951** Graduates from Crozer Theological Seminary in Chester, Pennsylvania, with a degree in divinity.
- **June 18, 1953** Marries Coretta Scott.
- **September 1954** Becomes pastor of Dexter Avenue Baptist Church, Montgomery, Alabama.
- **June 5, 1955** Receives a PhD in theology from Boston University.
- **December 1955** As head of the Montgomery Improvement Association, King becomes spokesman for the year-long Montgomery Bus Boycott protesting against segregation.
- **January 30, 1956** A bomb explodes at King's home in Montgomery.
- **November 13, 1956** The Supreme Court rules bus segregation illegal.
- **January 11, 1957** King is elected head of the civil rights organization that will become the Southern Christian Leadership Conference.
- **September 20, 1958** Stabbed by a woman during a book-signing in Blumstein's department store in Harlem, New York.
- **1959** Resigns as pastor at Dexter to focus on civil rights work; returns to Atlanta, Georgia.
- **October 1960** King is imprisoned for participating in a sit-in protest in Atlanta, Georgia; presidential candidate John F. Kennedy contrives his release.
- **1961** Attorney-General Robert Kennedy asks the FBI to put King under surveillance.
- **April 16, 1963** Imprisoned during civil rights protests in Birmingham, Alabama, King writes his "Letter from Birmingham Jail," affirming the need to defy unjust laws.
- **August 28, 1963** During the March on Washington for Jobs and Freedom, King delivers his "I have a dream…" speech from the steps of the Lincoln Memorial.
- **July 2, 1964** Witnesses the signing of the Civil Rights Act, outlawing discrimination.
- **December 10, 1964** At the age of 35, King becomes the youngest male recipient of the Nobel Peace Prize.
- **March 7–25, 1965** King's leadership is rejected by younger activists.
- **August 4, 1965** Voting Rights Act is passed.
- **January 22, 1966** Moves into a tenement in a black ghetto in Chicago to draw attention to the issue of black urban poverty.
- **April 4, 1967** Denounces the Vietnam War and describes the United States as "the greatest purveyor of violence in the world today."
- **April 4, 1968** King is assassinated at the Lorraine Motel in Memphis.

WINS NOBEL PRIZE 1964

« BEFORE

The existence of social hierarchies often disadvantages vulnerable groups, such as the poor. The idea that everyone should have equal rights arose in the 18th century.

POLITICAL RIGHTS

The world's oldest written constitution for an independent state is the **US Constitution** of 1787 **« 298–99**, which set out the duties of government and its responsibilities toward its citizens. In 1789, the French Revolutionary Assembly issued the **Declaration of the Rights of Man « 303**. It stated that "all men are created equal" and defined various democratic principles, such as equality before the law and freedom from arbitrary arrest. Women, however, were excluded. In 1791 the US Bill of Rights guaranteed rights, such as **freedom of speech**, but it did not apply to blacks or American Indians.

PHILOSOPHICAL RIGHTS

Individual social reformers and philosophers were also important in the growth of human rights. The political thinker Tom Paine helped to draft the US Constitution and wrote *The Rights of Man* (1791–92) in support of the French Revolution **« 302–03**. English philosopher John Stuart Mill defended the freedom of the individual against state control.

JOHN STUART MILL, PROPONENT OF SOCIAL REFORM AND HUMAN RIGHTS

RIGHTS ACTIVIST (1884–1962)

ELEANOR ROOSEVELT

Eleanor Roosevelt, wife of President Franklin D. Roosevelt, is often called America's most significant First Lady. She was active in the League of Women Voters and the Women's Trade Union League. After the president's death, she was elected chair of the UN Human Rights Commission and played a key role in drafting the "Declaration of Universal Human Rights" (1948). She hoped it would be a "Magna Carta of all men everywhere," the word "men" applying to both sexes.

Civil Rights

The demand for civil and human rights has been a major feature of political and social movements worldwide since the early 20th century. Among the many causes that have been fought for are the right of women to vote and equal rights for ethnic minorities.

Human rights are built on the idea that all people should enjoy minimum standards in many areas of life, including the right to liberty, freedom of expression and conscience, to be treated equally before the law, and not to be tortured or subjected to degrading treatment. In 1948 these ideals were published by the General Assembly of the United Nations in the "Universal Declaration of Human Rights." Other United Nations Conventions (agreements among member countries) have followed, including the elimination of racial discrimination (1969), outlawing torture (1987), and the rights of the child (1989).

By contrast, civil rights are written into the laws or constitution of a country to protect its citizens. They relate only to citizens in that country. Most democracies, including the United States, Canada, France, and Germany, have civil rights written into their constitutions, although this does not necessarily mean that in practice all people are treated equally. Nor do countries have to be full democracies to proclaim civil rights. In 1936, the Soviet Union proclaimed a new constitution outlining civil rights, but they only existed on paper and were never implemented.

The right to vote
A fundamental civil right is the right to full citizenship, but women and ethnic minorities have often had to fight hard to obtain it. In the early

Against the vote
Opponents of women's right to vote used any methods to attack the suffragettes. Posters lampooned them as harridans, who should be forcibly shackled and gagged.

> ## "Civil liberties victories never stay won, but must be fought for over and over again."
> IRA GLASSER, EXECUTIVE DIRECTOR OF THE AMERICAN CIVIL LIBERTIES UNION, 1978–2001

20th century, in both Britain and the US, the demand for the vote for women became a major issue.

In Britain the campaign began in 1867 when Parliament proposed to extend suffrage (the right to vote) to a wider range of men but still exclude women. For the next 50 years a growing tide of protests, demonstrations, and petitions made this one of the most divisive issues in modern British politics. In 1903, the militant Women's Social and Political Union (WPSU) was formed by Emmeline Pankhurst. Frustrated by the failure to achieve the vote by peaceful means, suffragettes, as these women became known, took direct action, including invading the Houses of Parliament. Many were imprisoned. The campaign finally achieved success in 1918 when women age 30 and over obtained the vote. Equal voting rights with men were granted in 1928.

A similar but more peaceful campaign began in the US in the 1840s. The first state to grant women the vote was Wyoming in 1869; nationally, women

SURVEILLANCE CAMERAS

CIVIL PARTNERSHIP CEREMONY

won the vote in 1920. In the end, in both countries, women got the vote as a direct acknowledgment of their crucial role in securing victory in World War I. However, voting alone did not confer equal citizenship. Discrimination in other areas continued, and from about 1970 a second women's rights movement fought for and succeeded in changing the law to ensure equality at work and elsewhere. This campaign showed that changes in the law mean little unless economic inequalities are also addressed. Even if they have the vote, women worldwide still experience discrimination, as do other minorities.

African-American and black rights
One of the best-known civil rights campaigns of modern times was waged in the US. During the 1950s and early 1960s, black Americans led by Dr. Martin Luther King Jr. (pp.432–33), fought for the end of segregation—whereby black people were discriminated against in many areas such as education and transportation—and full civil rights. Years of civil disobedience resulted in a series of important legal changes that ended segregation in many areas and removed literacy tests preventing black Americans from voting.

In South Africa, too, a bitter struggle began against apartheid after 1948. This government-enforced policy of segregation denied black Africans the vote and many other rights (see pp.454–55). When apartheid ended after 1991 and South Africa held its first fully democratic elections in 1994, the sight of thousands of black voters lining up to exercise their new right to vote reaffirmed the importance of a basic civil right many of us now take for granted.

Hunger strike medal of honor
In July 1909, Majorie Wallace Dunlop became the first suffragette to go on hunger strike. Many others followed her lead. In retaliation, the British government introduced the brutal process of force-feeding. Women who braved the experience wore hunger-strike medals.

Selling The Suffragette
Women had to overcome many barriers to claim their right to vote. In 1912 the Women's Social and Political Union (WSPU) launched its own newspaper, *The Suffragette*. Hundreds of long-skirted women sold the paper in public, challenging social convention and risking public hostility.

AFTER

Human rights remain a key issue, with many at risk or being eroded worldwide.

CHALLENGES TO CIVIL LIBERTIES
Civil liberties, such as the right to privacy, may be suspended during wartime. After the 9/11 attacks on New York **466–67 》** and the start of the "war on terror," countries such as Britain and the US passed **antiterrorist laws** that allow authorities to intercept electronic data, and to detain suspected terrorists for longer without charge. Some people think these laws **threaten hard-won civil rights**; others think they are justified to prevent terrorism.

CIVIL RIGHTS AROUND THE WORLD
Since the 1960s, many minority groups have struggled to put an end to discrimination. During the 1990s, Britain and the US introduced **disability acts**. Gay rights activists have struggled for years to achieve full citizenship. Denmark has recognized **civil unions** since 1989. Other European countries, such as France, Germany, Portugal, and Britain, slowly followed suit. In 2000, Vermont enacted the first US civil union.

1893 The year that New Zealand became the first country to grant women equal voting rights.

1902 The year that Australia granted equal voting rights to women.

Marching for rights
National Guard troops watch with bayonets raised as African-American sanitation workers march peacefully in Memphis, Tennessee in April 1968. This contrasts with a similar demonstration the day before, when a black teenager was killed by the police.

BEFORE

Ireland, a mainly Catholic country, had a fraught relationship with its Protestant neighbor, Britain, for many centuries.

THE BRITISH IN IRELAND
After victory in the English Civil War, **Oliver Cromwell ‹‹ 264–65** invaded and conquered the whole of Ireland, opening it up to colonization by English and Scottish Protestants. In 1782 Ireland received an independent parliament, but after revolts in 1798 this was abolished. Britain and Ireland were united in 1801.

THE EASTER RISING
Anger erupted in April 1916 in a rebellion known as the Easter Rising. Militant Irish Republicans seized several key locations in Dublin and issued the **Proclamation of the Republic**, declaring Ireland to be an independent state. After six days of fighting, the British suppressed the uprising and executed its leaders, which generated sympathy for the Republican cause and awakened nationalist sentiment.

MICHAEL COLLINS

IRISH FREE STATE
In 1921 Michael Collins, a Republican leader, was sent to London to negotiate a treaty with the British. Ireland was to be self-governing but kept within the British Empire. Six counties in the region of Ulster (Northern Ireland) remained part of the UK. In 1922 Collins founded the **Irish Free State** (later, the Irish Republic). A year of civil war followed, as many Republicans rejected partition.

THE NORTH
In the largely Protestant north, nationalists, in favor of a united Ireland, were seen as a threat. This led to preferential treatment of Protestant Unionists in jobs and housing. Despite brief campaigns by the paramilitary **Irish Republican Army** (IRA), formed in the 1920s, the province was stable. However, in 1966 Unionists formed the Ulster Volunteer Force (UVF) in response to the Republican threat and the violence escalated.

In September 1968, the Northern Ireland Civil Rights Association (NICRA), a predominantly Catholic organization, announced a march was to take place in the city of Derry on October 5, 1968 to demand an end to discrimination against Irish Catholics. A Protestant organization, the Apprentice Boys of Derry, announced they would also march at that time. NICRA was barred from marching by the British Government but decided to proceed. The Royal Ulster Constabulary (RUC), armed with truncheons, charged at the marchers. Images of the violence shocked many around the world. Northern Irish Students formed a more radical civil rights group called the People's Democracy (PD) based on socialist principles (see pp.336–37). Inspired by Martin Luther King Jr. (see pp.432–33), about 40 members of the PD marched from the city of Belfast to Derry on January 1, 1969 to highlight social injustices in Northern Ireland. The march was attacked by Unionists

SECTARIANISM Division of a society into religious factions, such as Protestant and Catholic, in which strong identification with the values within each faction leads to exclusion of those with different values.

along its route with iron bars and stones. These events precipitated a split in the IRA (see BEFORE): the Official IRA, and the Provisional IRA. The Provisional IRA was determined to use force to reunite Ireland, and launched an armed attack against British rule.

Peaceful protest
The Provisional IRA became closely involved in civilian demonstrations and riots against the British. The Unionist UVF began to use violence to "protect the Protestant community" from the Provisional IRA and launched offensives against Catholics and the Irish Republic (see BEFORE). The British Government responded by implementing Operation "Demetrius" in Northern Ireland on August 9, 1971. This introduced

Confrontation
Civil rights protesters vent their frustrations at British soldiers dressed in riot gear, across a barricade in Derry on Bloody Sunday. The soldiers were armed with guns containing rubber bullets. Tensions came to a head when stones were thrown at the soldiers. Rubber bullets were replaced with live ammunition, leaving 13 dead.

The Troubles

For about 30 years, from the 1960s to the 1990s, repeated acts of intense violence flared between Northern Ireland's mostly Catholic, nationalist community, who wanted to break from British rule, and the principally Protestant Unionist, pro-British, community—a period known as "the Troubles."

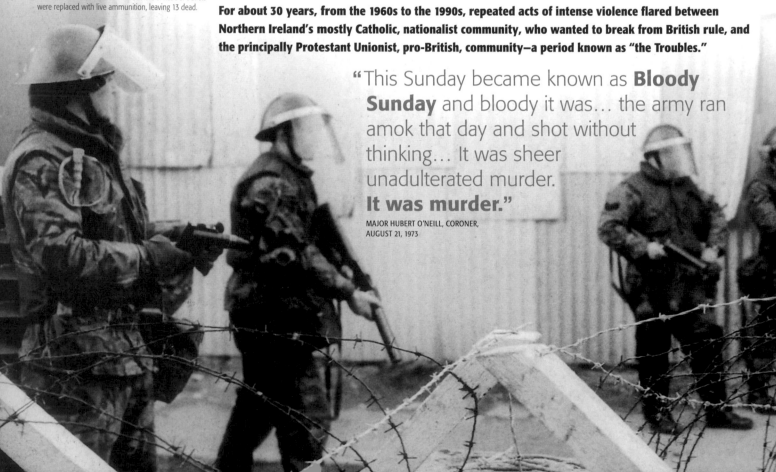

" This Sunday became known as **Bloody Sunday** and bloody it was… the army ran amok that day and shot without thinking… It was sheer unadulterated murder. **It was murder.**"

MAJOR HUBERT O'NEILL, CORONER,
AUGUST 21, 1973

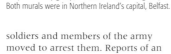

internment, which allowed the British army and RUC to arrest and imprison without trial those accused of being members of illegal paramilitary groups.

On Sunday, January 30, 1972, NICRA organized a march in the city of Derry against the internment policy, in which 10,000–20,000 people took part. They were prevented from entering the city by the British army, so most moved to "Free Derry Corner" to attend a rally. Some young men threw stones at

Marking territory
The Republican mural on the left commemorates the Easter Rising; the Unionist mural on the right shows the paramilitary group, the Ulster Freedom Fighters. Both murals were in Northern Ireland's capital, Belfast.

soldiers and members of the army moved to arrest them. Reports of an IRA sniper were allegedly passed to the British command and the order to switch from rubber bullets to live rounds was given. Within 30 minutes soldiers had shot dead 13 unarmed men and injured a further 14, many of whom were trying to flee.

Armed campaign
The events of "Bloody Sunday," as it came to be known, caused shock and revulsion worldwide. In Ireland the killings increased support for the IRA, especially among disaffected young people. It marked a major turning point in the fortunes of Northern Ireland. In March 1972, British Prime Minister Edward Heath decided to suspend the Northern Ireland Parliament, which was formed in 1920 and sat at Stormont in east Belfast. He

IRA bombing
This shows the aftermath of one of the Guildford bombs in 1974. The Horse and Groom pub was packed with young soldiers, many back from duty in Northern Ireland. Four men, known as the "Guildford Four" were later arrested and wrongly convicted of the act.

imposed direct rule from London and established the Northern Ireland Office to govern the province. Fresh rioting began and the IRA stepped up its armed campaign.

The Provisional IRA took its fight to force the British out of Northern Ireland to the mainland. On October 5, 1974 the IRA planted bombs in two pubs in the town of Guildford, popular with army personnel, killing 5 and injuring 65. On November 21, 1974 the IRA bombed two more pubs, this time in central Birmingham, killing 21 and injuring 182. In response, the British Government introduced the Prevention of Terrorism Act, which allowed suspects to be held without charge for up to seven days. Most suspects were sent to the Maze prison, at Long Kesh in County Antrim. In the late 1970s

several Republican prisoners began a bitter struggle for status as political prisoners. This culminated in the hunger strikes of 1981, in which ten inmates refused food and died of starvation in the prison hospital. Support for the political wing of the IRA, Sinn Féin, soared. This alarmed London, leading to political initiatives by successive governments, all hoping to find a peaceful solution to the crisis.

AFTER

After bombing campaigns on mainland Britain, both political leaders and paramilitary groups moved toward peace.

MAINLAND BOMBINGS
In the 1980s the IRA formed small groups in mainland Britain. They targeted politicians, and financial and shopping districts. These acts were designed to put **political and economic pressure** on the British government.

GOOD FRIDAY AGREEMENT
Changes in leadership in Britain, Dublin, and in Ulster Unionism led to the "Good Friday Agreement" in 1998. It recognized Northern Ireland's right to exist, while acknowledging the nationalist desire for a united Ireland. Voters elected a new **Northern Ireland Assembly** (NIA) to form a parliament at Stormont.

STORMONT

IRA DISBANDS
The NIA was suspended when the Provisional IRA delayed the decommission of its weapons. On August 15, 1998 an IRA bomb killed 29 people in County Tyrone. On **July 28, 2005** the IRA ceased its armed campaign, but dissident Republicans who rejected the peace settlement continued attacks at a much lower level.

A NEW ERA
In March 2007, the leaders of Sinn Féin (a Republican political party) and the Ulster Unionists, who had previously refused to work together, agreed to share power at Stormont. On May 8, 2007 the Assembly was restored.

Dictatorship and Democracy

In the latter part of the 20th century, Latin American countries veered between nationalist, authoritarian, revolutionary, and civilian regimes. Democracy and some stability have gradually been restored to some nations, but, while the region's economy has improved overall, inequality and poverty remain major challenges.

Chile's military coup, led by General Augusto Pinochet in 1973, was the first of several in 1970s Latin America (see pp.422–23). From 1976, Argentina was ruled by a succession of military figures, including General Leopardo Galtieri, who was among a number of Latin American leaders given training at the School of the Americas, a US army facility in Panama. Both the Pinochet and Galtieri regimes were characterized by the suppression of opposition—thousands of dissidents were tortured or disappeared without a trace.

The corrupt Somoza dynasty, which ruled in Nicaragua from 1936, faced growing opposition in the early 1970s from the International Socialist Sandinista group FSLN. Sandinista rebels were supported by the Catholic Church and much of the Nicaraguan population. In 1979, Anastasio Somoza was overthrown by popular revolution, and a *junta* (council) of National Reconstruction dominated by the FSLN took over the country.

In 1970s El Salvador, the elitist government of Arturo Molina was resented by a population living in abject poverty. Violence between right-wing paramilitary units known as "death squads" and left-wing revolutionary groups escalated into civil war in 1979. Fearing a communist takeover, the US funded the El Salvadoran military. Fighting and human rights abuses continued throughout the 1980s until

mounting foreign debt, and Argentina slid into recession. The economy finally began to stabilize in 2005.

In the 1980s, General Pinochet's regime in Chile introduced some liberalizing measures as the state moved toward a free-market economy.

> **DISSIDENT** An individual who disagrees, protests, or acts against established opinion, policy, or government.

Greater freedoms of speech led inevitably to calls for democracy, which was restored in 1989. Chile experienced impressive growth in the 1990s and is one of the more robust post-dictatorship economies.

BEFORE

Latin America has been shaped by the interests and intervention of foreign powers, first by Europe, and later, the United States.

THE GREAT DEPRESSION
Economic depression in Europe and North America in the 1930s had a **catastrophic effect** on Latin American economies, most of which were **dependent on exports** of raw materials. The plight of the poor in many countries led to a growth of revolutionary movements **<<422–23**.

INDUSTRIALIZATION
During the economic crisis of the 1930s, many governments in Latin America **nationalized resources** previously controlled by **foreign interests**, and began industrialization programs **<<422–23**.

GENERAL PINOCHET

THE COLD WAR
Rivalry between the Soviet Union and US after World War II **<<406–07** even extended to Latin America. The US supported the **Pinochet coup** in Chile, and the overthrow of left-wing regimes, while the Soviet Union backed **communist Cuba**. The 1961 Cuban Missile Crisis intensified this competition. The Soviet Union supported Cuba through an American economic embargo, and the US gave funding and military support to keep their **chosen regimes** in power.

"Sometimes **democracy** must be **bathed in blood**."

GENERAL AUGUSTO PINOCHET, ATTRIBUTED

in 1992, 12 years of violence ended with the El Salvador Peace Accords.

The return of democracy
In the 1980s and 1990s, the political tide turned again in Latin America: dictatorships were overthrown and democracy restored.

Democracy returned to Argentina in 1983. After a period of spiraling inflation, President Carlos Menem introduced wide-ranging reforms in the 1990s, privatizing state assets and imposing a fixed exchange rate. However, Menem and his successor Fernando de la Rúa failed to address

The oil-rich state of Venezuela had regained democratic rule in 1958, but the gap between rich and poor caused discontent. In 1998, President Hugo Chávez (see right) was elected, vowing to bring greater equality. He launched "Plan Bolivar 2000," which introduced social and welfare reforms and halted the privatization of state assets. Oil profits have helped ensure success for Chávez and growth in the economy.

US intervention
Frequently referred to as "America's backyard," Latin America has often seen US interference. In 1983 the US invaded the island nation of Grenada after reports that an airport there was secretly intended for Soviet use, and even after the end of the Cold War (see pp.406–07) US troops invaded Panama in 1989, and removed General Noriega's government due in part to alleged drug trafficking.

Some Latin American nations have tried to avoid US economic domination. In 2007, the "Bank of the South" was formed by Hugo Chávez to finance regional infrastructure projects and social programs.

The Mexico–US Border
The order for a fence 700 miles (1,126 km) long to separate the two countries was given by President George W. Bush in 2006 to prevent the flow of illegal immigrants into the United States.

AFTER

In the 21st century, a more politically stable Latin America is increasing its economic ambitions, and many of its leaders are calling for greater regional integration.

MIGRATION NORTH
Poverty in Latin America leads many people to migrate north in **search of a better life** in the US. The US Census shows that migration patterns have shifted radically since World War II, when most immigrants were European. Today the majority of the US's legal migrants are from Latin America, and many more enter illegally. A large proportion of US's estimated 12 million illegal immigrants crossed at the **Mexican border**.

GREATER POLITICAL STABILITY
Despite the problems in the region, in 2006, there were still **democratic elections** in 12 countries of Latin America , including the return of a socialist prime minister in Chile.

Protests against Pinochet
Chileans take to the streets with pictures of those who went missing during Pinochet's military rule, when more than 3,000 were arrested and murdered by the authorities. In 2001, relatives were finally given access to records and learned the fate of "the disappeared."

VENEZUELAN PRESIDENT (1954–)

HUGO CHÁVEZ

Elected president of Venezuela in 1998, Hugo Chávez introduced the "Bolivarian Revolution," a brand of democratic socialism, prioritizing social reform. An admirer of Fidel Castro, he was briefly removed from office in 2002 by the Venezuelan army, but was returned to power by a popular uprising. His radical foreign policy criticizes the US, and calls for improved trade and international aid. However, a 2007 referendum rejected his plans for wholesale constitutional reform.

BEFORE

In 1948 the state of Israel was created from land belonging to the Arab state of Palestine. The oil-rich Arab nations denied Israel's legitimacy and began a series of military reprisals to regain the land.

FORMATION OF OAPEC
The Organization of Arab Petroleum Exporting Countries was founded in 1968. Its member states, which include Iran, Iraq, and Saudi Arabia, were all developing nations seeking to assert their rights in a market dominated by foreign-owned multinational oil companies. As **oil reserves** in other parts of the world dwindled, **OAPEC became increasingly powerful**.

SIX-DAY WAR
In 1967 Egypt closed the Gulf of Aqaba to Israel. In the Six-Day War that ensued, **Israel** defeated **Egypt, Syria, and Jordan,** and occupied land later known as the **Occupied Territories**.

UNREST IN MIDDLE EAST
The territorial losses and humiliation of the Six-Day War **intensified Arab resentment** toward both the Israelis and the Western governments that supported them.

ISRAELI TANK IN SYRIA

The **Oil Crisis**

By the 1970s, rising industrial and domestic consumption of fuel created a growing dependence on imports of foreign oil for the industrialized Western powers. Oil was the fuel of the global economy and most of the world's oil reserves were concentrated in the Middle East.

In October 1973, Egypt and Syria, backed by Iraq, Jordan, and Saudi Arabia, invaded Israel on the holy Jewish holiday of Yom Kippur. The three-week Yom Kippur War represents a watershed in Middle Eastern history. With the element of surprise on their side and the advantage of improved arms, Arab troops fared better than in any previous Arab–Israeli conflict, gaining some of the territory lost during the Six-Day War (see BEFORE).

Oil supply cut

The Yom Kippur War also saw OAPEC flex its political muscle for the first time. Ten days into the war, OAPEC leaders King Faisel of Saudi Arabia and Egyptian President Anwar Sadat

Fuel shortage
An American gas station attendant ensures that motorists receive just their allocated ration of 10 gallons of gasoline per car during the oil crisis of 1973–74. The OAPEC oil embargo caused fuel shortages and a massive rise in fuel prices in the US, Europe, and Japan.

announced an embargo on shipments of crude oil to all Western nations that were providing supplies or aid to Israel. The embargo lasted six months—from October 1973 until March 1974. Its aim was to force Israel's allies to pressure it into giving up the occupied territories (see BEFORE).

The embargo targeted Israel's key ally, the US, but did not apply to all European nations. The Netherlands, which sent arms to Israel and allowed the US to use Dutch airfields for supply runs, faced a complete embargo. Supplies to the UK and France, which had embargoed arms and supplies to both Arabs and Israelis, were not cut off. However, the economic impact of restricting the flow of crude oil to the world market caused

Yom Kippur war
The Israeli army attacks Syrian positions in the Golan Heights on October 12, 1973. Six days earlier, the Syrians had invaded Israel, but they were quickly driven back beyond their own border.

oil prices to triple. Even if countries were not embargoed from receiving oil, many could not afford to buy it in anything like the same quantities. Without fuel to power production,

5 PERCENT the annual rise in oil usage in the early 1970s.

98 PERCENT the drop in oil imports to the US from OAPEC.

400 PERCENT the rise in the price of oil from 1973 to 1974.

industrial output slowed dramatically, inflation spiraled, and the world slipped into economic recession. It became all too clear that the economic boom experienced by Western nations in the postwar years had been entirely dependent on their ability to dictate low fixed-rate prices to the oil-supplying nations.

Energy crisis

When the embargo hit the US, inflation rose to over 10 percent, interest rates rocketed, and an enormous trade deficit developed. Schools and businesses adopted policies of regular closures to save on heating oil, while homeowners were called on to turn down their heating thermostats. Unemployment rates, a growing issue since the start of the 1970s, continued to rise as industries were forced to lay off workers. The price of gas for domestic consumption quadrupled during the embargo period, and up to 20 percent of US gas stations were without fuel during the crisis.

In an economy where 85 percent of the workforce drove to their place of work, people began to line up for hours at a time to refuel their cars. At President Nixon's request, gas was rationed to a maximum of 10 gallons per customer.

Price rises in crude oil had a huge impact in Europe, especially in the UK, which imported over 80 percent of its oil from the Middle East. Before the crisis struck, Edward Heath's Conservative government was already struggling with rising inflation and trade union unrest. In May 1973, 1.6 million workers went on strike to protest against the introduction of pay restraints. As the year progressed, relations between workers and government steadily worsened.

In November 1973, a ban on over-time by electricity and coal workers exacerbated the British fuel shortage.

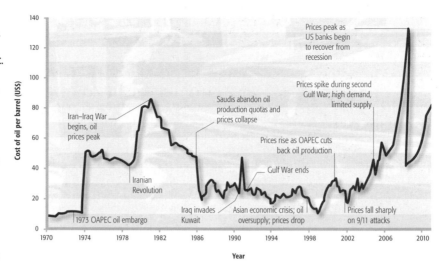

The politics of oil
This graph shows the rise and fall in oil production prices from 1970 and its relationship to specific events. As supplies of oil dwindled in other parts of the world, the value of oil reserves in the Middle East increased. Since oil underpins industrial and domestic energy production, any political instability in the region has repercussions elsewhere. Increased demand in fast-developing Asian economies has also pushed up the price of oil and other commodities.

Heath's government was forced to announce a state of emergency, limiting industrial and commercial users of electricity to a total of 5 days fuel supply every two weeks. When coal miners went on all-out strike in early 1974, the government introduced a compulsory three-day week to save on both energy consumption and the wage bill. The crisis ended with a settlement for the National Union of Mine Workers, which cost the country over $250 million and increased the

Coping with a "car-free" Sunday
During the oil crisis, an enterprising German hotel owner (above) circumvents the nationwide vehicle ban on Sundays by reverting to horse power. "The Big Freeze" is the cover story of the December 3, 1973 issue of *Time* magazine (right). Three months into the oil crisis, the article suggests it will be a cold holiday season for Americans.

national wage bill by 30 percent. With full-time coal production reestablished, Britain returned to a 5-day working week in March 1974, but restrictions on the use of electricity were retained for several months.

Coping with the crisis

A range of conservation measures were introduced by governments to cope with the oil crisis. Many lowered speed limits to 50 mph (80 km/h), which reduced oil consumption. In the US, the consumption of oil dropped by 20 percent, as the public made efforts to conserve both oil and money by switching to more affordable forms of energy, such as coal, or solar and wind power. The US also extended Daylight Saving Time and, like Germany, developed a policy of "car-free" Sundays. In Britain, the public became used to living and working by candlelight during a long winter of phased energy-conserving power cuts. Other restrictions included ending television broadcasts by 10:30 pm, turning off streetlights at midnight, and canceling soccer matches played under floodlights. Civic Christmas lights were allowed to remain switched on by special government dispensation.

OAPEC's embargo inflicted serious damage on the global economy and left the leaders of many of the industrialized nations determined to reduce their reliance on Middle Eastern oil. Many began to fund research into alternative energy sources such as wind, tidal, and solar energy. In the US, President Nixon approved the building of a Trans-Alaskan oil pipeline, designed to supply 2,000,000 barrels of oil a day to the American market. Big automobile manufacturers began to consider smaller, more economic alternatives to the large "gas-guzzling" cars of the 1950s and 1960s. Japan, in particular, pursued reforms in its energy policy to avoid a similar future crisis, developing its nuclear energy capacity and pioneering some of the world's most successful energy-efficient cars. Unlike other industrialized nations, Japan revived quickly after the crisis. This turnaround in economic fortune is generally credited to the Japanese government's investing in such industries as electronics (see pp.456–57) that are not dependent on oil.

AFTER

Since 1973, the US has pursued policies to protect itself from a repeat of the oil crisis.

MIDDLE EAST PEACE PROCESS
The oil embargo radically changed the OAPEC nations' **power and standing in world politics**. Western nations were forced to give Arab objections to the existence of Israel a fair hearing. From his inauguration in 1977, US president Jimmy Carter pursued **a peaceful resolution to Arab–Israeli conflict**. In March 1979, the signing of a bilateral peace treaty between Israel and Egypt was a first step along this difficult diplomatic road **≪ 415**.

US ENERGY POLICY
The National Energy Act of 1978 continued to exercise controls over industrial energy use, promoting greater use of renewable energy and introducing higher tax rates for fuel-inefficient vehicles. This led to the development of efficient hybrid cars that can run partly on electric motors.

HYBRID CAR

THE US IN THE MIDDLE EAST
US intervention in the Middle East was not confined to peacemaking. In the 1980s the US worked hard to gain interests in the oil reserves by supporting regimes such as that of Saddam Hussein against Iran **468–69 ≫**. The instability in Iraq after the 2003 invasion led to questions about America's long-term influence over the region's oil.

BEFORE

A desire to return to a purer, more traditional form of Islam (the Muslim faith) grew among Muslims tired of westernizing influences on their way of life.

DEOBANDI ISLAMIC MOVEMENT
Al Imam Mohammad Quasim Nanotwi established the **Deoband Madrassa** (religious school) in British-ruled India in 1866. The school taught **Shariah law** (see right) and aimed to **purify Islam** of "un-Islamic" practices, particularly the influences of British colonial culture. After the partition of India **≪ 410–11** in 1947, the Deoband Madrassa closed, and new madrassas in Pakistan were opened.

THE MUSLIM BROTHERHOOD
Founded by **Hasan al-Banna** in Egypt in 1928, the Muslim Brotherhood agitated for the introduction of Shariah law. The Brothers' leader bemoaned the sickness of the *Ummah*, or larger Muslim community, and gave the Brothers

COLONIAL RULE *jihadia* (**military training**) to help the "struggle in the way of God" against them. The Brotherhood's activities led to their being **outlawed in Egypt**. Saudi Arabia gave refuge to Brotherhood exiles.

The Iranian Revolution

The growth of Arab nationalism in the aftermath of World War I was accompanied by the rise of "Islamism" in some Arab nations. The Islamist movement aimed to overthrow secular, pro-Western governments in the Middle East and establish Islamic states governed by Shariah law.

Many citizens of the Middle East resented the post-World War I settlements, which gave Britain and France mandates to administer their nations. Leaders of Middle Eastern countries were chosen for their willingness to collaborate with the foreign powers, and many were corrupt. Ordinary people were given few, if any, democratic rights. While Britain did provide constitutions and elected assemblies, its advisers ensured that British interests were served in any governmental decisions.

In World War I, Persia was divided between Russia and Britain, but the Russians withdrew after the Bolshevik revolution of 1917 (see pp.376–77), leaving Britain sole rights to exploit Persian oil. In the early 1920s, the British identified Reza Khan, a senior figure in the Persian military, as a leader who could maintain the Anglo-Persian status quo. With British backing, Khan led an armed campaign to crush political opposition, declaring himself Shah of Persia in 1925.

Modernization and secularization

A fierce believer in Westernization, the Shah modernized the infrastructure of the country, which was renamed Iran in 1935. He abandoned Islamic education in favor of a more secular

Lavish lifestyle
Mohammed Reza Shah—shown here with his daughter, Princess Shahnaz, in 1957—had an opulent lifestyle, while the majority of his people lived in abject poverty. Cold War tensions and the need for Iranian oil led Western powers to ignore the Shah's misrule.

WAHHABISM A form of Islam named after Muhammed Ibn Abdul Wahhab (1703–91), who reintroduced Shariah law to the Arabian Peninsula. Shariah imposes religious rules on every aspect of life, including politics, sexuality, and social issues. Wahhabism became the formal doctrine of Saudi Arabia in 1800.

curriculum, discarded much of Shariah law, and discouraged Iranians from obeying the call to prayer or from making pilgrimages. The result was ever-greater social division. While the upper classes became more secular and Western in their outlook, the masses—who were forced to pay heavy taxes to fund the Shah's reforms—remained impoverished and deeply religious.

World War II and after

Reza Shah offered support to the Nazis in World War II, hoping that Germany would help Iran to rid itself of British influence. The Shah's Nazi sympathies threatened Allied access to Iranian oil, so when Germany invaded Russia in

Protest against the Shah
The corrupt and brutal regime of Mohammed Reza Shah produced waves of demonstration during 1978. Protesters thronged the streets clutching pictures of the exiled religious cleric Ayatollah Khomeini. In December, the Shah abandoned his attempts to hold on to power and fled Iran, leaving the way open for Khomeini to return to Iran.

1941, British and Russian troops invaded Iran. Reza Shah was deposed and replaced by his son, Mohammed Reza. Resentment of Western interference deepened.

In the postwar years, students spearheaded a backlash against secularism and corruption. In 1951, political unrest forced the Shah to loosen his grip on power and appoint Mohammed Mossadeq as Prime Minister. Mossadeq soon nationalized the assets of the Anglo-Iranian Oil Company. With the Cold War at its height (see pp.406–07), fears of growing Soviet influence in the Middle East led Britain and the US to block sales of Iranian oil. Iran's economy descended into crisis.

In 1953, Western intelligence services supported a military coup, which restored absolute power to Mohammed Reza Shah. The Shah's rule became increasingly dictatorial. While his security police ran a terror campaign against dissenters and many of the rural poor were suffering from malnutrition, the Shah led a lavish life on oil revenues, which grew from an annual $285 million in 1960 to $18,523 million by the mid-1970s.

Islamic revolution

In Iran's mosques, the teachings of an exiled ayatollah (high-ranking Muslim cleric) were gaining ground. Ayatollah Ruhollah Khomeini had been exiled in 1964 for calling the Shah a "puppet" of the West. His teachings called for an end to the Shah's reign, insisting that only clerics should rule, since they are the true representatives of God.

Iran hostage crisis
Student militants burn a US flag on the roof of the US embassy in Tehran during the early days of the 1979 hostage crisis, when embassy staff were held hostage by protesters.

By 1978, Khomeini had widespread support. Pro-Khomeini demonstrations were brutally suppressed, but unrest still spread from city to city as clerics, nationalists, and moderates united in a struggle for change. Although martial law was imposed, many troops refused to shoot at protesters. In December, the US tried to persuade the Shah to liberalize his regime, but revolution was now inevitable. The Shah and his family fled Iran on January 16, 1979.

Khomeini returned to Iran on February 1, 1979. After initial fighting between political factions, a popular referendum voted for the creation of an Islamic republic. A new constitution named Khomeini as Iran's supreme leader, clergy were appointed to run state institutions, and Shariah law was introduced.

Triumphant return
After 14 years in exile, Ayatollah Ruhollah Khomeini arrived in Tehran to an ecstatic reception. Khomeini rapidly set about creating a clerical state under Shariah Law.

The Iran Hostage Crisis

On October 22, 1979, US president Jimmy Carter allowed the Shah to enter the US for cancer treatment. Outraged Iranian students, who wanted the Shah

Since the Iranian Revolution, the world has seen tensions between Muslim groups, as well as continued hostility in some Islamic factions toward Western regimes.

THE MANY STRANDS OF ISLAM
Khomeini's traditionalism is not the only view of Islam. Like Christianity, Islam has a number of **different interpretations** and several distinct denominations, or groups. **Sunni** Muslims form the largest group, comprising about 85 percent of the world's Muslims; **Shia** form approximately 15 percent. Some Muslims follow a mystical form of Islam called **Sufism**. All denominations have a slightly different understanding of the **Qur'an**, the central religious text of Islam.

IRAN AFTER KHOMEINI
After the death of Ayatollah Khomeini in 1988 largely came to nothing, hopes for a moderation in the Islamic regime rose with the election of the reformist cleric **Mohammed Khatami** as president in 1997. However, his attempts at reform were hampered by political conservatives, hard-line clerics, and the state security apparatus, and in 2005 he was replaced by the ultraconservative nationalist, **Mahmoud Ahmadinejad**. Since the 1980s Iran has been accused of meddling in Syria to support the Islamist Hezbollah militia, and favoring Shia factions in post-Saddam Iraq. It has also pursued the **development of a nuclear program** despite fierce opposition from other countries that fear this is aimed at producing nuclear weapons.

THE POWER OF FAITH

returned to Iran to face trial, invaded the US embassy in Tehran, taking 63 Americans hostage. Although the Shah died less than a year later, Khomeini refused to release the hostages, holding 52 Americans captive for 444 days. The crisis finally concluded with the signing of the Algiers Accord in January 1981.

Khomeini's defiance of America was a key factor in Western governments' support for Saddam Hussein's invasion of Iran in 1980, and their willingness to provide him with weapons during the eight-year-long Iran–Iraq war (see p.468). By the time Khomeini died in June 1989, Iran was a well-established Islamic state.

> "In Islam, the legislative **power and competence** to establish laws belong exclusively to God."
>
> AYATOLLAH RUHOLLAH KHOMEINI

‹‹ BEFORE

Afghanistan is ethnically diverse, with a rugged geography. Dogged by clan and tribal issues, it has repeatedly been invaded.

A LANDLOCKED COUNTRY
Afghanistan lies at the **heart of Asia**, nestled between Iran in the west and Pakistan in the south and east. Its northern borders touch former Soviet countries such as Uzbekistan.

STABILITY AND UNREST
Between 1933–73, Afghanistan was stable under King Sahir Shah. In 1973, **a bloodless coup** saw his brother-in-law, Sardar Daoud Khan (below), seize control of the country. He was murdered in 1978 when the communist **People's Democratic Party of Afghanistan (PDPA)** launched the Great Saur Revolution.

COMMUNIST TAKEOVER
Supported by the USSR, the PDPA applied Marxist-style reforms **‹‹ 334–35**, such as state control of agriculture. In 1978, a treaty was signed allowing the use of Soviet troops if requested by Afghanistan.

PRIME MINISTER SARDAR DAOUD KHAN

When the People's Democratic Party of Afghanistan (PDPA) took power in 1978 (see BEFORE), conflict broke out immediately. After several days of internal power struggles, a party leader and Marxist scholar, Noor Mohammed Tureki, became the President of Afghanistan. There were primarily two Marxist groups in the country: the Khalq Party and the Parcham Party. Tureki was the leader of the former. To establish a communist government in Afghanistan, the Khalq and the Parcham parties agreed to split power, but only a few months later Tureki killed and jailed many Parchamis and pressed ahead with a rapid program of communist reform, including secularism, equal rights for women, and land redistribution; but within months insurrection was breaking out all over the country. In March 1979, a resistance group declared a *jihad*, or "holy war," against the godless regime

1 MILLION Afghans died in the war.

5 MILLION Afghans became refugees in nearby countries.

52 THOUSAND Soviet soldiers were killed or wounded.

in Kabul. In the same month more than 100 Soviet citizens were killed in Herat, western Afghanistan. In September 1979, Tureki tried to assassinate his prime minister, Hafizulla Amin. Amin had Tureki arrested, and took control of the government. He later announced that Tureki was dead.

American involvement
The United States had been keeping a careful eye on the new Soviet-backed regime. In the 1950s and 1960s, four US presidents faced the significant task of defending American interests in the Middle East and South Asia, particularly in the vast reservoirs of oil and natural gas in and around the Persian Gulf and the Arabian Peninsula. With the onset of

the Cold War in 1946 (see pp.406–07), the US perceived the Soviet Union to be their main threat. This perception was to continue for the next half-century. The US sought advice from politicians in anticommunist Muslim

Kalashnikov AK-47
The CIA, the US foreign intelligence agency, funneled extensive aid to the Mujahideen via Pakistan, including hundreds of thousands of AK-47s. Made in the USSR, they were cheap, reliable, and easily available.

Fighting back
From machine gun nests like this one above the Jagdalak Valley, insurgents attack Soviet forces, who were vulnerable in the mountainous terrain.

War in Afghanistan

When Soviet armed forces invaded neighboring Afghanistan in December 1979, they were supremely confident of seizing immediate control. However, the Russian troops found themselves bogged down in a ten-year war that proved to be a disaster for both countries. The war hastened the breakup of the Soviet Union, and plunged Afghanistan into a state of lawlessness.

and Arab states, such as Pakistan and Saudi Arabia. This was the beginning of a curious relationship between the US and Islam.

With the PDPA in power, US president Jimmy Carter and national security advisor Zbigniew Brzezinski authorized the covert funding and training of antigovernment forces. Military and intelligence services backed with Saudi Arabian finance and Pakistani logistical support, managed the training, equipping, and paying of

Soviet withdrawal
In May 1988, Afghanistan, Pakistan, the USSR, and the US signed agreements to end foreign intervention in Afghanistan, and the USSR began withdrawing its forces.

volunteers, the Mujahideen (Persian for "warriors"), who opposed the Marxists.

The Soviet presence in Afghanistan was increasing. Citing the 1978 Treaty of Friendship, allowing Soviet military intervention if requested (see BEFORE), the Soviets stormed into the capital city of Kabul on December 24, 1979. The

110,000–150,000 Soviet troops arriving in Afghanistan (assisted by 100,000 pro-communist Afghan troops) were met with Mujahideen resistance. Despite Russia's superior weapons, the rebels frequently eluded them in the hostile mountainous terrain.

Stalemate
The international response ranged from stern warnings to a boycott of the 1980 Moscow Olympics. The conflict settled into a stalemate, with Soviet and

government forces controlling the urban areas, while the rebels operated freely in the mountains. As the war progressed, the rebels improved their tactics and began using imported and captured weapons. Their leaders favored sabotage, such as blowing up government office buildings. On September 4, 1985, insurgents shot down a domestic plane as it took off from Kandahar airport, killing 52 people.

In February 1988, under increasing international pressure, Soviet President Gorbachev announced the withdrawal of troops, a task completed a year later.

The war left Afghanistan with severe political, economic, and ecological problems. Many had died or fled the country, and economic production was curtailed. The guerrilla forces that had triumphed were unable to unite, and Afghanistan was divided between regional warlords. These divisions set the stage for the rise of the Taliban later in the decade.

> "We now have the opportunity of giving to **the USSR its Vietnam War**."
>
> ZBIGNIEW BRZEZINSKI, U.S. NATIONAL SECURITY ADVISER, JANUARY 18, 1978

AFTER »

Following Soviet withdrawal from Afghanistan in 1989, the United States and its allies did little to rebuild the country, leaving a dangerous leadership vacuum.

THE WARLORDS
Mujahideen factions gained power, but ethnic fighting broke out, giving rise to **warlords**. Out of this chaos emerged the **Taliban**.

RISE OF THE TALIBAN
The Taliban, led by Mullah Omar, was **a political and religious force,** which was initially supported by US-backed Pakistan. After taking control of most of Afghanistan, it imposed a strict interpretation of **Islamic Sharia Law**. Girls' schools were closed and women were barred from working. Following the **September 11 attacks 466–67 »**, the US launched a military campaign to destroy the **Al-Qaeda terrorist**

network operating in Afghanistan, and with it the Taliban government.

THE WAR CONTINUES
In December 2001, major leaders from the Afghan opposition groups agreed to form a **democratic government**, and Hamid

HAMID KARZAI

Karzai was elected president in 2004. The Taliban regrouped on the border with Pakistan and has, since 2006, mounted severe attacks on NATO forces based in Afghanistan. Karzai's re-election in 2009, disputed by his political opponents, has done little to bring stability. By 2010, though the Taliban had yet to be defeated, the US and other NATO forces planned to withdraw.

ДОЛОЙ ЛЕНИНИЗМ

THE ERA OF STAGNATION
In 1964, **Leonid Brezhnev** succeeded **Nikita Khrushchev** as leader of the USSR and stayed in office until 1982. Under his leadership the **economy stagnated,** and slow growth was experienced in some sectors. There were **perennial shortages** of manufactured goods and food, and reduced consumer options caused frustration among the people.

LEONID BREZHNEV

DOUBLE STANDARDS IN THE SYSTEM
Although all Soviet citizens were officially equal, in reality, **the system was corruptible**; bribes secured better jobs or housing and **senior communist party officials** had access to **privileges** unattainable by ordinary people.

Perestroika

When Mikhail Gorbachev became leader of the Soviet Union in 1985, he acknowledged faults within the communist system and set out a new plan for political reform—*perestroika*. He aimed to renew the Soviet Union, but *perestroika* resulted in changes that altered the country beyond recognition.

orbachev was a child of communism, the first leader of the USSR to have been born after the revolution (see pp.376–77). He did not question Lenin's view that communism could only be achieved through disciplined, central organization, but aimed to address failings elsewhere in the Soviet system. Through *perestroika* (restructuring) he attempted to streamline the Soviet Communist Party (CPSU). Gorbachev also recognized that state repression of those who criticized the CPSU had created problems in Soviet society. He pledged a new openness—*glasnost*—

in political affairs; exiled intellectuals were allowed to return and political debate was encouraged.

At first, *glasnost* and *perestroika* were met with general excitement, although there was resistance from those who resented reforms aimed at reducing their power and privilege. By the end of 1986, however, with the economic situation worsening, Gorbachev's talk of progress began to sound like an empty promise. His economic reforms were too cautious. He introduced limited rights for private enterprise, but most production remained under control of the state, where restructuring

failed to stimulate growth. By 1987, *perestroika* had led to longer food queues and food shortages.

Glasnost had enabled all Soviet citizens to express their dissatisfaction with both the CPSU and the Soviet system. In 1988, Gorbachev began to face internal resistance as nationalist movements in Kazakhstan, Armenia, Azerbaijan, and the Baltic States (Estonia, Latvia, and Lithuania) demanded independence from the centralized Soviet government.

In 1989, hoping that the Soviet people would accept a new "humane communism," Gorbachev allowed

Down with Lenin
Gorbachev's decision to allow criticism of the communist system resulted in demands for an end to repressive one-party government. Protesters called for multi-party elections and democracy.

RUSSIAN PRESIDENT (1931–)

MIKHAIL GORBACHEV

Mikhail Gorbachev was born in Stavropol in southwestern Russia. He became active in politics at an early age and became leader of the Soviet Union in 1985. Gorbachev transformed Soviet relations with the Western world, and is widely credited with reversing the arms race and ending the Cold War (see pp.406–07). He attempted to solve Soviet economic and political problems through programs of domestic reform. After the collapse of the Soviet Union in 1991, he made several failed attempts to return to the political stage in Russia. He was awarded the Nobel Peace Prize in 1990.

"Upon the success of *perestroika* depends the **future of peace**."

MIKHAIL GORBACHEV, 1987

openly contested elections for some members of the Congress of People's Deputies (Soviet Parliament). However, he soon faced demands for greater concessions from a newly elected people's deputy, Boris Yeltsin.

Gorbachev and Yeltsin

Yeltsin had become popular in the Soviet Union because of his open criticism of Gorbachev and *perestroika*. In 1990, he was elected President of the Russian Federation, the largest Soviet republic. He used this position to attack Gorbachev and the CPSU, insisting that the party should no longer dominate government. His resignation from the party in July 1990 was a public challenge. Next to Yeltsin, Gorbachev looked suddenly weak and old-fashioned.

Throughout 1990, Gorbachev struggled to hold the Soviet Union together, sending troops into

Azerbaijan to suppress inter-ethnic fighting, and opposing independence in the Baltic States. On August 19, 1991, a committee of CPSU hardliners staged a coup, arresting Gorbachev and his advisors. They declared a state of emergency and announced their intention to reestablish old-style Soviet rule. Yeltsin rushed to the White House (the Russian Parliament building), and called on the people to come and protect their parliament. Support for Yeltsin ended the coup. Gorbachev was reinstated as president after four days, but Yeltsin was the true hero of the hour and Gorbachev's prestige was irreversibly damaged.

In September 1991, the Congress of People's Deputies granted independence to all Soviet republics, dissolving the USSR. With no union to rule over, Gorbachev had effectively been downsized. He resigned his post in December 1991.

The former USSR in 1991
After the USSR's collapse, the vast nation split into 15 separate states, the largest of which was the Russian Federation. These established independent governments and many began economic cooperation as members of the Commonwealth of Independent States (CIS).

The collapse of communism in Russia created economic instability and demands for independence in Chechnya.

YELTSIN IN POWER

Following the collapse of communism, Boris Yeltsin introduced a **market economy** in the Russian Federation. **Inflation soared** and domestic production plummeted. Russia was plunged into **recession** with greater material hardships than had been suffered under communism or *perestroika*. In 1993 the Congress of People's Deputies attempted to impeach Yeltsin, but he survived in office, eventually resigning in 1999, a **deeply unpopular figure**.

BORIS YELTSIN

WAR IN CHECHNYA

After 1991, the Russian Federation faced **independence** demands from its southern province of Chechnya. In 1994, Yeltsin sent troops into Grozny, the Chechen capital, to crush the rebels. The war lasted until 1996 with **serious casualties** on both sides. After Russian withdrawal, the unrest continued and a second war began in 1999.

FIGHTING IN CHECHNYA

KEY

▨ Territory controlled by USSR from 1945
▪ Russian Federation from 1991
◉ Commonwealth of Independent States, 1991

SWEDEN
FINLAND
Barents Sea
Kara Sea
Laptev Sea
Kolyma
ESTONIA
LATVIA
Tallinn
LITHUANIA
Kaliningrad
Riga
St. Petersburg (Leningrad)
Arkhangel'sk
Plesetsk
◉ BELARUS
Vilnius
Minsk
Ural Mountains
R U S S I A N   F E D E R A T I O N
Magadan
Chernobyl
Moscow
S i b e r i a
Tula
Nizhny Novgorod
Yashkar Ola
Lower Tunguska
Yakutsk
Sea of Okhotsk
◉ MOLDOVA
Kiev
Ryazan'
Ob'
Yenisey
Lena
UKRAINE
Voronezh
Perm'
Kazan
Yekaterinburg
West Siberian Plain
Tyumen'
Irtysh
Ob'
Odessa
Dnipropetrovs'k
Samara
Ufa
Tomsk
Lena
Donets'k
Volga
Chelyabinsk
Omsk
Krasnoyarsk
Amur
Svobodnyy
Black Sea
Rostov
Volgograd (Stalingrad)
Novosibirsk
Lake Baikal
Irkutsk
Blagoveshchensk
◉ GEORGIA
Akmola
◉ ARMENIA
Groznyy
Tbilisi
KAZAKHSTAN
Karaganda
Vladivostok
Yerevan
Caspian Sea
Aral Sea
Altai Mountains
MONGOLIA
CHINA
Baku
UZBEKISTAN
Lake Balkash
Sea of Japan
◉ AZERBAIJAN
Dashkhovuz
Almaty
TURKMENISTAN
Bukhara
Tashkent
Bishkek
Ashgabat
Samarkand
KYRGYZSTAN ◉
I R A N
Dushanbe
TAJIKISTAN ◉
AFGHANISTAN

0   1000 km
0   1000 miles

N

Raising the Iron Curtain

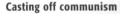

A new Hungary
Citizens wave pro-democracy banners as the Republic of Hungary is proclaimed on October 23, 1989—the anniversary of the 1956 Hungarian Uprising against the Soviet Union.

Following the defeat of Nazi Germany, tension between the superpowers split Europe into a communist "East" and a capitalist "West." Gorbachev's repeal of the "Brezhnev Doctrine" opened the floodgates for popular demands for reform, leading to the dismantling of the Iron Curtain across Eastern Europe.

It was the former British prime minister Winston Churchill (see pp.392–93) who likened the division of East and West in 1946 to "an iron curtain descended across the Continent." Inhabitants of Eastern Europe were prohibited from crossing into the West, and most people knew little about the way of life on the other side. The first indications that the curtain might rise came in 1985, when Mikhail Gorbachev was appointed General Secretary of the Soviet Communist Party. Gorbachev proposed to set Russia on a new course (see pp.446–47), but his vision required a transformation in East–West relations.

In 1983, US president Ronald Reagan's decision to fund a space-based missile defense system, known as Star Wars, suggested a continuing escalation of the arms race (the competitive stockpiling of more and more powerful weapons), but in 1986 Gorbachev stunned the international community with a call to eliminate all nuclear weapons by the year 2000. This move led to the Intermediate-Range Nuclear Forces (INF) Treaty in 1987—a first step toward dismantling the super-powers' massive nuclear arsenals.

Gorbachev's role in reversing the arms race won him worldwide acclaim. In 1988 he went on to push through his most radical reform of Soviet foreign policy: the abandonment of the "Brezhnev Doctrine," which prohibited Eastern Bloc (see BEFORE) and other satellite countries from reforming their political systems. This doctrine had led to military intervention in Czechoslovakia in 1968 and Afghanistan in 1979 (see pp.444–45).

Casting off communism

With the threat of Soviet interference removed, communist governments found it difficult to keep control.

A wave of popular protest developed within the Eastern Bloc countries, calling for an end to communist rule. By 1989, East Germany was faced with a rapidly depleting workforce as thousands of citizens decamped to West Germany via Hungary and Czechoslovakia. In November the government agreed to open its borders with West Germany, and

citizens poured across the border to greet their former countrymen. In 1990 politicians on both sides agreed to the reunification of Germany.

Solidarity wins out

In Poland, popular desire for change led to the emergence of the Solidarity Trade Union Movement in the early 1980s. The movement demanded workers' rights and the freedom to practice Catholicism—banned

BEFORE

As the Cold War intensified, the Soviet Union acted to increase its control of political policy in the satellite Eastern Bloc states.

EUROPE DIVIDED
After World War II, **new national boundaries were created and countries divided** as the victorious Allies determined the future shape of Europe. Stalin ensured that the Soviet Union incorporated eastern Poland and the Baltic States. **Germany and its capital, Berlin, were divided** into Eastern and Western sectors **≪ 426–27**.

COMMUNISM IN EASTERN EUROPE
By 1949, communist regimes had been established in Albania, Romania, Hungary, Bulgaria, Czechoslovakia, Poland, and East Germany. Although nominally independent, these nations were **dominated by the Soviet Union.** Collectively known as the **Eastern Bloc**, these Soviet satellite states were required to **mirror Soviet political structures** and to join the Soviet military alliance, the **Warsaw Pact**.

SOVIET IMPERIALISM
The Soviet Union did not tolerate rebellion or divergence from its party line. In 1953, Soviet troops suppressed riots and a general strike in East Germany, and when, in 1956, discontent with the Hungarian communist government led to nationwide revolt, the uprising was crushed with massive military force. In 1968, during a period known as the "**Prague Spring,**" Czechoslovakia introduced liberalizing measures. Forces from the Warsaw Pact invaded and reestablished communist party discipline.

Romanian revolution
People shelter behind army tanks in Bucharest during Eastern Europe's most violent transition to democracy. More than 1,000 Romanians were killed in clashes between demonstrators and security forces.

Turbulent times
A revolutionary holds a Romanian flag, the communist symbol defiantly torn from its center, and looks down on Palace Square in Bucharest, days before the overthrow of Ceaușescu's regime in December 1989.

DECISIVE MOMENT

THE FALL OF THE BERLIN WALL

The Berlin Wall was the most famous physical manifestation of the Iron Curtain. The East German government built the wall in 1961 to prevent skilled workers from crossing into West Berlin to work, describing it as an "anti-Fascist Protective Rampart." For the next 30 years movement of citizens between West and East was highly restricted. During this time it has been claimed that as many as 200 people were shot by East German guards as they tried to escape to the West. In the 1970s and 1980s, graffiti artists covered the western side of the wall with paintings and slogans protesting at the division of Berlin. On November 9, 1989, when the abandonment of border controls was announced, tens of thousands of celebrating Berliners converged on the wall. Over the following days, the city's inhabitants began to dismantle the wall with their own hands.

The transition to democracy triggered nationalist conflicts and economic hardship.

WAR IN YUGOSLAVIA
In 1992, waves of nationalist sentiment led to the violent dismemberment of the communist Federation of Yugoslavia **450–51 »**.

NATO IN EASTERN EUROPE
NATO 397 » has expanded since the fall of communism to include most former Warsaw Pact countries. Consultations on international security are held between NATO and non-members, including Russia and Ukraine.

THE ORANGE REVOLUTION
Thousands **took to the streets of Kiev**, Ukraine, to protest the disputed election in 2004. This forced a revote that brought pro-EU leader Viktor Yushchenko to power, but five years later the Orange coalition had collapsed and he was defeated in presidential elections by his former opponent from 2004.

CAMPING OUT IN KIEV

> "People have passed through a very dark tunnel at the end of which **there was a light**..."

VACLAV HAVEL, CZECH PRESIDENT, 1990

under the communist regime. The communist government attempted to repress Solidarity, but, by 1989, was forced to accept more open elections. Solidarity was elected as Poland's largest governing party by a huge majority, and its founder, Lech Walesa, served as president from 1990 to 1995.

Democracy spreads
1989 also saw the "Velvet Revolution" in Czechoslovakia, when mass protests secured the overthrow of the communist government. Alexander Dubček, hero of the Prague Spring (see BEFORE), was brought back from political isolation to serve in a new federal parliament. Hungary and Bulgaria also made peaceful transitions to democracy in the early 1990s. The Hungarian communist government tried offering reforms while maintaining a one-party system, but popular pressure led to the declaration of the Third Hungarian Republic and the promise of multi-party elections. Both Hungary and Bulgaria became parliamentary democracies in 1990.

Violent overthrow
Romania's communist leader, Nicolae Ceauşescu, ran a particularly repressive and ruthless regime. His overthrow in 1989 is the one instance of violent revolution during this period. Ceauşescu was arrested and subsequently shot by the army. He was succeeded by Ion Iliescu, a former member of the communist regime. Iliescu, a dominant political figure in Romania since the revolution, helped develop a brand of democratic socialism that retains some policies from the communist era. The last Eastern Bloc state to adopt parliamentary democracy was Albania, in 1992. Charges of corruption and economic mismanagement followed, but by 2007 that country seemed to be progressing toward full democracy.

CZECH WRITER AND STATESMAN (1936–)

VACLAV HAVEL

Born into a wealthy and cultured family, Havel's "bourgeois" roots meant that he was not entitled to a university education. In the 1960s Havel's first plays were produced on stage, but his work became increasingly subversive and he was imprisoned for dissent. Havel was elected president of Czechoslovakia after the Velvet Revolution. Profoundly convinced that a politician should follow his individual conscience, his decisions as president were often controversial. Havel resigned in 1992, but was reelected in 1993 and remained in office until 2003.

War in Yugoslavia

In 1991, Yugoslavia was torn apart by a dramatic and violent civil war, which ended with its breakup. The world witnessed some of the worst atrocities committed since World War II, NATO faced its gravest challenge concerning a sovereign nation, and Bosnia was transformed into a killing field.

« BEFORE

Yugoslavia did not exist until after the end of World War I. Unification came about as Serbs called for a "land of the south Slavs."

BIRTH OF A NATION

The Kingdom of Yugoslavia was formed out of the ashes of the **Austro-Hungarian Empire** in 1918 **« 372–73**. It included the formerly independent kingdoms of Serbia and Montenegro as well as the former Austro-Hungarian territories of Croatia, Slovenia, and Bosnia-Herzegovina.

JOSIP TITO'S DICTATORSHIP

Yugoslavia was invaded by Nazi Germany in World War II **« 392–405**. But the Germans faced **fierce resistance** from Yugoslav **communist partisans**, a resistance force under **Josip Tito**. Thanks to their ruthless tactics, and a flow of Russian, British, and American aid, Tito's partisans emerged at the end of the war as masters of the country.

In 1946, Tito reorganized the state into **six socialist republics**: Serbia, Croatia, Slovenia, Montenegro, Macedonia, and Bosnia-Herzegovina. There were also two semiautonomous regions within Serbia: Kosovo and Vojvodina. Until his death in 1980, Tito ruled Yugoslavia as a **one-party dictatorship**.

JOSIP TITO

DISINTEGRATION OF YUGOSLAVIA

For the rest of the 1980s, Yugoslavia was ruled by a committee composed of the presidents of the six republics and two regions. The country slipped into **economic crisis**, and **national and ethnic rivalries** between the republics intensified.

By the end of the 1980s, Communism was in a state of collapse across Europe **« 448–49**. In 1990 the republics held multi-party elections, which further inflamed the ethnic tensions.

The collapse of communism in Europe in the 1980s encouraged the growth of nationalism in all the Yugoslav republics (see BEFORE). In 1990, in the first multi-party elections held in Yugoslavia after the end of the communist era, both Slovenia and Croatia elected nationalist governments and national groups demanded independence throughout Yugoslavia. In Serbia, however, Slobodan Milosevic opposed these calls. As president of the largest of the Yugoslav republics, Milosevic was determined to maintain the unity of greater Yugoslavia, with Serbia as the dominant power.

For and against
A Bosnian poster calls the Bosnian Serb leader Karadzic a war criminal (left), but a protester demands Serbian leader Milosevic's release from jail, in 2001 (above).

Initial conflicts

Serbia's political posturing soon turned into violence. In 1989, Milosevic began a crackdown on the politically assertive Albanian Muslim majority in Kosovo, a semi-independent region in southern Serbia. In 1991, when the republic of Slovenia declared its independence from Yugoslavia, the Serb-dominated Yugoslav army intervened to prevent it from seceding. The Yugoslav army was badly prepared and had to withdraw, but when the Croatian republic also claimed independence, the Yugoslav army under Milosevic launched a full-scale offensive. The city of Vukovar in eastern Croatia was destroyed, and Serbs began mass executions of Croat men. International response was limited. The US officially recognized Slovenia and Croatia's independence, but did not intervene in the conflict. In late 1992, the United Nations (see right) brokered a ceasefire between the Serbs and the Croats.

War in Bosnia

Bosnia was the most ethnically diverse of the six Yugoslav republics, with 43 percent of the population Bosnian Muslim, 31 percent Serbian, and 17 percent Croatian. This ethnic mix proved extremely divisive: Bosnian Muslims and Croats favored independence, but Bosnian Serbs preferred to remain a part of the wider Yugoslavia. In 1992, following a referendum that was boycotted by the Bosnian Serbs, Bosnia declared itself independent from Yugoslavia.

Milosevic's Serbian forces responded by attacking the non-Serb population of Bosnia, and Bosnian Serbs laid siege to the capital Sarajevo. Many Bosnian Muslims were imprisoned in harsh Serb-run prison camps and Muslim women raped. The international media began to use the term "ethnic cleansing" to describe the systematic expulsion and killing of ethnic and religious groups as practiced by the Serbs in Bosnia.

The siege of Sarajevo
Under siege from Bosnian Serbs, the mainly Bosnian Muslim civilians of Sarajevo struggled for survival. Water, medicine, and food were in short supply. The threat from snipers was constant and venturing into the streets perilous. A ceasefire was declared in late 1995, although the siege was not officially lifted until February 1996.

> **"Our time… has shown us that man's capacity for evil knows no limits."**
> KOFI ANNAN, UNITED NATIONS SECRETARY GENERAL, 1997

DEMISE OF YUGOSLAVIA

From the initial calls for independence in 1991 to the peace accord in 1995, Yugoslavia was scene of many bloody battles and human rights violations.

January 1992 Macedonia declares independence.

April 1992 Bosnia and Herzegovina declare independence.

August 1993 Shocking **photographs** emerge of emaciated Muslims held in Bosnian Serb **prison camps**.

April–May 1993 UN Security Council declares six **"Safe Areas"** for Bosnian Muslims.

February 1994 Mortar explodes in a Sarajevo market; 68 killed and nearly 200 wounded, prompting international calls for military intervention against Serbs.

August–September 1995 US leads **NATO bombing campaign** in response to the horrors of Srebrenica, targeting Serbian military positions.

December 1995 Bosnia, Serbia, and Croatia sign the **Dayton Peace Accord** to end the war in Bosnia.

1991	1992	1993	1994	1995

June 1991 Slovenia and **Croatia declare independence** from Yugoslavia.

July 1991 Milosevic's **Serbian forces invade Croatia;** the city of Vukovar is bombarded and reduced to rubble.

April 1992 Open warfare begins as Bosnian Serbs commence four-year-long **siege of Sarajevo**.

1993–1995 Lack of military intervention by international community allows Serbs in Bosnia to commit **genocide** against Bosnian Muslims.

February 1994 NATO jets **shoot down four Serb aircraft** for violating UN no-fly zone.

July 1995 Serbs under command of General Ratko Mladic kill 8,000 men and boys in **Srebrenica** in a policy of "ethnic cleansing".

July 1995 Radovan Karadzic and Ratko Mladic are **indicted for war crimes**.

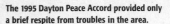

The 1995 Dayton Peace Accord provided only a brief respite from troubles in the area.

AFTERMATH
The Dayton Peace Accord ruled that Bosnia would be **split** into the **Bosnian Serb Republic** and the **Muslim–Croat Federation**. Radovan Karadzic and Ratko Mladic were both indicted for **war crimes**. Karadzic was captured in 2008 to face trial at the Hague, but Mladic remains at large.

KOSOVO
Hundreds of people were injured in ethnic violence in Kosovo following the **Kosovo War** (1996–99). A nervous peace now exists in the region.

WAR CRIMES
Slobodan Milosevic lost the Serbian presidential election in 2000. He refused to accept the result, but was **forced out of office** by strikes and massive protests. He was handed over to a **UN war crimes tribunal** in the Hague, in the Netherlands, and put on trial for **crimes against humanity and genocide**. He spent five years in prison and died of a heart attack shortly before the trial was concluded.

SERBIA-MONTENEGRO
In February 2003, what remained of Yugoslavia was replaced with a loose federation called **Serbia and Montenegro**. On June 3, 2006 Montenegro formally declared its independence.

IDEAS

UNITED NATIONS

The name "United Nations" was first used in World War II when 26 nations pledged to continue fighting against the Axis Powers: Germany, Italy, and latterly Japan. Based in New York, the United Nations officially came into existence on October 24, 1945, when its charter was ratified by China, France, the Soviet Union, the UK, and the US. The charter gives the UN Security Council the power to take collective action in maintaining international peace and security. Although soldiers deployed by the UN share a uniform, they remain members of their respective armed forces. In July 1998 in Rome, the 120 Member States of the UN adopted a treaty to establish a permanent international criminal court.

Although the international community imposed economic sanctions on Serbia, UN troops in Bosnia were prohibited from using military force. Throughout 1993, confident that the UN would not take military action, Serbs continued to commit atrocities. Over a million people were driven from their homes by Serb forces under Radovan Karadzic, president of the Bosnian Serb Republic.

UN intervention
In 1994, a marketplace in Sarajevo was struck by a Serb mortar shell, killing 68 people. Scenes of the carnage were relayed around the globe, intensifying calls for intervention. The US issued an ultimatum through the North Atlantic Treaty Organization (NATO) demanding that the Serbs withdraw their arms from Sarajevo. The Serbs complied and a NATO-imposed ceasefire was declared.

Diplomatic efforts, however, did not stop Serbs from attacking Muslim towns in Bosnia, many of which had been declared "Safe Havens" by the UN. In

Kosovo
NATO peacekeeping troops clamber through an abandoned house in Kosovo. Forces were sent in following the 1999 war between the Serbian government and Kosovan Albanians fighting for independence from Serbia.

one "Safe Haven" at Srebrenica, UN peacekeeping forces watched helplessly as Serbs under General Ratko Mladic slaughtered an estimated 8,000 men and boys—the worst mass murder in Europe since the end of World War II. Serb forces also took hundreds of UN troops hostage and used them as human shields, chained to military targets.

In August 1995, NATO war planes began a fierce air campaign against Serb troops throughout Bosnia, and the Serb leader Slobodan Milosevic finally agreed to peace talks. Three weeks later the Dayton Peace Accord was declared.

This was not the end of the wars in Yugoslavia, however. Fighting between ethnic Albanian minorities and the Macedonian and Serbian governments continued. In Kosovo, this led to a new NATO bombing campaign in 1999. Eventually, Serb forces withdrew from Kosovo and in 2006 the province formally declared its independence.

BEFORE

World War II left millions in Europe experiencing renewed hardship as governments faced the task of rebuilding their shattered nations. From 1947, US financial aid helped economic recovery.

POSTWAR REPARATIONS

In the aftermath of World War II, European governments **struggled to provide basic necessities** for their populations. Initially, Allied nations demanded reparation (compensation) payments from Germany, in the form of coal and other natural resources. German machinery plants and factories were dismantled and transported to Britain, France, and the Soviet Union. France wanted to ensure that Germany could never rearm again and took administrative control of key industrial regions. Germany faced two years of widespread hunger.

REBUILDING DRESDEN

THE MARSHALL PLAN

In 1947, US secretary of state **General George Marshall** introduced a plan to address **"the dislocation of the entire fabric of the European economy"** by proposing massive, long-term financial aid. Concerned that Communist revolutions in Eastern Europe would soon spread to West Germany and beyond, the ban on German industrial reconstruction was partially withdrawn. Over the next five years, the US poured billions of dollars into rebuilding Western Europe.

GEORGE MARSHALL

Symbol of unity
Twelve gold stars on the blue background of the European flag represent Europe as a whole and the equality of all nations within the union.

United Europe

After two devastating global conflicts, Europe had experienced more suffering than it could bear. In the decades following 1945, Europeans became inspired by a new vision of a united continent, where combined economic and political purpose would make wars between their nations unthinkable.

From 1945, Europeans began to demand reform in domestic government policies; welfare provision, such as free healthcare—an accepted ideal in Sweden by then—became a key feature of legislative changes across much of the continent. Widespread calls for a different approach to foreign relations led to some truly radical changes in political thinking, particularly in Germany and France. Konrad Adenauer, the chancellor of West Germany, skillfully pursued policies of reconciliation with Germany's European neighbors. In 1950, he sanctioned French political strategist Jean Monnet's proposal to integrate the French and German coal and steel industries, ensuring that neither country could rearm without the support of the other. Monnet's strategy, known as the "Schuman Plan," led to the founding of the European Coal and Steel Community (ECSC) in 1951, which pooled the coal and steel resources of France, Germany, Italy, Belgium, Luxembourg, and the Netherlands. Economic cooperation between these six nations was extended in 1957 with the formation of the European Economic Community (EEC), or Common Market. The EEC allowed free movement of goods, services, and labor between member states and developed mutually beneficial joint agricultural, welfare, and foreign trade policies.

Britain and the EEC

Britain rejected the opportunity to become an EEC founder member. However, the economic growth of the six nations soon outstripped that of the UK and, in 1961, Prime Minister Harold Macmillan began negotiations to join. Throughout the 1960s, Britain and the EEC argued over terms of British membership. Britain finally joined in 1973 when the OAPEC oil crisis (see pp.440–41), had precipitated a period

of stagflation—a combination of spiraling inflation, a slowdown in productivity, and rising unemployment. By the end of the decade, the newly elected British prime minister, Margaret Thatcher, was calling for reductions in EEC controls and a return to a free-market economy.

European Union

Continental Europe took a different view, seeking to strengthen rather than relax economic cooperation. In 1986, French President François Mitterrand and German Chancellor Helmut Kohl created the "Single European Act," establishing a single European market. In 1992, the "Maastricht Treaty" renamed the EEC the European Union (EU) and its powers were increased. By 2007 the EU had 27 member states, representing

European Union
German Chancellor Helmut Kohl and French President François Mitterrand after French approval of the Maastricht Treaty in September 1992 moved both men closer to achieving their vision of a united Europe.

494 million people with a combined GDP of $14.5 trillion. Beyond economic success, the EU has built on policies of reconciliation and nations have worked together to achieve unprecedented peace and unity in Europe.

VOTING IN THE COUNCIL OF THE EU
Government ministers from each EU member state vote on legislation, budget, and economic policy. The bigger the country's population, the more votes it has, although there is some weighting to favor less populous countries.

France	29	Bulgaria	10
Germany	29	Sweden	10
Italy	29	Denmark	7
United Kingdom	29	Finland	7
Poland	27	Ireland	7
Spain	27	Lithuania	7
Romania	14	Slovakia	7
Netherlands	13	Cyprus	4
Belgium	12	Estonia	4
Czech Republic	12	Latvia	4
Greece	12	Luxembourg	4
Hungary	12	Slovenia	4
Portugal	12	Malta	3
Austria	10	**Total**	**345**

> "We **never want to wage war again** against each other… That is the most important reason for a **United Europe**."
>
> FORMER GERMAN CHANCELLOR HELMUT KOHL, 1 MAY 2004

BRITISH PRIME MINISTER (1925–)

MARGARET THATCHER

Margaret Thatcher served as prime minister of Britain from 1979 until 1990. Her administration followed a disastrous period of recession in Britain, and Thatcher was elected on the promise of tough measures to improve economic performance. Her attitude to the European Union was famously confrontational, but she signed up for the Single European Act of 1986, which formally established the single European market and closer European political cooperation. Always a controversial figure, Thatcher once declared: "There is no such thing as society." She is remembered by many for bringing radical social and economic change to Britain, but many disliked her for her role in selling off state assets and weakening trade unions.

AFTER

EU governments can be torn between the needs of the union and national interests.

MIGRATION AND RACE RELATIONS
EU membership allows free cross-border movement for workers between most member states. This has led to a large influx of migrant workers from poorer EU states into richer ones, **creating racial tensions** and demands for restrictions from **right-wing political elements** in Britain, France, Germany, and other member nations.

FINANCIAL UNION
Although many countries joined **the euro** (the single currency) in 2002, some EU states have chosen to maintain their own currencies as they fear the **loss of national sovereign rights.**

EUROS

KEY
- EEC members, January 1981
- Joined January 1986
- Admitted October 1990
- Joined January 1995
- Joined May 2004
- Joined January 2007
- Other countries applying for membership

ICELAND

Germany
- **Joined** April 18, 1951
- **Key industry** Car manufacture

Sweden
- **Joined** January 1, 1995
- **Key industry** Forestry

Great Britain
- **Joined** January 1, 1973
- **Key industry** Finance

Faeroe Islands

0   500 km
0   500 miles

N

NORWAY

SWEDEN

FINLAND

IRELAND

UNITED KINGDOM

NETHERLANDS

DENMARK

ESTONIA

LATVIA

LITHUANIA

RUSSIAN FEDERATION

RUSSIAN FEDERATION

BELARUS

BELGIUM

GERMANY

POLAND

UKRAINE

Hungary
- **Joined** May 1, 2004 (festivities above)
- **Key industry** Transport equipment

Bay of Biscay

LUXEMBOURG

LIECHTENSTEIN

FRANCE

SWITZERLAND

AUSTRIA

CZECH REPUBLIC

SLOVAKIA

HUNGARY

MOLDOVA

SLOVENIA

ROMANIA

PORTUGAL

ANDORRA

SPAIN

SAN MARINO

MONACO

Corsica

Balearic Islands

Sardinia

CROATIA

BOSNIA AND HERZEGOVINA

SERBIA

KOSOVO (disputed)

MONT.

ALBANIA

MACEDONIA

BULGARIA

Black Sea

GEORGIA

ARMENIA

GIBRALTAR

Sicily

ITALY

GREECE

TURKEY

IRAQ

SYRIA

MALTA

Crete

CYPRUS

Countries of the EU
The European Union has continued to expand since its origins in 1945. This map shows states that have joined since 1981. Supported by the umbrella of economic unity, newer member states with developing economies hope to emulate the economic growth of the established nations. European industry is successful in areas from agriculture and tourism to finance and fashion.

Portugal
- **Joined** January 1, 1986
- **Key industry** Cork

Spain
- **Joined** January 1, 1986
- **Key industry** Tourism

France
- **Joined** April 18, 1951
- **Key industry** Agriculture

Italy
- **Joined** April 18, 1951
- **Key industry** Fashion

1914–PRESENT

CIVIL RIGHTS LEADER (1918–)

NELSON MANDELA

Nelson Rolihlahla Mandela was born in the Eastern Cape, South Africa. He served a 27-year prison sentence for his part in antiapartheid activities. Released from prison in 1990, he became South Africa's first black president in 1994. Mandela has unrivaled global status as a pioneer for peace and democracy.

"Never, never, and **never again** shall it be that this beautiful land will again experience **the oppression of one by another**..."

NELSON MANDELA, INAUGURAL ADDRESS, MAY 9, 1994

Dr. Hendrik Verwoerd, Prime Minister of South Africa from 1958 to 1966, created a system of apartheid (see right), which embodied his "white supremacist" belief that not all races were equal. His views echoed Adolf Hitler's philosophy of the Aryan master race (see pp.400–01). The extreme inequalities created in South African society under apartheid raised voices of protest not only among blacks, "coloreds," and sections of South Africa's white population, but also internationally.

The struggle
In 1960, 69 people died and 180 were injured when police turned their guns on a nonviolent demonstration organized by the antiapartheid group Pan Africanist Congress (PAC). This massacre in the township of Sharpeville triggered a shift to more militant tactics among activists. In 1961, Nelson Mandela became leader of the military wing of the African National Congress (ANC) political party, beginning a campaign of sabotage targeting government installations. Mandela and other members of the ANC were arrested in 1962 and subsequently sentenced to life imprisonment. At his trial, Mandela spoke of freedom, democracy, and equality for all South Africans. His long imprisonment became a subject of growing international condemnation.

The "Homeland System," introduced in the 1960s, aimed to complete the implementation of apartheid by creating independent homelands where blacks were forced to live. These areas were impoverished rural areas with no real capacity to function as separate states. The relocation of blacks to the homelands

Steve Biko
This 1977 cover of *Drum*, a South African magazine for black issues and culture, features antiapartheid activist Steve Biko. Biko died as a result of beatings sustained in police custody in 1977.

13 PERCENT of the country was divided into 10 homelands.

80 PERCENT of the population lived in these homelands.

meant that they were no longer South African and worked in the country as foreign migrants without citizens' rights.

Apartheid and Beyond

Apartheid was a brutal system that imposed the will of a minority on the majority of the South African population. When it ended in the 1990s, there followed an extraordinary attempt to come to terms with the past, as South Africans of all races cooperated in a process known as "Truth and Reconciliation."

BEFORE

South Africa's ruling powers maintained a divided population for much of 20th century.

THE PRE-APARTHEID ERA
Between 1910 and 1948, the South African Government pursued measures to deprive blacks and "coloreds" (those of mixed racial origins) of the right to vote or to own land. Acts such as the **Native Urban Areas Act** of 1923 resulted in "surplus" blacks being removed from cities, creating many "whites-only" areas.

THE NATIONAL PARTY
In 1948 the uncompromisingly **racist National Party** rose to power in South Africa and adopted a policy of "apartheid"

(see right), a legal system that completely segregated (separated) the political, social, and cultural lives of white and black South Africans.

APARTHEID LAW
Early apartheid measures included "blood laws," such as the Immorality Act and Population Registration Act (1950), which banned intermarriage and sexual relations between races. Public transportation and amenities were divided into **separate areas for whites and blacks**, and segregation of the education system and employment ensured that blacks had no prospects other than menial low-paid work.

OFFICIAL SEGREGATION

WHITES COLOUREDS
BLANKE SKLEURLINGE

| APARTHEID A policy of segregation and discrimination against the nonwhite population of South Africa. The term is from the Afrikaans for "separateness."

As the 1970s and 1980s progressed, violence escalated, including violence between rival black factions such as the ANC and the Inkatha Freedom Party. All dissent was suppressed by a police force and military who habitually committed atrocities, including torture. In 1986 the international community imposed economic sanctions on South Africa in an attempt to force an end to apartheid but, even with the majority of whites now opposed to the system, the government still failed to respond with significant reform.

A new beginning
It took a new administration to open the way for change. President F.W. de Klerk was elected in 1989 and lifted bans on the ANC and other opposition groups. On February 11, 1990, Nelson Mandela was released. Mandela and de Klerk achieved the transition of South Africa to democratic majority rule under difficult circumstances. They faced different views from tribal and political factions within the black community and opposition to change from some whites. Their solution was

to adopt a unified approach, and in 1994 Nelson Mandela was elected president of South Africa, becoming head of the Government of National Unity in which minority parties, including vice-president de Klerk's National Party, were represented.

The new government recognized that if unity was to be achieved between its divided communities, it must take action. The antiapartheid campaigner Archbishop Desmond Tutu was appointed head of the Truth and Reconciliation Commission (TRC), which was a historic attempt to address the violence and human rights abuses of the apartheid era. Over a three-year period the commission heard the testimonies of both the victims and the perpetrators of crimes. Although never intended as an instrument of punishment, the TRC

bore witness to the suffering of victims and could grant perpetrators amnesty from possible prosecution. In 1998 the TRC published its findings. Atrocities committed by all sections of society were condemned, including the actions of the black vigilante group Mandela United Football Club, led by Nelson Mandela's former wife, Winnie.

The extraordinary ambition of the TRC was to heal the wounds of a brutal past by acknowledging their truth. South African willingness to engage in this process won the nation worldwide respect. In his response to the commission's findings, Nelson Mandela called on people to "celebrate and strengthen what we have done as a nation as we leave our terrible past behind us forever."

Act of defiance
Archbishop Desmond Tutu addresses a gathering of the Defiance Campaign against Unjust Laws in Cape Town, in 1988. Many "defiers" were imprisoned for peaceful protest

ANC logo
On the flag, black represents those who fought for freedom; green, the land reclaimed from oppressors; and gold, South Africa's natural wealth. The shield and spear represent the early years of struggle, and the wheel is a symbol of unity.

The apartheid system has disappeared, but its effects are still felt in South Africa.

LEGACIES IN SOUTH AFRICA
The majority of the poor are black and the bulk of property remains in white ownership. The government, led since 1999 by **Thabo Mbeki**, has introduced various measures to create greater equality.

THABO MBEKI

ROLE IN AFRICA
South Africa's foreign policy now aims to **promote the economic, political, and cultural regeneration of Africa**, through the New Partnership for African Development (NEPAD). South Africa has also played an active role in seeking an end to crises in Burundi and the Democratic Republic of Congo.

AIDS
One of the major challenges facing South Africa is an **HIV/AIDS epidemic 464–65 »**, which is decimating the economically active population.

AIDS AWARENESS RIBBON

Freedom day
On April 27, 1994, millions of South Africans lined up to exercise their newly won right to vote in the first free election held after apartheid. A government of National Unity was elected.

Car manufacture
This is a highly automated production line at the Hyundai car plant in South Korea. Founded in 1947, the hugely successful Hyundai Group is a South Korean conglomerate that has pioneered robotic engineering techniques in car production.

Tiger Economies

After World War II, Japan made economic reforms, establishing itself as one of the world's richest nations. Similar economic transformations occurred in South Korea, Taiwan, Hong Kong, and Singapore, who are known collectively as the "tiger economies" or "Asian tigers."

« BEFORE

Japan's drive for growth led to the invasion of China and involvement in World War II.

THE MODERNIZATION OF JAPAN
Japan's **Meiji Restoration** « **356–57** triggered economic and social change in late-19th-century Japan. Increased trade with the West led to an era of rapid industrialization.

CONFLICT WITH CHINA
During the **Great Depression** « **384–85,** loss of foreign capital and raw material imports badly affected Japanese industry. The acquisition of

JAPANESE TROOPS, 1931

territories on the Asian mainland came to be seen as essential for economic survival. In 1931, Japan occupied the Chinese province of Manchuria. In 1937, a clash between Chinese and Japanese troops escalated into a renewed Sino-Japanese War.

JAPAN IN WORLD WAR II
In 1941, Japan began extending its empire in East Asia and the Pacific. After bombing **Pearl Harbor** « **402–03,** it invaded Indonesia, Burma, and other territories held by Europeans.

Worsening postwar relations between the Allies and the Soviet Union (see pp.406–07) combined with the rise of communist movements in territories including Vietnam, Korea, and Malaya (see pp.412–13), led many in the West to fear communist takeover in Asia and the Pacific. These fears increased when ongoing civil conflict in China ended with the founding of Mao Zedong's Communist People's Republic in 1949 (see pp.424–25). The new anxieties of the Cold War era led the US to provide economic support to noncommunist governments in the region.

The rise of Japan
After World War II, Allied forces led by US General MacArthur occupied Japan. for six years. MacArthur worked with Japanese Prime Minister Shigeru Yoshida to develop a blueprint for the future of Japan, drafting a new democratic constitution and reforming political and legal structures. Japan was barred from maintaining armed forces of its own; all energy was focused on rebuilding its economic potential. After the outbreak of the Korean War in 1950 (see pp.406–07), large US orders for Japanese-manufactured arms boosted

Japanese yen
The yen is the currency of Japan. First introduced by the Meiji government in 1870, the modern Japanese yen has a stable reputation and is widely chosen alongside the US dollar for foreign exchange reserves.

the economy. Although the US occupation was a time of economic privation for many Japanese, much of the country's later prosperity was based on the access granted to the American market, an arrangement that continued after occupation ended in 1952. From the mid-1950s, Japan's economy entered a period of rapid growth. Having established the heavy industries—coal, steel, and energy production—the government began to support development of shipbuilding and car manufacture. Through the 1960s industrial emphasis shifted to high-tech production of cameras and video recorders; and electronic devices using new microchip technology, including computers. Global companies such as Sony, Toyota, and Nissan emerged.

In spite of setbacks during the 1973 Oil Crisis (see pp.440–41) and a period of recession in the 1990s, Japan's

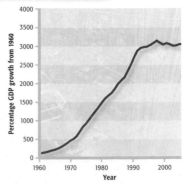

Japanese growth
This graph shows the astonishing growth in Japan's economy by charting the gross domestic product (GDP), which is the sum of the market value of all the goods produced within the country, from the 1960s.

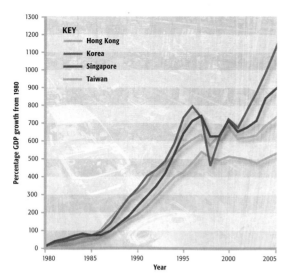

Rise of the tiger economies

The tiger economies grew rapidly from the 1980s but all suffered a drop after the Asian financial crisis of the late 1990s, as shown by the GDP growth charted left. All made a quick recovery, particularly Korea.

economy now ranks second only to that of the US. This transformation has been called miraculous, but was in fact the result of efficient government control of finance. Industries were systematically targeted for development, government loans made available to fledgling companies, and competition from foreign imports restricted. For many years postwar, economic growth was an absolute priority and expenditure in other areas, such as housing, was severely restricted. However, successive governments did prioritize education and Japan's skilled workforce has contributed to the success and technical excellence of Japanese products.

Asian tigers

Since the 1960s, South Korea, Taiwan, Singapore, and Hong Kong have achieved economic

growth of such speed that it earned them the nickname "tiger." The Asian tigers are among the only former territories of colonial empire to have substantially closed their income gap with established industrialized nations. A range of measures, including the creation of government banks, subsidized credit for industry, and incentives for foreign investors, fostered export-driven markets, where the marriage of foreign technology with cheap labor produced goods at reduced cost.

The tiger economies' dependence on exports makes them reliant on the behavior of the economies they supply. In 1997, the Asian financial crisis occurred when foreign investors withdrew funds from Thailand. The crisis deepened when investors panicked, thinking that if one country's economy was failing, then others must be affected, and rushed to dump Asian assets. Within months the crisis spread across the entire region.

Within a few years the markets rallied and fears of a long recession faded. The economic rise of South Korea began with an emphasis on light

Singapore Harbor
Cranes and cargo ships line Singapore City's bustling industrial waterfront. In the background stand the towers of the city's business district.

industry in the early years of growth, and shifted toward car manufacture and consumer electronics in the 1970s. The Asian financial crisis caused the collapse of South Korea's major car manufacturer KIA Motors, but assistance from the International Monetary Fund (IMF) and market-orientated reforms restored stability. In 2007, South Korea rose to become the world's ninth-largest economy. However, questions remain about South Korea's long-term prospects. An increasingly educated labor force is rising up against the regime's repressive labor laws. Commentators suggest that liberalizing reforms are needed to ensure continued growth.

In the 1950s, Taiwan, an island off the Chinese mainland, was a largely agricultural economy. From 1962, economic reforms encouraged industrial development and attracted foreign investment. Taiwan received support from the US, which was eager to bolster the regime against the threat of takeover by Communist China. Initially most of Taiwan's output was from labor-intensive industries such as textiles, but in the 1980s, focus shifted to production of high-tech products. Today Taiwan's economy dominates global production of computers.

After gaining independence from Britain in 1965, Singapore's government adopted an export-oriented policy framework, to encourage foreign investment. The strategy resulted in growth of 8 percent per year between 1960 and 1997. A skilled workforce and efficient infra-structure have attracted investment from over 7,000 multinational corporations, who account for over two-thirds of manufacturing output and direct export sales. Fields of production include electronics and pharmaceuticals.

Hong Kong was a British colony from 1842 to 1997. After 1950, the territory followed a similar pattern of industrialization, going on to become a market leader in toys and electronic equipment. Since 2005, the growing confidence of the Hong Kong stock exchange has been cementing its status as a financial hub in Southeast Asia.

Second wave

In the late 20th century, the Four Tigers were nearing fully developed economic status. Investment in education and training had created skilled, educated workforces who

INVENTION

BULLET TRAIN

The Japanese *Shinkansen* or Bullet Train was one of the earliest high-speed trains. Services started in 1964, running at speeds of up to 131 mph (210 km/h). Operated by Japan Railways, the trains run between most major Japanese cities, achieving speeds of up to 186 mph (300 km/h). Current research is aimed at reducing the noise of the trains, which create a loud boom on entering tunnels.

required better wages and working conditions, and investors began to turn to other Asian countries—Thailand, Malaysia, and Indonesia—in search of continued profits. During the 1990s, strong export-dependent economies evolved in these nations, securing foreign investment. Thailand and Indonesia were badly affected by the 1997 financial crisis. Since then, both governments have pursued "dual track" economic measures, which prioritize the development of domestic industry, as well as export-oriented production. At present, the new tigers all show rapid growth, and Malaysia seeks to emulate the original tigers by improving education and refocusing the economy toward higher-technology production.

Towering success
A symbol of Malaysia's economic miracle, the Petronas Towers in Kuala Lumpur, Malaysia, were designed by the architect Cesar Pelli and built in 1995–98. They are among the world's tallest buildings.

AFTER ››

The term "tiger" is adopted by other nations with rapid economic growth, but the impact of such growth on workers raises concerns.

LOW-WAGE WORKERS

Asian tiger governments have been accused of running their economies in the sole interests of investors, resulting in low pay for workers. A World Bank report noted that they were "less responsive than other developing economy governments" to having a minimum wage.

ASEAN

Founded in 1967 with five members, the Association of South East Asian Nations has grown to encompass almost all of Southeast Asia, increasingly adopting policies to produce a single market in the region. Rapid economic growth, particularly in Malaysia, Thailand, and Singapore, has allowed enormous strides in development.

Scientific discovery has always pushed back the frontiers of knowledge and solved pressing human problems, but technological progress also raises serious ethical dilemmas—from the morality of genetic technology, to questions of regulation, such as censorship of the Internet, or the ecological damage generated by industrialization. Scientific inventions have often generated changes undreamt of by their makers. Albert Einstein (see pp.416–17), the brilliant physicist who formulated the Theory of Relativity, saw his discovery used to create the atomic bomb. He later remarked, "It has become appallingly obvious

> "Almost everything that **distinguishes the modern world** from earlier centuries is attributable to **science.**"
>
> BERTRAND RUSSELL, BRITISH PHILOSOPHER, "A HISTORY OF WESTERN PHILOSOPHY," 1945

that our technology has exceeded our humanity."

Aerospace

Space travel is perhaps the greatest symbol of technological progress in the modern age. The race between the two opposing Cold War (see pp.406–07) superpowers, the US and the Soviet Union, for supremacy in space

gathered pace in the late 1950s and ended when Soviet astronaut Yuri Gagarin successfully orbited Earth in 1961. The next goal was to put a man on the Moon. This was achieved in 1969 when the US Apollo 11 spacecraft landed on the Moon, and millions across the world watched astronauts Neil Armstrong and Buzz Aldrin step onto the lunar surface. In 1975, the superpowers adopted a policy of cooperation and simultaneously launched crewed spacecraft, a mission known as the Apollo–Soyuz Test Project.

Volkswagen Beetle
The "Beetle" was first produced in Germany in 1938 as Adolf Hitler's affordable "people's car." Production of the classic VW Beetle peaked at 1.3 million in 1971 and ceased in 2003. It remains an icon of twentieth-century design.

NUCLEAR FISSION

Nuclear fission occurs when the nucleus of an atom splits into two or more smaller nuclei. It is used in the production of nuclear power and weapons. Scientists Otto Hahn and Fritz Strassman discovered the process during research carried out in 1938–39. In 1942, a team led by Enrico Fermi created the first controlled self-sustaining nuclear chain reaction. With World War II raging, governments funded scientists to develop an atomic bomb. In the US, physicist Robert Oppenheimer led the Manhattan Project, which built the bombs used on Japan (see p.405).

Modern Technology

Technological advances continue to transform daily life. Today we can understand the workings of the universe down to its tiniest particles and change the nature of living organisms. We live longer and travel farther and faster than the most optimistic of inventors would have predicted in earlier centuries.

Uses for smart alloys are being investigated by the aircraft industry, seeking ways to improve aircraft maneuverability, and by the medical profession—for example, by incorporating flexibility into the metal plates and pins that are used to support broken limbs while they heal.

Progress in the understanding of natural polymers (compounds made up of simple repeating molecular units), led to the development of synthetic polymers, which are used in plastic-based materials such as Plexiglas, polythene, and many modern textile fabrics. Commercial production of nylon, the first fiber to be made completely from petrochemicals (substances derived from petroleum), began in 1939. Nylon was the first of a new breed of manufactured fibres, which include polyester, Lycra, and Kevlar. In 1986, microfibers further revolutionized fabric technology, producing materials made from minute filaments that are as

⟪ BEFORE

Scientific discoveries have at times caused controversy, but advances in radio, computing, and new materials in the 19th century made future breakthroughs possible.

SCIENCE AND ETHICS
Throughout history, the scientist's quest for understanding has led many into serious trouble. In 1633, the Catholic Inquisition tried **Galileo** ⟪ 268–69 for heresy for suggesting that Earth moves around the Sun. **Charles Darwin's theories of evolution** ⟪ 340–41 challenged "creationist" views that God created the world, triggering a huge debate ⟪ 342–43.

COMPUTERS
In 1801, **Joseph Jacquard** invented a power loom, which could base its weave on patterns read from punched wooden cards. **Charles Babbage** ⟪ 344 built on this concept in the 1830s, to create the **difference calculator,** which could store and calculate numbers. In 1890,

BAKELITE TELEPHONE

Herman Hollerith used punchcard techniques in the Hollerith Desk, a prototype computer.

SYNTHETIC MATERIALS
Many materials used in modern technology were invented in the 19th century, including parkesine, the first manufactured plastic, in 1855, and cellulose triacetate, the earliest synthetic fiber, in 1869, a forerunner of rayon, nylon, and polyester. In 1907 Leo Baekeland created the first plastic made from synthetic materials and named it Bakelite.

TRANSATLANTIC RADIO

In 1901, **Guglielmo Marconi** ⟪ 344–45, inventor of the radio-telegraph system, made the first transatlantic radio transmission, across a distance of 2,100 miles (3,400 km).

MARCONI

Subsequent collaborations have included the European Space Station, *Mir,* and the International Space Station, which draws on the scientific and technological resources of 16 nations.

New materials
Most modern manufactured items are made from materials specially developed to be durable, portable, and efficient. The production of so-called "smart materials" has had a big impact in recent times. Smart materials have the capacity to alter their properties when external conditions change. They include smart alloys or "shape memory alloys," metals that "remember" their own geometry and can return to their original shape after being distorted.

First views of the moon
An American boy watches as the first televised pictures of the Moon's surface are beamed back to Earth in March 1965. The Ranger 9 uncrewed probe showed viewers unprecedented images of the lunar terrain.

⟫

Apollo rocket
At 9:32 am on July 16, 1969 a plume of flame signals liftoff of the Apollo 11 Saturn V space vehicle. US astronauts Neil Armstrong, Michael Collins, and Buzz Aldrin leave the Kennedy Space Center, heading for the Moon.

tough and resilient as other synthetics but much thinner and lighter. The lightness and durability of microfibers was first used in suits for astronauts, but is now found in sportswear. This trend for "high end" technology to filter down into everyday life is common. The polymer Teflon—discovered accidentally during a refrigeration experiment—is used to insulate coat bullets, but also forms the surface of a nonstick frying pan.

Technology in everyday life

Breakthrough inventions of the 20th and early 21st centuries have entered everyday usage as a result of mass production techniques. The invention of household machines has led to an increase in leisure time in developed countries and the very concept of progress has become synonymous with the ready availability of new technology. The development of the microchip has

had a huge impact on the way we communicate since being pioneered by Jack Kilby and Robert Noyce in the 1950s (see p.479). Miniaturized technology combined with the advent of the Internet has provided access to global instant communication.

> "The only way to discover the **limits of the possible** is to venture a little past them into the **impossible.**"
>
> ARTHUR C. CLARKE, WRITER, 1962

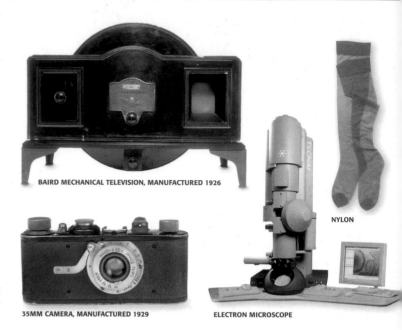

BAIRD MECHANICAL TELEVISION, MANUFACTURED 1926

35MM CAMERA, MANUFACTURED 1929

NYLON

ELECTRON MICROSCOPE

INVENTIONS
New technologies invented during the last 100 years have changed the world for ever.

1925 John Logie Baird creates the **first mechanical television**, successfully transmitting pictures in his London attic.

1930 Frank Whittle submits his plans for a **turbojet aircraft engine** to the RAF.

1934 Percy Shaw invents the **cat's-eye**, a safety device used in road construction.

1935 Wallace Carrothers and DuPont Labs invent **nylon**, the first truly **manmade fiber**.

1945 The atomic bomb is invented by scientists working on the US Manhattan Project.

1948 The **vinyl LP** is introduced. Records used to be made from glass or zinc. Vinyl improved durability and sound quality.

1954 Chaplin, Fuller, and Parson invent the first **solar panels** using photovoltaic cells to convert the Sun's energy into electrical energy.

1920 ⋯ **1930** ⋯ **1940** ⋯ **1950**

1920 The **electric food mixer** is produced by the Hobart Corporation, providing a smaller version of industrial mixers for use in the home.

1927 The first **flash bulb** is invented by Paul Vierkotter, allowing photographers to take pictures without natural light.

1931 Max Knott and Ernst Ruska invent the first **electron microscope**. It uses electrons to create a magnified image.

1934 Joseph Begun invents the first **tape recorder**, capable of storing and playing back sound.

1940s Carbon fiber is developed in a British laboratory. It is light, durable, and extremely versatile. Modern applications include engineering products and motor sports, sailing, and cycling equipment.

1953 The **portable transistor radio** is invented by Texas Instruments.

1959 Jack Kilby and Robert Noyce invent the **microchip**.

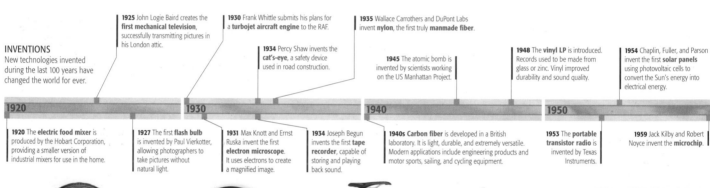

VINYL RECORD

CAT'S-EYE

CARBON FIBER BIKE

AUDIO TAPE PLAYER, MANUFACTURED 1950

ELECTRIC TOASTER, MANUFACTURED 1920

JET ENGINE

ENGINEER (1907–96)

FRANK WHITTLE

Frank Whittle joined the British Royal Air Force as an aircraft apprentice, at the age of 17. During his training he wrote a thesis proposing that piston aircraft engines be replaced by turbines. In 1936, Whittle set up the company Power Jets Ltd. and developed these ideas, creating the "Gloster Whittle," the first jet engine aircraft to fly in the UK. He worked with engineering manufacturers, such as Rolls Royce, and then became a research professor at the US Naval Academy.

SOLAR PANELS

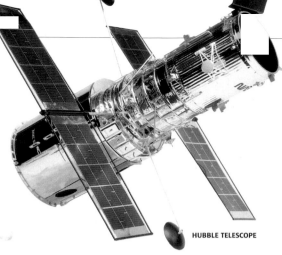
HUBBLE TELESCOPE

Scientists continue to dream of pushing back the realms of possibility in the 21st century.

SPACE EXPLORATION
The **space elevator** is a proposed structure that would consist of a cable anchored to Earth's surface and attached to a counterweight in space. Theoretically, vehicles could climb the cable and escape the planet's gravity without the use of rocket propulsion. Scientists are also pioneering the use of robots, such as the **Mars Exploration Rover**, to explore nearby planets.

MOVING MATTER
Scientists are also developing the process of **quantum tunneling** in the hope of achieving matter transportation.

MARS EXPLORER

ADDING MACHINE, MANUFACTURED 1950S

PORTABLE TRANSISTOR RADIO

DVD

1969 The Concorde flies for the first time. The commercial supersonic airliner entered service in 1976 and set many speed records, including the circumnavigation of the world in 31 hours, 27 minutes and 49 seconds.

1977 The Commodore PET (personal electronic transactor) was one of the first consumer-level computers to be launched, and it revolutionized home computing.

1983 The first cellular phones were sold in the 1980s but were conceived in 1947. At that time the technology required was nonexistent. Newer "smartphones," such as the BlackBerry, have computerlike functions, including email access.

1990 The **Hubble space telescope** is launched into Earth orbit. It has confirmed theories about the birth of planets and produced images of galaxies at various stages of development.

2001 Apple produces the **iPod**, a portable digital audio player. iPods have developed the technical capability to incorporate video and cell-phone technology. The technology was developed further with Apple's iPhone in 2007 and the iPad in 2010.

| 1960 | 1970 | 1980 | 1990 | 2000 |

1967 The first **handheld electronic calculator** provided features of earlier adding machines in a smaller and more portable form.

1980 Philips develops fluorescent energy-saving light bulbs. Low-wattage bulbs use up to 80 percent less energy and last up to 10 times as long as traditional light bulbs.

1983 British inventor James Dyson builds a prototype **cyclone-action vacuum cleaner**, with no dust bag.

1991 Kodak produces the **digital camera system**, having developed solid-state image sensors that converted light into digital pictures.

1995 The **DVD** (digitally versatile disc) is used for data storage, including high-quality sound and moving images.

ELECTRIC FOOD MIXER, MANUFACTURED 1950S

COMMODORE PET PERSONAL COMPUTER

COMPUTER MEMORY BOARD

DYSON VACUUM CLEANER

LOW-WATT LIGHT BULB

DIGITAL CAMERA

BLACKBERRY

APPLE IPOD

CONCORDE

‹‹ BEFORE

Developments in new agricultural techniques—such as the introduction of farm machinery, pesticides, and fertilizers—revolutionized food production in the 19th and early 20th centuries.

THE ADVENT OF MECHANIZATION

By the middle of the 19th century, steam engines were driving **farm machinery**. At the end of the 19th century the development of oil-powered **traction engines** led to a revolution in agricultural methods, allowing greater areas to be

TRACTOR STATION, 1930

farmed by fewer workers. In the Soviet Union, tractor stations rented machines to nearby **collectivized** farms—small peasant holdings that were joined together into vast cooperative farms under Stalin. The policy transformed agricultural production in the USSR **‹‹ 280–81**.

FERTILIZERS AND PESTICIDES

Decline of the natural fertility of the soil was already a major concern in the mid-19th century **‹‹ 290–91**. Both Europe and America had begun to depend on imports of **guano** (dried excrement of fish-eating birds) from South America. Guano improves crop yields by adding nitrogen and phosphorus to soil. The use of **pesticides** also increased during this period, with the discovery of pyrethrum oil and derris, both natural insecticides extracted from plants. Compounds of heavy metals, including copper and arsenic, were used to combat plant diseases.

Feeding the World

In the 1960s a "Green Revolution" in biotechnology boosted agricultural productivity. The efforts of agriculturalists and scientists resulted in improved fertilization and pest controls and the development of specially bred strains of high-yield, disease-resistant crops.

The founding of the United Nations' Food and Agriculture Organization (FAO) in 1945 signaled an international desire to create change in the postwar era through a sharing of knowledge and resources to improve crop performance and eliminate hunger. The FAO focused special attention on rural areas in developing nations, as this is where the majority of the poor and hungry were, and still are, located.

New methods

In the 1940s the biochemist Norman Borlaug (see right) initiated an experimental program to assist

America's breadbasket

Resembling a work of modern art, green crops cover what was once shortgrass prairie in Kansas. The crops are fed from underground water reserves and by circular sprinklers, which cause the round growth pattern.

poor Mexican farmers in increasing their wheat production. Borlaug concentrated on plant breeding. Over a 20-year period he developed a strain of high-yield dwarf wheat that was resistant to a variety of diseases and pests. Borlaug's wheat was cultivated in India and Pakistan with spectacular results. In 1960 the International Rice Research Institute was established in the Philippines to improve the production of rice, the staple diet of much of the world's population. The institute's work has helped rice farmers increase production by an average of 2.5 percent each year since 1965. These transformations in agriculture became known as the Green Revolution. Research continues to develop a range of rice varieties or "cultivars" to suit the needs of different regions including

> **INDIA AND PAKISTAN almost doubled their wheat production between 1965 and 1970.**

New Rice for Africa (NERICA)—a strain of rice suited to Africa's dry ecosystems

In the 1960s the insecticide DDT was the first of a range of new organic chemical insecticides that were widely used for their capacity to control multiple species of pests with a single treatment. These chemicals were put to use in developing countries. However, in 1962 the American biologist Rachel Carson cataloged the environmental impact of spraying DDT and said it may cause cancer. It was eventually banned worldwide. New methods, such as intensive irrigation, were introduced to maximize productivity on poor farming land.

However, the new agricultural methods have generated further problems. Pesticides, especially earlier,

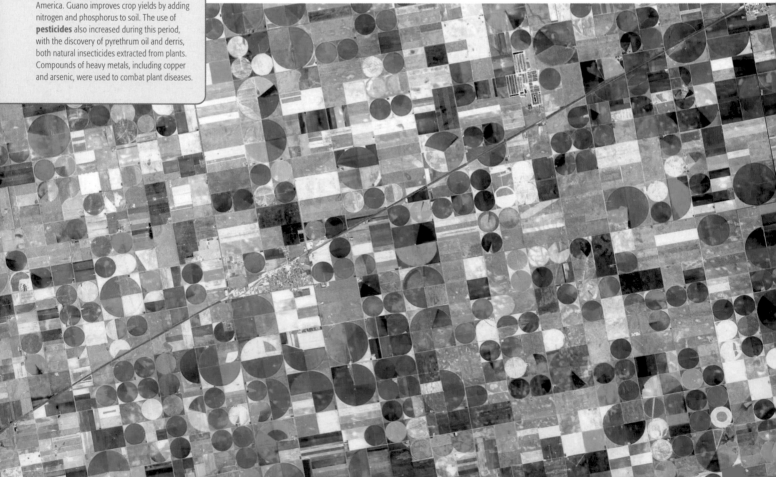

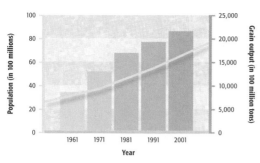

Rising demand
Despite fears that population growth would exceed our capacity to produce food, advances in farming methods have increased the productivity of the land. This graph charts world population against global grain output.

KEY
— Population
▪ Grain

Delivering aid
Drought-stricken Niger, in northwest Africa, faced widespread famine in 2005. Thousands of children died before foreign aid was received.

NORMAN BORLAUG

A key figure in the Green Revolution, Norman Borlaug was born into a farming family in Iowa. Borlaug studied forestry and microbiology before researching crop species and developing a new brand of high-yield wheat (see left). His goal was to feed the hungry people of the world. His groundbreaking work brought him many honors, including the Nobel Peace Prize in 1970.

cruder forms, killed not only the targeted pests but also other insects and organisms that previously acted as natural inhibitors of the pest population. Pests develop resistance to chemical treatments and the same is true of plant diseases. It is not uncommon for new plant varieties to become obsolete in the space of three to four years, which is the time it takes for diseases and insects to adapt and destroy the crop. One serious effect of this problem is that the poorest farmers of the developing world are spending a large percentage of their income on new chemicals as they struggle to combat pest and disease resistance.

Food supply

The distribution of food aid to poorer countries came into practice to combat food shortages after World War II. The Indian famine of 1944 and China's great famine of 1959–61, where 30 million starved to death, triggered an international undertaking to establish secure and sustainable

Rice research
Seedlings for "Golden Rice," a new rice variety modified to contain extra vitamin A, are grown in test tubes at an International Rice Research Institute laboratory.

forms of food supply. Nations producing a food surplus pledged to maintain food supplies in the event of widespread crop failure. The US, the European Union (see pp.452–53), Canada, Japan, and Australia have been the biggest suppliers of food aid, but worldwide demand has often outstripped the ability to supply it.

Food production has matched the growth in worldwide population, but hunger and malnutrition remain a problem in some areas. This is especially the case in Africa, where many people still live in fear of hunger and starvation, and an estimated 200 million people suffer from malnutrition. The governments of many African countries are dependent on food aid. In 2003 climate conditions led to crop failure and famine in southern Africa and in 2006 droughts created crises in Ethiopia, Kenya, and Somalia—stark evidence that the inequalities that the Green Revolution sought to erase persist.

Rising oil prices and a switch to growing biofuels led to big rises in basic food prices from 2007, provoking the "tortilla riots" in Mexico in 2007 and violent protests in many African countries in 2008.

While poorer regions are still dependent on one or two crops for survival, in the developed world an abundance and variety of food are available. Increased incomes have enabled an expanding middle class to adopt high-protein diets, and in the richest nations health risks associated with obesity are a growing problem. Many Western governments have felt compelled to introduce healthier eating initiatives to encourage the consumption of a balanced diet. Concerns have also been raised about the health risks created by chemical residues found in, or added to, produce. This has led to an increased demand for organic food, produced without the use of chemicals or artificial additives.

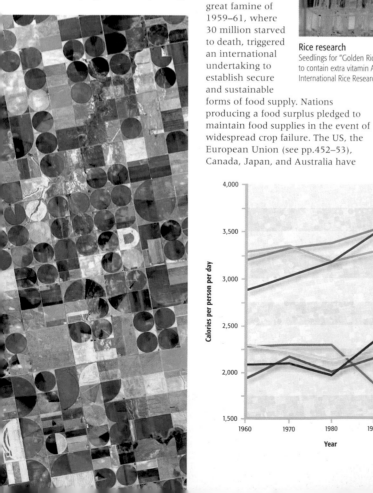

Food consumption
Although total food production has kept pace with the global rise in population (see above), the situation differs from country to country. Poorer nations have far less food available to their growing populations than more developed countries. This is reflected in the daily average caloric consumption (energy consumed from food) per person, as shown in this graph.

KEY
— Central African Republic
— Democratic Republic of Congo
— France
— India
— United Kingdom
— United States
— Vietnam

AFTER ≫

Genetic modification is one of the newest methods of creating stronger crops.

GENETIC MODIFICATION

GMOs are organisms whose genetic material has been modified by adding extra material to generate new and useful **inherited traits**. Developed in the 1990s, the technique was applied to various crops, principally corn and soybeans, but also tomatoes, wheat, and many others, in the hope of **GM FRUIT** creating crops with **better pest resistance**, disease resistance, shelf life, and taste. Concerns have arisen about the effects on **biodiversity** (the variety of species in a given ecosystem) that planting genetically-modified crops could have.

Scientific discoveries and improved sanitation in the 19th century laid the foundations for the medical revolution of the 20th.

SANITATION
In British cities c. 1830, **infant mortality** was about 50 percent–half of all children born died before 5 years of age. Most deaths were caused by water contaminated with sewage. In the second half of the 19th century, sewers were built and water was piped into cities. By 1914, infant mortality was less than 10 percent.

1890S DISINFECTANT ADVERTISEMENT

HOSPITAL HYGIENE
In the 1840s, the Hungarian physician **Ignaz Philipp Semmelweis** noticed that cases of puerperal ("childbed") fever, which killed thousands of mothers after giving birth, were reduced if nurses and doctors washed their hands between handling corpses and treating patients. His discovery led to better hospital hygiene. Carbolic acid was used to sterilize surgical equipment and wounds from the 1860s.

BACTERIA AND DISEASE
In the 1870s and 1880s, the German physician Robert Koch isolated the different bacteria that cause tuberculosis, cholera, and anthrax, allowing more effective **vaccines << 327** to be developed.

VITAMINS
In the early 1900s, scientists investigating the link between **diet and health** identified key nutrients in food. In 1912, **Cashmir Funk** named them "vitamines"; "vita" meaning life, and "amine" from compounds isolated in his experiments.

BRITISH SCIENTIST (1881–1955)

ALEXANDER FLEMING

Born in Scotland, the pharmacologist and biologist Alexander Fleming made huge contributions to the fields of bacteriology, immunology, and chemotherapy. He is famous for isolating the antibiotic substance penicillin from the fungus *Penicillium notatum*. He shared the 1945 Nobel Prize for medicine with Ernst Chain and Howard Florey.

Protecting the troops
Sailors in the British Royal Navy receive inoculations against cholera before deployment overseas during World War I.

World Health

The past century has produced astonishing advances in health and medicine. Some infectious illnesses have been eradicated, but there are still many killer diseases at large, especially in the developing world.

In the first few decades of the 20th century, Dr. Sara Josephine Baker pioneered the education of women in the basic hygiene and dietary care of their children in the slums of New York City. Baker's health education program led to a significant reduction in infant mortality rates, and by the 1950s most industrialized countries had adopted similar measures.

Health education, better sanitation, and rising living standards in industrialized countries combined to produce steady, if unspectacular, improvements in public health. However, some developments were more dramatic. In 1928, Alexander Fleming (see left) found that a rare strain of mold inhibited the growth of bacteria. This discovery enabled him to develop penicillin—an infection-fighting "antibiotic" drug. Mass production of penicillin began in 1945. By the 1950s, antibiotics were providing effective treatments for many terrible diseases, including syphilis, gangrene, and tuberculosis (TB).

In the second half of the 20th century, mass vaccination programs, funded by governments and the World Health Organization (WHO), further reduced

Changing attitudes
A 1950s ad (left) shows Hollywood star and future US president Ronald Reagan promoting cigarettes. Two decades later, a French cancer charity (right) warns of the health risks of smoking to pregnant women and their babies.

mortality rates. In 1980, the WHO announced the global elimination of smallpox. Polio, too, is close to being eradicated; in fact, the general trend for most infectious diseases is downward.

Furthermore, chemotherapy has made huge strides in the fight against cancer, and heart and organ transplants are now commonplace. Perhaps most amazingly, in vitro fertilization (IVF) can allow couples who would previously have been childless to have a family.

Rich and poor
Unfortunately, the great achievements in health care and medicine are not always passed on to the poor. The diphtheria, tetanus, whooping cough (DTP) vaccine has been available since the 1940s, and has largely eradicated these diseases in the developed world. However, in Africa, India, and Eastern Asia, less than 50 percent of children are covered by DTP programs. WHO

statistics show that children in the poorest countries have a mortality rate 2.5 times higher than their counterparts in developed nations.

The greatest killers in the developing world are waterborne illnesses such as typhoid, cholera, dysentery, and even diarrhea. In fact, nearly 40,000 people die each day from drinking water contaminated by sewage. Providing sanitation and clean drinking water is a major challenge for the governments of developing countries. Respiratory diseases such as bronchitis, emphysema, pneumonia, and lung cancer also take a heavy toll. These diseases are often linked to the inhalation of smoke from indoor cooking fires. A simple solution is to provide a smoke hood and a chimney, rather than an open

Global trends in HIV infection
Around 40 million people worldwide (nearly two-thirds of whom live in Africa) are infected with HIV, the virus that causes AIDS. Over 4 million new cases occurred in 2006 alone. "Cocktails" of antiretroviral drugs have improved health and life expectancy for people with HIV.

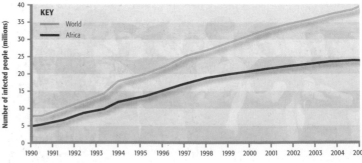

KEY
— World
— Africa

Number of infected people (millions)

40 / 35 / 30 / 25 / 20 / 15 / 10 / 5 / 0

1990 1991 1992 1993 1994 1995 1996 1997 1998 1999 2000 2001 2002 2003 2004 2005

Year

HUMAN GENOME

Genetics is the science of genes and heredity. Inside living cells are chromosomes. These carry genes—"instructions" that determine every aspect of an organism. Chromosomes are long molecules of deoxyribonucleic acid, or DNA. In 2000, scientists announced that they had worked out the structure of the human genome, the sequence of thousands of individual nucleic acids that make up a DNA molecule. Armed with this knowledge, doctors hope to use gene therapy to treat hereditary diseases (genetic disorders).

CHROMOSOMES OF A HUMAN MALE

Flu pandemic
In Seattle, WA, policemen wear protective masks during the outbreak of "Spanish Flu" in 1918. This was the most devastating pandemic in modern history.

3 Deaths per minute are related to inhaling cooking-fire smoke.

25 MILLION children worldwide have been orphaned by AIDS.

43 MILLION US citizens are clinically obese.

fire, but the first priority is education. Public health efforts in rich countries are increasingly focused on excessive consumption of food, alcohol, and tobacco. Incidence of obesity, diabetes, heart disease, and some cancers are seriously stretching healthcare systems.

Disease pandemics
Even if the disparity between health in rich and poor nations is addressed, the world's population will still be at risk from pandemics—epidemics that occur on a global scale. Just after World War I, a pandemic of "Spanish flu" (influenza) killed up to 20 million people—more than the war itself. AIDS (Acquired Immunodeficiency Syndrome), first identified in 1981, has claimed some 25 million lives. In 2009 a flu virus crossed the species barrier from pigs, causing thousands of deaths. "Swine flu," first identified in Mexico, led to a global panic, but petered out without causing the massive death toll initially predicted.

Fears of future pandemics have also been fueled by the fact that the effects of antibiotics on disease have begun to weaken as bacteria develop immunity to drugs. "Superbugs," such as MRSA, are emerging with resistance to even the most powerful antibiotics.

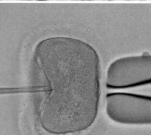

In vitro fertilization (IVF)
The first stage of the IVF artificial insemination process involves injecting sperm into an egg cell (shown above). The fertilized egg is then implanted into a woman's uterus so that a normal pregnancy process can occur.

Cholera in Bangladesh
A father cradles his dying son during the 1971 cholera outbreak in Bangladesh. Lack of sanitation and access to clean drinking water led to the deaths of 6,500 people.

AFTER

Whether it is anticipating new pandemics or battling existing diseases, there are many challenges facing 21st-century medicine.

NEW DRUGS, NEW VACCINES
The rise of **antibiotic-resistant "superbugs"** means that new drugs and treatments will be needed to combat bacterial infection. There is some experimental use of **bacteriophages**, which are viruses that attack bacteria. Other priorities include developing **vaccines against HIV/AIDS** and **malaria**. Malaria kills over 1 million people per year, and in some regions the malaria parasite that causes the disease is growing increasingly resistant to current drug treatments.

BACTERIOPHAGE

ADVANCES IN MEDICINE
Since the 1920s, tremendous advances have been made in medicine and surgery as scientists, researchers, and doctors seek solutions to world health problems.

1932 In Germany, Josef Klarer makes the first **sulfa drugs** (synthetic antibiotics).

1950 In the UK, Richard Doll publishes evidence that **smoking causes lung cancer**.

1960 The world's first internal **"pacemaker,"** a battery-powered device that stimulates and regulates the **human heartbeat**, is successfully implanted.

1967 South African heart surgeon Dr. Christiaan Barnard performs the world's first **human heart transplant** in South Africa.

1978 Louise Brown, the **first IVF child**, is born in the UK.

1990s Highly Active Anti-Retroviral Therapy **(HAART)**, using a "cocktail" of drugs, makes huge strides in suppressing **HIV/AIDS** in infected people.

1998 French surgeons perform the first successful **hand transplant**.

2000 After a decade of international effort, scientists announce that they have mapped the **human genome**—the sequence of nucleic acids in molecules of human **DNA**.

| 1920 | 1930 | 1940 | 1950 | 1960 | 1970 | 1980 | 1990 | 2000 |

1922 Canadian doctors pioneer **insulin treatment for diabetes**.

1928 Alexander Fleming isolates **penicillin**, the first **antibiotic agent**.

1954 The first successful **kidney transplant** is carried out by Joseph Murray in Boston, MA.

1960 The female oral **contraceptive pill** becomes available in the US.

1973 In the UK, Godfrey Hounsfield and Allan Cormack develop the **CAT or CT scan**, which produces X-ray **cross-sections of the body**.

1987 The first successful **lung transplant** is carried out by Joel Cooper in Baltimore, MD.

1990 Gene therapy successfully treats SCID, a rare genetic disorder of the immune system.

2005 Surgeons in France carry out a partial **face transplant**.

9/11

On September 11, 2001, 19 Islamic extremists launched attacks on the World Trade Center in New York City and the Pentagon in Washington, D.C., killing thousands. This strike by members of the Al-Qaeda terrorist network on symbols of Western power shocked the world. It lead to an American declaration of "War on Terror" to end international terrorism.

At 8:46 a.m. local time, American Airlines Flight 11 crashed into the north tower of the World Trade Center, killing the 92 people on board—and killing or trapping a further 1,366 people at or above the point of impact. News teams rushed to the scene. Initial reports described the crash as a terrible accident but when, just 16 minutes later, news cameras witnessed United Airlines Flight 175 crashing into the center's south tower, it was clear that the US was under attack.

The hijackers, who were mainly Saudi-Arabian nationals, had taken over the California-bound flights soon after takeoff from East Coast airports. They used knives, mace, and the threat of bombs to subdue crews and passengers, then directed the fuel-laden jets toward their targets.

In the north tower, all routes down were cut off. People trapped inside made desperate calls to loved ones, begging for help or simply saying farewell. Around the world, millions watched the awful sight of people hurling themselves from the burning building. In the south tower one staircase was undamaged. Just 18 of the 600 people trapped in the building walked to safety before the tower collapsed. At 10:28 a.m., the north tower also fell.

Flight controllers became aware that two more planes had been hijacked but were unable to locate them before 9:37 a.m., when American Airlines Flight 77 crashed into the Pentagon, headquarters of the US Department of Defense, killing a further 189 people. At 10:03 a.m., United Airlines Flight 93 crashed into a field near Shanksville, Pennsylvannia, killing all those on board. Cell phone records and evidence from black box recorders reveal that passengers, alerted to the fate of other hijacked planes by phone calls, planned to charge the cockpit and attack their hijackers. Although the passengers could not break into the cockpit, they did succeed in diverting the hijackers from their intended target, almost certainly the Capitol Building or White House in Washington, D.C. During the final minutes of the Flight 93 recordings the hijackers can be heard deciding to abort their mission and crash the plane. As the plane hurtles toward the ground, the terrorists are praying fervently.

New York terror attacks
The World Trade Center, a great symbol of American wealth and power, moments after hijackers crashed their planes into its twin towers.

> "Today, our fellow citizens, **our way of life,** our very freedom came under attack."
>
> PRESIDENT GEORGE W. BUSH ADDRESSING THE NATION, SEPTEMBER 11, 2001

BEFORE

The British mandate, which put Iraq under British administration, lasted from 1919 to 1932. The mandate was awarded to Britain under the terms of the Covenant of the League of Nations following World War I.

THE BRITISH MANDATE
Britain's controlling interest in the Iraqi oil business « 414 caused deep resentment among Iraqi nationalists, but Britain ensured that their oil concession continued post-mandate. During World War II the British prime minister, Winston Churchill, ordered troops into Iraq to safeguard Britain's oil supplies.

THE ARAB LEAGUE was founded by seven Arab nations—Egypt, Syria, Iraq, Lebanon, Jordan, Saudi Arabia, and Yemen—in 1945. Five years later, its members signed a Defense and Economic Co-operation Treaty.

SUEZ CRISIS
In 1956, the Egyptian president, **Gamel Abdel Nasser**, wrested control of the **Suez Canal** away from the French and British « 412–13. This encouraged Arab nationalists across the Middle East to push for independence. In 1961, Iraq nationalized the oil concession areas, ending foreign interests in the industry.

IRAN–IRAQ WAR
This conflict was triggered by a territorial dispute over the Shatt-al-Arab waterway between the two rival states. Iran's revolutionary leader,

Ayatollah Khomeini « 442–43, was unpopular with both oil-rich Arab states and Western leaders, who he denounced, sanctioning the seizure of the US embassy in Tehran by militants

IRAN–IRAQ WAR

in 1979. Saudi Arabia, the US, and others sold weapons to the Iraqi leader **Saddam Hussein** (see right), who waged chemical warfare against Iranian forces.

American carrier in the Suez Canal
The Suez Canal allows transportation between Europe and Asia without the need to circumnavigate Africa and is of great strategic significance. In the image above, a US aircraft carrier is covered by a gunner in an anti-submarine helicopter as it proceeds up the canal.

The Gulf Wars

Conflict erupted in the Persian Gulf in 1990 when the United Nations moved to oust Iraqi forces from neighboring Kuwait. A military operation led by US forces put an end to the occupation, but concerns about Iraqi leader Saddam Hussein led the US and Britain to enter a second war in the Gulf in 2003.

On August 2, 1990 Saddam Hussein (see right) invaded the oil-rich gulf state of Kuwait. The United Nation's Security Council demanded immediate and unconditional withdrawal, but Saddam, a brutal dictator who had recently appointed himself Iraq's "President for Life," ignored the UN and announced that Kuwait had become a part of Iraq. The US acted to avert the crisis with a show of strength, sending substantial numbers of troops to the gulf region. Many UN nations, including Britain and members of the Arab League (see BEFORE) followed suit. Saddam responded by placing captured foreign nationals of "hostile countries" at key strategic sites in Kuwait in the hope of deterring air attacks.

The First Gulf War
In late fall, the UN issued an ultimatum effectively authorizing the use of force if Saddam did not withdraw from Kuwait by January 15, 1991. He refused to comply. The First Gulf War began on January 17 when the US and coalition forces launched Operation "Desert Storm," attacking Iraq and Kuwait from the air. Saddam's response was to launch the first of several Scud missile attacks on the Israeli capital, Tel Aviv. As allied forces entered Kuwait, Iraq launched missiles on Saudi Arabia, but was ultimately no match for the fierce military onslaught of Desert Storm. In late February, after five weeks of war, US forces took Kuwait City and US president George Bush announced a cessation of hostilities.

Saddam Hussein showed no sign of being humbled by his defeat. As Iraqi troops withdrew, they placed land mines around Kuwaiti oil wells before setting them alight. It was an act of pure defiance. The Kuwait oil fires burned for several months, causing massive environmental damage.

After the conflicts Saddam was faced with uprisings in the southern Shi'a region of Iraq and in the Kurdish north. These revolts were speedily crushed. The extent of Saddam's brutality toward his own citizens was revealed years later when mass graves

were uncovered. In the aftermath of the war, the UN agreed that Saddam could remain in power, but economic sanctions would remain in place until Iraq destroyed both its stockpile and its manufacturing ability of weapons of mass destruction (WMD)—nuclear, chemical, and biological weapons. Over the succeeding years UN weapons inspectors visited Iraq to check this disarmament process. Saddam frequently obstructed the inspections, moving and concealing weapons, and in 1998 ordered the inspectors out of Iraq. The US and UK retaliated by launching Operation "Desert Fox," a bombing campaign aimed at destroying Iraq's weapons.

The horrific terrorist attacks on the United States in 2001 (see pp.466–67) led to a decisive shift in US tolerance of Saddam's defiant behavior. In his 2002 State of the Union address, President George W. Bush declared, "I will not wait on events while danger gathers." The US was now prepared to make preemptive strikes against its enemies to combat any further potential terrorist attacks. Bush instructed the Pentagon, the US department of defense, to develop plans for war on Iraq. The US was supported in its plans for "War on Terror" by the British government, but there was grave concern

Outdated weapons
Coalition forces in the 2003 Iraq War had state-of-the-art equipment; but Iraqi soldiers had outdated Soviet-made arms such as this RPG-7V grenade-launcher.

among other world leaders about the legality of American intentions. Arguments focused on whether Iraq actually still possessed WMD. George W. Bush insisted that they did, and he was supported in this view by the British prime minister, Tony Blair. In September 2002, Blair released a dossier detailing the government's assessment of Iraq's military capability. It claimed that Saddam had the capacity to deploy chemical and biological weapons within 45 minutes. The reliability of the dossier was rapidly called into question, as it was revealed to be based in part on research written 12 years previously,

SADDAM HUSSEIN

Saddam Hussein was born to a poor family in rural Iraq. In 1957 he joined the Ba'ath Party, and a year later he became involved in an unsuccessful plot to assassinate Iraq's then-leader, General Quassim. By 1972 Saddam had a major role in government. He became Iraq's leader and gradually took absolute power, using torture, violence, and coercion to subdue the population. He was captured by US troops after the fall of Baghdad and tried and executed for war crimes.

but President Bush continued to put pressure on the UN to sanction war against Iraq.

A second conflict
With events escalating toward conflict, the UN sent weapons inspectors back into Iraq in an attempt to discover the truth about Saddam's military capacity. In spite of the UN chief weapons inspector's appeal for more time to verify the facts, US patience had run out. On March 17 the UN was informed that the diplomatic process was over, and on March 20 the US-led coalition attacked

American helicopters in Kuwait
US gunship helicopters in the burning oil fields of Kuwait. The "scorched earth" policy was ordered by defeated Iraqi leader Saddam Hussein.

"Highway of Death"
This name was given to the road leading north out of Kuwait City, which is lined with the remains of destroyed cars and trucks. It was heavily bombed by the coalition while blocked with retreating Iraqi forces.

Iraq. The progress of the Second Gulf War, or Iraq War, was rapid and by April 9 the coalition forces took the Iraqi capital, Baghdad. Fully expecting that the war would soon be over, the US appointed a governing council to supervise the creation of a new Iraqi government. However, in many ways, the Iraq War was only just beginning.

Continuing violence
The toppling of Saddam Hussein created national chaos as fighting erupted between different religious and ethnic Iraqi factions. In July 2003 George W. Bush reported that his forces now faced a "low-intensity" war. A brutal and bloody conflict has ensued involving suicide bombings and guerrilla-style tactics. Although the US handed sovereignty back to Iraq in 2004 and Iraq subsequently elected a government, thousands of Iraqi civilians, police, allied soldiers, and political insurgents (rebels) have died since the fall of Baghdad.

A fight for power
Iraq's new government is Shi'a Muslim dominated, while insurgent groups are mainly Sunni Muslims. Shi'a Muslims are the second-largest denomination of the Islamic faith and adhere only to the teachings of Muhammad and the religious guidance of his family or his descendants. Sunni Muslims are the largest denomination of Islam and represent a branch of Islam that accepted the caliphate (leadership) of Abu Bakr, as Muhammad's friend and successor.

The ongoing violence in Iraq is not simply directed against the foreign troops still attempting to keep the peace on Iraqi soil, but is increasingly a fight for power between rival religious and political factions. The Islamic terrorist group Al-Qaeda, which carried out the 9/11 attacks (see p.467), is among the many factions operating in Iraq today.

The war with Iraq was controversial, and large demonstrations in Europe and the US protested against it. In Iraq itself, although the insurgency seemed to have subsided by 2010, violence continued in many provinces. The new US president, Barack Obama, withdrew US combat troops from Iraq by August 2010, but 50,000 US service personnel remained in an advisory capacity. Elections in 2010 produced a stalemate between pro-Sunni and pro-Shi'a groups and eight months after the vote a new government had still not been sworn in.

Dictator's downfall
When US Marines entered the center of Baghdad, signaling Iraqi defeat, Saddam Hussein's statue was pulled down outside the Palestine Hotel by crowds of people celebrating the ousting from power of the brutal dictator.

Iran's nuclear program under president Mahmoud Ahmadinejad and Islamic extremist activity remain causes of concern in the Middle East.

IRANIAN NUCLEAR AMBITIONS
Iran's determination to develop its nuclear capacity have raised **international concern**. In 2007, the United Nation's (UN) nuclear agency confirmed that Iran had enriched small amounts of uranium. Iran's president Mahmoud Ahmadinejad insisted that it was for peaceful purposes only. However, his hardline attitude toward attempts to regulate his nuclear program has led to speculation that Iran is seeking to develop atomic weapons and that military strikes may be organized against Iran to prevent this. The **UN Security Council** imposed sanctions on Iran for not halting the program.

ISLAMIC EXTREMISM
Recent years have seen a rise in Islamic extremist activity. Since the attacks on the US in 2001, terrorists have struck many times. In 2005 crowds at the Hindu festival of Diwali were bombed in Delhi, India. In Mumbai in 2008, a series of gun and bomb attakcs by terrorists killed around 175 people. This extremist activity is often attributed to the **anti-Western feeling** generated by the Iraq War, although in India attacks are often linked to the activities of pro-Pakistani Kashmiri separatists.

Globalization

A phenomenon of the modern world, globalization often refers to the rise of multinational corporations that wield extraordinary economic power. Global consumption of increasingly uniform products has led to concern that the cultural differences of nations will be eroded.

BEFORE

The disastrous effects of protectionist economic policies in the Great Depression Era led to changes in economic thinking.

THE IMF AND GATT AGREEMENTS
In 1944, representatives of 45 nations met in Bretton Woods, New Hampshire, and established the **International Monetary Fund (IMF)** to increase world trade through cooperation between nations. In 1947, the first General Agreement on Tariffs and Trade (GATT treaty) influenced over $10 billion worth of trade between its members.

G6
In 1975, France, Italy, Japan, Germany, Britain, and the US formed the **Group of Six**–a forum for international trade policy discussions. Known as **G8** after Canada and Russia joined, they represent 65 percent of the global economy.

Times Square
Animated neon and LED signs shimmer on the streets of New York, advertising global brands 24 hours a day. Some companies pay millions of dollars for an annual lease on a space in Times Square and tens of millions more to create an attention-grabbing advertisement.

" Under the impact of globalization... **everyday life** is becoming opened up from the **hold of tradition.**"

ANTHONY GIDDENS, SOCIOLOGIST, 1999

Distant production
In this toy factory in Guanyao, China, female workers assemble Barbie products. The Barbie doll was created by Mattel in the US in 1959 and is now produced and sold all over the world.

In his book *The Gutenberg Galaxy*, published in 1962, communications theorist Marshall McLuhan predicted that the world would soon become recreated as a "global village." Today, as US manufacturers make products in Southeast Asia for the European market and customer inquiries in Britain are dealt with through call centers in India, McLuhan's prophesy of an interdependent world seems truly visionary. The globalization of economies has allowed business to market products internationally, forming many global partnerships and alliances.

The global system
During the 20th century, national governments tended to provide "infrastructure" services such as transit systems, and energy supplies. By the 1980s, economists agreed that underinvestment in these infrastructures had led to problems of low productivity and poor service quality; state control of the infrastructure hampered economic growth. From the 1980s onward, governments began to liberalize their economies, privatizing state assets, and encouraging "open" competitive markets. These reforms contributed to major global economic change. The tonnage of goods traded worldwide is currently estimated to be 16 times greater than in 1950. The rapidly developing Chinese economy is often cited as an example of the benefits of globalization. Since China turned its back, economically at least, on the communist system and opened up its markets to international trade and investment, it is estimated that there has been a seven-fold increase in income per head.

The growth in global trade is due in part to international trade agreements, another

Global product
After the huge success of the iPod (see p.461), which launched in 2001 and sold over 42 million worldwide by early 2006, Apple went on to produce the iPhone.

major factor being the impact of technological advances. The advent of the Internet and digital communications systems has added new dimensions to the world's economic infrastructure. International trade can be conducted quickly and efficiently, and companies are expanding their operations across the globe.

Multinational growth
The rise of multinational corporations is a major feature of globalization. Many have annual turnovers larger than the value of the economies of many small countries.

A feature of the products and services provided by multinationals is that they offer customers an identical experience. This is particularly true of branded food companies, such as McDonalds, Coca-Cola, and Starbucks, and manufacturers of sports equipment, such as Nike and Reebok. The presence of these companies' logos, or "brands," promises the same product whether we purchase it in Melbourne, Mumbai, or Miami. This corporate branding of goods has been hugely successful. Worldwide, the possession of "designer label" goods is seen as a mark of success, a marketing triumph that has generated phenomenal profits for the multi-nationals. However, the uniformity of experience provided by such companies has resulted in complaints as local, regional, and even national cultural distinctions are being lost.

Many of those opposed to multinational industry also complain that their wealth gives them the power to influence the economic and political decisions of governments, particularly in the area of trade restrictions. Some companies have been guilty of exploiting cheap labor to produce items that are then sold at a profit to Western consumers.

Whatever their opinion of the globalization of the world economy, commentators are united in the view that the world has been transformed by its impact. The consequences of these rapid and massive changes are only just beginning to be understood.

IDEA
ANTIGLOBALIZATION

On November 30, 1999, riot police in Seattle, WA, used pepper spray and tear gas to disperse antiglobalization protesters at a World Trade Organization conference. Since the 1990s, the number of staged protests against global trade agreements has increased. Protesters are concerned that in order for governments and multinational companies to make a profit, there is a requirement that poor countries must remain the impoverished suppliers of raw materials and cheap labor.

AFTER

Globalization has contributed to a growing sense of global responsibility. Governments and multinational businesses are now doing more to combat Third World poverty and conserve the environment.

FIGHTING POVERTY
For many people the **inequalities between** the lives of **rich and poor are no longer acceptable** and multinational companies and governments are increasingly facing demands to address world poverty. Campaigns such as **"Make Poverty History"** promote issues including trade justice for poorer nations and the cancellation of Third World debts.

THE GLOBAL ENVIRONMENT
The continuing rise in temperatures throughout the world has placed the issue of **global warming** at the center of the political agenda **476–77 »**. Changes in Earth's climate are directly linked to higher levels of carbon dioxide in the atmosphere created by human activity. International agreements such as the **Kyoto Protocol**, enforced since 2005, and the Copenhagen Agreement of 2010, have attempted to promote cleaner manufacturing practices in industry in order to try to reduce greenhouse gas emissions.

◀◀ BEFORE

Until the late 1970s, China's communist leaders rejected a free market economy (in which production is controlled by the laws of supply and demand rather than the state) as against their socialist principles.

CHINA'S ECONOMY UNDER MAO
Under China's first communist leader, Mao Zedong ◀◀ 424–25, free enterprise was banned and peasants could not own their own land.

1,008 MILLION The size of China's population in 1982. It was about 540 million when the Communists took power in 1949.

LOW OUTPUT
When Mao died in 1976, China had roughly the same economic output as Canada, a country with a much smaller population of 23 million.

DENG XIAOPING
A member of the Chinese Communist Party from the 1920s, Deng Xiaoping (1904–97) took part in the Long March and the foundation of the **Chinese People's Republic ◀◀ 424–25**. By 1957 he was secretary-general of the Party, but during the Cultural Revolution he was subjected to public humiliation and sent to work in a factory. He later triumphed in the power struggle after Mao's death to lead the Communist Party and masterminded the **growth of China's economy** in the 1980s.

DENG XIAOPING

Superpower China

By embracing the free market, from the 1980s China achieved extraordinarily rapid economic growth and underwent a major social transformation. But politically the country remained under the strictly authoritarian rule of the Communist Party.

Within three years of Mao Zedong's death in 1976, China's communist government began to turn away from the economic policies based on collective ownership and centralized planning that had previously been believed essential to any communist system. Deng Xiaoping advocated economic growth as the supreme goal—to be achieved at any cost.

Special economic zones
A raft of measures in 1979 put the country on its new path. Four Special Economic Zones (SEZs) were established at the southern Chinese ports of Zhuhai, Shantou, and Xiamen, and foreign firms were invited to invest capital on favorable terms. Western capitalist businesses were given the opportunity to exploit cheap Chinese labor, while in return China gained foreign exchange with which to buy imported goods and was given access to new technology from the West. At the same time, in rural areas, where 80 percent of the population lived, families were encouraged to cultivate their own land for profit. When challenged by those who objected to capitalist free-market economics, Deng defended his new policies as a practical path to

prosperity: "It does not matter whether a cat is black or white," he stated, "as long as it catches mice it is a good cat." Many non-Chinese observers believed that economic freedom would be linked to political freedom.

But in 1989, when communist regimes were toppling in Europe (see pp.448–49), pro-democracy activists in China had their demands for reform brutally rejected. The 1989 massacre of demonstrators by the army in Beijing's Tiananmen Square (see p.425) was an unequivocal statement of the Chinese Communist Party's firm intention to keep its authoritarian grip on society.

Despite this political stance, there was no turning back from the economic reforms. Although proceeding in stages and strictly supervised by the state, the

> **"Poverty is not socialism. To be rich is glorious."**
> DENG XIAOPING, 1979

transition to a free market economy gathered pace through the 1990s. So thorough was the transformation that in 1997 China was able to absorb the British colony of Hong Kong, one of the major centers of global capitalism, without noticeably affecting the territory's business community. The success of the new policies in creating economic growth was huge—between 1979 and 2002 China's real Gross Domestic Product grew at 9.3 percent per year, the fastest growth rate of any major country.

By the beginning of the new millennium a considerable part of the Chinese population had become part of a modern consumer society. It was said that under Mao people had wanted the "Four Musts"—a bicycle, a radio, a watch, and a

sewing machine; but by the 1990s, they aspired to the "Eight Bigs"—a color television, a refrigerator, a stereo, a camera, a motorbike, a set of furniture, a washing machine, and an electric fan. By 2005 China had overtaken the United States in sales of televisions and cellular phones.

Gap between rich and poor

The transition to a free market caused massive social disruption. Corruption was rampant and a wide gulf opened between the winners and losers in the new economy. While successful Chinese businessmen drove around in Mercedes, millions of people in rural areas were subsisting on less than $1 a day, and pay for factory workers was pitifully low. Some 150 million Chinese peasants

The Three Gorges Dam
Spanning the Yangzi River, the world's largest hydroelectric river dam, when fully operational, will provide power and improve flood control. Its social costs included relocating a million people.

Tourism in China
In 2005, the number of foreign tourists (excluding overseas Chinese) visiting China was 20 million. By 2020 it may be the world's most popular destination.

2008 Beijing Olympics
China has enthusiastically embraced the opportunity to showcase its great achievements. "One World, One Dream" is the Games' motto.

> **If growth rates continue as they are, China will become the world's largest economy, overtaking the United States in about 2030.**
>
> ### HARMING THE PLANET
> Rapid economic growth in China has been accompanied by severe **environmental damage**.
>
> ### POPULATION GROWTH
> Since 1980, the Chinese government has exercised a **"one-child" policy**. Despite this, China's population is expected to stabilize at 1.5 billion by 2050.
>
> ### CHINESE MOONSHOT
> A crewed Chinese moon landing is projected for 2020 at the latest.

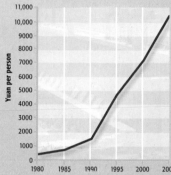

China's GDP takes a giant leap
China's level of economic output rose in the 1980s but took off spectacularly in the 1990s as the pace of economic reform quickened. There were fears the economy might "overheat," causing high inflation.

were displaced from the land, roaming the country in search of work. Many migrated to China's cities; others went abroad, making China one of the world's major sources of illegal migrant workers. Urban unemployment also soared as the government struggled to reduce the vast workforce relying on state employment. By the first decade of the 21st century, jobs in the state sector were disappearing at a rate of around 10 million a year.

Into the future

Deng Xiaoping died in 1997, the last Chinese leader of the heroic generation of the Long March. His successor, Jiang Zemin, reaffirmed communist rule, asserting that the Party had always represented the interests of the Chinese people. Yet the regime was threatened by the desire for Western-style freedoms among educated, well-to-do dissidents

and by the mass discontent of workers suffering from poverty and insecurity.

The government's trump card was its assertion of national pride. Prestige events, such as the launch of China's first crewed space flight in 2004 and the staging of the Olympic Games in Beijing in 2008—and an increasingly assertive foreign policy—appealed to most Chinese, who looked forward to their country being recognized as a major world power in the century ahead.

City of the future
Shanghai is the ninth-largest city in the world. The city's futuristic novelties include what will be the world's tallest building, the 101-story Shanghai World Financial Center (seen below at an early stage of construction), the Oriental Pearl TV Tower, and the first commercial "maglev" railroad—hovering over magnetic rails, the train can reach 268 mph (431 km/h).

Dynamic Populations

More than half the people of the world currently live in urban areas. With global urban population numbers rising by 180,000 each day, it is predicted that by 2050 two-thirds of the world's population will be city dwellers.

U rbanization became a worldwide phenomenon in the 20th century as the populations of less economically developed nations in South America, Asia, and Africa followed the Western trend for urban migration.

Urbanization is not constrained by national boundaries. Many migrants move countries in search of a better life, generally moving from developing countries to the developed world.

Growing concerns

People continue to be drawn to cities by the promise of economic and social opportunity. Cities are political, cultural, and commercial centers where much of a nation's essential work is done. However, expanding urban population numbers place heavy demands on the infrastructures of modern cities where poverty often exists side by side with great affluence. Lack of housing has contributed to increasing numbers of people living on the streets and there is serious concern about the spread of infectious diseases, including tuberculosis and HIV/Aids (see pp.464–65) among the poor and homeless.

Crime is another problem in most of the world's major cities. There is particular concern about violent crime among urban youth. Issues of poverty and social exclusion are thought to have contributed to growing youth violence and the use of firearms has led to the creation of "zones of lawlessness" in certain cities.

Third World cities are currently expanding at the fastest rate. Here, many migrants flee war or rural poverty to find themselves living in slums without hope of work, adequate shelter, sanitation, or clean water supplies. In sub-Saharan Africa, 70 percent of the urban population are slum-dwellers.

KEY
- City population in 1950 (millions)
- City population in 1975 (millions)
- City population in 2000 (millions)

Shifting city populations
The recorded rises in urban population numbers since 1950 reflect differing rates of industrialization across the globe. Urban explosion in Latin America, India, Asia, and China can be seen in the leap in population numbers since 1975.

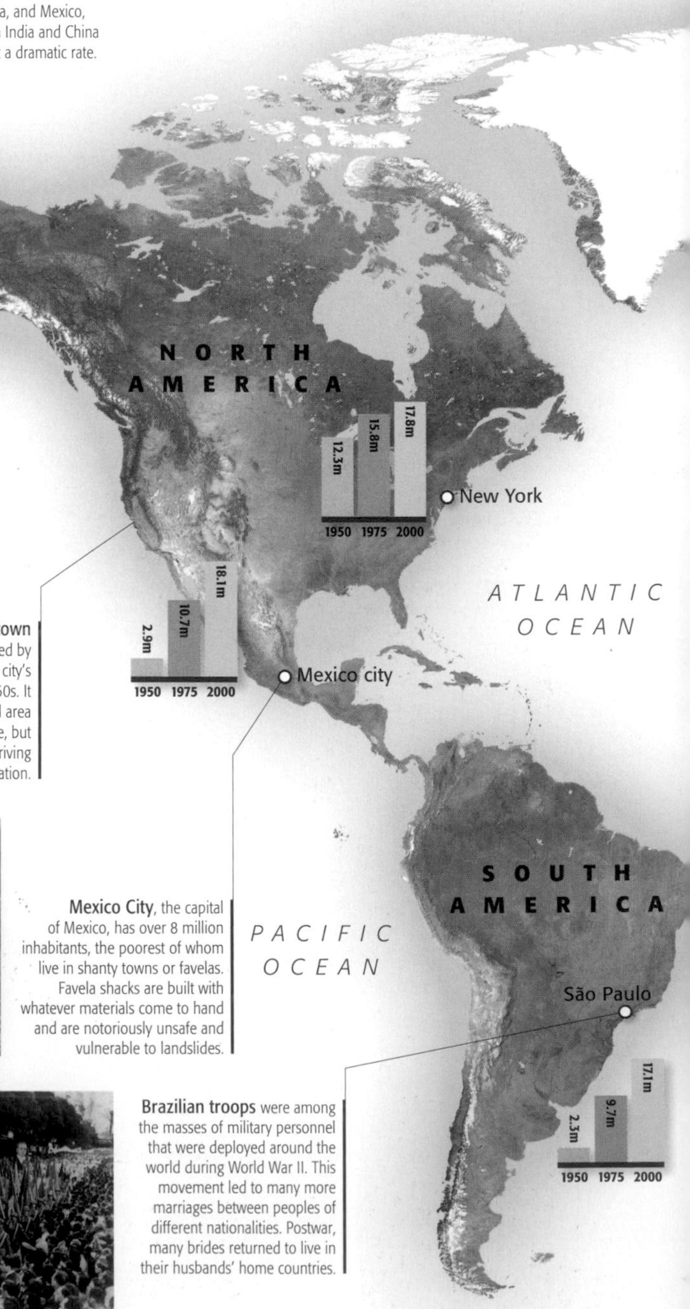

Urban growth
Comparative urban population numbers since 1990 show that European and Japanese urban population growth has slowed. Urbanization continues to increase in the US, Australia, and Mexico, and rates in India and China are rising at a dramatic rate.

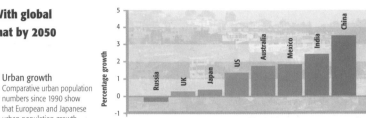
Average annual growth of urban population 1990–2003

BEFORE

During the Industrial Revolution there was a rapid mass migration of people from rural to urban areas across Europe and the US.

URBANIZATION
In 1800, one in four British people lived in cities, but by 1900 it was three in four. This process of migration, known as urbanization, occurred across Europe and North America during the Industrial Revolution ≪ 292–95. The sudden concentration of large numbers of people in cities and towns ≪ 322–25 created crowded and unsanitary conditions. The Western world gradually addressed these social problems, developing infrastructures that could provide the necessary support for their industrial workforces. Because opportunity for advancement was located in the city, urban populations continued to grow.

ARRIVING IN NEW YORK

San Francisco's Chinatown was a ghetto established by Chinese immigrants in the city's downtown area in the 1850s. It was once an impoverished area shunned by non-Chinese, but today it is a vibrant, thriving tourist destination.

Mexico City, the capital of Mexico, has over 8 million inhabitants, the poorest of whom live in shanty towns or favelas. Favela shacks are built with whatever materials come to hand and are notoriously unsafe and vulnerable to landslides.

Brazilian troops were among the masses of military personnel that were deployed around the world during World War II. This movement led to many more marriages between peoples of different nationalities. Postwar, many brides returned to live in their husbands' home countries.

NORTH AMERICA

12.3m 15.8m 17.8m
1950 1975 2000

New York

2.9m 10.7m 18.1m
1950 1975 2000

Mexico city

ATLANTIC OCEAN

PACIFIC OCEAN

SOUTH AMERICA

São Paulo

2.3m 9.7m 17.1m
1950 1975 2000

Immigrants from different cultural and ethnic groups have, for centuries, settled in London. New arrivals often populate inner-city areas, congregating in enclaves. Then, as they assimilate, these groups move out into more mixed communities, making way for the next wave of migrants.

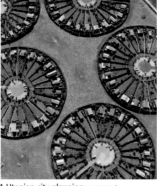

Utopian city planning movements in the interwar years aimed to improve the quality of city life. Architects and town planners created custom-built "new towns," often using experimental design, such as these circular housing developments in Denmark.

Irkutsk, Russia is typical of European industrial cities that sprang up before World War II, with large-scale factories and plants utilizing a large labor force. The city was transformed from a small town during the 1930s as Stalin's great industrialization programs took effect (see pp.380–81).

AFTER »

Urban growth is predicted to continue, and this will bring new challenges to overcome.

WORLD URBAN FORUM
In 2006, the UN established a forum to address the challenges of increasing urbanization. The stated priorities of the forum are to find **solutions for urban poverty** and to improve **access to basic facilities** such as shelter and sanitation for the urban poor.

ENVIRONMENTAL IMPACT
A major effect of growing urbanization is the increase in CO_2 **emissions** generated by both congestion and industry. Rapid industrialization in Third World cities is accelerating the rise in emissions and fueling concerns about climate change **476–77** »

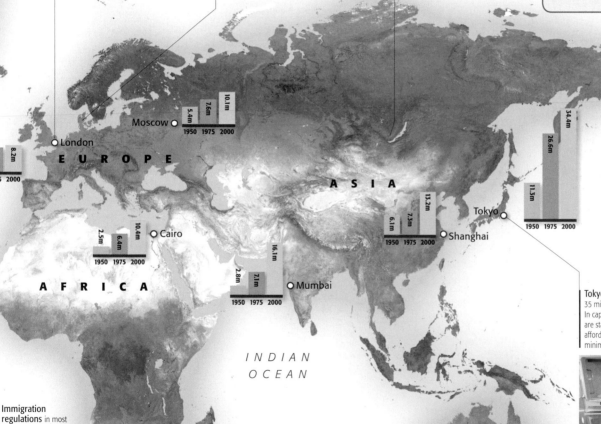

Moscow — 5.4m / 7.6m / 10.1m — 1950 1975 2000

London — 8.4m / 7.5m / 8.2m — 1950 1975 2000

E U R O P E

A S I A

Cairo — 2.5m / 6.4m / 10.4m — 1950 1975 2000

A F R I C A

Mumbai — 2.8m / 7.1m / 16.1m — 1950 1975 2000

Shanghai — 6.1m / 7.3m / 13.2m — 1950 1975 2000

Tokyo — 11.3m / 26.6m / 34.4m — 1950 1975 2000

PACIFIC OCEAN

INDIAN OCEAN

Immigration regulations in most countries of the developed world seek to control population numbers by limiting the number of people officially allowed to enter. Economic migrants, who are often fleeing terrible poverty, may take huge risks to circumvent these rules.

Large numbers of Europeans relocated to Australia after World War II, and in the 1970s the numbers of Asian migrants increased. It remains a popular destination today, particularly for workers seeking improved climate and lifestyles.

A U S T R A L I A

Melbourne — 1.3m / 2.9m / 4m — 1950 1975 2000

Tokyo has a population of more than 35 million, and space is at a premium. In capsule hotels, the sleeping quarters are stacked one above another, creating affordable accommodation from minimum space.

« BEFORE

Since the end of the last ice age, natural factors and human actions have had an impact on Earth's climate.

NATURAL CLIMATE CHANGES

The last ice age « 22–23 ended between 10,000 and 15,000 years ago, and since then the **world has been getting warmer**. Researchers have suggested a range of natural causes for this warming, including variations in Earth's orbit, fluctuations in the Sun's output, and volcanic activity.

CONGESTED ROADS

INDUSTRIAL EFFECTS

Since the Industrial Revolution « 292–93, the average global temperature has risen more quickly. Increased burning of fossil fuels, such as oil and coal, has led to **higher levels of carbon dioxide (CO_2)** in Earth's atmosphere, and so increased the "greenhouse effect."

THE GREENHOUSE EFFECT

In 1824, French mathematician and physicist **Joseph Fourier** observed that Earth's surface and atmosphere are warmed because the **Sun's heat is absorbed by naturally occurring "greenhouse" gases**, including methane (CO_4) and carbon dioxide (CO_2).

Since the Industrial Revolution (see pp.292–93), average global temperatures have risen by about 1.4°F (0.8°C). This warming has accelerated in the last four decades. From 1996 to 2009, 13 of the warmest years on record have been noted.

The current situation

In 2007, the Intergovernmental Panel on Climate Change (IPCC) published a report in which it projected probable rises in temperature of between 3.2 and 7°F (1.8–4°C) by the end of the 21st century. The panel declared themselves confident that the "net

84 PERCENT of Antarctic glaciers have retreated since 1950.

20 PERCENT reduction in polar ice caps since 1978.

10 PERCENT shrinkage in global snow and ice cover since 1960.

effect of human activity since 1750 has been one of warming." The IPCC was set up by the World Meteorological Organization (WMO) and the United Nations Environment Program (UNEP) to investigate climate change. Its conclusion that humans have caused climate change is based on the fact that the atmospheric concentration of carbon dioxide (CO_2) has increased by 31 percent since the preindustrial era, intensifying the greenhouse effect (see BEFORE).

Increased CO_2 emissions are a direct result of industrialization. Coal-burning power stations generate CO_2—as do air, sea, and road traffic; each of the 232 million cars in the US produces more than five tons of CO_2 every year.

Plants and trees naturally counteract emissions, by incorporating CO_2 into their tissues, and by releasing oxygen into the atmosphere, but 13 million hectares (32 million acres) of the

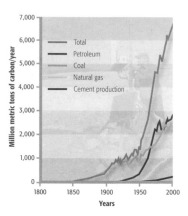

Fossil carbon emissions

The graph indicates the rise in carbon emissions in the atmosphere since 1850. Steady increases in industrial activity and in vehicle numbers, along with growing CO_2 emissions caused by burning fossil fuels and producing cement and natural gas, mean that global fossil carbon emissions are now more than 7 billion tons per year.

Climate Change

Earth's atmosphere has a natural capacity to warm the planet. Without this heat, the planet could not sustain life—but the world is rapidly getting warmer. Many experts believe human activity is to blame, calling for urgent action to prevent a global crisis and protect the planet for future generations.

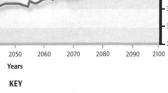

5.9 TONS **of carbon produced per person, per year in the US.**

2.9 TONS **of carbon produced per person, per year in the UK.**

0.3 TONS **of carbon produced per person, per year in India.**

world's forests are lost each year to industrial logging, so less and less carbon is being neutralized.

The oceans also absorb CO_2 and contain the largest store of the gas on Earth, but warming of the oceans reduces the sea's capacity to absorb carbon dioxide from the atmosphere. There has been widespread retreat of glaciers in nonpolar regions, and a

The Shining Mountain
According to some scientists, Mount Kilimanjaro's ice fields could be gone by the year 2020. The ice on the mountain's summit has dwindled by 82 percent over the past century, which is particularly remarkable given that it has survived previous climate shifts—including a severe 300-year-long drought 4,000 years ago. These images show the peak in February 1993 (top) and February 2000 (right).

decrease in global snow and ice cover since the late 1960s. Sea levels are rising, and may rise a further 20–16 in (25–40 cm) by 2100.

Experts also believe climate change is responsible for changes in rainfall patterns, which have created severe water shortages in many regions of the world—tens of millions have suffered from drought in Africa since the 1980s. Climate change probably contributes to the increased intensity of heatwaves and tropical storms, although no direct causal link has been established with such extreme weather events as Hurricane Katrina, which devastated the north-central Gulf Coast in 2006.

The implications

The IPCC and many other organizations predict dire consequences for the world, and especially for the poorest nations, if CO_2 emissions continue to rise. Increasing sea levels could displace tens

Lengthy fast
An adult female polar bear hauls herself out of the Arctic waters. The progressively earlier breakup of sea ice shortens the vital spring hunting season for female polar bears. As a result, weight loss is affecting their ability to reproduce, and the survival of their cubs.

of millions of people from low-lying areas such as the Ganges and Nile deltas.

Many animal species are in danger of extinction. The World Conservation Union (WCU) considers 688 African fish, bird, and mammal species to be under threat, and 201 of these are classed as "critically endangered." The reduction of Arctic summer sea ice is jeopardizing the survival of some species, including polar bears. The IPCC suggests that the summer sea ice will disappear entirely in the second half of the 21st century. The message from environmental lobby groups worldwide is that governments must act, and act now, to reduce CO_2 emissions. Industrialized countries are promoting personal carbon-offset programs in which people are encouraged to plant trees to offset their "carbon footprints." However, given the number of trees needed to offset the carbon emissions of just one car per year and fact that large

portions of the world's forests are disappearing, the fear is that climate change may now be progressing so rapidly that humans will soon be unable to stop it.

The scientific debate

The factors that affect climate are complex, and the scientific community is not universally persuaded that human beings are—or have been—a major cause of climate change. Natural climate variability is certainly a factor, but most scientists believe that Earth is undergoing significant warming as a direct result of human activities—and that this trend of global warming will continue.

32 MILLION acres of forest lost each year.

240 TREES needed to absorb the CO_2 emitted by one car each year.

10 PERCENT of the world's coral reefs now destroyed.

KEY
— CO_2 concentration
— Temperature

21st century warming
Current projections for global warming predict temperature rises of between 3.2 and 7°F (1.8–4°C) and a steady rise in atmospheric concentrations of CO_2. The increased levels of this gas in the atmosphere heighten the greenhouse effect, pushing temperatures upward.

" Future generations may well have occasion to ask themselves, **'What were our parents thinking?'** " AL GORE, FROM "AN INCONVENIENT TRUTH", 2006

HOW WE KNOW
MEASURING CLIMATE CHANGE

Scientists monitor glaciers in the Arctic and Antarctica to determine the current changes occurring in the polar regions. However, in order to assess climate change, they must form a picture of past climates. Clues to past climatic conditions are hidden in rocks and trees, but the most revealing indicators of the historical climate are preserved in ice (see pp.22–23). Scientists studying glaciers are able to analyze air bubbles trapped in the ice and determine the levels of gases in the atmosphere at the time the ice was formed, giving them information on how the atmosphere has changed over the centuries.

AFTER »

Given humankind's destructive impact on the environment, the race is on to find alternative sources of energy to replace power generation using fossil fuels.

TIDAL POWER
Investigations into harnessing tidal stream power, where energy is drawn from tidal currents, are showing promise, and prototype **wave energy converters** are also producing good results, but both these techniques are at an early stage of development. At La Rance, France, a tidal barrier built in the 1960s generates 240MW of power, but such barrages are expensive to build.

SOLAR POWER
Photovoltaic cells convert solar energy into electricity and provide a **clean source of electricity**, but the technology is expensive and cannot provide enough power for large commercial needs. In principle, however, much more solar energy falls on Earth than the amount of energy generated by burning fossil fuels; so solar power generation remains a key area of research.

WIND POWER
The conversion of wind energy into electricity currently provides just one percent of the electricity used worldwide. However, it is a popular form of **sustainable energy** in certain European nations. Nine percent of the electricity used in Spain and 20 percent of electricity used in Denmark is generated by wind power. This technology is not without drawbacks—the construction of the platforms for each turbine uses large amounts of cement, a major contributor to CO_2 emissions.

WIND TURBINES

<<

BEFORE

Developments in communication and transportation in the 19th and early 20th centuries wrought new social, political, and economic ties between people living thousands of miles apart.

BETTER COMMUNICATION NETWORKS
British engineers **George Stephenson and Isambard Kingdom Brunel** contributed to the development of efficient rail transport systems, making travel across countries and continents faster and more affordable. Improvements to the size and speed of ocean-going ships increased the transport of freight around the world, while the success of wire-based telephone and telegraph systems allowed **instant communication** across physical space for the first time.

THE BIRTH OF TOURISM
Until the late 19th century, **tourism**, or recreational travel, was **the preserve of the better off**, but many more people were taking vacations by the 1900s. Companies such as Thomas Cook & Son, the first travel agent, began to organize **package tours**, including a "round-the-world trip."

Shrinking World

Our experience of the world has been radically altered by modern technology. A journey that once took weeks by land or sea can now be flown in a matter of hours, and messages are transmitted around the world at the click of a mouse, giving us the impression that the world is becoming smaller.

Since World War I, advances in technology have transformed global communications and transportation systems, allowing both economic and personal connections to flourish on a worldwide scale. Without these technological developments, many features of modern life, including the phenomena of globalization (see pp.470–71) and global tourism, would not have occurred.

Revolutionizing travel
The 20th-century boom in travel was largely due to advances in the design of the internal combustion engine, which still powers most motor vehicles, ships, airplanes, and helicopters. The Ford Motor Company (see right) began to mass-produce combustion engines in 1906, pioneering "assembly lines" to

Transatlantic liners
Cunard Cruise Liners represented the height of luxurious travel for tourists crossing between Europe and the US during the interwar years.

speed up car production. Today motor manufacturing is a multi-billion-dollar industry. Global statistics predict that by 2030 there will be 1.2 billion motor vehicles in use worldwide.

As motor vehicles improved, so did road networks. The first "high-speed" intersection-free road, the *Automobil-Verkehrs- und Übungsstraße* (AVUS), was constructed in Berlin in 1912. Soon, multilane highways, such as Route 66, which runs from Chicago to Los Angeles, shortened travel times, allowing the transport of people and goods over longer distances. In recent years, high-speed rail links have seen

Passenger jets
Lining up on the runway at Gatwick Airport near London, UK, a passenger jet takes off every few minutes while others land nearby. Over a million people pass through the airport every year.

major investment. A world speed record was set when the French *train à grande vitesse* (TGV) reached speeds of 357 mph (575 km/h). These new trains promise to halve current journey times; a 315-mile (500-km) trip from Paris to Stuttgart will take just 3 hours and 40 minutes.

Advances in maritime engineering have produced faster, larger ships that are able to transport millions of tons of cargo around the world. Improved refrigeration techniques allow perishable foodstuffs to be carried by both sea and air, making products that were once a luxury readily available.

The development of cheaper and faster modes of travel has brought previously inaccessible parts of the world within reach of ordinary people. In the century following the Wright Brothers' first powered flight in 1904, aeronautical science has revolutionized aircraft design. Today, wide-bodied, high performance jet airliners carry millions of passengers every year.

Going places
Tourism is one of the world's most rapidly growing industries, driven by higher levels of disposable income in some societies, as well as developments in technology and the transport infrastructure. Taking vacations became the social norm in the developed world as terms of employment began to include periods of paid leave in the early decades of the 20th century. At first, people tended to vacation in domestic locations, but from the 1950s, mass tourism, particularly between European destinations, became common. Long-haul travel between

INDUSTRIALIST (1863–1947)
HENRY FORD

Henry Ford founded the Ford Motor Company in 1903. From 1909, he began mass production of the Model T Ford, using assembly line methods and wage incentives. Soon the company was producing a complete car in 1 hour and 33 minutes and its price fell from $1,000 to $360. Ford became the world's leading car manufacturer. He opposed World War I and sponsored an international conference to try to negotiate an armistice. In the 1930s, he was violently opposed to unions and was the last car manufacturer to recognize union workers in his factories.

Satellite communications
A Western journalist transmits a report by satellite phone from the hills of Northern Afghanistan. Portable satellite communications devices can provide news of events from around the world as they occur.

continents remained expensive until the 1980s, when improved airline passenger capacity and shortened journey times

"... people's lives change so fast, that a person is **born into one kind of world** [and] **grows up in another**..."

MARGARET MEAD, US ANTHROPOLOGIST

led to an increase in long-haul traffic. This upward trend has continued, with growing numbers of people traveling between continents for their vacations. In recent years, tourism has become

more specialized. With the growth in "niche markets" catering for special interests such as extreme sports, the market has both grown and fragmented. Destinations that were once the preserve of intrepid explorers, such as the Galápagos Islands (see pp.340–41), are now tourist hotspots. Nowhere is inaccessible—even Mount Everest, the summit of which was only reached for the first time by Edmund Hilary and Tenzing Norgay in 1953, has become a tourist destination.

Instant communication
The technological revolution gathered pace from the late 1950s with the invention of the microchip (see pp.460–61). This transformed the modern world. Microtechnology has touched most fields of manufacturing and engineering, from weapons design to medical robotics. The impact on human communications has been huge. Microchips provide the "brains" for computers, personal communicators, and cellular phones, allowing instant global communication and the storage of vast amounts of information. Data that previously filled libraries can now be stored on one tiny chip. The creation of the Internet (see right) allowed this information to be shared among computer users worldwide.

It is often said that the 21st century will be the "Communications Age",

an age centered on shared information between individuals, businesses, and nations. In the past, geographical distance impeded communication, but technology has broken down these barriers. The Communications Age

2 BILLION people worldwide regularly access the Internet.

offers the chance for knowledge to be shared across the world. After more than a century in which international conflicts have wrought so much carnage, some have begun to promote a new ideal for this age: that of the global citizen.

The seemingly insatiable public appetite for travel to exotic locations shows no sign of fading in the 21st century. Not content with gaining access to the remotest corners of Earth, there is now a new demand for vacations that are literally out of this world.

SPACE TOURISM
The British entrepreneur Richard Branson has poured millions of dollars into the Virgin Spaceship to take passengers into space. Wealthy individuals and corporations are already booking "**personal spaceflights**" with the Russian Space Agency. Tourists have to undergo rigorous physical training and medical tests before being declared fit to travel. To date, five people have vacationed in space, paying as much as $25 million for the privilege. The first tourist, California financier Dennis Tito, described his eight-day voyage as "a trip to paradise."

INVENTION
THE WORLD WIDE WEB

British physicist Tim Berners Lee invented the World Wide Web in the late 1980s and early 1990s. Lee developed the concept of "hypertext" in order to share research with fellow scientists across a single computer network. His original ideas led to the popularization of the Internet as people used this technology to build websites, which could be accessed from computers anywhere in the world. Lee currently heads the World Wide Web consortium that concentrates on improving Internet technology and accessibility.

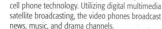

Personal communicators
These video phones are the latest development in cell phone technology. Utilizing digital multimedia satellite broadcasting, the video phones broadcast news, music, and drama channels.

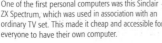

Personal computers
One of the first personal computers was this Sinclair ZX Spectrum, which was used in association with an ordinary TV set. This made it cheap and accessible for everyone to have their own computer.

Global Positioning System
This GPS receiver picks up signals transmitted by global navigation satellites to determine its location and direction. GPS technology has become an important tool for mapmaking, land surveying, and navigation.

NATIONAL HISTORIES

This section traces the individual histories of the world's 195 countries, from the oldest surviving republic to the UN's latest member, and shows how modern states have emerged from the ashes of empires and world wars.

North and Central America

The continent of North America stretches from the Arctic Ocean in the north to the isthmus connecting Central America in the south with South America, and includes the many islands of the Caribbean. The US, Canada, and many of the islands are predominantly English-speaking. Mexico is the world's most populous Spanish-speaking nation. Once entirely colonized by European countries, all but a few islands are now independent.

United States

The US is the world's fourth largest country, and politically dominates most of the Americas.

c.35000BCE Possible first date for human explorers to cross the land bridge from Siberia and begin to hunt and roam in the far northwest of the continent.

c.13000BCE Earliest evidence of colonization in the northwest of the continent as the last Ice Age ends.

c.9000BCE Hunter-gatherers spread to the Great Plains and the southern deserts.

c.3000BCE First farmers grow crops in the southwest.

c.100BCE The Hopewell people settle in the Ohio Valley and begin to build burial mounds.

c.400 Hohokam people begin building villages in the southwest. Soon after this, hunters on the Great Plains first use bows and arrows to kill buffalo.

c.600 People in the Mississippi River valley begin to build small towns and burial mounds.

c.700 The city of Cahokia is built in the northern Mississippi River valley. A vast, earthen temple mound, used for religious purposes, dominates the city.

800 Corn becomes an important source of food in the eastern woodlands; within 200 years, permanent villages are built throughout the region. Hardier strains of corn and beans increase food production in the Mississippi valley, allowing the population to increase.

900 The first farming villages are constructed on the Great Plains.

900 The Anasazi people of Chaco Canyon in New Mexico build a network of villages linked by roads. At Pueblo Bonito they construct a D-shaped, four-story apartment building capable of housing up to 1,200 people in 800 rooms.

c.1000 Vikings build a settlement in what is now Newfoundland, the first contact between Europe and the Americas.

1200 Cahokia is at the height of its power, with more than 10,000 people.

1492 Christopher Columbus makes the first of his four voyages to the Americas.

1498 On his second voyage, Italian John Cabot explores the coast of North America as far south as Delaware.

1499 Italian navigator Amerigo Vespucci voyages to South America and the Caribbean. He is the first European navigator to realize that the lands Columbus had reached were not in Asia but part of a new continent. He called this land mass *Mundus Novus* ("new world"). When the German cartographer Martin Waldseemüller wrote a geography book in 1507, he named this world "the land of Amerigo, or America, after Amerigo, its discoverer..." At first, this name applied to South America only, but in 1538 Flemish mapmaker Gerardus Mercator became the first person to designate both North and South America on a world map.

1524–25 Italian navigator Giovanni da Verrazano, exploring under French auspices, sails down the Atlantic coast as far as Cape Fear, North Carolina. On the way he passes into what is now New York Harbor, through narrows that today bear his name.

1526 The Spanish establish a settlement at San Miguel de Gualdape in what is now Georgetown, South Carolina. Among their number are a few African slaves. The colony only lasts a year, as half of the Spanish die. The Africans revolt, set fire to the settlement, and live among the American Indians as the first black settlers in North America. As the Spanish continue their exploration of the region, more African slaves escape.

1527–28 Pánfilo de Narváez, a Spanish conquistador, explores the west coast of Florida and the Gulf of Mexico. His expedition ends in disaster and only four men survive by making an eight-year trek on foot to another Spanish settlement.

1539–42 Hernando de Soto follows on from the Narváez expedition and roams around unsuccessfully in search of gold, crossing the Mississippi during his travels.

1565 A Spanish expedition led by Pedro Menendez sets up the colony of St. Augustine on the west coast of Florida, the oldest permanent US city founded by Europeans. Among their number are African slaves. The nearby French colony at Fort Caroline, established in 1564, is destroyed by the Spanish as a potential threat to their transatlantic fleets carrying gold bullion to Spain.

1584 An English colony is established by explorer Sir Walter Raleigh on Roanoke Island and is resettled in 1587. It vanishes without trace by 1590.

1607 The first successful English colony, Jamestown, named after English king James I, is established in Virginia. The Dutch sail up the Hudson River to establish Fort Nassau in what is now Albany in 1614. They later settle in New York and in 1626 purchase Manhattan Island from the American Indians. In 1638 the Swedes establish their own colony of New Sweden on the Delaware River, although it is seized by the Dutch in 1655.

1619 Twenty Africans, among them three women, arrive in Jamestown, Virginia aboard a Dutch ship and are sold as indentured servants, the foreunners of slaves. When William Tucker is born around 1623, he becomes the first African–American born in the 13 colonies.

1620 The Pilgrims arrive at Cape Cod, Massachusetts.

1620s The transatlantic slave trade gathers pace as France joins England and the Netherlands in the trade. African slaves are brought to New York (1626), Maryland and Massachusetts (1634), New Hampshire (1645), and other English colonies. By 1649 there are 300 African slaves in Virginia, and at least 2,000 by 1671. By 1675 the total number of African slaves in the North American colonies grows to more than 5,000.

1665 Following the second Anglo-Dutch War, control of the New Netherlands passes to the English crown. The colony and the city of New Amsterdam are both renamed New York. The English are now the dominant colonial power on the eastern seaboard, establishing 13 colonies from New Hampshire and Massachusetts in the north to Georgia in the south. The French control the Mississippi River valley, the Great Lakes, and the St. Lawrence River valley of Canada, while the Spanish control Florida, the southwest, and the west coast of North America.

1671 Thomas Batts and Robert Fallam, two English explorers, are the first Europeans to find a way through the Appalachian Mountains. They follow the Staunton River through the Blue Ridge and emerge on the westerly flowing New River, following it to the Ohio River. Soon, other explorers are discovering new routes through the mountain range.

1680–82 Robert de la Salle, a French trader, explores south from French Canada and sails the length of the Mississippi River to the Gulf of Mexico, claiming the entire region for France.

1681 Pennsylvania is established as a Quaker colony by William Penn.

1689–97 King William's War, the American extension of the War of the League of Augsburg between France and, among others, England, sees the French and their Huron allies raid New England. Further conflict between the two colonial powers breaks out during Queen Anne's War, known in Europe as the War of the Spanish Succession (1702–13), during which the French raid Connecticut.

The Pilgrims
A 19th-century image depicts the relieved English pilgrims landing at Plymouth Rock, Massachusetts, in December 1620—a seminal moment in American history. The pilgrims were a group of puritans intent on preserving their cultural identity. Luckily, they found an abandoned settlement.

The White House
Work on the US president's official residence began in 1792 after a design by Irish architect James Hoban was chosen by George Washington from among nine competition entries. The building was first occupied in 1800. After being burned by the British in 1814, it was restored and painted white.

1708 Black slaves outnumber white inhabitants in the Carolinas for the first time. Over the next 50 years, thousands of slaves arrive in the colonies each year.

1709 Work begins on a slave market at the end of Wall Street in New York City.

1713 England assumes a dominant role in the transatlantic slave trade after Queen Anne's War.

1738 Escaped slaves establish the first free black township in the Americas at Fort Mose in Florida.

1744–48 After a lengthy period of sometimes uneasy peace, France and Britain continue their rivalry in North America during King George's War (known in Europe as the War of the Austrian Succession). After unsuccessful British and Iroquois raids on New France (along the St. Lawrence River in Canada), the French and their Huron allies raid Maine and New York. Hostilities continue after the war in the Ohio River valley, where the French try to halt British expansion westward by destroying Fort Pickawillany in 1752.

1750 The slave population of the English colonies reaches 236,400, of whom more than 200,000 live south of Pennsylvania. A decade later, their total population reaches 325,806.

1755–63 The French and Indian War is the most decisive phase of the lengthy Anglo-French conflict in North America and is the American counterpart of the Seven Years War in Europe. The French are at a disadvantage because their total number of colonists in North America is only one-tenth that of the British colonies, while Britain's Royal Navy is able to stop trade and troop reinforcements from reaching French colonies. Initially the French have some successes, but after their defeat in Canada in 1759, the British are supreme. Under the Treaty of Paris that ends the war, Britain gains control over French Canada and that portion of Louisiana lying east of the Mississippi River. Spain surrenders Florida to the British.

1763 Britain sets a Proclamation Line defining the limit to the westward expansion of its 13 American colonies. The 1774 Québec Act extends British Canada's boundaries south to the Ohio and Mississippi rivers. Both measures are widely seen as restrictive limits on colonial freedom and expansion.

1765 The British government imposes direct taxation on its American colonies for the first time in order to pay for the recent war and the cost of keeping a large army in the Americas. The Stamp Act, which placed a tax on newspapers and other items, is widely resented and, after much opposition, is repealed in 1766.

1766 The Declatory Act affirms Britain's right to legislate in its 13 American colonies.

1769–74 In just five years, ships from Irish ports alone bring 44,000 new colonists to British North America. By 1774 there are more than 2 million Europeans on the continent. Scots, Irish, Germans, and others swell the numbers. Not all of them support the British crown.

1770 British troops kill three and mortally wound five Bostonians, adding to the tension between Britain and its increasingly rebellious colonists.

1773 Massachusetts citizens board three ships in Boston Harbor and throw their cargo overboard in protest against the imposition of a tea tax.

" We hold these **truths** to be self-evident, that all men are created **equal**"

US DECLARATION OF INDEPENDENCE
JULY 4, 1776

1775–81 The American Revolution breaks out as colonists clash with British troops at Lexington and Concord near Boston on April 19, 1775. Forces of the 13 rebel colonies, led after June by George Washington, struggle at first but eventually overwhelm the British, with French and Spanish support. The victory of the French fleet over the British off the Chesapeake Capes forces the surrender of the British at Yorktown in 1781.

1776 The Declaration of Independence is drafted by Thomas Jefferson. It states, among other things, that people have "certain unalienable rights, that among these are life, liberty, and the pursuit of happiness."

1783 Under the Treaty of Paris, Britain recognizes the independence of the United States. Florida is restored to Spain. The western border of the new state stretches to the Mississippi River.

1787 A Constitutional Convention, held in Philadelphia, revises the Articles of Confederation, originally agreed in 1777, by drafting a new constitution for the federation of the 13 states.

1787–90 The new constitution is ratified by the 13 states; it is officially accepted on June 21, 1788, after the number of states ratifying it reaches nine, the required two-thirds level of approval.

1789 George Washington is elected first president of the United States in February, and the first Congress meets in New York City, the designated seat of federal government. The Supreme Court is established in September.

1790, 1791 The District of Columbia is established under Acts of Congress on land ceded by the states of Maryland and Virginia, to become the new site of the federal capital. The site, on the Potomac River, is chosen by George Washington. In 1800 the federal government moves from Philadelphia to begin work in Washington; the same year, John Adams becomes the first president to live in the White House.

1791 Ten amendments to the constitution guaranteeing freedom of speech, assembly, and other rights, come into effect as the Bill of Rights.

1797 George Washington steps down as president after two terms (he was reelected in 1792) and is succeeded by his vice president, John Adams. Washington dies in 1799 at his home at Mount Vernon, Virginia.

1801 Thomas Jefferson is elected third president after a dead heat in the electoral college with Aaron Burr. The matter is decided by the House of Representatives, who make their choice after 36 ballots.

DECISIVE MOMENT

THE US CONSTITUTION

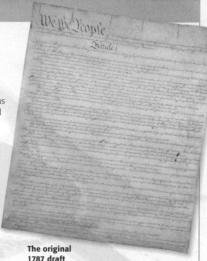

The US Constitution (right) was drawn up by the Constitutional Convention in Philadelphia in 1787 and agreed on September 17. It came into force after nine states had ratified it by June 21,1788.

The constitution opens with the famous preamble: "We, the people of the United States, in order to form a more perfect union, establish justice, insure domestic tranquility, provide for the common defense, promote the general welfare, and secure the blessings of liberty to ourselves and our posterity, do ordain and establish this constitution for the United States of America."

The document then spells out in seven articles how the new country is to be governed. It establishes the three branches of government—the legislative (congress), the executive (the presidency), and the judiciary (the courts)—and builds in checks and balances so that each acts as a restraint on the actions of the other two. Congress is to consist of two houses: the lower House of Representatives, whose elected members are drawn from each state in proportion to its population, and the upper Senate, consisting of two elected members from each state. Alongside the federal structure of government established by the constitution, state and local governments complete the American system of democratic government.

The original 1787 draft

Article V of the constitution allows for it to be amended. This has occurred 27 times, most recently in 1992. Notable amendments are the first ten, known together as the Bill of Rights, which were added in 1791.

Subsequent important amendments include the 13th, abolishing slavery in 1865; the 15th, establishing equal voting rights for blacks and whites in 1870; the 18th, prohibiting the sale of alcohol in 1919; and the 19th, granting votes to women in 1920. The 21st amendment of 1933 repealed the 18th, allowing Americans to drink legally once again.

Slater's Mill, 1793
An English immigrant, Samuel Slater, established this water-powered textile mill in Pawtucket, Rhode Island. The valley of the Connecticut River soon became America's first major industrial region.

1803 Louisiana purchase: France, having regained Louisiana from Spain in 1800, sells it to the US for about $15 million. The purchase effectively doubles the size of the United States, extending its western borders to the Rocky Mountains.

1801–05 Barbary Wars: US naval forces clash with the "Barbary States" of North Africa (Algiers, Moroccco, and Libya) over raids on American shipping and the states' demands for bribes to cease the attacks and to release captured sailors. A peace treaty, signed in June 1805 and ratified by the Senate in 1806, largely ends the conflict.

1804–06 Meriwether Lewis, secretary to President Jefferson, and William Clark are sent by the president to explore the newly acquired territory of Lousiana. They set off up the Missouri River from St. Charles, Missouri, in the hope of finding a route along the Columbia River to the Pacific coast. Although they reached the Pacific in 1805, the route they find is not easy. They do, however, make useful contact with many native peoples.

1809 Jefferson is succeeded as president first by James Madison and then, in 1817, by James Monroe, both associated with Jefferson's Democratic–Republican movement. This movement stresses states' rights as opposed to the federalist views of the second president, John Adams.

1810 US annexes west Florida.

1812–14 US at war with Britain because of Britain's refusal to recognize American commercial neutrality during Britain's lengthy war with Napoleonic France. The US tries but fails to dislodge the British from Canada; in response the British invade and in 1814 burn Washington. A peace treaty is signed in Ghent, in what is now Belgium, but news arrives too late to prevent General Andrew Jackson's forces from inflicting a massive defeat on the British at New Orleans in January 1815.

1817 Mississippi is admitted as the 20th state of the Union, followed by Illinois in 1818 and Alabama in 1819.

1817–18 First war against the Seminole people of Florida. After a second war in 1835–42, many Seminoles are forcibly relocated to Oklahoma.

1818 The lengthy border between the US and Canada west of the Great Lakes to the Rocky Mountains is fixed at the 49th parallel, with the US gaining the Red River Colony in what is now Northern Dakota and Minnesota.

1819 Spain cedes Florida to the US.

1820 The Missouri compromise allows slavery in the new state of Missouri but outlaws it north and west of the Missouri River. There were fears when Missouri applied for statehood in 1819 that the balance of 11 slave-owning and 11 free states already in the Union would be upset. The northern states strongly object to slavery, but the Constitutional

Convention of 1787, while prohibiting the import of slaves, protected slavery from federal interference. The Missouri compromise allowed the slave state of Missouri to join at the same time as the free state of Maine, thus balancing both interests within the Union.

1823 The Monroe Doctrine asserts US supremacy in the western hemisphere and warns European powers against any attempts at colonization in the Americas.

1825 John Quincy Adams becomes the sixth president after a contested election in which Andrew Jackson, hero of New Orleans, received more popular votes but lost when the election became a contingent election decided by the House of Representatives.

1828 The Democrat–Republican movement becomes the Democratic Party as Andrew Jackson is elected president. The party holds its first national presidential nominations in 1832.

1830 The Indian Removal Act allows for the permanent removal of American Indians from their land; an act of 1834 sets up the Indian Territory in what is now Arkansas. Cherokees, Seminoles, Creeks, and others are all forcibly moved.

1836 Texas declares independence from Mexico. After a Texan garrison is massacred at the Alamo in San Antonio, the Texans defeat a Mexican army at San Jacinto, winning their independence.

1841 William Henry Harrison is inaugurated as the ninth president on March 4 but dies a month later. Vice president John Tyler succeeds him.

1842 Under the Webster–Ashburton Treaty the northeast border of the US with British Canada is finally settled.

1845 Texas is annexed to the US.

1845 Congress fixes the date of future presidential elections on the Tuesday following the first Monday in November.

1846 Britain and the US agree to divide Oregon Country between them along the 49th parallel. President James Polk had claimed the whole of the territory up to the southern border of Russian Alaska with a cry of "54° 40′ or fight!" Had he won, the US would have excluded British Canada from the Pacific coastline.

1846–48 Mexico is defeated in the US–Mexican war. Under the Treaty of Guadalupe Hidalgo, Mexico renounces claims to Texas and cedes California and most of New Mexico to the US.

1848 Gold is discovered in the Lower Sacramento valley in California, prompting a massive goldrush.

1848 Seneca Falls Convention: the first national meeting held to discuss women's rights calls for women's suffrage.

1850 California joins as a free state, becoming the 31st state in the Union.

1853 Under the terms of the Gadsden purchase the US acquires parts of southern New Mexico and Arizona so that the Southern Pacific Railroad can be built from Texas to California.

1854 The Republican Party is formed upon the principle of opposing the extension of slavery.

1854 The Kansas–Nebraska Act sets up two new territories and gives settlers the right to decide whether or not to allow slavery. In effect the act ends the Missouri compromise, as both territories were meant to be free from slavery.

1857 The Dred Scott ruling by the Supreme Court declares that neither Congress nor the people of a territory could abolish slavery. This make the Missouri compromise unconstitutional and destroys the balance between free and slave states

1859 John Brown tries to organize a slave rebellion in Virginia. He is caught, tried for treason, and hanged.

1860 Abraham Lincoln is elected as first Republican president, winning all but one of the northern free states but failing to win a single slave state. South Carolina becomes the first state to secede from the Union over the issue of slavery.

1861–65 Civil War. The conflict begins when seven (later 11) secessionist states form the Confederate States of America. The Confederate States eventually surrender on April 9, 1865 at Appomattox, Virginia, following the fall of Charleston and Richmond.

1861 On February 9, Jefferson Davis, former US Army officer and Secretary of

Lewis and Clark
Officially known as the "Corps of Discovery," Lewis and Clark's expedition to explore Louisiana included Sacagawea, a young woman of the Shoshone American Indian nation, who proved invaluable as an interpreter. She is shown here standing behind Lewis and Clark.

" A house divided against itself **cannot stand**. I believe this government cannot endure permanently **half slave and half free**."

ABRAHAM LINCOLN, ILLINOIS REPUBLICAN STATE CONVENTION, JUNE 16, 1858

Union soldier's cap
The narrow-brimmed hat known as a "forage cap" was worn by most Union troops. Union forces had standardized, mass-produced clothing and gear; the Confederates usually had to improvise.

the Army, takes office as President of the Confederate States of America. On April 12, Confederate troops fire on Union-held Fort Sumter in the harbor at Charleston, South Carolina. The first major battle of the war, First Bull Run, fought in Virginia, ends in a Union defeat.

1862 On April 6–7, A Union army under Ulysses S. Grant is nearly overwhelmed at Shiloh, Tennessee. A Union offensive up the peninsula between the James and York rivers, aimed at taking the Confederate capitol, Richmond, ends in defeat, but Union naval forces succeed in capturing New Orleans, Louisiana. In June, Robert E. Lee takes command of the Confederacy's Army of Northern Virginia. Lee invades Maryland, but is halted at Antietam. Congress passes the Homestead Act, which grants 640 acres of western land to any head of household who settles on it for five years

1863 On January 1, the Emancipation Proclamation is issued by Abraham Lincoln, freeing slaves in the Confederacy. At the end of the Civil War, slavery is abolished by the 13th Amendment to the Constitution. The 14th Amendment of 1868 gives former slaves US citizenship, while the 15th Amendment of 1870 guarantees their right to vote. American Indians have to wait until 1924 to become citizens. Lee again invades the North, and the Army of Northern Virginia and the Army of the Potomac clash at Gettysburg, Pennsylvania (July 1–3), which ends in a Union victory. Rioting breaks out in New York City over the new draft law, which introduces conscription.

1864 In the spring, Union commander Grant begins an offensive against Richmond. In September, the Union's western army, under General William T. Sherman, captures Atlanta, Georgia. The victory helps Lincoln win reelection to a second term in the presidential election in November. Sherman sets out on a "March to the Sea," taking Savannah on the Atlantic coast (December 21).

1865 A peace conference in February fails when the Union refuses to accept

independence for the Confederacy. At the beginning of April, Grant resumes the offensive toward Richmond.

1865 On April 15 Abraham Lincoln is assassinated; vice president Andrew Johnson takes over as president.

1866–77 Reconstruction of the South as former Confederate states are slowly allowed back into the Union. An amnesty is granted to former Confederates who pledge allegiance to the Union.

1866 Ku Klux Klan founded to oppose civil rights for former slaves.

1867 Russia sells Alaska to the US for $7.2 million.

1868 For the first time a sitting president, Andrew Johnson, is impeached (tried) by Congress, for trying to obstruct Reconstuction. The measure passes the House of Representatives but does not achieve the necessary Senate majority.

1869 The Union Pacific and Central Pacific railroads meet at Promontory Point, Utah, thus completing the first transcontinental railroad. A ceremonial golden spike is driven into the railroad.

1869 Wyoming becomes the first US territory to grant women the vote.

1870 US population reaches 40 million.

1870 John D. Rockefeller founds the Standard Oil Company of Ohio, soon to become America's largest oil company.

1871 The city of Chicago, almost entirely built of wood, is destroyed in a massive fire that kills several hundred people, makes 90,000 homeless, and destroys some $200 millon worth of property. After the fire, the city is rebuilt in stone and steel, and the world's first skyscrapers are constructed.

1876 Alexander Graham Bell patents the telephone. In 1885 Bell forms the American Telephone and Telegraph Co.

1876–77 The Great Sioux War breaks out on the northern Great Plains after the Sioux resist gold prospectors entering their lands. Although they massacre General George Custer and 200 troops at Little Bighorn, they are eventually forced to surrender.

1882 Immigration controls limit entry of Chinese, as well as "convicts, lunatics, and other undesirables."

1885 Grover Cleveland becomes the first Democratic president since James Buchanan in 1857. Although he loses the office in 1889, he wins reelection in 1893, the first and only time that a US president has served nonconsecutive terms.

	PRESIDENTS OF THE UNITED STATES			
	PRESIDENT	**PARTY**	**DATES**	**VICE PRESIDENT**
1	George Washington	None	1789–97	John Adams
2	John Adams	F	1797–1801	Thomas Jefferson
3	Thomas Jefferson	DR	1801–09	Aaron Burr 1801–05 George Clinton 1805–09
4	James Madison	DR	1809–17	George Clinton 1809–12 No vice president 1812–13 Elbridge Gerry 1813–14 No vice president 1814–17
5	James Monroe	DR	1817–25	Daniel D. Tomkins
6	John Quincy Adams	DR	1825–29	John C. Calhoun
7	Andrew Jackson	D	1829–37	John C. Calhoun 1829–32 No vice president 1832–33 Martin Van Buren 1833–37
8	Martin Van Buren	D	1837–41	Richard M. Johnson
9	William Henry Harrison	W	1841	John Tyler
10	John Tyler	W	1841–45	No vice president
11	James K. Polk	D	1845–49	George M. Dallas
12	Zachary Taylor	W	1849–50	Millard Fillmore
13	Millard Fillmore	W	1850–53	No vice president
14	Franklin Pierce	D	1853–57	William R. King 1853 No vice president 1853–57
15	James Buchanan	D	1857–61	John C. Breckinridge
16	Abraham Lincoln	R	1861–65	Hannibal Hamlin 1861–65 Andrew Johnson 1865
17	Andrew Johnson	D/NU	1865–69	No vice president
18	Ulysses S. Grant	R	1869–77	Schuyler Colfax 1869–73 Henry Wilson 1873–75 No vice president 1875–77
19	Rutherford B. Hayes	R	1877–81	William A. Wheeler
20	James Garfield	R	1881	Chester A. Arthur
21	Chester A. Arthur	R	1881–85	No vice president
22	Grover Cleveland	D	1885–89	Thomas A. Hendricks 1885 No vice president 1885–89
23	Benjamin Harrison	R	1889–93	Levi P. Morton
24	Grover Cleveland	D	1893–97	Adlai E. Stevenson
25	William McKinley	R	1897–1901	Garret A. Hobart 1897–99 No vice president 1899–1901 Theodore Roosevelt 1901
26	Theodore Roosevelt	R	1901–09	No vice president 1901–05 Charles W. Fairbanks 1905–09
27	William Howard Taft	R	1909–13	James S. Sherman 1909–12 No vice president 1912–13
28	Woodrow Wilson	D	1913–21	Thomas R. Marshall
29	Warren G. Harding	R	1921–23	Calvin Coolidge
30	Calvin Coolidge	R	1923–29	No vice president 1923–25 Charles G. Dawes 1925–29
31	Herbert Hoover	R	1929–33	Charles Curtis
32	Franklin Delano Roosevelt	D	1933–45	John N. Garner 1933–41 Henry A. Wallace 1941–45 Harry S. Truman 1945
33	Harry S. Truman	D	1945–53	No vice president 1945–49 Alben W. Barkley 1949–53
34	Dwight D. Eisenhower	R	1953–61	Richard M. Nixon
35	John F. Kennedy	D	1961–63	Lyndon B. Johnson
36	Lyndon B. Johnson	D	1963–69	No vice president 1963–65 Hubert Humphrey 1965–69
37	Richard M. Nixon	R	1969–74	Spiro T. Agnew 1969–73 No vice president 1973 Gerald Ford 1973–74
38	Gerald Ford	R	1974–77	No vice president 1974 Nelson A. Rockefeller 1974–77
39	Jimmy Carter	D	1977–81	Walter Mondale
40	Ronald Reagan	R	1981–89	George Herbert Walker Bush
41	George H. W. Bush	R	1989–93	J. Danforth Quayle
42	Bill Clinton	D	1993–2001	Albert Gore, Jr.
43	George W. Bush	R	2001–09	Dick Cheney
44	Barack Obama	D	2009–	Joseph Biden
45	Election due November 2012			

F *Federalist,* **DR** *Democratic–Republican,* **D** *Democratic,* **R** *Republican,* **W** *Whig,* **NU** *National Union*

1886 **Growing industrial militancy** in Chicago as workers demonstrate for an eight-hour day. Police intervene, causing the Haymarket Riot. Industrial protests against low wages, long hours, poor conditions, and lack of union recognition soon spread throughout America.

1889 **North and South Dakota** become the 39th and 40th states of the Union. Montana, Washington, Idaho, and Wyoming join within a year.

1890 **The massacre at** Wounded Knee, South Dakota, is the last major military conflict between American Indian and US forces.

1890 **Antitrust Law is** passed to curb big-business power.

1890 **The Irish** population of New York is now twice that of Dublin. In 1892 the Ellis Island immigration reception center in New York is opened.

1896 **Utah admitted** as the 45th state of the Union after its Mormon inhabitants promise to relinquinsh polygamy.

1896 **The Supreme Court** affirms the "separate but equal" doctrine allowing racial segregation.

1898 **The Spanish-American** war ends with the US gaining control of Guam, the Philippines, and Puerto Rico.

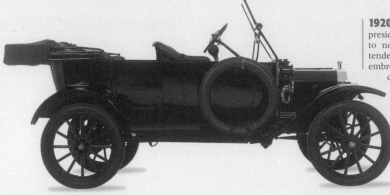

Mass-production
The first Model T Fords were individually built in the factory at Detroit, but in 1913 they became the first cars to be mass-produced on an assembly line, a process that reduced their cost considerably.

Movie capital
The attraction of more sunlight, varied settings, and lower wages turned Hollywood, a suburb of Los Angeles, California, into the center of the US film production industry after 1910. British actor Charlie Chaplin (above) was an early star.

1901 **United States Steel Corporation** beomes the first billion-dollar company.

1901 **President William McKinley is** assassinated by an anarchist in Buffalo, New York. Theodore Roosevelt becomes president.

1905 **More than 1 million** immigrants enter America in a year. By 1910 the US population rises to 92 million.

1908 **Model T Ford** production begins.

1909 **The NAACP**—the National Association for the Advancement of Colored People—is formed in New York to promote civil rights.

1912 **New Mexico and Arizona** join as the 47th and 48th states of the Union.

1912 **Woodrow Wilson** is elected president. Theodore Roosevelt, who had stood down in favor of William Taft in the 1908 election, stands against him, splitting the Repubican vote and letting the Democrats in.

1913 **The Federal Reserve Bank Act** sets up a series of 12 district reserve banks overseen by a federal board. This has the power to control the supply of money and raise or lower interest rates to prevent financial collapse.

1914 **US troops intervene** in the Mexican civil war, landing Marines in the port city of Veracruz in April.

1914 **Ludlow Massacre:** a strike by Colorado coal miners turns deadly when troops fire on the strikers' camp, killing 24.

1916 **Pancho Villa,** Mexican rebel leader, raids Columbus, New Mexico; 18 Americans are killed. In response, the National Guard is mobilized along the US-Mexican border and a force under General John J. Pershing is sent into Mexico itself, but Villa eludes capture.

1917 **US enters World War I** on the Allied side against Germany. Wilson had declared American neutrality when war broke out in 1914 and won reelection in 1916 on the slogan "He kept us out of the war." The mood of the country became increasingly anti-German, however, after the sinking in 1915 of the SS *Lusitania* off the coast of Ireland. In February 1917 Germany announces it will attack all foreign ships in an effort to starve Britain and France of much-needed supplies. Germany also tries to divert American attention away from Europe by inciting Mexico to invade the US. When this policy is revealed by the publication of a secret telegram sent by German foreign secretary Arthur Zimmerman to his minister in Mexico, the US declares war, on April 6.

1918 **The arrival of** 500,000 fresh US troops in France by May 1918 and a further 313,400 in July tips the balance in the Allies' favor. As German morale collapses, an armistice is declared in November 1918. Approximately 56,000 US troops are killed and 204,000 injured in the war.

1918 **The Fourteen Points** for peace are proposed by President Wilson, including the setting up of the international League of Nations to prevent future wars.

1919 **When Senate refuses** to ratify the peace treaties drafted at Versailles and join the League of Nations, Wilson tours the country rallying support for his policies. In September he collapses and later suffers a stroke, ending any chance of the US agreeing to join the League.

1920 **The 18th Amendment** to the Constitution outlaws the sale of alcohol throughout the country, ushering in Prohibition. The ban has the effect of driving drinking underground into illegal speakeasies and the hands of criminal gangs, as well as supporting a massive illegal trade in bootleg liquor. Neighboring Canada and Mexico both benefit from cross-border smuggling.

1920 **The 19th Amendment** to the Constitution grants all women the vote.

1920 **Warren G. Harding** is elected president on a program of "a return to normalcy," appealing to isolationist tendencies in the country. He is soon embroiled in the "Teapot Dome" corruption scandal over the management of naval oil reserves, but dies in office in 1923. He is succeeded by vice president Calvin Coolidge, who presides over a long period of unsustainable economic growth during the "jazz age."

1921 **William Taft,** president from 1909 to 1913, is named Chief Justice of the Supreme Court, the only man ever to head both the executive and judicial branches of the federal government.

1921 **The Emergency Quota** Act, and 1924's Johnson–Reed Act, both introduce quotas for immigrants based on the population of ethnic groups in the 1910 and 1890 censuses. Small quotas are allowed for Syria, Turkey, and Palestine, but all other Asian immigration to the US is now banned.

1925 **The Scopes Trial** takes places in Dayton, Tennessee, of a teacher charged with, and then convicted of, teaching evolution rather than creationism.

1927 **The first "talkie"**—*The Jazz Singer*—staring Al Jolson, opens in New York. The previous year, *Don Juan* had become the first movie with a synchronized musical score. Within a few years, the era of the silent movie is over.

1928 **Herbert Hoover, a** Republican, is elected 31st president by a landslide, promising that there will be "a chicken in every pot and a car in every garage."

US WRITER (1902–68)

JOHN STEINBECK

The third American writer to win the Nobel Prize for Literature (1962), Steinbeck's novels describe the plight of ordinary Americans struggling to survive difficult times with empathy and insight. Born in California, Steinbeck hit his literary stride during the Great Depression with the short novel *Of Mice and Men* (1937) and the novel considered to be his masterpiece, *The Grapes of Wrath* (1940), which told the story of the Joads, a family fleeing the dust bowl for California.

"I pledge you, I pledge myself, to a **new deal** for the **American people**."

FRANKLIN D. ROOSEVELT, PRESIDENTIAL NOMINATION ACCEPTANCE SPEECH, CHICAGO, JULY 2, 1932

1929 First Academy Awards ("Oscars") are presented in Hollywood.

1929 New York stock market collapses on Black Tuesday, October 29, leading to major national and then international economic depression.

1930 The US population hits 123 million, up 30 million since 1910.

1931 The Empire State Building opens in New York and remains the world's tallest building for more than 40 years.

1932 Franklin D. Roosevelt wins the election as Democratic candidate over the incumbent Republican president Herbert Hoover.

1933 Roosevelt becomes president, stating at his inauguration that "the only thing we have to fear is fear itself." Faced with near economic collapse and a run on the banking system, he calls an immediate session of Congress. In an unprecedented 100 days of legislation, he tackles banking, industry, agriculture, labor, and agricultural relief in order to promote economic recovery. Among the many new institutions he sets up to reduce unemployment are the Federal Relief Emergency Administration, the Civilian Conservation Corps, the Tennessee Valley Authority, and the Civic Works Administration.

1933 Roosevelt makes the first of his nationwide radio "fireside chats" to the American people in March, using this and later broadcasts to explain his policies and reassure the people about their future.

1933 The 21st Amendment to the Constitution repeals the 18th Amendment of 1919 and ends Prohibititon.

1934 Drought turns much of the midwest into a dust bowl, while farm prices have dropped by half over the previous four years. Many farmers are forced to sell their land and leave.

1935 The Supreme Court rules that the National Industrial Recovery Act, which regulates wages, hours, working conditions, and collective bargaining in factories, is unconstitutional.

1935 The Social Security Act provides old age pensions and unemployment benefits, and help for children with disabilities. The Act is one of the most important pieces of social legislation passed in the US and remains the basis for most federal welfare provisions today.

1936 The Supreme Court invalidates the New Deal Agricultural Adjustment Act.

Roosevelt's subsequent attempt to reform the court's membership fails, tarnishing his reputation.

1936 Roosevelt wins a landslide reelection victory, carrying every state except Maine and Vermont and winning the greatest electoral majority since 1820. The Democrats achieve large majorities in both houses of Congress. He takes office in 1937, stating that "I see one-third of a nation ill-housed, ill-clad, ill-nourished."

1939 US remains neutral as World War II breaks out in Europe in September.

1940 US gains the right to acquire leases on British bases in the Americas, such as those in Newfoundland, Bermuda, and the Caribbean, in order to defend itself against possible attack. The first peacetime program of compulsory military service is introduced, providing for the registration of all men between ages 21 and 35. Other measures are taken to prepare the country for a possible war against Germany or Japan.

1940 President Roosevelt becomes the first American to be elected to a third term as president.

1941 Mount Rushmore Memorial, bearing the portraits of presidents Washington, Jefferson, Theodore Roosevelt, and Lincoln, is completed.

1941 Lend-Lease Act gives arms and other war supplies to Britain by sale, transfer, exchange, or lease. Soon-to-be supplied items are the mass-produced Liberty ships, each one taking at most 42 days to build.

Liberty ships
The Liberty merchant ships were prefabricated in sections for assembly in a shipyard: 600 were built in 1942 alone. Each took vital supplies to Britain.

1941 US troops land in Iceland to prevent its occupation by Germany for use as a naval or air base against the US.

1941–46 The Manhattan Project, code name for the program to build an atomic bomb, begins after Albert Einstein (at the urging of several other scientists) warns President Roosevelt that Nazi Germany may be developing such a weapon. The program, led by army general Leslie Groves and civilian scientist J. Robert Oppenheimer, involves a massive yet secret effort that ultimately costs $2 billion. The first bomb is successfully tested at Alamagordo, New Mexico, on July 16, 1945.

1941 Pearl Harbor: On the morning of December 7, Japanese planes launch a surprise attack on the US naval base at Pearl Harbor in Hawaii, later attacking the

American Philippines, Guam, and Midway. President Roosevelt calls it "a date which will live in infamy." The US declares war on Japan; Germany and Italy—Japan's allies—declare war on the US.

1942 In the Pacific, US forces are pushed on the defensive until they stop the Japanese advance at the Battle of the Coral Sea in May, then turn the tide at Midway in June. Both battles are fought at sea using aircraft carriers operating over vast distances. In November, US and Allied troops land in North Africa to fight against German and Italian troops.

1943 As US troops fight their way across the Pacific, US and Allied troops invade Italy in July. Conferences between the Allied leaders in Québec, Tehran, and Cairo map out the war strategy.

US OVERSEAS TERRITORIES

INCORPORATED TERRITORIES

PUERTO RICO
The Commonwealth of Puerto Rico is the easternmost of the Greater Antilles chain in the Caribbean. Its population density is higher than in any US state.
15th century Puerto Rico is discovered by Columbus and colonized by Spain.
1868 Revolt against colonial rule leads to unsuccessful declaration of independence.
1898 During the Spanish-American War US troops occupy Puerto Rico; the island is ceded by Spain to the US.
1917 Puerto Ricans gain US citizenship.
1932 Name changes from Porto Rico to Puerto Rico.
1947 Limited self-government granted.
1952 Puerto Rico is granted commonwealth association with the US.
1967 A plebiscite on relations with the US results in a 60 percent vote for continuing autonomous commonwealth status.
1968 The pro-statehood New Progressive Party (NPP) under Luis A. Ferre wins the governorship election.
1991 A referendum on the island's future relationship with the US results in a majority in favor of closer integration.
1992 NPP wins governorship and legislative elections.
1993, 1998 Nonbinding referenda produce narrow results in favor of retaining commonwealth status.
2001 Pro-statehood NPP governor replaced by anti-statehood Sila Calderón—the first female governor of Puerto Rico.

NORTHERN MARIANA ISLANDS
The Commonwealth of the Northern Mariana Islands lies in the western Pacific.
1889 Spain sells islands to Germany.
1914 Occupied by Japan at start of World War I and later administered under a League of Nations mandate.
1944 Occupied by US troops.
1947 Become part of US-administered Trust Territory of the Pacific Islands.
1978 Commonwealth status established.
1986 Islanders gains US citizenship.

UNINCORPORATED TERRITORIES

AMERICAN SAMOA
Island group in the southern Pacific.
1899 US and Germany agree to divide Samoan islands between them.
1960 Samoan legislature gains limited law-making authority.

GUAM
Volcanic island at the southern end of the Northern Marianas.
1521 Magellan discovers Guam and claims it for Spain.
1899 Spain cedes island to US.
1950 US Interior Department runs the island; Guamanians gain full US citizenship.

US VIRGIN ISLANDS
Group of islands east of Puerto Rico.
1493 Discovered by Columbus and claimed for Spain.
1672 Danes first settle in islands.
1754 Danish colony established.
1917 Purchased by US for $25 million because of their strategic position on sea routes to the Panama Canal.
1932 Islanders given US citizenship.
1954 US Interior Department runs islands.

OTHER ISLANDS
Howland, Baker & Jarvis Islands, Palmyra Atoll Four small Pacific islands, southwest of Hawaii, administered by the US Department of the Interior (DOI).
Johnson Atoll Two small Pacific islands 680 miles (1,100 km) southwest of Hawaii, administered by the DOI.
Kingman Reef Small Pacific reef, 930 miles (1,500 km) southwest of Hawaii, administered by the US Navy.
Midway Islands Two small islands at the the western end of the Hawaiian chain, administered by the DOI.
Navassa Island Small Caribbean island, 30 miles (48 km) west of Haiti, administered by the DOI.
Wake Island Three small Pacific islands 2,300 miles (3,700 km) west of Hawaii, administered by the DOI.

1943 **After victory in North Africa** the Allies take Sicily and then invade mainland Italy, beginning a long campaign; Rome will not fall until June 1944. The US Army Air Forces continue their strategic bombing campaign against Germany.

1944 **D-Day:** US and Allied troops take part in the largest-ever amphibious landings on the beaches of Normandy in France as they begin the liberation of Europe from Nazi rule.

1944 **In the Pacific,** US forces continue to move closer to Japan, capturing islands in an air-land-sea campaign to bring the Japanese homeland within range of the US Army Air Forces' new B-29 bombers. In October US troops land in the Philippines.

1944 **Roosevelt wins** an unprecedented fourth term as president; Harry S. Truman is elected vice president.

1945 **At Yalta in the Crimea,** Roosevelt, Stalin, and Churchill meet for the last time to plan for the post-war world.

1945 **US and Allied forces** make a final push into Germany following the failure of a major German winter offensive in Belgium (the "Battle of the Bulge"). American units seize an intact bridge across the Rhine River in March, allowing the encirclement of the Ruhr region.

1945 **Following the unexpected** death of Roosevelt in April, Harry S. Truman becomes president. Within a month, the defeat of Nazi Germany brings the war in Europe to an end. At Potsdam, Germany, in late July, the Allied leaders demand the unconditional surrender of Japan.

1945 **President Truman** makes the decision to drop two atomic bombs on the Japanese cities of Hiroshima and Nagasaki, bringing the war in Asia to an end in September. US troops under General Douglas MacArthur occupy Japan and begin to demobilize Japanese troops and reconstruct the country along democractic principles.

1945 **The United Nations charter** is signed by 51 nations in San Francisco. The US is one of the first signatories, supporting the UN as it had failed to support the League of Nations after World War I. The first UN meeting is in London, but it agrees to seek a permanent home in New York, where it meets for the first time on October 23, 1946.

1947 **The Marshall Plan** provides aid to stricken and devastated Europe.

1947 **The House Un-American Activites** Committee begins an investigation into supposed communist infiltration of the movie industry.

1948 **The US armed forces** are integrated for the first time.

1948 **Harry S. Truman wins** a surprise election victory over his Republican rival, Thomas Dewey.

1949 **US joins the** North Atlantic Treaty Organization (NATO), a mutual defense alliance of western democratic nations, the first time the US has entered into such an alliance in peacetime.

1950 **Senator Joseph McCarthy** leads an anticommunist witchhunt. He overreaches himself when, in 1954, he attacks the president, and is condemned by the Senate for misconduct.

Give 'em Hell, Harry!
Harry S. Truman's 1948 victory was a great political upset; before the polls closed, many newspapers (like the one held aloft by a grinning Truman the following morning) prematurely announced a Republican victory.

> " **Ask not what your country can do for you**—ask what you can do for **your country**."
>
> JOHN F. KENNEDY, INAUGURAL ADDRESS, WASHINGTON, DC, JANUARY 20, 1961

1950–53 **Korean War:** US and allies fight under the UN to prevent a communist takeover of Korea.

1952 **Dwight D. Eisenhower,** the Republican former Supreme Allied Commander in Western Europe during World War II, is elected president; Richard Nixon is vice president.

1954 **Supreme Court rules** racial segregation in schools is unconstitutional. African–Americans, seeking rights, begin a campaign of civil disobedience.

1955 **Rock 'n' roll hits America** as Bill Haley tops the charts with "Rock Around the Clock." The next year, Elvis Presley tops the charts for the first time.

1955–56 **Boycott of racially segregated** buses led by Martin Luther King succeeds in Montgomery, Alabama.

1957 **US troops** enforce desegregation of schools in Little Rock, Arkansas.

1959 **Alaska and Hawaii** become the 49th and 50th states of the Union. No new states have been admitted since.

1960 **John F. Kennedy** wins election as president by a narrow majority against his Republican opponent, Richard Nixon. A US-backed invasion of Cuba to overthrow Fidel Castro fails.

1961 **The US manned space program** begins when Commander Alan Shepard is launched into space. President Kennedy pledges to land a man on the moon by the end of the decade.

1962 **Soviet missile bases** are sited on Cuba; the threat of nuclear war is averted when the USSR decides not to launch the missiles.

1963 **Martin Luther King, Jr.** leads a massive civil rights demonstration in Washington, during which he makes his famous "I have a dream" speech.

1963 **Kennedy is assassinated** in Dallas, Texas; Lyndon B. Johnson, Kennedy's vice president, becomes president.

1964 **Civil Rights Act** outlaws racial discrimination in jobs and services.

1964 **US involvement in** Vietnam steps up after an incident in the Gulf of Tonkin, where the Vietnamese supposedly attack two American destroyers.

1964 **Lyndon B. Johnson** wins huge election victory over Republican Barry Goldwater.

1966 **As America commits** more troops to Vietnam, protests against the war build up and race riots break out in many US cities.

1968 **Martin Luther King, Jr.,** is assassinated in Memphis, Tennessee. Robert Kennedy is assassinated in Los Angeles while running for president.

1968 **As the Vietnam** conflict intensifies during the Tet Offensive, and opposition to the war grows, President Johnson decides not to run for reelection; Richard Nixon wins the election for the Republicans, but continues the US policy in Vietnam.

1969 **Woodstock rock festival:** more than 400,000 people attend a rock festival in upstate New York, one of the seminal events of the 1960s.

Nixon in China
In 1972 President Nixon attempted to normalize relations with communist China by making a historic visit. He did not know until he landed whether he would be allowed to meet Mao.

1969 **Man on the moon:** Neil Armstrong becomes the first man to walk on the moon when he steps off Apollo 11 on July 20, 1969: "That's one small step for a man, one giant leap for mankind."

1970 **Four students are shot dead** by National Guardsmen at Kent State University in Ohio, while protesting against the war in Vietnam.

1971 **The 26th Amendment** to the Constitution lowers the voting age to 18 in all elections. A proposed amendment guaranteeing women's rights is passed by Congress in 1973 but falls three states short of ratification in 1982.

1972 Nixon makes a historic visit to communist China and meets Chairman Mao, the first meeting between the leaders of the two countries since the communists took over China in 1949.

1973 Roe v. Wade: a historic Supreme Court decision strikes down state abortion laws as violations of the right to privacy, thus making abortions legal in the US.

1973 Withdrawal of US troops from Vietnam; 58,000 US troops have been killed in the conflict. Two years later, the North Vietnamese take over the south and reunify the country.

1973 Vice president Spiro T. Agnew resigns after a charge of income tax evasion. House minority leader Gerald Ford is appointed vice president.

1974 Richard Nixon resigns following the Watergate scandal over the break-in at Democratic Party headquarters at the Watergate Hotel in Washington, DC, during the 1972 election. Nixon authorized the break-in and then tried to cover up the evidence. The House of Representatives begins impeachment proceedings, but Nixon decides to resign. Gerald Ford succeeds him, becoming the first president never to have been elected as either president or vice president.

1975 Gerald Ford is the object of two assassination attempts in a three-week period in September. He is unharmed in both incidents.

1975 A US Apollo and a Soviet Soyuz spacecraft dock in orbit.

1975 Bil Gates and Paul Allen start Microsoft to develop software for personal computers.

1976 Democrat Jimmy Carter is elected president. Carter, a former governor of Georgia, is the first candidate from the Deep South to be elected president since the Civil War.

1981 IBM PC
IBM's decision to license the PC's technology to other computer-makers led to the proliferation of inexpensive "PC clones," speeding up the adoption of computers in offices and homes.

THE 50 STATES OF THE UNION					
NAME	DATE OF ADMISSION	ORDER OF ADMISSION	STATE CAPITAL	AREA (mi²)	POPULATION (2009 EST)
Alabama (AL)	1819	22	Montgomery	50,744	4,708,708
Alaska (AK)	1959	49	Juneau	571,951	698,473
Arizona (AZ)	1912	48	Phoenix	113,635	6,595,778
Arkansas (AR)	1836	25	Little Rock	52,068	2,889,450
California (CA)	1850	31	Sacramento	155,959	36,961,664
Colorado (CO)	1876	38	Denver	103,717	5,024,748
Connecticut (CT)	1788	5	Hartford	4,844	3,518,388
Delaware (DR)	1787	1	Dover	1,954	885,122
Florida (FL)	1845	27	Tallahassee	53,927	18,537,969
Georgia (GA)	1788	4	Atlanta	57,906	9,829,211
Hawaii (HI)	1959	50	Honolulu	6,423	1,295,178
Idaho (ID)	1890	43	Boise	82,747	1,545,801
Illinois (IL)	1818	21	Springfield	55,584	12,910,409
Indiana (IN)	1816	19	Indianapolis	35,867	6,423,113
Iowa (IA)	1846	29	Des Moines	55,869	3,007,856
Kansas (KS)	1861	34	Topeka	81,815	2,818,747
Kentucky (KY)	1792	15	Frankfort	39,728	4,314,113
Louisiana (LA)	1812	18	Baton Rouge	43,562	4,492,076
Maine (ME)	1820	23	Augusta	30,862	1,318,301
Maryland (MD)	1788	7	Annapolis	9,774	5,600,388
Massachusetts (MA)	1788	6	Boston	7,840	5,699,478
Michigan (MI)	1837	26	Lansing	56,804	9,969,727
Minnesota (MN)	1858	32	St. Paul	79,610	5,266,214
Mississippi (MS)	1817	20	Jackson	46,907	2,951,996
Missouri (MO)	1821	24	Jefferson City	68,886	5,987,580
Montana (MT)	1889	41	Helena	145,552	974,989
Nebraska (NE)	1867	37	Lincoln	76,872	1,796,619
Nevada (NV)	1864	36	Carson City	109,826	2,643,085
New Hampshire (NH)	1788	9	Concord	8,968	1,324,575
New Jersey (NJ)	1787	3	Trenton	7,417	8,717,925
New Mexico (NM)	1912	47	Santa Fe	121,356	2,009,671
New York (NY)	1788	11	Albany	47,214	19,541,453
North Carolina (NC)	1789	12	Raleigh	48,711	9,380,884
North Dakota (ND)	1889	39	Bismarck	68,976	646,844
Ohio (OH)	1803	17	Columbus	40,948	11,542,645
Oklahoma (OK)	1907	46	Oklahoma City	66,667	3,687,050
Oregon (OR)	1859	33	Salem	95,997	3,825,657
Pennsylvania (PA)	1787	2	Harrisburg	117,347	12,604,767
Rhode Island (RI)	1790	13	Providence	1,045	1,053,209
South Carolina (SC)	1788	8	Columbia	30,109	4,561,242
South Dakota (SD)	1889	40	Pierre	75,885	812,383
Tennessee (TN)	1796	16	Nashville	41,217	6,296,254
Texas (TX)	1845	28	Austin	261,797	24,782,302
Utah (UT)	1896	45	Salt Lake City	82,144	2,784,572
Vermont (VT)	1791	14	Montpelier	9,250	621,760
Virginia (VA)	1788	10	Richmond	39,594	7,882,590
Washington (WA)	1889	42	Olympia	66,544	6,664,195
West Virginia (WV)	1863	35	Charleston	24,077	1,819,777
Wisconsin (WI)	1848	30	Madison	54,310	5,654,774
Wyoming (WY)	1890	44	Cheyenne	97,100	544,270
District of Columbia (DC)	–	–	–	69	599,657

1976 US celebrates 200 years of independence.

1977 Apple Computer founders Steve Jobs and Steve Wozniak introduce the Apple II. Easy to use and expandable, it helps create a market for personal computers in homes, offices, and schools.

1977 US agrees to hand back the Canal Zone to Panama in 1999.

1977 A 24-hour blackout strikes New York City on July 13.

1977 A new cabinet department—the Department of Energy—is created.

1978 US-sponsored Camp David accords between Egypt and Israel.

1978 Proposition 13, A statewide referendum that leads to a drastic reduction in property taxes, passes in California and is seen as a sign of a move to the right in American politics.

1979 The Chrysler Corporation asks the federal government for a $1 billion loan to avoid bankruptcy.

1979 The US Treasury issues the nation's first $1 coin, bearing the likeness of women's rights pioneer Susan B. Anthony. The coin never wins widespread acceptance.

1979 Nuclear disaster at Three Mile Island power station in Harrisburg, Pennsylvania, as a faulty cooling system leads to a meltdown inside the reactor and the release of some radiation: it is the worst nuclear accident in US history.

1979 Iranian militants occupy the US embassy in Tehran and take 52 hostages, who are eventually released after 444 days in captivity.

1980 A botched attempt at rescuing the US hostages in Tehran on April 8 leads to the death of eight servicemen in the Iranian desert.

1980 The US and the People's Republic of China establish diplomatic relations.

US PRESIDENT (1911–2004)

RONALD REAGAN

Ronald Reagan was the 40th President of the United States (1981–89). Born to a family of modest means in Illinois, he was a Hollywood actor before entering politics. In 1962 he switched allegiance from the Democrats to the Republicans, winning the California governorship in 1966 and the US presidency in 1980.

A genial and relaxed personality, Reagan is credited with revitalizing America's economy after a recession. Nicknamed "Reaganomics," his policies consisted of job creation, tax cuts, deregulation, but soaring budget deficits. Reagan was reelected by a landslide in 1984, after record-breaking economic growth.

Though virulently anticommunist, his good relationship with Soviet premier Mikhail Gorbachev helped bring a peaceful end to the Cold War.

1980 **Ronald Reagan wins** election for the Republicans.

1981 **John Hinckley, Jr.,** shoots and wounds Ronald Reagan outside a Washington, DC, hotel.

1981 **Columbia, the world's** first reusable space shuttle, makes its maiden flight.

1981 **Sandra Day O'Connor,** a Republican, becomes the first female US Supreme Court Justice.

1983 **Military invasion of** Grenada to overthrow left-wing government.

1984 **Reagan wins** a landslide victory against the Democrat Walter Mondale.

1985 **Relations with the USSR** improve as President Reagan and Mikhail Gorbachev hold the first of three summits.

1986 **Iran–Contra affair** is revealed: the US government has illegally supplied arms to Iran and used the profits to fund the Contra rebels fighting the elected left-wing government of Nicaragua.

Oprah Winfrey
One of the most influential (and wealthiest) media figures in the world, Winfrey overcame poverty to create a media empire including a talk show, a magazine, and stage and screen productions.

1987 **Intermediate-Range Nuclear Forces** Treaty signed by US and USSR: all intermediate-range missiles are destroyed, the first time a complete class of missiles has been destroyed.

1987 **The Space Shuttle** *Challenger* explodes shortly after launch on January 28, killing all seven astronauts aboard. The crew included New Hampshire schoolteacher Christa McAuliffe.

1987 **US warplanes bomb** Tripoli, Libya, after a bomb believed to have been planted by Libyan agents kills three people, including two US servicemen, in a Berlin nightclub.

1987 **On "Black Monday,"** October 19, stocks fall steeply, leading to Wall Street's biggest one-day loss in decades.

1988 **In the Persian Gulf,** a missile from the US warship *Vincennes* is mistakenly launched at an Iranian civil airliner. All 290 people aboard are killed.

1988 **Space Shuttle flights,** halted since the *Challenger* disaster, resume with the launch of the shuttle *Discovery*.

1989 **US overthrows** General Noriega of Panama and arrests him on drug charges.

1989 **The oil tanker** *Exxon Valdez* runs aground in Prince William Sound, Alaska, spilling more than 1 million barrels of oil in what is perhaps the worst environmental disaster in US history.

1991 **US-led Gulf War** liberates Kuwait from Iraqi occupation. The conflict begins in August 1990 when Iraqi forces invade the neighboring country, which Iraqi dictator Saddam Hussein claims is Iraq's "19th Province." The first phase of the war, Operation Desert Shield, is the buildup of US and other coalition forces (including those from several Arab nations) in Saudi Arabia. The second phase, Operation Desert Storm, begins with a massive air offensive, followed by a land campaign that lasts three days before the Iraqis retreat from Kuwait. Saddam Hussein remains in power, however.

1992 **Black youths riot** in Los Angeles and other cities after an all-white jury acquits four white Los Angeles police officers of beating a black motorist, Rodney King, despite video evidence. In three days of violence in Los Angeles, more than 50 people are killed and the city sustains about $1 billion in property damage.

1992 **Democratic candidate** Bill Clinton defeats George Bush in his bid for reelection. Al Gore becomes vice president. (Running as an Independent, billionaire businessman H. Ross Perot receives almost 19 percent of the popular vote.) Bush's popularity had soared following the successful conclusion of the Gulf War, but an economic recession (and Bush's violation of his pledge not to raise taxes) hampered him in the months prior to the election.

1993 **Martin Luther King, Jr.'s** birthday becomes a public holiday in all 50 states.

1994 **Health care reform** legislation is defeated in Congress.

1994 **North American Free Trade** Agreement with Canada and Mexico goes into effect.

1994 **Special counsel investigation** of Whitewater affair begins over the Clintons' financial dealings in Arkansas.

In midterm elections, the Republicans gain majorities in both houses of Congress. Newt Gingrich, architect of the victories with his "Contract with America," becomes Speaker of the House.

1995 **Oklahoma City bombing by** right-wing activist Timothy McVeigh; over 160 die when a truck bomb is detonated outside the city's federal office building.

1996 **Clinton and Gore reelected.**

1997 **Madeleine Albright** becomes the first woman to head the State Department.

1998 **Scandal over Clinton's** affair with a White House intern leads to impeachment proceedings for suspected perjury and abuse of power.

1998 **US embassies** in Kenya and Tanzania are bombed by Islamic militants; the US launches air strikes on Sudan and Afghanistan in revenge.

1999 **Clinton is acquitted** in his impeachment trial as the Senate finds him not guilty of perjury by 55 votes to 45.

1999 **In the Kosovo War,** warplanes and missiles from US and other NATO forces attack Yugoslavia.

1999 **Columbine High School** in Colorado is the scene of a horrific school shooting;

> " I can hear you. The rest of the world hears you. And the people who **knocked these buildings down** will hear all of us soon."

PRESIDENT GEORGE W. BUSH TO RESCUE WORKERS AT GROUND ZERO, SEPTEMBER 14, 2001

Ceremony at Ground Zero
On September 11, 2002, relatives of those who died in the attack on the World Trade Center gathered to mark the first anniversary of 9/11. Among those killed on 9/11 were 343 New York City firefighters and 50 New York City and Port Authority police officers.

two students kill 12 of their fellow students and a teacher before turning their guns on themselves.

2000 **In the presidential election,** Al Gore, the Democratic candidate, eventually concedes to Republican candidate George W. Bush, son of the former president. Gore receives more popular votes than Bush, but the contest is decided by a few thousand highly controversial ballots cast in Florida, home state of Governor Jeb Bush, George Bush's brother.

2000 **The growth of the Internet** fuels the booming economy, as shown by online service America Online's purchase of "old media" conglomerate Time Warner for $160 billion in the largest corporate merger to date. By the end of the year, however, the so-called "Internet Bubble" has largely burst, driving many companies out of business and others (like AOL Time Warner) to suffer big drops in share value.

2001 **9/11:** In the world's worst terrorist attack, Al-Qaeda kills nearly 3,000 people as two hijacked planes are flown into the twin towers of the World Trade Center in New York and a third hits the Pentagon in Virginia. A fourth hijacked plane crash-lands in a field in Pennsylvania. In the aftermath of the attack, President Bush launches a "war on terror."

2001 **Anthrax spores are** sent through the mail. They kill five people and sicken 13 others. The culprit or culprits remain unknown.

2001 **In October** the US and its allies launch air strikes against Afghanistan, and launch a ground offensive a month later. This offensive topples the country's Taliban regime, which is accused of harboring the Al-Qaeda leader Osama bin Laden. Suspected Al-Qaeda members and others are held in the US naval base at Guantánamo Bay, Cuba. They are classified as "illegal combatants," and denied the rights of prisoners of war under the Geneva Convention.

2002 **The murder rate falls** to its lowest level for 30 years, but gun crime remains high. The US holds more than 2 million people in prison, almost a quarter of the world's total. African–Americans comprise 12 percent of the US population but 44 percent of its prisoners.

2002 **WorldCom** bankruptcy is the largest-ever corporate collapse.

2002 **The Republicans gain firm** control of both houses of Congress, allowing the president to push through various controversial policies.

2003 **For the second time,** a US space shuttle is lost with all its crew as *Discovery* breaks up over Texas while preparing to land.

2003 **Austrian-born movie star** Arnold Schwarzenegger, a Republican, becomes governor of California.

2003 **Bush launches a war** against Iraq to overthrow Saddam Hussein, whom he accuses of possessing weapons of mass destruction and of supporting international terrorism. US, UK, and other allied troops occupy the country and hold democractic elections, but a large-scale uprising against the occupation and sectarian violence soon result in a state of near civil war, with rising US and UK casualties. Saddam Hussein is captured, and found guilty by an Iraqi court of crimes against humanity; he is executed in December 2006.

2004 **Massachusetts** legalizes same-sex marriage. By now several states legally recognize same-sex civil unions or domestic partnerships, but the use of the term "marriage" to describe these is highly controversial.

2004 **George W. Bush wins** a narrow reelection victory against the Democratic candidate, John Kerry. While Kerry is a Vietnam veteran, a conservative media campaign questioning his wartime service hurts his candidacy, as does the perception among some voters that he doesn't offer a credible plan for ending the conflict in Iraq.

2005 **Hurricane Katrina** leaves New Orleans devastated, as the city's protective levees are breached. There is widespread criticism of the federal government's slow response to the crisis, which leaves hundreds of thousands of people—most of them poor and African–American—homeless and destitute.

2006 **The geographical shift** in America's population toward the south and southwest of the country continues, and Arizona now has the fastest growing population in the country. The state capital, Phoenix, is now the fastest-growing city in the US and sprawls over an area larger than Los Angeles.

2006 **The Democrats** win back control of both houses of Congress as public opinion begins to turn against Bush as the insurgency in Iraq intensifies.

2006 **On October 23,** at 7:46 a.m. Eastern Time, the 300 millionth American is born somewhere in the country. The population has increased by 50 percent, from 200 million, in the last 39 years. Due to legal and illegal immigration, the percentage of foreign-born Americans is now at least 11 percent nationwide, according to the 2000 Census.

2007 **Virginia issues the first** official apology for slavery made by any US state. It expresses "profound regret" for slavery and the exploitation of American Indians by white settlers. The apology is all the more important as Virginia was at the heart of the Confederacy during the Civil War.

2007 **January: US Representative** Nancy Pelosi is sworn in as the first female Speaker of the House of Representatives.

2007 **February: Barack Obama,** US senator from Illinois, announces he will

Pro-immigration rally
New Yorkers demonstrate in support of immigration reform in March 2007. There are now an estimated 10–12 million illegal immigrants in the US, with the largest percentage from Mexico.

seek the Democratic nomination for president in the 2008 election. With former first lady and current US senator from New York Hilary Clinton also seeking the party's nomination, the upcoming election is widely seen as being the first in US history in which a woman or an African–American stands a good chance of reaching the White House.

2007 **April: At Virginia Polytechnic** Institute and State University in Blacksburg, Virginia, student Cho Seung Hui uses two handguns to kill 32 people. He commits suicide at the end of the rampage. The massacre is not only the worst school shooting in US history, but also the country's deadliest single episode of gun violence.

2007 **April: Dow Jones** Industrial Average closes above 13,000 for the first time.

2007 **May: Congress approves** a $100 billion spending package to continue financing the war in Iraq. The bill passes without setting a timetable for US withdrawal from Iraq.

2008 **The United States** is hit by its worst economic crisis since the Great Depression as problems in the subprime mortgage market spill over and affect the banking system more generally. The investment bank Lehman Brothers goes bankrupt, while the giant Fannie Mae and Freddie Mac mortgage-underwriting companies are taken under government control. The government pushes through an Economic Stabilization act and guarantees billions of dollars of support for other banks to prevent a complete meltdown of the global banking system.

2009 **The Democrat Barack Obama,** elected in November 2008, takes office as the 44th president of the United States in January. He is the first African–American to hold such high office. His first priority is the managing of the economic crisis, but he seeks also to mark a change from American foreign policy under George W. Bush by reaching out to Muslim countries, offering a dialogue with Iran. In October he is awarded the Nobel Peace Prize. He pledges an increase in US troop levels in Afghanistan and pushes through a substantial health care reform bill.

2010 **In April, an explosion** on the Deepwater Horizon oil rig in the Gulf of Mexico, operated by BP, leads to a massive seepage of oil and months of struggle to contain the spill. By the time the well is sealed in September, around 5 million barrels of oil have leaked out. Intense political pressure on BP in the US results in the company pledging a $20 billion fund to compensate those affected by the disaster.

≪236–37 Pilgrim Fathers
≪280–81 The Slave Trade
≪298–99 American Declaration of Independence
≪314–15 The American Civil War
≪418–19 The American Dream
≪430–31 The Vietnam War
≪466–67 9/11

Surge in Iraq
Despite widespread political opposition to a continued US presence in Iraq, in January 2007 President Bush committed an additional 22,000 troops in a bid to secure Baghdad from sectarian violence. Here, fresh US troops await deployment.

Canada

The second-largest country by area in the world, Canada has been independent since 1931.

900s–1000s The eastern coast of present-day Canada is explored and briefly settled by Norse explorers from Greenland.

1497–98 Italian navigator John Cabot explores the coast between Labrador and Chesapeake Bay.

1600s The exploration and settlement of Newfoundland and Québec is carried out.

1608 Québec City is founded.

1610 English Explorer Henry Hudson discovers Hudson Bay.

1629 English forces occupy the French stronghold of Québec City.

1632 Control of New France (the area around present-day Québec) and of Acadia (present-day Nova Scotia and New Brunswick) is granted to France by King Charles I of England.

1663 New France becomes a French Royal colony.

1713 Newfoundland and mainland Acadia are awarded to Britain under the terms of the Peace of Utrecht.

1743–48 King George's War: Britain captures French naval base at Louisbourg on Isle Royale, while French raid New York.

1755–63 The French and Indian War, the American equivalent of the Seven Years War, is concluded by the Treaty of Paris, which awards to Britain all French possessions in Canada except the islands of Saint Pierre and Miquelon off the coast of Newfoundland.

1758 The first elected legislative assembly in British North America meets at Halifax, Nova Scotia.

1774 Québec Act recognizes Roman Catholicism, and French language, culture, and traditions.

1775–83 During the American Revolution, Canada becomes a refuge for loyalists to British Crown.

1867 Federation of Canada is created under British North America Act, uniting Nova Scotia, New Brunswick, Québec, and Ontario.

1870 Manitoba joins the federation, followed by British Columbia in 1871 and Prince Edward Island in 1873.

1885 Transcontinental railroad completed.

1897 Klondike gold rush begins.

1914–18, 1939–45 Canada supports Allies in both world wars.

1931 Autonomy within British Commonwealth.

1949 Founding member of NATO. Newfoundland joins federation.

1968 Liberal Party under Pierre Trudeau in power. Separatist Parti Québécois (PQ) is formed to demand political separation from the federation with economic association.

1969 English and French made the official languages in Canada by the Official Languages Act.

1970s Extremist groups resort to violence to promote Québec's independence.

1976 In Québec, PQ wins elections.

1980 Separation of Québec rejected at referendum. Pierre Trudeau is prime minister again.

1982 UK transfers all powers relating to Canada in British law.

1984 Trudeau resigns. Elections won by Progressive Conservative Party (PCP); Brian Mulroney is prime minister until 1993.

1987 Meech Lake Accord on provincial–federal relationship. It was rejected in 1990.

1989 Canadian–US Free Trade Agreement.

1992 Charlottetown Agreement on provincial–federal issues rejected in a referendum. Canada, Mexico, and US finalize terms for North American Free Trade Agreement (NAFTA).

1993 Crushing election defeat of PCP, which now holds only two seats in parliament, and the rise of regional parties; Jean Chrétien leads Liberal government.

1994 PQ regains power in Québec. NAFTA takes effect.

1995 Narrow "no" vote in a second Québec sovereignty referendum.

1995 Fishing dispute with EU.

1997 Regional considerations again dominate federal elections; Liberals retain power; election victory based on support in Ontario.

1997 Calgary Conference establishes a Canadian unity framework and recognizes Québec's "unique character"; all provinces take part except Québec.

1997 Supreme Court ruling on land rights establishes the principle of "Aboriginial title," opening the way for the return of all ancestral lands claimed by indigenous Canadian and Inuit nations.

1998 The federal government formally apologizes to Canadian Indians for past mistreatment.

1998 PQ only narrowly holds power in Québec.

1999 Nunavut gains the status of a territory, the first part of Canada to be governed by indigenous Inuits.

2000 Federal Clarity Act sets strict criteria for the validation of any pro-independence referendum.

2003 PQ ousted by Liberals in Québec after nine years in power. Chrétien stands down as federal prime minister in favor of Paul Martin.

2004 Early elections: Liberals again retain power, forming a minority government with the federal Bloc Québécois and New Democratic Parties.

2006 In the general election, the Liberals narrowly lose power after financial scandals in government; the newly revived Conservatives under Stephen Harper take power for the first time in 12 years.

2008 Stephen Harper's Progressive Conservative government is reelected.

« 232–33 The Great Food Exchange
« 434–35 Civil Rights

DECISIVE MOMENT

CONSTITUTIONAL CRISIS OVER QUEBEC, 1981

French-speaking Québec's often-fraught relationship with English-speaking Canada reached a new low on November 4, 1981, when Prime Minister Pierre Trudeau met with every provincial premiere except Québec's Réne Lévesque to seek their signatures on a new Canadian constitution. Québec still hasn't signed the document, and 14 years later the Québécois rejected independence in a referendum by a 1 percent majority. For the first time a clear majority of French-speakers voted for secession, and Québec's future remains uncertain.

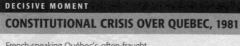

Québec's flag
Formally adopted in 1948, the provincial blue and white flag of Québec is a modern version of the *Fleurdelisé*, an old French-Canadian flag. The *fleur-de-lis* or lily was the traditional symbol of royalist France.

Mexico

A large, mostly Spanish-speaking nation that won independence from Spain in 1821.

c.1325 The Mexica (Aztecs) start construction of the city of Tenochtitlán (modern-day Mexico City) on Lake Texcoco. By the 15th century, the Aztec Triple Alliance of Tenochtitlán, Texcoco, and Tlacopán dominates the Valley of Mexico, and its power reaches the Pacific and Atlantic coasts.

1519–21 Hernán Cortés lands in Mexico and takes control of the Aztec empire ruled by Emperor Moctezuma.

1522 Cortés is named captain-general of Spanish-controlled American territories known as New Spain.

1535 The Viceroyalty of New Spain, incorporating the Captaincy-General, is established. By 1546 the Spaniards have discovered large silver mines at Zacatecas.

1808 The Viceroy of New Spain is ousted but the territory remains in royalist hands (supporting Ferdinand VII of Spain whom Napoleon had deposed) until 1821.

1810 Father Miguel Hidalgo leads abortive rising against Spanish.

1821 Spanish viceroy forced to leave by Mexican rebel Agustín de Iturbide, who is proclaimed emperor of Mexico.

1822 Federal Republic established.

1823 Texas opened to US immigration.

1830 Mexican troops fail to control increased immigration from the US.

1836 Texas declares its independence from Mexico and is recognized by the US and Spain.

1845 US annexes Texas.

1846 War breaks out with US following its annexation of Texas.

1848 Mexico loses modern-day New Mexico, Arizona, Nevada, Utah, California, and part of Colorado to the US by the Treaty of Guadalupe Hidalgo.

1853 Mexico sells strip of land to the US in the Gadsden Purchase, allowing the US Southern Pacific Railroad to cross from Texas into southern California; the land now forms the southern part of Arizona and New Mexico.

1857–61 War of Reform won by anticlerical Liberals.

1862 France, Britain, and Spain launch military expeditions to Mexico.

1863 French troops capture Mexico City. Maximilian of Austria established as Mexican emperor.

Face of the "Porfiriato"
General Porfirio Díaz (1830–1915) seized power in 1876. His government, known as the *Porfiriato*, was economically successful, but his rigging of the 1910 general election led to his overthrow in 1911.

1867 **Mexico City recaptured by** Benito Juárez. Maximilian shot.

1876 **Porfirio Díaz president.** Economic growth; rail system built.

1901 **First year of** oil production.

1910–20 **Mexican Revolution provoked** by the perceived exclusion from power of the middle classes and desire for land reform among peasants; 250,000 killed in this long-running and brutal civil war.

1911 **Díaz overthrown by** Francisco Madero. Guerrilla war breaks out in north. Emiliano Zapata leads peasant revolt in the south.

1913 **Madero murdered.** He is replaced by his chief of staff, General Victoriano Huerta. He faces opposition from Zapata in the south, Pancho Villa in the north, and from within his own elite from Venustiano Carranza.

1914 **President Wilson** of the US intervenes in the civil war by deposing General Huerta, whom he distrusts: Wilson also sends warships to Tampico and troops to Veracruz in order to safeguard US interests in Mexico.

1917 **New constitution limits** power of the Church. Mineral and subsoil rights reserved for the nation. Carranza becomes first president under the new constitution.

1919 **Zapata is assassinated** under Carranza's orders. Carranza is himself murdered a year later on the orders of his own army commander, Álvaro Obregón, who assumes the presidency. Villa is murdered in 1923.

1926–29 **Cristero rebellion led by** militant Catholic priests.

1929 **National Revolutionary Party** (later the Institutional Revolutionary Party, PRI) is formed.

1934 **General Cárdenas president.** Land reform accelerated, cooperative farms established, railroads nationalized, and US and UK oil companies expelled.

1940s **US war effort** helps Mexican economy grow.

1946 **Election of Miguel Alemán** as PRI president is opposed unsuccessfully by the last military rebellion in Mexico's history. Alemán's pro-business administration begins period of economic prosperity known as the "Mexican Miracle."

1968 **An uprising** by students in Mexico City results in a bloody massacre.

1970 **Accelerating population** growth reaches 3 percent a year.

1982 **Mexico declares** it cannot repay its foreign debt of over $800 billion.

1984 **Government contravenes** constitution by relaxing laws on foreign investment.

1985 **Earthquake in Mexico City.** Official death toll 7,000. Economic cost estimated at $425 million.

1988 **Carlos Salinas de Gortari**, minister of planning during the earthquake, is elected president.

1990 **Privatization program begins.**

1994–95 **Guerrilla rebellion in** southern Chiapas state by the Zapatista National Liberation Army (EZLN) for Amerindian rights is brutally suppressed by the army with at least 100 killed. Mexico joins North American Free Trade Agreement (NAFTA). PRI presidential candidate Luis Colosio murdered. Ernesto Zedillo replaces him and is elected. Economic crisis.

1997 **Watershed elections;** end of PRI's monopoly on power in Congress.

1999 **Austerity budget** and controversial bail-out of the banking system approved with the support of the National Action Party (PAN).

2000 **PAN** wins presidency and elections, ending 70 years of PRI rule. President Vicente Fox takes office, promising an end to corruption.

2001 **EZLN guerrillas** make 16-day motorcade from Chiapas to Mexico City to push for an indigenous rights law.

2006 **In contested elections**, PRI collapses to become the third political force after PAN and the Party of the Democratic Revolution (PRD). In the concurrent presidential election, PAN's Felipe Calderón wins by a tiny margin over the PRD's Andrés Manuel López Obrador.

2009 **H1N1 "Swine flu"** is first identified in Mexico and spreads worldwide.

«210–13 Pre-Columbian Americas
«214–15 Aztec to Inca
«318–19 Latin America Liberated

Guatemala

The largest and most populous of the states on the Central American isthmus.

c.250–900 CE **Maya city-states** flourish in modern-day southern Mexico and Central America. Maya civilization collapses as the cities are abandoned in the 8th and 9th centuries.

1524 **The Spaniards set** foot in Guatemala and in 1526 incorporate it into the Viceroyalty of New Spain.

1821 **As a regional** capital of the Viceroyalty of New Spain, Guatemala proclaims its independence.

1823 **Guatemala, along with** El Salvador, Honduras, Nicaragua, and Costa Rica reaffirm their independence as the United Provinces of Central America.

1838 **Guatemala leaves the** United Provinces to become an independent republic.

1944 **General Jorge Ubico Castañeda**, who took power in 1931, is overthrown in a popular uprising. Liberal reformer Juan José Arévalo wins the subsequent 1945 election.

1951 **Jacobo Arbenz Guzmán** is elected president and in 1952 introduces land reform and social reform measures.

1954 **US-backed coup** topples reformist Arbenz government.

1966–84 **Counter-insurgency war;** "pacification" of the highland Amerindians by the army; 200,000 die.

1986 **Return of civilian** rule; Marco Vinicio Cerezo Arévalo elected president.

US-sponsored coup
The CIA backed the coup of 1954 that overthrew President Arbenz after plantations run by the US-owned United Fruit Company were expropriated. The coup (above) led to 30 years of military rule.

1991 **Jorge Antonio Serrano** elected president but flees country after abortive "self-coup" in 1993.

1996 **President Álvaro Arzú elected;** peace deal with the Guatemalan National Revolutionary Unity (URNG) guerrillas ends 36 years of civil war.

1999 **Truth Commission** blames army and paramilitary allies for almost all human rights abuses during the civil war.

2005 **Floods and mudslides** caused by tropical storm Stan kill 1,500 people.

2007 **Alvaro Colom** of the center-left National Unity of Hope Party is elected president.

«74–75 People of the Jaguar
«210–13 Pre-Columbian Americas
«214–15 Aztec to Inca

Belize

Formerly British Honduras, Belize was the last country in the region to gain independence.

1670 **Spain, the colonial** power in Central America, recognizes certain British rights in the uninhabited area then bordered by the Sarstoon River.

1798 **Spain, which continues** to claim sovereignty, is defeated at the battle of St. George's Cay.

1802 **British sovereignty over** the colony is recognized by the Peace of Amiens.

1821 **Guatemala claims sovereignty** over the territory.

1862 **The area becomes** a British crown colony known as British Honduras.

1919 **Demands for more** rights by black Belizeans returning from World War I.

1936 **New constitution with** limited franchise introduced.

1950 **People's United Party** formed; voting age qualification for women reduced from 30 to 21.

1954 **Full adult suffrage.**

1972 **Guatemala threatens invasion.** Britain sends troops.

1981 **Full independence.**

1998 **People's United Party** wins crushing general election victory.

2000 **Guatemala revives claim** to half of the country.

2003 **Guatemala rejects** draft treaty aimed at settling border dispute.

«230–31 Contact Americas
«230–31 The Great Food Exchange

Honduras

Still recovering from a devastating hurricane in 1998, while it nurtures a fragile democracy.

1821 **After forming part** of the Captaincy-General of Guatemala, Honduras becomes independent from Spain and part of Mexico until 1823, and then part of the United Provinces of Central America until 1838.

1838 **Declares full independence.**

1890s **US banana plantations** set up.

1932–49 **Dictatorship of General** Tiburcio Carías Andino of National Party of Honduras (PNH).

1954 **Liberal Party of Honduras's** (PLH) president-elect Villeda Morales is deposed but reelected in 1957 (serving to 1963).

1963 **Military coup.**

1969 **Six-day Soccer War** with El Salvador sparked by a controversial World Cup match.

1980–83 **PLH wins elections** but General Gustavo Alvarez holds real power. Military maneuvers with US. Trade unionists arrested; death squads operate.

1984 **Return to democracy.**

1988 **Twelve thousand** Contra rebels are forced out of Nicaragua into Honduras.

1995 **Military defies** human rights abuse charges.

1998 **Hurricane Mitch wreaks** havoc, causing the deaths of at least 5,600 people and damage estimated at $3 billion.

1999 **Appointment of first** civilian defense minister, consolidating the transition to civilian rule.

1999 **Miskito Amerindians,** about 45,000, and the English-speaking *garífuna* (black) population on the Caribbean coast unite to oppose a constitutional amendment allowing foreigners to buy land in coastal areas, traditionally their communal lands.

2006 **Manuel Zelaya** of the Liberal Party becomes president after a bitterly contested election. He wins on a platform of tackling gang violence and drug trafficking.

2009 **Zelaya is deposed** by the military and replaced by Roberto Micheletti, the Speaker of Congress. The US rejects the coup and the Organization of American States (OAS) suspends Honduras. Zelaya attempts a return but is not reinstated, so goes into exile in the Dominican Republic. Porfirio Lobo Sosa wins the November elections and becomes president.

« 210–13 Pre-Columbian Americas
« 214–15 Aztec to Inca
« 232–33 The Great Food Exchange

El Salvador

The smallest and most densely populated republic in Central America.

1522 **A Spanish expeditionary** force disembarks in the Gulf of Fonseca and calls the territory Cuscatlan.

1525 **San Salvador is** founded by Diego de Alvarado before being transferred to its present location in 1528.

1821 **The territory,** which forms part of the Captaincy-General of Guatemala, proclaims its independence from Spain as part of the United Provinces of Central America. Years of internal conflict ensue.

1838 **The Act of Independence** is signed in Guatemala.

1841 **El Salvador finally leaves** the United Provinces.

1849 **El Salvador** is confirmed as an independent sovereign republic.

1932 **Army crushes popular** insurrection led by Farabundo Martí.

1944–79 **Army rules through** National Conciliation Party (PCN).

1979 **Reformist officers overthrow** PCN government.

1981 **Left-wing Farabundo Martí** National Liberation Movement (FMLN) launches civil war.

1989 **Right-wing Arena** (Nationalist Republican Alliance) party wins the presidential election.

1992 **UN-brokered peace** between the government and the FMLN, which is now recognized as a political party.

1997 **Leftists wins mayoralty** of San Salvador and half the state capitals.

1999 **Arena's Francisco Flores** wins presidential election, reducing the FMLN to a distant second. Flores promises to reduce poverty and redistribute income.

2000 **FMLN wins** assembly elections, retaining power in 2003.

2001 **Devastating earthquakes** kill hundreds; dollarization of economy.

2004 **Arena** retains the presidency, won by Elías Antonio (Tony) Saca, a popular former sports correspondent.

2009 **Mauricio Funes of the** FMNL wins general election, becoming El Salvador's first left-wing president since the end of the civil war. The FMNL has the most seats in parliament.

« 230–31 Contact Americas
« 232–33 The Great Food Exchange
« 438–39 Dictatorship and Democracy

Nicaragua

A country recovering from years of civil war between the government and US-backed guerrillas.

1544 **Nicaragua is incorporated** into the Captaincy-General of Guatemala.

1821 **Nicaragua becomes** independent from Spain and is incorporated into the United Provinces of Central America.

1838 **When the United Provinces** fall apart, Nicaragua becomes a republic.

1856 **US adventurer** William Walker proclaims himself president as part of a move to establish a slave republic in Central America.

1905 **The Altamirano–Harrison** treaty between the UK and Nicaragua recognizes full Nicaraguan sovereignty over the Atlantic coast, where the UK had a protectorate until 1894.

1909 **US marines** land in Bluefields and bring to power Juan Estrada, who signs pacts placing Nicaragua effectively under US administration. The Marines intervene in Nicaragua again in 1912–25 and in 1926–33.

1936 **Anastasio Somoza** takes power after the National Guard forces President Sacasa's resignation, instituting a 53-year family dictatorship.

1956 **On Somoza's** assassination he is succeeded by his son Luis and, in 1967, by his other son Anastasio.

1962 **Foundation of** the Sandinista National Liberation Front (FSLN).

1974 **The FSLN offensive** against the Somoza government gathers force, intensifying into civil war by 1978.

1979 **President Somoza flees** into exile. The Sandinistas take power and redistribute land to landless peasants.

1981 **Rebel Contra guerrillas** based in Honduras and funded by the US begin military campaign against the Sandinista government.

Hurricane Mitch
A devastating blow to Nicaragua came in October 1998, when Hurricane Mitch wrecked the country, destroying the tourist industry and causing at least 3,800 deaths and many more injuries.

1984 **Sandinista leader Daniel Ortega** elected president.

1986 **Nicaragua wins** case at International Court of Justice against US violations of its sovereignty.

1988 **Hurricane Mitch** wrecks country.

1990 **Civil war ends.** Multi-party elections result in the surprise defeat of Ortega and the victory of Violeta Chamorro, widow of a Somoza opponent assassinated in 1978, at the head of anti-Sandinista coalition.

1996 **Arnoldo Alemán** of the Constitutional Liberal Party again defeats Ortega and the Sandinistas, who go on to lose again in 2001.

2006 **Daniel Ortega** returns to power in presidential election.

« 230–31 Contact Americas
« 232–33 The Great Food Exchange
« 438–39 Dictatorship and Democracy

Costa Rica

Costa Rica is the most stable Central American country, with a highly developed welfare state.

1502 **Columbus lands during** the course of his last voyage. In the second half of the century the territory is annexed to the Captaincy-General of Guatemala and becomes a European-oriented society of small landowners.

1821–38 **Upon independence** Costa Rica forms part of the United Provinces of Central America until its dissolution.

1948 **Disputed elections lead** to civil war; ended by Social Democratic Party (later the National Liberation Party, the PLN) forming a provisional military government under José Figueros Ferrer. The army is then abolished and a highly developed welfare state is introduced.

1949 **New constitution** is promulgated, forbidding national armies. A civil guard and police force keep order.

1987 **Central American Peace** Plan initiated by President Óscar Arias of the PLN in an effort to bring peace to the region; he wins the Nobel Peace Prize that year.

2006 **Former president** Óscar Arias returns to power promising a fresh start after a series of corruption scandals.

2007 **Costa Rica votes** for ratification of the Central American Free Trade Area (CAFTA).

2010 **Laura Chinchilla** becomes Costa Rica's first female president.

« 230–31 Contact Americas
« 232–33 The Great Food Exchange
« 438–39 Dictatorship and Democracy

Panama

Long dominated by the US, which recently handed over control of the canal for the first time.

1513 **Vasco Núñez de Balboa** sights the Pacific from Panama, which, due to its position between the two oceans, becomes a commercial center of geopolitical importance until the end of the 18th century.

1717 **As a province** of Colombia, Panama is transferred from the Viceroyalty of Peru to the Viceroyalty of Granada.

1821 **On independence** from Spain, Panama becomes part of Gran Colombia.

1830 **On the breakup** of Gran Colombia, Panama remains part of Colombia.

1889 **French attempt** to build canal ends in failure with 22,000 workers dead.

1903 **With US support** Panama revolts against Colombia, declaring independence. It immediately grants the US rights over an Atlantic–Pacific corridor through its territory so that a canal can be built between the Caribbean and Pacific Ocean.

1914 **The Panama Canal** is completed and formally opens on August 15.

1968 **Accession of** Brigadier-General Omar Torrijos Herrera to power in a coup.

1977 **Torrijos and US** President Carter sign new Panama Canal treaties transferring control of the canal to Panama on December 31, 1999.

1979 **Treaties officially** ending US control over the Panama Canal Zone enter into force.

1987 **A state of emergency** is imposed after antigovernment protests over the alleged rigging of the 1984 elections by the power behind the civilian government, General Manuel Noriega.

1989 **Three days after** presidential elections, Noriega annuls the results.

1989 **Noriega formally assumes** power as head of state with wide powers.

1989 **The US installs** the apparent victor in the 1989 election, Guillermo Endara, as head of state and invades with 23,000 troops to depose Noriega, whom it accuses of drug activities.

1990 **Noriega surrenders** to the US authorities and is taken as a prisoner to the US for trial on drug charges.

1990 **The National Guard** and defense forces are disbanded and replaced by the 11,800-strong Panamanian Public Force, comprising the National Police, the National Air Service, and the National Maritime Service.

DECISIVE MOMENT

THE PANAMA CANAL, 1914

The Panama Canal opened on August 15, 1914. Using an ingenious system of locks to carry ships up over the isthmus, the canal dramatically affected shipping, shortening the sea journey between America's east and west coasts and obviating the need for a perilous rounding of Cape Horn at the tip of South America. The canal resulted in a massive increase in international trade and improved the fortunes of Panama. In 1999, full control of the canal (and its revenues) reverted to Panama.

1994 **The Democratic Revolutionary Party** (PRD), Noriega's old party but now largely pro-US, wins presidential and legislative elections.

1999 **All remaining US troops** leave the country when the Canal Zone is finally handed back to Panama.

1999 **Spill-over from the Colombian** civil war leads to increasing number of border incidents in the south of the country.

1999 **Mireya Moscoso** of the Arnulfista Party (PA) is elected first woman president. Lacking a legislative majority, she struggles to meet her promises to help the poor.

2004 **Martin Torrijos** of the PRD wins the presidency after campaigning to fight corruption and unemployment while improving the social security system.

2005 **Torrijos begins social security** reforms by raising pension contributions and increasing the retirement age; popular protests break out.

2006 **Proposals to widen** the Panama Canal to take larger ships are approved in a national referendum.

2009–10 **Former Panamanian** president Manuel Noriega is extradited from the US to France.

2010 **The candidate of** the conservative opposition Alliance for Change, Ricardo Martinelli, wins presidential election. Trial of Manuel Noriega begins in Paris.

≪280–81 The Slave Trade
≪318–19 Latin America Liberated

Cuba

The largest island in the Caribbean, Cuba is the only communist state in the Americas.

1492 **First Europeans arrive** with Christopher Columbus and claim the island for Spain.

1511 **Cuba is settled** and colonized by Spaniards.

1762 **The British occupy** Havana, returning it to Spain the next year under the Treaty of Paris. Cuba prospers under a slave-labor economy with access to North American markets. A strong Spanish garrison inhibits moves to independence.

1868 **End of the** slave trade.

1868–78 **A major rebellion** against Spanish rule initiates a 10-year guerrilla war, which ends in defeat.

1895 **José Martí lands** along with a small band of rebel exiles to start war of independence. Martí is killed on the first day of fighting and thousands of Cubans subsequently die in Spanish concentration camps.

1898 **In support of** Cuban rebels, the US declares war on Spain to protect strong US financial interests in Cuba.

1899 **US occupies Cuba** and installs military interim government.

1901 **US is granted** intervention rights and military bases, including Guantánamo Bay naval base.

1902 **Tomás Estrada Palma** takes over as first Cuban president. US leaves Cuba, but intervenes in 1906–09 and 1919–24.

1925–33 **Dictatorship of President** Gerardo Machado.

1933 **Years of guerrilla** activity end in revolution. Fulgencio Batista takes over as military dictator.

1955 **Fidel Castro exiled** after two years' imprisonment for subversion.

1956–58 **Castro returns to** lead a guerrilla war in the Sierra Maestra.

1959 **Batista flees.** Castro takes over with his brother Raúl, Che Guevara, and Camilo Cienfuegos as his deputies. Wholesale nationalizations; Cuba reorganized on Soviet model.

1961 **US breaks off** relations. US-backed invasion of Bay of Pigs by anti-Castro Cubans fails. Cuba declares itself a Marxist-Leninist state.

1962 **US economic and** political blockade. Missile crisis: Soviet deployment of nuclear weapons in Cuba leads to extreme Soviet–US tension; war averted by Khrushchev ordering withdrawal of the weapons.

1965 **Che Guevara resigns** to pursue foreign liberation wars.

1972 **Cuba joins COMECON** (the communist economic bloc).

1976 **New socialist constitution.** Cuban troops fight in Angola until 1991.

1977 **Sends troops to** fight in Ethiopia.

1980 **About 25,000 Cubans,** including many "undesirables" (criminals and others), are permitted to leave for the US.

1982 **US tightens sanctions** and bans flights and tourism to Cuba.

1991 **As USSR collapses,** Cuba loses valuable trading partner; rationing is tightened as economy weakens. Policy of encouraging tourism to save economy.

2002 **US base at** Guantánamo Bay used as US prison in "war on terror."

2006 **After an illness** and surgery, Castro transfers power to his brother Raúl.

2008 **Castro announces** he will step down as president. His brother, Raúl takes over and a slow process of liberalization begins. The EU formally lifts sanctions against the country. In September, Cuba is devastated by Hurricanes Gustav and Ike, leaving 200,000 homeless.

≪280–81 The Slave Trade
≪422–23 Viva la Revolución

CUBAN DICTATOR (1926–)

FIDEL CASTRO

Revolutionary leader of Cuba since 1959, Fidel Castro was a lawyer from a wealthy family who took up arms against the Batista regime. Attacked by many for the lack of democracy and human rights in Cuba, Castro's policies have nevertheless given Cubans one of the highest life expectancies in Latin America and a high literacy rate. Despite this, thousands have risked their lives to flee Cuba in search of a better life in the US.

Jamaica

First a Spanish possession and then a British colony, the island of Jamaica won its independence in 1962.

1494 Columbus lands at Dry Harbour, now Discovery Bay, on his second voyage.

1509 Columbus's son Diego Colón takes the island and appoints Juan de Esquivel as the first governor.

1655 An English expedition under Admiral Penn lands. Spain capitulates. Island becomes haven for buccaneers. Sugar cane, cotton, and cattle are established in a slave-labor economy.

1660 The Spanish are finally expelled.

1670 Jamaica is formally ceded to England.

1820s Jamaica becomes one of the world's leading sugar-exporting nations.

1866 Jamaica becomes a British colony.

1938 Norman Manley forms the People's National Party (PNP) as a democratic socialist party. The PNP is the oldest political party in the English-speaking Caribbean.

1942 The discovery of bauxite and its subsequent development displaces sugar as the main industry.

1958–61 Jamaica forms part of the West Indies Federation.

1959 Internal self-government begins.

1962 Independence under the Jamaica Labour Party (JLP), a moderately conservative party, led by Alexander Bustamente.

1972 PNP elected under Michael Manley, its founder's son; reforms fail and street violence begins.

1980 Unpopular IMF austerity measures lead to JLP election win under Edward Seaga.

1989 PNP returned under Michael Manley; austerity continues.

Portia Simpson-Miller
Prime minister of Jamaica since 2006, Portia Simpson-Miller is the third female head of government in the anglophone Caribbean.

1992 Percival Patterson becomes prime minister upon Michael Manley's retirement.

1999 Violent protests over fuel tax increases.

2006 Portia Simpson-Miller of the PNP becomes first female prime minister.

《 **280–81** The Slave Trade

Haiti

A chronically poor nation occupying the western third of the island of Hispaniola.

1492 During his first voyage to the Americas, Columbus reaches Hispaniola.

1697 The buccaneer-based French community of Saint-Domingue is recognized by Spain under the Treaty of Ryswick and flourishes as a rich French plantation colony, with an estimated 500,000 slaves by 1789.

1791 A massacre of French by slaves signals the beginning of a bitter 13–year civil war under Haitian leader Toussaint L'Ouverture. The Haitians strongly resist French, Dutch, and English troops.

1804 Jean-Jacques Dessalines proclaims the independence of Haiti as the first black republic in the Americas and subsequently appoints himself emperor.

1806 Henri Christophe takes part in plot to overthrow Dessalines and is appointed president in 1807, becoming King Henri I in 1811 until his suicide in 1829.

1822–44 Haitians invade the neighboring Spanish colony of Santo Domingo and rule repressively.

1915–34 US occupation.

1957–71 François "Papa Doc" Duvalier's brutal dictatorship.

1971–86 Duvalier's son Jean-Claude, "Baby Doc," rules until forced to flee.

1990 Jean-Bertrand Aristide of left-wing Lavalas party elected; exiled in 1991 coup.

1994–95 US forces oust military. Aristide reinstated; new elections held.

1996 René Préval is elected president.

2000–04 Aristide returns as president, but is ousted by members of the military.

2006 New elections result in the former president René Préval taking office.

2008 Widespread food rioting caused by price increases leads to the fall of Prime Minister Alexis's government.

2009 World Bank and IMF cancel 80 percent of Haiti's debt.

2010 Magnitude 7.0 earthquake near Port-au-Prince kills around 300,000 people.

《 **228–29** Columbus Lands in the Caribbean
《 **280–81** The Slave Trade

Dominican Rep

Sharing the island of Hispaniola with Haiti, this was the first place to be settled by the Spanish.

1492 Columbus reaches the island of Hispaniola. The first area actually to be settled by Spaniards, it becomes the center of Spanish activity and rule in the region, producing gold, sugar, and finally cattle.

1697 The island is divided between Spain and France.

1795 French domination is extended to the Spanish section of Hispaniola, but this is occupied by native Haitian forces under Toussaint L'Ouverture. Between 1809 and 1844 French troops are ejected.

1844 The Dominican Republic achieves independence with the formal but arbitrary division of the two parts of the island.

1861 Spanish colonial rule is reestablished at the request of President Pedro Santana as a bulwark against Haitian attempts to take back the Dominican Republic.

1865 The country finally becomes independent from Spain but further years of instability ensue.

1916–24 The Dominican Republic is occupied by US troops; the US retains customs control until 1940.

1930 General Rafael Trujillo is elected president and establishes a brutal and repressive dictatorship, dominating political life directly or indirectly until his assassination in 1961.

1965 Civil war. US intervention.

1966 Pro-American Joaquín Balaguer starts the first of seven presidential terms over the next 30 years.

1996 Lionel Fernández of the moderate Dominican Liberation Party (PLD) succeeds Balaguer and pledges reforms to stamp out corruption.

1998 Major hurricane damage.

2000 Hipolito Mejía of the center-left Dominican Revolutionary Party (PRD) wins the presidency, but his popularity is soon eroded by high inflation, electricity shortages, and major bank collapses.

2004 Fernández is reelected and introduces austerity measures to stabilize the economy and reduce inflation.

《 **228–29** Columbus Lands in the Caribbean
《 **280–81** The Slave Trade

Bahamas

An English-speaking archipelago in the Atlantic, with a strong economy based on tourism.

1492 Columbus first sets foot on San Salvador (possibly Watling Island).

1647 Islands settled by Puritan refugees from Bermuda.

1690 The islands are granted by the British to the owners of Carolina.

1717 The British Crown assumes direct control, and the first British governor arrives the following year.

1781 Spain seizes the islands.

1783 The islands are recaptured by the British and confirmed as British territory.

1920–33 US prohibition laws turn Bahamas into bootlegging center.

1959–62 Introduction of male suffrage; women gain the vote.

1973 Independence from Britain.

1983 Narcotic-smuggling scandals involving the government.

1992 Free National Movement takes power, ending 25 years of Progressive Liberal Party (PLP) rule.

2002 PLP returns to power under Perry Christie.

2009 Free National Movement under Hubert Ingraham takes power.

《 **228–29** Columbus Lands in the Caribbean

Antigua & Barbuda

British influence remains strong in this former colony in the middle of the Leeward Islands.

1632 After settlement by the Spanish and French in the 16th and early 17th centuries, a permanent British settlement is established under Sir Thomas Warner.

1667 After a brief interlude of French occupation, the Treaty of Breda returns Antigua to Britain.

1860 Barbuda, hitherto owned by the British Codrington family, is formally incorporated into the colony

1951 Universal adult suffrage introduced.

1981 Independence from Britain under Vere Bird; union with Antigua opposed by the Barbudan secessionist movement.

1983 Islands support US invasion of Grenada.

Tourism
Antigua is a popular tourist destination, especially for cruise ships visiting the historic Nelson's Dockyard in English Harbour (above).

1994 Lester Bird succeeds his father as prime minister.

2004 United Progressive Party takes power for the first time.

2009 Financial crisis after Allen Sanford, the island's biggest investor, is charged with fraud.

« 228–29 Columbus Lands in the Caribbean
« 280–81 The Slave Trade

St. Kitts & Nevis

These popular tourist destinations lie at the northern end of the Leeward Islands.

1623 The British first settle on St. Kitts, and on Nevis in 1628; the islands become a British colony in 1783.

1932 Pro-independence St. Kitts-Nevis-Anguilla Labour Party set up.

1967 Internal self-government.

1980 Anguilla formally separates from St Kitts & Nevis.

1983 Independence from Britain.

1998 Nevis referendum rejects secession.

Dominica

Small Caribbean island named after Sunday, the day Christopher Columbus first landed there.

1493 Columbus lands on Dominica.

1759 The island is seized by the British after control has been fiercely contested by British, French, and Caribs in the 17th and 18th centuries. The production of sugar cane is established using slave labor, followed by cotton and coffee.

1805 Dominica becomes a British colony.

1951 Universal suffrage is introduced.

1958–62 Dominica is a member of the West Indies Federation.

1962 A new constitution is introduced as Dominica and other Windward Islands achieve separate status.

1967 Full internal autonomy as a West Indies Associated State, with Edward Le Blanc as prime minister. UK responsible for defense and foreign relations.

1974 On his retirement, Le Blanc is succeeded by Patrick John, who conducts independence negotiations.

1975 Morne Trois Pitons national park established.

1978 Independence from UK. Patrick John is first prime minister.

1980 Eugenia Charles, the Caribbean's first woman prime minister, is elected.

1981 Two coup attempts, backed by Patrick John, are foiled.

1995 Main opposition party defeats Eugenia Charles, who retires.

2004 Roosevelt Skerrit becomes, at 31, the world's youngest serving PM.

2009 Hurricane Dean wipes out 90 percent of Dominica's banana crop.

« 228–29 Columbus Lands in the Caribbean
« 280–81 The Slave Trade

St. Lucia

Ruled by both France and Britain, St. Lucia retains the character of both countries.

1814 Ownership of the island is finally settled in Britain's favor.

1964 Sugar-growing ends on the island.

1979 Gains independence. Tourist boom.

1990 Establishes body with Dominica, Grenada, and St. Vincent to discuss forming a Windward Islands Federation.

2000 Blacklisted by the OECD as an international tax haven.

St. Vincent

St. Vincent & the Grenadines lie towards the southern end of the Windward Islands.

1627 British and French settlers occupy the islands.

1773 The Caribs recognize British rule, but rebel in 1795–7, aided by the French.

1951 Universal suffrage is introduced.

1969 Internal self-government is achieved.

1979 Full independence from Britain. La Soufrière volcano erupts.

1984 New Democratic Party, founded by James Mitchell in 1975, wins first of four terms. Mitchell resigns in 2002.

2001 Unity Labour Party wins a landslide election victory; Ralph Gonsalves becomes prime minister.

« 280–81 The Slave Trade

Barbados

The most easterly of the Windward Islands, Barbados was referred to as "Little England."

1627 Barbados becomes English colony.

1800s Barbados becomes a prosperous sugar-producing colony with more than 80,000 slaves.

1834 The abolition of slavery is a major factor precipitating economic decline.

1951 Universal adult suffrage introduced.

1966 Independence from Britain.

1983 Supports and provides a base for the US invasion of Grenada.

1994–2003 Barbados Labour Party wins three successive general elections.

2008 Democratic Labour Party under David Thompson wins election.

2009 Clico, a Trinidad-based insurance company, collapses, almost toppling Thompson, who dies in office in 2010.

« 280–81 The Slave Trade

Grenada

The most southerly Windward Island, Grenada is a major nutmeg producer.

1498 Columbus visits the island, which he names Concepción.

1650 The island is occupied by forces of the governor of French Martinique.

1674 French control is imposed. Sugar mills are established.

1762 The British take control and introduce a slave-labor economy producing cotton, cocoa, and nutmeg.

1951 Universal suffrage introduced.

1958–62 Grenada forms part of the West Indies Federation.

1967 Internal self-government.

1974 Gains independence from Britain.

1979 Coup makes Maurice Bishop prime minister. Growing links with Cuba.

1983 US invasion establishes pro-US administration.

1995 Keith Mitchell elected prime minister.

2004 Hurricane Ivan devastates island.

2008 Keith Mitchell loses election in surprise National Democratic party win.

« 280–81 The Slave Trade

Trinidad & Tobago

This two-island republic lies very close to the Venezuelan coast of South America.

1498 Columbus visits Trinidad and claims both islands for Spain.

1781 French capture Tobago.

1799 Britain seizes Trinidad and, in 1814, France cedes control over Tobago.

1888 Trinidad and Tobago united.

1956 Eric Williams founds People's National Movement (PNM) and wins general election with support from Afro-Caribbeans; the minority Asian population supports the opposition.

1958–1961 Member of West Indian Federation.

1962 Independence from Britain.

1980 Tobago gets its own House of Assembly and internal autonomy in 1987.

1995 Basdeo Panday becomes the first Asian-origin prime minister.

2010 Kamla Persad-Bissessar becomes the first female prime minister.

« 280–81 The Slave Trade

Oil wealth
Commercial production of oil began on Trinidad in 1908 and now accounts for 70 percent of export earnings. Gas production is also important.

South America

The 12 countries of South America–the world's fourth-largest continent–were colonial outposts of European powers until the early 19th century. A series of wars with local nationalist movements resulted in independence for most of the continent by the 1820s.

Colombia

A state plagued by violence ever since independence, Colombia is slowly stabilizing.

1525 Spain begins the conquest of Colombia, subjugating the Cibcha people who live in Colombia and Panama.

1530s Gonzalo Jiménez de Quesada explores what is now Colombia while searching for the legendary El Dorado.

1717 Santa Fé de Bogota becomes capital of the new Viceroyalty of New Granada.

1811 Independence from Spain is declared in Cundinamarca.

1819 Simón Bolívar–"the Liberator"– defeats the Spanish at Boyacá. Republic of Gran Colombia formed including present-day Venezuela, Ecuador, and Panama.

1830 Venezuela and Ecuador split away during revolts and civil wars. Colombia independent as "New Granada."

1849 The centralist Conservative and federalist Liberal parties are established.

1861–86 Period in which the Liberals hold monopoly on power.

1863 Changes name to United States of Colombia.

Against the state
The combination of left-wing guerrilla groups, such as the M-19, and drug cartels made Colombia one of the world's more dangerous countries in the 1980s and 1990s.

1886–1930 Period of one-party Conservative rule.

1899–1902 Liberal "War of 1,000 Days" revolt fails; 120,000 die.

1903 US helps Panama secede so that it can build the canal across the isthmus; the new country is not recognized by Colombia until 1921.

1930 Liberal President Olaya Herrera is elected by a coalition in the first peaceful change of power.

1946 Conservatives take over.

1948 Shooting of Liberal leader and the subsequent El Bogotazo riot spark civil war lasting until 1957; 300,000 killed.

1953–57 Military dictatorship of Rojas Pinilla.

1958 Conservatives and Liberals agree to alternate government in a National Front until 1974. Other parties are banned.

1965 Left-wing guerrilla movements, the National Liberation Army (ELN) and the Maoist Popular Liberation Army, are formed.

1966 Armed Revolutionary Forces of Colombia (FARC) guerrilla group is formed.

1968 Constitutional reform allows new parties, but two-party parity continues. Guerrilla groups proliferate from now on.

1984 Minister of Justice assassinated for enforcing antidrug campaign.

1985 M-19 guerrillas blast their way into Ministry of Justice; 11 judges

and 90 others are killed. The Patriotic Union (UP) Party is formed.

1986 Liberal Virgilio Barco Vargas wins presidential elections, ending power-sharing. UP wins 11 seats in parliament. Right-wing paramilitary groups start a murder campaign against UP politicians. Violence by both left-wing groups and death squads run by drug cartels continues.

1989 M-19 signs peace agreement with government and becomes a legal party.

1990 UP and PL presidential candidates are murdered. Liberal César Gaviria is elected on an antidrug platform.

1991 New constitution legalizes divorce and prohibits extradition of Colombian nationals. Indigenous peoples' democratic rights are guaranteed, but territorial claims are not addressed.

1992–93 Medellín drug cartel leader Pablo Escobar is captured. He escapes and is shot dead by the police.

1995–96 President Ernesto Samper is cleared of charges of receiving Cali cartel drug funds for elections.

1998 Andrés Pastrana Arango of the Conservative Party succeeds Samper.

2001 US-backed spraying of illegal coca plantations begins in south; destruction of food crops by herbicides provokes resentment among peasant farmers.

2002 Peace talks with FARC and ELN are abandoned, and the military invades the demilitarized haven granted to FARC as part of the peace deal. Right-wing independent candidate Álvaro Uribe Vélez wins the presidential election.

2003 Right-wing paramilitaries United Self-Defense Forces of Colombia (AUC) begin to disarm.

2006 President Uribe wins second four-year term in office.

2009–10 Accusations that the Venezuelans are giving refuge to FARC guerrillas almost lead to open war.

2010 Juan Manuel Santos wins presidential elections.

Venezuela

The first colony to win independence from Spain. Vast reserves of oil have been discovered there.

1498–1500 Columbus sails along the Venezuelan coast on his third voyage. The region is inhabited by Carib, Arawak, and Chibcha peoples.

1777 Venezuela becomes a Captaincy-General within the Spanish Viceroyalty of New Granada.

1806–21 War of Liberation, headed by Simón Bolívar, in which 25 percent of the Venezuelan population dies.

1811 Independence is formally declared, but Venezuela again falls under Spanish rule in 1812.

1813 Bolívar sets up a government in Caracas but is driven out by the Spanish the following year.

1816 Bolívar returns from exile with an expeditionary force and establishes capital at Angostura (now Ciudad Bolívar).

1819 A congress at Angostura establishes Gran Colombia: Venezuela, New Granada (Panama and Colombia), and Ecuador.

1821 Battle of Carabobo overthrows Spanish rule and leads to consolidation of independence within Gran Colombia.

1830 Gran Colombia collapses. José Antonio Páez rules Venezuela; coffee planters are effectively in control.

1870 Antonio Guzmán Blanco comes to power. Construction begins on a new railway system and Guzmán develops agriculture and education.

1902 Venezuela defaults on loans taken out to modernize its infrastructure. Its ports are blockaded by British, Italian, and German warships in response.

1908 General Juan Vicente Gómez becomes dictator. The oil industry is developed and Venezuela becomes world's largest exporter of oil.

1935 Gómez falls from power. Increasing mass participation in political process.

1945 Military coup: Rómulo Betancourt takes power as leader of a civilian–military junta.

1948 Democratic Action Party (AD) wins elections, with novelist Rómulo Gallegos as presidential candidate. A military coup overthrows him and Carlos Delgado Chalbaud becomes president with US and military backing.

1958 General strike. Admiral Larrázabal leads a military coup. In free elections, Betancourt, newly returned from exile, wins presidential election for the AD. Anticommunist campaign mounted.

DECISIVE MOMENT

BATTLE OF CARABOBO, 1821

On June 24, 1821, independence fighters led by Simón Bolívar defeated Spanish royalists on the plains to the west of Caracas. Bolívar is shown here accepting the standard after a victory that all but freed Venezuela from Spanish control, with independence finally assured two years later. Breaking the terms of an armistice he had signed with the Spanish government in November 1820, Bolívar had attacked the royalist garrison on Lake Maracaibo. The two armies met on the plains of Carabobo, where Bolívar's forces routed the remaining Spaniards under General Miguel de la Torre; only 400 escaped out of 5,000.

1960 **Movement of the** Revolutionary Left (MIR) splits from the AD and begins antigovernment activities.

1960 **Venezuela becomes** a founding member of the Organization of the Petroleum Exporting Countries (OPEC).

1962 **Communist-backed guerrilla** warfare attempts repetition of Cuban revolution in Venezuela, but fails to gain sufficient popular support.

1963 **Raúl Leoni (AD)** is elected president in the first-ever democratic transfer of power. Antiguerrilla campaign continues.

1966 **Unsuccessful coup attempt** by supporters of former president Pérez Jiménez.

1969 **Rafael Caldera Rodríguez** of the Social Christian Party (COPEI) becomes president. Continues Leoni's policies.

1973 **Oil and steel** industries nationalized during the world oil crisis. Venezuelan currency peaks against the US dollar.

1978 **Elections won by** COPEI's Luis Herrera Campíns. Disastrous economic programs harm economy.

1983 **Election victory under** Jaime Lusinchi (AD). A sharp fall in world oil prices leads to cuts in state welfare and social unrest.

1988–89 **Carlos Andrés Pérez** wins elections for AD. Venezuela takes out an IMF loan and initiates an austerity program. In the Caracas food riots, 1,500 die. Martial law is declared.

1992 **Hugo Chávez** leads a failed coup attempt. He later forms the Fifth Republic Movement (MVR) to gain power.

1993–95 **Andrés Pérez ousted** on charges of corruption. Caldera Rodríguez is reelected amid growing social unrest.

1998–99 **Hugo Chávez's MVR-led** coalition defeats the COPEI-led coalition in elections. Chávez embarks on a "Bolivarian Revolution" of social and political reform, using oil revenues to fund education and health programs.

2006 **Chávez wins presidential election,** taking almost two-thirds of the vote.

2007 **Plans are announced** to nationalize the energy supply and telecommunications industries. Chávez narrowly loses referendum on extending his constitutional changes.

2010 **The opposition makes** gains in parliamentary elections, although Chávez still commands a majority in Congress.

«230–31 Contact Americas
«280–81 The Slave Trade
«318–19 Latin America Liberated

Oil wealth
Venezuela has the largest proven oil reserves of any country outside the Middle East, much of it centered around Lake Maracaibo (above). High oil revenues have funded President Chávez's ambitious program of social reform.

Guyana

A former British colony, Guyana is the only English-speaking nation on the continent.

1499 **The coast is** explored by Alonso de Ojeda on Columbus's third voyage.

1530s **The search for** El Dorado centers on the Amazon and Orinoco areas.

1616 **A Dutch expedition** under Adrian Groenewegen establishes a fort at Kykoveral, where Dutch settlers arrive in 1624. Both England and France establish colonies in the region.

1648 **Under the Treaty** of Munster, Spain recognizes Berbice and Essequibo, including Demerara, as Dutch colonies.

1667 **By the Treaty of Breda,** the Dutch gain all English colonies in Guyana.

1814 **The Dutch colonies** come under English control and in 1831 are united as British Guiana, the first and only British colony in South America.

1850s **The UK imports** laborers from India to add to the large number of freed slaves originally brought over from Africa from the 17th century onward.

1879 **Gold is discovered,** prompting UK expansion and a boundary dispute with Venezuela only settled in 1904; Venezuela still claims western Guyana.

1953 **First universal elections** won by the People's Progressive Party (PPP) under Cheddi Jagan; parliament later suspended by UK.

1964 **People's National Congress (PNC)** dominates ruling coalition parties.

1966 **Independence from UK** as a republic within the Commonwealth.

1973 **PPP boycotts parliament,** accusing the PNC of electoral fraud.

1992 **Fair elections won** by PPP: Jagan is reelected president.

1997–98 **Jagan dies in** office. The PNC rejects his widow Janet's election victory. A political crisis erupts until she is accepted as president.

1999 **Caricom**—the Caribbean Community and Common Market—brokers a peace deal. Janet Jagan resigns due to illness.

2001 **Political violence flares** again when Bharrat Jagdeo of the PPP wins the presidential election. Tensions remain high until the PNC leader, Desmond Hoyte, dies in 2003.

2006 **Bharrat Jagdeo** wins a new presidential term.

«280–81 The Slave Trade

Suriname

This former Dutch colony is the smallest country in South America but ethnically very diverse.

1667 **Dutch rule begins** after the Treaty of Breda between the Netherlands and England recognizes Dutch rule in Guiana.

1975 **Independence from the Netherlands.**

1980 **Military coup:** rule by Lieutenant Colonel Desi Bouterse. A National Military Council is established to run the country. Further coup attempts occur in 1981 and 1982.

1982 **Political opponents are executed.** The Dutch suspend aid for six years.

1986–92 **Maroon rebels** of the Suriname Liberation Army wage war.

1987 **A new constitution** is approved in a referendum.

1988 **Elections return** Suriname to democracy.

1990 **A further military coup** deposes the government. A peace agreement is signed with the rebels in 1992.

1991–96 **A coalition** New Front for Democracy and Development (NF) government representing Creoles, South Asians, and Javanese peoples takes power under Ronald Venetiaan of the Suriname National Party.

1992 **Bouterse quits as** head of the army, easing tensions in the country.

1996 **Jules Wijdenbosch** of the opposition National Democratic Party (NDP) and an ally of Bouterse wins power but refuses to extradite Bouterse to the Netherlands on drug charges.

2000 **Opposition NF wins** elections under Ronald Venetiaan. He cuts public spending, and starts a process of reform.

2004 **The Dutch guilder** is replaced by the Suriname dollar; reforms restructure the important banana industry.

2004 **UN mediates in** a maritime border dispute with Guyana.

2005 **Ronald Venetiaan** wins reelection to the presidency.

2007 **At least 250,000** Surinamese now live abroad. Most live in the Netherlands, boosting the national economy with remittances. Of the home population of 450,000, more than 90 percent live near the coast, the rest in scattered villages in the interior.

2010 **Former President Bouterse** wins presidential elections.

«230–31 Contact Americas
«280–81 The Slave Trade

Ecuador

Ecuador straddles the equator. The country also includes the Galápagos Islands in the Pacific.

1478 **The area of present-day** Ecuador is incorporated into the Inca Empire by Topa Yupanqui. Centered around Quito, the region rapidly develops into an important commercial center.

c.1527 **On the death of Inca** Huayna Capac, the Inca Empire is divided in two between Huáscar in Cuzco and his younger brother Atahuallpa, who is based in Quito. Atahuallpa defeats Huáscar in 1532 in a battle outside Cuzco to become sole ruler, only to be captured by Pizarro later that year. The war of succession fatally weakens the Inca Empire, which falls to the Spanish invaders.

1528 **Francisco Pizarro sails** along the coast as far as the border of present-day Ecuador and Peru.

1533 **Sebastián de Benalcazar,** one of Pizarro's lieutenants, leads expedition to the region, which is claimed for Spain.

1563 **The Audiencia of Quito** is established within the Viceroyalty of Peru. It is transferred to the jurisdiction of the Viceroyalty of New Granada in 1739.

1809 **An abortive rebellion** fails.

1822 **Quito is taken** from the Spanish by Antonio José de Sucre at the Battle of Pichincha. Simón Bolívar incorporates Ecuador into Gran Colombia, along with Colombia, Panama, and Venezuela.

1830 **Gran Colombia dissolves,** and Ecuador becomes an independent state under Juan José Flores, a Conservative.

1832 **Ecuador tries but fails** to win Popayán province from Colombia; annexes Galápagos Islands.

1850s **The Conservatives,** who support the Catholic church, and the radical Liberals, who support economic reform, begin lengthy battle for power.

1925 **The army** replaces the coastal banking interests as the ultimate source of power in the country.

1941–42 **Loss of mineral-rich** El Oro region to Peru.

1944–47 **José María Velasco Ibarra** stages a coup and becomes president for the second time.

1948 **Reforming president** Galo Plaza Lasso wins in free elections and introduces wide-ranging political reforms.

1948–60 **Ecuador develops** its banana plantations.

1952 **Velasco Ibarra** returns to power. He improves schools and roads.

1955–60 **Camilo Ponce Enríquez** is first Conservative president in 60 years.

1960 **The government renounces** peace treaty that gave El Oro region to Peru.

1963–66 **Military junta rules.**

1968 **Velasco Ibarra** is elected president for the fifth time. Faced with dissent, he takes absolute power in 1970.

1972 **Oil production starts.** Velasco Ibarra is ousted in a military coup.

1979 **Return to democracy** as the military end their rule.

1992 **Amerindians win land** in Amazonia.

1997 **President Abdala Bucaram** deposed by Congress after his administration seeks to implement popular reforms.

1998–99 **Jamil Mahuad** of the Popular Democratic Party wins elections.

2000 **After massive depreciation** of the sucre, it is replaced by the US dollar.

2000 **Army sides with** Amerindian protestors. Vice president Gustavo Noboa replaces Mahuad.

2002 **Lucio Gutiérrez, leader** of the 2000 coup, is elected president.

2005 **Gutiérrez is removed by Congress;** elections in 2006 won by Rafael Correa.

2007 **In a referendum,** voters approve a new constituent assembly.

2008 **Ecuador announces it** will default on billions of dollars of debt.

2009 **President Correa wins** second term.

« 210–13 Pre-Columbian Americas
« 318–19 Latin America Liberated

Banana republic
Ecuador is the world's biggest producer of bananas and supports a major fishing industry. The country is also a net exporter of oil obtained from Amazonia, east of the Andes.

Peru

Once the heart of the Inca Empire, Peru has a large indigenous population of Quechua speakers.

c.1000–200 BCE **Chavin civilization** flourishes. It is followed by the Nazca, c.200 BCE–800 CE, who first develop large-scale irrigation systems.

1300s CE **Under the reign** of the fourth emperor, Mayta Capac, the Inca begin to attack their neighbors and extend their power beyond their base in the Cuzco valley. By the 15th century, the Inca Empire reaches as far as present-day central Chile, and the Inca language, Quechua, has been imposed on all its subjects.

Inca gold
This figure is typical of Inca craftsmanship. The Spanish melted down many such objects found in the Inca capital, Cuzco, for shipment to Spain.

1528 **Francisco Pizarro sails** along the coast as far as the frontier of present-day Peru and Ecuador.

1532 **Pizarro lands and** captures the Inca ruler Atahuallpa. The Incas are massacred at Cajamarca. Atahuallpa is executed in 1533. The invaders advance to the capital, Cuzco, and strip it of gold.

1542 **Viceroyalty of Peru** is established.

1780–81 **Tupac Amaru II** leads an unsuccessful revolt against Spanish rule.

1821 **Independence is proclaimed** in Lima after its capture by Argentine liberator José de San Martín, who has just liberated Chile from Spanish rule.

1824 **Spain suffers final** defeats at battles of Junín and Ayacucho by Simón Bolívar and Antonio José de Sucre, liberators of Venezuela and Colombia. Peru now gains full independence.

1836–39 **Peru and Bolivia** join in a short-lived confederation, ended when Chile intervenes, fearing that the new state is a threat to its interests.

1844–51 **General Ramón Castilla** is president; he returns to power in 1855–62. Under his rule, Peru enjoys stability and economic development: the guano and nitrate deposits are exploited for the first time, and transportation links are improved.

1860 **New constitution** introduced that remains in force until 1920.

1866 **Peruvian–Spanish War** as Spain attempts to regain Peru.

1872–76 **Manuel Pardo** is the first democratically elected president.

1879–84 **War of the Pacific:** Chile defeats Peru and Bolivia. Peru loses territory in south.

1908–12 **Augusto Leguía y Salcedo** rules as a dictator. He comes to power again in 1919 and rules until 1930.

1911 **The lost Inca city Machu Picchu** is discovered by Hiram Bingham.

1924 **Dr. Víctor Raúl** Haya de la Torre founds nationalist and radical American Popular Revolutionary Alliance (APRA) in exile in Mexico.

1930 **Leguía is ousted:** APRA moves home to Peru as first political party.

1931–45 **APRA is** banned.

1939–45 **A moderate, pro-US** civilian government comes to power.

1948 **General Manuel Odría** takes power and APRA is banned again.

1956 **Civilian government** is restored.

1962, 1963 **Two military coups.**

1963 **Election of** Fernando Belaúnde Terry, a moderate reformer. Land reform begins to redistribute land to poor peasant farmers, but the military is used to suppress a communist-inspired insurgency.

1968 **A left-wing military** junta takes over. It attempts to alleviate poverty and adopts a policy of widespread nationalization.

1975–78 **New right-wing military junta** runs the country.

1980 **Belaúnde reelected.** The Maoist guerrilla group Sendero Luminoso (Shining Path) begins an armed struggle.

1981–98 **Border war with** Ecuador over the El Oro region, the Amazonian territory given to Peru by a 1942 treaty.

1982 **Deaths and "disappearances"** start to escalate as the army cracks down on guerrillas and the drug trade.

1985 **First-ever electoral win for** APRA, under Alán García Pérez.

1987 **Peru goes bankrupt** as García's government fails; plans to nationalize banks are blocked by the new Libertad movement led by novelist Mario Vargas Llosa.

1990 **Over 3,000 political** murders a year as violence engulfs the country. Alberto Fujimori, an independent, is elected president on an anticorruption platform and introduces austerity program.

1992 **Fujimori's "self-coup":** Fujimori summarily closes Congress. A referendum

CAPTURE OF COMRADE GONZALO, 1992

The self-styled Comrade Gonzalo, Abimael Guzmán, was captured in Lima on September 12, 1992. A philosophy teacher, Guzmán founded the Maoist guerrilla group Shining Path in 1970, drawing support from among the marginalized rural poor. Shining Path embarked on a campaign of bombings and murders throughout the 1980s, in which an estimated 140,000 people were killed. His capture was a severe blow to the group, which thereafter declined as a threat. The end of Shining Path power allowed Peru to promote tourism for the first time in years.

Behind bars
The Fujimori government displayed a defiant Guzmán for the benefit of the world's press. Without his charismatic leadership Shining Path soon lost momentum.

approves a new constitution allowing him to stand again as president. In 1995 Fujimori is reelected president.

1996–97 Left-wing Tupac Amarú guerrillas seize hundreds of hostages at Japanese ambassador's residence in a four-month siege.

2000 Fujimori resigns amid a corruption scandal, despite having won controversial third term earlier in the year; he seeks refuge in Japan.

2001 Fresh presidential elections, won by Alejandro Toledo of the Perú Posible (PP) party. Toledo thus becomes the nation's first Amerindian president.

2003 Beatriz Merino is appointed first woman prime minister.

2006 García returns to power.

2007 Former president Alberto Fujimori is extradited from Chile to face corruption charges (sentenced in 2009 to 25 years).

Bolivia

The continent's poorest country, which is named after the "Liberator," Simón Bolívar.

1532 Spanish conquer the area that is now Bolivia, which is part of the Inca empire. The indigenous people are finally defeated by the Spanish in 1538. The region is governed as part of Upper Peru.

1545 Cerro Rico, the Silver Mountain, is discovered at Potosí. Within three decades, Potosí is the largest city in the Americas with 120,000 inhabitants. Silver mining provides Spain with a large income.

1559 Placed within the Charcas Audiencia attached to the Viceroyalty of Peru, which includes modern-day Bolivia and much surrounding land. This leads to disputes and wars after independence.

1776 Upper Peru becomes part of Viceroyalty of Río de la Plata centered around Buenos Aires.

1809 Simón Bolívar inspires first revolutionary uprisings in Latin America at Chuquisaca (Sucre), La Paz, and Cochabamba, but they fail.

1824 Spaniards suffer final defeat by Bolívar's general, José de Sucre.

1825 Independence.

1826 Bolivia draws up its first, republican, constitution; the country is named after Simón Bolívar, and Chuquisaca is renamed Sucre, after the liberating general.

1836–39 Union with Peru fails, leading to a long period of internal disorder.

1864–71 Ruthless rule of Mariano Melgarejo. Three Amerindian revolts over the seizure of ancestral lands are crushed.

1879–84 Bolivia is defeated by Chile in the War of the Pacific. Bolivia loses coastal Atacama and its rich nitrate deposits to Chile and is left landlocked.

1880–1930 Period of stable governments. Exports from mining bring prosperity.

1903 Acre province is ceded to Brazil. The rubber-rich area had long been contested by the two nations.

1904 Ismail Montes starts the first of his two terms as president (1904–09, 1913–17). He officially ends the War of the Pacific with Chile and starts a

program of wide-ranging social, administrative, and economic reforms, building new railroads and developing the mining industry.

1914 Republican Party founded.

1920 Amerindian rebellion.

1923 Miners' uprising suppressed.

1932–35 Chaco War with Paraguay, the bloodiest conflict in the world between the two world wars. Bolivia loses three-quarters of the Chaco region in 1938. Rise of radicalism and the labor movement.

1951 Víctor Paz Estenssoro of the nationalistic, pro-miner, Nationalist Revolutionary Movement (MNR) is elected president, but is prevented from taking office by a military coup.

1952 Revolution: Paz Estenssoro of the MNR takes power with the help of national police and a militia recruited from the mines. Land reforms improve Amerindians' status. Education is reformed, universal suffrage is introduced—giving full rights to the Amerindian community—and the tin mines are nationalized.

1956 MNR candidate Hernán Siles Zuaso wins presidential election; he is succeeded in 1960 by returning president Paz Estenssoro.

1964 Military takes over in coup after economic collapse.

1967 Che Guevara is killed while trying to mobilize Bolivian workers.

1969–79 Military regimes rule with increasing severity. A coup in 1979 fails, leading to interim civilian rule.

1980 Military takes over again.

1982 President-elect Siles Zuazo finally heads leftist civilian MIR government. Inflation runs at 24,000 percent.

1985 Paz Estenssoro's MNR wins elections. Austerity measures bring annual inflation down to 20 percent.

1989 Movement for the Revolutionary Left (MIR) takes power after narrow electoral victory. President Paz Zamora makes pact with 1970s dictator General Hugo Banzer, leader of the nationalist Democratic Action (ADN) party.

1990 4 million acres (1.6 million hectares) of rainforest are recognized as Amerindian territory.

1993 MNR voted back to power.

1997 Banzer wins the presidential elections.

1999 Opposition demands inquiry into Banzer's role in regional military repression in 1970s.

2000 Government's water supply privatization plans and coca eradication program provoke uprisings by peasants and coca growers.

2001 Banzer resigns due to ill-health.

2002 MNR wins elections under Sánchez de Lozada, who is forced out in 2005.

2006 Evo Morales Ayma of the Movement toward Socialism (MAS) becomes the first indigenous president. A new constitution guarantees greater rights to the indigenous majority. Land reform bill aimed at redistribution is passed. Gas is nationalized.

2009 Evo Morales wins second term.

2010 Electricity-generation industry is nationalized.

Bolivian *marchistas*
These miners, along with other so-called *marchistas*, descended on La Paz on November 30, 2006, to demonstrate in favor of President Morales's land reforms. Millions of acres will be redistributed under new laws.

Brazil

South America's only Portuguese-speaking nation was a 19th-century empire in its own right.

1494 **The Treaty of Tordesillas** sets a boundary between Portuguese and Spanish possessions, which awards Portugal roughly the eastern half of South America.

1500 **Pedro Alvares Cabral** reaches the Brazilian coast.

1532 **First permanent** Portuguese settlement at São Vicente in São Paulo; settlement also begins in the northeast.

1549 **Salvador is founded** as the country's first capital and 12 captaincies are established to govern the country, stretching inland from the coast.

1549 **A Captain-General** is sent out to establish a centralized government at Bahia. He is accompanied by Jesuits who play a key role in the unification of the colony and the exploration of the interior.

1555 **French Protestant Huguenots** establish themselves on an island in Rio de Janeiro harbor. They are expelled in 1567 by Mem de Sá, who founds the city of Rio de Janeiro.

1580–1640 **Brazil becomes part of** the Spanish empire when Spain takes over Portugal.

1630–54 **The Dutch control** a large sugar-growing region in the northeast. The Portuguese cannot expel them as their country is now part of Spain; in the end, the Dutch are expelled by a naval force sent from Rio de Janeiro.

1630–95 **Freed slave settlements** oppose the colonialists, particularly at Palmares in the north, under African leader Zumbi.

1763 **Rio de Janeiro** becomes the national capital.

1789 **Inconfidência rebellion,** led by Tiradentes, fails to establish Brazilian independence.

1807 **The French under Napoleon** invade Portugal. King João VI flees to Brazil with a British naval escort. In return, Brazil's ports are opened up to foreign trade.

1821 **King João returns** to Portugal; his son Pedro is made regent of Brazil.

1822 **Pedro declares** his independence from Portugal and is made Emperor Pedro I of Brazil. Pedro uses a former British admiral and a former French general to help him drive the Portuguese out of the country. Although no set battles are fought, both sides use guerrilla tactics in the war before the Portuguese eventually withdraw. Portugal recognizes the new country's independence in 1825.

1828 **Brazil loses Spanish-speaking** Uruguay after a three-year war with Argentina.

1831 **Military revolt after war** with Argentina. Emperor Pedro I abdicates and is succeeded by his five-year-old son, Pedro II.

1835–45 **Rio Grande** province in the south of the country secedes.

1850 **Brazil abolishes** the transatlantic slave trade.

1865–70 **Brazil wins the war** of the Triple Alliance with Argentina and Uruguay against Paraguay, gaining some territory from Paraguay in the south.

1871 **A law for the** gradual emancipation of slaves is passed.

1888 **While Pedro II** is away in Europe, his daughter Isabella governs the country and slavery is completely abolished. The landowners and military turn against the emperor.

1889 **The first republic** is established, seen as a necessary step by modernizers. Pedro II goes into exile in Paris. Prosperity increases as a result of international demand for coffee.

1891 **Federal constitution established.** Rivalry between the states and the influence of the army in government cause political tensions.

1903–05 **Gains land** from Venezuela and Colombia in the northwest, and from Bolivia in the west.

1914–18 **World War I** in Europe causes coffee exports to slump, but stimulates other sectors and brings an economic boom.

1920s **Working-class and intellectual** movements call for an end to oligarchic rule.

1929 **After the Wall Street Crash,** 29 million bags of coffee go unsold.

> " **By my blood, by my honor, and by God, I will make Brazil free. It is time! Independence or death.** We are separated from Portugal."

PEDRO I OF BRAZIL, SPEAKING AT THE IPIRANGA RIVER, SEPTEMBER 7, 1822

1930 **Coffee prices collapse.** Revolt led by Dr. Getúlio Vargas, the "Father of the Poor," who becomes president. There is rapid industrial growth as measures are taken to reverse the country's growing economic dependence on coffee through import substitution industrialization.

1937 **Vargas's position as** benevolent dictator is formalized in the *Estado Nôvo*, the "New State," a centralized and corporatist state based on the fascist model. Vargas, although a dictator, wins applause for his nationalist policies and economic success.

1942 **Brazil declares war** on Germany. The economy booms as raw materials such as rubber are in great demand.

1945 **Vargas is forced out** by the military. General Eurico Gaspar Dutra is elected president, but the economy falters as inflation soars.

1951 **Vargas is reelected president.**

1954 **State oil monopoly** is created. Social security laws are passed.

1954 **The US opposes Vargas's** socialist policies. The right, backed by the military, demands his resignation. Faced with economic problems and political infighting, he commits suicide. He leaves behind a letter blaming "dark forces" (meaning the US and its local supporters) for blocking his efforts to make reforms.

1956–60 **President Juscelino Kubitschek,** backed by the Brazilian Labor Party (PTB), attracts foreign investment for new industries, especially from the US.

1960–61 **Conservative Jânio da Silva** Quadros is elected president with the greatest popular margin in Brazil's history. He tries to break dependence on US trade, but his autocratc and unpredictable manner arouses opposition and undermines his reforms, and he is forced to resign after only seven months in office.

1960 **Brasília, built in** three years, becomes new capital. PTB leader João Goulart is elected president.

1961–63 **Presidential powers** are briefly curtailed as the right wing reacts to Goulart's policies. The presidential system is reinstated after a plebiscite.

1964 **Bloodless military coup** under army chief General Castelo Branco, backed by the US, deposes Goulart. The 1946 liberal constitution is suspended.

1965 **Branco assumes dictatorship** after antimilitary parties win election in two states. He bans all existing political parties, but creates two official new ones. He is followed by a succession of military rulers. Fast-track economic development, the so-called "Brazilian Miracle," is counterbalanced by ruthless suppression of left-wing activists.

DECISIVE MOMENT

STUDENT RIOTS, 1968

Inspired by rioters around the world, notably in France and Mexico, students took to the streets of São Paulo on September 3, 1968, to protest the military dictatorship that had seized power in 1964. Their actions provoked a brutal clampdown by the authorities. In the following years, hundreds died in left- and right-wing guerrilla warfare. State censorship of the media was tightened and many of Brazil's intellectuals were forced into exile. Emergency measures were kept in place until 1978, and the military remained in power until 1985.

Students on the rampage
A police van is enthusiastically trashed before it is torched by a protester during riots in São Paulo. Brazil's military dictators suppressed the protests with extreme brutality.

President "Lula"
The first working-class president in Brazil's history, Luiz Inácio Lula da Silva came to power in 2003 pledging to abolish hunger by putting three meals a day on the plates of every Brazilian. In 2006 he was reelected with more than 60 percent of the vote, despite a corruption scandal that tarnished his reputation as a reformer.

1968 **In the face of student protests** and criticism from the church against military rule, the new military ruler, Marshall Costa E. Silva, dismisses Congress and assumes one-man rule.

1969 **General Emílio Garrastazú Médici** becomes president. Left- and right-wing terrorism, including the capture of several diplomats, becomes a feature of Brazilian politics.

1973 **World oil crisis** marks the end of the economic boom. Brazil's foreign debt is now the largest in world.

1978 **All emergency legislation** is ended.

1979 **More political parties** are allowed as military rule is relaxed and moves are made toward democracy.

1979–85 **Period of massive** industrial and economic growth.

1980 **Huge migrations into** Rondônia state begin.

1985 **Civilian senator Tancredo Neves** appointed president after vote of electoral college but dies before taking office. Illiterate adults are given the vote. José Sarney takes over.

1987 **Gold found on Yanomami** lands in Roraima state in the Amazon region. Illegal diggers rush in by the thousands, threatening the way of life of the indigenous Yanomami.

1988 **New constitution** provides for freedom of assembly, the right to strike, and a reduction in the working week, and promises massive social spending but fails to address land reform. Chico Mendes, the rubber-tappers' union leader and leading environmentalist, is murdered.

1989 **Brazil's first environmental** protection plan is drawn up. Annual inflation reaches 1,000 percent.

1990 **Fernando Collor de Mello** wins first fully democratic presidential elections, and, after increasing international pressure, sponsors programs to decrease the rate of deforestation in the Amazon basin and protect the autonomy of the native Yanomami people.

1992 **Earth Summit** is held in Rio de Janeiro, the world's first such summit. Collor de Mello resigns and is impeached for corruption; he is the first Brazilian president to be impeached by Congress.

1993 **Brazilians vote in a referendum** to retain the direct election of the president.

1994–95 **Plan Real ends** hyperinflation. Congress resists constitutional reforms, but approves privatizations of state monopolies.

1999 **Fernando Henrique Cardoso,** in power since 1995, is reelected president. Real devalued in economic crisis.

2000 **Economy recovers.** Ruling parties divide over elections of the heads of Congress.

2001–02 **Recovery of the economy** threatened by financial crisis in Argentina.

2003 **At his fourth attempt,** Luiz Inácio Lula da Silva, the leader of the left-wing Workers' Party (PT) wins the presidential election and becomes the country's first working-class president. He is elected on a social platform to fight poverty and hunger, but in office his policies resemble those of his predecessors.

2004 **Brazil launches** its first space rocket. Bids for a permanent seat on the UN Security Council.

2006 **Brazil announces** that it expects to become energy self-sufficient by the end of the year. Brazil's ethanol industry (making car fuel from sugar cane) makes it a world leader in cutting carbon emissions. Lula is reelected president despite accusations of corruption.

2007 **Criminal proceedings** relating to the Mensalão "votes for cash" scandal continue.

2008 **Brazil declines invitation** to join OPEC.

2010 **Dilma Rousseff of** the Worker's Party wins second-round run-off election and becomes Brazil's first female president.

Paraguay

Landlocked and with few natural resources, Paraguay has a long history of despotic rule.

1526 **Spanish first explore** the upper reaches of the Paraguay River and surrounding region.

1537 **Sailing up the** Paraná River in search of silver and a way across the continent, the Spaniards establish a fort at Asunción, which becomes the capital of La Plata province. The Guaraní, settled agriculturalists who live in the Paraguay river basin, help the Spanish conquer the southern Chaco area, home to nomadic hunters who raid Guaraní settlements.

1617 **Hernando Arias de Saavedra,** governor of Río de la Plata province, splits Paraguay away from Argentina.

1721–31 **Temporary independence** from Spain as José de Antequera leads a revolt.

1767 **The Jesuits,** who arrived in 1588 and organized the Amerindians into mission communities, are expelled.

1776 **Region made part** of the Viceroyalty of Río de la Plata.

1810 **Manuel Belgrano** is unsuccessful in carrying over the Argentinian revolt against Spanish rule into Paraguay.

1811 **The Spanish administration** is quietly deposed. Paraguay is now independent. Over the next 50 years, it is ruled by dictatorships and cut off from the outside world. It is protected from the unrest affecting its neighbors and becomes an economic power.

1814–40 **José Gaspar Rodríguez Francia** —"El Supremo"—rules the country with corruption-free but harsh rule. He is the first of three dictators that dominate the history of the country.

General Stroessner
Dictator from 1954 until he was deposed in 1989, General Alfredo Stroessner was the son of German immigrants and a virulent anticommunist who used torture and kidnappings to sustain his rule.

1844–62 **Carlos Antonio López** becomes dictator. His son Francisco succeeds him, but brings about disaster with the War of the Triple Alliance.

1864–70 **Paraguay loses** the War of the Triple Alliance against Argentina, Brazil, and Uruguay and eventually loses land to Brazil and Argentina, with a further loss in 1880 to Bolivia. More than two-thirds of its population (300,000) are killed in the war, plunging the country into a lengthy period of economic decline. Recovery is slow as warring *caudillos* set up short-lived dictatorships.

1932–35 **The Chaco War** against Bolivia over the disputed Chaco territory, where the supposed discovery of oil held out the promise of great wealth in this once-barren region.

1938 **Boundary with Bolivia** is fixed; Paraguay awarded large tracts of land. The country emerges victorious but exhausted after the conflict.

1940–48 **A rapid turnover** of governments ends when Higinio Moríngo holds power. His repressive, dictatorial rule is challenged by numerous uprisings.

1954–89 **Rule of Alfredo Stroessner.** His repressive military regime stifles opposition and rigs elections to win repeated electoral success.

1973 **Brazil and Paraguay** agree to build a massive hydroelectric project on the Paraná River at Itaipú; it is the world's second-largest such project.

1989 **Despite winning an eighth** term in 1988, General Stroessner is overthrown in a coup and is replaced by the coup's leader, General Andrés Rodríguez.

1993 **First coup attempt** by General Lino Oviedo, the former army chief, fails, as do further attempts in 1996 and 2000.

1994–95 **Congress tries** but fails to limit the powers of the military after the president, Juan Carlos Wasmosy, endorses the military's political and institutional role.

1998–99 **Colorado Party (PC)** president Raúl Cubas resigns after Congress votes to impeach him for the assassination of the vice president, Luis Argaña; Cubas and Oviedo leave the country.

2003 **Nicanor Duarte Frutos** of the PC wins presidential election.

2004 **Oviedo returns from exile** hoping to stand in the 2008 presidential election, but is arrested on arrival.

2008 **Fernando Lugo,** a former Roman Catholic bishop becomes president, ending Colorado Party's 60 years of rule. He accuses his predecessor Lino Oviedo of plotting against him and is embroiled in a controversy over his alleged fathering of children while a bishop.

Chile

A long, narrow country west of the Andes that has made a peaceful return to democracy.

1540 **A Spanish expedition** led by Pedro de Valdivia crosses the Andes from Peru and founds several cities, including Santiago in 1541. Lautaro, the leader of the Araucanian Indians, who offer fierce resistance, is killed in 1557. Valdivia is killed by the Araucanians in 1554.

1817 **José de San Martín,** revolutionary leader in Argentina against Spanish rule, leads an army aross the Andes and routs the Spaniards at the Battle of Chacabuco.

1817–18 **Bernardo O'Higgins** leads the republican Army of the Andes in victories against royalist Spanish forces.

1818 **The Battle of Maipu** pits the independence army, assisted by San Martín's liberation forces, against the remaining Spanish forces and ensures Chilean independence.

1818–23 **As autocratic leader** of the new republic, Bernardo O'Higgins, formerly Viceroy of Peru and known as "the Liberator," lays the political foundations of an oligarchic state that are later consolidated in the constitution of 1833.

1829–30 **After a civil war** between Liberals and Conservatives, Conservative alliance led by Diego Portales seizes power.

1836–39 **During a war** against Peru, which Chile wins, Portales is assassinated.

1879–84 **Chile emerges enriched** from the Pacific War, waged against Bolivia and Peru over control of nitrate-producing areas and the port of Antofagasta. Chile extends its territory northward and ends Bolivia's access to the coast.

1886–91 **Presidency of** José Manuel Balmaceda, a Liberal, is characterized by a struggle between presidential and congressional authority, and ends in a bloody civil war in 1891.

1902 **Chile extends southward** into Patagonia and on to the island of Tierra del Fuego, shared jointly with Argentina.

1920 **Election of** President Arturo Alessandri—"The Lion"—who introduces social and labor reforms. His policies are blocked by the legislature, and he resigns in 1924 but is recalled in 1925 after the army intervenes to support him; a revised constitution bolsters his powers.

1929 **Chile loses a chunk of northern** territory to Peru in brief war.

1932 **A coup installs** the 100-day "Socialist Republic" of Carlos Davila.

1936–46 **Communist, Radical,** and Socialist parties form the Popular Front coalition, taking power in 1938.

Bernardo O'Higgins
The illegitimate son of an Irishman in Spanish government service, O'Higgins spent his childhood in Europe but returned to Chile in 1802 committed to its independence.

1946–64 **Right-wing** presidents follow US policy and marginalize the left.

1970 **Salvador Allende is** the world's first democratically elected Marxist president.

1973 **Allende dies in** US-backed military coup. Brutal dictatorship of General Augusto Pinochet begins, who imprisons, tortures, and kills many of his opponents.

1988 **Referendum votes no** to Pinochet staying in power.

1989 **Democracy peacefully restored;** Pinochet steps down after Patricio Aylwin of the Christian Democratic Party (PDC) wins an election victory.

1998 **Pinochet is detained** while on a visit to the UK, pending extradition to Spain on human rights abuse charges. He is released on health grounds.

2000 **Ricardo Lagos of the Socialist Party** (PS) sworn in as president. Pinochet, who has returned to Chile, is deemed unfit to face trial, and is released.

2004 **Divorce is legalized.**

2006 **Michelle Bachelet (PS)** wins election as first woman president. Pinochet dies at age 91.

2010 **Sebastian Pinera** wins elections, becoming the first right-wing president for 20 years. Central Chile earthquake kills hundreds. After an explosion, 33 miners are trapped underground, but are all safely rescued after 69 days.

« 214–15 Aztec to Inca
« 318–19 Latin America Liberated
« 422–23 Viva la Revolución
« 438–39 Dictatorship and Democracy

Uruguay

A republic originally set up to act as a buffer state between Argentina and Brazil.

1624 **Spanish found first permanent** settlement at Soriano in southwest of the country; the Portuguese then found a settlement in 1680, and fortify a hill in present-day Montevideo in 1717, starting a colonial rivalry between the two nations over control of Uruguay.

1726 **Spaniards found Montevideo.** By end of the century, the whole country is divided into large cattle ranches.

1811 **Patriotic rancher** and local caudillo, José Gervasio Artigas, declares Montevideo independent from Brazil.

1812–20 **Uruguayans, known as** Orientales ("Easterners," from the eastern side of the River Plate), fight wars against Argentinian and Brazilian invaders.

1821 **Brazil annexes** Montevideo.

1827 **General Lavalleja defeats** Brazilians with Argentine help.

1828 **Seeing trade benefits** that an independent Uruguay would bring as a buffer state between Argentina and Brazil, Britain mediates and secures Uruguayan independence.

1836 **Start of large-scale** European immigration.

1838–65 **La Guerra Grande** civil war between Blancos (Whites, future conservative party) and Colorados (Reds, future liberals).

1865–70 **Colorado president** General Venancio Flore, takes Uruguay into the War of the Triple Alliance against Paraguay.

1872 **Peace under military** rule. Blancos strong in country; Colorados in cities.

1890s **Violent strikes by** immigrant trade unionists against landed elite enriched by massive European investment in ranching.

1903–07 **Reformist Colorado,** José Batllé y Ordóñez, is president.

1911–15 **Batllé's second term** in office. Batllismo creates the first welfare state in Latin America, with pensions and free education and health service; also implements nationalizations, church is disestablished, and death penalty abolished.

1933 **Following a military coup,** opposition groups are excluded from politics.

1939–45 **Uruguay remains neutral** during World War II.

1942 **President Alfredo Baldomir** dismisses the government and tries to bring back proper representation.

1951 **New constitution replaces** president with nine-member council. Decade of great prosperity follows until world agricultural prices plummet.

1958 **Blancos win elections** for the first time in 93 years.

1962 **Tupamaros urban guerrilla** group founded. Its campaign lasts until 1973.

1966 **The presidency is reinstated.**

1967 **Jorge Pacheco becomes** president, introducing tough anti-inflation policies.

1973 **Military coup:** the army promises to encourage foreign investment. Political freedoms are denied and the left is brutally repressed. 400,000 emigrate.

1984–85 **Military steps down:** Julio Sanguinetti (Colorado) wins a new presidential election.

1986 **Those guilty of** human rights abuses are granted amnesty.

1989 **Referendum endorses amnesty** in interest of stability. Elections won by Lacalle Herrera and Blancos.

Living off the land
Sometimes described as a large cattle ranch with a country attached, Uruguay is a successful wool and meat exporter. Livestock products bring in more than a third of current export earnings. On the country's vast *estancias* (above), the gaucho way of life predominates.

1994 Sanguinetti reelected.

1995 Uruguay joins Mercosur common market with Brazil, Paraguay, and Argentina.

1999 Presidential election won by Colorado candidate Jorge Batlle.

2000 Foot-and-mouth disease forces temporary suspension of beef exports.

2004 Presidential election won by Tabaré Vázquez, heading a four-party coalition including the Socialist Party of Uruguay, who thus becomes the first left-wing president. Poverty-tackling measures such as a minimum wage are introduced.

2006 Uruguay pays off debt to the IMF.

2009 Discovery of large natural gas fields off Uruguay's Atlantic coast is announced.

2010 Former left-wing rebel José Mujica is elected president.

≪280–81 The Slave Trade

Argentina

Once one of the richest countries in the world, Argentina is in crisis since defaulting on its debt.

1516 Juan de Solís is killed by the indigenous inhabitants after landing in what is now Argentina.

1526 Sebastian Cabot builds a fort on the estuary of the Río de la Plata.

1536 Pedro de Mendoza establishes the port of Santa María del Buen Aire on the site of the modern-day capital.

1590s Amerindians prevent the Spaniards from settling in the east of Argentina, but are finally subdued.

1776 Buenos Aires is separated from the Viceroyalty of Peru and becomes the seat of the Viceroyalty of Río de la Plata.

1816 Independence is achieved as the United Provinces of the River Plate. Conflict ensues between Unitarians advocating a centralized state ruled from Buenos Aires and the provincial Federalists of the interior.

1827 Bernardino Rivadavia, the republic's first president, resigns after his progressive Unitarian constitution is rejected by the provinces.

1829 Juan Manuel de Rosas, a Federalist caudillo with a broad base of support, is appointed governor of Buenos Aires province. His dictatorship extends the power of Buenos Aires.

1835–52 Rosas dictatorship does much to unify the country. His rule is authoritarian, even requiring the wearing of red to show support for the regime.

1853 Federal system set up.

1857 Europeans start settling the pampas: six million arrive by 1930, turning the region into one of the world's granaries and providing the mainstay of Argentina's export trade.

1862–80 Under three reforming governments, schools are built, public works started, and liberal reforms introduced.

1869 At the end of the War of the Triple Alliance against Paraguay, Argentina gains some land in the north from Paraguay.

1877 First refrigerated ship starts frozen beef trade to Europe.

1878–83 War against the pampas Amerindians leads to their almost total extermination.

1881 Argentina extends its rule southward through Patagonia to Tierra del Fuego.

1902 Boundary dispute with Chile over Tierra del Fuego is largely settled.

1916 Radical Hipólito Yrigoyen wins first democratic presidential elections and introduces much social legislation. He loses power in elections in 1922.

1928 Yrigoyen returns to power, but is ousted in a military coup in 1930; by now Conservatives in the country have adopted fascist leanings.

1938 The Radicals return to power, but serious illness causes their president, Roberto Ortiz, to retire; he is succeeded by the Conservative Ramón Castillo.

1943 Castillo is overthrown in a military coup; Juan Perón reorganizes trade unions as labor minister.

1946 Perón is elected president, with military and labor backing.

1949 A new constitution strengthens the presidency, allowing Perón to run for office again. He founds the Peronista political party.

1952 Eva Perón, "Evita," the charismatic wife of Juan Perón, dies of leukemia at the age of 33.

1955 Military coup ousts Perón after economy falters. Inflation, strikes, and unemployment destabilize the country. The military hands over power in 1958 to an elected president.

1963 After further military intervention and the banning of Peronista and Communist parties from standing in the election, Arturo Illía, a moderate liberal, takes power. He releases political prisoners and introduces some stability. Illía is overthrown in a military coup in 1966.

1972 Perón returns from exile in Madrid and in 1973 is reelected president with his third wife, Isabel, as vice president.

JUAN PERON

Juan Perón first came to prominence as part of a group of proto-fascist army colonels who overthrew the government in 1943. As secretary of labor and later vice president, he backed welfare legislation, winning the approval of the trade unions, who became the backbone of his later support.

In 1946 Perón was elected president. He pursued a path between capitalism and communism and was strongly nationalistic, anti-US, and anticommunist.

In power Perón became increasingly authoritarian, jailing opponents and censoring the press. While his wife Evita launched a public charm offensive, he purged the trade unions of communists and reorganized them along fascist lines. His rule aroused strong opposition: the Catholic church excommunicated him and he was overthrown in a coup in 1955.

Perón's second term as president from 1973–74 was not a success, but Peronism continues to be major political force.

1974 Juan Perón dies and is succeeded by his widow, Isabel, who is unable to exercise control over the country.

1976 Military junta seizes power: political parties are banned and brutal repression sees between 15,000 and 30,000 opponents of the regime disappear.

1981 General Leopoldo Galtieri becomes president, heading a three-man junta.

1982 Galtieri orders the invasion of the British-held Falkland Islands (Malvinas) and South Georgia. The UK retakes them in a war costing around 1,000 lives.

1983 Pro-human rights candidate Raúl Alfonsín wins presidency. Hyperinflation.

1989–92 Carlos Menem, a Peronist, is president; inflation down to 18 percent.

1995 Economy enters recession.

1999 Fernando de la Rúa is elected president leading a center-left alliance.

2000 Vice President Carlos "Chaco" Alvarez resigns over Senate bribes-for-votes scandal. Slump in beef exports after outbreak of foot-and-mouth disease. IMF grants Argentina aid of nearly $40 billion.

2001 Strikes in protest against proposed austerity measures. The government defaults on debt repayments. Restrictions on bank withdrawals provoke a general strike. De la Rúa resigns.

2002 Peronist Eduardo Duhalde takes over the presidency—the fifth president in 12 days. Savings are wiped out as the peso is devalued, ending parity with the US dollar. Unemployed protesters, known as *piqueteros*, take to the streets.

2003 Néstor Kirchner becomes president. He restructures Argentina's debts and stabilizes economy.

2005 Workers from Zanon factory in Neuquén present a petition in Buenos Aires asking to keep control of their factory. Since 2001, over 200 factories have been reopened by their workers.

2007 Christina Fernandez de Kirchner, wife of former president Néstor Kirchner, is elected president.

2010 Argentina is first Latin American country to legalize same-sex marriages. Former president Kirchner dies.

≪422–23 Viva la Revolución
≪438–39 Dictatorship and Democracy

Europe

The world's second-smallest continent has a great variety of landscapes, climates, and ethnic groups. Twice in the last century, conflict in Europe led to world war, but the continent is now largely at peace, with many countries members of the European Union.

United Kingdom

A small island kingdom that once ruled the largest empire in the history of the world.

43 CE Britain (Britannia) is invaded and conquered by the Romans.

410 The last Roman legions leave Britain. Over the next century Anglo-Saxon invaders push the native Celtic population out of the south and east of the island.

597 St. Augustine settles in Canterbury and begins to convert the kingdom of Kent to Christianity.

617 Northumbria establishes supremacy over the other six kingdoms of England.

757–96 Offa is king of Mercia and builds a defensive dike on the border between England and Wales.

793 Viking raids on Britain from Denmark and Norway begin.

802–39 Egbert is king of Wessex and, after defeating the Mercians in 825 and receiving the submission of Northumbria in 829, is recognized by his fellow kings as the first king of all England.

871–99 Alfred the Great is king of Wessex. In 891 Alfred orders the compilation of the *Anglo-Saxon Chronicle*, a record of the events of England that is continually updated until the 1100s. For his victories against the Danes, his wise rule, and his artistic patronage, Alfred is known as "the Great," the only English king ever to be known by this title.

878 By the Treaty of Wedmore, Alfred divides England in two with the Danes. After the capture of London in 886, he is recognized as king of all England.

899 Edward the Elder and his successors as kings of Wessex expel most Danes and regain control of much of England.

1002 After a long period of peace, Viking raids are renewed by Sweyn Forkbeard, king of Denmark, who becomes king of England in 1013.

1016–42 England becomes part of a vast Scandinavian kingdom comprising Denmark, Norway, and much of Sweden, ruled over by Canute and his two sons.

1066 Norman conquest of England commences following the defeat of King Harold II (1066) at Hastings by the invading army of Duke William of Normandy. As William I, or "William the Conqueror" (1066–87), he crushes a succession of rebellions and starts an ambitious castle-building program, including the Tower of London.

1085 William orders the compilation of the Domesday Book, a record of the population, extent, value, state of cultivation, ownership, and tenancy of all the land in England.

1154–89 Henry II is the first Plantagenet king, controlling an Angevin empire through marriage and conquest that stretches from the Scottish border down to the Pyrenees in southern France.

1171 Supported by the pope, Henry invades Ireland to control potentially rebellious English and Irish nobles. The Irish kings and nobles pledge allegiance to Henry, marking the start of more than 700 years of English rule over Ireland.

1189 Richard I, "the Lionheart," ascends the throne and spends almost all his 10-year reign abroad, fighting to regain Jerusalem during the crusades. Killed fighting in France, he is succeeded by his brother John (1199–1216).

1215 The Magna Carta, or Great Charter, is signed at Runnymede by King John and the English barons. This protects the nobility's rights against the excessive use of royal power in matters of taxation, justice, religion, and foreign policy. The charter lays down the respective rights and responsibilities of laymen and the church in relation to the power of the crown. Important at the time, the charter's relevance lessened as feudalism declined, and under the Tudors it was forgotten. It is now considered a milestone in English constitutional history.

1265 Representatives from the boroughs, as well as lords, clergy, and knights are summoned by Simon de Montfort to the first English parliament. The Model Parliament summoned by Edward I (1272–1307) in 1295 is even more representative in its composition.

1277 Edward I (1272–1307) invades Wales and overcomes Welsh resistance led by Prince Llywelyn II by 1282. In 1284 he ends Welsh independence by the Statute of Rhuddlan.

1301 Edward I makes his son Edward (later Edward II, 1307–27) the first Prince of Wales, a title given to all male heirs to the throne ever since.

1337–1453 The 100 Years War between England and France begins as Edward III lays claim to the French throne. Edward and his son, the Black Prince, win major victories at Crécy (1346) and Poitiers (1356). A treaty in 1360 gives Edward much land in return for renouncing his claim, but the French renew war in 1369 and drive the English out of many of their possessions by 1374.

1348–50 The Black Death sweeps across Europe and kills between one-third and one-half of the English population.

1381 Sparked by the imposition of a poll tax in 1380, serfs rebel in the Peasants' Revolt, led by Wat Tyler.

1399 Richard II is deposed by his cousin, Henry of Lancaster (Henry IV, 1399–1413), and murdered at the start of a period of conflict between the royal houses of Lancaster and York—the Wars of the Roses—that lasts until 1485.

1400–15 Owain Glyndwr leads major revolt in Wales against English rule.

1415 Henry V (1413–22) revives the 100 Years War and wins a major victory at Agincourt. Under the 1420 Treaty of Troyes, he becomes regent of France and heir to the French throne. However, he dies in 1422 before he can succeed. After 1429 the French, led by Joan of Arc, push the English out of France, finally ending the war in 1453.

1483 After the death of his father Edward IV (1461–70, 1471–83), the boy king Edward V disappears while in the Tower of London, presumed murdered by his uncle, Richard III.

1485 Richard III (1483–85) is defeated and killed at Bosworth Field by the Lancastrian Henry Tudor, who becomes Henry VII (1485–1509).

1509–47 Henry VIII is king, ruling at first through Cardinal Wolsey.

1534 Following the pope's refusal to annul his marriage to Catherine of Aragon to allow him to marry Anne Boleyn, Henry VIII breaks with Roman Catholic Church, and becomes Supreme Head of the Church. After the end of his marriage to Anne Boleyn in 1536, he subsequently marries four more times.

1536–43 Although Wales has been subjugated since 1284, a political union of Wales with England is forged, giving the Welsh representation in parliament.

1536–39 The monasteries are dissolved in order to fund the government. An authorized Bible in English is published for the first time in 1539.

1541 Having broken the power of Ireland's feudal lords, Henry VIII adopts the title of King of Ireland.

1547–53 During the reign of Edward VI, England becomes a Protestant nation with an English Bible and prayer book.

1553 Mary, daughter of Catherine of Aragon and Henry VIII, becomes Mary I. She tries but fails to bring England back into the Catholic fold, burning many Protestants at the stake. Her childless marriage to Philip II of Spain, the leading Catholic monarch in Europe, makes her unpopular, as does loss in 1558 of Calais, the last English possession in France.

DECISIVE MOMENT

DEFEAT OF LLYWELYN THE LAST, 1282

Wales has a much older history as a nation than England. Driven out of England by the Anglo-Saxons in the 5th and 6th centuries, the Celts formed a number of principalities in Wales that were united in the early 1200s. When Edward I came to the English throne in 1272, he summoned the Welsh prince, Llywelyn II, to pay homage. When Llywelyn refused, Edward invaded in 1277 and exacted the homage. Llywelyn rebelled in 1282 and Edward invaded again. After the prince was killed that year in an ambush, Welsh morale was crushed and Edward swiftly reinforced his conquest by building castles such as Harlech (below) to subdue his new realm. The defeat established an English hegemony over Wales that endures today.

1558 Mary is succeeded by her sister, Elizabeth (1558–1603), who restores a moderate Protestant church.

1587 Attempts to restore a Catholic to the throne founder when Mary, Queen of Scots, who was being held prisoner by Elizabeth, is executed after three plots to bring her to the throne are unmasked.

1588 The English navy defeats the Spanish Armada, which is sent by Philip II of Spain to invade England.

1600 East India Company is chartered to trade with the East Indies and later India.

1603 On Elizabeth's death, James VI, Stewart (Stuart) king of Scotland from 1567, becomes James I of England, thus uniting the crowns, although not the governments, parliaments, churches, or laws, of England and Scotland.

1605 Gunpowder plot to blow up the king while he is attending parliament is foiled, an event still celebrated each year.

1607 First successful English colony in the Americas set up in Jamestown, Virginia. In all, 13 colonies are established along the eastern seaboard of America, as well as colonies in Canada and the Caribbean. The creation of a British Empire during and after the 1600s brings huge wealth into the country.

1625 Charles I becomes king. A believer in the Divine Right of Kings, he rules without parliament from 1629–40.

1639 Civil War begins in Scotland over religious differences between the king and the Scottish church. A Catholic rebellion in Ireland in 1641 and civil war in England between king and parliament in 1642 turn the conflict into a three-kingdom war. In 1648 Charles is decisively defeated at Preston by the parliamentary army, led by Oliver Cromwell, and in early 1649 is put on trial for treason.

1649 Charles is executed and a commonwealth, or republic, is established. Catholic opposition in Ireland is brutally crushed by Oliver Cromwell, who acts as Lord Protector from 1653 until his death in 1658. An attempt by Charles's son Charles II to regain the throne in 1650–51 is defeated. The English republic, however, is not a success, because it fails to gain support or establish lasting institutions.

1660 Two years after Cromwell's death, monarchy is restored under Charles II.

1666 Great Fire of London destroys most of city. Christopher Wren rebuilds many old churches in the new baroque style.

1685–88 James II suspends laws against Catholics and attempts to restore Catholicism to England.

1688 In the bloodless "Glorious Revolution," James II is overthrown and succeeded as monarch by his daughter Mary II, who is married to the Dutch

UNITED KINGDOM

INDEPENDENT SCOTLAND

The northernmost kingdom of the British Isles, united with the English crown since 1603 and part of the United Kingdom since 1707.

Scotland timeline

450 BCE First Celts settle in Scotland.
c.400 CE St. Ninian brings Christianity.
560s St. Columba founds a monastery on Iona. By this time, Scotland is divided into four kingdoms: Dalraida in the west, the Pictish kingdom in the north, Strathclyde in the southwest, and Lothian in the east.
834–59 Kenneth MacAlpin conquers the Picts and unites northern Scotland.
900s Vikings conquer Orkney and Shetland.
1034–35 Malcolm II annexes Lothian in 1018 and gains Strathclyde in 1019, uniting all of Scotland.
1071–72 William the Conqueror invades Scotland and compels Malcolm III to recognize him as overlord.
1138 David I invades England but is defeated at Northallerton.
1173–74 William the Lyon invades England but is captured by Henry II and surrenders Scottish independence to him.
1189 Richard I of England recognizes Scottish independence in return for money to fund the Third Crusade.
1217 Peace treaty with England guarantees almost 20 years of peace.
1237 Treaty of York defines English border.
1263 Alexander III defeats Vikings at Largs and expels them from Scottish mainland.

The Scottish Parliament

After the accession of James VI to the English crown in 1603, Scotland kept its parliament until the Act of Union in 1707. It regained it in 1999, when a new building including this accomodation block, was erected in Edinburgh.

1290 After infant queen Margaret dies on way home to Scotland, Scots nobles ask Edward I to choose a king; he chooses John Balliol in 1292.
1295 "Auld Alliance" of Scotland and France.
1296 Edward I invades, deposes John Balliol, and rules the country. In 1297 Scots rise in revolt under William Wallace.
1305 William Wallace killed by English.
1306 Robert Bruce rises in revolt and is crowned king.
1314 Scottish victory at Bannockburn over Edward II of England leads to English recognition of Scottish independence in 1328.
1320 Declaration of Arbroath from Scottish nobles to the pope affirms its independence.
1346 David II invades England but is defeated; he is held captive until 1357.
1371 Robert Stewart, hereditary High Steward of Scotland and grandson of Robert Bruce, is crowned first Stewart king.
1406 The future James I is taken prisoner by pirates on his way home from France and is held prisoner in England for 18 years. When he eventually returns to Scotland in 1424, he proves a capable and enlightened monarch.
1412 First Scottish university is founded at St. Andrews, followed by Glasgow in 1450 and Aberdeen in 1495.
1437 James I is murdered; his son, James II, rules until 1460 and encourages the Renaissance in Scotland.

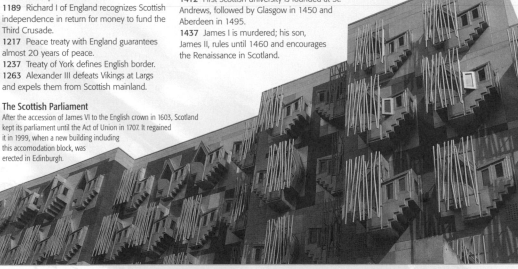

1472 Scotland gains Orkney and Shetland.
1513 James IV dies at the Battle of Flodden while invading England; most of the Scottish nobility is wiped out.
1542 Scots again defeated by the English at Solway Moss; James V dies and his one-week-old daughter, Mary, becomes queen.
1548 Mary leaves for France to be educated, and in 1558 marries the French dauphin, becoming Queen of France the next year.
1560 The Reformation Parliament makes Scotland a Protestant nation.
1561 Mary returns to Scotland after the death of her husband. After the death of one husband in suspicious circumstances, and a quick marriage to another man, Mary is thrown out by the Scottish lords in 1567, and flees to England, where she is held captive by her cousin Elizabeth I. Her son is James VI.
1587 Mary is tried for treason and executed by Elizabeth.
1603 James VI inherits English throne from Elizabeth as James I.

Protestant William of Orange. With the passage of a Bill of Rights in 1689, Catholics are barred from the throne and a constitutional form of government is established, with parliamentary consent becoming necessary for the king to levy taxes, suspend laws, or raise a peacetime army.

1690 In Ireland a Catholic uprising led by James II is defeated at the Battle of the Boyne. The Catholic siege of Protestants in Londonderry is lifted.

1694 On the death of Mary II, William rules alone.

1701 Act of Settlement confirms Mary's sister Anne as heir to the throne, to be followed by the descendents of the Protestant Electress Sophia of Hanover, a granddaughter of James I.

1702–13 England fights in the War of the Spanish Succession against Louis XIV of France, winning battles at Blenheim (1704) and Oudenarde (1708) under John Churchill, Duke of Marlborough.

1707 Act of Union established between England and Scotland, creating the United Kingdom. Scotland retains its separate legal system and Presbyterian Church, but the Scottish parliament is abolished.

1714 The Hanoverian succession is assured when George I assumes the throne. A Jacobite rebellion in 1715 led by the son of James II is easily defeated.

1721 Robert Walpole becomes the First Lord of the Treasury (regarded as the first prime minister).

1727–60 George II is king; he is the last British monarch to fight in battle, at Dettingen in 1743.

1745 Rebellion by Scottish Jacobites, led by "Bonnie Prince Charlie," grandson of James II. He invades England but is routed at the Battle of Culloden in 1746.

1760–1820 Reign of George III, during which he suffers from porphyria, a disease that makes him appear mad. In 1811 his son is made Prince Regent to govern the country until his father dies.

1763 Victory in the Seven Years War against France brings British control of Canada, America, and much of India.

1775–83 Britain loses its North American colonies in the American Revolution.

"Want is one only of five giants on the road of **reconstruction**... the others are Disease, Ignorance, Squalor, and Idleness. "

WILLIAM BEVERIDGE, ARCHITECT OF THE WELFARE STATE, 1942

UNITED KINGDOM

BRITISH OVERSEAS TERRITORIES

ANGUILLA
Island in northeast Caribbean.
1650 First colonized by British settlers.
1825 Administered by St. Kitts.
1967 Reverts to direct British rule.

BERMUDA
Islands in west Atlantic.
1609 First colonized by British.
1968 Internal self-government.
1995 Rejects independence from UK.

BRITISH ANTARCTIC TERRITORY
British territorial claim in Antarctica.
1962 Separate from Falklands Dependency.

BRITISH INDIAN OCEAN TERRITORY
Uninhabited military bases used by US.
1965 Created by taking islands from Mauritius and Seychelles to form US and UK naval and air base; all residents expelled.

BRITISH VIRGIN ISLANDS
Island group in northern Caribbean.
1648 Settled by Dutch; by British in 1666.
1672 Made a British crown colony.

CAYMAN ISLANDS
Island group in western Caribbean.
1670 Recognized as British possessions.
1863 Administered by Jamaica, but remain British on Jamaican independence in 1962.

FALKLAND ISLANDS
Islands off the coast of Argentina.
1592 First visited by English sailors.
1765–66 British settlement is established, which Spain recognizes in 1771, but withdrawn in 1774 for economic reasons. A Spanish garrison is also withdrawn in 1811, leaving islands uninhabited.
1820 Buenos Aires government sends ship to the islands to proclaim its sovereignty as successor to former Spanish colonial power.
1829 United Provinces of La Plata appoints a governor to the islands.
1833 UK sovereignty established after UK warships expel Argentinians in 1831–32.
1982 Argentinian forces invade and occupy Falklands and install Argentinian governor. UK dispatches a task force, forcing Argentinian surrender after six weeks of fighting; about 1,000 people are killed.

1995 Agreement reached with Argentina on division of oil and gas exploration revenues in offshore waters; breaks down in 2007.

GIBRALTAR
Rocky peninsula of southern Spain.
1704 British seize Gibraltar from Spain during War of the Spanish Succession.
1713 Treaty of Utrecht cedes rock to Britain.
1830 Gibraltar becomes a crown colony.
1963 Spain revives claim to Gibraltar and begins to blockade the rock.
1967 In a referendum, Gibraltarians vote overwhelmingly to maintain links with UK.
1969 New constitution allows full internal self-government and guarantees sovereignty over Gibraltar will not be relinquished to Spain against wishes of Gibraltarian people.
1977 Talks between UK and Spain include, for the first time, Gibraltarian representatives.
1985 Spain–Gibraltar border fully reopened.
2006 Gibraltar, Spain, and UK meet as equals for first time and agree to confidence-building measures; new constitution gives more powers to Gibraltar.

MONTSERRAT
Volcanic island in eastern Caribbean.
1632 First colonized by British.
1958 British crown colony.
1995–97 Soufrière Hills volcanic eruption causes evacuation of most of island.

PITCAIRN ISLAND
Isolated Pacific islands with population of 48.
1790 Occupied by HMS *Bounty* mutineers.

ST. HELENA
Island group including Ascension and Tristan da Cunha.
1659 Administered by East India Company.
1821 Napoleon dies in exile on St. Helena.
1961 Volcanic eruption causes complete evacuation of Tristan da Cunha for two years.

SOUTH GEORGIA & SANDWICH ISLANDS
Island group north of Antarctica.
1775 Claimed for Britain by Captain Cook.

TURKS & CAICOS ISLANDS
Island group south of Bahamas in Caribbean.
1766 British take control.
1973 Separated from the Bahamas.

1775 James Watt invents the first effective steam engine; other inventions follow and the Industrial Revolution gathers pace in Britain.

1793–1815 Britain goes to war with revolutionary and Napoleonic France. Horatio Nelson defeats the French at the naval battles of the Nile (1798) and Trafalgar (1805), where he loses his life.

The Duke of Wellington, successful commander of forces in the Peninsular War of 1808–14 that evicts the French from Spain and Portugal, finally defeats Napoleon at Waterloo in 1815.

1801 Act of Union with Ireland creates the United Kingdom of Great Britain and Ireland.

1807 The slave trade, but not slavery, is abolished throughout the British Empire.

1820–30 The Prince Regent is king as George IV. He is succeeded by his brother, William IV.

1825 Stockton to Darlington railway opens, the world's first public railroad line.

1829 After considerable agitation, the Catholic Relief Act is passed, allowing Roman Catholics to stand for parliament.

1829 Robert Peel founds the Metropolitan Police Force in London.

1832 The Great Reform Act is passed, conferring voting rights on middle-class men and redistributing parliamentary seats on a fairer basis. Working-class men are enfranchised by the Reform Acts of 1867 and 1884, while the property qualification for all members of parliament is abolished in 1858 and the secret ballot introduced in 1872. However, women are not yet allowed to vote or stand for parliament.

1833 Slavery is finally abolished throughout the British Empire.

1834 Poor Law Act is passed, creating workhouses for the poor.

1834 The Tolpuddle Martyrs are transported to Australia for attempting to form a trade union.

1835 The Municpal Reform Act is passed, requiring members of town councils to be elected by taxpayers.

1837–1901 Victoria is queen, succeeding her uncle, William IV. She becomes the longest-serving British monarch.

1838 The six-point People's Charter is issued by the Chartists, who campaign for further reform of the voting system.

1840 Penny post introduced, the first flat-rate postal service in the world.

1846 Home Secretary Robert Peel repeals the Corn Laws, imposed from 1815 to control the import and export of grain.

1851 Great Exhibition held in London.

1861 Prince Albert, consort of Queen Victoria, dies. Victoria goes into mourning for 13 years, refusing to appear in public.

1867 Canada becomes the first dominion or independent state in British Empire.

1868 William Gladstone becomes prime minister, heading the first of his four reforming governments.

1877 Queen Victoria is declared Empress of India, as Britain approaches its zenith as an imperial power.

1906 Reformist Liberal government introduces old-age pensions and national insurance. To pay for this, it taxes the rich, causing a major constitutional crisis with the aristocratic House of Lords, solved by the 1911 Parliament Act, which drastically reduces its powers.

1914 World War I begins.

1918 Armistice ends the war; 750,000 dead and many millions injured.

1918 Women over the age of 30 can now vote and stand for parliament. The first woman takes her seat in 1919. Women finally gain voting equality in 1928.

1924 First, minority, Labour government is elected under Ramsay MacDonald.

1926 General Strike in support of the miners fails in its objectives.

1936 Edward VIII abdicates over marriage to Mrs. Simpson, a divorcee. His brother becomes king as George VI.

1939 UK declares war on Germany after it invades Poland at start of World War II.

1940 Winston Churchill becomes prime minister.

1942 The Beveridge Report proposes the creation of a welfare state at the end of the war to support people "from the cradle to the grave."

1945 World War II ends with victory, at the cost of 330,000 British lives.

1945 Labour government of Clement Attlee wins massive majority over Churchill's Conservatives.

1946 Nationalization of Bank of England, railroads, coal, and public utilities.

Clement Attlee
Prime minister from 1945–51, Attlee transformed Britain by introducing the National Health Service and by nationalizing industries.

1947 **Independence** of the Indian subcontinent begins the dismemberment of the British Empire.

1948 **National Health Service** establishes free medical treatment for all.

1949 **Founding member of** NATO.

1951 **The Festival of Britain** provides relief from post-war austerity measures.

1951 **Conservatives** return to power.

1952 **Elizabeth II** becomes queen.

1956 **Suez crisis:** UK and France collude with Israel to invade Egypt but are forced out under US pressure.

1957 **UK grants independence** to Ghana, its first African colony to be decolonized. By 1980, almost all former British colonies gain their independence.

1973 **UK joins** the European Economic Community (EEC, now EU).

1975 **First North Sea oil** is piped ashore.

1979 **Margaret Thatcher** becomes first British woman prime minister and holds power until 1990; she ushers in 18 years of Conservative government.

1982 **Argentina invades** Falkland Islands, which are retaken by a UK task force.

1986 **Financial services** deregulated in "Big Bang" as British economy booms.

1990 **Rioters in London** protest against the Poll Tax, which replaced rates to finance local councils. Thatcher is toppled by her party and replaced by John Major.

1997 **Landslide election victory** for Labour Party under Tony Blair.

1999 **Devolution gives** Scotland its own parliament and Wales its own assembly.

2001 **Labour wins a second term** with a huge majority and goes on to win a third in 2005. The UK joins the US in the invasion of Afghanistan after the 9/11 terror attacks against the US.

2003 **UK and the US** invade Iraq and overthrow Saddam Hussein, a move that is hugely divisive in Britain.

2005 **On July 7,** four Al-Qaeda inspired militants detonate bombs on the London Underground and on a London bus, killing 52 passengers.

2007 **Blair stands down** as prime minister and Gordon Brown replaces him.

2008 **The global economic crisis** hits Britain badly. The government is forced to nationalize the Northern Rock building society in February and in October the HSBC and Lloyds TSB banks are taken under majority government control. The additional government expenditure sees Britain's budget deficit rise to 11.4 percent of GDP by 2010.

UNITED KINGDOM

NORTHERN IRELAND

Northern Ireland consists of six counties in the north of Ireland that remained part of the UK when the 26 southern counties became independent. The province is often called Ulster, one of the four ancient kingdoms of Ireland.

1920 Government of Ireland Act partitions Ireland, with a Protestant north.
1921 Northern Irish parliament first meets.
1969 Widespread rioting after Protestants attack Catholic districts: British army is deployed as violence erupts across the province, marking the start of "the Troubles."
1972 Northern Irish parliament suspended; direct British rule imposed.
1985 Anglo-Irish agreement between Britain and Ireland to work for peace.
1998 Good Friday agreement sets up a devolved assembly.
2005 IRA declares armed struggle is over.
2007 DUP and Sinn Féin agree to share power; devolved assembly finally meets.

Orange Marching Season
Every July 12, members of the Protestant Orange Order march to commemorate the Battle of the Boyne in 1691, when Protestant William of Orange defeated Catholic James II.

2010 **General election:** With no overall majority, the Conservative leader David Cameron negotiates a formal coalition with the Liberal Democrats.

《 192–93 The Battle of Hastings
《 264–65 The English Civil War
《 292–93 The Industrial Revolution
《 348–49 Queen Victoria
《 412–13 End of the Colonial Era

Ireland

Centuries of struggle against English rule brought independence for most of Ireland in 1922.

c.300 BCE **Ireland is invaded** by Gaelic-speaking Celts.

432 CE **Christianity is introduced** to Ireland by St. Patrick (c.389–461), who becomes the country's patron saint.

795 **First Viking raid** on Ireland; the Vikings settle along the coast, founding Dublin in 811.

1014 **At the battle** of Clontarf, Viking power is broken and the four traditional Irish kingdoms of Ulster, Leinster, Munster, and Connaught are briefly united under Brian Boru.

1171 **During the reign** of English king Henry II (1154–89), Anglo-Norman adventurers conquer parts of Ireland, having received authorization from Pope Adrian IV (an Englishman) to subjugate Ireland. By the 1175 Treaty of Windsor, the High King of Ireland recognizes the English King as his overlord.

1264 **First meeting** of Irish parliament.

1494 **Under the terms** of Poynings' Law, English laws apply to Ireland.

1541 **Having broken the** power of Ireland's feudal lords, Henry VIII (1509–47) adopts the title of King of Ireland.

1559–1607 **Against the backdrop** of attempts by Elizabeth I (1558–1603) to impose Protestantism, a succession of unsuccessful rebellions against the English are launched in Ulster (1559–66, 1593–1603) and Munster (1569–72). In 1607, 100 Irish Catholic lords flee to Rome. Scottish Presbyterian settlers move to Ulster, taking land from Irish Catholics.

1609 **First Ulster plantations** created.

1641 **Catholics launch** a rebellion against English rule which is eventually crushed at Drogheda in 1649 by Oliver Cromwell.

1652 **Act of Settlement** displaces Irish Catholics to poor land in Connaught.

1690 **Irish Catholics** who support the deposed English Catholic king James II (1685–88) are defeated by William of Orange at the Battle of the Boyne.

1704 **Under the terms** of a new penal code, Catholics are deprived of the right to acquire property and in 1728 the right to vote. The "Protestant Ascendancy" lasts for most of the 18th century.

1778 **Irish MP Henry Gratton** secures the removal of most anti-Catholic land laws.

1795 **Ulster Protestants** set up the Loyal Orange Institution—the Orange Order—to defend land rights against Catholics.

1798 **United Irishmen** rebellion against British rule, led by Wolfe Tone, crushed.

1801 **The Act of Union** between Great Britain and Ireland comes into force. The Irish parliament is abolished and Ireland obtains representation at the Westminster parliament. Catholics are not allowed to sit in the House of Commons until 1829.

1845–51 **Famine. One million** die and more than one million emigrate.

1858 **Irish Republican Brotherhood,** or Fenians, formed to fight for an independent Irish republic.

1869 **Irish church** disestablished.

1870 **First land reform** act begins to tackle issues of absentee landlords, lack of tenant security, and unfair rents.

1882 **Irish MPs in London** form the Irish Parliamentary Party to fight for home rule.

1896, 1893 **Home Rule Bills** to give Ireland its own parliament are defeated.

1905 **Sinn Féin founded**.

1912 **An attempt to introduce** new Home Rule Bill brings Ireland to the brink of civil war as unionists and nationalists set up armed militias.

1916 **Easter Rising in** Dublin by the Irish Republican Brotherhood soon crushed. The British execute the leaders, increasing support for the Republican cause.

1918 **Sinn Féin** wins landslide in general election; its MPs do not take their seats but set up independent Dáil Eireann (Assembly of Ireland) in Dublin and declare Irish independence in 1919.

1919–21 **Anglo-Irish war** between Irish Republican Army (IRA) and British army.

1921 **Anglo-Irish Treaty** sets up Irish Free State in 1922, with six northern counties in the UK.

1922–23 **Civil war** between pro- and anti-Treaty forces.

1937 **Full sovereignty** as Eire.

1949 **Eire becomes** Republic of Ireland and leaves the British Commonwealth.

1973 **Ireland joins** the EEC (now EU).

1990 **Mary Robinson** elected first woman president.

1995 **Referendum favors divorce.**

2002 **Ireland adopts the euro.**

2008 **Voters reject the Lisbon Treaty** causing a crisis in the EU. The treaty is passed in a second referendum in 2009.

2009 **Global economic crisis** affects Ireland badly, with unemployment reaching 11 percent.

2010 **Ireland accepts** EU and IMF bailout of its banking system, amounting to 85 billion euros. Prime Minister Brian Cowen calls early general election, won the following year by Fine Gael, which enters coalition with Labour Party.

《 134–35 Celtic Warriors
《 436–37 "The Troubles"

France

Europe's first modern republic, and a prime mover for European integration.

600 BCE Greeks found colony of Massalia on the Mediterranean coast and other trading colonies. They trade tin and other commodities up the Rhône and into northern and western France with the Celts and other peoples.

121 BCE Southern France is occupied by the Romans and becomes the province of Gallia Narbonensis.

105 BCE Two Roman armies are destroyed by the Cimbri and Teutones—Germanic tribes—at Arausio in the Rhône valley in 105 BCE. The Cimbri move on to invade Spain, but the Roman dictator Marius rallies his troops and defeats the Cimbri at Aquae Sextiae in 102 BCE.

58–51 BCE The Romans, under Julius Caesar, conquer Gaul, an area roughly equivalent to modern France, defeating Vercingetorix at Alesia in 52 BCE. The new territory is divided into Gallia Lugdunensis in the north, Gallia Belgica in the northeast, and Aquitania in the west. A rebellion against Roman rule in 26 CE is crushed.

253 CE Frankish tribes from Germany first cross the Rhine into Gaul.

260 Postumus usurps power in Gaul and creates an independent Roman empire including Britannia and Hispaniae (Spain), which lasts until 274. He secures power by defending his Gallic Empire's frontiers against barbarian attack.

406 A coalition of Vandals, Suevi, and Alans invades Gaul before crossing into Spain. They are followed into Gaul by Franks, Burgundians, and Alemanni.

418–62 The Romans settle, invading Visigoth tribes in Aquitaine.

Church to the kings of France
Built on the eastern half of the Île de la Cité in Paris between 1163 and 1257, Notre Dame is one of Europe's finest examples of early Gothic architecture. As the "parish church of the kings of France," it also saw the coronation of Henry VI of England, crowned king of France in 1431.

451 Attila the Hun invades Gaul but is defeated by a coalition of Romans, Franks, and Visigoths.

486 Roman power in Gaul ("Francia") finally collapses when Syagrius, the last Roman commander, is defeated by Clovis I, the first of the Merovingian kings, at Soissons. Clovis's reign marks the foundation of the Frankish empire that soon covers western and northern France, except Brittany, and extends east into the Low Countries and Germany. The Burgundians control the south and east, and the Visigoths the far southwest.

496 Clovis and the Franks convert to Christianity. This wins them the support of their Gallo-Roman subjects and of eastern Roman emperors. Gradually eliminating rivals, the Frankish kingdom becomes the strongest power in Europe by 600.

507 Clovis defeats the Visigoths at Vouillé, driving them into Spain.

511 Clovis dies and his kingdom is divided among his four sons, as is the Germanic custom. This has the effect of weakening the kingdom, resulting in instability, civil war, and assassinations.

561 The kingdom is divided again, between the sons of Clothar I.

639 With the death of King Dagobert, a succession of weak Merovingian kings sees power pass to the mayor of the palace, a high-ranking court official.

670 As Frankish power declines, Aquitaine breaks away and is not taken back into the kingdom until 768.

679–714 Pepin II of Herstal is the most successful mayor of the palace. He is effective ruler of the entire kingdom.

732 Mayor Charles Martel defeats an invading Muslim army at Poitiers, ending Muslim expansion in western Europe.

741 Pepin III succeeds Charles Martel. In 751 he makes an alliance with the papacy. In return for military help, Pope

FRANCIS I

Francis I succeeded to the French crown in 1515 upon the death of his wife's father, Louis XII, since women were prohibited from inheriting the throne. Francis was France's first Renaissance king, surrounding himself with musicians and poets at his court, where visitors included Leonardo da Vinci.

While his reign proved the catalyst for a flowering of the arts, Francis's political record was more mixed. He was defeated by Habsburg emperor Charles V at the Battle of Pavia in 1525 and forced to surrender any claims in Italy after a period of imprisonment. However, one of Francis's lasting legacies was the historic accommodation he reached with the Ottoman Turks, who became allies of France during the Italian War (1542–46).

Zacharias authorizes him to depose the Merovingian king and assume the kingship of the Franks himself as the first Carolingian king.

768 On the death of Pepin III, the kingdom is divided between his two sons, Charlemagne and Carloman. When Carloman dies in 771, Charlemagne is sole ruler. He conquers the Lombard kingdom of Italy in 774 and doubles the size of his kingdom by 800, extending its borders from northern Spain to the Elbe in Germany. His capital at Aachen is the intellectual center of Europe.

799 Fiercely independent Brittany is conquered by Charlemagne, although it rebels in 812.

800 King Charlemagne is crowned Emperor of the West by Pope Leo III and effectively establishes the Carolingian empire.

806 Charlemagne sets up a chain of customs posts in eastern Germany to control trade with the Slavs.

814 Charlemagne dies and is succeeded by Louis the Pious, who dies in 840. Civil war breaks out between his younger sons for the succession.

843 Treaty of Verdun divides Charlemagne's empire into three: West Francia (France), East Francia (Germany), and Italy. The empire is briefly reunited under Charles the Fat (884–87) but it finally breaks up into five kingdoms as Burgundy and Provence break away.

911 Charles the Simple allows Norse raiders to settle in Normandy.

987 The Capetian dynasty, which lasts until 1328 and succeeds that of the Carolingians, is founded by Hugh Capet (987–996), although it is not until the late 12th century that the Capetian realm attains its greatest territorial extent.

1066 Duke William of Normandy invades England and seizes the throne, starting 400 years of conflict over lands owned by the English kings in France.

1154 Henry II of England rules the vast Angevin empire in France, a territory far bigger than that of the French king.

1180–1223 Philip Augustus is king and revives the monarchy. He defeats an Anglo-German invasion at Bouvines in 1214, recovering all English lands in France except Gascony, and makes France the strongest nation in Europe.

1309 The papacy is moved from Rome to Avignon in France by Pope Clement V. From 1378, during the period of the Great Schism, there are two rival popes, until the Roman party achieves sole recognition in 1417 and returns the papacy to Rome.

1328 Philip VI is first Valois king.

1337 The Hundred Years War, between France and England, begins when Edward III of England lays claim to the French throne. Edward and his son, the Black Prince, win major victories at Crécy (1346) and Poitiers (1356).

1347 Calais surrenders to the English after a long siege; the town remains an English possession until 1558.

1348–50 The Black Death sweeps across Europe and kills between one-third and one-half of the French population.

1360 Under the Treaty of Bretigny, Edward III renounces his claim to the French throne in return for Aquitaine and Gascony.

1363 Duchy of Burgundy is created out of royal lands, and extends its power by gaining lands in the Rhine valley and Flanders. The dukes often ally with the English against the French kings.

1369 The French renew war and drive the English out of most of their positions by 1374.

1415 Henry V of England revives the Hundred Years War and wins a major victory at Agincourt. Under the 1420 Treaty of Troyes, he becomes regent of

France and, by marrying King Charles VI's daughter, heir to the French throne. He dies before he can succeed to the French throne.

1415 Led initially by Joan of Arc, the French push the English out of France, recapturing Normandy in 1449, Gascony in 1450, and finally ending the war with the recapture of Aquitaine in 1453.

1419–67 Reign of Duke Philip the Good of Burgundy, who acquires further territory in the Netherlands. His successor, Charles the Bold (1467–77), unites his territories, but the French king Louis XI (1461–81) seizes French Burgundy while the rest becomes part of the Habsburg family lands.

1494 Charles VIII invades Italy, starting a long series of wars with the Habsburg emperors. In 1525 the capture of Francis I by Spanish troops at Pavia and his subsequent imprisonment in Spain brings the wars to a climax. Francis renounces French claims in Italy, notably Milan, but hostilities are renewed and are only settled at the Treaty of Cateau-Cambrésis in 1559.

1517 The Reformation starts in Europe. Many French people convert to Protestantism (known in France as Huguenotism).

1562–98 In the French Wars of Religion, Protestant Huguenot and Catholic nobles fight for supremacy following the death of the last Valois king, Henry II, in 1559.

1572 Four thousand Huguenots are killed on the orders of Catherine de Medici, the regent of France, in the St. Bartholomew's Day massacre.

1594 Henry IV, who has converted to Catholicism in 1593 on the grounds that "Paris is worth a mass," is crowned the first of the Bourbon kings. The Huguenots are granted freedom of worship in the 1598 Edict of Nantes.

1608 The foundation of Québec in Canada leads to the creation of a large French empire in North America.

1610 Henry IV is assassinated. He is succeeded by Louis XIII, whose first minister, Cardinal Richelieu, consolidates the monarchy's standing both at home and abroad.

1627–28 French Huguenots rise in revolt but are crushed at La Rochelle.

1628 During the 30 Years War (1618–48), France goes on the offensive against Spain and the Holy Roman Empire in Germany, with the intent of dismembering the powerful Habsburg empire. France defeats Spanish attacks and gains Roussillon from Spain in 1642. In 1640 the French support Portuguese and Catalan revolts against Spanish rule, and they aid the Neapolitan revolt in 1647.

1643 Louis XIV, the "Sun King," ascends the throne at the age of five. Cardinal Mazarin acts on his behalf as first minister.

1659 The foundation of Fort St. Louis on the Senegal River marks the start of France's colonial empire in West Africa.

1661 The young king takes full power. During his reign, the absolutism of the *ancien régime* reaches its peak. At home the arts flourish under his patronage. Abroad he establishes French hegemony over much of Western Europe in a series of victorious military campaigns, pushing France's borders north into Flanders and east to the Rhine. However, from 1700, as Europe unites in resistance, his position begins to be undermined.

1664 French East India Company founded and begins to set up trading colonies on the east coast of India.

1685 Revocation of the Edict of Nantes sends many Huguenots into exile in England and Germany.

1701–13 War of the Spanish Succession breaks out when Louis tries to place his grandson Philip on the throne of France. Philip is eventually recognized as Bourbon king of Spain, but renounces any future claim to the throne of France.

1715 Death of Louis XIV. His successor, Louis XV (1715–74), lacks interest in government and politics and is less successful in campaigns abroad and in countering growing opposition at home.

1740 The War of the Austrian Succession follows the death of the last male Habsburg emperor, Charles VI. France and Prussia unsuccessfully support the claim of the Elector of Bavaria to the Habsburg throne against that of Charles's daughter Maria Theresa, whose claim is upheld at the Treaty of Aix-la-Chapelle (1748).

1756–63 The Seven Years War continues disputes left unresolved by the Treaty of Aix-la-Chapelle as Britain and France seek to win maritime and colonial supremacy in North America, the West Indies, and India. As a result of British success in the war, France is obliged to cede almost all of its possessions in North America, the West Indies, and India to Britain, and lands west of the Mississippi to Spain, and is left with little of its large American empire remaining.

1766 France annexes Duchy of Lorraine, consolidating its eastern border on the Rhine.

1776–83 Expensive support for the Americans in their Revolution helps undermine the *ancien régime*.

1789 For the first time since 1614, Louis XVI (1774–92) summons the advisory Estates-General in an attempt to secure revenue for the bankrupt government. As the nobles and clergy (the first and second estates) lose control to the "third estate" (the commoners), a national assembly is formed by the third estate and demands reform of the monarchy. Louis XVI's indecisive response sparks the storming of the Bastille on July 14. The National Assembly issues the "Declaration of the Rights of Man." Further hesitation on Louis XVI's part prompts the women of Paris to march to Versailles in October to demand bread; they take the royal family to Paris as hostages.

1790 A new constitution is proclaimed, but in 1791 the king and his family attempt to flee the country in disguise. However, they are brought back as prisoners and Louis is forced to accept the new constitution.

1792 Royalist emigrés begin to muster support abroad as Austria and Prussia declare war on behalf of the king. Britain, Spain, and Holland declare war in 1793. The Paris mob storms the royal palace of the Tuileries. The Paris Commune led by Georges Danton seizes power and a national convention replaces the national assembly and abolishes the monarchy.

1793 Louis XVI is tried, convicted, and executed. Control of the country passes from the moderate Girondins to the extremist Jacobins, led by Maximilien François Robespierre as the "Reign of Terror" begins with a series of mass executions.

1794 Robespierre's Committee of Public Safety is overthrown in a coup and Robespierre is executed. A new constitution in 1795 establishes the more moderate Directory which, however, becomes increasingly corrupt.

1799 Napoleon Bonaparte, a successful general from Corsica, overthrows the Directory and in a coup assumes dictatorial powers as First Consul.

1804 At his coronation in Paris, Napoleon takes the crown from the pope and proclaims himself Emperor of the French. At home he introduces many reforms, including the legal "Code Napoléon"; abroad he defeats the Austrians and Russians at Austerlitz in 1805 and the Prussians at Jena in 1806.

1812 Napoleon's invasion of Russia leads to defeat at the hands of the Russian winter and to the Austro-Prussian capture of Paris in 1814. He is deposed and sent into exile on Elba. The Bourbon monarchy is reinstated, with Louis XVIII, younger brother of Louis XVII, as king.

1815 Napoleon returns from exile for a final "hundred days" that end in defeat by British and Prussian forces at the Battle of Waterloo. Louis XVIII returns again.

Paris Commune
This medal was awarded to a supporter of the short-lived Paris Commune of 1871, formed in the period of turmoil following the Franco-Prussian war.

1830 Louis XVIII's brother Charles X, who ascended the throne in 1824, is forced to abdicate in the "July Revolution" and Louis-Philippe I of Orléans is installed as the "citizen king."

1830 The capture of Algiers marks the beginning of France's second colonial empire, in North Africa.

1848 At a time of food shortages, Louis Philippe is toppled by popular riots in a revolution and a Second Republic is proclaimed. Charles-Louis Napoleon, nephew of Napoleon Bonaparte, is elected president with more than 70 percent of the total vote.

1851 Napoleon seizes power in a coup d'état with the support of monarchists and the army.

1852 Charles-Louis Napoleon takes the title Emperor Napoleon III. He proclaims a Second Empire based on plebiscitary autocracy and becomes involved in wars with Russia in the Crimea in 1854–56 and with Austria in 1859, gaining Savoy and Nice from Piedmont in 1860.

1863 Napoleon III supports an ill-fated venture to install a puppet emperor in Mexico. French prestige suffers when Maximilian I is executed in 1867.

1870 Napoleon III declares war on Prussia to gain diplomatic dominance in Europe. French armies are quickly defeated at Metz and Sedan, where Napoleon is captured. The Third Republic is proclaimed and continues resistance until Prussian forces enter Paris in January 1871. France is obliged to cede Alsace and Lorraine to Germany.

Napoleon III
Nephew of Napoleon Bonaparte, Charles-Louis Napoleon twice tried to overthrow Louis-Philippe but was elected president of France in 1848, seized power in 1851, and became emperor the following year.

1870 **In Paris**, a revolutionary commune holds power, but is brutally suppressed at the cost of 20,000 lives by Louis Adolphe Thiers, who serves as president from 1871 until 1873. Instability is endemic in the new republic: over the next 70 years there are 109 separate governments.

1881 **Tunisia becomes** a French protectorate; in 1887 a protectorate is established in Indochina.

1894 **France signs a military** alliance with Russia against growing German power in Europe.

1899 **After a near conflict** at Fashoda, Sudan, France, and UK reach agreement over spheres of influence in Africa.

1904 **Entente Cordiale** with UK resolves colonial differences over Morocco, Egypt, Suez Canal, and Madagascar, and develops into a diplomatic alliance.

1905 **Church and state** are separated in the wake of the Dreyfus Affair in which a Jew, Captain Alfred Dreyfus, is unjustly convicted of treason in 1894 and only acquitted in 1906.

1907 **UK signs an** agreement with Russia, extending its alliance with France to form the Triple Entente.

1912 **France and Spain** establish protectorates over Morocco.

1914 **Germany declares** war on France as World War I breaks out. Germany invades France before it turns to face Russia. UK joins the war as an ally of France, and sends a large army. The German advance toward Paris is stopped at the Marne, and by the end of 1914 a stalemate develops along the western front. About 550,000 French soldiers are killed in the Battle of Verdun (February 1915–December 1916), and 200,000 in the second Battle of the Aisne (April–May 1917).

FRANCE
FRENCH OVERSEAS DEPARTMENTS & TERRITORIES

CLIPPERTON ISLAND
French Dependency off coast of Mexico, named after a pirate, John Clipperton.
1855 Claimed by France.

EUROPA AND OTHER ISLANDS
Five groups of islands off the west coast of Madagascar and claimed by that country.
1960 Administered by France.

FRENCH GUIANA
Mainland colony in South America.
1568 Gaspar de Sostelle and 126 families attempt to settle but are driven out by the indigenous population.
1676 The territory is recaptured by France from the Dutch.
1817 Territory becomes a French colony and is later used as a penal colony.
1946 Made an Overseas Department.

FRENCH POLYNESIA
Island group in South Pacific.
1521 Ferdinand Magellan reaches Pukapuka in the Tuamotu Archipelago, which is already inhabited by Polynesians.
1768 Tahiti is visited by Louis-Antoine de Bougainville.
1842 France makes Tahiti a protectorate.
1880 Tahiti and its dependants become a French colony. The rest of the island groups are annexed by 1900.
1946 French Polynesia becomes an Overseas Territory.
1963 French government announces plans to begin a nuclear testing program. First test takes place at Mururoa Atoll.
1995 Underground nuclear test on Mururoa Atoll prompts a series of demonstrations and riots in Tahiti.
1995 The last of five Greenpeace vessels accused of entering the 12-mile (20-km) exclusion zone around the atolls is seized by French commandos.
1996 Nuclear tests suspended.

GUADELOUPE
Large island in the eastern Caribbean.
1493 Claimed for Spain by Columbus.
1635 French colony established.
1946 Becomes an Overseas Department.

MARTINIQUE
Large island in the Caribbean.
1502 Claimed for Spain by Columbus.
1635 French colony established.
1946 Becomes an Overseas Department.

MAYOTTE
Island in western Indian Ocean.
1843 French colony, part of the Comoros.
1974 When Comoros is independent, Mayotte becomes Departmental Collective.

NEW CALEDONIA
Large island in southwest Pacific Ocean.
1840 First European settlers arrive.
1853 French colony.
1958 Becomes an Overseas Territory.
1998 Becomes a Territorial Collective; a referendum on independence will be held between 2013 and 2018.

REUNION
Island in Indian Ocean.
1638 French possession as Ile Saint Paul (later Ile Bourbon).
1946 Becomes an Overseas Department.

ST. PIERRE & MIQUELON
Islands off the east coast of Canada.
1816 French colony.
1985 Becomes a Territorial Collective.

SOUTHERN & ANTARCTIC TERRITORIES
Islands in the south Indian Ocean plus the French Antarctic claim.
1955 Organized as an Overseas Territory.

WALLIS & FUTUNA
Islands in the central Pacific Ocean.
1961 Become an Overseas Territory.

CHARLES DE GAULLE

The man commonly referred to in France as Général de Gaulle was a French military leader and statesman.

Prior to World War II, de Gaulle was an armored warfare tactician. After war broke out, he reached the rank of brigadier general, becoming leader of the Free French government in London and of the French Resistance. Following liberation in 1944, he led the French provisional government.

Called to form a government in 1958, de Gaulle was the Fifth Republic's first president, 1958–69. His political ideology, known as Gaullism, has had a lasting influence on French politics.

" The cause of France is not lost… Whatever happens, **the flame** of French resistance must not and **shall not die**. "

GENERAL DE GAULLE, BROADCASTING FROM LONDON, JUNE 18, 1940

1918 **The Allies break through** German lines in the summer of 1918 and force an armistice in November.

1919 **The peace treaties** signed at Versailles outside Paris return Alsace and Lorraine to France, award France mandates over Saarland in Germany, and satisfy French demand for German reparations. By later agreements, France receives mandates over Lebanon and Syria, and territories in West Africa.

1919–39 **Economic recession** and political instability as the Third Republic has 44 governments.

1923 **French troops** occupy the Ruhr to enforce German reparation payments. They withdraw in 1925 as the Locarno Pact confirms the existing Franco–German border and promises better relations between the two powers.

1933 **Hitler comes to power** in Germany and begins to dismantle the Versailles settlement. UK and France appease Germany at Munich in 1938, but offer support to Poland when Hitler occupies neighboring Czechoslovakia in 1939.

1939 **German invasion of Poland** starts World War II. France and UK declare war.

1940 **Germany invades and forces** a French capitulation; a collaborationist regime under Marshal Pétain, hero of the defense of Verdun in 1916, is set up in Vichy in the south as the Germans control the north and west of the country. General de Gaulle leads the "Free French" from London.

1943–44 **France recognizes** the independence of Syria and Lebanon.

1944 **Liberation of France** as Allied troops invade Normandy on D-Day. De Gaulle takes over as leader of the provisional goverment.

1945 **World War II ends:** France joins in the four-power occupation of Germany.

1946–58 **Fourth Republic** is set up but is plagued by political instability.

1949 **France joins NATO.**

1950 **Schuman plan for the** union of French and West German iron, steel, and coal industries in order to prevent another war between the two nations leads to the establishment of the European Coal and Steel Community (ECSC) with West Germany,

Liberation
On August 26, 1944, crowds cheered Allied troops in a victory parade down the Champs Élysées. The German garrison surrendered the previous day.

Italy, the Netherlands, Belgium, and Luxembourg in 1952, the first step on the road toward European union.

1954 After a massive defeat at Dien Bien Phu at the hands of Vietnamese nationalists, France pulls out of southeast Asia and recognizes the independence of a divided Vietnam, Laos, and Cambodia. France hands over its remaining possessions in the subcontinent to India. War of Independence breaks out in Algeria against French rule.

1956 Morocco and Tunisia gain their independence.

1956 France and UK take part in an abortive war to reverse Egypt's nationalization of the Suez Canal.

1957 France signs the Treaty of Rome with its five ECSC partners to create the European Economic Community.

1958 Fifth Republic is formed after the Fourth Republic collapses as army defiance in Algeria threatens civil war. De Gaulle becomes president.

1960 All French colonies in Africa except two gain their independence. The Comoros Islands become independent in 1975, Djibouti in 1977.

1962 Algerian independence is won after bitter war with France comes to an end.

1966 France withdraws from NATO military command as it pursues an increasingly independent foreign policy.

1968 General strike and student demonstrations over wages and education policy lead to turmoil across France. The National Assembly is dissolved but the Gaullists win the general election.

STUDENT PROTESTS, 2006

On March 18, 2006, some 700,000 protesters converged on Paris and clashed violently with riot police. The demonstrators were objecting to a controversial bill to deregulate the labor market by making it easier to fire people under 26. The bill was perceived as grossly unfair because it made young people's jobs insecure. A month after the protest President Chirac scrapped the bill. Giving in to the protesters was seen by many observers as a missed opportunity for France to implement badly needed economic reforms and to free its labor market from stifling regulation.

Revolutionary spirit
Young protesters storm the Place de la Nation in Paris and throw the government into turmoil.

1969 De Gaulle resigns after defeat in referendum on regional reform and is replaced as president by Georges Pompidou, who dies in office in 1974.

1970 Death of de Gaulle.

1974 Valéry Giscard d'Estaing is elected president in a center-right coalition.

1981 The Socialist Party (PS) candidate François Mitterrand is elected president.

1983–86 After pursuing protectionist socialist economic policies, the government begins to deregulate the economy.

1986 "Cohabitation" between socialist president and a new right-wing government led by Jacques Chirac.

1988 Mitterrand wins second term. A PS-led coalition returns to goverment.

1991 Edith Cresson becomes France's first woman prime minister.

1992 France signs Maastricht treaty on European Union.

1993 Center-right coalition wins election.

1995 Jacques Chirac, the right-wing candidate, is elected president, ending 14 years of socialist presidency.

1995–96 Series of nuclear tests in French Polynesia conducted despite international condemnation.

1996 Unpopular austerity measures introduced to prepare the economy for European monetary union.

1997 Center-right loses elections: a PS-led government takes office with Lionel Jospin as prime minister.

1998–99 Extensive privatization program is initiated.

2000 Thirty-five-hour week becomes law. Chirac embroiled in corruption scandal.

2001 Compulsory military service is abolished.

2002 Euro replaces the franc.

2002 Jacques Chirac is reelected president. The National Front leader Jean-Marie Le Pen's strong showing in first round of voting sends shockwaves throughout France and leads to mass protests. These elections are first with presidential and parliamentary elections fought on the same five-year timetable, ending difficulties of cohabitation.

2002 Widespread public-sector worker strikes over privatization program bring country to a standstill.

2003 France is heavily critical of the US–UK invasion of Iraq. An estimated 11,000 elderly people die in severe heatwave in August.

2004 Protests by France's sizeable Muslim community when French MPs vote to ban the headscarf in schools.

2005 Referendum rejects proposed EU constitution. Prime minister Jean-Pierre Raffarin resigns. Unrest among deprived immigrant youths sparks riots that spread throughout cities. State of emergency is declared.

2006 New youth employment laws spark mass demonstrations across France. The legislation is dropped when the protests continue. Tough new restrictions on immigration make it harder for unskilled migrants to settle in France.

2007 Nicolas Sarkozy wins presidential election for the right, defeating Ségolène Royale of the Socialists in the second round, as Jacques Chirac steps down from power.

2008 Société Général loses 5 million euros due to unauthorized trading by a single rogue trader.

2010 The French government's order to dismantle illegal Roma Gypsy camps is controversial in other EU countries, who claim this contravenes directives on freedom of movement. President Sarkozy's party suffers heavy losses in regional elections, losing in 20 out of 22 regions.

The casino lifestyle
Monaco's fortunes were transformed when Prince Charles III, after whom the main town of Monte Carlo is named, opened a casino (above) in 1878, attracting both big money and tourism.

Monaco

A tiny principality on the Mediterranean coast, used as a tax haven by Europe's super-rich.

1191 Ancient port of Monaco is ceded by Henry VI, Holy Roman Emperor, to Genoa.

1297 The Grimaldis, an ancient Genoese family, establish themselves as the principality's hereditary rulers.

1641 Becomes a French protectorate.

1793 During the French Revolution, Monaco is annexed.

1814 Under the Treaty of Paris the Grimaldis regain power.

1860 Independent under French protection.

1911 First constitution drafted.

1929 First Monaco Grand Prix.

1949 Rainier III accedes to the throne.

1962 End of absolute authority of the prince; women obtain the vote.

1963 Democratic legislative elections held for first time.

1982 Princess Grace, a former Hollywood film star and wife of Prince Rainier, dies following a car accident.

1993 Monaco joins UN, becoming the smallest member state.

2002 Constitution revised. A new succession law is passed, designed to keep the Grimaldi family on the throne if Crown Prince Albert has no heir.

2005 Prince Albert succeeds his father.

Spain

Following a long period of decline, Spain has made a successful transition from dictatorship to democracy.

218 BCE The boundary between Roman and Carthaginian Spain lies along the Ebro River.

206 BCE Spain is conquered by the Romans under Scipio Africanus after his legions have driven out the Carthaginians.

133 BCE The final Celtic resistance to Roman rule is broken when the northern city of Numantia falls after a 20-year war.

419 CE At the end of the Roman Empire, a Visigothic kingdom is established in most of Spain with a Suevic kingdom in the northwest and some Vandal settlements in the far south.

554 Civil war in the Visigothic kingdom gives the Byzantine emperor Justinian the opportunity to reconquer southern Spain.

571 Visigoths recapture Córdoba and the rest of the southern state.

585 Visigoths conquer the Suevic kingdom and rule all of Spain.

587 Visigothic king Recared I converts to Catholicism.

711 The Visigoths are defeated by the Moors from North Africa, who introduce Islam to Spain.

718 The Asturian kingdom of northern Spain wins a decisive victory against the Moors at Covadonga, halting their expansion across the peninsula. The kingdom contines to grow at Muslim Spain's expense over the next century.

756 Spain becomes independent from the rest of the Muslim world when Abd-ar-Rahman founds the Umayyad Emirate at Córdoba. The emirate becomes a caliphate in 929. By this time, Córdoba, the capital city of the Umayyad Emirate, is the largest and one of the most prosperous cities in Western Europe.

778 Charlemagne, king of the Franks, defeats the Moors at Roncesvalles in the Basque country and extends Frankish rule over most of northeast Spain.

812 Discovery of what are claimed to be the bones of St. James the Apostle in Compostela; the town soon becomes second only to Rome as a major pilgrim destination.

900s A series of major Muslim raids are conducted into the kingdom of Asturias and León and the Byzantine-held Balearic Islands, which fall to the Muslims in 903.

962 The Christian reconquest of Spain is launched.

El Escorial

Philip II ordered the building of El Escorial, near Madrid, as a monastery and burial place for Spain's kings. It was begun in 1563 by Juan Bautista de Toledo, a Renaissance Spanish architect who had worked in Italy, and completed in 1584.

1008–31 Civil war breaks out in the Umayyad caliphate.

1100s Arabs introduce the art of papermaking to Europe at the port of Valencia.

1143 Alfonso VII of León recognizes the independence of Portugal.

1212 The extent of Moorish rule is reduced after the Moors suffer a major defeat at the battle of Las Navas de Tolosa. Spain now consists of the kingdoms of León and Navarre in the north, Castile in the center, Aragon in the east, and the Almohad Caliphate in the south. The Muslim Emirate of Mallorca rules the Balearic Islands.

1254 Muslim university founded at Seville. Under Muslim rule, towns such as Seville and Toledo are important centers of Islamic scholarship, enabling the knowledge of classical learning, preserved in Arabic translations and texts, to enter the cathedral schools of Western Europe. Muslim Spain also supports a thriving Jewish population that is tolerated by the Muslim authorities.

1360 Muslim rule in Spain is reduced to just the Emirate of Granada in the far south; the Balearic islands are now under Aragonese rule (since 1287).

1385 A Castilian attempt to conquer Portugal is defeated, preserving Portugal's independence.

1442 Aragon acquires Naples in southern Italy to add to its Mediterranean empire of the Balearics, Sardinia, and Sicily.

1469 The future united kingdom of Spain is created by the marriage of Isabella of Castile to Ferdinand of Aragon.

1474 Isabella becomes queen of Castile on the death of her half-brother Henry IV. Her claim is contested by Henry's heiress, Juana la Beltraneja, but is enforced through the skilful generalship of her husband, Ferdinand.

1478 The Spanish Inquisition is formed to test the sincerity of Jewish converts to Christianity. It is not officially abolished until 1834, and acquires a sinister reputation for its work.

1479 Ferdinand becomes king of Aragon. With Isabella, they begin to rule their two kingdoms jointly in 1481.

1492 Spanish forces expel the Moors from Granada, completing the Christian reconquest of Spain.

Moorish ceramics

This delicately patterned ceramic dish dates from the period of the emirate of Granada. Moorish arts and architecture achieved a high degree of sophistication during the 13th and 14th centuries.

1492 Isabella supports Christopher Columbus financially in his voyage to the "New World."

1493 Spain gains Roussilon province in the Pyrenees from France.

1494 Charles VIII of France invades Italy, starting a series of wars with Spain for control of Italy.

1496 Spain establishes Caribbean colony of Santo Domingo in Hispaniola.

1497 Spain takes Melila in North Africa, going on to acquire Oran in 1509, Algiers and Bougie in 1510, and Tunis in 1535.

1504 On Isabella's death, Ferdinand is recognized as regent for their daughter, Joanna the Mad.

1508–15 Spain colonizes Puerto Rico, Cuba, and Jamaica. In Cuba, the original indigenous peole are reduced from 50,000 to about 5,000 in 1550, due to deaths from European diseases against which they have no immunity.

1515 Ferdinand incorporates Navarre into Castile, thus becoming the first king of a united Spain.

1516 Charles of Habsburg becomes Charles I of Spain on the death of his father, Ferdinand. In 1519 he becomes Holy Roman Emperor Charles V, but is

> " I have placed under the **dominion of the King and Queen...** a second world through which **Spain,** which was reckoned a poor country, has become the richest. "
>
> CHRISTOPHER COLUMBUS, IN A LETTER WRITTEN IN 1500

involved in lengthy battles with Protestant princes in the empire, and in wars with France, to the neglect of Spain.

1519–24 **Hernán Cortés** conquers Aztec Empire for Spain.

1520–22 **Comunero popular** uprising in northern Spain is crushed.

1531–35 **Francisco Pizarro** conquers Inca empire for Spain.

1538 **Spanish control** is established in Colombia with the foundation of Santa Fé de Bogotá.

1554 **Philip, heir to the throne,** marries Mary Tudor, queen of England, and is king of England until her death in 1558. Ascends the Spanish throne as Philip II in 1556.

1556 **Charles V abdicates,** and the Holy Roman Empire is divided between Austrian Habsburg and Spanish lands. His brother Ferdinand rules the Austrian Habsburg lands and becomes Holy Roman Emperor, while his son Philip II rules Spain along with Sardinia, Naples and Sicily, the Duchy of Milan, Franch-Comté, and the Netherlands and Luxembourg. Charles retires to a monastery in Spain.

1559 **Treaty of Cateau–Cambrésis** ends Italian wars with France.

1561 **Madrid is** established as the Spanish capital.

1563–84 **Philip II builds** the vast palace of el Escorial, outside Madrid.

1565 **Spanish build forts** in Florida to defend Spanish bullion fleets sailing home from Mexico and Panama.

1566 **Protestant Dutch rise** up against Spanish rule, and are helped by Elizabeth I of England.

1568–71 **Moriscos** (Moors converted to Christianity) revolt in southern Spain but are crushed by Philip II.

1571 **Spanish capture** Manila and it becomes capital of Spanish Philippines.

1574 **The fall of** Spanish-controlled Tunis to an Ottoman fleet ends Spanish hopes of maintaining a significant military presence in North Africa. Tunis was first recaptured by the Ottomans in 1569, but recaptured by the Spanish in 1572, only to be lost again two years later.

1578 **Spanish troops** reconquer most of southern Netherlands.

1579 **Northern provinces of** the Netherlands formally unite under the Union of Utrecht to fight Spanish rule.

1580 **Portugal comes under** the control of the Spanish crown after the death of the childless king, Henrique. Philip II invades to enforce his claim, winning the Battle of Alcantara. Spain is now at the height of its imperial power in Europe.

Baroque king
King Philip IV, seen here in a portrait by Diego Velázquez, Spain's outstanding painter of the age, was an active patron of the arts. But during his reign Spain declined as a major European power.

1581 **Spain makes** peace with the Ottoman Turks in the Mediterranean.

1588 **Philip sends** an armada to invade England after its Protestant queen, Elizabeth, executes her Catholic cousin and rival for the throne, Mary, Queen of Scots.

1598 **Death of Philip II;** acccession of Philip III.

1609 **Twelve–year truce** is signed between Spain and the United Netherlands.

1618–48 **Period of** the 30 Years War, during which Spain is involved in almost constant warfare in Europe, largely against France and the Protestant rulers of Germany and northern Europe.

1621 **Philip IV becomes king**.

1628 **French offensives begin** against Spanish territories. The French campaigns are directed by Cardinal Richelieu, chief minister to Louis XIII, who sets out to attack and dismember the Habsburg Empire in Europe.

1640 **France supports** rebellions in Portugal and Catalonia against Spanish rule. The subsequent French invasion of Catalonia leads to a long, inconclusive conflict in the region.

1643 **France inflicts major** defeat of Spanish forces at Rocroi in the Spanish Netherlands.

1642 **French capture strategic** naval base of Dunkirk in Spanish Netherlands.

1647 **France encourages** revolt in Naples to weaken Spanish rule in Italy.

1648 **Spain loses Portugal** and the United Provinces at the end of the 30 Years War, marking the beginning of Spain's imperial decline.

1655 **Spain loses** Jamaica to Britain.

1658 **England seizes** Dunkirk from Spain and in 1662 sells it to France.

1659 **Treaty of the Pyrenees** ends lengthy war with France and cedes control of Rousillon to France.

1665 **Philip IV dies** and is succeeded by his only surviving child and heir, the sickly Charles II.

1667 **France starts lengthy** campaign to gain the Spanish Netherlands.

1672 **France attacks** the Netherlands and occupies most of it by 1678.

1688–97 **War of the League of Augsburg:** Spain, Sweden, the Palatinate, Bavaria, and Saxony oppose France.

1701–14 **The War of** the Spanish Succession breaks out after the death of the childless Charles II, the last Habsburg ruler of Spain, in 1700. Louis XIV of France claims the throne for his Bourbon grandson, Philip, while Britain and others propose the Habsburg Archduke Charles of Austria. Spain and its European possessions become a battleground for competing Portuguese, British, French, and Austrian forces. The war is most bitter in Spain itself: pro-Bourbon Castile is pitted against pro-Habsburg Catalonia.

1704 **British seize** Gibraltar and later Menorca.

1710 **Madrid briefly occupied** by the anti-Bourbon alliance.

1713 **Treaty of Utrecht** ends the War of the Spanish Succession. The French Bourbon candidate becomes Philip V of Spain, but renounces any claim to the French throne. Spain loses southern Netherlands, Milan, Naples, and Sardinia to Austria; Britain keeps Gibraltar and

Menorca, and the right to supply slaves to Spain's American colonies. Spain is now a minor power in a Europe dominated by France, Britain, and Austria.

1716 **Spain occupies part** of modern Texas in response to French expansion from Louisiana.

1717 **Philip V of Spain** tries to supplant Austrian rule in the former Spanish possessions in Italy. He is defeated in 1720.

1731–48 **In a complex** diplomatic shuffle with Austria over possessions in Italy, Spain gains Naples, Sicily, and Parma.

1763 **Spain gains all land** west of the Mississippi river from France; it is transferred back to France in 1800.

1778 **Spain gains island** of Fernando Pó in Africa's Gulf of Guinea from Portugal.

1779–83 **After a lengthy siege,** Spain fails to recapture Gibraltar from Britain. In America, Spain regains Florida from the British, acquired in 1763.

1782 **Spain regains Menorca** from Britain, only to lose it again in 1798.

1807 **Napoleon invades Portugal** to force it to accept the continental trading system designed to exclude British goods. The conflict spreads to Spain the next year and Napoleon places his brother Joseph Bonaparte on the throne, thus provoking a Spanish rebellion and British intervention in the Peninsular War. The British evict the French by 1814.

1811–28 **Spain loses most** of its American colonies, keeping just Cuba and Puerto Rico.

1815 **At the Congress of Vienna,** Spain loses all its Italian possessions.

1833–86 **Disputed succession** leads to a series of Carlist revolts and counter-coups, after the conservative Don Carlos is excluded from the succession by his brother Ferdinand VII in 1830.

DECISIVE MOMENT

PEACE OF UTRECHT, 1713

The Peace of Utrecht comprised a series of treaties signed in the Dutch city of Utrecht in 1713. By ending the War of the Spanish Succession, the Peace was one of the great achievements of 18th-century diplomacy.

The treaties were signed by the representatives of Louis XIV of France and Philip V of Spain on the one hand, and of Queen Anne of Britain, the Duke of Savoy, and the United Provinces on the other. The main loser was Spain, whose European empire was carved up: Savoy received Sicily and parts of the Duchy of Milan, while Holy Roman Emperor Charles VI received the Spanish Netherlands, the Kingdom of Naples,

Treaty between Britain and Spain

Sardinia, and most of the Duchy of Milan. By the treaty concluded between Spain and Britain on July 13, 1713 (above), Britain received Gibraltar and Menorca.

ATTEMPTED COUP, 1981

At 6:30 pm on February 23, 1981, Spain's parliament was seized by 200 soldiers of the Guardia Civil. Under Spain's 1978 constitution King Juan Carlos had handed power to an elected legislature and became a nonruling monarch. This caused animosity within the armed forces, which led to the attempted military coup. But within hours the coup collapsed when the king himself appeared on television, calling for public support for the democratic government.

Fascism's last gasp
Colonel Antonio Tejero (right) fires shots into the air as he announces the coup, telling deputies to await the arrival of a "competent military authority" who never came.

1873–74 A republic is briefly declared.

1874 Constitutional monarchy restored under Alfonso XII.

1881 Trade unions legalized.

1884 Spain acquires Rio de Oro in the Western Sahara.

1886 Death of Alfonso XII; he is succeeded by his son Alfonso XIII.

1898 Defeat in war with US results in loss of Cuba, Puerto Rico, and the Philippines; islands in the western Pacific are transferred to Germany.

1912 Spain acquires protectorate in Morocco.

1914–18 Spain neutral in World War I.

1921 Spanish army routed by Berbers in Spanish Morocco.

1923 Coup by General Primo de Rivera is accepted by King Alfonso XIII. Military dictatorship runs Spain in an increasingly authoritarian way.

1930 Primo de Rivera is dismissed by Alfonso XIII.

1931 Second Republic proclaimed under the radical Miguel Azaña. Alfonso XIII flees Spain. Spain is now split between right-wing nationalists, monarchists, Carlists, a growing Fascist movement based on the Falange Party, and the Roman Catholic Church, and a left wing of republicans, socialists, communists, anarchists, radicals, trade unionists, and Catalan and Basque separatists.

1932 Statute of autonomy granted to Catalonia; it is revoked after the general election the following year.

1932 Government introduces agrarian law to improve wages and working conditions on the land against fierce resistance from traditional landowners.

1933 Center-right coalition wins general election.

1934 Asturias uprising quashed by army.

1936 Civil war begins after Popular Front—a republican coalition—wins elections. Right-wing military uprising against the republic coordinated by General Francisco Franco, who is subsequently appointed leader of the nationalists and invades from Morocco. Germany and Italy support the Nationalists, the USSR supports the Republicans, with individual socialists and communists from across Europe joining the International Brigades. UK and France try to impose an arms ban on both sides.

1937 German Condor Legion bombs ancient Basque capital of Guernica as the Nationalists overrun the Basque country.

1939 Nationalists first capture Barcelona and then Madrid, ending the Civil War, which claims more than 600,000 lives. Franco imposes authoritarian, conservative, and Catholic rule, and crushes all dissent, making his Falange Party the sole legal political party.

1940 Franco meets Hitler, but does not enter World War II.

1946 UN condemns Franco regime.

1948 Spain excluded from the Marshall Plan to rebuild Europe after the war.

1950 UN lifts veto on Spanish membership.

1951 US changes policy toward Spain, now seeing Franco as a bulwark against communism, and begins to provide aid.

1953 Concordat with Vatican. Franco grants US military bases in Spain.

1955 Spain joins UN.

1959 Stabilization Plan is basis for rapid economic growth in the next decade.

1961 Basque separatist group ETA begins violent campaign for independence.

1969 Franco names Juan Carlos, grandson of Alfonso XIII, as his successor.

1973 Basque separatists assassinate prime Minister Carrero Blanco; replaced by Arias Navarro.

1975 Death of Franco: proclamation of King Juan Carlos I.

1976 King appoints Adolfo Suárez as prime minister.

1977 First democratic elections since 1936 are won by Suárez's Democratic Center Union.

1978 New constitution declares Spain a parliamentary monarchy and is approved by a public referendum.

1981 Leopoldo Calvo Sotelo replaces Suárez. King foils attempted fascist coup in the Cortés. Spain joins NATO.

1982 Felipe González wins victory for Spanish Socialist Workers' Party (PSOE).

The Guggenheim
Opened to the public in 1997 and dedicated to modern and contemporary art, the Guggenheim Museum formed part of a large and successful regeneration plan for the northern city of Bilbao.

1986 Spain joins European Community. González wins referendum on keeping Spain in NATO.

1992 Olympic Games held in Barcelona, Expo '92 in Seville; both huge successes.

1996 PSOE loses election; José María Aznar of the Conservative Popular Party (PP) is prime minister. He takes a hard line on Basque separatism and skilfully manages a rapidly improving economy.

1998 Former PSOE minister and two others found guilty of involvement in Basque kidnappings.

1999 The Basque terrorist organization ETA ends ceasefire.

2000 Aznar and PP win general elections.

2001 Conscription is abolished.

2002 Euro introduced.

2004 Islamic terrorists bomb trains in Madrid in retaliation against Spanish support for the US invasion of Iraq: 200 people are killed. The Aznar government loses general election three days later to the PSOE, led by José Luis Zapatero, who pulls Spanish troops out of Iraq.

2005 ETA car bomb explodes in Madrid. The goverment offers peace talks to ETA about the future of the Basque region. ETA declares a "permanent ceasefire" in 2006 but it is broken the same year by a car bomb at Madrid airport.

2007 More than 22,000 immigrants arrive from West Africa.

2008 Socialists are reelected to Parliament with increased representation.

2009 In Basque regional elections, a non-nationalist regional government is returned for the first time in more than 30 years.

2010 ETA announces a new ceasefire but it is dismissed by the government.

Andorra

A tiny, Catalan-speaking country in the Pyrenees bordered by France and Spain.

218 BCE The Andosini, a tribe subdued by the Carthaginian general, Hannibal, are the first recorded inhabitants of the state.

768–814 CE During the reign of Charlemagne, the country is established as a buffer state against Spanish Muslims.

1278 The Bishop of the Spanish diocese of Urgel and the Count of Foix are designated co-princes of Andorra. The rights vested in the house of Foix pass by marriage to the Kings of Navarre and, in 1589 on the accession of Henri of Navarre as Henri IV, to the crown of France.

1814 Independence confirmed.

1933–34 French occupation after the proclamation of independent King Boris I.

1982 First General Council or parliament is appointed.

1991 EU customs union comes into effect.

1993 Andorra joins the UN.

1994 Government falls; replaced by center-right Liberal cabinet.

2002 Andorra adopts the euro.

2009 Andorra agrees to ease banking secrecy rules.

Portugal

An Atlantic-facing country with natural borders and a long maritime and imperial history.

100S BCE Portugal is conquered by Roman forces, becoming the provinces of Lusitania and Gallaecia. When the empire falls, Portugal is conquered by the Visigoths and the Sueves after 409 CE.

711 The Moors arrive on the Iberian peninsula; the south of Portugal becomes Muslim; the north remains Christian.

1139 Afonso Henriques declares himself king of Portugal, formerly a county of the Spanish kingdom of León and Castile.

1147 Lisbon falls to Christian forces.

1254 First parliament convened at Leiria.

1272 Afonso III expels the last of the Moors from the Algarve.

1290 First university founded in Lisbon.

1369–85 Castilian rule is reestablished, but is ended at the Battle of Aljubarrota (1385) where English archers are crucial.

1387 Anglo–Portuguese alliance is cemented by marriage of King João I to an English princess.

1415 Portugal founds the first modern European colony in Africa at Ceuta.

1418 Prince Henry the Navigator, son of João I, sponsors a series of voyages of exploration into the Atlantic and south along the coast of Africa.

1419 Portugal takes Madeira, followed by the Azores in 1427, Cape Verde Islands in 1456, Guinea in 1480, and São Tomé and Principe islands in 1483.

1445 A slave market and fort are established by the Portuguese in Arguin Bay in present-day Mauritania.

1470s Lisbon becomes a major slave port. By 1539 over 12,000 slaves are being sold in the city's markets each year.

1494 Under the Treaty of Tordesillas, Pope Alexander VI divides the "New World" recently discovered by Columbus between Portugal and Spain.

1497–99 Vasco da Gama voyages around the Cape of Good Hope to India.

1500 Pedro Álvares Cabral accidentally discovers Brazil on journey to India; Brazil soon develops into a large colony.

1510 Portuguese establish a colony at Goa in India and Macao in China in 1557. Territories are also acquired in Angola and Mozambique and the east Indies.

1578 King Sebastião is killed at the Battle of Alcazarquivir in Morocco. He is succeeded by his brother Henrique.

1580 Philip II of Spain claims the Portuguese crown on the death of Henrique and invades.

1580–1640 Portugal united with Spain.

1598–1663 Many overseas territorial possessions lost to the Dutch.

1640 Portugal regains its independence from Spain after an uprising led by the Duke of Braganza, crowned João IV.

1755 Earthquake destroys Lisbon.

1793 Joins coalition against revolutionary France.

1807 France invades; royal family flees to Brazil.

1808 British troops arrive under Wellington: start of the Peninsular War, which lasts until 1812.

1820 Uprisings in Porto and Lisbon. Liberal revolution.

1821 King João VI returns from exile in Brazil and accepts the first Portuguese constitution. In 1822 his son and regent, Dom Pedro, declares independence as Emperor Pedro I of Brazil.

1834 Dom Pedro returns to Portugal to end civil war and installs his daughter as Queen Maria II.

1890 Planned land connection between Portuguese colonies of Angola and Mozambique thwarted by the British.

1908 Assassination of Carlos I and the heir to the throne.

1910 Abdication of Manuel II and proclamation of the republic.

1916 Portugal fights with the Allies in World War I.

1926 Army overturns republic.

1928 António Salazar joins government as finance minister.

1932 Salazar becomes prime minister.

1933 Constitution of the "New State," instituting right-wing dictatorship.

1936–39 Salazar assists Franco in Spanish Civil War.

1939–45 Portugal remains neutral during World War II, but lets the Allies use air bases in Azores.

1947 Attempted revolt is crushed. Labor leaders and rebel army officers are deported to Cape Verde.

1949 Portugal becomes founding member of NATO.

1961 India annexes Goa and other Indian colonies. Guerrilla warfare breaks out in Angola, Mozambique, and Guinea.

1970 Death of Salazar. Succeeded by Marcelo Caetano.

1974 Carnation Revolution: Left-wing Armed Forces Movement overthrows Caetano in bloodless revolution.

1974–75 Portuguese colonies of Guinea-Bissau, Mozambique, Cape Verde Islands, São Tomé and Príncipe, and

António Salazar
A profoundly religious and conservative man, Salazar presided over a corporatist and reactionary state that suppressed all political opposition.

Angola gain independence. Some 750,000 expatriates return to Portugal.

1975 Communist takeover foiled by Mário Soares's Socialist Party (PS). Portuguese withdraw from East Timor.

1976 General António Eanes elected president. Adoption of new constitution. Soares appointed prime minister.

1980 General Eanes reelected.

1982 Civilian government restored.

1983 Soares becomes caretaker prime minister; PS is majority party.

1985 Anibal Cavaco Silva becomes prime minister of minority Social Democratic Party (PSD) government.

1986 Soares elected president. Portugal joins European Union.

1987 Cavaco Silva wins absolute majority in parliament.

1995 PS wins elections; António Guterres becomes prime minister.

1996 Former PS leader Jorge Sampaio elected president.

1999 Portugal returns Macao, the last European colony in Asia, to China.

2002 Portugal adopts the euro. José Manuel Barroso of the Socialist Party forms center-right coalition government.

2007 Portugal votes to legalize abortion.

2008 Portuguese parliament votes to reform spelling of the language to bring it in line with Brazilian practices.

2009 Socialists under Jose Socrates reelected with reduced minority.

2010 Protests and strikes break out against the government's austerity program.

《224–25 Voyages of Discovery
《238–39 Trade and Empire
《268–69 The Lisbon Earthquake
《280–81 The Slave Trade
《412–13 End of the Colonial Era

PORTUGUESE KING (1554–78)

SEBASTIÃO I

The tragedy of King Sebastião is one of the seminal events of Portuguese history. At the age of 24, he received permission from the pope to lead a crusade against the infidel in Morocco. Landing on the North African coast, he unwisely led his troops inland, and, on August 4, 1578, was met by a well-equipped Muslim army at the Battle of Alcazarquivir. The Portuguese force was routed, and Sebastião was never seen again. Doubts over his fate gave rise to the legend of the king who would one day return.

Italy

A Mediterranean country that once controlled an empire stretching from Scotland to Egypt.

753 BCE The traditional date for the founding of Rome by Romulus and Remus.

510 BCE Rome becomes a republic after the expulsion of king Tarquinius Superbus; over the next two centuries the military might of Rome gradually conquers the surrounding peoples in central Italy.

390 BCE Gauls capture Rome and burn most of it to the ground. After they leave, the Romans rebuild their city and protect it with the Servian Wall.

272 BCE After the conquest of Taranto in the south, all of central and southern Italy is united under Roman rule.

264–146 BCE Rome fights for domination of the western Mediterranean with Carthage, a Phoenician city in North Africa, which is eventually defeated in the three lengthy Punic Wars (264–241 BCE, 218–202 BCE, 149–146 BCE); Rome proceeds to conquer Greece and most of the Mediterranean region.

49–44 BCE Julius Caesar is dictator of Rome.

27 BCE Octavian, adoptive son of Caesar, is proclaimed imperator, or supreme commander, thereby effectively destroying the institutions of the republic and inaugurating imperial rule. In 23 BCE he is awarded the title Augustus ("the deeply respected one") by the Senate.

79 CE Mount Vesuvius erupts, burying the two cities of Pompeii and Herculaneum.

117–138 During the reign of Emperor Hadrian, the Roman Empire includes the Iberian peninsula, Gaul (present-day France), Britannia (present-day Britain), Greece, all of central Europe south of the Rhine and Danube rivers, Asia Minor, Armenia, Syria (including Palestine), Egypt, and North Africa.

284–305 Emperor Diocletian sets up the four-man Tetrarchy to govern in order to make it easier to govern the empire; he also increases the size and efficiency of the army to deal with the growing external threat. During his reign, the empire is both prosperous and peaceful.

306–37 Emperor Constantine reunites the empire.

313 Religious freedom is guaranteed throughout the empire by the Edict of Milan; Christianity becomes the dominant religion and Rome becomes the seat of the papacy. Emperor Constantine also establishes a new eastern capital of the empire at Constantinople.

The civilized invaders
Many of the tribes that invaded the Roman Empire quickly absorbed Roman culture and beliefs. This mausoleum was built in Ravenna by the Ostrogoths for their leader Theodoric.

363 After the death of the Emperor Julian, who tried but failed to reintroduce the old Roman pagan gods, Christianity returns as the main religion.

375 As the Huns continue to press westward, the Visigoths cross the Danube into the empire. After they defeat and kill Emperor Valens at Adrianople in 378, they are allowed to settle in what is now Bulgaria.

395 Visigoths rebel under their leader Alaric, and raid the Balkans and northern Italy. After the death of Theodosius I, the empire is now permanently split between eastern and western halves.

410 Visigoths sack Rome.

418 The Visigoths establish an independent kingdom in Aquitaine in Gaul, and large parts of Spain are now under Vandal, Alan, or Suevi control. By the time the Vandals cross to North Africa in 1429 and capture Carthage, the western Roman Empire is on the point of collapse. Many of these invading tribes, however, are already Christian or soon convert to Christianity, adopting Roman customs and culture and taking over many of the institutions and practices of the empire.

476 The Roman Empire collapses in the west as the last emperor, Romulus Augustulus, abdicates, although the empire continues to survive in the east.

492 Italy falls to the Ostrogoths. Theodoric founds Kingdom of Italy with its capital at Ravenna.

533–53 Byzantine emperor Justinian I achieves reconquest of Italy, but at great cost to surviving Roman cities.

568 Italy invaded by another Germanic tribe, the Lombards. They never conquer the whole peninsula; Byzantines retain control of parts of Italy from Ravenna.

774 The Franks under Charlemagne conquer the Lombard kingdom in northern Italy; Charlemagne is crowned emperor by the pope in Rome in 800.

962 The coronation in Rome by Pope John XII of Otto I of Germany as emperor marks the beginning of the Holy Roman Empire. Developments over the next three centuries are molded by the struggle for supremacy between papacy and empire, mirrored locally in the struggle between Guelphs (the papal party) and Ghibellines (supporters of the emperor).

1060–1139 The Normans conquer Sicily and southern Italy. The kingdom of Sicily, later known as Naples or the Two Sicilies, is established in 1130 and remains under Norman rule until the Hohenstaufen dynasty of Holy Roman Emperors takes over in 1179.

1300s In the absence of a strong central authority following the withdrawal of the German emperors, northern Italy fragments into a number of small but increasingly powerful city-states, notably the republics of Venice, Florence, and Genoa and the duchies of Milan, Mantua, and Savoy-Piedmont; these cities, among the most important trading and financial centers of Europe, are in the vanguard of the Renaissance, the great cultural revival of the 14th–16th centuries. Writers such as Boccaccio and Dante, artists and sculptors such as Giotto, Fra Angelico, Donatello, Raphael, and Michaelangelo, and architects such as Alberti and Brunelleschi receive patronage from the various Italian princes and dukes and transform the Italian cities and courts into the leading artistic and cultural centers of Europe.

1494–1525 In a series of wars, Valois France and Habsburg Spain, each supported by Italian allies, vie for domination of Italy. The wars end in defeat for France and also mark the decline of the city-states, which suffer major devastation and are adversely affected by the new economic conditions created by the severance of traditional land and sea routes across the Mediterranean to the east and the opening of the new Atlantic route.

1559 The Treaty of Cateau-Cambrésis ends the Spanish-French wars in Italy. France gains some land, but Spain is the big winner, controlling Milan, Naples, Sicily, and Sardinia, and now dominates the Italian peninsula and the western Mediterranean. The Reformation has little effect in Italy, which remains staunchly Catholic.

1618–48 Although not directly involved in the 30 Years War, the Italian states are caught up in the fighting as France threatens the Italian possessions of Habsburg Spain. In 1629 France threatens Mantua and in 1637 Milan. A revolt in Naples against Spanish rule in 1647 is actively supported by French troops.

1701–14 The Spanish Habsburg domination of Italy ends. After the War of the Spanish Succession its position is usurped by Habsburg Austria, which acquires Milan, Naples, Sicily, and Sardinia.

1731–48 Further readjustments between Spain and Austria give Spain control of Naples, Sicily, and Parma, and Austria control of Milan and Tuscany. Sardinia and Piedmont are united as one kingdom.

1796–97 French revolutionary forces under Napoleon Bonaparte conquer most of Italy. Napoleon redraws the country's map and absorbs Piedmont, Genoa, Tuscany, and the Papal States directly into France, and creates a kingdom of Italy in the north and Naples in the south. Sicily is now independent of Naples.

1814 After the defeat of France, the Congress of Vienna redraws the map of Italy, giving Austria control over Venice, Milan, Parma, Modena, Lucca, and Tuscany. Sardinia–Piedmont and the Papal States remain independent, while the Kingdom of the Two Sicilies gains its independence.

1831 Giuseppe Mazzini forms the Young Italy movement and becomes one of the intellectual fathers of the Risorgimento ("resurgence"), the national movement aiming for the unification of Italy. Nationalist revolts or popular uprisings against Austrian, papal, or illiberal Italian rule break out in Turin, Milan, Genoa, Modena, Parma, Naples, and many other Italian cities from 1830 onward, although all are easily crushed by authoritarian powers.

1848 In the Year of Revolutions that break out across Europe, Sardinia–Piedmont adopts a liberal constitution that is extended throughout Italy following unification.

1848–49 Nationalists rise against the Austrian rulers in the north and against the papacy. A Roman republic is established by radicals, including Guiseppe Garibaldi, but the republic is crushed by French troops called in to restore Pope Pius IX to power. In the north, nationalist troops are defeated by Austrian troops at the battle of Novara; Austria regains control of its Italian possessions.

Renaissance man
Michelangelo (left) was a painter, sculptor, architect, poet, and engineer. Along with Leonardo da Vinci, he epitomized the Italian Renaissance.

1849 **Victor Emmanuel II** becomes king of Sardinia–Piedmont and appoints Count Camillo di Cavour as prime minister. They institute liberal domestic reforms and increasingly act as the leaders of the Italian nationalist and unification movement.

1854–56 **Count Cavour** sends Piedmontese forces to fight with the UK and France against Russia in the Crimean War, as a way of enlisting their help for future Italian unification, as he realizes that Italy will not be united under its own efforts.

1882 **Italy joins** Austria–Hungary and Germany in the Triple Alliance.

1889–96 **As part of** its efforts to acquire a colonial empire, Italy conquers Eritrea and Somalia in east Africa, but is defeated by Ethiopia (then known as Abyssinia) at the battle of Adowa in 1896, a rare defeat of a European by an African nation.

1911–12 **Taking advantage of the** Ottoman Empire's weakness, Italy seizes Libya and the Dodecanese islands in the Aegean in a brief war.

> " I can offer you neither honors nor wages; I offer you **hunger, thirst,** forced marches, battles, and death. Anyone who loves his country, **follow me**. "

GIUSEPPE GARIBALDI, ROME, 1849

1859–70 **The unification of** Italy is achieved under the leadership of Victor Emmanuel II of Sardinia–Piedmont (proclaimed King of Italy in March 1861), Count Cavour, and the forces of Giuseppe Garibaldi. Most of northern Italy is united by Sardinia–Piedmont after the War of Unification against Austria in 1859, won at the Battle of Magenta with the help of French troops. In return, France gains Savoy and Nice from Piedmont. Garibaldi and his redshirts conquer Sicily and Naples in 1860 and then head north toward Rome before handing over their conquests to Victor Emmanuel II. Venice is ceded by Austria after a brief war in 1866, and Rome is occupied by Italian troops in 1870. As the country is unified, the national capital shifts from Turin to Florence in 1865 and then to Rome in 1870. Despite this unification under a single monarch, however, Italy remains more a union of provinces than a single country, with strong regional differences existing between the industrial and rich north and the agricultural and poor south.

1915 **Having abandoned** the Triple Alliance, Italy joins World War I on the side of the Entente powers and attacks Austria–Hungary, fighting 11 battles along the river Isonzo east of Venice (1915–17) and then suffering a major defeat at Austrian and German hands at Caporetto in 1917. British and French troops are rushed to Italy to save it from collapse. In the closing months of the war, the Italians score a major victory over Austria–Hungary at Vittorio Veneto.

1919 **Under the Treaty of Saint** Germain-en-Laye, Italy is awarded South Tyrol and Trieste but is forced to give up claims on the Adriatic coast, which is given to the new state of Yugoslavia. It also gains land in Libya from British-held Egypt and from French West Africa. Italy, however, is dissatisfied with the peace settlement, believing it has received insufficient land or prestige as a result of having fought on the winning side of the war.

Proclamation at Teano
On October 26, 1860, Giuseppe Garibaldi (below, center) greeted Victor Emanuel II at Teano and hailed him king of Italy. Thus Garibaldi sacrificed republican hopes for the sake of unity under a monarchy.

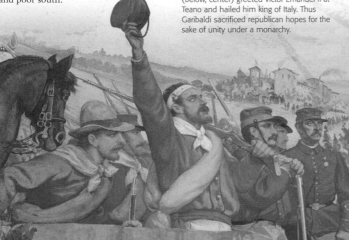

1919 **Italy and Yugoslavia** dispute ownership of the Adriatic port of Fiume, which is occupied by the Italian nationalist D'Annunzio until he is ejected in 1921. The port is eventually incorporated into Italy in 1924. Italy also gains the Adriatic port of Zara in 1920.

1919–22 **Nationalist and labor** unrest provokes strikes in many Italian cities, notably Bologna, Florence, and Rome, as fascists, socialists, and communists battle for control.

1921 **Benito Mussolini,** a former socialist, merges numerous right-wing and anti-communist groups to form the Fascist Party, which takes a leading role in the industrial and civil disturbances occurring across Italy.

1922 **Benito Mussolini asked** to form a government by King Victor Emmanuel III, prompted by his threat to "March on Rome" to demand that a fascist government be formed in order to forestall civil war and a communist revolution. Mussolini becomes Il Duce, or leader, and heads a coalition of fascists and nationalists. He begins to crack down on parliamentary dissent.

1923 **Corfu incident:** after an Italian general and four assistants were shot while determining the Greek–Albanian border, Mussolini orders a naval bombardment and occupation of the Greek island of Corfu. After international pressure, Italy withdraws, although it receives a large indemnity from Greece.

1925 **Italy continues to** expand its African empire, gaining the Jubaland Strip from British-run Kenya, followed by more land from Egypt in 1926 and terrritory to the south of Libya from the UK and France in 1934–35.

1928–29 **One-party rule** is introduced.

1929 **Lateran Treaties with** the Vatican recognize the sovereignty of the Holy See.

1935–36 **Italy invades and** occupies Ethiopia.

1936 **Rome–Berlin Axis** formed with Nazi Germany. In 1937 Italy also joins the Anti-Comintern Pact with Germany and Japan.

1936–39 **Italy gives massive** military and financial support to General Franco's Nationalists fighting to overturn the Republican government of Spain during the Spanish Civil War.

1939 **Italy invades** and annexes the Adriatic state of Albania.

1940 **Italy enters** World War II on the German side and invades Greece and Egypt, although it is quickly thrown out of both. In 1941 it participates in the German invasion of the USSR, as well as acquiring control of parts of southeast France, western Yugoslavia and Croatia, the Adriatic coast, and much of Greece. It soon loses its empire in East Africa to Allied forces, and only holds out in Libya with German support until 1943, when it is evicted from North Africa.

1943 **Italy invaded by Allies.** The king deposes Mussolini and signs an armistice with the Allies. Mussolini is imprisoned but is helped to escape to the north, where he sets up a republican, fascist government. Italy declares war on Germany, which promptly occupies most of Italy and and continues to fight the Allies on Italian soil.

1944 **Germans put up** fierce resistance, especially at Monte Cassino. Allied landings at Anzio lead to the occupation of Rome.

1945 **Mussolini and his** mistress are captured and executed by Italian partisans.

1946 **Referendum votes in** favor of Italy becoming a republic.

1947 **Italy signs peace** treaty, ceding border areas to France and Yugoslavia, the Dodecanese to Greece, and giving up all its colonies in Africa.

1947 **Marshall Aid** helps rebuild Italy after the war and aids growth.

1948 **Christian Democrats** (DC) under De Gasperi head coalition.

1949 **Founder member** of NATO.

1950 **Agreement with US** on US bases to be located in Italy.

1951 Joins European Coal and Steel Community.

1953–2001 The prime minister changes 35 times during this period, a sign of the shifting political allegiances and the revolving-door principle of Italian government. Amintore Fanfani is prime minister on five separate occasions between 1954 and 1987, often for no more than a few months at a time, and also serves as interim president in 1978.

1957 Treaty of Rome signed as Italy becomes a founder member of the EEC. Aided by funds from that organization, industrial growth accelerates.

The Treaty of Rome
At the signing of the Treaty of Rome on March 25, 1957, Italy became one of the founder members of the European Economic Community, the organization that gave rise to today's European Union. Italy has remained a fervent member ever since, as its economy, industry, and infrastructure have all benefited massively from membership.

1963 DC government under Aldo Moro forms coalition with Socialist Party (PSI).

1970 Red Brigades, an extreme-left terrorist group, are formed.

1972 Support for extreme right reaches post-war peak (9 percent). Rise in urban terrorism by extreme left and right.

1976 Communist Party (PCI) support reaches a peak of 34 percent under Enrico Berlinguer, a proponent of moderate communist policies.

1978 Aldo Moro abducted and murdered by Red Brigades.

1980 Extreme-right bombing of Bologna station kills 84, wounds 200.

1983–87 Center-left coalition formed under Bettino Craxi of the PSI.

1990 Reactionary Northern League led by Umberto Bossi attacks immigration policies and subsidies for the south and demands independence for the rich north of the country; this demand is later toned down to demand more autonomy and financial control.

1992 Corruption scandal, involving bribes for public contracts, uncovered in Milan. Government members of all parties are accused of receiving kickbacks. Former prime minister Craxi is convicted, while another former prime minister, Giulio Andreotti, is brought to trial accused of dealing with the Sicilian Mafia.

1994 DC support collapses: a coalition government is formed between the newspaper magnate Silvio Berlusconi's Forza Italia, the Northern League, and neo-fascist Northern Alliance.

1995–96 Technocrat government under Lamberto Dini tackles the budget, pensions, media, and regional issues, after the Northern League leaves Berlusconi's government, causing it to fall.

1996 Center-left Olive Tree alliance wins general election; Romano Prodi becomes prime minister and successfully steers the economy so that Italy qualifies for euro membership in 1999.

1999 Prodi government falls; he is replaced by Massimo D'Alema as prime minister.

2000 D'Alema replaced by Giuliano Amato.

2001 Berlusconi returns to power to lead a right-wing coalition in general election.

2002 Italy joins the euro, but it struggles to solve its economic problems.

2005 Conscription into the armed services ends.

2006 Berlusconi narrowly loses the general election to the center-left Union coalition led by Romano Prodi. When he leaves office, Berlusconi has been the longest-serving Italian prime minister since 1945. The new government has a working majority of 67 in the Chamber of Deputies but only 2 in the Senate.

2007 Prodi resigns after failing to obtain Senate support for the continuation of US bases in the country,

but is asked to form a new government by the president.

2008 Berlusconi is reelected for a third term as prime minister.

2009 An earthquake hits Abruzzo, leaving hundreds dead.

≪106–07 The Rise of Rome
≪108–09 Julius Caesar
≪110–13 From Republic to Empire
≪150–51 Decline and Fall
≪188–91 Medieval Europe
≪250–53 The Renaissance
≪254–55 Leonardo da Vinci
≪386–87 Fascism

Vatican City

The world's smallest state and one of the only two theocracies; the other is Iran.

324–49 Roman emperor Constantine the Great builds a basilica over the traditional burial place of St. Peter, replacing the earlier 2nd-century shrine.

756 Donation of Pippin provides legal basis for papal dominion in central Italy.

1417 After the pope's return from Avignon in France at the end of the 39-year Great Schism, they take up residence in the Vatican Palace.

1869–70 First Vatican Council expounds doctrine of papal infallibility.

1870 Italian forces enter Rome, ending papal temporal power in Italy. The pope is left as a self-imposed captive in Rome.

1929 Lateran Treaty: Italy accepts the Vatican City as an independent state,

consisting of St. Peter's Basilica, ten other buildings in Rome, and the pope's summer residence at Castel Gandolfo. The Holy See is located in the Vatican City.

1939–58 Pope Pius XII is heavily criticized for failing to take action over the Holocaust during World War II.

1958–63 Reforming papacy of Pope John XXIII.

1963–78 Paul VI is pope; he is succeeded by John Paul I, who dies within a month.

1978 Polish cardinal Karol Wojtyla becomes Pope John Paul II, the first non-Italian pope since 1523.

1981–82 Attempts on pope's life.

1984 Catholicism disestablished as the Italian state religion.

1985 Catholic catechism revised for the first time since 1566.

1994–95 Opposition to abortion and contraception reiterated.

1998 Statement repenting Catholic passivity during the Holocaust.

2000 Jubilee Year: a papal apology is made for Catholic violence and oppression over two millennia.

2001 John Paul II is first pope to enter a mosque.

2005 John Paul II dies; Cardinal Joseph Ratzinger of Germany is elected Pope Benedict XVI after four ballots of the College of Cardinals and establishes himself as a conservative in theological affairs.

St. Peter's Basilica
Most of the great architects, artists, and sculptors of the Renaissance were involved in the design and building of St. Peter's, which took more than a century to complete. The basilica and its public square lie at the heart of the Vatican City.

The mountainous republic
San Marino is dominated by Monte Titano, on which stands La Cesta fortress. Most of the country can be seen from the top. San Marino was the world's smallest republic from 301 CE to 1968, losing the title to the newly independent Pacific island, Nauru.

San Marino

The world's oldest republic and one of its smallest. It is entirely surrounded by Italy.

300s **San Marino** is founded by a Christian stonecutter from Dalmatia, who takes refuge here. A large community is resident in the country by the 400s and manages to retain its independence.

1243 **First Captains General** (joint heads of state) are appointed.

1631 **Independence** is recognized by the papacy.

1797 **After Napoleon invades** Italy, San Marino refuses the expansion he offers at the expense of the surrounding Papal States.

1815 **Congress of Vienna** at the end of the Napoleonic Wars recognizes the independence of the state.

1849 **San Marino offers** refuge to Italian patriot Giuseppe Garibaldi after his failed attempt to expel the Austrians from Italy.

1862 **San Marino signs** friendship treaty with Italy but refuses to join the newly united nation. The treaty has been renewed several times since.

1915–18 **San Marino fights** for Italy in World War I.

1940 **Remains neutral** during World War II, and houses around 100,000 refugees.

1944 **Allied aircraft bomb** the country as they fight the Germans in Italy.

1945–57 **First period of** Communist (PCS) Party rule.

1957–78 **Coalition of Christian** Democrats (PDCS) and Social Democrats comes to power. In 1973 the Social Democrats are replaced by the Socialists (PSS) and the tiny Movement for Statutory Liberties party.

1960 **Women obtain the vote.**

1973 **Women granted** the right to hold public office.

1978–86 **Coalition of** San Marino Communist Party (PCS) and Socialists (PSS) in power.

1986 **Financial scandals** lead to a grand coalition of the PDCS and PCS parties, reelected in 1988.

1988 **Joins Council of** Europe.

1990 **PCS renames itself** the PPDS.

1992 **San Marino** joins the UN.

1992 **The collapse** of communism in Europe sees the Communist Party ousted from the coalition and replaced by the Socialists.

2001 **Communist Party** reforms itself as the Party of Democrats (PdP) and takes 20 percent of the vote in a general election won by the Christian Democrats with 41 percent and the Socialists with 24 percent.

2002 **Introduction of euro.**

Malta

A small island republic in the Mediterranean, once the stronghold of the Knights of St. John.

870 CE **Arab Saracens** seize Malta, which had been successively ruled by the Phoenicians, Carthaginians, Greeks, and Romans.

1091 **Malta is conquered** by the Norman-ruled kingdom of Sicily, and is governed by Sicilian rulers until 1530.

1282 **Malta comes under** Spanish Aragonese rule when Sicily chooses the Aragonese king Peter III to rule them.

1530 **Malta is entrusted** to the Knights of St. John of the Hospital (the Hospitallers) by the Habsburg Emperor Charles V.

1565 **Malta withstands a** lengthy Ottoman siege.

1798 **Napoleon Bonaparte drives** out the Hospitaller Knights. The Maltese rise in rebellion and the island is blockaded by the British.

1800 **The British take** control of Malta.

1802 **The Maltese people** freely request the protection of the British crown, providing their rights and privileges can be preserved.

1814 **British possession** is confirmed by the Treaty of Paris and the 1815 Congress of Vienna.

1921 **Malta is granted** a representative assembly, although this autonomy is revoked at the beginning of World War II.

1929 **Tension grows between** the UK, the Roman Catholic Church, and Italy under Mussolini, who makes territorial claims to the island.

1939–45 **Malta comes under** sustained air and sea attack by the Axis powers throughout World War II and is in a state of constant siege. In 1942 the UK awards Malta and its people the George Cross—the highest civilian award for bravery—for their resistance. The Allies invade Sicily from Malta in 1943.

1947 **Internal self-government.**

1959 **Self-government** is revoked after talks over possible integration with the UK break down. It is restored in 1962. Malta is the only British colony where integration with the UK is seriously considered.

1947 **Internal self-government.**

1964 **Full independence from** UK within the Commonwealth.

1971–87 **Dom Mintoff's** Malta Labour Party (MLP) in power; it promotes Malta's nonaligned status, ends the UK's naval presence on the island, forges closer ties with Libya, which advises and trains its army, and nationalizes many important industries.

1974 **Malta becomes** a republic within the Commonwealth.

1987–96 **Edward Fenech Adami** of the Nationalist Party (NP) is prime minister and begins talks for Malta to join the EU. His government favors a free-market approach to the economy, deregulating the banking, telecommunications, and trade sectors, introducing much-needed economic and administrative reforms.

1996 **A modernized MLP** under Alfred Sant returns to power; it weakens trade union links and stalls the nation's EU application, but its small parliamentary majority undermines its work.

1998 **Early elections bring** pro-EU Fenech Adami back to power.

2003 **In a referendum,** Maltese vote in favor of EU membership. Fenech Adami wins another term as NP prime minister.

2004 **Fenech Adami becomes** president; Lawrence Gonzi takes over as prime minister.

2004 **Malta finally** joins the European Union.

2008 **Malta adopts** the euro.

« 110–13 From Republic to Empire
« 150–51 Decline and Fall?

DECISIVE MOMENT

THE SIEGE OF MALTA, 1526

Forced out of Rhodes by the Turks in 1522, the Knights of St. John created a fortress in Malta (right). In 1565 the Turks sent a 30,000-strong army to take the island. The harbor was guarded by the fort of St. Elmo, which held out until June 23. The capture cost the Turks 8,000 casualties. The assault then moved to the inner fortifications but was repulsed by savage fighting. The arrival of a relief force on September 7 convinced the Turks to cut their losses, which had mounted to 24,000. The siege checked the Ottoman advance in the Mediterranean.

Switzerland

A mountainous republic at the center of western Europe but politically separate from it.

1291 After the Habsburgs curtail the autonomy of the Swiss cantons, Unterwalden, Schwyz, and Uri set up the Perpetual League to pursue Swiss liberty.

1499 Now joined by other cantons, the Swiss succeed in gaining virtual independence with the Habsburgs retaining only a titular role.

1648 Peace of Westphalia ending the 30 Years War recognizes the full independence of the Swiss Confederation.

1798 Invaded by Napoleon, who creates Helvetic Republic, which lasts until 1803.

1815 Congress of Vienna after Napoleon's defeat confirms Swiss independence and establishes its neutrality. Geneva, Neuchâtel, and Valais join the Swiss Confederation.

1848 New constitution gives central government more powers, but guarantees the cantons' powers.

1857 King of Prussia renounces territorial claims over Neuchâtel.

1874 Referendum established as important decision-making tool in government.

1914–18 Plays humanitarian role in World War I.

1919 Proportional representation ensures future political stability.

1920 Joins League of Nations, based in Geneva.

1939–45 Switzerland remains neutral in World War II and refuses to join the UN in 1945.

The Red Cross
This field ambulance bearing the Red Cross was used in World War I. The foundation of the Red Cross in Geneva in 1863 by Swiss social activist Henri Dunant, and the signing of the 1864 Geneva Convention on the conduct of war, made Geneva a center of international diplomacy.

1959 Founder member of European Free Trade Area. The present four-party coalition comes to power.

1967 Right-wing groups make electoral gains, campaigning to restrict entry of foreign workers.

1971 Most women granted the right to vote in federal elections.

1986 Referendum opposes joining UN. Immigrant numbers are restricted.

1988 Kopp resigns over allegedly violating secrecy of information laws. She is aquitted in 1990, but the case reveals that the Public Prosecutor's office holds secret files on 200,000 people. Violent protests. State security laws amended.

1992 Joins IMF and World Bank.

1998 $1.25 billion compensation paid to relatives of Holocaust victims whose funds were deposited in Swiss banks.

1999 Ruth Dreifuss is first woman president.

2000 Referendum endorses close trade links with EU, but full membership is rejected in a referendum in 2001.

2002 Abortion decriminalized. Switzerland joins UN.

2009 Switzerland announces it will relax banking secrecy laws.

《 306–07 The Napoleonic Wars

Liechtenstein

A tiny principality wedged between Austria and Switzerland, with which it has close ties.

1342 Graf Hartmann von Montfort becomes owner of the Castle of Vaduz and in 1396, still under the control of the Montfort family, Vaduz is confirmed as a fief of the Holy Roman Empire.

1416 The last Montfort count bequeaths Vaduz to Baron von Brandis of Emmental, who in 1419 also gains control of the domain of Schellenberg to the north of Vaduz.

1719 Following the purchase of Vaduz by Prince Johann Adam Andreas von Liechtenstein in 1712, the Holy Roman Emperor Charles VI raises the status of Vaduz and Schellenberg to that of an independent principality.

1806 Liechtenstein declares its full sovereignty as the Holy Roman Empire is dissolved. A Rheinbund league of German princes, which is formed at the suggestion of Napoleon Bonaparte, does not outlast Napoleon, and in 1815 Liechtenstein joins the German Confederation, remaining a member until its dissolution in 1866.

1852 A customs union is formed with Austria and the Austrian currency becomes the legal tender. This lasts until the dismemberment of the Austro–Hungarian Empire in 1918.

1866 Liechtenstein formally achieves independence following the dissolution of the German Confederation.

1868 Liechtenstein's standing army is abolished.

1921 New constitution grants joint authority to a hereditary prince and a Landtag (parliament). Liechtenstein adopts Swiss currency.

1923 Customs union with Switzerland.

1938 Prince Franz Josef II maintains neutrality during World War II.

1990 Joins UN.

1995 Joins European Economic Area and World Trade Organization.

1997 End of the coalition dominant since 1938. Mario Frick now heads a Fatherland Union government.

2000 Swiss army inadvertently invades Liechtenstein when a training mission gets lost and crosses an unmarked border.

2003 Referendum votes to give Prince Hans-Adam II sweeping political powers.

Slovenia

The richest republic of the former Yugoslavia was also the first to declare independence.

14 CE The Roman general Gaius Octavius (later Emperor Augustus) founds a city on the site of Ljubljana.

900 CE The Magyars take Ljubljana, which passes into the hands of the dukes of Carinthia in the 12th century.

1277 The Habsburgs control the region; while under Austrian rule Ljubljana becomes center for Slovenian nationalism.

1809 Napoleon captures the territories held by Austria and reorganizes them into the Illyrian Provinces, with Ljubljana as the seat of government. Serfdom is abolished and the peasants are given their lands. Austria regains control in 1814.

1855 Slovenian nationalists develop a cooperative movement in the countryside that provides credit and other services to help Slovenes break free of Germanic institutions.

1867 Austria–Hungary reorganizes the Slavs under its control after its defeat by Prussia. Slovenes are linked to Austria.

1918 Serbian Prince Alexander unites Serbia, Montenegro, Croatia, Bosnia, and Slovenia into the Kingdom of Serbs, Croats, and Slovenes, after the defeat of the Central Powers. Alexander becomes king in August 1921.

1929 Alexander imposes a dictatorship to end Serbian, Croatian, and Slovene nationalism and renames the country Yugoslavia. However his rule merely increases Serbian domination, bureaucracy, and repression by the police. Alexander is assassinated in 1934.

1941–45 Germany occupies Slovenia in World War II and divides it with Italy.

1945 Josef Tito's communists take power in Yugoslavia. When he dies in 1980, Yugoslavia begins to fall apart.

1989 Parliament confirms the right to secede and calls multiparty elections.

1990 Control over the army asserted; a referendum approves secession.

1991 Independence declared as Slovenia is the first Yugoslav republic to secede. The Yugoslav federal army repelled. Fewer than 100 die in the clashes.

1993 Joins IMF and IBRD.

Slovenians celebrate
Upon seceding from Yugoslavia on June 25, 1991, Slovenia was invaded by the federal army and a 10-day war ensued. Armed resistance, roadblocks, and desertions put an end to the attack.

2004 Slovenia joins the EU and NATO.

2007 Slovenia is first of the new EU member states to adopt the euro.

2010 Referendum backs international arbitration on border dispute with Croatia.

《 262–63 The 30 Years War

Austria

Once a dominant force in Central Europe, and since 1995 a member of the European Union.

15 BCE Austria south of the Danube is conquered by the Romans and incorporated within the Roman Empire.

790 CE **The area becomes** the eastern frontier province (Ostmark) of the Frankish Empire and later part of Charlemagne's Holy Roman Empire.

976 **Emperor Otto II** gives the province to a member of the Babenburg family, who rule it for the next 270 years.

1278 **Count Rudolf of Habsburg,** Holy Roman Emperor from 1273, invades Austria and Styria. In 1282 he declares the title of Duke of Austria to be hereditary, thus founding the Habsburg domination of Austria that is to last until 1918. Over the next two centuries, the Habsburgs steadily increase their lands through strategic marriages, gaining Burgundy, the Netherlands, and eventually Spain and southern Italy, as well as lands belonging to Hungary.

1516–56 **Under Charles V** the Habsburg Empire reaches its zenith, stretching from the Americas to the Low Countries, with Austria acquiring control over much of Bohemia in 1526 and forming a bulwark of Christian resistance against the Ottoman Turks.

1529 **The Ottomans besiege** Vienna but fail to capture it.

1556 **On the abdication** of Charles V, the vast Habsburg empire is split in two, with Austria controlling lands in Germany and the rest going to Habsburg Spain.

1648 **The Treaty of Westphalia,** signed at the conclusion of the 30 Years War involving Catholic Austria, France, and Spain and Protestant Germany, England, Scandinavia, and Holland, marks the decline of the Holy Roman Empire as a political unit, with German states securing their sovereignty. It heralds the start of the Habsburgs' long decline in relation to France and Prussia.

1683 **The Ottomans again** besiege Vienna; the country is saved by a multinational army of Germans and Poles led by Jan Sobieski. From now on, Austria takes the offensive against the Ottomans and steadily advances at their expense into the Balkans, gaining Hungary in 1699.

1713 **The Treaty of Utrecht,** negotiated at the end of the War of the Spanish Succession, confirms Habsburg claims to the former Spanish Netherlands, as well as gaining Milan and, for a time, Naples, Sardinia, and Sicily in Italy. Austria acquires Tuscany in 1737, confirming its hold on Italy.

1748 **The Treaty of** Aix-la-Chapelle brings to an end the War of Austrian Succession, which broke out in 1740 following the death of Charles VI, the last male Habsburg heir. It recognizes his daughter, Maria Theresa, as ruler of the Habsburg lands, although Silesia is ceded to Prussia.

1772–97 **Successive partitions** of Poland with Russia and Prussia take place. In 1772 Austria gains Galicia in the first partition. In 1795 it gains "lesser Poland,"

including Cracow, in the third partition. The end of Poland as an independent nation is confirmed by treaty in 1797.

1793 **Austria declares war** against revolutionary France in support of Louis XVI, whose wife, Marie Antoinette, is an Austrian princess.

1805 **The Austrians** and Russians are defeated at the battle of Austerlitz by Napoleon, who incorporates many Austrian territories into France, or the new Confederation of the Rhine. In 1806 Franz I of Austria (who had declared himself emperor the year before) is obliged to renounce his title as Holy Roman Emperor as the empire is dissolved by Napoleon. In 1809–13 Austria is allied with France after a massive defeat at Wagram, but changes sides to defeat Napoleon at the Battle of the Nations at Leipzig in 1813. The Congress of Vienna of 1814–15, which settles the map of post-Napoleonic Europe, brings territorial gains to Austria, most significantly in northern Italy, and makes Austria titular head of the German Confederation, largely due to the astute diplomacy of Chancellor Metternich.

1848 **Popular revolutions within** the Habsburg domains lead to Metternich's resignation, the abdication of Emperor Ferdinand, and, with Russian help in Hungary, the succession to the throne of his nephew Franz Josef (1848–1916).

Marie Theresa
Only 23 when she came to the throne in 1740, Marie Theresa became one of the outstanding enlightened rulers of the 18th century, famed for her courage and determination.

THE ASSASSINATION OF DOLLFUSS, 1934

Engelbert Dollfuss (1892–1934) became chancellor of Austria in May 1932. His fear of socialist revolt led him in March 1933 to suspend parliament and, in February 1934, to use the army against the socialists in Vienna. In May he introduced a fascist-style constitution, but he was an isolated figure, hated by the left and by the Nazis who wanted a union with Germany. On July 25, 1934, he was shot dead by Nazi agents who had entered the Chancellery. His body is seen here being carried out. Dollfuss's death weakened Austria, and opened the way to Hitler's takeover in 1938.

1859–60 **Austria loses** most of its Italian possessions as Italy unifies.

1866 **After Prussia** unilaterally ends the German Confederation, it declares war on Austria and defeats it in the Seven Weeks War, excluding it from German affairs. Austria loses the Duchy of Holstein to Prussia and Venetia to Italy.

1867 **An Austro–Hungarian** "dual monarchy," with independent parliaments for each country, is established by Franz Josef; the two countries keep a common army, currency, and customs union.

1908 **Austria annexes** Bosnia–Herzegovina in the Balkans, heightening international tension.

1914 **The start of** World War I is precipitated by assassination of Archduke Franz Ferdinand, heir to the Austrian Habsburg throne, by a Serbian extremist. Austria–Hungary invades Serbia, but is unsuccessful until the following year when its armies are supported by German troops.

1918 **At the end** of World War I the Austrian Republic is proclaimed following the abdication of Emperor Charles and the collapse of the Austro–Hungarian empire.

1919 **The Treaty of** St. Germain between Austria and the Allies reduces Austria to a rump state as a result of territorial concessions made to the new states of Czechoslovakia, Hungary, Poland, and Yugoslavia. Anschluss or union with Germany is forbidden.

1933 **Parliamentary government is** suspended by the Christian Social Chancellor Engelbert Dollfuss.

1934 **Dollfuss starts imprisoning** social democrats, communists, and National Socialist (Nazi) Party members. The Nazis attempt a coup and assassinate Dollfuss.

1938 **Anschluss as Austria** is incorporated into Germany by Hitler and renamed Ostmark. Chancellor Kurt Schuschnigg imprisoned.

1945 **At the end of World War II,** Austria is occupied by Soviet, UK, US, and French forces. Elections result in a coalition of

the Austrian People's Party (OVP) and the Social Democrats (SPO).

1950 **Attempted coup by** Communist Party fails. Marshall Aid helps economic recovery.

1955 **Austrian State Treaty** signed, terminating the occupation and recognizing Austria as a neutral sovereign state.

1971 **SPO government formed** under Bruno Kreisky, who dominates Austrian politics for 12 years.

1986 **Kurt Waldheim, former** UN secretary general, is elected president, despite war crimes allegations. Jörg Haider becomes leader of the right-wing Freedom Party (FPO), prompting the SPP to pull out of government. Elections produce a stalemate and a return to the "grand coalition" of the OVP and SPO in 1987, which lasts until 1999.

1992 **Thomas Klestil** of the OVP elected president. Elections confirm some traditional OVP supporters defecting to the FPO.

1995 **Austria joins** the EU.

1998 **Klestil reelected president.**

1999 **Haider's FPO wins** 40 percent of votes in Carinthia regional poll and ties for second with OVP in general election in October; the SPO remains as the largest party.

2000 **OVP accepts FPO** into coalition, with Wolfgang Schüssel as chancellor, prompting a political crisis as EU imposes diplomatic sanctions.

2002 **Austria** adopts the euro.

2008 **Far-right-wing** parties including Jörg Haider's People's Party win 29 percent of the vote in parliamentary elections. Haider is killed in a car crash.

« 134–35 Celtic Warriors.
« 186–87 The Black Death
« 262–63 The 30 Years War
« 296–97 The First Global Conflict
« 306–07 The Napoleonic Wars

Germany

An economic giant at the heart of Europe and one of the main supporters of the European Union.

400s BCE **Germanic peoples** from southern Scandinavia spread south into Germany, displacing the native Celts and occupying the whole country from the Rhine across to the Danube by c.360 CE.

9 CE **The extension of** the Roman Empire east of the Rhine is thwarted by a Germanic tribe, the Cherusci, under the leadership of Arminius at the battle of Teutoburgerwald. Roman rule over those tribes living west of the Rhine had already been accomplished by Julius Caesar in 56 BCE. From then on, Romans make no serious attempts to conquer the Germans again, although they do send punitive expeditions across the Rhine against troublesome tribes.

74 CE **Romans begin annexation** of Agri Decumates, the triangle of land between the Rhine and Danube rivers, and fortify its frontier with the Germans along the Roman Limes. They hold this southwestern part of Germany until 260.

200s **German tribes** merge to form powerful confederations, notably the Frankish confederacy.

250s **Franks, Burgundians,** Alemanni, and other German tribes begin to raid the Roman Empire.

370s **The westward movement** of the Huns causes many Germanic tribes to cross the Rhine into the Roman Empire. By the time the Roman Empire in the west finally collapses in 476, the powerful Frankish kingdom in the west and the Burgundian kingdom in the southwest of Germany are established.

561 **Franks rule** most of central, western, and southern Germany and steadily expand their realm into a vast empire.

800 **The Frankish Empire** reaches its apogee when Charlemagne is crowned Emperor of the West by Pope Leo III. However, the empire does not survive for long after Charlemagne's death in 814.

HOLY ROMAN EMPEROR (1122–90)

FREDERICK I BARBAROSSA

Frederick I Barbarossa was the German emperor who challenged papal authority and established German dominance over much of Europe. He was elected king in 1152 and immediately challenged the authority of the pope. Crowned emperor in 1155, he embarked on a series of six military campaigns against the Lombard leagues in northern Italy. In 1177, Barbarossa finally recognized Alexander III as the true pope, and was reconciled to him. Within the empire, Barbarossa struggled violently with Henry the Lion, duke of Bavaria, who was eventually stripped of his possessions. Barbarossa drowned crossing the Saleph River (in present-day Turkey) on the Third Crusade.

Civil war breaks out in 827 between his sons, and continues until the empire is divided into three parts: the German-speaking lands of East Francia are separated from what later becomes France in the Partition of Verdun in 843.

911 **Duke Conrad, successor** to Louis the Child, the last of the German Carolingians, is elected the first Saxon king of the Germans.

915 **Magyars raid Germany,** although they are eventually heavily defeated at Lechfeld in 955. At the same time, Vikings from Scandinavia raid the north coasts and sail up the rivers searching for plunder.

936 **Otto I** becomes king of the Saxon dynasty and begins to establish a powerful Saxon kingdom, defeating the independent German dukes of south Germany and fighting Magyar and Viking raiders. His kingdom includes most of western Germany and the Low Countries, although expansion eastward along the Baltic is only temporary, the lands being lost again in 982.

962 **Otto I** is crowned Holy Roman Emperor by the pope, thus making the German kings emperors of much of western Europe.

973 **After the death** of Otto, his successors continue to expand the Holy Roman Empire south and east to include the whole of Germany, the Low Countries, Austria, Switzerland, northern Italy, and southeast France. The German emperors have control over ecclesiastical appointments of bishops, abbots, and others, and grant lands as fiefs to these churchmen for them to administer, thus retaining control as the lands pass back to the crown on the death of the celibate churchmen. This system works as long as the emperor can keep control over the ecclesiastical appointments and acts as a balance against the powerful landholdings of the hereditary nobility.

1056 **On the death** of Henry III, his son Henry IV becomes king but because he is a minor, power is held by

a weak regency. The papacy takes the opportunity to reassert its authority over church appointments: the Investiture Contest (1075–1122) gives the papacy greatly enhanced power over appointments and thus weakens the emperor.

1152 **Frederick I Barbarossa** of the Hohenstaufen dynasty briefly revives German and Holy Roman imperial power at the expense of the papacy, while the crusading Teutonic Knights continue to expand the empire eastward along the Baltic coast. However, Frederick is challenged by powerful territorial princes, notably Henry the Lion of the Welf family, while his attempt to tighten imperial control in Italy is defeated by the Lombard League of northern cities at Legarno in 1176. Open warfare between the Guelphs, led by Henry the Lion and allies of the pope, and the Ghibellines, the imperial party, erupts. By the time of Frederick's death in 1190, the area covered by modern Germany is on the way to becoming a patchwork of nominally independent states.

1212 **Frederick II** attempts to consolidate imperial power, but is opposed by the papacy and the Italian cities. His reign ends in failure upon his death in 1250. An interregnum from 1254–73 sees great political instability as rivals fight it out for the imperial crown. In 1266 the Saxon dynasty is overthrown. However, many new German cities are established in Poland during the 13th century as the empire continues to expand to the east.

1241 **Lübeck and Hamburg** form a trading alliance that gives rise to the Hanseatic League, which during the later Middle Ages functions as an independent political power with its own armed forces.

1273 **Count Rudolf of Habsburg** establishes himself as King of the Germans and Holy Roman Emperor. This marks the start of the Habsburg dynasty's domination of Austria and Germany.

1325 **The Wittelsbach** family gains the upper hand over the Habsburgs, only to lose it to the Luxembourgs in 1346. Habsburg power is not restored until 1438, when Albert II is elected emperor.

1348–50 **Black Death** decimates German population.

1356 **Emperor Charles IV** issues the Golden Bull ending papal role in imperial elections. Seven electors now choose the emperor: the Duke of Saxony, the King of Bohemia, the Count Palatine of the Rhine, the Margrave of Brandenburg, and the bishops of Cologne, Mainz, and Trier.

1377–89 **Habsburg, Wittelsbach,** and Luxembourg princes combine to reduce the independence of the cities of southern Germany and the Rhineland.

1477 **The Habsburg heir** Maximilian I marries Mary of Burgundy, thus acquiring the Low Countries as well as Burgundy. When he becomes emperor in 1493, Habsburg power in Europe grows considerably as more lands are acquired by marriage and diplomacy.

1516 **Charles V, grandson** of Maximilian, acquires Spain and its vast European empire. On the death of Maximilian in 1519, he acquires the Habsburg lands and becomes Holy Roman Emperor. The Habsburgs now dominate Europe.

Trading power
This seal of the Hanseatic League dates from 1329. The League, an alliance of city guilds, established a powerful trading monopoly over most of northern Europe between the 13th and 17th centuries.

1517 **The German theologian** Martin Luther nails his 95 theses on the door of a Wittenberg church, challenging the established Catholic hierarchies and especially the practice of selling indulgences to raise funds. The debate he starts soon spreads around Germany.

1521 **Luther is excommunicated** by the pope and outlawed by the emperor at the Diet of Worms; these events mark the real start of the Protestant Reformation in Europe.

1524–26 **Influenced by radical** Protestant preachers and frustrated by economic hardship, Germany's lower classes rise up in a peasants' revolt. However, they are crushed by the army of Philip of Hesse, a Protestant who enjoys Luther's support, and 100,000 are slaughtered.

1530 **German Protestants publish** 28 articles of faith to prevent a split with the Catholic church; by now the princes of Saxony, Hesse, Brandenburg, and Brunswick are Lutherans as the Reformation spreads throughout northern Germany; most of southern Germany remains Catholic. Warfare between the emperor and Protestant states is common.

1534 **Anabaptists seize Munster,** prophesying the end of the world.

1547 **Emperor Charles V** defeats the Protestant Schmalkaldic League of Protestant princes at Mühlberg, but fails to stem the growing tide of Protestantism throughout Germany.

1555 **Under the terms** of the Peace of Augsburg, it is agreed by the Holy Roman Emperor that each German prince should be left free to impose the faith of his choice within his territories.

1556 **Charles V abdicates:** his vast empire is split in half, with the German

The Frankfurt Assembly
Representatives from all German states met in Frankfurt in the revolutionary year 1848 with the aim of uniting the country in a democratic way. They offered the role of king to Frederick William IV of Prussia, who refused what he called "a crown from the gutter."

part and the Holy Roman Empire going to his brother, Ferdinand I; his Habsburg son Philip II inherits Spain.

1560s Calvinism spreads northward from Switzerland and establishes itself in Nassau, the Palatinate, and Ansbach, as well as making inroads into Hesse-Kassel and Brandenburg. Although Calvinism is excluded from the tolerance extended by the Peace of Augsburg, its main principle—allowing individual princes to decide their faith—allowed it to take root.

1618 The 30 Years War begins. Fought mainly between Catholic and Protestant states within Germany, the conflict starts in Bohemia but ends temporarily in 1623 with Protestant defeat and the occupation of the Lower Palatinate by imperial and Spanish troops. Intervention by Denmark in 1625 and then by Sweden in 1630 tilts the balance back in favor of Protestant states, but the intervention of France, a Catholic nation, against both imperial and Spanish Habsburgs in 1635 turns the conflict into a power struggle for control of Europe.

1648 By the Treaties of Westphalia that end the war, the Holy Roman Emperor recognizes the full religious and political sovereignty of the German states; territory is ceded to Sweden in the north and to France in the west. By the end of the war, Germany is economically devastated, and is now divided into numerous small kingdoms, principalities, and bishoprics. It becomes a backwater within Europe, fought over by Habsburgs, the French, and others. The Habsburgs continue to rule the empire, which now exists in name only, as real power, such as it is, is with the numerous small states.

1714 George, Elector of Hanover, becomes king of Great Britain; the electorate (after 1815, the kingdom) remains in personal union with Britain until 1837, when the Salic Law forbids the accession of Victoria to the throne and the two countries separate.

1740 Frederick II "the Great" of the Hohenzollern dynasty becomes king of Prussia. During his reign he establishes Prussia as a major power

in northern Germany, gaining Silesia during the War of the Austrian Succession in 1740–48 (which Austria fails to regain in the Seven Years War of 1756–63) and gaining Pomerania and East Prussia in the first partition of Poland in 1772. A benevolent despot at home, Frederick II concedes full religious tolerance, abolishes torture, and liberates state serfs.

1792 Prussia, along with Austria, declares war on revolutionary France as part of the First Coalition. By 1800, France's armies have pushed the French eastern border up to the Rhine.

1793–95 In the second partition of Poland in 1793, Prussia, now ruled by Frederick William II, gains "greater Poland," which includes Posen (Poznan) and Lodz, as well as Danzig (Gdansk). In 1795, in the third partition, Prussia gains Warsaw. The end of Poland is confirmed in a 1797 treaty.

1806 Following the defeat of the Habsburg monarch Francis I at Austerlitz in December 1805, Emperor Napoleon Bonaparte declares the Holy Roman Empire (or First German Reich) dissolved and creates a new Rhenish League—the Confederation of the Rhine—under his protectorship. This comprises 16 princedoms and cities including Bavaria, Hesse, Saxony, Westphalia, and Württemberg. Most of the rest of western Germany is absorbed directly into France.

1806 The Prussian army is defeated at Jena in October; the following year, Prussia allies with France.

1813 The Rhenish League breaks up after Napoleon is defeated at the Battle of the Nations at Leipzig in October 1813 following his retreat from Russia. It is replaced at the Congress of Vienna in 1814–15 by a new German confederation comprising 39 substantially independent states and with a diet (parliament) under the nominal presidency of Austria, although dominated by both Austria and Prussia, now the main power in northern Germany.

1834 To increase its relative authority inside the German Zollverein, Prussia founds a German *Zollverein* (customs union) by merging the various existing north German *Zollvereinen* under its leadership. This abolishes the complicated system of intra-German tariffs and allows the relatively free trade of goods across much of northern Germany, promoting trade and industry. The individual states do, however, retain their own currencies. It also consolidates Prussian power, as Austria remains in favor of protection and outside the union. By 1852 the *Zollverein* includes all German states except Austria, the two Mecklenburgs, and various Hanseatic cities.

1848 Popular revolutions break out in many German states, temporarily overthrowing the monarchies. In Frankfurt a constituent assembly is elected and discusses the drafting of a national and liberal constitution for a united Germany. However, its offer of the German imperial crown to King Frederick William IV of Prussia is rejected by him, and opposed by Austria, while non-German minorities and German radicals refuse to accept the parliament. By 1849 Austrian and Prussian forces have repressed the revolutions and the old order is restored.

"Place in the hands of the king of Prussia the strongest possible military power, then he will be able to carry out the policy… through blood and iron."

OTTO VON BISMARCK IN THE PRUSSIAN HOUSE OF DEPUTIES, JANUARY 28, 1886

1862 Otto von Bismarck becomes Chancellor of Prussia, a post he holds until 1890. First he gains Schleswig from Denmark in 1864 and then in the Seven Weeks War of 1866 defeats Austria at the Battle of Sadowa, forcing her out of German affairs. This results in the 1866 Peace of Prague which gives Prussia control of most of Germany north of the Main River. In 1867 a North German Confederation is formed which unites all the north German states but excludes the southern states of Baden, Bavaria, Hesse–Darmstadt, Lichtenberg, Württemberg, and Austria.

1870s A period of rapid expansion sees Germany become one of the major economic powers in the world.

1870–71 In a brief war with France, the French emperor Napoleon III is captured at Sedan and Paris besieged. By the Treaty of Frankfurt, France surrenders its two eastern provinces of Alsace and Lorraine.

1871 In January 1871 King Wilhelm I of Prussia is proclaimed emperor of Germany in the Hall of Mirrors in Versailles Palace, outside Paris. The new German empire has a federal constitution with many powers conceded to individual German states. These states keep their own monarchies and institutions, which leads to conflict between them and the imperial crown and parliament.

1873 Bismarck negotiates the League of the Three Emperors with Austria–Hungary and Russia; it lasts until 1890, when tensions between Austria and Russia over Bulgaria cause it to collapse.

1878 Major European powers meet in Berlin under Bismarck's leadership to impose peace in the Balkans after the Russo-Turkish War of 1877–78. A second major congress in 1884–85 draws up the colonial map of Africa; by this stage, Germany is the diplomatic leader of Europe.

1879 Dual Alliance is agreed with Austria–Hungary.

1882 Triple Alliance is agreed with Austria–Hungary and Italy.

1884–85 Germany gains the African colonies of Togoland, Cameroon, South-West Africa, and German East Africa—its "place in the sun." It also gains Qingdao in China in 1897 and Samoa in the South Pacific in 1899, as well as islands in the western Pacific.

Franco-Prussian war
An artillery unit of the 400,000-strong French army is here seen manning an outdated muzzle-loading cannon. During the conflict this proved no match for the power and range of the new German breach-loading cannon.

1888 Kaiser Wilhelm II succeeds to the throne, with aspirations for German world role. Bismarck dismissed.

1898, 1900 Two German naval laws confirm the growth of the German navy as a rival to Britain's Royal Navy.

1905–06 German colonial claims in Morocco lead to tension with France and the UK. A second crisis in 1911, when Germany sends a gunboat to Agadir, is resolved in France's favor.

1914 Germany enters World War I on the side of Austria–Hungary and Ottoman Turkey as one of the Central Powers, fighting against the Allied Powers of the UK, France, Italy, Russia, Serbia, and Japan. Hopes for a quick victory on the Western Front are not fulfilled when Germany is obliged to retreat after the first Battle of the Marne in September 1914 and troops become bogged down in trench warfare along the Western Front with great loss of life. In April 1917 the US joins the war on the Allied side. There is greater success for Germany in the east where defeats for Russia precipitate two revolutions after which the new Bolshevik government withdraws from the war and accepts the degrading Peace of Brest-Litovsk in March 1918, surrendering much land.

1918 Despite now being able to concentrate its forces on the Western Front after the defeat of Russia, Germany is beaten back and forced to concede defeat in an armistice signed on November 11, 1918, after 1,774,000 German soldiers' lives have been lost. Facing a mutiny by military and naval forces and popular disillusionment with the war, Kaiser Wilhelm II's abdication is announced on November 9 and he flees into exile in Holland. Later that day a republic is proclaimed in Berlin with a government headed by Friedrich Ebert, the leader of the German Social Democratic Party.

U-boats surrender, 1918
Here, German U-boats are impounded by the Allies at the end of World War I. Germany fought an effective U-boat campaign, sinking 50 British cruisers in the first 10 weeks of the war.

1919 Ebert crushes a "Spartakist" revolt in Berlin, led by the German Communist Party (KPD) founded by Karl Liebknecht and Rosa Luxemburg in January 1919. Ebert is elected president and the constitution of a liberal democratic Weimar Republic is approved later in the same year.

1919 By the Treaty of Versailles Germany agrees to cede territory to France, Belgium, Denmark, and the new states of Poland, Czechoslovakia, and Lithuania. It is forbidden Anschluss, or union, with Austria, and loses all its colonies to League of Nation mandates. The Saarland is placed under the League of Nations, demilitarized, and occupied by Allied troops for 15 years. Germany is forced to accept its guilt in causing the war, pay financial reparations to the Allies, and limit the size of its armed forces.

1923 In retaliation for Germany's non-payment of reparations, French and Belgian troops occupy the Ruhr, withdrawing in 1924 after Germany accepts the Dawes Plan on reparations.

1923 Adolf Hitler, leader of the nationalist, anti-Semitic National Socialist German Workers' Party (NSDAP, or Nazis) stages an abortive putsch in Munich, as hyperinflation rages. He is imprisoned for eight months in 1924, during which time he writes *Mein Kampf* ("My Struggle").

1925 Field Marshal Paul von Hindenburg becomes president, ushering in a period of somewhat greater political stability. The arts flourish in Berlin, and Germany is admitted to the League of Nations in 1926 (of which it remains a member until Hitler's withdrawal in October 1933). However, the Weimar Republic proves too weak to weather the global economic recession that hits Germany after 1929 and soon causes mass unemployment.

1930 In the general election, support for the NSDAP increases sevenfold (to 18.3 percent) compared with the last election two years earlier.

1932 In a general election in July, the NSDAP wins 37.4 percent of the vote and replaces the SPD as the largest single party, although in a further election in November, its share of the vote falls to 33.2 percent. The Reichstag (parliament) finds itself increasingly unable to retain control of the situation as street violence escalates and Nazi supporters clash with their communist, socialist, and trade union opponents.

1933 President Hindenburg appoints Hitler chancellor at the head of a minority government in January. In March, after blaming the communists for an arson attack on the Reichstag, Hitler secures passage of an Enabling Act granting him dictatorial powers for four years. In July, Germany becomes a one-party state.

1934 In the "Night of the Long Knives," Nazis kill thousands of opponents within and outside the party. When Hindenburg dies in August 1934 Hitler assumes the presidency, although retaining the title "Führer" (leader).

Badge of rank
This Nazi Party badge with golden oak leaves was worn by high-ranking members only, many of them answerable solely to Hitler. By making himself the final arbiter between competing subordinates, Hitler increased his power.

1935 Nuremberg Laws strip Jews of their German citizenship and forbid marriages between Jews and German citizens. Jews are also removed from the armed services, the civil service, and, in 1938, all Jewish businesses are "Aryanized"—that is, transferred to "German" ownership with minimal compensation paid.

1935 The Saar, under League of Nations control since the end of World War I, again becomes part of Germany after a plebiscite shows overwhelming support for reintegration. In March of the following year, in violation of the 1919 Treaty of Versailles, German troops reoccupy the demilitarized Rhineland.

1936 The Olympic Games are held in Berlin and used to showcase Nazi ideals and propaganda.

1938 In the Anschluss, German troops enter Austria and incorporate it into the Third Reich. At the Munich conference in September, UK and France agree to Hitler's occupation of the Sudetenland border region in Czechoslovakia. By March 1939 all of Czechoslovakia is under Nazi control, with Slovakia becoming a puppet state.

1938 Jewish homes, businesses, and synagogues are attacked throughout Germany in the "Kristallnacht" (night of broken glass) pogrom.

1939 Germany seizes Memel from Lithuania.

1939 After secretly signing the Molotov–Ribbentrop nonaggression pact with the USSR on August 23, Germany invades Poland on September 1. Britain and France, treaty-bound to defend Poland, declare war on Germany on September 3, thus beginning World War II.

1940 Successful "Blitzkrieg" invasions of Norway, Denmark, Holland, France, and Belgium by June 1940 see Germany occupying most of Western Europe.

1941 Hitler opens a new eastern front, first invading Yugoslavia and Greece in April and then in June launching an offensive against the USSR. By the end of the year Leningrad is under siege and German forces are just miles from Moscow.

1942–43 In North Africa, the army of Field Marshal Erwin Rommel is gradually beaten back during 1942 and defeated at El Alamein in October. On the eastern front 300,000 German soldiers die defending Stalingrad and Field Marshal Paulus is forced to surrender in February 1943. Although Hitler

does not immediately appreciate the significance of the Japanese attack on Pearl Harbor in December 1941 which brings the US into the war, the addition of US forces on the Allied side eventually turns the tide in the Allies' favor.

1943 British and US air forces launch raids on German cities and industries.

1944 D-Day: Allied forces land in Normandy, France, in June, liberating Paris in August, Brussels in September, and crossing the Rhine in March 1945, while in the East, Soviet forces advance through Eastern Europe toward Berlin.

1945 Faced with military defeat on both the eastern and western fronts, Hitler commits suicide in his Berlin bunker on April 30. Two days later, Berlin falls to Soviet forces. On May 7 the German army capitulates to the Allies.

1945 The Allied Control Commission assumes control of Germany, which is divided into four (British, French, Soviet, and US) occupation zones, with four-power control over Berlin. Germany loses part of East Prussia to the USSR, and the rest of East Prussia and large parts of eastern Germany to Poland. In all, 3,250,000 German soldiers and 500,000 German civilians have died during World War II. Around 6,000,000 Jews (half of whom died at the Auschwitz–Birkenau concentration camp in Poland) have been massacred during the Holocaust. In November, trials of Nazi war criminals commence at Nuremberg.

1948–49 As Cold War tensions rise, a Soviet attempt to blockade West Berlin leads to a massive Allied airlift that keeps the city alive until the blockade is lifted. Berlin remains a source of tension between the two sides.

1948 A constituent assembly meeting in Bonn drafts the Basic Law for the three

Konrad Adenauer
Having been dismissed from office and imprisoned by the Nazis, Konrad Adenauer (1876–1967) was an ideal candidate for chancellor of West Germany in 1949. He integrated the nation into Western Europe and cultivated a friendship with France.

German contrition
In December 1970 the West German chancellor Willy Brandt visited Poland; at the Warsaw Ghetto memorial, he expressed sorrow for Nazi war crimes, and knelt in homage to the victims.

western zones of occupation, which will become their future constitution.

1949 Germany is divided as the three western zones are merged into the German Federal Republic, with its capital in Bonn, while the Soviet zone becomes the communist German Democratic Republic with its capital in East Berlin. Konrad Adenauer is the first West German chancellor (until 1963). Walter Ulbricht is General Secretary of the East German Communist Party until 1971, when he is succeeded by Erich Honecker.

1951 West Germany joins its historic enemy, France, as well as Italy and the Low Countries, in the European Coal and Steel Community, the first step to creating the European Union. Further steps toward European integration begin.

1953 Strikes and rioting in East Berlin against communist rule as thousands of refugees pour through the border into West Berlin seeking a better life.

1955 West Germany joins NATO; East Germany joins the Warsaw Pact as Cold War divisions harden in Europe.

1957 West Germany signs the Treaty of Rome setting up the European Economic Community.

1961 Berlin Wall built to seal off West Berlin; the US responds by moving a large tank division into the city. The visit of US president John F. Kennedy to the city in June 1963, when he gives his famous *Ich bin ein Berliner* ("I am a Berliner") speech further raises morale in the city.

1963 Konrad Adenauer steps down as West German chancellor and is succeeded by Ludwig Erhard.

1966–69 West German grand coalition of CDU and SPD parties, headed by Kurt Georg Kiesinger.

1969–82 SPD-led West German coalition governments with the Free Democratic Party (FDP) under Willy Brandt (1969–74) and Helmut Schmidt (1974–82).

1970 West Germany signs peace treaties with the USSR and Poland, recognizing their post-war borders and ending German claims to territories it lost at the end of World War II. For his work in promoting peace in Europe, and for his policy of "Ostpolitik," "east policy" or detente with Eastern Europe, Brandt is awarded the 1971 Nobel Peace Prize.

1972 West and East Germany sign a treaty of mutual recognition. Agreements with the USSR about access to West Berlin reduce tensions in and around the city.

1973 Both Germanies join the UN.

1974 Willy Brandt is forced to resign after an East German spy is found working as a personal aide in his office.

1982 Helmut Kohl becomes West German chancellor at the head of a CDU–FDP coalition.

1988 In a speech to the UN, the Soviet leader Mikhail Gorbachev signals the end of Soviet domination of Eastern Europe, including East Germany, by withdrawing Soviet troops and giving states "freedom of choice" over their future.

1989 As Hungary dismantles its fortified border with Austria, thus breaking down the Iron Curtain, thousands of East Germans pour through seeking a new life in the West. At first the East German government does not reduce its hardline rule, but it is told to change by Gorbachev. As massive, peaceful protests break out across East Germany, notably in Dresden, the border is opened and Berliners begin to dismantle the Berlin Wall.

1990 Reunification of Germany as the USSR and the other wartime allies raise no objections. East and West Germany sign a treaty extending the West German currency and its economic, monetary, and social legislation to East Germany. The East German parliament votes for union as the five East German länder (states) join the Federal Republic. The first all-German elections held since 1933 result in a Kohl-led government.

1996 Rising concern over jobs as Germany struggles to reintegrate the poor parts of former East Germany into the economy, despite massive investment in the region to overcome years of communist rule and environmental degradation.

1998 Gerhard Schröder heads a coalition of SPD and Greens.

1999 For the first time since World War II, German troops take part in military activities abroad, participating in the NATO action against Serbia. In 2001 Germany is given command of the NATO peacekeeping mission in Macedonia, while German troops are also involved in

GERMANY
EAST GERMANY

The five former eastern provinces of Germany were occupied by Soviet forces after World War II. A people's assembly meeting in East Berlin in 1948–49 prepared a constitution for the new state, which came into being on October 7, 1949, as the German Democratic Republic.

The new state embarked on a program of "socialist construction" led by the Socialist Unity Party of Walter Ulbricht. Industry was nationalized and agriculture collectivized, while reparations were made to the USSR for the cost of the war. The resulting hardship led to riots and strikes in 1953, which were put down with Soviet troops and tanks.

During the 1950s, economic differences between East and West Germany grew, leading many East Germans to flee through West Berlin in search of a better life. This outlet to the West was sealed in 1961 with the building of the Berlin Wall.

Relations between East and West Germany improved during the 1970s, with the East German parliament removing all references to reunification of Germany from its constitution in 1974. However, a new exodus of East Germans through Hungary to the west as the Iron Curtain collapsed in 1989 threatened communist rule. Non-communists entered the government, but the fall of the Berlin Wall and the collapse of communism in Eastern Europe spelled the end of East Germany, which united with the west in 1990. Below, East Berliners mark May 1 with a march celebrating the heroes of communism.

peacekeeping in Afghanistan after 2002. Germany has also been a leading light in the EU's Rapid Reaction Force, providing almost half its personnel.

1999 The Federal Assembly and the rest of the German government move from Bonn back to Berlin.

2000 Helmut Kohl is disgraced in a party funding scandal.

2002 Germany abandons the deutschmark—the symbol of its post-war regeneration—in favor of the euro.

2002 Edmund Stoiber, leader of the CDU's sister party, the Bavarian Christian Social Union (CSU), challenges Schröder for the chancellorship, but fails in the general election to defeat the governing "red–green" coalition.

2003 Germany is extremely critical of the US–UK invasion of Iraq.

2005 In federal elections, no single party wins a majority, or is able to form a working coalition with the minority parties. The two main parties join a grand coalition led by Angela Merkel, the CDU leader and first woman to become German chancellor.

2007 Germany holds both the rotating presidency of the EU and heads the G8 group of leading industrial nations, giving it unprecedented influence on the international stage.

2008 A huge fiscal stimulus package is agreed to counter the effects of the international financial crisis.

2009 Angela Merkel of the CDU-CSU wins the general election, with an increased number of seats but not an overall majority. She forms a coalition government with the Free Democrats (FDP). The German economy shrinks by 5 percent over the year.

Netherlands

A low-lying country that once controlled a wealthy international trading empire.

400s CE **After the departure** of the Romans, three Germanic tribes (Franks in the south, Frisians in the north, Saxons in the east) assert control.

768–814 **During the reign** of Charlemagne, the Franks conquer the whole of the Netherlands; after his death the region becomes part of the Middle Frankish kingdom and then of the East Frankish kingdom, later the Holy Roman Empire.

1000s **Decline of central** authority leads to a feudal fragmentation and the formation of autonomous states; the county of Holland, in the west, becomes the dominant power in the region.

1433 **Holland becomes** a Burgundian possession by inheritance, and part of the Habsburg Empire in 1482.

1515–55 **During the reign** of Charles V, all the remaining autonomous territories become Habsburg possessions; the Netherlands is thus united for the first time; on Charles's abdication they come under Spanish Habsburg rule.

1567 **Resistance to Philip II** of Spain, fueled in part by the rise of Protestantism, leads to a popular revolt led by William (the Silent) of Orange, sections of the nobility, and the powerful merchant class.

1581 **The seven northern provinces** formally declare their independence from Spain and form the Republic of the United Provinces of the Netherlands.

1602 **Dutch East India Company** is founded, locating its headquarters at Batavia, now Jakarta, in 1619. The company develops a major maritime trading empire in the East Indies.

1609 **Twelve-year truce** with Spain begins, but founders over demand for recognition of religious freedoms.

DUTCH REVOLT LEADER (1533–84)

WILLIAM I OF NASSAU

William I of Orange-Nassau, also known as William the Silent, became Prince of Orange in 1544. He was the main leader of the Dutch revolt against the Spanish that started the 80 Years War and ended with the independence of the United Provinces in 1648. Unhappy with the treatment of Dutch Protestants, William joined the Dutch uprising. He was the most politically capable of the rebels, leading them to several military victories against the Spanish. Declared an outlaw by Philip II of Spain in 1580, he was murdered in Delft by a supporter of the king.

Golden Age

These elegant merchants' houses date from Amsterdam's 17th-century "Golden Age," when the city was the wealthiest in the world and at the hub of international trade.

1614 **Dutch traders begin** to trade and form colonies on the Hudson River in North America; the colonies are seized by Britain in 1664.

1648 **The Peace of Munster** confirms Dutch independence, ending the so-called 80 Years War of independence.

1652–74 **The Dutch fight three** wars with Britain over control of maritime trade.

1689–1702 **William of Orange,** the hereditary stadtholder, or provincial leader, becomes king of England and campaigns against Louis XIV of France.

1713 **The Treaty of Utrecht**, ends both the War of the Spanish Succession and Dutch involvement in European power struggles.

1795 **French forces invade;** local groups proclaim the Batavian Republic, modeled on revolutionary France.

1806 **Holland again becomes** a kingdom under Louis Bonaparte, but is annexed by France four years later.

1813 **Dutch oust French** and choose to become a constitutional monarchy.

1815 **Congress of Vienna:** United Kingdom of Netherlands formed that includes Belgium and Luxembourg.

1830 **Belgium revolts** and secedes; its independence is recognized by the Netherlands in 1839.

1848 **New constitution:** ministers to be accountable to parliament.

1897–1901 **Wide-ranging social** legislation enacted.

1898 **Wilhelmina succeeds** to throne, ending Luxembourg union where male hereditary Salic Law is in force.

1914–18 **Dutch neutrality respected** in World War I.

1919 **Women fully enfranchised.**

1940 **Dutch assert neutrality** in World War II, but Nazi Germany invades and meets fierce resistance to the occupation.

1942 **Japan invades Dutch** East Indies.

1944–45 **"Winter of starvation"** in German-occupied western provinces.

1945 **Liberation.** International Court of Justice set up in the Hague in 1946.

1946–58 **Labor Party** (PvdA) under Willem Drees leads center-left coalitions as the country rebuilds after the war.

1948 **Juliana becomes queen.**

1948 **Customs union with** Belgium and Luxembourg (Benelux) comes into operation.

1949 **Most of the East Indies** colonies gain independence as Indonesia after a four-year guerrilla war.

1957 **Founder member of** the EEC.

1960 **Economic union with** Belgium and Luxembourg comes into effect.

1963 **The final Dutch colony** in the East Indies—Western New Guinea—is relinquished to Indonesia.

1973 **PvdA wins power** after 15 years in opposition and leads a center-left coalition.

1977–81 **Coalition** formed by the Christian Democrats (CDA) and the People's Party (VVD).

1980 **CDA alliance of** the "confessional" parties forms a single party.

1980 **Beatrix** becomes queen.

2000 **Licensed brothels** legalized.

2002 **Adopts the euro.**

2002 **Government resigns** after the Dutch army is blamed for not preventing the Srebrenica massacre in Bosnia.

2002 **Right-wing** populist Pim Fortuyn

is assassinated; his party becomes second largest in parliament and joins the government. The coalition collapses in 2003.

2005 **Dutch voters** reject a proposed EU constitution.

NETHERLANDS

DUTCH DEPENDENCIES

The Dutch once had a major trading empire in Asia, South Africa, and the Americas. With Suriname's independence in 1975, that empire has now all but gone.

ARUBA
Island off the coast of Venezuela.
1499 Island first claimed by Spain.
1636 Acquired by the Dutch. At first is left to the indigenous Arawaks.
1848 Becomes part of the Netherlands Antilles.
1954 Netherlands Antilles gain internal self-government.
1986 Aruba becomes a separate Dutch dependency.
1994 The transition to independence is halted over lack of economic viability and fears for the island's security.

NETHERLANDS ANTILLES
Island group consisting of Curaçao and Bonaire off Venezuela, and Saba, Sint Maarten, and St. Eustasius—shared with French Guadeloupe—in east Caribbean.
1845 Netherlands Antilles formed.
1954 Gain internal self-government.
2000 Sint Maarten votes for autonomy.
2004 Bonaire and Saba vote for direct administration by the Dutch government, as does St. Eustasius in 2005.
2005 Curaçao votes for autonomy.
2010 Netherlands Antilles are dissolved. Curaçao and Sint Maarten become constituent countries of the Netherlands. The other islands become part of the province of North Holland.

2010 **Coalition government** collapses over presence of Dutch troops in Afghanistan. An indecisive election gives center-right Liberal party most seats. Dutch troops are withdrawn from Afghanistan in August.

《208–09 Cities and Trade
《238–39 Trade and Empire
《276–77 The Birth of Capitalism
《350–51 Colonial Resistance

Belgium

A largely low-lying country that has been a frequent battleground over the centuries.

51 BCE **The Romans complete** the conquest of the Celtic and Germanic tribes in the area covering present-day Belgium; the region becomes one of the provinces of Gaul.

Antwerp
The Flemish city of Antwerp rose to prominence in the 15th century as Bruges declined in importance. The world's first stock exchange was opened here in 1460 and the city became Europe's chief commercial and financial center in the 1500s, helped by the arrival of Jewish diamond craftsmen expelled from Portugal.

481–511 Under Clovis, the Franks establish a kingdom centered in what is now southern Belgium and northern France; under his successors the Frankish kingdom expands to cover most of Western Europe, reaching its apogee under Charlemagne.

889 Following several divisions, western Belgium (the county of Flanders) becomes part of the West Frankish kingdom or France, while the rest of the country (the duchy of Lower Lorraine) becomes part of the East Frankish kingdom or Germany (later the Holy Roman Empire).

1100s Feudal fragmentation leads to the rise of six main regional states: the county of Flanders in the west, the duchy of Brabant in the center, the bishopric of Liège in the east, the county of Hainault in the southwest, and the duchy of Luxembourg in the southeast. The towns of Flanders and Brabant are among the most prosperous in Europe, with wealth derived from the trade in wool.

1384 Philip the Bold, Duke of Burgundy, inherits Flanders; over the next 60 years Burgundy acquires all the other important territories in the region except for Liège, thereby creating an unprecedented degree of unity within the Low Countries.

1477 The Burgundian territories pass to the House of Habsburg.

1555–56 On the abdication of Habsburg Emperor Charles V, the Austrian and Spanish Habsburg lines are separated. The Low Countries become a province of Spain.

1567 Resistance to Spanish rule, fueled in part by the rise of Protestantism, leads to a popular revolt led by sections of the nobility and the powerful merchant class.

1579 The southern provinces (broadly speaking present-day Belgium) form the Union of Arras, reaffirming loyalty to the Habsburgs and Catholicism; the northern provinces (the future Netherlands) declare their independence from Spain in 1581.

1585 The Dutch impose a blockade on Antwerp, starting a long-term decline of the Southern Netherlands.

1648 The Treaty of Münster reaffirms Spanish rule over the Southern Netherlands.

1713 Under the Treaty of Utrecht, the Southern Netherlands are transferred to Austrian Habsburg rule.

1792–95 French and Austrian troops fight for control of the Austrian Netherlands. The territory is annexed by France.

1814–15 Congress of Vienna: European powers decide to merge Belgium with the Netherlands under King William I of Orange.

1830 Revolt against Dutch leads to the declaration of independence.

1831 European powers install Leopold Saxe Coburg as King of the Belgians

1839 Dutch recognize the independence of Belgium.

1865 Leopold II crowned king.

1884–85 Berlin Conference gives Leopold the Congo as a personal colony.

1908 After an international outcry over conditions in the Congo, the Belgian government has to take over the colony.

1909 On the death of Leopold II, his nephew succeeds as Albert I.

1914 German armies invade. Belgium occupied until 1918.

1919 Under League of Nations mandate, Belgium acquires Burundi and Rwanda.

1921 Belgo-Luxembourg Economic Union formed: Belgian and Luxembourg currencies are locked.

1934 Leopold III becomes king.

1936 Belgium declares neutrality.

1940–44 Germany occupies Belgium.

1948 Customs union with Netherlands and Luxembourg (Benelux) formed.

1950 King wins referendum on his retaining the throne, but rumors over wartime collaboration persist. In 1951 he abdicates in favor of his son, Baudouin.

1957 Signs Treaty of Rome as one of six founding members of EEC.

1992 Christian Democrat and Social Democrat government led by Jean-Luc Dehaene takes over federal government.

1980 New constitution devolves government by language: French, Flemish (Dutch), and German.

1993 Culmination of reforms creating a federal state with greater powers for regions and city governments.

1993 King Baudouin dies and is succeeded by Albert II.

End of the line
This railway station sign greeted the hundreds of thousands of troops arriving at the front in Belgium during World War I. Four major battles were fought at Ypres, including the third, Passchendaele, in 1917, with disastrous loss of life.

1995 Allegations of corruption and murder involving French-speaking Socialist Party force resignations of Walloon premier, federal deputy premier, and Willy Claes as NATO secretary general. In 1999 Claes is found guilty of bribery in connection with a defense contract.

1996 The murder of young girls arouses fears of a pedophile ring. Accusations of incompetence of authorities.

1999 New coalition government is formed, including Greens for first time, as environmental issues become important.

2009 Nine months after an indecisive general election, Yves Leterme, leader of the Flemish Christian Democrats, returns for a second term.

2010 The government collapses when Flemish liberals walk out over Francophone voting rights. Flemish separatists become the largest party in the subsequent general election.

« 150–51 Decline and Fall
« 208–09 Cities and Trade

Luxembourg

A grand duchy in western Europe with great wealth based on banking and other services.

406–07 CE An invasion by Germanic tribes ends the Roman occupation of the Rhine frontier area.

963 Luxembourg becomes an autonomous county within the Holy Roman Empire and a Duchy within the Empire from 1354.

1308–1437 The House of Luxembourg provides four Holy Roman Emperors.

1443 Luxembourg becomes one of the Burgundian lands in the Low Countries.

1477 Luxembourg passes to the Habsburgs. It is ruled by the Spanish Habsburgs from 1555 until 1713.

1713 Under the Treaty of Utrecht the southern Netherlands pass to Austrian Habsburg rule.

1815 Luxembourg becomes an independent Grand Duchy within the German Confederation, with the king of the Netherlands as head of state.

1831 Much of western (French-speaking) Luxembourg takes part in Belgian revolt against Dutch rule.

1839 The Treaty of London recognizes Belgian possession of western Luxembourg; independence of the remainder is affirmed.

1867 A congress in London confirms Luxembourg's perpetual neutrality; a Prussian garrison is withdrawn and King William III of the Netherlands is obliged to keep the Grand Duchy.

1890 Link with Dutch throne ends.

1921 Economic union with Belgium.

1940–44 German occupation.

1948 Benelux treaty creating a customs union comes into effect.

1957 Signs Treaty of Rome as one of six founding members of EEC.

1995–99 Prime Minister Jacques Santer is president of the European Commission until he is forced to resign amid corruption allegations.

2000 Grand Duke Jean abdicates in favor of his son, Henri.

2002 Euro introduced.

2008 The role of the monarchy is reduced to a ceremonial one after an attempt by Grand Duke Henri to block a bill legalizing euthanasia.

« 262–63 The 30 Years War

Iceland

Europe's westernmost country was colonized by Vikings and maintains its Scandinavian connection.

874 **Iceland is settled** by Vikings of Norwegian origin.

930 **The Althing, the** world's oldest sovereign parliament, is founded.

1262 **The independent commonwealth** of Iceland declares allegiance to Norway.

1380 **Iceland comes under** Danish rule when Norway unites with Denmark.

1800 **The Althing, which** lost influence under Danish rule, ceases to exist.

1814 **Norway and Sweden** enter a union; Iceland remains Danish.

1843 **Althing is** reconstituted. When Denmark becomes a constitutional monarchy in 1849, pressure grows for a constitution for Iceland.

1874 **Christian IX** promulgates Icelandic constitution, granting limited home rule.

1914 **Iceland becomes autonomous**.

1915 **Universal suffrage** is introduced.

1918 **The Act of Union** establishes internal home rule under the Danish crown, which continues to control defense and foreign policy matters.

1940–44 **Occupied by UK** and US.

1944 **Independence as a republic.**

1951 **US air base** built at Keflavík despite strong local opposition.

1972–76 **Extends fishing limits** to 200 miles (320 km); two "cod wars" with UK.

1985 **Declares nuclear-free** status.

President Vigdís
In 1980 Vigdís Finnbogadóttir, a former artistic director of the Reykjavíc Theater Company, became the world's first elected woman head of state, holding office until 1996.

2008 **Financial crisis** forces government to nationalize all three major banks. Central banks of Sweden, Norway, and Denmark put in place a 1.5 billion euro package to keep Icelandic economy from collapsing. Interest rates soar to 18 percent and government falls. Social Democrats under Johanna Sigurdardottir take power.

2009 **Iceland applies to join** the EU.

2010 **Eruption of volcano** over the Eyjafjallajokull glacier spreads an ash cloud over Europe, which severely disrupts air traffic for weeks.

Norway

A mountainous country in Scandinavia that was ruled from Denmark for hundreds of years.

800s **Norwegians join other** Viking groups in seaborne migrations and conquests across Europe and west to Iceland, Greenland, and North America.

872 **Harald I Fairhair** unifies the small Norwegian kingdoms and proclaims himself king of the Norwegians.

1015–28 **Norway becomes** Christian under Olaf II.

1396–1814 **Under the Union** of Kalmar, Danish monarch rules Norway.

1536 **Norway is proclaimed** a province of Denmark, but retains some traditional institutions. Evangelical Lutheranism is declared the established church.

1814 **Personal Union** of Danish and Norwegian crowns ends; Norway adopts a new constitution. The Storting (parliament) elects the Danish prince Christian Frederik as king. However, Denmark had ceded Norway to Sweden by the Treaty of Kiel. A brief rebellion led by Christian Frederik is ended by a Swedish invasion; the elderly Carl XIII of Sweden is elected king of Norway. Norway keeps its constitution, parliament, and government.

1905 **As tension with** Sweden grows, the Storting declares a plebiscite and obtains overwhelming support for independence; Sweden agrees to dissolve the union. Prince Carl of Denmark becomes King Håkon VII of Norway.

1935 **Norwegian Labor Party** (DNA) forms reforming government.

1942–45 **Nazi occupation:** Vidkun Quisling leads collaborationist regime.

1945 **DNA resumes power.**

1949 **Founder member of** NATO.

1957 **King Håkon dies.** Succeeded by son, Olaf V.

1960 **Becomes member of** European Free Trade Area (EFTA).

NORWAY
OVERSEAS TERRITORIES

BOUVET & ST. PETER ISLANDS
Islands in south Atlantic and Pacific oceans.
1739 Discovered by Jean Bouvet de Lozier.
1825 Claimed by Britain.
1930 Dependency of Norway.
1931 Peter I island in far south of Pacific Ocean is made a dependency.

JAN MAYEN
Island in the Greenland Sea.
1614 Dutch whaler Jan Mayen visits and names island.
1921 Norway establishes weather and radio station on this uninhabited island.
1929 Incorporated into Norway.

QUEEN MAUD LAND
Norwegian claim in Antarctica.
1939 Norwegian sovereignty.
1957 Given dependency status.

SVALBARD
Archipelago in the Arctic Ocean.
1194 First discovered by Norsemen.
1596 Rediscovered by the Dutch navigator Willem Barents.
1600s Importance of whale hunting gives rise to rival Dutch, British, and Danish claims to islands.
1920 Spitsbergen Treaty grants sovereignty to Norway but allows treaty signatories to exploit coal deposits.

1962 **Unsuccessfully applies to** join the European Economic Community (EEC).

1965 **DNA electoral defeat** by Center Party (SP) coalition led by Per Borten.

1967 **Second bid for** EEC membership.

1972 **EC membership rejected** in popular referendum by 3 percent majority. Center coalition government takes power with Lars Korvald as prime minister.

1975 **Norway meets** UN target of 0.7 percent of GNP in development aid each year, and has done so for every year since then. Aid goes to Africa, South and Central Asia, and now Eastern Europe.

1981 **Gro Harlem Brundtland** becomes first woman prime minister, but loses power to the first majority Conservative government in 53 years. She regains power in 1986–89 and again in 1990–96.

1985 **Norway agrees to suspend** commercial whaling, but has since lifted the bans on fishing minke whales and on exporting whale products.

1986 **Over 100,000 demonstrate for** better working conditions.

1989 **USSR agrees** to exchange of information after fires on Soviet nuclear submarines off Norwegian coast.

1991 **Olaf V dies**; he is succeeded by his son, King Harald V.

1993 **Oslo accords** between Israel and the Palestinians result from secret Norwegian diplomacy.

1994 **European Economic Area** comes into effect. Referendum rejects EU membership.

2002 **Norway acts** as peacekeeper in the Sri Lankan civil war.

« 202–03 Raiders and Traders

Sweden

An affluent Scandinavian country that was a major European power in the 17th century.

600s **The Svear** (from which "Sweden" is derived) extend their rule over much of central Sweden.

800s **The Svear and Gota** ("Goths") join other Viking groups in waves of seaborne migrations and conquest, which extend across Europe and beyond and last until the 11th century.

1100s **Christianity becomes the** dominant religion throughout Sweden; Erik IX (1150–60) and his successors incorporate Gotland island into the kingdom, which by this stage covers most of present-day southern Sweden.

1319–64 **Under Magnus II** Sweden establishes control over Finland and Norway, but loses Gotland in 1361.

1396 **Union of Kalmar:** Sweden and Denmark are joined in personal union under Queen Margrethe I of Denmark.

1523 **With tension between** Sweden and Denmark growing, the Swedish estates elect a local noble, Gustav Vasa, as king, dissolving the Union of Kalmar.

1527 **Evangelical Lutheranism** is established as the state religion.

1560–95 **Sweden** gains Lapland and northern Finland.

1561 **Sweden gains Estonia,** acquiring Karelia, Ingria, and Livonia (Latvia) by 1629.

1611 **During the reign** of Gustavus II Adolphus (1611–32) Sweden takes an active part in the 30 Years War (1618–48) and becomes the dominant regional power and a major European power. In 1632 Gustavus II Adolphus is mortally wounded at the battle of Lützen, near Leipzig, although Sweden is victorious.

1632 **Gustavus II Adolphus** is succeeded by his six-year-old daughter Kristina. His chancellor, Axel Oxenstierna, continues to manage affairs of state during her minority. She is an enthusiastic patron of the arts and the Swedish court attracts some of the best minds in Europe. Having converted to Catholicism, she abdicates in 1654 and dies in Rome in 1689.

1658 **Sweden gains the Skane** and Blekinge regions of southern Sweden and also, for two years, Trondheim from Denmark–Norway.

1660 **The Peace of** Copenhagen confirms Sweden's empire, which includes Finland, Estonia, Ingria, Livonia, and Pomerania, and several other possessions in Germany.

1679 **Under the "reduction"** Charles XI (1660–97) breaks the power of the nobility and establishes an absolute monarchy with the support of the Riksdag (parliament).

1721 **The Treaty of** Nystad, at the end of the Great Northern War (1700–21), marks the end of Sweden as a major power; it loses its Baltic empire to Russia.

1723 **A constitution is** adopted that subordinates the crown to parliament, although absolute rule is partially reasserted under Gustav III, who rules from 1771 until 1792.

1809 **Sweden is obliged** to cede Finland to Russia; a new parliamentary constitution is adopted later in the year.

Gustavus II Adolphus
King of Sweden from 1611–32, Gustavus led a formidably experienced and well-equipped army into Germany in 1630 that turned the tide of the 30 Years War against the Catholic nations.

1814–15 **Congress of Vienna.** Sweden cedes territory to Russia and Denmark.

1865–66 **Riksdag (parliament)** reformed into a bicameral structure.

1905 **Norway gains** independence from Sweden.

1914–18 **Sweden remains neutral** during World War I but supplies Germany, leading to an Allied blockade.

1917 **The new Liberal** government limits exports contributing to German war effort.

1919 **Universal adult suffrage.**

1921 **Finland gains Åland** Islands as retribution for Sweden's war role.

1932 **Severe recession.** Social Democrat (SAP) government under Per Albin Hansson is elected.

1939–45 **Sweden neutral** in World War II, but grants transit rights to German forces.

1945–69 **Continuing Social Democratic** (SSA) rule makes Sweden the world's most advanced welfare state.

1950 **Gustav VI Adolf** becomes king.

1953 **Nordic Council member.**

1960 **Joins European** Free Trade Area.

1969 **Olof Palme** becomes prime minister, losing power in 1976.

1973 **Carl XVI Gustav** on throne.

1975 **Major constitutional reform:** the Riksdag becomes unicameral with a three-year term. Role of monarchy reduced to ceremonial functions.

1982 **Olof Palme forms** government.

1986 **Palme shot dead.** His deputy, Ingvar Carlsson, succeeds him as prime minister. Police fail to find the killer.

1990 **Carlsson introduces** moderate austerity package, cuts government spending, raises indirect taxes.

1991 **SSA remains** largest party after a general election but is unable to form a government; Carlsson resigns. Carl Bildt, leader of the Moderate Party (MS), forms coalition of nonsocialist parties.

1992 **Austerity measures succeed** in reducing inflation but SSA refuses to support further spending cuts.

1995 **Joins EU.**

1996 **Carlsson resigns; replaced** by Göran Persson (to 2006).

1999 **Swedish cabinet** first in world to have a majority of women. Foreign minister Anna Lindh is stabbed to death.

2003 **Referendum rejects** the euro.

2006 **Moderate Party** under Frederick Reinfeldt returns to power.

2010 **Anti-immigration** Swedish Democrats become the first far-right party to enter the Swedish parliament.

«186–87 The Black Death
«202–03 Raiders and Traders
«262–63 The 30 Years War
«272–73 Masters of War

Denmark

The most southerly Scandinavian nation, once united with Norway, Iceland, and Sweden.

800s **The Dan people** or Danes, who originally came from southern Sweden, join other Viking groups in seaborne conquest across Europe and beyond.

c.980 **Harald Bluetooth** establishes unified Danish kingdom.

1000s **Christianity is** main religion.

1016–35 **Canute the Great** unites all of Scandinavia and England under his rule.

1157–82 **Denmark's ascendancy within** Scandinavia is reasserted during the reign of Valdemar the Great.

1396 **Union of Kalmar** unites Norway, Iceland, and Sweden (including Finland) in a personal union under Danish crown; Sweden and Finland secede in 1523.

1448 **Christian I ascends** throne as the first monarch of Oldenburg royal house.

1533–36 **A civil war** leads to the establishment of Evangelical Lutheranism as the state religion.

1660 **A new constitution** sponsored by Frederick III breaks privileges of nobility and establishes an absolute monarchy.

1814 **Denmark,** an ally of France, loses its remaining German possessions and cedes Norway to Sweden.

1849 **First democratic** constitution.

1864 **Denmark forced to** cede Schleswig and Holstein after losing war with Prussia.

1914–18 **Neutral in** World War I.

1920 **Northern Schleswig votes** to return to Danish rule.

Model occupation
German troops invaded Denmark on April 9, 1940. Unlike other occupied countries, Denmark's institutions continued to function as normal. The Nazis considered it a model occupation until a wave of strikes and protests prompted them to take full command.

1924 **First Social Democratic** (SD) government takes power and introduces advanced social welfare legislation.

1939–45 **World War II:** Denmark is neutral, but Germany invades in 1940. When the Nazis impose anti-Semitic laws, Danish seafarers ferry all but 500 of Denmark's 8,400 Jews to Sweden.

1944 **Iceland declares independence** from Denmark.

1945 **After the defeat** of Germany, SD leads post-war coalition governments.

1953 **A single-chamber,** proportionally elected parliament is created.

1960 **Denmark joins** the European Free Trade Association (EFTA).

1975–82 **SD's Anker Jorgensen** heads series of coalitions.

1982–93 **Poul Schlüter** is the first Conservative prime minister since 1901, in coalition with the Liberals.

2000 **Referendum rejects joining** euro.

2006 **Cartoons of Prophet** Muhammad published in a Danish newspaper spark protests in Muslim countries.

2009 **Denmark hosts the** UN climate change summit at Copenhagen.

«202–03 Raiders and Traders
«256–59 The Reformation
«262–63 The 30 Years War

DENMARK
SELF-GOVERNING TERRITORIES

FAEROE ISLANDS
Group of islands in the North Atlantic.
700s Irish monks first settle the Faeroes; Norwegian Vikings follow in 800.
1035 Formally a Norwegian possession.
1396 Along with Norway, the Faeroes become part of Denmark, and remain so when Norway joins Sweden in 1814.
1816 Faeroes are made an administrative district of Denmark.
1852 The regional parliament is restored but only as a consultative body.
1940–45 British troops occupy Faeroes.
1948 Denmark grants home rule.
1972 Islands vote not to join EC.

GREENLAND
World's largest island, in the North Atlantic.
989 Settled by Eric the Red.
1262 Greenland formally becomes a Norwegian possession.
1396 Along with Norway, Greenland becomes part of Denmark.
1953 New Danish constitution fully integrates Greenland into Danish kingdom.
1973 Joins EC with Denmark despite voting no in a referendum.
1979 Denmark grants home rule.
1985 Leaves the European Community.
2008 Referendum votes for greater autonomy from Denmark.

Finland

A sparsely populated, forested country that has had an uneasy relationship with Russia.

1150s Finns convert to Christianity.

1323 Treaty of Pähkinäsaari: Finland part of Swedish kingdom.

1581 Finland is made a grand duchy under the Swedish crown.

1700–21 Sweden is defeated by Russia in the Great Northern War and is obliged to cede Finnish Karelia to Russia.

1809 Treaty of Fredrikshamn: Sweden cedes Finland to Russia. Finland becomes a grand duchy, enjoying autonomy.

1812 Helsinki becomes the capital.

1863 Finnish becomes an official language alongside Swedish.

1865 Grand Duchy acquires its own monetary system.

1879 Conscription law lays the foundation for a Finnish army.

1899 Czar Nicholas II begins process of russification. The Labor Party is founded.

1900 Gradual imposition of Russian as the official language.

1901 Finnish army disbanded, Finns ordered into Russian units. Disobedience campaign prevents men being drafted.

1903 Labor Party becomes Social Democratic Party (SDP).

1905 National strike forces restoration of 1899 status quo.

1906 Universal suffrage introduced.

1910 Responsibility for important legislation passed to Russian Duma.

1917 Russian revolution allows Finland to declare independence.

1918 Civil war between Bolsheviks and right-wing government. General Carl Gustav Mannerheim leads government to victory at Battle of Tampere.

1919 Finland becomes a republic: Kaarlo Ståhlberg elected president.

1920 Treaty of Tartu: USSR recognizes Finland's borders.

1921 Åland Islands become part of Finland.

1939 Nazi–Soviet Pact gives the USSR a free hand in Finland. A Soviet invasion of Finland is met with strong resistance.

1940 Treaty of Moscow. Finland cedes a tenth of its national territory.

1941 Finnish troops join Germany in its invasion of the USSR.

1944 Red Army invades and Finland, led by Marshal Mannerheim, signs armistice.

1946 President Mannerheim resigns; Juho Paasikivi president.

1948 Friendship treaty with the USSR: agrees to resist any attack on USSR made through Finland by Germany or its allies.

1952 Payment of $570 million in war reparations completed.

1956–91 Coalition governments between SDP and Agrarians hold power.

1989 The USSR recognizes Finnish neutrality for the first time.

1992 Finland signs 10-year agreement with Russia which, for first time since World War II, has no military provisions.

1995 Finland joins EU.

2000 Tarja Halonen is first woman head of state.

2002 Finland adopts the euro.

2008 Former president Marttii Ahtisaari receives the 2008 Nobel Peace Prize.

« 186–87 The Black Death

FINNISH WAR LEADER (1867–1951)

MARSHAL MANNERHEIM

Baron Carl Gustav Emil Mannerheim was a Finnish field marshal. Born into a noble Swedish–Finnish family, Mannerheim rose to the rank of general in the czarist army of Russian-occupied Finland. In 1918 he led his forces against the Finnish Bolsheviks, and in the following year became regent of Finland. Defeated in the elections of 1919, he retired and became a philanthropist. But in 1931 he returned to the fore as head of the Finnish defense council and commanded the Finnish forces against the USSR in the Winter War of 1939–40 and again in 1941–44. In August 1944 he became president and ended the war with the USSR. Ill health drove him to resign in 1946.

Estonia

The most northerly of the three Baltic states, and closely linked to Finland in language and culture.

1219 Reval (now Tallinn) is founded by Danish invaders, who convert the pagan Estonians. Sweden takes control 1561.

1721 By the Treaty of Nystadt, Russia acquires Estonia from Sweden, under whose rule Estonia has become Lutheran.

1881 A policy of russification in public life, including the construction of an Orthodox cathedral in Tallinn in 1900, strengthens national consciousness.

1917 The Russian provisional government allows the creation of a unified Estonian district and elections to an Estonian National Council. The council moves to secede from Russia after the October Revolution when a Bolshevik government is imposed. Declares independence February 1918.

Historic Tallinn
This ancient city has always been an important center for Baltic Sea trade. During the 13th century it was the northernmost member of the Hanseatic League, the mercantile alliance of trading cities.

1919 Assisted by the British fleet and Finnish volunteers Estonia forces the Red Army out of the country; independence is confirmed by the Treaty of Tartu in 1920.

1934–38 President Paets declares a state of emergency and rules by decree.

1940 Soviet forces annex Estonia.

1941–44 Germany occupies Estonia.

1944 Thousands of Estonians fight with the Finns against Soviet forces.

1949 Soviet leader Stalin deports 95,000 Estonians to labor camps as the country is reabsorbed into the USSR.

1985 Reform in the USSR is not matched by hardliners in Estonian Supreme Soviet.

1988 The Estonian Supreme Soviet declares sovereignty.

1989 Estonian made official language.

1990 Elections to the Estonian Supreme Soviet result in a nationalist majority. Independence is declared in 1991.

1992 First multi-party elections.

1994 Last Soviet troops withdraw.

2004 Estonia joins the EU and NATO.

2007 Rift with Russia over the removal of a Russian war memorial from Tallinn.

Latvia

A Baltic nation with sizeable Russian and other minority populations.

1237 The Swordbrothers and Teutonic knights merge (as the Livonian Order) after the territory of modern-day Latvia is subjugated by Germans.

1558 Russia declares war on the Livonian Order over access to the Baltic, capturing 20 Livonian strongholds (but renounces its claim in 1582).

1609 Livonia is ceded to Sweden by Vasili IV Shuisky of Russia in return for troops during the Russian Time of Troubles.

1721 Russia acquires Livonia and Estonia from Sweden under Treaty of Nystadt.

1773 On the second partition of Poland, the Polish part of current-day Latvia becomes part of the Russian Empire.

1917 Opposes Russian Bolshevik Revolution. Declares independence.

1918–20 Invaded by Bolsheviks and German forces.

1920 Latvian independence recognized by Russia.

1940 Incorporated into USSR under the Nazi–Soviet Pact.

1990 Popular Front of Latvia (PLF) wins elections and declares independence from the USSR.

1991 USSR recognizes independence.

1998 Naturalization procedure is eased to help the Russian and other minorities gain Latvian citizenship.

1998–2002 Political instability with four different prime ministers.

1999 Vaira Vik-Freiberga becomes the first woman president. The last Russian military installation in Latvia—the Skrunda radar station—is dismantled.

2000 Latvian proclaimed the only state language, and is used in all schools from 2004. This strains relations with Russia.

2004 Latvia joins the EU and NATO. Latvia elects Indulis Emsis as the world's first Green prime minister.

2007 Latvia signs a border demarcation treaty with Russia.

2009 **The IMF puts in place** a 1.7 billion euro rescue package for Latvia.

2009 **Government collapses** as unemployment soars to 20 percent. Valdis Domrovskis of the center-right New Era party becomes prime minister.

« 186–87 The Black Death
« 446–47 Perestroika

Lithuania

A Baltic country at various times fought over by Russia, Germany, and Poland.

1322 **Gediminas establishes the** capital at Vilnius, and conquers areas of present-day Belarus. His son Algirdas expands Lithuania into present-day Ukraine.

1386 **Poland and Lithuania** unite; at the height of their power in the 15th century, the domains of the Jagiellonian kings stretch from the Baltic to the Black Sea.

1569 **Union of Lublin** binds Lithuania and Poland with a common Diet and a single capital, Warsaw.

1795 **Three partitions** of Poland result in Lithuania becoming Russian territory. Poles and Lithuanians join the uprisings against Russian rule in 1831 and 1863.

1915 **Occupied by German** troops.

1918 **Independence declared.**

1926 **Military coup:** one-party rule under Antanas Smetona.

1940 **Annexed by** USSR.

1941–44 **Nazi occupation.**

1945 **Incorporated into USSR.**

The last pagan
The marriage of Lithuanian Grand Prince Jagiello (above) and Queen Jadwiga of Poland in 1386 united the two countries; Jagiello, a pagan, converted to Catholicism, as did his people.

1991 **Achieves full** independence. Russian troops leave by 1993.

2004 **Lithuania joins** the EU and NATO.

2007 **Lithuania's** application to join the euro is turned down.

2009 **Economic crisis** as Lithuania's GDP declines 12.6 percent in a single year.

« 186–87 The Black Death

Poland

A once-powerful Catholic nation that has been repeatedly partitioned and invaded.

966 **King Mieszko,** who had united three Slavonic tribes and founded the Polish Piast dynasty, becomes a Christian.

1386 **Poland and Lithuania** are united by the marriage of Queen Jadwiga of Poland and Grand Prince Jagiello of Lithuania. In the 15th century the Jagiellonian domains, the largest in Europe, stretch from the Baltic to the Black Sea.

1572 **Sigismund August II,** the last of the Jagiellonian dynasty, dies, after having concluded in 1569 the Union of Lublin, strengthening the common state of Poland and Lithuania. The two capitals of Cracow and Vilnius are replaced by a single capital city, Warsaw, in 1596.

1764 **Stanislas August Poniatowski** is appointed to the Polish throne through the influence of Russian Czarina Catherine II after nearly two centuries of intermittent war between Poland and its neighbors—Russia, Sweden, and the Ottoman Empire.

1772 **The first partition** of Poland takes place between Prussia, Austria, and Russia by the Treaty of St. Petersburg.

1791 **A new liberal** constitution, forced through by Stanislas, reduces the traditional powers of the nobility. The nobles call on Russia for aid.

1793 **Second partition** of Poland: the Treaty of Grodno divides more Polish territory between Russia and Prussia.

1795 **Austria, Prussia,** and Russia negotiate the third partition of Poland, and in 1797 proclaim the abolition of Poland (Finis Poloniae), following Stanislas August's abdication in 1795.

1807–13 **Following the Treaty** of Tilsit between Napoleon and Czar Alexander I, Poland is resurrected as the French vassal state of the Duchy of Warsaw.

1815 **The Treaty of Vienna** allocates to Russia a large portion of the Duchy.

1830–31 **Insurrection in Warsaw.** The Polish Diet creates a national government. Russian troops invade and take Warsaw and direct rule from Russia is imposed.

THE CREATION OF SOLIDARITY, 1980

The independent trade union Solidarity emerged out of a wave of strikes in the Gdansk shipyards in August 1980. Led by Lech Walesa, an electrician, it soon became a vehicle for Poles to demand widespread economic, social, and political changes and eventually to threaten communist rule itself.

Outlawed in 1982 after martial law was imposed, Solidarity re-emerged in the late 1980s as communism collapsed. It became a political party in 1989, electing Walesa as president of Poland in 1990. Solidarity's success sparked 1989's anti-communist revolutions throughout eastern Europe.

1846 **Austria annexes Cracow,** established as a republic by Treaty of Vienna.

1863 **An uprising against** Russian rule is suppressed with Prussian help, ending the liberal reforms of 1861–62.

1918 **A Polish state is recreated** out of Germany, Russia, and Austria–Hungary, after Germany's defeat in World War I.

1921 **Democratic constitution.**

1926–35 **Pilsudski heads military** coup: nine years of authoritarian rule.

1939 **Germany invades** and divides Poland with Russia.

1941 **First Nazi concentration camps** built on Polish soil.

1943 **Jews in the Warsaw** Ghetto rise up against German persecution.

1944 **Warsaw uprising** against the Germans fails as the advancing Soviet army decides not to intervene.

1945 **Yalta and Potsdam** conferences set present borders and determine political allegiance to USSR.

1947 **Communists manipulate elections** to gain power, banning opposition parties.

1970 **Food price increases** lead to riots in the Baltic port cities. Hundreds are killed. The government of Wladyslaw Gomulka falls.

1980 **Strikes force the** government to negotiate with Solidarity: Gdansk Accords grant the right to form free trade unions.

1981 **General Wojciech Jaruzelski** becomes prime minister.

1981–83 **Martial law: Solidarity** movement forced into underground

existence, and many of its leaders, including Lech Walesa, are interned. Walesa awarded Nobel Peace Prize.

1986 **Amnesty for political** prisoners.

1988 **Renewed industrial unrest.**

1989 **Ruling communists** hold talks with Solidarity, which is legalized again. Partially free elections are held: first post-war noncommunist government formed.

1990 **Lech Walesa** is elected president.

1991 **Free elections lead** to fragmented parliament.

1993 **Elections: reformed communists** head coalition. Last Russian troops leave.

1994 **Launch of mass** privatization.

1995 **Leader of reformed** communists Aleksander Kwasniewski is president.

1996 **Historic Gdansk shipyard** declared bankrupt and closed down.

1997 **Parliament finally adopts** new post-communist constitution. Legislative elections end former communist majority.

1999 **Poland joins NATO.**

2004 **Joins the** EU.

2007 **The archbishop of Warsaw** resigns after revelations he helped the secret police under the communist regime.

2010 **National crisis** after President Lech Kaczynski dies in a plane crash. His brother Jaroslaw loses presidential election to Bronislaw Komorowski of the center-right Civil Platform party.

« 188–91 Medieval Europe
« 306–07 The Napoleonic Wars
« 448–49 Raising the Iron Curtain

Czech Republic

The landlocked Czech Republic comprises the ancient territories of Bohemia and Moravia.

962 CE **The coronation of** Otto I marks the beginning of the Holy Roman Empire, of which Bohemia is a founding member.

973 **The bishopric of** Prague is created.

1200s **Under Ottakar I,** Bohemia becomes a kingdom, the only one within the Holy Roman Empire.

1222 **Ottakar I annexes** Moravia after the death of his brother Vladislau, margrave of the territory.

1310 **John of Luxembourg** marries Elisabeth, the sister of Wenceslas III of Bohemia, and becomes King of Bohemia.

1344 **Prague becomes an** archbishopric four years before the founding of the Charles University in Prague. Around this time, Prague is considered the third most important city of Europe, after Constantinople and Paris.

1346 **The Czech king** Charles (son of John of Luxembourg) is crowned Holy Roman Emperor as Charles IV, marking the apogee of the Bohemian kingdom.

1415 **The Czech priest** and scholar Jan Hus is burnt at the stake after leading a religious reformation. The execution sparks nearly 20 years of civil war.

1419 **Hussites seeking to** reform Czech society throw prominent Catholic nobles from a Prague castle window in the first "defenestration of Prague."

1526 **Bohemia comes under** the rule of the Austrian Habsburgs.

1618 **Rising tensions between** Catholics and Protestants result in another defenestration that marks the beginning of the 30 Years War.

1620 **Protestant nobles seeking** to break Habsburg rule are beaten at the Battle of the White Mountain outside Prague.

CZECH STATESMAN (1921–92)

ALEXANDER DUBCEK

A Slovak communist and a fighter in the Slovak Resistance in 1944, Alexander Dubcek (1921–92) led the Slovak Communist Party from 1958 until he took over the leadership of Czechoslovakia in January 1968.

As leader of the "Prague Spring" of 1968, he tried to introduce communism with a human face, relaxing its totalitarian grip on power without ending its rule. The policy failed when Warsaw Pact troops invaded in August and he was arrested, and later expelled from the party. After the Velvet Revolution of 1989, he became speaker of the federal assembly.

1740 **Prussia invades Silesia,** which has belonged to Bohemia since the 14th century. The 1745 Treaty of Dresden confirms Prussian control over Silesia, except for a small part in the east known as Austrian Silesia.

1781 **Under Habsburg King** Josef II, an edict of tolerance benefits both Protestants and Jews. Serfdom is also abolished, although the feudal system is not. German is decreed the sole administrative language of Bohemia and Moravia.

1848 **Czech nationalist** Frantisek Palacky and the Czech authorities refuse to participate in the elections held within the German Confederation (of which Bohemia forms a part) in contrast to the Germans in Bohemia and Moravia who wish to be part of a unified Germany.

1918 **After the defeat** of Austria–Hungary in World War I, Czechoslovakia is established as a democratic state comprising the Czech Lands of Bohemia and Moravia, and Slovakia. Tomas Masaryk becomes president.

1938 **German-speaking Sudetenland** is incorporated into Nazi Germany after a Munich meeting between Hitler and British prime minister Neville Chamberlain.

1939 **Hitler annexes** the rest of Czechoslovakia and creates a German "protectorate" of Bohemia and Moravia. The Diet of Bratislava declares Slovakian independence under the protection of the German Reich and the leadership of a former priest, Jozef Tiso.

1942 **The assassination of** Nazi "protector" Reinhard Heydrich prompts reprisals, including the murder of the male population of the village of Lidice.

1945 **Edvard Benes,** president of the government-in-exile in London, reaches an agreement in Moscow with the exiled communist leader Klement Gottwald on the formation of a multi-party National Front.

1946 **The communists poll** 38 percent of the vote in a general election. Gottwald, as leader of the largest party, is invited to lead an all-party coalition government.

1948 **President Benes swears** in a new communist-dominated cabinet led by Gottwald, which takes power in the "Prague coup" after intimidation by the Communist Party (CPCz) leads non-communists to resign from government.

1948 **The Social Democratic** Party is merged with the CPCz.

1948 **A new constitution** declares Czechoslovakia a people's democracy.

1950 **The start of** a wave of political show trials ushers in purges and executions of party members and officials.

1968 **The "Prague Spring,"** an attempt at liberalization led by Alexander Dubcek, is ended as the USSR and other Warsaw Pact countries invade.

1989 **As communist rule weakens** throughout eastern Europe, Civic Forum, led by playwright Vaclav Havel, takes to the streets in mass, peaceful demonstrations to demand the end of communist rule and free elections. The "Velvet Revolution" achieves its aims and the free elections are won by Civic Forum with Havel as president.

1992 **A two-party system** is established as Civic Forum falls apart. Vaclav Klaus of the right-of-center Civic Democratic Party (ODS) becomes prime minister in 1997, facing the opposition left-of-center Czech Social Democratic Party (CSSD).

1993 **Amicable division of Czechoslovakia** into the Czech Republic and Slovakia.

1998 **Start of EU** membership negotiations

1999 **Joins NATO.**

2003 **Vaclav Havel** steps down as president and is succeeded by former prime minister Vaclav Klaus.

2004 **Last conscripts join** the army as it slims down to become a professional force. Czech Republic joins the EU.

2005 **Stanislav Gross** resigns as prime minister after allegations about his financial affairs.

2006 **Elections result** in a hung parliament. A center-right coalition is approved by parliament in 2007.

2008 **Czech Republic agrees** to host part of new US missile defense system.

2010 **Left-wing Social Democrats** win most votes in general election, but the second-place Civil Platform (OSD) forms a coalition government with smaller parties.

« 306–07 The Napoleonic Wars
« 448–49 Raising the Iron Curtain

Slovakia

Once part of Czechoslovakia, the country is now an independent state.

900s **The Slav peoples** of the region fall under Hungarian rule, and remain part of the Hungarian or Austro–Hungarian empire until 1918.

1918 **Becomes part of new state** of Czechoslovakia.

1939–45 **After the dismemberment** of Czechoslovakia by Nazi Germany, Slovakia becomes a puppet pro-Nazi state under Jozef Tiso.

Puppet priest
A Nazi officer looks on approvingly as Father Jozef Tiso (1887–1947), head of the pro-Nazi Slovak puppet state, gives a speech during World War II. Tiso was executed for treason in 1947.

1944 **Slovak National Uprising** by Slovak partisans against German rule is savagely crushed with huge loss of life.

1945 **Czechoslovak state restored.**

1948 **Communists seize power.**

1989 **"Velvet Revolution" introduces** democracy.

1992 **Vladimir Meciar** of the Movement for a Democratic Slovakia, wins election proposing independence for Slovakia.

1993 **Separate** Slovak and Czech states are established after the two nations part peacefully in the so-called "Velvet Divorce."

1998 **Coalition wins election.** It includes Hungarian Coalition Party representing the 10-percent Hungarian minority, thus reducing ethnic tension in the country.

2004 **Slovakia** joins EU and NATO.

2009 **Slovakia** adopts the euro. Laws passed fining anyone using a minority language inside government buildings.

« 186–87 The Black Death
« 448–49 Raising the Iron Curtain

Hungary

A landlocked, ethnically diverse nation whose boundaries have been redrawn many times.

400s–600s CE **The central Carpathian** basin is successively invaded by Huns and Avars, who are then conquered by Charlemagne in the late 700s.

800s CE **The Magyars,** a Finno-Ugric people from beyond the Ural mountains, move westward and conquer the region.

c.900 **Semi-legendary prince** Árpád, leader of the Magyars, founds a dynasty that lasts until 1301.

955 **Magyars are heavily defeated** by the Holy Roman Emperor Otto I at the Battle of Lechfeld. As part of the truce, Catholic missionaries arrive to convert the Magyars.

1001 **Saint Stephen,** who unifies the Magyars and completes Hungary's conversion to Christianity, is crowned the first King of Hungary. He rules until 1038.

1100 **Hungarian rule now** extends to include Slovakia, Ruthenia, and Transylvania.

1115–1420 **Hungary and Venice** clash 21 times for control over ports on the Adriatic.

1453 **Ottoman Turkish** assaults on Hungary increase after the fall of Constantinople, but in 1456 Janos Hunyadi, military regent of Hungary, breaks the siege of Belgrade and the Turks are kept at bay until 1521.

1458–90 **The reign of** Matthias Corvinus, second son of Janos Hunyadi, marks the golden age of Hungarian history. Mining of the country's gold, silver, and copper deposits makes it one of the richest countries in Europe, while success against the Turks brings it Bosnia (1461), Moldavia and Wallachia (1467), Moravia and Silesia (1478), and a large part of Austria itself by 1485.

1526 **A peasant revolt** allows the Ottoman Turks to enter the country and win a massive victory at Mohács, where King Louis II is killed. Hungary loses its independence, which it does not regain until 1918. The Turks now control central Hungary (including Buda from 1541), while the west of the country submits to the Austrian Habsburgs. Transylvania is effectively ruled by the Ottomans.

1558 **Tensions rise between** Catholic "royal Hungary" and Transylvania, where freedom of worship for both Catholics and Lutherans is guaranteed by the Diet of Torda. These are especially high at the time of the 30 Years War (1618–48).

1606 **Treaty of Zsitvatorok,** designed to establish borders between Habsburg and Ottoman empires, fails to bring peace.

1699 **Treaty of Karlowitz** confirms the expulsion of the Turks from Hungary.

1703 **In Transylvania Ferenc II** Rakoczi leads a revolt, which is crushed by the Austrians, whose rule is confirmed in the Peace of Szatmar of 1711.

1780 **Emperor Josef II,** who rules until 1790, attempts reforms, including the abolition of serfdom, but is thwarted by the Hungarian aristocracy. The Hungarian language is officially recognized. Hungarian literature and sciences contribute to a growing Hungarian nationalism.

1848 **Revolution forces** Emperor Ferdinand to make government accountable to parliament. Nationalist grievances lead to civil war. Ferdinand is persuaded to abdicate and is succeeded by his nephew, Franz-Josef.

1849 **Franz-Josef** is deposed and Lajos Kossuth, one of the leaders of the revolution, is declared provisional governor. Austria appeals to Russia for assistance. Some 200,000 Russian troops crush the revolt and Kossuth flees the country.

1861 **The Hungarian Diet** demands equality between Austria and Hungary.

1867 **A dual monarchy** of Austria–Hungary is created after Austria's defeat the previous year in a war against Prussia.

The two semi-independent states are held together by the emperor, who is king of Hungary, his court, common armed forces, and a common currency and customs union, but there is no single government and very different constitutions. Count Gyula Andrassy becomes the first Hungarian prime minister.

1914 **Austria–Hungary provokes** World War I after the murder of the Austrian Archduke Franz Ferdinand in Sarajevo leads it to declare war on Serbia; Germany comes to Austria–Hungary's support.

1918 **Hungarian Republic is created** as Austria–Hungary is defeated and falls apart at the end of World War I.

1919 **Béla Kún leads** a short-lived communist government. Romania intervenes militarily and hands power to Admiral Horthy, who acts as regent for the Hungarian claimant Charles, but refuses to hand over power to him when he returns to claim his throne in 1921.

1938–41 **Hungary gains territory** by the Vienna Award from Czechoslovakia, Yugoslavia, and Romania in return for supporting Nazi Germany.

1940 **Hungary signs Tripartite Pact** with Germany and its allies against the USSR, but remains out of the war.

1944 **Nazi Germany preempts** the Soviets by invading Hungary. The deportation of Jews and Roma to extermination camps begins. When the Soviet Red Army enters in October, Horthy is forced to resign.

1945 **Liberation by the** Red Army: a Soviet-formed provisional government is installed. Ferenc Nagy of the Smallholders Party becomes prime minister and tries to resist the communist takeover.

1947 **Communists emerge as** the largest party in the second post-war election.

1949 **New constitution:** Hungary formally becomes a People's Republic.

1950–51 **First Secretary Mátyás Rákosi** uses authoritarian powers to collectivize agriculture and industrialize the economy.

1953 **Imre Nagy, Rákosi's** rival, becomes premier and reduces political terror.

1955 **Nagy deposed by** Rákosi.

1956 **Rákosi is forced out** by the Soviets in an attempt to appease Hungarian unrest; student demonstrations demanding the withdrawal of Soviet troops and Nagy's return turn into a popular uprising. Nagy is reappointed premier and János Kádár becomes First Secretary. When Nagy announces Hungary will leave the Warsaw Pact, Soviet forces enter the country. About 25,000 are killed as Kádár takes over as premier.

1958 **Nagy is executed.**

1968 **Kádár introduces** "New Economic Mechanism" to bring market elements

Popular uprising
Soviet troops rolled into Budapest in November 1956 to put down an anti-Soviet uprising. The rebels seen here climbing onto a Soviet tank would soon be brutally rounded up and interned.

to socialism in order to liberalize communist rule gradually.

1986 **Police suppress commemoration** of the 1956 uprising. Democratic opposition demands that Kádár resign.

1987 **Party reformers establish** the Hungarian Democratic Forum (MDF) as a political movement.

1988 **Kádár is ousted;** environmental protests force the suspension of plans for Nagymaros Dam on the Danube.

1989 **End of one-party** state as parliament votes to allow independent parties. Posthumous rehabilitation of Nagy, who is given a state funeral. Round table talks between the government and opposition.

1990 **József Antall's MDF** wins multi-party elections decisively. Hungary moves from communism to free-market capitalism.

1991 **Warsaw Pact is dissolved** as the last Soviet troops leave Hungary.

1994 **Former communist** party, now the Hungarian Socialist Party (MSzP), wins general election under Gyula Horn. An austerity program prompts protests.

1998 **Right-of-center** coalition is formed.

1999 **Joins NATO.** Hungary's airspace is used in the NATO bombing of Yugoslavia during the Kosovo crisis.

2001 **The Status Law granting** special rights to ethnic Hungarians living mainly in Serbia and Romania causes tensions with its neighbors.

2004 **Hungary joins** the EU.

2009 **Hungary receives** $25 billion economic package from EU and IMF following global economic crisis.

2010 **The conservative** opposition Fidesz party wins a landslide victory in parliamentary elections, gaining over two-thirds of the seats.

« 188–91 Medieval Europe
« 206–07 The Rise of Ottoman Power
« 246–47 The Ottoman Empire
« 448–49 Raising the Iron Curtain

HUNGARIAN KING (1443–90)

MATTHIAS CORVINUS

The son of military leader Janos Hunyadi, Matthias I was elected king of Hungary in 1458 in the face of rival claims from his uncle, Holy Roman Emperor Frederick III.

Matthias, nicknamed "Corvinus" after the raven on his emblem, did much to centralize the state during his reign, increasing taxes to pay for a standing army. He also championed the arts and sciences, which flourished in his court. Matthias successfully expanded Hungarian territory, taking many of Habsburg Frederick III's lands. After his death in 1490, however, all these gains were quickly lost.

Romania

A large Balkan country, divided by the Carpathian mountains, with a latinate culture and language.

106 CE **The Roman emperor** Trajan conquers the area now forming Romania, and establishes the province of Dacia. Roman rule lasts until 272. The Latin-derived language and the country's name are hallmarks of lasting Roman influence.

600s **Invasions first of** Slavs and later of Magyars, who occupy and settle in Transylvania.

1000s **Hungary conquers Transylvania.** In the 13th and 14th centuries, separate Romanian principalities emerge in Wallachia and Moldavia but are then conquered by the Turks: Wallachia pays tribute to the Ottoman Empire from 1417, Moldavia from 1456, and Transylvania from 1526.

1699 **The Habsburgs win** control of Transylvania under the Treaty of Karlowitz. Wallachia and Moldavia, however, remain vassals of the Turks.

1828–34 **Moldavia and Wallachia** occupied by Russia.

1848 **Demands for independence** from the various Romanian provinces are swiftly crushed by the Ottoman imperial authorities.

1858 **The Paris Convention,** after the Crimean War, recognizes Wallachian and Moldavian independence within the Ottoman Empire, as the notion of Romanian unity and independence gains strength.

1859 **Unification of Moldova** and Wallachia forms the basis of a future Romania.

1877–78 **At the end of the Russo-Turkish** War, Romania gains its independence, with the reigning prince, Charles of Hohenzollern-Sigmaringen, ruling as King Carol I from 1881–1914.

1883 **Romania is closely** identified with the Triple Alliance of Germany, Austria–Hungary, and Italy. Its royal dynasty is a branch of the German imperial family.

1913 **Gains southern** Dobruja region from Bulgaria at the end of the Second Balkan War.

1914–27 **Ferdinand I** is king.

1914 **At the outbreak of World War I,** Romania remains neutral despite close ties with Germany, but is courted by the Allies who offer the territory of Transylvania as an inducement.

1916–18 **Enters World War I** on Allied side, but is quickly invaded and occupied by Austrian and Bulgarian troops. By the end of the war, Romania has lost

335,700 men, or 44 percent of all its soldiers, with another 120,000, or 16 percent, injured.

1918 **Gains Bessarabia** from Russia after Moldavians appeal to Romania for help against the Bolsheviks.

1920 **Treaty of Trianon**—the post-war peace treaty with Hungary—transfers Transylvania to Romania, which thus gains a sizeable Hungarian minority population.

1924 **Communists banned in** unstable political arena.

1927 **On the death of Ferdinand II,** his heir, Carol, is in France, having been disinherited in 1925. Carol's six-year-old son takes the throne under a regency.

1930 **Carol returns** to claim his throne as Carol II.

1938 **Carol II establishes** royal autocracy.

1940 **Territory forcibly ceded** to the USSR, Bulgaria, and Hungary after pressure from USSR and Germany. Coup by fascist Iron Guard as King Carol abdicates in favor of son, Michael. Ion Antonescu comes to power.

1940 **Signs Tripartite Pact** with Germany and in 1941 enters World War II on Axis side, hoping to recover Bessarabia.

1944 **Romania switches sides** as Soviet troops reach border.

1945 **Soviet-backed regime** installed: the Romanian Communist Party plays an increasing role.

1946 **Romania regains Transylvania** from Hungary and Dobruja from Bulgaria, but not Bessarabia. Communist-led National Democratic Front wins majority in disputed elections.

1947 **King Michael is forced** to abdicate as Romania becomes a communist republic.

1948–53 **Centrally planned economy** is put in place.

1953 **Leaders of Jewish** community are prosecuted for Zionism.

1955 **Joins Warsaw Pact.**

1958 **Soviet troops withdraw.**

1964 **Prime Minister Gheorghiu-Dej** declares national sovereignty; he proposes joint planning by all communist countries to lessen Soviet economic control.

1965 **Nicolae Ceausescu becomes party** secretary after death of Gheorghiu-Dej.

1968–80 **Ceausescu condemns Soviet** invasion of Czechoslovakia, and pursues an increasingly independent foreign policy.

1989 **Demonstrations against** communist rule lead to savage crackdown with many killed. The armed forces join with opposition in National Salvation Front (NSF) to form a government: Ion Iliescu is declared president. Ceausescu and his wife are summarily tried and shot.

1990 **NSF wins election:** political prisoners are freed but many are later reinterned.

1991 **New constitution, providing** for market reform, is approved.

1994 **General strike demands** faster economic reform.

1996 **Reconciliation treaty** with Hungary.

1996 **Center-right coalition** wins elections as Iliescu is defeated.

1997 **Treaty recognizes Ukraine's** sovereignty over territory ruled by Romania in 1919–40.

2000 **Ion Iliescu** wins elections as the center parties collapse; the nationalist Greater Romania Party is second.

2004 **Romania** joins NATO.

2007 **Romania** joins the EU.

2008 **EU warns Romania** over its high level of corruption and threatens to withhold economic subsidies.

2010 **Romanian goverment** agrees to host US missile shield.

≪≪ 448–49 Raising the Iron Curtain

COMMUNIST DICTATOR (1918–89)

NICOLAE CEAUSESCU

Nicolae Ceausescu was the independent-minded communist leader of Romania from 1965 onward. He stressed the sovereignty of his country against the USSR, although he kept Romania in both the Warsaw Pact and Comecon. His obsession with paying off the national debt impoverished the country, and his cult of personality, repression of minorities, and grandiose public works programs made him deeply unpopular. When Romania turned against the communists in 1989, he and his hated wife were summarily tried and executed on Christmas Day.

Moldova

Formerly part of Romania and then the USSR, Moldova has decided to remain independent.

100s CE **The territory forms** part of the kingdom of Dacia.

500s **Slavs migrate to** the area.

1300s **Dragos becomes the** first prince of Moldavia, having migrated with his followers from the northern Carpathians. In 1349 first independent Moldavian state emerges, but is soon a subject of Poland.

1457–1504 **Stephen the Great** defeats a Turkish army at Rahova, but in 1484 his army is defeated and by 1514 Stephen's son Bogdan III pays tribute to Turkey. By the end of the 16th century, Bessarabia (Eastern Moldavia) is under Turkish control; Western Moldavia eventually becomes part of Romania.

1812 **Russia annexes Bessarabia.** Many Moldavians flee west, fearing the introduction of serfdom.

1917 **After the Bolshevik** revolution, a national council declares Bessarabia an autonomous republic of the Federation of Russian Socialist Republics.

1918 **Romanian troops** drive out the Russians and Bessarabia joins Romania.

1924 **A Moldavian** ASSR is established within the Ukranian SSR by the USSR.

1940 **Romania cedes Bessarabia** to the USSR as part of the Nazi–Soviet Pact.

1941–44 **Bessarabia again under** Romanian control.

1944 **Returns to Soviet** control.

1990 **Declares sovereignty** as USSR collapses. Transdniestria (on eastern bank of the Dniester) also declares sovereignty.

1989 **Romanian is reinstated** as the official language.

1991 **Independence as Moldova.** Gagauzia in the south declares independence, but accepts autonomy in 1994.

1993 **Pro-unification parties'** general election defeat leads to the rejection in a 1994 referendum of reunification with Romania.

2001 **Transdniestrian authorities** halt the withdrawal of Russian forces.

2006 **Transdniestia referendum** backs independence from Moldova.

2009 **Protests lead to** new elections after victory of ruling Communist party. In the revote a right-wing coalition is victorious, but in 2010 the Constitutional Court dissolves parliament and orders fresh elections to be held.

Bulgaria

A mountainous Slav country on the Black Sea that was once at the heart of the Byzantine Empire.

681 **Byzantium cedes the** territories north of the Balkan ridge to Khan Asparuh and the first Bulgarian state, with its capital at Pliska, emerges, peopled by Bulgars, tribes of Slavic and Turkic origin who have settled in the region over the preceding 200 years.

865 **During the reign** of Boris I, Bulgaria accepts Christianity; the church follows the Slavonic liturgy, introduced by disciples of Cyril and Methodius. An expansion of the kingdom under Boris's son Simeon from 893 is accompanied by a flourishing in the arts.

1242 **A golden** age, during which the Bulgarian state again expands to the dimensions of Simeon's empire (with its capital at Tarnovo), is ended by the Mongol invasion, causing the Bulgarian state to splinter.

1393–96 **Bulgaria is conquered** by the Turks. The Bulgarian Patriarchate is suppressed, and the church turns toward the Greek Orthodox Church. Turkish domination lasts almost 500 years, and Turks settle in several regions of Bulgaria.

1876 **An uprising against** the Turks, originating in Bosnia in 1875, is brutally suppressed, attracting sympathy for the Bulgarian cause from the Great Powers.

1878 **After the defeat** of the Ottoman Empire in the Russo-Turkish War of 1877–78, the Treaty of San Stefano is signed. It would have created a new, greater Bulgarian state stretching from the Danube to the Aegean. Britain and Austria–Hungary force Russia to reconsider, and the new Bulgaria is divided into three parts by the Treaty of Berlin concluded a few months later: a Bulgarian principality, north of the

Converting the pagans
Saints Cyril and Methodius, portrayed here in an Orthodox church icon, set out in 863 to convert pagan Slavs to Orthodox Christianity, which became the dominant religion of Bulgaria.

Balkan mountains; Eastern Rumelia south of the Balkan mountains and under Turkish rule; and Macedonia and Eastern Thrace.

1885 **Eastern Rumelia is** added to the Bulgarian principality by force. A dispute between Bulgaria and Russia results in the abdication of the Bulgarian ruler Alexander of Battenberg (elected in 1879), and the election in 1887 by the National Assembly of the pro-Austrian Ferdinand of Saxe-Coburg to the throne.

1908 **After Austria–Hungary** annexes Bosnia–Herzegovina, Bulgaria declares itself an independent kingdom, and Ferdinand proclaims himself czar.

1912 **Bulgaria, Serbia, Greece,** and Montenegro defeat Turkey in the First Balkan War, and divide Turkish Macedonia between them. Bulgaria feels aggrieved by the settlement and in 1913 attacks its former allies, who are now joined by Romania and Turkey, but is quickly defeated, losing Dobruja to Romania in the north, Thrace in the southeast to Turkey, and most of its gains in Macedonia to Greece and Serbia.

1915–18 **Bulgaria enters** World War I on the side of the Central Powers to avenge its defeat in the 1913 Balkan War, and declares war on Serbia.

1919 **By the Treaty** of Neuilly, the defeated Bulgaria loses all of Thrace, and thus its coastline on the Aegean, to Greece, and hands over territory in Macedonia to Yugoslavia.

1920 **The left-wing** Agrarian Party wins power. The Communist Party, also strong in the country's first parliament, refuses to participate in government.

1923 **Prime Minister** Aleksandur Stamboliski is killed in a coup. Insurrections by the agrarians and communists fail. Terrorist organizations become active. A succession of coalition governments lasts until a military government seizes power in a coup.

1934 **King Boris III** establishes his personal dictatorship.

1941 **Boris signs Tripartite Pact** with Nazi Germany and its allies and permits the German army to occupy its territory. Bulgaria joins the Axis powers and takes part in the occupation of Yugoslavia, for which it is granted much of Macedonia.

1943 **After Boris III dies** suddenly, the six-year-old Simeon II succeeds him.

1944 **Allies firebomb Sofia** as the Soviet army invades. An antifascist Fatherland Front coalition, including the Agrarian and Bulgarian Communist (BCP) parties, takes power in a bloodless coup. Kimon Georgiev is prime minister.

1946 **Referendum abolishes** the monarchy and a republic is proclaimed. A general election results in a BCP majority.

DECISIVE MOMENT

CONGRESS OF BERLIN, 1878

Bulgarians celebrate their national day on March 3. On this day in 1878 the Treaty of Stefano was signed, ending the Russo-Turkish War and granting independence to Ottoman-controlled Bulgaria. The idea for the new state was short-lived, however. On June 13 the major European powers met in Berlin to rewrite the settlement (below). The UK wanted to limit Russian influence in the Mediterranean by propping up the failing Ottomans. Meanwhile, Austria–Hungary wished to extend its influence in the Balkans. As a result, Bulgaria was vastly reduced, losing Macedonia and Eastern Rumelia in the resulting Treaty of Berlin. The aspirations of the peoples of the Balkans themselves were all but ignored in the new treaty, sowing the seeds for future crises in the region.

1946 **The country is renamed** the People's Republic of Bulgaria.

1947 **Prime Minister** Georgi Dmitrov discredits Agrarian Party leader Nikola Petkov, who is arrested and sentenced to death. A Soviet-style constitution is adopted and a one-party state established. Nationalization of the economy begins.

1949 **Dmitrov dies** and is succeeded as prime minister by Vasil Kolarov. After he dies in 1950, he is replaced by "Little Stalin," Vulko Chervenkov, who begins a BCP purge and mass collectivization.

1953 **Joseph Stalin dies** and Chervenkov's power begins to wane.

1954 **Chervenkov yields** position of First Secretary to Todor Zhivkov, who sets out to make Bulgaria an inseparable part of the Soviet system.

1955–60 **Zhivkov exonerates victims** of Chervenkov's purges.

1965 **Plot to overthrow** Zhivkov is discovered by Soviet agents.

1968 **Bulgarian troops aid** Soviet army in invasion of Czechoslovakia.

1971 **New constitution: Zhivkov** becomes Chairman of the State Council and resigns as premier.

1978 **Purge of BCP:** about 30,000 members expelled.

1984 **Turkish minority** is forced to take Slavic names.

1989 **About 300,000 Bulgarian Turks** are forced out by Bulgarian discrimination. Zhivkov is ousted as BCP leader; replaced by Petar Mladenov. Mass protest in Sofia for democratic reform. The Union of Democratic Forces (UDF) is formed.

1990 **Economic and political collapse:** BCP loses constitutional role as leading political party and changes name to Bulgarian Socialist Party (BSP). A general election produces no overall result but Zhelyu Zhelev, UDF leader, becomes president, with the BSP in government. The country is renamed Republic of Bulgaria and communist symbols are removed from the national flag.

1991 **New constitution adopted:** UDF wins elections.

1992 **Continued unrest** as the UDF resigns after losing a vote of confidence and the BSP and Movement for Rights and Freedoms (MRF) form a coalition government. Zhivkov is convicted of corruption and human rights abuses.

1993 **Privatization** program begins.

1994 **General elections return** BSP to power.

1996 **Financial crisis.** Presidential elections won by opposition UDF candidate, Peter Stoyanov.

1997 **General election won** by UDF with Ivan Kostov as prime minister.

2001 **Despite economic upturn,** voters turn to new party headed by the ex-king, who becomes prime minister under the name of Simeon Sakskoburggotski.

2004 **Joins** NATO.

2007 **Joins** EU.

2008 **EU suspends** aid to Bulgaria over levels of corruption there and failure to tackle organized crime.

«110–13 From Republic to Empire
«150–51 Decline and Fall?
«198–99 The Byzantine Empire

Croatia

Formerly part of Hungary and then Yugoslavia, Croatia is now a fully independent state.

168 BCE **Romans conquer** the kingdom of Illyria, which becomes the Province of Illyricum (later split into Pannonia and Dalmatia).

40 CE **Visigoths begin to settle** on the coast, with Ostrogoths settling farther inland. The whole country then becomes part of the Ostrogothic kingdom.

640 **Croats conquer** the Avars. A Croat duchy is formed, the Croats accepting rule by the Franks in the following century. Byzantines settle along the coast.

925 **Duke Tomislav takes** the title King of Croatia, which is recognized by the papacy. A truce in the conflicts with the Byzantine Empire and its maritime successors, the Venetians, is followed by expansion down the coast in Dalmatia.

1060 **Croatia accepts** the Roman Catholic rite at the Council of Split, which bans services in Church Slavonic (the language of the Eastern Orthodox church).

1089 **The assassination** of King Demetrius Zvonimir leads to anarchy. Croatia is conquered by Hungary, Zvonimir's widow being the sister of the Hungarian king. In 1102 Croatia unites with Hungary, although it retains some measure of autonomy.

1526 **The Turks defeat** the Hungarians at Mohács, and occupy most of Croatia. In 1527 Croatian nobles elect Ferdinand of Austria as their king. Croatia is thus split between the Austro–Hungarian and the Ottoman Empires.

1699 **The Ottomans** are forced to cede Ottoman-controlled Croatia to Austria–Hungary under the Treaty of Karlowitz, after their failure to capture Vienna in 1683. Recolonization of Croatia with Christians takes place, including establishing pockets of Serbian population in Croatia.

1809 **Napoleon captures the** Croatian territory held by Austria–Hungary and reorganizes it into an Illyrian province, along French lines, giving an impetus to Croatian national sentiment. Austria–Hungary regains control in 1813.

1843 **Hungary imposes a** language law making Magyar the official language in Croatia amid increased Croatian nationalism. The Croatian parliament makes Croat the official language in 1847. In 1849 Croatia becomes an Austrian crown land after a revolt in Austrian-controlled Hungary in 1848 is crushed, with the assistance of Croatian (and Russian) troops.

1867 **Croatia becomes** an autonomous land under Hungarian control once more, as Austria and Hungary divide their Slav

Mayhem at Mohács
Here, Turkish leader Suleyman the Magnificent rides to victory over the Hungarians at the Battle of Mohács in 1526. As a result, the Turks occupied most of Croatia for more than 170 years.

lands after the Habsburgs' defeat by Prussia, and establish the dual monarchy of Austria–Hungary. In 1868 the Hungarians recognize the existence of the Croatian nation, albeit subordinate to Hungary, with its official language, parliament, and ruler, invoking the 12th-century agreement to this effect.

1875 **An insurrection against** Turkish rule in Herzegovina spreads to Bosnia and provokes a crisis in the region as it spreads to Croatia, where there is agitation for Bosnia to be incorporated into Croatia. This leads to anti-Hungarian rioting in 1883.

1881 **Military frontier** areas are integrated back into civilian rule.

1912 **After nearly** a decade of nationalist disturbances and the emergence of a majority Serbo–Croat coalition for Yugoslav unity, which takes power in Croatia in 1906, the Hungarian government suspends the Croatian constitution and imposes a dictatorship.

1914 **World War I** breaks out, triggered by the murder of the Austrian archduke Franz Ferdinand, heir to the Austrian emperor, in Sarajevo, the Bosnian capital. Austria–Hungary clamps down on Croatian nationalism. A group of Croatian exiles in London helps in 1915 to form the Yugoslav Committee and continues to demand union with Serbia.

1918 **With Austria–Hungary** on the point of collapse at the end of World War I, the Croatian Diet declares independence from Hungary and appeals for help from the Serbian army. In December the Serbian prince, Alexander, proclaims the united kingdom of Serbs, Croats, and Slovenes.

1920 **Elections to a** Constituent Assembly result in a centrist government led by the Serb Nikola Pasic. A unitary constitution, promulgated in 1921, is opposed by Croat parliamentarians.

1929 **Alexander imposes a** dictatorship to end Serbian, Croatian, and Slovene nationalism and renames the country Yugoslavia. However his rule merely increases Serbian domination, bureaucracy, and repression by the police. Alexander is assassinated in 1934.

1941–45 **Following the Nazi occupation** of Yugoslavia, Croatia is placed under joint Italian and German control with a puppet government run by the fascist Ustase Party. The Ustase persecute the Serbs and others, killing several hundred thousand of them in Jasenovac and other concentration camps. Serb Chetnik resistance fighters retaliate by killing many Croats in Bosnia and elsewhere.

1945 **At the end of the war,** Josef Tito, a Croat and the leader of the communist partisans that had largely liberated the country from German control, takes power in Yugosalvia. Up to 200,000 Ustase troops and civilians attempt to flee

Evil of the Ustase
Croatian fascists, the Ustase, summarily execute ethnic Serbs in Croatia during World War II. The Ustase were especially brutal, even by fascist standards, killing thousands and leaving a legacy of anti-Croat feeling, particularly in Serbia.

to safety in Austria, but are caught by Tito's troops; at least 110,000 are killed. Croatia becomes one of the six federal republics within Yugoslavia.

1980 **After the death of Tito,** Yugoslavia begins to unravel as nationalist tensions, and rivalry between Serbs and Croats, rise to the surface of politics.

1988 **The federal Yugoslav** government falls when its budget proposals are defeated in the National Assembly. Pressure from Croatia and Slovenia over greater republican autonomy is opposed by hardliners in Serbia, who demand a strong centralized state.

1990 **The League of Communists** of Yugoslavia votes to abolish its leading role as democratization sweeps across the communist world. However the communist parties of the six republics differ sharply over how to achieve reform.

1990 **The nationalist Croatian** Democratic Union (HDZ), led by Franjo Tudjman, wins multi-party elections in Croatia. Nationalist parties win elections in Slovenia, Macedonia, and Bosnia–Herzegovina.

1991 **Serbia and its** allies refuse to support the election of the vice-president of Croatia, Croatian nationalist Stjepan Mesic, as president of the collective state. On June 25 Croatia declares its independence. Serb forces invade Western Slavonia and other regions, while the rebel Serb republic of Krajina, in the west of Croatia, is proclaimed. Bosnian Serbs occupy Eastern Slavonia.

1992 **Independence is assured** as Serb forces withdraw, but leave a force in Western Slavonia in the center of the country. Franjo Tudjman is president and involves Croatia in the Bosnian war.

1995 **Krajina and Western** Slavonia are recaptured from Yugoslav forces.

1998 **Eastern Slavonia** is finally reintegrated into Croatia as agreement is reached with the Bosnian Serbs.

1999 **Death of Tudjman;** hardline nationalism begins to lose ground.

2000 **Center-left** Social Democratic Party (SDP) of Stjepan Mesic wins elections and steers Croatia toward Western Europe.

2003 **HDZ returns to power,** but continues pro-Western policies.

2003 **Croatia applies for** EU membership.

2007 **The ruling HDZ party** wins election. An ethnic Serb is appointed to a key position (deputy prime minister) for the first time.

2009 **Croatia joins NATO.** Talks on joining the EU resume after Slovenia drops its objections.

« 110–13 From Republic to Empire
« 246–47 The Ottoman Empire
« 450–51 War in Yugoslavia

Bosnia & Herzegovina

A mountainous country that, after a civil war, is in effect an international protectorate.

168 BCE **The Romans subjugate** Illyria, including the territory of modern-day Bosnia–Herzegovina.

476 CE **After the collapse of** the Western Roman Empire the area is conquered, in turn, by the Byzantine Empire, the Huns, Bulgars, and the Avars, who bring Slavs to the area as vassals.

1180 **Kulin, a member** of the heretical Christian Bogomils, rules a prosperous Bosnia, despite a Catholic crusade that is waged by Hungary on the church's behalf against Bogomilism in the Balkans.

1254 **Bela IV asserts** the authority of the Hungaro–Croatian kings over part of Bosnia.

1322 **Stepan II Kotromanic becomes** ruler of a Bosnia subject to Hungary.

1353 **Kotromanic's nephew Tvrtko** succeeds his uncle and, with Serbia in decline, increases Bosnia's territory. In 1377 he is crowned king of Serbia, Bosnia, Croatia, and the coast, despite failing to prevent an Ottoman Turkish victory over the Serbs at Kosovo in 1389.

1463 **Ottomans conquer Bosnia** and, in 1492, capture Herzegovina (which takes its name from the title herceg—duke— assumed by its ruler Stevan Vukcic in 1448). Significant sections of the population convert to Islam. Bosnia becomes a key outpost for the Turks in their European wars.

1697 **The Hungarian prince** Eugene captures Sarajevo from the Turks. Under the Treaty of Karlowitz in 1699 Bosnia is divided between the Ottoman and Habsburg Empires.

1831 **Hussein Kapetan,** the "Dragon of Bosnia," rebels against the Turks. After occupying territory in Macedonia and Bulgaria, he is defeated and exiled.

1875 **An insurrection against** Turkish rule in Herzegovina spreads to Bosnia and is supported by Serbs and Montenegrins. Serbia, which has long aspired to unification with Bosnia, declares war on the Turks, but is swiftly defeated. Austria–Hungary occupies Bosnia–Herzegovina and the Sandzak of Novi Pazar, a narrow strip of land separating Serbia from Montenegro, after Turkey's defeat in the Russo-Turkish war of 1877–78.

1908 **Austria–Hungary annexes** Bosnia–Herzegovina, with tacit agreement from Russia, weakened by the 1905 revolution and war with Japan. The Sandzak is restored to the Ottoman Empire. Without Russian support, can do nothing and the annexation is recognized by the major European powers in April 1909.

1914 **Gavrilo Princip,** a Bosnian Serb revolutionary of the Black Hand secret society, assassinates the Austrian archduke Franz Ferdinand, heir to the emperor Franz-Josef, and his wife in Sarajevo, the Bosnian capital. An Austrian ultimatum is rejected by Serbia and the war between them spreads across Europe.

1918 **National committee is** formed in Sarajevo after the defeat of Austria–Hungary. Bosnia is united with Serbia in the kingdom of Serbs, Croats, and Slovenes. A period of democracy follows, marred by ethnic disputes.

1929 **Dictatorship is imposed** by King Alexander in attempt to end nationalism. The country is renamed Yugoslavia.

1941 **Germany invades Yugoslavia.** Bosnia and Herzegovina are assigned to Croatia, under the rule of the fascist Ante Pavelic and his Ustase Party. Rival partisan groups form to offer resistance: the Serbian royalist Chetniks and the communist Partisans under Josef Broz Tito, leader of the Communist Party of Yugoslavia, which forms a provisional government in 1943.

1945 **Tito's provisional government** abolishes the monarchy and in 1946 proclaims the Federal People's Republic of Yugoslavia, in which Bosnia and Herzegovina is one of the six constituent republics. In the 1960s, the Muslims are deemed to constitute a "nation."

1972 **Trials of nationalists** begin in Sarajevo in the wake of an increase in ethnic tension throughout Yugoslavia.

1980 **Tito dies** and is replaced by an eight-person, rotating collective leadership from each republic and province. In Bosnia–Herzegovina the local regime is characterized by corruption and authoritarianism.

1990 **Bosnian nationalists** defeat communists in multi-party elections, which are won by the Party of Democratic Action (SDA), led by Alija Izetbegovic, who becomes president after independence.

1991 **Slobodan Milosevic** of Serbia and Franjo Tudjman agree secretly to divide Bosnia between their two countries.

1991 **Bosnian parliament** announces republican sovereignty but remains within Yugoslavia.

1992 **Bosnians vote in** a referendum for independence, which is recognized by the the EU and US. Serbs declare "Republika Srpska," an independent Serbian republic, in Bosnia. A three-sided civil war begins with Muslims defending themselves against both Croat and Serb forces. Elsewhere an uneasy coalition of Muslims and Serbs fight the Croats. The war is marked by Serb and Croat brutality.

1992 **The UN intervenes** by taking over Sarajevo airport to fly in relief supplies,

WAR CRIMES TRIBUNAL IS ESTABLISHED, 1993

On May 25, 1993, the UN Security Council approved the foundation of the International Criminal Tribunal for the former Yugoslavia, with the aim of prosecuting crimes committed in the Bosnian war. The Bosnian Serb commander Dusko Tadic (right) was sentenced to 20 years in prison for crimes against the Muslims in Omarska and other detention camps. The court has given a voice to thousands of victims who have testified as witnesses against defendants.

and imposes sanctions. It also condemns "ethnic cleansing" by Serbs of Muslims and Croats from parts of Bosnia, and approves the use of force to restore peace.

1993 **UN establishes** "safe havens" for Muslims.

1994 **Muslims and Croats** form federation in Herzegovina, while NATO begins air strikes against Bosnian Serb positions.

1995 **Bosnian Serb troops** kill 8,000 Muslims in Srebrenica. Croatian–Bosnian offensive wins back significant areas.

1995 **A peace deal brokered** by US President Clinton is reached at Dayton, Ohio, between the presidents of Serbia, Bosnia, and Croatia. The agreement sets up two separate states within Bosnia—the Muslim–Croat Federation, and Republika Srpska—operating underneath a three-community rotating presidency and a two-chamber representative federal parliament. A UN High Representative retains ultimate control of the country.

1995 **The NATO international** IFOR contingent takes over peace-keeping duties from the UN, and is replaced in 1996 by SFOR, a "Stabilization Force."

1996 **First international war** crimes trial since 1945 opens in the Hague.

1998–2000 **Elections show** continued support for nationalist parties.

2001 **Ethnic Croats briefly** establish autonomy in Herzegovina (in south).

2004 **EU takes** over peace-keeping duties, although the UN retains control.

2005 **Leaders of the three** main ethnic groups agree to a series of constitutional reforms to enhance the authority of the Bosnian government, streamlining the federal presidency and parliament, and reducing the powers of the federal states.

2006 **Bosnia joins** NATO's Partnership for Peace program, a precursor to full NATO membership.

2008 **Former Bosnian** Serb leader Radovan Karadzic is arrested in Belgrade and sent to the Hague for trial (which begins in 2009). In Bosnia, nationalist parties win largest vote share in elections, cementing ethnic divisions.

2010 **Parties favoring** Bosnian unity do well in Croat and Bosnian Muslim areas in general elections, but nationalist parties top the polls in Serb areas.

《 198–99 The Byzantine Empire
《 246–47 The Ottoman Empire
《 450–51 War in Yugoslavia

Rebuilding bridges

In 1993 the destruction by Bosnian Croats of the 16th-century bridge linking Croat and Muslim communities on either side of the River Neretva in Mostar symbolized the collapse of Bosnia itself. The bridge (below) has been painstakingly restored.

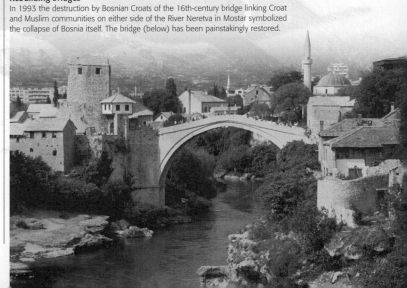

Serbia

Formerly the most powerful republic within Yugoslavia and now an independent nation.

168 BCE   The Romans subjugate the Illyrians. By 9 CE the territory is divided and renamed Pannonia and Moesia. The Western Roman Empire declines in the 4th century and the territory is conquered, in turn, by the Eastern Roman Empire (the Byzantines), the Huns and Bulgars, and the Avars, who bring Slavs to the area as vassals.

626 CE   The Byzantine Empire defeats the Avars and takes over much of Serbia.

879   Croats in the north and west break away from Byzantium and turn to Catholic Rome, but are invaded by Hungary in 1089. Eastern Orthodox Serbs in the south and west become part of the Bulgarian Empire at the beginning of the 900s but gain some autonomy under Stephen Vojislav in the 1030s.

1101   Civil war breaks out in Serbia after the death of King Constantin Bodin.

1165   The Nemanjic dynasty establishes a Serbian empire, which lasts until the death of King Stefan Uros V in 1371.

1389   The Battle of Kosovo Polje means the end of Serbian independence, as Prince Lazar Hrebljanovic is defeated by the Ottoman Turks.

1459   The Turks complete the conquest of the former Serbian Empire.

1699   The Ottoman Empire is forced to cede Croatia and most of northern Serbia to Austria–Hungary under the Treaty of Karlowitz, after failing to capture Vienna. The Ottomans recapture Serbia in 1739.

1804   Anti-Turkish revolts, led by Karageorge, break out in Serbia, and last until 1813 when they are crushed.

1817   Milos Orbenovic, leader of an insurrection against Ottoman rule since 1815, achieves autonomy for Serbia within the Ottoman Empire.

1829   Serbian autonomy is established by the Treaty of Adrianople, which ends a Russo-Turkish war. Milos Obrenovic is recognized as hereditary prince of autonomous Serbia. He attempts to expand Serbia, before abdicating in 1839 in the face of opposition. A period of factional fighting is followed by a coup in 1842 that brings Alexander Karageorgevic (son of Karageorge) to power.

1858   Milos returns to power after Alexander Karageorgevic is deposed. His son Michael succeeds him in attempting to modernize the Serbian government, before being assassinated in 1868.

1876   Serbia and Montenegro declare war on Turkey in support of Bosnian

insurrectionists. Russia declares war in their support in 1877 and, after the Turkish defeat, Serbia becomes an independent principality under the Treaty of San Stefano. Under the 1878 Treaty of Berlin, Serbia loses some territory back to Turkey but gains land in the southeast from Bulgaria. A period of nationalist and international conflict follows in the region.

1882   Prince Milan Obrenovic is proclaimed king.

1903   Serbian king Alexander is murdered by officers in his Belgrade palace after years of factionalism and corruption in government which began during the reign of his father, King Milan. His successor, King Peter, begins liberalization and allows parliamentary government.

1908   Austria–Hungary annexes Bosnia, with tacit Russian agreement. Serbia protests but, without its Russian ally's support, can do nothing.

1912   First Balkan War begins after Serbia, Montenegro, Bulgaria, and Greece form the Balkan League and declare war on Turkey. Serbia increases its territory to the south after the defeat of Turkey, and then gains more land from Bulgaria after its defeat in Second Balkan War of 1913.

1914   World War I is triggered by the assassination by Gavrilo Princip, a Serbian revolutionary, of the Austrian archduke Franz Ferdinand, heir to the Austrian throne, in Sarajevo. An Austrian ultimatum is rejected by Serbia and the war between them spreads across Europe.

1918   Serbian king Alexander Karageorgevic unites the weakened Serbia, Montenegro, and Slovenia into the Kingdom of Serbs, Croats, and Slovenes, after the defeat of Austria–Hungary.

1920   Elections to a Constituent Assembly result in a centrist government led by the Serbian Nikola Pasic. A unitary constitution, promulgated in 1921, is consistently opposed by Croat parliamentarians.

1929   Alexander imposes a dictatorship to end Serbian, Croatian, and Slovene

THE BATTLE OF KOSOVO, 1389

Here, Serb cavalry make an ill-fated charge toward the Turkish lines at the Battle of Kosovo, which resulted in a Serb rout on June 28, 1389. The defeat ended Serb independence for almost 500 years, but Kosovo has remained the heartland of Serb nationalism ever since, even though the region today has fewer than 100,000 Serbs living among two million Kosovo Albanians. Such nationalist sentiments explain the brutal Serbian reaction to growing calls for an independent Kosovo in the 1990s.

nationalism and renames the country Yugoslavia. However his rule merely increases Serbian domination, bureaucracy, and repression by the police.

1934   Alexander is assassinated in France. Yugoslavia is ruled by regents on behalf of the child king Peter.

1941   Germany invades Yugoslavia after the overthrow of a Yugoslav government, which had signed the Tripartite Pact with the Axis powers, and its replacement with a pro-British alternative. The country is partitioned. Rival partisan groups resist the Nazis—Serbian royalist Cetniks and the communist Partisans under Josef Tito, Communist Party of Yugoslavia leader.

1942   Communists set up an Anti-Fascist National Liberation Council, which becomes the provisional government in 1943 and takes power after the Nazi defeat in 1945.

1945   Tito's provisional government abolishes the monarchy and in 1946 proclaims the Federal People's Republic of Yugoslavia with six constituent republics, including Serbia. The majority Albanian region of Kosovo and the Hungarian-speaking province of Vojvodina in the north are given the status of autonomous regions within Serbia.

1948   Tito takes Yugoslavia out of the Soviet bloc after he is accused of "nationalist deviationism" over his reluctance to allow Yugoslavia to become a Moscow satellite. A Soviet economic blockade is imposed. Tito seeks economic help from the US and Western Europe.

1953   Bicameral National Assembly adopts new constitution guaranteeing sovereignty to the six Yugoslav republics.

1980   After the death of Tito, Yugoslavia begins to unravel as nationalist tensions, and rivalry between Serbs and Croats rise to the surface of politics.

1987   Slobodan Milosevic becomes leader of Serbian Communist Party and, in 1989, president of Serbia.

1988   Yugoslav federal government falls when its budget proposals are defeated in

the parliament. Pressure from Croatia and Slovenia for greater autonomy is opposed by hardliners in Serbia, who demand a strong centralized state.

1990   Referendum in Serbia approves constitutional changes, which end the autonomy of Kosovo and Vojvodina. Unrest follows the implementation of the new constitution.

1990   Elections are held in Macedonia, and later in Bosnia–Herzegovina, which result in nationalist victories. Communists retain power in Serbia and Montenegro.

1991   Croatia and Slovenia proclaim independence, followed by Macedonia. Fighting in Slovenia as the Serb-dominated Yugoslav National Army (JNA) attempts to take control of the republic.

1991   Hostilities begin in Croatia between Serb militants, backed by the JNA, and the Croatian military. The fighting is punctuated by a series of shortlived ceasefires, brokered by the EU.

1991   A rump presidency, comprising Serbia (with Kosovo and Vojvodina) and Montenegro assumes federal power. Yugoslav navy blockades Croatian ports.

1992   Bosnia–Herzegovina proclaims independence; civil war breaks out. UN imposes sanctions on Yugoslavia for its role in provoking the war.

1992   New Federal Republic of Yugoslavia (FRY), consisting of Serbia (with Kosovo and Vojvodina) and Montenegro is formed. Elections in Kosovo, declared illegal by the Serbian authorities, result in victory for a Democratic Alliance of Kosovo, whose leader, Ibrahim Rugova, is elected president and proclaims independence.

1992   Slobodan Milosevic is reelected as Serbian president. His Socialist Party of Serbia (SPS) strengthens its position in the Serbian legislature.

1995   Milosevic signs Bosnian peace accord.

1996   UN sanctions formally lifted.

1997   Concessions made by Milosevic after massive protests, acknowledging malpractice in municipal elections. Milosevic becomes federal president.

1998   Conflict in Kosovo escalates as freedom fighters confront Yugoslav army.

1999   Talks between Kosovan leaders and Yugoslavia break down in Paris; Serb "ethnic cleansing" of Kosovan areas precipitates mass exodus. NATO bombs Yugoslav position to force them out of Kosovo, which is now policed by the international force KFOR. Kosovo is now under UN adminstration.

2000   Defeat of Milosevic in first round of presidential election. Opposition candidate Vojislav Kostunica sweeps to power after anti-Milosevic protests.

2001 **Kosovo elects** its own assembly.

2001 **Milosevic arrested;** he is extradited to face war crimes tribunal in the Hague, but dies in 2006 before the case ends.

2003 **Country adopts** Union of Serbia and Montenegro as official title.

2006 **Montenegro votes to** leave the union with Serbia and become an independent nation.

2007 **UN special envoy Martti Ahtisaari** recommends almost total independence for Kosovo as a ward of the EU.

2008 **Kosovo declares independence** from Serbia on February 17.

2008 **The pro-EU** Democratic party and the nationalist Socialist Party form a coalition government.

2009 **Serbia applies** to join the euro.

« 198–99 The Byzantine Empire
« 246–47 The Ottoman Empire
« 450–51 War in Yugoslavia

Montenegro

Once part of Yugoslavia, it became the world's 194th independent state in 2006.

1300s **Montenegro consists** of the small, inland principality of Zeta within Serbia.

1463 **Turks complete** conquest of former Serbian Empire, leaving only Montenegro semi-independent, under Ivan IV.

1499 **Montenegro is placed** under Ottoman suzerainty and from 1566 is governed by the prince-bishop of Cetinje.

1696–1735 **Under Danilo I**, the episcopal succession is made hereditary in the Petrovic-Njegos family, passing from uncle to nephew as the bishops could not marry. In 1715 Danilo I inaugurates a traditional alliance with Russia.

1699 **Ottomans recognize** Montenegrin independence by the Treaty of Karlowitz, and it is confirmed again in 1799.

1878 **Congress of Berlin** recognizes Montenegrin independence; Montenegro gains a narrow outlet to the Adriatic.

1910 **Nicholas I** proclaims himself king.

1913 **Gains territory** from Ottoman Turkey at end of First Balkan War and now shares a land border with Serbia.

1914 **Joins Serbia** in World War I against Austria–Hungary but is invaded and occupied in 1915.

1918 **National assembly** proclaims union with Serbia as part of the Kingdom of the Serbs, Croats, and Slovenes, known from 1929 as Yugoslavia.

1919 **Nationalist revolt against** a Serbian takeover is suppressed by 1924.

1946 **Becomes one of the six** republics within the Federal People's Republic of Yugoslavia under Tito's communist leadership, and gains more land along the Dalmatian coast.

1990 **Communists retain** power in elections as Yugoslavia collapses.

1992 **New Federal Republic** of Yugoslavia (FRY), consisting of Montenegro and Serbia (with Kosovo and Vojvodina) is formed.

1996 **Montenegro severs ties with** Serbia and adopts the German mark and, after 2002, the euro, as its currency.

2006 **Montenegrins vote** in a referendum for independence from Serbia, although the 55-percent threshold is passed by only 2,300 votes.

2008 **Applies to join** the euro.

« 450–51 War in Yugoslavia

Macedonia

A poor former Yugoslav state that has struggled as an independent nation since 1991.

300s BCE **First kingdom of Macedonia** covers territory now occupied by northern Greece and southern Albania, former Yugoslavia, and Bulgaria. Under Philip II and Alexander the Great, Macedonia expands into the Middle East, but disintegrates after Alexander's death, becoming a Roman province in 146 BCE.

400s CE **Slavs occupy Macedonia.**

800s **Macedonia becomes part** of the Bulgarian Empire following two centuries of dispute with the Byzantine Empire.

963 **Macedonia forms part** of the empire of Samuil, which regains territory from the Byzantines, but collapses in 1018.

1380 **Turks occupy** Macedonia, which has an ethnic mix of Slavs, Greeks, and Albanians. Turkish rule leads to decline of Christian population through emigration.

1878 **Russia's victory over** Turkey leads to Bulgarian, Serb, and Greek claims to the remaining Turkish-held Macedonia. Internal Macedonian Revolutionary Organization (VMRO) formed in 1893 calls for "Macedonia for the Macedonians" and a Balkan federation.

1903 **Bulgarian insurgents** spark an uprising in Macedonia, which is brutally suppressed. Some 1,700 noncombatant Macedonian Slavs are shot by the Turks.

1912–13 **Two Balkan wars** lead to a new partition of Macedonia between Greece, Bulgaria, and Serbia. At the end of World

War I in 1918, Serbian-held Macedonia becomes part of Yugoslavia.

1924 **VMRO manifesto** for an autonomous Macedonia leads to a wave of assassinations of opposing federalists by the VMRO. The Yugoslav government crushes the VMRO in 1934.

1941 **Germany occupies** Yugoslavia. Macedonia is largely occupied by Bulgaria. Communist Partisan leader Tito organizes Macedonian liberation movement.

1946 **Macedonia becomes one** of the six republics within the Federal People's Republic of Yugoslavia.

1989–90 **Multi-party elections** held as Yugoslavia collapses.

1991 **Independence declared:** EU recognition is delayed by Greece.

1993 **Macedonia recognized** by EU as the Former Yugoslav Republic of Macedonia. Joins UN.

1995 **Accord with Greece** as it lifts its trade embargo.

1999 **Upheaval in Kosovo** spills over into Macedonia, a quarter of whose population is Albanian.

2001 **Armed insurrection** by Albanian militants inside Macedonia seeking greater autonomy leads to involvement of NATO peacekeeping force.

2004 **Elections grant** more autonomy to predominantly Albanian areas; Macedonia applies to join the EU.

2008 **Greece blocks** an invitation to Macedonia to join NATO over the country's use of the name "Macedonia," which it claims implies designs on Greek territory.

« 96–97 Alexander the Great
« 198–99 The Byzantine Empire
« 246–47 The Ottoman Empire

Kosovo

Albanian-speaking part of Yugoslavia, it won partially recognized independence in 2008.

1180–90 **Ottoman Turks** defeat Serbs at the Battle of Kosovo Polje.

1912–13 **The Balkan Wars end** with the recognition of Albanian independence. Most of Kosovo awarded to Serbia.

1946 **New Yugoslav constitution** confirms Kosovo's status as autonomous region, with limited self-government.

1981 **Death of Marshal Tito** leads to uncertainty. Riots break out in Kosovo.

1987 **The new Serbian leader** Slobodan Milosevic leads a rally in Kosovo of Serb nationalists calling for the closer integration of Kosovo into Serbia.

1991 **The separatist Kosovo** assembly holds a referendum, which votes 99.8 percent for an independent Kosovo.

1998 **Clashes between** the KLA (Kosovo Liberation Army) and the Serb police lead to a violent crackdown with Yugoslav army forces joining in the repression.

1999 **Failure of peace talks.** NATO launches air strikes against Yugoslavia. Huge numbers of ethnic-Albanian refugees flee Kosovo. In June, Milosevic agrees to withdraw military forces and a UN-backed force, KFOR, enters Kosovo.

2008 **Kosovo declares** its independence. It is rejected by Serbia, but recognized by the United States and most of the EU.

2008 **Powers transferred** from the UN authorities to the Kosovan government.

2010 **The International Court** of Justice finds Kosovo's 2008 independence was legal under international law.

Macedonians shatter ceasefire
On June 22, 2001, Macedonia broke an 11-day-old ceasefire with Albanian rebels seeking greater autonomy, shelling alleged insurgent positions such as this mosque in Aracinovo. The conflict ended in September when NATO troops disarmed the rebels.

Albania

An impoverished, former hardline communist state on the Adriatic struggling to tackle great poverty.

168 BCE **The Romans conquer** the territory of the Illyrians along the Adriatic coast, which includes present-day Albania.

300S CE **Successive waves** of invasions of the Balkans precipitate major population movements. The remaining Illyrians seek refuge in the mountains of Albania.

700S **Foreign powers** (including Byzantium, Bulgaria, Serbia, Epirus, Sicily, and Venice) fight each other for control of Albania. The country is divided into feuding principalities.

1380S **Ottoman Turks** subject local princes to their rule.

1443–68 **Under George Kastrioti,** known as Skanderbeg ("Lord Alexander"), the Albanians rebel against Ottoman rule. A Turkish reconquest, completed in 1501, leads to a strong Islamization.

1760 **Mehmed Bushati,** Pasha of Scutari, throws off Turkish suzerainty. The defeat of his grandson Mustapha in 1831 breaks Bushati power. In the south Ali Pasha of Tepelen establishes an independent state; the Turks overthrow him in 1822.

1878–81 **Rebellion first** supports the Ottomans by resisting Treaty of Berlin settlement, but then seeks Albanian independence.

Albania's Stalin
Enver Hoxha (1908–85) led the communist resistance to Italian rule and, after 1944, ran Albania on strict Stalinist principles, pursuing a policy of isolation from the rest of the world.

1912 **After 40 years** of nationalist agitation, Albania asserts its independence from Turkish rule in the First Balkan War (1912–13) and is recognized as a Muslim principality by the 1913 Treaty of London.

1914–18 **Albania** remains neutral in World War I.

1921 **After a long dispute** between Italy, Greece, and Yugoslavia, its neighbors recognize the borders established in 1913.

1924 **After a rebellion** by the landowner Ahmed Zogu, Albania becomes a republic in 1925 with Zogu as president. In 1928 he assumes the title King Zog I.

1939 **Italy invades Albania.** King Zog flees to England.

1941 **Enver Hoxha** builds up the Workers' Party as the main, communist resistance movement to Italian rule.

1944 **A communist state, led** by Enver Hoxha, is established on liberation.

1949 **Albania joins** the USSR-dominated Comecon trading association.

1955 **Founding member of** Warsaw Pact communist military alliance.

1956 **Hoxha refuses to accept** Soviet criticisms of Stalin, and breaks with the USSR, moving toward China.

1961 **Albania excluded from** Comecon and, in 1968, withdraws from the Warsaw Pact. Foreign travel is banned, and thousands are killed in political purges.

1976 **After the death of Mao,** Hoxha severs links with China. Albania is now completely isolated from the communist world and from western Europe.

1985 **Hoxha dies** and is succeeded by his deputy, Ramiz Ali.

1990 **Political reforms** introduced, but slow progress leads to demonstrations.

1991 **In the first** multi-party elections since the 1920s, the communists are returned to power, changing their name to the Socialist Party.

1992 **The opposition Democratic Party** wins elections and Sali Berisha becomes the first non-communist president.

1997 **Economic chaos** as the failure of a pyramid selling scheme causes revolt. King Zog's son, Leka, fails in bid to become king.

1999 **Refugees cross** the border from Kosovo.

2007 **Former president Berisha** of the Democratic Party takes power, ending eight years of Socialist rule.

2009 **Albania joins NATO;** Democratic Party wins elections by a narrow margin.

« 246–47 The Ottoman Empire

Cyprus

Island in the eastern Mediterranean divided by the Turkish occupation of the north.

333 BCE **Alexander the Great's** Macedon army captures the island, which in 294 BCE becomes an Egyptian dependency.

58 BCE **Cyprus passes into** Roman hands.

688 CE **Agreement between** Byzantium and Muslim Umayyad caliphate leaves island neutral until its reoccupation by Byzantium in 965.

A divided island
Icons such as this one fill Greek Orthodox churches in the southern half of Cyprus. Since 1974, the island has been divided into the Greek south and the Turkish north.

1191–92 **Brief English rule** under Richard the Lionheart at the end of the Third Crusade. Richard marries Berengaria of Navarre on the island in 1191 and she is crowned Queen of England and Cyprus.

1489 **The Venetians annex** the island.

1571 **The Ottoman conquest** marks the start of 300 years of Muslim Turkish rule.

1878 **Congress of Berlin:** UK takes over the administration of Cyprus under continued Turkish sovereignty.

1914 **The UK annexes Cyprus** when Turkey joins the Central Powers in World War I.

1923 **Greece and Turkey** acknowledge British sovereignty over Cyprus under the Treaty of Lausanne.

1925 **Island becomes a British** Crown Colony.

1931 **Greek Cypriot demands** for union with Greece culminate in rioting. Direct rule from London is imposed.

1955 **The National Organization of** Cypriot Fighters (EOKA), Greek Cypriots seeking political unity with Greece (*enosis*), begins a guerrilla war, which lasts until 1959. The Cypriot Nationalist leader is Archbishop Makarios III.

1959 **The Zurich** and London agreements provide for Cyprus to become independent under a power-sharing agreement between the Greek and Turkish communities, with trilateral guarantees (from Greece, Turkey, and the UK). UK keeps military bases at Akrotiri and Dhekelia. Makarios is elected president in December 1959.

1960 **Cyprus gains independence** from the UK within the Commonwealth.

1963 **Turkish Cypriots abandon** parliament in protest at Greek domination. As fighting between the two communities intensifies, the UN sends in troops to keep the peace in 1964.

1974 **President Makarios deposed** by the Greek military junta in an attempt to enforce *enosis*. Turkey invades to protect the Turkish community, and partitions the island along what becomes the Green Line; 200,000 Greek Cypriots flee the Turkish north, while 65,000 Turkish Cypriots flee in the other direction.

1983 **Self-proclamation of** the Turkish Republic of Northern Cyprus (TRNC) with Rauf Denktash as president, recognized only by Turkey. More than 100,000 mainland Turks now settle in the north.

1991 **UN refuses to** recognize the TRNC.

1998 **Talks on EU** membership start, following an application in 1990 to join.

1998 **Turkish Cypriot leader** Rauf Denktash proposes a federation that recognizes "the equal and sovereign status of Cyprus's Greek and Turkish parts"; the proposal is rejected by both the Greek and Cypriot governments.

2002 **UN proposes** a peace plan for a common Cypriot state with two component states; the talks collapse in 2003, although the TRNC opens up the Green Line as a goodwill gesture.

2004 **In referendums, the UN plan** is accepted by Turkish but rejected by Greek Cypriots.

2004 **Cyprus joins** the EU, but the Turkish north is excluded.

2006 **In talks,** President Papadopolous and Turkish Cypriot leader Mehmet Ali Talat agree to increased contact.

2007 **Greek and Turkish Cypriots** demolish barriers dividing the center of Nicosia.

2008 **Cyprus adopts the euro.** Opposition communist leader Demtris Christofias wins presidential elections.

2010 **Pro-independence** candidate Dervis Eroglu wins presidential election in TRNC, dealing a blow to reunification talks.

Greece

The cradle of democracy, occupying the south of the Balkan peninsula and over 1,400 islands.

2300–1400 BCE Minoan culture flourishes on Crete and *c.*1400 BCE is superseded by mainland Mycenaeans.

490 BCE The Athenians defeat the Persian forces of King Darius at Marathon, marking the rise of the city-state of Athens and the golden age of Classical Greece.

356–323 BCE Philip of Macedon and his son Alexander the Great complete the conquest of the whole country. Alexander overthrows the Persian Empire and extends Greek rule as far as India. On his death his empire is divided into four.

146 CE The destruction of Corinth by Roman forces leads to the inclusion of the whole country in the Roman Empire.

395 CE As the Roman Empire is permanently divided, Greece falls into the Eastern (later Byzantine) half.

1387–1460 Ottomans conquer Greece.

1821 A Greek nationalist movement declares independence. Ottomans attempt to regain power, but the Greeks appeal for help from France, Britain, and Russia.

1828 Russia declares war on the Ottoman Empire in support of the Greeks: the Treaty of Adrianople of 1829 ending the war recognizes Greek autonomy.

1832 The London Conference establishes Greek independence and installs Otto, son of King Ludwig of Bavaria, as king.

1863 Greece gains the Ionian Islands and Cythera from the UK and Thessaly in 1881 from the Ottomans.

The Greek War of Independence
Inspired by the revolutions in America and France, the Greeks rose against their Turkish overlords in 1821, but suffered a disastrous defeat when the Turks besieged the port of Missolonghi in 1825 (above). The turning point in the war came with the destruction of a joint Ottoman–Egyptian fleet at Naravino Bay in 1827 by British, French, and Russian forces.

1908 Crete, autonomous in the Ottoman Empire, declares union with Greece.

1912 Italy seizes the Dodecanese Islands from the Ottoman Empire.

1912–13 In the two Balkan Wars, Greece gains Macedonia, southern Epirus, and eastern Aegean islands.

1913 George I is assassinated and is succeeded by Constantine I. His pro-German sympathies bring him into conflict with prime minister Eleftherios Venizelos, who takes Greece into World War I on the side of the Allies in 1917. Constantine abdicates in favor of his son Alexander, regains the throne on Alexander's death in 1920, but abdicates in 1922; he is succeeded by George II.

1919 Treaty of Neuilly awards Western Thrace to Greece, shutting Bulgaria off from the Adriatic.

1920–22 Greek attempts to gain Greek-speaking territory in Asia Minor after the collapse of the Ottoman Empire end in disaster; Greece recognizes Turkish rule over most of the disputed territory under 1923 Treaty of Lausanne. A mass migration of ethnic Turks into Turkey and ethnic Greeks into Greece ensues.

1924 A republic is declared and political instability leads to military intervention.

1935 A plebiscite following Venizelos's electoral defeat results in a vote to restore George II. After an inconclusive election in 1936, a right-wing dictatorship under General Joannis Metaxas is established.

1941 Germany occupies Greece: rival royalist and communist-dominated National Liberation Front (EAM) resistance movements fight back. As the German army retreats in late 1944, the two groups fight for control of Greece.

1946 The monarchy is restored.

DECISIVE MOMENT
OUTBREAK OF THE GREEK CIVIL WAR, 1944

On December 3, 1944, a bitter civil war erupted in Athens between the communist (ELAS) and royalist (EDES) guerrilla groups that had jointly resisted the Germans during the wartime occupation. After the German withdrawal an uneasy coalition existed between the two that soon broke as ELAS guerrillas overran the whole of Greece except Athens and Salonika.

Although ELAS conceded defeat in 1945, the group went underground and resumed full-scale guerrilla war in 1946. By the time the royalists eventually won in 1949, mainly due to massive US aid, more than 30,000 people had been killed in many acts of brutality and sabotage (below). For the Greeks the civil war left a deeper psychological scar than World War II. The left remained alienated and outside Greek politics until 1981, while many resistance fighters who had played an honorable part in the defeat of Germany lost their lives.

1946–49 Civil war: victory for royalists led by Marshall Aleksandros Papagos.

1947 Italy cedes Dodecanese to Greece.

1952 After a period of unstable governments, Papagos and his Greek Rally party win elections that also give women the vote for the first time.

1955 Papagos dies: the leadership of Greek Rally, now the National Radical Union, passes to Constantine Karamanlis.

1963–64 Opposition Center Union of George Papandreou wins power.

1967 Colonel George Papadopolous seizes power in a coup; the king is exiled.

1973 Greece is declared a republic, with Papadopoulos as president.

1974 Greece leaves NATO in protest over the Turkish occupation of northern Cyprus. The "Colonels' regime" falls, having failed to help Cyprus; New Democracy (ND) wins elections with Constantine Karamanlis as premier.

1980 Karamanlis becomes president; Greece rejoins NATO.

1981 The Pan-Hellenic Socialist Movement (PASOK) wins elections with Andreas Papandreou as the first socialist premier.

1981 Greece joins the European Community (now EU).

1989 Two inconclusive elections lead to the formation of an all-party coalition.

1990 New Democracy wins elections but faces strikes against economic reforms.

1993 PASOK wins election: Andreas Papandreou returns as premier.

1996 Papandreou resigns as prime minister; succeeded by Kostas Simitis.

1999 Earthquakes in both Greece and Turkey gain a sympathetic response from both sides.

2002 Greece adopts the euro.

2004 Athens hosts the Olympic Games.

2004 ND, headed by Costas Karamanlis, defeats PASOK.

2007 Wildfires sweep through Greece, killing dozens. New Democracy narrowly wins reelection, despite criticism of its handling of the fires.

2009 Opposition PASOK wins snap election over the economy and George Papandreou becomes prime minister.

2010 Loss of confidence in Greek economy leads to funding crisis. Government debt reaches 120 percent of GDP. The EU establishes a fund to bail out Greece (and any other failing states' economies).

Russian Federation

A vast nation, stretching across Europe and Asia, with a long history of authoritarian rule.

862 **Rurik the Viking** establishes order among quarreling Slav tribes in Novgorod. According to legend, he is invited to rule over them. Varangians—the Swedish Vikings—use the river routes of the Dnieper for trade as far afield as Constantinople, the Byzantine Empire and the Middle East.

882 **Oleg, Rurik's successor,** occupies Kiev, and further descendants of Rurik, including the regent Olga, who around 955 is baptized in Constantinople, unite the Kievan and Novgorod states.

988 **Prince Vladimir, Olga's** grandson, is baptized and converts the Kievan lands (Rus) to Eastern Orthodox Christianity. He marries Anne, sister of the Byzantine Emperor Basil II.

1237–40 **The Mongols (Tatars)** conquer Rus, and rule for nearly 250 years. The polity of Rus has disintegrated since its golden age under Prince Yaroslav the Wise into quarreling princedoms ruled by members of the same dynasty.

1328 **The Tatar Khan** gives Ivan Kalita, prince of Moscow, the right of seniority over the other Russian princes and Moscow emerges as the most powerful Russian princedom. In 1326 the Metropolitan of Russia moves his seat to Moscow, after residing in Vladimir since the fall of Kiev.

1453 **Constantinople, the center** of eastern Christianity, falls to the Turks. Moscow comes to regard itself as Constantinople's successor, "the third Rome" and center of Orthodox Christianity. Ivan III of Muscovy marries the niece of the last Byzantine emperor and calls himself Czar (a corruption of the Latin Caesar). When Novgorod falls to Moscow in 1471, the Russian princedoms are united.

1480 **Ivan III ceases to** pay tribute to the Tatars, making Muscovy an independent although isolated nation.

Imperial power
The Winter Palace in St. Petersburg was completed in 1762 for Catherine the Great. The assault on the palace by Bolshevik forces in 1917 was one of the seminal events of the Russian Revolution.

Ivan III
Grand Prince of Moscow from 1462, Ivan assumed the title Sovereign of all Russia in 1493, and, in marrying a Byzantine princess, acquired the emblem of the two-headed eagle of Byzantium.

1501 **Ivan III invades** Poland–Lithuania. His successor Vasili II gains Smolensk in 1514.

1533 **Ivan IV** (Ivan Grozny or "the Terrible"), grandson of Ivan III, ascends to the throne at the age of three. His reign effectively begins in 1547, when he becomes the first ruler to be crowned czar. He conquers the Khanates of Kazan in 1552 and of Astrakhan in 1556, steadily expanding Russian territory south toward the Caspian and Black seas and opening up trade routes down the Volga and across the Urals to Central Asia. In 1565 he makes much of northern Russia around Novgorod his own personal state (the Oprichnina), bringing him into conflict with the boyars (high noblemen). He seizes the boyars' lands and hands them to a service nobility dependent on the czar. The remaining free peasant communities are all destroyed. The second half of his rule is marked by repression of the boyars, many of whom are executed for treason.

1571 **Crimean Tatars** sack Moscow in the civil war caused by Ivan's policy of forced russification and Christianization.

1581 **Russian conquest** of Siberia begins under Ivan IV. Fur trappers and traders establish a series of trading fairs in southern Siberia; the trade in furs is heavily regulated, and brings in great wealth.

1582 **Poland and Sweden** repel Russia's attempt to gain a Baltic coastline.

1595 **Russian control** over eastern Ukraine is secured.

1598 **Boris Godunov,** brother-in-law of Feodor I, Ivan's son, is elected czar. On his death in 1605, the "Time of Troubles" begins—a turbulent period resulting from the lack of a natural successor to the throne, a rise in social discontent, and war in Russia sparked by Swedish and Polish aggression that decimates western Russia.

1611 **Ingria and Karelia** are ceded to Sweden, which occupies the Novgorod area until 1617, when Russia abandons claims to Estonia and Livonia (Latvia) by the Treaty of Stolbovo.

1613 **Mikhail Romanov, first** of the dynasty that will rule until 1917, is elected czar after the Poles are driven out of Moscow. He is succeeded in 1645 by his son Alexis.

1637 **Russian explorers** reach the Pacific coast of Siberia.

1655 **Russian forts are built** along the Amur river inside Manchu China. By the 1689 Treaty of Nerchinsk, Russia abandons the vast region north of the Amur river to Manchu China.

1667 **Poland cedes** Smolensk and Kiev to Russia.

1670 **The first of a series** of rebellions shake Russian rule in the south, including the Cossack rebellion led by Stenka Razin ("Little Stephen") which is eventually crushed. Uprisings by Don and Dnieper Cossacks against Polish rule allow Russia to extend its territories south to the Ottoman client state of the Crimea and west to Kiev.

1682 **Peter I** (Peter the Great) becomes czar after a confused period of palace coups and struggles for the succession. Initially he is joint czar with his mentally challenged half-brother Ivan V under the regency of their elder sister, Sophia. He becomes sole czar in 1696. Peter introduces, by force where necesssary, Western culture, customs, education, economy, and government to Russia. In 1703 he founds St. Petersburg, which in 1712 becomes the Russian capital. War with Sweden prompts Peter to create Russia's first navy and its first modern army. He dies in 1725, having had his son

executed and established the right of the sovereign to choose a successor. Palace coups establish or end the next eight reigns until 1801.

1696 **Peter the Great** takes the strategic fortress of Azov from the Ottomans, gaining Russian access to the Black Sea for the first time. Defeat by the Ottomans at Prut in the Balkans in 1711 ends plans to expand into the Balkans and Russia is forced to hand Azov back, only regaining it in 1736.

1700–21 **Great Northern War** between Sweden and those, including Russia, seeking to deprive it of its Baltic and north German territories. Russia is defeated by Sweden at Narva in 1700 but defeats the Swedish king, Charles XII, at Poltava in Ukraine in 1709. The treaties that end the war in 1720–21 give Russia control over Estonia, Ingria, and part of Karelia, giving it access to the Baltic Sea.

1712 **Seat of government** moved from Moscow to St. Petersburg.

1723–32 **Russia occupies** the Persian-held south and west coasts of the Caspian Sea, before being forced out by the Persians under Nadir Shah.

> " I shall be an autocrat: that's my trade. **And the good Lord** will forgive me: **that's his**."
>
> ATTRIBUTED TO CATHERINE THE GREAT
> (REIGNED 1762–96)

1762 **The German-born** Catherine II (Catherine the Great) becomes empress after leading a palace coup against her husband, Peter III. Her reign extends Russian territory at the expense of Poland and Turkey, and although initially the ideas of the Enlightenment are welcomed in the Russian state, they are suppressed after the French Revolution of 1789. Catherine dies in 1796.

1772 **First partition of Poland** with Austria and Prussia brings gains of territory west of Smolensk. The second partition in 1793 brings west Ukraine; the third in 1795 brings Lithuania and most of Belarussia.

1773 **The Don Cossack** Emelian Pugachev leads a rebellion against the Russian feudal system, and takes control of a large part of eastern Russia. He is defeated the following year.

1783 **Catherine annexes** the Khanate of the Crimea and orders the construction of a huge naval base at Sevastopol on the Black Sea.

1784 **Russian traders from Siberia** cross the Bering Strait into America and establish the first settlement in Alaska near Kodiak.

1796 **On the death of** Catherine the Great, her son Paul I becomes czar. He is assassinated in 1801, after a conspiracy is hatched among sections of the increasingly alienated nobility. He is succeeded by his son Alexander I.

1801 **The Orthodox Christian kingdom** of Georgia voluntarily unites with Russia.

1809 **Russia gains** Finland from Sweden.

1812 **Napoleon invades Russia** and within three months has entered Moscow, but the same night a terrible fire razes the city. Czar Alexander I refuses to surrender; the French, cut off from their supply lines, are forced to retreat through the Russian winter, pursued by the Russian army.

1814 **Alexander I leads** Russian, Austrian, and Prussian armies into Paris. The Congress of Vienna of 1815 redraws the political map of Europe, giving Russia control over the whole of Poland and establishing Russia as a major force in European affairs. Antiautocratic ideas gain popularity among the young nobility during the military campaigns in the west.

1822–65 **Kazakh khanates** are gained by Russia.

1825 **On Alexander's sudden** death, young army officers (the "Decembrists") stage a revolt in favor of the abolition of serfdom and constitutional reform, including a constitutional monarchy. The uprising is suppressed and the new czar, Alexander's brother, Nicholas I, begins a 30-year reign of reactionary policies, characterized by militarism and bureaucracy, which earns him the nickname "the gendarme of Europe."

1830–31 **Insurrection in Poland** is brutally suppressed.

1848 **Revolutions elsewhere in** Europe prompt Nicholas to impose new censorship, new restrictions on academic freedom in Russia's relatively young universities, and a prohibition on foreign travel. Russian troops are sent at Austria's request to put down the revolution in Hungary.

1853–56 **The Crimean War** against Turkey, France, and the UK ends in defeat for Russia. The conflict was prompted by Nicholas's decision to occupy the Balkan provinces of Moldavia and Wallachia in 1853 and Russian threats to British interests in the Mediterranean and to the sovereignty of the Ottoman Empire. Nicholas dies in March 1855 and is succeeded by his son, Alexander II.

1858–60 **Russia gains land** north of the Amur River and the coastal region of Ussuri, giving it access to the warm-water port of Vladivostok. By 1875 it has gained the whole of the large offshore island of Sakhalin.

1859–78 **Russia extends** its territory south into the Caucasus, gaining western Georgia and the whole of Armenia.

1860 **Russian revolutionary movements** emerge, including the influential Narodniks (Populists), who preach that intellectuals could inspire "the people" with revolutionary ideas because the peasantry embody socialism in their communally arranged households. However, in 1874–77 the failure of a Populists' crusade to win the hearts of Russia's peasants leads some factions to turn to terrorism.

1861 **Alexander orders the** emancipation of the serfs and begins a period of reform of local government (creating the *zemstvo* system of rural councils), the judiciary, and financial institutions, although the reforms are limited by remaining within an autocratic framework. Massive discontent remains, however, as the serfs have to pay redemption fees for the land they tilled. The discontent is held in check by the secret police and army.

1866–76 **Russia expands** into the khanates of Bukhara, Khiva, and Kokand.

1867 **Russia sells Alaska** to the US for $7.2 million.

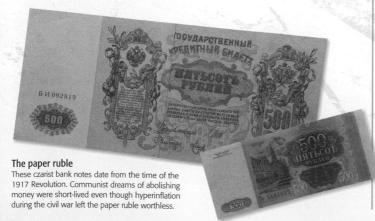

The paper ruble
These czarist bank notes date from the time of the 1917 Revolution. Communist dreams of abolishing money were short-lived even though hyperinflation during the civil war left the paper ruble worthless.

DECISIVE MOMENT

THE FIRST SOVIET, 1922

The Union of Soviet Socialist Republics (USSR) was created after the adoption of its founding treaty by the Congress of Soviets—workers' elected councils—in Moscow on December 30, 1922. Delegates came from four republics—Russia, Ukraine, Belorussia, and Transcaucasia. By 1941, there were 15 constituent republics in the union, each with their own rights but subject to direction from the governing body of the Union, the central Presidium. The 1936 constitution set up various councils and an assembly of deputies; in reality, all policy from 1923 was determined by the general secretary of the party, Joseph Stalin.

Lenin speaks
Vladimir Lenin, seen here galvanizing troops during the 1917 Revolution, was a strong advocate of a federal USSR.

1881 **Russians crush Turkmen resistance** at Goktepe.

1881 **Alexander II is assassinated** in St. Petersburg by the terrorist group Narodnaya Volya (The People's Will), an offshoot of the Populist movement. Alexander III establishes a period of reaction, russification, and militant Orthodoxy. Pogroms against Jewish communities begin.

1884 **Russia** completes its conquest of Central Asia by acquiring the city of Merv.

1891–1916 **Trans-Siberian Railroad** is constructed from Moscow to Vladivostok.

1894 **The last Russian** czar, Nicholas II, accedes to the throne. In the 1890s, Russian industry grows by an average of 8 percent a year, creating a significant and highly localized working class. Marxism begins to attract considerable strength among intellectuals and radicals.

1904–05 **Russian war against** Japan, caused by rivalry in Manchuria and Korea, ends in defeat for Russia and the loss of southern Sakhalin.

1905 **Discontent with war** against Japan, high taxation, and industrial distress erupts in revolution. A mutiny on the battleship *Potemkin* in the Black Sea fleet spreads to other units in the army and navy, and there is a general strike, forcing Czar Nicholas to grant a constitution, a legislative Duma, and a prime minister.

1909–14 **Rapid economic expansion.**

1914 **Russia enters World War I** against Germany, but suffers huge losses, although it has some successes against Austria–Hungary.

1917 **The February Revolution** leads to the abdication of Nicholas II. A provisional government is established. In the October Revolution, the Bolsheviks seize power with Lenin as leader.

1918 **Treaty of Brest-Litovsk,** signed with Germany, ends war. Russia loses Finland, the Baltic States, Poland, Belorussia, Ukraine, and states in the Caucasus.

1918 **Nicholas II** and family are shot.

1918–21 **Civil war** breaks out as the Bolshevik Red Army and counter-revolutionaries struggle for control. Bolshevik control is confirmed in 1921.

1920–21 **Ukraine, Belorussia, Caucasus** states, and Central Asia are reconquered.

1921 **"New Economic Policy"** relaxes state controls after peasant riots and shortages of food. It allows some private commerce and free trade.

1922 **USSR is established.**

1924 **Lenin dies.** The ensuing leadership struggle is eventually won by Stalin.

1928 **First Five-Year Plan:** forced industrialization and collectivization as the New Economic Policy is abandoned in favor of total state control of industry and agriculture.

1929 **Trotsky,** founder of the Red Army and political opponent of Stalin, is exiled.

1936–38 **Show trials and** campaigns by Stalin against actual and suspected members of the opposition send millions to labor camps in Siberia and elsewhere. Up to 7 million are arrested and 3 million killed through execution or internment.

Russia's natural wealth
Gas pipelines such as this one stretch from Siberia to Europe. In 2006 Russia supplied one-third of Europe's oil and 40 percent of its gas. Russia has occasionally used these resources for political ends, cutting off supplies to Georgia and Ukraine.

1939 **Nazi–Soviet Pact** gives USSR the Baltic states, eastern Poland, and Bessarabia.

1941 **Germany attacks the USSR** and its armies advance rapidly, catching Stalin unprepared.

1943 **Great Soviet** victory at Stalingrad halts the Germans, as its besieged army surrenders.

1944–45 **Soviet offensive penetrates** the Balkans and crosses Germany to Berlin.

1945 **Germany is defeated.** Under the Yalta and Potsdam agreements between the USSR, US, and UK, eastern and most of southeastern Europe fall within the Soviet zone of influence.

1947 **Cold War begins** with the US and its Western allies. Stalin, fearing the penetration of Western capitalist values, persecutes returning soldiers.

1953 **Stalin dies** and is eventually replaced by Nikita Khrushchev.

1956 **Khrushchev makes** a "secret speech" at the Twentieth Party Congress denouncing the cult of Stalin. Reforms remove the worst excesses of Stalinist power and repression.

1957 **USSR launches** *Sputnik I*, the first artificial satellite in space.

1961 **Yuri Gagarin is first** man in space.

1962 **Cuban missile crisis** brings the world close to nuclear war. Khrushchev backs down and does not send missiles.

1964 **Khrushchev is ousted** in a coup and replaced by Leonid Brezhnev, who ushers in a period of economic stagnation and political reaction.

1975 **Helsinki Final Act** confirms European frontiers as at the end of World War II.

1979 **Soviet troops enter Afghanistan** in support of the communist government.

1982 **Brezhnev dies,** and is followed by two elderly successors, Andropov and Chernenko, who both die in office.

1985 **Mikhail Gorbachev comes to power** and begins the process of perestroika, "restructuring" the economy. The first of three US–USSR summits results in arms reduction treaties. Nationalist conflicts surface in the republics.

1988 **Law of Cooperatives** permits limited private ownership of businesses.

1990 **Gorbachev becomes Soviet** president. There is the first part-elected parliament.

1991 **Boris Yeltsin is elected** president of Russia. Yeltsin and Muscovites resist a hardline communist coup against Gorbachev, who bans the Communist Party. As Russia and the other republics leave the USSR and set up the Commonwealth of Independent States (CIS), the USSR collapses.

1992 **The country moves rapidly** from communism to free-market capitalism involving a series of cut-rate privatizations of state-owned companies. Russia takes up the seat of the former USSR on the UN Security Council.

1993 **Yeltsin decrees the dissolution** of Supreme Soviet and uses force to disband parliament. Elections return conservative state Duma (parliament).

1994–96 **Russian military offensive** against Chechnya.

1995 **Communists win** parliamentary elections.

1996 **Yeltsin is reelected despite** strong communist challenge.

1998 **Economic turmoil forces** devaluation of the ruble. There is severe recession and rampant inflation.

1998–99 **Yeltsin repeatedly changes** prime ministers in a succession of crises.

1999 **Parliamentary elections:** Yeltsin resigns and the prime minister, Vladimir Putin, becomes acting president.

1999–2000 **Terrorist violence blamed** on Islamic separatists in Dagestan and Chechnya. In a renewed military offensive against Chechnya, the Chechen capital Grozny falls to Russian forces.

2000 **Putin wins presidential** election and consolidates power. He attacks the "oligarchs" who made fortunes in the privatizations of former state enterprises. The Russian economy begins to improve.

2000 **Kursk nuclear** submarine sinks in the Barents Sea with loss of the entire 118-man crew.

2001 **Mergers make Putin's** United Russia Party the largest grouping in parliament.

2002 **Russia reaches agreement** with US on strategic nuclear weapons reduction. Russia and NATO establish a council to cooperate on countering terrorism.

2002 **Chechen separatists** storm a Moscow theater and seize hostages: 128 hostages are killed during the rescue. Two years later, hundreds of children die in the Beslan school massacre.

2004 **Putin is reelected** president.

2006 **Russia cuts** gas supplies to Ukraine over prices. The Kremlin says this is an economic decision, while Kiev claims political motives. Relations with Georgia deteriorate after Russian officers are arrested on suspicion of spying.

2006 **Campaigning journalist** Anna Politkovskaya is murdered.

2007 **Former president** Boris Yeltsin dies of heart failure.

2007 **President Putin's** United Russia party wins a landslide election victory.

2008 **Dimitri Medvedev** wins presidential election. Vladimir Putin becomes prime minister. Tensions with Georgia over the separatist South Ossetia region lead to war. Russian forces pull back from positions in Georgia, but retain a strong presence in South Ossetia. Russia threatens to deploy missiles in its Kaliningrad enclave in response to US intentions to establish a missile shield in Europe.

2010 **Heatwave devastates** the Russian wheat crop. Suicide bomb kills 39 on the Moscow subway.

《296–97 The First Global Conflict
《376–77 The Russian Revolution
《406–07 The Cold War
《444–45 War in Afghanistan
《446–47 Perestroika

Ukraine

The second-largest country in Europe after Russia, Ukraine means "on the border."

800s CE **Varangian Vikings** establish themselves in Kiev and unite the Slavs in the powerful Kievan Rus.

Ukrainian famine
This starving Ukrainian peasant was photographed around 1933. Stalin's decision to requisition all grain for export led to the worst man-made famine in history. At least seven million died of hunger.

DECISIVE MOMENT

CHECHNYA DECLARES INDEPENDENCE, 1991

On November 1, 1991, Chechnya, a Soviet republic, declared its independence as the USSR collapsed. The Chechens of the northern Caucasus have a proud history as an independent people, but were no match for the Russian army that invaded the country in 1994 and smashed the capital, Grozny (left).

A peace agreement was signed in August 1996. Fighting resumed in 1999 and has continued ever since, with great brutality from the Russian forces, who now identify the Chechens as Muslim terrorists rather than as a people seeking to rule themselves.

1240 **Kiev is captured** by the Mongols.

1300s **Poland captures** Galicia while Lithuania expands eastward into the region; by 1386 Ukraine is part of the Lithuanian–Polish commonwealth.

1772, 1793 **In the first two partitions** of Poland, Galicia becomes part of Austria, Ukraine part of the Russian Empire.

1917 **An independent Ukrainian republic** is declared. The following year, Austrian Ukraine proclaims itself a republic and is federated with its Russian counterpart.

1919 **The Red Army invades.** Ukrainian Soviet Socialist Republic is proclaimed.

1920 **Poland invades and western** Ukraine comes under Polish occupation.

1922 **Ukrainian SSR** becomes one of the founder members of the USSR.

1922–30 **Cultural revival under** Lenin's "Ukrainianization" policy.

1932–33 **Ukrainianization policy** is reversed. Stalin collectivizes agriculture, inducing famine to eliminate Ukraine as source of opposition; seven million die.

1939 **The USSR invades** Poland after the Nazi–Soviet Pact and incorporates its ethnic Ukrainian territories into Ukraine.

1941 **Germany invades the USSR.** Roughly 7.5 million Ukrainians die by 1945.

1942 **Nationalists form Ukrainian** Insurgent army, which wages war against both Germans and Soviets.

1954 **Russia cedes Crimea** to Ukraine.

1972 **Arrests of intellectuals** and dissidents by Soviets, as Volodymyr Shcherbitsky, a hardline Brezhnevite, replaces reformer Petr Shelest as head of Communist Party of Ukraine (CPU).

1986 **In the world's worst nuclear** disaster, a reactor at Chernobyl explodes, sending a radioactive plume across Europe, but missing nearby Kiev.

1989 **First major coalminers'** strike in Donbass; pro-Gorbachev Volodymyr Ivashko heads CPU.

1990 **Ukrainian parliament declares** Ukrainian SSR a sovereign state.

1991 **Ukraine declares full** independence, a move approved in a referendum by 90 percent of voters. Leonid Kravchuk becomes president. The CPU is banned.

1993 **Major strike in** Donbass results in a costly settlement, which exacerbates the budget deficit and stimulates hyperinflation. The CPU is reestablished.

1994 **Leonid Kuchma** defeats Kravchuk to become first democratically elected president of Ukraine.

1996 **New constitution** comes into force.

1997 **Friendship treaty signed** with Russia. The accord allows the use of Ukrainian ports by Russia and division of the Black Sea fleet. A cooperation deal signed the following year.

1999 **Kuchma reelected despite** opposition claims of fraud.

2000 **Chernobyl site closed.**

2001 **Growing protests** after Kuchma is linked with the murder of journalist Georgiy Gongadze. Kuchma replaces the reformist government of Viktor Yushchenko after parliamentary defeat.

2004 **Kuchma's chosen successor** Viktor Yanukovich wins contested elections. Victor Yushchenko falls seriously ill and it is confirmed that he has been poisoned with dioxin. Mass protests in Kiev during the Orange Revolution lead to a revote in December and victory for Yushchenko.

2006 **Yanukovich wins** parliamentary elections and becomes prime minister. He clashes with Yushchenko on most policies.

2007 **President Yushchenko** attempts to dissolve parliament to force new elections, leading to constitutional crisis.

2009 **Russia cuts off** gas supplies to Ukraine for a week.

2010 **Viktor Yanukovich** wins run-off presidential election against prime minister Yuliya Timoshenko (Viktor Yushchenko is eliminated in the first round). The Ukrainian parliament ratifies a 25-year extension of the Russian lease on the Black Sea bases.

《 138–39 Nomads of the Steppes
《 186–87 The Black Death

Belarus

Belarus—the name means "White Russia"—became independent only reluctantly in 1991.

900s–1100s CE **Emergence of** the principality of Polotsk on the territory of modern Belarus.

1324 **The area is** incorporated into the Grand Duchy of Lithuania. Minsk becomes an important commercial and cultural center.

1386 **The Grand Duchy** of Lithuania unites with Poland: Belorussia, as it was then known, becomes part of the Lithuanian–Polish commonwealth, participating in wars against the Teutonic Order, the Russians, the Tatars, and the Turks.

1772–95 **The partition of** Poland leads to the region being taken over by Russia.

1835 **Nicholas I decrees** that Minsk shall be a place where Jews can live.

1863 **An uprising** against Russian rule, led by Kastus Kalinowski, is put down and Kalinowski is executed.

1905 **The Russian** Revolution leads to a renewal of the Belorussian national movement. The revolutionary Hromada (community) Party demands autonomy for Belorussia, but wins little support.

1918 **After the Bolshevik Revolution** of 1917, the Belorussian Bosheviks stage a coup and declare independence as the Belorussian Soviet Socialist Republic (BSSR). Germans occupy Minsk.

1919 **Poland invades Belorussia.**

1920 **Minsk is retaken** by the Red Army. Eastern Belorussia is reestablished as a Soviet Socialist Republic.

1921 **Under the Treaty of Riga,** Western Belorussia is incorporated into Poland.

1922 **BSSR becomes part** of USSR.

1929 **Stalin implements collectivization** of agriculture.

1939 **Western Belorussia is** reincorporated into the USSR when the Soviet Red Army invades Poland.

1941–44 **Germany occupies Belarus**, and over two million people, including most of the large Jewish population, die.

1965 **K. T. Mazurau,** Communist Party of Belorussia (PKB) leader, becomes first deputy chair of Soviet government.

1986 **Radioactive fallout after** Chernobyl affects 70 percent of country.

Protest at dictator's "reelection"
Demonstrators gather in Minsk in March 2006, demanding a fresh vote after hardline communist president Aleksandr Lukashenko won a landslide victory. The elections were widely condemned as rigged.

1988 **Evidence is revealed** of mass executions (over 300,000) by the Soviet military between 1937 and 1941 near Minsk: popular outrage fuels the formation of the nationalist Belarussian Popular Front (BPF).

1989 **Belarussian is adopted as** the republic's official language.

1990 **PKB prevents BPF** from participating in elections to Supreme Soviet. BPF members join other opposition groups in the Belarussian Democratic Bloc (BDB). After the BDB wins 25 percent of seats, the PKB bows to opposition pressure and issues the Declaration of the State Sovereignty of BSSR.

1991 **Eighty-three percent vote in** referendum to preserve union with USSR, but as the USSR falls apart, the country declares independence as the Republic of Belarus. Belarus, Russia, and Ukraine later establish the Commonwealth of Independent States.

1992 **Supreme Soviet announces** that Soviet nuclear weapons must be cleared from Belarus by 1999.

1993 **Belarussian parliament ratifies** nuclear nonproliferation treaties.

1994 **A new presidential constitution** is approved; Aleksandr Lukashenko defeats prime minister Vyacheslav Kebich in elections. Monetary union with Russia.

1995 **First full-fledged** post-Soviet parliament elected. Friendship and cooperation pact signed with Russia.

1996 **Referendum approves** constitutional changes, thereby strengthening Lukashenko's powers.

2000–01 **In parliamentary elections** Lukashenko wins again after a clampdown on PKB's political opponents.

2006 **Lukashenko wins** third term as president in a disputed election. Defeated candidate is jailed for "hooliganism."

2008 **The governing party** wins all 110 seats in parliamentary elections.

《 186–87 The Black Death

Africa

The world's second-largest continent was home to sophisticated medieval empires. Since the 16th century, however, it has been ravaged successively by European imperialists, the slave trade, post-colonial dictators, civil wars, AIDS, and poverty.

Armed uprising
Protesters brandish weapons in a demonstration against French rule on August 19, 1955, in Khenifra. Moroccan and Algerian nationalists clashed with French troops here and in 13 other strategically important towns. Over 1,000 were killed in a weekend of fighting.

Morocco

A kingdom in the northwest that has been ruled over by a succession of Islamic dynasties.

500s BCE Originally inhabited by Berbers, the region along the North African coast as far as Lixus (Larache) was first colonized by the Phoenicians. By the 500s BCE their descendants, the Carthaginians, controlled most of the trading ports from Libya to Lixus and Mogador (Essaouira) in Morocco.

264–146 BCE Rome's Punic Wars against Carthage (in Tunisia) eventually result in the sacking of Carthage in 146 BCE and the extension of the Roman Empire along the entire North African coast.

429 CE Vandal tribes cross from Spain to North Africa and begin occupying the area from Tangier to Carthage.

711 Arab armies bring Islam to Morocco and establish the Idrissid kingdom, which rules from 744 to 788.

1053 Establishment of Almoravid dynasty under Yusuf Ibn Tashfin, who conquers West Africa and Morocco. By the time of his death in 1106, he also holds sway over Muslim Spain.

Battle of Alcazarquivir
At Alcazarquivir in 1578 Portugal made an ill-fated attempt to suppress resistance to Portuguese rule in Morocco. The result was a rout and the death of the Portuguese king, Sebastião I (above).

1147 The Almohads replace the Almoravids. Their Moroccan territories are captured by the Marinids in 1269.

1415 Portuguese take Ceuta, the first of many European colonies in Africa. In 1497, the Spanish take Melilla.

1666 The Alaouite dynasty is founded after Moulay Rashid seizes control of Fes from the Saadians. When he dies in 1672 disorder reigns and it is only in 1677 that his son Moulay Ismail regains control of the region. A large slave army wins back all Spanish coastal enclaves except Ceuta and Melilla.

1860 Spain acquires the port of Ifni.

1884 Spain acquires Rio de Oro (Western Sahara).

1904 France and Spain conclude a secret agreement to partition Morocco.

1906 At the Algeciras conference, France and Spain promise to respect Morocco's independence but are given the power over Moroccan customs and police.

1911 In the Agadir Incident, Germany sends a gunboat to Agadir, officially to protect German interests against French expansion. Negotiations lead to Germany recognizing France's rights in Morocco in return for ceding territory in Congo.

1912 A French protectorate is established under the Treaty of Fez after Sultan Abd ul-Hafiz uses French troops to quash rivals; Spain establishes protectorates in the north and far south of the country.

1921 Abd-el-Krim defeats the Spanish at Battle of Annual. Abd-el-Krim sets up a Berber republic in the Rif mountains and is eventually defeated by a vast French and Spanish army in 1926; a guerrilla campaign continues until 1933.

1927 Sidi Muhammad Yousif becomes Sultan Muhammad V of Morocco.

1953 Sultan Muhammad is forced to abdicate by the French because of his support for independence.

1955 Sultan Muhammad returns from exile to conclude independence deal.

1956 France recognizes Moroccan independence under Sultan Mohammed Ibn Yousif. Spain renounces control over most of its territories.

1961 Hassan II succeeds his father.

1969 Spain returns Ifni to Morocco.

1975 International Court of Justice grants right of self-determination to Western Saharan people after Spain announces it will leave the colony.

1976 Morocco and Mauritania occupy and partition Western Sahara; Polisario guerrillas begin a campaign to expel them and win independence for the region.

1979 Mauritania renounces all claims to its part of Western Sahara, which is added to Morocco's territory.

1987 Defensive wall is complete around Western Sahara to keep out Polisario fighters based in Algeria.

1989 Arab Maghreb Union (AMU) creates a no-tariff zone between Morocco, Algeria, Tunisia, Libya, and Mauritania.

1991 Morocco accepts UN plan for a referendum in Western Sahara.

1992 New constitution grants majority party in parliament the right to choose the government.

1993 First general election for nine years. After parties refuse his invitation, king appoints a nonparty government.

1994 King Hassan replaces veteran prime minister Karim Lamrani with Abdellatif Filali.

1995 Islamist opposition leader Mohamed Basri returns to Morocco after 28 years of exile.

1998 Socialists enter government with Abderrahmane Youssoufi as prime minister.

1999 King Hassan dies: Mohammed VI enthroned. Liberalization announced.

2000–01 UN plan for Western Sahara founders; UN proposes a 10-year trial period as part of Morocco.

2002 Confrontation with Spain over control of a rocky islet off the north coast.

2003 Militant Islamic group explode a massive bomb in Casablanca.

« 158–59 Diffusion of Knowledge
« 174–77 The Ascent of Islam

Algeria

Africa's second-largest country has suffered a turbulent post-colonial history.

40 CE Ptolemy, king of Mauretania, is murdered on the orders of Roman emperor Caligula; the kingdom is split into two Roman provinces that become a major source of grain for the empire.

429 CE The Vandals invade and end Roman rule.

683 Arab invasions bring Islam to Algeria.

944 Foundation of Algiers.

1516 Barbarossa, or Khair-ed-din the "red beard," a Barbary pirate, captures Algiers for the Ottoman Empire.

1830 French troops invade, bringing Ottoman rule to an end, although opposition from the Berbers, led by Abd al-Kadir, is fierce and the region is not fully subjugated until 1847.

1881 The three "departments" of Algiers, Oran, and Constantine are incorporated as part of metropolitan France, although from 1900 a governor-general rules with greater local autonomy.

1942 **Allied forces** seize control of Algeria from the French Vichy administration. Algeria becomes a base for the Free French movement.

1947 **An Algerian national** assembly is established, although restrictive voting qualifications mean that few Muslims have the vote.

1954 **The first of** a series of guerrilla attacks marks the start of independence struggle led by the National Liberation Front (Front de Libération Nationale, FLN). French forces numbering 450,000 are deployed in an attempt to retain control of the country.

1958 **French Algerian generals,** fearing that the French government will negotiate with the FLN, stage a coup. As a result Charles de Gaulle returns to power. After a referendum in metropolitan France and its colonies, including Algeria, where Muslim women are allowed to vote for the first time, the Fifth French Republic is established with de Gaulle as president. Meanwhile, the FLN sets up a "free Algerian" government in Cairo with Ferhat Abbas as prime minister.

1959 **In the face** of continued heavy fighting, de Gaulle proposes a referendum on independence for Algeria. French colonists and military personnel opposed to Algerian independence set up the Organization of the Secret Army (Organisation de l'armée secrète, OAS).

1961 **The French government** and the Algerian provisional government agree to begin negotiations on independence. An OAS-led coup in Algeria collapses after four days.

1962 **Negotiations result in** the signing of a formal ceasefire agreement in Evian, France, and in agreements on the holding of a referendum on independence. The French people approve these agreements in a referendum in 1963.

1962 **In a referendum,** 91.2 percent of total registered electorate votes in favor of independence, which is declared on July 3. Ahmed Ben Bella is elected prime minister and, after the approval by referendum of a constitution, he is elected first president of Algeria.

1965 **Military junta topples** the government of Ahmed Ben Bella. Revolutionary council set up.

1966 **Judiciary is "Algerianized."** Tribunals try "economic crimes."

1971 **Oil industry is nationalized.** President Boumedienne continues with land reform, a national health service, and "socialist" management.

1976 **National Charter establishes** a socialist state.

1980 **Ben Bella is released** after 15 years' detention. France gives incentives for the return home of 800,000 Algerian immigrants.

1987 **Limited economic liberalization.** A cooperation agreement is signed with the USSR.

1988 **Amid anti-FLN violence,** a state of emergency is declared.

1989 **Constitutional reforms diminish the** power of the FLN: new political parties are founded, including the Islamic Salvation Front (FIS).

1990 **Political exiles are permitted** to return. FIS wins municipal elections.

1991 **FIS leaders Abassi** Madani and Ali Belhadj arrested. The FIS wins most seats in elections to the National People's Assembly.

1992 **Second round of elections** is canceled. President Chadli is overthrown by the military. President Boudiaf is

assassinated. Madani and Belhadj are given 12 years in jail.

1993 **Political violence led** by extreme rebel Armed Islamic group (GIA).

1995 **Democratic presidential elections** are won by Liamine Zéroual.

1996 **Murders continue, notably** of Catholic clergy and a GIA leader.

1997 **Madani is released** from jail but debarred from active politics.

1999 **Abdelaziz Bouteflika elected** president in poll boycotted by opposition.

2000 **FIS voluntarily disarms**.

2001 **Hundreds die** in Berber protests.

2002 **Berber language** Tamazight is recognized as a national, although not an official, language.

2004 **President Bouteflika** is reelected.

2005 **Charter for Peace and Reconciliation** is approved in a referendum.

2006 **A six-month amnesty** is offered to Islamic militants.

2007 **33 people killed** in bus blasts in Algiers.

2009 **President Bouteflika** wins a third presidential term.

《 158–59 Diffusion of Knowledge
《 174–75 The Ascent of Islam
《 412–13 End of the Colonial Era

Tunisia

North Africa's smallest country has been a province of several ancient empires.

c.1100 BCE **Phoenician traders establish** a port at Utica and gain control of the coastal region from the Berbers.

814 BCE **Carthage founded** by Phoenician Queen Elyssa (Dido). By the sixth century BCE Carthage has a population of 400,000 and controls the coastal trading ports from Leptis (in modern Libya) to Lixus and Mogador in Morocco.

264 BCE **First Punic War** marks the start of three Roman wars against Carthage, culminating in the sacking of Carthage in 146 BCE and Roman occupation.

439 CE **Vandal tribes** capture Carthage, ending Roman occupation.

534 **Byzantine rule** is reestablished.

698 **Arab invaders seize Carthage** and establish a new city at Tunis.

1230 **The Hafsid dynasty** is founded. Tunis becomes the capital.

1574 **Tunisia becomes** a province of the Ottoman Empire.

1883 **La Marsa Treaty** makes Tunisia a French protectorate.

1920 **Destour (Constitution) Party** calls for self-government.

1935 **Habib Bourguiba forms** Neo-Destour (New Constitution) Party.

1943 **Defeat of Axis** powers by British and American troops restores French rule.

1955 **Internal autonomy. Bourguiba** returns from exile.

1956 **Independence. Bourguiba elected** prime minister. Personal Statutes Code gives rights to women.

1957 **The Bey is deposed.** Tunisia made a republic with Bourguiba as president.

1964 **Neo-Destour made** sole legal party; renamed Destour Socialist Party (PSD).

1969 **Agricultural collectivization,** begun 1964, is abandoned.

1974 **Bourguiba is elected president**-for-life by National Assembly.

1974–76 **Hundreds imprisoned for** belonging to "illegal organizations."

1978 **Trade union movement,** UGTT, holds 24-hour general strike.

1983–94 **Palestine Liberation** Organization has headquarters in Tunis.

1987 **Fundamentalist leader** Rachid Ghannouchi is arrested. Ben Ali takes over the presidency after doctors certify Bourguiba senile. PSD renamed Constitutional Democratic Rally (RCD).

1988 **Most political prisoners** released. Reforms introduce multi-party system.

1991 **Abortive coup is blamed** on fundamentalist party al-Nahda, which is banned.

1996 **Opposition leader** Mohammed Moada of the Movement of Social Democrats (MDA) is imprisoned.

1999 **Ben Ali** and the RCD again dominate elections.

2006 **Government campaigns** against the wearing of headscarves by women.

2007 **Islamist militants** clash with security forces in Tunis.

2009 **President Ben Ali** wins a fifth term.

2011 **Ben Ali** is forced to stand down after massive street protests and flees to Saudi Arabia.

《 158–59 Diffusion of Knowledge
《 174–75 The Ascent of Islam
《 200–01 The Crusades
《 246–47 The Ottoman Empire

The Barbary pirates
Pirates operating out of ports on the Barbary coast terrorized the Mediterranean for centuries. The French tried to suppress them with battleships in 1688 (above), but it was not until 1815 that the threat was lifted.

Libya

An Arab country that was a pariah state for decades until trade sanctions were lifted in 2004.

c.700 BCE Phoenician traders establish settlements in Tripolitania, in the northwest, while Cyrenaica in the northeast is settled by Greeks.

1st century BCE Coastal region becomes part of Roman Empire. Roman rule is subsequently extended inland to Fezzan.

647 CE Arab invasions end Byzantine rule.

1158 Almohads from Morocco establish control over Tripolitania and rule for the next 350 years. Cyrenaica comes under Egyptian control.

1510 Tripoli is captured by Spanish King Ferdinand.

1551 Sinan Pasha recaptures Tripoli, establishing Ottoman rule. Turkish pashas rule from Tripoli.

1711 Ahmad Karamanli kills Ottoman pasha. Governorship of Tripoli becomes hereditary office of the Karamanli family.

1835 Ottoman forces are dispatched to Tripoli as a result of a disputed succession within the Karamanli family. Karamanli leader is deposed. Within a few years a militant Muslim sect known as the Sanusi or Senussi is founded.

1911 Italy attacks Tripoli and Libyan ports. In 1912 the Ottoman Empire yields control of Libya to Italy in the Treaty of Ouchy.

1914 Italian military supremacy is established in most of the country, but there are continuing attacks from rebel Senussi in the south.

1932 The Italians reestablish control after the defeat of Senussi forces seeking self-government. Italian colonists begin to arrive.

Roman Libya
This magnificent Roman amphitheater stands amid the ruins of Leptis Magna, one of three Roman cities that gave their name to Tripolitania, and thus to modern Tripoli, the capital of Libya.

1943 British forces finally capture Tripoli and set up a military administration.

1951 The United Republic of Libya (comprising Tripolitania, Cyrenaica, and Fezzan) is proclaimed with Mohammed Sayed Idris el-Senussi, the Emir of Cyrenaica, as king.

1969 King Idris is deposed in a bloodless coup by the Revolutionary Command Council led by Colonel Muammar Gaddafi. Tripoli Charter sets up an alliance with Egypt and Sudan.

1970 UK and US military ordered out. Property of Italians and Jews is confiscated. Western oil company assets are nationalized.

1973 Libya forms abortive union with Egypt. Gaddafi launches the "Cultural Revolution"; occupies Aozou Strip in Chad.

1974 Libya forms union with Tunisia.

1977 Official name changed to the Great Socialist People's Libyan Arab Jamahiriyah.

1984 Gunman at Libyan embassy in London kills a policewoman; UK severs diplomatic relations with Libya (until 1999). Libya signs Oudja Accord with Morocco for an Arab African Federation.

1985 Libya expels 30,000 foreign workers; Tunisia cuts diplomatic links.

1986 US aircraft bomb Libya, killing 101 people and destroying Gaddafi's residence in punishment for Libya's alleged support of international terrorism.

1988 Pan-Am airliner explodes over Lockerbie, Scotland. Libyan involvement is alleged.

1989 Arab Maghreb Union established with Algeria, Morocco, Mauritania, and Tunisia. Libya and Chad ceasefire in Aozou Strip.

1992–93 UN sanctions imposed as Libya fails to hand over Lockerbie suspects.

1994 Religious leaders obtain the right to issue religious fatwas for first time

since 1969. The contested Aozou strip is finally returned to Chad.

1996 US imposes penalties on companies investing in Libya's energy sector.

1999 Lockerbie suspects handed over for trial in the Netherlands under Scottish law; UN sanctions are eased as a result.

2001 Lockerbie trial verdict: one suspect is convicted and the other is released. Sanctions are eased further.

2003 Libya announces it will end its development of weapons of mass destruction and pay compenstion to victims of its 1980s terrorist campaigns; sanctions are finally lifted in 2004.

2006 US restores full diplomatic ties with Libya.

2009 Abdelbaset Ali al-Megrahi, convicted of involvement in the Lockerbie bombing, is transferred from prison in Scotland to Libya on health grounds.

2011 Street protests lead to civil war. In Benghazi and eastern Libya the opposition takes control. UN no-fly zone imposed.

« 158–59 Diffusion of Knowledge
« 174–75 The Ascent of Islam
« 178–79 Islamic Treasures

Niger

Once the heartland of Africa's mighty medieval empires, but today one of its poorest countries.

1200s–1500s Empires of Mali and Songhay rise to power in the region.

1300s Agadez becomes an important center of trans-Sahara trade.

1883–1904 France overcomes the powerful Islamic Sokoto Empire and establishes control over the country, finally occupying Agadez after strong Tuareg resistance.

1916–17 The Tuareg occupy Agadez and control the Air Mountains.

1950s Two political movements emerge, the radical Sawaba party of Djibo Bakary and the conservative Niger Progressive Party (PPN) of Hamani Diori. Sawaba is banned in 1959.

1960 Independence from France: Diori becomes president.

1968 French open uranium mines.

1973 Sixty percent of livestock die in a severe drought.

1974 Military coup under General Seyni Kountché.

1984 Niger River dries up in a drought. Uranium boom ends.

1987 Kountché dies. General Ali Saibou eases transition to democracy.

1990–95 Tuareg rebellion.

1992 Multi-party constitution leads to democratic elections in 1993.

1996 Military coup. A new constitution in 1999 leads to multi-party elections won by Mamadou Tandja.

2004 Mamadou Tandja wins second presidential term.

2005 Ceremony at which 7,000 slaves are to be freed is canceled as the government denies the existence of slavery. Widespread protests at tax increases on basic foods.

2009 President Tandja suspends the constitution and pushes through a referendum allowing him to stand for a third term. He then wins elections which are boycotted by the opposition.

2010 President Tandja is ousted in military coup.

« 360–61 The Scramble for Africa

Chad

A poor, largely desert nation ruled by ancient African kingdoms before being colonized by France.

800s Kanem–Bornu Empire is founded in the north of what is now Chad.

1500s–1600s Baguirmi and Ouaddai kingdoms hold sway over the region.

1878 Rabah Zobeir begins the conquest of Chad from Sudan.

1900 French defeat Zobeir at Kusseri.

1959 Preindependence elections result in victory for François (later Ngarta) Tombalbaye, who becomes prime minister.

1960 Independence from France.

1973 Libyans seize Aozou strip in north.

1975 Coup by General Félix Malloum.

1979–82 North-south civil war.

1982 Hissène Habré, a northerner, defeats Oueddei; he holds power to 1990.

1990 Idriss Déby seizes power and holds power in successive elections.

1994 Libya relinquishes Aozou strip.

1996 National ceasefire; new constitution.

1999–2003 Rebellion in north is ended with peace deal.

2005 Chad declares war on Sudan for trying to destabilize Chad's border region in the wake of the Darfur crisis.

2006 **Hundreds die** in an attempted coup against President Déby.

2008 **Rebel offensive** reaches outskirts of N'Djamena before it is repelled.

2010 **The Chad-Sudan border** is opened again after a seven-year closure.

« 280–81   The Slave Trade

Sudan

Africa's largest country, divided between a Muslim north and an animist and Christian south.

c.1580–1050 BCE **New Kingdom** in Egypt expands its frontiers up the Nile River south into Nubia (the north of modern Sudan). By the 11th century BCE, Egyptian control of Nubia is weakened and a separate kingdom is established in Kush, farther to the south, which between 770–716 BCE conquers Egypt.

641 CE **Muslim Arabs conquer** what is now Sudan. At this time the name "Sudan" is generally used to refer to the whole belt of territory immediately south of the Sahara, known in Arabic as "bilad al-Sudan" or the "land of the black men."

1821 **Northern Sudan is** conquered by the viceroy of Egypt, Mohammed Ali. Trade routes are opened up through the southern Sudd swamps. Slave trade kills much of the southern population.

1874–80 **The Sudan** is administered for the Egyptian viceroy by the British General Gordon.

1881 **Muhammad Ahmed el-Mahdi** declares a holy war against the Egyptian administration in Khartoum.

1882 **British take over Egypt.**

1883 **Muslim revolt** led by the Mahdi, whose forces capture Khartoum in 1885.

1898 **Mahdists are defeated** by the British at Omdurman.

1954 **Becomes self-governing.**

1955 **Rebellion in the south** starts 17-year-long civil war.

1956 **Gains independence as republic.**

1958–64 **Military rule.**

1965 **Civilian revolution:** elections held.

1969 **Military coup led by** Colonel Jaafar Nimeiri.

1972 **South gets limited** autonomy.

1973 **Sudanese Socialist Union** is sole party.

1983 **Southern rebellion resumes.**

1984 **Devastating drought.**

1989 **General Omar Bashir** takes over.

1991 **Sharia penal code** is instituted.

2001 **Bashir ousts fundamentalist** al-Turabi from leadership. New attempts to make peace with southern rebels.

2003 **Pro-government** Arab "Janjaweed" militias carry out systematic killings of African villagers in the Darfur region, an act seen by many as genocide.

2005 **New constitution** grants the south degree of autonomy. Former rebel leader John Garang becomes vice president, but dies in a helicopter crash.

2006 **Fighting continues** in Darfur as the smaller rebel groups reject the peace settlement.

2007 **A United Nations** peacekeeping mission for Darfur is established.

2009 **The International Criminal Court** issues a warrant for the arrest of President Bashir of Sudan on charges of genocide.

2010 **The Justice and Equality Movement** (JEM), the main rebel group in Darfur, signs peace accord with the government.

2011 **Referendum in the south** votes overwhelmingly for secession.

« 174–75   The Ascent of Islam
« 360–61   The Scramble for Africa

Egypt

Home to one of the world's oldest civilizations, which emerged along the Nile.

c.3000 BCE **With the foundation** of the Old Kingdom, the fertile lands of Upper and Lower Egypt along the Nile are united for the first time.

c.2060–1785 BCE **The Middle Kingdom** expands trade with Asia, but Egyptian expansion up the Nile into Nubia is then stalled by nomadic Hyksos invaders from the east in 1730 BCE.

c.1580–1050 BCE **The New Kingdom** resumes expansion of Egypt's frontiers to the south and into Mesopotamia.

525–402 BCE **Persians conquer** Egypt, and again in 343–332 BCE.

332 BCE **Alexander the Great** conquers Egypt and moves the capital to Alexandria on the Mediterranean, founded in 331 BCE.

304 BCE **After the death of Alexander** in 323 BCE, Egypt eventually passes to one of his generals, who rules as Ptolemy I.

51 BCE **Last of the** Ptolemaic dynasty, Cleopatra, becomes ruler of Egypt.

31 BCE **Naval battle of** Actium: Cleopatra defeated by the Romans. After her suicide

---

On July 26, 1956, Egypt's president, Gamal Abdel Nasser, nationalized the Suez Canal, the shares in which were owned by UK and French investors. Fearful that Egypt's assertion of sovereignty would result in an Arab attack, Israel invaded Sinai. When both sides refused to halt military action, UK and French forces attacked Port Said on October 6 (right) in order to seize the canal. Pressure from the UN and US forced a humiliating ceasefire on the UK and France. The UN stationed troops to keep Israel and Egypt apart. The crisis marked the end of British influence in the region.

---

in 30 BCE, Egypt becomes part of the Roman and successor Byzantine empires.

641–42 CE **Byzantine Empire loses** Egypt to Muslim invaders from Arabia, who introduce Arabic and Islam.

868–905 **Tulunid dynasty wrests** control of Egypt from the Abbasid Caliphate.

969 **Shia Fatimids** make Cairo their capital.

1169–71 **Saladin takes Egypt** and founds the short-lived Ayyubid dynasty.

1250 **Mamluks, slave soldiers,** mainly of Circassian origin, take power.

1517 **Cairo is captured** by Turks; Egypt becomes part of the Ottoman Empire.

1798 **Napoleon invades Egypt,** but his fleet is destroyed by the British at the Battle of the Nile at Aboukir Bay.

1805 **Mohammed Ali,** an Albanian in the Turkish army, seizes power. Ottomans recognize him as Viceroy of Egypt.

1869 **The Suez Canal** is opened.

1882 **British forces occupy** Cairo. Egypt effectively under British rule, although still part of the Ottoman Empire.

1914 **Britain makes Egypt** a protectorate.

1922 **Britain grants** Egypt limited independence. Sultan Ahmed Fuad becomes King Fuad and rules until his death in 1936, when he is succeeded by his son King Farouk.

1924 **The first democratic** election held under the 1923 constitution brings Wafd Party leader Saad Zaghlul to power.

1936 **The Anglo-Egyptian** treaty ends the British military presence in Egypt. During World War II Britain defends Egypt; Axis forces are repulsed at El Alamein in November 1942.

1948 **The first Arab-Israeli** war ends in defeat for Egypt.

1952 **Free Officers' Movement,** led by General Neguib, forces Farouk to abdicate. Constitution is suspended.

1953 **A republic** is proclaimed with Neguib as president.

1954 **Gamal Abdel Nasser** deposes Neguib and becomes president.

1956 **Suez Crisis over** nationalization of Suez Canal. Israeli, British, and French forces withdraw after pressure from UN.

1960–70 **Building of Aswan** Dam.

1967 **Sinai is lost** in the Six Day War with Israel.

1970 **Nasser dies** of a heart attack and is succeeded by Anwar Sadat.

1972 **Soviet military advisers** are dismissed from Egypt.

1974–75 **US brokers partial** Israeli withdrawal from Sinai.

1977 **Sadat visits Jerusalem** for first-ever meeting with Israeli prime minister.

1978 **Camp David accords,** brokered by US, signed by Egypt and Israel.

1981 **Sadat is assassinated** by Islamist extremists; succeeded by Hosni Mubarak.

1986 **President Mubarak meets** Israeli prime minister Shimon Peres to discuss Middle East peace.

1994–98 **Islamist extremist terror** campaign, killing civilians and tourists.

2005 **Mubarak is reelected** for fifth consecutive term as president.

2006 **1,000 people die** in Red Sea ferry sinking.

2011 **Mubarak resigns after** 18 days of street protests in Cairo. The Armed Forces Supreme Council takes power.

« 56–57   The Divine Pharaohs
« 64–65   Egypt in Order and Chaos
« 66–67   Rameses II
« 68–69   Realm of Osiris
« 70–71   Ancient Egyptian Life
« 72–73   Building for Eternity
« 118–19   Greek and Roman Egypt
« 158–59   Diffusion of Knowledge
« 412–13   End of the Colonial Era

Mauritania

A Muslim nation with a black minority on the Atlantic coast at the western end of the Sahara.

1896 Colonized by France.

1960 Independence from France. A one-party state is established under Moktarould Daddah.

1979 Peace with Polisario in war waged over control of Western Sahara.

1984 Moaouia Taya takes power in coup, and wins reelection after 1992.

2005 Taya overthrown as president; first free elections in 2007 won by Sidi Ouid Abadallahi.

2007 Parliament outlaws slavery.

2008 The Dakar motor rally is canceled after the murder of four tourists.

2008 President Abdallahi, Mauritania's first democratically elected president, is overthrown in a military coup.

Mali

Formerly French Sudan, the country is now named after the great medieval empire of the region.

700s–1050 Mali is part of the empire of Ghana.

1200–1500 Empire of Mali grows rich on gold and trans-Saharan trade.

1450s Empire of Songhay flourishes in the eastern regions.

1800s Fula and Toucouleur jihads spread from east and west.

1881–93 The French colonize the area.

1898 The French destroy Samori Toure's Mandinka state.

Timbuktu
This remote city in northern Mali has been a major trans-Saharan trading post for centuries and was once a center of Islam. This engraving dates from the 1800s when the first Europeans arrived.

1960 Independence.

1968–90 Moussa Traoré is dictator.

1991 Traoré is toppled and imprisoned.

1992 First multi-party elections.

2009 Government forces capture main bases of Tuareg rebels.

Burkina Faso

A former French colony in the Sahel that is threatened by desertification.

1000s Rise of the Mossi kingdom.

1300s Arrival of Islam.

1890s French conquest overcomes Mossi resistance. Protectorate established 1895.

1920 Upper Volta is created as a colony separate from French Sudan.

1958 Upper Volta granted self-governing status within the French Community.

1960 Independence from France: Maurice Yameogo becomes the first president and bans opposition parties.

1970 New constitution allows for power-sharing between politicians and the army.

1983–87 Thomas Sankara holds power: his People's Salvation Council (PSC) begins radical reforms.

1984 Renamed Burkina Faso.

1987 Blaise Compaoré rules country.

2005 Compaoré wins third straight term in office.

Cape Verde Islands

A former Portuguese archipelago, Cape Verde has been democratic and stable since 1991.

1456 Alvise Cadamosto a Venetian captain working for the Portuguese, visits the Cape Verde archipelago.

1462 Portuguese seafarers begin the process of settlement of the uninhabited islands. Slaves are brought from mainland to work the small parcels of arable land.

1600–1760 Ribeira Grande (on Santo Antão) becomes an important entrepot for trans-Atlantic slave trade.

1869 Emancipation of slaves begins.

1956 The African Party for the Independence of Guinea-Bissau and Cape Verde (PAIGC) is established by Amilcar Cabral and Aristides Pereira.

1961 Joint struggle for independence of Cape Verde and Guinea-Bissau begins.

1975 Independence from Portugal.

1991 First multi-party elections.

2006 About 7,000 NATO troops take part in war games on São Vicente island.

Senegal

An ethnically diverse state with a strong economy based around the port of Dakar.

1000s Rise of the Jolof Empire.

1100–1300 Becomes part of the Mali Empire.

1444 Portuguese, then Dutch and French establish trading posts on coast.

1895 Senegal becomes part of French West Africa.

1904 Dakar becomes capital of French West Africa.

1960 Independence from France.

1966–76 One-party state.

1981 Multi-party democracy restored.

2000 For first time since independence, Senegalese Socialist Party loses power to opposition. Abdoulaye Wade becomes president. Referendum approves new democratic constitution.

2002 1,800 passengers are killed in Joola ferry disaster.

2007 President Wade is reelected.

Gambia

A narrow ribbon of land along the river Gambia heavily dependent on peanut exports.

1200s First southward migration of significant numbers of Fula.

1661 British capture James Island.

1816 Britain acquires site of Bathurst (now Banjul) after a struggle for control among European seafaring countries.

1888 Gambia becomes a British crown colony.

1959 Dawda Jawara founds People's Progressive Party; he takes power in 1962 and rules democratically until 1994.

1965 Independence from Britain.

1970 Republic is set up with Jawara as president.

1981 Senegalese troops help crush army coup attempt.

1982–89 Federation with Senegal.

1994 Jawara is ousted in an army coup.

1996 Yahya Jammeh wins presidential election, but three major parties are excluded from elections.

2001 $2 million antipoverty program is launched by the government.

Guinea-Bissau

An impoverished, low-lying country that has suffered frequent military coups and rebellions.

1000s Four main ethnic groups—the Balante, Fulani, Manydyako, and Molinke—live in the country.

1446 Portuguese explorer Nuno Tristão visits the area.

1616 Portugal installs a military garrison at Cacheu to control the slave trade.

1879 Bissau and Cacheu united as Portuguese Guinea.

1956 Amilcar Cabral forms the African Party for the Independence of Guinea-Bissau and Cape Verde (PAIGC).

1959 Striking dockers are massacred in Bissau. PAIGC sets up its headquarters in Conakry, Guinea.

1960s PAIGC occupies large areas of the country.

1973 Amilcar Cabral is assassinated in Conakry.

1973 PAIGC declares the country independent, with Luis Cabral as president of the State Council.

1974 Formal independence from Portugal as the Portuguese Empire collapses. The PAIGC takes power.

1980 Military coup, in part inspired by resentment about continuing domination of Cape Verdeans in government.

1984 New constitution establishes the state on Marxist–Leninist principles.

1990 Multi-party politics accepted.

1994 Elections won by PAIGC.

1998 Army rebellion by Ansumane Mané leads to international intervention by other West African states.

1999 A transitional government is set up; the opposition Party for Social Renewal (PRS) defeats PAIGC in elections.

2000 Kumba Yalla becomes president. Mane is killed in a failed coup attempt.

2003 Yalla overthrown in military coup: elections in 2004 return PAIGC to power.

2006 Appeals for international help to stop human-traffickers smuggling migrants from Guinea-Bissau to Europe.

2009 President Vieira and the chief of the army are assassinated. In the subsequent presidential election, which is won by Malam Bacai Sanha, police shoot and kill one of the other candidates.

Guinea

A former one-party state whose transition to democracy has often been disrupted.

1200s Gold-producing area of Wangara becomes an important center in the development of the Islamic Mali Empire.

1460s Portuguese sailors first explore the Guinea coast; by the 1600s, British, French, and Portuguese merchants are acquiring slaves in the region.

1700s Revival of Islam under the Fula people of the Futa Jallon region.

1870s Almamy Samori Touré consolidates his Mandinka empire of Wassulu, which becomes a symbol of resistance to French colonization.

1881 France signs treaty with Futa Jallon.

1891 War breaks out between Samori's forces and the French. Samori offers to cede his empire to the UK.

1892 The French invade Futa Jallon.

1898 The French defeat Samori. Colonization begins.

1904 Guinea becomes part of French West African Federation.

1947 Ahmed Sekou Touré and others form the Democratic Party of Guinea (PDG).

1958 Guinea is the only French colony to vote "no" on President de Gaulle's offer of a French community; French withdraw and Guinea becomes independent with Sekou Touré as president.

1984 Sekou Touré dies. The army stages a coup and dissolves national assembly.

1992 Multi-party democracy introduced.

1993–95 Disputed elections won by former military leader Lansana Conté.

1998 Conté reelected president.

2000 Attacks from Sierra Leone and Liberia. Guinea in a state of civil war: 250,000 refugees caught up in the fighting.

2003 Opposition boycotts the presidential election after Conté alters the constitution to allow for his reelection.

DECISIVE MOMENT

MONROVIA FOUNDED, 1821

On February 6, 1820, the ship *Elizabeth* left New York for the West African coast. Its passengers were the first US freed slaves bound for Monrovia, a city founded the following year by the American Colonization Society, which had purchased part of British Sierra Leone. Efforts to send freed slaves back to Africa had begun in the American colonies in the 1770s. Some proslavers wanted to send the freed slaves back in order to preserve an exclusively slave-owning white society, while some Christians hoped they would act as missionaries. By 1847 some 22,000 had settled in Monrovia (below).

2009 Military seizes power after the death of president Conté. 150 people shot dead in protests against the military junta.

« 182–83 South of the Sahara
« 280–81 The Slave Trade

Liberia

A once-proud and independent state reduced to anarchy by civil wars.

1821 American Colonization Society begins settling liberated US slaves along the coast.

1847 Foundation as an independent state.

1890s Government asserts the present boundaries in response to UK and French colonial expansion.

1944 William Tubman becomes president.

1971 William Tolbert succeeds Tubman.

1980 Tolbert is assassinated: Samuel Doe takes power in a coup.

1990 Outbreak of civil war: ECOMOG peacekeeping force backed by Nigeria and Ghana sent to restore order.

1990 Doe is assassinated: Charles Taylor and other warlords jostle for power.

1997 Charles Taylor becomes president: other groups continue to oppose him.

2001 Borders with Guinea and Sierra Leone are closed as civil war escalates.

2003 Taylor is ousted.

2005 Ellen Johnson-Sirleaf is elected Africa's first woman head of state.

2007 Charles Taylor appears before war crimes tribunal at the Hague.

« 182–83 South of the Sahara
« 280–81 The Slave Trade

Sierra Leone

A desperately poor nation whose diamond industry has often brought conflict and armed rebellion.

1100s Temnes and others are settled in the country.

1462s Portuguese sailor Pedro de Cintra visits the area.

1787 British administer coastal colony around Freetown, settled by freed slaves.

1896 British protectorate is declared.

1961 Independence from Britain.

1978 Becomes a single-party republic.

1991 Revolutionary United Front (RUF) rebellion leads to a decade of civil war.

1999 Power-sharing agreement to end civil war lasts for one year, but UN and British intervention secures a ceasefire.

2002 Ahmad Kabba of the Sierra Leone People's Party wins reelection.

2004 UN-backed war crimes tribunal begins operation (it winds down in 2009).

2006 President Kabbah announces 90 percent of Sierra Leone's international debt has been written off by creditors.

« 280–81 The Slave Trade

Ivory Coast

One of the larger nations in the region and an island of stability until the late 1990s.

1300s Mandinkas arrive in the area.

1600s European slaving activities begin.

1842 French obtain trading rights on the coast.

1893 Becomes a French colony.

1903–35 Plantations developed.

1910 Rebellion by the southern Abe people is harshly suppressed.

1960 Independence from France: Félix Houphouët-Boigny becomes president.

1970 Oil production starts.

1990 First contested polls: Houphouët-Boigny wins.

1993 Houphouët-Boigny dies.

2002–03 Military uprising turns into major rebellion before peace is established.

2004 Power-sharing deal falters.

2005 United Nations mediators appoint Charles Bonny as prime minister.

2006 Bonny's government resigns over leak of toxic waste fumes at an Abidjan dump, which kills three people.

2007 New power-sharing deal signed.

2010 Disputed election ends with Laurent Gbagbo and Alassane Ouattara both claiming victory. Country on the brink of civil war.

« 182–83 South of the Sahara
« 280–81 The Slave Trade

Ghana

The first black African nation to gain its independence from a European empire.

1100s Akan peoples begin to settle the northern forests of present-day Asante.

1482 Portuguese seafarers build a castle at the spot now known as Elmina.

1700s The Akwamu Empire reaches its fullest expansion; its power is gradually replaced by the Asante kingdom.

1806–14 The Asante assert military superiority over the coastal Fanti people.

1874 UK forces devastate Kumasi in the first of the Asante Wars and establish the British Gold Coast.

1949 Kwame Nkrumah forms the Convention People's Party (CPP).

1952 After electoral victories for his CPP, Nkrumah becomes Prime Minister.

1957 As Ghana, the country gains independence under Nkrumah.

1964 Single-party rule is introduced.

1972–79 Corrupt rule of General Acheampong, who is executed in 1979.

1979 Flight Lieutenant Jerry Rawlings stages coup. He wins multi-party elections in 1992 and 1996.

2000 The opposition New Patriotic Party under John Kufuor wins power.

2008 John Atta Mills becomes president.

« 280–81 The Slave Trade

Togo

A narrow country wedged between Ghana and Benin and dominated by the large port of Lomé.

1884 Togo becomes a German protectorate. After Germany's defeat in World War I, it is divided between France and Britain.

1960 French sector becomes independent as Togo, while the British part is joined to Ghana.

1967 Gnassingbé Eyadéma takes power in a coup and is Africa's longest-serving ruler by the time of his death; he rules by repression and brutality.

2005 Eyadéma dies. He is replaced by his son Faure, who wins elections widely condemned as rigged.

2006 Government and opposition parties agree to a transitional government.

Benin

A former slave-trading state and French colony wedged between Togo and Nigeria.

1400s Kingdom of Benin established under the Obas.

1500s Portuguese seafarers commence trade with coastal rulers.

1620 The Fon, indigenous slave traders, found kingdom of Dahomey.

1850s After the abolition of the slave trade, palm oil becomes the main export.

1863 Porto Novo becomes a French protectorate.

1890–94 Armed conflict between Dahomey and France, ending with French victory.

1892 French establish protectorate.

1901 Present borders of Dahomey, as it was then known, fixed by France.

1904 Becomes part of French West Africa.

1960 Full independence from France.

1972 Military coup: Marxism–Leninism is official ideology. It is dropped in 1989.

1975 Renamed Benin.

1990 Benin introduces multi-party democracy. President Kerekou is beaten by Nicephore Soglo in elections in 1991 and respects the result. Kerekou is re-elected in 1996 amid accusations of fraud.

« 280–81 The Slave Trade

Nigeria

Africa's most populous state and once home to the ancient kingdom of Benin.

800 BCE Nok people develop first organized society in the region.

1000 CE Kanem becomes major state, which grows rich on trans-Sahara trade.

1400s Oyo and Benin states flourish in the south, the Ife in the west, while the Igbo live in small villages in the southeast. First Portuguese landings.

1500s Songhai Empire controls the north until conquered by Morocco in 1591.

1700s With Britain taking the lead, the slave trade develops to the point where 15,000 slaves are being exported annually from the Bight of Benin and a further 15,000 from the Bight of Biafra.

1861 The British annex Lagos and the process of formal colonization begins.

1886 Royal Niger Company given official responsibility for British sphere of influence along the Niger and Benue rivers. British armed forces coerce local rulers into accepting British rule.

1900 The Royal Niger Company's charter is revoked.

1900 British Protectorate of Northern Nigeria is established.

1906 Lagos is incorporated into the Protectorate of Southern Nigeria.

1909 West Africa Frontier Force (WAFF) is established; the subjugation of the north of the region begins.

1914 Protectorates of Northern and Southern Nigeria are joined to form the colony of Nigeria.

1960 Independence from Britain as a federated state.

1961 Northern part of UN Trust Territory of the Cameroons is incorporated as part of Nigeria's Northern Region.

1966 First military coup, led by Major General Ironsi. Thousands of Igbo in Northern Region are massacred.

1966–75 General Gowon in power.

1967–70 Civil war: Lieutenant Colonel Ojukwu calls for secession of oil-rich east under its new name, Biafra. Over one million Nigerians die before secessionists are defeated by federal forces.

1978 Political parties are legalized. Must represent national, not tribal, interests.

1979 Elections won by Alhaji Shehu Shagari and the National Party of Nigeria (NPN); return to civilian government.

Beauty in bronze
The kingdom of Benin flourished in southern Nigeria from the 1200s to the 1600s. Its craftworkers used the lost-wax process to cast beautiful portrait heads like this one in bronze.

1983 Military coup. Major General Mohammed Buhari heads the Supreme Military Council.

1985 Major General Ibrahim Babangida heads a bloodless coup, promising a return to democracy.

1993 Elections annulled; Babangida resigns; military sets up Interim National Government (ING). The army, headed by General Sani Abacha, takes over.

1995 Ban on parties is lifted. Military tribunal convicts former head of state General Olusegun Obasanjo and 39 others for plotting coup. Execution of novelist Ken Saro-Wiwa and eight other Ogoni activists: Commonwealth suspends Nigeria's membership.

1998 Abacha dies; his successor announces a timetable for restoring civilian rule by 1999.

1999 Elections for state governors, legislature, and presidency won by Olusegun Obasanjo. Commonwealth membership restored.

2000 Ethnic violence escalates, threatening national unity.

2001 Bauchi becomes the tenth state to introduce sharia law; divisions widen between the Muslim north and Christian south.

2006 Militants in Niger Delta attack oil pipelines. Nigeria cedes sovereignty over disputed Bakassi peninsula to Cameroon.

2007 Umaru Yar'Adua of the PDP wins presidential elections.

2008 200 people killed in Muslim–Christian rioting in central town of Jos.

2010 Further religious clashes kill 300. Vice President Goodluck Jonathan becomes president after Umar Yar'Adua dies following a long illness and prolonged absence in Saudi Arabia.

« 280–81 The Slave Trade
« 320–21 Completing the Map

Cameroon

Dubbed "Africa in miniature" on account of its 230 different peoples and varied habitats.

1100s Expansion of the Kanem-Bornu Empire to include the northern regions.

1472 Portuguese explorers arrive; later development of slave trade by Europeans.

1884 Germany declares Kamerun protectorate.

1922 Most of the territory is mandated to France, with the remainder to Britain.

1960 Gains independence from France; northern part joins Nigeria in 1961.

1984 Country is renamed Cameroon.

1992 First democratic elections for 30 years return ruling party to power.

2000 World Bank funding is approved for oil and pipeline project.

2008 Last part of disputed Bakassi Peninsula handed over by Nigeria.

« 280–81 The Slave Trade

Equatorial Guinea

The only Spanish-speaking state in Africa, with the potential of great wealth from oil.

1778 Portugal hands over Fernando Po (Bioko) and Annobon islands to Spain. Spain later develops a trading post on islands off the coast of Rio Muni.

1858 Spain permanently occupies Bioko, developing cocoa plantations.

1900 Treaty of Paris confirms Spanish rule over Rio Muni. Forestry concessions and oil palm plantations are developed in Rio Muni, with small cocoa and coffee plantations later.

1959 Fernando Po and Rio Muni are incorporated into metropolitan Spain; the inhabitants gain full Spanish citizenship.

1968 Independence, with Francisco Macias Nguema, from Esangui Fang clan, as president. Macias abandons democracy, and installs a repressive regime.

1991 Multi-party constitution.

1992 **Oil production starts.**

2004 **Foreign mercenaries** are arrested in suspected coup plot.

2006 **Government resigns** en masse following allegations of corruption.

2008 **British mercenary** Simon Mann extradited to Equatorial Guinea to face charges relating to 2004 coup attempt. He is sentenced to 34 years in prison but released in 2009.

« 182–83 South of the Sahara

São Tomé & Príncipe

Two islands in the Gulf of Guinea that were controlled by Portugal for more than 500 years.

1470 **Portuguese reach** uninhabited islands and import African slaves to work on sugar and cocoa plantations.

1975 **Independence** as a Marxist one-party state; plantations nationalized.

1990 **New democratic constitution** introduces multi-party democracy.

1995 **Príncipe is granted** autonomy.

2001 **Fradique de Menezes wins** the presidency and promises greater cooperation with parliament. He survives an attempted coup in 2003.

2010 **Opposition Independent** Action Party (ADI) wins parliamentary elections.

« 280–81 The Slave Trade

Gabon

An equatorial country that has made the post-colonial transition to multi-party democracy.

1472 **Portuguese trading ships** make the first European contact.

1600s **European merchants trade** tobacco, cloth, and arms for ivory, slaves, and rubber. The Fang, moving south from the savannah lands of Cameroon, expel the indigenous peoples.

1849 **Libreville is founded** by Vili slaves freed by the French.

1880 **Count Savorgnan de Brazza** signs a treaty with King Makoko of the Teke that gives France rights over a vast tract of central Africa, although most of this area was not under the control of Makoko.

1960 **Independence from France:** Léon M'ba is president.

1964 **Military coup. French** intervene to reinstate M'ba.

1967 **Albert-Bernard** (later Omar) Bongo becomes president.

1968 **Single-party state** instituted.

1990 **Multi-party democracy.**

2006 **Gabon enters talks** with Equatorial Guinea over disputed oil-rich waters.

2009 **Omar Bongo dies** after 42 years as president. His son Ali Ben Bongo wins presidential election amidst allegations of fraud.

« 280–81 The Slave Trade

Central African Rep

A landlocked, unstable country that has been plagued by military coups and rebel insurgencies.

1500s **Slave raids from** the north and west are common.

1800s **Baya arrive** from Cameroon, fleeing the Fulani; later in the century, the Banda flee Islamic slavers in Sudan.

1889 **French establish** a base at Bangui.

1905 **Oubangui-Chari territory** is united with Chad. Later revolts by the plantation forced-labor workers are suppressed.

1950 **First parliamentary deputy,** Barthelemy Boganda, founds Movement for Social Evolution in Black Africa.

1958 **Internal self-government** is granted with Boganda as prime minister.

1960 **Independence** under David Dacko (Boganda having died in a plane crash).

1966 **Coup by** Jean-Bédel Bokassa, who in 1977 proclaims himself emperor.

Emperor Bokassa I
Dictator of the Central African Republic from 1966, Jean-Bédel Bokassa (1921–96) crowned himself emperor in 1977. He was overthrown in 1979 and put on trial for the brutal excesses of his regime.

1979 **French help overthrow** Bokassa and reinstate Dacko.

1981 **General Kolingba** ousts Dacko.

1996 **Government of national** unity formed following army rebellion; further coups continue to destabilize the country.

2005 **Thousands flee** lawless north into neighboring Chad.

2007 **Rebel leaders** sign a peace accord with President Bozize in Libya.

2008 **Two of three** main rebel groups sign a peace accord with the government.

2009 **A national unity government** is formed, including former rebels.

Congo

An oil- and timber-rich country appallingly governed in the years since independence.

1400s **Two kingdoms** occupy present-day Congo: Loango in the south, Makoko farther inland; the northern forest regions are the home of Binga pygmies.

1880 **French explorer** Count Savorgnan de Brazza visits the region. He establishes a treaty with Makoko, chief of Teke, which he claims gives rights to the region.

1891 **Congo is founded** on the north bank of Stanley Pool on the Zaire River.

1910 **French Congo** is integrated into French Equatorial Africa.

1940 **The French governor,** Félix Éboué, supports de Gaulle and rejects France's Vichy government.

1944 **De Gaulle holds** conference in Brazzaville to reorganize African colonies.

1956 **Abbé Fulbert Youlou** founds Democratic Union for the Defense of African Interests (UDDIA).

1958 **Admission of Congo** to Franco-African Community as an autonomous state.

1960 **Independence** from France as Republic of Congo.

1968–91 **Declared a one-party** Marxist–Leninist state.

1992–97 **Political violence, coups,** and rebellions weaken the country.

1997–2003 **Violence erupts when the** president tries to disarm militias ahead of elections; a peace deal with Ninja rebel militia eventually brings some stability.

2009 **President Dennis Nguess** is elected for second term in elections boycotted by the opposition.

« 412–13 End of the Colonial Era

Dem Rep Congo

Africa's third-largest country, bankrupted since independence by its long-serving dictator.

1400s **Kongo emerges** as a powerful kingdom on the coast.

1885 **King Leopold of Belgium's** claim to the Congo as his personal fiefdom is recognized at the Berlin Conference.

1908 **Belgium takes over** Congo Free State from Leopold.

1957 **Limited African rule** introduced.

1960 **Independence of Republic** of Congo with Patrice Lumumba as prime minister. Katanga (Shaba) secedes; Belgian troops are sent in; Lumumba is arrested.

1961 **Lumumba is murdered.** In 2002, the Belgian government admits that it killed him and apologizes.

1963 **Katanga secession collapses.**

1965 **Joseph Désiré Mobutu** seizes power and starts stealing the country's wealth.

1970 **Mobutu elected president;** his Popular Revolutionary Movement (MPR) becomes sole legal party.

1971 **Country is renamed Zaire.**

1982 **Opposition parties** set up Union for Democracy and Social Progress (UDPS).

1990 **Mobutu announces** transition to multi-party rule after security forces kill prodemocracy demonstrators.

1996 **Major insurgency launched** in east by Alliance of Democratic Forces for the Liberation of the Congo (AFDL).

1997 **Forces led by** Laurent Kabila sweep south and west. Mobutu flees and dies in exile. The country is renamed the Democratic Republic of the Congo.

2000 **UN approves peacekeeping** mission; arrival stalled by Kabila, who is assassinated in 2001.

2006 **Serious unrest** as opposition rejects the victory in presidential elections of Laurent Kabila's son, Joseph.

2006 **Forces of renegade general** Laurent Nkunda and government troops clash in North Kivu province.

2008 **Peace agreement is signed** between government and Nkunda's rebel forces.

2008 **Heavy clashes erupt** in the east of the country between Rwandan Hutu militia and General Nkunda's forces.

2009 **Government offensive defeats** Nkunda, who is arrested in Rwanda.

« 412–13 End of the Colonial Era

Eritrea

The newest nation in Africa only emerged as an independent republic in 1993.

1885 Italy occupies Massawa and begins colonization of Eritrea. In the centuries before this Eritrea successively passed under the control of Arabs, Ottomans, and Egyptians.

1895 Italy launches an attempted invasion of Ethiopia from Eritrea.

1896 Italian forces are defeated at the battle of Adowa.

1936 Eritrea becomes part of large Italian empire in East Africa after Italy successfully invades, conquers Ethiopia, and merges it with Italian Somaliland.

1941 The administration of Eritrea is taken over by the UK after the defeat of Italian forces in East Africa during World War II. The new administration permits political activity.

1950 The UN General Assembly gives Eritrea self-government within a federal union with Ethiopia, which rejects it.

1952 Eritrea absorbed by Ethiopia.

1961 Beginning of armed struggle against Ethiopian rule by the Eritrean People's Liberation Front (EPLF).

1991 EPLF takes Asmara, the capital, and helps overthrow the military government in Ethiopia.

1993 Formal independence.

1998 Border war with Ethiopia over a small area of disputed territory around the towns of Badme and Sheraro; over 70,000 troops are killed on both sides.

2000 OAU peace treaty is signed.

2001 Ethiopia completes troop withdrawal from Eritrea; a buffer zone is created to separate the two armies.

2001 The two countries agree to abide by the decision of an international boundary commission.

2003 Boundary commission awards Badme to Eritrea: Ethiopia refuses to accept the decision it has signed.

2005 Eritrea expels UN observers.

2006 UN accuses Eritrea of arming the rival Islamist administration in neighboring Somalia.

2007 Eritrea accepts the findings of an independent boundary commission on its disputed border with Ethiopia.

2009 Fighting breaks out between Eritrean and Djiboutian forces at disputed Ras Doumeira border.

Djibouti

Little more than a port with a desert hinterland, Djibouti has historically depended on shipping.

1862 France gains control of the trading port of Obock in northern Djibouti.

1897 In a treaty signed between the emperor of Ethiopia and France, Djibouti is designated "the official outlet for Ethiopian commerce."

1909–17 The Franco–Ethiopian Railway Company (CFE) builds a railway from Djibouti to Addis Ababa.

1977 Independence from France.

1981–92 One-party state.

1991 Front for the Restoration of Unity and Democracy (FRUD), an Afar guerrilla group, launches armed insurrection.

1994 Peace agreement with FRUD.

2000 Civil war ends.

2002 US sets up a base in support of its war on terror.

2002 President Ismail Guelleh wins reelection as sole candidate.

2003 Multi-party elections held.

2006 A UN report accuses Djibouti of arming Islamist rebels in Somalia.

2009 Outbreak of fighting at disputed border with Eritrea.

Ethiopia

The only African state to avoid colonization, Ethiopia was the cradle of an ancient civilization.

500 BCE Foundation of kingdom of Axum, the nucleus of later Ethiopia.

328 CE Christianity adopted as state religion of Axum.

1270 Overthrow of Zagwe dynasty by Amhara princes. Foundation of Solomonid dynasty.

1528–43 Muslim invasion led by Ahmad Gran eventually repelled with Portuguese assistance.

1855 Amhara chief overthrows puppet emperor at Gondar and proclaims himself Emperor Tewodoros (Theodore) II. In 1868 he commits suicide rather than surrender to British expeditionary force.

1889 Menelik II becomes emperor and begins imperial expansion east and south.

1896 Italian invasion defeated at Adowa.

1913 Menelik II dies. In 1916 his son, Lij Iyasu, is deposed for converting to Islam and proposing alliance with Turkey. Menelik's daughter, Zauditu, becomes empress with Ras Tafari as regent.

1930 Zauditu dies. Ras Tafari Makonnen crowned Emperor Haile Selassie.

1936 Italians occupy Ethiopia. League of Nations fails to react.

1941 British oust Italians and restore Haile Selassie.

1952 Eritrea is federated with Ethiopia.

1963 Organization of African Unity is fomed with headquarters in Addis Ababa.

1972–74 Famine kills 200,000.

1974 Strikes and army mutinies against Haile Selassie's autocratic rule. Derg (Military Committee) stages coup.

1975 Ethiopia becomes socialist state, with nationalizations, worker cooperatives, and health reforms.

1977 Colonel Mengistu Haile Mariam takes over. Somali invasion of Ogaden defeated with Soviet and Cuban help.

1978–79 Thousands of political opponents killed or imprisoned.

1984 One million people die in famine after drought and years of war. Live Aid concert raises funds for relief. Drought returns in 1987.

1988 Eritrean and Tigrean People's Liberation Fronts (EPLF and TPLF) begin new offensives. Mengistu's budget is for "Everything to the War Front."

1989 Military coup fails. TPLF in control of most of Tigre. TPLF and Ethiopian People's Revolutionary Movement form alliance—EPRDF.

1991 Mengistu accepts defeat and flees country. EPRDF enters Addis Ababa, sets up provisional government.

1993 Transitional rule ends. EPRDF wins landslide in multi-party elections and sets up first democratic government. New

nine-state federation is formed as Eritrea gains its independence.

1998–2000 Tensions with Eritrea escalate into a border war.

2001 Ethiopia withdraws troops from Eritrea, but refuses to accept boundary commission's award to Eritrea in 2003.

2006 Ethiopia sends troops to help overthrow Islamic forces in Somalia.

2007 Ethiopia rejects findings of international border commission on disputed border with Eritrea.

2009 Ethiopia withdraws its troops from Somalia.

2010 Menes Zelewi reelected president for fourth term amid allegations of fraud.

« 182–83 South of the Sahara

Somalia

An ethnically homogenous, poor state in the Horn of Africa torn apart by clan warfare.

1884, 1889 The lands of the Somalis become British and Italian colonies.

1960 Unification at independence.

1964–87 Conflict with Ethiopia over Ogaden region.

1969 Siad Barre is dictator.

1991 Siad Barre ousted. Civil war and clan chaos result in mass starvation. In the north, Somaliland declares secession.

1993 US rangers are killed when Somali militias shoot down two US Black Hawk helicopters in Mogadishu.

1995 UN withdraws as international community abandons country.

2001 Transitional national government established. It governs from Djibouti (and later Kenya) as it is unable to control Mogadishu.

ETHIOPIAN EMPEROR (1892–1975)

HAILE SELASSIE I

Haile Selassie I was the emperor of Ethiopia (1930–74), a throne supposedly descended from King Solomon. When Italy invaded Ethiopia in 1935, he led his troops in the field, but in 1936 was forced to flee and twice appealed in vain to the League of Nations for action against Italy. In 1940, Haile Selassie returned to Africa with British aid, and in 1941 regained his throne. In the 1960s and 1970s he worked for pan-African aims, particularly through the Organization of African Unity, but in 1974 the army seized control and arrested him. He was killed in prison on the orders of the coup leaders in 1975.

2006 Islamic Courts Union takes the capital, Mogadishu, and brings some order to the country. Ethiopian troops and US gunships intervene to attack the Islamists, who flee in 2007.

2007 African Union forces arrive in Somalia.

2008 Somali-based pirates hijack Saudi Arabian oil supertanker *MV Sirius Star*.

2009 Radical Islamist group Al-Shabbab makes gains as Ethiopian army withdraws.

2005 Violent protesters in Nairobi reject proposed new constitution.

2008 Tribal violence kills over 1,000 after a disputed presidential election. Power-sharing agreement between president Mwai Kibaki and Raile Odinga.

2010 Referendum passes constitutional changes to limit presidential authority and devolve more power to the regions.

« 182–83 South of the Sahara
« 412–13 End of the Colonial Era

2008 Government and LRA sign a ceasefire, but fighting continues.

2010 Bomb attacks in Kampala kill 74 people. The Somali Islamist militia Al-Shabbab claims responsibility.

« 412–13 End of the Colonial Era

Kenya

A diverse nation of 70 different peoples, Kenya has had a difficult post-colonial history.

1200 A distinctive Swahili culture of mixed Arabs, Africans, and Persians thrives on the coast, while Bantu, Cushitic, and Nilotic speakers live inland.

1498 Portuguese explorer Vasco da Gama visits the powerful city of Mombasa.

1502–09 Portuguese take over Swahili ports on the coast.

1698 Omanis from the Arabian peninsula control the entire coast, moving their capital from Muscat to Zanzibar in 1840.

1920 Kenya becomes a British colony.

1944 Kenyan African Union (KAU) formed. Jomo Kenyatta leads it from 1947.

1952–56 Mau Mau, Kikuyu-led violent campaign to restore African lands.

1953 KAU banned and Kenyatta is jailed until 1961, when he is released and takes up the presidency of KANU.

1963 Independence. The following year a republic is set up. Kenyatta is president and Odinga vice president.

1969 Jaramogi Mboya murdered, Odinga arrested as opposition to KANU grows.

1978 Kenyatta dies: vice president Daniel arap Moi succeeds him.

1990 Government implicated in deaths of foreign minister Robert Ouko and Anglican archbishop. Riots. Odinga and others form FORD, outlawed by government.

1991 Arrest of FORD leaders and attempts to stop prodemocracy protests.

1997 December, Moi wins further term in widely criticized elections.

1999 Moi appoints paleontologist Richard Leakey to lead drive against corruption; Leakey resigns in 2001.

2002 Mwai Kibaki becomes first non-KANU president on promise to end corruption. Corruption worsens.

Uganda

A country on the East African Plateau torn apart by ethnic strife and bad government.

1700s Buganda replaces Bunyoro as the major kingdom in the region.

1890 The UK and Germany agree that Buganda is of interest to the UK, and Tanganyika to Germany.

1894 A British protectorate is established over Buganda. Bunyoro, Toro, Ankole, and Busoga follow in 1896.

1953–55 The Kabaka of Buganda, Mutesa II, is exiled to the UK for opposing British plans for a unitary state.

1962 Uganda is independent, with Milton Obote as prime minister and the Kabaka as head of state.

1962–71 Milton Obote in power.

1966 New constitution ends Buganda's autonomy; in 1967 traditional kingships are abolished; the Kabaka goes into exile.

1971 Idi Amin seizes power in a military coup; he expels the Asian community in 1972, leading to economic collapse. After he invades Tanzania in 1978 to claim new territory, Tanzania invades Uganda in 1979 and ends his brutal rule.

1980–85 Milton Obote returns to rule the country for a second time. Yoweri Museveni sets up National Resistance Army to overthrow Obote.

1986 Museveni seizes power and establishes the "no party" system that removes ethnic clashes from politics.

1993 Traditional kingships restored.

1996 Museveni wins first free presidential election.

1999 Agreement with Sudan allows troops to enter Sudan in pursuit of rebel Lord's Resistance Army (LRA) fighters.

2002 Uganda withdraws its forces after intervening in Congo's civil war.

2006 Government and LRA sign truce aimed at ending long-running conflict.

Tanzania

A peaceful but poor nation with a strong Swahili culture and tradition.

800s Arab merchants establish a trading settlement at Kilwa, while Persian merchants settle on Zanzibar and Pemba.

1200 A distinctive Swahili culture of Arabs, Africans, and Persians thrives.

1500–09 Portuguese take over Swahili ports on the coast.

1650s Omanis take over Zanzibar; it eventually becomes the capital of their maritime empire in 1840.

1873 The UK forces the Sultan of Zanzibar to close his slave market.

1885 Tanganyika a German colony; the British take over Zanzibar in 1890.

1919 Tanganyika a British mandate.

1961 Tanganyika independent, followed by Zanzibar in 1963.

1962 Julius Nyerere becomes president and introduces policy of African socialism.

1964 Sultanate of Zanzibar overthrown in left-wing revolution; Tanganyika and Zanzibar merge to become Tanzania.

1985 President Mwinyi begins relaxation of socialist policies after Nyerere retires.

1995 Multi-party elections. Benjamin Mkapa becomes president.

2005 Jakaya Kikwete wins presidency.

2010 Tanzania joins the new East African Common Market.

Rwanda

An ethnically divided country and the scene of an appalling act of genocide in 1994.

1000s Arrival of Hutu agriculturalists, followed by Tutsi cattle-owners in 1400s. They remain distinct ethnic groups.

1897 Traditional kingdom of Rwanda is absorbed into German East Africa.

1922 Belgium takes over Rwanda from Germany under mandate.

Rwandan crisis
Within 100 days in 1994 some 800,000 Tutsis were murdered by Hutu militias. The militias then fled to neighboring Zaire, taking with them about 2 million Hutu refugees (above).

1962 Independence under a Hutu-led government.

1994 Hutu president Habyarimana dies in plane crash blamed on Tutsis. Genocidal violence killing 800,000 people is then unleashed by Hutu extremists against Tutsis and moderate Hutus.

2000 Paul Kagame is elected president.

2005 Mass release of 36,000 prisoners who have confessed to the genocide.

2008 Paul Kagame's RPF wins elections.

2009 Rwanda's education system switches from French to English. Rwanda is admitted to the Commonwealth.

Burundi

A small nation torn between its Hutu majority and dominant Tutsi minority peoples.

1897 Burundi kingdom absorbed into German East Africa.

1922 Belgium takes over. Country is merged with Rwanda as Ruanda-Urundi.

1959 Split from Rwanda is followed by independence from Belgium in 1962.

1966 Army overthrows monarchy.

1972 Tutsis massacre 150,000 Hutus.

1993 Ndadaye, the first Hutu president, is killed in Tutsi-dominated army coup.

2000 Arusha peace accord between Tutsis and Hutus, power-sharing agreed.

2003 Major rebel assault against Bujumbura as power-sharing deal falters.

2005 A new power-sharing constitution.

2008–09 Renewed fighting between government forces and FNL rebels.

Angola

A former Portuguese colony ripped apart by constant civil war since independence.

200s BCE **Bantu-speakers** migrate south into the region.

1482 **Portuguese under Diego Cão** reach Angola and establish forts along the coast.

1575 **Luanda founded** by the Portuguese; Portugal later sends troops to collect minerals and slaves, shipping the slaves to its colony in Brazil through Luanda.

1891 **The frontiers** of Angola are fixed, following the 1884–85 Congress of Berlin. The Portuguese introduce forced labor.

1945 **After World War II,** Portuguese emigration to Angola increases.

1956 **The antitribal** Popular Movement for the Liberation of Angola (MPLA) is formed with the aim of ending colonial rule. Led by Agostinho Neto, it later receives support from Soviet bloc countries.

1961 **Rebellions in Luanda** and northern Angola against colonial rule, followed by severe repression and the launching by the MPLA of the anticolonial armed struggle in the rural areas.

1962 **The northern-based** National Front for the Liberation of Angola (FNLA) starts insurgency under Holden Roberto: it appeals to tribal allegiances and eventually has support from the US and Zaire.

1966 **Formation of National Union** for the Total Independence of Angola (UNITA), the third major nationalist movement, led by Jonas Savimbi. By 1990 it controls large parts of the country from its base in Jamba. It receives substantial assistance from the US and South Africa.

1974 **Coup in Lisbon** leads to the end of Portuguese colonial wars. Independence is scheduled for 1975, and a transitional government is formed by the three nationalist movements. This breaks down and conflict ensues between them.

1975 **The MPLA** proclaims the People's Republic of Angola with Neto as president. MPLA forces defeat the FNLA in the north and stop South African invasion in support of UNITA some 185 miles (300 km) south of Luanda with the help of Cuban troops.

1979 **José Eduardo dos Santos** (MPLA) becomes president.

1991 **UN-brokered peace** but an MPLA election victory provokes UNITA to resume fighting the following year.

1994 **Lusaka peace agreement.**

1998 **Civil war erupts again.**

2000 **Fighting spreads as** UNITA increases guerrilla activity.

2002 **UNITA leader** Jonas Savimbi killed.

2002 **A ceasefire** between UNITA rebels and the government brings peace; more than half a million Angolans have died in the fighting since independence.

2008 **First parliamentary elections** in 16 years are held.

2010 **Angola hosts** the African Nations soccer tournament. Attack on Togo team bus kills driver and injures several players.

« 182–83 South of the Sahara

Zambia

A landlocked southern African country whose fortunes remain tied to the copper industry.

1890s **British magnate** Cecil Rhodes acquires treaty rights over Barotseland.

1900 **British South Africa Company** gains mining rights in the region.

1911 **Renamed** Northern Rhodesia.

1924 **Becomes a** British protectorate.

1953–63 **Part of the Federation** of Rhodesia and Nyasaland.

1964 **Independent** as Zambia with Kenneth Kaunda of the United National Independence Party (UNIP) as president.

1972 **UNIP one-party** government.

1982–91 **Austerity measures** and corruption; pressure grows for democracy.

1991 **Multi-party democracy;** Frederick Chiluba of the Movement for Multi-Party Democracy (MMD) defeats Kaunda.

2001 **Levy Mwanawasa of the** MMD wins presidential elections.

2007 **President Mwanawasa** wins a second term, but dies in August 2008 after a stroke. Rupiah Banda replaces him.

2009 **Frederick Chiluba** is arrested and charged with corruption.

Malawi

A narrow, landlocked country dominated by Lake Malawi, Africa's third-largest lake.

1891 **Malawi becomes** the British protectorate of Nyasaland after long period of Scottish missionary activity.

1953–63 **Colony incorporated** into the Federation of Rhodesia and Nyasaland.

1964 **Independence as Malawi** under Hastings Banda. Two years later Malawi becomes a one-party state.

1992 **Antigovernment riots;** illegal prodemocracy groups unite.

1993 **Referendum for multi-party system.**

1994 **Bakili Muluzi's opposition** United Democratic Front (UDF) wins first democratic elections.

1999 **Muluzi reelected president.** In 2006 he is arrested on corruption charges.

2002 **Severe cholera epidemic.**

2004 **Bingu wa Mutharika** wins presidency.

« 182–83 South of the Sahara

Mozambique

A poor country wrecked by civil war that once played a major part in Portugal's slave trade.

1498 **Vasco da Gama's** arrival at Mozambique Island. Almost half a century later the first Portuguese trading center at Quelimane becomes a center for slave trading to Brazil.

1684 **The Mwene Matapa** kingdom recognizes Portuguese sovereignty. Later the Changamire of the Rozvi kingdom conquer the Mwene Matapa and push the Portuguese south of the Zambezi River.

1752 **After reestablishing control** north of the Zambezi, the Portuguese appoint a colonial governor, having previously run the country as part of Portuguese India.

1780s **The slave trade becomes** a major factor in the economy. The Portuguese introduce a system of forced labor when slavery is ended in the late 19th century.

1842 **Portugal outlaws** the slave trade in Mozambique.

1932 **Portuguese colonial** government takes control of those parts of the country run by private Portuguese companies.

1951 **Mozambique becomes an** overseas province of Portugal. In the next 20 years Lisbon introduces settlement schemes.

1962 **The Front for** the Liberation of Mozambique (Frelimo) is formed and starts a war of liberation against Portugal.

1975 **Mozambique gains** independence; Frelimo leader Samora Machel becomes president.

1976 **The Renamo resistance movement** is set up inside Mozambique by the white Rhodesian government in order to destabilize its neighbor, which is supporting the ZANU and ZAPU fight against white rule in Rhodesia.

1976–80 **Mozambique closes** the Rhodesian border to prevent aid reaching Renamo. This leads to numerous reprisals inside the country by Renamo.

1977 **Frelimo constitutes itself** as a Marxist–Leninist party.

1980 **After white minority** rule ends in former Rhodesia, South Africa takes over the backing of Renamo.

1982 **Zimbabwean troops** arrive to guard the vital Mutare–Beira rail link.

1984 **Nkomati Accord:** South Africa agrees to cease funding Renamo if Mozambique ceases aid to the ANC; however, fighting continues.

1986 **Renamo declares war** on Zimbabwe; Tanzanian troops arrive to reinforce Frelimo.

1986 **President Machel** dies in a mysterious plane crash in South Africa; he is succeeded by Joaquim Chissano.

1988 **Nkomati Accord is** reactivated. Mozambique workers allowed back to work in South African mines.

1989 **War and malnutrition** claim one million lives.

1989 **Frelimo drops Marxism–Leninism** and in the new constitution of 1990 supports multi-party elections and the free-market economy.

NDONGO QUEEN (C.1583–1663)

NJINGA MBANDE

Portuguese attempts to colonize the interior of Angola brought them into conflict with the strongly independent Ndongo kingdom. After a period of uneasy peace, fighting broke out in 1617. A peace deal was struck in 1621 when King Ngola Mbande sent his sister Njinga to negotiate with the Portuguese.

On the king's death in 1624, Njinga became queen. She continued to fight the Portuguese, but when they overran her kingdom in 1629, she fled to neighboring Mtamba, captured its ruler, Queen Mwongo, and took control. She ruled her new country successfully and independently until her death in 1663.

Portuguese legacy
An elegant cathedral in Quelimane is a relic of Portuguese colonial rule. Portuguese is the official language of Mozambique. The most common local dialect is Chuabo.

1990 **Renamo** loses the support of South Africa as apartheid ends, and in 1994, the ANC—Frelimo supporters—takes power.

1992 **Chissano signs** Rome peace agreement with Renamo.

1994 **Democratic elections** return Frelimo to power. They introduce major reforms to modernize the economy.

1995 **Mozambique** joins the Commonwealth, the only non-British former colony to be a member.

1997 **The G7 group of** major industrial countries chooses Mozambique as the flagship for its international debt-relief initiative.

2000–01 **Devastating floods** displace many thousands of people and harm the economy. The country is then affected by a severe drought in 2002.

2004 **Armando Guebuza wins** presidential election for Frelimo.

2007 **Chinese president** Hu Jintao visits and promises massive investment.

2009 **President Guebeza** is reelected with over 75 percent of the vote. The opposition party Renamo alleges fraud.

2010 **Riots against food prices** break out. Police shoot a number of protesters dead.

Madagascar

One of the world's poorest countries, which won independence from France in 1960.

400s **The first settlers** arrive from Indonesia. They are later joined by Bantu migrants from Africa.

1500 **Portuguese explorer** Diego Dias visits Madagascar.

1883–85 **The first Franco–Malagasy** war leads to the establishment of a French protectorate.

1895 **The French invade** and capture the main city of Antananarivo.

1896 **Madagascar becomes a** French colony. The Merina monarchy that rules the interior of the island is abolished as the French subdue the island.

1898–1906 **A revolt against** French rule is brutally suppressed.

1947–48 **French troops kill** thousands in nationalist uprisings.

1960 **Independence from France.**

1975 **Radical socialist** Didier Ratsiraka takes power. A new constitution sets up a "Democratic Republic" in which only a single party is permitted from 1977.

1990–92 **After months of unrest** and mass strikes, a new democratic constitution is established that sets up the Third Republic, restores civilian rule, and introduces multi-party democracy.

1991 **Opposition Forces Vives** (CFV), coalition of political parties, is set up, led by Albert Zafy.

1993 **Zafy's CFV defeats** Ratsiraka's coalition government in free elections.

1996 **Zafy impeached.**

1997 **Ratsiraka elected president.**

1998 **New constitution is adopted.**

2002 **Opposition leader** Marc Ravalomanana claims victory in the 2001 presidential election. In response, the incumbent president, Didier Ratsiraka, sets up a rival government in the port city of Tamatave. As fighting breaks out, the High Court rules in Ravalomanana's favor and Ratsiraka goes into exile.

2003 **Ratsiraka sentenced** in absentia to ten years' hard labor for embezzlement.

2006 **Ravalomana wins** reelection.

2008 **Cyclone Ivan** leaves over 300,000 homeless.

2009 **Violent protests** in Antananarivo after closure of opposition TV station. The government dismisses Andry Rajoelina, mayor of Antananarivo, and the military mutiny in favor of him. After a standoff, President Ravalomana resigns and is replaced by Rajoelina.

2009 **A power-sharing deal** between two sides is brokered, but breaks down.

2010 **AU and EU impose sanctions** against Madagascar. Ex-president Ravolomana is sentenced to life imprisonment for the shooting of protesters.

Comoros

An archipelago republic off the east coast with a chaotic political system and frequent coups.

1886 **Comoros becomes a** French protectorate after years of rule by a matrilineally inherited sultanate with strong cultural ties to the Arab world.

1947 **Comoros acquires** the status of a French overseas territory.

1961 **Internal self-government.**

1974 **Referendum** for independence. Island of Mayotte votes to remain French.

1975 **Independence** from France.

1975–96 **French mercenary** Bob Denard overthrows four governments.

1992 **Chaotic first** multi-party polls.

1997 **Both Anjouan** and Mohéli islands declare independence.

2002 **President Azzali Assoumani,** who seized power in 1999, promises a "Union of the Comoros," but tensions continue.

2006 **Muslim cleric** Ahmed Abdallah Sambi wins federal presidential elections.

2007 **Anjouan president Bacar** refuses to stand down; the island effectively secedes.

2008 **AU and Comoros troops** invade Anjouan and retake it.

2009 **Mayotte votes to integrate** with France in a referendum not recognized by the Comoran government.

Mauritius

An island republic in the Indian Ocean and one of the world's most densely populated countries.

1598 **Mauritius colonized** by the Dutch.

1722 **First French settlers** arrive.

Port Louis
This 18th-century picture shows a view of Port Louis, Mauritius, which was founded by the French in 1735 as a supply port for European ships making the long voyage around the Cape of Good Hope.

1814 **Islands acquired** by the British.

1968 **Independence from Britain.**

1992 **Becomes a republic.**

2000 **Coalition government set up** that alternates the main parties in power.

Seychelles

A group of 115 islands in the Indian Ocean that have been independent since 1976.

1742 **The islands are** explored by France, which claims possession of them in 1756.

1770 **The first French settlers** arrive to exploit the abundant supplies of tortoises and timber; they later introduce slavery.

1814 **The Treaty of Paris** transfers control of the islands from France to Britain.

1903 **Seychelles becomes a** crown colony.

1964 **Political parties formed,** led by France Albert René (pro-independence) and James Mancham (pro-UK rule).

1965 **The Desroches,** Aldabra, and Farquhar island groups are leased to the US; the British return the islands upon independence in 1976.

1976 **Independence from Britain:** coalition formed with Mancham as president and René as prime minister.

1977 **René takes over** in a coup.

1979 **One-party socialist** rule established.

1979–87 **Several coup attempts**.

1993 **Democratic elections** are held for the first time since 1976; René remains president as head of the Seychelles People's Progressive Front (SPPF).

1998 **René's SPPF** adopts plans for an international trading zone with free ports.

2004 **René's vice president,** James Michel, assumes the presidency (reelected 2006).

Namibia

A former German colony that was dominated by South Africa until winning independence in 1990.

1890 An Anglo–German agreement acknowledges German control of South West Africa and Britain's annexation of Walvis Bay in 1886 for Cape Colony. German colonists take best farming land and displace the indigenous people.

1904–08 Germans ruthlessly suppress rising by the Hereros and Namaqua, killing about 80,000 in open genocide; a harsh forced-labor regime is introduced.

1915 German forces surrender to South African troops.

1920 League of Nations awards South Africa the mandate to administer the territory "as an integral part of the Union of South Africa." South Africa extends the German policy of reserves for the indigenous population, 17 of which are established by 1939.

1946 UN General Assembly rejects South African request to incorporate South West Africa into its own territory; South Africa refuses to agree a trusteeship agreement.

1950 International Court of Justice rules that South Africa has no right to change the international status of the territory. Two further ICJ rulings, in 1955 and 1956, uphold the UN's right to supervise the administration.

1960 South West Africa People's Organization (SWAPO) is formed under Sam Nujoma and Herman Toivo ja Toivo. Based on the Ovamboland People's Organization, formed earlier with the aim of ending the contract labor system, SWAPO has broader objectives; it seeks to mobilize all the people of Namibia against South African rule.

1966 Apartheid laws imposed: SWAPO begins armed struggle.

1968 Country is renamed Namibia by UN General Assembly.

1972 UN recognizes SWAPO.

1990 After concerted international pressure and years of armed struggle, Namibia gains independence from South Africa; Sam Nujoma is elected president.

1994 South Africa relinquishes Walvis Bay.

1999 Sam Nujoma wins third term.

2004 Hifikepunye Pohamba is president.

2005 Government begins expropriation of white-owned farms.

2009 President Pohamba is reelected.

« 182–83 South of the Sahara

Botswana

An arid and landlocked country wealthy from diamonds and minerals but weakened by AIDS.

1813 The London Missionary Society establishes a mission, the first permanent settlements having been established by the Kwena (a Tswana people), who had come from South Africa a century earlier.

1885 The UK establishes the Bechuanaland Protectorate at request of local people to preempt annexation by South Africa.

1900 Administration passes to the High Commissioner for Basutoland, Bechuanaland, and Swaziland, with minimal interference in tribal affairs and only limited sales of land to white settlers and companies.

1920 Elected European and separate nominated African advisory councils are formed; the latter serves as a forum for African opposition to South African pressure for incorporation.

1948 Incorporation into South Africa is ruled out when the National Party comes to power there, but South Africa by now dominates the economy, which is little more than a labor reserve for South African mines and farms.

1950 As a result of South African pressure, tribal chief Seretse Khama is exiled by the UK administration following his marriage to a white Englishwoman. He is only allowed to return six years later on condition that he renounces the chieftainship of the Bamangwato.

1951 Joint advisory council is formed.

1961 Legislative council is set up.

1965 Bechuanaland (later Botswana) Democratic Party (BDP), led by Seretse Khama, wins first general election and all subsequent general elections.

1966 Independence declared.

1980 Vice President Quett (later Ketumile) Masire succeeds the late Seretse Khama as president.

1992–93 Strikes and corruption scandals prompt resignations of senior BDP figures.

1994 BDP support eroded in election.

1998 Vice President Festus Mogae succeeds Masire as president.

2001 Botswana has world's highest HIV infection rate of 38.3 percent of the population.

2008 BDP wins elections and Seretse Khama, son of the first president, is returned as president.

« 182–83 South of the Sahara

Zimbabwe

A formerly rich country reduced to poverty and economic collapse by its long-serving dictator.

500s Bantu speakers migrate south into the country, displacing earlier iron-working cultures.

1400s Great Zimbabwe grows rich on cattle grazing, gold mining, and trade with merchants on the coast.

1830s Shona peoples displaced by incoming Ndebele invaders, who force them to pay tribute.

1890 British South Africa Company of Cecil Rhodes founds Fort Salisbury as settlers begin to colonize the country.

1896–97 Shona and Ndebele revolt unsuccessfully against British rule.

1911 Rhodesia divided into southern and northern halves.

1923 After settlers vote against joining South Africa, Southern Rhodesia becomes a self-governing British colony.

1953 Southern Rhodesia joins Northern Rhodesia (now Zambia) and Nyasaland (now Malawi) in the Federation of Rhodesia and Nyasaland.

1961 Joshua Nkomo forms Zimbabwe African People's Union (ZAPU).

1962 ZAPU banned. Segregationist Rhodesian Front (RF) wins elections.

1963 African nationalists in Northern Rhodesia and Nyasaland demand dissolution of federation, which

Great Zimbabwe
Ruins are all that remain of Great Zimbabwe, the city that lay at the heart of the vast Munhumatapa Empire (c.1450–1629), which once incorporated present-day Zimbabwe and Mozambique.

is then dissolved. Zimbabwe African National Union (ZANU) is formed by the Reverend Sithole and Robert Mugabe.

1964 New RF prime minister Ian Smith rejects British demands for majority rule.

1965 RF reelected: Ian Smith declares unilateral independence from the UK, which imposes economic sanctions. ZANU and ZAPU begin guerrilla war.

1976 ZANU and ZAPU unite as Patriotic Front (PF) and are backed by frontline African states of Mozambique, Tanzania, Botswana, and Zambia.

1979 After four years, talks at Lancaster House in London reach agreement on a new constitution for majority rule. Britain resumes colonial rule.

1980 Independence as Zimbabwe. After a violent election campaign, Mugabe becomes prime minister.

1983–84 Unrest in Matabeleland, ZAPU–PF's power base.

1985 Elections return ZANU–PF, with manifesto to create one-party state; many ZAPU–PF members arrested.

1987 ZAPU–PF banned. Provision for white seats in parliament abolished. ZANU–PF and ZAPU–PF sign unity agreement. Mugabe elected president, with Nkomo as vice-president.

1990 Elections won by ZANU–PF. Mugabe reelected president.

1998 Nationwide strikes and protests against Mugabe's authoritarian rule. The Opposition Movement for Democratic Change (MDC) is founded the following year.

2000 Expropriations of white-owned farms by squatters lead to collapse in food production and rising inflation.

2006 Economic situation worsens. Inflation exceeds 1,000 percent.

2007 Morgan Tsvangirai, head of the MDC, is severely beaten by police.

2008 In presidential elections, opposition leader Morgan Tsvangirai wins most votes in first round to face run-off with Robert Mugabe. Tsvangirai boycotts the second round, alleging intimidation and Mugabe is declared the winner. Subsequent negotiations between the two lead to a power-sharing agreement.

2009 Tsvangirai is sworn in as prime minister, but the relationship between him and Mugabe is troubled, with allegations of violence orchestrated by ZANU and violations of the constitution.

2010 Annual rate of inflation, which had reached 231 million percent in 2008, declines to 4.1 percent.

« 182–83 South of the Sahara
« 320–21 Completing the Map

South Africa

A country ruled by a white minority through an oppressive system of apartheid until 1993.

600s After migrating slowly south, Bantu-speaking peoples settle in today's Transvaal, Natal, and Eastern Cape; Khoisan-speaking herders and hunter-gatherers live in the rest of the country.

1652 The Dutch East India Company establishes a provisioning station at Table Bay in the Cape, the first white settlement.

1779 Competition for grazing and arable land between the Dutch and the Xhosa develops into a series of frontier wars that continue for the next century.

1795 British first take the Cape; after a further period of Dutch rule (1803–06), the UK formally acquires the colony in 1814.

1835 Land-hungry Boer settlers, frustrated by Xhosa resistance and resenting British domination, begin their Great Trek north. Despite fierce battles with the Zulus and others, they expand white occupation into what is now the Transvaal, Natal, and Orange Free State.

1852 The Transvaal and, in 1854, the Orange Free State both gain their independence. Natal (proclaimed a colony in 1843) remains under British rule and is populated by British settlers.

1871 Four years after the discovery of diamonds, the UK annexes the diamond fields. This is followed in 1877 by the annexation of the Transvaal with its gold fields. Exploitation of diamonds and gold leads to economic boom and development of the migrant labor system, with African areas becoming "labor reservoirs."

1880–81 In the First South African (Boer) War, the Boers rise in revolt and defeat the British at Majuba Hill in 1881, winning back their independence. The British also fight and defeat the Zulus, but suffer a huge defeat at Isandlwana in 1879.

1896 Jameson Raid: a mounted column of British South Africa Company troops are captured by Boer forces.

1899–1902 Second South African (Boer) War is launched by Boer leader Paul Kruger with attacks on Natal and Cape Colony. After initial Boer successes the Boer capital, Pretoria, is captured in June 1900 and Boer guerrilla resistance is broken down. British keep Boer civilians in concentration camps.

1902 Treaty of Vereeniging incorporates Transvaal and Orange Free State once again into the British Empire.

1910 Union of South Africa set up; white monopoly of power is formalized.

1912 African National Congress (ANC) is formed.

The Boers
Descendants of the Dutch colonists, the Boers were hardy farmers and tough fighters, maintaining their independence until overcome by the British in 1902. This picture, taken in 1910, shows the wagons they used for defense if attacked.

1948 National Party (NP) takes power; apartheid segregationist policy introduced.

1958–66 Hendrik Verwoerd prime minister: "Grand Apartheid" policy is implemented.

1959 Pan Africanist Congress (PAC) is formed.

1960 Sharpeville massacre: police shoot demonstrators protesting against the pass laws; ANC and PAC banned.

1961 South Africa becomes a republic and leaves the Commonwealth.

1964 ANC leader Nelson Mandela jailed.

1976 Soweto uprisings by black students; hundreds killed.

1978 P. W. Botha in office.

1984 New constitution: Indians and blacks get some representation.

1985 State of emergency introduced.

1989 F. W. De Klerk replaces Botha as president.

1990 De Klerk legalizes ANC and PAC and frees Nelson Mandela.

1990–93 International sanctions gradually withdrawn.

1991 Convention for a Democratic South Africa (CODESA) starts work.

1993 Mandela and De Klerk win Nobel Peace Prize as apartheid is peacefully dismantled.

1994 Multi-racial elections won by the ANC; Mandela is elected president.

1998 Truth and Reconciliation Report condemns both apartheid crimes and ANC excesses.

1999 ANC election victory; Thabo Mbeki succeeds Mandela as president.

2002 World summit on sustainable development held in Johannesburg. Court orders the government to provide anti-AIDS drugs at all hospitals.

2004 ANC wins over two-thirds of the vote in elections; Mbeki is reelected.

2006 Ex-deputy president Jacob Zuma is aquitted on rape charges and reinstated as deputy leader of the ANC.

2008 A wave of anti-foreigner violence sweeps country, directed at Zimbabweans, Malawians, and Mozambicans. Many die. Thabo Mbeki is forced to resign as president over claims he interfered in corruption case against Jacob Zuma.

2009 Jacob Zuma is elected president.

2010 South Africa hosts the soccer World Cup.

« 434–35 Civil Rights
« 454–55 Apartheid and Beyond

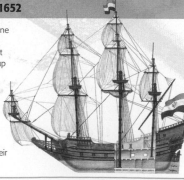

DECISIVE MOMENT

THE ARRIVAL OF THE DUTCH, 1652

The arrival of Jan van Riebeeck, five ships (one shown here), and about 90 people in Table Bay on April 6, 1652, had a profound impact on southern Africa. The colonists at first set up a provisioning station for Dutch East India Company ships, but subsequently ventured inland to farm the rich pastures. By the end of the 18th century, Cape Colony was home to the largest concentration of Europeans in Africa. The arrival of the British in 1795, however, changed the situation, as the Dutch were now the colonized and felt their Presbyterian culture to be under threat.

Swaziland

A landlocked kingdom bordered on three sides by South Africa, on whom it is largely dependent.

1902 British protectorate established.

1968 Independence from UK.

1973 King Sobhuza bans political activity.

1978 New constitution confirms king's executive and legislative control.

1982 King Sobhuza dies. Queen Mother becomes regent for Prince Makhosetive. Power struggle between modernists and traditionalists in royal Dlamini clan.

1986 Makhosetive crowned King Mswati III at the age of 18.

1992 Limited electoral reforms, although political parties are still banned.

2002 Mass pro-democracy protests.

2005 The king signs a new constitution that enshrines human rights. The document has taken eight years to draft.

2008 Elections are boycotted by the opposition. An attempted bomb attack is blamed on them and the leader of the Pudemo party is detained.

Lesotho

A mountainous and landlocked monarchy entirely surrounded by South Africa.

1868 British protectorate established after Moshoeshoe I is forced to cede fertile areas to Boers. After administration by Cape Colony between 1871–83, Britain resumes direct responsibility.

1884 Becomes the British Crown Colony of Basutoland.

1966 Independent kingdom.

1986 Military coup.

1990 King Moshoeshoe II exiled; his son installed as Letsie III.

1993 Free elections: Moshoeshoe II returns in 1994 and is restored as king.

1996 Letsie III succeeds to throne.

1998 New Lesotho Congress for Democracy wins polls. South Africa intervenes after coup attempt, and reconciles king and parties.

2004 Prime minister Mosisili appeals for food aid. Hundreds of thousands face shortages after three-year drought.

2007 General strike called by opposition.

Asia

The world's largest continent, Asia extends from the Arctic to the equator and from the Mediterranean to the Pacific. The first complex civilization arose in Asia, in ancient Mesopotamia (present-day Iraq), as did all the world's major religions.

Turkey

This secular republic bridging Europe and Asia emerged from the ashes of the Ottoman Empire.

667 BCE **The city of Byzantium** is founded by Greek colonists from Megara.

330 CE **Byzantium is refounded** by Emperor Constantine I as Nova Roma, the new capital of the eastern Roman Empire, and is later renamed Constantinople.

1453 **Constantinople is seized** by the Ottoman Turks and renamed Istanbul, becoming the capital of their empire.

1500s **Ottoman Empire** reaches its peak under Sultan Suleyman I, controlling much of southeast Europe, the Middle East, and North Africa.

1821 **Greek War of Independence** begins.

1832 **Greece is granted** independence by the Treaty of Constantinople.

1853–56 **Crimean War** with Russia, won by the Ottomans with foreign aid.

1908 **The Young Turk Revolution** sees parliament reinstated, as discontent with the Sultan's rule grows.

1911 **Ottomans are defeated** by Italy and are forced out of Libya. Albania declares its independence.

1914 **Ottoman Empire** enters World War I on the side of the Central Powers.

1915 **Approximately 800,000** Armenians are massacred by Turkish authorities.

1920 **Following defeat** in World War I, the Ottoman Empire is broken up, Turkey is forced to sign the Treaty of Sèvres, which includes the establishment of independent Armenian and Kurdish states, and pay reparations. A war of independence is launched.

1923 **Sultan Muhammad VI** is deposed, and Turkey is declared a republic with Kemal Atatürk as president and Ankara as its new capital. Treaty of Lausanne ends war with Allies, replacing the Treaty of Sèvres. Under a forced exchange, 1.3 million Greeks leave Turkey and 400,000 Turks leave Greece.

1924 **Religious courts** abolished.

1928 **Islam no longer** state religion.

1934 **Women given** the vote.

1938 **President Atatürk** dies. Succeeded by Ismet Inönü.

1945 **Turkey joins UN**.

1952 **Joins NATO**.

1960 **Army stages coup** against ruling Democratic Party and suspends National Assembly.

1961 **Turkey returns** to civilian rule under a new constitution.

1963 **Association agreement** with the European Economic Community (EEC).

TURKISH STATESMAN (1881–1938)

MUSTAFA KEMAL ATATÜRK

The father of the modern Republic of Turkey, Mustafa Kemal forged a secular state from the ashes of the Ottoman Empire, leading the fight against the post–World War I settlement imposed by the Allies and overthrowing the sultan. As president, Kemal introduced a European-style legal system and disestablished Islam as the state religion.

Kemal introduced surnames as part of his Westernizing agenda, and in 1934 he took the name Atatürk, which means "father of the Turks." He is still revered by many Turks as the man who restored pride to a shattered nation.

1974 **Turkish forces invade** northern Cyprus in response to intercommunal strife between Greek and Turkish populations on the island.

1980 **Martial law** is imposed after a coup.

1982 **New constitution** approved by referendum.

1983 **General election** won by Turgut Özal's ANAP (Motherland Party).

1984 **Turkey recognizes** Turkish Republic of Northern Cyprus. Kurdish separatist PKK (Kurdistan Workers' Party) launches guerrilla war in southeast.

1987 **Turkey applies** to join EEC.

1990 **US-led coalition** launches air strikes on Iraq from Turkish bases.

1991 **Elections won by DYP** (True Path Party). Süleyman Demirel premier.

1992 **Joins Black Sea Alliance**.

1993 **Demirel elected president.** Tansu Çiller becomes DYP leader and heads coalition.

1995 **Major offensive** is launched against Kurdish guerrillas in the southeast. Çiller coalition collapses and Islamist Welfare Party (RP) wins election, but center-right DYP–ANAP coalition takes office.

1996 **RP leader** Necmettin Erbakan heads first Islamist government since 1923.

1997 **Mesut Yilmaz reappointed** to head minority ANAP government.

1998 **RP is banned** by constitutional court. Mesut Yilmaz resigns as prime minister after corruption allegations. He is replaced by Bulent Ecevit.

1999 **Democratic Left Party (DSP)** wins most seats in general election. Captured Kurdish guerrilla leader Abdullah Ocalan sentenced to death. His sentence is later commuted to life imprisonment. Izmit earthquake kills 14,000.

2000 **National Assembly refuses** to reelect Demirel for a second term. He is replaced by Ahmet Necdet Sezer.

2001 **Acute financial crisis.** Prisoners and their relatives die in hunger strikes over conditions in high-security prisons.

2002 **Islamist Justice Party** (AK) wins landslide victory in elections. Abdullah Gul becomes prime minister.

2003 **Laws are passed** easing restrictions on the use of the Kurdish language. AK leader Recep Tayyip Erdogan becomes prime minister after entering parliament through a by-election.

2007 **Turkish-Armenian** community leader Hrant Dink is assassinated.

2007 **The religious AK party** wins elections. Abdullah Gul becomes president.

2008 **President Gul** signs constitutional amendments rescinding a ban on the wearing of Islamic headscarves by women in universities.

2010 **A court in Istanbul** indicts 200 military officers for plotting to overthrow the government. In a referendum, voters back reforms to give the government increased power over army and judiciary.

Georgia

A small ex-Soviet state in the Caucasus plagued by civil war since gaining independence.

300s BCE **First records** of a Georgian kingdom (of Kartli) after Alexander the Great's conquest of the Persian Empire.

318 CE **Georgia is converted** to Christianity. Over the following 300 years a conflict between Byzantium and Persia leads to the division of the country.

1014 **King Bagrat III** dies after uniting eastern and western Georgia. A golden age follows during the reign of Queen Tamara (1184–1213).

1236 **The Mongols conquer** eastern Georgia, although the western territory of Imeretia remains independent.

1453 **The fall** of Constantinople leaves Georgia isolated from western Christianity. Muslim invaders partition the country.

1783 **Russia guarantees** its independence, but Persia invades Georgia in 1795.

1801 **Russia annexes** Persian-ruled provinces of Kartlia and Kakhetia.

1810 **Western Georgia,** occupied by the Ottomans, is annexed by the Russians.

1826–28 **Russia again defeats** Persia in a war over Georgia.

1864 **Georgian peasants receive** limited freedoms.

1881 **A policy of russification** leads to an increase in radicalism.

1918 **Georgia proclaims** its independence under a Menshevik government and is briefly partly occupied by UK forces.

1921 **The Red Army** invades Georgia, ordered in by Joseph Stalin, despite a treaty of recognition between the two countries.

1922–36 **Georgia is incorporated** into the Transcaucasian Soviet Federative Socialist Republic (TSFSR).

1989 **Pro-independence riots** in Tbilisi are put down by Soviet troops.

Eduard Shevardnadze
The last foreign minister of the USSR and president of Georgia 1995–2003, Shevardnadze forged his reputation fighting corruption, yet was forced out in the Rose Revolution for vote-rigging.

1990 **Georgia declares** sovereignty and secedes from the USSR.

1991 **Georgia declares independence.** Zviad Gamsakhurdia elected president.

1992 **Gamsakhurdia flees Tbilisi.** Shevardnadze chair of State Council.

1992–93 **Fighting breaks out** in Abkhazia between government troops and separatists. Ten thousand are killed.

1994 **Ceasefire is established** between government and Abkhaz separatists.

1995 **Shevardnadze survives** assassination attempt, elected president.

1999 **Opening of pipeline** from Caspian Sea to Black Sea.

2000 **Shevardnadze** is reelected. The withdrawal of Russian troops begins.

2003 **In the so-called** Rose Revolution, Shevardnadze is peacefully removed from office amid accusations of corruption.

2004 **Mikhail Saakashvili** is president after new elections. Leader of the autonomous region of Ajaria, Aslan Abashidze, rebels. He backs down after a stand-off and is forced into exile.

2005 **Plans to grant autonomy** to South Ossetia and Abkhasia within the Georgian state are announced.

2006 **South Ossetians** vote in favor of independence from Georgia.

2008 **Russia intervenes** in Georgia, claiming it is protecting the rights of South Ossetia. Its army occupies South Ossetia and parts of Georgia itself, and advances close to Tbilisi. President Medvedev withdraws troops from Georgia, but leaves them in South Ossetia.

« 90–91 Frontiers of Power

Armenia

A former Soviet republic that suffered centuries of domination, often brutal, by neighboring states.

500s–400s BCE **The Armenians are** conquered by Persia and then by Alexander the Great.

1st century BCE **Under Tigranes II,** Armenia becomes a powerful state, establishing an empire for itself.

69 BCE **Roman general Lucullus** invades Armenia, which is thereafter disputed between Rome and the Parthian (later Sassanian) Persian empire.

301 CE **Armenia converts** to Christianity, the first sovereign nation to do so.

628 CE **Becomes province** of Byzantium.

885 CE **Armenia regains** independence, which it maintains until conquered by the Seljuk Turks in the 11th century.

1639 **Partition of Armenia** as the west becomes part of Turkey and the east is incorporated into the Persian Empire.

1828 **Eastern Armenia** part of the Russian Empire after the Russo-Persian war.

1877–78 **Massacre of Armenians** during Russo-Turkish war.

1894–96 **Some 200,000 people** in Turkish Armenia massacred by the Turks.

1915 **Ottomans exile 1.75** million Turkish Armenians, and kill at least half of them.

1916 **Czarist Russia** conquers Armenia.

1918 **Armenia becomes** an independent republic.

1920 **Invaded by Turkey** and Russia. Socialist republic is declared.

1922 **Becomes a Soviet republic.**

1980s **Encouraged by the USSR's** policy of glasnost, demonstrations in Yerevan become more and more frequent.

1988 **An earthquake** in northern Armenia kills 25,000. The Medzamor nuclear power plant is declared unsafe and closed. Armenian population of Nagorno-Karabakh vote to secede from Azerbaijan, leading to civil conflict.

1990 **Elections are won** by Armenian nationalists. Independence is declared.

1991 **Armenia joins** the Commonwealth of Independent States (CIS) with Levon Ter Petrosian elected president.

1992 **Armenia admitted** to the UN.

1995 **Medzamor nuclear plant** reopens owing to an energy crisis, despite warnings that it is still unsafe.

1994 **The region** of Nagorno-Karabakh in Azerbaijan proclaims itself a republic with ethnic Armenian forces in control.

1998 **Ter Petrossian** resigns over opposition to his desire to compromise over Nagorno-Karabakh. Nationalist Robert Kocharyan replaces him.

1999 **Gunmen open fire** in the Armenian parliament, killing the prime minister, the speaker, and six others.

2007 **A bill allowing dual citizenship** is passed, paving the way for the naturalization of an estimated 8 million people in Armenia's diaspora.

2009 **Turkey and Armenia** agree to normalize relations (but ratification of the agreement is suspended in 2010 by the Armenian parliament).

« 98–99 The Greeks in Asia

First Christian state
Two years after Armenia became the first state to adopt Christianity as its official religion in 301 CE, Saint Gregory the Illuminator founded this cathedral at Echmiadzin, Armenia's holiest city. Gregory also founded the Armenian Apostolic Church.

Azerbaijan

The first Soviet republic to declare independence, oil reserves are the key to its future prosperity.

300s CE **The area which** is now Azerbaijan falls under the domination of the Persian Sassanian dynasty.

641 **Muslims conquer** the region.

1000s **Seljuk Turks dominate** the region until overrun by the Mongols under Genghis Khan in the 13th century, and Tamerlane in the 14th century.

1728 **Treaty of Constantinople** affirms Ottoman control over the region after 300 years of rivalry between Turkey and Persia.

1828 **The Treaty of Turkmenchai** divides the region along the Araks River between Persia (to the south) and Russia.

1918 **UK forces** help install an independent, nationalist government in Azerbaijan. Azerbaijan declares neutrality in the Russian Civil War.

1920 **Red Army invades.**

1922 **Azerbaijan is incorporated** in Transcaucasian Soviet Federative Socialist Republic (TSFSR).

1930 **Forced collectivization** of agriculture.

1936 **TSFSR is disbanded** and Azerbaijan becomes a full union republic (ASSR).

1945 **Attempted annexation** of Azeri region of Iran.

1990 **Nagorno-Karabakh** attempts secession. Soviet troops move in.

1991 **Azerbaijan gains** independence.

1993 **Heydar Aliyev** is elected president.

1994 **Ceasefire** in war with Armenia over Nagorno-Karabakh.

1995 **A rebellion by** the special police led by Rovshan Jovadov is crushed.

2001 **Azerbaijan becomes** a full member of the Council of Europe.

2002 **Construction work begins** on an oil pipeline from Azerbaijan to Turkey.

2003 **Heydar Aliyev dies.**

2004 **Ilham Aliyev,** son of Heydar, is elected president.

2005 **Ruling New Azerbaijan Party** wins elections amid allegations of fraud.

2008 **Ilham Aliyev** wins a second term in elections boycotted by the opposition.

« 98–99 The Greeks in Asia
« 246–47 The Ottoman Empire

Syria

An Arab one-party state that has had turbulent foreign relations since independence in 1941.

600s BCE Area part of Assyrian Empire.

1st century BCE Area part of Roman Empire.

634 CE Muslim forces conquer Syria, defeating the Byzantines.

997 CE Northern Syria falls to the Byzantines and the south is ruled by the Egyptian Fatimid dynasty.

1098 Antioch captured by crusaders.

1260–1516 The Mamluks control Syria.

1516 Syria falls to the Ottomans.

1918 Arab troops led by Emir Faisal enter Damascus after 400 years of Ottoman rule.

1920 Faisal proclaimed king. After San Remo Conference awards Syria to France, he is ousted by French forces who proclaim new state of Greater Lebanon.

1925–26 Uprising against French rule.

1941 British and French occupy Syria and promise end to the French mandate.

1958–61 Syria united with Egypt in the United Arab Republic.

1963 Ba'athist military junta seizes power. Major General Amin al-Hafez becomes president.

1966 Hafez ousted by military coup supported by radical Ba'ath Party members.

1967 Israel overruns Syrian positions above Lake Tiberias, seizes Golan Heights, and occupies Quneitra.

1970 Hafez al-Assad seizes power.

1973 New constitution secures Ba'ath Party dominance. More territory temporarily lost to Israel in war.

1976 With a peacekeeping mandate from Arab League, Syria intervenes to quell fighting in Lebanon.

1977 Relations broken off with Egypt after President Sadat's visit to Jerusalem.

1978 Assad returned for second term.

1980 Membership in extremist Muslim Brotherhood made capital offense.

1981 Israel annexes Golan Heights.

1982 Islamic extremist uprising in Hama crushed; thousands killed. Israel invades Lebanon; Syrian missiles in Bekaa Valley are destroyed.

1985 Assad reelected president.

1986 Syrian complicity alleged in planting a bomb on Israeli airliner in London.

1989 Diplomatic relations reestablished with Egypt.

1991 Syrian troops take part in US-led invasion of Kuwait. The Damascus Declaration, an aid and defense pact with Egypt, Saudi Arabia, Kuwait, UAE, Qatar, Bahrain, and Oman, is signed.

1999 Assad reconfirmed as president.

2000 Death of Hafez al-Assad. He is succeeded by his son Bashar.

2001 Syrian troops leave Beirut.

2003 Israel bombs "terrorist camps" in Syria.

2006 Thousands flee into Syria to escape Israel's attack on Lebanon.

2006 Iraq and Syria restore diplomatic relations after a break of nearly 25 years (but they are broken off again in 2009–10).

2009 Syrian stock exchange starts trading.

2010 US restores sanctions against Syria, accusing it of supporting terrorist groups such as Hezbollah.

«54–55 The Cradle of Civilization
«80–81 Rulers of the Iron Age

French fortress
The crusader castle Krak des Chevaliers, built in the 12th century, was the power center of the French Knights Hospitaller in the Holy Land and one of the greatest crusader fortresses of medieval Christendom. It eventually fell to the Arab leader Baibars after a short siege in 1271.

Lebanon

Once a refuge for persecuted religious and political groups, Lebanon was shattered by civil war.

600s BCE Area part of Assyrian Empire.

1st century BCE The area becomes part of the Roman Empire.

900s Muslim sects begin their penetration of the Lebanese mountains.

1516-17 The Ottomans conquer Lebanon.

1633 Ottoman Sultan Murad IV takes control of Lebanon.

1860 The Druzes and Maronites clash and massacres are carried out by both sides.

1920 France creates Greater Lebanon, which includes Tripoli, Tyre, and Beirut.

1941 The Free French proclaim Lebanon independent. Full autonomy comes in 1946 when last French troops withdraw.

1958 President Kamil Shamoun requests the presence of US troops.

1975 Civil war erupts between Christian and Muslim militias.

1978 Israel invades and occupies territory. Israel invades again in 1982.

1983 More than 300 US and French troops are killed by two bombs in Beirut planted by militant Shia groups.

1989 Taif Agreement ends civil war.

1991 Militias are disbanded but radical Islamist group Hezbollah and Christian South Lebanon Army (SLA) do not comply.

1992 First election in 20 years. Rafiq al-Hariri prime minister.

1996 Israeli attack kills over 100 civilians at the UN base in Qana.

1998 Émile Lahoud becomes president.

2000 Israeli forces withdraw from southern Lebanon.

2005 Former prime minister Rafik Hariri is killed by a car bomb. Calls for Syria to withdraw its troops intensify.

2006 Israel launches strikes against Lebanon after Hezbollah captures two Israeli soldiers. Truce declared after 34 days of war.

2007 Lebanese army lays siege to a Palestinian refugee camp for four months. More than 300 die.

2008 A new cabinet is formed by Prime Minister Fouad Siniora; Hezbollah ministers have enough posts to afford them a veto.

2009 The International tribunal set up to try suspected killers of assassinated PM

Hariri opens in the Hague. Pro-Western party led by Saad Hariri wins most seats in general election.

«80–81 Rulers of the Iron Age
«414–15 The Promised Land

Jordan

An independent kingdom since 1946, most of whose people live along the east bank of the Jordan River.

1918 King Faisal establishes autonomous Arab government in Damascus.

1920 The Palestine mandate, covering present-day Israel, Jordan, and the West Bank, is awarded to the UK. King Faisal is forced out of Damascus.

1921 Hashemite King Abdullah is proclaimed ruler of Transjordan.

1948 State of Israel created in British-mandate Palestine. Thousands of Palestinians flee Arab–Israeli fighting to the West Bank and Jordan.

1949 The remainder of Palestine becomes the "Hashemite Kingdom of Jordan."

1950 Jordan annexes the West Bank and East Jerusalem.

1953 Hussein is proclaimed king after the assassination of his uncle Abdullah.

1967 Israel seizes West Bank territories during the Six-Day War.

1970 A massive crackdown on the Palestine Liberation Organization (PLO) results in thousands of casualties in a civil war known as Black September.

1986 King Hussein breaks all political links with the PLO.

1988 Jordan cedes claims to the West Bank to the PLO. Hussein publicly backs the Palestinian uprising, or intifada, against Israeli rule.

1989 First general election held since 1967 but contested only by independent candidates as political parties are banned.

1990 Severe economic and diplomatic strain affects country—a result of Iraq's invasion of Kuwait.

1994 Peace treaty with Israel ends a 46-year state of war.

1999 King Hussein dies and is succeeded by King Abdullah II.

2002 Agreement with Israel to pipe water from the Red Sea to the shrinking Dead Sea. The project is the two countries' largest joint venture.

2005 Explosions kill 56 people, mostly Jordanians, at three hotels in Amman. Al-Qaeda in Iraq claims responsibility.

2007 Pro-government groups do well in general elections; the opposition Islamic Action Front loses ground.

« 150–51 Decline and Fall

Israel

A country created in 1948, fulfilling the Zionist ambition for a Jewish state.

c.990 BCE Jerusalem captured by King David; Israel unified as one nation.

332 BCE Alexander the Great conquers the Persian Empire and takes control of Palestine. Begins Hellenization of area.

63 BCE Jerusalem conquered by Rome.

66–70 CE Jewish revolt against Rome. Fortress of Masada falls in 73 BCE.

1099 Crusaders take Jerusalem after a siege. More than 20,000 Jews and Muslims slaughtered or sold as slaves.

1897 At the Basle Congress in Switzerland, journalist Theodor Herzl defines the aim of Zionism as striving to create Jewish state.

1916 The Sykes–Picot Agreement is signed between Britain and France. Palestine is promised to Britain.

1917 In the Balfour Declaration, the British government agrees to the establishment of a national home for the Jewish people providing that the rights of non-Jews are unaffected.

1920 The San Remo Conference gives the mandate for Palestine to Britain.

1929 Arabs and Jews clash during violent protests in Palestine.

1936 The Arab population of Palestine goes on a six-month strike followed by a large-scale rebellion.

1939 The British government proposes a bill that envisages Palestine as a state in which Arabs and Jews share government.

1942 David Ben-Gurion, chairman of the Jewish Agency Executive, calls for the emigration of Jews to Palestine and the establishment of a Jewish State.

1947 The UN General Assembly adopts a plan for Palestine which divides the country into six parts, with three of the larger parts allocated to the Jews. The Arabs refuse to accept it; clashes follow, and 1,700 people are killed.

1948 Clashes between Arabs and Jews turn into a full-scale war. A provisional Jewish government is established with Ben-Gurion as prime minister. The State of Israel is officially declared, as 400,000 Arabs flee. It is immediately recognized by the US and USSR.

1949 The first general election is held for a single-chamber Knesset (parliament) elected by proportional representation.

1956 President Nasser of Egypt nationalizes the Suez Canal. Israel invades Sinai and Anglo-French forces invade Port Said in Egypt.

1957 Under US pressure, Israeli forces withdraw from the territories invaded in the Suez conflict.

1964 Egypt and other Arab states set up Palestine Liberation Organization (PLO).

1965 Fatah, the secular political party of the PLO, carries out its first guerrilla action against Israel.

1967 Six-Day War begins with Israel attacking Egypt. Israel takes West Bank, Gaza, Sinai, and Golan Heights.

1968–70 Israel establishes Jewish

> " **Israel has created a new image** of the Jew in the world—the image of… a people that can **fight** with **heroism**. "

DAVID BEN-GURION

GOLDA MEIR

One of the founders of the State of Israel, Golda Meir was born in Kiev, Russia. Poverty forced her family to emigrate to Wisconsin in 1906, where Golda became a Zionist. In 1922 she moved to Palestine to live on a kibbutz. She became active in trade union politics before being elected to the knesset and serving as Minister of Labor 1949–56 and Foreign Minister 1956–66. On the sudden death of Levi Eshkol in 1969, she succeeded him as prime minister at age 70. Despite victory in the Yom Kippur War (1973), she faced internal political squabbles and decided to resign in 1974.

PALESTINE AND THE OSLO ACCORDS, 1993

The Oslo agreement, which set up a Palestine National Authority and gave the Palestinians control over a limited portion of Gaza and the West Bank, was signed in Norway in September 1993 and tantalizingly offered the promise of a lasting peace. With little progress made toward reclaiming the territory lost to Israel in 1948, the Arab states in 1964 established the Palestine Liberation Organization as a force to help liberate the Occupied Territories. The PLO—some of whose fighters are depicted here—came to act as a proxy government-in-exile for the Palestinians. Despite a history of violent opposition to Israel, the PLO entered unprecedented talks with Yitzhak Rabin's moderate Labor government in an attempt to negotiate a "land for peace" deal.

settlements in the occupied territories. Yasser Arafat named chairman of PLO.

1973 Egypt and Syria attack Israel. Yom Kippur War ends in victory for Israel.

1977 Egyptian president Anwar Sadat addresses Israeli Knesset (parliament).

1978 Camp David accords with Egypt. Menachim Begin and Sadat sign Israeli–Egyptian Peace Treaty in Washington, DC. Sinai returned to Egypt.

1981 The US sponsors ceasefire between Israel and the PLO that lasts until June 1982. Israel annexes Syria's Golan region.

1982 Israel invades Lebanon.

1987 Palestinians launch first intifada

(uprising). Hamas, a hardline, armed Islamist movement, emerges.

1990 Government collapses over proposed negotiations with Palestinians. Influx of Jews from former Soviet Union.

1992 Yitzhak Rabin (Labor) becomes prime minister.

1992 Israel and the PLO sign Declaration of Principles ("Oslo Accords").

1994 Palestinian autonomy begins in Gaza and Jericho. First Palestinian suicide bombing against Israeli civilians is carried out in response to a massacre of Palestinians at Hebron by an Israeli settler. Israel and Jordan sign peace treaty.

1995 Prime minister Rabin is murdered in Tel Aviv by an Israeli extremist. He is replaced by Shimon Peres.

1996 First Palestinian elections. Arafat wins. Benjamin Netanyahu (Likud) defeats Peres to become prime minister.

1999 Ehud Barak (Labor) is elected prime minister.

2000 Israeli forces withdraw from southern Lebanon. Violent Israeli–Palestinian clashes begin a second intifada.

2001 Hardliner Ariel Sharon (Likud) is elected prime minister.

2002 Israel reoccupies most Palestinian areas evacuated as part of the Oslo process. Arafat is forced into house arrest. Israel begins construction of a security wall within the West Bank.

2004 Arafat dies in Paris.

2005 Mahmoud Abbas elected President of the Palestinian Authority. Israel evacuates all Israeli settlements in Gaza. Sharon forms new Kadima Party in response to opposition to his plans to withdraw Israeli settlers.

2006 Hamas wins a majority in Palestinian elections. Ehud Olmert (Kadima) becomes prime minister after Sharon suffers a stroke. Israel launches a 34-day war against Hezbollah in Lebanon.

2008 The Winograd commission on the 2006 Lebanon wars finds there were serious failings in the country's leadership. The Israeli army launches a major incursion into the Gaza Strip.

2009 Benyamin Netanyahu, leader of Likud, is elected prime minister.

2010 Israeli armed forces attack a flotilla carrying aid bound for Gaza.

« 78–79 Bronze Age Collapse
« 200–01 The Crusades
« 400–01 The Holocaust
« 414–15 The Promised Land

Saudi Arabia

An oil-rich kingdom with laws based on the ultra-conservative principles of Wahhabi Islam.

400s CE Arabia is invaded by Ethiopians and Sassanians from Persia.

c.610 CE Muhammad begins preaching in Mecca. He moves against the ruling Quraysh and takes the city in 630. Mecca becomes the center of Islam, but the Arabian peninsula is otherwise sidelined under the Umayyad and Abbasid Caliphates and the Ottoman Sultanate.

1871 The Ottomans take control of the province of Hasa.

1891 Saud family are exiled to Kuwait.

1902 Abd al-Aziz (Ibn Saud) returns from exile and captures Riyadh.

1913–26 Ibn Saud and the Ikhwan sweep across Arabia, taking Hasa in 1913, Mecca in 1924, and Medina in 1925. In 1921 he takes the title Sultan of Najd, and in 1926 he is named King of the Hijaz.

1928–30 The Ikhwan rebel and are defeated after two years of civil war.

1932 Ibn Saud unifies his domain as Saudi Arabia.

1937 Oil reserves are discovered near Riyadh. Production begins within a year.

1953 King Saud succeeds to the throne.

1964 King Saud abdicates in favor of his brother Faisal.

1967 Saudi Arabia joins Jordan and Iraq against Israel in Six-Day War.

1973 Saudi Arabia imposes oil embargo on Western supporters of Israel.

1975 King Faisal assassinated by a nephew; succeeded by his brother Khalid.

1979 Muslim fundamentalists led by Juhaiman ibn Seif al-Otaibi seize Grand Mosque in Mecca.

1982 King Fahd succeeds on the death of his brother King Khalid.

1990–91 US, UK, French, Egyptian, and Syrian forces assemble in Saudi Arabia for the Gulf War against Iraq. Public executions are halted.

1993 King Fahd appoints 60-man Consultative Council (Majlis ash-Shoura).

1996 King Fahd briefly hands control to Crown Prince Abdullah after a stroke.

2001 Relations with US are strained after 15 Saudis take part in the 9/11 attack.

2005 King Fahd dies and is succeeded by Crown Prince Abdullah.

2005 First-ever national municipal elections are held (but the franchise is restricted to men).

2006 360 pilgrims are killed in a crush during the Hajj.

2009 The trials of 330 suspected Islamist terrorists conclude.

« 174–77 The Ascent of Islam
« 246–47 The Ottoman Empire
« 440–41 The Oil Crisis

DECISIVE MOMENT
IBN SAUD DEFEATS THE IKHWAN, 1930

In January 1930, a two-year civil war ended when the leaders of a military force known as the Ikhwan were captured by the British and handed over to Ibn Saud, the first king of Saudi Arabia.

Ibn Saud had established the Ikhwan in 1912 as an elite fighting unit educated in the Wahhabi tradition of Islam. But he had trained them too well. As he swept to victory against Ottoman rule, Ibn Saud began to cooperate with foreign powers, in particular the British. The Ikhwan saw this as a betrayal and in 1928 they had rebelled. His defeat of the Ikhwan crushed all opposition and established the rule of the House of Saud.

Ikhwan on the move
Riding camels with banners flying, the Ikhwan were ferocious Bedouin soldiers driven by an Islamic fundamentalist zeal.

Yemen

In the poorest country in the Middle East, unified in 1990, tensions between north and south persist.

630 CE Muslim forces occupy Yemen.

1839 UK occupies Aden.

1849 Ottomans take control of north.

1918 North Yemen gains independence. Ruled by Imam Yahya.

1937 Aden made a crown colony.

1962 Imam deposed in a coup, Yemen Arab Republic (YAR) in north.

1962–70 Northern civil war between royalists and republicans.

1963 British-ruled Aden and Protectorate of Southern Arabia unified.

1967 British troops leave Aden.

1970 South Yemen renamed People's Democratic Republic of Yemen (PDRY) after radical Marxists seize power.

1972 War between YAR and PDRY ends in a peace settlement.

1978 A coup in PDRY brings radical Abdalfattah Ismail to power.

1980 Ismail replaced by moderate Ali Nasir Muhammad.

1986 Coup attempt in PDRY leads to civil war. Rebels take control of Aden.

1987 Oil production starts in YAR.

1990 Formal unification in May. Ali Saleh president of Republic of Yemen.

1991 Yemen opposes the US-led action against Iraq.

1997 President Saleh's GPC wins an absolute majority in general election.

2000 USS Cole is badly damaged by suicide attack in Aden harbor.

2004–05 Supporters of dissident cleric Hussein al-Houthi rebel in the north. Uprising ends with a pardon to the rebels.

2006 President Saleh is reelected.

2008 Clashes with Al-Houthi rebels and with protesters in Sana. Attack on the US embassy in Sana kills 18 people.

2009 A government offensive against the northern rebels; Saudi Arabian army involved in fighting the Yemeni rebels.

2010 A ceasefire is signed with northern rebels who release nearly 200 prisoners.

« 158–59 Diffusion of Knowledge
« 174–77 The Ascent of Islam

Oman

The oldest independent state in the Arab world, and until recently one of the most isolated.

700s CE Establishment of an independent Ibadi Imamate in Oman.

1507 Portuguese take control of Oman.

1650 Imam Nasir Ibn Murshid of the Yaariba dynasty expels the Portuguese.

1730 The Omanis conquer Portuguese settlements on the East Coast of Africa.

1743 The Persians capture Muscat.

1749 Ahmad Ibn Said is elected Imam as the Persians are expelled, and founds the Al-Said dynasty, which rules to the present day.

1913 Control of the country fractures. The interior is ruled by the Ibadite imams, while the sultan controls the coast.

1920 The sultan recognizes the autonomy of the interior in a peace agreement brokered by the British.

1932 Sultan Said bin Taimur comes to power. He adopts an isolationist, anti-Western approach.

1959 Bin Taimur regains control of the interior, responding to popular demands for complete independence.

1964 Oil reserves are discovered. Extraction begins three years later.

1965 Leftist forces in the southern region of Dhofar begin an uprising.

1970 Sultan Qaboos bin Said seizes power from his father in a bloodless coup. He begins a program of liberalization.

1975 Dhofar revolt is finally suppressed with the aid of troops from Jordan and Iran.

1991 Consultative Council set up as Sultan Qaboos allows limited elections.

1997 Women are allowed to stand and vote in elections to the Consultative Council. The first two women are elected.

1999 Oman and neighboring United Arab Emirates (UAE) sign an agreement ending a long-standing border dispute.

2003 Consultative Council members elected for first time, as all citizens over the age of 21 are allowed to vote. The vote had previously been limited to tribal leaders, chosen intellectuals, and businessmen.

2004 Oman appoints its first female minister.

« 158–59 Diffusion of Knowledge
« 174–77 The Ascent of Islam

Boom-time city
Unlike the other Emirates, Dubai's wealth is not historically dependent on oil revenues. As service industries develop, construction of prestige high-rise developments continues to boom.

UAE

The oil-rich Emirates have developed rapidly over the past 30 years, but remain autocratic regimes.

1820 **The area becomes** known as the Trucial Coast after the UK signs a treaty with local rulers to combat piracy.

1892 **Deal between** Trucial States and UK: each emirate controls internal affairs while the UK controls foreign policy.

1952 **The seven emirates** come together in the Trucial Council.

1959 **Significant oil strikes** in the region.

1968 **Bahrain and Qatar** join the Trucial States, only to leave three years later.

1971 **The UK withdraws** as protecting power and the UAE federation is formed, comprising Abu Dhabi, Ajman, Dubai, Fujairah, Sharjah, and Umm al-Qaywayn. Sheikh Zayed Bin-Sultan Al Nuhayyan presides over the federation.

1972 **Ras al-Khaymah** joins the federation.

1987 **Failed coup** in Sharjah.

1991 **UAE offers bases** to the West after Kuwait is invaded. BCCI bank, owned by Abu Dhabi's ruling family, collapses.

1993 **Immigrants from Asia** and Africa now three-quarters of the population.

2000 **Sharia law** is introduced in Fujairah and an Indonesian woman is sentenced to be stoned to death.

2004 **Sheikh Zayed** dies and is replaced by his son, Sheikh Khalifa.

2006 **The UAE holds** its first-ever national elections, with the franchise limited to a hand-picked electorate. They elect half the members of the Federal National Council, an advisory body.

2009 **The international** financial crisis causes the UAE to withdraw from the planned Gulf Monetary Union. The government-owned conglomerate Dubai World almost collapses. Only $4.1 billion bailout from Abu Dhabi saves it.

2010 **The Burj Khalifa** tower opens in Dubai as the world's tallest building.

« 158–59 Diffusion of Knowledge
« 174–77 The Ascent of Islam

Bahrain

This island state in the Persian Gulf has diversified from oil into financial services.

1521 **The Portuguese assume** control.

1602 **Persia** occupies Bahrain.

1783 **The Iranians are** expelled by the Arabian Utub tribe, whose principal family, the al-Khalifas, still rule today.

1861 **The ruling sheikh** of Bahrain agrees to abstain from war, piracy, and slavery in return for British military support.

1880 **Administrative control and** foreign relations are granted to the UK.

1913 **UK and the Ottoman** Empire sign a treaty recognizing Bahrain's independence.

1931 **Oil is discovered** in Bahrain, and extraction begins a year later.

1939 **The British decide** that the Hawar Islands belong to Bahrain and not Qatar.

1967 **The UK relocates** its naval base in the region from Aden to Bahrain. The following year, it announces its intention to close all bases "east of Suez" by 1971.

1971 **Independence from Britain** under Sheikh Isa Bin-Salman Al Khalifah.

1975 **Emir dissolves** the National Assembly and rules by decree.

1981 **Founding member of** GCC.

1990–91 **Bahrain supports UN** action expelling Iraq from Kuwait.

1994–96 **Shia unrest.**

1999 **Accession to throne** of Sheikh Hamad bin Isa al-Khalifa.

2001 **Transition to democracy.** Bahrain becomes a constitutional monarchy with an elected lower chamber of parliament.

2002 **Parliamentary elections** are held for the first time in 30 years.

2006 **Shia opposition** wins 40 percent of votes in election. Jawad bin Salem al Oraied, a Shia, becomes prime minister.

2010 **Twenty Shia** political leaders are arrested, accused of plotting to overthrow the Bahraini monarchy.

« 158–59 Diffusion of Knowledge
« 174–77 The Ascent of Islam

Qatar

A former center of pearl fishing that has been transformed by the discovery of oil.

1700s **Pearling and trading** settlements are established along the coast.

1867 **Doha is all but destroyed** in a conflict with neighboring Bahrain. The UK recognizes Qatar as a separate entity from Bahrain.

1939 **Oil reserves are discovered** but exploitation is delayed by World War II. Post-war, oil quickly replaces pearling and fishing as Qatar's main source of income.

1971 **Independence from the** UK.

1972 **Accession of Amir** Khalifa, who deposes his father.

1995 **Sheikh Hamad overthrows** his father Shaikh Khalifa in a bloodless coup.

1996 **Satellite TV channel** Al-Jazeera, a news channel, is launched. Funded by the emir, it broadcasts to much of the Arab world, providing an Arab perspective on world affairs.

1999 **First-ever polls,** to elect new municipal council, mark the beginning of a program of democratization.

2000 **Thirty-three** rebels are sentenced to life imprisonment for their part in the failed 1996 coup. Among them is the emir's cousin, an ally of the emir's deposed father.

2001 **Long-standing border** disputes with Saudi Arabia and Bahrain are settled.

2004 **Relations with Russia** deteriorate when former Chechen president Zelimkhan Yanderbiyev is killed in an explosion in Doha.

« 158–59 Diffusion of Knowledge
« 174–77 The Ascent of Islam

Kuwait

A small oil-producing kingdom surrounded by large and powerful neighbors.

750–1258 **The Abbasid Caliphate** of Baghdad controls Kuwait.

1258–1546 **Kuwait under** Mongol rule.

1546–1918 **Ottomans govern** Kuwait.

1756 **Al-Sabah ruling** dynasty is founded.

1899 **Sheikh Mubarak** grants the UK control of the country's foreign relations.

1918 **Ottoman Empire** dismantled. Kuwait becomes a British protectorate. New Iraqi state makes first claims over Kuwait.

1938 **Oil extraction** begins.

1961 **Independence from UK.**

1976 **Emir suspends National** Assembly.

1990 **Iraq invades,** starting the Gulf War.

1991 **An international coalition** led by the US forces the Iraqis to withdraw, but oil wells are set aflame and no oil can be produced until 1992. Under international pressure, the emir promises democratic reforms.

1992 **National Assembly elections** held.

1994 **Iraq recognizes** Kuwait's sovereign status.

2003 **The roles of** prime minister and heir to throne are separated for first time since independence. Islamist candidates make gains in general election.

2006 **Women are able** to vote for parliament for the first time.

2006 **Sheikh Saber** dies and is succeeded by Sheikh Sabah al-Ahmed.

2008 **Radical Islamists** win more than half the seats in general election.

« 80–81 Rulers of the Iron Age
« 468–69 The Gulf Wars

Fields of fire
Here Kuwaiti oil fields set aflame by retreating Iraqi troops blacken the sky with smoke. About 50 oil wells were lit after the 1990 Iraqi invasion. The cost of the clean up ran into billions of dollars.

Iraq

Iraq has struggled to assert its independence in a troubled history marred by foreign invasions.

c. **3000 BCE** **Sumerian civilization** flourishes in Mesopotamia, the area of modern Iraq.

c. **1700 BCE** **Hammurabi of** Babylon establishes an empire in Mesopotamia.

700s–600s BCE **Assyrians** rule much of Iraq from Nineveh.

539–538 BCE **Persian king** Cyrus the Great seizes Babylon.

331 BCE **Alexander the Great** takes Babylon during his conquest of the Persian empire. Iraq is ruled by his Greek successors until the 2nd century BCE, and then by the Parthians and Sassanian Persians.

Golden goat
This gold and lapis lazuli ornament was dicovered in the 1920s in the Royal Tombs of Ur by British archaeologist Leonard Woolley. It dates from about 2500 BCE when Sumerian culture was at its zenith.

637 CE **Muslim Arab** armies take over Iraq after the battle of Jalula.

762 **Baghdad founded** on the banks of the Tigris by Caliph Al-Mansour as his new capital. Iraq becomes political and cultural center of the Abbasid caliphate.

900s–1000s **Baghdad falls** to the Shi'ite Buwaihids.

1000s **The Seljuk** Turks dominate Iraq.

1534 **The Ottoman Sultan** Suleyman conquers Baghdad. Iraq is under Ottoman control for four centuries, save for a brief Safavid Persian occupation in the 1600s.

1914 **The Ottoman Empire** sides with Germany during World War I. British troops invade Iraq to deprive the Central Powers of vital staging post.

1915–16 **British defeated** at Siege of Kut.

1916 **Sykes–Picot** agreement between Britain and France on the future of the Middle East after the war's end.

1917 **British troops** capture Baghdad.

1920 **League of Nations** awards mandate over Iraq to Britain, leading to an uprising in Iraq.

1921 **Amir Faisal Ibn Hussein** becomes first king of Iraq following a plebiscite.

1922 **An Anglo-Iraqi** Treaty is signed, guaranteeing the UK special interests in exchange for the establishment of a constituent assembly in Iraq.

1932 **King Faisal formally** proclaims Iraq an independent and sovereign state.

1948 **Iraqi troops are** sent to Israel to fight in the Arab–Israeli war.

1956 **Iraq joins** the Baghdad Pact, a pro-US alliance of West Asian powers.

1958 **King Faisal II** is killed in a coup. Brigadier Abd-Al-Karim Kassem becomes president.

1961 **Start of Kurdish** rebellion in north Iraq. Baghdad claims sovereignty over Kuwait on the eve of Kuwait's independence.

1963 **Kassem overthrown** in a coup led by the Arab Socialist Ba'ath Party, but the Ba'athists are in turn ousted by Colonel Abd as-Salem Muhammad Aref. Kuwait's sovereignty is recognized.

1966 **Aref is succeeded** by his brother, Abd ar-Rahman.

1968 **Ba'athists, under Ahmad** Hassan al-Bakr, take power.

1970 **Revolutionary Command Council** establishes manifesto on Kurdish autonomy.

1972 **Nationalization of Western-** controlled Iraq Petroleum Company. Treaty of Friendship and Cooperation signed with the Soviet Union.

1978 **Iraq and Syria** form economic and political union.

1979 **Saddam Hussein replaces** al-Bakr as president.

1980 **Outbreak of** the Iraq–Iran war, in a border dispute with the new Revolutionary Islamic government in Tehran. The Iranians seek to topple the Sunni Saddam, who they see as oppressing Iraq's Shia majority.

1981 **Israeli jets attack** and cripple Iraqi nuclear research facility at Osirak near Baghdad.

Abbasid splendor
From the mid-8th century, Baghdad under the Abbasids became the capital of the Islamic world, adorned with a number of splendid mosques.

1982 **Shia leader** Mohammed Baqir al-Hakim, exiled in Tehran, forms Supreme Council of the Islamic Revolution in Iraq.

1988 **Iraq and Iran** agree ceasefire. Iraqi government forces use chemical weapons in attack on Kurdish village of Halabja.

1990 **British journalist** Farzad Bazoft hanged for spying. Iraq and Iran restore diplomatic relations. Iraq invades Kuwait. UN authorizes the use of force to enforce Iraqi withdrawal.

1991 **Gulf War.** US-led military coalition launches massive air and ground offensives, which drive the Iraqis out of Kuwait. The Iraqi regime puts down Shia rebellion. Establishment of safe haven for Kurds in northern Iraq.

1992 **Western powers proclaim** air exclusion zone over southern Iraq.

1994 **Outbreak of Kurdish** civil war. Iraq recognizes Kuwaiti sovereignty.

1995 **Government minister** Gen. Hussein Kamil defects to Jordan. He is murdered on his return to Iraq in February 1996.

1996 **First legislative elections** since 1989 are won by ruling Ba'ath Party. UN supervises limited sales of Iraq oil to purchase humanitarian supplies. Iraqi forces launch offensive into Kurdish safe haven, capturing Irbil. US expands southern air exclusion zone to just south of Baghdad.

1998–99 **UN weapons inspection** teams are refused reentry into Iraq; US and UK mount punitive air strikes to destroy Iraq's nuclear, biological, and chemical weapons programs.

1999 **Grand Ayatollah** Muhammad Sadiq al-Sadr, leader of Iraq's Shias, is assassinated in Najaf.

2002 **United Nations** weapons inspectors return to Iraq as UN Security Council warns of grave consequences if it does not cooperate with their investigation.

2003 **American-led coalition** invades Iraq on March 20, capturing Baghdad less than three weeks later. Saddam eludes capture until December. A US-led administration is installed in Baghdad, the Ba'ath party is made illegal, and the armed forces are dissolved.

2004 **Anti-US insurgency** mounts, with increasing attacks against coalition forces. Initially largely Sunni-led, Shia militias now join the movement to oust the US. US restores Iraqi sovereignty to government under Iyad Allawi. Major US offensive against insurgents in Fallujah.

2005 **Voting takes place** for a Transitional National Assembly. Increase in car bombings by insurgents. Kurdish leader Jalal Talabani becomes president of Iraq. New constitution approved by Iraqi voters. Trial of Saddam Hussein for crimes against humanity begins. Parliamentary elections leave Shia-led United Iraqi Alliance as largest party.

2006 **Jawad al-Maliki** becomes prime minister. Insurgency-related deaths mount dramatically: an independent study estimates that 600,000 Iraqis have died since the 2003 invasion. Leader of Al-Qaeda in Iraq, Abu Musab al-Zarqawi, is killed in US air strike. Saddam Hussein is sentenced to death and hanged.

2007 **United States** announces new security plan for Baghdad, but a series of car bombs in the capital kills hundreds. Former Vice President Taha Yassin Ramadan is executed. Calls for US withdrawal mount.

2007 **Britain hands over** control of security in Basra province to Iraqi government.

2008 **United States** hands over security control in Anbar provine to the Iraqi government: it is the first Sunni province to be handed over to Iraqi security forces. The Iraqi parliament approves a security pact by which all American forces are to leave Iraq by the end of 2011.

2009 **Prime Minister** al-Maliki's political bloc wins a big victory in local elections. President Obama announces withdrawal of most US forces by late August 2010.

2010 **"Chemical" Ali-Hassan al Majid** is executed. Legislative elections produce no clear outcome and allegations of fraud; it takes seven months for al-Maliki to be reappointed as prime minister. The last US combat brigade leaves Iraq in August.

> "The great **duel**, the **mother of all battles** has begun. The dawn of victory **nears**..."
>
> IRAQI PRESIDENT SADDAM HUSSEIN ON THE IMPENDING AMERICAN OFFENSIVE TO RETAKE KUWAIT, 1991

Iran

Known as Persia until 1935, Iran blends theocratic government with modern nationalism.

533 BCE **Cyrus the Great** unites the Medes and Persians to form the first great Persian Empire, which is ruled by the Achaemenid dynasty and is conquered by Alexander of Macedon (Alexander the Great) in 331 BCE.

224 CE **The Sassanian Empire** is founded, posing a serious military threat to the eastern Roman Empire. The ancient Zoroastrian religion becomes predominant.

637–641 CE **The Sassanian Empire** is conquered by Muslim Arabs. Persia is Islamized, but fragments politically.

1502 **The Safavid Empire** is founded by Ismail Safavi, and Persia again becomes a political entity, and a military rival to Ottoman Turkey. Shia Islam becomes the established religion of the state.

1587–1629 **Under Shah Abbas I** Safavid Persia reaches the apogee of its power. The royal capital of Isfahan is adorned with mosques and new public buildings.

1779 **Fath Ali Sha founds** the Qajar dynasty, which rules Persia until 1926.

1814 **The Treaty of Tehran** is concluded with Great Britain to protect Persian territories from unprovoked aggression.

1906 **Demands for reform** lead to the so-called Constitutional Revolution and the establishment of a Constituent National Assembly (or Majlis), freedom of the press, and security of property tenure.

1908 **The Anglo-Persian** Oil Company is founded.

1920 **Bolshevik Russian forces** invade the Caspian province of Gilan.

1921 **Reza Khan,** the leader of the Persian Cossack Brigade, seizes power. A peace treaty is signed with Soviet Russia.

1925 **Reza Khan becomes** shah and establishes the Pahlavi dynasty. He embarks on a major reform program of modernization and Westernization, but becomes increasingly reliant on Germany for support. In 1935 he changes the country's name from Persia to Iran.

1941 **The United Kingdom** and the Soviet Union invade Iran, and in September the Shah is forced to abdicate in favor of his son, Muhammad Reza Pahlavi.

1951 **The nationalist regime** of Mohammad Mossadeq comes to power. The oil industry is nationalized, causing grave friction with the US and UK.

1953 **An American-backed coup** overthrows Mossadeq. The Shah returns with Anglo-American backing.

1957 **SAVAK, the Shah's** secret police, is established to control opposition.

1964 **Shia religious leader** Ayatollah Khomeini is exiled to Iraq.

1971 **Shah celebrates the 2500th** anniversary of Persian monarchy in a spectacular series of celebrations at the ancient Achaemenid capital of Persepolis.

1977 **Khomeini's son dies.** Anti-Shah demonstrations break out during the funeral and subsequent mourning.

1978 **Riots and strikes** against the Shah's government mount in Iran. Martial law is declared. Khomeini settles in Paris.

1979 **Shah goes into** exile. Ayatollah Khomeini returns from exile and declares an Islamic republic. Radical students seize 63 hostages at US embassy in Tehran.

1980 **Shah dies** in exile. Iraq invades Iran, starting an eight-year war. Iranians suffer large initial losses.

1981 **US hostages released.** Hojatoleslam Ali Khamenei elected president.

1982 **Iranians recapture** most of ground lost to Iraq and push into Iraqi territory.

1985 **Khamenei reelected** president.

1987 **Around 275 Iranian** pilgrims are killed in riots during the annual Hajj pilgrimage to Mecca.

1988 **Iranian airliner** is shot down by USS *Vincennes*; 290 people are killed. Ceasefire ends Iran–Iraq war.

1989 **Khomeini issues fatwa** condemning British author Salman Rushdie to death for alleged blasphemy in *The Satanic Verses*. Khomeini dies. President Ali Khamenei appointed supreme religious leader of Iran. Hashemi Rafsanjani elected president.

SHAH REZA KHAN

Reza Khan joined the Persian Cossack Brigade at the age of 15. He rose to be the Brigade's leader and in 1921 supported a coup that reduced the last Qajar shah to a puppet. By 1923, he had become prime minister of the new regime.

Reza consolidated his power, suppressed all opposition, and in 1925 had himself declared the first shah of the new Pahlavi dynasty. He introduced a series of economic reforms that required external finance. This served to increase foreign influence in the country. He actively promoted social reform, forbidding traditional dress and the wearing of the veil by women. By the 1930s, Reza's government had become increasingly despotic and unpopular. His pro-Axis stance during World War II led the UK and USSR to occupy Iran in 1941, depose him, and install his son Mohammad Reza Pahlavi as shah. Reza Khan died in exile in South Africa.

1990 **Earthquake in northern** Iran kills 45,000 people. Iran remains neutral following Iraq's invasion of Kuwait.

1992 **Majlis elections** give a majority to reformist candidates favoring Rafsanjani.

1993 **Rafsanjani reelected** president despite campaign by Ayatollah Khamenei to eradicate Western influences.

1995 **Imposition of US** sanctions on Iran over alleged Iranian sponsorship of international terrorist groups.

1996 **Majlis elections.** Conservative Society for Combatant Clergy loses ground to more liberal factions.

1997 **Earthquake south of** Mashhad kills 1,500 people. Mohammad Khatami elected president, and begins to implement reformist agenda.

1999 **First nationwide** local elections since 1979. President Khatami visits Italy—first Iranian

leader to be received by a Western government since 1979.

2000 **Sweeping election** victory for reformists. Despite this, conservatives control many of the levers of power and there is a crackdown on reformist press.

2002 **US President** George W. Bush calls Iran a member of the "Axis of Evil."

2003 **Earthquake destroys** the medieval mud-brick city of Bam, killing over 40,000. Massive student demonstrations in Tehran end in brutal crackdown.

2004 **Conservatives win** elections to the Majlis after controversy over disqualification of reformist candidates.

2005 **Conservative mayor** of Tehran, Mahmoud Ahmadinejad, wins presidential election. He promises economic reform.

2006 **Iran announces** it has enriched uranium. UN imposes limited sanctions against Iran.

2007 **Nuclear crisis continues** as Iran declares it has begun full-scale nuclear fuel production, reinforcing fears that it aims to develop nuclear weapons.

2008 **Conservatives win** more than two-thirds of seats in parliamentary elections. Iran tests a long-range missile capable of hitting Israel.

2009 **Ahmadinejad reelected.** Violent protests alleging election fraud and a major crackdown on protesters ensues.

2010 **Iran reaches a deal** to send nuclear fuel abroad for enrichment, to Turkey and Brazil. The UN Security Council votes for expanded sanctions against Iran.

Death of Khomeini
Ruhollah Khomeini's death in 1989 deprived the Iranian revolution of the spiritual leadership he had exercised for more than a decade. His passing opened the way for more liberal movements to shape Iran's future.

Kazakhstan

The last Soviet republic to declare its independence, Kazakhstan has mineral and agricultural wealth.

1500S **Kipchaks and other** Turkic, Mongol, and Iranian groups break away from the Mongol Golden Horde and migrate to the territory now known as Kazakhstan, forming three nomadic states: the Senior Zhouz (Horde) in the southeast, the Middle Zhouz in the northern and central areas, and the Junior Zhouz in the northwest.

1846 **The Senior Zhouz** joins the Russian Empire. By 1865 the whole of present-day Kazakhstan is in Russian hands.

1889 **Russian eastward expansion** leads to a law on designated areas for state-aided settlement, including regions of present-day Kazakhstan.

1916 **Rebellion against Russian** rule is brutally suppressed.

1917 **Russian Revolution inspires** civil war in Kazakhstan between Bolsheviks, anti-Bolsheviks, and Kazakh nationalists. Russian settlement intensifies after 1917 as Kazakhstan is subjected to industrial and agricultural development. Nationalists set up an autonomous republic.

1920 **Bolsheviks take control:** Kirghiz Autonomous Soviet Socialist Republic is set up within Russian Soviet Federative Socialist Republic, later the USSR.

1925 **The Kirghiz ASSR is renamed** the Kazakh ASSR as the Soviet Central Asian territories are reorganized into three autonomous regions and two republics.

1930S **Stalin's collectivization** program leads to an increase in Russian settlement and the deaths of an estimated one million Kazakhs.

1936 **Kazakhstan becomes** a full union republic of the USSR as Kazakh SSR.

1941–45 **Large-scale deportations** to Kazakhstan of Germans, Jews, Crimean Tatars, Chechens, Ingush, and others felt to be a threat or to be disloyal to the USSR during World War II.

1950S **Nuclear test site** set up at Semipalatinsk; 500 nuclear explosions follow before testing ends in 1991.

1954–60 **Soviet policy** to plow the "Virgin Lands" for grain is most vigorously followed in Kazakhstan, despite the environmental consequences.

1986 **Riots in Almaty,** the then capital, after an ethnic Russian, Gennadi Kolbin, is appointed head of the Kazakhstan Communist Party (CPK) to replace an ethnic Kazakh, Dinmukhamed Konayev.

1989 **Kolbin is replaced** by Nursultan Nazarbayev, an ethnic Kazakh.

DECISIVE MOMENT

FIRST MAN IN SPACE, 1961

On April 12, 1961, Yuri Gagarin, pictured right in his spacesuit, became the first man in space. His flight, a single orbit of the Earth lasting 1 hour, 48 minutes, began on top of a 4.5 ton *Vostok* ("East") rocket launched from the Soviet space center at Baikonur in Kazakhstan.

The Baikonur cosmodrome is the world's oldest: construction began in 1955, and several historic flights were launched from there, including the very first artificial satellite, *Sputnik I*, in 1957. After Kazakhstan became independent in 1991, Russia negotiated an agreement to continue to use the center until 2050.

1990 **CPK wins elections** to supreme soviet by an overwhelming majority: Nazarbayev is appointed first president of Kazakhstan as the country declares sovereignty within the USSR.

1991 **Kazakhstan votes to** preserve the USSR as a union of sovereign states. As the USSR breaks up, it is the last of the 15 constituent republics to declare its independence and join the Commonwealth of Independent States (CIS). The CPK restructures itself as the Socialist Party of Kazakhstan (SPK).

1992 **Opposition demonstrations against** the dominance of reformed communists in the supreme soviet, now the supreme Kenges. Nationalist groups form Azat, the Republican Party. Kazakhstan is admitted to the United Nations.

1993 **A new constitution** is adopted and a new currency, the tenge, is introduced.

1994 **Legislative elections are annulled** after widespread voting irregularities.

1995 **Kazakhstan, along with** Belarus and Ukraine, gets rid of the former Soviet nuclear arsenal.

1995 **Adoption of a new** constitution broadening presidential powers and allowing the president to dissolve parliament and rule by decree.

1997 **Capital moved from** the southern city of Almaty north to Akmola (renamed Astana in 1998), partly to control the local Russian population in the region.

1998 **Legislature approves constitutional** amendments, including the holding of an early presidential election.

1999 **Nazarbayev is reelected president** for a further seven-year term in elections widely believed to be fraudulent.

2000 **Legislation grants** Nazarbayev with lifelong powers and privileges.

2003 **Sale of former** collectivized farmland is legalized as part of a program of economic liberalization and privatization.

2005 **Nazarbayev is reelected** for a

---

further seven-year term with more than 90 percent of the vote. Opposition leader Zamanbek Nurkadilov is murdered.

2007 **The Kazakh parliament** votes to allow president Nazarbayev an unlimited number of terms. His party wins all seats in the lower house in general elections.

2007 **The Chinese and Kazakh** presidents unveil the Kazakh section of a natural gas pipeline from China to Central Asia.

« 138–39 Nomads of the Steppes
« 184–85 The Silk Road

Uzbekistan

A territory fought over by many ancient empires and today the most populous Central Asian republic.

500S BCE **Cyrus the Great,** founder of the Persian Empire, conquers Central Asia.

327 BCE **Alexander the Great** conquers the states of Sogdiana and Bactria.

500S CE **The Turks control** Central Asia but are driven out by the Arabs in the 7th and 8th centuries, returning in the 10th century.

1500S **The Shaybani Uzbeks** rule an unstable region, from Bukhara and Samarkand.

1700S–1800S **Uzbekistan ruled** by Muslim khanates of Bukhara, Khokand, and Khiva.

1865 **Expanding Russian Empire** captures Uzbek city of Tashkent.

1876 **Expansionist Russia completes** the annexation of the khanates of Bukhara, Khiva, and Khokand.

1916 **An armed uprising** against Russian domination in Samarkand is crushed.

1917 **The Russian Revolution** leads to demands for an independent Bukhara. Soviet power established in Tashkent.

1921 **Turkestan Autonomous** Soviet Socialist Republic (ASSR), incorporating present-day Uzbekistan, is proclaimed.

1923–41 **A new written language** replaces the old Turkic language. Initially it is written in Arabic, but later it is changed to the Roman alphabet and finally to Cyrillic.

1924 **Basmachi rebels, who** resisted Soviet rule, are crushed. The Uzbek SSR is founded; until 1929, it includes the Tajik ASSR.

1925 **Anti-Islam campaign** bans religious schools and closes mosques.

1936 **Karakalpak ASSR** (formerly part of the Russian Soviet Federative Socialist Republic) incorporated into Uzbek SSR.

1937 **Uzbek communist leadership** is purged by Stalin.

1941–45 **World War II gives rise** to an industrial boom.

1959 **Sharaf Rashidov becomes** the First Secretary of the Communist Party of Uzbekistan (CPUz). He retains the position until 1983.

Cities of the Silk Road
The spectacular Shirdar Madrasa at Samarkhand is one of the great Islamic schools of the world. Uzbekistan lies on the ancient Silk Road connecting China with Central Asia and the Mediterranean. Merchants created cities such as Samarkhand along the route.

1982–83 **Yuri Andropov becomes** Soviet president. His anticorruption purge results in the emergence of a new generation of Central Asian officials.

1989 **First non-communist political** movement, Unity Party (Birlik), is formed but not officially recognized. A Birlik campaign leads to Uzbek being declared the official language.

1990 **Islam Karimov becomes** executive president of the new Uzbek Supreme Soviet. Inter-ethnic fighting in the Fergana Valley causes 320 deaths.

1991 **As the USSR collapses,** Uzbekistan declares its independence and adopts the Republic of Uzbekistan as its official name. Uzbekistan joins the Commonwealth of Independent States (CIS). The Communist Party of Uzbekistan is restructured as the People's Democratic Party of Uzbekistan (PDP) with Islam Karimov confirmed as president.

1992 **Price liberalization provokes** student riots in Tashkent. A new post-Soviet constitution is adopted along Western democratic lines, but all religious and nationalist parties are banned. Uzbekistan sends troops to Tajikistan to suppress violence and strengthen border.

1993 **Growing harassment of** opposition political parties, the nationalist Erk (Freedom) and religious Birlik (Unity).

1995 **Karimov's PDP wins** legislative elections. Referendum extends Karimov's presidential term until 2000.

1996 **Islamic Movement** of Uzbekistan (IMU) formed to fight for Islamic republic.

1999 **Bomb attacks by** IMU lead to crackdown and arrests of hundreds of opposition activists.

2000 **Karimov is reelected** as president in elections widely viewed as rigged.

2001 **US sets up** up an air base at Khanabad to help it fight the Taliban in Afghanistan, but its aid to Uzbekistan is stopped in 2004 because of human rights abuses. The Uzbek government closes the base in 2005.

2002 **Presidential term** extended from five to seven years.

2005 **Government troops shoot** about 750 unarmed people in Andijan in the Fergana Valley demonstrating in support of 23 local people charged with "extremism," that is, membership of a banned Islamic organization.

2007 **President Karimov** is elected for new seven-year term in disputed election.

2008 **Uzbekistan announces** it is to allow US forces to use the Termez air base, following their expulsion from the base at Khanabad in 2005.

《 138–39 Nomads of the Steppes
《 184–85 The Silk Road

Turkmenistan

A poor and isolated Central Asian nation with a long history of despotic rule.

1229 **Genghis Khan conquers** the region.

1600s **The territory, occupied** by Turkmen tribes, is fought over by Persia, the khanates of Khiva and Bukhara, and Afghanistan.

1881 **Russian forces, led** by General Skobelev, conquer Turkmen stronghold of Gok-Teppeh, killing over 14,000 people. Ashgabat is founded by the Russians in the Akhal-Teke oasis. It becomes first a military stronghold, then a trading center.

1884 **The oasis city** of Merv is conquered by Russia. The invasion, which takes Russian forces to the borders of Afghanistan and Persia by 1900, results in Turkmen tribes fleeing to Persia.

1918–19 **After the Russian** Revolution, an independent Turkmen administration is supported by a British garrison.

1920 **Bolsheviks capture** Turkmen territory.

1921 **Turkestan is reconstituted** as an Autonomous Soviet Socialist Republic with the Russian Soviet Federative Socialist Republic (RSFSR).

1924 **Creation of Turkmen** Soviet Socialist Republic.

1948 **Earthquake rocks Ashgabat,** killing 100,000.

1985 **Saparmurad Niyazov** becomes president of the Communist Party.

1990 **Niyazov is elected** president of the Turkmenistan SSR.

1991 **Independence from USSR:** Niyazov becomes president of new state, bans Communist Party and forms the Democratic Party of Turkmenistan, the country's only legal party.

1992 **Niyazov is reelected** unopposed as president.

1994 **After parliament votes** to extend Niyazov's term of office to 2002, a referendum shows that 99.99 percent of voters are in favor.

1995 **Turkmenistan's declaration** of neutrality is recognized by the UN.

1999 **Niyazov's term of office** is extended indefinitely by parliament.

2000 **All government** officials forced to speak Turkmen as other native languages are banned from public use.

2002 **Niyazov revises** the calendar, naming months after himself, his mother, and *Ruhnama,* his spiritual guidebook.

SAPARMURAD NIYAZOV

Saparmurad Niyazov styled himself Turkmenbashi, the "father of all Turkmen." In power from 1990 to his death in 2006, he fostered an extreme personality cult in his country and enacted a number of highly eccentric laws. His portrait adorns buildings, while towns, streets, and even months of the year have been renamed in his honor. His spiritual guide to living, *Ruhnama,* was adopted as the national guidebook to be studied by all students. Most dramatically, a giant gold statue of him stands in the center of the capital, Ashgabat, revolving every 24 hours so that the Sun always shines on his face.

2002 **Opposition parties** in exile form Turkmen Democratic Opposition in Vienna. A coup attempt later in the year is blamed on the group, leading to mass repression and imprisonment of opponents.

2003 **The government removes** the right of Russians—who form 10 percent of the population—to hold dual citizenship, and gives them two months to decide which passport to keep.

2006 **Human rights activist** Ogulsapar Muradova dies in prison. Niyazov dies of a heart attack.

2007 **Gurbanguli Berdymukhamedov,** former health minister and deputy prime minister, is elected president with 89 percent of the vote.

2008 **A new constitution** establishes a directly elected parliament. The Gregorian calendar is readopted.

2009 **Gas pipeline** opens to China.

2010 **The gold statue** of former president Niyazov is removed from Ashgabat.

《 138–39 Nomads of the Steppes
《 184–85 The Silk Road

Kyrgyzstan

A small, mountainous state with a largely rural population and a large Russian minority.

700s **Kyrgyz people begin to settle** and trade in the valley of the Chu River, site of the present-day capital Bishkek.

1855 **Borombei Bekmuratov, chief** of the nomad Bugu tribe east of Issyk Kul, accepts dependence on the Russian Empire.

1876 **Kyrgyz lands** annexed into the Russian Empire.

1924 **Incorporated into** the USSR.

1991 **Independence from USSR** under President Askar Akayev.

2005 **Akayev swept aside** in the Tulip Revolution after he attempts to rig presidential elections. Kurmanbek Bakiyev elected president.

2006 **President Bakiyev** establishes a new constitution limiting his powers.

2007 **The opposition** fails to win a single seat in elections amid fraud allegations.

2009 **President Bakiyev** announces closure of the US air base at Manas.

2009 **Bakiyev** swept from power. Roza Otunbayeva becomes president.

《 138–39 Nomads of the Steppes

Tajikistan

A mountainous state whose languages and traditions are similar to those of Iran.

1876 **Russians conquer** the region.

1924 **Soviets take over** Tajikistan.

1929 **Tajikistan becomes** a full republic of the USSR as Tajik SSR.

1940 **Cyrillic** script is introduced.

1989 **Tajik becomes** official language.

1991 **Independence from USSR;** the previous communist leader, Rakhmon Nabiev, wins elections.

1992 **Demonstrators force Nabiev** from power. Civil war breaks out as Islamic Revival Party fights for an Islamic republic. Another former communist, Imomali Rakhmonov, wins power.

1997–98 **Peace accord with** rebels as Islamists join goverment.

2006 **Rakhmonov** wins reelection in an election considered corrupt by foreign observers. (Reelected 2010.)

《 184–85 The Silk Road

Afghanistan

The world's poorest state, gripped by armed conflict, Islamic fundamentalism, and civil war since 1979.

530s BCE Cyrus the Great makes Afghanistan part of the Persian Empire.

327 BCE Alexander the Great conquers most of the Afghan satrapies.

50 CE Afghanistan becomes part of the Kushan Empire.

250 Afghanistan becomes part of the Persian Sassanian Empire.

652 Arab armies invade, bringing Islam with them.

820s Local Arab or Persian families rule most of the country.

997 Mahmud of Ghazni extends his power as far as the Punjab in India.

1219 Genghis Khan invades.

1369 Timur (Tamerlane) invades and makes the country part of his empire.

1504 Babur, a descendant of Genghis Khan and Timur, makes Kabul the capital of an independent principality and goes on to establish the Mughal Empire in northern India.

1530 On the death of Babur, Afghanistan is divided between an Uzbek north, Mughal east, and Persian west.

1747 Ahmed Shah Durrani, a Pashtun leader, is elected emir by the tribal council and establishes the last great independent Afghan Empire.

1809 Afghanistan signs a treaty of friendship with Britain in which the Afghan ruler Shah Shoja promises to oppose the passage of foreign (Russian) troops through his territory.

1823 After the death of the last Durrani emir, no new ruler emerges until 1826, when Dost Muhammad becomes emir. During his reign, the UK and Russia begin to compete for influence in the region during the so-called "Great Game."

1839–42 Following the failure of a British mission to Kabul led by Captain Alexander Burnes in 1837, British forces invade Afghanistan during the first Anglo-Afghan war in an attempt to overthrow Dost Muhammad. He is at first deposed but restored after a major Afghan revolt in Kabul, the capital.

1855 Dost Muhammad signs treaty of friendship with the UK.

1878–81 The second Anglo-Afghan war follows British failure to establish full control over Afghanistan's foreign relations, after the Afghan ruler grants territory to Russia.

1879 Under the Treaty of Gandmak signed with Emir Yaqub Ali Khan, various Afghan areas are annexed by the UK. Yaqub Ali Khan is later exiled and a new treaty is signed in 1893 with Emir Abdul Rahman, establishing the Durand Line, a contentious boundary between Afghanistan and British India that splits Pashtun lands in two.

1895 The UK and Russia create the "Afghan Finger," or Wakhan Corridor, a sliver of land that stretches through the Pamir Mountains to China, which they attach to Afghanistan, thus keeping the rival British and Russian empires apart.

1901 Habibullah becomes emir.

1904 The western border with Persia is finally settled.

1907 The Anglo-Russian Entente guarantees Afghanistan's independence with British control of its foreign affairs.

1919 Habibullah is assassinated; his successor, Amunallah, attempts to free his country from British influence and invades India. A third, brief Afghan War breaks out that ends when the British bomb Kabul and Jalalabad. By the Treaty of Rawalpindi, the British recognize Afghanistan's full independence.

1928 Amanullah begins to reform the country, reducing the power of religious leaders and giving women more freedom, banning the veil and ending polygamy; he now styles himself king.

1929 Amanullah abdicates as a revolt breaks out against his reforms; he is replaced by an illiterate Tajik warlord, Bacha-i Saqao, who seizes the throne. Later that year, Amanullah's cousin, Nadir Khan, seizes power and becomes king.

1932 The country's first university is founded in Kabul.

1933 Nadir Khan is assassinated; his son, Zahir Shah, becomes king.

> ## "We will not accept a government of **wrong-doers**. We prefer death than to be part of an **evil government**."
>
> MULLAH OMAR, TALIBAN LEADER, AFTER HIS DEFEAT, 2001

1946 Afghanistan joins the UN.

1953 Mohammad Daud Khan is named prime minister.

1956 First Five-Year Plan to modernize the country with Soviet aid as Daud Khan becomes increasingly pro-Soviet.

1963 Daud resigns after the king rejects his proposals for democratic reforms.

1964 King Zahir Shah introduces limited democratic reforms as he attempts to become a constitutional monarch.

1965 Elections are held, but the monarchy retains power. The Marxist Party of Afghanistan (PDPA) is formed and banned. PDPA splits into the Parcham (flag) and Khalq (masses) factions.

1973 Daud mounts a coup with Parcham support, and declares a republic. The Mujahideen rebellion begins.

1978 Mohammad Taraki takes power and introduces communist rule.

1979 Taraki is ousted by the hardline Hafizullah Amin. Amin is then killed in a coup backed by the USSR that sends in 80,000 troops to support the new moderate Parcham PDPA government of Babrak Karmal. The Mujahideen rebellion is stepped up into full-scale guerrilla war with US backing.

1986 Muhammad Najibullah replaces Karmal as head of government.

1988 Peace accord with USSR.

1989 Last Soviet troops withdraw.

1992 Najibullah overthrown by the Mujahideen, but civil war soon erupts between the different groups.

1994 The radical Islamist Taliban movement captures Kandahar and makes it its stronghold. Osama bin Laden returns to the country to set up Al-Qaeda bases.

1996 Taliban seizes Kabul and impose strict Islamic regime; the Northern Alliance leads resistance to the Taliban.

1998 Earthquake in north kills thousands.

2000 Country suffers worst drought in 30 years. The UN imposes sanctions in response to Taliban support for bin Laden.

2001 Ancient Buddhist statues in Bamiyan destroyed.

2001 Following the 9/11 attacks in New York, US-led coalition forces attack Afghanistan in a concerted effort to flush out Al-Qaeda terrorists and bring down the Taliban government. Hamid Karzai heads new coalition government. US and other foreign troops occupy the country.

2004 The Loya Jirga (Grand Council) of tribal leaders establishes a new constitution. Hamid Karzai wins presidential election.

2005 The Taliban regroups and goes on the offensive, exploiting popular resentment at foreign occupation.

2006 NATO takes over responsibility for security across the whole of Afghanistan.

2007 A series of offensives in Helmand province takes place, aimed at dislodging the Taliban. The opium crop is reported to be at an all-time high.

2008 Germany, France, and Britain increase troop numbers. A bomb attack on the Indian embassy in Kabul kills 50.

2009 A major US offensive in Helmand takes place. Hamid Karzai is reelected president amidst allegations of ballot rigging. President Obama announces plans to increase US troop levels by 30,000.

2010 Further NATO offensives take place in Helmand.

Ill-fated Afghan adventures
British troops are seen here mobilizing in Kabul during the second Afghan War of 1878–81. Britain fought three wars in Afghanistan to protect British India and keep the Russians at bay but failed to subdue the rebellious Afghans.

Pakistan

A populous and politically unstable Muslim state that was part of British India until 1947.

2600s BCE Indus valley civilization flourishes, building the great cities of Harappa and Mohenjo-Daro.

500 BCE Persian Achaemenid Empire stretches as far east as Indus river.

326 BCE Alexander the Great conquers Punjab region. The country is then ruled by the Seleucid Empire, the Mauryas, an Indo-Greek Bactrian kingdom, Scythian nomads, and the Parthians.

100s CE Kanishka dynasty of Kushan rulers control the country from their capital at Peshawar.

711 Muslim Arabs conquer Sindh, controlling most of northwest India by 900. The Ghaznavid Empire rules the region until 1186, when the empire is overthrown by Muhammad of Ghur, who conquers northern India. During the 13th century, the region falls under the control of the Muslim Sultanate of Delhi and, by 1600, the Mughal Empire.

1843 The British annex Sind province and, in 1846–49, the Punjab.

1857 Lahore, Peshawar, and other cities rise up against British rule during the Sepoy Rebellion.

1877 Most of present-day Pakistan becomes part of British India when Queen Victoria is made empress of India.

1893 The British settle the western frontier with Afghanistan along the Durand Line, bisecting Pashtun lands.

1897 More than 35,000 troops are needed by the British to quell an uprising by Pathan tribes in the northwest.

1901 British set up Northwest Frontier Province to try to contain rebellious tribes of the region.

1906 Muslim League founded as an organ of Indian Muslim separatism, to counter the all-India beliefs of the Indian National Congress.

1930 The poet Muhammad Iqbal introduces the idea of a Muslim nation distinct from Hindu India, an idea taken up by Indian Muslim students in Britain, who are the first to use the word Pakistan, meaning "land of the pure" in Urdu.

1940 Muslim League, led by Muhammad Ali Jinnah, demands a Muslim state in India in those areas where Muslims predominate. Three states in the northwest of India—Baluchistan, Northwest Frontier Province, and Sind— have huge Muslim majorities, while three more states—the Punjab in the west and Assam and Bengal in the east—are more

PAKISTANI STATESMAN (1876–1948)
MUHAMMAD ALI JINNAH

The founding father of Pakistan, Muhammad Ali Jinnah was a far-from-devout Muslim—he drank alcohol and ate pork—who had left the all-India Congress Party in 1934 to join the Muslim League. His aim was to campaign for a Muslim state in India.

In 1940 he led calls for the partition of India and the creation of the Muslim state of Pakistan. He cleverly aligned the League with Britain during World War II, but lost British support when he adopted direct action in 1946. He thus failed to achieve the six-province state he had wanted, but oversaw the independence of Pakistan when the British partitioned India on its independence in 1947. He served as first governor general of Pakistan, but died 13 months later.

evenly divided between Muslim and Hindu. Jinnah demands all six.

1944 Talks between Jinnah and Mahatma Gandhi on the future of India and its possible partition collapse.

1946 Muslim League wins most Muslim constituencies in elections. On August 16 Jinnah calls a direct action day in support of his demands, causing riots in Calcutta and elsewhere with at least 5,000 dead.

1947 Partition of India: the British viceroy of India, Lord Louis Mountbatten, announces the partition of India into largely Muslim and Hindu states: the state parliaments of Punjab and Bengal, and the Muslim Sylhet district of Assam, must decide which country to join or whether to partition themselves between the two. At independence on August 15, Pakistan is set up with Jinnah as the first governor general. Punjab and Bengal vote for partition; Sylhet votes to join Pakistan. Pakistan is thus created in two parts— East and West—separated by 994 miles (1,600 km) of Indian territory. Millions of Muslims and Hindus displaced by large-scale migration.

1948 First Indo-Pakistan war over Kashmir, a predominantly Muslim state whose Hindu ruler hesitated to join either new state at independence. Muslim tribesmen backed by Pakistan invade the state to force it to join Pakistan, prompting India to intervene. The two countries divide Kashmir between them.

1949 New Awami League (AL) demands East Bengal's autonomy. The proposed liberal constitution is opposed by orthodox Muslims, and the prime minister is assassinated in 1951.

1956 Constitution establishes Pakistan as an Islamic republic; East Bengal is now known as East Pakistan.

1958 Martial law: General Muhammad Ayyub Khan takes over. In 1962 he introduces a new constitution creating an Islamic republic with two provinces— West and East Pakistan—and two languages—Urdu and Bengali. The new city of Islamabad is made the capital.

1965 Second Indo-Pakistan war over Kashmir and the disputed Rann of Kutch.

1970 Ayyub Khan resigns as General Agha Yahya Khan takes over. First direct elections won by Awami League; West Pakistani parties reject results, leading to a military crackdown in East Pakistan.

1971 East Pakistan secedes as Bangladesh. Pakistan People's Party (PPP) leader Zulfikar Ali Bhutto is president.

1972 Simla peace agreement with India commits the two countries "to settle their differences by peaceful means."

War with India
The two nations have gone to war twice over Kashmir, and once over Bangladesh. These Pakistani troops fought in the second war over Kashmir in 1965.

1973 Bhutto, now prime minister, initiates Islamic socialism.

1977 General election causes riots over allegations of vote rigging; General Zia ul-Haq stages a military coup.

1979 Bhutto is executed after being found guilty of ordering the murder of a political opponent.

1986 Bhutto's daughter Benazir returns from exile to lead PPP.

1988 Zia is killed in a plane crash. Benazir Bhutto wins general election.

1990 President dismisses Benazir Bhutto. Nawaz Sharif becomes prime minister.

1991 Muslim sharia law incorporated in legal code.

1993 President Khan and Prime Minister Sharif resign. After elections, Benazir Bhutto returns to power.

1996 President dismisses Bhutto again.

1997 Pakistan Muslim League wins landslide election victory; Nawaz Sharif elected prime minister.

1998 Nuclear tests are carried out as Pakistan acquires nuclear weapons.

1999 Military coup by General Pervez Musharraf; Sharif is found guilty of treason and exiled. Serious clashes with Indian troops around Kargil in Kashmir.

2001 National assembly suspended; Musharraf appoints himself president. A referendum in 2002 allows him to hold power until 2007.

2001 US-led invasion of Afghanistan places Pakistan in frontline of the international "war on terror."

2003 Relations with India improve; the leaders of both nations hold talks in 2005.

2005 An earthquake in Kashmir leaves thousands dead.

2007 Benazir Bhutto, standing in presidential elections, is assassinated. Pervez Musharraf is elected for second presidential term.

2008 Opposition parties win a clear majority in parliamentary elections. Ali Asif Zardari, the widower of Benazir Bhutto, is elected president.

2009 The government agrees to implement Sharia law in northwestern Swat valley to head off increasing militant control there. After this fails, the government launches offensive in Swat. The Pakistani Taliban leader Baitullah Mehsud is killed by a US drone attack.

2010 The worst flood in 80 years leads to over 1,500 deaths.

« 78–79 Bronze Age Collapse
« 410–11 The Partition of India

India

A vast subcontinent that has been home to some of the world's oldest civilizations.

2600 BCE **Indus Valley** civilization flourishes.

1500 BCE **Aryan invaders destroy** the Indus civilization. The Vedic age develops the Brahmanic caste system of Hinduism.

320–185 BCE **The Mauryan Empire** unifies most of India and establishes Buddhism as the state religion.

320 CE **Foundation of the** Gupta dynasty and the beginning of the "Classical Age."

455 CE **The arrival of** the Huns and the overthrow of the Guptas.

606–47 **Harsha Vardhana** unites northern India in the Harsha Empire. Kannauj is its capital. After the fall of the Harsha Empire, Kannauj becomes capital of the Pratihara Empire.

711 **Muslim armies** conquer Sind.

750–1150 **Buddhism flourishes** in eastern India.

800s **Expansion of the Chola Empire** in southern India. By the 11th century, it includes the Maldives, parts of Burma, Malaya, and Sumatra.

800–1200 **Period of Rajput** kingdoms in Rajputana (present-day Rajasthan), northwest India.

1000–25 **Mahmud of** Ghazni invades from Afghanistan into northern India.

1018 **City of** Kannauj falls to Turkish invaders.

1192 **Rajput king** Prithviraj III is defeated by Muslim forces. This marks the end of the Rajput period.

1192–1398 **The Muslim Delhi** Sultanate is established in the Indo-Gangetic plain of northern India.

1200s **Chola Empire** begins to shrink as neighboring kingdoms take its land.

Bronze Chola god

This 11th-century Chola bronze depicts the Hindu god Rama. Hinduism was the religion of the Chola Empire; its kings were thought to be descendants of the god Shiva. Other religions were tolerated.

1279 **Rajendra III**, the last Chola king, dies. The Chola Empire is overthrown by rival kingdoms.

c.1300 **Muslim sultans** of Delhi attack southern India, extending their kingdom.

1336 **Hindu kingdom** of Vijayanagar is founded in southern India. It halts Muslim expansion in the south.

1398 **Delhi is sacked** by the Mongol army of Timur (Tamerlane).

1526 **The establishment of** the Mughal Empire, which reaches its peak during the reign of Emperor Akbar (1556–1605).

1632 **Construction of the Taj** Mahal, a mausoleum commissioned by Emperor Shah Jahan for his favorite wife, Mumtaz Mahal, is begun at Agra.

1659 **Shivaji Bhonsle** leads a small, ill-equipped Maratha army to defeat a much greater Adilshahi force at the Battle of Pratapgarh.

1674 **Maratha Empire** is established by Shivaji Bhonsle in central and nothern India. It dominates the region until 1818.

1707 **The death of** Emperor Aurangzeb marks the onset of Mughal decline.

1757 **British military victory** in Bengal by the East India Company's private army, led by Robert Clive, heralds the consolidation of British power in India.

1777 **The first Anglo-Maratha** war begins between the East India Company and the Maratha Empire. Further wars start in 1803 and 1817.

1857 **Sepoy rebellion** spreads across India and is suppressed the following year.

1858 **Formal dissolution of** Mughal Empire and the assumption of direct control by the British government.

1877 **Queen Victoria** is proclaimed empress of India.

1885 **The Indian** National Congress is formed as a forum for the nationalist movement.

1919 **Act of parliament** introduces "responsible government."

1920–22 **Mahatma Gandhi's** first civil disobedience campaign.

1935 **Government of India Act** grants autonomy to provinces.

1936 **First elections under** new constitution.

1942–43 **"Quit India"** movement launched by the Indian National Congress.

DECISIVE MOMENT

THE SEPOY REBELLION, 1857–58

The Sepoy Rebellion was a widespread revolt against British rule that began among Indian soldiers in the East India Company. It was sparked by the introduction of the Enfield rifle, for which troops had to bite the ends off cartridges that were allegedly greased with pig and cow lard, contact with which was regarded as an insult to Muslims and Hindus alike. More generally, however, the rebellion stemmed from discontent with insensitive British attempts to Westernize India. Troops in Meerut who refused the rifles in April 1857 were severely punished. In response their comrades shot their British officers and marched on Delhi, where the local Indian garrison joined a spreading revolt that was not suppressed until nearly a year later. After the rebellion, which many in India now consider to have been a first war of independence, the British stepped back from imposing measures and began a process of consultation with Indians over policy. Seen here are rebels tied to cannons as punishment.

1947 **End of British** rule and partition into a Hindu-majority India and a Muslim-dominated Pakistan. Jawaharlal Nehru becomes first prime minister of independent India.

1948 **Assassination of Mahatma** Gandhi by a Hindu extremist. War with Pakistan over Kashmir.

1950 **India becomes** a republic.

1951–52 **First general election** is won by Congress Party under Nehru.

1957 **Congress Party** is reelected. First elected communist state government is installed in Kerala.

1960 **Bombay is divided** into the states of Gujarat and Maharashtra.

1962 **Congress Party reelected.** India loses war with China over Aksai Chin.

1964 **Nehru dies.** Lal Bahadur Shastri becomes prime minister.

1965 **Second war with** Pakistan over Kashmir.

1966 **Prime minister** Lal Bahadur Shastri dies; Indira Gandhi (daughter of Jawaharlal Nehru) is chosen as a compromise candidate to replace him.

1969 **Congress Party splits** into two factions. The larger faction is led by Indira Gandhi.

1971 **Indira Gandhi's** Congress (R) Party wins elections. Third war with Pakistan, over the creation of Bangladesh. Twenty-year friendship treaty signed with USSR.

1972 **Simla Agreement** signed with Pakistan, laying down principles for peace.

1974 **Explosion of first** nuclear device in underground test.

1975 **Indira Gandhi** declares a state of emergency after being found guilty of electoral malpractice.

1975–77 **Program of** compulsory birth control introduced. Nearly 1,000 political opponents are jailed.

1977 **Congress Party loses** general election. People's Party (JD) takes power.

1978 **New political splinter** group, Congress (Indira)—C(I)—Party is established and led by Indira Gandhi.

1980 **Congress (I)** wins general election.

1984 **Indian troops storm** Golden Temple in Amritsar to capture militants seeking Sikh self rule. Indira Gandhi assassinated by her Sikh bodyguards; her son Rajiv becomes prime minister and C(I) leader. Gas explosion at US-owned Union Carbide plant in Bhopal kills 2,000.

1987 **Indian peacekeeping force** is deployed in Sri Lanka to combat Tamil Tigers. It loses 1,200 men.

1989 **General election:** National Front forms minority government with support of nationalist BJP. The C(I) Party is implicated in the Bofors corruption scandal as Rajiv Gandhi and others are accused of receiving kickbacks from a defense contractor.

1990 **Peacekeeping force** is withdrawn from Sri Lanka. BJP leader Lal Advani is arrested for inciting intercommunal violence. Muslim separatist groups begin a campaign of violence in Kashmir. Congress (I) returns to power in coalition with JD.

1991 **Congress (I) withdraws** from government. Rajiv Gandhi is assassinated during the ensuing election campaign by a suicide bomber connected to Sri Lankan Tamil Tigers; Narasimha Rao becomes prime minister of a Congress (I) minority government. A program of economic liberalization is initiated.

1992 **Hindu extremists demolish** Babri Masjid mosque at Ayodhya, triggering widespread Hindu–Muslim violence; 1,200 people die.

1993 **Resurgence of** Hindu–Muslim riots. Bomb explosions in Mumbai.

1994 **Rupee is made fully** convertible. C(I) is routed in key state elections amid allegations of corruption. Talks with China are held in New Delhi aimed at reducing tensions at the border.

1995 **Punjab chief minister** is assassinated by Sikh extremists.

1996 **Corruption scandal triggers** political crisis. Hindu nationalist BJP is the largest party but fails to win vote of confidence; leftist United Front coalition government takes office.

1997 **United Front government** falls as C(I) withdraws support.

1998 **General election;** BJP led by Atal Bihari Vajpayee forms coalition

government. Sonia Gandhi, widow of Rajiv Gandhi, becomes president of C(I). India detonates a nuclear bomb to widespread international condemnation.

1999 **India and Pakistan** test nuclear missiles and clash violently in Kashmir. BJP returned to power in elections triggered by a vote of no confidence. A cyclone kills about 10,000 in eastern state of Orissa.

2000 **Population reaches** one billion. US President Bill Clinton makes historic visit.

2001 **Earthquake kills more** than 25,000 people in Gujarat. BJP government implicated in major bribery scandal connected to illegal arms sales. Kashmiri militants mount an armed attack on the parliament in Delhi. India launches satellite into space.

2002 **Indian government** accuses Pakistan of direct responsibilty for terrorist attacks by Kashmiri separatists. Bloody inter-religious rioting breaks out in Gujarat. About 1,000 are killed. India test-fires a nuclear-capable missile.

2003 **India and Pakistan** declare a ceasefire in Kashmir. Direct air links between the two countries resume.

2004 **Surprise victory for** Congress Party in general elections. Manmohan Singh is sworn in as prime minister.

2005 **Monsoon rains** in Mumbai kill more than 1,000. First bus service in 60 years operates between India and Pakistan. An earthquake in Kashmir kills more than 1,000. Kashmiri rebels detonate bombs in Delhi, killing 62.

2006 **Attacks by Islamic** militants intensify, including over 180 killed by bombs on rush-hour trains in Mumbai.

2007 **India and Pakistan** sign agreement to reduce risk of accidental nuclear war.

2007 **Pratibha Patil becomes** India's first female president.

2008 **Nearly 200 people** are killed in attacks by militant gunmen in Mumbai.

2009 **The Congress Party** wins increased number of seats in the general election, but falls just short of an absolute majority.

《58–59 Mysteries of the Indus
《124–25 India's First Empire
《180–81 The Delhi Sultanate
《244–45 The Great Mughals
《352–53 The British Raj
《408–09 Mahatma Gandhi
《410–11 The Partition of India

Nepal

A Himalayan kingdom with an agricultural economy and a turbulent political history.

1769 **Formation of the** Nepali state by King Prithvinarayan Shah, Raja of Gorkha, following his conquest of three Nepal Valley kingdoms.

1814–16 **Anglo-Nepalese war** ends in a treaty that establishes Nepal's boundaries and recognizes its autonomy.

1816 **Establishment of quasi-British** protectorate ruled by hereditary Ranas.

1923 **Treaty with Britain** recognizes Nepali independence.

1951 **End of Rana rule.** Sovereignty of crown is restored; Nepalese Congress Party (NCP) forms the government.

1959 **First multi-party constitution.**

1960 **Constitution is suspended** by King Mahendra, who seizes political control.

1962–90 **Under the panchayat** nonparty system, the king exercises sole power.

1972 **Birendra succeeds to** the throne.

1980 **Panchayat system** confirmed by referendum.

1985 **NCP begins a campaign of** civil disobedience to campaign for the restoration of the multi-party system.

1990 **Prodemocracy protests** are violently suppressed. King Birendra agrees to a new democratic constitution.

1994 **Minority communist** government.

1995–98 **Weak** coalition governments. Maoist insurrection breaks out seeking the overthrow of the monarchy.

1999 **NCP election victory.** Maoist insurgency continues in rural areas.

2001 **Royal family massacred** in palace shootings by Crown Prince Dipendra. Gyanendra is crowned amid unrest.

2003 **Rebels implement** ceasefire, but pull out of peace talks with government.

2005 **King Gyanendra** dismisses prime minister and assumes direct power.

2006 **Parliament reinstated** by king following weeks of strikes and protests. Parliament curtails king's powers and holds peace talks with rebels.

2007 **Maoists sit** in parliament under the terms of a temporary constitution.

2007 **Parliament approves** the abolition of the monarchy.

2008 **Former Maoists emerge** as the largest party after parliamentary elections. Nepal becomes a republic. The Maoist leader Prachanda forms a government.

2009 **Maoists leave** the government in an argument over army reforms.

Bhutan

A forested Himalayan kingdom isolated from the outside world for most of its history.

1616 **Unification of** the state by Prince-Abbot Shabdrung Ngawang Namgyal.

1731 **Tibet imposes suzerainty** on Bhutan and this is passed on in turn to China.

1770s–80s **UK involvement** in Bhutan begins with missions sent by Warren Hastings after conflict between Bhutan and Cooch Bihar.

1864 **Border war** with the UK leaves Bhutan with loss of territory.

1907 **Monarchy established.** Ugyen Wangchuck is chosen as hereditary ruler.

1949 **India is given** influence over Bhutan's foreign affairs.

1952 **National Assembly inaugurated.**

1968 **King forms first** cabinet.

1971 **Joins UN.**

1972 **King Jigme Wangchuk** begins policy of modernization.

1990 **Ethnic Nepalese launch** campaign for civil rights. Thousands flee to Nepal.

1998 **King proposes to** reform government and cedes some powers.

1999 **First TV service** inaugurated.

2003 **Bhutanese soldiers** fight Indian separatist rebels.

2007 **Agreement with India** gives Bhutan more influence over foreign policy.

2008 **The royalist** Bhutan Harmony Party wins all but three seats in the country's first parliamentary elections.

《184–85 The Silk Road

INDIAN STATESWOMAN (1917–84)

INDIRA GANDHI

Prime minister of India from 1966–77, and again from 1980 until her assassination in 1984, Indira Gandhi was the daughter of India's first prime minister, Jawaharlal Nehru, and the mother of another, Rajiv Gandhi. She was elected to parliament in 1964.

In office, Gandhi began an ambitious program of modernization but in 1975 was convicted of electoral offenses relating to the 1971 election. She responded by clamping down on her opposition and the conviction was later overturned. She lost the 1977 election and was out of office until reelected in 1980. In 1984 she used the military to suppress Sikh rebels; a few months later, Gandhi was murdered by her Sikh bodyguards.

Sri Lanka

An ancient civilization ravaged by civil war as the Tamil population attempts to secede.

400s BCE **Indo-Aryan** migrants from northern India settle on the island. Emergence of the Sinhalese as the most powerful of the numerous clans.

200s BCE **Tamils migrate** to the island from India.

1017 CE **Sri Lanka is conquered** by the Chola Empire.

***c.*1070** **Cholas expelled**.

1200s **Arab traders** establish bases on the island.

1411 **Cheng Ho,** a Chinese admiral, captures the island's king and takes him to China.

1505 **Portuguese fleet** lands in Sri Lanka, then known as Ceylon.

1656–1796 **Period of** Dutch control.

Artistic sophistication
This elegant 8th-century gilded figure of the Buddhist goddess Tara is a superb example of Sri Lankan bronze casting.

1802 **Ceylon becomes a** British crown colony by Peace of Amiens, formalizing British control of areas occupied in 1796.

1815 **British occupy Kandy,** winning control over the whole island, and start bringing in Tamil laborers from southern India to work tea, coffee, and coconut plantations.

1833 **English made** the official language.

1931 **Constitutional reforms are** introduced with the assurance of self-government in the near future and universal suffrage.

DECISIVE MOMENT
CHILDREN PROTEST, 2003

On October 6, 2003, an unprecedented demonstration broke out among school children in Valachchenai in the east of Sri Lanka. Despite fears of violent reprisals, they sat in the roads and blocked traffic in protest at the abduction of 23 of their classmates by the Tamil Tigers. The abduction took place just hours after the Tigers had agreed a program with the children's charity Unicef to return child soldiers to their families. The demonstration drew world attention to the plight of children, such as this one (right), forced to fight as soldiers by the Tiger rebels.

1948 **Island** is granted full independence.

1949 **Indian Tamil workers** are stripped of suffrage and citizenship rights.

1956 **Solomon Bandaranaike** is elected prime minister. He makes Sinhala sole official language.

1959 **Bandaranaike** assassinated. He is succeeded by his widow, Sirimavo, the world's first woman prime minister.

1972 **Name changed to** Sri Lanka, and Buddhism promoted as main religion, antagonizing Hindu Tamils.

1975 **Tamil Tigers formed** amid mounting tension in Tamil north and east.

1977 **Separatist Tamil United** Liberation Front party wins all seats in Tamil areas.

1983 **Tamil Tigers begin** civil war.

1985 **First attempts at** peace talks between Tamil Tigers and government end in failure.

1987 **Indo–Sri Lankan** peace agreement leads to dispatch of Indian peacekeeping force to Tamil areas.

1990 **Indian force** leaves. Violence between army and Tamil Tigers escalates.

1993 **President Premadasa killed** by Tamil suicide bomber.

1994 **Left-wing PA** wins election; Chandrika Kumaratunga president.

1995–2001 **War in north and east.**

1999 **Kumaratunga is wounded** in assassination attempt. She is reelected.

2002 **Ceasefire signed.** Civilian flights to Jaffna in Tamil north resume and road links reopen. Tamil Tigers drop demand for a separate state.

2004 **Renegade Tigers** regain control of east. More than 30,000 killed by tsunami.

2006 **Tigers begin** a bombing campaign in breach of the 2002 ceasefire. Intense fighting with government forces. Peace talks resume in Geneva but break down.

2007 **Government troops** clear eastern coastal areas of rebels. Thousands of civilians flee the fighting. President Mahinda Rajapaksa's government finally wins a parliamentary majority after 25 opposition MPs defect to its side. Tigers launch first jet air strike.

2008 **Sri Lankan government** renounces the truce with the Tamil Tigers and launches a major offensive.

2009 **Government forces** capture Kilinochchi, Tamil Tiger administrative headquarters, and the remaining Tamil Tiger positions, ending the civil war. The Tamil Tiger leader Velupillai Prabhakaran is killed in the fighting.

2010 **President Rajapaksa** wins a new presidential term, but the result is rejected by his opponent General Fonseka.

Maldives

An island nation making a difficult transition to democracy after years of colonial rule.

1153 **According to legend,** the Maldive king is converted to Islam by an itinerant Muslim holy man.

1558–73 **The islands are** occupied by the Portuguese, who are evicted by Bidu Muhammad Takurufana al Azam, a hero of Maldivian history.

1887 **British protectorate over** the islands formalizes British control.

1932 **First democratic constitution:** the sultanate becomes an elected position.

1965 **Full independence** from the UK.

1968 **Sultanate abolished.** Ibrahim Nasir elected first president of new republic.

1978 **Maumoon Abd al-Gayoom** becomes president on Nasir's retirement.

1980s **Development of** tourist industry fuels economic growth.

1988 **Coup attempt involving** Sri Lankan mercenaries is defeated.

1994 **Nonparty legislative elections.**

1998 **New constitution; Gayoom** is reelected for fifth five-year term.

2002 **Government takes legal** action against US for failing to endorse Kyoto Protocol on carbon emissions.

2003 **Amnesty International** accuses Maldives of torture and political repression. Antigovernment riots occur in Male. Gayoom is reelected for sixth term.

2004 **Gayoom promises** to allow formation of political parties and to limit the presidential term of office. Prodemocracy demonstration turns

---

violent and a state of emergency is declared. Scores are killed and several islands devastated by tsunami.

2005 **Unanimous vote in** parliament to allow multi-party politics.

2006 **Gayoom pardons** senior opposition leader Jennifer Latheef, imprisoned on terrorism charges.

2008 **Gayoom** defeated by Mohammed Nasheed in presidential elections.

Bangladesh

A young, flood-prone country that surrounds the confluence of the Ganges and Jamuna rivers.

1905 **Muslims persuade British** rulers to partition the state of Bengal and create a Muslim-dominated East Bengal.

1906 **Muslim League is established** in Dhaka.

1912 **Partition of 1905** is reversed.

1947 **British withdraw from** India. Partition establishes a largely Muslim state of East (present-day Bangladesh) and West Pakistan, separated by 1,000 miles (1,600 km) of Indian, and largely Hindu, territory.

1949 **Awami League founded** to campaign for autonomy from West Pakistan.

1968 **General Yahya Khan** heads government in Islamabad.

1970 **Elections give Awami** League, under Sheikh Mujib Rahman, a clear majority in East Pakistan. Rioting and guerrilla warfare follow Yahya Khan's refusal to convene the assembly. The year ends with the worst recorded storms in Bangladesh's history—between 200,000 and 500,000 are killed.

1971 **Civil war starts** as Sheikh Mujib Rahman and Awami League declare unilateral independence. Sheikh Mujib is arrested and taken to West Pakistan. East Pakistan army mutinies. Ten million Bangladeshis flee to India. Pakistani troops are defeated in 12 days by Mukhti Bahini—the Bengal Liberation Army.

1972 **Sheikh Mujib returns** and is elected prime minister. Country changes name to Bangladesh. Nationalization of key industries, including jute and textile. Bangladesh achieves international recognition and joins Commonwealth. Pakistan withdraws in protest.

1974 **Severe floods damage** rice crop.

1975 **Sheikh Mujib is assassinated** in a military coup. General Zia ur-Rahman takes power and institutes a single-party state. Martial law is imposed.

1976 **Banning of trade** union federations.

1977 General Zia assumes the presidency. Islam is adopted as the first principle of the constitution.

1979 Martial law lifted following victory of Zia's Bangladesh National Party (BNP) in elections.

1981 General Zia is assassinated in failed military coup. Succeeded by Abdus Sattar.

1982 General Ershad takes over in coup.

1983 Ershad assumes the presidency, an act confirmed in a referendum in 1985.

1986 Awami League (AL) and BNP fail to unseat Ershad in elections.

1987 Ershad announces state of emergency after opposition demonstrations and strikes.

1988 Islam becomes the constitutional state religion. Floods cover three-quarters of country. Opposition boycotts elections.

1990 Ershad resigns following mass demonstrations.

1991 Elections won by BNP. Khaleda Zia becomes prime minister. Ershad is imprisoned for corruption. The role of the president is reduced to ceremonial functions. Cyclonic floods kill 150,000.

1994 Author Taslima Nasreen, accused of blasphemy, flees to Sweden.

1996 General election, boycotted by opposition parties, returns BNP to power. Opposition parties reject result and force fresh elections. Sheikh Hasina Wajed of the AL takes power.

1997 Ershad is released from prison. Opposition begins campaign of strikes against the government.

1998 Two-thirds of country devastated by worst-ever floods. Fifteen former army officers are sentenced to death for involvement in assassination of President Mujib in 1975.

2000 In a row with Pakistan over the 1971 war, Bangladesh demands an apology for alleged genocide.

2001 Elections won by BNP. Supreme Court declares the issuing of religious decrees (fatwas) to be a criminal offense. Awami League leader Hasina steps down, becoming first prime minister to complete a five-year term. Khaleda Zia's BNP wins at polls.

2002 President Musharraf of Pakistan visits Bangladesh and expresses regret for Pakistani excesses during the 1971 war. Five hundred people are killed when a ferry sinks in a storm.

2004 Opposition calls 21 general strikes in a campaign to oust the government. Constitution is amended to reserve 45 seats for female MPs. Bomb attacks by Islamic extremists continue. Floods in Dhaka are the worst in decades.

2005 More than 140 people are killed when a ferry capsizes in Dhaka; months later 150 are killed in a week in three ferry accidents; more than 600 died in similar ferry disasters in 2002 and 2003. Islamic extremist bombing campaign continues.

2006 AL ends year-long parliamentary boycott. Amid violent antigovernment demonstrations, President Ahmed assumes caretaker role as prime minister Zia completes her term and steps down.

2007 State of emergency declared during violence prior to election. Six Islamic extremists convicted of bombings in 2005 are hanged. Sheikh Hasina is charged with conspiring to murder a political rival; Khaleda Zia is put under house arrest.

2007 Cyclone Sidr hits Bangladesh, killing thousands of people.

2008 After more than a year of military rule, elections are held. Sheikh Hasina's Awami League wins a landslide victory.

« 410–11 The Partition of India

Burma

A former British colony ruled since 1962 by the military, who renamed it Myanmar in 1989.

1000s Burma is first united under King Anarutha (1044–77), the founder of the Pagan dynasty.

1287 Burma is overrun by the forces of Kublai Khan.

1535–45 Burma is reunited under King Tabinshweti, founder of Toungoo dynasty.

1714–60 Under Alaungpaya, founder of the Kongaung dynasty, the Burmese kingdom is at its height, stretching as far as parts of Thailand and India.

1824–86 Burma fights three separate wars against the British over the boundaries of Britain's Indian Empire.

1886 Burma becomes a province of British India.

1930–31 Economic depression triggers popular unrest.

1937 Separated from India as a British crown colony.

1942 Japan invades.

1945 Anti-Fascist People's Freedom League (AFPFL), led by Aung San, helps the Allies reoccupy country.

1947 Burmese independence. Aung San wins elections, but is assassinated.

1948 Independence under new prime minister, U Nu, who initiates socialist policies. Revolts by ethnic separatists, notably the Karen liberation struggle.

Royal opulence
The Kanbawzathati palace in the ancient Burmese capital of Hanthawaddy is a testimony to the wealth of King Bayinnaung of the Toungoo dynasty (reigned 1551–81). He unified the country and conquered the Shan states and Siam (now Thailand). The king was a prolific builder and a patron of the arts.

1958 Ruling AFPFL splits into two.

1960 U Nu's faction wins elections.

1962 General Ne Win stages military coup. "New Order" policy of "Buddhist Socialism" deepens Burma's international isolation. Mining and other industries nationalized. Free trade prohibited.

1964 Socialist Program Party declared sole legal party.

1976 Ethnic liberation groups gain control of 40 percent of country.

1982 Nonindigenous people barred from public office.

1988 Thousands die in student riots. Ne Win resigns. Martial law declared. Aung San Suu Kyi, daughter of General Aung San, and others form National League for Democracy (NLD). General Saw Maung leads military coup. State Law and Order Restoration Council (SLORC) takes power.

1989 Army arrests NLD leaders. Country officially renamed Union of Myanmar.

1990 Elections permitted. NLD wins landslide but SLORC refuses to concede power. More NLD leaders arrested.

1991 Aung San Suu Kyi is awarded Nobel Peace Prize.

1992 General Than Shwe takes over as SLORC leader.

1995 Aung San Suu Kyi is released.

1997 Ruling SLORC renamed State Peace and Development Council (SPDC). US imposes sanctions and bans further investment in Burma.

1998 NLD sets deadline for convening parliament; military junta refuses.

1999 Aung San Suu Kyi rejects conditions set by SPDC for visiting the UK to see her husband, Michael Aris, who dies of cancer.

2000 Secret talks begin between Aung San Suu Kyi and SPDC. Aung San Suu Kyi under house arrest again.

2003 Aung San Suu Kyi taken into "protective custody" following clashes between her supporters and the government. Khin Nyunt becomes prime minister. He is ousted in 2004.

2007 Nationwide protests break out led by Buddhist monks, but mass arrests put them to an end.

2008 New constitution allocates a quarter of seats in parliament to the military. Cyclone Nargis kills over 100,000 people.

2009 Aung San Suu Kyi is sentenced to a further 18 months house arrest.

2010 The government-backed United Solidarity and Development Party (USDP) wins a landslide election victory. A week after the election, Aung San Suu Kyi is released from house arrest.

« 172–73 Lost Empires
« 184–85 The Silk Road

BURMESE POLITICIAN (1945–)
AUNG SAN SUU KYI

Aung San Suu Kyi, the Burmese opposition leader, began her nonviolent struggle for democracy in 1988 following the slaughter of student protesters by Burma's military authorities. Placed under long periods of house arrest she has refused the military's offer to free her if she leaves Burma. In 1990, the military ignored the 80 percent of parliamentary seats that her party (the NLD) won in that year's election.

China

The world's most populous country, and for centuries the world's most advanced civilization.

6th–5th century BCE Confucius (*c*.551–*c*.479 BCE) passes his teachings down to his disciples to be recorded in the *Analects*. Confucian thought is supplemented by the teachings of Mencius in the 4th century BCE. Lao Zu (possibly mythical) creates the philosophy later set down in the *Dao De Jing* as Taoist thought. Han Fei Zi establishes the legalist school.

221 BCE **China is unified** for the first time under an imperial dynasty, the Qin, with its capital in Chang'an (present day Xi'an). The first emperor, Shi Huangdi, infamous for his hardline suppression of subversion and mass execution of intellectuals, is also credited with the instigation of the Great Wall. Script and weights and measures are standardized.

206 BCE **Liu Bang leads** a peasant uprising to overthrow the Qin dynasty and establish the Han, under which China remains unified almost continually for more than four centuries. Stability allows major advances to be made in political thought, economics, invention, and administration, and Chinese territory is enlarged through several successful military campaigns.

6 CE **The declining Han** dynasty is usurped by Wang Mang who establishes the short-lived Xin dynasty.

25 CE **The Han dynasty** is restored with its capital farther east in Luoyang, for which reason the second Han period is known as the Eastern Han.

220 CE **The Eastern Han** fails to produce the stability and achievements of the earlier Western Han due to a succession of young and weak emperors, and the country splits into three warring kingdoms: Shu, Wei, and Wu.

265 CE **The Northern and** Southern dynasties period begins. During this period northern China is ruled by six different dynasties and the south by three.

589 **Yang Jian, regent** of the Northern Zhou dynasty conquers the Southern Chen dynasty and establishes the Sui, building a new capital in Luoyang. The Sui dynasty instigates many of the institutions developed to great success in the Tang: the administration, tax, forced labor, penal, and examination systems. The Grand Canal is constructed. Excessive demands on the peasants for forced labor under the second emperor of the Sui bring about a peasant revolt in 611 CE that heralds the end of the dynasty.

618 **Li Yuan leads** an army revolt and captures Chang'an, hereafter capital of the Tang, but in 626 CE passes the throne to his second son, Li Shimin, who becomes the famous Emperor Tai Zong of the Tang.

The political institutions of the Sui are reformed along less repressive lines and the empire consolidated. "Land equalization" is carried out. The Tang is referred to in Chinese history as a golden age, mostly for its arts (especially poetry and painting), which flourish under imperial patronage, and for unprecedented territorial expansion, but also for its political and religious tolerance.

755 **Poor government leads** to social disorder and An Lushan leads a rebellion, which takes eight years to quell. The Tang recovers sufficiently for almost another century of stability (mid-Tang), but social order declines due to power struggles within the court throughout the late Tang period (820–907 CE).

906 **The collapse of** the Tang produces 54 years of disunity when rule passes between five separate dynasties (Later Liang, Later Tang, Later Jin, Later Han, and Later Zhou). Parts of North China come under the rule of 10 non-Chinese kingdoms.

960 **Zhou Kuangyin, commander** of the Later Zhou's imperial army, leads a revolt to seize power, founds the Song dynasty, creating the capital in Kaifeng, and conquers the other Chinese states over a period of 15 years. In spite of rigorous attempts at centralizing control and defending itself against external attack, the Song never achieves the unity of the Tang. Political and military instability breeds philosophical and religious ferment, including the development of neo-Confucian thought, which draws from ideas in both Confucian traditions and Buddhism.

1127 **The Jurchen conquest** of northern China combines with factional struggles and peasant rebellions to effect the collapse of the Northern Song dynasty, which reestablishes itself in Hangzhou as the Southern Song. Northern China falls under the control of the Jurchen Jin dynasty. Military conflict continues between the two regimes. The writing of Ci poetry reaches its peak in the south. Mongol armies under Ghengis Khan begin their gradual conquest of China.

1275 **Venetian explorer** Marco Polo arrives in China. He will spend 17 years there in the service of Kublai Khan.

1279 **The Mongol conquest** of China is completed under Kublai Khan, and the Yuan dynasty established, bringing the capital to the site of present-day Beijing for the first time. Under the Mongols, agriculture, communications, and local administration are strengthened, drama flourishes, and advances are made in science and technology. A policy of tolerance is adopted toward religion. Like many dynasties before it, the Mongol dynasty deteriorates through corruption and is overthrown by peasant rebellions.

Chariot ornament
In the 4th century BCE, about the time this ornament adorned a Chinese war chariot, Sun Tzu wrote his treatise *The Art of War*, which included the maxim "all war is based on deception."

1368 **Zhu Yuanzhang** establishes the Ming dynasty, moving the capital to Nanjing, then back to Beijing in 1421.

1421 **Policies are adopted** to restore order in the countryside: land is allocated to refugees and taxation eased. The bureaucracy is reorganized. Indiscriminate executions and the establishment of a secret service ensure the unopposed rule of the emperor, and heavy censorship and editing of texts is instigated. The novel is introduced as a new form of literature and *The Water Margin* and *Journey to the West* ("Monkey") achieve particular acclaim. The dynasty is consistently shaken by peasant uprisings, and weakened by the excessive power of the eunuchs in the court. It is, however, Manchu invaders who bring about the fall of the Ming Dynasty.

1582 **Portuguese traders arrive** at Guangzhou.

1644 **The Manchus conquer** China, expand the region to an unprecedented extent, and modify the Qing institutions. They allow the Han to participate in government, while holding on to power. Wearing of the hair in a queue is made compulsory as is neo-Confucianism, though most of the emperors are also Buddhist adherents. While czarist Russia encroaches on Chinese territory in the north, European merchants begin to arrive by sea along the south coast and establish trade links.

Magnificence of the Manchu
Kangxi (above) was the second Manchu emperor. During his reign (1661–1722), he opened China up to foreign trade and encouraged Western ideas. He added parts of Russia and Tibet to the empire.

1736 **Emperor Qianlong comes** to power, a patron of Buddhism under whose reign huge amounts of resources are spent on imperial leisure.

1839–60 **Opium Wars with** Britain and France. Alarmed at the rise in opium use, the Chinese government attempts to limit its import. China is defeated by the British in 1842, and forced to open ports to foreigners. The Manchu are also forced to hand over Hong Kong to the British. China is again defeated in 1860, this time by a combined Anglo-French force. With restrictions lifted, the opium trade thrives and the number of users grows rapidly.

1850–64 **Hung Hsiu-chuan** proclaims a new dynasty in the Taiping uprising, seizing control of the city of Nanjing and establishing a Christian regime. He declares himself to be the younger brother of Jesus Christ. With the help of UK and US forces, Nanjing is recaptured by the Manchu government in 1864 after a conflict that leaves about 20 million dead. Although victorious, the Manchus' authority is undermined in many parts of China.

1883–85 **In the Tonkin War,** the French take over control of northern Vietnam from China.

1895 **China is defeated** by Japan in a war over control of the Korean peninsula.

1900 **The Boxer Rebellion,** an attempt to expel all foreigners, is suppressed. Foreign troops are now stationed at every important junction between Beijing and Shanghai as the Manchu government is fatally weakened.

1911 **Manchu Empire overthrown** by nationalists led by Sun Yat-sen. Republic of China declared.

1912 **Sun Yat-sen** forms the National People's Party (Kuomintang).

1916 **Nationalists factionalize. Sun** Yat-sen sets up government in Guangdong. Rest of China under control of rival warlords.

1921 **The Chinese Communist Party** (CCP) is founded in Shanghai at its first national congress, held in a small house and attended by 13 people.

1922 **Under pressure from** the CCP to formalize his movement's political doctrine, Sun Yat-sen begins a series of lectures outlining his Three Great Principles, which champion nationalism, democracy, and socialism.

1923 **The CCP joins Soviet**-backed Guomindang to fight the warlords.

1925 **Chiang Kai-shek** becomes Kuomintang leader on death of Sun Yat-sen.

1927 **Chiang turns on** the CCP. The CCP leaders escape to rural south.

CHINESE NATIONALIST LEADER (1866–1925)

SUN YAT-SEN

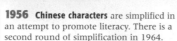

Often referred to as "the Father of Modern China," Sun Yat-sen was the leader of the National People's Party (Kuomintang). Sun became the first president of the Republic of China in 1912 when he returned from 16 years of exile to overthrow the failing Manchu dynasty. He quickly lost power again and spent the following years fighting the warlords who controlled much of the country, making an alliance with the newly formed Communist Party. He died from cancer before he was able to consolidate his power and reunify China.

Sun became the symbol of Chinese modernization after his death due to his unrivaled knowledge of the West and determination to develop China. Uniquely, he is now revered in both mainland China and Taiwan.

1930–34 Mao Zedong formulates his strategy of a peasant-led revolution.

1931 Japan invades Manchuria.

1934 Chiang forces the CCP out of its southern bases. Start of the 7,450-mile (12,000-km) Long March as the Red Armies of the CCP retreat.

1935 Long March ends in Yanan, Shaanxi province, as the CCP relocates its power base from the southeast to the northwest. Of the 100,000 who had started the march, only 8,000 remain. Mao, who lost a brother and two young children in the Long March, becomes leader of the CCP.

1937–45 In a war against Japan, the CCP Red Army fights in the north, the Kuomintang in the south. Japan is defeated.

1945–49 War between Red Army and Kuomintang. US-backed Kuomintang retreats to Taiwan.

1949 Mao proclaims the People's Republic of China on October 1.

1950 Chinese invasion of Tibet. Mutual assistance treaty with USSR.

1950–58 Land reform culminates in the setting up of communes. First five-year plan (1953–58) fails.

Little red thoughts
Teenage members of the Red Guard (above) read the thoughts of Chairman Mao from the Little Red Book. They were encouraged to humiliate their elders in a campaign against the "Four Olds."

1956 Chinese characters are simplified in an attempt to promote literacy. There is a second round of simplification in 1964.

1958 "Great Leap Forward" to boost production fails. Farming is collectivized and this contributes to millions of deaths during the 1959–61 famine. Just two years into the five-year plan, it is abandoned. Mao resigns as CCP chairman and is succeeded by Liu Shaoqi.

1959 Revolt in Tibet is put down and the Dalai Lama flees to India, where he sets up a government-in-exile.

1960 Sino–Soviet split as Mao considers that the Soviet Revolution has lost its way.

1961–65 A more pragmatic economic approach is adopted, led by Liu and Deng Xiaoping.

1962 Border conflict between China and India leaves 2,000 dead and China in continued occupation of the disputed Himalayan region of Aksai Chin.

1964 Mao's Little Red Book, containing a collection of his sayings, is first published. China conducts its first test of a nuclear weapon in the Lop Nur desert.

1966 The Cultural Revolution is initiated by Mao to restore his supreme power. It is intended to last 10 years. Schools are shut down and the youthful Red Guards are encouraged to attack all authority and bourgeois ideas. Party officials and community leaders are subjected to public criticism and humiliation as work all but grinds to a halt, and many thousands die. The cult of personality surrounding Mao is intensified and the Red Guards splinter into factions, each claiming to represent the will of Mao.

1966–68 Campaign against the "Four Olds": old ideas, old customs, old culture, old habits. Temples are ransacked, books are burned, and intellectuals are persecuted. By 1968, industrial production has dipped to barely 12 percent of the levels of 1966.

1967 Army intervenes to restore order amid countrywide chaos. The Red Guards

are dispersed as the Cultural Revolution is brought to an end. Liu and Deng are purged from the party.

1969 Mao regains chair of the CCP. Lin Biao is designated his successor, but is quickly attacked by Mao. Chinese and Soviet forces clash on an island in the Ussuri river.

1970 China launches its first satellite, Dong Fang Hong I (The East is Red I).

1971 Lin Biao dies in plane crash.

1972 US President Nixon visits China and meets Mao, as a more open foreign policy is initiated by Zhou Enlai.

1973 Mao's wife Jiang Qing, Zhang Chunquio, and other "Gang of Four" members are elected to the CCP politburo. Deng Xiaoping rehabilitated.

1976 Zhou Enlai dies. Mao strips Deng of all his posts. Following a long period of illness, Mao dies at age 82. On his death, the Gang of Four attempt to seize power, but is thwarted by supporters of Deng. The Gang of Four is arrested (and put on trial in 1981). A massive earthquake at Tangshan in Hebei province leaves at least 250,000 dead.

1977 Deng regains party posts and begins to extend power base.

1978 Economic modernization launched. Farmers are allowed to farm for profit.

1978–79 The Democracy Wall movement in Beijing provides an outlet for protesters seeking greater democratic freedom during a period known as the "Beijing Spring." Criticism of the Gang of Four and acknowledged past mistakes

is encouraged, but when the present system is criticized, the Wall is closed.

1979 Diplomatic relations are established with the US and President Jimmy Carter visits China. Sino-Vietnamese War leaves 80,000 dead. Pinyin is adopted as the official system of transcribing Chinese into Latin alphabets.

1980 Deng emerges as China's paramount leader. Economic reform gathers pace, but hopes for political change are suppressed. First Special Economic Zone (SEZ) established in Shenzhen. A "one child" family planning policy is adopted at a national level.

1984 Industrial reforms announced.

1986–90 Implementation of Open-Door policy to encourage foreign trade and investement.

1987 CCP secretary general Hu Yaobang is forced to resign over his liberal stance and moves to rehabilitate victims of the Cultural Revolution.

1989 Prodemocracy demonstrations in Tiananmen Square, which are initially aimed at the posthumous rehabilitation of Hu Yaobang. After initial hesitation by the government, the uprising is ordered to be crushed by the army, with the loss of 1,000–5,000 lives. Beijing is placed under martial law and China briefly faces international isolation.

1990 Shanghai stock exchange restarts operations after a 41-year closure.

1992 China ratifies the Nuclear Non-Proliferation Treaty. Russia and China sign a declaration restoring friendly ties.

DECISIVE MOMENT

LHASA UPRISING, 1959

On March 10, 1959, simmering tension between Tibetans and their Chinese rulers exploded in an uprising in the Tibetan capital, Lhasa. Thousands took to the streets surrounding the Potala Palace (below) to protest against the influx of Chinese settlers, which had begun when Chinese troops entered eastern Tibet in October 1950.

Tibet had declared its independence in 1911 when the Manchu had fallen, and governed itself for 40 years, but its poorly equipped army had been no match for the invading Chinese in 1950. This proved true again and the uprising was crushed, leaving thousands dead. The Dalai Lama, spiritual leader

of Tibet, was forced to flee across the Himalayas on foot. He set up a government-in-exile in India and has campaigned for an independent Tibet ever since.

Following the uprising, the Chinese government, which formally recognizes Tibet as an autonomous region, began a crackdown on Tibetan religion and culture. In the 1970s, repression eased but riots broke out again in the late 1980s and martial law was imposed in 1988.

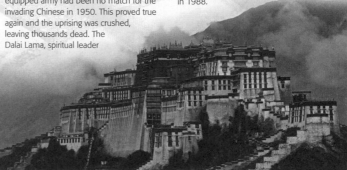

1992–95 Trials of prodemocracy activists continue. Plans for market economy accelerated.

1993 Jiang Zemin replaces Yang Shangkun as president, espousing the policy of a "Socialist Market Economy."

1995–96 Chinese missile tests in the Strait of Taiwan lead to serious crisis and allegations that China is seeking to influence the results of the 1996 Taiwanese presidential elections.

1997 Deng Xiaoping dies at age 92. The UK hands back sovereignty over Hong Kong to China. The five-yearly party congress confirms Jiang's leadership and backs his reformist policies.

1998 Zhu Rongji becomes prime minister and announces economic reforms that will lead to the closure or amalgamation of loss-making state enterprises and a reduction in the civil service by up to 4 million jobs. The East Asian economic crisis leads to a sharp downturn in growth, but China avoids significant capital flight or currency devaluation.

1999 The Portuguese-administered territory of Macao is returned to China. There is friction over a Taiwanese claim of statehood. NATO accidentally bombs the Chinese embassy in Belgrade leading to international crisis. The quasi-religious Falun Gong sect is declared a threat to stability and outlawed.

2000 Taiwanese presidential election causes tension. US normalizes trade relations. As part of an official clampdown on corruption, a former deputy chairman of the National People's Congress is executed for accepting a bribe.

2001 Major diplomatic incident with US when a Chinese pilot is killed and a US spy-plane is forced down on Hainan Island. China carries out military exercises simulating an invasion of Taiwan. Beijing is awarded the 2008 Olympic Games. China joins the World Trade Organization after a 15-year campaign to secure its entry to the world trading body.

2002 Vice President Hu Jintao becomes Head of the CCP, replacing Jiang Zemin. US President George W. Bush visits China on the 30th anniversary of the visit by his predecessor Richard Nixon.

2003 Outbreak of Severe Acute Respiratory Syndrome (SARS) in China. The extremely infectious disease spreads throughout East and Southeast Asia and as far as Europe and the US, sparking concerns about a global pandemic and leaving nearly 800 dead before the outbreak is contained. Hu Jintao is elected as president by the National People's Congress. China's first manned spacecraft is launched, with astronaut Yang Liwei on board. Construction begins on the Three Gorges Dam on the Yangtze River.

2004 China signs economic agreement with Association of Southeast Asian Nations (ASEAN) trading bloc.

CHINA
SPECIAL ADMINISTRATIVE REGIONS AND DISPUTED TERRITORIES

HONG KONG ISLAND was ceded to Britain in 1842. Further mainland territory was aquired in 1860 (the Kowloon peninsula) and 1898 (the New Territories). Hong Kong was returned to Chinese rule in 1997.

1842 The UK defeats China in the Opium War of 1839–42; as a result, Hong Kong is ceded to the UK under the Treaty of Nanjing.
1860 Defeat in the Second Opium War (1856–60) leads to cession of Kowloon.
1898 Continued aggression pressures the Manchu government to sign the second Peking Convention, granting a 99-year lease of the New Territories to the UK.
1941–45 The Japanese invade and occupy Hong Kong.
1949 The communist takeover of mainland China halts British plans to allow greater autonomy to Hong Kong.
1967 Hong Kong trade is disrupted by civil disturbances created by the influence of the Cultural Revolution in China.
1981 The British Nationality Act, granting British Nationality (Overseas) but not right of abode in the UK to Hong Kong Chinese creates great controversy.
1984 The Sino-British Joint Declaration is signed. It grants China sovereignty over Hong Kong after 1997, guaranteeing a high degree of autonomy in economic affairs and the continuation of the present legal and capitalist economic systems.
1997 Hong Kong handed back to China, now known as a Special Administrative Region of China.
2008 Prodemocracy parties win more than a third of seats, giving them veto over constitutional changes.

MACAO occupies a narrow peninsula on the opposite side of the Pearl River estuary from Hong Kong. The last European colony in Asia, Macao was handed back to China by Portugal in 1999.

1513 The first Portuguese ship arrives in the Pearl River estuary.
1557 Portugal begins paying tribute to China in return for using Macau as an intermediary port for ships traveling to Japan. An international merchant community establishes itself.
1800s Hong Kong replaces Macau as the major trading port of the region.
1955 Macau is made an overseas province by Portugal.
1984 For the first time, the Chinese majority are given the vote.
1987 Portugal agrees to return Macau to China in 1999 on terms similiar to those agreed with the UK over Hong Kong.
1999 Macau becomes a Special Administrative Region of China.

TAIWAN The island lies off the southeast coast of mainland China. Mountains cover two-thirds of the island. The fertile lowlands are densely populated. In 1949, when the communists ousted Chiang Kai-shek's Kuomintang (KMT) from power on the mainland, he established the Republic of China on the island. De facto military rule has been democratized progressively since 1986, and the KMT's grip was shaken by defeat in the 2000 presidential election. Mainland China still considers Taiwan a renegade province, and only a few countries officially recognize the regime there.

1590 Portuguese sailors reach the island and name it Formosa (beautiful).
1642 The Dutch take control.
1683 The Manchus claim the island as part of Qing China.
1895 Following China's defeat in the Sino-Japanese War, control of the island passes to Japan.
1945 Taiwan is returned to China.
1949 Chiang Kai-shek establishes the Republic of China on the island.
1971 The People's Republic of China replaces Taiwan at the UN.
1975 Chiang Kai-shek dies. His son Chiang Ching-kuo becomes KMT leader.
1986 KMT ends martial law and permits visits to the Chinese mainland for "humanitarian" purposes for first time in 38 years. In 1988, mainland Chinese are allowed to visit Taiwan on same basis. Formation of political parties is permitted.
1990 KMT formally ends its state of war with People's Republic of China.
1996 Lee Teng-hui wins first direct presidential elections.
1999 Thousands die in earthquake.
2000 Chen Shui-bian of DPP wins presidency, overturning KMT dominance.
2003 Taipei 101, the world's tallest building, is completed. There is a severe outbreak of the viral disease SARS.
2005 Lien Chan becomes the first KMT leader since 1949 to visit mainland China.
2008 The KMT wins a landslide victory in parliamentary elections. Ma Ying-Jeou of the KMT is elected president. Former president Chen is arrested on charges of money laundering.
2010 China and Taiwan sign free trade pact.

2005 First direct flights between People's Republic of China and Taiwan since 1949. Violent anti-Japanese protests break out in Chinese cities over the coverage of Japan's occupation of China in a Japanese school textbook. Lien Chian, chairman of the Kuomintang party of Taiwan, visits mainland China and meets CCP leader Hu Jintao, the highest-level meeting between Beijing and Taipei politicians since 1949. China and Russia hold first joint military exercises. The highly pathogenic H5N1 strain of avian flu is detected in migratory birds in Qinghai, China. China and Russia sign an agreement settling a long-running dispute over their common eastern border.

Former reformist leader Zhao Ziyang dies after years of house arrest following the Tiananmen Square massacre.

2006 Work on the Three Gorges Dam is finished. A railway line linking China and Tibet is completed. The official news agency announces the worst drought in 50 years.

2007 China carries out a successful missile test in space, destroying a Chinese weather satellite. Prime Minister Wen Jiabao addresses the Japanese parliament, the first Chinese head of government to do so, as the two countries agree to a process of reconciliation.

2008 A huge earthquake in Sichuan kills tens of thousands; China and Russia sign a treaty to end their 40-year border dispute; Beijing hosts the Olympic Games. A scandal erupts as 50,000 Chinese children fall ill after drinking tainted milk.

2009 China and Russia sign a 20-year deal to supply oil to China. Serious ethnic disturbances erupt in Xinjiang.

2010 Imprisoned Chinese dissident Liu Xaobao is awarded the Nobel Peace Prize.

《60–61 Bronze Age China
《126–27 The Unification of China
《128–29 The Centralized State
《160–61 China's Golden Age
《162–63 The Song Dynasty
《166–67 The Ming Dynasty
《184–85 The Silk Road
《240–41 The Three Emperors
《354–55 The Opium Wars
《424–25 China's Long March
《472–73 Superpower China

Hong Kong is returned to China
On July 1, 1997, Hong Kong (left) reverted from British to Chinese sovereignty. Under the policy of "one country, two systems," the island remains a center of international finance and trade.

Mongolia

A remote, sparsely populated country that once ruled the largest-ever Asian empire.

1206 Ghengis Khan unifies the Mongol tribes and launches a campaign of conquest that is continued by his son and grandson to create a huge empire.

1636 The Manchu conquer southern Mongolia, creating Inner Mongolia. Outer Mongolia is offered Manchu protection in 1691.

1911 Outer Mongolia declares its independence as Manchu dynasty falls.

1919 China reoccupies Outer Mongolia.

1921 With Red Army support, Mongolian revolutionaries drive out the Chinese.

1924 The Mongolian People's Republic, an independent communist state, is declared.

1966 Soviet troops are secretly stationed in Mongolia. They stay until 1986.

1990 Political parties are legalized after street demonstrations.

1992 Former communists, MPRP, returned to power in first democratic elections, but lose elections in 1996.

1999–2001 Severe winters cause widespread hardship.

2008 President Enkbyar declares a state of emergency after rioting in the capital.

2010 Extremely cold winter kills so many livestock that UN establishes a program to pay herders to collect the carcasses.

« 164–65 Genghis Khan

North Korea

An isolationist communist regime presides over the impoverished north of the Korean peninsula.

676 CE The Korean peninsula is unified under the Kingdom of Silla. Towards the end of the 700s, the kingdom begins to break apart as a result of uprisings and conflicts within the aristocracy.

935 CE Kingdom of Goryo is established, once more uniting the peninsula.

1231 Mongols invade Goryo.

1392 Yi Song-gye, a general under the Goryo regime, deposes the king and founds the Yi dynasty. Two years later, the capital is moved to Seoul.

1636 Korea is invaded by the Manchus, who later go on to conquer China, ruling as the Qing dynasty.

1894–95 Japan defeats the Chinese in Korea, beginning the Sino-Japanese War.

1904–05 Following the Russo-Japanese War, Japan conquers Korea.

1910 Japan annexes Korea.

1919 Independence protests are violently suppressed by the Japanese.

1930S Northern Korea's industry is developed by the Japanese to supply material for expansion into China.

1945 Following World War II Korea splits at 38ºN. North is occupied by the USSR.

1946 KWP (Korean Workers' Party) is founded. One of its leaders is Kim Il-sung, who has received Red Army training.

1948 Democratic People's Republic of Korea created with Kim Il-sung as leader.

1950–53 The Korean War begins when Kim Il-sung invades South Korea with the intention of uniting the country. North Koreans take much of the south, before US intervention drives them back. At least 3 million people die.

1950S Kim Il-sung starts to develop an extreme personality cult.

1988 North Korea begins a repressive process of "ideological rectification."

1991 North and South Korea join the UN, and sign basic agreements to foster economic and cultural exchanges.

1994 Kim Il-sung dies. He is declared "Eternal President" four years later. His son, Kim Jong-il, succeeds him.

1996 Famine follows widespread floods.

1997 Famine worsens: estimates of the dead range from 100,000 up to 3 million. Kim Jong-il becomes party leader.

1998 North Korean mini-submarine is captured in South Korean waters.

2000 Kim Jong-il meets South Korean president Kim Dae-jung in Pyongyang. As a result, a limited number of North Koreans meet relatives from the south, separated since 1950–53, in a reunion.

2002 Tensions with the US are heightened as President Bush names North Korea as part of an "Axis of Evil."

2006 North Korea tests long-range missiles and claims to have tested a nuclear weapon.

2007 In a deal struck in Beijing, North Korea agrees to close its main nuclear reactor in exchange for aid.

2007 Devastating floods hit North Korea.

2008 Relations between North and South deteriorate. North Korea says it is slowing down the dismantling of its nuclear program.

Border line

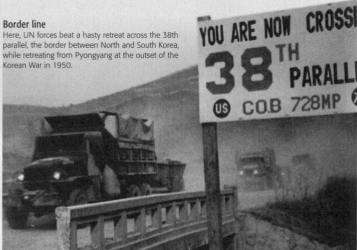

Here, UN forces beat a hasty retreat across the 38th parallel, the border between North and South Korea, while retreating from Pyongyang at the outset of the Korean War in 1950.

2009 North Korea launches a long-range missile test, and carries out an underground nuclear test. Both tests draw international condemnation.

2009 A currency reform provokes unprecedented levels of public protests.

2009 Sinking of a South Korean warship, allegedly by northern forces, raises tension. The North Korean Army bombards a South Korean island near Seoul, the worst attack since the Korean War.

« 90–91 Frontiers of Power

South Korea

The southern half of the peninsula has prospered significantly since the 1950 Korean War.

1945 US and Soviet armies arrive. Korea split at 38ºN. South comes under de facto US rule.

1948 Republic of South Korea is created. Syngman Rhee becomes the first president of an authoritarian regime.

1950 North Korea invades, sparking Korean War. The US, with UN backing, enters on the South's side; China unofficially assists the North.

1951 Fighting stabilizes at 38th parallel.

1953 Following an armistice, a de facto border is established at the ceasefire line.

1960 Syngman Rhee resigns in the face of popular revolt (the "April Revolution").

1961 Military coup leads to authoritarian junta led by Park Chung-hee.

1963 After pressure for a civilian government, Park is reelected as president (also in 1967 and 1971). Strong manufacturing base and exports drive massive economic development.

1965 Links with Japan are restored.

1966 Hundreds of thousands of troops are deployed in South Vietnam.

1972 Martial law. A new constitution confers greater presidential powers.

1979 Park is assassinated. General Chun Doo-hwan, intelligence chief, leads coup.

1980 Chun chosen as president. Kim Dae-jung arrested.

1987 Sixth Republic includes genuine multi-party democracy.

1988 Seoul hosts the Olympics.

1991 South Korea joins UN.

1992 Diplomatic links with China are established. Kim Young-sam is the first civilian president in 30 years.

1998 Kim Dae-jung becomes president and pursues a "sunshine policy" of offering aid to North Korea.

2000 Kim Dae-jung meets Kim Jong-il in a summit in Pyongyang. Kim Dae-jung awarded Nobel Peace Prize.

2002 South Korea cohosts the World Cup with Japan, reaching the semifinals.

2003 In the biggest mass-crossing of the border since the war, hundreds of South Koreans visit Pyongyang.

2007 South Korea resumes high-level talks with North Korea. Lee Myung-Bak wins presidential elections.

2009 North and South Korean warships exchange fire across their disputed maritime frontier.

2010 South Korea breaks off trade with North after the sinking of the warship Chaeson. North Korean army shells South Korean Yeonpyeong island, leading to dangerous rise in tension.

« 90–91 Frontiers of Power
« 170–71 Korea in the Middle Ages
« 184–85 The Silk Road
« 456–57 Tiger Economies

Japan

An island monarchy that has renounced its martial past to become the world's third-largest economy.

c.350 CE Japan is unified under the rule of the powerful Yamato clan.

538 CE Buddhism is introduced to Japan, through China and Korea.

604 CE Prince Shotoku issues the Constitution of 17 Articles, setting out ethical maxims of government, which shows Buddhist and Confucian influence.

645 Fujiwara Kamatari institutes a reformed system of government based upon the Chinese model of a complex, centralized administration.

670–714 The main temple in the Horyu-ji temple complex, the Golden Hall, is built by carpenters from Korea.

710 Heijoko (Nara) becomes the first permanent capital, modeled on the Chinese city of Chang'an.

794 The Heian period begins. The power of the emperors falls into hands of the Fujiwara clan. The capital moves to Heiankyo (modern Kyoto).

c.1020 Murashi Shikibu writes *The Tale of Genji*, thought to be the first-ever novel.

1150s–80s Civil war between rival clans results in the Fujiwara clan losing their grip on power.

1159 Following the battle known as the Heiji Disturbance, the Taira clan emerge as the most powerful family.

1185 A military government is consolidated under the leader of the Minamoto clan, Minamoto Yorimoto, after his defeat of the Taira clan.

1192 Minamoto Yorimoto forces the emperor to give him the title of shogun.

1274 The first Mongol invasion is defeated. The samurai resist the Yuan army, which is made up of Mongol, Chinese, and Korean soldiers.

Samurai fortress
Himeji Castle, begun in 1333, has all the defensive and architectural features of a Japanese medieval fortress, including gun emplacements and stone-dropping holes.

DECISIVE MOMENT

THE CLOSED COUNTRY EDICT, 1635

By the early 17th century, there were about half a million Christians in Japan, the largest number in any Asian country. Distrust of Europeans and fear of the subversive power of Christianity led the Tokugawa Shogunate to implement a series of anti-Christian and anti-foreigner measures, culminating in 1635 with the Closed Country Edict. Addressed to two commissioners in the southern port Nagasaki, a stronghold of Christianity, the Edict forbade Japanese ships to leave for foreign countries, and ordered the execution by sword of anyone returning from abroad. The decision sealed the fate of Japan for the next 220 years as it entered a period of introspective isolation, untouched by foreign influence.

Samurai katana, 17th century

1281 The second Mongol invasion is repulsed after a typhoon wipes out the Mongol armada. This typhoon is called a *kamikaze*, or divine wind, sent by the gods to save Japan from the invaders.

1336 The Muromachi period, which lasts until 1573, begins. It is a period of devastating civil wars and the breakdown of central government, but also of growth in the arts and commerce.

1424 Zeami Kiyotsugu writes *Kakyo* (The Mirror of the Flower), in which he lays down the principles of Noh theater.

1467 The Onin War, triggered by a dispute over the accession within the Ashikaga shogunate, begins. It turns into a civil war that lasts for 100 years.

c.1542 The Portuguese land in Japan, probably the first Europeans to do so. They introduce the musket.

1592 The Japanese invade Korea and are defeated.

1597 A second Japanese invasion of Korea also ends in failure. Hideyoshi Toyotomi orders the execution by crucifixion of nine Catholic missionaries and 17 Japanese converts.

1600 In the Battle of Sekigahara, Tokugawa Ieyasu defeats Ishida Mitsunari to become master of Japan.

1603 Ieyasu is appointed Shogun by the imperial court. He is now officially the man authorized to keep the peace in the emperor's name. The Tokugawa Shogunate will rule Japan for the next 265 years.

1635 Tokugawa Iemitsu, grandson of Ieyasu, issues an edict forbidding Japanese citizens to leave the country. Japan shuts itself off from the world.

1639 The Portuguese are excluded from Japan by Iemitsu, and Christianity is strictly prohibited. The period of *sakoku* (closed country) begins, with trade restricted to limited dealings with the Dutch and Chinese through Nagasaki.

1666 Samurai warrior Matsuo Basho becomes a *ronin* (a masterless samurai) when his lord dies. He renounces his warrior status to devote himself to poetry, perfecting the "new style" in the 17-syllable haiku form.

1830s Widespread famine leads to increasing popular unrest.

1836 An uprising in Gunnai district of Kai province (Yamanashi prefecture), attracts more than 50,000 participants and for a time reduces the center of Kai to anarchy. This is a direct challenge to the authority of the Tokugawa administration, the *bafuku*.

1841 Mizuno Tadakuni, the chief senior councillor, institutes the Tempo reforms aimed at rebuilding shattered communities after the famine, and also at curtailing samurai power.

1843 Tadakuni is forced from power. He predicts that, thanks to his reforms, the Tokugawa shogunate will survive for another 30 years. In fact it lasts just 25 more years.

1844–46 British and French warships visit the Ryukyu Islands and Nagasaki seeking to open up commercial relations with Japan.

1853 Commodore Matthew Perry of the US Navy enters Edo (Tokyo) harbor, and demands the opening of trade relations.

1854 A trade treaty is signed with the US, opening two ports to American shipping. Treaties with the UK, Russia, France, and others follow.

1859 The Shogun is assassinated by nationalists in a reaction against treaties with foreigners.

1863 Japanese fire on foreign vessels, leading to Anglo-Satsuma War.

1864 UK, US, French, and Dutch naval fleets force Japan to abide by the treaties.

1868 The Meiji Restoration results in the overthrow of the Tokugawa regime and the restoration of imperial power.

1871 The old feudal order is dismantled and all class privileges are removed, including the samurai class's monopoly of arms. A national army is formed.

1872 Modernization along western lines begins in earnest. Japan's strong military tradition becomes state-directed.

1877 The Satsuma clan revolt. Angry at the idea of a conscript army, they march on Kumamoto Castle and the whole army is sent in to crush them. Armed only with swords and a few Enfield rifles, the Satsuma are slaughtered—400 are left alive out of 20,000. The defeat marks the end of the samurai order.

1889 A constitution modeled on that of Bismarck's Germany is adopted, with a bicameral legislature and a constitutional monarchy. Only 1 percent of the population qualifies for office.

1894–95 War with China ends in Japanese victory. China is forced to withdraw from Korea, and cede the Liaotung Peninsula to Japan. Large-scale heavy industry is developed and foreign trade increases sharply.

1904–05 War with Russia ends in Japanese victory. Formosa (Taiwan) and Korea come under Japanese control.

1914 Japan joins World War I on the Allied side, seeing limited naval action.

1919 The Versailles peace conference gives Japan territorial gains in the Pacific.

1921 Prime Minister Hara Takashi is assassinated by a right-wing fanatic. Japan signs a naval arms limitation treaty

The shock of the new
When a US coal-fired gunship carrying modern weaponry entered Edo harbor on July 8, 1853 (above), the Japanese realized how backward their 220-year policy of isolation had made them. The country soon embarked on a rapid process of Westernization.

with the US, replacing an agreement with the UK and marking a shift in power in the Pacific.

1923 **Yokohama earthquake** kills 140,000 people.

1927 **Japan enters a period** of radical nationalism, and introduces the notion of a "coprosperity sphere" in southeast Asia under Japanese control. This is interpreted in the US as a threat to its Pacific interests.

1931 **Chinese Manchuria** is invaded and the puppet state of Manchukuo is set up.

1932 **The country's** political leaders hand over power to the militarists.

1936 **Japan signs a pact** with Nazi Germany.

1937 **Japan launches** a full-scale invasion of China proper.

1938 **All political parties** are placed under one common banner. Japan is now effectively ruled by militarists.

1939 **In an undeclared** border war with the USSR, Japan is defeated.

1940 **Japan occupies** French Indochina.

1941 **The US imposes** a trade embargo, including oil, on Japan, thereby threatening to derail its military machine. Japan responds in December by launching an attack on the US fleet at Pearl Harbor, Hawaii, and invading US, UK, and Dutch possessions in the Pacific.

1942 **Japan loses** the decisive naval battle of Midway.

1945 **Huge US bombing** campaign culminates in dropping of atomic bombs on Hiroshima and Nagasaki. The USSR declares war on Japan. Emperor Hirohito surrenders. Japan is placed under the control of a US military government with General Douglas MacArthur installed as Supreme Commander in Japan.

1946 **In a radio broadcast** to the nation on January 1, Emperor Hirohito renounces his traditional divine status.

1947 **A new Japanese constitution** is ratified. The emperor is retained as head of state in a ceremonial role. Pacifism is written into the constitution, as Japan renounces the use of force to resolve international disputes.

1948 **Tojo Hideki,** prime minister during World War II, is executed along with six others for war crimes. High executives of the largest industrial firms are removed from their positions.

1950 **US army contracts** resulting from the Korean War lead to rapid expansion of the Japanese economy.

1952 **The Treaty of San Francisco** officially marks the end of World War II and Japan regains independence. Industrial production recovers to 15 percent above 1936 levels. A 20-year period of rapid economic growth begins.

1955 **A new political party,** the Liberal-Democratic Party (LDP), is formed from a merger of several conservative parties. The LDP governs for the next 38 years.

1956 **Japan joins the UN** and reestablishes relations with the USSR.

1964 **Tokyo hosts the Olympics.** The first Shinkansen (bullet train) service linking Tokyo to Osaka is opened to coincide with the Olympics. Japan is admitted to the OECD.

1970 **Acclaimed writer Yukio Mishima** seizes control of a military headquarters in Tokyo, and commits *seppuku* (ritual suicide) to protest the Westernization of Japan. The Osaka World Exhibition showcases Japan's technological prowess.

1972 **Prime Minister Tanaka Kakuei** visits Beijing and Japan officially recognizes the People's Republic of China.

1973 **Economic growth stalls** as the price of oil quadruples. It is decided to concentrate investment in high-tech industries to reduce the country's dependence on oil imports.

1976 **LDP shaken** by the Lockheed bribery scandal, when it is revealed that senior Japanese politicians accepted

money in return for aircraft contracts. Prime Minister Tanaka Kakuei resigns. In the subsequent election, the LDP remains in power but loses its outright majority.

1979 **The second world oil crisis** affects Japan much less and growth continues at 6 percent per year.

1980 **The LDP regains** an overall majority in national elections.

1982 **Honda** establishes its first car factory in the US, in Marysville, Ohio.

1988 **Japan becomes** the world's largest aid donor and overseas investor.

1989 **Emperor Hirohito dies** and is succeeded by his son, Akihito. The Recruit–Cosmos bribery scandal leads to the resignation of prime minister Noburo Takeshita. He is replaced by Sosuke Uno, who is in turn forced to resign over a sexual scandal. The Tokyo stock market crashes shortly after the Nikkei 225 had reached a record high of 39,000.

1990 **An immigration law** comes into effect opening up the Japanese labor market to foreign workers for the first time ever. This is an attempt to solve the country's chronic labor shortages.

1991 **Japan pledges** billions of dollars in support of Operation Desert Storm in Kuwait and Iraq. The Nikkei 225 falls to 15,000, less than half its highest value.

1991–92 **The LDP is torn** by factional disputes, further financial scandals, and the issue of electoral reform.

1993 **Reformists split** from the LDP and create new parties. In elections, the LDP loses power. Morihiro Hosokawa becomes prime minister at the head of a seven-party coalition. Arrests of 165 political leaders and 445 business people for suspected electoral fraud.

1994 **Hosokawa resigns.** The withdrawal of the Social Democratic Party of Japan (SDPJ) causes the coalition government

to collapse. A new three-party coalition includes the LDP and SDPJ. Tomiici Murayama becomes first socialist prime minister in 50 years.

1995 **The Kobe earthquake** kills more than 5,000 people, and leaves over 300,000 homeless. Members of the religious group Aum Shinrikyo attack the Tokyo subway with deadly gas, killing 12 people and injuring hundreds.

1996 **LDP forms a minority** government.

1997 **Severe economic recession** rocks Southeast Asia. As the major creditor country of the region, Japan suffers.

1998 **Crisis over reform** of the banking and financial system.

2000 **Prime Minister Keizo Obuchi** falls into a coma, and is replaced by Yoshiro Mori. LDP with coalition partners retains majority in June general election. Unemployment over 5 percent for the first time since the end of World War II.

2001 **The LDP turns to** populist right-winger Junichiro Koizumi as prime minister. He controversially pays homage at a shrine to Japan's war dead. Tanaka Makiko becomes Japan's first woman foreign minister.

2002 **Japan cohosts** the soccer World Cup with South Korea, the first World Cup to be held in Asia.

2003 **Japan sends troops** to support the US-led invasion of Iraq, the first time Japanese soldiers have been deployed in a war zone since the end of World War II.

2005 **Prime Minister Junichiro Koizumi** calls a general election two years early after bills to privatize Japan Post are voted down in the upper house. The ruling LDP is reelected in a landslide victory.

2006 **Shinzo Abe** becomes prime minister. Japan establishes its first formal Defense Ministry since World War II.

2007 **The ruling LDP** suffers severe defeat in upper house elections; Yasuo Fukuda becomes prime minister.

2009 **Global financial crisis:** Japan's economy shrinks 3.3 percent in a single quarter. The Democratic Party of Japan wins landslide election victory, ending 50 years of LDP rule. Yukio Hatoyama of the DPJ becomes prime minister.

2010 **Hatoyama quits as PM** and is replaced by Finance Minister Naoto Kan.

2011 **A massive earthquake** off the northeast coast of Honshu is followed by a devastating tsunami. Nuclear power plant at Fukushima suffers serious damage and radiation leaks.

Michinomiya Hirohito
Emperor of Japan from 1926 until his death in 1989, the myopic Hirohito was worshipped as a living god until 1946. His broadcast on August 15, 1945, signaled Japan's surrender in World War II.

Thailand

The Kingdom of Thailand is the only country in Southeast Asia never colonized by Europeans.

1350 **The Thai kingdom** of Ayutthaya succeeds the state of Sukhotai.

1569 **The Burmese** defeat Ayutthayan forces and rule the kingdom for 15 years.

1767 **The Burmese occupy** the Thai capital of Ayutthaya once again, this time bringing an end to Ayutthayan rule.

1782 **Rama I** founds the Chakri dynasty that still rules the country, and makes Bangkok the capital of Siam.

1826 **Rama III** concludes a treaty establishing trade with the West but maintaining independence.

1851 **King Mongkut succeeds** his elder brother Rama III to the throne.

1855 **Mongkut signs** the Bowring trade treaty with the UK, which ensures that Siam retains its independence.

1868–1910 **King Chulalongkorn** embarks on a program of Westernization.

1907 **Siam cedes** western Khmer (Cambodia) and southern Laos to France.

1925 **King Prajadhipok begins** a period of absolute rule.

1932 **In a bloodless** coup, the power of the monarchy is curtailed and a parliament is created, elected by universal suffrage.

1939 **Siam is renamed** Thailand.

1941 **Japan invades** and the government is effectively controlled by the Japanese.

1944 **Pro-Japanese** prime minister Phibun is voted out of office.

1945 **Exiled King Ananda** returns.

1946 **Ananda is assassinated.** King Bhumibol accedes to the throne.

1947 **A military coup** restores former dictator Phibun to power.

1951–57 **The US pours aid** into Thailand, seen by the US as a key ally in the Cold War.

1957 **The constitution is abolished** in another military coup.

1965 **Thailand allows the US** to use Thai bases during the Vietnam War.

1968 **New constitution endorses** an elected parliament.

1971 **Army suspends constitution.**

1973–76 **Student riots** lead to a restoration of democracy.

1976 **Renewed military takeover.**

1980–88 **General Prem Tinsulanonda** is prime minister.

1988 **General Chatichai Choonhaven**, the right-wing leader of the Thai Nation Party (CT), is named prime minister.

1991 **Military coup instals** civilian Anand Panyarachun as caretaker premier.

1992 **General Suchinda** is named premier. Following demonstrations, the king forces him to step down and reinstalls Anand.

1995 **The CT** wins the general election.

1996 **Early elections;** Chaovalit Yongchaiyuth of the New Aim Party becomes prime minister.

1997 **Amid a financial** and economic crisis, the Chaovalit government falls. The Democratic Party's Chuan Leekpai becomes prime minister.

2001 **Thai Rak Thai (TRT),** led by Thaksin Shinawatra, wins elections.

2004 **Five thousand killed** by a tsunami on December 26.

2006 **Thaksin Shinawatra** is overthrown by the military and sent into exile.

2007 **Rak Thai party** banned. A new pro-Shinawatra party, the People's Power Party, wins most votes in general election.

2008 **Facing trial for corruption,** Shinawatra flees to Britain. People's Alliance for Democracy (PAD) protesters occupy government buildings in Bangkok and block flights from Bangkok airport. Opposition leader Abhisit Vejjajiva becomes prime minister.

2010 **Pro-Thanksin Shinawatra** Red Shirt protesters in Bangkok are defeated.

« 172–73 Lost Empires

Peaceful coup d'état
Tanks roll into Bangkok on September 19, 2006. The army suspended the constitution and declared martial law, but pledged to restore democracy. Many supported the coup.

Laos

Since 1975 Laos has been a communist state but market-oriented reforms are under way.

1893 **A Franco-Siamese** treaty establishes French control over all territory east of the Mekong River.

1899 **Creation of Laos** under the French.

1941 **Japanese seize power** from the Vichy French in Indochina.

1946 **French rule resumed.**

1950 **Lao Patriotic Front** (LPF) set up to oppose French rule. It gains the support of the newly formed communist Lao People's Party (LPP).

1954 **Laos gains independence** as a constitutional monarchy backed by France and the US.

1963 **LPF begins an armed** struggle against royal government through its armed wing, the Pathet Lao.

1964 **US bombs** North Vietnamese sanctuaries in Laos.

1973 **The Laos People's** Revolutionary Party (LPRP, formerly the LPF) and royal government form a coalition after the withdrawal of US forces from Indochina.

1975 **LPRP seizes power,** abolishes the monarchy, and proclaims the Lao People's Democratic Republic. Premier Kaysone Phomvihane adopts policies for a "socialist transformation" of the economy.

1977 **A treaty** providing for mutual security is signed with Vietnam.

1978 **Popular unrest** and resistance to collectivization. The former king and crown prince are arrested and die in captivity. Almost 50,000 Laotians flee to neighboring Thailand.

1986 **Fourth Party Congress** introduces market-oriented economic reforms.

1989 **National elections are held.** All candidates approved by LPRP.

1990 **Counter-offensives** are carried out against right-wing, largely Hmong guerrilla bases in the outer provinces.

1997 **Laos accedes to ASEAN.**

1999 **Popular protests** demand greater political freedom.

2004 **Laos hosts** the annual ASEAN summit for the first time.

2006 **Over 400 ethnic Hmong,** hiding in the jungle since the end of the Vietnam War, surrender to the authorities.

« 350–51 Colonial Resistance
« 412–13 End of the Colonial Era

Cambodia

An ancient kingdom, Cambodia is slowly recovering from decades of violent civil conflict.

802 CE **Jayavarman II** founds Khmer Empire, which becomes centered on the temple and city complex of Angkor Wat.

1431 **Siamese kingdom** of Ayutthaya captures Ankor Wat and royal court moves to Phnom Penh.

1863 **Cambodia becomes** French protectorate headed by King Norodom; becomes part of French Indochina in 1887.

1953 **Cambodia becomes independent.**

1954 **At Geneva** peace conference, French and Vietnamese nationalists agree to withdraw forces from Cambodia.

1955 **King Sihanouk abdicates** to pursue a political career, taking the title Prince.

1970 **Right-wing coup** led by prime minister Lon Nol deposes Sihanouk. Exiled Sihanouk forms Royal Government of National Union of Cambodia (GRUNC), backed by communist Khmer Rouge.

1975 **GRUNC troops capture** Phnom Penh. Khmer Rouge assumes power with Prince Sihanouk as head of state. Huge numbers die under extremist regime.

1976 **Country renamed** Democratic Kampuchea. Sihanouk resigns. Pol Pot becomes prime minister.

1978 **Vietnam invades,** supported by communists opposed to Pol Pot.

1979 **Vietnamese capture** Phnom Penh. Khmer Rouge ousted by Kampuchean People's Revolutionary Party (KPRP). Khmer Rouge starts guerrilla war.

1982 **Government-in-exile,** headed by Prince Sihanouk, is recognized by UN.

1989 **Withdrawal of Vietnamese** troops.

1990 **UN-monitored** ceasefire.

1991 **Signing of Paris** peace accords. Sihanouk reinstated as head of state.

1993 **Elections** won by royalist Funcinpec. Sihanouk takes the title King.

1997 **Coup by prime minister** Hun Sen.

1998 **Pol Pot** dies; Khmer Rouge disarms.

1999 **Cambodia admitted to** ASEAN.

2001 **Law approved** on trials of Khmer Rouge leaders for atrocities.

2004 **Sihanouk abdicates** and is replaced as head of state by his son Sihamoni.

2007 **Nuon Chea,** the most senior surviving Khmer Rouge leader, is arrested.

2008 **Hun Sen's CPP** wins a general election amid fraud allegations.

2010 **The former Khmer Rouge** prison commandant Duch is found guilty of crimes against humanity and sentenced to 35 years imprisonment.

« 172–73 Lost Empires
« 412–13 End of the Colonial Era

Vietnam

Partitioned in 1954, Vietnam was unified in 1976 after military victory by the communist North.

939 CE **After 1,000 years** of Chinese domination, a semi-independent Vietnamese state is created around the Red River delta by Ngo Quyen.

1516 **A group of Portuguese** adventurers are first Europeans to reach Vietnam.

1862 **Southern Vietnam (Cochin China)** becomes a French colony, followed by central and northern Vietnam (Annam and Tonkin) in 1883.

1920 **Quoc ngu** (Roman script) replaces Chinese script.

1930 **Ho Chi Minh** founds the Indochina Communist Party.

1940 **Japanese invasion.**

1941 **Viet Minh resistance** founded in exile in China.

1945 **Viet Minh take** Saigon and Hanoi. Emperor abdicates. Democratic Republic of Vietnam proclaimed.

1946 **First Indochina War with France.**

1954 **French are defeated** at Dien Bien Phu. Vietnam is divided at 17°N. USSR supports the North, while the US arms the South.

1960 **Groups opposed** to the Dien Bien Phu regime in South Vietnam unite as the Viet Cong.

1961 **US pours in** military advisers. US Congress approves war in 1964.

1965 **General Nguyen Van Thieu** takes over military government of South. First US combat troops arrive.

1965–68 **Operation Rolling Thunder**—intense bombing of the North by US.

1967 **Antiwar protests start** in US.

1968 **In the Tet (New Year) Offensive**, 105 towns are attacked in South with infiltrated arms. Viet Cong suffers serious losses. Peace talks begin.

1969 **Ho Chi Minh dies**, succeeded by Le Duan. War intensifies in spite of continuing peace talks.

1970 **US begins secret** attacks in Laos and Cambodia and new mass bombing of North to keep arms from reaching Viet Cong.

1972 **Eleven-day Christmas Campaign** is heaviest US bombing of war.

1973 **Paris Peace Agreements** signed, but fighting continues.

1975 **Fall of Saigon** to combined forces of North and Provisional Revolutionary (Viet Cong) Government of South.

1976 **Vietnam united** as the Socialist Republic of Vietnam. Saigon renamed Ho Chi Minh City.

1978 **Invasion of Cambodia** to oust Pol Pot regime (by January 1979).

1979 **Nine-Day War** with China. "Boat people" crisis. At a UN conference, Vietnam agrees to allow legal emigration.

1986 **Death of Le Duan**. Nguyen Van Linh initiates liberal economic policy of *doi moi* (renovation).

1992 **Revised constitution** allows foreign investment, but essential role of Communist Party is unchanged.

1995 **US–Vietnamese relations** normalized. Vietnam joins ASEAN.

2000 **Bill Clinton** becomes the first US president to visit Vietnam since the war.

2007 **Joins** World Trade Organization.

2007 **President Nguyen Minh Triet** is the first Vietnamese head of state to visit US since the end of the Vietnam War in 1975.

2008 **Vietnam and China** sign an agreement to end their long-running border dispute.

« 172–73 Lost Empires
« 350–51 Colonial Resistance
« 412–13 End of the Colonial Era
« 430–31 The Vietnam War

Malaysia

The Federation of Malaysia comprises Peninsular Malaysia, Sarawak, and Sabah.

1400s **Conversion of Malay** peoples to Islam begins.

1826 **British settlements** of Malacca, Penang, and Singapore joined together as Straits Settlements colony.

1957 **Malaya** gains independence.

1963 **Federation of Malaysia** founded.

1965 **Singapore leaves federation**, reducing Malaysian states to 13.

1970 **Malay-Chinese** ethnic tension forces resignation of prime minister

Tunku Abdul Rahman. New prime minister, Tun Abdul Razak, creates the National Front (BN) coalition.

1976–78 **Guerrilla attacks** by banned Communist Party of Malaya (CPM), based in southern Thailand.

1976 **Tun Abdul Razak** dies and is succeeded by his deputy.

1977 **Unrest in Kelantan** following expulsion of its chief minister from the Pan-Malaysian Islamic Party (PAS).

1978 **Elections consolidate BN** power. Government rejects Chinese university.

1978–89 **Unrestricted asylum given** to Vietnamese refugees.

1981 **Mahathir Muhammad** becomes prime minister.

1987 **Detention without trial** of 106 politicians from all parties suspected of Chinese sympathies. Media censored.

1989 **Disaffected members** of ruling UMNO party join opposition PAS. CPM signs peace agreement with Malaysian and Thai governments.

1997 **Major financial** crisis.

1998 **Prime Minister** Mahathir Muhammad fires his deputy and presumed successor, Anwar Ibrahim, on charges of sexual misconduct.

2001 **Ethnic clashes** between Malays and ethnic Indians.

2005 **A crackdown** on illegal immigration sees an exodus of hundreds of thousands of illegal workers.

2006 **Construction of a bridge** linking Malaysia to Singapore is shelved.

2008 **The ruling National Front** loses its two-thirds majority in parliament, its worst election result in decades.

« 172–73 Lost Empires
« 282–83 Exploring the Pacific
« 412–13 End of the Colonial Era

VIETNAMESE REVOLUTIONARY (1890–1969)

HO CHI MINH

Ho Chi Minh founded the Indochina Communist Party in 1930. During World War II he led the Viet Minh guerrillas and established a government in Hanoi in 1945. When the French tried to regain control he proclaimed independence and led the resistance that forced the French to withdraw. President of North Vietnam from 1955, he successfully countered US involvement in Vietnam in the 1960s, by which time he was in failing health. "Uncle Ho" came to symbolize the communists' willingness to endure a war of attrition. He died six years before the US finally withdrew from South Vietnam.

Singapore

A former British colony with an authoritarian government and strict social controls.

1819 **Sir Stamford Raffles,** a British East India Company official, establishes a trading station on Singapore island.

1824 **The Malays cede** the whole island to the East India Company in perpetuity.

1869 **Suez Canal opens** and trade with Europe booms.

1941 **Singapore falls** to the Japanese.

1946 **Singapore** becomes separate colony under UK rule.

1954 **The People's Action** Party (PAP) is formed under Lee Kuan Yew.

1959 **Self-government is won.** Lee Kuan Yew becomes first prime minister.

1963 **Joins** the Federation of Malaysia.

1965 **Singapore declares** itself an independent republic.

1984 **Opposition candidates** win two seats in general election: first non-PAP MPs since 1966.

1990 **Lee Kuan Yew** steps down after 31 years. Goh Chok Tong becomes new prime minister.

1993 **Ong Teng Cheong** first directly elected president.

1995 **Briton Nick Leeson** is sentenced to six years in prison for his disastrous dealing on the Singapore stock exchange.

2004 **Lee Hsien Loong**, eldest son of Lee Kuan Yew, becomes prime minister.

2006 **President Lee Hsien Loong** wins general election for the PAP.

« 172–73 Lost Empires
« 350–51 Colonial Resistance

Philippines

Formerly a Spanish colony, the archipelago state of the Philippines is now dominated by the US.

1521 **A Spanish expedition** led by the Portuguese explorer Ferdinand Magellan lands in the Philippines. Magellan himself is later killed in the Philippines.

1565 **Miguel Lopez de Legazpi** founds a Spanish settlement in the Philippines.

1571 **Manila is captured** by the Spanish.

1892 **The Katipunan** ("Sons of the People") movement is founded under the leadership of Andres Bonifacio.

1896 **Katipunan launches** the Philippine revolution. Pro-independence writer, José Rizal, is executed by the Spanish.

1897 **Bonifacio is executed** on the orders of a military court appointed by a rival rebel leader, Emilio Aguinaldo. Later that year Aguinaldo is exiled to Hong Kong.

1898 **In the Spanish-American War,** US forces destroy the Spanish fleet. Spain cedes the Philippines to the US.

1901 **Aguinaldo is captured** after returning from exile. He later fights against the occupying forces.

1935 **The Sakdalistas**, a movement formed to combat inequitable land distribution and excessive taxes, begins an uprising which is quickly put down.

1935 **The Commonwealth** of the Philippines is created in preparation for complete independence. Manuel Quezon is its president.

1941 **The Philippines** is invaded by Japanese forces.

1942 **The Hukbalahap,** or Huks, is formed, a militant peasant movement that fights against the Japanese. After the war the US and Philippine authorities try to suppress the movement.

1944 **US forces land** on the Philippines.

1946 **The Philippine Republic** is inaugurated, with independence from the US. Manuel A. Roxas is its first president.

1965 **Ferdinand Marcos** elected president.

1969–72 **Marcos reelected** amid malpractice allegations.

1972 **Marcos declares martial law.** Opposition leaders arrested; National Assembly suspended; press censored.

1977 **Ex-Liberal Party** leader Benigno Aquino sentenced to death. Criticism forces Marcos to delay execution.

1978 **Elections won by** Marcos's New Society (KBL).

Elected kleptocrat
Ferdinand Marcos was elected to office in 1965, but stayed in power between 1972 and 1981 by imposing martial law and imprisoning, torturing, or murdering opponents. He was finally ousted in 1986 and sent into exile in the US. Marcos is thought to have plundered a personal fortune of $10 billion while in office.

1980 **Aquino allowed** to travel to US for medical treatment.

1981 **Martial law ends.** Marcos is reelected president.

1983 **Aquino shot dead** on return from US. Inquiry blames military conspiracy.

1986 **After a disputed election,** the army rebels, and Aquino's widow, Corazon, comes to power. Marcos is exiled to US.

1988 **Marcos and wife** Imelda are indicted for massive racketeering.

1989 **Marcos dies in the US**.

1990 **Imelda Marcos is acquitted** of fraud charges in US. Earthquake in Baguio City leaves 1,600 dead.

1991 **Mount Pinatubo erupts.** US leaves Clark Air Base.

1992 **General Fidel Ramos** wins the presidential election. US withdraws from Subic Bay base.

1996 **Peace agreement** with Muslim MNLF secessionists.

1998 **Joseph Estrada** becomes president.

2000 **Estrada is impeached** on charges of corruption and violating the constitution.

2000 **Gloria Arroyo,** Estrada's deputy, is sworn in as president.

2002 **A series of bomb attacks** is blamed on Islamic extremists.

2005 **Peace talks** take place between the government and Islamic separatists.

2007 **The military** is accused of the murder of hundreds of left-wing activists.

2008 **A deal to put an end** to fighting with the MILF separatist in Mindanao breaks down over objections of Christian communities. In renewed outbreaks, 30 people are killed.

2009 **Talks resume** with MILF rebels.

2010 **Benigno Aquino** is elected president.

« 172–73 Lost Empires
« 282–83 Exploring the Pacific

Brunei

A former British colony, this oil-rich Muslim sultanate is ruled by an authoritarian royal family.

1200s **Islam arrives** in Brunei.

1200s–1300s **Brunei is brought** under the control of the Javanese Majapahit Empire.

1400s **Brunei controls** Sarawak, Sabah, the Celebes, and parts of Borneo and the Philippines.

1841 **After a revolt** against Sultan Omar Ali Saifuddin II, Sarawak is ceded to the British soldier who had helped crush the uprising, James Brooke.

1846 **Brunei cedes** Labuan to British.

1888 **Brunei is declared** a British protectorate.

1929 **Oil extraction begins.**

1959 **First constitution** enshrines Islam as the state religion.

1962 **Prodemocracy rebellion.** The sultan rules by decree.

1984 **Independence** from the UK. Brunei joins ASEAN.

1990 **Ideology** of Malay Muslim Monarchy introduced by Sultan Bolkiah.

1991 **Imports of alcohol** banned.

1992 **Joins Non-Aligned** Movement.

1998 **Sultan's son,** Al-Muhtadee Billah, is made crown prince.

2004 **Parliament is reopened** 20 years after it was closed.

2007 **Brunei signs** a "Rainforest Declaration" (along with Indonesia and Malaysia) intended to protect those countries' tropical forests.

Indonesia

A Muslim nation of 17,500 islands, Indonesia is the fourth most populous country in the world.

1st century CE **The peoples of** the Indonesian archipelago first come into contact with the Hindu-Buddhist culture of India.

600s–700s **The Buddhist,** Sumatra-based Sri-Vijaya Empire emerges as the earliest known Indonesian kingdom; it subsequently extends from Sumatra over Malaya and southern Thailand.

1100s **Islam begins** its penetration of Indonesia.

1293 **The Sri-Vijaya Empire** is succeeded by the Hindu-Buddhist Java-based Majapahit Empire.

1300s **Small Islamic principalities** begin to emerge along the sea-lanes and coastal areas.

1512 **Portuguese arrive** on Ternate and then their traders gain control of the Moluccan clove trade.

1602 **The Dutch United East India** Company (VOC) establishes a monopoly over the regional spice trade.

1799 **The VOC charter** expires and the Dutch government takes control of the archipelago.

1825–30 **The Java Wars** are the first unsuccessful indigenous rebellion against Dutch rule.

1830 **The Dutch implement** the Culture System, forcing the cultivation of commercial crops for export.

1901 **The Dutch introduce** limited educational and administrative opportunities for indigenous people.

1910 **Dutch expansion** to the Outer Islands is completed. All of present-day Indonesia is under Dutch control.

1930s **Dutch repress nationalists.**

1942–45 **Japanese occupation.** Sukarno works with Japanese while promoting independence.

1945 **Declaration** of independence.

1945–49 **Nationalist** guerrilla war.

1949 **Dutch grant** independence under President Sukarno.

1950 **Chancellor Soumokil** declares the Molucca Islands' independence. The army is sent in and crushes the rebellion.

1955 **Bandung plays host** to a meeting of heads of government that gives rise to the Non-Aligned Movement.

1957 **Sukarno introduces** authoritarian "Guided Democracy," based on indigenous procedures.

1958 **Leaders in western Sumatra** mount a direct challenge to Jakarta and declare themselves the Revolutionary Government of the Republic of Indonesia. The rebellion is quickly suppressed.

1962 **The Dutch** agree to hand over Irian Jaya (West Papua) to Indonesia after a transition period administered by the UN. Indonesia hosts the Fourth Asian Games.

1963 **Indonesia** assumes control of Irian Jaya. Indonesia announces policy of "Konfrontasi" with Malaysia.

1965 **Communist PKI alliance** with military ends. Army crushes abortive coup and acts to eliminate PKI. Up to 1 million people are killed. Indonesian oil deposits are nationalized.

1966 **Sukarno hands over emergency** power to General Suharto, who reverses many of Sukarno's policies. Indonesia rejoins the UN.

1967 **Indonesia plays leading role** in the creation of the Association of Southeast Asian Nations (ASEAN).

1968 **Suharto** becomes president.

1971 **Students protest** against the corrupt generals ruling the country.

1975 **Invasion of East Timor,** which becomes the 27th province in 1976.

1979 **The Transmigrasi project** is initiated, and over 2 million people are transported to other islands to ease overcrowding on Java.

1984 **Muslim protests** in Jakarta.

1989 **Unrest in Java and Sumbawa.** Indonesia and Australia sign an agreement over the exploitation of resources in the seas between the two countries.

1991 **Troops massacre** proindependence demonstrators in East Timor.

1996 **Antigovernment** demonstrations in Jakarta.

1997 **Economic recession,** as a result of which the Indonesian rupiah plummets in value. The region suffers from widespread smog caused by forest fires.

1998 **Suharto resigns** amid unrest. Replaced by B. J. Habibie. Five students are killed in violent clashes with anti-insurrection forces.

1999 **Free elections** won by opposition leader Megawati Sukarnoputri. East Timor referendum backing independence triggers violent backlash. UN appoints transitional authority. Abdurrahman Wahid elected president, Megawati named vice president. Wahid offers Aceh greater autonomy.

2001 **Wahid removed,** amid allegations of corruption and incompetence, to be replaced by Megawati.

2002 **East Timor** becomes independent. A bomb attack in Bali kills 202 people. A peace treaty is signed in Geneva between the government and the Free Aceh Movement (GAM).

2003 **Peace talks** break down, and a military offensive is mounted against GAM. Three men are sentenced to death for their role in the Bali bombing.

2004 **Former general** Susilo Bambang Yudhoyono wins first-ever elections to choose a president directly. Tsunami leaves over 200,000 dead or missing. The region of Aceh is by far the worst hit.

2005 **Peace is agreed** between the government and GAM. GAM disarms and government troops withdraw from Aceh.

2006 **A powerful** earthquake and tsunami kill thousands on Java.

2007 **The alleged leader** of the Islamist militant group Jemaah Islamia is captured.

2008 **Former president Suharto** dies. A joint Indonesian–East Timorese Truth Commission report blames Indonesia for human rights violations on East Timor in 1999. President Yudhoyono issues a statement expressing "regret." Three militants convicted for the 2002 Bali bombings are executed.

2009 **President Yudhoyono** is reelected. His Democratic Party receives an increased vote share in the general election.

East Timor

After a bloody conflict, the former Portuguese colony won independence from Indonesia in 1999.

1200s–1400s The Javanese-based Majapahit Empire extends its control over the Indonesian archipelago, including Timor.

1500s **The Portuguese** arrive and settle on the island of Timor, using it as a trading post and a source of sandalwood.

1613 **Dutch capture** Portuguese base on Solor and expand their control over western Timor, confining the Portuguese to the eastern half of the island.

1859 **A treaty between** the Dutch and Portuguese codifies the relationship between the two colonial powers of Timor. The final boundaries are not delineated until 1914.

1942–45 **The Japanese occupy** the island of Timor. At the end of World War II, the Portuguese regain sovereignty over the East.

1974 **Revolution in Portugal** brings down the military dictatorship, resulting in the collapse of Portugal's overseas empire.

1975 **The moderate** Democratic Union of Timor (UDT) stages a coup in East Timor, demanding independence from Portugal. Civil war breaks out between the UDT and the anti-Indonesian movement FRETILIN.

1975 **FRETILIN proclaims** the independence of the Democratic Republic of East Timor. Indonesian forces invade East Timor. The Portuguese break off diplomatic relations with Indonesia.

1976 **UN Security Council** adopts a resolution calling on Indonesia to withdraw all its forces from East Timor without delay.

1976 **President Suharto** declares East Timor to be a province of Indonesia.

1986 **FRETILIN and UDT** agree to coordinate their efforts to resist the Indonesians.

1988 **Indonesian government** allows foreign access to East Timor for the first time in 13 years.

1991 **Indonesia agrees to** allow a delegation from Portugal to visit East Timor. Trip is canceled after Indonesia objects to a member of the delegation.

1991 **Indonesian troops open fire** on a crowd of mourners in Dili, killing at least 50 people. Australia and Indonesia

conclude an agreement over the Timor Gap, an area of rich oil deposits.

1992 **FRETILIN leader** José Xanana Gusmão captured near Dili.

1993 **Gusmão** given life sentence.

1994 **Indonesian military** holds talks with the imprisoned Gusmão on possibility of UN referendum on East Timor.

1996 **East Timor's** international profile is raised when exiled resistance leader José Ramos Horta and Bishop of Dili Carlos Belo are jointly awarded the Nobel Peace Prize.

1998 **Indonesian president** Suharto resigns.

1999 **Pro-Indonesian militias** stoke violence against independence activists. People of East Timor vote overwhelmingly for independence. UN peacekeeping force takes over. Ramos Horta returns to East Timor from exile. Xanana Gusmão is released.

2002 **Gusmão** is named president of a fully independent East Timor.

2004 **Production at Bayu Undan** offshore gasfield begins.

2005 **UN peacekeepers leave.**

2006 **Agreement with Australia** divides resources in the Timor Sea. Serious clashes in Dili involving former members of the army.

2006 **Foreign troops** arrive in Dili to end widespread violence involving former soldiers. Prime minister Alkatin resigns over his handling of the unrest and Jose Ramos-Horta takes over as prime minister.

2007 **Ramos-Horta** wins presidential elections. Xanana Gusmão is named the new prime minister.

2008 **Ramos-Horta** is seriously wounded in an attack on the presidential palace by rebels. The joint Indonesian–East Timorese Truth Commission report blames Indonesia for human rights violations on East Timor in 1999.

DECISIVE MOMENT

EAST TIMOR VOTES FOR INDEPENDENCE, 1999

On August 30, 1999, in a vote with a staggering 99 percent turnout, four out of every five East Timorese voters chose independence from Indonesia. The vote dramatically marked the end of Indonesia's 23-year occupation of the country. The struggle for independence had cost more than 100,000 lives. Euphoric crowds took to the streets of Dili to celebrate (right) but violent clashes instigated by the Indonesian military broke out soon afterward. An Australian-led peacekeeping force restored order and international outrage soon led to Indonesia withdrawing its troops.

Oceania

The widely scattered territories of Oceania stretch across the Pacific Ocean but are home to only 0.5 percent of the world's population. Australia and New Zealand dominate Oceania. In both countries the British colonial legacy remains strong.

Australia

The world's smallest continent, which was colonized by the British in the 18th century.

45000 BCE **Archaeological evidence** suggests that Aborigines—who crossed over the then land bridge from Southeast Asia—lived in Australia from this time.

1606 **Dutch explorer** William Jansz goes ashore on the west coast of Cape York.

1642 **Dutch explorer** Abel Tasman lands in Van Diemen's Land (now Tasmania).

1688 **The first British** explorer, William Dampier, lands on Australia's northwest coast.

1770 **Captain James Cook** charts the east coast, landing at Botany Bay. He raises the British flag on an island off Cape York, claiming the territory for Britain.

1788 **Eleven ships from** Britain land their passengers—including more than 700 convicts—at Port Jackson (now Sydney). Penal colony set up in New South Wales.

1790 **Free settlers** begin arriving.

1803 **Penal colony** set up on Van Diemen's Land (later Tasmania).

1813 **Explorers first cross** the Blue Mountains, part of the Great Dividing Range down the east coast of Australia.

1825 **Colony of Van Diemen's Land** founded, followed by Western Australia in 1829, South Australia in 1836, Victoria in 1851, and Queensland in 1859.

1828–30 **Charles Sturt** maps the Murray and Darling river basins; he treks into central Australia in 1844–45.

1840 **Transportation of convicts** to New South Wales is ended.

1850 **British Parliament** passes the Australian Colonies Government Act. This allows colonies to set up legislatures.

1851 **Gold is discovered** at Bathurst in New South Wales and Ballarat in Victoria. The ensuing gold rush attracts thousands.

1853 **Transportation from the UK** to Tasmania is ended.

1853–67 **Transportation is temporarily** introduced to Western Australia.

1855 **New South Wales, Victoria,** South Australia, and Tasmania gain self-government, followed by Queensland in 1859 and Western Australia in 1890.

1859 **South Australian government** offers a prize to the first person to cross the unexplored continent from south to north. Robert O'Hara Burke and William Wills set out from Melbourne in 1860 and almost reach the north coast, but turn back and die on the way home in 1861.

1861 **After two previous attempts,** John McDouall Stuart sets out from Adelaide and reaches Darwin in the north in 1862.

1891 **The first Australian** Federal Convention meets. Delegates draw up a draft constitution to federate the states.

1901 **The Commonwealth** of Australia comes into being. A parliament is created with a House of Representatives and a Senate. The British monarch is head of state and appoints a Governor-General. The Immigration Restriction Act limits non-European immigration, beginning the "White Australia Policy."

1911 **Canberra founded** as federal capital.

1914–18 **Australia fights** with Britain and its allies in World War I. Its troops capture German colonies in the Pacific and fight in Turkey and Europe.

Canberra
Rivalry between Melbourne and Sydney led to the decision in 1911 to build a new national capital midway between the two. Building began in 1923 and the federal parliament (above) opened in 1927.

1915 **Australian troops suffer** heavy casualties at Gallipoli in Turkey.

1929 **Industrial upheaval** and financial collapse caused by the Great Depression.

1939 **Prime Minister Robert Menzies** announces that Australia will follow the UK into war with Germany.

1942 **Fall of Singapore** to Japanese army. As a Japanese invasion of Australia seems imminent, the government turns to the US for help.

1950–53 **Australian troops committed** to UN forces fighting in Korea against North Korean communists.

1951 **ANZUS military** assistance treaty is signed with the US. Under the treaty, Australia is committed to participate in the Vietnam War in the 1960s.

1956 **Olympic Games** held in Melbourne.

1962 **Menzies government commits** Australian aid to war in Vietnam.

1966 **Adopts decimal currency.**

1967 **Aborigines are granted** full citizenship rights, but their land rights are not recognized.

1972 **Gough Whitlam** is elected as Labour prime minister and ceases aid to South Vietnam.

1975 **Whitlam government dismissed** by Governor-General Sir John Kerr for failing to gain parliamentary approval for the national budget. Malcolm Fraser forms coalition government.

1992 **Paul Keating replaces** Bob Hawke as Labour prime minister and announces a "Turning toward Asia" policy.

1993 **After the High Court's** Mabo Judgment had recognized Aboriginal rights in 1992, the Native Title Act provides compensation for Aboriginal rights extinguished by existing land title.

AUSTRALIA

EXTERNAL TERRITORIES

AUSTRALIAN ANTARCTIC TERRITORY
1933 Set up under imperial order.

COCOS (KEELING) ISLANDS
Two atolls in the western Indian Ocean.
1609 Discovered by William Keeling.
1857 Britain annexes the islands.
1955 Transferred to Australia.

CHRISTMAS ISLAND
Isolated peak in the Indian Ocean.
1888 Annexed by Britain.
1957 Transferred to Australia.

NORFOLK ISLAND
Island off east coast of Australia.
1788–1814, 1825–56 Penal colony.
1913 Designated an Australian Territory.

HEARD & McDONALD ISLANDS
Remote islands in south Indian Ocean.
1947 Britain gives islands to Australia.

ASHMORE & CARTIER ISLANDS
Islands in the Indian Ocean.
1933 Designated an Australian Territory.

CORAL SEA ISLANDS
A group of islands off northeast coast.
1969 Designated an Australian territory.

1996 **Liberal John Howard** becomes prime minister. The shooting of 35 people by a gunman in Port Arthur, Tasmania, prompts tightening of gun control laws.

1999 **Referendum rejects proposals** to replace Queen Elizabeth II as head of state by a president elected by parliament.

2000 **Olympic Games** are held in Sydney.

2002 **Eighty-eight Australian tourists** are killed in Bali bombings by Islamists.

2003 **Troops are deployed** in the Gulf, provoking protests. The Senate passes a no-confidence motion against Howard for his handling of the Iraq crisis.

2006 **A deal is signed** with East Timor over oil and gas rights in the Timor Sea.

2007 **The Labour Party** under Kevin Rudd win landslide election victory. Rudd signs the Kyoto Protocol, reversing the policy of the previous Liberal PM John Howard.

2008 **The government** apologizes for past wrongs done to indigenous population.

2009 **Bushfires** in Victoria kill 180 people.

2010 **Kevin Rudd resigns** as prime minister. Julia Gillard becomes first female prime minister and narrowly wins subsequent election, forming a minority administration—the first since 1942.

« 290–91 The Food Revolution
« 320–21 Completing the Map
« 350–51 Colonial Resistance

New Zealand

South Pacific islands first settled 1,000 years ago by the Maori, who call the country Aotearoa.

1000–1200 The Maori reach New Zealand from eastern Polynesia.

1642 The Dutch explorer Abel Tasman sights the west coast of the South Island.

1769 Captain James Cook makes the first of three visits to New Zealand.

1840 British sovereignty is proclaimed with the signing of the Treaty of Waitangi by a British representative and leaders of some Maori tribes. Settlers from the UK arrive at Port Nicholson (now Wellington).

1852 The British parliament passes a Constitution Act, which creates a House of Representatives and Legislative Council.

1860 The Taranaki war begins when British troops try to remove Maori people from land allegedly bought by the Crown.

1863 War between the Maori and British troops breaks out over land in Waikato. The land is eventually confiscated.

1867 Four Maori seats are established in the House of Representatives.

1890 A Liberal government is elected, with John Ballance as premier.

1893 Women are given the vote.

1894 The Liberal government, now under the leadership of Richard John Seddon, passes legislation providing for industrial arbitration, better factory conditions, and old-age pensions.

1907 New Zealand becomes an independent dominion, self-governing from 1926 although remaining subordinate to the UK parliament.

1947 Gains full independence when it adopts the 1931 Statute of Westminster.

1962 Western Samoa (now Samoa) gains independence from New Zealand.

1975 Conservative National Party (NP) wins elections. Economic austerity program is introduced.

1984 Labour Party (LP) elected with David Lange prime minister. Auckland harbor headland restored to Maoris.

1985 New Zealand bans nuclear vessels from ports and waters. French agents sink Greenpeace ship *Rainbow Warrior* in Auckland harbor.

1986 US suspends military obligations under military ANZUS Treaty.

1987 LP wins elections and implements widespread privatization. Nuclear ban is enshrined in legislation.

The Maori
The first settlers in New Zealand were the Maori from Polynesia, who make up about one-eighth of New Zealand's 3.9-million residents. In recent years they have waged successful claims for the return of their traditional lands.

1989 Cabinet split: Lange resigns and is succeeded by Geoffrey Palmer.

1990 Palmer resigns. LP defeated by NP in elections. James Bolger prime minister.

1992 Maori win South Island fishing rights.

1993 Docking of first French naval ship for eight years. NP returned with single-seat majority in election.

NEW ZEALAND
OVERSEAS TERRITORIES

New Zealand is an unwilling colonial power and has no wish to keep overseas territories. Their economic weakness forces New Zealand to take responsibility for their foreign policy and defense.

TOKELAU
Three small atolls to the north of Samoa.
1926 Sovereignty transferred from UK.

ROSS DEPENDENCY
New Zealand's Antarctic territory.
1923 Created by imperial order.
1959 Territorial claims frozen.

SELF-GOVERNING OVERSEAS TERRITORIES
COOK ISLANDS
A group of atolls and volcanic islands in the South Pacific.
1888 British protectorate is set up.
1901 Annexed as part of New Zealand.
1965 Islands become a self-governing territory in association with New Zealand.

NIUE
The world's largest coral island.
1900 Annexed by the UK and transferred to New Zealand in 1901.
1974 Is granted self-governing status.

1993 Majority vote in referendum to adopt proportional representation.

1994 Senior-level US contacts are restored; US agrees not to send nuclear-armed ships to New Zealand ports. Maori reject government 10-year land claims settlement of NZ$1 billion.

1995 Waitangi Day celebrations are abandoned after Maori protests. Crown apologizes to the Maori and signs Waikato Raupatu Claims Settlement Act.

1996 NP forms coalition to preserve overall legislative majority after first general election under new PR system.

1997 NP forms coalition with New Zealand First (NZF) party. Jenny Shipley becomes first woman prime minister.

1998 Shipley sacks NZF leader Winston Peters as deputy prime minister, and forms a minority government when coalition splits. Waitangi Tribunal orders the government to return to the Maori NZ$6.1 million-worth of confiscated land.

1999 LP led by Helen Clark wins general election. She is reelected in 2002 and again in 2005. NZ troops join UN peacekeeping force in East Timor.

2006 Maori Queen, Te Arikinui Dame Te Atairangikaahu, dies at age 75.

2008 John Key's National Party wins a general election, ending nine years of Labour rule. Fiji and New Zealand expel each other's top diplomats in a row over Fiji's postponement of elections. Full diplomatic ties are restored only in 2010.

2011 City of Christchurch on South Island hit by major eathquake.

«216–17 Polynesian Expansion
«282–83 Exploring the Pacific
«350–51 Colonial Resistance

Papua New Guinea

The world's most linguistically diverse country with more than 750 languages spoken.

1526 Portuguese explorer Jorge de Meneses lands on the northwest coast.

1545 Spanish first claim the whole island of New Guinea.

1828 The Dutch claim the western part of the island as part of the Dutch East Indies; it now forms part of Indonesia.

1884 The UK lays claim to the southeast coast of New Guinea island, and to the islands to the east, which it annexes in 1888. Germany claims the northeast coast and nearby islands.

1902 Australia takes over British sector, which is renamed Papua in 1906.

1914 German sector occupied by Australia.

1920 Former German New Guinea is mandated by the League of Nations to Australia; the mandate is renewed after World War II by the UN.

1942–45 Japanese occupation.

1964 National Parliament created.

1971 Renamed Papua New Guinea.

1975 Independence under Michael Somare, leader since 1972.

1988 Bougainville Revolutionary Army (BRA) begins guerrilla campaign to achieve independence for their island.

1994 Peace treaty between the government and BRA rebels sets up a provisional Bougainville government; fighting resumes in 1995.

1997 El Niño effect causes severe drought and storms.

1997 Sir Julius Chan resigns as prime minister over the use of Western-led mercenaries to put down the rebellion in Bougainville. Permanent ceasefire achieved in Bougainville in 1998.

2000 Loloata Understanding promises autonomy for Bougainville.

2001 Peace agreement with Bougainville ratified after three-year ceasefire.

2005 New autonomous Bougainville government is sworn into office after largely peaceful elections.

2007 Parliament legalizes casinos and online gambling in a bid to boost economy.

2009 Papua New Guinea suffers its first recorded outbreak of cholera.

«282–83 Exploring the Pacific

Palau

A republic in the western Pacific consisting of more than 300 islands, of which only nine are inhabited.

1500s **Palau colonized** by Spain, which only acquires full sovereignty in 1886.

1899 **Spain sells Palau** to Germany.

1914 Japan occupies Palau.

1921 **League of Nations** grants a mandate over Palau to Japan.

1944 **US troops** occupy Palau near the end of World War II.

1947 **UN Trust Territory** of the Pacific Islands—including Palau—is established.

1979 **Palau votes against** joining the new Federated States of Micronesia and becomes autonomous in 1981.

1982 **Palau signs Compact** of Free Association with the US.

1994 **Palau becomes independent** in free association with the US.

2006 **Government moves** to new capital Melekeok.

2009 **Palau accepts** six Chinese ethnic Uighurs freed from Guantanamo Bay.

《216–17 Polynesian Expansion

Micronesia

Micronesia comprises the former Caroline Islands—except Palau—in the western Pacific.

1500s **Islands colonized** by Spain.

1899 **Spain sells the islands** to Germany.

1914 **At start of World War I,** Japan occupies Caroline Islands.

1920 **League of Nations** grants a mandate over the islands to Japan.

1945 **US troops** occupy the Caroline Islands at the end of World War II.

1947 **UN Trust Territory** of the Pacific Islands—including the Caroline Islands—is established, administered by the US.

1979 **Federated States of Micronesia** is formed.

1986 **A compact of Free** Association with the US becomes operational as the islands gain independence.

2004 **Nearly all of Yap's** infrastructure is destroyed by Typhoon Sudal.

《216–17 Polynesian Expansion

Nauru

The island nation of Nauru is the world's smallest republic, with only 12,570 inhabitants.

1798 **Earlier colonized** by Melanesians and Polynesians, Nauru is discovered by British navigator Captain John Fearn.

1888 **Nauru is annexed** by Germany.

1900 **Phosphate** is found on the island; extraction begins in 1906 in a joint UK–German venture.

1914 **Nauru is captured** by Australian forces at the start of World War I.

1920 **League of** Nations mandate places Nauru under control of Australia, New Zealand, and the UK, with the island's administration conducted by Australia.

1942 **The Japanese occupy** Nauru. More than a thousand islanders are deported to Truk in Micronesia where 500 die from bombing and starvation.

1945 **Nauru is occupied** by Allied troops.

1947 **Australia, New Zealand,** and UK administer Nauru under UN trusteeship.

1968 **Nauru gains independence.**

1970 **Gains control of** phosphate industry.

1993 **Australia and UK agree** to provide compensation for environmental damage caused by phosphate extraction.

1999 **Joins UN.**

2001 **As the phosphate** runs out, the island relies on Australian aid, agreeing to hold Australian asylum seekers. Nauru's offshore banks are closed after US allegations of money laundering.

2004 **State of emergency is declared** after parliament fails to pass the budget.

2008 **Australia halts its policy** of sending asylum seekers to Nauru.

2010 **Referendum rejects proposed** changes to the constitution.

《216–17 Polynesian Expansion

Nauru, world's smallest republic
The tiny island republic is almost circular, with a 10-mile (16-km) ring road around the outside. Everyone lives on the narrow coastal strip, as the interior is uninhabitable former mining land.

Marshall Islands

A collection of 34 widely scattered atolls in the central Pacific, of which 24 are inhabited.

1788 **British explorer John Marshall** visits the islands, giving them their name.

1886 **Islands become** a German colony.

1914 **Japan occupies** the islands and governs them after 1920 under a League of Nations mandate.

1944 **US troops occupy** the islands and use them from 1946 for nuclear tests.

1946 **First nuclear test** at Bikini Atoll. Tests continue until 1958.

1986 **Compact of Free** Association with US as the islands become independent. The UN trust is ended in 1990.

2001 **Compensation to the people** of Bikini Atoll for the damage caused by US nuclear testing is agreed to in principle.

2008 **A state of emergency** is declared as waves flood major urban centers.

《216–17 Polynesian Expansion

Kiribati

One half of the former Gilbert & Ellice Islands, Kiribati is pronounced "Keer-ee-bus."

1605 **The Spanish explorer,** Quiros, sights one of the islands in Kiribati, already inhabited by Micronesian people.

1892 **The British establish** a protectorate over the phosphate-producing Gilbert & Ellice Islands.

1916 **The Gilbert & Ellice** Islands are declared a British colony.

1942–43 **The Gilbert Islands** are occupied by the Japanese. Tarawa Atoll is the site of a fierce battle between US and Japanese troops.

1957 **First British nuclear** tests take place near Christmas Island (now Kiritimati).

1979 **Independence as two** states: Kiribati (the Gilberts) and Tuvalu (the Ellices).

1981 **Kiribati wins damages** for phosphate mining from UK.

1986 **Kiribati signs** lucrative fishing deal with the US in return for aid.

2002 **Announces legal action** against US for environmental problems stemming from US refusal to sign Kyoto Protocol.

《216–17 Polynesian Expansion

Solomon Islands

A large archipelago scattered over the western Pacific; most islands are coral reefs.

1568 **Spanish first** make contact with the islands, which are inhabited by Melanesian people.

1893 **UK makes the southern** Solomons a protectorate, adding further islands in 1898–99, and acquiring some northern islands from Germany in 1900.

1942–43 **During Japanese occupation,** a lengthy battle with US forces takes place around Guadalcanal Island.

1978 **Independence from UK.**

1998 **Ethnic conflict between** Guadalcanal and Malaita islanders as 20,000 Malaitans are forced from their homes on Guadalcanal by native militias. In 2000 Malaita rebels stage an unsuccessful coup and hold the prime minister at gunpoint for two days.

2003 **After further ethnic** conflict, an Australian-led Regional Assistance Mission arrives to restore order and reform the country's chaotic finances.

2005 **Harold Keke,** a leader of an anti-Malaitan militia in the 1998-2003 Guadalcanal conflict, is convicted of the 2002 murder of an MP.

2009 **A Truth and Reconciliation** Commission is established to investigate fighting between ethnic militias on Guadalcanal in 1997–2003.

《216–17 Polynesian Expansion

Vanuatu

A sprawling archipelago of 82 islands in the South Pacific, of which only 12 are of any size.

1605 **The Spanish explorer,** Quiros, visits the islands.

1800s **The Melanesian** inhabitants are visited by European missionaries and merchants seeking to cut the sandalwood trees. Cotton planters follow.

1906 **In response to calls** from Australia to annex the islands, the UK and France agree on joint rule of the New Hebrides, as they are now called.

1938 **The John Frum** cargo cult emerges, promising the return of goods "stolen by foreigners." Its leaders are jailed, but in 1956 it is recognized as a religion.

1980 **Independence as the Republic** of Vanuatu. The name means "Our Land Forever." The northern island of Espiritu Santo attempts to secede.

1999 **A tsunami causes** extensive damage.

2003 **Economic reforms** take Vanuatu off the international blacklist of tax havens.

2009 **Prime minister** Edward Natapei is temporarily removed from office after missing three sittings of parliament without submitting written explanation.

2010 **Natapei is ousted** following a vote of no-confidence. He is replaced by his deputy Sato Kilman.

《216–17 Polynesian Expansion

Tuvalu

One of the world's smallest and most isolated states, Tuvalu consists of nine atolls.

1892 **Britain annexes** the Ellice Islands.

1916 **The Ellice Islands** are joined to the Gilbert Islands.

1974 **Ellice Islanders vote** to separate from the Gilberts.

1978 **Independence** from the UK as Tuvalu.

1987 **Tuvalu Trust Fund** is set up to provide future income for the islands.

1998 **Lucrative deal** for the sale of the country's ".tv" internet suffix.

2000 **Joins UN** as the 189th member.

2001 **New Zealand** agrees to take Tuvalu citizens if the islands, none of which is higher than 15 ft (4.5 m) above sea level, are flooded as a result of global warming.

《216–17 Polynesian Expansion

Samoa

The nine Polynesian volcanic islands of Samoa lie in the heart of the South Pacific.

1830 **Colonial rivalry** begins for control of the islands. The chiefs of the islands sign treaties with various European powers in 1838–39.

1889 **After continuing** rivalry between the UK, Germany, and the US for influence, the three powers agree by the Treaty of Berlin to guarantee Samoa's independence and neutrality.

1899 **The Samoan Islands** are divided between German Western and US Eastern Samoa.

1914 **New Zealand troops** occupy Western Samoa at the start of World War I. New Zealand remains the colonial power until independence in 1962.

1962 **Western Samoa becomes** the first independent Polynesian nation.

1990 **Cyclone Ofa leaves** 10,000 people homeless.

1991 **Universal suffrage is introduced:** previously, only the 1,800 elected chiefs could vote.

1997 **The country's name** is changed to the Independent State of Samoa.

2007 **King Malietoa Tanumafili** dies after ruling Samoa for 45 years.

2009 **Samoa switches** to driving on the left-hand side of the road. Tsunami kills 200 people.

《216–17 Polynesian Expansion

Fiji

A volcanic archipelago in the south Pacific ripped apart by racial tensions in recent years.

1643 **Abel Tasman,** the Dutch explorer, sights the Fijian islands.

1800 **The first Europeans** begin to settle in Fiji: sailors, escaped convicts from Australia, traders, and missionaries.

Island immigrant
Between 1879 and 1916, the British brought in laborers from India to work on the copra and sugar cane plantations. By 1945 Indians like this farmer outnumbered ethnic Melanesian Fijians.

1874 **Fiji becomes a** British colony.

1937 **Fiji's legislative council** becomes partly elected, partly nominated.

1970 **Independence** from the UK.

1987 **Election win for** Indo-Fijian coalition leads to coups to secure minority ethnic Fijian rule. Fiji becomes a republic and is ejected from Commonwealth.

1989 **Mass Indo-Fijian** emigration.

1990 **Constitution discriminating against** Indo-Fijians introduced.

1997 **Census shows ethnic** Fijians outnumber Indo-Fijians. Fiji rejoins the Commonwealth. New constitution changes the name to the Fiji Islands.

1999 **General election won** by Labour Party. Mahendra Chaudhry becomes the first Indo-Fijian prime minister.

2000 **After a civilian-led coup,** a new ethnic Fijian government is formed.

2006 **Fiji is suspended** from the Commonwealth after another coup.

2009 **The Appeal Court** rules the suspension was illegal. President Ilolo repeals the constitution, dismisses all judges, appoints himself head of state, and reappoints Frank Bainimarama as prime minister. The Commonwealth imposes full suspension on Fiji.

《216–17 Polynesian Expansion
《282–83 Exploring the Pacific

Tonga

Tonga is unique in the Pacific as it has retained its monarchy and was never colonized.

300 BCE **Tonga settled** by Polynesians.

1643 **Abel Tasman** visits the islands, followed by Captain Cook in 1773.

1820 **Taufa'ahau Tupou (George I)** becomes king of his native Ha'apai and unifies the other islands by 1843.

1860 **Tonga becomes** Christian.

1862 **King grants** freedom to the people from the arbitrary rule of minor chiefs.

1875 **First constitution is established.**

1900 **Amid concern over German** ambitions in the region, the Treaty of Friendship and Protection is signed with the UK.

1958 **Greater autonomy** from the UK is enshrined in a Friendship Treaty.

1965 **Taufa'ahau Tupou IV** accedes on the death of his mother, Salote Tupou III.

1970 **Full independence within** British Commonwealth.

1996 **Limited general election** sees strong showing by prodemocracy candidates.

2000 **King appoints** his conservative third son, 'Ulukalala Lavaka Ata, as prime minister for life, but he resigns in 2006.

2001 **The official court jester,** a US businessman and financial adviser, loses $26 million of public money.

2006 **Resignation of** 'Ulukalala Lavaka Ata, as prime minister. Feleti Sevele becomes the first non-noble prime minister in his place. King Taufa'ahau Tupou IV dies. He is succeeded by Crown Prince Tupouto'. A state of emergency is declared after riots protesting the lack of democracy.

2009 **A committee** on constitutional reform recommends the institution of a popularly elected parliament and the reduction of the monarchy's role to a ceremonial one.

《216–17 Polynesian Expansion

Antarctica

The world's fifth-largest continent, Antarctica is almost entirely covered with thick ice.

1820 **Russian explorer** Thaddeus von Bellingshausen is first European to sight Antarctica.

1839–43 **British explorer** James Clark Ross discovers new territory around what is now called the Ross Sea.

1909 **British explorer** Ernest Shackleton's expedition gets to within 97 nautical miles (180 km) of the Pole.

1911 **Expedition** led by Norwegian explorer Roald Amundsen is first to reach the South Pole.

1912 **British explorer** Robert Scott reaches the South Pole one month after Amundsen; Scott and his team die two months later on the return journey.

1929 **US aviator Richard Byrd** is the first person to fly over the South Pole.

1957–58 **International Geophysical Year** launches scientific exploration of Antarctica.

1959 **Antarctic Treaty signed** by 12 countries: international governance is set up and all seven national territorial claims are frozen.

1978 **Convention limiting seal** hunting comes into force.

1979 **Air New Zealand** flight 901 crashes into Mount Erebus. All 257 aboard killed.

1985 **Ozone layer depletion** above Antarctica is discovered.

1994 **Establishment of Antarctic** whale sanctuary.

1998 **Agreement on** 50-year ban on mineral extraction comes into force.

2007 **There are currently** 46 signatory nations to the Antarctic Treaty, of which 18 have observer status.

《320–21 Completing the Map

INDEX AND ACKNOWLEDGMENTS

Index

Page references in *italics* denote illustrations.

Acknowledgments

Dorling Kindersley would like to thank the following people for their help in the preparation of this book: Richard Beatty and Sarah Levete for proof reading; John Breen, Michael Brett, Amy-Sue Bix, Howard Hotson, Rosamond McKitterick, and Chris Scarre for advice on content; Joanna Chisholm, Tarda Davison-Aitkins, Julie Ferris, Ben Hoare, Margaret Hynes, Neil Lockley, and Debra Wolter for editorial assistance; Smiljka Surla for design assistance; Laragh Kedwell for DTP support; Claire Morrey, Christine Pascall, and Joanne Grey at English Heritage for access to Dover Castle; Adam Howard at Invisiblecities Ltd for artworks (model by Andy Kay); Ailsa Heritage for advice on maps.

Dorling Kindersley would also like to thank the following people for their help in the preparation of updates to the book: consultant Philip Parker; Ferdie McDonald and Manisha Majithia for editorial; Gadi Farfour and Steve Woosnam-Savage for design; Dawn Bates for proofreading; John Searcy for Americanization.

PICTURE CREDITS

The publisher would like to thank the following for their kind permission to reproduce their photographs:
Romaine Werblow at DK Images, Sonia Harder at AKG Images, Everyone at The Art Archive, Jenny Page at The Bridgeman Art Library and Nejla Burnazoglu.

(**Key**: a-above; b-below/bottom; c-center; f-far; l-left; r-right; t-top)

Abbreviations:
AKG akg-images **Alamy** - Alamy Images; **AA&A** - Ancient Art & Architecture Collection; **AA** - The Art Archive; **BAL** - The Bridgeman Art Library; **BM** - The Trustees of the British Museum; **DK** - DK Images; **Getty** - Getty Images; **LoC** - Library Of Congress, Washington, D.C.; **NHM** - The Natural History Museum, London; **S&S** - Science & Society Picture Library; **WFA** - Werner Forman Archive.

1 DK: Oxford University Museum of Natural History. **2-3 Alamy:** Visual Arts Library (London). **4-5 Getty:** National Geographic / Richard T. Nowitz. **6 akg-images:** Erich Lessing (tr). **Alamy:** Chris Knapton (bl); Tribaleye Images / J. Marshall (br). **DK:** Oxford University Museum of Natural History (tl). **WFA:** Egyptian Museum, Cairo (c). **7 Alamy:** Classic Image (tr); IML Image Group Ltd (bl). **BAL:** Edinburgh University Library, Scotland, With kind permission of the University of Edinburgh (br). **WFA:** Private Collection (ca). **8 Alamy:** ArkReligion.com (bl). **BAL:** Musée du Louvre, Paris (br). **Corbis:** Bettmann (cr). **S&S:** National Railway Museum (tc). **9 Corbis:** (bl). **Getty:** National Geographic / Justin Guariglia (br). **10-11 Corbis:** Derek Croucher. **12 DK:** Oxford University Museum of Natural History. **14 Alamy:** Black Star (Goats). **AA&A:** (Mammoth House). **BAL:** Museum of Fine Arts, Houston, Texas, Museum purchase with funds provided by the Museum Collectors (Jomon Pottery). **Corbis:** Wolfgang Kaehler (Olduvai). **DK:** Courtesy of the Natural History Museum, London (Handaxe, Lucy); Oxford University Museum of Natural History (Neanderthal Skull, Homo sapiens Skull). **Getty:** National Geographic / Joy Tessman (Hunter); Carsten Peter (Ice Age). **Panos Pictures:** Georg Gerster (Village). **14-15 Corbis:** Sygma / Charles Jean Marc (Background). **15 AKG:** (Bandkeramik Pottery). **Alamy:** Chris Knapton (Stonehenge); Tom Schmelzer (Cattle); Stock Connection Blue (Maize). **Corbis:** The Art Archive (Varna Gold); Gianni Dagli Orti (Warka Vase). **DK:** Judith Miller / Ancient Art (Tel Halaf); Courtesy of The Science Museum, London (Obsidian). **WFA:** Ashmolean Museum, Oxford (Nekhen Ivory). **16 Corbis:** Wolfgang Kaehler. **17 Alamy:** Steve Bloom Images (tl). **DK:** Courtesy of the Natural History Museum, London (cr). **18 NHM:** (Homo Habilis Front & Side). **Science Photo Library:** John Reader (tr). **18-19 DK:** Oxford University Museum of Natural History (All other images). **19 NHM:** (Paranthropus boisei Side). **20 Getty:** National Geographic / Sisse Brimberg (t). **Science Photo Library:** MSF / Javier Trueba (bc). **21 DK:** Courtesy of the Manchester Museum (cra). **Science Photo Library:** Sovereign, ISM (br). **University of Bergen, Norway:** Christopher Henshilwood (bl). **22 Corbis:** Roger Ressmeyer (cra). **Getty:** Carsten Peter (b). **23 Alamy:** Tom Till (tr). **Getty:** National Geographic / James P. Blair (br). **NASA:** JPL (cr). **24 Getty:** Science Faction / Roger Ressmeyer / Fred Hirschmann (cla). **25 Alamy:** Ilya Genkin (bc); Robert Harding Picture Library Ltd (crb). **Corbis:** The Art Archive (tc); Gianni Dagli Orti (clb). **Getty:** AFP / STR (tr); National Geographic / Ira Block (bl). **26 AA&A:** (tl). **NHM:** (cr). **26-27 Getty:** National Geographic / Chris Johns (b). **27 Corbis:** Lowell Georgia (fcla); Gianni Dagli Orti (cr). **28 Corbis:** Michael Amendolia. **29 Corbis:** Bettmann (cra); Free Agents Limited (cr); Warren Morgan (bc); Reuters (tl); Reuters / Stephen Hird (cla). **DK:** Courtesy of The American Museum of Natural History (br). **30 DK:** Courtesy of The Museum of London (ca, b/Harpoon Point, b/Fishing Spear, b/Flint Arrow, b/Mesolithic Arrow). **31 Getty:** National Geographic / Joy Tessman (tl); National Geographic / David A. Harvey (br). **WFA:** Field Museum of Natural History, Chicago (tr); University of British Columbia, Vancouver, Canada (cl). **32 National Geographic Image Collection:** Kenneth Garrett (b). **33 Alamy:** LOOK Die Bildagentur der Fotografen GmbH (tc). **AA:** Egyptian Museum Turin / Dagli Orti (cr); Dagli Orti (br). **Corbis:** Rob Howard (bc). **34 Alamy:** Visual Arts Library (London) (10). **AA:** Moravian Museum Brno / Dagli Orti (8); Museo Tridentino Scienze Naturali Trento / Dagli Orti (2). **Deutsches Archäologisches Institut:** (9). **DK:** Courtesy of The Museum of London (3, 11); Courtesy of the Natural History Museum, London (1, 4, 7, 12 Barbed); Courtesy of The Science Museum, London (12 Serrated). **Getty:** AFP / Anna Zieminski (5). **National Geographic Image Collection:** (6). **35 AA:** Musée du Louvre, Paris / Dagli Orti (14). **BAL:** Brooklyn Museum of Art, New York, Charles Edwin Wilbour Fund (16); Iraq Museum, Baghdad, Photo © Held Collection (21). **BM:** (15). **DK:** The British Museum, London (13); Courtesy of the University Museum of Archaeology and Anthropology, Cambridge (18, 19). Photo **Scala, Florence:** The Metropolitan Museum of Art, New York / Art Resource (20). **36 Alamy:** Martin Shields (bc); Stock Connection Blue (tr); Worldwide Picture Library (cb). **37 Alamy:** Black Star (cl); Israel Images (tr); Charles Mistral (tl); Tom Schmelzer (c). **38 BAL:** Museum of Fine Arts, Houston, Texas, Museum purchase with funds provided by the Museum Collectors (bc). **DK:** © CONACULTA-INAH-MEX. Authorized reproduction by the Instituto Nacional de Antropologia e Historia (tl). **39 AA:** Dagli Orti (br). **DK:** The British Museum (tr). **Panos Pictures:** Georg Gerster (l). **40 Alamy:** Robert Estall Photo Agency (clb). **Corbis:** Adam Woolfitt (bl). **DK:** Courtesy of the University Museum of Archaeology and Anthropology, Cambridge (cla). **41 Alamy:** Chris Knapton (t). **Corbis:** Richard A. Cooke (bl). Panos **Pictures:** Georg Gerster (br). **42 AA:** Musée du Louvre, Paris / Dagli Orti (c). **DK:** Courtesy of The Science Museum, London(cla). **43 AA:** Devizes Museum / Eileen Tweedy (tr). **BAL:** South Tyrol Museum of Archaeology, Bolzano, Wolfgang Neeb (bc). **Corbis:** The Art Archive (tl); Jonathan Blair (cr). **44 Corbis:** Gianni Dagli Orti (cl). **DK:** Judith Miller / Ancient Art (ca). **WFA:** Ashmolean Museum, Oxford (br); British Museum, London (bl). **45 Corbis:** Yann Arthus-Bertrand (tl); Sandro Vannini (br). **DK:** Judith Miller / Ancient Art (tr). **46 WFA:** Egyptian Museum, Cairo. **48 AKG:** (Sargon). **AA:** Musée du Louvre, Paris / Dagli Orti (Gudea); National Museum, Karachi / Dagli Orti (Seal); Dagli Orti (Ship Building). **Corbis:** Brooklyn Museum (Pepi); Christie's Images (Cycladic Figure); Reuters / Sengo Perez (Caral); Michael S. Yamashita (Ur). **DK:** The British Museum, London (Standard of Ur). **Getty:** The Image Bank / Michael John O'Neill (Great Pyramid). **Photo Scala, Florence:** The Metropolitan Museum of Art, New York / Art Resource (Tablet). **48-49 AKG:** Andrea Jemolo (Background). **49 Alamy:** Helene Rogers (Knossos); Visual Arts Library (London) (Phaistos Disk). **AA:** Egyptian Museum Turin / Dagli Orti (Vizier); Dagli Orti (Akrotiri). **Corbis:** Yann Arthus-Bertrand (Hattusas). **DK:** The British Museum, London (Shang Bronze). **Jürgen Liepe:** Egyptian Museum, Cairo (Nubian Army). **Photo Scala, Florence:** The Metropolitan Museum of Art, New York / Art Resource (Hittite Statue). **50 AKG:** Erich Lessing (Kudurru). **Alamy:** Visual Arts Library (London) (Letter). **AA&A:** (Philistine Head). **AA:** Egyptian Museum, Cairo / Dagli Orti (Akhenaten). **BAL:** Ashmolean Museum, University of Oxford (Vase). **Corbis:** Archivo Iconografico, S.A. (Agamemnon). **DK:** Courtesy of The British Library, London (Oracle Bones); The British Museum, London (Book of the Dead). **Getty:** Robert Harding World Imagery / Gavin Hellier (Hatshepsut Temple). **WFA:** (Rameses III). **50-51 AKG:** Andrea Jemolo (Background). **51 AKG:** Erich Lessing (Assyrian Relief, Sargon II). **Alamy:** Visual Arts Library (London) (Phoenician Script); Ken Welsh (Carthage). **Corbis:** Danny Lehman (Olmec Head). **DK:** The British Museum, London (Zhou Bronze). **National Geographic Image Collection:** O. Louis Mazzatenta (Chariot Burial). **New Carlsberg Glyptotek, Copenhagen:** Ole Haupt (Kawa Stele). **Panos Pictures:** Georg Gerster (Kurgans). **52 DK:** The Science Museum, London (tr, bc). **Rex Features:** Sipa Press (cla). **WFA:** Egyptian Museum, Cairo (clb). **53 AKG:** Erich Lessing (tl). **AA:** Musée Condé Chantilly / Dagli Orti (br). **S&S:** (cr). **The Wellcome Institute Library, London:** (bl). **54 AKG:** (bl). **AA&A:** (cl). **BAL:** Private Collection, Photo © Heini Schneebeli (tl). **DK:** The British Museum, London (tc). **55 AKG:** Erich Lessing (bl). **Alamy:** Visual Arts Library (London) (crb). **AA:** Musée du Louvre, Paris / Dagli Orti (cra). **DK:** The British Museum, London (tl). **56 AKG:** Erich Lessing (c). **AA:** Dagli Orti (cra). **Corbis:** Sandro Vannini (cla). **DK:** The British Museum, London (bl). **57 Alamy:** Tor Eigeland (cra). **AA:** Musée du Louvre, Paris / Dagli Orti (cl). **Corbis:** Brooklyn Museum (crb). **DK:** The British Museum, London (bl). **Getty:** The Image Bank / Michael John O'Neill (tl). **58 AKG:** Gérard Degeorge (tr). **AA:** National Museum, Karachi / Dagli Orti (cl). **BAL:** Ashmoleon Museum, University of Oxford (crb). **DK:** Courtesy of The National Museum, New Delhi (c). **59 Getty:** Robert Harding World Imagery / Ursula Gahwiler. **60 Corbis:** Asian Art & Archaeology, Inc. (cl). **60-61 DK:** The British Museum, London (c). **61 DK:** Courtesy of The British Library, London (cr, bc); Courtesy of the University Museum of Archaeology and Anthropology, Cambridge (c). **National Geographic Image Collection:** O. Louis Mazzatenta (tr). **62 DK:** The British Museum, London (bl). **Photo Scala, Florence:** The Metropolitan Museum of Art, New York / Art Resource (br). **The Schøyen Collection, Oslo and London:** MS 4631 (tl). 63 **Alamy:** Visual Arts Library (London) (tr). **AA:** Egyptian Museum Turin / Dagli Orti (tl). **Corbis:** Gianni Dagli Orti (crb, cb). **DK:** The British Museum, London (c); Courtesy of the London College of Printing (br). **64 AA:** Egyptian Museum Turin / Dagli Orti (ca). **Corbis:** Gianni Dagli Orti (cl). **Jürgen Liepe:** Egyptian Museum, Cairo (crb). **65 Alamy:** Lebrecht Music and Arts Photo Library (cra); Tribaleye Images / J. Marshall (l). **BAL:** Musée du Louvre, Paris, Peter Willi (br). **66 Alamy:** The Print Collector (c). **AA:** Musée du Louvre, Paris / Dagli Orti (bc). **Corbis:** Zefa / Paul C. Pet (l). **67 AA:** Dagli Orti (tc). **Corbis:** Roger Wood (crb). **Getty:** The Bridgeman Art Library (bc). **68 AA:** Musée du Louvre, Paris / Dagli Orti (cl). **DK:** The British Museum, London (tl, cr). **69 AA:** Egyptian Museum, Cairo / Dagli Orti (br). **DK:** The British Museum, London (tl, tr, bl). **70 AKG:** (9). **AA:** Egyptian Museum, Cairo / Dagli Orti (2). **DK:** Courtesy of the Ashmolean Museum, Oxford (5); The British Museum, London (1, 3, 4, 6, 7, 10, 12, 13, 14). **Photo Scala, Florence:** The Metropolitan Museum of Art, New York / Art Resource (8, 11). **71 DK:** The British Museum, London (17, 18, 19, 20, 21, 22). **Photo Scala, Florence:** The Metropolitan Museum of Art, New York / Art Resource (15, 16). **72 Deutsches Archäologisches Institut:** (cla). **72-73 Getty:** Robert Harding World Imagery / Gavin Hellier (b). **73 Alamy:** ImageState (cra). **AA:** Private Collection / Dagli Orti (br). **Corbis:** Michael S. Yamashita (cla). **Panos Pictures:** Georg Gerster (cl). **74 AA:** Xalapa Museum Veracruz, Mexico / Dagli Orti (bl). **Corbis:** Danny Lehman (c); Reuters / Sengo Perez (cla). **75 AA:** National Anthropological Museum, Mexico / Dagli Orti (bl). **John W. Rick:** (tc). **76 Alamy:** Wolfgang Kaehler (tr); Visual Arts Library (London) (bl). **BAL:** Ashmolean Museum, University of Oxford (br). **Corbis:** The Art Archive (cl); Christie's Images (cla). **77 Alamy:** Ian Dagnall (cb); Helene Rogers (bl). **AA:** Dagli Orti (cr). **78 AKG:** Erich Lessing (tl). **Photo Scala, Florence:** The Metropolitan Museum of Art, New York / Art Resource (cl). **WFA:** (r); E. Strouhal (bl). **79 Alamy:** Visual Arts Library (London) (br). **AA&A:** (cra). **Corbis:** Yann Arthus-Bertrand (cb). **80 AKG:** Erich Lessing (tl, bc, bl). **Corbis:** Gianni Dagli Orti (br). **81 AKG:** Erich Lessing (c). **AA:** The British Museum, London / Dagli Orti (tl). **82 Alamy:** Ken Welsh (tc). **Corbis:** Werner Forman Archive (cl). **New Carlsberg Glyptotek, Copenhagen:** Ole Haupt (cr). **Photo Scala, Florence:** The Metropolitan Museum of Art, New York / Art Resource (bl). **83 Alamy:** Visual Arts Library (London) (cr). **BM:** (tl). **Corbis:** Gianni Dagli Orti (c). **DK:** The British Museum, London (tr). **Réunion des**

Musées Nationaux Agence Photographique: Hervé Lewandowski (tc). **84 akg-images:** Erich Lessing. **86 AKG:** Erich Lessing (Hallstatt Wagon). **Alamy:** Visual Arts Library (London) (Hesiod). **AA:** Bardo Museum, Tunis / Dagli Orti (Homer's Odyssey); Musée du Louvre, Paris / Dagli Orti (Susa Frieze); National Archaeological Museum, Athens / Dagli Orti (Kouros Figure). **BAL:** Iraq Museum, Baghdad (Ishtar Gate). **BM:** (Cyrus Cylinder). **Corbis:** Archivo Iconografico, S.A. (Confucius); Werner Forman Archive (Persepolis Relief). **DK:** The British Museum, London (Greek Vase). **WFA:** David Bernstein Fine Art, New York (Paracas Textile). **86-87 Alamy:** Visual Arts Library (London) (Background). **87 Alamy:** Andrew Holt (Parthenon Horse); Peter Horree (Alexander the Great); Visual Arts Library (London) (Pazyryk Carpet); World Religions Photo Library (Sanchi Stupa). **AA:** Archaeological Museum, Teheran / Dagli Orti (Seleucid Bronze); Musée du Louvre, Paris / Dagli Orti (Sacrifice to Mars). **BAL:** Bildarchiv Steffens (Monte Alban); Vatican Museums and Galleries, Vatican City (School of Athens). **BM:** (Carthage Coin). **Corbis:** Keren Su (Terracotta Army). **WFA:** Hermitage Museum, St. Petersburg (Scythian Horseman). **88 AKG:** Erich Lessing (Gundestrup Cauldron). **AA&A:** PRISMA (Julius Caesar). **AA:** (Cleopatra). **Getty:** Robert Harding World Imagery / Lee Frost (Nemrut Dagi); Robert Harding World Imagery / Neale Clark (Petra). **Panos Pictures:** Georg Gerster (Teotihuacan, Apamea Colonnade). **WFA:** Museo Archeologico Nazionale, Naples (Pompeii Portrait); Museum für Völkerkunde, Berlin (Moche Pot). **88-89 Alamy:** Visual Arts Library (London) (Background). **89 AKG:** (Chinese Writing, Battle of Milvian). **AA&A:** (Sassanian Plate). **AA:** Gioviana Archives, Florence / Dagli Orti (Attila the Hun). **BAL:** Boltin Picture Library (Irish Brooch); National Museum of India, New Delhi (Buddha Head). **BM:** (Hun Coin). **Corbis:** Bettmann (Mayan Relief); Burstein Collection (Kushan Head); Pierre Colombel (Silk Road). **90 AA:** Archaeological Museum, Florence / Dagli Orti (tr); Musée Rolin Autun / Dagli Orti (tl). **BAL:** Iraq Museum, Baghdad (bl). **Corbis:** Francis G. Mayer (bc/left); Roger Wood (bc/right). **Getty:** De Agostini Picture Library (tc). **WFA:** Theresa McCullough Collection, London (br). **91 AA:** Real biblioteca de lo Escorial / Dagli Orti (cr). **BAL:** The British Museum, London (cra). **Still Pictures:** Transit (bl). **92 AA:** Archaeological Museum, Istanbul / Dagli Orti (tl). **Panos Pictures:** Insight / Marcus Rose (b). **93 AA:** Musée du Louvre, Paris / Dagli Orti (bl). **BM:** (c). **Corbis:** Bettmann (br). **WFA:** Archaeological Museum, Teheran (cl). **94 AKG:** Orsi Battaglini (bl); Electa (tl). **Alamy:** Andrew Holt (tr). **DK:** Archaeological Receipts Fund (TAP) (br); D'Ephorate of Prehistoric and Classical Antiquities. Archaeological Receipts Fund (bc). **95 AA:** Museo Nazionale Palazzo Altemps, Rome / Dagli Orti (tc). **96 Alamy:** Peter Horree. **97 AKG:** (bc). **Alamy:** Mary Evans Picture Library (c). **Corbis:** Bettmann (cra); John Heseltine (tl). **98 Corbis:** Werner Forman Archive (clb). **Getty:** Robert Harding World Imagery / Lee Frost (t). **99 AA:** Musée Guimet, Paris / Dagli Orti (tr). **Corbis:** Archivo Iconografico, S.A. (br). **Wikipedia, The Free Encyclopedia:** (cl). **100 AKG:** (crb). **AA:** Agora Museum, Athens / Dagli Orti (cl, clb). **Corbis:** Gianni Dagli Orti (bl). **DK:** The British Museum, London (cla). **101 Panos Pictures:** Georg Gerster. **102 Alamy:** The Print Collector (br). **AA:** Archaeological Museum, Aleppo / Dagli Orti (bl); Bardo Museum, Tunis / Dagli Orti (ca). **103 AKG:** (br). **AA:** The British Library, London (tr); National Archaeological Museum, Athens (bl). **Corbis:** Archivo Iconografico, S.A. (tl). **104 The British Library, London:** (bc). **Corbis:** Araldo de Luca (tr). **DK:** The British Museum, London (cla). **WFA:** Dr. E. Strouhal (bl). 105 **AKG:** The British Library, London (tr). **The Wellcome Institute Library, London:** (br). **106 AA:** Museo Capitolino, Rome / Dagli Orti (br). **DK:** The British Museum, London (cl, cla). **WFA:** (bl). **106-107 AA:** Musée du Louvre, Paris / Dagli Orti (t). **107 Alamy:** Mary Evans Picture Library (crb). **DK:** The British Museum, London (clb). **108 AA&A:** PRISMA (c). **BAL:** Bibliothèque Nationale, Paris, Archives Charmet (bl). **109 AKG:** (cr). **Alamy:** CuboImages srl (c); Hideo Kurihara (tc). **AA:** Galleria d'Arte Moderna, Rome / Dagli Orti (bc). **The British Library, London:** (cla). **110 Alamy:** Art Kowalsky (bl); David Robertson (cl). Visual Arts Library (London) (tl); Ken Welsh (clb). **BM:** (tr). **Corbis:** Zefa / José Fusta Raga (br). **WFA:** Museo Archeologico Nazionale, Naples (bc). **111 Alamy:** Robert Harding Picture Library (br). **Getty:** Photographer's Choice / Michael Dunning (cb). **Panos Pictures:** Georg Gerster (tl). **112 AKG:** (bl). **Alamy:** Ace Stock Limited (br). **DK:** The British Museum, London (tc). **113 Alamy:** Brian Hoffman (ca); Martin Jenkinson (tl). **AA:** Archaeological Museum, Naples / Dagli Orti (b/Bracelet); Musée du Louvre, Paris / Dagli Orti (br); Museo della Civilta Romana, Rome / Dagli Orti (cr). **DK:** The British Museum, London (Spoon, b/Ladle, b/Grooming Kit, b/ Coins). **114 AA:** Archaeological Museum, Châtillon-sur-Seine / Dagli Orti (clb). **DK:** The British Museum, London (crb, br). **Panos Pictures:** Georg Gerster (tr). **115 DK:** Courtesy of the Ermine Street Guard. **116 AA:** National Archaeological Museum, Athens / Dagli Orti (bl). **Corbis:** Araldo de Luca (r). **DK:** The British Museum, London (cl). **117 Alamy:** Ken Welsh (br). **BAL:** Villa Farnesina, Rome (cr). **DK:** The British Museum, London (tc). **118 AKG:** Erich Lessing (bl). **BAL:** Musée de la Vieille Charite, Marseille / Giraudon (tl). **Stéphane Compoint:** (cra). **Corbis:** Alinari Archives (crb). **119 AA:** Museo Prenestino, Palestrina / Dagli Orti. **120 Alamy:** North Wind Picture Archives (bc). **AA:** (r). **BM:** (clb). **121 AKG:** (br); Hilbich (tc). **AA:** Musée du Louvre, Paris / Dagli Orti (cr, bc). **BAL:** Musée du Louvre, Paris / Giraudon / Lauros (cl). **122 Alamy:** Visual Arts Library (London) (crb). **AA&A:** (cb). **AA:** Archaeological Museum, Teheran / Dagli Orti (clb). **BM:** (cla). **Corbis:** Pierre Colombel (tl). 123 BAL. **124 AKG:** Jean-Louis Nou (bc). **Alamy:** IML Image Group Ltd (tr); Sherab (br). **125 Alamy:** Bildarchiv Monheim GmbH (br); World Religions Photo Library (ca). **BAL:** National Museum of India, New Delhi (crb). **Corbis:** Charles & Josette Lenars (tr). **126 Corbis:** Keren Su. **127 AA&A:** (tr). **AA:** The British Library, London (bc). **Corbis:** Bettmann (br). **DK:** The British Museum, London (cla). **128 BAL:** Bibliothèque Nationale, Paris (tr). **DK:** The British Museum, London (bl); The British Library, London (br). **129 AKG:** (bc). **AA:** Jan Vinchon Numismatist, Paris / Dagli Orti (cra). **130 Alamy:** Visual Arts Library (London) (cla, clb). **BAL:** Vatican Museums and Galleries, Vatican City (r). **131 AA:** Archaeological Museum, Naples / Dagli Orti (bl); Museo Civico, San Gimignano / Dagli Orti (br). **BAL:** Musée d'Archeologie et d'Histoire, Lausanne (crb); Museo Archeologico Nazionale, Naples (cla). **Corbis:** Archivo Iconografico, S.A. (cr). **132 AKG:** (bl). **AA&A:** (br). **AA:** Archaeological Museum, Bagdad / Dagli Orti (tr). **BM:** (cla). **133 AA:** Bodleian Library, Oxford (cra). **Getty:** Robert Harding World Imagery / Neale Clark (tl). **134 AKG:** Erich Lessing (cl). **Alamy:** Mary Evans Picture Library (bl). **Corbis:** Araldo de Luca (tc). **134-135 AKG:** (bc). **135 AKG:** Erich Lessing (cla). **BAL:** Boltin Picture Library (tr). **BM:** (tc). **136 AKG:** Erich Lessing (3, 5). **BM:** (1). **Corbis:** Werner Forman Archive / National Museum of Ireland (7). **DK:** The British Museum, London (2); Courtesy of The Museum of London (6); Courtesy of the University Museum of Archaeology and Anthropology, Cambridge (8, 10, 12). **WFA:** The British Museum, London (4,11); National Museum, Copenhagen (9). **137 AKG:** Erich Lessing (15, 19 Right). **Alamy:** Visual Arts Library (London) (16). **AA:** Jan Vinchon Numismatist, Paris / Dagli Orti (19 Left). **DK:** The British Museum, London (13, 21); Courtesy of the University Museum of Archaeology and Anthropology, Cambridge (17). **WFA:** National Museum of Ireland (18, 20, 22); National Museum of Wales (14). **138 Alamy:** Visual Arts Library (London) (bl). **Panos Pictures:** Georg Gerster (tl). **WFA:** Hermitage Museum, St. Petersburg (tr). **138-139 Corbis:** Michael Setboun (b). **139 AKG:** Mark De Fraeye (cla). **BM:** (tr). **Corbis:** Burstein Collection (tc). **140 BAL:** Bildarchiv Steffens (bl). **Panos Pictures:** Georg Gerster (cra). **WFA:** David Bernstein Fine Art, New York (tl); Museum für Völkerkunde, Berlin (c, crb). **141 Corbis:** Bettmann. **142 AKG:** Andrea Baguzzi (r); Erich Lessing (bl). **143 AKG:** (bl); Erich Lessing (cl). **BM:** (br). **WFA:** The British Museum, London (ca). **144 AA:** Museo Civico, Orvieto (tl). **Getty:** AFP / Menahem Kahana (b). **145 Alamy:** Visual Arts Library (London) (cr). **146 Alamy:** The Print Collector (br). **AA:** Musée Guimet, Paris / Dagli Orti (bl). **Corbis:** Nathan Benn (tc). **DK:** The British Museum, London (tl, tr). **147 Alamy:** Steve Allen Travel Photography (tl). **Corbis:** JAI / Michele Falzone (fbr); Patrick Ward (ca). **Getty:** National Geographic / Martin Gray (cra); Riser / China Tourism Press (bl); Taxi / Gavin Hellier (br). **Panos Pictures:** Dominic Harcourt-Webster (fbl). **148-149 AKG. 150 Alamy:** Visual Arts Library (London) (tr). **AA:** Gioviana Archives, Florence / Dagli Orti (bl). **BM:** (cla). **150-151 AKG:** Erich Lessing (bc). **151 DK:** The British Museum, London (br). **152 WFA:** Private Collection. **154 AKG:** The British Library, London (Lindisfarne Gospels); Erich Lessing (Jayavarman VII). **Alamy:** Visual Arts Library (London) (Charlemagne). **AA:** The British Library, London (Harun al-Rashid). **Corbis:** Christie's Images (Ceramic Horse); Richard T. Nowitz (Dome of the Rock). **DK:** Courtesy of the Royal Museum of Scotland, Edinburgh (Portrait Beaker). **Still Pictures:** Frans Lemmens (Camel Train). **WFA:** The British Museum, London (Mayan Relief). **Wikipedia, The Free Encyclopedia:** Bilkent University / Department of History (Battle of Badr). **154-155 WFA:** Yamato Bunkaken, Nara (Background). **155 Alamy:** John Goulter (King Alfred). **AA:** Musée Guimet, Paris / Dagli Orti (Chola Bronze); Private Collection, Paris / Dagli Orti (Fujiwara Fan). **BAL:** Private Collection / Archives Charmet (Chinese Fireworks). **Corbis:** Ted Spiegel (Viking Longship). **Dennis Cox / ChinaStock:** Sun Kerang (Movable Type). **DK:** Courtesy of the National Maritime Museum, London (Astrolabe). **National Archives and Records Administration, USA:** (Battle of Lechfeld). **156 AKG:** Robert Aberman (Great Zimbabwe). **Alamy:** Jim Lane (Francis of Assisi); Mary Evans Picture Library (Saladin). **AA:** Turkish and Islamic Art Museum, Istanbul / Dagli Orti (Seljuk Turks). **BAL:** Centre Historique des Archives Nationales, Paris / Lauros / Giraudon (Templars Seal); Private Collection (Genghis Khan). **Getty:** Lonely Planet Images / Richard l'Anson (Qutab Minar). **Kenny Grant:** (Angkor Wat). **WFA:** Cathedral Treasury, Limburg (Byzantine Relic). **Wikipedia, The Free Encyclopedia:** (Battle of Hastings). **156-157 WFA:** Yamato Bunkaken, Nara (Background). **157 AKG:** (Black Death, Kublai Khan); The British Library, London (Bruges). **Alamy:** Vehbi Koca (Ottoman Helmet); Lebrecht Music and Arts Photo Library (Alhambra). **AA&A:** (Mongol Invasion). **AA:** Bibliothèque Nationale, Paris (Marco Polo). **Corbis:** Christie's Images (Benin Bronze); Gordon R. Gainer (Henry the Navigator). **DK:** Judith Miller / Sloan's (Ming Vase). **WFA:** The British Museum, London (Jade Mask). **158 Alamy:** Gus (bc); Visual Arts Library (London) (tl, ca). **AA:** Rheinische Landesmuseum, Trier / Dagli Orti (clb). **159 AKG:** The British Library, London (tl). **Alamy:** Visual Arts Library (London) (bl). **AA:** The Bodleian Library, Oxford (br). **BAL:** S. Ambrogio, Florence (tr). **160 BAL:** Musée Guimet, Paris / Archives Charmet (bl). **DK:** Judith Miller / Ancient Art (tl). **WFA:** (br). **161 Corbis:** Christie's Images (clb). **DK:** The British Library, London (br); Judith Miller / Sloans & Kenyon (cra). **Terra Galleria Photography:** Quang-Tuan Luong (tl). **162 AA:** Musée Guimet, Paris / Dagli Orti (clb). **Dennis Cox / ChinaStock:** Sun Kerang (crb). **162-163 AA:** National Palace Museum, Taiwan (t). **163 AKG:** (crb). **BAL:** Private Collection / Archives Charmet (bl). **164 BAL:** Bibliothèque Nationale, Paris (clb); The British Museum, London (bl); Private Collection (r). **165 AKG:** (bc). **Alamy:** Visual Arts Library (London) (br). **AA:** Biblioteca Nazionale Marciana, Venice / Harper Collins Publishers (tl). **DK:** Courtesy of the University Museum of Archaeology and Anthropology, Cambridge (c). **166 DK:** Judith Miller / Sloan's (bc). **WFA:** Private Collection, London (clb). **166-167 Still Pictures:** UNEP (t). **167 Alamy:** View Stock (bl). **Getty:** AFP / Goh Chai Hin (c). **168 AA&A:** (bl). **AA:** Private Collection, Paris / Dagli Orti (cra). **Corbis:** Sakamoto Photo Research Laboratory (cla). **WFA:** Burke Collection, New York (br). **169 AA:** (tr). **DK:** Board of Trustees of the Royal Armouries (l). **170 King Sejong the Great Memorial Society:** (tr, br). **171 Corbis:** Christie's Images (c). **Getty:** AFP / Kim Jae-Hwan (bl). **King Sejong the Great Memorial Society:** (cr, br). **172 Alamy:** Visual Arts Library (London) (tl). **Panos Pictures:** Georg Gerster (clb). **WFA:** (cra). **172-173 Kenny Grant:** (b). **173 AKG:** Erich Lessing (cb). **Alamy:** Ken Welsh (cra). **174 AA:** Museum of Islamic Art, Cairo (bc). **DK:** Courtesy of the Pitt Rivers Museum, University of Oxford (cla). **175 Corbis:** Richard T. Nowitz (tr). **DK:** Courtesy of the National Maritime Museum, London (crb). **Wikipedia, The Free Encyclopedia:** Bilkent University / Department of History (bc). **176 AKG:** (cl). **AA:** The British Library, London (br). **177 Alamy:** Lebrecht Music and Arts Photo Library (tl); Nicholas Pitt (cra); Andrew Watson (cl). **AA:** Turkish and Islamic Art Museum, Istanbul / Dagli Orti (bc). **Getty:** Lonely Planet Images / Richard l'Anson (c). **Magnum Photos:** Abbas (crb). **Wikipedia, The Free Encyclopedia:** (tc). **178 Photo Scala, Florence:** The Metropolitan Museum of Art, New York / Art Resource (1, 2, 3, 4, 5, 7, 8). **179 DK:** The British Museum, London (11, 14). **Photo Scala, Florence:** The Metropolitan Museum of Art, New York / Art Resource (6, 9, 10, 12, 13, 15, 16, 17). **180 AA:** Musée Guimet, Paris / Dagli Orti (cla). **Corbis:** Charles & Josette Lenars (cra). **181 Alamy:** Trip (c). **BAL:** Bonhams, London (tl). **Corbis:** Macduff Everton (b). **182 AKG:** Robert Aberman (br). **BAL:** Heini Schneebeli (cra). **Corbis:** Cordaiy Photo Library Ltd / Colin Hoskins (clb). **Still Pictures:** Frans Lemmens (cla). **WFA:** Robert Aberman (bl, crb). **183 AKG:** Erich Lessing (bl). **Corbis:** Christie's Images (crb); Sandro Vannini (cra). **WFA:** The British Museum, London (tl). **184 Alamy:** Images&Stories (tr). **AA:** Bibliothèque Nationale, Paris (bl). **WFA:** (cla). **185 Alamy:** Iain Masterton (br); World Religions Photo Library (tl). **Corbis:**

Michael S. Yamashita (tr). **186 Corbis:** Reuters / Kin Cheung (crb). **Science Photo Library:** Dr. Gary Gaugler (bc). **Wikipedia, The Free Encyclopedia:** Royal Ontario Museum, Toronto (cl). **187 AKG. 188 BAL:** Archives du Ministère des Affaires Étrangères, Paris / Archives Charmet (br). **Getty:** Imagno (c). **189 Alamy:** John Goulter (br); Visual Arts Library (London) (tl). **National Archives and Records Administration, USA:** (tr). **190 DK:** By kind permission of the Trustees of The Wallace Collection, London (tc). **191 Alamy:** Mary Evans Picture Library (tl). **BAL:** Chetham's Library, Manchester (cr). **DK:** By kind permission of the Trustees of The Wallace Collection, London (bc). **192-193 Wikipedia, The Free Encyclopedia. 194 Alamy:** Visual Arts Library (London) (cl). **BAL:** Santa Maria Novella, Florence (br). **Corbis:** Michel Setbourn (c). **195 Alamy:** Visual Arts Library (London) (tr). **Corbis:** Jan Butchofsky-Houser (br). **196 Alamy:** Jim Lane (br); Visual Arts Library (London) (tl). **AA:** The British Library, London (c). **197 Alamy:** Classic Image (cra). **198 AA:** Dagli Orti (bl). **Corbis:** Paul H. Kuiper (tr). **WFA:** Cathedral Treasury, Limburg (c). **199 AKG:** Erich Lessing (cr, bl). **200 DK:** (c); The British Museum, London (cl). **201 Alamy:** Mary Evans Picture Library (tr). **AA:** Biblioteca Capitolare, Padua / Dagli Orti (tl). **BAL:** Centre Historique des Archives Nationales, Paris / Lauros / Giraudon (bl). **202 Alamy:** Visual Arts Library (London) (tl). **DK:** Danish National Museum (br/Spear); Courtesy of The Museum of London (br/Sword); Courtesy of the Universitets Oldsaksamling, Oslo (cl). **The Fitzwilliam Museum, Cambridge:** Department of Coins and Medals (bc). **203 Corbis:** Ted Spiegel (c). **DK:** The British Museum, London (cr); Courtesy of the Statens Historiska Museum, Stockholm (tl, cl, tc); Courtesy of the Universitetets kulturhistoriske Museer / Vikingskipshuset / Frits Solvang (b). **204-205 BAL:** Edinburgh University Library, Scotland, With kind permission of the University of Edinburgh. **206 Alamy:** Vehbi Koca (c). **AA:** Turkish and Islamic Art Museum, Istanbul / Dagli Orti (cl). **207 Alamy:** Visual Arts Library (London) (bl). **AA&A:** (br). **BM:** (bc). **Corbis:** The Art Archive (t). **208 Alamy:** Peter Horree (ca). **AA:** Dagli Orti (cl, cb). **Corbis:** Archivo Iconografico, S.A. (bl). **209 AKG:** The British Library, London (l); Electa (tr). **BAL:** Hermitage, St. Petersburg (br). **Corbis:** Zefa / José Fusta Raga (c). **210 Alamy:** AA World Travel Library (bc). **AA:** National Anthropological Museum, Mexico / Dagli Orti (br). **WFA:** The British Museum, London (cra, cl). **211 AA. 212 Corbis:** Nathan Benn (bc); Werner Forman Archive (tc). **213 Alamy:** Robert Fried (t). **Still Pictures:** Jim Wark (bl). **214 DK:** The British Museum, London (14); © CONACULTA-INAH-MEX. Authorized reproduction by the Instituto Nacional de Antropologia e Historia (1, 2, 6, 7, 8, 11, 12). **215 DK:** The British Museum, London (10); Courtesy of the Royal Museum of Scotland, Edinburgh (9, 13); © CONACULTA-INAH-MEX. Authorized reproduction by the Instituto Nacional de Antropologia e Historia (3, 4, 5, 15, 16, 17). **216 BM:** (ca). **DK:** International Sailing Craft Association, Lowestoft (cr). **NHM:** (cl). **216-217 Getty:** Altrendo Images (b). **217 BM:** (tr). **National Maritime Museum, London:** (tc). **218 Alamy:** Classic Image. **220 AKG:** (Columbus, Isabella). **Alamy:** Visual Arts Library (London) (Martin Luther). **AA:** Marine Museum, Lisbon / Dagli Orti (Magellan). **BAL:** Museo de America, Madrid / Giraudon (Seville). **Corbis:** Bettmann (Leonardo da Vinci). **DK:** Courtesy of The British Library, London (Gutenberg Bible); Courtesy of the Saint Bride Printing Library, London (Printing Press). **WFA:** N.J. Saunders (Inca Depot). **220-221 Corbis:** Sandro Vannini (Background). **221 AKG:** (Smallpox); Cameraphoto (Lepanto); VISIOARS (Tea Ceremony). **Alamy:** The Print Collector (Elizabeth I); V&A Images (Censer). **AA:** Bibliothèque des Arts Décoratifs, Paris / Dagli Orti (Mercator Map). **Corbis:** Francis G. Mayer (Henry VIII); Ali Meyer (Suleyman). **DK:** Courtesy of the University Museum of Archaeology and Anthropology, Cambridge (Gold Armlets). **National Maritime Museum, London:** (Mariner's Mirrour). **WFA:** Auckland Institute and Museum, Auckland (Eel Trap). **222 Alamy:** The Print Collector (Adolphus, Newton Telescope); Swerve (Pilgrim House); Visual Arts Library (London) (Versailles). **AA:** Galleria degli Uffizi, Florence / Dagli Orti (Louis XIV); Terry Engell Gallery / Eileen Tweedy (Mayflower). **BAL:** Archives du Ministère des Affaires Étrangères, Paris / Archives Charmet (Treaty of Westphalia); Private Collection (Bartolomeo Book). **Corbis:** Stefano Bianchetti (Copernicus Map). **DK:** Scottish United Services Museum, Edinburgh Castle / National Museums of Scotland (Mortar Gun). **LoC:** The Foundation Press, Inc., Cleveland, Ohio (First Thanksgiving). **222-223 Corbis:** Sandro Vannini (Background). **223 Alamy:** Mary Evans Picture Library (Lloyd's List). **BAL:** Bibliothèque Nationale, Paris (Diderot Encyclopedia); Private Collection / Michael Graham-Stewart (Slave Ship). **The British Library, London:** (Colonies Map). **Corbis:** Bettmann (Newton, Lisbon Earthquake). **Getty:** Hulton Archive (Blackbeard, Banknote). **National Maritime Museum, London:** (Harrison Clock). **224 AA:** Marine Museum, Lisbon / Dagli Orti (bc). **Corbis:** Gordon R. Gainer (cl). **225 DK:** Courtesy of the National Maritime Museum, London (cr). **226 AKG:** (r). **AA:** Museo Colonial Antigua, Guatemala / Dagli Orti (bl). **BAL:** Fitzwilliam Museum, University of Cambridge (cl). **227 AA:** Academia BB AA S Fernando, Madrid / Dagli Orti (tl); Museo del Prado, Madrid (ca); Museo Navale, Pegli / Dagli Orti (cr). **The Bridgeman Art Library:** Prado, Madrid, Spain (bc). **228-229 AKG. 230 AA:** Museo Ciudad, Mexico / Dagli Orti (cl); Private Collection / Ellen Tweedy (cr). **Corbis:** Sygma / Lorpress / J.C. Kanny (clb). **231 Alamy:** Humberto Olarte Cupas (bl); The Print Collector (cra). **DK:** Courtesy of the Charlestown Shipwreck and Heritage Centre, Cornwall (br); Courtesy of the University Museum of Archaeology and Anthropology, Cambridge (tc). **WFA:** N.J. Saunders (clb). **232 AKG:** (cr). **LoC:** The Foundation Press, Inc., Cleveland, Ohio (tc). **232-233 Alamy:** Mike Hill (b). **233 Alamy:** Edward Parker (tl). **BAL:** Private Collection (c). **DK:** Courtesy of the National Maritime Museum, London (cra). **234 Alamy:** Visual Arts Library (London) (br). **Getty:** Time & Life Pictures / Mansell (t). **235 Alamy:** Eye Ubiquitous (bc); V&A Images (cl). **BAL:** Museo de America, Madrid / Giraudon (tr). **Corbis:** Arte & Immagini srl (cra). **236 Alamy:** North Wind Picture Archives (bl). **AA:** Terry Engell Gallery / Eileen Tweedy (t). **Corbis:** The Mariners' Museum (bc). **237 Alamy:** Swerve (bl, bc). **The British Library, London:** (tr). **BM:** (c). **Corbis:** Photo Images / Lee Snider (cr). **238 BM:** (cr). **DK:** Courtesy of the Musée de Saint-Malo (tr). **Getty:** Hulton Archive (tc). **National Maritime Museum, London:** (bl). **238-239 Corbis:** Stapleton Collection (b). **239 Alamy:** Mary Evans Picture Library (tl). **240 The British Library, London:** (tc). **241 DK:** The British Museum, London (crb); Judith Miller / Wallis and Wallis (c/Jade, c/Porcelain); Courtesy of the National Maritime Museum, London (l). **Réunion des Musées Nationaux Agence Photographique:** Thierry Ollivier (cra). **242 Corbis:** Christie's Images (b). **243 AKG:** VISIOARS (tr). **BAL:** Leeds Museums and Art Galleries (City Museum, br). **Corbis:** Werner Forman (bl). **DK:** The British Museum, London (fbr); Courtesy of the Pitt Rivers Museum, University of Oxford (tl). **WFA:** Noh Theatre Collection, Kongo School, Kyoto (bc). **244 Corbis:** Angelo Hornak (cl). **245 Alamy:** Tibor Bognar (tr). **BAL:** Private Collection, Dinodia (cr). **246 Alamy:** Images&Stories (cla). **Corbis:** Werner Forman (bc). **DK:** By kind permission of the Trustees of the Wallace Collection (c, clb). **247 Alamy:** ArkReligion.com (l). **AA:** Turkish and Islamic Art Museum, Istanbul / Dagli Orti (cr). **Wikipedia, The Free Encyclopedia:** (br). **248-249 AKG:** Cameraphoto. **250 AKG:** Rabatti - Dominqie (bc). **Alamy:** Lebrecht Music and Arts Photo Library (c). **AA:** Duomo, Florence / Dagli Orti (tr). **BAL:** Bibliothèque Nationale, Paris (bl). **Corbis:** Sandro Vannini (cr). **251 Alamy:** Visual Arts Library (London) (br). **AA:** Galleria degli Uffizi, Florence / Dagli Orti (cl). **Corbis:** Jim Zuckerman (bl). **252 Corbis:** Archivo Iconografico, S.A. (bl); By kind permission of the Trustees of the National Gallery, London (tr). **253 Alamy:** INTERFOTO Pressebildagentur (cr). **AA:** Bibliothèque des Arts Décoratifs, Paris / Dagli Orti (tr). **BAL:** The British Museum, London (c). **Corbis:** Archivo Iconografico, S.A. (tl). **DK:** Courtesy of the Saint Bride Printing Library, London (bc). **254 Corbis:** Alinari Archives (b/Signature); Bettmann (r); Dennis Marsico (bl); Ted Spiegel (clb). **255 Alamy:** imagebroker (c); INTERFOTO Pressebildagentur (cr); Visual Arts Library (London) (b). **256 AKG:** (tl). **Alamy:** Anatoly Pronin (cl); Visual Arts Library (London) (bl). **256-257 DK:** Courtesy of The British Library, London (c). **257 Corbis:** Summerfield Press (cr). **258 AKG:** (r). **Corbis:** Archivo Iconografico, S.A. (bl). **259 BAL:** Bibliothèque Nationale, Paris / Lauros / Giraudon (cl); Church of St. Ignatius, Rome / Alinari (tr). **260 Alamy:** The Print Collector (r). **BAL:** Walker Art Gallery, National Museums, Liverpool (clb). **Corbis:** Francis G. Mayer (bl). **261 AA:** National Maritime Museum, London / Harper Collins Publishers (tl); Eileen Tweedy (crb). **BAL:** Ashmolean Museum, University of Oxford (bc). **Corbis:** Bettmann (ca); Baldwin H. Ward & Kathryn C. Ward (bl). **262 AKG:** Erich Lessing (cl). **Corbis:** (tl). **DK:** By kind permission of the Trustees of The Wallace Collection, London (cr). **263 Alamy:** Visual Arts Library (London) (t). **BAL:** Archives du Ministère des Affaires Étrangères, Paris / Archives Charmet (br). **264 Alamy:** David Stares (cl). **BAL:** The British Library, London (r). **265 Alamy:** Glenn Harper (cr). **BAL:** Private Collection / Bonhams, London (bc); Houses of Parliament, Westminster, London (tr). **DK:** English Civil War Society (english-civil-war-society.org) (tc). **266 Corbis:** Stefano Bianchetti (bc); Massimo Listri (cl). **DK:** Courtesy of the National Maritime Museum, London (r); The Science Museum, London (tl). **267 Alamy:** The Print Collector (tr). **Corbis:** Bettmann (tc). **DK:** Courtesy of The Science Museum, London (tl). **Photo Scala, Florence:** Biblioteca Nazionale, Florence (cr). **268-269 Corbis:** Bettmann. **270 AA:** National Gallery of Scotland (cla). **Corbis:** Archivo Iconografico, S.A. (bc); Michel Setboun (clb). **270-271 BAL:** Bibliothèque Nationale, Paris (c/1); Musée de la Ville de Paris, Musée Carnavalet, Paris / Lauros / Giraudon (c/2); Stapleton Collection (c/3). **271 Alamy:** INTERFOTO Pressebildagentur (bc). **Corbis:** Bob Krist (cr). **272 AKG:** Nimatallah (tc). **Alamy:** The Print Collector (bc). **272-273 National Maritime Museum, London:** (b). **273 DK:** Scottish United Services Museum, Edinburgh Castle / National Museums of Scotland (t, c). **274 DK:** By kind permission of the Trustees of The Wallace Collection, London (7, 8, 9, 10). **275 DK:** By kind permission of the Trustees of The Wallace Collection, London (14); Courtesy of Warwick Castle, Warwick (15-21). **276 BAL:** The British Museum, London (br). **Corbis:** Bettmann (ca). **DK:** The British Museum, London (clb). **277 Alamy:** Andrew Holt (br). **BM:** (c). **DK:** The British Museum, London (tr). **Getty:** Hulton Archive (tl). **278 AA:** Galleria degli Uffizi, Florence / Dagli Orti (r). **BAL:** Bibliothèque Nationale, Paris / Archives Charmet (bc). **279 AKG:** (bc). **Alamy:** Visual Arts Library (London) (tl, tc). **AA:** Musée de Tessé, Le Mans / Dagli Orti (cra); Dagli Orti (c). **280 DK:** Wilberforce House, Hull Museums (bl). **280-281 BAL:** Private Collection / Michael Graham-Stewart (c). **281 BAL:** Peter Newark American Pictures (cr). **Corbis:** Bojan Brecelj (br). **DK:** Wilberforce House, Hull Museums (tc). **282 National Maritime Museum, London:** (tc). **282-283 Corbis:** Historical Picture Archive (b). **283 Getty:** Iconica / John W. Banagan (crb). **WFA:** Auckland Institute and Museum, Auckland (clb). **284 S&S:** National Railway Museum. **286 AKG:** (Battle of Zorndorf). **Alamy:** Visual Arts Library London (Tennis Court Oath). **AA:** The British Museum, London (Adam Smith); Musée des Beaux Arts, Nantes / Dagli Orti (Frederick the Great). **BAL:** The British Library, London (East India Co); Capitol Collection, Washington, D.C. (Declaration of Independence); National Gallery of Victoria, Melbourne / Gilbee Bequest (Captain Cook). **Corbis:** (Treaty of Paris). **National Maritime Museum, London:** (Chronometer). **S&S:** Science Museum Pictorial (Bridgewater Canal). **Wikipedia, The Free Encyclopedia:** (Articles of Confederation). **286-287 iStockphoto.com:** Vladimir Pomortsev (Background). **287 AKG:** Laurent Lecat (Napoleon's Sword). **Alamy:** Visual Arts Library (London) (Marie Antoinette Execution, Robespierre). **AA:** Museo Historico Nacional, Buenos Aires / Dagli Orti (Bolivar); Eileen Tweedy (Anglo-Burmese War). **BAL:** Archives du Ministère des Affaires Étrangères, Paris / Archives Charmet (Treaty of Vienna); Private Collection / Index (Battle of Maipu); Musée de la Marine, Paris / J.P. Zenobel (Battle of Trafalgar); Private Collection / Agnew's, London (Napoleon); Private Collection / Michael Graham-Stewart (Abolition of Slave Trade). **S&S:** The Science Museum, London (Morton Seed Drill). **288 AKG:** (Communist Manifesto). **Alamy:** Visual Arts Libary, London (Goethe). **AA:** Private Collection (Sepoy Mutiny). **BAL:** Musée du Louvre, Paris (Liberty); Private Collection (Great Exhibition). **DK:** Rough Guides / Angus Osborn (Pistol). **Getty:** Imagno (Bismarck). **LoC:** (Garibaldi). **The National Archives:** (Nanking Treaty). **NHM:** (Galapagos Specimen). **288-289 iStockphoto.com:** Vladimir Pomortsev (Background). **289 Alamy:** Mary Evans Picture Library (Young Turks); Popperfoto (Boer War). **Corbis:** (Mexican Revolution); Hulton-Deutsch Collection (Eiffel Tower). **DK:** Courtesy of the National Motor Museum, Beaulieu (Benz Velo); Courtesy of The Science Museum, London (Bell Telephone, Phonograph). **Getty:** Lambert (Einstein); Pascal Sebah (Sphinx). **The Wellcome Institute Library, London:** (X-Ray). **290 BAL:** Peter Newark American Pictures (tr). **Corbis:** Yann Arthus-Bertrand (cla). **S&S:** Royal Photographic Society (b). **291 Alamy:** Mary Evans Picture Library (tc); The Print Collector (br). **Getty:** Riser / Fernando Bueno (cra). **S&S:** The Science Museum, London (cla, bl). **292 Corbis:** Minnesota Historical Society (tr). **S&S:** Science Museum Pictorial (clb). **293 AA:** Private Collection / Marc Charmet (cra). **Corbis:** (tl). **DK:** Courtesy of The Science Museum, London (bc). **Getty:** Topical Press Agency (c). **294 Corbis:** Hulton-Deutsch Collection (tl). **Getty:** General Photographic

Agency (clb); Topical Press Agency (cr); Roger Viollet / Boyer (cla). **295 Corbis:** Charles E. Rotkin (br). **Getty:** Hulton Archive / Alex Inglis (tl); London Stereoscopic Company (tc). **296 AA:** Museum der Stadt, Wien / Dagli Orti (tl). **296-297 AKG:** (b). **297 AA:** Musée des Beaux Arts, Nantes / Dagli Orti (ca). **Getty:** Hulton Archive (cra). **298 Alamy:** Danita Delimont (bc); North Wind Picture Archives (cla). **Wikipedia, The Free Encyclopedia:** (tr). **299 BAL:** Capitol Collection, Washington, D.C. (b); Collection of the New-York Historical Society (tc). **DK:** Confederate Memorial Hall, New Orleans (tr). **300-301 Alamy:** Visual Arts Library (London). **302 Alamy:** Visual Arts Library (London) (cl, b). **303 Alamy:** Visual Arts Library (London) (cla). **AA:** (bc). **Magnum Photos:** Bruno Barbey (crb). **304 BAL:** Archives du Ministère des Affaires Étrangères, Paris / Archives Charmet (clb); Private Collection / Agnew's, London (r). **Corbis:** Hulton-Deutsch Collection (bc). **305 AKG:** VISIOARS (cla). **Alamy:** North Wind Picture Archives (ca); The Print Collector (bc). **BAL:** Bibliothèque des Arts Décoratifs, Paris / Archives Charmet (tc). **Corbis:** Elio Ciol (cr/Above). **DK:** The British Museum, London (cr/Below). **306 AKG:** Laurent Lecat (tl). **BAL:** Musée de la Marine, Paris / J.P. Zenobel (b). **307 AKG:** (crb). **Alamy:** The Print Collector (bc). **308 BAL:** Wilberforce House, Hull City Museums and Art Galleries (tr). **Corbis:** Historical Picture Archive (bl). **309 Alamy:** Mary Evans Picture Library (cr); The Print Collector (tl). **BAL:** The British Library, London (bc); Private Collection / Michael Graham-Stewart (tc, cl). **310 Corbis:** (cla, bl); Bettmann (br). **DK:** Courtesy of the American Museum of Natural History (tc). **311 BAL:** Peter Newark American Pictures (tl). **Corbis:** Bettmann (tr). **LoC:** Underwood & Underwood (cr). **National Archives and Records Administration, USA:** (bc). **312-313 DK:** Courtesy of the American Museum of Natural History (1-17). **314 AA:** Culver Pictures (ca). **LoC:** (bl). **314-315 LoC:** Timothy H. O'Sullivan (b). **315 Corbis:** Smithsonian Institution (cl). **DK:** Confederate Memorial Hall, New Orleans (c). **LoC:** (cra). **316 AA:** Culver Pictures (bl). **BAL:** Peter Newark American Pictures (cl). **Corbis:** Bettmann (cb). **LoC:** Alexander Gardner (tr). **317 BAL:** Collection of the New-York Historical Society (bc). **Corbis:** (cr); Profiles in History (tc). **DK:** Rough Guides / Angus Osborn (cb). **LoC:** Alexander Gardner (tl). **318 BAL:** Private Collection / Index (br). **Corbis:** (t). **319 Alamy:** Marco Regalia (tl). **AA:** Museo Historico Nacional, Buenos Aires / Dagli Orti (tr). **Corbis:** Bettmann (cr). **320 Alamy:** The Print Collector (tr); Visual Arts Library (London) (tc). **National Maritime Museum, London:** (c). **320-321 Getty:** Hulton Archive (b). **321 Alamy:** Mary Evans Picture Library (crb). **BAL:** Royal Geographical Society, London (tl/Map). **DK:** Royal Geographical Society, London (tl/Pith Helmet). **NASA:** (cra). **322-323 Corbis:** (b). **324 The Art Institute Of Chicago:** Ryerson & Burnham Libraries (tl). **Corbis:** Austrian Archives (tr). **Getty:** Central Press (bc); Hulton Archive (cr, bl); Hulton Archive / Thomas Annan (tc). **325 Alamy:** Peter Treanor (cr). **Magnum Photos:** Stuart Franklin (tr). **National Archives and Records Administration, USA:** (tc). **326 AKG:** (cla). **Corbis:** Bettmann (b). **S&S:** The Science Museum, London (tr). **327 Corbis:** Hulton-Deutsch Collection (cra). **DK:** The Science Museum, London (bc). **The Wellcome Institute Library, London:** (tc). **328 Alamy:** Mary Evans Picture Library (bc). **BAL:** Musée du Louvre, Paris / Peter Willi (cl). **328-329 BAL:** Musée du Louvre, Paris (c). **329 AKG:** (cr). **330 Alamy:** Mary Evans Picture Library (br). **BAL:** Archives du Ministère des Affaires Étrangères, Paris / Archives Charmet (cl). **LoC:** (ca). **332 Corbis:** Hulton-Deutsch Collection. **333 Getty:** Imagno (clb). **iStockphoto.com:** Lance Bellers (crb). **Kansallisarkisto, National Archives of Finland:** Reko Etelävuori (cra). **LoC:** Frances Benjamin Johnston (tc). **334 AKG:** (bc). **AA:** Karl Marx Museum, Trier (r). **Getty Images:** AFP(clb). **335 AKG:** (cl, bc, cra). **Alamy:** The Print Collector (tl). **Corbis:** Bettmann (tc). **336 Alamy:** Bill Bachman (cl). **BAL:** Bibliothèque des Arts Décoratifs, Paris / Archives Charmet (cr); The Science Museum, London (bc). **Getty:** MPI (bl). **337 BAL:** Private Collection / Archives Charmet (l, br). **Getty:** Hulton Archive (cr). **338 Alamy:** Visual Arts Libary, London (br). **AA:** The British Museum, London (clb). **Corbis:** Christie's Images (c). **339 AKG:** (tl). **Alamy:** Patrick Ashby (tr); Lebrecht Music and Arts Photo Library (bl). **Corbis:** Christie's Images (bc). **340 Alamy:** Visual Arts Library (London) (tl). **NHM:** (bl, c, r). **341 Alamy:** Mary Evans Picture Libray (bl); Popperfoto (cr). **BAL:** The British Library, London (cl). **DK:** Judith Miller / Gardiner Houlgate (br). **342 Alamy:** Mary Evans Picture Library (tr); North Wind Picture Archives (tl). **Corbis:** Jim Zuckerman (br). **DK:** Courtesy of the National Maritime Museum, London (clb). **343 Alamy:** Mary Evans Picture Library (tl); Phototake Inc. (tr). **Getty:** Lambert (bc). **S&S:** The Science Museum, London (cra). **344 BAL:** The British Museum, London (cl). **DK:** Museum of Artillery, The Rotunda, Woolwich, London (b/Gatling Gun); Courtesy of The Science Museum, London (b/Bell Telephone, b/Can Opener, b/ Gramophone). **S&S:** The Science Museum, London (b/Tin Can). **345 DK:** Courtesy of the National Motor Museum, Beaulieu (Benz Velo); Courtesy of the Robert Opie Collection, The Museum of Advertising and Packaging, Gloucester (Brownie Camera); Courtesy of the Phoenix Mueum of History, Arizona / Alan Keohane (Cash Register); Courtesy of The Science Museum, London (Leclanché Cell, Diving Helmet); Courtesy of The Shuttleworth Collection, Bedfordshire (Wright Flyer). **LoC:** (Edison). **S&S:** The Science Museum, London (Filament Bulb, Typewriter). **346 DK:** Judith Miller / Wallis and Wallis (bc). **347 AKG:** (bl). **348 Alamy:** Mary Evans Picture Library (bl). **AA:** (r). **BAL:** Ashmolean Museum, University of Oxford (clb). **349 Alamy:** Alan King (crb). **BAL:** Cotehele House, Cornwall (ca); Private Collection (tl). **DK:** Courtesy of the Royal Green Jackets Museum, Winchester (cl). **Getty:** Hulton Archive (bl). **350 AA:** Travelsite / Global (bc). **BAL:** National Gallery of Victoria, Melbourne / Gilbee Bequest (tl); National Library of Australia, Canberra (bl). **351 AA:** Eileen Tweedy (tr). **Corbis:** Bettmann (br); North Carolina Museum of Art (c). **352 AA:** Private Collection (bl). **BAL:** The British Library, London (cla). **DK:** Courtesy of the National Railway Museum, New Delhi (cb). **353 AKG:** François Guénet (bl). **Corbis:** Hulton-Deutsch Collection (tl); Sygma / Jean Pierre Amet (bc). **354 Corbis:** Hulton-Deutsch Collection (ca). **Getty:** Hulton Archive (b). **National Maritime Museum, London:** (tr). **355 Corbis:** Leonard de Selva (bc); Hulton-Deutsch Collection (crb). **The National Archives:** (t). **356 Corbis:** Bettmann (b); Sakamoto Photo Research Laboratory (cla). **357 Corbis:** Asian Art & Archaeology, Inc. (tl, br); **Getty images** (cr). **358 Corbis:** Bettmann (bl). **DK:** Courtesy of the Ashmolean Museum, Oxford (cla). **Getty:** Imagno (tc). **359 Alamy:** Mary Evans Picture Library (tl). **Corbis:** (cr). **Getty:** General Photographic Agency (bc). **360 AA:** John Meek (bl). **DK:** Courtesy of the Royal Geographic Society, London (tl). **Wikipedia, The Free Encyclopedia:** (tr). **361 Alamy:** Popperfoto (cra). **BAL:** Private Collection / Archives Charmet (tl). **Getty:** Pascal Sebah (cb). **Inkartha Freedom Party (www.ifp.org.za):** (br). **362 Corbis:** Bettmann. **364 AKG:** (Inflation). **Alamy:** David J. Green (Poppy); The Print Collector (Lenin). **AA:** Culver Pictures (Flu); Imperial War Museum, London (Over the Top). **Corbis:** Rykoff Collection (Assassination). **DK:** Courtesy of the Imperial War Museum, London (Red Army Badge); Courtesy of the Museum of the Revolution, Moscow (Banner, Stalin). **Getty:** Hulton Archive (Michael Collins); Time Life Pictures / Margaret Bourke-White (Collective Farm). **364-365 Corbis:** Digital Art (Background). **365 AKG:** (Hitler). **Alamy:** Popperfoto (Gandhi). **Corbis:** Bettmann (Nuremberg, Pearl Harbour). **DK:** Courtesy of the Imperial War Museum, London (Jude Star). **Getty:** FPG (Hiroshima); MPI / Dorothea Lange (Depression). **Imagine China:** (Mao). **David King Collection:** (Soviet Poster). **Magnum Photos:** Robert Capa © 2001 By Cornell Capa (Spanish Civil War). **366 Alamy:** Popperfoto (Peron). **AA:** Eileen Tweedy (Korean War). **Corbis:** Bettmann (Berlin Wall, JFK Funeral, Moon Landing); Hulton-Deutsch Collection (Suez Crisis). **Getty:** Time Life Pictures / Larry Burrows (Vietnam). **Magnum Photos:** Rene Burri (Guevara); Nicolas Tikhomiroff (Algerian Independence). **S&S:** The Science Museum, London (Contraceptive Pill). 366-367 **Corbis:** Digital Art (Background). **367 African Pictures:** Baileys African History Archive (Biko). **Alamy:** Peter Jordan (Thatcher). **Corbis:** Bettmann (Iranian Revolution); Michael Freeman (Pinochet Protest); Reuters (Afghan War); Reuters / Charles Platiau (Romanian Revolution); Peter Turnley (Gorbachev). **Getty:** Reportage / Tom Stoddart (Berlin Wall). **Magnum Photos:** Jean Gaumy (Iranian Troops); Gilles Peress (Bloody Sunday). **S&S:** The Science Museum, London (Computer). **368 Alamy:** ImageState (AIDS); Jesper Jensen (Wind Farm). **Corbis:** In Visu / Christophe Calais (Sadam Statue); Lester Lefkowitz (Times Square); Peter Turnley (Mandela, Yeltsin). **Getty:** Liaison / Stephen Ferry (Arafat & Rabin); Spencer Platt (9/11); Science Faction / Louie Psihoyos (Petronas Towers). **Rex Features:** Andrew Testa (Kosovo). **368-369 Corbis:** Digital Art (Background). **369 Getty:** National Geographic / Justin Guariglia. **370-371 Corbis:** Rykoff Collection. **372 AA:** The British Library, London (cla). **372-373 AA:** Imperial War Museum, London (b). **373 Getty:** Hulton Archive (tr). **374 AA:** Imperial War Museum, London. **375 Alamy:** David J. Green (crb). **AA:** Museum of the City of New York (c). **376 AA:** (tr). **Corbis:** Swim Ink 2, LLC (bl). **377 Alamy:** The Print Collector (bl). **Corbis:** Bettmann (c). **DK:** Courtesy of the Imperial War Museum, London (cr); Courtesy of the H. Keith Melton Collection (br); Courtesy of the Museum of the Revolution, Moscow (tc). **Getty:** Hulton Archive (tr). **378 Alamy:** Popperfoto (cl, tr). **379 Alamy:** The Print Collector (bc). **BAL:** Private Collection / Archives Charmet (crb). **Corbis:** (cl). **DK:** Courtesy of the Museum of the Revolution, Moscow / Andy Crawford (cr). **David King Collection:** (tc, cla). **380 Alamy:** Visual Arts Library (London) (cla). **Getty:** Time Life Pictures / Margaret Bourke-White (b). **381 Alamy:** Mary Evans Picture Library (bl). **AA:** Culver Pictures (tr). **BAL:** Private Collection (crb). **Corbis:** Bettmann (cl). **DK:** Courtesy of the Museum of the Revolution, Moscow (tl). **382-383 David King Collection:** (1-18). **384 AKG:** (cl). **Corbis:** Bettmann (c). **385 DK:** Rough Guides / Greg Ward (br). **Getty:** MPI / Dorothea Lange (tl). **386 AA:** John Meek (bl); Dagli Orti (crb). **Getty:** Pierre Petit (cla). **386-387 Corbis:** Bettmann (tc). **387 Alamy:** Mary Evans Picture Library (clb). **AA:** Private Collection / Marc Charmet (tr). **Corbis:** Hulton-Deutsch Collection (br). **388 Corbis:** Archivo Iconografico, S.A. (tl). **Magnum Photos:** Robert Capa © 2001 By Cornell Capa (bl, crb). **389 AKG:** (c). **AA:** Private Collection / Marc Charmet (ftl); Reina Sofia Museum, Madrid, Guernica, 1937 by Pablo Picasso (1881-1973). Oil on Canvas. 351 x 782 cm © Succession Picasso / DACS (tr). **BAL:** Private Collection (crb). **Corbis:** (tl); Hulton-Deutsch Collection (bl). **390 AKG:** (r). **Alamy:** Mary Evans Picture Library (bl). **BAL:** Private Collection (cl); Private Collection / Archives Charmet (c). **391 AKG:** Ullstein Bild (cl). **Alamy:** Popperfoto (bc). **AA:** John Meek (tc). **Corbis:** Leonard de Selva (crb). **392 AA:** Imperial War Museum, London (tr). **BAL:** Peter Newark Historical Pictures (bl). **Getty:** Hulton Archive (cla). **393 Alamy:** Lebrecht Music and Arts Photo Library (c). **BAL:** Peter Newark Military Pictures (br). **Corbis:** Hulton-Deutsch Collection (tl). **394-395 Magnum Photos:** Soviet Group / Georgi Zelma. **396 AKG:** (tl). **Corbis:** (cl); Bettmann (b). **397 AKG:** (cra). **398-399 Magnum Photos:** Robert Capa © 2001 By Cornell Capa. **400 AKG:** Ullstein Bild (cl). **Alamy:** Mary Evans Picture Library (c). **Corbis:** Bettmann (tr). **DK:** Courtesy of the Imperial War Museum, London (cr). **400-401 Corbis:** Reuters / Auschwitz Museum (b). **401 AKG:** (c, clb). **Corbis:** Bettmann (cl). **Getty:** AFP / Simon Christophe (cr). **402 Corbis:** David J. & Janice L. Frent Collection (crb). **Getty:** Keystone (cra). **403 Alamy:** David South (cr). **Corbis:** Bettmann (tl, br); Hulton-Deutsch Collection (bc). **404-405 Corbis:** Peace Memorial Museum / EPA. **406 AA:** Eileen Tweedy (cr). **Corbis:** (cl); Bettmann (b). **David King Collection:** (tl). **407 Magnum Photos:** Rene Burri (c). **NATO Media Library:** (cra). **408 Alamy:** Popperfoto (clb, r). **DK:** Courtesy of The British Library, London (bl). **409 Alamy:** The Print Collector (c). **Corbis:** Bettmann (tl, cra); Ted Streshinsky (bc). **DK:** Courtesy of the John Frost Historical Archive (br). **410-411 Corbis:** Bettmann (b). **411 Getty:** AFP (cl); Keystone (ca). **412 Alamy:** Popperfoto (cr). **Corbis:** Hulton-Deutsch Collection (bc). **413 Magnum Photos:** Henri Cartier-Bresson (clb); Nicolas Tikhomiroff (t). **PA Photos:** AP Photo / Olivier Asselin (br). **414 Getty:** GPO (cla). **Magnum Photos:** Robert Capa © 2001 by Cornell Capa (ca). **415 AKG:** Bildarchiv Pisarek (c). **Getty:** Hulton Archive (cla); Liaison / Stephen Ferry (br); Time Life Pictures / John Phillips (tc). **Magnum Photos:** Robert Capa © 2001 By Cornell Capa (bl). **416 Alamy:** The Print Collector (bl). **Corbis:** Bettmann (tr). **Wikipedia, The Free Encyclopedia:** (bc). **417 Corbis:** Bettmann (cra, cl). **Getty:** Time Life Pictures (cb). **NASA:** W. Couch (University of New South Wales) , R. Ellis (Cambridge University) (tc). **418 The Advertising Archives:** (tr, cra, crb). **Corbis:** (cl). **419 Corbis:** James Leynse (br); Genevieve Naylor (cl). **Getty:** Lambert (t); Time Life Pictures / Hank Walker (bc). **Magnum Photos:** Dennis Stock (cr). **420-421 Corbis:** Bettmann. **422 Alamy:** Danita Delimont. **423 Alamy:** Popperfoto (tr). **Corbis:** Bettmann (bc). **Magnum Photos:** Rene Burri (cr). **424 BAL:** Private Collection (br). **Corbis:** (cla). **Imagine China:** (tr). **425 Alamy:** AA World Travel Library (c). **Corbis:** Bettmann (tr, crb). **426-427 Corbis:** Bettmann. **428 Alamy:** Pictorial Press Ltd (c). **Corbis:** Bettmann (bl). **Getty:** Frank Driggs Collection (cl). **S&S:** The Science Museum, London (cra). **429 Alamy:** Pictorial Press Ltd (cra). **The Kobal Collection:** SNC (tl). **Magnum Photos:** David Hurn (b). **430 Getty:** Time Life Pictures / Larry Burrows (tr). **LoC:** L.A. Shafer (cla). **Magnum Photos:** Bruno Barbey (br). **431 AA:** US Naval Museum, Washington D.C. (bc). **Getty:** Hulton

Archive (ca); Hulton Archive / Three Lions (tc). **432 Corbis:** Raymond Gehman (bc); Flip Schulke (clb). **Magnum Photos:** Bob Adelman (tr). **433 Alamy:** Popperfoto (br); The Print Collector (crb). **Corbis:** Bettmann (tc); David J. & Janice L. Frent Collection (cl); Reuters / William Philpott (bc). **434 Alamy:** Popperfoto (r); The Print Collector (cl). **Corbis:** Hulton-Deutsch Collection (bl). **435 Alamy:** Roger Bamber (cr); Mary Evans Picture Library (ca). **AA:** London Museum / Eileen Tweedy (bl). **Corbis:** Bettmann (br). **iStockphoto.com:** Philipp Baer (tr). **436 Getty:** Hulton Archive (tc). **Magnum Photos:** Gilles Peress (b). **437 Alamy:** Joe Fox (tl); Tim Graham (br); TNT Magazine (tr). **Getty:** Evening Standard / Maurice Hibberd (cl). **438 Corbis:** Karen Kasmauski (bc); **Getty:** AFP / Cris Bouroncle (bl); AFP / Pedro Rey (br). **439 Corbis:** Michael Freeman. **440 Corbis:** Bettmann (cra); Vittoriano Rastelli (cla). **Getty:** Time Life Pictures / Ted Thai (b). **441 AKG:** (cl). **Getty:** Time Life Pictures / Time Inc. (cb). **Toyota (GB) PLC:** (br). **442 Alamy:** Popperfoto (cra). **BAL:** Private Collection / Archives Charmet (cl). **Corbis:** Bettmann (b). **443 Corbis:** Bettmann (tc); Michel Setboun (cb). **Getty:** Robert Nickelsberg (cr). **444 PA Photos:** AP Photo (cl). **444-445 Corbis:** Reuters (b). **445 Corbis:** Reuters / Jean-Marc Loos (br). **Getty:** Liaison / Robert Nickelsberg (tc). **446 Getty:** Keystone (bl); Time Life Pictures / Igor Gavilov (t). **447 Corbis:** Sygma / Patrick Chauvel (cr); Peter Turnley (cl, tr). **448 Corbis:** Reuters / Charles Platiau (cb); Sygma / Bernard Bisson (tr); Peter Turnley (bc). **449 Getty:** AFP / Pascal George (br); Reportage / Tom Stoddart (tc). **Magnum Photos:** Thomas Dworzak (cr). **450 Corbis:** Reuters / Ivan Milutinovic (ca); Reuters / Zika Milutinovic (cl). **Magnum Photos:** Abbas (c). **451 Corbis:** Chris Rainier (tl). **Getty:** AFP / Dimitar Dilkoff (cr). **Rex Features:** Action Press (br); Andrew Testa (cla). **452 Alamy:** Peter Jordan (br); Alex Segre (bl). **Getty:** AFP / Joel Robine (c); Hulton Archive / Keystone Features / Fred Ramage (cla); Time Life Pictures / Francis Miller (clb). **453 Alamy:** Imagebroker (fbr); Nature Picture Library (bl). **Corbis:** Charles O'Rear (fbl). **Getty:** AFP / Ben Stansall (cla); AFP / Attila Kisbenedek (cr); Aurora / Jose Azel (tr); Photographer's Choice / Werner Dieterich (br). **454 African Pictures:** Baileys African History Archive (tc). **Corbis:** Peter Turnley (cl). **Magnum Photos:** Ian Berry (bc). **455 African National Congress:** (tc). **African Pictures:** iAfrica Photos / Eric Miller (c). **Alamy:** ImageState (c). **Getty:** AFP / Alexander Joe (cra). **Magnum Photos:** Ian Berry (b). **456 Corbis:** Hulton-Deutsch Collection (bl). **Getty Images:** AFP (cr). **Rex Features:** Sipa Press (t). **457 Alamy:** Maximilian Weinzierl (cl). **Corbis:** Craig Lovell (cra). **Getty:** Science Faction / Louie Psihoyos (bl). **458 Alamy:** Popperfoto (bl). **Corbis:** Bettmann (crb). **DK:** Judith Miller / Luna (clb). **Getty:** Aurora / Peter Essick (cr). **459 NASA. 460 Alamy:** Popperfoto (Whittle). **DK:** Courtesy of Glasgow Museum (TV); Courtesy of The Science Museum, London (Tape Recorder, Cats Eye). **461 Alamy:** Mark Boulton (Lightbulb); Hugh Threlfall (DVD). **Courtesy of Apple. Apple and the Apple logo are trademarks of Apple Computer Inc., registered in the US and other countries:** (iPod). **Courtesy of Canon (UK) Ltd:** (Camera). **Corbis:** Roger Ressmeyer (Solar Energy). **DK:** Courtesy of the Design Museum, London (Food Mixer); Courtesy of Dyson (Dyson); Courtesy of the Imperial War Museum, Duxford (Concorde); Courtesy of The Science Museum, London (Transistor Radio, Memory Board). **NASA:** (Mars Rover). **Research In Motion Limited:** (Blackberry). **S&S:** The Science Museum, London (Computer). **462 AA:** Culver

Pictures (cl). **NASA:** GSFC / METI / ERSDAC / JAROS, and U.S. / Japan ASTER Science Team (b). **463 Corbis:** Sygma / Micheline Pelletier (cra). **Getty:** AFP / Issouf Sanogo (tc). **Panos Pictures:** Chris Stowers (c). **Still Pictures:** Leonard Lessin (br). **464 Alamy:** Popperfoto (bl). **BAL:** Peter Newark American Pictures (cl); Private Collection / Archives Charmet (cr). **Corbis:** Bettmann (tc). **The Wellcome Institute Library, London:** (cla). **465 Alamy:** Popperfoto (clb). **AA:** Culver Pictures (tl) **Science Photo Library:** CNRI (tr); Eye of Science (crb). **Still Pictures:** Jochen Tack (cb). **466-467 Getty:** Spencer Platt (t). **468 Corbis:** Sygma (cr). **Getty:** USAF (bl). **Magnum Photos:** Jean Gaumy (clb). **469 Corbis:** In Visu / Christophe Calais (c); Peter Turnley (tl). **Magnum Photos:** Abbas (b). **470 Corbis:** Lester Lefkowitz. **471 Courtesy of Apple. Apple and the Apple logo are trademarks of Apple Computer Inc., registered in the US and other countries:** (c). **Corbis:** Reuters / Andy Clark (cr). **Rex Features:** Emma Sklar (tl). **472-473 Getty:** Wally McNamee (cl). **472-473 Getty:** National Geographic / Justin Guariglia (b). **473 Corbis:** Xiaoyang Liu (tc). **Getty:** National Geographic / Todd Gipstein (tl); Guang Niu (ca). **474 Corbis:** Bettmann (bl); Hulton-Deutsch Collection (bc). **Getty:** FPG / Keystone (t). **Still Pictures:** UNEP / Monica Terrazas Glavan (cb). **475 Alamy:** Andrew Fox (tl). **AA:** Eileen Tweedy (bc). **Corbis:** Gideon Mendel (tr); Tom Nebbia (tc); Roger Ressmeyer (br). **Getty:** AFP / Desiree Martin (bl). **476 Corbis:** Derek Trask (cla). **FLPA:** Minden Pictures / Flip Nicklin (b). **477 Alamy:** Nick Cobbing (bc); Jesper Jensen (crb). **NASA:** Jim Williams, GSFC Scientific Visualization Studio, and the Landsat 7 Science Team (cl). **478 Alamy:** Roger Bamber (t). **Corbis:** Stapleton Collection (bc). **479 © CERN Geneva:** (fbr). **Corbis:** Reuters / Samsung Electronics (fbl). **DK:** Judith Miller / Hugo Lee-Jones (bl). **Courtesy of Garmin (Europe) Ltd:** (br). **Getty:** (tc); Scott Peterson (c). **480 Alamy:** ImageState. **482 Alamy:** Mary Evans Picture Library (tl). **483 LoC:** Benjamin Henry Latrobe (tl). **National Archives and Records Administration, USA:** Records of the Continental and Confederation Congresses and the Constitutional Convention, 1774–1789, Record Group 360 (crb). **484 Alamy:** Dennis Hallinan (tl). **Getty:** MPI (bl). **486 DK:** Courtesy of the National Motor Museum, Beaulieu (tr). **Corbis:** Hulton-Deutsch Collection (br). **Getty:** AFP (bl). **487 Corbis:** Bettmann (bl). **488 Alamy:** Underwood Archives (bl). **Corbis:** (cr). **489 S&S:** The Science Museum, London (bl). **490 Getty:** AFP / Amy Sancetta (br); Evan Agostini (bl). **LoC:** (tc). **491 Corbis:** Owen Franken (br). **Getty:** AFP / Timothy A. Clary (tc). **492 iStockphoto. com:** Paul Vasarhelyi (b). **493 Corbis:** Bettmann (bc). **LoC:** George Grantham Bain Collection (tl). **494 Corbis:** Sygma / Bernard Bisson (bc). **495 Alamy:** Popperfoto (br). **Corbis:** (c). **496 Getty:** AFP / Fabrice Coffrini (bl). **497 Alamy:** BL Images Ltd (tl); Jenny Matthews (br). **498 Corbis:** Sygma / Les Stone (cr). **499 AA:** Museo Bolívar, Caracas / Dagli Orti (tc). **Corbis:** Yann Arthus-Bertrand (bl). **500 Corbis:** Owen Franken (bc); Lorpresse / J.C. Kanny (cr). **501 Getty:** AFP / Ali Burafi (br); AFP / Hector Mata (cl). **502 Corbis:** Bettmann (br). **Getty:** AFP / SA Evaristo (tl). **504 Corbis:** (tc). **Getty:** Time Life Pictures / Hart Preston (br). **505 Corbis:** Horacio Villalobos (cr). **506 Alamy:** Guy Edwardes Photography (br). **507 Alamy:** Worldwide Picture Library (cr). **508 Getty:** Picture Post / Kurt Hutton (bc). **509 Alamy:** Popperfoto (br). **Corbis:** Michael St. Maur Sheil (tc). **510 Alamy:** Visual Arts Library (London) (tr). **511 Alamy:** Lebrecht Music and Arts Photo

Library (br). **DK:** Courtesy of Patrice Reboul (tr). **512 Alamy:** The Print Collector (br). **Getty:** Roger Viollet (tr). **513 Alamy:** Jon Arnold Images (tr). **Corbis:** Jerome Sessini (bl). **514 AA:** Instituto de Valencia de Don Juan, Madrid / Dagli Orti (c). **Getty:** Robert Harding World Imagery (tr). **515 BAL:** Archives du Ministère des Affaires Étrangères, Paris / Archives Charmet (br). **Corbis:** Geoffrey Clements (tl). **516 Alamy Images:** The Steve Bicknell Style Library (bc). **Corbis:** Central Press (tc). **517 Alamy:** Visual Arts Library (London) (bc). **Corbis:** Bettmann (tr). **Getty:** Central Press (tc). **518 Corbis:** Ruggero Vanni (tc). **519 Corbis:** Popperfoto (tr). **Getty:** Massimo Listri (bl). **520 Getty:** AFP (cl). **521 Alamy:** Tibor Bognar (tl). **DK:** Courtesy of the Vatican Museums and Galleries, Rome (br). **522 Corbis:** Peter Turnley (cr). **523 Getty:** Henry Guttmann (tr); Time Life Pictures / Mansell (bl). **524 AKG:** (tr). **Alamy:** Visual Arts Library (London) (bc). **525 BAL:** Historisches Museum, Frankfurt / Archives Charmet (tl). **Corbis:** Hulton-Deutsch Collection (tr). **526 AKG:** (tc). **Getty:** Time Life Pictures / Thomas D. Mcavoy (br); Topical Press Agency / JJ Lambe (bl). **527 Getty:** AFP (tl). **Magnum Photos:** Thomas Hoepker (cr). **528 Alamy:** Carole Hewer (tl). **Getty:** Mary Evans Picture Library (bc). **529 AKG:** Sotheby's (tl). **DK:** Courtesy of the Imperial War Museum, London (c). **530 Corbis:** Bob Krist (bl). **531 AKG:** (tc). **AA:** Gripsholm Castle, Sweden / Dagli Orti (cl). **532 Alamy:** Jon Arnold Images (c). **Corbis:** Bettmann (bc). **533 BAL:** Bibliothèque Polonaise, Paris / Bonora (bl). **Corbis:** Peter Turnley (tr). **534 Getty:** Hulton Archive (bc); Hulton Archive / Keystone (cr). **535 AKG:** Ullstein Bild (tr). **Alamy:** Visual Arts Library (London) (bc). **536 Corbis:** Bettmann (bc). **537 AKG:** (cra). **Corbis:** José F. Poblete (bl). **538 Alamy:** Visual Arts Library (London) (tc). **Corbis:** Reuters (br). **539 Alamy:** Martin Mayer (br). **Corbis:** Reuters / Hans Steinmeier (tc). **540 AKG:** (tc). **541 Getty:** Darko Bandic (br). **542 BAL:** Museum of the Monastery of Kykkos, Cyprus / Lauros / Giraudon (c). **Corbis:** Bettmann (bl). **543 Corbis:** Bettmann (cr); Stapleton Collection (bc). **544 Corbis:** Richard T. Nowitz (bl). **Getty:** Hulton Archive (tc). **545 Corbis:** Bettmann (tr). **546 Corbis:** Sygma / Fabian Cevallos (tl). **Getty:** AFP / Pascal Guyot (bl); London Express (br). **547 Getty:** AFP / Viktor Drachev (br). **548 Corbis:** Bettmann (tr, bl). **549 AA:** Musée du Château de Versailles / Dagli Orti (bl). **550 Getty:** Iconica / Sergio Pitamitz (bl). **551 Corbis:** Hulton-Deutsch Collection (tr). **552 AA:** Musée des Arts Africains et Océaniens / Dagli Orti (bl). **553 Alamy:** INTERFOTO Pressebildagentur (c). **555 Corbis:** Sygma / Richard Melloul (c). **556 Getty:** Time & Life Pictures / Alfred Eisenstardt (tl). **557 Getty:** AFP / Alexander Joe (tr). **558 Corbis:** Stapleton Collection (bl). **559 Alamy:** Zute Lightfoot (cl). **AA:** Eileen Tweedy (br). **560 Getty:** Robert Harding World Imagery / I. Vanderharst (bc). **561 AKG:** (tc). **AA:** John Meek (br). **562 Alamy:** Popperfoto (bl). **563 AA:** Dagli Orti (bc). **Getty:** Time Life Pictures / Shelly Katz (tl). **564 AA:** Manuel Cohen (bl). **565 Alamy:** Popperfoto (bl). **Getty:** Paula Bronstein (br). **566 Alamy:** Royal Geographic Society (bl). **567 Magnum Photos:** Steve McCurry (bl). **Still Pictures:** (tl). **568 AA:** Dagli Orti (tr). **DK:** The British Museum, London (cl). **569 Corbis:** Bettmann (tr). **Magnum Photos:** Jean Gaumy (bc). **570 Getty:** AFP (tc); Lonely Planet Images / Martin Moos (br). **571 Corbis:** Bruno Fert (c). **572 Corbis:** Hulton-Deutsch Collection (bc). **573 Corbis:** Bettmann (bb). **Getty:** Time Life Pictures / Margaret Bourke-White (cr). **574 AKG:** (cr). **Corbis:** Philadelphia Museum of Art (bl). **575 Alamy:** Sunil Malhotra (bl). **576 BM:**

(cl). **Magnum Photos:** Steve McCurry (bl). **577 Alamy:** Paul Strawson (tr). **Corbis:** Howard Davies (br). **578 DK:** The British Museum, London (tc). **Wikipedia, The Free Encyclopedia:** (bc). **579 Alamy:** Yu Guiyou (tc). **Panos Pictures:** Jeremy Horner (br). **580 DK:** Rough Guides / Karen Trist (bc). **Getty:** AFP (tl). **581 Corbis:** (tr). **583 AA:** The British Museum, London (tl). **Corbis:** Bettmann (bc). **584 Getty:** AFP (bc). **585 Alamy:** Popperfoto (tc). **586 Corbis:** Bettmann (tc). **587 Getty:** Paula Bronstein (br). **588 Corbis:** José Fuste Raga (cr). **589 Getty:** Liaison / Paula Bronstein (tc). **590 Getty:** AFP / Torsten Blackwood (bc). **591 Alamy:** Danita Delimont (c).

All other images © Dorling Kindersley
For further information see:
www.dkimages.com